HARRAP'S
Mini Pocket
FRENCH AND ENGLISH
DICTIONARY

HARRAP'S
Mini Pocket
FRENCH AND ENGLISH DICTIONARY

FRENCH–ENGLISH, ENGLISH–FRENCH
IN ONE VOLUME

ABRIDGED BY

PATRICIA FORBES, B.A. (Oxon)

AND

MARGARET LEDÉSERT, M.A. ♀

FROM
*Harrap's New Shorter French
and English Dictionary*

HARRAP LONDON

First published as
Harrap's New Pocket French and English Dictionary
in 1969

First published in this edition
in Great Britain 1977
by George G. Harrap & Co. Ltd
182–184 High Holborn, London WC1V 7AX

Reprinted 1977; 1978

© *George G. Harrap & Co. Ltd* 1977

ISBN 0 245 53135 1

PRINTED IN GREAT BRITAIN BY OFFSET LITHOGRAPHY BY
BILLING AND SONS LTD, GUILDFORD, LONDON AND WORCESTER

PREFACE

THIS work is a completely new version of HARRAP'S POCKET FRENCH
AND ENGLISH DICTIONARY, originally compiled by the late R. P. Jago,
and aims at offering the user a useful modern vocabulary of French and
English words, including French-Canadianisms, Americanisms and
Australianisms. The main body of the work does not include place
names or proper names, which are listed in separate appendices.

As far as the English language is concerned, the standard spellings
current in England have been used throughout. Common alternative
spellings are given in the English-French part, though it should be
noted that for words with the alternate suffixes -ise or -ize and -isation
or -ization, -ize and -ization have been adopted throughout. The
attention of the North-American user is directed towards a few salient
differences in spelling:

(a) the English use of -our in words which in American usage are
spelt with -or (e.g. Eng: colour, U.S: color).

(b) the use of the final -re in words where American usage favours
-er (e.g. Eng: theatre, U.S: theater).

(c) the doubling of the l before an ending beginning with a vowel,
irrespective of accentuation (e.g. Eng: woollen, U.S: woolen; Eng:
travelling, U.S: traveling).

(d) the single l before a final syllable beginning with a consonant,
where the American usage is ll (e.g. Eng: skilful, U.S: skillful; Eng:
enrolment, U.S: enrollment).

(e) the use of a c in certain words where American usage favours
an s (e.g. Eng: defence, U.S: defense).

The phonetics of both French and English words are given according
to the symbols of the International Phonetic Association

An outstanding feature of the dictionary is the number of examples
given to show the various uses of the more important words. In order
to do this and to keep the length to reasonable dimensions a number
of space-saving devices have been adopted:

1. When in an example a headword is repeated in exactly the same
form it is represented by the initial letter, though plural nouns or

5

Preface

verb conjugations in which the form differs from the infinitive are given in full.

e.g. **pave,** *v.tr.* paver (une rue) . . . **to p. the way,** préparer le terrain.

2. In the French-English part a certain number of adverbs and simple derivatives follow the headword; the form of these is indicated simply by the ending and no translation is given if no difficulty in meaning is involved. *e.g.* **prison,** *s.f.* prison. *s.* **-nier, -nière,** prisoner; **observ/er,** *v.tr.* to observe . . . *s.f.* **-ation.**

3. In the English-French part nouns, verbs, adjectives or adverbs which have the same form are shown together under one headword, with the distinguishing divisions I, II, III, etc. Derivatives, whether hyphenated or not, are listed under the main headword, but the words appear in full in order that the stressed syllable may be shown.

e.g. **peel,** I. *s.* pelure *f* . . . II. *v.* 1. *v.tr.* peler (un fruit) . . . **'peeler,** *s.* éplucheur *m* . . . **'peelings,** *s.pl.* épluchures *f.*

Derivatives appear in alphabetical order with the exception of adverbs, which are usually designated as -ly, -ily, etc., and which come immediately after the adjective.

The following conventions have also been observed:

(*a*) Nouns have been described as 'substantives', being listed as *s.m.* or *s.f.* in the French-English part. In the English-French part the gender is given after the French word. Nouns which have irregular plurals, or French adjectives with irregular plurals or feminine forms are marked †; for these words the user should refer to the grammar notes at the beginning of each part. An exception to this rule is made for French hyphenated nouns; as the rules governing the plurals are complicated the plural is given under the headword. The user is therefore advised to consult the French headword for the plural of a compound noun occurring in the translation in the English/French part.

(*b*) Irregular verbs are marked ‡, and for these also the user should refer to the grammar notes.

(*c*) Owing to the different systems of administration, etc., in the different countries it is not always possible to give true translations for different functions or offices. In such cases the sign = has been used to indicate the nearest equivalent.

We should like to thank all who have helped us in our revision work and in the reading of the proofs, notably Mr R. P. L. Ledésert, *Licencié en Droit, Licencié ès Lettres,* Miss M. Holland Smith, Mr F. G. S. Parker, M.A., Mrs F. Collin, M.A. (Montréal), Mr P. H. Collin, M.A., Mrs E. A. H. Strick, M.A., and Mr R. Usher, M.B.E., M.A.

Patricia Forbes
Margaret Ledésert

PRÉFACE

CET ouvrage est une version entièrement nouvelle du HARRAP'S POCKET FRENCH AND ENGLISH DICTIONARY, par R. P. Jago, dont le but est d'offrir à l'usager un vocabulaire utile et moderne du français et de l'anglais, y compris de nombreux canadianismes français, des américanismes et des mots utilisés en Australie. Nous n'avons donné ni noms géographiques ni noms propres dans l'ouvrage même mais ceux-ci figurent dans les appendices.

L'orthographe des mots anglais respecte l'usage britannique. Les variantes usuelles figurent dans la partie anglais-français; il faut cependant signaler que pour la double forme des suffixes -ise ou -ize, et -isation ou -ization l'orthographe -ize et -ization a été adoptée dans les deux parties du dictionnaire.

Nous attirons l'attention du lecteur habitué à l'usage américain sur quelques différences particulièrement frappantes:

(a) l'emploi anglais de -our dans des mots pour lesquels l'américain emploierait l'orthographe -or (ex. angl: colour, U.S: color).

(b) l'emploi de la finale -re dans des mots pour lesquels l'usage américain donne la préférence à la forme -er (ex. angl: theatre, U.S: theater).

(c) le redoublement de la lettre l devant une voyelle (ex. angl: woollen, U.S: woolen; angl: travelling, U.S: traveling).

(d) l'emploi de l'l simple devant une syllabe finale commençant par une consonne, alors que l'usage américain est ll (ex. angl: skilful, U.S: skillful; angl: enrolment, U.S: enrollment).

(e) l'emploi d'un c dans certains mots pour lesquels l'américain donne la préférence à l's (ex. angl: defence, U.S: defense).

Pour la transcription phonétique des mots français et anglais, nous employons les signes de l'Association phonétique internationale.

Les nombreux exemples donnés pour illustrer l'usage des mots les plus importants est l'une des caractéristiques essentielles de ce dictionnaire. Cependant, afin d'éviter d'accroître démesurément le volume de l'ouvrage un certain nombre de règles typographiques ont été adoptées pour gagner de la place.

7

Préface

1. Quand, dans un exemple, un mot principal est répété sans changement, il est représenté par la lettre initiale, alors que les noms au pluriel ou les formes des verbes pour lesquels l'orthographe change (ce qui n'est pas toujours le cas en anglais), sont écrites en toutes lettres. *ex.* pave, *v.tr.* paver (une rue) . . . to p. the way, préparer le terrain.

2. Dans la partie français-anglais un certain nombre d'adverbes e t de dérivés simples sont insérés à la suite du mot principal, avec ou sans traduction suivant la difficulté de la traduction. *ex.* **prison,** *s.f.* prison. *s.* -nier, -nière, prisoner; **observ/er,** *v.tr.* to observe . . . *s.f.* -ation.

3. Dans la partie anglais-français les noms, verbes, adjectifs ou adverbes ayant la même forme sont groupés sous le même mot principal, et séparés par les sous-titres I, II, III, etc. Les dérivés, écrits avec ou sans trait d'union, suivent le mot principal; ils sont écrits en toutes lettres afin de pouvoir indiquer la syllabe accentuée. *ex.* peel. **I.** *s.* pelure *f* . . . **II.** *v.* **1.** *v.tr.* peler (un fruit) . . . 'peeler, *s.* éplucheur *m* . . . 'peelings, *s.pl.* épluchures *f.*

Les dérivés sont classés par ordre alphabétique, à l'exception des adverbes en -ly, qui suivent directement les adjectifs.

En outre, les conventions suivantes one été respectées:

(*a*) Les noms ont été classés comme substantifs et leur genre défini *s.m.* ou *s.f.* dans la partie français-anglais. Dans la partie anglais-français le genre est indiqué après le mot français. Les noms dont le pluriel est irrégulier et les adjectifs français, dont le féminin ou le pluriel ne se forme pas par la simple addition d'un -e ou d'un -s sont accompagnés du signe † qui renvoie le lecteur aux notes grammaticales placées au début de chaque partie, français-anglais et anglais-français. Une exception à cette règle générale est faite pour les noms composés français, dont le pluriel suit le mot principal en raison des règles compliquées qui régissent le pluriel de ces noms.

(*b*) Les verbes irréguliers sont indiqués par le signe ‡ qui renvoie le lecteur aux notes grammaticales.

(*c*) Etant donné les différences dans les structures administratives et autres des deux pays, il n'est pas toujours possible de traduire exactement les diverses charges, fonctions, etc. Dans de tels cas, le signe = a été utilisé pour indiquer l'équivalent le plus proche.

Nous tenons à remercier tous ceux qui nous ont aidées au travail de révision et à la lecture des épreuves: Mr R. P. L. Ledésert, *Licencié en Droit, Licencié-ès-Lettres,* Miss M. Holland Smith, Mr F. G. S. Parker, M.A., Mrs F. Collin, M.A. (Montréal), Mr P. H. Collin, M.A., Mrs E. A. H. Strick, M.A., et Mr R. Usher, M.B.E., M.A.

Patricia Forbes
Margaret Ledésert

ABBREVIATIONS
USED IN THE DICTIONARY

a.	adjective	adjectif
A. & A:	art and architecture	beaux arts et architecture
abs.	absolute use of verb	emploi absolu du verbe
Adm:	administration	administration
adv.	adverb	adverbe
Agr:	agriculture	agriculture
Anat:	anatomy	anatomie
approx.	approximately	sens approché
art.	article	article
Atom Ph:	atomic physics	sciences atomiques
Austr:	Australia; Australian	Australie; australien
Aut:	cars, motoring	automobilisme, voitures
aux.	auxiliary	auxiliaire
Av:	aviation, aircraft, aeronautics	aviation, avions, aéronautique
Bot:	botany	botanique
Can:	Canada; Canadian	Canada; canadien
Ch:	chemistry	chimie
Cin:	cinema	cinéma
Civ.E:	civil engineering	génie civil
Cl:	clothing	vêtements
coll.	collective	collectif
Com:	commerce	commerce
comp.	comparative	comparatif
conj.	conjunction	conjonction
Cu:	cooking, food	cuisine, comestibles
def.	definite	défini
dem.	demonstrative	démonstratif
E:	engineering, mechanics	mécanique, industries mécaniques
Ecc:	ecclesiastical	église et clergé
El:	electricity	électricité
Eng:	English; England	Angleterre; anglais
esp.	especially	surtout
etc.	et cetera	et cætera
excl.	exclamation, exclamatory	exclamation, exclamatif
f.	feminine	féminin
F:	colloquial	familier
Fb:	football and rugby	football et rugby
Fin:	finance	finances
Fish:	fish; fishing	poissons; pêche
Fr:	French; France	français; France
Fr. C:	French Canadian	canadien français
fu.	future	futur
Geog:	geography	géographie
Gram:	grammar	grammaire
H:	household	économie domestique
Her:	heraldry	blason
Hist:	history	histoire
imp.	imperative	impératif
imperf.	imperfect	imparfait
impers.	impersonal	impersonnel
Ind:	industry, industrial	industrie, industriel
indef.	indefinite	indéfini
interrog.	interrogative	interrogatif
inv.	invariable	invariable
Jur:	law	droit, terme du palais
Ling:	linguistics	linguistique
Lit:	literary use; literature	forme littéraire, littérature
m.	masculine	masculin
Med:	medicine	médecine
Meteo:	meteorology	météorologie
Mil:	military	militaire

Abbreviations

Min:	minerals; mining	minéraux; minerais; exploitation des mines
Mth:	mathematics	mathématiques
Mus:	music	musique
Nau:	nautical; navy	terme nautique; marine
neg.	negative	négatif
occ.	occasionally	parfois
p.	(*i*) participle, (*ii*) past	(*i*) participe, (*ii*) passé
P:	uneducated expression, slang	populaire, argot
Pej:	pejorative	péjoratif
pers.	person; personal	personne; personnel
Ph:	physics	physique
Phot:	photography	photographie
pl.	plural	pluriel
P.N:	public notice	avis au public
Pol:	politics	politique
poss.	possessive	possessif
p.p.	past participle	participe passé
pred.	predicative	attributif
prep.	preposition	préposition
Pr. n.	proper name	nom propre
pron.	pronoun	pronom
pr. p.	present participle	participe présent
P.T.T:	post, telegraph, telephone	postes et télécommunications
Psy:	psychology	psychologie
qch.	(something)	quelque chose
qn	(someone)	quelqu'un
Rad:	radio	radio
Rail:	railways	chemins de fer
Rec:	gramophones, tape-recording	phonographes, magnétophones
rel.	relative	relatif
R.t.m.	registered trade mark	marque déposée
s.	noun	substantif
Sc:	science	sujets scientifiques
Sch:	scholastic	scolaire
Scot:	Scotland; Scottish	Écosse; écossais
sg.	singular	singulier
s.o.	someone	(quelqu'un)
Sp:	sport, games	sport, jeux
sth.	something	(quelque chose)
sub.	subjunctive	subjonctif
Techn:	technical terms	terme(s) technique(s), de métier
Th:	theatre	théâtre
T.V:	television	télévision
U.S:	United States; American	États-Unis; américain
usu.	usually	d'ordinaire
v.	verb	verbe
v.i.	intransitive verb	verbe intransitif
v. ind. tr.	verb indirectly transitive	verb transitif indirect
v. pr.	pronominal (reflexive) verb	verbe pronominal
v. tr.	transitive verb	verbe transitif
Z:	zoology	zoologie

PART I
FRENCH-ENGLISH: FRANÇAIS-ANGLAIS

GRAMMAR NOTES

I. FEMININE AND PLURAL FORMS

1. General rules: To form the feminine of an adjective, add -e; if the masculine form ends in -e, the feminine form is the same as the masculine. *N.B.* If the adjective ends in -é, -e is added to form the feminine, *e.g.* carré, carrée. To form the **plural** of a noun or adjective, add -s to the singular form; if the noun or adjective ends in -s, -x, or -z, the plural form is the same as the singular. Adjectives and nouns which do not follow these general rules are marked †, and the summaries below give the principal rules governing these.

2. Irregular feminines of adjectives

(*a*) masculine ending -if, feminine -ive. *e.g.* actif, active; vif, vive.

(*b*) masculine ending -eux, feminine -euse. *e.g.* heureux, heureuse. *Exception:* vieux, *f.* vieille, *m.* form before vowel sound vieil.

(*c*) masculine ending -eau or -ou, feminine -elle, -olle; *m.* ending before vowel sound -el, -ol. *e.g.* beau, bel, belle; nouveau, nouvel, nouvelle; fou, fol, folle. *N.B.* No alternative *m* form for jumeau, as this adjective always comes after the noun it qualifies.

(*d*) masculine ending -er, feminine -ère; some adjectives ending in -et also add the grave accent. *e.g.* léger, légère; premier, première; complet, complète; discret, discrète; incomplet, incomplète; inquiet, inquiète; secret, secrète.

(*e*) for most adjectives ending in -l, -n, -s, and -t, double the consonant and add -e to form the feminine. *e.g.* cruel, cruelle; gentil, gentille; nul, nulle; gras, grasse; gros, grosse; las, lasse; muet, muette; net, nette; sot, sotte; bon, bonne. *Note also:* faux, fausse; roux, rousse.

(*f*) masculine ending -u, feminine -uë. *e.g.* aigu, aiguë; ambigu, ambiguë.

(*g*) for irregular adjectives which are also nouns, the feminine form is given under the headword, *e.g.* pécheur, consolateur.

(*h*) irregular forms not in the above categories: bénin, bénigne; blanc, blanche; favori, favorite; franc, franche; grec, grecque; long, longue; malin, maligne; public, publique; sec, sèche; turc, turque.

3. Plurals of nouns and adjectives

(*a*) for most nouns or adjectives ending in -au or -eu, add -x, to form the plural. *e.g.* manteau, manteaux; jumeau, jumeaux; eau, eaux;

cheveu, cheveux. *Exceptions:* bleu, bleus; pneu, pneus; landau, landaus.

(*b*) singular -al, plural -aux. *e.g.* cheval, chevaux; journal, journaux; loyal, loyaux; mal, maux. *Exceptions:* bal, bals; banal, banals; carnaval, carnavals; chacal, chacals; naval, navals; fatal, fatals; glacial, glacials; régal, régals; the plural of idéal is usually idéaux, but sometimes idéals.

(*c*) most nouns ending in -ou, plural -ous: *e.g.* trou, trous. *Exceptions:* bijou, bijoux; caillou, cailloux; chou, choux; genou, genoux; hibou, hiboux; pou, poux.

(*d*) for a few nouns ending in -ail, plural form -aux: bail, baux; corail, coraux; émail, émaux; soupirail, soupiraux; travail, travaux; vitrail, vitraux; the plural of ail is aulx or ails.

(*e*) nouns with highly irregular or double plurals: (*i*) aïeul, aïeuls (= *great-grandparents*), aïeux (= *ancestors*); (*ii*) ciel, cieux, but ciels in meaning of skies in a painting; (*iii*) œil, yeux.

(*f*) as the rules are complicated, the plurals of hyphenated nouns are given under the headwords.

(*g*) Note the following plurals (originally written as two words): madame, mesdames; mademoiselle, mesdemoiselles; monsieur, messieurs; monseigneur, messeigneurs.

(*h*) qualified colour adjectives are invariable: *e.g.* une robe gris clair; des yeux blue foncé.

II. VERB CONJUGATION

1. Regular verbs

Infinitive	-ER Verbs *donn/er*	-IR Verbs *fin/ir*	-RE Verbs *vend/re*
1. Present	je donne	je finis	je vends
	tu donnes	tu finis	tu vends
	il donne	il finit	il vend
	nous donnons	nous finissons	nous vendons
	vous donnez	vous finissez	vous vendez
	ils donnent	ils finissent	ils vendent
2. Imperfect	je donnais	je finissais	je vendais
	tu donnais	tu finissais	tu vendais
	il donnait	il finissait	il vendait
	nous donnions	nous finissions	nous vendions
	vous donniez	vous finissiez	vous vendiez
	ils donnaient	ils finissaient	ils vendaient
3. Past Historic	je donnai	je finis	je vendis
	tu donnas	tu finis	tu vendis
	il donna	il finit	il vendit
	nous donnâmes	nous finîmes	nous vendîmes
	vous donnâtes	vous finîtes	vous vendîtes
	ils donnèrent	ils finirent	ils vendirent
4. Future	je donnerai	je finirai	je vendrai
	tu donneras	tu finiras	tu vendras
	il donnera	il finira	il vendra
	nous donnerons	nous finirons	nous vendrons
	vous donnerez	vous finirez	vous vendrez
	ils donneront	ils finiront	ils vendront

Grammar notes

5. Present Subjunctive	je donne	je finisse	je vende
	tu donnes	tu finisses	tu vendes
	il donne	il finisse	il vende
	nous donnions	nous finissions	nous vendions
	vous donniez	vous finissiez	vous vendiez
	ils donnent	ils finissent	ils vendent
6. Imperative	donne	finis	vends
	donnons	finissons	vendons
	donnez	finissez	vendez
7. Present Participle	donnant	finissant	vendant
8. Past Participle	donné	fini	vendu

The table above shows the conjugation of the principal tenses of the three main groups of verbs. Among the -er verbs there are some slight modifications which do not qualify the verbs in question to be classified as irregular, and which are listed below.

(a) verbs in -ger (e.g. manger) *All* these verbs take an extra e before endings beginning with o or a.

Present: je mange, nous mangeons; *Imperfect:* je mangeais, nous mangions; *Past Historic:* je mangeai, etc.; *Present participle:* mangeant.

(b) verbs in -cer (e.g. commencer) *All* these verbs change c to ç before endings beginning with o or a. *Present:* je commence, nous commençons; *Imperfect:* je commençais, nous commencions; *Past Historic:* je commençai, etc.; *Present Participle:* commençant.

(c) When the infinitive ends in e + single consonant + er (e.g. appeler, acheter) the verbs fall into two groups:

(i) some (e.g. appeler) double the consonant before the unpronounced endings of the present tense, and in the future: *Present:* j'appelle, nous appelons, ils appellent; *Future:* j'appellerai. Like appeler: atteler; épeler; épousseter; renouveler.

(ii) Others (e.g. acheter) add a grave accent. *Present:* J'achète, nous achetons, ils achètent. *Future:* j'achèterai. Like acheter: congeler; dégeler; geler; mener; modeler; peler; peser.

(d) When the infinitive ends in é + single consonant + er (e.g. espérer) the acute accent changes to grave in the present tense, but the acute accent is maintained in the future.

Present: j'espère, nous espérons, ils espèrent. *Future* j'espérerai.

(e) Verbs in -yer (e.g. essuyer) The y changes to i before the unpronounced endings of the present tense: j'essuie, nous essuyons; ils essuient: *Future:* j'essuierai.

2. Irregular verbs

Irregular verbs are listed alphabetically below. As verb endings in the imperfect, future and present subjunctive (with few exceptions) are

15

invariable, and those of the past historic (with a few exceptions) fall into three groups, only the first person singular has been given for these tenses. For the present tense the first person singular and plural are generally adequate, though other persons are given for highly irregular verbs. The imperative is given only if it differs from the present tense. Only those tenses in which irregularities occur are listed; for other tenses see the type -ER, -IR, and -RE verbs.

1. = Present. 2. = Imperfect. 3. = Past historic. 4. = Future. 5. = Present subjunctive. 6. = Imperative. 7. = Present participle. 8. = Past participle. n. = nous. v. = vous. * verbs conjugated with être.

ABATTRE, *like* battre. **ABSOUDRE**. 1. j'absous, n. absolvons; 2. j'absolvais; 3. *rarely used*; 5. j'absolve; 7. absolvant; 8. absous, absoute. **ABSTRAIRE**. 1. j'abstrais, n. abstrayons; 2. j'abstrayais; 3. *none*; 5. j'abstraie; 7. abstrayant; 8. abstrait. **ACQUÉRIR**. 1. j'acquiers, n. acquérons; 2. j'acquérais; 3. j'acquis; 4. j'acquerrai; 5. j'acquière; 7. acquérant; 8. acquis. **ACCUEILLIR**, *like* cueillir. **ADJOINDRE**, *like* atteindre. **ADMETTRE**, *like* mettre. *** ALLER**. 1. je vais, tu vas, il va, n. allons, ils vont; 4. j'irai; 5. j'aille, nous allions, ils aillent; 6. va, allons, allez. **APERCEVOIR**, *like* recevoir. **APPARAÎTRE**, *like* connaître. **APPARTENIR**, *like* tenir. **APPRENDRE**, *like* prendre. **ASSEOIR**. 1. j'assieds, n. asseyons, ils asseyent; 2. j'asseyais; 3. j'assis; 4. j'assiérai; 5. j'asseye; 7. asseyant; 8. assis. (*similarly* * s'asseoir). **ASTREINDRE**, *like* atteindre. **ATTEINDRE**. 1. j'atteins; n. atteignons, ils atteignent; 2. j'atteignais; 3. j'atteignis; 4. j'atteindrai; 5. j'atteigne; 7. atteignant; 8. atteint. **AVOIR**. 1. j'ai, tu as, il a, n. avons, v. avez, ils ont; 2. j'avais; 3. j'eus; 4. j'aurai; 5. j'aie, il ait, n. ayons, ils aient; 6. aie, ayons, ayez; 7. ayant; 8. eu. **BATTRE**. 1. je bats; n. battons; 5. je batte. **BOIRE**. 1. je bois; n. buvons, ils boivent; 2. je buvais; 3. je bus; 5. je boive, n. buvions; 7. buvant; 8. bu. **BOUILLIR**. 1. je bous, n. bouillons; 2. je bouillais; 3. *not used*; 5. je bouille; 7. bouillant. **BRAIRE** (*defective*). 1. il brait, ils braient; 4. il braira, ils brairont. **CIRCONCIRE**. 1. je circoncis; n. circoncisons; 3. je circoncis; 8. circoncis. **CIRCONSCRIRE**, *like* écrire. **CIRCONVENIR**, *like* venir. **COMBATTRE**, *like* battre. **COMMETTRE**, *like* mettre. **COMPARAÎTRE**, *like* connaître. **COMPRENDRE**, *like* prendre. **COMPROMETTRE**, *like* mettre. **CONCEVOIR**, *like* recevoir. **CONCLURE**. 1. je conclue, n. concluons. **CONCOURIR**, *like* courir. **CONDUIRE**. 1. je conduis, n. conduisons; 3. je conduisis; 8. conduit. **CONNAÎTRE**. 1. je connais, il connaît, n. connaissons; 3. je connus; 5. je connaisse; 7. connaissant; 8. connu. **CONQUÉRIR**, *like* acquérir. **CON-**

SENTIR, *like* mentir.   **CONSTRUIRE**, *like* conduire.   **CON-TENIR**, *like* tenir.   **CONTRAINDRE**, *like* atteindre.   **CON-TREDIRE**, *like* dire *except* 1. v. contredisez.   **CONTREFAIRE**, *like* faire.   **CONTREVENIR**, *like* tenir.   **CONVAINCRE**, *like* vaincre.   **CONVENIR**, *like* tenir.   **COUDRE**. 1. je couds, n. cousons, ils cousent; 3. je cousis; 5. je couse; 7. cousant; 8. cousu.   **COURIR**. 1. je cours, n. courons; 3. je courus; 4. je courrai; 5. je coure; 8. couru.   **COUVRIR**. 1. je couvre, n. couvrons; 2. je couvrais; 5. je couvre; 8. couvert.   **CRAINDRE**, *like* atteindre.   **CROIRE**. 1. je crois, n. croyons; 2. je croyais; 3. je crus; 5. je croie, n. croyions; 7. croyant; 8. cru.   **CROÎTRE**. 1. je crois, il croît, n. croissons; 2. je croissais; 3. je crûs; 4. je croisse; 7. croissant; 8. crû, crue.   **CUEILLIR**. 1. je cueille, n. cueillons; 2. je cueillais; 4. je cueillerai; 5. je cueille; 7. cueillant.   **CUIRE**. 1. je cuis, n. cuisons; 2. je cuisais; 3. je cuisis; 5. je cuise; 7. cuisant; 8. cuit.   **DÉBATTRE**, *like* battre.   **DÉCEVOIR**, *like* recevoir.   **DÉCOUVRIR**, *like* couvrir.   **DÉCROÎTRE**, *like* croître.   **DÉFAILLIR** (*defective*). 1. je défaille, n. défaillons; 2. je défaillais; 3. je défaillis; 5. je défaille; 6. *none*; 7. défaillant; 8. défailli (*rare*).   **DÉFAIRE**, *like* faire.   **DÉTENIR**, *like* tenir.   **DÉTRUIRE**, *like* conduire.   * **DEVENIR**, *like* tenir.   **DEVOIR**. 1. je dois, n. devons; 2. je devais; 3. je dus; 4. je devrai; 5. je doive, nous devions; 6. *not used*; 7. devant; 8. dû, due, *pl.* dus, dues.   **DIRE**. 1. je dis, n. disons, v. dites; 2. je disais; 3. je dis; 5. je dise; 4. disant; 8. dit.   **DISPARAÎTRE**, *like* connaître.   **DISSATISFAIRE**, *like* faire.   **DISSOUDRE**, *like* absoudre.   **DISTRAIRE**, *like* abstraire.   **DORMIR**, *like* mentir.   **ÉCHOIR** (*defective, used only in*) 1. il échoit; 3. il échut, ils échurent; 4. il échoira; 7. échéant; 8. échu.   **ÉCRIRE**. 1. j'écris, n. écrivons; 2. j'écrivais; 3. j'écrivis; 5. j'écrive; 7. écrivant; 8. écrit.   **ÉLIRE**, *like* lire.   **ÉMET-TRE**, *like* mettre.   **ÉMOUVOIR**, *like* mouvoir.   **ENCOURIR**, *like* courir.   **ENDUIRE**, *like* conduire.   **ENFREINDRE**, *like* atteindre.   * **S'ENFUIR**, *like* fuir.   * **S'ENSUIVRE**, *like* suivre, *but impersonal* (il *form only*).   **ENTREPRENDRE**, *like* prendre.   **ENTRETENIR**, *like* tenir.   **ENTREVOIR**, *like* voir.   **ENVOYER**. 4. j'enverrai.   * **S'ÉPRENDRE**, *like* prendre.   **ÉTEINDRE**, *like* atteindre.   **ÊTRE**. 1. je suis, tu es, il est, n. sommes, v. êtes, ils sont; 2. j'étais; 3. je fus; 4. je serai; 5. je sois, n. soyons, ils soient; 6. sois, soyons, soyez; 7. étant; 8. été.   **EXCLURE**, *like* conclure.   **EXTRAIRE**, *like* abstraire.   **FAILLIR** (*defective, used only in*) 3. je faillis; 4. je faillirai; *perfect:* j'ai failli.   **FAIRE**. 1. je fais, n. faisons, v. faites, ils font; 2. je faisais; 3. je fis; 4. je ferai; 5. je fasse; 7. faisant; 8. fait.   **FALLOIR** (*impersonal*). 1. il faut; 2. il fallait; 3. il fallut; 4. il faudra; 5. il faille; 6. *none*; 7. *none*; 8. fallu.   **FRIRE** (*defective, used only in*) 1. je

17

fris, tu fris, il frit; 4. je frirai, etc.; 6. fris; 8. frit (*for other persons and tenses use* faire frire).   HAÏR. 1. je hais, il hait, n. haïssons. INDUIRE, *like* conduire.   INSCRIRE, *like* écrire.   INSTRUIRE, *like* conduire.   INTERDIRE, *like* dire, except 1. v. interdisez.   INTERROMPRE, *like* rompre.   INTERVENIR, *like* tenir.   JOINDRE, *like* atteindre.   LIRE. 1. je lis, n. lisons; 2. je lisais; 3. je lus; 5. je lise; 7. lisant; 8. lu.   LUIRE. 1. je luis, n. luisons; 2. je luisais; 3. je luisis; 5. je luise; 7. luisant; 8. lui.   MAUDIRE. 1. je maudis, n. maudissons; 2. je maudissais; 3. je maudis; 4. je maudirai; 5. je maudisse; 7. maudissant; 8. maudit. MÉCONNAÎTRE, *like* connaître.   MÉDIRE, *like* dire, except 1. v. médisez.   MENTIR. 1. je mens; n. mentons; 2. je mentais; 5. je mente; 7. mentant.   METTRE. 1. je mets, n. mettons; 2. je mettais; 5. je mette; 7. mettant; 8. mis.   MOUDRE. 1. je mouds, n. moulons; 2. je moulais; 3. je moulus; 5. je moule; 7. moulant; 8. moulu.   *MOURIR. 1. je meurs, n. mourons, ils meurent; 2. je mourais; 3. je mourus; 4. je mourrai; 5. je meure, n. mourions; 7. mourant; 8. mort.   MOUVOIR. 1. je meus, n. mouvons, ils meuvent; 2. je mouvais; 3. je mus (*rare*); 4. je mouvrai; 5. je meuve, n. mouvions.   *NAÎTRE. 1. je nais, il naît, n. naissons; 2. je naissais; 3. je naquis; 4. je naîtrai; 5. je naisse; 7. naissant; 8. né. NUIRE. 1. je nuis, n. nuisons; 2. je nuisais; 3. je nuisis; 7. nuisant; 8. nui.   OBTENIR, *like* tenir.   OFFRIR, *like* couvrir. OMETTRE, *like* mettre.   OUVRIR, *like* couvrir.   PAÎTRE (*defective*). 1. je pais, il paît, n. paissons; 2. je paissais; 3. *none*; 4. je paîtrai; 5. je paisse; 7. paissant; 8. *none*.   PARAÎTRE, *like* connaître.   PARCOURIR, *like* courir.   *PARTIR, *like* mentir.   *PARVENIR, *like* tenir.   PEINDRE, *like* atteindre. PERCEVOIR, *like* recevoir.   PERMETTRE, *like* mettre. PLAINDRE, *like* atteindre.   PLAIRE. 1. je plais, n. plaisons; 2. je plaisais; 3. je plus; 5. je plaise; 7. plaisant; 8. plu.   PLEUVOIR (*impers.*). 1. il pleut; 2. il pleuvait; 3. il plut; 4. il pleuvra; 5. il pleuve; 6. *none*; 7. pleuvant; 8. plu.   POINDRE (*defective*, *3rd pers. sing. only*). 1. il point; 2. il poignait; 4. il poindra (*no other tenses used*).   POURSUIVRE, *like* suivre.   POURVOIR, *like* voir, *except*: 4. je pourvoirai.   POUVOIR. 1. je peux, *or* je puis, tu peux, il peut, n. pouvons, ils peuvent; 2. je pouvais; 3. je pus; 4. je pourrai; 5. je puisse; 6. *not used*; 7. pouvant; 8. pu.   PRÉDIRE, *like* dire, *except*: 1. v. prédisez.   PRENDRE. 1. je prends, n. prenons, ils prennent; 2. je prenais; 3. je pris; 5. je prenne; 7. prenant; 8. pris.   PRESCRIRE, *like* écrire.   PRESSENTIR, *like* mentir.   PRÉVENIR, *like* tenir.   PRÉVOIR, *like* voir *except*: 4. je prévoirai.   PRODUIRE, *like* conduire.   PROMETTRE, *like* mettre.   PROSCRIRE, *like* écrire.   *PROVENIR, *like* tenir.   PUER. *Regular, but defective; no past historic*

or imperative. **RASSEOIR**, *like* asseoir. **RECEVOIR.**
1. je reçois, n. recevons, ils reçoivent; 2. je recevais; 3. je reçus; 4. je recevrai; 5. je reçoive, n. recevions, ils reçoivent; 7. recevant; 8. reçu.
RECONNAÎTRE, *like* connaître. **RECONSTRUIRE**, *like* conduire. **RECOURIR**, *like* courir. **RECOUVRIR**, *like* couvrir.
RECUEILLIR, *like* cueillir. **REDIRE**, *like* dire. **RÉDUIRE**, *like* conduire. **REFAIRE**, *like* faire. **REJOINDRE**, *like* atteindre. **RELIRE**, *like* lire. **REMETTRE**, *like* mettre.
* **RENAÎTRE**, *like* naître. **RENDORMIR**, *like* mentir.
* **REPARTIR**, *like* mentir. **RÉPARTIR**, *like* finir. **RE-PENTIR**, *like* mentir. **REPRENDRE**, *like* prendre. **RE-PRODUIRE**, *like* conduire. **RÉSOUDRE**, *like* absoudre. **RESSENTIR**, *like* mentir. **RESSORTIR**, *like* mentir. **RE-STREINDRE**, *like* atteindre. **RETENIR**, *like* tenir. * **RE-VENIR**, *like* tenir. **REVIVRE**, *like* vivre. **REVÊTIR**, *like* vêtir. **RIRE.** 1. je ris, n. rions; 2. je riais; 3. je ris; 5. je rie, n. riions; 7. riant; 8. ri. **ROMPRE**, 1. il rompt. **ROUVRIR**, *like* couvrir. **SATISFAIRE**, *like* faire. **SAVOIR.** 1. je sais, n. savons, il savent; 2. je savais; 3. je sus; 4. je saurai; 5. je sache; 6. sache, sachons, sachez; 7. sachant; 8. su. **SÉDUIRE**, *like* conduire. **SERVIR**, *like* mentir. **SORTIR**, *like* mentir. **SOUFFRIR**, *like* couvrir. **SOUMETTRE**, *like* mettre. **SOUSCRIRE**, *like* écrire. **SOUSTRAIRE**, *like* abstraire. **SOUTENIR**, *like* tenir. **SUBVENIR**, *like* tenir. **SUFFIRE.** 1. je suffis, n. suffisons; 2. je suffisais; 3. je suffis; 5. je suffise; 7. suffisant; 8. suffi. **SUIVRE.** 1. je suis, n. suivons; 2. je suivais; 3. je suivis; 5. je suive; 7. suivant; 8. suivi. **SURPRENDRE**, *like* prendre.
* **SURVENIR**, *like* tenir. **SURVIVRE**, *like* vivre. **TAIRE.**
1. je tais, n. taisons; 2. je taisais; 3. je tus; 5. je taise; 7. taisant; 8. tu. **TEINDRE**, *like* atteindre. **TENIR.** 1. je tiens, n. tenons, ils tiennent; 2. je tenais; 3. je, tu, tins, il tint, n. tînmes, v. tîntes, ils tinrent; 4. je tiendrai; 5. je tienne; 7. tenant; 8. tenu. **TRADUIRE**, *like* conduire. **TRAIRE**, *like* abstraire; *no past historic.* **TRAN-SCRIRE**, *like* écrire. **TRANSMETTRE**, *like* mettre. **TRANSPARAÎTRE**, *like* connaître. **TRESSAILLIR**, *like* couvrir *except* 8. tressailli. **VAINCRE.** 1. je vaincs, il vainc, n. vainquons; 2. je vainquais; 3. je vainquis; 5. je vainque; 7. vainquant; 8. vaincu. **VALOIR.** 1. je vaux, n. valons; 2. je valais; 3. je valus; 4. je vaudrai; 5. je vaille; 6. *not used*; 7. valant; 8 valu. * **VENIR**, *like* tenir. **VÊTIR.** 1. je vêts, n. vêtons; 2. je vêtais; 5. je vête; 7. vêtant; 8. vêtu. **VIVRE.** 1. je vis, n. vivons; 2. je vivais; 3. je vécus; 5. je vive; 7. vivant; 8. vécu. **VOIR.** 1. je vois, n. voyons; 2. je voyais; 3. je vis; 4. je verrai; 5. je voie, n. voyions; 7. voyant; 8. vu. **VOULOIR.** 1. je veux, n. voulons, ils veulent; 2. je voulais; 3. je voulus; 4. je voudrai; 5. je veuille; 6. veuille, veuillons, veuillez; 7. voulant; 8. voulu.

PRONUNCIATION

A table of the phonetic symbols used to represent the pronunciation of the French words is given below, with examples of the words in which they occur. The following consonants, for which the phonetic symbol is the same as the letter of the written word, and which therefore cause no pronunciation difficulties, have not been listed:

b, d, l, m, n, r, t, v.

The stressed syllables are not indicated: the general rule is that in a word of more than one syllable the stress falls on the last syllable except where the vowel of that syllable is a mute e, when the stress is on the preceding syllable. But it must be borne in mind that the stress is much lighter than in English.

TABLE OF PHONETIC SYMBOLS

VOWELS

[i]	vite, cygne		[y:]	mur, sûr
[i:]	rire, lyre		[ø]	feu, ceux, nœud
[e]	été, donner, j'ai		[ø:]	meule, jeûne
[ɛ]	elle, très, peine, mais, Noël		[œ]	jeune, œuf, cueillir
[ɛ:]	terre, père, paire		[œ:]	fleur, sœur, œuvre
[a]	chat, là, femme, toit [twa]		[ə]	le, ce, entremets
[a:]	rare, tard, noir [nwa:r]		[ɛ̃]	vin, plein, main, chien, examen, faim, thym
[ɑ]	pas, âge, le bois [bwa]		
[ɑ:]	sable, âge, tâche		[ɛ̃:]	prince, ceindre, plaindre
[ɔ]	donne, album		[ɑ̃]	enfant, temps, paon
[ɔ:]	fort		[ɑ̃:]	danse, centre, ample
[o]	dos, impôt, chaud		[ɔ̃]	mon, plomb, nom
[o:]	fosse, fausse, rôle		[ɔ̃:]	honte, nombre, comte
[u]	tout, goût, août		[œ̃]	lundi, à jeun, parfum
[u:]	cour, autour		[œ̃:]	humble
[y]	cru, eu			

CONSONANTS

[f]	feu, bref, phrase		[k]	camp, képi, quatre, écho
[p]	pain, absolu		[g]	garde, guerre, second
[s]	sou, rébus, cire, scène, action, six		[ɲ]	campagne
[z]	cousin, zéro, deuxième		[ks]	accident, extrême
[ʃ]	chose, chercher, schisme		[gz]	exister
[ʒ]	gilet, manger, jeter			

SEMI-CONSONANTS

[j]	yacht, piano, ration, voyage, travailler, cahier		[w]	ouate, ouest, noir [nwa:r], pingouin
			[ɥ]	muet, huit, lui

DIPHTHONGS

[i:j]	fille, famille		[a:j]	ferraille
[ɛ:j]	soleil, veille, paye		[ɑ:j]	il bâille, rail
[aj]	bail, travail, médaille		[œj]	fauteuil, œil, je cueille

A

A, a [α], *s.m.* (the letter) A, a.
à [a], *prep.* (contracts with *le* into au, with *les* into aux). I. 1. (*direction*) aller à l'école, to go to school; voyage à Paris, journey to Paris; au voleur! stop thief! 2. (*time*) du matin au soir, from morning till evening; à jeudi! see you on Thursday! 3. (*point in space*) à la gare, at the station; au jardin, in the garden. 4. (*point in time*) à deux heures, at two o'clock; à mon arrivée, on my arrival. 5. à pied, on foot; vendre au kilo, to sell by the kilo; manger à sa faim, to eat one's fill. 6. (*indirect object*) donner qch. à qn, to give sth. to s.o.; penser à qch., to think of sth. 7. tasse à thé, teacup; chambre à deux lits, room with two beds; homme aux cheveux noirs, man with black hair; un livre à moi, a book of mine. 8. c'est à vous de décider, it is for you to decide; c'est à vous! your turn! II. (*introducing infin.*) 1. il apprend à lire, he is learning to read. 2. j'ai une lettre à écrire, I have a letter to write; machine à coudre, sewing-machine. 3. je suis prêt à vous écouter, I am ready to listen to you. 4. laid à faire peur, frightfully ugly; un bruit à tout casser, a shattering noise.
abaiss/er [abɛse], *v.tr.* 1. to lower. 2. to reduce. 3. to humble. *s.m.*-ement.
  s'abaisser à faire qch., to stoop to doing sth.
abandon [abɑ̃dɔ̃], *s.m.* 1. surrender. 2. forsaking, desertion. 3. à l'a., neglected. 4. lack of restraint.
abandonn/er [abɑ̃dɔne], *v.tr.* 1. to forsake, desert, abandon, to leave. 2. to surrender, give up.
  s'abandonner. (*a*) to neglect oneself. (*b*) to give way (to grief).
abasourd/ir [abazurdiːr], *v.tr.* to astound, stagger. *s.m.* -issement.
abat-jour [abaʒuːr], *s.m.inv.* (lamp) shade.
abattage [abataːʒ], *s.m.* felling.
abattement [abatmɑ̃], *s.m.* (*a*) prostration; (*b*) despondency, low spirits.
abattis [abati], *s.m.pl.* giblets.
abattoir [abatwaːr], *s.m.* slaughter-house.
‡abattre [abatr], *v.tr.* 1. (*a*) to knock down; to overthrow; (*b*) to fell. 2. to slaughter. 3. to bring down. 4. to dishearten.
  s'abattre. 1. to collapse. 2. s'a. sur qch., to pounce upon sth.
abattu [abaty], *a.* dejected, *F:* fed-up.
abbaye [abei], *s.f.* abbey, monastery.
abbé [abe], *s.m.* 1. abbot. 2. priest.
abbesse [abɛs], *s.f.* abbess.
abcès [apsɛ], *s.m.* abscess.
abdication [abdikasjɔ̃], *s.f.* abdication.
abdiquer [abdike], *v.tr.* to abdicate.

abdomen [abdɔmɛn], *s.m.* abdomen.
abeille [abɛːj], *s.f.* bee.
abîme [abiːm], *s.m.* abyss, chasm.
abîmer [abime], *v.tr.* to spoil, damage.
  s'abîmer, to get spoiled.
abject [abʒɛkt], *a.* abject; mean. *adv.* -ement.
abjurer [abʒyre], *v.tr.* to abjure.
aboi [abwa], *s.m.* aux abois, at bay.
aboiement [abwamɑ̃], *s.m.* bark, barking.
abolir [abɔliːr], *v.tr.* to abolish, suppress.
abolition [abɔlisjɔ̃], *s.f.* abolition.
abominable [abɔminabl], *a.* abominable. *adv.* -ment.
abominer [abɔmine], *v.tr.* to abominate.
abondance [abɔ̃dɑ̃ːs], *s.f.* 1. abundance, plenty. 2. parler d'a., to speak extempore.
abond/ant [abɔ̃dɑ̃], *a.* abundant, plentiful. *adv.* -amment.
abonder [abɔ̃de], *v.i.* to abound (en, in).
abonné [abɔne], *s.* 1. subscriber. 2. season-ticket holder.
abonnement [abɔnmɑ̃], *s.m.* 1. subscription. 2. (carte d') a., season ticket.
abonner (s') [sabɔne], *v.pr.* to subscribe.
abord [abɔːr], *s.m.* 1. access. 2. avoir l'a. facile, to be approachable. 3. *adv. phr.* d'a., at first; dès l'a., from the outset.
abordable [abɔrdabl], *a.* 1. approachable; *F:* prix a., a reasonable price. 2. affable, kindly; peu a., stand-offish, grumpy.
aborder [abɔrde], *v.i.* to land. *v.tr.* (*a*) to accost (s.o.); (*b*) to tackle (a question); (*c*) to board (ship).
about/ir [abutiːr], *v.i.* 1. a. à, dans, en, qch., to end at, in, sth.; to lead to sth.; n'a. à rien, to come to nothing. 2. *abs.* to succeed. *s.m.* -issement, outcome.
‡aboyer [abwaje], *v.i.* to bark.
‡abrasif [abrazif], *a, & s.m.* abrasive.
abrégé [abreʒe], *s.m.* summary, précis.
‡abréger [abreʒe], *v.tr.* 1. to shorten; to cut short. 2. to abbreviate.
abreuver [abrœve], *v.tr.* 1. to water (horses). 2. to flood, irrigate.
abreuvoir [abrœvwaːr], *s.m.* horse pond, drinking-trough.
abréviation [abrevjasjɔ̃], *s.f.* abbreviation.
abri [abri], *s.m.* shelter; à l'a., sheltered.
abricot [abriko], *s.m.* apricot.
abricotier [abrikɔtje], *s.m.* apricot tree.
abri-garage [abrigaraʒ], *s.m.* car port. pl. *abris-garages*.
abriter [abrite], *v.tr.* to shelter, shield.
‡abroger [abrɔʒe], *v.tr.* to repeal (law).
abrupt [abrypt], *a.* 1. steep. 2. abrupt, blunt. *adv.* -ement.
abrutir [abrytiːr], *v.tr.* to stupefy, daze; être abruti, to be exhausted, *F:* whacked.

abrutissement [abrytismā], s.m. 1. degradation. 2. brutishness.

absence [apsā:s], s.f. absence.

absent [apsā], a. (a) absent; (b) missing.

absenter (s') [sapsāte], v.pr. 1. to absent oneself. 2. to stay away.

abside [apsid], s.f. d. & A: apse.

absolu [apsɔly], a. absolute; positive. adv. **-ment**.

absolution [apsɔlysjɔ̃], s.f. absolution.

absorbant [apsɔrbā], a. 1. absorbent. 2. absorbing, engrossing.

absorber [apsɔrbe], v.tr. to absorb.

‡**absoudre** [apsudr], v.tr. to absolve.

‡**abstenir (s')** [sapstəni:r], v.pr. to abstain.

abstinence [apstinā:s], s.f. abstinence.

abstraction [apstraksjɔ̃], s.f. abstraction; faire a. de qch., to disregard sth.

abstraire [apstrɛ:r], v.tr. to abstract.

abstrait [apstrɛ], a. 1. abstracted. 2. abstract (idea), abstruse (question).

absurde [apsyrd], a. absurd. adv. **-ment**.

absurdité [apsyrdite], s.f. absurdity.

abus [aby], s.m. 1. (a) abuse, misuse; (b) a. de confiance, breach of trust. 2. corrupt practice. 3. error.

abuser [abyze]. 1. v.i. (a) a. de qch., to misuse sth.; a. du tabac, to smoke too much; (b) a. de qn, to take advantage of sth., s.o.; abs. j'ai peur d'a., I'm afraid of bothering you. 2. v.tr. to deceive.

s'abuser, to delude oneself, to be mistaken.

‡**abusif** [abyzif], a. 1. emploi a., misuse. 2. excessive; mère abusive, possessive mother. adv. **-ivement**.

acacia [akasja], s.m. acacia.

académicien [akademisjɛ̃], s.m. academician.

académie [akademi], s.f. academy.

académique [akademik], a. academic.

acajou [akaʒu], s.m. mahogany.

accablant [akablā], a. 1. overwhelming. 2. overpowering (heat).

accablement [akabləmā], s.m. dejection.

accabler [akable], v.tr. to overpower, overwhelm, crush.

accalmie [akalmi], s.f. lull.

accaparer [akapare], v.tr. to monopolize.

‡**accéder** [aksede], v.i. to have access (à, to).

accélérateur [akselerato:r], s.m. accelerator.

accélération [akselerasjɔ̃], s.f. acceleration.

‡**accélérer** [akselere], v.tr. to accelerate.

accent [aksā], s.m. accent, stress.

accentuer [aksātɥe], v.tr. 1. to stress 2. emphasize. s.f. **-ation**.

s'accentuer, to become more pronounced, more marked.

acceptable [akseptabl], a. acceptable.

accepter [aksepte], v.tr. to accept.

accès [aksɛ], s.m. 1. access, approach. 2. Med: fit, attack.

accessible [aksesibl], a. accessible, F: get-at-able.

accession [aksesjɔ̃], s.f. 1. accession. 2. adherence (to a party).

accessoire [akseswa:r]. 1. a. accessory. 2. s.m. accessory; pl. Th: properties.

accident [aksidā], s.m. accident; a. du travail, industrial injury; a. d'avion, plane crash; nous sommes arrivés sans a., we arrived safely.

accidenté, -ée [aksidāte]. 1. a. uneven (ground); hilly (region); F: damaged (car). 2. s. victim of an accident.

‡**accidentel** [aksidātɛl], a. accidental. adv. **-ellement**.

acclamation [aklamasjɔ̃], s.f. acclamation.

acclamer [aklame], v.tr. to acclaim, cheer.

acclimater [aklimate], v.tr. to acclimatize. s.f. **-ation**.

s'acclimater à, to get used to (a climate, an idea).

accommodant [akɔmɔdā], a. good-natured, easy-going.

accommodement [akɔmɔdmā], s.m. compromise, arrangement.

accommoder [akɔmɔde], v.tr. 1. (a) to make comfortable; (b) to suit. 2. to dress (food).

s'accommoder. 1. s'a. de qch., to make the best of sth. 2. s'a. à qch., to adapt oneself to sth.

accompagnateur, -trice [akɔ̃paɲatœ:r, -tris], s. Mus: accompanist.

accompagnement [akɔ̃paɲmā], s.m. 1. accompanying (s.o.). 2. Mus: accompaniment.

accompagner [akɔ̃paɲe], v.tr. to accompany; to escort, go with (s.o.).

accomplir [akɔ̃pli:r], v.tr. 1. to accomplish, to fulfil. 2. to finish. s.m. **-issement**.

accord [akɔ:r], s.m. 1. agreement; d'a., in agreement; d'a.! agreed! 2. chord. 3. Mus: être d'a., to be in tune; Rad: to be tuned in.

accordéon [akɔrdeɔ̃], s.m. accordion; en a., (i) pleated (skirt); (ii) F: crumpled (mudguard).

accorder [akɔrde], v.tr. 1. to reconcile. 2. to tune. 3. to grant. s.m. **-age**; s.m. **-ement**, tuning.

s'accorder. 1. to agree. 2. to tune (up).

accoster [akɔste], v.tr. 1. to accost, to come up to (s.o.). 2. (of boat) to berth. s.m. **-age**.

accoucher [akuʃe], v.i. Med: to give birth to (a baby). s.m. **-ement**, childbirth.

accouder (s') [sakude], v.pr. to lean on one's elbows.

accoupler [akuple], v.tr. to couple; El: to connect. s.m. **-ement**.

‡**accourir** [akuri:r], v.i. to come running (up).

accoutrement [akutrəmã], *s.m. Pej:* dress, *F:* get-up.

accoutumance [akutymã:s], *s.f. Med:* tolerance (to a drug); habit.

accoutumer [akutyme], *v.tr.* to accustom.
  s'accoutumer, to get accustomed.

accréditer [akredite], *v.tr.* 1. to accredit. 2. to credit, believe.

accroc [akro], *s.m.* 1. tear, rent. 2. hitch, difficulty.

accrocher [akrɔʃe], *v.tr.* (*a*) to hook; *F:* a. une voiture, to collide with a car; (*b*) to hang up (the phone); (*c*) *Rad: abs.* to tune in.
  s'accrocher à, to fasten on to, cling to.

accroissement [akrwasmã], *s.m.* growth; increase.

‡**accroître** [akrwa:tr], *v.tr.* to increase.
  s'accroître, to grow.

accroupir (s') [sakrupi:r], *v.pr.* to squat.

accueil [akœ:j], *s.m.* reception, welcome.

‡**accueillir** [akœji:r], *v.tr.* to receive, greet.

accumulateur [akymylatœ:r], *F:* accu [aky], *s.m.* accumulator, battery.

accumul/er [akymyle], *v.tr.* to accumulate. *s.f.* -ation.

accusateur, -trice [akyzatœ:r, -tris]. 1. *a.* accusing. 2. *s.* accuser.

†**accusatif** [akyzatif], *a. & s.m.* accusative.

accusation [akyzasjɔ̃], *s.f.* accusation.

accusé, -ée [akyze] 1. *a.* pronounced; nez a., prominent nose. 2. *s.* accused. 3. *s.m.* a. de réception, acknowledgement of receipt.

accuser [akyze], *v.tr.* 1. to accuse. 2. to acknowledge (a fact, a receipt). 3. to show up, accentuate.

acerbe [asɛrb], *a.* 1. tart, sour. 2. harsh.

acéré [asere], *a.* sharp, keen.

acétate [asetat], *s.m.* acetate.

acétique [asetik], *a. Ch:* acetic.

acétocellulose [asetɔsɛlylo:z], *s.f. Ind:* cellulose acetate.

acétylène [asetile(:)n], *s.m.* acetylene.

achalandé [aʃalãde], *a.* magasin bien a., (i) well patronized shop; (ii) *F:* well stocked shop.

acharné [aʃarne], *a.* 1. eager, keen. 2. stubborn, desperate.

acharnement [aʃarnəmã], *s.m.* (*a*) desperate eagerness; (*b*) relentlessness.

acharner (s') [saʃarne], *v.pr.* 1. s'a. après qn., to be dead set against s.o. 2. s'a. sur, to work unceasingly at.

achat [aʃa], *s.m.* purchase.

acheminer [aʃmine], *v.pr.* to be, go, on one's way (sur, vers, towards).

‡**acheter** [aʃte], *v.tr.* to buy, purchase; a. qch. à qn., to buy sth. from s.o.

acheteur, -euse [aʃtœ:r, -ø:z], *s.* purchaser.

achèvement [aʃevmã], *s.m.* completion.

‡**achever** [aʃve], *v.tr.* 1. to end, finish (off), complete. 2. to put (animal) out of its pain.

acide [asid]. 1. *a.* acid, sour. 2. *s.m.* acid.

acidité [asidite], *s.f.* acidity, sourness.

acier [asje], *s.m.* steel.

acné [akne], *s.f.* acne.

acompte [akɔ̃:t], *s.m.* instalment, payment on account.

aconit [akɔnit], *s.m. Bot:* aconite.

à-côté [akote], *s.m.* 1. aside (remark). 2. *pl.* side-issues, sidelights.

à-coup [aku], *s.m.* jerk, sudden stoppage; par à-coups, by fits and starts.

acoustique [akustik]. 1. *a.* acoustic. 2. *s.f.* acoustics.

acquéreur, -euse [akerœ:r, -ø:z], *s.* purchaser.

‡**acquérir** [akeri:r], *v.tr.* to acquire, obtain, get, win, gain, secure.

acquiescement [akjɛsmã], *s.m.* consent, assent.

acquiescer [akjɛse], *v.i.* to acquiesce.

acquis [aki], *a.* acquired; fait a., accepted fact.

acquisition [akizisjɔ̃], *s.f.* acquisition.

acquit [aki], *s.m.* receipt; pour a., paid.

acquittement [akitmã], *s.m.* 1. discharge, payment. 2. acquittal.

acquitter [akite], *v.tr.* 1. to acquit. 2. (*a*) to discharge (a debt); (*b*) to receipt (a bill).
  s'acquitter. 1. s'a. d'un devoir, to discharge a duty. 2. to acquit oneself (bien, mal, well, badly).

âcre [ɑ:kr], *a.* acrid, bitter, pungent.

acrimonie [akrimɔni], *s.f.* acrimony.

†**acrimonieu/x** [akrimɔnjø], *a.* acrimonious. *adv.* -sement.

acrobate [akrɔbat], *s.m. & f.* acrobat.

acrobatique [akrɔbatik], *a.* acrobatic.

acte [akt], *s.m.* 1. action, deed. 2. *Jur:* (*a*) deed, title; (*b*) a. judiciaire, writ; (*c*) record. 2. *Th:* act.

acteur [aktœ:r], *s.m.* actor.

†**act/if** [aktif]. 1. *a.* active, brisk, alert. 2. *s.m.* assets, credit. *adv.* -ivement.

action [aksjɔ̃], *s.f.* 1. action; act. 2. *Fin:* share; compagnie par actions, jointstock company. 3. action, lawsuit, trial.

actionnaire [aksjɔnɛ:r], *s.m. & f.* shareholder.

actionner [aksjɔne], *v.tr.* 1. to sue. 2. to set in motion.

activer [aktive], *v.tr.* to quicken, urge on.
  s'activer, to bestir oneself.

activité [aktivite], *s.f.* activity; en a., in progress, at work.

actrice [aktris], *s.f.* actress.

actuaire [aktɥɛ:r], *s.m.* actuary.

actualité [aktɥalite], *s.f.* 1. actuality, reality. 2. *pl.* actualités, current events; *T.V: Cin:* news.

†**actuel** [aktɥɛl], *a.* of the present day, existing, current. *adv.* -lement.

acuité [akɥite], *s.f.* acuteness, sharpness.

adaptation [adaptasjɔ̃], *s.f.* adaptation; *Cin:* treatment; *Rad:* matching.

adapter [adapte], *v.tr.* to fit; to adapt.

addenda [adɛ̃da], *s.m.inv.* addendum.

addition [ad(d)isjɔ̃], *s.f.* 1. addition. 2. bill. *U.S:* check.

†additionnel [ad(d)isjɔnɛl], *a.* additional.

additionner [ad(d)isjɔne], *v.tr.* to add (up).

adhérent [adeʀɑ̃], *a. & s.* adherent.

‡adhérer [adere], *v.i.* to adhere, stick (to); (*of wheels*) to grip. 2. a. à, to join (a party).

†adhésif [adezif], *a. & s.m.* adhesive.

adhésion [adezjɔ̃], *s.f.* 1. adhesion, sticking. 2. a. à, joining (a club).

adieu [adjø], *s.m.* farewell; faire ses adieux, to say goodbye.

†adipeux [adipø], *a.* adipose, fatty.

adjacent [adʒasɑ̃], *a.* next (à, to); bordering (à, on).

†adjectif [adʒɛktif]. 1. *a.* adjectival. 2. *s.m.* adjective.

‡adjoindre [adʒwɛ̃:dr], *v.tr.* 1. to unite (à, with). 2. to add.

adjoint, -ointe [adʒwɛ̃, -wɛ̃:t], *s.* assistant; deputy.

adjudant [adʒydɑ̃], *s.m.* (*a*) company sergeant-major; (*b*) a.-major, adjutant.

adjudicataire [adʒydikatɛ:r], *s.* highest bidder.

adjudicateur, -trice [adʒydikatœ:r, -tris], *s.* adjudicator, awarder (of contract, etc.).

adjudication [adʒydikasjɔ̃], *s.f.* (*a*) adjudication, award; (*b*) (*at auction*) knocking-down; par voie d'a., (i) by tender, (ii) by auction.

‡adjuger [adʒyʒe], *v.tr.* to allocate, award.

‡admettre [admɛtr], *v.tr.* to admit. 1. to let in. 2. to permit. 3. to acknowledge.

administrateur, -trice [administratœ:r, -tris], *s.* administrator.

†administratif [administratif], *a.* administrative.

administration [administrasjɔ̃], *s.f.* 1. administration. 2. government service.

administrer [administre], *v.tr.* to administer, to govern.

admirable [admirabl], *a.* admirable. *adv.* -ment.

admirateur, -trice [admiratœ:r, -tris], *s.* admirer.

admiration [admirasjɔ̃], *s.f.* admiration.

admirer [admire], *v.tr.* to admire.

admissible [admisibl], *a.* admissible. *s.f.* -ilité.

admission [admisjɔ̃], *s.f.* admission.

adolescence [adolessɑ̃s], *s.f.* adolescence.

adolescent, -ente [adolessɑ̃-ɑ̃:t], *a.* adolescent, *F:* teenager.

adonner (s') [sadone], *v.pr.* s'a. à qch., to devote oneself to sth., to take up (a profession, sport), to take to (drink).

adopter [adopte], *v.tr.* to adopt.

†adoptif [adoptif], *a.* adopted.

adoption [adopsjɔ̃], *s.f.* adoption.

adorable [adorabl], *a.* adorable, charming. *adv.* -ment.

ador/er [adore], *v.tr.* to adore, worship. *s.f.* -ation.

adossé [adose], *a.* back to back.

adosser [adose], *v.tr.* to place back to back. s'adosser, to lean (back) (à, contre, against).

adoucir [adusir], *v.tr.* 1. to soften; to sweeten. 2. to alleviate. 3. to mollify. s'adoucir, to grow softer, milder.

adouciss/ement [adusismɑ̃], *s.m.* 1. softening. 2. alleviation (of pain). *s.m.* -age. *s.m.* -eur, water-softener.

adrénaline [adrenalin], *s.f. Med:* adrenalin.

adresse [adrɛs], *s.f.* 1. address, destination. 2. (*a*) skill, dexterity; (*b*) shrewdness.

adresser [adrese], *v.tr.* to address. s'adresser. 1. to apply (à, to); "s'a. ici," 'enquire here.' 2. s'a. à qn, to ask s.o.

adroit [adrwa], *a.* 1. dextrous, skilful. 2. shrewd. *adv.* -ement.

adulte [adylt], *a. & s.m. & f.* adult.

adultère [adyltɛ:r], *s.m.* adultery.

‡adultérer [adyltere], *v.tr.* to adulterate.

‡advenir [advəni:r], *v.i.* (*used only in the 3rd pers.*) to occur, happen, to come (about); advienne que pourra, come what may.

adverbe [advɛrb], *s.m.* adverb.

†adverbial [advɛrbjal], *a.* adverbial.

adversaire [advɛrsɛ:r], *s.m.* opponent.

adverse [advɛrs], *a.* adverse, unfavourable.

adversité [advɛrsite], *s.f.* misfortune, distress.

aérage [aera:ʒ], *s.m.*, **aération** [aerasjɔ̃], *s.f.* ventilation.

‡aérer [aere], *v.tr.* to ventilate.

†aérien [aerjɛ̃], *a.* aerial; air-; overhead.

aéro-club [aeroklœb], *s.m.* flying-club.

aérodrome [aerodro:m], *s.m.* aerodrome.

aérodynamique [aerodinamik]. 1. *a.* streamlined. 2. *s.f.* aerodynamics.

aérogare [aerogar], *s.f.* air terminal.

aéroglisseur [aeroglisœ:r], *s.m.* hovercraft.

aérogramme [aerogram], *s.m. Fr.C:* airletter.

aéronaute [aerono:t], *s.m. & f.* aeronaut.

aéronautique [aeronotik]. 1. *a.* aeronautical. 2. *s.f.* aeronautics.

aéronaval [aeronaval]. 1. *a.* aeronautical. 2. *s.f.* l'aéronavale = Fleet Air Arm.

aéronef [aeronɛf], *s.m.* aircraft.

aéroport [aeropɔr], *s.m.* airport.

aéroporté [aeropɔrte], *a.* airborne.

aéropostal [aeropostal], *a.* airmail.

aéroroute [aerorut], *s.f.* airway.

aérosol [aerosɔl], *s.m.* aerosol.

aérotransporter [aerotrɑ̃spɔrte], *v.tr.* to carry by air, to fly (goods, people).

affabilité [afabilite], *s.f.* affability.

affable [afa:bl], *a.* gracious, affable.

affaibl/ir [afebli:r], *v.tr.* to weaken. *s.m.* -issement.

　　s'affaiblir, to become weak.

affaire [afɛ:r], *s.f.* **1.** (a) business, affair; savoir son a., to know what one is doing; (b) question, matter; a. d'intérêt, money matter; une grande a., a big concern; (c) thing (required) faire l'a., to answer the purpose; son a. est faite, he is done for; (d) (serious) business, matter; la belle a.! pooh, is that all! s'attirer une (mauvaise) a., to get into trouble. **2.** (a) deal, transaction; bonne a., good bargain; (b) avoir a. à, avec, qn, to have to deal with s.o. **3.** *pl.* (a) things, belongings; (b) business, trade.

affairé [afɛre], *a.* busy.

affaissement [afɛsmã], *s.m.* **1.** subsidence. **2.** depression, despondency.

affaisser (s') [safɛse], *v.pr.* to subside, collapse.

affamé [afame], *a.* hungry, starving.

affectation [afektasjɔ̃], *s.f.* affectation; (a) affectedness; (b) pretence.

affecter [afɛkte], *v.tr.* **1.** to allocate, earmark (sth.). **2.** to pretend. **3.** to have a liking for. **4.** (a) to affect, move (s.o.'s feelings). **(b)** to have an effect on (health).

affection [afɛksjɔ̃], *s.f.* affection. **1.** fondness. **2.** *Med:* complaint.

affectionné [afɛksjɔne], *a.* affectionate, loving.

affectionner [afɛksjɔne], *v.tr.* to be fond of.

†affectueu/x [afɛktɥø], *a.* affectionate. *adv.* -sement.

afferm/ir [afɛrmi:r], *v.tr.* to strengthen. *s.m.* -issement.

　　s'affermir, to become stronger; to harden, to set.

affichage [afiʃa:ʒ], *s.m.* bill-posting; *Sp:* tableau d'a., telegraph board.

affiche [afiʃ], *s.f.* poster.

afficher [afiʃe], *v.tr.* **1.** to stick (up), display. **2.** to make a show of.

　　s'afficher, to show off.

affilé [afile], *a.* sharp.

affil/er [afile], *v.tr.* to sharpen. *s.m.* -age.

affilier [afilje], *v.tr.* to affiliate (à, to, with).

　　s'affilier à un parti, to join a party.

affiner [afine], *v.tr.* to improve, refine.

affinité [afinite], *s.f.* affinity (entre, between).

†affirmat/if [afirmatif]. **1.** *a.* affirmative, positive; signe a., nod. **2.** *s.f.* l'affirmative, the affirmative. *adv.* -ivement.

affirmer [afirme], *v.tr.* to affirm, assert.

affleurer [aflœre], *v.tr.* to be level, flush, with (sth.).

affliction [afliksjɔ̃], *s.f.* affliction.

‡affliger [afliʒe], *v.tr.* **1.** to afflict (de, with). **2.** to distress.

　　s'affliger, to grieve (de, at).

affluence [aflyãs], *s.f.* **1.** flow. **2.** abundance; wealth. **3.** crowd; heures d'a., rush hours.

affluent [aflyã], *s.m. Geog:* tributary.

affluer [aflye], *v.i.* **1.** to flow. **2.** to abound. **3.** to flock.

affolé [afɔle], *a.* crazy, distracted.

affolement [afɔlmã], *s.m.* **1.** distraction, panic. **2.** racing (of engine).

affoler [afɔle], *v.tr.* to madden.

　　s'affoler. **1.** to panic. **2.** to become infatuated (de, with).

affranch/ir [afrɑ̃ʃi:r], *v.tr.* **1.** to set free. **2.** to stamp (letter). *s.m.* -issement.

‡affr/éter [afrete], *v.tr.* **1.** *Nau:* (a) to freight (ship); (b) to charter (ship, plane). *s.m.* -ètement. *s.m.* -éteur.

affreu/x [afrø], *a.* frightful. *adv.* -sement.

affront [afrɔ̃], *s.m.* insult, snub.

affront/er [afrɔ̃te], *v.tr.* to face, tackle (s.o., sth.). *s.m.* -ement.

affût [afy], *s.m.* être, se mettre, à l'a. de, to lie in wait for. **2.** gun-carriage.

affûter [afyte], *v.tr.* to sharpen (tool).

afin [afɛ̃], *adv.* **1.** a. de + *inf.* to, in order to. **2.** a. que + *sub.*, so that, in order that.

africain, -aine [afrikɛ̃, -ɛn], *a. & s.* African.

afro-asiatique [afroazjatik], *a.* Afro-asian.

agaçant [agasã], *a.* **1.** annoying, irritating. **2.** provocative.

‡agac/er [agase], *v.tr.* **1.** to grate upon (nerves, ears). **2.** to provoke, irritate (s.o.). *s.m.* -ement, irritation.

agacerie [agasri], *s.f.* provocation.

agate [agat], *s.f.* agate.

âge [ɑ:ʒ], *s.m.* **1.** age; (a) quel â. avez-vous? how old are you? **2.** le bas â., infancy; (c) old age. **2.** generation. **3.** period; le moyen â., the Middle Ages.

âgé [aʒe], *a.* **1.** â. de dix ans, ten years old. **2.** elderly.

agence [aʒã:s], *s.f.* agency.

agenc/er [aʒãse], *v.tr.* to arrange, to adjust. *s.m.* -ement.

agenda [aʒɛ̃da], *s.m.* memorandum-book.

agenouiller (s') [saʒnuje], *v.pr.* to kneel (down).

agent [aʒã], *s.m.* (a) agent; a. d'affaires, man of business; (b) a. (de police), policeman; (c) a. de change, stock-broker.

agglomérant [aglɔmɛrã], *s.m.* (road) binding material.

agglomération [aglɔmerasjɔ̃], *s.f.* **1.** agglomeration. **2.** built-up area.

aggloméré [aglɔmere], *s.m.* **1.** compressed fuel. **2.** breezeblock.

aggrav/er [agrave], *v.tr.* **1.** to aggravate (disease); to worsen. **2.** to increase. *s.f.* -ation.

　　s'aggraver, to grow worse.

agile [aʒil], a. agile, nimble. adv. -ment.

agilité [aʒilite], s.f. agility, nimbleness.

agiot/er [aʒjɔte], v.i. to speculate. s.m. -eur.

ag/ir [aʒi:r], v.i. to act. 1. faire a. qch., to set sth. going; a. bien, mal, to behave well, badly. 2. to act, take effect. a. -issant, active.
 s'agir (de), v.impers. (a) to concern; de quoi s'agit-il? what's it all about? F: what's up? (b) il s'agit de faire qch., it's a matter of doing sth.

agitateur, -trice, [aʒitatœ:r, -tris], s. agitator.

agitation [aʒitasjɔ̃], s.f. agitation. 1. (a) shaking, waving, wagging; (b) discussion; (c) l'a. ouvrière, labour unrest. 2. (a) perturbation; (b) restlessness.

agité [aʒite], a. 1. rough (sea). 2. agitated; troubled (sleep). 3. excited.

agiter [aʒite], v.tr. 1. (a) to agitate, to wave, to wag; (b) to shake. 2. to stir up, excite. 3. to debate.
 s'agiter. (a) to be in movement; (b) to become excited.

agneau [aɲo], s.m. lamb.

agonie [agɔni], s.f. death agony; être à l'a., to be at one's last gasp.

agonisant [agɔnizɑ̃]. 1. a. dying. 2. s.m. dying person.

agoniser [agɔnize], v.i. to be dying.

agrafe [agraf], s.f. hook, fastener; clasp.

agraf/er [agrafe], v.tr. to hook, clip, do up (a dress, etc.). c.f. -euse, stapler.
 s'agrafer à qn, qch., to hang on to s.o., sth.

agrand/ir [agrɑ̃di:r], v.tr. (a) to make larger; to enlarge; (b) to magnify. s.m. -issement.
 s'agrandir, to grow larger; to expand.

agréable [agreabl], a. agreeable, pleasant, nice; pour vous être a., to oblige you. adv.-ment.

agréé [agree], a. 1. approved. 2. Fr.C: comptable a., chartered accountant.

agréer [agree], v.tr. to accept; agréez mes salutations empressées, (I am) yours sincerely.

agrégé, -ée [agreʒe], a. & s. qualified (graduate schoolmaster, -mistress).

agrément [agremɑ̃], s.m. 1. pleasure; charm; jardin d'a., flower garden. 2. assent, approval.

agrémenter [agremɑ̃te], v.tr. to embellish, ornament (de, with).

agrès [agrɛ], s.m.pl. tackle, rigging; (gym) apparatus.

agresseur [agresœ:r], s.m. aggressor.

†agress/if [agresif], a. aggressive. adv. -ivement.

agression [agresjɔ̃], s.f. aggression.

agricole [agrikɔl], a. agricultural.

agriculteur [agrikylt:r], s.m. farmer.

agriculture [agrikylty:r], s.f. agriculture, farming.

agripper [agripe], v.tr. to clutch, grip. s'agripper, to cling (à, to).

agronomie [agrɔnɔmi], s.f. Agr: agronomics.

agrumes [agry:m], s.m.pl. citrus fruit.

aguerri [ageri], a. seasoned, trained.

aguets [agɛ], s.m.pl. aux a., on the watch.

ahuri [ayri], a. bewildered, confused.

ahur/ir [ayri:r], v.tr. to bewilder. s.m. -issement, bewilderment.

aide¹ [ɛ(:)d], s.f. help, aid; prep. phr. à l'a. de, with the help of.

aide² s.m. & f. assistant.

aide [ɛde], v.tr. to help, aid.

aide-ouïe [ɛdwi], s.m.inv. hearing aid.

aïeul [ajœl], s.m. 1. (pl. aïeuls) grandfather. 2. (pl. aïeux) ancestor.

aigle [ɛgl]. 1. s.m. & f. eagle. 2. s.m. lectern.

aiglefin [ɛgləfɛ̃], s.m. haddock.

aigre [ɛgr], a. (a) sour, acid; (b) sour, crabbed; (c) shrill. adv. -ment.

aigrelet [ɛgrəlɛ], a. a sourish, tart.

aigreur [ɛgrœ:r], s.f. sourness, tartness.

aigr/ir [ɛgri:r]. 1. v.tr. to embitter. 2. v.i. to turn sour. s.m. -issement.

†aigu [egy], a. 1. sharp, pointed. Mth: angle a., acute angle. 2. acute; keen. 3. shrill. 4. Gram: accent a., acute accent.

aiguille [egɥi:j], s.f. 1. needle. 2. (a) a. de pin, pine-needle; (b) Rail: point. 3. spire. 4. hand (of clock).

aiguillon [egɥijɔ̃], s.m. 1. (a) goad; (b) incentive. 2. sting (of wasp).

aiguillonner [egɥijɔne], v.tr. to goad. 2. to incite.

aiguiser [eg(ɥ)ize], v.tr. (a) to whet; to sharpen; (b) to point.

†ail [a:j], s.m. garlic.

aile [ɛl], s.f. 1. wing. 2. wing (of aircraft); sail (of windmill); blade (of propeller); wing (of car).

ailé [ɛle], a. winged, feathered.

aileron [ɛlrɔ̃], s.m. 1. (a) pinion; (b) fin. 2. Av: aileron; Aut: fin.

ailier [ɛlje], s.m. Sp: wing (player).

ailleurs [ajœ:r], adv. 1. elsewhere. 2. adv. phr. d'a., besides, moreover.

aimable [ɛmabl], a. 1. amiable; kind; peu a., ungracious. 2. lovable. adv. -ment.

aimant¹ [ɛmɑ̃], a. loving, affectionate.

aimant², s.m. magnet.

aimer [ɛme], v.tr. 1. (a) to like; to be fond of; (b) a. mieux, to prefer. 2. a. (d'amour), to love.

aine [ɛn], s.f. Anat: groin.

aîné [ɛne], a. (a) elder; eldest; s. il est mon a., he is older than I am; (b) senior.

aînesse [ɛnɛs], s.f. primogeniture; droit d'a., birthright.

ainsi [ɛ̃si]. 1. adv. so; like this, like that; s'il en est a., if so; et a. de suite, and so on; pour a. dire, so to speak. 2. conj. so, thus. 3. conj.phr. a. que, (just) as; as also.

air [ɛːr], s.m. I. (a) air, atmosphere; en plein a., in the open air; à a. conditionné, air-conditioned; (b) en l'a., in the air; paroles en l'a., idle talk. II. 1. (a) appearance, look; (b) avoir l'a., to look, seem; il a un drôle d'a., he looks odd. 2. manner, way. III. tune, air.

airain [ɛrɛ̃], s.m. bronze, brass; homme d'a., man of iron.

aire [ɛːr], s.f. 1. surface; floor; a. d'une grange, threshing-floor. 2. area. 3. eyrie. 4. les aires du vent, the points of the compass.

airelle [ɛrɛl], s.f. bilberry, U.S: huckleberry.

aisance [ɛzɑ̃ːs], s.f. ease; easy circumstances.

aise [ɛːz], 1. s.f. ease, comfort; être à l'a., to be comfortable; to be well-off; à votre a.! just as you like! (à l'a.) être bien a., very glad. 2. a. (a) easy, free; comfortable; (b) well-to-do. 2. easy (task).

aisé [ɛze], a. 1. (a) easy, free; comfortable; (b) well-to-do. 2. easy (task). adv. -ément.

aisselle [ɛsɛl], s.f. armpit.

ajisme [aʒism], s.m. Youth Hostel movement.

ajiste [aʒist], s.m. & f. (youth) hosteller.

ajonc [aʒɔ̃], s.m. furze, gorse.

ajouré [aʒure], a. perforated, pierced.

ajourn/er [aʒurne], v.tr. to postpone. s.m. -ement.

ajouter [aʒute], v.tr. to add.

ajust/er [aʒyste], v.tr. 1. (a) to adjust; (b) a. son fusil, to take aim with one's rifle; a. qn, to aim (a gun) at s.o.; (c) tapis ajusté, fitted carpet. 2. to put right. s.m. -ement.

alacrité [alakrite], s.f. alacrity, eagerness.

alarme [alarm], s.f. alarm.

alarmer [alarme], v.tr. 1. to give the alarm to. 2. to frighten, alarm.
s'alarmer, to take fright (de, at).

albanais, -aise [albanɛ, -ɛːz], a. & s. Albanian.

albâtre [albɑːtr], s.m. alabaster.

albatros [albatros], s.m. albatross.

albinos [albinos], s. & a. inv. albino.

album [albɔm], s.m. 1. album, sketchbook. 2. trade catalogue.

albumine [albymin], s.f. Ch: albumin.

alcalin [alkalɛ̃], a. & s.m. alkaline.

alcaliniser [alkalinize], v.tr. Ch: to alkalize.

alcool [alkɔl], s.m. alcohol; spirit(s); a. à brûler, methylated spirit. s.m. -isme.

alcoolique [alkɔlik]. 1. a. alcoholic, spirituous. 2. s. drunkard.

alcootest [alkɔtɛst], s.m. breathalyser (test).

alcôve [alkoːv], s.f. alcove, (bed-)recess.

aléa [alea], s.m. risk, hazard; chance. a. -toire, risky.

alène [alɛn], s.f. awl.

alentour [alɑ̃tuːr]. 1. adv. around, round about; le pays d'a., the surrounding country. 2. s.m.pl. vicinity.

alerte [alɛrt]. 1. int. to arms! 2. s.f. alarm, warning. 3. a. alert, brisk.

alerter [alɛrte], v.tr. to warn, to alert.

alevin [alvɛ̃], s.m. Fish: fry.

alezan [alzɑ̃], a. & s. chestnut (horse).

alfa [alfa], s.m. alfa(-grass), esparto.

algèbre [alʒɛbr], s.f. algebra.

algérien, -ienne [alʒerjɛ̃, -jɛn], a. & s. Algerian.

algérois, -oise [alʒerwa, -waːz], a. & s. (inhabitant) of Algiers.

algue [alg], s.f. seaweed.

aliénation [aljenasjɔ̃], s.f. 1. alienation (of property). 2. estrangement. 3. a. mentale, insanity.

aliéné, -eé [aljene], a. & s. lunatic.

†aliéner [aljene], v.tr. to alienate.

align/er [aline], v.tr. to align, draw up. s.m. -ement.
s'aligner, to fall into line.

aliment [alimɑ̃], s.m. food. a. -aire, alimentary.

alimentation [alimɑ̃tasjɔ̃], s.f. (a) food supply; rayon d'a., food department; (b) F: grocer's shop; (c) nutrition, diet.

alimenter [alimɑ̃te], v.tr. to feed, nourish.

alinéa [alinea], s.m. paragraph.

alité [alite], a. confined to (one's) bed, F: laid up.

alizé [alize], s.m. trade wind.

allait/er [alete], v.tr. to suckle. s.m. -ement.

allant [alɑ̃], a. active, busy. s.m. avoir de l'a., to have plenty of go.

‡all/écher [al(l)eʃe], v.tr. to allure, entice, tempt. s.m. -èchement.

allée [ale], s.f. 1. allées et venues, coming and going. 2. (a) walk; path; (b) alley.

‡all/éger [al(l)eʒe], v.tr. to relieve (pain). s.m. -égement, relief.

allégorique [allegɔrik], a. allegorical.

allègre [alleːgr], a. lively, gay, cheerful.

allégresse [al(l)egrɛs], s.f. gladness.

‡alléguer [al(l)ege], v.tr. to allege, plead.

allemand, -ande [almɑ̃, -ɑ̃ːd], a. & s. German.

‡aller [ale]. I. v.i. (aux: être). 1. to go. 2. (a) to be going (well); ça ira! we'll manage! (b) (of clock, etc.) to go, work; (c) comment allez-vous? how are you? 3. (of clothes) a. (à qn) (i) to suit; (ii) to fit; F: ça va! all right. 4. (a) (+ inf.) a. voir qn, to go and see s.o.; (b) (aux. use, pr. & imperf. only) to be about (to do sth.); il va s'en occuper, he is going to see about it. 5. y a. (a) j'y vais! on y va! coming! (b) allons-y! well, here goes! vas-y! allez-y! go on! 6. v.impers. il va de soi, it goes without saying; il y allait de la vie, it was a matter of life and death. 7.

int. allons! come! allons donc! (i) come along! (ii) nonsense! II. *s.m.* 3. going: (billet d')a. et retour, return ticket. 2. pis a., last resort; makeshift; au pis a., if the worst comes to the worst.

s'en aller, to go away, to depart.

aller/gie [aler3i], *s.f. Med:* allergy. a. **-gique, allergic.**

alliage [alja:3], *s.m.* alloy.

alliance [aljã:s], *s.f.* 1. alliance. 2. wedding-ring.

allié, -iée [alje]. 1. *a.* allied. 2. *s. (a)* ally; *(b)* relation by marriage.

allier [alje], *v.tr.* 1. to ally, unite. 2. to alloy, mix.

alligator [al(l)igato:r], *s.m.* alligator.

allô, allo [alo], *int. P.T.T:* hullo! hallo!

allocation [allɔkasjɔ̃], *s.f.* 1. allocation. 2. allowance, grant.

allocution [allɔkysjɔ̃], *s.f.* short speech, address.

‡allonger [alɔ̃ʒe], *v.tr.* 1. to lengthen. 2. to stretch out. 3. to prolong.

allumage [alyma:3], *s.m.* lighting (of lamp); *Aut:* ignition.

allume-feu [alymfø], *s.m.inv.* fire-lighter, kindling.

allume-gaz [alymga:z], *s.m.inv.* gas-lighter.

allumer [alyme], *v.tr.* 1. to light; *abs.* to light up. 2. to inflame.

s'allumer, to kindle, to catch alight.

allumette [alymet], *s.f.* match.

allure [aly:r], *s.f.* 1. *(a)* walk, bearing; *(b)* pace; *(c)* speed; à toute a., at full speed. 2. *(a)* demeanour; *(b)* aspect, look.

allusion [allyzjɔ̃], *s.f.* allusion; hint.

†alluvial [allyvjal], *a.* alluvial.

almanach [almana], *s.m.* almanac.

aloi [alwa], *s.m.* standard, quality; de bon a., genuine.

alors [alɔ:r], *adv.* 1. then; at the time. 2. therefore, so. 3. *conj.phr.* a. que, when; a. même que, (i) at the very time when; (ii) even though. 4. then, next.

alouette [alwet], *s.f. Z:* lark.

alourd/ir [alurdi:r], *v.tr.* 1. to make heavy. 2. to weigh down (s.o.). *s.m.* **-issement.**

s'alourdir, to grow heavy; to grow stupid.

†aloyau [alwajo], *s.m. Cu:* sirloin.

alpaga [alpaga], *s.m.* alpaca.

alpestre [alpɛstr], *a.* alpine.

alphab/et [alfabe], *s.m.* alphabet. *a.* **-étique,** alphabetical.

alpin/isme [alpinism], *s.m.* mountaineering. *s.m. & f.* **-iste.**

alsacien, -ienne [alzasjɛ̃, -jɛn], *a. & s.* Alsatian.

altérable [alterabl], *a.* liable to deterioration.

altération [alterasjɔ̃], *s.f.* 1. change; deterioration. 2. adulteration.

altercation [alterkasjɔ̃], *s.f.* dispute.

‡altérer [altere], *v.tr.* 1. to change (voice); to impair (health). 2. to tamper with. 3. to make thirsty.

†alternatif [alternatif], *a.* 1. *(a)* alternate; *(b) El:* alternating (current). 2. alternative. 3. *s.f.* alternative, alternative.

alterner [alterne], *v.i. (a)* to alternate; *(b)* to take turns.

altesse [altes], *s.f.* (Royal, etc.) Highness.

alt/ier [altje], *a.* haughty, proud. *adv.* **-ièrement.**

altitude [altityd], *s.f.* altitude, height.

alto [alto], *s.m.* 1. *Mus:* alto. 2. viola. 3. tenor saxhorn.

altru/isme [altryism], *s.m.* altruism. *a. & s.* **-iste.**

aluminium [alyminjɔm], *s.m.* aluminium.

alun [alœ̃], *s.m.* alum.

alun/ir [alyni:r], *v.i.* to land on the moon. *s.m.* **-issage,** landing on the moon.

amabilité [amabilite], *s.f.* 1. amiability; kindness. 2. *pl.* civilities.

amadouer [amadwe], *v.tr.* to coax.

amaigr/ir [amegri:r], *v.tr.* to make thin. *s.m.* **-issement.**

s'amaigrir, to grow thin.

amalgam/e [amalgam], *s.m.* amalgam. *s.f.* **-ation.**

amalgamer [amalgame], *v.tr.* to amalgamate.

s'amalgamer, to blend.

amand/e [amã:d], *s.f.* almond. *s.m.* **-ier,** almond-tree.

amant, -ante [amã, ã-:t], *s.* lover, *f.* mistress.

amarre [ama:r], *s.f.* (mooring) rope.

amarr/er [amare], *v.tr.* to moor. *s.m.* **-age.**

amas [ama], *s.m.* heap, pile.

amass/er [amase], *v.tr.* 1. to pile up. 2. to amass. 3. to gather together. *s.m.* **-age.**

amateur [amatœ:r], *s.* 1. lover (of sth.); a. de cinéma, film enthusiast. 2. amateur.

amateurisme [amatœrism], *s.m. Sp:* amateurism.

amazone [amazon], *s.f.* 1. *(a) Geog:* l'A., the (River) Amazon; *(b)* horsewoman. 2. riding-habit.

ambages [ɔ̃ba:3], *s.f.pl.* circumlocution; parler sans a., to speak to the point.

ambassade [ɔ̃basad], *s.f.* embassy.

ambassadeur [ɔ̃basadœ:r], *s.m.* ambassador.

ambassadrice [ɔ̃basadris], *s.f.* ambassadress; (woman) ambassador.

ambiance [ɔ̃bjã:s], *s.f. (a)* environment; *(b)* atmosphere, tone.

†ambigu [ɔ̃bigy], *a.* ambiguous. *adv.* **-ment.**

ambiguïté [ɔ̃biguite], *s.f.* ambiguity.

†ambitieu/x [ɔ̃bisjø], *a.* ambitious. *adv.* **-sement.**

ambition [ɔ̃bisjɔ̃], *s.f.* ambition.

ambitionner [ɔ̃bisjone], *v.tr.* to covet.

ambre [ɑ̃:br], *s.m.* 1. a. gris, ambergris. 2. a. (jaune), amber.

ambulance [ɑ̃bylɑ̃:s], *s.f.* ambulance.

ambulant [ɑ̃bylɑ̃], a. itinerant; marchand a., pedlar, street hawker.

âme [ɑːm], *s.f.* 1. soul; être l'â d'une entreprise, to be the moving spirit of an undertaking.

amélior/er [ameljɔre], *v.tr.* to ameliorate. *s.f.* -ation.
  s'améliorer, to improve.

amen [amen], *int.* amen.

‡**aménag/er** [amenaʒe], *v.tr.* to fit up. *s.m.* -ement, fittings.

amende [amɑ̃:d], *s.f.* 1. fine. 2. faire a. honorable, to apologize.

amend/er [amɑ̃de], *v.tr.* to amend. -ement, improvement.
  s'amender, to improve.

‡**amener** [amne], *v.tr.* to bring; a. à faire qch., to induce to do sth.

aménité [amenite], *s.f.* amenity; charm.

amenuiser (s') [samønyize], *v.pr.* to become thinner, smaller.

amer[1] [amɛːr]. 1. a. bitter. *s.m.* bitter(s). adv. -èrement.

amer[2], *s.m.* sea-mark, landmark.

américain, -caine [amerikɛ̃, -ken], a. & s. American.

américaniser (s') [samerikanize], *v.pr.* to become americanized.

amer/rir [ameri:r], *v.i.* to alight (on sea); to splash down. *s.m.* -issage, splash-down.

amertume [amertym], *s.f.* bitterness.

améthyste [ametist], *s.f.* amethyst.

ameublement [amœbləmɑ̃], *s.m.* 1. furnishing. 2. furniture.

ami [ami], 1. *s.* friend; mon ami, (i) my dear fellow; (ii) my dear. 2. a. friendly (de, to).

amiable [amjabl], a. amicable; vente à l'a., private sale.

amiante [amjɑ̃:t], *s.m.* asbestos; carton d'a., asbestos board.

†**amical** [amikal], a. friendly. adv. -ement.

amibe [amib], *s.f.* amoeba.

amidon [amidɔ̃], *s.m.* starch.

amidonner [amidɔne], *v.tr.* to starch.

aminc/ir [amɛ̃si:r], *v.tr.* to make thinner, slim. a. -issant. *s.m.* -issement.

†**amiral** [amiral], *s.m.* admiral.

amirauté [amirote], *s.f.* admiralty.

amitié [amitje], *s.f.* 1. friendship, affection. 2. (a) kindness, favour; (b) pl. avec mes sincères amitiés, with kind regards; amitiés à tout le monde, love to all.

ammoniaque [amɔnjak], *s.f.* ammonia.

amnistie [amnisti], *s.f.* amnesty.

amocher [amɔʃe], *v.tr.* F: to damage (sth.); P: to beat (s.o.) up.

amoindr/ir [amwɛ̃dri:r], *v.tr.* to reduce; to belittle. 2. *v.i.* & pr. to diminish. *s.m.* -issement, reduction.

amoll/ir [amɔli:r], *v.tr.* 1. to soften. 2. to weaken, enervate. *s.m.* -issement.

‡**amonc/eler** [amɔ̃sle], *v.tr.* to pile up, heap up. *s.m.* -ellement, heap.

amont [amɔ̃], *s.m.* en a., upstream.

amorce [amɔrs], *s.f.* 1. (a) fuse; (b) percussion cap; (c) priming (of pump). 2. bait.

‡**amor/cer** [amɔrse], *v.tr.* 1. to prime (pump). 2. (a) to bait; (b) to allure. *s.m.* -çage.

amorphe [amɔrf], a. amorphous.

amort/ir [amɔrti:r], *v.tr.* 1. to deaden (pain); to break (fall). 2. to redeem, pay off. a. -issable, redeemable. *s.m.* -issement. *s.m.* -isseur, shock absorber.

amour [amu:r], *s.m.* 1. love, affection. 2. mon a., my love, my sweetheart. 3. cupid.

†**amoureu/x** [amurø]. 1. a. loving; être a. de, to be in love with. 2. *s.m.* lover. adv. -sement.

amour-propre [amurprɔpr], *s.m.* (a) self-respect; pride; (b) self-esteem, vanity.

amov/ible [amɔvibl], a. 1. removable. 2. detachable, interchangeable. *s.f.* -ibilité.

ampère [ɑ̃pɛ:r], *s.m.* El: ampere, F: amp.

ampèremètre [ɑ̃permɛt:r], *s.m.* ammeter.

amphibie [ɑ̃fibi]. 1. a. amphibious; Mil: etc: opération a., combined operation. 2. *s.m.* amphibian.

ample [ɑ̃pl], a. 1. ample. 2. roomy. adv. -ment.

ampleur [ɑ̃plœ:r], *s.f.* fullness; volume.

amplificateur [ɑ̃plifikatœ:r], *s.m.* amplifier.

amplifier [ɑ̃plifje], *v.tr.* to amplify.

ampoule [ɑ̃pul], *s.f.* 1. (electric) bulb. 2. blister. 3. Med: ampoule.

amput/er [ɑ̃pyte], *v.tr.* to amputate. *s.f.* -ation.

amusant [amyzɑ̃], a. amusing, funny.

amuse-gueule [amy:zgœl], *s.m.* F: cocktail snack. pl. amuse-gueules.

amus/er [amyze], *v.tr.* to amuse, entertain. *s.m.* -ement.
  s'amuser, to enjoy oneself.

amygdal/e [amigdal], *s.f.* tonsil. *s.f.* -ite, tonsillitis.

an [ɑ̃], *s.m.* year; tous les ans, every year; le jour de l'an, New Year's Day.

anachronisme [anakrɔnism], *s.m.* anachronism.

anagramme [anagram], *s.f.* anagram.

analo/gie [analɔʒi], *s.f.* analogy. a. -gue, similar.

analphabète [analfabet], a. & s. illiterate.

analyse [anali:z], *s.f.* analysis.

analys/er [analize], *v.tr.* to analyse. a. -able.

analytique [analitik], a. analytical. adv. -ment.

ananas [anana], *s.m.* pineapple.

anarchie [anarʃi], *s.f.* anarchy.

anathème [anatem], *s.m.* ban, curse.

anatom/ie [anatɔmi], *s.f.* anatomy. a. -ique.

†**ancestral** [ɑ̃sestral], a. ancestral.

ancêtre [ɑ̃sɛːtr], *s.m. & f.* ancestor, ancestress.

anchois [ɑ̃ʃwa], *s.m.* anchovy; **beurre d'a.**, anchovy paste.

†**ancien** [ɑ̃sjɛ̃], *a.* 1. ancient, old. 2. former, old, ex-. 3. senior. *adv.* -**nement**, formerly.

ancienneté [ɑ̃sjɛnte], *s.f.* 1. antiquity. 2. seniority; length of service.

ancr/e [ɑ̃ːkr], *s.f.* anchor; **jeter, mouiller, l'a.**, to anchor. *s.m.* -**age**, anchorage.

âne [ɑːn], *s.m.* 1. ass; donkey; **en dos d'â.**, hump-backed (bridge). 2. dunce.

anéant/ir [aneɑ̃tiːr] *v.tr.* to destroy. *s.m.* -**issement**, destruction.

anecdote [anɛgdɔt], *s.f.* anecdote.

ném/ie [anemi], *s.f.* anaemia. *a.*-**ique**.

anémier (s') [sanemje], *v.pr.* to become anaemic.

anémone [anemɔn], *s.f.* anemone.

ânerie [ɑnri], *s.f.* foolish act, remark.

ânesse [ɑnɛs], *s.f.* she-ass.

anesthés/ier [anɛstezje], *v.tr.* to anaesthetize. *s.m.* -**iste**.

anesthésique [anɛstezik], *a. & s.m.* anaesthetic.

ange [ɑ̃ːʒ], *s.m.* angel; **être aux anges**, to walk on air.

angélique [ɑ̃ʒelik], *a.* angelic. *adv.* -**ment**.

angélus [ɑ̃ʒelyːs], *s.m.* angelus(-bell).

angine [ɑ̃ʒin], *s.f.* quinsy; tonsillitis; **a. de poitrine**, angina.

anglais, -aise [ɑ̃glɛ, -ɛːz]. 1. *a.* English; British; **filer à l'anglaise**, to take French leave. 2. *s.* English(wo)man; Briton. 3. *s.m.* English.

angle [ɑ̃ːgl], *s.m.* 1. angle. 2. corner.

anglican, -ane [ɑ̃glikɑ̃, -an], *a. & s.* anglican; **l'église anglicane**, the Church of England.

anglo-normand, -ande [ɑ̃glɔnɔrmɑ̃, ɑ̃ːd], *a. & s.* Anglo-Norman; **les îles anglo-normandes**, the Channel Islands.

anglophile [ɑ̃glɔfil], *a. & s.* anglophile.

anglophobe [ɑ̃glɔfɔb]. 1. *a.* anglophobic. 2. *s.* anglophobe.

anglophone [ɑ̃glɔfɔn], *a.* English-speaking.

anglo-saxon, -onne [ɑ̃glɔsaksɔ̃, -ɔn], *a. & s.* Anglo-saxon; English-speaking (person).

angoissant [ɑ̃gwasɑ̃], *a.* distressing; tense.

angoisse [ɑ̃gwas], *s.f.* anguish; distress.

angoisser [ɑ̃gwase], *v.tr.* to distress.

anguille [ɑ̃giːj], *s.f.* eel.

angulaire [ɑ̃gylɛːr]. 1. *a.* angular; **pierre a.**, corner-stone. 2. *s.m.* **grand a.**, wide-angle lens.

†**anguleux** [ɑ̃gylø] *a.* angular; rugged.

anicroche [anikrɔʃ], *s.f.* difficulty, hitch.

aniline [anilin], *s.f.* aniline.

†**animal** [animal]. 1. *s.m.* animal. 2. *a.* (*a*) animal; (*b*) sensual, brutal.

anim/er [anime], *v.tr.* 1. to animate. 2. to actuate. 3. to enliven. *s.f.* -**ation**. **s'animer**. 1. to come to life. 2. to become lively.

animosité [animozite], *s.f.* animosity, animus.

anis [ani], *s.m. Bot:* anise; **graine d'a.**, aniseed.

anisette [anizɛt], *s.f.* anisette (drink).

ankyloser (s') [sɑ̃kiloze], *v.pr.* to stiffen, to get stiff.

annal/es [annal], *s.f.pl.* annals; (public) records. *s.m.* -**iste**.

anneau [ano], *s.m.* 1. ring. 2. (*a*) link; (*b*) coil (of serpent).

année [ane], *s.f.* year; **à l'a.**, by the year; **étudiants de première a.**, first-year students.

année-lumière [anelymjɛːr], *s.f.* light-year. *pl.* **années-lumière**.

annexe [an(n)ɛks], *s.f.* 1. annexe (to building). 2. (*a*) rider; schedule; appendix; (*b*) enclosure (with letter). 3. *a.* **lettre a.**, covering letter.

annexer [an(n)ɛkse], *v.tr.* 1. to annex. 2. to append, attach, enclose.

annihil/er [an(n)iile], *v.tr.* to destroy. *s.f.* -**ation**, destruction.

anniversaire [anivɛrsɛːr]. 1. *a. & s.m.* anniversary. 2. *s.m.* birthday.

annonce [anɔ̃ːs], *s.f.* 1. (*a*) announcement; (*b*) call (at cards); (*c*) indication. 2. advertisement.

annoncer [anɔ̃se], *v.tr.* 1. to announce; (*at cards*) **a. son jeu**, to declare. 2. to advertise. 3. (*a*) to foretell; (*b*) to indicate.

annonceur, -euse [anɔ̃sœːr, -øːz], *s.* advertiser.

annonciation [anɔ̃sjasjɔ̃], *s.f.* (feast of the) Annunciation.

annot/er [an(n)ɔte], *v.tr.* to annotate. *s.f.* -**ation**.

annuaire [an(n)ɥɛːr], *s.m.* 1. year-book. 2. calendar. 3. (telephone) directory.

†**annuel** [an(n)ɥɛl], *a.* annual, yearly. *adv.* -**lement**.

annuité [an(n)ɥite], *s.f.* annuity.

annulaire [an(n)ylɛːr]. 1. *a.* annular, ring-shaped. 2. *s.m.* ring-finger.

annul/er [an(n)yle], *v.tr.* to annul. *s.m.* -**ement**, *s.f.* -**ation**.

anobl/ir [anɔbliːr], *v.tr.* to ennoble. *s.m.* -**issement**.

anode [anɔd], *s.f. El:* anode.

anodin [anɔdɛ̃]. 1. *a.* soothing; mild, harmless. 2. *s.m.* palliative; pain-killer.

anomalie [anɔmali], *s.f.* anomaly; **a. congénitale**, (physical) deformity.

ânonner [anɔne], *v.tr.* to hum and haw; to mumble.

anonyme [anɔnim]. 1. *a.* (*a*) anonymous; (*b*) **société a.**, limited company. 2. *s.m.* anonymity. *adv.* -**ment**.

anorak [anɔrak], *s.m.* anorak, wind-cheater.

†**anormal** [anɔrmal], *a.* abnormal. *adv.* -**ement**.

anse [ɑ̃s], *s.f.* 1. handle (of jug, basket). 2. bight, bay.

antagonisme [ãtagɔnism], s.m. antagonism.

antagoniste [ãtagɔnist]. 1. a. antagonistic. 2. s. antagonist, opponent.

antarctique [ãtar(k)tik], a. antarctic.

antécédent [ãtesedã]. 1. a. antecedent; previous. 2. s.m. (a) Gram: antecedent; (b) pl. previous history; antecedents.

†antédiluvien [ãtedilyvjɛ̃], a. antediluvian.

antenne [ãten], s.f. 1. Rad: aerial; a. de télévision, T.V. aerial; a. (de) radar, (radar) scanner. 2. antenna, feeler.

antérieur [ãterjœ:r], a. 1. anterior (à, to); earlier. 2. fore-(limb). adv. -ement, previously.

anthologie [ãtɔlɔʒi], s.f. anthology.

anthracite [ãtrasit], s.m. anthracite.

anthropoïde [ãtrɔpɔid], a. & s.m. anthropoid.

anthropologie [ãtrɔpɔlɔʒi], s.f. anthropology. s.m. -ogiste, -ogue, anthropologist.

anti-aérien [ãtiaerjɛ̃], a. anti-aircraft (gun, etc.).

anti-atomique [ãtiatɔmik], a. antinuclear.

antibiotique [ãtibjɔtik], a. & s.m. antibiotic.

antibrouillard [ãtibruja:r], a. & s.m. Aut: (phare) a., fog-lamp.

†anticancéreux [ãtikãserø], a. centre a., cancer hospital.

antichambre [ãtiʃã:br], s.f. waiting-room.

antichoc [ãtiʃɔk], a. inv. shock-proof.

anticiper [ãtisipe], v.tr. to anticipate. s.f. -ation.

anticoagulant [ãtikɔagylã], a. & s.m. anticoagulant.

antidérapant [ãtiderapã], a. non-skid.

antidétonant [ãtidetɔnã], a. & s.m. anti-knock (petrol).

antidote [ãtidɔt], s.m. antidote.

antigel [ãtiʒel], s.m. anti-freeze.

antigivrage [ãtiʒivra:ʒ], s.m. anti-icing.

antigrippal [ãtigripal], a. anti-flu.

antilope [ãtilɔp], s.f. antelope.

antimite [ãtimit]. 1. a. mothproof. 2. s.m. moth-killer.

antimoine [ãtimwan], s.m. antimony.

antiparasite [ãtiparazit], s.m. El: suppressor.

antipath/ie [ãtipati], s.f. antipathy. a. -ique, antipathetic.

antipodes [ãtipɔd], s.m.pl. Antipodes.

antiquaire [ãtike:r], s.m. antique dealer.

antique [ãtik], a. (a) ancient; (b) antique.

antiquité [ãtikite], s.f. 1. antiquity. 2. pl. antiques.

antirouille [ãtiru:j], s.m. rust preventive.

antiseptique [ãtiseptik], a. & s.m. antiseptic.

antithèse [ãtite:z], s.f. antithesis.

antitoxique [ãtitɔksik], a. & s.m. Med: antitoxic.

---

†antituberculeux [ãtityberklø], a. antitubercular; centre a., tuberculosis centre.

antre [ã:tr], s.m. cavern; den, lair.

anxiété [ãksjete], s.f. anxiety.

†anxieu/x [ãksjø], a. anxious, uneasy. adv. -sement.

août [u], s.m. August; au mois d'a., en a., in (the month of) August; le premier, le sept, a. (on) the first, the seventh, of August.

apais/er [apeze], v.tr. 1. to appease, calm. 2. to allay; to quell. s.m. -ement.
s'apaiser, to calm down.

apanage [apana:ʒ], s.m. attribute (de, of).

aparté [aparte], s.m. aside.

apathie [apati], s.f. apathy; listlessness.

apathique [apatik], a. apathetic; listless. adv. -ment.

‡apercevoir [apersəvwa:r], v.tr. to perceive, see.
s'apercevoir de, to perceive, notice; to become aware of.

aperçu [apersy], s.m. 1. glimpse. 2. outline, sketch, summary.

apéritif [aperitif], s.m. drink, aperitif.

à-peu-près [apøpre], s.m.inv. approximation, vague answer.

apicult/ure [apikylty:r], s.f. bee-keeping. s.m. -eur.

apitoyer [apitwaje], v.tr. to move (to pity); to incite to pity.
s'apitoyer sur le sort de qn, to commiserate with s.o.

aplan/ir [aplani:r], v.tr. 1. to flatten; to smooth away. 2. to level. s.m. -issement, flattening; levelling.

aplat/ir [aplati:r], v.tr. to flatten. s.m. -issement, flattening, crushing.
s'aplatir. 1. to go flat. 2. to grovel.

aplomb [aplɔ̃], s.m. 1. d'a., upright; plumb. 2. assurance, self-possession.

apogée [apɔʒe], s.m. apogee; height.

apologie [apɔlɔʒi], s.f. defence, vindication. NOTE: never = EXCUSE, q.v.

apoplectique [apɔplektik], a. & s. apoplectic.

apoplexie [apɔpleksi], s.f. apoplexy.

apostat [apɔsta], a. & s. apostate; turn-coat.

apostolique [apɔstɔlik], a. apostolic.

apostrophe [apɔstrɔf], s.f. apostrophe.

apôtre [apo:tr], s.m. apostle.

‡apparaître [apare:tr], v.i. 1. to appear; to come into sight. 2. to become evident.

apparat [apara], s.m. pomp, display.

appareil [apare:j], s.m. (a) apparatus, outfit; (b) device, appliance; (c) instrument; F: être à l'a., to be on the phone; a. (photographique), camera; a. à coussin d'air, hovercraft.

appareill/er [apareje], v.tr. 1. to install, fit up, equip. 2. abs: to get under way. s.m. -age.

apparence [aparɑ̃:s], *s.f.* **1.** appearance; look. **2.** sauver les apparences, to keep up appearances.

appar/ent [aparɑ̃], *a.* **1.** (*a*) visible; apparent; (*b*) obvious. **2.** apparent, not real. *adv.* **-emment.**

apparenté [aparɑ̃te], *a.* related, akin.

apparier [aparje], *v.tr.* to match.

apparition [aparisjɔ̃], *s.f.* **1.** appearance; publication. **2.** apparition, ghost.

appartement [apartəmɑ̃], *s.m.* flat, *U.S:* apartment.

‡appartenir [apartəni:r], *v.i.* **1.** to belong. **2.** *v. impers.*; il lui appartient de, it falls to him to.

appât [apɑ], *s.m.* (*a*) bait; (*b*) lure.

appauvr/ir [apovri:r], *v.tr.* to impoverish. *s.m.* **-issement.**

appel [apɛl], *s.m.* **1.** appeal. **2.** call; summons. **3.** roll-call.

‡appeler [aple], *v.tr.* **1.** to call (to). **2.** (*a*) to call in, send for; **a.** qn en justice, to sue s.o.; (*b*) être appelé à qch., to be destined for sth. **3.** to call; to name. **4.** (*a*) to appeal to, call on; (*b*) to call for. **5.** *v.i.* en **a.** à qn, to appeal to s.o.

　s'appeler, to be called, named.

appellation [apɛllasjɔ̃], *s.f.* (*a*) name, term; (*b*) trade name; **a.** contrôlée, guaranteed vintage (wine).

append/ice [ap(p)ɛdis], *s.m.* appendix. *s.f.* **-icite,** appendicitis.

appentis [apɑ̃ti], *s.m.* outhouse.

appesantir [apəzɑ̃ti:r], *v.tr.* **1.** to weigh down. **2.** to dull.

appétissant [apetisɑ̃], *a.* appetizing.

appétit [apeti], *s.m.* **1.** appetite. **2.** desire.

applaud/ir [aplodi:r], *v.tr.* **1.** *v.tr.* to applaud. **2.** *v.ind.tr.* **a.** à qch., to approve sth. *s.m.* **-issement,** applause.

applic/ation [aplikasjɔ̃], *s.f.* application. *a.* **-able.**

appliqué [aplike], *a.* studious; painstaking.

appliquer [aplike], *v.tr.* to apply.

　s'appliquer, to work hard.

appointements [apwɛ̃tmɑ̃], *s.m.pl.* salary.

apporter [aporte], *v.tr.* to bring.

apposer [apoze], *v.tr.* to affix, place, put.

appréciable [apresjabl], *a.* appreciable.

†appréciateur [apresjatœ:r], *a.* appreciative.

appréciation [apresjasjɔ̃], *s.f.* **1.** valuation. **2.** appreciation. **3.** rise in value.

apprécier [apresje], *v.tr.* **1.** (*a*) to appraise; (*b*) to estimate. **2.** to appreciate.

appréhender [apreɑ̃de], *v.tr.* to apprehend.

†appréhensif [apreɑ̃sif], *a.* apprehensive (de, of).

appréhension [apreɑ̃sjɔ̃], *s.f.* **1.** understanding. **2.** dread (de, of).

‡apprendre [aprɑ̃:dr], *v.tr.* **1.** (*a*) to learn; (*b*) to hear of. **2.** (*a*) qch. à qn, (*a*) to teach s.o. sth.; (*b*) to tell s.o. sth.

apprent/i [aprɑ̃ti], *s.* (*a*) apprentice; (*b*) novice. *s.m.* **-issage,** apprenticeship.

apprêter [aprɛte], *v.tr.* to prepare; to make ready.

　s'apprêter, to get ready.

apprivoisé [aprivwaze], *a.* tame.

apprivois/er [aprivwaze], *v.tr.* to tame. *s.m.* **-ement,** taming, domestication.

†approbateur [aprobatœ:r], *a.* approving.

approbation [aprobasjɔ̃], *s.f.* approval.

approchant [aprɔʃɑ̃], *a.* approximating, similar (de, to).

approche [aprɔʃ], *s.f.* **1.** approach, drawing near; d'une **a.** difficile, difficult of access. **2.** *pl.* approaches.

approch/er [aprɔʃe]. **1.** *v.tr.* (*a*) to bring, draw, near (de, to); approchez votre chaise, draw up your chair; (*b*) to approach. **2.** *v.i.* (*a*) to approach; (*b*) nous approchons de Paris, we are getting near Paris. *a.* **-able.**

　s'approcher, to come near; to approach; **s'a.** de qch., to come up to sth.

approfondi [aprɔfɔ̃di], *a.* careful; thorough (study, etc.).

approfondir [aprɔfɔ̃di:r], *v.tr.* **1.** to deepen. **2.** to go thoroughly into.

approprié [aproprie], *a.* appropriate.

appropr/ier [aproprie], *v.tr.* **1.** s'a. qch., to appropriate sth. **2.** to arrange, adapt (sth). *s.f.* **-iation.**

approuver [apruve], *v.tr.* **1.** to approve of, be pleased with; **a.** de la tête, to nod approval. **2.** to agree to.

approvision/er [aprovizjone], *v.tr.* to supply (de, with); to provision. *s.m.* **-ement,** stock.

　s'approvisionner, to lay in stores.

†approximat/if [aproksimatif], *a.* approximate. *adv.* **-ivement.**

appui [apɥi], *s.m.* **1.** prop, stay. **2.** support; à hauteur d'a., breast-high.

appuyer [apɥije], *v.tr.* **1.** to support, to prop (sth.) up. **2.** **a.** la main sur la table, to rest, lean, one's hand on the table. **3.** *abs.* **a.** sur, to press (the button); to stress (a word).

　s'appuyer, to lean, rest.

âpre [ɑ:pr], *a.* **1.** rough, harsh. **2.** biting, sharp. **3.** keen (competition). *adv.* **-ment.** *s.f.* **-té,** harshness.

après [aprɛ]. **I.** *prep.* **1.** (*order in time, space*) (*a*) after; jour a. jour, day after day; (*b*) je viens a. lui, I come next to him. **2.** courir a. qn, to run after s.o. **3.** *prep. phr.* d'a., according to; after. **4. a.** avoir dîné, after dining. **II.** *adv.* (*a*) afterwards, later; le jour (d')a., the next day; et a.? what then? (*b*) *conj.phr.* a. que, after, when.

après-demain [aprɛdmɛ̃], *adv.* the day after tomorrow.

après-guerre [aprɛgɛ:r], *s.m.inv.* post-war period.

après-midi [aprɛmidi], *s.m.inv.* afternoon.

à-propos [apropo], *s.m.* aptness (of a remark).

apte [apt], *a.* 1. fitted, qualified. 2. apt.

aptitude [aptityd], *s.f.* aptitude, fitness.

aquaplane [akwaplan], *s.m. Sp:* surfboard; aquaplane.

aquarelle [akwarɛl], *s.f.* water-colour.

aquarium [akwarjɔm], *s.m.* aquarium.

aquatique [akwatik], *a.* aquatic.

aqueduc [ak(ə)dyk], *s.m.* aqueduct.

aquilin [akilɛ̃], *a.* aquiline; nez a., Roman nose.

arabe [arab]. 1. *a.* & *s.* (a) Arab; (b) Arabian. *a.* & *s.m.* Arabic.

arable [arabl], *a.* arable.

arachide [araʃid], *s.f.* peanut, groundnut.

araignée [arɛne], *s.f.* spider.

arbitraire [arbitrɛːr], *a.* arbitrary. *adv.* -ment.

arbitre [arbitr], *s.m.* (a) arbitrator; (b) umpire; referee; (c) arbiter.

arbitr/er [arbitre], *v.tr.* 1. to arbitrate. 2. to umpire, referee. *s.m.* -age, arbitration.

arborer [arbɔre], *v.tr.* to hoist (flag).

arbre [arbr], *s.m.* 1. tree. 2. shaft, axle.

arbrisseau [arbriso], *s.m.* shrubby tree.

arbuste [arbyst], *s.m.* bush.

arc [ark], *s.m.* 1. bow; tir à l'a., archery. 2. arch. 3. *Mth: El:* arc.

arcade [arkad], *s.f.* (a) archway; (b) pl. arcade.

arc-boutant [arkbutã], *s.m.* flying buttress. *pl. arcs-boutants.*

arc-bouter [arkbute], *v.tr.* to buttress. s'a.-bouter, to brace oneself.

arceau [arso], *s.m.* arch (of vault).

arc-en-ciel [arkãsjɛl], *s.m.* rainbow. *pl. arcs-en-ciel* [arkã-].

archaïque [arkaik], *a.* archaic.

archange [arkãːʒ], *s.m.* archangel.

arche [arʃ], *s.f.* arch (of bridge).

archéo/logie [arkeɔlɔʒi], *s.f.* archaeology. *s.m.* -logue, -logist.

archer [arʃe], *s.m.* archer, bowman.

archet [arʃɛ], *s.m.* bow (of violin).

archevêque [arʃəveːk], *s.m.* archbishop.

archi- [arʃi], *prefix.* (*intensive*) archifou, stark mad; archiplein, packed tight.

archipel [arʃipɛl], *s.m.* archipelago.

architecte [arʃitɛkt], *s.m.* architect; a.-urbaniste, town-planner.

architecture [arʃitɛktyːr], *s.f.* architecture.

archives [arʃiːv], *s.f.pl.* archives; records.

archiviste [arʃivist], *s.m.* & *f.* archivist; keeper of records. 2. filing clerk.

arctique [arktik], *a.* arctic.

ard/ent [ardã], *a.* 1. burning, scorching; charbons ardents, live coals. 2. ardent. *adv.* -emment.

ardeur [ardœːr], *s.f.* 1. heat. 2. ardour.

ardoise [ardwaːz], *s.f.* slate.

ardu [ardy], *a.* 1. steep, difficult. 2. arduous, hard.

are [aːr], *s.m.* 100 square metres.

arène [arɛn], *s.f.* arena, *esp.* bull-ring.

aréole [areɔl], *s.f.* halo, nimbus.

arête [arɛt], *s.f.* 1. (fish-)bone. 2. line; edge; ridge.

argent [arʒã], *s.m.* 1. silver. 2. money.

argenterie [arʒãtri], *s.f.* (silver-)plate.

argentin [arʒãtɛ̃], *a.* silvery; tinkling.

argile [arʒil], *s.f.* clay.

argot [argo], *s.m.* slang.

‡arguer [argɥe]. 1. *v.tr.* to infer, assert. 2. *v.i.* to argue.

argument [argymã], *s.m.* argument; outline; synopsis.

argumenter [argymãte], *v.i.* to argue.

aride [arid], *a.* a arid, dry, barren. *s.f.* -ité.

aristocrat/e [aristɔkrat], *s.m.* & *f.* aristocrat. *a.* -ique.

aristocratie [aristɔkrasi], *s.f.* aristocracy.

arithmétique [aritmetik], *s.f.* arithmetic.

arlequin [arlɔkɛ̃], *s.m.* harlequin.

armateur [armatœːr], *s.m.* (ship-)owner.

armature [armatyːr], *s.f.* 1. framework. 2. *El:* armature. 3. *Mus:* key-signature.

arme [arm], *s.f.* 1. arm, weapon; maître d'armes, fencing-master; place d'armes, parade-ground; prise d'armes, ceremonial parade. 2. *pl. Her:* arms.

armée [arme], *s.f.* army; a. de l'air, Air Force.

arm/er [arme]. I. *v.tr.* 1. to arm (de, with). 2. to strengthen, reinforce. 3. to equip (ship). 4. to cock (fire-arm). II. *v.i.* to arm. *s.m.* -ement.

armistice [armistis], *s.m.* armistice.

armoire [armwaːr], *s.f.* 1. wardrobe. 2. cupboard.

armoiries [armwari], *s.f.pl.* (coat of) arms.

armur/e [armyːr], *s.f.* armour. *s.m.* -ier, gunsmith; armourer.

aromat/e [aromat], *s.m. Cu:* spice. *a.* -ique, aromatic.

arôme [aroːm], *s.m.* aroma.

arpent/er [arpãte], *v.tr.* to stride along; to pace up and down. *s.m.* -eur (land-)surveyor.

arqué [arke], *a.* arched, curved.

arquer [arke], *v.tr.* to bend; a. le dos, to hump one's back.

arrache-pied (d') [daraʃpje], *adv.phr.* without interruption.

arracher [araʃe], *v.tr.* to tear (out); to pull (up); s'a. les cheveux, to tear one's hair.

‡arrang/er [arãʒe], *v.tr.* to arrange. 1. to set in order. 2. to contrive. 3. to settle. *s.m.* -ement. s'arranger. 1. to manage, contrive. 2. to come to an agreement.

arrérages [arera:ʒ], *s.m.pl.* arrears.

arrestation [arestasjɔ̃], *s.f.* arrest.

arrêt [arɛ], *s.m.* 1. stop, stoppage; cran d'a., safety-catch; point d'a., stopping place. *P.N:* a. fixe, bus stop. 2. (a) decree; (b) judgment; sentence. 3. arrest.

arrêté [arɛte]. 1. a. fixed, decided (ideas). 2. s.m. decision, decree.

arrêter [arɛte]. I. v.tr. 1. to stop; to detain. 2. to arrest, seize. 3. to decide; a, un jour, to fix a day. II. v.i. to stop, halt.
s'arrêter, to stop.

arrhes [aːr], s.f.pl. (money) deposit.

arrière [arjɛːr]. 1. adv. (en) a. (a) behind. prep.phr. en a. de qch., behind sth.; (c) backwards; faire marche a., to reverse. 2. a.inv. back. Aut: feu a., rear light. 3. s.m. (a) back; (b) stern. 4. s.m Fb: back.

arriéré [arjere], a. 1. in arrears; over-due. 2. backward (child); old-fashioned (pers., idea).

Note. In the following compounds ARRIÈRE is inv., the noun takes the plural. For phonetics, consult the second component.

arrière-boutique, s.f. back-shop.
arrière-cour, s.f. back-yard.
arrière-garde, s.f. rear-guard.
arrière-goût, s.m. after-taste.
arrière-grands-parents, s.m.pl. great-grandparents.
arrière-pensée, s.f. (a) mental reservation; (b) ulterior motive.
arrière-plan, s.m. background.
arrière-saison, s.f. late season.
arrière-scène, s.f. back of the stage.

arrim/er [arime], v.tr. to stow (cargo). s.m. -age. s.m. -eur.

arrivée [arive], s.f. arrival; Sp: (winning)-post.

arriv/er [arive], v.i. (aux. être). 1. (a) to arrive, come; (b) a. à, to reach; (c) il faudra bien en a. là, it must come to that. 2. to succeed. 3. to happen. s.m. & f. -iste, thruster.

arrogance [arɔgɑ̃ːs], s.f. arrogance.

arrog/ant [arɔgɑ̃], a. arrogant, over-bearing. adv. -amment.

‡arroger (s') [sarɔʒe], v.tr.pr. to arro-gate, assume, to oneself.

arrondi [arɔ̃di], a. rounded.

arrond/ir [arɔ̃diːr], v.tr. to round (off).
s'arrondir, to become round; to fill out.

arrondissement [arɔ̃dismɑ̃], s.m. (a) administrative area; (b) (urban) postal district.

arros/er [aroze], v.tr. (a) to water; (b) to irrigate (a meadow). s.m. -age, watering.

arrosoir [arozwaːr], s.m. watering-can.

†arsenal [arsənal], s.m. arsenal.

arsenic [arsənik], s.m. arsenic.

art [aːr], s.m. 1. art; arts d'agrément, accomplishments. 2. skill; ouvrages d'a., construction works.

artère [artɛːr], s.f. 1. Anat: artery. 2. main road, thoroughfare.

†artériel [arterjɛl], a. arterial.

arthrit/e [artrit], s.f. Med: arthritis. a. & s. -ique.

artichaut [artiʃo], s.m. (globe) artichoke.

article [artikl], s.m. 1. (a) article, clause. (b) item; (c) (newspaper) article. 2. article, commodity; pl. goods. 3. Gram: article.

articul/er [artikyle], v.tr. to articulate. s.f. -ation.

artifice [artifis], s.m. 1. artifice; contri-vance. 2. feu d'a., fireworks.

†artificiel [artifisjɛl], a. artificial. adv. -lement.

artill/erie [artijri], s.f. artillery. s.m. -eur, gunner.

artisan [artizã], s.m. artisan, craftsman.

artiste [artist]. 1. s.m. & f. (a) artist (in-cluding musician, etc.); (b) performer; (c) artiste. 2. a. artistic.

artistique [artistik], a. artistic. adv. -ment.

aryen, -yenne [arjɛ̃, -jɛn], a. & s. Aryan.

as [aːs], s.m. ace.

ascendant [as(s)ɑ̃dɑ̃]. 1. a. ascending, upward. 2. s.m. ascendancy.

ascenseur [asɑ̃sœːr], s.m. lift, U.S: ele-vator.

ascension [asɑ̃sjɔ̃], s.f. ascent, ascension; climb. s.m. & f. -niste, mountaineer.

ascète [asɛt], s.m. & f. ascetic.

ascét/ique [asetik], a. & s. ascetic. s.m. -isme, asceticism.

ascorbique [askɔrbik], a. acide a., vitamin C.

asdic [asdik], s.m. Nau: asdic.

asiate [azjat], s. (of pers.) Asian.

asiatique [azjatik], a. & s. Asiatic.

asile [azil], s.m. shelter, refuge; a. des marins, Sailors' Home.

aspect [aspɛ], s.m. 1. sight, aspect. 2. appearance.

asperge [aspɛrʒ], s.f. asparagus.

‡asperger [aspɛrʒe], v.tr. to sprinkle with (holy) water.

aspérité [asperite], s.f. asperity. 1. ruggedness, roughness. 2. harshness.

asphalte [asfalt], s.m. asphalt.

asphyx/ier [asfiksje], v.tr. to asphyxiate.

aspirant [aspirã], s.m. (a) aspirant; candidate; (b) Nau: midshipman; Mil: officer cadet.

aspirateur [aspiratœːr], s.m. vacuum cleaner.

aspir/er [aspire]. 1. v.ind.tr. to aspire. 2. v.tr. (a) to inspire, inhale; (b) to suck up. s.f. -ation.

aspirine [aspirin], s.f. aspirin.

assagir (s') [sasaʒiːr], v.tr. to become wiser; to sober down.

‡assaill/ir [as(s)ajiːr], v.tr. to assault, attack. s.m. -ant, assailant.

assain/ir [aseniːr], v.tr. to make healthier. s.m. -issement, cleansing.

assaisonn/er [asɛzɔne], v.tr. to season (food). s.m. -ement, seasoning.

assassin [asasɛ̃], s. assassin; murderer.

assassin/er [asasine], v.tr. to assassinate. s.m. -at, murder, assassination.

assaut [aso], *s.m.* 1. assault, attack, onslaught. 2. match, bout.

‡**ass/écher** [aseʃe], *v.tr.* to dry, drain. *s.m.* -**èchement**, draining, drainage.

assemblée [asãble], *s.f.* assembly; (public, political) meeting.

assembl/er [asãble], *v.tr.* 1. to assemble; to convene. 2. to assemble (a machine). *s.m.* -**age**.
   s'assembler, to meet together.

assentiment [asãtimã], *s.m.* assent, consent.

‡**asseoir** [aswaːr], *v.tr.* 1. to set, seat. 2. to lay (foundations).
   s'asseoir, to sit down.

assermenté [asɛrmãte], *a.* sworn (in).

asserv/ir [asɛrviːr], *v.tr.* to enslave. *s.m.* -**issement**, bondage.

assesseur [asesœːr], *s.m.* assessor.

assez [ase], *adv.* 1. enough, sufficient; **j'en ai a.!** I've had enough of it. 2. rather, fairly.

assid/u [asidy], *a.* assiduous. *adv.* -**ûment**.

assiduité [asidɥite], *s.f.* assiduity.

‡**assiég/er** [asjeʒe], *v.tr.* 1. to besiege. 2. to beset, crowd round. *s.m.* -**eant**, besieger.

assiette [asjet], *s.f.* 1. (a) stable position; **ne pas être dans son a.**, to be out of sorts; (b) position, site. 2. support, basis. 3. plate; *F:* **l'a. au beurre**, cushy job.

assign/er [asiɲe], *v.tr.* 1. to assign. 2. to summon, subpoena. *s.f.* -**ation**, writ.

assimil/er [as(s)imile], *v.tr.* 1. to assimilate. 2. to liken, compare (à, to, with). *s.f.* -**ation**.

assis [asi], *a.* seated, sitting.

assise [asiːz], *s.f.* 1. seating; foundation. 2. *pl.* assizes.

assistance [asistãs], *s.f.* 1. audience; spectators. 2. assistance, help.

assistant, -ante [asistã, ã-tt], *s.* (a) bystander, onlooker, spectator; (b) member of the audience.

assister [asiste], 1. *v.i.* to be present (à, at). 2. *v.tr.* to help, assist.

association [asɔsjasjɔ̃], *s.f.* 1. association (of ideas). 2. (a) society, company; association; (b) partnership.

associé [asɔsje], *s.* partner.

associer [asɔsje], *v.tr.* to associate, connect.
   s'associer. 1. to share (à, in). 2. to enter into partnership; to associate.

assombr/ir [asɔ̃briːr], *v.tr.* (a) to darken, obscure; (b) to cast a gloom over. *s.m.* -**issement**.
   s'assombrir. (a) to cloud over; (b) to become gloomy.

assomm/er [asɔme], *v.tr.* 1. to fell (an ox). 2. *F:* to bore (s.o.). *a.* -**ant**, *F:* boring.

assommoir [asɔmwaːr], *s.m.* 1. club, bludgeon. 2. *F:* low pub.

assorti [asɔrti], *a.* 1. matched, paired. 2. assorted, mixed.

assort/ir [asɔrtiːr], *v.tr.* to assort, match. *s.m.* -**iment**.

assoup/ir [asupiːr], *v.tr.* to make drowsy. *s.m.* -**issement**, drowsiness.
   s'assoupir, to doze off.

assourd/ir [asurdiːr], *v.tr.* 1. to deafen. 2. to deaden (sound). *a.* -**issant**, deafening. *s.m.* -**issement**, deadening.

assouv/ir [asuviːr], *v.tr.* to appease (hunger). *s.m.* -**issement**.
   s'assouvir, to satiate oneself.

assujett/ir [asyʒetiːr], *v.tr.* to subdue; to curb; to compel. *s.m.* -**issement**.

assumer [asyme], *v.tr.* to assume; to take upon oneself.

assurance [asyrãːs], *s.f.* 1. assurance. 2. insurance; assurances sociales, national insurance.

assuré [asyre]. 1. *a.* firm, sure; assured, confident; **voix mal assurée**, unsteady voice. 2. *s.* policy-holder; **a. social**, member of the national insurance scheme. *adv.* -**ment**, certainly.

assur/er [asyre], *v.tr.* 1. (a) to make firm; to secure; (b) to ensure. 2. to assure; to declare. 3. to insure. *s.m.* -**eur**, insurer.
   s'assurer. 1. to make sure. 2. to make sure of, to secure. 3. to get insured.

astérique [asterisk], *s.m.* asterisk.

asthmatique [asmatik], *a.* asthmatic.

asthme [asm], *s.m.* asthma.

asticot [astiko], *s.m.* maggot; *Fish:* gentle.

astiqu/er [astike], *v.tr.* to polish, furbish. *s.m.* -**age**.

†**astral** [astral], *a.* astral.

astre [astr], *s.m.* heavenly body; star.

‡**astreindre** [astrɛ̃ːdr], *v.tr.* to compel; to tie down.

astringent [astrɛ̃ʒã], *a. & s.m.* astringent.

astro/logie [astrɔlɔʒi], *s.f.* astrology. *s.m.* -**logue**, astrologer.

astronaute [astronoːt], *s.m.* astronaut. *s.f.* -**ique**, space travel.

astronef [astrɔnef], *s.m.* space ship.

astrono/mie [astronɔmi], *s.f.* astronomy. *s.m.* -**me**, astronomer. *a.* -**mique**, astronomic(al). *adv.* -**iquement**.

astuce [astys], *s.f.* 1. astuteness; wile. 2. *F:* gadget.

†**astucieu/x** [astysjø], *a.* astute, artful. *adv.* -**sement**.

atelier [atəlje], *s.m.* (a) (work)shop, workroom; (b) studio.

athé/e [ate]. 1. *a.* atheistic. 2. *s.* atheist. *s.m.* -**isme**.

ath/lète [atlɛt], *s.m.* athlete. *a.* -**létique**, athletic. *s.m.* -**létisme**, athletics.

atlantique [atlãtik], *a.* l'**océan A.**, **l'A.**, the Atlantic (Ocean).

atlas [atlaːs], *s.m.* atlas.

atmos/phère [atmosfɛːr], *s.f.* atmosphere. *a.* -**phérique**.

atoll [atɔl], *s.m.* atoll; coral island.

atome [atoːm], *s.m.* atom.

atomique [atɔmik], *a.* atomic; **pile a.,** atomic pile; **bombe a.,** atom bomb; **sous-marin a.,** nuclear submarine.

atomiser [atɔmizœr], *v.tr.* spray(er).

atout [atu], *s.m.* trump.

âtre [ɑːtr], *s.m.* fire-place, hearth(-stone).

atroce [atrɔs], *a.* atrocious; agonizing. *adv.* **-ment.**

atrocité [atrɔsite], *s.f.* 1. atrociousness. 2. atrocity.

attabler (s') [satable], *v.pr.* to sit down to table.

attache [ataʃ], *s.f.* 1. fastening; tying up. 2. tie, fastening; leash.

attaché [ataʃe]. 1. *a.* (*a*) fastened, tied-up; (*b*) attached, devoted. 2. *s.m.* (military) attaché.

attache-lettre [ataʃletr], *s.f.* paper clip. *pl.* **attache-lettres.**

attacher [ataʃe], *v.tr.* to attach; to fasten, bind. *s.m.* **-ement,** affection. **s'attacher.** 1. to attach oneself; to cling. 2. to apply oneself, to stick, to (a task).

attaque [atak], *s.f.* attack, onslaught.

attaquer [atake], *v.tr.* to attack. **s'attaquer** à, to make an attack (à, on).

attardé [atarde], *a.* 1. belated; late. 2. *s.m.* **les attardés,** the mentally retarded.

attarder [atarde], *v.tr.* to keep (s.o.) late. **s'attarder,** to linger, loiter.

‡**atteindre** [atɛːdr], *v.tr.* (*a*) to reach; to overtake; to attain; (*b*) to hit; **être atteint** (i) **au bras,** to be wounded in the arm; (ii) **d'une maladie,** to be attacked by a disease.

atteinte [atɛːt], *s.f.* 1. reach; **hors d'a.,** out of reach. 2. blow, hit; **porter a. à,** to injure.

‡**attel er** [atle], *v.tr.* 1. to harness. 2. to couple. *s.m.* **-age,** team.

attenant [atnɑ̃], *a.* contiguous (à, to), adjoining.

attendre [atɑ̃ːdr], *v.tr.* 1. to wait for, to await; **se faire a.,** to be late; **attendez donc! wait a bit!;** *en attendant,* meanwhile; *conj.phr.* **en attendant que,** till. 2. to expect. **s'attendre à,** to expect.

attendr i [atɑ̃dri], *a.* fond; compassionate.

attendr/ir [atɑ̃driːr], *v.tr.* to soften. *s.m.* **-issant,** moving. *s.m.* **-issement,** pity. **s'attendrir,** to be moved (to pity).

attendu [atɑ̃dy]. 1. *prep.* considering; owing to. 2. *conj.phr.* **a. que,** considering that.

attentat [atɑ̃ta], *s.m.* outrage; crime.

attente [atɑ̃ːt], *s.f.* 1. wait(ing); **salle d'a.** waiting-room. 2. expectation.

attenter [atɑ̃te], *v.ind.tr.* to make an attempt (à, on).

†**attent/if** [atɑ̃tif], *a.* attentive; careful. *s.m.* **-ivement.**

attention [atɑ̃sjɔ̃], *s.f.* attention; care; **faites a.!** take care! **a.!** look out!

atténu/er [atenɥe], *v.tr.* to attenuate, lessen. *s.f.* **-ation.**

atterré [atere], *a.* crushed, stunned (by news).

atterrer [atere], *v.tr.* to overwhelm, astound; to strike with consternation.

atterr/ir [ateriːr], *v.i. Av:* to land. *s.m.* **-issage,** landing.

attest/er [ateste], *v.tr.* to testify to. *s.f.* **-ation.**

attiéd/ir [atjediːr], *v.tr.* to make tepid. *s.m.* **-issement,** cooling (off).

attirail [atiraj], *s.m.* gear; outfit.

attirer [atire], *v.tr.* 1. (*a*) to attract, draw; (*b*) **s'a. un blâme,** to incur a reprimand. 2. to lure, entice.

attisée [atize], *s.f. Fr.C:* (bright) fire.

attiser [atize], *v.tr.* to poke (fire).

attitré [atitre], *a.* regular, appointed (agent).

attitude [atityd], *s.f.* attitude.

attraction [atraksjɔ̃], *s.f.* 1. (*a*) attraction (of magnet); (*b*) attractiveness. 2. *pl. Th:* music-hall show.

attrait [atrɛ], *s.m.* attraction, lure.

attrape [atrap], *s.f.* trick, catch.

attrape-nigaud [atrapnigo], *s.m.* booby-trap. *pl.* **attrape-nigauds.**

attraper [atrape], *v.tr.* to catch. 1. (*a*) to (en)trap; (*b*) to trick, cheat. 2. (*a*) to seize; (*b*) to hit; (*c*) **a. un rhume,** to catch (a) cold.

attrayant [atrɛjɑ̃], *a.* attractive.

attribu/er [atribɥe], *v.tr.* 1. to assign. 2. to attribute; to impute. 3. to claim. *a.* **-able.**

attribut [atriby], *s.m.* attribute.

attribution [atribysjɔ̃], *s.f.* 1. attribution. 2. sphere of duties; functions.

attrister [atriste], *v.tr.* to sadden.

attroupement [atrupmɑ̃], *s.m.* (unlawful) assembly, *F:* mob.

au [o] = **à le.**

aubaine [obɛn], *s.f.* windfall, godsend; *Fr.C: F:* bargain.

aube¹ [ob], *s.f.* 1. dawn. 2. *Ecc:* alb.

aube², *s.f.* paddle, blade (of wheel, of turbine); vane (of fan).

aubépine [obepin], *s.f.* hawthorn.

auberg/e [obɛrʒ], *s.f.* inn. *s.m. & f.* **-iste,** innkeeper.

aucun [okœ̃]. 1. *pron.* (*a*) anyone, any; (*b*) no one; not any; **je n'ai a. soupçon,** I haven't the slightest suspicion. 2. *a.* any. *adv.* **-ement,** not at all.

audace [odas], *s.f.* 1. boldness, daring. 2. impudence.

†**audacieu/x** [odasjø], *a.* 1. bold, daring. 2. impudent. *adv.* **-sement.**

au-dessous [odsu], *adv.* 1. below (it); underneath. 2. *prep.phr.* **au-d. de,** below, under; beneath.

au-dessus [odsy], *adv.* 1. above (it); over. 2. *prep.phr.* **a.-d. de,** above; over.

au-devant [odvɑ̃], *adv.* (only in such phrases as) 1. **aller a.-d.,** to go to meet (sth.). 2. *prep.phr.* **aller a.-d. de** qn, to go to meet s.o.; **aller a.-d. des désirs de** qn, to anticipate s.o.'s wishes.

audible [ɔdibl], a. audible.

audience [ɔdjɑ̃:s], s.f. (a) hearing; (b) sitting, court.

†audio-visuel [ɔdjovizɥɛl], a. audio-visual.

auditeur, -trice [oditœ:r, -tris], s. hearer, listener; Rad: programme des auditeurs, request programme.

auditoire [oditwa:r], s.m. audience.

auge [o:ʒ], s.f. feeding-trough.

augment/er [ɔgmɑ̃te], v.tr. & i. to increase. s.f. -ation.

augurer [ɔgyre], v.tr. to augur, forecast.

auguste [ɔgyst], a. majestic.

aujourd'hui [oʒurdɥi], adv. today; nowadays.

aumône [omo:n], s.f. alms.

aumônier [omonje], s.m. chaplain.

aune [o:n], s.f. alder.

auparavant [oparavɑ̃], adv. before(hand), previously.

auprès [oprɛ], adv. 1. close to. 2. prep. phr. a. de; (a) close to, by; with; (b) compared with.

auquel [okɛl]. See LEQUEL.

auréole [oreɔl], s.f. halo.

aurore [ɔrɔ:r], s.f. (a) dawn, daybreak; (b) a. boréale, aurora borealis.

auspices [ɔspis], s.m.pl. auspices; omen(s).

aussi [osi]. 1. adv. (a) as; (in comparisons) a. grand que, as tall as; (b) also, too; (c) conj.phr. aussi bien que, as well as. 2. conj. (a) therefore, so; (b) a. bien, moreover, besides.

aussitôt [osito], adv. (a) immediately, at once; a. dit, a. fait, no sooner said than done; (b) conj.phr. a. que, as soon as.

austère [ɔstɛ:r], a. austere. adv. -ment.

austérité [ɔsterite], s.f. austerity.

†australien, -ienne [ɔstraljɛ̃, -jɛn], a. & s. Australian.

autant [otɑ̃], adv. 1. as much, so much; as many, so many. 2. a. que, as much as, as many as; (b) as far as, as near as. 3. a. de, as much, so much, so many. 4. (a) conj.phr. d'a., more especially as; (b) d'a. plus, (all) the more.

autel [otɛl], s.m. altar.

auteur [otœ:r], s.m. 1. author, perpetrator; être l'a. d'un accident, to be the cause of an accident. 2. author, writer; droit d'a., copyright; droits d'a., royalties.

authenti/cité [otɑ̃tisite], s.f. authenticity. a. -que, authentic.

auto [oto], s.f. (motor)car.

autobiograph/ie [otobjɔgrafi], s.f. autobiography. a. -ique, autobiographical.

autobus [otobys], s.m. bus.

autocar [otoka:r], s.m. (motor)coach, (country) bus.

autochenille [otoʃni:j], s.f. (a) caterpillar tractor; (b) half-track vehicle.

autocopier [otokɔpje], v.tr. to duplicate (circulars, etc.).

autocrate [otokrat], s.m. autocrat.

autocratie [otokrasi], s.f. autocracy.

autocratique [otokratik], a. autocratic. adv. -ment.

autocuiseur [otokɥizœ:r], s.m. Cu: pressure-cooker.

autodébrayage [otodebrɛja:ʒ], s.m. Aut: automatic clutch.

autodétermination [otodetɛrminasjɔ̃], s.f. self-determination.

auto-école [otoekɔl], s.f. school of motoring. pl. auto-écoles.

autogare [otoga:r], s.f. coach-, bus-station.

autographe [otograf]. 1. a. autograph(ic). 2. s.m. autograph.

automate [otomat], s.m. automaton.

automation [otomasjɔ̃], s.f. automation.

automatique [otomatik], a. automatic. adv. -ment.

automatiser [otomatize], v.tr. to automatize.

†automnal [otɔmnal], a. autumnal.

automne [otɔn], s.m. autumn, U.S: fall.

automobile [otomobil]. 1. a. canot a., motor-boat; salon a., motor show. 2. s.f. (motor) car.

automobiliste [otomobilist], s.m. & f. motorist.

automoteur, -trice [otomotœ:r, -tris]. 1. a. self-propelling. 2. s.f. automotrice, rail-car.

autopropulsé [otoprɔpylse], a. self-propelled.

autopsie [otopsi], s.f. post-mortem (examination).

autorail [otora:j], s.m. rail-car.

autoris/er [otorize], v.tr. to authorize; to sanction. s.f. -ation, permit.

autoritaire [otoritɛ:r], a. authoritative, dictatorial. adv. -ment.

autorité [otorite], s.f. authority.

autoroute [otorut], s.f. motorway, U.S: expressway.

auto-stop [otostɔp], s.m. hitch-hiking; faire de l'a.-s., to hitch-hike.

autour [otu:r], adv. 1. round; about. 2. prep.phr. a. de, round, about.

autre [o:tr], a. & pron. 1. (a) other, further; (b) nous autres Anglais, we English; (c) d'un jour à l'a., any day; de temps à a., now and then; (d) l'un et l'a., both; (e) l'un ou l'a., either; ni l'un ni l'a., neither; (f) les uns . . . les autres . . , some . . . some . . .; (g) l'un l'a., each other. 2. (a) other, different; j'en ai vu bien d'autres, I've been through worse than that; (b) nul a., personne (d')a., nobody else; F: à d'autres! nonsense! (c) indef.pron.m. a. chose, something else; c'est tout a. chose! that's quite a different matter! adv. -ment, otherwise.

autrefois [otrəfwa], adv. formerly.

†**autrichien, -ienne** [otriʃjɛ̃, -jɛn], a. & s. Austrian.

autruche [otryʃ], s.f. ostrich.

autrui [otrɥi], pron.indef: others; other people.

auvent [ovɑ̃], s.m. porch roof.

aux [o] = à les.

auxiliaire [oksiljɛ:r]. 1. a. auxiliary. 2. s. auxiliary; assistant.

auxquels, -elles [okɛl]. See LEQUEL.

avachi [avaʃi], a. slack, sloppy.

aval [aval], s.m. en a., downstream.

avalanche [avalɑ̃:ʃ], s.f. avalanche.

avaler [avale], v.tr. to swallow; to devour.

avance [avɑ̃:s], s.f. 1. advance, lead. 2. projection. 3. (a) advance, loan. (b) pl. advances. 4. adv.phr. (a) payer d'a., to pay in advance; (b) payable à l'a., payable in advance; (c) l'horloge est en a., the clock is fast; nous sommes en a., we are early.

avancé [avɑ̃se], a. advanced; (of pupil) forward; à une heure avancée, at a late hour.

†**avanc/er** [avɑ̃se]. I. v.tr. 1. to advance, put forward. 2. to make earlier. 3. a. de l'argent, to advance money. 4. to promote. II. v.i. 1. to advance, move forward; to progress. 2. (a) to be ahead of time; (b) to project. s.m. -ement.

s'avancer. 1. to move forward, to advance. 2. to progress. 3. to jut out.

avanie [avani], s.f. insult; snub.

avant [avɑ̃]. I. 1. prep. before. 2. (a) prep.phr. a. de + inf., before; a. de partir, before leaving; (b) conj.phr. a. que + sub., before; a. que vous (ne) partiez, before you leave. 3. adv. before. 4. adv. forward. 5. adv.phr. en a., in front; forward; prep.phr. en a. de, ahead of. II. s.m. 1. front. 2. Sp: forward.

avantage [avɑ̃ta:ʒ], s.m. 1. advantage; avoir l'a., to have the best of it. 2. (tennis) (ad)vantage.

†**avantager** [avɑ̃taʒe], v.tr. to favour.

†**avantageu/x** [avɑ̃taʒø], a. advantageous. adv. -sement.

NOTE. In the following compounds AVANT is inv., the noun or adj. takes the plural. For phonetics, consult the second component.

avant-bras, s.m. forearm.

avant-centre, s.m. Sp: centre-forward.

avant-cour, s.f. fore-court.

avant-coureur, s.m. forerunner.

†**avant-dernier,** a. last but one.

avant-garde, s.f. advanced guard; avant-garde.

avant-goût, s.m. foretaste.

avant-hier, adv. the day before yesterday.

avant-plan, s.m. foreground.

avant-première, s.f. Cin: etc: preview.

avant-propos, s.m. preface.

avant-veille, s.f. two days before.

avar/e [ava:r]. 1. a. miserly; sparing. 2. s. miser. s.f. -ice, avarice. adv. -ement.

†**avaricieu/x** [avarisjø], a. avaricious, stingy. adv. -sement.

avarie [avari], s.f. damage, injury.

avarier [avarje], v.tr. to damage, spoil.

avec [avɛk]. 1. prep. with. 2. adv. with (it).

aven [avɛn], s.m. Geog: swallow-hole, aven.

avenant [avnɑ̃], a. 1. attractive, pleasing. 2. à l'a., in keeping; to match.

avènement [avɛnmɑ̃], s.m. accession.

avenir [avni:r], s.m. future; dans l'a., at some future date; à l'a., in future.

aventure [avɑ̃ty:r], s.f. 1. adventure. 2. chance, hazard; à l'a., at random. 3. dire la bonne a., to tell fortunes.

aventur/ier [avɑ̃tyrje], s.m. -ier, adventurer.

s'aventurer, to venture.

†**aventureux** [avɑ̃tyrø], a. venturesome.

avenue [avny], s.f. avenue; drive.

avéré [avere], a. authenticated; avowed.

averse [avɛrs], s.f. sudden shower.

aversion [avɛrsjɔ̃], s.f. aversion; dislike; prendre en a., to take a dislike to.

averti [avɛrti], a. experienced; wide-awake; well-informed.

avert/ir [avɛrti:r], v.tr. to warn, notify. s.m. -issement, warning.

avertisseur [avɛrtisœ:r], s.m. alarm; a. d'incendie, fire-alarm; Aut: hooter.

†**aveu** [avø], s.m. confession.

aveugl/e [avœgl], a. blind; s. blind man; blind woman. adv. -ement.

aveugl/er [avœgle], v.tr. (a) to blind; (b) to dazzle. s.f. -a. -ant, s.m. -ement.

aviateur, -trice [avjatœ:r, -tris], s. aviator; airman, airwoman.

aviation [avjasjɔ̃], s.f. aviation; champ d'a., airfield.

aviculture [avikylty:r], s.f. poultry-farming.

avid/e [avid], a. greedy; eager. s.f. -ité, greed. adv. -ement.

avil/ir [avili:r], v.tr. to degrade. a. -issant. s.m. -issement.

avion [avjɔ̃], s.m. aircraft; (a) de ligne, airliner; (on letter) par a. (by) air-mail.

aviron [avirɔ̃], s.m. oar; scull; Fc: paddle (of canoe); cercle d'a., rowing-club.

avis [avi], s.m. 1. (a) opinion, judgment; à mon a., in my opinion; j'ai changé d'a., I have changed my mind; (b) advice. 2. notice, announcement.

avisé [avize], a. prudent; far-seeing.

aviser [avize], v.tr. to advise; to inform. s'aviser, to bethink oneself; s'a. de, to take it into one's head to.

avitaminose [avitaminoːz], s.f. Med: vitamin deficiency.

avocat [avɔka], s. barrister; counsel.

avoine [avwan], *s.f.* oats; farine d'a., oat-meal.

‡**avoir** [avwa:r]. I. *v.tr.* (*the aux. of all tr. and many intr. vbs.*) 1. (*a*) to have, possess; a. beaucoup d'amis, to have many friends; (*b*) a. dix ans, to be ten years old. 2. to get, obtain; a. le prix, to win the prize; a. Paris, to get Paris, (i) on the phone, (ii) on the radio. 3. to feel unwell; qu'avez-vous? what's the matter with you? qu'est-ce qu'il a? (i) what's wrong with him? (ii) *F:* what's bitten him? what's up with him? 4. a. qch. à faire, to have sth. to do. 5. *impers.* y avoir; (*a*) il y a, there is, there are; il n'y a pas de quoi, don't mention it; (*b*) qu'est-ce qu'il y a? what's the matter? (*c*) il y a deux ans, two years ago. 6. (*aux. use*) j'ai fini, I have finished. II. *s.m.* property; *Com:* doit et a., debit and credit.

avoisinant [avwazinã], *a.* neighbouring.

avoisiner [avwazine], *v.tr.* to border on.

avortement [avɔrtə], *v.i.* to miscarry. *s.m. -ement;* (i) miscarriage; (ii) abortion.

avoué [avwe], *s.m.* = solicitor.

avouer [avwe], *v.tr.* 1. to acknowledge. 2. to confess.

avril [avril], *s.m.* April; poisson d'a., April fool; le premier a., April fool's day.

axe [aks], *s.m.* 1. axis. 2. axle.

axiom/e [aksjɔːm], *s.m.* axiom. *a. -atique.*

azote [azɔt], *s.m.* nitrogen.

azur [azy:r], *s.m.* azure, blue; la Côte d'A., the Riviera.

B

B, b [be], *s.m.* (the letter) B, b.

babill/er [babije], *v.i.* to chatter. *s.m. -age. s. -ard, -arde,* chatterbox.

bâbord [babɔːr], *s.m. Nau:* port (side).

babouin [babwɛ̃], *s.m.* baboon.

bac¹ [bak], *s.m.* (*a*) ferry-boat; (*b*) ferry.

bac², *s.m. Sch: F:* = G.C.E.

baccalauréat [bakalɔrea], *s.m.* = General Certificate of Education.

bâche [baʃ], *s.f.* tarpaulin.

bachelier, -ière [baʃəlje, -jɛːr], *s. Sch:* one who has passed the baccalauréat.

bachot [baʃo], *s.m. Sch: F:* = G.C.E.

bacille [basil], *s.m.* bacillus.

bâcl/er [bakle], *v.tr.* to scamp (work). *s.m. -age,* scamping (of work).

bactér/ie [bakteri], *s.f.* bacterium, *pl. -ia. s.m. -icide.*

bactériolog/ie [bakterjɔlɔʒi], *s.f.* bacteriology. *a. -ique. s. -iste.*

badaud [bado], *s.* saunterer, stroller.

badigeonn/er [badiʒɔne], *v.tr.* to distemper. *s.m. -age,* distempering.

badin/er [badine], *v.i.* to jest. 2. *v.tr.* to tease. *s.m. -age.*

bafouer [bafwe], *v.tr.* to scoff, jeer, at.

bafouill/er [bafuje], *v.tr. & i.* to splutter, to stammer; (*of engine*) to miss, to splutter. *s.m. -age. s. -eur, -euse.*

bagage [baga:ʒ], *s.m.* 1. baggage. 2. *pl.* luggage.

bagarre [bagar], *s.f.* brawl.

bagarrer (se) [səbagare], *v.pr.* to scuffle, to brawl.

bagatelle [bagatel], *s.f.* trifle, bagatelle.

bagne [baɲ], *s.m.* convict prison.

bagnole [baɲɔl], *s.f. F:* (motor) car.

bague [bag], *s.f.* (jewelled) ring.

baguette [baget], *s.f.* rod, wand.

bah [ba], *int.* nonsense!

bahut [bay], *s.m.* cupboard, cabinet.

baie¹ [bɛ], *s.f. Geog:* bay.

baie², *s.f.* (window) bay.

baie³, *s.f.* berry.

baignade [bɛɲaːd], *s.f.* (*a*) bathe; (*b*) bathing-place.

baigner [beɲe]. 1. *v.tr.* (*a*) to bathe; to dip; (*b*) (*of sea*) to wash (coast); (*c*) to bath (child). 2. *v.i.* to soak, se baigner, to bathe.

baigneur, -euse [beɲœːr, -øːz], *s.* 1. bather. 2. bath attendant.

baignoire [beɲwaːr], *s.f.* 1. bath. 2. *Th:* ground-floor box.

‡**bail** [baːj], *s.m.* lease.

bâill/er [baːje], *v.i.* to yawn. *s.m. -ement.*

bâillonn/er [bɑjɔne], *v.tr.* to gag. *s.m. -ement.*

bain [bɛ̃], *s.m.* bath; (*a*) salle de bains, bathroom; (*b*) *pl.* watering-place; spa; (*c*) bathe.

bain-marie [bɛ̃mari], *s.m. Cu:* double saucepan. *pl. bains-marie.*

baïonnette [bajɔnet], *s.f.* bayonet.

baiser [beze]. I. *v.tr. b.* qn sur la joue, to kiss s.o. on the cheek. II. *s.m.* kiss.

baissant [bɛsɑ̃], *a.* declining; setting.

baisse [bes], *s.f.* 1. subsidence; ebb. 2. fall, drop (in prices).

baisser [bese]. 1. *v.tr.* to lower; to let down. 2. *v.i.* (*a*) to fall; to sink. II. *s.m. b.* du rideau, fall of the curtain. se baisser, to stoop.

bal [bal], *s.m.* ball, dance. *pl. bals.*

balad/er [balade], *v.i. & pr. F:* to stroll, to saunter; se b. en auto, to go for a drive. *s.f. -euse,* inspection lamp.

balafre [balafr], *s.f.* 1. slash, gash. 2. scar.

balafrer [balafre], *v.tr.* 1. to gash, slash. 2. visage balafré, scarred face.

balai [bale], *s.m.* broom; b. mécanique, carpet-sweeper; manche à b., (i) broomstick; (ii) *Av:* joy-stick.

balance [balɑ̃ːs], *s.f.* 1. balance; (pair of) scales. 2. balancing; balance.

‡balanc/er [balɑ̃se]. I. v.tr. 1. to balance. 2. to swing, rock. s.m. -ement. II. v.i. to swing.

se balancer, to swing; to rock.

balançoire [balɑ̃swaːr], s.f. (child's) swing.

‡balay/er [baleje], v.tr. to sweep (up); T.V: to scan. s.m. -age, scanning.

balayeur, -euse [balejœːr, -øːz], s. 1. sweeper. 2. s.f. balayeuse, (machine) street-sweeper.

balayures [balejyr], s.f.pl. sweepings.

balbuti/er [balbysje], v.i. 1. to stammer. 2. v.tr. to stammer out. s.m. -ement.

balcon [balkɔ̃], s.m. 1. balcony. 2. Th: dress-circle.

baleine [balɛn], s.f. 1. whale. 2. whalebone.

baleinier, -ière [balenje, -jɛːr]. 1. s.m. whaler. 2. s.f. baleinière, whale-boat.

balise [baliz], s.f. 1. beacon; sea-mark. 2. Av: ground light.

balis/er [balize], v.tr. (a) to buoy, mark out (channel); (b) to mark out (runway); piste balisée, flare-path. s.m. -age.

balistique [balistik], s.f. ballistics.

balivernes [balivɛrn], s.f.pl. F: twaddle.

ballade [balad], s.f. ballad.

ballant [balɑ̃], a. swinging, dangling.

balle [bal], s.f. 1. ball. 2. bullet. 3. bale.

ballerine [balrin], s.f. ballerina.

ballet [balɛ], s.m. ballet.

ballon [balɔ̃], s.m. 1. balloon. 2. football.

ballot [balo], s.m. bundle, bale.

ballottage [balɔtaːʒ], s.m. Pol: second ballot.

ballott/er [balɔte]. 1. v.tr. to toss (about). 2. v.i. to toss (on the water). s.m. -ement.

balnéaire [balneɛːr], a. station b., watering-place.

balourd [baluːr], s. awkward person. s.f. -ise, blunder.

baltique [baltik], a. Baltic.

balustrade [balystrad], s.f. 1. balustrade. 2. (hand-)rail; railing.

balustres [balystr], s.m.pl. banisters.

bambou [bɑ̃bu], s.m. bamboo(-cane).

†banal [banal], a. commonplace.

banalis/er [banalize], v.tr. to render commonplace. s.f. -ation.

banalité [banalite], s.f. 1. banality, triteness. 2. commonplace remark.

bana/ne [banan], s.f. banana. s.m. -nier, (i) banana-tree; (ii) banana boat.

banc [bɑ̃], s.m. 1. bench, form; pew; b. des prévenus, dock; b. du jury, jury-box. 2. b. de sable, sand-bank. 3. shoal (of fish).

bancaire [bɑ̃kɛːr], a. (concerning banking.

†bancal [bɑ̃kal], a. (a) bandy-legged; (b) rickety.

bandage [bɑ̃daːʒ], s.m. 1. bandage. 2. tyre.

bande¹ [bɑ̃d], s.f. (a) band, strip; (b) Rad: b. de fréquence, frequency band; (c) Cin: etc: b. sonore, sound track; b. magnétique, recording tape; (d) (iron) tyre; (e) b. illustrée, strip cartoon; (f) (at billiards) cushion.

bande², s.f. 1. band, party, troop. 2. flight, flock; pack.

band/er [bɑ̃de], v.tr. 1. to bandage, bind (up). 2. to bend (a bow).

bander² (se), v.pr. to band together.

bandit [bɑ̃di], s.m. (a) bandit; (b) ruffian.

bandoulière [bɑ̃duljɛːr], s.f. shoulder-strap; en b., slung (across the back).

banlieue [bɑ̃ljø], s.f. suburbs; outskirts. s.m. -sard, suburbanite.

bannière [banjɛːr], s.f. banner.

bann/ir [baniːr], v.tr. to banish; to exile. s.m. -issement, banishment.

banque [bɑ̃ːk], s.f. bank. s.f. -route, bankruptcy.

banquet [bɑ̃kɛ], s.m. banquet, feast.

banquette [bɑ̃kɛt], s.f. bench, seat.

banquier [bɑ̃kje], s.m. banker.

banquise [bɑ̃kiz], s.f. ice-floe, ice-pack.

bans [bɑ̃], s.m. pl. banns.

baptême [batɛːm], s.m. baptism, christening; nom de b., Christian name.

baptiser [batize], v.tr. to baptize.

baquet [bakɛ], s.m. tub, bucket.

bar [baːr], s.m. (public) bar.

baragouin/er [baragwine], v.tr. & i. to talk gibberish; to jabber. s.m. -age.

baraque [barak], s.f. (a) hut, shanty; (b) booth (at fair). s.m. -ement, hutting.

baratte [barat], s.f. churn.

baratt/er [barate], v.tr. to churn.

barbant [barbɑ̃], a. P: tiresome, boring.

barbare [barbaːr]. 1. a. (a) barbaric; (b) barbarous. 2. s.m. barbarian. adv. -ment.

barbarie [barbari], s.f. barbarity, cruelty.

barbe [barb], s.f. beard; rire dans sa b., to laugh up one's sleeve; se faire la b., to shave; P: quelle b.! what a bore! la b.! shut up!

barbelé [barbəle]. 1. a. barbed. 2. s.m. barbed wire.

barbiche [barbiʃ], s.f. goatee (beard).

barbier [barbje], s.m. barber.

barbot/er [barbɔte], v.i. to paddle. s.m. -age.

barbouill/er [barbuje], v.tr. to daub; to smear (de, with).

se barbouiller, to dirty one's face.

barbu, -ue [barby]. 1. a. bearded. 2. s.f. Fish: barbue, brill.

barde [bard], s.m. bard, poet.

barème [barɛm], s.m. 1. ready-reckoner. 2. printed table (of fares).

barguign/er [bargiɲe], v.i. F: to shilly-shally. s.m. -age. s. -eur, -euse.

baril [bari], s.m. barrel, cask, keg.

bariol/er [barjɔle], v.tr. to variegate; to paint gaudily. s.m. -age.

baro/mètre [baromɛtr], s.m. barometer. a. -métrique.

baron, -onne [barɔ̃, -ɔn], s. baron; baroness.

baronnet [barɔnɛ], s.m. baronet.

baroque [barɔk]. 1. a. quaint, odd. 2. a. & s.m. baroque (style).

barque [bark], s.f. boat.

barrage [baraːʒ, ba-], s.m. 1. barring. 2. (a) barrier; dam, weir; (b) Mil: barrage.

barre [baːr], s.f. 1. (a) bar, rod; (b) bar, barrier; (c) bar (of river). 2. helm (of ship). 3. line, dash, stroke. 4. stripe.

barreau [baro], s.m. 1. small bar; rail. 2. Jur: bar.

barrer [bɔre], v.tr. 1. (a) to fasten with a bar; (b) to bar, obstruct; to dam; P.N: rue barrée, no thoroughfare. 2. b. un chèque, to cross a cheque. 2. b. to cross out. 4. Nau: to steer.

barrette [barɛt], s.f. biretta.

barricade [barikad], s.f. barricade.

barricader [barikade], v.tr. to barricade.

barrière [barjɛːr], s.f. 1. barrier. 2. gate; toll-gate.

barrique [barik], s.f. large barrel; cask.

baryton [baritɔ̃], a. & s.m. baritone.

baryum [barjɔm], s.m. Min: barium.

bas, basse [bɑ, bɑːs]. I. a. 1. low. 2. mean, base, low. adv. -sement, basely. II. adv. 1. low (down). 2. met b. to lay down; to overthrow; (of animal) to drop (young). 3. parler tout b. to speak in a whisper. III. s.m. 1. lower part; adv.phr. en b. (down) below; downstairs; adv.phr. à b. down; à b. les mains! hands off! 2. stocking. IV. basse, s.f. Mus: bass.

basané [bazane], a. sunburnt, tanned.

bas-côté [bakote], s.m. 1. aisle (of church). 2. shoulder, side (of road).

bascule [baskyl], s.f. rocker; see-saw; (balance à) b. weighing machine; camion à b., tip(ping) lorry.

bascul/er [baskyle], v.tr. & i. (a) to rock, swing; (b) to tip (up). s.m. -age.

base [bɑːz], s.f. 1. base. 2. basis, foundation.

baser [baze], v.tr. to base, found.

bas-fond [bafɔ̃], s.m. 1. low ground; swamp. 2. shallow, shoal.

basque [bask], a. & s. Basque.

basse-cour [baskuːr], s.f. farmyard, poultry-yard. pl. basses-cours.

bassesse [basɛs], s.f. 1. baseness, lowness. 2. low, mean action.

bassin [basɛ̃], s.m. 1. basin, bowl, pan. 2. reservoir. 3. dock. 4. b. houiller, coalfield.

basson [basɔ̃], s.m. 1. bassoon. 2. bassoonist.

bastingage [bastɛ̃gaːʒ], s.m. bulwarks.

bataclan [bataklɑ̃], s.m. paraphernalia; tout le b., the whole caboodle.

bataille [bataːj], s.f. battle.

†batailleur [batajœːr], a. fighting, pugnacious.

bataillon [batajɔ̃], s.m. battalion.

bâtard [bataːr], a. & s. bastard; chien b., mongrel.

bâtardeau [batardo], s.m. coffer-dam, caisson.

bateau [bato], s.m. boat; le train du b., the boat-train.

bateau-citerne [batositɛrn], s.m. tanker. pl. bateaux-citernes.

batelier [batəlje], s. boatman; waterman.

bathyscaphe [batiskaf], s.m. bathyscaph.

bâti [bati], s.m. frame(-work).

batifol/er [batifole], v.i. to frolic, lark about. s.m. -age. s. -eur, -euse.

bâtiment [batimɑ̃], s.m. 1. building, edifice. 2. ship, vessel.

bâtir [batiːr], v.tr. to build, erect.

batiste [batist], s.f. cambric.

bâton [batɔ̃], s.m. stick, staff; mettre des bâtons dans les roues, to put a spoke in (s.o.'s) wheel; to interfere.

bâtonner [batɔne], v.tr. to beat, cudgel.

battant [batɑ̃]. I. a. 1. a beating; pluie battante, driving rain; tout b. neuf, brand-new. II. s.m. 1. clapper, tongue. 2. leaf, flap.

batterie [batri], s.f. 1. battery. 2. (a) set, collection; (b) b. électrique, electric battery. 3. battery (for chickens).

batteur, -euse [batœːr, -øːz], s. 1. beater. 2. s.f. batteuse, threshing-machine.

†batt/re [batr], v.tr. & i. to beat, to defeat; to fly (a flag); to shuffle (cards); b. la mesure, to beat time; b. des mains, to clap one's hands. s.m. -ement.
se battre, to fight.

baume [boːm], s.m. balm, balsam.

bauxite [boksit], s.f. Min: bauxite.

bavard [bavaːr]. I. a. talkative, garrulous. 2. s. chatterbox.

bavard/er [bavarde], v.i. 1. to chatter. 2. to gossip. s.m. -age, gossip.

bave [baːv], s.f. slaver, dribble.

bavette [bavɛt], s.f. 1. bib. 2. Cu: top of the sirloin.

bazar [bazaːr], s.m. bazaar, cheap shop.

béant [beɑ̃], a. gaping; yawning (chasm).

béat [bea], a. sanctimonious, smug. adv. -ement.

béatifier [beatifje], v.tr. to beatify.

béatitude [beatityd], s.f. 1. (a) beatitude; (b) bliss. 2. smugness, complacency.

†beau [bo]. I. a. 1. beautiful, handsome; le b. sexe, the fair sex. 2. fine; noble; (a) un bel esprit, a wit; (b) avoir b. jeu, to have every opportunity; le b. côté, the bright side; (c) smart, spruce; le b. monde, society; (d) b. temps, fine weather; (e) (intensive) au b. milieu, right in the middle. 3. adv.phrs. bel et bien, entirely, quite; tout b.! easy! gently! de plus belle, more than ever. 4. n.phrs. (a) l'échapper belle, to have a narrow escape; (b) il fait b. (temps), it is fine (weather); (c) avoir b. faire

qch., to do sth. in vain. II. beau, belle, *s.* 1. beauty. 2. *s.m.* beautiful things. 3. *s.f. Sp:* la belle, the deciding game.

beaucoup [boku]. 1. *s.m.inv.* (*a*) much, *F:* a lot; (*b*) (a great) many; b. de, much; (a great) many; (*c*) adv.phr. de b., much, by far. 2. *adv.* much.

beau-fils [bofis], *s.m.* 1. son-in-law. 2. stepson. *pl. beaux-fils.*

beau-frère [bofrɛːr], *s.m.* brother-in-law. *pl. beaux-frères.*

beau-père [bopɛːr], *s.m.* 1. father-in-law. 2. stepfather. *pl. beaux-pères.*

beauté [bote], *s.f.* 1. beauty, loveliness; institut de b., beauty parlour. 2. beauty; beautiful woman.

beaux-arts [bozaːr], *s.m.pl.* fine arts.

bébé [bebe], *s.m.* baby.

bec [bɛk], *s.m.* 1. beak; bill; coup de b., peck; du b. et des ongles, tooth and nail. 2. (*a*) spout; (*b*) b. de gaz., gas-burner.

bécane [bekan], *s.f. F:* bike.

bécasse [bekas], *s.f.* woodcock.

bécassine [bekasin], *s.f.* snipe.

bêche [bɛʃ], *s.f.* spade.

bêch/er [beʃe], *v.tr.* to dig. *s.* -age, digging, *s.* -eur, -euse, digger.

‡becqueter [bekte], *v.tr.* (*of birds*) (*a*) to pick up; (*b*) to peck.

bedeau [bado], *s.m.* verger.

bédouin -ine [bedwɛ̃, -in], *a.* & *s.* Bedouin.

beffroi [befrwa], *s.m.* belfry.

‡bég/ayer [begɛje], *v.i.* & *tr.* to stutter, stammer. *s.m.* -aiement, stammer(ing).

bègue [bɛg], *s.* stammerer.

beige [bɛːʒ], *a.* beige.

beignet [bɛɲɛ], *s.m.* fritter.

bel. See BEAU.

bêl/er [bele], *v.i.* to bleat. *s.m.* -ement.

belette [bəlɛt], *s.f.* weasel.

belge [bɛlʒ], *a.* & *s.* Belgian.

bélier [belje], *s.m.* ram.

belladone [bɛl(l)adɔn], *s.f.* belladonna, deadly nightshade.

belle. See BEAU.

belle-famille [bɛlfami:j], *s.f. F:* the 'in-laws.' *pl. belles-familles.*

belle-fille [bɛlfi:j], *s.f.* 1. step-daughter. 2. daughter-in-law. *pl. belles-filles.*

belle-mère [bɛlmɛ:r], *s.f.* 1. step-mother. 2. mother-in-law. *pl. belles-mères.*

belle-sœur [bɛlsœ:r], *s.f.* sister-in-law. *pl. belles-sœurs.*

belligérant [bɛl(l)iʒerɑ̃], *a.* & *s.m.* belligerent.

†belliqueux [bɛl(l)ikø], *a.* warlike.

belvédère [bɛlvedɛːr], *s.m.* 1. view-point. 2. summer-house.

bémol [bemɔl], *s.m. Mus:* flat.

bénédicité [benedisite], *s.m.* grace (at a meal).

bénédictin, -ine [benediktɛ̃, -in], 1. *a.* & *s.* Benedictine (monk, nun). 2. *s.f.* Benedictine (liqueur).

bénédiction [benediksjɔ̃], *s.f.* blessing.

bénéfice [benefis], *s.m.* 1. profit, gain. 2. benefit. 3. benefice.

bénéficier [benefisje], *v.i.* to profit (de, by).

bénévole [benevɔl], *a.* 1. benevolent; kindly. 2. gratuitous. *adv.* -ment.

bénignité [beniɲite], *s.f.* (*a*) kindness; (*b*) mildness.

†bén/in [benɛ̃], *a.* (*a*) benign; (*b*) mild. *a.f.* -igne. *adv.* -ignement.

bénir [beni:r], *v.tr.* 1. (*a*) to bless; (*b*) to thank. 2. to consecrate.

bénit [beni], *a.* consecrated, blessed; eau bénite, holy water.

bénitier [benitje], *s.m.* holy-water stoup.

benne [bɛn], *s.f. Min:* skip, tub; camion à b. basculante, tip-lorry.

benzine [bɛ̃zin], *s.f. Ch:* benzine.

béquille [beki:j], *s.f.* 1. crutch. 2. (motor cycle) stand.

berceau [bɛrso], *s.m.* cradle.

‡berc/er [bɛrse], *v.tr.* 1. to rock. 2. to lull; to send to sleep. *s.f.* -euse, lullaby.

se bercer. 1. to rock, sway. 2. se b. d'une illusion, to cherish an illusion.

béret [berɛ], *s.m.* beret.

berge [bɛrʒ], *s.f.* (steep) bank.

berg/er, -ère [bɛrʒe, -ɛːr], *s.* 1. shepherd; shepherdess; *s.f.* bergère, easy-chair. *s.f.* -erie, sheepfold.

bergeronnette [bɛrʒərɔnɛt], *s.f.* wagtail.

berlinois, -oise [bɛrlinwa, -wɑːz], *a.* of Berlin. 2. *s.* Berliner.

béryl [beril], *s.m.* beryl.

besicles [bəzikl], *s.f.pl. F:* goggles, specs.

besogne [b(ə)zɔɲ], *s.f.* work; task, job.

†besogneux [bəzɔɲø], *a.* needy, impecunious.

besoin [bəzwɛ̃], *s.m.* 1. necessity, requirement; (*a*) au b., if necessary; when required; (*b*) avoir b. de, to need, want. 2. poverty.

†bestial [bɛstjal], *a.* bestial, brutish. *adv.* -ement.

bestiaux [bɛstjo], *s.m.pl.* cattle, livestock.

bestiole [bɛstjɔl], *s.f.* tiny beast; insect.

bétail [betaj], *s.m. coll.* cattle; livestock.

bête [bɛːt], *s.f.* 1. animal; dumb creature; b. de trait, draught animal; b. à bon Dieu, ladybird. 2. (*a*) simpleton; faire la b., *F:* to act dumb; (*b*) a. stupid, foolish. *adv.* -ment.

bêtise [betiːz], *s.f.* 1. stupidity, silliness. 2. nonsense; faire des bêtises, to play the fool. 3. blunder; piece of stupidity.

béton [betɔ̃], *s.m.* 1. concrete; b. armé, ferro-concrete.

bétonn/er [betɔne], *v.tr.* to concrete. *s.* -age. *s.f.* -ière, concrete-mixer.

betterave [bɛtraːv], *s.f.* beet(root).

beugl/er [bøgle], *v.i.* to low; to bellow. *s.m.* -ement.

beurr/e [bœːr], *s.m.* butter. *s.m.* -ier, butter dish.

beurrer [bœre], *v.tr.* to butter.

bévue [bevy], *s.f.* blunder, mistake.

biais [bjɛ]. ·1. *a.* oblique, slanting. 2. *s.m.* bias, slant; en b., askew; regarder de b., to look sideways at.

bibelot [biblo], *s.m.* curio; trinket.

biberon [bibrɔ̃], *s.m.* feeding-bottle.

Bible [bibl], *s.f.* Bible.

bibliobus [biblibys], *s.m.* mobile library.

bibliographie [bibliɔgrafi], *s.f.* bibliography. *a.* **-ique**.

bibliophile [bibliɔfil], *s.m.* book-lover.

bibliothécaire [bibliɔtekɛːr], *s.m.* librarian.

bibliothèque [bibliɔtɛk], *s.f.* 1. library. 2. bookcase.

biblique [biblik], *a.* biblical.

biche [biʃ], *s.f.* hind, doe.

bicolore [bikɔlɔːr], *a.* two-coloured.

bicoque [bikɔk], *s.f. F:* shanty.

bicyclette [bisiklɛt], *s.f.* bicycle, cycle.

bidon [bidɔ̃], *s.m.* (*a*) can, drum, tin (for oil, petrol); (*b*) *Mil:* water-bottle.

bidonville [bidɔ̃vil], *s.m.* shantytown.

bielle [bjɛl], *s.f. Aut: etc:* crank-arm; tête de b., big end.

bien [bjɛ̃]. I. *adv.* 1. well; vous avez b. fait, you did right; aller b., to be well; très b.! well done! 2. (*with adj. function*) (*a*) right, proper; (*b*) comfortable; vous voilà b.! you're in a fine fix! (*c*) être b. avec, to be on good terms with. 3. (*emphatic*) (*a*) right, really, quite; je l'avais b. dit! didn't I say so? b. entendu, of course; (*b*) (=TRÈS) very; (*c*) (= BEAUCOUP) much, many. 4. *adv.phr.* tant b. que mal, somehow (or other). 5. *conj.phr.* b. que, though. 6. *int.* eh b.! well! II. *s.m.* 1. good; grand b. vous fasse! much good may it do you! 2. possession, property; **biens immeubles**, real estate; **biens de consommation**, consumer goods.

bien-être [bjɛ̃nɛːtr], *s.m. no pl.* (*a*) well-being; comfort; (*b*) welfare.

bienfaisance [bjɛ̃fəzɑ̃ːs], *s.f.* charity; **bureau de b.**, relief committee.

bienfaisant [bjɛ̃fəzɑ̃], *a.* 1. beneficent, charitable. 2. beneficial, salutary.

bienfait [bjɛ̃fɛ], *s.m.* kindness, service; gift.

bienfaiteur, -trice [bjɛ̃fɛtœːr, -tris], *s.* benefactor, benefactress.

†bienheureux [bjɛ̃nœrø], *a.* 1. blissful, happy. 2. blessed.

†biennal [bien(n)al], *a.* two-yearly (exhibition, etc.).

bienséance [bjɛ̃seɑ̃ːs], *s.f.* propriety.

bientôt [bjɛ̃to], *adv.* (very) soon; before long; à b.! good-bye, see you again soon.

bienveillance [bjɛ̃vejɑ̃ːs], *s.f.* benevolence; kindness.

bienveillant [bjɛ̃vejɑ̃], *a.* kind, benevolent (envers, pour, to).

bienvenu, -e [bjɛ̃vəny], *a. & s.* welcome.

bienvenue [bjɛ̃vəny], *s.f.* welcome; souhaiter la b. à qn, to welcome s.o.

bière¹ [bjɛːr], *s.f.* beer.

bière², *s.f.* coffin.

biffer [bife], *v.tr.* to cross out, cancel. *s.m.* **-age**, crossing out, cancellation.

bifteck [biftɛk], *s.m.* (beef)steak; *F:* la course au b., the rat race.

bifurquer [bifyrke], *v.tr. & i.* (*of road, rail, tree*) to fork. *s.f.* **-cation**, fork, junction.

bigamie [bigami], *s.f.* bigamy.

bigarrer [bigare], *v.tr.* to variegate, mottle. *s.f.* **-ure**, (colour-)medley.

bigorneau [bigɔrno], *s.m.* winkle.

bigot [bigo]. 1. *a.* (over-)devout. 2. *s.* bigot.

bigoudi [bigudi], *s.m.* hair-curler.

†bijou [biʒu], *s.m.* piece of jewellery; jewel, gem.

bijouterie [biʒutri], *s.f.* 1. jeweller's shop. 2. jewellery; jewels. *s.m.-* **tier**, jeweller.

bikini [bikini], *s.m. Cl:* bikini.

bilan [bilɑ̃], *s.m.* balance-sheet.

†bilatéral [bilateral], *a.* bilateral.

bile [bil], *s.f.* (*a*) bile, gall; (*b*) bad temper; s'échauffer la b., to worry.

†bilieux [biljø], *a.* 1. bilious. 2 (*a*) short tempered, testy; (*b*) morose.

bilingue [bilɛ̃ːg], *a.* bilingual.

billard [bijaːr], *s.m.* 1. billiards. 2. billiard-table; *F:* operating-table. 3. billiard-room.

bille [bij], *s.f.* 1. billiard-ball. 2. marble. 3. ballpoint (pen). 4. roulement à billes, ball-bearing.

billet [bijɛ], *s.m.* 1. note, short letter. 2. notice; invitation-card. 3. ticket. 4. (*a*) promissory note, bill; (*b*) b. de banque, bank-note.

billevesée [bilvəze, bij-], *s.f.* crack-brained notion; nonsense.

billion [biljɔ̃], *s.m.* billion.

billot [bijo], *s.m.* block of wood.

bimbeloterie [bɛ̃blɔtri], *s.f.* 1. toy manufacture. 2. toys, knick-knacks.

†bimensuel [bimɑ̃sɥɛl], *a.* fortnightly. *adv.* **-ellement**.

bimoteur [bimɔtœːr], *a.m.* twin-engine.

biner [bine], *v.tr.* to hoe. *s.m.* **-age**, hoeing. *s.f.* **-ette**, hoe.

biochimie [biɔʃimi], *s.f.* biochemistry.

biographe [biɔgraf], *s.m.* biographer. *s.f.* **-graphie**. *a.* **-graphique**.

biologie [biɔlɔʒi], *s.f.* biology. *a.* **-logique**, biological. *s.m.* **-logiste**.

biparti [biparti], *a.* bipartite.

bipède [biped], *s.m.* biped.

biphasé [bifaze], *a. El:* two-phase (current).

biplace [biplas], *a. & s.m.* two-seater.

bique [bik], *s.f.* nanny-goat.

biréacteur [bireaktœːr], *s.m. Av:* twin-jet plane.

birman, -ane [birmɑ̃, -an], *a. & s.* Burmese.

bis¹ [bi], a. greyish-brown.
bis² [bis], adv. twice. 1. no. 10 bis = no. 10A. 2. repeat. 3. encore!
†bisannuel [bizanɥɛl], a. biennial.
biscornu [biskɔrny], a. 1. mis-shapen. 2. crotchety; queer (ideas).
biscuit [biskɥi], s.m. biscuit, U.S: cookie.
bismuth [bismyt], s.m. bismuth.
bisséqué [biseke], a. bisected.
bissextile [bisekstil], a.f. année b., leap-year.
bistro(t) [bistro], s.m. P: pub.
bitum/er [bityme], v.tr. 1. to asphalt (road, etc.). 2. to tar. -age.
bivouac [bivwak], s.m. bivouac.
bizarre [bizaːr], a. peculiar, odd, queer. adv. -ment.
bizarrerie [bizarəri], s.f. 1. peculiarity, oddness. 2. whimsicalness.
black-out [blakaut], s.m. black-out.
blafard [blafaːr], a. pallid, wan.
blague [blag], s.f. 1. (tobacco-)pouch. 2. (a) humbug; sans b.? really? (b) joke.
blagu/er [blage]. -1. v.i. to joke. 2. v.tr. make fun of (s.o., sth.). a. & s. -eur, -euse.
blaireau [blɛro], s.m. 1. badger. 2. shaving-brush.
blâme [blɑːm], s.m. blame; censure.
blâm/er [blɑme], v.tr. 1. to blame; to find fault with. 2. to reprimand. a. -able, blameworthy.
blanc, blanche [blɑ̃, blɑ̃ːʃ]. I. a. 1. white. 2. light-coloured; pale. s. un b. white man. 3. clean, pure. 4. blank; nuit blanche, sleepless night. II. s.m. 1. white. 2. blank. 3. (a) saigner à b., to bleed white; (b) cartouche à b., blank cartridge. 4. breast (of chicken). 5. linen drapery; vente de b., white sale. III. blanche, s.f. Mus: minim.
blanchaille [blɑ̃ʃaːj], s.f. whitebait.
blanchâtre [blɑ̃ʃɑːtr], a. whitish.
blancheur [blɑ̃ʃœːr], s.f. 1. whiteness. 2. purity.
blanch/ir [blɑ̃ʃiːr]. 1. v.tr. (a) to whiten; (b) to bleach; (c) to wash, launder; (d) to whitewash. 2. v.i. to turn white. -issage, s. -isseur, -isseuse.
blanchisserie [blɑ̃ʃisri], s.f. (a) laundering; (b) laundry; b. automatique, launderette.
blanquette [blɑ̃kɛt], s.f. 1. Cu: white (veal) stew. 2. (varieties of) white wine.
blasé [blɑze], a. blasé, surfeited.
blason [blɑzɔ̃], s.m. (a) coat of arms; (b) heraldry.
blasphème [blasfɛm], s.m. blasphemy.
‡blasphémer [blasfeme], v.i. to blaspheme.
blatte [blat], s.f. cockroach.
blé [ble], s.m. wheat.

blême [blɛm], a. 1. (a) livid; (b) cadaverous. 2. pale; wan.
blêm/ir [blemiːr], v.i. to turn pale, livid. s.m. -issement.
blessant [blesɑ̃], a. offensive, cutting (remark).
blessé, -ée [blese], s. wounded person.
bless/er [blese], v.tr. 1. to wound, hurt. 2. to offend. s.f. -ure, wound. se blesser, to take offence (de, at).
†blet, blette [blɛ, blɛt], a. over-ripe, sleepy.
bleu [blø]. 1. a. blue. 2. s.m. (a) blue; (b) bruise; (c) blue (cheese). 3. s. recruit. 4. s.m. (a) blueprint; (b) pl. bleus, boiler suit. a. -âtre, bluish.
bleu/ir [bløiːr]. 1 v.tr. to blue; to make blue. 2. v.i. to become blue. s.m. -et, cornflower.
blind/er [blɛ̃de], v.tr. Mil: etc: to armour (-plate) (ship, tank, car). s.m. -age.
bloc [blɔk], s.m. 1. block, lump. 2. coalition; faire b., to unite. 3. pad (of paper). 4. unit; Cin: b. sonore, sound unit; H: b. cuisine, kitchen unit.
blocus [blɔkyːs], s.m. blockade.
blond [blɔ̃]. 1. a. fair, flaxen; blond; bière blonde = light ale. 2. s. blond(e).
bloquer [blɔke], v.tr. (a) to block, obstruct, jam; (b) to blockade.
blottir (se) [səblɔtiːr], v.pr. to cower, to hide.
blouse [bluːz], s.f. overall; blouse.
blouson [bluzɔ̃], s.m. (lumber-)jacket, wind-cheater.
bluet [blɥɛ], s.m. cornflower.
bobine [bɔbin], s.f. bobbin, spool, reel.
bocal, -aux [bɔkal], s.m. (a) (wide-mouthed) bottle; (b) goldfish bowl.
bock [bɔk], s.m. glass of beer.
bœuf [bœf, pl. bø], s.m. 1. ox, bullock. 2. beef.
bohème [bɔɛm], a. & s. Bohemian; une vie de b., a free and easy life.
bohémien, -ienne [bɔemjɛ̃, -jɛn], a. & s. 1. Geog: Bohemian. 2. gipsy.
‡boire [bwaːr]. I. v.tr. 1. to drink; b. un coup, to have a drink; b. un affront, to pocket an insult. 2. abs. il boit, he drinks. II. s.m. drink.
bois [bwa], s.m. 1. wood, forest; petit b., spinney. 2. wood, timber. 3. woodcut. 4. pl. antlers. 5. b. de lit, bedstead. 6. Mus: les b., the woodwind.
boisé [bwaze], a. wooded (country). 2. panelled (room).
boiserie [bwazri], s.f. woodwork, panelling.
boisson [bwasɔ̃], s.f. beverage; drink.
boîte [bwa(ː)t], s.f. 1. box; b. en fer blanc, tin, can; conserves en b., tinned, canned, food. 2. Aut: b. de vitesses, gearbox; El: b. à fusibles, fuse-box. 3. b. de nuit, night-club.
boit/er [bwate], v.i. to limp. a. & s. -eux, -euse, limping, lame (person).
bol [bɔl], s.m. bowl, basin.

bombard/er [bɔ̃barde], *v.tr.* to bomb. *s.m.* -ement, bombing. *s.m.* -ier, bomber.

bombe [bɔ̃b], *s.f.* 1. bomb; b. H., H.-bomb. 2. b. glacée, ice-pudding. 3. faire la b., to be on the spree.

bombé [bɔ̃be], *a.* convex, bulging.

bomber [bɔ̃be]. 1. *v.tr.* (*a*) la poitrine, to throw out one's chest; (*b*) to bend, arch. 2. *v.i.* to bulge (out).

bon, bonne [bɔ̃, bɔn]. I. *a.* 1. good, honest. 2. good, nice; cela est b. à dire, it's easier said than done. 3. clever, capable. 4. right, correct. 5. good, kind (pour, envers, to). 6. good, advantageous; c'est b. à savoir, it's worth knowing; b. marché, cheap. 7. good, suitable; b. à manger, good to eat. 8. good, favourable; souhaiter la bonne année à qn, to wish s.o. a happy New Year. 9. good, sound, safe; en b. état, in good, working, order. 10. *adv.* tenir b., to hold one's own; sentir b., to smell nice; il fait b. ici, it is comfortable here. 11. pour de b., for good (and all). 12. *int.* good! agreed! II. *s.m.* 1. order, voucher; b. de caisse, cash voucher. 2. bond, bill. III. bonne, *s.f.* maid; bonne d'enfants, nanny.

bonbon [bɔ̃bɔ̃], *s.m.* sweet.

bond [bɔ̃], *s.m.* 1. bound, leap, jump, spring. 2. (*of ball*) bounce.

bonde [bɔ̃d], *s.f.* 1. (*a*) bung; (*b*) plug. 2. bung-hole, plug-hole.

bondé [bɔ̃de], *a.* chock-full, crammed.

bond/ir [bɔ̃diːr], *v.i.* 1. to leap, bound. 2. to bounce. *a.* -issant.

bonheur [bɔnœːr], *s.m.* 1. good fortune, good luck, success; jouer de b., to be in luck. 2. happiness.

bonhomie [bɔnɔmi], *s.f.* good nature.

bonhomme [bɔnɔm], *s.m.* simple, good-natured man; b. de neige, snowman. *pl.* bonshommes [bɔ̃zɔm].

boniment [bɔnimɑ̃], *s.m.* patter.

bonjour [bɔ̃ʒuːr], *s.m.* good day, good morning, good afternoon.

bonne, *s.f.* see BON.

bonne-maman [bɔnmamɑ̃], *s.f.* F: granny. *pl.* bonnes-mamans.

bonnement [bɔnmɑ̃], *adv.* (*only in*) tout b., simply, plainly.

bonnet [bɔnɛ], *s.m.* cap; F: gros b., big-wig.

bonneterie [bɔntri], *s.f.* hosiery, knitwear.

bonnetier [bɔntje], *s.* hosier.

bon-papa [bɔ̃papa], *s.m.F:* grandad. *pl.* bons-papas.

bonsoir [bɔ̃swaːr], *s.m.* good evening, good night.

bonté [bɔ̃te], *s.f.* 1. (*a*) goodness, kindness; (*b*) *pl.* kindnesses. 2. goodness, excellence.

borax [bɔraks], *s.m. Ch:* borax.

bord [bɔːr], *s.m.* 1. (*a*) side (of ship); faux b., list; (*b*) tack, leg; (*c*) les hommes du b., the ship's company. 2. edge; border; brim. 3. shore; bank (of river); b. de la mer, seaside.

bordeaux [bɔrdo], *s.m.* Bordeaux (wine); b. rouge, claret.

border [bɔrde], *v.tr.* (*a*) to border; to edge; (*b*) to tuck up (in bed).

bordereau [bɔrdəro], *s.m. Com:* memo, consignment note; b. de paie, wages docket; b. de crédit, credit note.

bordure [bɔrdyːr], *s.f.* 1. border, rim. 2. frame.

borgne [bɔrɲ], *a.* 1. one-eyed. 2. disreputable.

borique [bɔrik], *a.* boric (acid).

borne [bɔrn], *s.f.* 1. (*a*) boundary-stone; b. kilométrique = milestone; (*b*) *pl.* boundaries, limits. 2. *El:* terminal.

borner [bɔrne], *v.tr.* 1. to form the boundary of. 2. to limit, restrict; esprit borné, narrow mind. se borner, to restrict oneself.

bosquet [bɔskɛ], *s.m.* grove, thicket.

bosse [bɔs], *s.f.* 1. hump. 2. bump; swelling. 3. dent. 4. boss.

‡bossel/er [bɔsle], *v.tr.* 1. to emboss. 2. to dent. *s.m.* -age. *s.f.* -ure, dent.

bossu [bɔsy]. 1. *a.* hunch-backed; humped (animal). 2. *s.* hunchback.

bot [bɔ], *a.* pied bot, club-foot.

botan/ique [bɔtanik], 1. *a.* botanical. *s.f.* botany. *s.m. & f.* -iste.

botte [bɔt], *s.f.* 1. bunch; truss, bundle. 2. (high) boot; Wellington. *s.f.* -tine, boot. *s.m.* -tier, bootmaker.

bouc [buk], *s.m.* billy-(goat).

bouche [buʃ], *s.f.* mouth. 1. bonne b., tit-bit; F: faire la petite b., to pick at one's food; b. bée, open-mouthed. 2. b. à feu, piece of artillery; b. d'eau, hydrant.

bouche-à-bouche [buʃabuʃ], *s.m.inv.* kiss of life.

bouchée [buʃe], *s.f.* mouthful.

bouch/er¹, *v.tr.* to stop (up); se b. le nez, to hold one's nose. *s.m.* -age.

bouch/er², *s.* butcher. *s.f.* -erie, butcher's shop.

bouche-trou [buʃtru], *s.m.* stop-gap; makeshift. *pl.* bouche-trous.

bouchon [buʃɔ̃], *s.f.* 1. stopper, plug, bung. b. de liège, cork.

boucle [bukl], *s.f.* 1. buckle, shackle. 2. loop; bow. 3. ring; boucles d'oreilles, earrings. 4. curl.

boucler [bukle], *v.tr.* (*a*) to buckle; to fasten; (*b*) to loop, tie up; b. la boucle, to loop the loop; (*c*) to curl.

bouclier [bukli(j)e], *s.m.* buckler, shield.

bouddhiste [budist], *a. & s.* Buddhist.

boud/er [bude]. 1. *v.i.* to sulk. 2. *v.tr.* to be sulky with. *s.f.* -erie, sulking. *a. & s.m.* -eur, -euse, sulky.

boudin [budɛ̃], s.m. 1. (black-)pudding. 2. (a) corkscrew curl; (b) flange (on wheel).

bou/e [bu], s.f. 1. mud. 2. sediment, deposit. s.m. -eur, dustman. a. †-eux, muddy.

bouée [bue], s.f. buoy; b. de sauvetage, life-buoy.

bouffée [bufe], s.f. puff (of smoke); whiff.

bouffer [bufe], v.tr. 1. to puff out. 2. P: to bolt (food).

bouffi [bufi], a. puffy, swollen; bloated. s.f. -ssure, swelling.

bouffon [bufɔ̃], s.m. buffoon. s.f. -nerie.

‡**bouger** [buʒe], v.i. & tr. to budge, stir, move.

boug/ie [buʒi], s.f. 1. candle. 2. candle-power. 3. b. (d'allumage), sparking-plug. s.m. -eoir, candlestick.

bougon, -onne [bugɔ̃, -ɔn]. 1. s. grumbler, grouser. 2. a. grumpy.

bougonner [bugɔne], v.i. to grumble.

bouillabaisse [bujabes], s.f. Provençal fish soup, bouillabaisse.

bouillant [bujɑ̃], a. 1. boiling. 2. fiery, hot-headed, impetuous.

bouillie [buji], s.f. gruel; porridge.

‡**bouill/ir** [bujiːr], v.i. to boil. s.f. -oire, kettle. s.f. -otte, hot-water bottle.

bouillon [bujɔ̃], s.m. 1. bubble. 2. Cu: stock.

bouillonn/er [bujɔne], v.i. to bubble, boil up. s.m. -ement.

boulang/er [bulɑ̃ʒe], s. baker. s.f. -erie, baker's shop.

boule [bul], s.f. 1. ball, sphere, globe. 2. jouer aux boules, to play bowls.

bouleau [bulo], s.m. birch(-tree).

bouledogue [buldɔg], s.m. bulldog.

boulette [bulɛt], s.f. 1. pellet. 2. Cu: rissole. 3. F: faire une b., to drop a brick.

boulevard [bulvaːr], s.m. boulevard.

boulevers/er [bulverse], v.tr. to upset; to overthrow; to throw into confusion. a. -ant, upsetting. s.m. -ement, upset.

boulon [bulɔ̃], s.m. bolt, pin.

boulot [bulo], s.m. F: work; job.

bouquet [bukɛ], s.m. 1. (a) bunch of flowers, bouquet; (b) clump (of trees). 2. aroma; bouquet.

bouquin [bukɛ̃], s.m. old book; F: book.

bouquin/er [bukine], v.i. 1. to collect (old) books. 2. to pore over (old) books; F: to read. s. -eur, -euse.

bouquiniste [bukinist], s.m. second-hand bookseller.

†**bourbeux** [burbø], a. muddy.

bourbier [burbje], s.m. slough, mire.

bourde [burd], s.f. 1. lie, falsehood. 2. blunder, bloomer.

bourdon [burdɔ̃], s.m. 1. great bell. 2. bumble-bee.

bourdonn/er [burdɔne], v.i. to buzz, hum. v.tr. to hum (tune). s.m. -ement, buzzing, humming.

bourg [buːr], s.m. small market-town.

bourgade [burgad], s.f. large village.

bourgeois [burʒwa]. I. s. middle-class man, woman; P: la bourgeoise, the missus. II. a. 1. middleclass. 2. homely, simple. 3. common, unrefined. adv. -ement.

bourgeoisie [burʒwazi], s.f. middle class.

bourgeon [burʒɔ̃], s.m. bud.

bourgeonner [burʒɔne], v.i. to bud, shoot.

bourgogne [burgɔɲ], s.m. (also vin de B.) Burgundy (wine).

bourrade [burad], s.f. blow; thrust.

bourrasque [burask], s.f. squall.

bourreau [buro], s.m. executioner.

bourrelet [burlɛ], s.m. 1. pad, wad, cushion. 2. rim, flange (of wheel).

bourr/er [bure], v.tr. to stuff, pad. s.m. -elier, harness-maker.

bourrique [burik], s.f. (a) she-ass; donkey; (b) dunce.

bourru [bury], a. rough, rude, surly.

bourse [burs], s.f. 1. purse, bag, pouch. 2. scholarship. 3. stock exchange; b. du travail, Labour Exchange.

boursier, -ière [bursje, -jɛːr], s. scholarship holder.

boursouffl/er [bursufle], v.tr. to puff up, to swell. s.f. -ure, swelling.

bouscul/er [buskyle], v.tr. to jostle, hustle. s.f. -ade, scuffle, rush.

bousill/er [buzije], v.tr. F: to bungle, to botch (up), to scamp (a job). s.m. -age. s.m. -eur.

boussole [busɔl], s.f. compass.

bout [bu], s.m. 1. extremity, end; au b. du compte, after all; être à b., to be exhausted; venir à b. de, to succeed in. 2. end, tip; endpiece; à b. portant, point-blank. 3. bit, fragment; scrap; b. de cigare, cigar stub.

boutade [butad], s.f. 1. whim, caprice. 2. sudden outburst. 3. flash of wit.

bouteille [butɛj], s.f. bottle.

bouti/que [butik], s.f. shop; stall; boutique. s. -quier, -quière, shop-keeper.

bouton [butɔ̃], s.m. 1. bud. 2. button; stud; pl. cuff links. 3. knob, handle; appuyez sur le b., press the button. 4. pimple. 5. b. d'or, buttercup.

boutonn/er [butɔne], v.tr. to button (up). s.f. -ière, button-hole.

bouture [butyːr], s.f. slip, cutting (of plant).

bouvreuil [buvrœːj], s.m. bullfinch.

bovin [bɔvɛ̃], a. bovine.

box [bɔks], s.m. 1. horse-box, loose-box. 2. Aut: lock-up garage. pl. boxes.

boxe [bɔks], s.f. boxing. s.m. -eur, boxer.

†**boyau** [bwajo], s.m. 1. bowel, gut. 2. hose-pipe. 3. narrow thoroughfare.

bracelet [braslɛ], s.m. bracelet; watch-strap.

braconn/er [brakɔne], v.tr. & i. to poach. s.m. -age, poaching. s.m. -ier, poacher.

brai [brɛ], s.m. pitch, tar.

braill/er [brɑje], v.i. to bawl, shout. s. -ard, -arde.

†**brai/re** [brɛːr], v.i. to bray. s.m. -ment.

braise [brɛːz], s.f. (glowing) embers.

brancard [brɑ̃kaːr], s.m. stretcher. s.m. -ier, stretcher-bearer.

branchage [brɑ̃ʃaːʒ], s.m. coll: branches (of trees).

branche [brɑ̃ʃ], s.f. 1. branch; bough. 2. leg (of compasses).

branch/er [brɑ̃ʃe], v.tr. El: to connect (up); to plug in; to put through (on phone). s.m. -ement.

branchies [brɑ̃ʃi], s.f.pl. gills (of fish).

brand/ir [brɑ̃diːr], v.tr. to brandish, flourish. s.m. -issement.

branle [brɑ̃ːl], s.m. mettre en b., to set going.

branl/er [brɑ̃le]. 1. v.tr. to swing, shake. 2. v.i. to shake; to be loose. a. -ant, rickety. s.m. -ement, oscillation.

braqu/er [brake], v.tr. (a) to point, aim (sur, at); (b) b. les yeux sur, to stare at; (c) v.i. voiture qui braque bien, car with a good lock.

bras [brɑ], s.m. 1. (a) arm; saisir qn à bras-le-corps, to grapple with s.o.; b. dessus b. dessous, arm in arm; (b) pl. hands, workmen. 2. arm (of a chair).

brasier [brazje], s.m. (a) fire of live coals; (b) source of intense heat.

brassard [brasaːr], s.m. armlet, arm-badge.

brasse [brɑːs], s.f. 1. fathom. 2. (swimming) stroke; breast-stroke.

brassée [brase], s.f. armful.

brass/er [brase], v.tr. 1. to brew. 2. to mix, stir (up). s.m. -age.

brasserie [brasri], s.f. 1. brewery. 2. brewing. 3. = restaurant (with bar).

brasseur, -euse [brasœːr, -øːz], s.m. 1. brewer. 2. b. d'affaires, business tycoon.

bravade [bravad], s.f. bravado, bluster.

brave [braːv], a. 1. brave, bold; un (homme) b., a brave man. 2. good, worthy; un b. homme, a worthy man. adv. -ment.

braver [brave], v.tr. to brave. 1. to face bravely. 2. to defy, dare.

bravo [bravo]. 1. int. bravo! hear, hear! 2. s.m. cheer, cheering.

bravoure [bravuːr], s.f. bravery, gallantry.

brebis [brəbi], s.f. 1. ewe. 2. sheep.

brèche [brɛʃ], s.f. breach, gap; notch.

bredouille [brəduːj], a.inv. être b., to have failed completely.

bredouill/er [brəduje], v.i. & tr. to mumble; to stammer. s. -eur, -euse.

†**bref** [brɛf]. 1. a. brief, short. 2. adv. briefly, in short.

brésilien, -ienne [breziljɛ̃, -jɛn], a. & s. Brazilian.

bretelle [brətɛl], s.f. 1. strap, sling. 2. pl. braces, U.S: suspenders.

breton, -onne [brətɔ̃, -ɔn], a. & s. Breton.

breuvage [brœvaːʒ], s.m. beverage, drink.

brevet [brəvɛ], s.m. 1. b. d'invention, (letters) patent. 2. diploma, certificate.

†**breveter** [brəvte], v.tr. to patent.

bréviaire [brevjɛːr], s.m. breviary.

brévité [brevite], s.f. shortness.

bribes [brib], s.f.pl. scraps, fragments.

bricole [brikɔl], s.f. usu. pl. trifle(s).

bricol/er [brikɔle], v.i. to do odd jobs. s.m.,-eur, -euse. s.m. -age.

bride [brid], s.f. (a) bridle; (b) rein(s); à b. abattue, at full speed.

brider [bride], v.tr. to bridle; to curb.

bridge [bridʒ], s.m. Sp: bridge.

†**bridg/er** [bridʒe], v.i. to play bridge. s. -eur, -euse, bridge-player.

briève/té [brievte], s.f. brevity. adv. -ment, briefly.

brigade [brigad], s.f. brigade.

brigadier [brigadje], s.m. (a) corporal (of mounted arms); (b) sergeant (of police).

brigand [brigɑ̃], s.m. brigand; ruffian. s.m. -age.

brill/ant [brijɑ̃]. 1. a. brilliant. 2. s.m. (a) brilliance, brightness; (b) polish, shine. 3. s.m. brilliant. adv. -amment.

briller [brije], v.i. to shine.

brin [brɛ̃], s.m. 1. blade (of grass). 2. bit, fragment. 3. strand (of rope).

brindille [brɛ̃diːj], s.f. sprig, twig.

brioche [briɔʃ], s.f. brioche.

brique [brik], s.f. brick.

briquet [brikɛ], s.m. cigarette-lighter.

brisant [brizɑ̃]. 1. a. shattering. 2. s.m. (a) reef; shoal; (b) breaker.

brise [briːz], s.f. breeze.

brisé [brize], a. broken; b. de fatigue, tired out.

brise-lames [brizlɑm], s.m.inv. break-water.

bris/er [brize], v.tr. (a) to break, smash. (b) to crush; (c) to break off. s.f. -ure. se briser, to break.

brise-vent [brizvɑ̃], s.m.inv. wind-break.

britannique [britanik], a. British.

broc [bro], s.m. pitcher; jug.

brocant/eur, -euse [brokɑ̃tœːr, -øːz], s. second-hand dealer. s.m. -age.

brocart [brokaːr], s.m. brocade.

broche [broʃ], s.f. 1. spit. 2. peg, pin. 3. spindle. 4. brooch.

broch/er [broʃe], v.tr. to stitch (book); livre broché, paper-bound book. s.m. -age.

brochet [broʃɛ], s.m. pike.

brochette [broʃɛt], s.f. skewer.

brochure [broʃyːr], s.f. pamphlet.

brod/er [brode], v.tr. to embroider. s.f. -erie, embroidery.

broiement [brwamɑ̃], s.m. crushing.

broncher [brɔ̃ʃe], v.i. 1. to stumble. 2. to move, stir; sans b., without flinching.

†**bronchial** [brɔ̃jjal], *a.* bronchial.
bronchite [brɔ̃jit], *s.f.* bronchitis.
bronze [brɔ̃:z], *s.m.* bronze.
bronzer [brɔ̃ze], *v.tr.* to tan, sunburn.
brosse [brɔs], *s.f.* brush.
bross/er [brɔse], *v.tr.* to brush; se b. les dents, to clean one's teeth. s.m. -age.
brouette [bruet], *s.f.* wheelbarrow.
brouhaha [bruaa], *s.m.* hubbub.
brouillard [bruja:r], *s.m.* fog.
brouille [bruje], *a.* 1. mixed, confused; œufs brouillés, scrambled eggs. 2. être b. avec qn, to be on bad terms with s.o.
brouill/er [bruje], *v.tr.* 1. to mix up; to jam (a message). 2. to set at logger-heads. *s.m.* Rad: -age, jamming. se brouiller. 1. to become confused. 2. to quarrel; to fall out.
brouillon [brujɔ̃], *s.m.* rough copy, draft.
broussaille [brusa:j], *s.f.* brushwood; cheveux en b., unkempt hair.
brouter [brute], *v.tr.* to graze.
‡**broyer** [brwaje], *v.tr.* to pound, to grind.
bru [bry], *s.f.* daughter-in-law.
bruine [brɥin], *s.f.* fine rain; drizzle.
bruiner [brɥine], *v.impers.* to drizzle.
bruissement [brɥismɑ̃], *s.m.* humming (of bees); murmuring (of brook); rustling.
bruit [brɥi], *s.m.* 1. (a) noise; din; report (of a gun); (b) noise, fuss. 2. rumour.
brûlant [brylɑ̃], *a.* burning; scalding; scorching; on fire.
brûlé [bryle]. 1. *a.* burnt. 2. *s.m.* odeur de b., smell of burning.
brûle-pourpoint (à) [abrylpurpwɛ̃], *adv. phr.* point-blank.
brûler [bryle]. 1. *v.tr.* to burn. 2. to scorch; (a) b. les feux, to shoot the (traffic) lights; (b) (of frost) to bite, nip (buds). II. *v.i.* 1. to burn; to be on fire. 2. b. de curiosité, to be burning with curiosity.
brûlure [bryly:r], *s.f.* 1. burn, scald. 2. frost-nip.
brume [brym], *s.f.* thick mist.
†**brumeux** [brymœ], *a.* misty.
brun, brune [brœ̃, bryn]. 1. *a.* brown; dark (complexion). 2. *s.m.* brown. 3. *s.f.* à la brune, at dusk. *a.* -âtre, brownish.
brunir [bryni:r]. 1. *v.i.* to become dark. 2. *v.tr.* to brown, darken.
brusque [brysk], *a.* 1. abrupt, blunt. 2. sudden; Aut: tournant b., sharp bend. *adv.* -ment.
brus/quer [bryske], *v.tr.* 1. to be abrupt with. 2. to precipitate. *s.f.* -querie, abruptness.
brut, -e [bryt], *a.* 1. brutish. 2. raw; crude. 3. gross (weight). 4. dry (champagne). 5. *s.m.* brute.
†**brutal** [brytal], *a.* (a) brutal, savage; (b) coarse, rough. *adv.* -ement.

brutaliser [brytalize], *v.tr.* to ill-treat.
brutalité [brytalite], *s.f.* brutality.
bruy/ant [brɥijɑ̃], *a.* 1. noisy. 2. loud. *adv.* -amment.
bruyère [brɥije:r], *s.f.* 1. (a) heather; (b) heath(-land). 2. briar (root, pipe).
buanderie [bɥɑ̃dri], *s.f.* wash-house.
bûche [by(:)ʃ], *s.f.* (a) (fire-)log; (b) fool.
bûcher[1] [byʃe], *s.m.* 1. wood-shed. 2. (a) pile of faggots; (b) funeral-pyre.
bûch/er[2], *v.tr. & i.* Sch: P: to swot. *s.-eur, -euse,* swot.
bûcheron [byʃrɔ̃], *s.m.* (a) woodcutter; (b) lumberman.
budget [bydʒɛ], *s.m.* budget; estimates. F: boucler le b., to make ends meet.
buée [bɥe], *s.f.* steam, vapour; mist (on windscreen).
buffet [byfe], *s.m.* 1. sideboard. 2. buffet; refreshment room.
buffle [byfl], *s.m.* buffalo.
buis [bɥi], *s.m.* 1. box(tree). 2. box (-wood).
buisson [bɥisɔ̃], *s.m.* bush.
bulb/e, *s.m. or f.* Bot: bulb. *a.* -eux, bulbous.
bulldozer [byldoze:r], *s.m.* bulldozer.
bulgare [bylgar], *a. & s.* Bulgarian.
bulletin [byltɛ̃], *s.m.* 1. bulletin; report; b. météo(rologique), weather report. 2. ticket, receipt; b. de vote, voting paper; b. de commande, order form.
bureau [byro], *s.m.* 1. writing-table; desk. 2. (a) office; b. de poste, post office; b. de tabac, tobacconist's shop; (b) board, committee.
bureaucrate [byrɔkrat], *s.m.* bureaucrat.
bureaucratie [byrɔkrasi], *s.f.* bureaucracy, F: red tape.
burette [byret], *s.f.* 1. cruet. 2. oil-can.
burlesque [byrlesk], *a.* 1. burlesque. 2. comical, ludicrous.
buse[1] [by:z], *s.f.* 1. buzzard. 2. fool.
buse[2], *s.f.* nose-piece, nozzle (of tube).
busqué [byske], *a.* aquiline, hooked (nose).
buste [byst], *s.m.* bust.
bustier [bystje], *s.m.* strapless brassiere.
but [by(t)], *s.m.* 1. mark (to aim at); objective. 2. goal. 3. object, aim. 4. *adv.phr.* de but en blanc, point-blank.
buta/ne [bytan], *s.m.* Ch: butane. *s.m. -nier,* tanker.
buté [byte], *a.* obstinate.
buter [byte], *v.i.* to strike, knock. se buter; se b. à. (a) to come up against; (b) to be set on (doing sth.).
butin [bytɛ̃], *s.m.* plunder. loot.
butte [byt], *s.f.* 1. knoll, mound. 2. être en b. à, to be exposed to (ridicule, etc.).
buvard [byva:r]. 1. *a. & s.m.* (papier) b., blotting-paper. 2. *s.m.* blotter.
buvette [byvet], *s.f.* refreshment bar.
buveur, -euse [byvœr, -ø:z], *s.* drinker.
byzantin [bizɑ̃tɛ̃], *a.* Byzantine.

C

C, c [se], *s.m.* (the letter) C, c.

ça. See CELA.

çà [sa]. **1.** *adv.* çà et là, here and there. **2.** *int.* ah çà! now then!

cabane [kaban], *s.f.* hut, shanty; *Fr.C:* c. à sucre, saphouse.

cabaret [kabarε], *s.m.* **1.** (*a*) = public house; (*b*) night club; cabaret. **2.** *Fr.C:* tray.

cabestan [kabεstã], *s.m.* capstan; windlass.

cabillau(d) [kabijo], *s.m.* fresh cod.

cabine [kabin], *s.f.* cabin; (*a*) beach-hut, bathing hut; c. (téléphonique), phone box; *Rail:* c. d'aiguillage, signal box; *Av:* c. étanche, pressure cabin; *Cin:* c. de projection, projection room; *Nau:* la c., the saloon; c. de luxe, stateroom; (*c*) cage (of lift).

cabinet [kabinε], *s.m.* **1.** small room; c. de toilette, small room with washbasin; *F:* les cabinets, the lavatory, *F:* the loo; c. de travail, study; *Phot:* c. noir, dark room. **2.** office; (doctor's) consulting room. **3.** *Pol:* cabinet.

câble [kɑːbl], *s.m.* cable.

câbl/er [kɑble], *v.tr.* (*a*) to cable (message); (*b*) *El:* to connect up. *s.m.* -age, wiring.

cabot/age [kabɔtaːʒ], *s.m.* coastal trade. *s.m.* -eur, coaster.

cabrer (se) [səkabre], *v.pr.* (*of horse, etc.*) to rear; *Av:* to pull up, nose up; *F:* (*of pers.*) to jib (at sth.).

cacah(o)uète [kakawεt], *s.f.* peanut.

cacao [kakao], *s.m.* cocoa.

cacatoès [kakatɔεs], *s.m.* cockatoo.

cache [kaʃ], *s.f.* hiding-place; cache.

cache-cache [kaʃkaʃ], *s.m.* hide-and-seek.

cachemire [kaʃmiːr], *s.m. Tex:* cashmere.

cache-nez [kaʃne], *s.m.inv.* muffler, scarf.

cacher [kaʃe], *v.tr.* to hide, secrete; (*b*) to conceal (sth. from view), to mask (feelings).

se cacher, to hide; se c. à qn, to hide from, to avoid, s.o.; se c. de qn, to conceal one's feelings from s.o.

cachet [kaʃε], *s.m.* **1.** (*a*) seal; (*b*) (trade) mark; stamp. **2.** *Med:* cachet. **3.** (*of clothes*) avoir du c., to be stylish.

†cacheter [kaʃte], *v.tr.* to seal (up).

cachette [kaʃεt], *s.f.* hiding-place; en c., secretly; on the quiet.

cachot [kaʃo], *s.m.* dungeon.

cactus [kaktys], *s.m.* cactus.

cadastre [kadastr], *s.m. Adm:* national land survey service.

cadavre [kadaːvr], *s.m.* corpse; carcass (of animal).

cadeau [kado], *s.m.* present; gift.

cadenas [kadna], *s.m.* padlock.

cadence [kadãːs], *s.f.* rhythm.

cadet, -ette [kadε, -εt], *a. & s.* (*a*) younger (child); *Sp:* junior; (*b*) youngest (member of the family).

cadran [kadrã], *s.m.* **1.** dial; c. solaire sundial. **2.** face (of clock).

cadre [kaːdr], *s.m.* **1.** (*a*) (picture) frame; border; (*b*) limits, framework; dans le c. des Nations unies, within the framework of the United Nations. **2.** (bicycle, etc.) frame. **3.** *usu.pl.* trained personnel; managerial staff.

†caduc [kadyk], *a.* **1.** decaying, crumbling (building). **2.** *Bot:* deciduous.

cafard [kafaːr], *s.m.* (*a*) cockroach; (*b*) *F:* avoir le c., to be fed up.

caf/é [kafe], *s.m.* **1.** coffee; c. au lait, c. crème, white coffee; c. complet, continental breakfast. **2.** = public house. *s.* **-etier, -etière,** café-owner. *s.f.* **-etière,** coffee-pot.

caféine [kafein], *s.f.* caffeine(e).

cage [kaːʒ], *s.f.* **1.** cage. **2.** well (of stairs); shaft (of lift).

†cagneux [kaɲø], *a.* knock-kneed.

cagnotte [kaɲɔt], *s.f.* pool, kitty.

cahier [kaje], *s.m.* exercise book.

cahot [kao], *s.m.* jolt; bump.

cahot/er [kaote], *v.tr. & i.* to bump along. *s.m.* **-ement.** *a.* **-eux, -euse.**

caille [kaːj], *s.f.* quail.

cailler [kaje], *v.tr., i., & pr.* to clot, curdle; to congeal.

†caillou [kaju], *s.m.* pebble.

caillout/er [kajute], *v.tr.* (*a*) to ballast, metal (road); (*b*) to pave (with pebbles). *s.m.* **-age.** *a.* **†-eux,** stony. *s.m.* **-is,** road-metal.

caiss/e [kεs], *s.f.* **1.** cage **1.** (*a*) (packing-)case; (*b*) box, chest. **2.** body (of vehicle). **3.** (*a*) cash-box; till; c. enregistreuse, cash-register; (*b*) pay-desk; (*c*) counting-house; (*d*) petite c., petty cash; (*e*) fund; (*f*) c. d'épargne, savings bank. **4.** grosse c., big drum. *s.* **-ier, -ière,** cashier.

caisson [kεsɔ̃], *s.m. Civ.E:* caisson; *Med:* mal des caissons, the bends.

cajol/er [kaʒɔle], *v.tr.* to cajole, coax. *s.* **-eur, -euse.** *s.f.* **-erie.**

calam/ité [kalamite], *s.f.* calamity, disaster; *a.* **†-iteux,** disastrous.

calandre [kalãːdr], *s.f.* (*a*) roller; (*b*) mangle; (*c*) *Aut:* radiator grill.

calandrer [kalãdre], *v.tr.* to mangle (clothes).

calcaire [kalkεːr], *a. & s.m.* limestone; eau c., hard water.

calciner [kalsine], *v.tr.* to char, burn.

calcium [kalsjɔm], *s.m.* calcium.

calcul [kalkyl], *s.m.* **1.** (*a*) calculation, reckoning; (*b*) arithmetic. **2.** *Med:* stone (in bladder).

calculateur, -trice [kalkylatœːr, -tris], *s.* **1.** (*pers.*) calculator; statistical assistant. **2.** calculating machine; computer.

calculer [kalkyle], *v.tr.* to calculate.

cale [kal], s.f. 1. hold (of ship). 2. (a) wedge, chock; (b) prop, strut. 3. c. sèche, dry dock.

caleçon [kalsɔ̃], s.m. (under-) pants; trunks.

calendrier [kalɑ̃dri(j)e], s.m. calendar.

calepin [kalpɛ̃], s.m. notebook.

caler [kale], v.tr. 1. to chock (up). 2. Aut: to stall (engine); to jam (valve); v.i. (of engine) to stall.

calibre [kalibr], s.m. 1. calibre, bore (of fire-arm). 2. gauge.

calibr/er [kalibre], v.tr. to gauge. s.m. -age.

calice [kalis], s.m. 1. chalice. 2. Bot: calyx.

califourchon (à) [kalifurʃɔ̃], adv.phr. astride.

câlin [kalɛ̃], a. affectionate, wheedling.

câlinerie [kalinri], s.f. 1. caressing. 2. caress.

†câilleux [kalø], a. horny, callous(ed).

calmant [kalmɑ̃], 1. a. calming; soothing. 2. s.m. Med: sedative.

calme [kalm], a. & s.m. calm, adv. -ment.

calmer [kalme], v.tr. to calm, quiet; to soothe.
  se calmer, to become calm; (of storm) to abate.

calomnie [kalɔmni], s.f. slander, libel.

calomni/er [kalɔmnje], v.tr. to slander, libel. a. & s. -ateur, -atrice. a. †-eux.

calorie [kalɔri], s.f. calorie.

‡calorifug/er [kalɔrifyʒe], v.tr. to insulate, lag (pipe, etc.). s.m. -eage, insulating.

calotte [kalɔt], s.f. skull-cap; c. glaciaire, ice cap.

calque [kalk], s.m. tracing; traced design.

calqu/er [kalke], v.tr. to trace (sur, from). s.m. -age.

calvaire [kalvɛːr], s.m. Calvary.

calvinisme [kalvinism], s.m. Ecc: Calvinism.

calvitie [kalvisi], s.f. baldness.

camarade [kamarad], s.m. & f. comrade; (school) friend.

cambouis [kɑ̃bwi], s.m. dirty oil or grease.

cambriol/er [kɑ̃briɔle], v.tr. to burgle. s.m. -age, burglary. s.m. -eur, burglar.

caméléon [kamele3], s.m. chameleon.

camélia [kamelja], s.m. camellia.

camelot [kamlo], s.m. street hawker; cheapjack.

camelote [kamlɔt], s.f. F: junk.

caméra [kamera], s.f. cine-camera.

camion [kamjɔ̃], s.m. lorry, U.S: truck. s.m. -nage, haulage. s.m. -neur, lorry-U.S: truck-, driver.

camion-citerne [kamjɔ̃sitɛrn], s.m. tanker (-lorry). pl. camions-citernes.

camionnette [kamjɔnɛt], s.f. (delivery) van, U.S: light truck.

camisole [kamizɔl], s.f. 1. Fr.C: vest, U.S: undershirt. 2. c. de force, straitjacket.

camomille [kamɔmiːj], s.f. camomile.

camoufl/er [kamufle], v.tr. to camouflage. s.m. -age.

camp [kɑ̃], s.m. 1. camp. 2. party; side.

campagnard, -arde [kɑ̃paɲaːr, -ard]. 1. a. country; rustic. 2. s. countryman, -woman.

campagne [kɑ̃paɲ], s.f. 1. country(side). 2. campaign.

campanule [kɑ̃panyl], s.f. Bot: campanula.

camp/er [kɑ̃pe]. 1. v.i. to camp. 2. v.tr. to encamp (troops). s.m. -ement. (i) camping; (ii) camp. s. -eur, -euse, camper.

camphre [kɑ̃ːfr], s.m. camphor.

camping [kɑ̃piŋ], s.m. 1. camping. 2. camp site; holiday camp.

campus [kɑ̃pys], s.m. c. (universitaire), (university) campus.

canadien, -ienne [kanadjɛ̃, -jɛn]. a. & s. Canadian. s.f. lumber jacket.

canaill/e [kanaːj], s.f. rabble. s.f. -erie, dirty trick.

†canal [kanal], s.m. 1. channel. 2. canal.

canalis/er [kanalize], v.tr. 1. to canalize (river). 2. to pipe (water, oil). s.f. -ation.

canapé [kanape], s.m. 1. sofa, couch. 2. (cocktail) canapé.

canard [kanaːr], s.m. 1. duck; drake. 2. false report, hoax.

canarder [kanarde], v.tr. to snipe at (s.o.).

canari [kanari], s.m. canary.

cancan [kɑ̃kɑ̃], s.m. tittle-tattle.

canc/er [kɑ̃sɛːr], s.m. cancer. a. †-éreux. a. -érigène, carcinogenic. s.m. -érologue, cancer specialist.

candeur [kɑ̃dœːr], s.f. ingenuousness.

candidat [kɑ̃dida], s.m. candidate, applicant. s.f. -ure.

candide [kɑ̃did], a. ingenuous, artless. adv. -ment.

cane [kan], s.f. duck. s.m. -ton, duckling.

canevas [kanva], s.m. canvas.

caniche [kaniʃ], s.m. & f. poodle.

canif [kanif], s.m. penknife.

canin [kanɛ̃], a. canine; exposition canine, dog-show.

caniveau [kanivo], s.m. gutter; dip (in road).

canne [kan], s.f. 1. cane, reed; c. à sucre, sugar-cane. 2. walking-stick. 3. c. à pêche, fishing-rod.

cannelle [kanɛl], s.f. cinnamon.

cannelure [kanlyːr], s.f. groove, slot.

cannibal/e [kanibal], s.m. & f. cannibal. s.m. -isme.

cano/ë [kanɔe], s.m. canoe. s.m. -éisme, canoeing. s. -éiste, canoeist.

canon¹ [kanɔ̃], s.m. 1. gun, cannon. 2. barrel (of rifle). s.f. -nade, gunfire. s.m. -nier, gunner.

canon², s.m. 1. canon, rule. 2. Mus: round, catch.

canot [kano], s.m. (open) boat; dinghy. s.m. -age, rowing.

canotier [kanɔtje], s.m. 1. oarsman. 2. straw hat, boater.

cantate [kɑ̃tat], s.f. cantata.

cantatrice [kɑ̃tatris], s.f. (professional) singer.

cantine [kɑ̃tin], s.f. canteen.

cantique [kɑ̃tik], s.m. (a) canticle; (b) hymn.

canton [kɑ̃tɔ̃], s.m. canton; district.

cantonade [kɑ̃tɔnad], s.f. Th: wings; parler à la c., to speak 'off.'

canton/ner [kɑ̃tɔne], v.tr. to billet (troops). s.m. -ement, billeting.

cantonnier [kɑ̃tɔnje], s.m. roadman.

caoutchouc [kautʃu], s.m. 1. rubber; c. mousse, foam rubber. 2. raincoat. 3. (a) elastic; (b) rubber band.

caoutchout/er [kautʃute], v.tr. to treat with rubber, to rubberize (sth.).

cap [kap], s.m. 1. cape, headland. 2. head (of ship); course.

capable [kapabl], a. capable. adv.-ment.

capacité [kapasite], s.f. capacity.

cape [kap], s.f. (hooded) cloak, cape; rire sous c., to laugh up one's sleeve.

capitaine [kapiten], s.m. (a) captain; Nau: c. de vaisseau, captain; Av: c. aviateur, flight lieutenant; (b) chief, head, leader.

†capital [kapital]. 1. a. (a) capital (punishment); (b) essential; principal; la ville capitale, s.f. la capitale, the capital (city); (c) lettre capitale, s.f. capitale, capital (letter). 2. s.m. capital, assets; c. social, registered capital. s.m. isme. s.m. & f. -iste.

capitul/er [kapityle], v.i. to capitulate. s.f. -ation.

†caporal [kapɔral], s.m. corporal; Av: leading aircraftman.

capot [kapo], s.m. 1. cover, hood, casing; Aut: bonnet, U.S: hood. 2. Nau: companion (hatch).

capote [kapɔt], s.f. 1. Mil: great-coat. 2. Aut: hood, U.S: top. 3. (chimney) cowl.

capot/er [kapɔte], v.i. to capsize; to overturn. s.m. -age.

câpre [kɑːpr], s.f. Bot: caper.

caprice [kapris], s.m. caprice, whim.

†capricieu/x [kaprisjø], a. capricious. adv. -ement.

capsule [kapsyl], s.f. capsule.

capt/er [kapte], v.tr. 1. to obtain (by undue influence); to pick up (transmission); to intercept; P.T.T: to tap (wires). 2. to harness (river); El: to pick up, collect (current). s.m. -age.

capti/f, -ive [kaptif, -iv], a. & s. captive; prisoner. s.f. -vité, captivity.

captiver [kaptive], v.tr. to captivate.

capture [kaptyːr], s.f. capture.

capturer [kaptyre], v.tr. to capture.

capuchon [kapyʃɔ̃], s.m. 1. (a) hood; (b) cowl. 2. cap (of fountain-pen).

capucine [kapysin], s.f. nasturtium.

caquet [kake], s.m. cackle, cackling (of hens); chatter.

‡caquet/er [kakte], v.i. 1. to cackle. 2. to chatter. s.m. -age. s. -eur, -euse.

car¹ [kaːr], conj. for, because.

car², s.m. (motor-)coach; (country) bus.

carabine [karabin], s.f. rifle.

caractère [karakteːr], s.m. 1. character; imprimé en gros caractères, printed in large type. 2. (a) characteristic; (b) official capacity. 3. (a) nature, disposition; (b) personality, character.

caractéris/er [karakterize], v.tr. to characterize. a. & s.f. -tique, characteristic.

carafe [karaf], s.f. decanter; carafe.

carambolage [karɑ̃bɔlaːʒ], s.m. (a) cannon (at billiards); (b) Aut: F: pile-up (in a road smash).

carat [kara], s.m. carat.

caravane [karavan], s.f. caravan. s.m. F: -ier, caravaner. s.m. F: -(n)ing, caravan(n)ing.

carbonate [karbɔnat], s.m. Ch: carbonate; c. de soude, washing soda.

carbone [karbɔn], s.m. carbon; papier c., carbon paper.

carbonique [karbɔnik], a. carbonic; neige c., dry ice.

carbonis/er [karbɔnize], v.tr. to burn, to char; être carbonisé, to be burnt to death (in accident). s.f. -ation.

carburant [karbyrɑ̃], s.m. motor fuel.

carburateur [karbyratœːr], s.m. carburettor.

carcasse [karkas], s.f. carcass; framework.

cardiaque [kardjak]. 1. a. heart (murmur, attack). 2. s. heart patient, case.

†cardinal [kardinal]. 1. a. cardinal (number). 2. s.m. Ecc: cardinal.

cardio/logie [kardjɔlɔʒi], s.f. Med: cardiology. s.m. -logue, cardiologist.

carême [karem], s.m. Lent.

‡carén/er [karene], v.tr. to streamline. s.m. -age, streamlining.

caresse [kares], s.f. caress.

caresser [karese], v.tr. 1. to caress, fondle. 2. to cherish (hope).

carg/o [kargo], s.m. cargo boat. s.f. -aison, freight.

caricature [karikatyːr], s.f. caricature.

caricatur/er [karikatyre], v.tr. to caricature. s.m. -iste.

carié [karje], a. (of tooth) decayed.

carillon [karijɔ̃], s.m. chime(s).

carillonn/er [karijɔne], v.i. (a) to ring a peal; (b) to chime. s.m. -ement, pealing. s.m. -eur, bell-ringer.

carmin [karmɛ̃], s.m. carmine.

carnassier [karnasje], a. & s.m. carnivorous (animal).

†carnaval [karnaval], s.m. carnival.

carnet [karne], s.m. note-book; c. de chèques, cheque book.

carnivore [karnivɔːr], *a. & s.* carnivorous (animal).

carotte [karɔt], *s.f.* carrot; *P:* trick, sell.

carpe [karp], *s.f.* carp.

carpette [karpɛt], *s.f.* rug.

carré [kare]. 1. *a.* (*a*) square; partie carrée, foursome; (*b*) blunt (answer). 2. *s.m.* (*a*) *Mth:* square; (*b*) landing (of staircase); *Nav:* c. des officiers, wardroom; (*c*) *Cl:* c. de soie, silk square. *adv.* -ment.

carreau [karo], *s.m.* 1. (*a*) (flooring) tile; (*b*) (window) pane. 2. (at cards) diamonds.

carrefour [karfuːr], *s.m.* cross-roads.

carrelage [karlaːʒ], *s.m.* tiling.

carrelet [karlɛ], *s.m.* plaice.

carrière¹ [karjɛːr], *s.f.* 1. career. 2. donner libre c. à ses idées, to give one's ideas free play.

carrière², *s.f.* (stone) quarry.

carrosserie [karɔsri], *s.f. Aut:* body, coachwork.

carrure [karyːr], *s.f.* breadth across the shoulders; avoir une belle c., to be strongly built.

cartable [kartabl], *s.m. Sch:* satchel.

carte [kart], *s.f.* 1. (piece of) cardboard; card; c. à jouer, playing-card; c. d'identité, identity card; c. de lecteur, reader's ticket; c. d'abonnement, season ticket; donner c. blanche (à qn), to give (s.o.) a free hand; c. (postale), postcard. 2. map. 3. menu.

carter [kartɛːr], *s.m. Aut:* casing; fond de c., sump.

carton [kartɔ̃], *s.m.* 1. cardboard. 2. cardboard box.

cartouch|e [kartuʃ]. 1. *s.m.* scroll; cartouche. 2. *s.f.* cartridge. *s.f.* -ière, cartridge-belt.

cas [ka], *s.m.* case; c. urgent, emergency; faire c. de, to value; en ce c., in that case; en tout c., in any case.

casanier, -ière [kazanje, -jɛːr], *a. & s.* stay-at-home.

cascade [kaskad], *s.f.* cascade, waterfall.

case [kaːz], *s.f.* 1. hut, cabin. 2. (*a*) compartment, pigeonhole; (*b*) square (of chessboard).

caser [kaze], *v.tr.* (*a*) to put away; to file; (*b*) to find a job for (s.o.).
se caser, to settle down; *F:* to marry.

caserne [kazɛrn], *s.f.* barracks.

casier [kazje], *s.m.* (*a*) set of pigeonholes; (*b*) c. à bouteilles, bottle rack, crate.

casino [kazino], *s.m.* casino.

casque [kask], *s.m.* helmet.

casquette [kaskɛt], *s.f.* cap.

cassant [kasɑ̃], *a.* 1. (*a*) brittle; (*b*) crisp (biscuit). 2. curt, abrupt.

cassation [kasasjɔ̃], *s.f.* annulment; Cour de c., Supreme Court of Appeal.

casse [kaːs], *s.f.* breakage, damage; *F:* il y aura de la c., there'll be trouble.

casse-cou [kasku], *s.m.inv.* 1. deathtrap. 2. dare-devil.

casse-croûte [kaskrut], *s.m.inv.* snack.

casse-noisette(s) [kasnwazɛt], *s.m.inv.* (pair of) nut-crackers.

casse-pieds [kaspje], *s.m.inv. F:* (of pers.) bore, nuisance.

cass|er [kase], *v.tr.* 1. to break, snap. 2. *Mil:* to cashier. 3. to squash. *s.f.* -ure, fracture.
se casser, to break, snap.

casserole [kasrɔl], *s.f.* (sauce)pan.

cassette [kasɛt], *s.f.* money-box.

cassis [kasi(s)], *s.m.* black-currant.

caste [kast], *s.f.* caste; esprit de c., class consciousness.

castor [kastɔːr], *s.m.* beaver.

†**casuel** [kazɥɛl], *a.* accidental.

cataclysme [kataklism], *s.m.* disaster.

catacombes [katakɔ̃b], *s.f.pl.* catacombs.

catadioptre [katadiɔptr], *s.m. Aut:* rear reflector.

catalogue [katalɔg], *s.m.* catalogue.

catalogu|er [katalɔge], *v.tr.* to catalogue. *s.m.* -age.

cata|**lyse** [kataliz], *s.f. Ch:* catalysis. *s.m.* -lyseur, catalyst. *a.* -lytique.

cataphote [katafɔt], *s.m. R.t.m.* cat's eye (reflector).

cataplasme [kataplasm], *s.m.* poultice.

catapulte [katapylt], *s.f.* catapult.

catapultage [katapyltaːʒ], *s.m. Av:* catapult launching.

cataracte [katarakt], *s.f.* cataract.

catarrhe [kataːr], *s.m.* catarrh.

catastrophe [katastrɔf], *s.f.* catastrophe.

catch [katʃ], *s.m.* all-in wrestling. *s.m.* -eur, all-in wrestler.

catéchiser [kateʃize], *v.tr.* 1. *Ecc:* to catechize. 2. to reason with; to indoctrinate.

catéchisme [kateʃism], *s.m.* catechism.

catégorie [kategɔri], *s.f.* category.

catégorique [kategɔrik], *a.* categorical; refus c., flat refusal. *adv.* -ment.

cathédrale [katedral], *s.f.* cathedral.

cathod|e [katɔd], *s.f. El:* cathode. *a.* -ique.

catholique [katɔlik]. 1. *a.* orthodox; *F:* ce n'est pas c., it sounds fishy. 2. *a. & s.* (Roman) Catholic.

cauchemar [koʃmaːr], *s.m.* nightmare.

cause [koːz], *s.f.* 1. cause; good reason; *prep.phr.* à c. de, on account of. 2. *Jur:* suit, action; en connaissance de c., with full knowledge of the case.

causer¹ [koze], *v.tr.* to cause.

caus/er², *v.i.* to chat. *s.m.* -eur, -euse.

causerie [kozri], *s.f.* (a) talk; (*b*) chat.

caustique [kostik], *a. & s.* caustic.

cautériser [koterize], *v.tr.* to cauterize.

caution [kosjɔ̃], *s.f.* 1. security, guarantee; bail; sujet à c., unconfirmed (news). 2. surety, guaranty. *s.m.* -nement, surety-bond.

cavalcade [kavalkad], s.f. 1. cavalcade. 2. pageant.

cavalerie [kavalri], s.f. cavalry.

caval/ier, -ière [kavalje, -jɛ:r]. 1. s. rider; horseman. 2. s.m. (a) Mil: trooper; (b) (chess) knight; (c) partner (to lady). 3. s.m. Techn: staple. 4. a. off-hand (manner). adv. **-ièrement.**

cav/e [ka:v], s.f. cellar. s.m. **-eau,** (burial) vault.

cavern/e [kavern], s.f. cave, cavern. a. †**-eux,** hollow (voice).

caviar [kavja:r], s.m. caviar.

cavité [kavite], s.f. cavity, hollow.

ce[1] [s(ə)], dem.pron.neut. (c' before parts of être beginning with a vowel it), that. 1. (as neuter subject of être, devoir être, pouvoir être): (a) (with adj. or adv. complement) c'est faux! it's not true! est-ce assez? is that enough? (b) (with s. or pron. as complement) (with 3rd pers. pl. complement, colloquial usage allows the sing.): c'est moi, c'est nous, ce sont eux; F: c'est eux, it is I, we, they, F: me, us, them; inv.phr. si ce n'est, except, unless (c) ce . . . ici = CECI; (d) ce . . . là = CELA; (e) c'est que; (introducing a statement) c'est qu'il fait froid! it is cold and no mistake! (f) est-ce que (eska); (introducing a question) est-ce que je peux entrer? may I come in? 2. (used as object to dire, faire, etc.) ce disant, so saying. 3. (a) (used as neuter antecedent to a rel. pron.) ce qui, ce que, etc. = what; (b) ce qui, ce que, etc. = which; (c) tout ce qui, que, everything, all (that). 4. (= CELA) sur ce, thereupon.

ce[2], cet, cette, ces [sə, sɛt, sɛt, se or sɛ], unstressed dem.a. (the form cet is used before a s. or adj. beginning with a vowel or 'h mute') this, that, pl. these, those. 1. ce dernier, the latter. 2. ce . . . -ci, this; ce . . . -là, that; prenez cette tasse-ci, take this cup.

ceci [səsi], dem.pron.neut. this (thing); écoutez bien ceci, now listen to this.

cécité [sesite], s.f. blindness.

‡**céder** [sede]. 1. v.tr. (a) to give up, yield; (b) to transfer. 2. v.i. to yield, give away.

cédille [sedij], s.f. cedilla.

cèdre [sɛ:dr], s.m. cedar(-tree, -wood).

ceinture [sɛ̃ty:r], s.f. 1. (a) girdle; belt; sash; c. de sauvetage, life-belt; c. de sécurité, safety-belt; (b) waist. 2. girdle.

ceinturer [sɛ̃tyre], v.tr. 1. to girdle, surround. 2. Sp: to tackle (a player).

cela [səla, sla], F: **ça** [sa], dem.pron. neut. (a) that (thing); qu'est-ce que c'est que c.? what is that? (b) that, it; (cela is the pron. used as neuter subject to all vbs. other than être; used with être is more emphatic than ce) c. ne vous regarde pas, that's no business of yours; (c) c'est ça, that's it, that's

right; il n'y a que ça, there's nothing like it; Com: et avec c., madame? and what else, madam?

célèbre [selɛbr], a. celebrated (par, for).

‡**célébr/er** [selebre], v.tr. to celebrate. s.f. **-ation.**

célébrité [selebrite], s.f. celebrity.

céleri [selri], s.m. celery; pied de c., head of celery.

célérité [selerite], s.f. speed.

céleste [selɛst], a. celestial, heavenly; bleu c., sky blue.

célibat [seliba], s.m. celibacy.

célibataire [selibatɛ:r], a. unmarried, single. s.m. bachelor. s.f. spinster.

celle. See CELUI.

cellophane [selɔfan], s.f. R.t.m: cellophane.

cellulaire [selylɛ:r], a. 1. cellular (tissue, etc.). 2. voiture c., police van.

cellul/e [selyl], s.f. cell. s.f. **-ite,' Med:** cellulitis.

celluloïd [selylɔid], s.m. R.t.m: celluloid.

cellulose [selylo:z], s.f. cellulose.

celui, celle, pl. **ceux, celles,** [səlɥi, sɛl, sø, sɛl], dem.pron. 1. (a) (completed by an adj. clause) the one; those; (b) he, she, those; c. qui mange peu dort bien, he who eats little sleeps well. 2. (followed by de) mes livres et ceux de Jean, my books and John's. 3. celui-ci, ceux-ci, this (one), these; the latter; celui-là, ceux-là, that (one); those; the former.

cément/er [semɑ̃te], v.tr. Ind: to case-harden (steel). s.f. **-ation.**

cendre [sɑ̃:dr], s.f. ash(es), cinders; Mer-credi des Cendres, Ash Wednesday.

cendré [sɑ̃dre], a. (ash-)grey; ashy; cheveux blond cendré, ash blond hair.

cendrée [sɑ̃dre], s.f. piste en c., cinder-track; dirt-track.

cendrier [sɑ̃drie], s.m. (a) ashpan; (b) ashtray.

cénotaphe [senɔtaf], s.m. cenotaph.

censé [sɑ̃se], a. supposed; je ne suis pas c. le savoir, I'm not supposed to know. adv. **-ment,** supposedly.

censeur [sɑ̃sœ:r], s.m. 1. critic. 2. censor. 3. Sch: vice-principal (of lycée).

censure [sɑ̃sy:r], s.f. 1. censorship. 2. censure, blame.

censurer [sɑ̃syre], v.tr. 1. to censure. 2. to censor.

cent[1] [sɑ̃], num.a. (takes a pl. s when multiplied by a preceding number and not followed by another numeral; inv. when used as an ordinal) (a) (one) hundred; deux cents hommes, two hundred men; deux cent trois pages, two hundred and three pages; faire les c. pas, to pace up and down. 2. s.m.inv. a hundred; sept pour c., seven per cent.

centaine [sɑ̃tɛn], s.f. a hundred (or so).

centenaire [sɑ̃tnɛːr]. 1. *a.* ancient. 2. *s.m. & f.* centenarian. 3. *s.m.* centenary.
centième [sɑ̃tjɛm], *num.a. & s.* hundredth.
centigrade [sɑ̃tigrad], *a.* centigrade.
centime [sɑ̃tim], *s.m.* centime.
centimètre [sɑ̃timɛtr], *s.m.* 1. centimetre. 2. tape-measure.
†**central** [sɑ̃tral]. 1. *a.* central. 2. *(a) s.m.* c. téléphonique, telephone exchange; *(b) s.f.* **centrale**, power-station; **centrale thermique, nucléaire, maré-motrice**, thermal, nuclear, tidal, power-station.
centre [sɑ̃ːtr], *s.m.* centre; middle.
centr/er [sɑ̃tre], *v.tr.* to centre (sur, on); to adjust (tool, etc.); *Sp:* c. le ballon, to centre the ball. *s.m.* -age. *s.m.* -eur.
centuple [sɑ̃typl], *a. & s.m.* hundredfold.
cep [sɛp)], *s.m.* vine-stock.
cèpe [sɛp], *s.m.* boletus, *F:* penny bun (mushroom).
cependant [s(ə)pɑ̃dɑ̃]. 1. *adv.* meanwhile. 2. *conj.* yet, still, nevertheless.
cercle [sɛrkl], *s.m.* 1. *(a)* circle; *(b)* club. 2. hoop, ring.
cercler [sɛrkle], *v.tr.* to encircle, to ring.
cercueil [sɛrkœːj], *s.m.* coffin.
céréale [sereal], *s.f. & a.* cereal.
†**cérébral** [serebral], *a.* cerebral.
cérémon/ie [seremɔni], *s.f.* ceremony; visite de c., formal call. *a.* †-ial, ceremonial. *a.* †-ieux, ceremonious.
cerf [sɛːr], *s.m.* stag.
cerf-volant [sɛrvɔlɑ̃], *s.m.* 1. stagbeetle. 2. *Sp:* kite; *pl.* cerfs-volants.
ceris/e [s(ə)riːz]. 1. *s.f.* cherry. *s.m. & a.inv.* cerise. *s.m.* -ier, cherry-tree.
cerner [sɛrne], *v.tr.* to encircle, surround; avoir les yeux cernés, to have rings under one's eyes.
certain [sɛrtɛ̃]. 1. *a. (a)* certain, sure; *(b)* il est c. de réussir, he is sure he will succeed; *(c)* fixed, stated (date, price). 2. *indef. a. & pron.* some, certain; d'un c. âge, elderly. *adv.* -ement.
certes [sɛrt], *adv.* (oui) c.! yes indeed!
certificat [sɛrtifika] *s.m.* certificate; testimonial; c. d'origine, pedigree (of dog, etc.).
certifier [sɛrtifje], *v.tr.* to certify, attest; to witness (signature).
certitude [sɛrtityd], *s.f.* certainty.
cerveau [sɛrvo], *s.m. (a) Anat:* brain; **rhume de c.**, cold in the head; *(b)* intellect, brains; c. brûlé, hot-head.
cervelas [sɛrvəla], *s.m.* saveloy.
cervelle [sɛrvɛl], *s.f.* 1. *Anat:* brain(s) (as matter); brûler la c. à qn, to blow s.o.'s brains out; *Cu:* c. de veau, calves' brains. 2. mind, brains; se creuser la c., to rack one's brains (pour, to).
ces. See CE[2].
césarienne [sezarjɛn], *a.f. Med:* caesarean (operation).

cesse [sɛs], *s.f.* cease, ceasing; sans c., unceasingly.
cess/er [sɛse], *v.tr. & i.* to cease, leave off, stop; faire c., to put a stop to; c. de faire, qch. to cease doing sth. *s.f.* -ation, cessation; suspension.
cession [sɛsjɔ̃], *s.f.* transfer. *s.m.* -naire, transferee.
c'est-à-dire [sɛtadiːr], *conj.phr.* that is (to say).
cet, cette. See CE[2].
ceux. See CELUI.
chacun [ʃakœ̃], *pron.* 1. each; each one. 2. everybody, everyone.
chagrin [ʃagrɛ̃]. 1. *s.m.(a)* grief, sorrow; *(b)* vexation, annoyance. 2. *a. (a)* distressed; *(b)* peevish, fretful.
chagriner [ʃagrine], *v.tr.* 1. to grieve, distress. 2. to annoy.
chahut/er [ʃayte], *v. 1. n.i. F:* to kick up a shindy; to lark about. 2. *v.tr.* to rag (s.o.). *s.m.* -age. *s.* -eur, rowdy.
chai [ʃɛ], *s.m.* wine and spirits storehouse.
chaîne [ʃɛːn], *s.f.* 1. *(a)* chain; *Nau:* cable; *Ind:* travail à la c., work on an assembly line; *(b)* shackles, fetters. 2. chain (of mountains). 3. *Tex:* warp.
chair [ʃɛːr], *s.f.* flesh. 1. en c. et en os, in the flesh; être (bien) en c., to be plump. 2. *Cu:* c. à saucisse, sausage meat; c. à canon, cannon-fodder; *(b)* pulp (of fruit).
chaire [ʃɛːr], *s.f.* 1. pulpit. 2. *(a)* chair, desk (of lecturer); *(b)* professorship.
chaise [ʃɛːz], *s.f.* chair, seat.
chaise-longue [ʃɛzlɔ̃ːg], *s.f.* chaise longue. *pl.* chaises-longues.
chaland [ʃalɑ̃], *s.m.* lighter, barge.
châle [ʃɑːl], *s.m.* shawl.
chalet [ʃalɛ], *s.m. (a)* chalet; *(b)* country cottage.
chaleur [ʃalœːr], *s.f. (a)* heat, warmth; *(b)* ardour, zeal.
†**chaleureu/x** [ʃalœrø], *a.* warm; cordial. *adv.* -sement.
chaloupe [ʃalup], *s.f.* launch; long-boat; *Fr. C:* rowing-boat, *U.S:* row-boat.
chalumeau [ʃalymo], *s.m.* 1. straw (for drinking). 2. blow-lamp.
chalut [ʃaly], *s.m.* drag-net; trawl. *s.m.* -ier, trawler.
chamailler (se) [ʃəfamɑje], *v.pr. F:* to squabble.
chambranle [ʃɑ̃brɑ̃ːl], *s.m.* frame (of door).
chambre [ʃɑ̃ːbr], *s.f.* 1. room; c. à deux lits, double room; c. d'ami, guest room; c. d'enfants, nursery. 2. *Adm:* chamber, house; c. de commerce, chamber of commerce. 3. *Aut:* c.à air, inner tube; *Phot:* c. noire, dark-room.
chambrée [ʃɑ̃bre], *s.f. Mil:* barrack-room.
chambrer [ʃɑ̃bre], *v.tr.* to take the chill off (red wine).
chameau, -elle [ʃamo, -ɛl], *s.m.* camel.
chamois [ʃamwa], *s.m.* chamois; peau de c., chamois, *F:* shammy, leather.

champ [ʃɑ̃], s.m. 1. (a) field; (b) c. de foire, fairground; c. d'aviation, airfield; c. de tir, rifle-range. 2. (a) field of action; scope; le c. est libre, the coast is clear; (b) c. magnétique, magnetic field.

champagne [ʃɑ̃paɲ]. 1. s.m. champagne. 2. s.f. fine c., liqueur brandy.

champêtre [ʃɑ̃pɛːtr], a. rustic, rural; garde c., rural policeman.

champignon [ʃɑ̃piɲɔ̃], s.m. 1. (a) c. comestible, (i) edible fungus, (ii) mushroom; (b) c. vénéneux, poisonous fungus. 2. Aut: F: accelerator.

champion, -ionne [ʃɑ̃pjɔ̃, -jɔn], s. champion. -nat, championship.

chance [ʃɑ̃ːs], s.f. 1. chance. 2. luck, fortune; avoir de la c., to be lucky.

‡chancel/er [ʃɑ̃sle], v.i. to stagger, totter. -lement.

chancel/ier [ʃɑ̃səlje], s.m. chancellor. s.f. -lerie, (i) chancellery (ii) chancery (of embassy).

†chanceux [ʃɑ̃sø], a. 1. hazardous. 2. lucky.

chandail [ʃɑ̃daːj], s.m. sweater, pullover.

chandelier [ʃɑ̃dəlje], s.m. candlestick.

chandelle [ʃɑ̃dɛl], s.f. 1. (tallow) candle; voir trente-six chandelles, to see stars. 2. (of aircraft) monter en c., to rocket.

change [ʃɑ̃ːʒ], s.m. exchange; bureau de c., foreign exchange office. 2. F: donner le c. à qn, to side-track s.o.

changeant [ʃɑ̃ʒɑ̃], a. changing; fickle.

‡chang/er [ʃɑ̃ʒe]. 1. v.tr. to change, exchange. 2. v.tr. to change, alter. 3. v.i. to (undergo a) change. s.m. -ement. s.m. -eur, money-changer. se changer. 1. to change; to alter. 2. to change one's clothes.

chanoine [ʃanwan], s.m. Ecc: canon.

chanson [ʃɑ̃sɔ̃], s.f. song.

chansonnier, -ière [ʃɑ̃sɔnje, -jɛːr], s. 1. (a) song-writer; (b) variety singer. 2. s.m. song-book.

chant [ʃɑ̃], s.m. 1. singing; song. melody, air.

chant/er [ʃɑ̃te], v.tr. to sing; faire c. qn, to blackmail s.o. s.m. -age, blackmail.

chanteur, -euse [ʃɑ̃tœːr, -øːz], s. singer, vocalist; maître c., blackmailer.

chantier [ʃɑ̃tje], s.m. yard; work(ing) site; dépôt; P.N: road works; c. de (construction), (i) works site; (ii) builder's yard.

chantonner [ʃɑ̃tɔne], v.tr. & i. to hum.

chantre [ʃɑ̃ːtr], s.m. Ecc: chorister.

chanvre [ʃɑ̃ːvr], s.m. hemp.

chao/s [kao], s.m. chaos, confusion. a. -tique, chaotic.

chap/eau [ʃapo], s.m. 1. hat; int. F: well done! saluer qn d'un coup de c., to raise one's hat to s.o.; c. bas, hat in hand. 2. cover; lid; cap. s.m. -elier, hatter. s.f. -ellerie, hat-trade, shop.

chapelet [ʃaplɛ], s.m. (lesser) rosary; égrener son c., to tell one's beads.

chapelle [ʃapɛl], s.f. chapel; c. de la Vierge, Lady Chapel.

chapelure [ʃaplyːr], s.f. Cu: breadcrumbs.

chaperon [ʃaprɔ̃], v.tr. to chaperon (a girl).

chapiteau [ʃapito], s.m. capital (of column).

chapitre [ʃapitr], s.m. 1. Ecc: chapter; salle du c., chapter house. 2. (a) chapter (of book); (b) head(ing); item

chapon [ʃapɔ̃], s.m. capon.

chaque [ʃak], a. each, every.

char [ʃaːr], s.m. 1. wagon; cart. 2. Mil: c. (de combat), tank. 3. Fr. C: car.

charbon [ʃarbɔ̃], s.m. (a) c. de bois, charcoal; être sur des charbons ardents, to be on tenterhooks; (b) carbon; (c) coal. s.m. -nage, coal-mining; pl. collieries.

charbonnier, -ière [ʃarbɔnje, -jɛːr]. 1. s.m. Nau: collier. 2. s. coal-merchant. 3. a. coal-mining (industry).

charcuterie [ʃarkytri], s.f. 1. delicatessen, pork butcher's shop. 2. delicatessen.

charcutier, -ière [ʃarkytje, -jɛːr], s. pork butcher.

chardon [ʃardɔ̃], s.m. thistle.

chardonneret [ʃardɔnrɛ], s.m. goldfinch.

charge [ʃarʒ], s.f. 1. load, burden. 2. charge, load; c. admissible, safe load. 3. (a) charge, responsibility; femme de c., housekeeper; (b) Adm: office. 4. charge, expense; charges sociales, national insurance contributions; être à la c. de qn, to be dependent on s.o. 5. Aut: etc: c. utile, carrying capacity. 6. Mil: charge. 7. Jur: charge, indictment; témoin à c., witness for the prosecution.

chargé [ʃarʒe], a. loaded, laden; jour c., busy day; temps c., overcast weather. 2. s.m. Sch: c. de cours, (university) lecturer.

‡charg/er [ʃarʒe], v.tr. 1. to load (de, with); to fill (pipe). 2. to instruct. 3. to charge. 4. Jur: to indict (s.o.) s.m. -ement, load; freight. se charger de, to undertake.

chariot [ʃarjo], s.m. 1. (a) wagon; (b) truck, trolley. 2. (a) carriage (of typewriter); (b) Av: c. d'atterrissage, undercarriage.

charitable [ʃaritabl], a. charitable (envers, to). adv. -ment.

charité [ʃarite], s.f. 1. charity. 2. act of charity.

charlatan [ʃarlatɑ̃], s. charlatan, quack. s.m. -isme.

charme [ʃarm], s.m. charm.

charm/er [ʃarme], v.tr. to charm. a. -ant, charming.

charnière [ʃarnjɛːr], s.f. hinge.

charnu [ʃarny], a. fleshy.

charpente [ʃarpɑ̃t], s.f. frame(work).

charpent/ier [ʃarpɑ̃tje], s.m. carpenter. s.f. -erie, carpentry.

charrett/e [ʃaret], *s.f.* cart; c. à bras, hand-cart; barrow. *s.m.* -ier, carter.

charrier [ʃarje], *v.tr.* to cart, carry.

charrue [ʃary], *s.f.* plough.

charte [ʃart], *s.f.* charter; la c. de l'Atlantique, the Atlantic Charter.

chartreux, -euse [ʃartrø, øːz]. 1. *s.m. & f.* Carthusian monk, nun. 2. *s.f.* (a) Carthusian monastery, charterhouse; (b) chartreuse (liqueur).

chas [ʃa], *s.m.* eye (of needle).

chasse [ʃas], *s.f.* 1. hunting; (game) shooting; c. sous-marine, underwater fishing; aller à la c., to go shooting. 2. c. d'eau, (W.C.) flush.

châsse [ʃaːs], *s.f.* reliquary, shrine.

chasse-neige [ʃasneːʒ], *s.m.inv.* 1. snow-plough. 2. (skiing) virage en c.-n., stem-turn.

chasser [ʃase]. 1. *v.tr.* (a) to chase, hunt; (b) to drive away; to dismiss; c. un clou, to drive in a nail. 2. *v.i.* to hunt; to shoot.

chasseur, -euse [ʃasœːr, -øːz], *s.* 1. (a) huntsman; hunter; (b) sportsman (with gun). 2. *s.m.* commissionaire; porter; page-boy. 3. *s.m. Av:* fighter.

châssis [ʃasi], *s.m.* (a) frame; (b) *Aut:* chassis.

chaste [ʃast], *a.* chaste, pure. *adv.* -ment. *s.f.* -té, purity.

chat, f. chatte [ʃa, ʃat], *s.* cat; *F:* mon petit chat, ma petite chatte, darling.

châtaign/e [ʃatɛɲ], *s.f.* chestnut. *s.m.* -ier, chestnut tree.

châtain [ʃatɛ̃], *a.inv.* (chestnut-)brown.

château [ʃato], *s.m.* 1. c. (fort), castle; châteaux en Espagne, castles in the air. 2. (a) country seat; mansion; (b) palace. 3. c. d'eau, water tower.

chateaubriand, -briant [ʃatobriɑ̃], *s.m. Cu:* porterhouse steak.

chat-huant [ʃaɥɑ̃], *s.m.* tawny owl. *pl. chats-huants.*

châti/er [ʃatje], *v.tr.* to punish, chastise; to chasten. *s.m.* -ment, punishment.

chatoiement [ʃatwamɑ̃], *s.m.* shimmer, sheen.

chaton [ʃatɔ̃], *s.m.* 1. kitten. 2. catkin.

chatouill/er [ʃatuje], *v.tr.* to tickle. *s.m.* -ement. *a.* †-eux, ticklish; sensitive.

‡**chatoy/er** [ʃatwaje], *v.i.* (a) to shimmer; (b) to glisten, sparkle. *a.* -ant, iridescent.

chatte. See CHAT.

chatterton [ʃatɛrtɔ̃], *s.m. El:* adhesive (insulating) tape.

chaud [ʃo]. 1. *a.* warm; hot; pleurer à chaudes larmes, to weep bitterly; il fait c., it is warm (weather). 2. *s.m.* avoir c., (of pers.) to be warm. *adv.* -ement.

chaudière [ʃodjɛːr], *s.f.* 1. copper (for washing). 2. boiler.

chaudron [ʃodrɔ̃], *s.m.* cauldron. *s.m.* -nier, boiler-maker.

chauffage [ʃofaːʒ], *s.m.* warming, heating; c. central, central heating.

chauffard [ʃofaːr], *s.m. F:* road hog.

chauffe [ʃof], *s.f.* 1. heating. 2. stoking.

chauffe-eau [ʃofo], *s.m.inv.* water-heater.

chauffer [ʃofe]. 1. *v.tr.* (a) to warm, heat; se c., to warm oneself; (b) chauffé au rouge, red-hot; (c) *F:* c. un examen, to swot for an exam. 2. *v.i.* to get warm, hot.

chauffeur, -euse [ʃofœːr, -øːz], *s.* 1. stoker, fireman. 2. *Aut:* driver; chauffeur, chauffeuse.

chaume [ʃoːm], *s.m.* (a) thatch; (b) stubble. *s.f.* -ière, thatched cottage.

chaussée [ʃose], *s.f.* 1. (a) sea-wall; (b) causeway. 2. (a) roadway; (b) high road.

chausse-pied [ʃospje], *s.m.* shoe-horn; *pl. chausse-pieds.*

chauss/er [ʃose], *v.tr.* to put on (footwear); être bien chaussé, to be well shod. *s.f.* -ette, sock.

chaussure [ʃosyːr], *s.f.* shoe; *pl.* footwear.

chauve [ʃoːv]. 1. *a.* (a) bald; (b) bare, denuded (hill, etc.). 2. *s.m.* bald person.

chauve-souris [ʃoːvsuri], *s.f. Z:* bat. *pl. chauves-souris.*

chaux [ʃo], *s.f.* lime; blanchir à la c., to whitewash.

chavirer [ʃavire], *v.i. & tr.* to capsize, upset.

chef [ʃef], *s.m.* 1. head; chief; principal; leader; scout-master; *Sp:* c. d'équipe, captain; c. de gare, stationmaster; c. de train, guard. 2. authority; de son (propre) c., (i) on one's own (authority); (ii) in one's own right.

chef-d'œuvre [ʃedœːvr], *s.m.* masterpiece. *pl. chefs-d'œuvre.*

chef-lieu [ʃefljø], *s.m.* chief town (of department). *pl. chefs-lieux.*

cheftaine [ʃeftɛn], *s.f.* (guide) captain; Brown Owl; (woman) cubmaster.

chemin [ʃmɛ̃], *s.m.* 1. (a) way, road; c. faisant, on the way; se mettre en c., to set out; (b) road, path, track; c. vicinal, by-road. 2. c. de fer, railway.

cheminée [ʃmine], *s.f.* 1. (a) fireplace; (b) (manteau de) c., mantelpiece. 2. (a) chimney; (b) funnel (of locomotive).

cheminot [ʃmino], *s.m.* railwayman.

chemise [ʃmiːz], *s.f.* 1. (a) shirt; (b) c. de nuit, nightdress. 2. folder; portfolio; dust-jacket (of book).

†**chenal** [ʃ(ə)nal], *s.m.* channel.

chêne [ʃɛn], *s.m.* oak.

chenet [ʃ(ə)nɛ], *s.m.* fire-dog; andiron.

chenille [ʃ(ə)niːj], *s.f.* 1. (a) caterpillar; (b) track (of tracked vehicle). 2. *Tex:* chenille.

chèque [ʃɛk], *s.m.* cheque; c. barré, crossed cheque; c. de voyage, traveller's cheque.

chèque-fleurs [ʃɛkflœːr], s.m. flower token. pl. chèques-fleurs.

chèque-repas [ʃɛkrəpa], s.m. luncheon voucher. pl. chèques-repas.

cher, chère[1] [ʃɛːr], a. 1. Dear, beloved; s. mon c., my dear fellow; ma chère, my dear. 2. dear, expensive. s.f. -té, expensiveness.

chercher [ʃɛrʃe], v.tr. 1. to look for; to seek. 2. aller c., to (go and) fetch; envoyer c., to send for. 3. c. à faire qch., to attempt to do sth.

chercheur, -euse [ʃɛrʃœːr, -øːz], s. seeker, searcher; investigator; (scientific) research worker.

chère[2] [ʃɛːr], s.f. bonne c., good food.

chèrement [ʃɛrmɑ̃], adv. dearly.

chéri, -ie [ʃeri]. 1. a. cherished, dear. 2. s. darling.

chérir [ʃeriːr], v.tr. to cherish; to love dearly.

chérubin [ʃerybɛ̃], s.m. cherub.

†chétif [ʃetif], a. 1. weak, puny, sickly, stunted. 2. poor, miserable, wretched.

†cheval, -aux [ʃəval], s.m. 1. horse; à c., on horseback; être à c. sur, to sit astride. 2. c. de bois, vaulting horse. 3. horse-power.

chevalerie [ʃ(ə)valri], s.f. 1. knighthood. 2. chivalry. a. -esque, chivalrous.

chevalet [ʃ(ə)vale], s.m. (a) trestle; (b) easel; (c) bridge (of violin).

chevalier [ʃ(ə)valje], s.m. (a) knight; c. d'industrie, adventurer, crook, sharper; (b) rider, horseman.

chevalin [ʃəvalɛ̃], a. equine; boucherie chevaline, horse-butcher's shop.

cheval-vapeur [ʃəvalvapœːr], s.m. horse-power. pl. chevaux-vapeur.

chevauchée [ʃ(ə)voʃe], s.f. 1. ride. 2. cavalcade.

chevauch/er [ʃ(ə)voʃe]. 1. v.i. (a) to ride (on horse); (b) to overlap. 2. v.tr. to straddle; to be astride. a. -ant, overlapping.

chevet [ʃ(ə)ve], s.m. head (of bed); livre de c., bedside book.

chev/eu, -eux [ʃ(ə)vø], s.m. 1. (a single) hair; couper un c. en quatre, to split hairs. 2. les cheveux, the hair. a. -elu, hairy; cuir c., scalp. s.f. -elure, (head of) hair.

cheville [ʃ(ə)viːj], s.f. 1. peg, pin; c. en fer, bolt. 2. plug. 3. ankle.

chèvre [ʃɛːvr], s.f. goat. s.m. -feuille, honeysuckle.

chevreau [ʃəvro], s.m. Z: kid.

chevreuil [ʃəvrœːj], s.m. roe-deer; Cu: venison.

chevron [ʃəvrɔ̃], s.m. 1. rafter. 2. Tex: en c., in herring-bone pattern. 3. Mil: long-service stripe.

chevrot/er [ʃəvrɔte], v.i. to sing, speak, in a quavering voice; to quaver. s.m. -ement.

chevrotine [ʃəvrɔtin], s.f. buck-shot.

chez [ʃe], prep. 1. c. qn, at s.o.'s house; je vais c. moi, I am going home; c. l'épicier, at the grocer's; (on letters) c. Mme Martin, care of, c/o, Mrs Martin. 2. with, among; c. les animaux, in the animal kingdom.

chic [ʃik]. 1. s.m. (a) skill, knack; (b) smartness, stylishness. 2. a.inv. in f., var. in pl. (a) smart, stylish; (b) F: fine, first-rate; un c. type, a good sort; sois c.! be a sport!

chican/e [ʃikan], s.f. 1. chicanery. 2. Techn: baffle(-plate). s.f. -erie, quibbling. a. †-eur, quibbling. s. -eur, -euse, quibbler.

chiche [ʃiʃ], a. mean, stingy. adv. -ment.

chicorée [ʃikɔre], s.f. chicory (for coffee); endive. c. (frisée), endive.

chien, f. chienne [ʃjɛ̃, ʃjɛn], s. 1. dog; f. bitch; entre c. et loup, in the twilight; quel temps de c.! what beastly weather! 2. (a) hammer (of gun); (b) c. d'arrêt, pawl, catch.

chien-loup [ʃjɛ̃lu], s.m. Alsatian (dog). pl. chiens-loups.

chiffon [ʃifɔ̃], s.m. 1. rag. 2. chiffon.

chiffonn/er [ʃifɔne], v.tr. to rumple, crumple. s.m. -ier, rag-and-bone man.

chiffre [ʃifr], s.m. 1. (a) figure, number; marqué en chiffres connus, marked in plain figures; (b) amount, total; c. d'affaires, turnover. 2. cipher, code.

chiffr/er [ʃifre]. 1. v.i. to calculate, reckon. 2. v.tr. (a) to number (pages, etc.); (b) to code (a message); (c) to mark (linen, etc.). s.m. -age.

chiffre-taxe [ʃifrataks], s.m. postage-due stamp. pl. chiffres-taxes.

chignon [ʃiɲɔ̃], s.m. knot of hair, bun.

chimie [ʃimi], s.f. chemistry.

chimique [ʃimik], a, chemical; un produit c., a chemical. adv. -ment.

chimiste [ʃimist], s.m. (research) chemist.

chimpanzé [ʃɛ̃pɑ̃ze], s.m. chimpanzee.

chinois, -oise [ʃinwa, -waːz]. 1. a. Chinese. 2. s. Chinaman, Chinese woman; les C., the Chinese. 3. s.m. Ling: Chinese.

chinoiserie [ʃinwazri], s.f. 1. Chinese curio. 2. F: monkey trick.

chinook [ʃinuk], s.m. Meteor: chinook (wind).

chiot [ʃjo], s.m. pup(py).

chip/er [ʃipe], v.tr. F: to pinch, to swipe (sth.). s. -eur, -euse.

chips [ʃips], s.m.pl. Cu: potato crisps.

chiquenaude [ʃiknoːd], s.f. fillip, flick.

chiroman/cie [ʃirɔmɑ̃si], s.f. palmistry. s. -cien, -cienne, fortune teller.

chirurg/ie [ʃiryrʒi], s.f. surgery. a. †-ical. a. -ique.

chirurgien [ʃiryrʒjɛ̃], s.m. surgeon; c. dentiste, dental surgeon.

chiure [ʃjyːr], s.f. fly-speck, -mark.

chlore [klɔːr], s.m. chlorine. s.m. -ure, chloride.

chlorhydrique [klɔridrik], a. hydrochloric (acid).

chloroforme [klɔrɔfɔrm], s.m. chloroform.

choc [ʃɔk], s.m. shock.

chocolat [ʃɔkɔla], s.m. chocolate.

chœur [kœːr], s.m. 1. chorus. 2. choir; enfant de c., altar boy.

choisir [ʃwaziːr], v.tr. to choose, select.

choix [ʃwa], s.m. choice, selection; Com: au c., all one price.

choléra [kɔlera], s.m. cholera.

cholestérol [kɔlesterɔl], s.m. Med: cholesterol.

chôm/er [ʃome], v.i. 1. fête chômée, public holiday. 2. to be unemployed. s.m. -age, unemployment. s. -eur, -euse, unemployed (person).

chopine [ʃɔpin], s.f. half-litre mug.

choquant [ʃɔkɑ̃], a. shocking, offensive.

choquer [ʃɔke], v.tr. 1. to strike, knock; c. les verres, to clink glasses. 2. to shock, offend (s.o.).

†choral [kɔral], a. choral.

chorée [kɔre], s.f. Med: chorea, F: St. Vitus' dance.

chorégraph/e [kɔregraf], s. Th: choreographer. s.f. -ie, choreography.

choriste [kɔrist], s.m. Ecc: chorister; Th: chorus singer.

chose [ʃoːz], s.f. thing; dites bien des choses de ma part à . . ., remember me to . . .; Monsieur C., Mr. What's-his-name.

†chou [ʃu], s.m. 1. cabbage; c. de Bruxelles, Brussels sprout; mon petit c., my dear, darling. 2. c. à la crème, cream bun, puff.

choucas [ʃuka], s.m. jackdaw.

choucroute [ʃukrut], s.f. sauerkraut.

chou-fleur [ʃuflœːr], s.m. cauliflower. pl. choux-fleurs.

chow-chow [tʃuʃou], s.m. Z: chow. pl. chow-chows.

‡choyer [ʃwaje], v.tr. to pet, coddle.

chrétien, -ienne [kretjɛ̃, -jɛn], a. & s. Christian. s.f. -té, Christendom.

Christ [krist], s.m. le Christ, Christ. s.m. -ianisme, Christianity.

chromatique [krɔmatik], a. chromatic.

chrome [kroːm], s.m. 1. chromium. 2. chrome (yellow).

chrom/er [krome], v.tr. Ind: to chrome. s.m. -age, chromium plating.

chronique [krɔnik], a. chronic.

chroniqu/e² [krɔnik], s.f. 1. chronicle. 2. news. s. -eur, -euse, reporter.

chronologique [krɔnɔlɔʒik], a. chronological. adv. -ment.

chrono/mètre [krɔnɔmɛtr], s.m. chronometer. s.m. -métrage, timing. v.tr. Sp: -métrer, to time. s.m. Sp: -métreur, timekeeper.

chrysalide [krizalid], s.f. chrysalis, pupa.

chrysanthème [krizɑ̃tɛ(ː)m], s.m. chrysanthemum.

chuchot/er [ʃyʃɔte], v.i. & tr. to whisper. s.m. -ement, s.f. -erie.

chut [ʃyt, ʃt], int. hush! ssh!

chute [ʃyt], s.f. 1. (a) fall; faire une c., to have a fall; c. d'eau, waterfall; c. de prix, drop in prices; (b) (down)fall. 2. c. des reins, small of the back. 3. Ind: shoot.

ci [si], dem.pron.inv. (still used in) comme ci, comme ça, so so.

cible [sibl], s.f. target.

ciboul/e [sibul], s.f. spring onion. s.f. -ette, chives.

cicatrice [sikatris], s.f. scar.

cicatriser [sikatrize]. 1. v.tr. to scar, mark (face, etc.). 2. v.t. & pr. to heal (up).

ci-contre [sikɔ̃tr], adv. (a) opposite; in the margin; (b) annexed; (c) on the other side (of page).

ci-dessous [sidsu], adv. hereunder; undermentioned; below.

ci-dessus [sidsy], adv. above(-mentioned).

cidre [si(ː)dr], s.m. cider.

ciel, pl. cieux [sjɛl, sjø], s.m. 1. (a) sky, heaven; à c. ouvert, out of doors; opencast (mine); (b) (pl. often ciels) climate, sky (in picture). 2. heaven; (juste) c.! (good) heavens!

cierge [sjɛrʒ], s.m. wax candle; taper.

cieux. See CIEL.

cigale [sigal], s.f. Z: cicada.

cigar/e [sigaːr], s.m. cigar. s.f. -ette, cigarette.

ci-gisant, ci-gît [siʒiːz, siʒi], (on gravestone) here lie(s) . . .

cigogne [sigɔɲ], s.f. stork.

ci-inclus [siɛ̃kly], a. (inv. when it precedes the s.) enclosed; the enclosed copy; ci-incluse, the enclosed copy; ci-i., copie . . ., herewith copy . . . .

ci-joint [siʒwɛ̃], a. (inv. when it precedes the s.) herewith.

cil [sil], s.m. (eye)lash.

cime [sim], s.f. summit; top.

ciment [simɑ̃], s.m. cement; c. armé, reinforced concrete.

ciment/er [simɑ̃te], v.tr. to cement. s.m. -age.

cimetière [simtjɛːr], s.m. cemetery, graveyard.

cinéaste [sineast], s.m. Cin: film producer or technician.

cinéma [sinema], s.m. cinema.

cinémascope [sinemaskɔp], s.m. cinemascope.

cinémathèque [sinematek], s.f. film library.

cinérama [sinerama], s.m. R.t.m. Cinerama.

cinglant [sɛ̃glɑ̃], a. lashing (rain); cutting, biting.

cinglé [sɛ̃gle], a. P: cracked, daft, nuts.

cingler [sɛ̃gle], v.tr. to lash, cut.

cinq [sɛ̃k], num.a.inv. & s.m.inv. (as cardinal a. before a. or s. beginning with a consonant pronounced [sɛ̃]) five;

(*but*) c. hommes [sɛkɔm], five men;
c. garçons [sɛ̃ garsɔ̃], five boys; (*but*)
le c. mars [lə sɛ̃kmars], March 5th.
cinquantaine [sɛ̃kɑ̃tɛn], *s.f.* (about) fifty.
cinquante [sɛ̃kɑ̃t], *num.a.inv.* fifty.
cinquantième [sɛ̃kɑ̃tjɛm], *num.a. & s.*
fiftieth.
cinquième [sɛ̃kjɛm], *num.a. & s.* fifth.
cintre [sɛ̃:tr], *s.m.* 1. curve, bend. 2.
arch (of tunnel). 3. coat-hanger.
cintré [sɛ̃tre], *a.* (*a*) arched; (*b*) curved;
(*c*) taille cintrée, nipped-in waist.
cirage [sira:ʒ], *s.m.* shoe, floor, polish.
‡**circon/cire** [sirkɔ̃si:r], *v.tr.* to circumcise. *s.f.* -cision, circumcision.
circonférence [sirkɔ̃ferɑ̃:s], *s.f.* circumference.
circonflexe [sirkɔ̃flɛks], *a.* circumflex
(accent).
circonlocution [sirkɔ̃lɔkysjɔ̃], *s.f.* circumlocution.
‡**circonscri/re** [sirkɔ̃skri:r], *v.tr.* to cir-
cumscribe. *s.f.* -ption, (electoral) district.
circonspect [sirkɔ̃spɛ], *a.* circumstance, event. *a.* †-iel.
circonstanc/e [sirkɔ̃stɑ̃:s], *s.f.* circumstance, event. *a.* †-iel.
‡**circonvenir** [sirkɔ̃vni:r], *v.tr.* to circum-
vent, thwart; to outwit.
circuit [sirkɥi], *s.m.* circuit.
circul/er [sirkyle], *v.i.* 1. to circulate,
flow. 2. to move about; "circulez!"
'pass along!' *a.* & *s.f.* -aire, circular.
s.f. -ation, traffic.
cire [si:r], *s.f.* wax.
ciré [sire], *a.* 1. polished; toile cirée,
American cloth. 2. *s.m. Nau:* oilskins.
cir/er [sire], *v.tr.* to wax; c. des chaussures, to polish shoes. *s.f.* -euse,
electric polisher.
cirque [sirk], *s.m.* 1. circus. 2. *Geog:*
corrie, cirque.
cisaille [siza:j], *s.f.* shears.
ciseau [sizo], *s.m.* 1. chisel. 2. *pl.* (*a*)
scissors; (*b*) shears.
‡**cisel/er** [sizle], *v.tr.* to chase (gold); to
chisel (wood). *s.m.* -age. *s.m.* -eur.
citadelle [sitadɛl], *s.f.* citadel, stronghold.
citadin [sitadɛ̃], *s.m.* town-dweller.
cité [site], *s.f.* 1. city; (*a*) (large) town; (*b*)
housing estate.
cit/er [site], *v.tr.* 1. to quote. 2. to
summon. 3. to mention (in dis-
patches). *s.f.* -ation.
citerne [sitɛrn], *s.f.* cistern, tank.
citoyen, -enne [sitwajɛ̃, -ɛn], *s.* citizen.
citrique [sitrik], *a.* citric (acid).
citron [sitrɔ̃], *s.m.* lemon. *s.f.* -nade,
lemonade. *s.m.* -nier, lemon tree.
citrouille [sitru:j], *s.f.* pumpkin.
civet [sivɛ], *s.m.* (game) stew; c. de
lièvre = jugged hare.
civière [sivjɛ:r], *s.f.* 1. hand-barrow. 2.
stretcher, litter. 3. bier.
civil [sivil], *a.* 1. civil (rights, etc.). 2.
s.m. un c., a civilian; en c.,* in plain
clothes. 3. *a.* polite. *s.f.* -ité,
courtesy.

civilement [sivilmɑ̃], *adv.* 1. se marier
c., to be married in a registry office.
2. politely.
civilis/er [sivilize], *v.tr.* to civilize. *a.*
†-ateur, civilizing. *s.f.* -ation.
civique [sivik], *a.* civic (duties, etc.); *Sch:*
instruction c., civics.
civisme [sivism], *s.m.* good citizenship.
claie [klɛ], *s.f.* hurdle.
clair [klɛːr]. 1. *a.* clear; (*a*) unclouded;
limpid; (*b*) obvious, plain; (*c*) bright;
light. 2. *adv.* plainly, clearly. 3. *s.m.*
(*a*) light; au c. de lune, by moonlight;
(*b*) message en c., message in clear (i.e.
not in code). *adv.* -ement.
claire-voie [klɛrwa], *s.f.* lattice-work
(fence, gate). *pl. claires-voies.*
clairière [klɛrjɛːr], *s.f.* clearing, glade.
clairon [klɛrɔ̃], *s.m.* (*a*) bugle; (*b*)
bugler.
clairsemé [klɛrsəme], *a.* scattered,
sparse.
clairvoyance [klɛrvwajɑ̃:s], *s.f.* 1. per-
spicacity, clear-sightedness. 2. second
sight.
clairvoyant [klɛrvwajɑ̃]. 1. *a.* perspica-
cious, clear-sighted. 2. *a.* & *s.* clairvoyant.
clameur [klamœːr], *s.f.* clamour, outcry.
clandestin [klɑ̃dɛstɛ̃], *a.* clandestine,
secret.
clapet [klapɛ], *s.m.* valve; c. à charnière,
clack-valve.
clapier [klapje], *s.m.* rabbit-hutch.
clapot/er [klapɔte], *v.i.* (*of sea*) to be
choppy. *s.m.* -ement, *s.m.* -is, lap(ping)
(of waves).
claque [klak], *s.f.* 1. smack, slap. 2. *Th:*
hired clappers.
claqu/er [klake]. 1. *v.i.* (*a*) to clap; (*of
door*) to bang; (*of teeth*) to chatter;
(*b*) *F:* to die; (*of engine, etc.*) to conk
out. 2. *v.tr. & i.* (*a*) to slam (the
door); to crack (a whip); (*b*) to slap
(child); (*c*) to burst (tyre); to tear
(muscle). *s.m.* -ement.
clarifier [klarifje], *v.tr.* to clarify.
clarinette [klarinɛt], *s.f.* clarinet.
clarté [klarte], *s.f.* 1. clearness, clarity
(of glass, of the mind). 2. light,
brightness.
classe [klɑːs], *s.f.* 1. class, division. 2.
(*a*) class, form; (*b*) aller en c., to go
to school.
class/er [klɑse], *v.tr.* 1. to class(ify). 2.
(*a*) to sort out; (*b*) to file. *s.m.*
-ement. *s.m.* -eur, file.
classifi/er [klasifje], *v.tr.* to classify. *s.f.*
-cation.
classique [klasik], *a.* 1. classic (al);
stand-ard (work); *F:* c'est un coup c., that's
an old dodge. 2. *s.m.* classic.
clause [kloːz], *s.f.* clause (in contract).
claustrophobie [klɔstrɔfɔbi], *s.f.* claustrophobia.
clavicule [klavikyl], *s.f.* collar-bone.
clavier [klavje], *s.m.* keyboard.

clé, clef, [kle], s.f. 1. key; (a) fermer à c., to lock; (b) key (to a cipher); clue. 2. *Mus:* clef. 3. wrench, spanner.

clématite [klematit], s.f. clematis.

clémence [klemã:s], s.f. 1. clemency (pour, envers, to, towards). 2. mildness.

clément [klemã], a. 1. clement (pour, envers, to, towards). 2. mild.

cleptoman/e [klɛptɔman], s.m. & f. kleptomaniac. s.f. -ie, kleptomania.

clerc [klɛːr], s.m. clerk (to lawyer).

clergé [klɛrʒe], s.m. clergy, priesthood.

†clérical [klerikal], a. clerical.

cliché [kliʃe], s.m. 1. *Phot:* negative. 2. cliché, stock phrase.

client, -ente [kliɑ̃, -ɑ̃:t], s. client, customer.

clientèle [kliɑ̃tɛl], s.f. practice (of doctor); custom(ers) (of shop, hotel, etc.).

clign/er [kliɲe], v.tr. & i. 1. c. les yeux, to blink. 2. c. de l'œil, to wink. s.m. -ement.

clignotant [kliɲɔtã], a. 1. blinking; twinkling. 2. s.m. *Aut:* winking-light direction indicator, *F:* winker.

clignot/er [kliɲɔte], v.i. (a) to blink; (b) to twinkle. s.m. -ement.

climat [klima], s.m. climate. a. -ique.

climatis/er [klimatize], v.tr. to air-condition. s.f. -ation, air-conditioning. s.m. -eur, air conditioner.

clin d'œil [klɛ̃dœːj], s.m. wink; en un c. d'œil, in the twinkling of an eye.

clinique [klinik]. 1. a. clinical (instruction, etc.). 2. s.f. nursing-home.

clinquant [klɛ̃kã], s.m. tinsel.

clique [klik], s.f. clique, gang, set.

‡cliquet/er [klikte], v.i. to clank; to jingle. s.m. -is, jingling.

clochard [klɔʃaːr], s.m. *F:* tramp, *U.S:* hobo.

cloche [klɔʃ], s.f. 1. bell. 2. (a) bellglass, cloche; (b) dish-cover.

clocher¹ [klɔʃe], s.m. belfry, steeple.

clocher², v.i. to limp, hobble; *F:* il y a quelque chose qui c., there's sth. wrong.

clochette [klɔʃɛt], s.f. small bell; handbell.

cloison [klwazɔ̃], s.f. 1. partition, division. 2. *Nau:* bulkhead.

cloître [klwaːtr], s.m. cloister(s).

clopin-clopant [klɔpɛ̃klɔpã], adv. *F:* aller c.-c., to limp along, hobble about.

clopiner [klɔpine], v.i. *F:* to hobble, limp.

cloque [klɔk], s.f. 1. swelling, blister. 2. *Agr:* rust, blight.

clos [klo]. 1. a. (a) closed; shut up; à la nuit close, after dark; (b) concluded. 2. s.m. enclosure.

clôture [kloty:r], s.f. 1. enclosure, fence. 2. (a) closing; (b) conclusion. 3. closing, winding up (of account).

clôtur/er [klotyre], v.tr. 1. to enclose. 2. (a) to close down; (b) to end. 3. to wind up, close (accounts).

clou [klu], s.m. 1. (a) nail; (b) star turn. 2. c. de girofle, clove. 3. *Aut: etc:* vieux c., old crock.

clouer [klue], v.tr. 1. to nail. 2. cloué sur place, rooted to the spot.

clout/er [klute], v.tr. to stud (boot); to fix (horse-shoe); passage clouté, pedestrian crossing. s.m. -age.

clown [klun], s.m. clown, buffoon.

coagul/er (se) [sǝkɔagyle], v.pr. to coagulate, clot; to curdle. s.f. -ation.

coali/ser (se) [sǝkɔalize], v.pr. to form a coalition, to unite. s.f. -tion.

coass/er [kɔase], v.i. (of frog) to croak. s.m. -ement, croaking.

cobalt [kɔbalt], s.m. cobalt.

cobaye [kɔbaj], s.m. guinea-pig.

cocaïne [kɔkain], s.f. cocaine.

cocarde [kɔkard], s.f. cockade, rosette: *Av:* company crest (on airliners).

coche [kɔʃ], s.f. notch, nick.

cochère [kɔʃɛːr], a.f. porte c., main gateway.

cochon [kɔʃɔ̃], s.m. 1. (a) pig, hog; (b) *P:* (of pers.) swine. 2. c. d'Inde, guinea-pig.

cocktail [kɔktɛl], s.m. (a) cocktail; (b) cocktail party.

coco [kɔko], s.m. 1. noix de c., coconut. 2. liquorice water. s.m. -tier, coconut palm.

cocon [kɔkɔ̃], s.m. cocoon.

cocotte-minute [kɔkɔtminyt], s.f. *R.t.m:* pressure-cooker. pl. cocottes-minute.

code [kɔd], s.m. code. 1. statute-book; *Aut:* c. de la route, highway code; se mettre en c., to dip one's headlights. 2. (telegraphic, etc.) code.

codicille [kɔdisil], s.m. codicil.

codirecteur, -trice [kɔdirɛktœːr, -tris], s. co-director.

coefficient [kɔefisjã], s.m. coefficient; *Ind:* c. de sécurité, safety factor.

coéquipier [kɔekipje], s.m. *Sp:* fellow member (of team).

cœur [kœːr], s.m. heart. 1. (a) maladie de c., heart disease; en c., heart-shaped; (b) avoir mal au c., to feel sick; cela soulève le c., it's sickening, nauseating. 2. soul, feelings; (a) en avoir le c. net, to clear the matter up; parler à c. ouvert, to speak freely; (b) apprendre par c., to learn by heart. 3. courage, spirit. 4. (a) travailler de bon c., to work with a will; (b) à vous de tout c., yours affectionately. 5. middle, midst. 6. (at cards) hearts.

coffr/e [kɔfr], s.m. chest, bin. s.m. -age, framework, shuttering.

coffre-fort, s.m. safe. pl. coffres-forts.

‡co/gérer [kɔʒere], v.tr. to manage (a business) jointly. s. -gérant, gérante, joint manager, manageress. s.f. -gestion, joint management.

cognac [kɔɲak], s.m. cognac; brandy.

cognée [kɔɲe], s.f. axe; hatchet.

cogner [kɔɲe], *v.tr.* to knock, thump; to hit (s.o.); *v.i.* (*of engine*) to knock.

cohérence [kɔerɑ̃s], *s.f.* coherence.

cohérent [kɔerɑ̃], *a.* coherent.

cohésion [kɔezjɔ̃], *s.f.* cohesion.

cohue [kɔy], *s.f.* crowd, mob.

coiffer [kwafe], *v.tr.* 1. to cover (the head). 2. c. qn, to do s.o.'s hair. **se coiffer.** 1. to put one's hat on. 2. to do one's hair.

coiffeur, -euse [kwafœːr, -øːz]. 1. *s.* hairdresser. 2. *s.f.* dressing table.

coiffure [kwafyːr], *s.f.* 1. headgear. 2. hair style. 3. hairdressing.

coin [kwɛ̃], *s.m.* 1. (*a*) corner; l'épicier du c., the local grocer; (*b*) c. du feu, inglenook; au c. du feu, by the fireside. 2. wedge. 3. stamp, die.

‡**coincer** [kwɛ̃se]. 1. *v.tr.* to wedge, chock (up); *F:* c. qn, to corner s.o.; to arrest s.o. 2. *v.i. & pr.* (*of machinery*) to jam, stick.

coïncider [kɔɛ̃side], *v.i.* to coincide. *s.f.* -dence. *a.* -dent.

coing [kwɛ̃], *s.m.* quince.

coke [kɔk], *s.m. Ind:* coke.

col [kɔl], *s.m.* 1. neck (of bottle). 2. collar; faux c., detachable collar. 3. *Geog:* pass, col.

coléoptère [kɔleɔptɛːr], *s.m.* beetle.

col/ère [kɔlɛːr]. 1. *s.f.* anger. 2. *a.* angry; irascible. *a.* †-éreux, -érique, quick tempered.

colimaçon [kɔlimasɔ̃], *s.m.* snail; escalier en c., spiral staircase.

colique [kɔlik], *s.f.* colic; *F:* stomach ache.

colis [kɔli], *s.m.* 1. parcel, package; par c. postal, by parcel post. 2. (article of) luggage.

collabor/er [kɔlabɔre], *v.i.* to collaborate. *s.* -ateur, -atrice. *s.f.* -ation.

collant [kɔlɑ̃]. 1. *a.* (*a*) sticky; (*b*) close-fitting. 2. *s.m.* (pair of) tights.

†**collatéral** [kɔlateral], *a.* collateral.

colle [kɔl], *s.f.* 1. paste; glue; size. 2. *F: Sch:* poser; poser une c., to ask a tricky question.

†**collect/if** [kɔlektif], *a.* collective, joint. *s.f.* -ivité, community.

collection [kɔleksjɔ̃], *s.f.* 1. collecting. 2. collection.

collectionn/er [kɔleksjɔne], *v.tr.* to collect. *s.* -eur, -euse, collector.

col/lège [kɔlɛːʒ], *s.m.* 1. college. 2. school. *a.* -légien, -légienne.

collègue [kɔlɛg], *s.m. & f.* colleague.

coller [kɔle], *v.tr.* to paste, stick, glue (à, to, on); *F:* to stump, floor (s.o.). 2. *v.i.* to stick, adhere, cling (à, to); *F:* ça ne colle pas, it doesn't work.

collier [kɔlje], *s.m.* 1. necklace. 2. c. de chien, dog-collar.

colline [kɔlin], *s.f.* hill.

collision [kɔl(l)izjɔ̃], *s.f.* collision; entrer en c. avec, to run into (s.o, sth.); *Sc:* c. de neutrons, knock-on; c. nucléaire, nuclear collision.

colloque [kɔlɔk], *s.m.* conference.

colomb/e [kɔlɔ̃:b], *s.f.* pigeon, dove. *s.m.* -ier, dovecote.

colon [kɔlɔ̃], *s.m.* colonist, settler. *a.* †-ial.

colonel [kɔlɔnel], *s.m.* colonel; *Av:* group captain.

colonie [kɔlɔni], *s.f.* colony, settlement.

colonis/er [kɔlɔnize], *v.tr.* to colonize. *s.f.* -ation.

colonne [kɔlɔn], *s.f.* column.

color/er [kɔlɔre], *v.tr.* to colour, tint; teint coloré, florid complexion. *s.f.* -ation, colouring; colour.

colorier [kɔlɔrje], *v.tr.* to colour (drawing).

coloris [kɔlɔri], *s.m.* colour(ing); *Com:* carte de c., shade card.

†**colossal** [kɔlɔsal], *a.* colossal, huge.

coma [kɔma], *s.m.* coma.

colporter [kɔlpɔrte], *v.tr.* (*a*) to hawk (goods); (*b*) to spread abroad (news).

combat [kɔ̃ba], *s.m.* 1. combat, fight; hors de c., disabled; out of action. 2. contest.

combattant [kɔ̃batɑ̃], *s.m.* combatant; anciens combattants, ex-servicemen.

‡**combattre** [kɔ̃batr]. 1. *v.tr.* to combat, to fight (against). 2. *v.i.* to fight, strive.

combien [kɔ̃bjɛ̃], *adv.* 1. (*exclamative*) (*a*) how (much)! (*b*) how many! c. de gens! what a lot of people! c. de (*interrogative*) (*a*) how much? (*b*) how many? c. vous dois-je? how much do I owe you? c. de fois? how many times? how often?

combinaison [kɔ̃binɛzɔ̃], *s.f.* 1. (*a*) combination; arrangement; (*b*) plan, scheme. 2. (*a*) overalls, dungarees; flying suit; (ii) (woman's) slip.

combinard [kɔ̃binar], *s.m. P:* racketeer; slick customer.

combine [kɔ̃bin], *s.f. F:* scheme, racket; fiddle; il faut savoir la c., you have to know the trick.

combiner [kɔ̃bine], *v.tr.* 1. to combine, unite; to arrange. 2. to contrive.

comble[1] [kɔ̃:bl], *s.m.* 1. pour c. de malheur, as a crowning misfortune; *F:* ça c'est le c.! that's the limit, the end! 2. (*a*) de fond en c., from top to bottom; (*b*) highest point; height (of happiness); depth (of despair).

comble[2], *a.* packed; salle c., full house.

combler [kɔ̃ble], *v.tr.* 1. to fill. 2. to heap (up); c. de bienfaits, to heap kindness on; il est comblé, he is entirely happy.

combustible [kɔ̃bystibl], *s.m.* fuel.

combustion [kɔ̃bystjɔ̃], *s.f.* combustion, burning.

coméd/ie [kɔmedi], *s.f.* comedy; c'est une vraie c., it's as good as a play. *s.* -ien, -ienne, actor, actress.

comestible [kɔmɛstibl]. **1.** *a.* edible, eatable. **2.** *s.m.* (article of) food.

comète [kɔmɛt], *s.f.* comet.

comique [kɔmik]. **1.** *(a)* a comic; *(b)* *s.m.* comedian. **2.** *a.* comical, funny. *adv.* -ment.

comité [kɔmite], *s.m.* committee, board; c. d'entreprise, joint production committee.

commandant [kɔmɑ̃dɑ̃]. **1.** *a.* commanding (officer). **2.** *s.m.* Nau: commander; Mil: major; Av: squadron-leader.

commande [kɔmɑ̃:d], *s.f.* **1.** order; fait sur c., made to order; payable à la c., cash with order. **2.** E: controls; c. du changement de vitesse, gear lever.

commandement [kɔmɑ̃dmɑ̃], *s.m.* **1.** command, order. **2.** (position of) command, authority.

commander [kɔmɑ̃de]. **1.** *v.tr.* *(a)* to command, order; *(b)* to be in command of; *(c)* to command (respect); *(d)* E: to dominate (the valley); *(d)* E: to control, operate; to drive. **2.** *v.ind.tr.* c. à, to control (one's impatience).

commandit/er [kɔmɑ̃dite], *v.tr.* to finance (enterprise). *s.m.* -aire, sleeping partner.

commando [kɔmɑ̃do], *s.m.* Mil: commando.

comme [kɔm]. **I.** *adv.* **1.** *(a)* as, like; faites c. moi, do as I do; *(b)* c'est tout c., it amounts to the same thing. **2.** (*exclamative*) how! c. il est maigre! how thin he is! **II.** *conj.* **1.** as; seeing that; c. vous êtes là, since you are here. **2.** (just) as.

commémor/er [kɔmmemɔre], *v.tr.* to commemorate. *a.* †-atif. *s.f.* -ation.

‡commenc/er [kɔmɑ̃se], *v.tr.* & *i.* to begin, start. *s.m.* -ement, beginning.

comment [kɔmɑ̃], *adv.* **1.** how; c. allez-vous? how are you? c. (dites-vous?) I beg your pardon? c. faire? what is to be done? **2.** (*exclamation*) what! why! mais c. donc! why, of course!

commentaire [kɔmɑ̃tɛ:r], *s.m.* **1.** commentary. **2.** comment.

comment/er [kɔmɑ̃te], *v.tr.* & *i.* to comment (up)on. *s.* -ateur, -atrice.

commerçant, -ante [kɔmɛrsɑ̃, -ɑ̃:t]. **1.** *a.* commercial; business; rue commerçante, shopping street. **2.** *s.* merchant, tradesman; être c., to be in business.

commerce [kɔmɛrs], *s.m.* **1.** commerce; trade; faire le c. de, to deal in. **2.** intercourse, dealings.

‡commercial [kɔmɛrsjal]. **1.** *a.* commercial; trading, business. **2.** *s.f.* commerciale, estate car. *adv.* -ement.

com/mère [kɔmɛːr], *s.f.* gossip, busybody. *s.m.* -mérage, gossip.

‡commettre [kɔmɛtr], *v.tr.* to commit.

commis [kɔmi], *s.m.* **1.** clerk. **2.** c. voyageur, commercial traveller.

commisération [kɔmmizerasjɔ̃], *s.f.* commiseration, pity.

‡commisérer [kɔmizere], *v.i.* to commiserate, sympathize.

commis/saire [kɔmisɛːr], *s.m.* commissioner; steward (of meeting); purser (of ship); c. de police = police superintendent. *s.m.* -sariat, central police station.

commission [kɔmisjɔ̃], *s.f.* **1.** commission. **2.** message, errand. **3.** committee. *s.m.* -naire.

commod/e [kɔmɔd]. **1.** *a.* *(a)* convenient; *(b)* comfortable (house); *(c)* accommodating. **2.** *s.f.* chest of drawers. *adv.* -ément.

commodité [kɔmɔdite], *s.f.* convenience; comfort.

commo/tion [kɔm(m)osjɔ̃], *s.f.* **1.** commotion, disturbance. **2.** concussion; electric shock. *a.* **c.** électrique, electric shock. -tionné, Med: shocked, F: concussed.

commun [kɔmœ̃], *a.* *(a)* common; mutual; *(b)* universal, general; *(c)* usual, everyday; *(d)* vulgar. *adv.* -ément.

communauté [kɔmynote], *s.f.* **1.** community (of interests). **2.** society.

commune [kɔmyn], *s.f.* **1.** la Chambre des Communes, (British) House of Commons. **2.** Fr. Adm: commune.

communica/tion [kɔmynikasjɔ̃], *s.f.* communication. **1.** P.T.T.: fausse c., wrong number. **2.** message. *a.* †-tif, talkative.

communi/er [kɔmynje], *v.i.* Ecc: to communicate. *s.* -ant, -ante.

communion [kɔmynjɔ̃], *s.f.* communion.

communiqué [kɔmynike], *s.m.* official statement; c. de presse, press release.

communi/quer [kɔmynike], *v.tr.* & *i.* to communicate. *a.* -cant, communicating (rooms).

commun/isme [kɔmynism], *s.m.* communism. *s.* -iste, -ante, fellow-traveller. *s.m.* & *f.* -iste.

commutateur [kɔmytatœːr], *s.m.* El: switch.

compact [kɔpakt], *a.* compact, dense.

compagne [kɔpaɲ], *s.f.* (female) companion.

compagnie [kɔpaɲi], *s.f.* **1.** company; tenir c. à qn, to keep s.o. company; fausser c. à qn, to give s.o. the slip. **2.** company; party. **3.** Durand et C. (*usu.* Cie), Durand and Co. **4.** Mil: company. **5.** herd (of deer); covey (of partridges).

compagnon [kɔpaɲɔ̃], *s.m.* companion, comrade; c. de bord, shipmate.

comparaison [kɔparɛzɔ̃], *s.f.* comparison; *prep.phr.* en c. de, compared with.

‡comparaître [kɔparɛːtr], *v.i.* Jur: to appear.

†**comparat/if** [kɔ̃paratif], *a. & s.m.* comparative. *adv.* -**ivement.**

compar/er [kɔ̃pare], *v.tr.* to compare. *a.* -**able.**

compartiment [kɔ̃partimã], *s.m.* compartment; partition.

compas [kɔ̃pa], *s.m.* 1. (pair of) compasses; c. à calibrer, cal(l)ipers. 2. c. de mer, mariner's compass.

compassion [kɔ̃pasjɔ̃], *s.f.* compassion, pity.

compat/ible [kɔ̃patibl], *a.* compatible. *s.f.* -**ibilité.**

compatissant [kɔ̃patisã], *a.* compassionate; tender-hearted.

compatriote [kɔ̃patriɔt], *s.m. & f.* compatriot.

compens/er [kɔ̃pãse], *v.tr.* to compensate; to make up for. *a. & s.m.* †-**ateur.** *s.f.* -**ation.**

compère [kɔ̃pɛːr], *s.m.* Th: compère (in revue); stooge (for clown).

compétence [kɔ̃petãs], *s.f.* 1. competence; ability; skill. *a.* -**ent,** competent.

compil/er [kɔ̃pile], *v.tr.* to compile. *s.* -**ateur,** -**atrice,** compiler. *s.f.* -**ation.**

complaisance [kɔ̃plɛzãs], *s.f.* 1. obligingness; auriez-vous la c. de . . . , would you be so kind as to . . . . 2. (self-)satisfaction.

complais/ant [kɔ̃plɛzã], *a.* (a) obliging; (b) complacent, self-satisfied. *adv.* -**amment.**

complément [kɔ̃plemã], *s.m.* complement.

†**compl/et** [kɔ̃plɛ]. 1. *a.* (a) complete, entire; (b) full. 2. *s.m.* (a) suit (of clothes); (b) *adj.phr.* au c., full (up). *adv.* -**ètement.**

‡**compléter** [kɔ̃plete], *v.tr.* to complete.

complex/e [kɔ̃plɛks]. 1. *a.* complex, complicated. 2. *s.m.* complex. *s.f.* -**ité.**

complexion [kɔ̃plɛksjɔ̃], *s.f.* constitution, temperament.

complic/e [kɔ̃plis], *s.* accomplice. *s.f.* -**ité,** complicity.

compliment [kɔ̃plimã], *s.m.* 1. compliment. 2. *pl.* kind regards, greetings; congratulations.

complimenter [kɔ̃plimãte], *v.tr.* to compliment; to congratulate (de, sur, on).

compli/quer [kɔ̃plike], *v.tr.* to complicate. *s.f.* -**cation.**

complot [kɔ̃plo], *s.m.* plot, conspiracy.

comploter [kɔ̃plote], *v.tr.* to plot, to scheme.

componction [kɔ̃pɔ̃ksjɔ̃], *s.f.* compunction; scruple, regret.

comport/er [kɔ̃pɔrte], *v.tr.* 1. to allow (of). 2. to call for, require. 3. to comprise. *s.m.* -**ement,** behaviour. **se comporter,** to behave.

composé [kɔ̃poze]. 1. *a.* (a) compound, combined; (b) composed; demure. 2. *s.m.* compound.

compos/er [kɔ̃poze], *v.tr.* 1. (a) to compose; to form; (b) P.T.T.: c. le numéro, to dial the number; (c) to

compose, arrange. 2. *v.i.* to compound. *s.* -**iteur,** -**itrice,** (i) composer; (ii) compositor. *s.f.* -**ition.** **se composer,** to consist (de, of).

compot/e [kɔ̃pɔt], *s.f.* stewed fruit. *s.m.* -**ier,** fruit-dish.

†**compréhensif** [kɔ̃preãsif], *a.* 1. comprehensive (statement). 2. understanding (mind).

compréhen/sion [kɔ̃preãsjɔ̃], *s.f.* understanding. *a.* -**sible.**

‡**comprendre** [kɔ̃prãːdr], *v.tr.* 1. to comprise, include; y compris, including. 2. to understand; cela se comprend, of course.

compression [kɔ̃presjɔ̃], *s.f.* 1. compression, squeezing. 2. reduction (of staff, etc.).

comprimé [kɔ̃prime]. 1. *a.* compressed (air). 2. *s.m. Med:* tablet, pill.

comprimer [kɔ̃prime], *v.tr.* 1. to compress. 2. to repress (tears).

‡**compromettre** [kɔ̃prɔmɛtr], *v.tr. & i.* to compromise; être compromis, to be implicated (dans, in).

compromis [kɔ̃prɔmi], *s.m.* compromise; mettre une affaire en c., to submit a matter for arbitration.

comptabilité [kɔ̃tabilite], *s.f.* 1. bookkeeping. 2. counting house.

comptable [kɔ̃tabl], *s.m.* accountant, book-keeper; expert c. = chartered accountant.

comptant [kɔ̃tã]. 1. *a.* argent c., ready money. 2. *adv.* payer c., to pay cash.

compte [kɔ̃ːt], *s.m.* 1. account; (a) reckoning; en fin de c., all things considered; (b) pour mon c., for my part; (c) rendu, report, review; se rendre c. de, to realize; (d) count; (missiles) c. à rebours, countdown.

compter [kɔ̃te]. 1. *v.tr.* (a) to count (up), reckon (up); *prep.phr.* à c. de, (reckoning) from; (b) c. faire qch., to reckon on doing sth. 2. *v.i.* (a) **vous pouvez y c.,** you may depend upon it; (b) to reckon.

compte-tours [kɔ̃ttuːr], *s.m.inv. Aut:* revolution counter.

compteur [kɔ̃tœːr], *s.m.* meter; *Aut:* c. de trajet, trip-recorder; c. de vitesse, speedometer; *Fr. C:* c. de stationement, parking meter.

comptoir [kɔ̃twaːr], *s.m.* 1. counter. 2. *Fin:* c. d'escompte, discount bank.

comput/er [kɔ̃pyte], *v.tr.* to compute. *s.f.* -**ation.**

comte [kɔ̃ːt], *s.m.* count; (*in Eng.*) earl.

comtesse [kɔ̃tɛs], *s.f.* countess.

concass/er [kɔ̃kase], *v.tr.* to crush, pound, grind (ore, pepper, etc.). *s.m.* -**age.** *s.m.* -**eur,** crushing-mill.

concave [kɔ̃kaːv], *a.* concave.

‡**concéder** [kɔ̃sede], *v.tr.* 1. to concede. 2. to admit.

concentr/er [kɔ̃sãtre], *v.tr.* to concentrate. *s.f.* -**ation.**

conception [kɔ̃sɛpsjɔ̃], s.f. 1. conception; c. dirigée, birth control. 2. (a) idea; (b) design.

concerner [kɔ̃sɛrne], v.tr. (used in 3rd pers. only) to concern, affect; cela vous concerne, it concerns you.

concert [kɔ̃sɛːr], s.m. Mus: concert.

concerter (se) [səkɔ̃sɛrte], v.pr. se c. to take counsel, to consult, Pej: to connive (avec qn, with s.o.).

concession [kɔ̃sɛsjɔ̃], s.f. concession. s.-naire, licence-holder, concessionaire.

‡**concevoir** [kɔ̃sǝvwaːr], v.tr. 1. to conceive (child). 2. to imagine (idea); to form (plan); to understand. a. -able.

concierge [kɔ̃sjɛrʒ], s.m. & f. (house-) porter; caretaker.

concil/ier [kɔ̃silje], v.tr. to conciliate, reconcile. s.f. -iation.
se concilier, to agree (avec, with).

concis [kɔ̃si], a. concise, terse.

concision [kɔ̃sizjɔ̃], s.f. conciseness, brevity.

concitoyen, -enne [kɔ̃sitwajɛ̃, -ɛn], s. fellow-citizen.

‡**conclu/re** [kɔ̃klyːr], v.tr. 1. to conclude. 2. to decide, infer. a. -ant. a. †-sif. s.f. -sion.

concombre [kɔ̃kɔ̃ːbr], s.m. cucumber.

concorde [kɔ̃kɔrd], s.f. concord, harmony.

concord/er [kɔ̃kɔrde], v.i. to agree, tally (avec, with). s.f. -ance, agreement.

‡**concourir** [kɔ̃kuriːr], v.i. 1. to combine, unite; to co-operate. 2. to compete.

concours [kɔ̃kuːr], s.m. 1. concourse, gathering. 2. co-operation. 3. competition; Sp: field events; c. hippique, horse show.

‡**concret** [kɔ̃krɛ], a. concrete, solid; cas c., actual case.

concrétiser [kɔ̃kretize], v.tr. to put (idea) into concrete form.

concurrence [kɔ̃kyrɑ̃ːs], s.f. 1. concurrence. 2. competition, rivalry.

concurren/t, -ente [kɔ̃kyrɑ̃, -ɑ̃ːt]. 1. a. co-operative; (b) competitive. 2. s. competitor. adv. -ement.

condamné, -ée [kɔ̃dane], s. condemned person.

condamn/er [kɔ̃dane], v.tr. to condemn. 1. (a) to sentence; le médecin l'a condamné, the doctor has given him up; (b) c. une porte, to block up a door. 2. to censure. s.f. -ation.

condens/er [kɔ̃dɑ̃se], v.tr. to condense; lait condensé, condensed milk; evaporated milk. s.m. Techn: -ateur, condenser. s.f. -ation.

condescend/re [kɔ̃desɑ̃ːdr], v.i. to condescend. s.f. -ance, condescension.

condiment [kɔ̃dimɑ̃], s.m. condiment, seasoning.

condition [kɔ̃disjɔ̃], s.f. 1. (a) state; (b) pl. conditions, circumstances. 2.

condition, stipulation; pl. terms; à c. de, provided that.

†**conditionnel** [kɔ̃disjɔnɛl], a. & s.m. conditional.

condition/er [kɔ̃disjɔne], v.tr. 1. to condition. 2. to pack(age) (goods). s.m. -ement, (i) packaging; (ii) air-conditioning. s.m. -eur, air-conditioner. s. -eur, -euse, packer.

condoléance [kɔ̃dɔleɑ̃ːs], s.f. condolence; (expression of) sympathy.

conducteur, -trice [kɔ̃dyktœːr, -tris]. 1. s. (a) leader, guide; (b) driver. 2. a. conducting. s.m. conductor (of heat).

‡**conduire** [kɔ̃dɥiːr], v.tr. 1. to conduct; to lead. 2. to drive; to steer. 3. to convey; to conduct (electricity, etc.). 4. to manage, supervise (house); c. un orchestre, to conduct an orchestra.
se conduire, to behave.

conduit [kɔ̃dɥi], s.m. passage, conduit, pipe; c. principal, main.

conduite [kɔ̃dɥit], s.f. 1. (a) conducting; leading (of s.o.); (b) driving; (c) Aut: drive; c. intérieure, saloon. 2. direction (of affairs). 3. conduct, behaviour.

cône [koːn], s.m. cone.

confection [kɔ̃fɛksjɔ̃], s.f. 1. making; manufacture. 2. ready-made clothes.

confectionn/er [kɔ̃fɛksjɔne], v.tr. to make (up); to construct (article); confectionné, ready-made (article). s.m. -ement.

confédération [kɔ̃federasjɔ̃], s.f. (con)federation.

confédéré [kɔ̃federe], a. confederate.

‡**confér/er** [kɔ̃fere]. 1. v.tr. to confer, award (privilege, etc.). 2. v.i. to confer (avec, with). s.f. -ence, lecture. s. -encier, -encière, lecturer.

confesse [kɔ̃fɛs], s.f. confession.

confess/er [kɔ̃fɛse], v.tr. 1. to confess, own up to (sth.). 2. (of priest) to confess (penitent). s.m. -eur, confessor. s.f. -ion.

confiance [kɔ̃fjɑ̃ːs], s.f. 1. confidence, trust. 2. confidence, sense of security; c. en soi, self-assurance.

confiant [kɔ̃fjɑ̃], a. 1. confiding, trustful. 2. confident. 3. self-confident.

confidence [kɔ̃fidɑ̃ːs], s.f. confidence.

confident, -ente [kɔ̃fidɑ̃, -ɑ̃ːt], s. confidant, f. confidante. a. †-iel. adv. -iellement.

confier [kɔ̃fje], v.tr. 1. to trust, entrust. 2. to confide, disclose.
se confier, to confide (à, in).

configuration [kɔ̃figyrasjɔ̃], s.f. configuration; lie (of the land).

confiner [kɔ̃fine]. 1. v.i. c. à, to border upon. 2. v.tr. to confine, imprison.

confirm/er [kɔ̃firme], v.tr. to confirm. a. †-atif. s.f. -ation.

confis/erie [kɔ̃fizri], s.f. (a) confectioner's shop; (b) confectionery. s. -eur, -euse, confectioner.

confis/quer [kɔ̃fiske], v.tr. to confiscate. s.f. -cation.

confit [kɔ̃fi], a. crystallized (fruit); s.m. conserve (of goose, etc.).

confiture [kɔ̃fityːr], s.f. jam.

conflit [kɔ̃fli], s.m. conflict; clash.

confluent [kɔ̃flyɑ̃], s.m. confluence (of rivers).

confondre [kɔ̃fɔ̃ːdr], v.tr. to confound. 1. (a) to mingle; (b) to mistake, confuse. 2. to disconcert, to put (s.o.) to confusion.
se confondre. 1. to intermingle, to blend. 2. se c. en excuses, to apologize profusely.

conform/e [kɔ̃fɔrm], a. conformable; consistent (à, with); identical; copie c., exact copy. adv. -ément.

conform/er [kɔ̃fɔrme], v.tr. (a) to form, shape; (b) to conform. s.f. -ité.
se conformer, to conform.

confort [kɔ̃fɔːr], s.m. comfort(s).

confortable [kɔ̃fɔrtabl], a. comfortable, snug. adv. -ment.

confrère [kɔ̃frɛːr], s.m. colleague; fellow-member.

confrérie [kɔ̃freri], s.f. (usu. religious) confraternity.

confront/er [kɔ̃frɔ̃te], v.tr. to confront (avec, with). s.f. -ation.

confus [kɔ̃fy], a. 1. confused; indistinct. 2. confused, abashed. adv. -ément.

confusion [kɔ̃fyzjɔ̃], s.f. confusion. 1. (a) disorder; (b) mistake. 2. embarrassment.

congé [kɔ̃ʒe], s.m. 1. leave, être en c. to be on holiday; congé(s) payé(s), holidays with pay. 2. dismissal, F: the sack.

congédi/er [kɔ̃ʒedje], v.tr. to dismiss, discharge. s.m. -ement.

‡cong/eler [kɔ̃ʒle], v.tr. to freeze; viande congelée, frozen meat. s.f. -élation; (a) freezing; (b) cold storage.

congestion [kɔ̃ʒɛstjɔ̃], s.f. congestion; c. cérébrale, apoplexy, F: stroke.

congestionné [kɔ̃ʒɛstjɔne], a. flushed, red (face).

congre [kɔ̃ːgr], s.m. conger-eel.

congr/ès [kɔ̃grɛ], s.m. congress. s.m. -essiste, member of congress.

conifère [kɔnifɛːr]. 1. a. a coniferous. 2. s.m.pl. conifers.

conique [kɔnik], a. a cone-shaped, conical.

conjectur/er [kɔ̃ʒɛktyre], v.tr. to conjecture.

conjoint [kɔ̃ʒwɛ̃], a. 1. united, joint. 2. married; s.m. Jur: les conjoints, husband and wife. adv. -ement.

conjonction [kɔ̃ʒɔ̃ksjɔ̃], s.f. union, connection. 2. Gram: conjunction.

†conjugal [kɔ̃ʒygal], a. conjugal; vie conjugale, married life. adv. -ement.

conjug/uer [kɔ̃ʒyge], v.tr. 1. Gram: to conjugate. 2. (a) to combine; (b) to pair (off). s.f. -aison, conjugation.

conjuré [kɔ̃ʒyre], s. conspirator.

conjur/er [kɔ̃ʒyre], v.tr. & i. 1. to plot. 2. to ward off (danger). s.f. -ation.

connaiss/ance [kɔnesɑ̃s], s.f. 1. acquaintance. 2. knowledge; understanding. 3. consciousness. s. -eur, -euse, expert.

‡connaître [kɔnɛːtr], v.tr. to know. 1. to be acquainted with (s.o., sth.); connu! I've heard that one before! 2. to have a thorough knowledge of (sth.).
se connaître. 1. se c. à, en, qch., to know all about sth. 2. il ne se connaît plus de joie, he is beside himself with joy.

connexion [kɔn(n)ɛksjɔ̃], s.f. connection.

connivence [kɔnivɑ̃ːs], s.f. connivance.

conquérant [kɔ̃kerɑ̃], a. conquering; air c., swagger; Guillaume le C., William the Conqueror.

‡conquérir [kɔ̃keriːr], v.tr. (a) to conquer; (b) to win (over).

conquête [kɔ̃kɛːt], s.f. conquest.

consacrer [kɔ̃sakre], v.tr. 1. (a) to consecrate; to devote (time to sth., etc.). 2. to sanctify, to sanction; expression consacrée, stock phrase.

conscience [kɔ̃sjɑ̃s], s.f. 1. consciousness. 2. (a) conscience; (b) conscientiousness.

†consciencieu/x [kɔ̃sjɑ̃sjø], a. conscientious. adv. -sement.

consci/ent [kɔ̃sjɑ̃], a. conscious (de, of); fully aware (of). adv. -emment.

conscription [kɔ̃skripsjɔ̃], s.f. conscription.

conscrit [kɔ̃skri], s.m. conscript.

consécration [kɔ̃sekrasjɔ̃], s.f. consecration; dedication.

†consécutif [kɔ̃sekytif], a. consecutive.

conseil [kɔ̃sɛːj], s.m. counsel; (piece of) advice. 2. Jur: counsellor, counsel. 3. council, committee; c. d'administration, board of directors.

conseiller¹ [kɔ̃seje], v.tr. to advise; recommend.

conseiller², -ère, s. 1. adviser. 2. councillor.

‡consent/ir [kɔ̃sɑ̃tiːr], v.i. to consent, agree. s.m. -ement, consent.

conséquence [kɔ̃sekɑ̃s], s.f. (a) consequence, result; en c., accordingly; (b) importance, consequence.

conséqu/ent [kɔ̃sekɑ̃]. 1. a. (a) consistent; (b) following. 2. adv.phr. par c., consequently, accordingly. adv. -emment.

conservateur, -trice [kɔ̃sɛrvatœːr, -triːs]. 1. s. keeper; warden; curator; Pol: conservative. 2. a. preservative (process, etc.).

conservatoire [kɔ̃sɛrvatwaːr], s.m. school, academy (of music, drama).

conserve [kɔ̃sɛrv], s.f. preserved, canned, food; conserves au vinaigre, pickles.

conserv/er [kɔ̃sɛrve], v.tr. 1. to preserve, can (food). 2. to keep, retain. s.f. -ation. s.f. -erie, canning factory.

considérable [kɔ̃siderabl], a. considerable. adv. -ment.

considération [kɔ̃siderasjɔ̃], s.f. 1. consideration, thought. 2. reason, motive. 3. regard.

‡considérer [kɔ̃sidere], v.tr. 1. to consider, think. 2. to think highly of (s.o.).

consignataire [kɔ̃siɲatɛːr], s. Com: consignee.

consignateur [kɔ̃siɲatœːr], s.m. Com: consignor; shipper.

consigne [kɔ̃siɲ], s.f. 1. order(s). 2. cloakroom; left-luggage office.

consign/er [kɔ̃siɲe], v.tr. to consign (goods, etc.). s.f. -ation, consignment.

consist/ance [kɔ̃sistɑ̃ːs], s.f. (a) consistency; (b) stability. a. -ant, firm.

consister [kɔ̃siste], v.i. to consist (en, of).

consol/er [kɔ̃sɔle], v.tr. to console, comfort. a. & s. -ateur, -atrice. s.f. -ation.

se consoler (d'une perte), to get over (a loss).

consolid/er [kɔ̃sɔlide], v.tr. to consolidate, strengthen. s.f. -ation.

se consolider, to grow firm.

consommateur, -trice [kɔ̃sɔmatœːr, -tris], s. (a) consumer (of products); (b) customer (in café).

consommation [kɔ̃sɔmasjɔ̃], s.f. 1. consummation, accomplishment (of work). 2. consumption. 3. drink.

consommé [kɔ̃sɔme]. 1. a. consummate (skill, etc.). 2. s.m. consommé, clear soup.

consom/mer [kɔ̃sɔme], v.tr. 1. to consummate. 2. to consume, use up.

consonne [kɔ̃sɔn], s.f. consonant.

consortium [kɔ̃sɔrsjɔm], s.m. Ind: consortium.

conspir/er [kɔ̃spire], v.i. to conspire, plot (contre, against). a. & s. -ateur, -atrice. s.f. -ation.

constance [kɔ̃stɑ̃ːs], s.f. constancy.

const/ant [kɔ̃stɑ̃], a. 1. (a) steadfast; (b) unshaken. 3. constant, uniform. adv. -amment.

constat/er [kɔ̃state], v.tr. 1. to establish, to find out. 2. to state. s.f. -ation, verification.

constellation [kɔ̃stellasjɔ̃], s.f. constellation.

constern/er [kɔ̃sterne], v.tr. to dismay. s.f. -ation.

constip/er [kɔ̃stipe], v.tr. to constipate. s.f. -ation.

constitu/er [kɔ̃stitɥe], v.tr. to constitute; (a) to form; (b) to set up. a. -ant, constituent.

constitution [kɔ̃stitysjɔ̃], s.f. 1. institution (of committee, etc.). 2. constitution. 3. composition. a. †-nel.

construct/ion [kɔ̃stryksjɔ̃], s.f. construction. s.m.-eur. a. †-if.

‡construire [kɔ̃strɥir], v.tr. to construct; to build; to make.

consul [kɔ̃syl], s.m. consul. a. -aire. s.m. -at, consulate.

consult/er [kɔ̃sylte], v.tr. to consult. a. †-atif, advisory. s.f. -ation.

consumer [kɔ̃syme], v.tr. to consume, se consumer, to waste away.

contact [kɔ̃takt], s.m. 1. contact, touch; prise de c., preliminary conversation. 2. El: connection; établir le c., to switch on. 3. verre de c., contact lens.

contacter [kɔ̃takte], v.tr. F: to contact (s.o.).

contagi/on [kɔ̃taʒjɔ̃], s.f. contagion. a. †-eux, contagious, F: catching.

contamin/er [kɔ̃tamine], v.tr. to contaminate. s.f. -ation.

conte [kɔ̃ːt], s.m. (a) story, tale; (b) yarn.

contempl/er [kɔ̃tɑ̃ple], v.tr. to contemplate. a. †-atif. s.f. -ation.

contemporain, -aine [kɔ̃tɑ̃pɔrɛ̃, -ɛn], a. & s. contemporary.

contenance [kɔ̃tnɑ̃ːs], s.f. 1. capacity; c. d'un champ, area of a field. 2. countenance, bearing; faire bonne c., to put a good face on it.

‡contenir [kɔ̃tniːr], v.tr. 1. to contain. 2. to restrain; to control.

se contenir, to keep one's temper.

content [kɔ̃tɑ̃], a. (a) content; (b) pleased (de, with); (c) glad.

content/er [kɔ̃tɑ̃te], v.tr. to content, satisfy. s.m. -ement, satisfaction (de, with).

se contenter, to be satisfied.

†contentieux [kɔ̃tɑ̃sjø]. 1. a. contentious. 2. s.m. Adm: legal department (of bank, etc.).

contenu [kɔ̃tny]. 1. a. restrained; pent-up. 2. s.m. contents (of parcel, etc.).

cont/er [kɔ̃te], v.tr. to tell, relate. s. -eur, -euse, (story-)teller.

conteste [kɔ̃test], s.f. sans c., indisputably.

contest/er [kɔ̃teste]. 1. v.tr. to contest, dispute. 2. v.i. to dispute. a. -able, debatable. s.f. -ation.

contexte [kɔ̃tekst], s.m. context.

†contigu [kɔ̃tigy], a. contiguous, adjoining. s.f. -ité, contiguity.

contin/ence [kɔ̃tinɑ̃ːs], s.f. continence, chastity. a. -ent¹, chaste.

continent² [kɔ̃tinɑ̃], s.m. 1. continent. 2. land mass.

contingent [kɔ̃tɛ̃ʒɑ̃], s.m. (a) Mil: contingent; le c. annuel, the annual call-up; (b) quota; ration.

contingent/er [kɔ̃tɛ̃ʒɑ̃te], v.tr. 1. to fix quotas for (imports, etc.). 2. to distribute (films) according to a quota. s.m. -ement.

continu [kɔ̃tiny], a. continuous, unceasing.

continu/er [kɔ̃tinɥe], v.tr. & i. to continue; to carry on; to go on (doing sth.); continuez! go on! s.f. -ation. a. †-el. adv. -ellement, continually. s.f. -ité, continuity.

contorsion [kɔ̃tɔrsjɔ̃], s.f. contortion. s.
-niste, contortionist.

contour [kɔ̃tu:r], s.m. 1. outline. 2.
contour.

contourn/er [kɔ̃turne], v.tr. 1. to shape.
2. to pass round 3. to distort. s.m.
-ement.

contracter[1] [kɔ̃trakte], v.tr. 1. (a) to
contract (alliance); (b) to incur (debt);
c. une assurance, to take out an
insurance policy. 2. to contract
(habit); to catch (disease).

contract/er[2], v.tr. to contract, draw together. s.f. **-ion**, contraction; shrinking.
　　se contracter, to contract; to shrink.

contradic/tion [kɔ̃tradiksjɔ̃], s.f. 1.
contradiction. 2. inconsistency; discrepancy. a. **-toire**, contradictory.

‡**contraindre** [kɔ̃trɛ̃:dr], v.tr. to constrain.
1. to restrain. 2. to compel.

contraint [kɔ̃trɛ̃], a. constrained; forced;
stiff.

contrainte [kɔ̃trɛ̃:t], s.f. constraint. 1.
restraint. 2. compulsion.

contraire [kɔ̃trɛ:r], a. 1. (a) contrary;
opposite; jusqu'à avis c., until further
notice; (b) au c., on the contrary.
2. adverse. adv. **-ment**.

contrari/er [kɔ̃trarje], v.tr. 1. to thwart,
oppose. 2. to annoy. s.m. **-ant**, annoying. s.f. **-été**, annoyance.

contraste [kɔ̃trast], s.m. contrast.

contraster [kɔ̃traste], v.i. & tr. to contrast.

contrat [kɔ̃tra], s.m. contract, agreement.

contravention [kɔ̃travɑ̃sjɔ̃], s.f.Jur: minor
offence.

contre [kɔ̃:tr]. 1. prep. against; (a) c.
toute attente, contrary to all expectations; (b) s'abriter c. la pluie, to shelter
from the rain; (c) (in exchange) for;
(d) to; cinq c. un, five to one; (e) close
to, by; sa maison est tout contre, his
house is close by. 2. adv. against.
3. s.m. par c., on the other hand.

　　NOTE. In the hyphenated nouns and
adjectives below contre remains inv.;
for phonetics and irreg. pl. forms
consult the second component.

contre-amiral, s.m. rear-admiral.
contre-attaque, s.f. counter-attack.
contre-attaquer, v.tr. to counter-attack.
contrebande [kɔ̃trəbɑ̃:d], s.f. 1. contraband, smuggling. 2. contraband
goods. s.m. **-ier**, smuggler.
contrecarrer [kɔ̃trəkare], v.tr. to cross,
thwart.
contre-cœur (à), adv.phr. unwillingly,
reluctantly, grudgingly.
contre-coup, s.m. (a) rebound; (b)
after-effects.
‡**contredire** [kɔ̃trədi:r], v.tr. to contradict.
contredit [kɔ̃tradi], adv.phr. sans c.,
assuredly, unquestionably.

contre-écrou, s.m. lock-nut.
contre-espion, s.m. counter-spy. s.m.
-nage, counter-espionnage.
contrefaçon [kɔ̃trəfasɔ̃], s.f. counterfeit,
forgery.
‡**contrefaire** [kɔ̃trəfɛ:r], v.tr. 1. (a) to
imitate; (b) to pretend. 2. to counterfeit.
contrefait [kɔ̃trəfɛ], a. 1. pretended. 2.
counterfeit, forged. 3. deformed.
contrefort [kɔ̃trəfɔ:r], s.m. 1. A: & A:
buttress. 2. spur (of mountain); pl.
foot-hills.
contre-jour (à), adv.phr. against the light;
assis à c.-j., sitting in one's own
light.
contremaître, -tresse [kɔ̃trəmɛ:tr, -trɛs],
s. foreman, forewoman; overseer.
contremander [kɔ̃trəmɑ̃de], v.tr. to
countermand, cancel, revoke; to call
off (strike).
contre-partie, s.f. 1. (a) opposite view-
point; (b) other party (in transaction).
2. duplicate, counterpart.
contreplaqué [kɔ̃trəplake], a. laminated;
(bois) c., plywood.
contrepoids [kɔ̃trəpwa], s.m. counterpoise, counterweight.
contre-poil (à), adv. phr. the wrong way
(of nap, hair); F: prendre qn à c.-p.,
to rub s.o. up the wrong way.
contrepoison [kɔ̃trəpwazɔ̃], s.m. antidote.
contresens [kɔ̃trəsɑ̃:s], s.m. 1. misinter-
pretation. 2. à c.-s., in the wrong way,
sense, direction.
contresigner [kɔ̃trəsiɲe], v.tr. to countersign.
contretemps [kɔ̃trətɑ̃], s.m. (a) mishap,
hitch; (b) delay, inconvenience.
contre-torpilleur, s.m.Nau: destroyer.
‡**contrevenir** [kɔ̃trəvni:r], v.ind.tr. to
contravene.
contribu/er [kɔ̃tribɥe], v.i. to contribute.
s.m. & f. **-able**, taxpayer. s.f.
-tion, tax; share.
contrit [kɔ̃tri], a. contrite, penitent.
contrôle [kɔ̃tro:l], s.m. 1. roll; list. 2.
testing. 3. inspection; auditing. 4.
c. des naissances, birth control.
contrôl/er [kɔ̃trole], v.tr. 1. to inspect;
to verify (to check. 2. to hold in check.
s. **-eur, -euse**, inspector; ticket-
collector.
controverse [kɔ̃trəvɛrs], s.f. controversy.
contusion [kɔ̃tyzjɔ̃], s.f. contusion,
bruise.
contusionner [kɔ̃tyzjɔne], v.tr. to bruise.
‡**convaincre** [kɔ̃vɛ̃:kr], v.tr. 1. to convince. 2. to convict.
convalescence [kɔ̃valessɑ̃:s], s.f. convalescence. a. & s. **-cent, -cente**.
convenable [kɔ̃vnabl], a. 1. suitable;
proper. 2. decent; seemly. adv.
-ment.
convenance [kɔ̃vnɑ̃:s], s.f. 1. suitability,
fitness. 2. propriety, decency.

‡**convenir** [kɔ̃vniːr], *v.i.* 1. (a) to suit; fit; (b) (*impersonal use*) il convient de, it is advisable to. 2. (a) to agree; c. de qch., to agree about sth; il fut convenu, it was agreed; (b) c. de qch., to admit sth.

convention [kɔ̃vɑ̃sjɔ̃], *s.f.* 1. convention; les conventions sociales, social conventions. 2. covenant, agreement. *a.* †-nel, conventional.

convenu [kɔ̃vny], *a.* agreed.

‡**converger** [kɔ̃vɛrʒe], *v.i.* to converge.

convers/er [kɔ̃vɛrse], *v.i.* to converse, talk. *s.f.* -ation.

conversion [kɔ̃vɛrsjɔ̃], *s.f.* conversion.

converti, -e [kɔ̃vɛrti], *s.* convert.

convert/ir [kɔ̃vɛrtiːr], *v.tr.* to convert. *s.m.* El: -isseur, transformer. **se convertir,** to become converted.

convexe [kɔ̃vɛks], *a.* convex.

conviction [kɔ̃viksjɔ̃], *s.f.* 1. conviction; firm belief. 2. Jur: pièce à c., exhibit.

convive [kɔ̃viːv], *s.m. & f.* (a) guest (at table); (b) table-companion.

convoi [kɔ̃vwa], *s.m.* convoy.

convoit/er [kɔ̃vwate], *v.tr.* to covet, desire. *s.f.* -ise, covetousness.

convo/quer [kɔ̃vɔke], *v.tr.* to summon. *s.f.* -cation, summons.

convuls/er [kɔ̃vylse], *v.tr.* to convulse. *a.* †-if. *adv.* -ivement. *s.f.* -ion.

convulsionner [kɔ̃vylsjɔne], *v.tr.* to cause an upheaval in.

‡**coopér/er** [kɔɔpere], *v.i.* to co-operate. *s.f.* -ation. *a.* †-atif. *s.f.* -ative, co-operative store.

coordination [kɔɔrdinasjɔ̃], *s.f.* co-ordination.

coordonner [kɔɔrdɔne], *v.tr.* to co-ordinate.

copain [kɔpɛ̃], *s.m.* F: friend, pal.

copeau [kɔpo], *s.m.* shaving; chip.

copie [kɔpi], *s.f.* copy; Adm: pour c. conforme, certified true copy.

copier [kɔpje], *v.tr.* to copy.

†**copieu/x** [kɔpjø], *a.* copious. *adv.* -sement.

copilote [kɔpilɔt], *s.m. Av:* co-pilot.

copine [kɔpin], *s.f. F:* (girl) friend.

copiste [kɔpist], *s.m. & f.* copier; faute de c., clerical error.

copra(h) [kɔpra], *s.m.* copra; huile de c., coconut oil.

copulation [kɔpylasjɔ̃], *s.f.* copulation.

coq [kɔk], *s.m.* (a) cock, U.S: rooster; jeune c, cockerel; Sp: poids c., bantam-weight; (b) cock, male (of birds); c. de bruyère, (great) grouse.

coque [kɔk], *s.f.* 1. (a) shell (of egg); un œuf à la c., a (soft-)boiled egg; (b) shell, husk (of nut). 2. hull (of ship). *s.m.* -tier, egg-cup.

coquelicot [kɔkliko], *s.m.* (red) poppy.

coqueluche [kɔklyʃ], *s.f.* whooping cough.

coqu/et, -ette [kɔkɛ], *a.* 1. (a) coquettish; (b) smart, dainty. 2. *s.f.* -flirt. *adv.* -ettement. *s.f.* -etterie.

coquillage [kɔkijaːʒ], *s.m.* 1. shell-fish. 2. (empty) shell (of shell-fish).

coquille [kɔkij], *s.f.* shell.

coquin, -ine [kɔkɛ̃, -in], *s.* rogue, rascal; petite coquine! little wretch!

cor [kɔr], *s.m.* 1. horn; cor de chasse, hunting-horn. 2. corn (on the toe).

†**corail** [kɔraj], *s.m.* coral.

corbeau [kɔrbo], *s.m.* 1. crow; raven. 2. A. & A: corbel, bracket.

corbeille [kɔrbɛːj], *s.f.* (open) basket.

corbillard [kɔrbijaːr], *s.m.* hearse.

cord/e [kɔrd], *s.f.* 1. (a) rope, cord, line; c. à linge, clothes-line; (b) usé jusqu'à la c., threadbare. 2. chord. 3. cordes vocales, vocal cords. *s.m.* -age, rope(s), gear.

cordeau [kɔrdo], *s.m.* 1. tiré au c., perfectly straight. 2. fuse.

cordée [kɔrde], *s.f. Sp:* roped (climbing) party.

†**cordial** [kɔrdjal]. 1. *s.m.* cordial; restorative, hearty. 2. *a.* cordial, hearty. *adv.* -ement. *s.f.* -ité, cordiality.

cordon [kɔrdɔ̃], *s.m.* 1. (a) cord; c. de la porte, (*concierge's*) door-pull; (b) ribbon (of an order). 2. cordon (of police).

cordonn/ier [kɔrdɔnje], *s.m.* shoemaker, cobbler.

coriace [kɔrjas], *a.* tough.

corne [kɔrn], *s.f.* 1. (a) horn; (b) (snail's) feeler; (beetle's) antenna. 2. dog's-ear (of a book).

corneille [kɔrnɛːj], *s.f.* crow, rook; c. des clochers, jackdaw.

cornemuse [kɔrnəmyːz], *s.f.* bagpipes.

corner [kɔrne], *v.tr.* (a) to trumpet; (b) Aut: to sound the horn; to hoot.

cornet [kɔrne], *s.m.* 1. c. à pistons, cornet. 2. (a) c. de glace, ice-cream cornet; (b) c. à dés, dice-box; c. de papier, screw of paper.

corniche [kɔrniʃ], *s.f.* 1. cornice. 2. ledge; (route en) c., cliff road, corniche road.

cornichon [kɔrniʃɔ̃], *s.m.* gherkin.

cornu [kɔrny], *a.* horned (beast).

cornue [kɔrny], *s.f. Ch:* retort.

corollaire [kɔrɔllɛːr], *s.m.* corollary.

corolle [kɔrɔl], *s.f.* corolla.

corporation [kɔrpɔrasjɔ̃], *s.f.* corporation, public body. *a.* †-if.

†**corporel** [kɔrpɔrel], *a.* corporeal; corporal.

corps [kɔːr], *s.m.* 1. body; saisir qn à bras-le-c., to grapple with s.o. 2. corpse. 3. Sc: c. simple, element; c. composé, compound. 4. main part (of sth.); Nau: perdu c. et biens, lost with all hands. 5. Mil: corps.

corps-de-garde [kɔːrdəgard], *s.m.inv. Mil:* guardroom.

corpul/ence [kɔrpylɑ̃ːs], *s.f.* stoutness. *a.* -ent, fat.

correct [kɔr(r)ɛkt], *a.* correct; accurate. *adv.* -ement.

correction [kɔr(r)ɛksjɔ̃], s.f. 1. correction. 2. reproof. 3. correctness.

†**correctionnel** [kɔr(r)ɛksjɔnɛl], a. Jur: délit c., minor offence.

correspondance [kɔrɛspɔ̃dɑ̃:s], s.f. 1. agreement. 2. Rail: connection. 3. (a) dealings (with s.o.); (b) correspondence.

correspondre [kɔrɛspɔ̃:dr], v.i. 1. to tally, agree (à, with). 2. to correspond.

corrida [kɔrida], s.f. bull-fight.

corridor [kɔridɔ:r], s.m. corridor, passage.

‡**corriger** [kɔriʒe], v.tr. 1. to correct. 2. to punish (child).

corro/der [kɔrɔde], v.tr. to corrode. a. & s.m. **-sif**. s.f. **-sion**.

corrompre [kɔr(r)ɔ̃:pr], v.tr. to corrupt; to deprave; homme corrompu, corrupt, depraved, man.
se **corrompre**, (of meat, etc.) to become tainted.

corrup/tion [kɔr(r)ypsjɔ̃], s.f. corruption. a. & s. **-teur, -trice**. a. **-tible**.

corsage [kɔrsa:ʒ], s.m. blouse.

corse [kɔrs], a. & s. Corsican.

corset [kɔrsɛ], s.m. corset. s. **-ier, -ière**, corset-maker.

cortège [kɔrtɛ:ʒ], s.m. 1. train, retinue. 2. procession; c. funèbre, funeral procession.

corvée [kɔrve], s.f. F: thankless job; quelle c.! what a bind!

coryza [kɔriza], s.m. Med: cold in the head.

cosmétique [kɔsmetik], a. & s.m. cosmetic.

cosmique [kɔsmik], a. cosmic.

cosmopolite [kɔsmɔpolit], a. & s. cosmopolitan.

cosse [kɔs], s.f. pod, husk, hull.

cossu [kɔsy], a. F: well-to-do (person).

costaud [kɔsto], a. & s.m. F: hefty, tough (person).

costume [kɔstym], s.m. costume, dress; c. de bain, bathing suit, swimsuit.

cote [kɔt], s.f. 1. quota. 2. (a) Com: quotation (of prices, etc.); (b) odds (on a horse).

côte [kot], s.f. 1. rib; à c., side by side; tissu à côtes, corded, ribbed, material. 2. (a) slope (of hill); vitesse en c., (hill-)climbing speed; (b) hill; à mi-c., half-way up, down (the hill). 3. coast, shore.

côté [kote], s.m. 1. side; à mes côtés, by my side; appartement c. midi, flat with southern aspect; d'un c., on the one hand; prendre qch. du bon c., to take sth. well; de tous (les) côtés, on all sides. 2. adv.phr. (a) de c., on one side; sideways; (b) à c. de, by the side of; next to.

coteau [kɔto], s.m. hill, hillside.

côtelette [kotlɛt], s.f. cutlet; chop.

coter [kɔte], v.tr. 1. to assess; Sch: to give a mark to (an exercise). 2. point coté, spot height (on map). 3. Com: to quote (shares, etc.); cheval très coté, well-backed horse; (of pers.) être bien coté, to be appreciated, valued.

coterie [kɔtri], s.f. (political, literary) set.

cotis/er [kɔtize], v.tr. to contribute. s.f. **-ation**, contribution, subscription. s. **-ant**, subscriber.

†**côtier** [kotje], a. coastal (trade, etc.); fleuve c., short river.

coton [kɔtɔ̃], s.m. cotton; fil de c., sewing cotton. s.m. **-nier**, cotton plant.

‡**côtoyer** [kotwaje], v.tr. to keep close to; to skirt.

cotylédon [kɔtiledɔ̃], s.m. Bot: cotyledon.

cou [ku], s.m. neck; la peau du cou, the scruff of the neck.

couchage [kuʃa:ʒ], s.m. (matériel de) c., bedding; sac de c., sleeping bag.

couchant [kuʃɑ̃]. 1. a. soleil c., setting sun. 2. s.m. (a) sunset; (b) le c., the west.

couche [kuʃ], s.f. (a) bed, layer; c. (de bébé), (baby's) napkin, F: nappy; c. de fumier, hotbed; semer sur c., to sow in heat; (b) coat (of paint).

coucher [kuʃe]. I. v. 1. v.tr. to put to bed. 2. v.i. c. à un hôtel, to sleep at an hotel. II. s.m. 1. l'heure du c., bedtime. 2. setting (of sun).
se **coucher**, (a) to go to bed; (b) to lie down; (c) (of sun) to set.

couchette [kuʃɛt], s.f. berth (on train, ship).

coucou [kuku], s.m. 1. (a) cuckoo; (b) cuckoo-clock. 2. cowslip.

coude [kud], s.m. 1. elbow; coup de c., nudge. 2. bend, elbow (of road); knee (of pipe).

cou-de-pied [kudpje], s.m. instep. pl. **cous-de-pied**.

‡**coud/oyer** [kudwaje], v.tr. to elbow. s.m. **-oiement**, elbowing.

†**coudre** [kudr], v.tr. to sew, stitch; machine à c., sewing-machine.

coudrier [kudrie], s.m. hazel(-tree).

couenne [kwan], s.f. (a) (thick) skin of pig; (b) bacon rind; pork crackling.

couiner [kwine], v.i. to squeak, to squeal; to whimper.

couler [kule]. 1. v.tr. (a) to pour; (b) to sink. 2. v.i. (a) to flow, run; nœud coulant, slip-knot; (b) c. bas, to founder.
se **couler**, to glide, slip.

couleur [kulœr], s.f. 1. (a) colour, tint; (b) complexion; perdre ses couleurs, to turn pale; (c) pl. colours, flag. 2. paint. 3. (at cards) suit.

couleuvre [kulœvr], s.f. non-(non-poisonous) snake; grass-snake.

coulisse [kulis], s.f. 1. groove. 2. Th: les coulisses, the wings; dans les coulisses, behind the scenes.

couloir [kulwa:r], s.m. corridor.

coup [ku], s.m. 1. (a) knock, blow; rap (on the door); tenir le c., F: to stick it; c. de couteau, stab; (b) c. de feu, shot; (c) c. de vent, gust of wind. 2. stroke (normal action of sth.); (a) sur le c. de midi, on the stroke of twelve; (b) c. de pied, kick; Sp: c. d'envoi, kick-off; (c) c. de chance, stroke of luck; (d) clap, peal (of thunder). 3. influence; agir sous le c. de la peur, to act out of fear. 4. (a) deed; c. de tête, impulsive act; tout d'un c., at one go; tout à c., suddenly; c. sur c., in rapid succession.

coupable [kupabl]. 1. a. guilty. 2. s. culprit. adv. -ment.

coupant [kupã]. 1. a. cutting, sharp. 2. s.m. (cutting) edge.

coupe[1] [kup], s.f. (a) c. de champagne, champagne glass; (b) Sp: cup.

coupe[2], s.f. 1. (a) cutting; c. de cheveux, haircut; (b) cut (of a coat). 2. (at cards) cut, cutting.

coupé [kupe], a. cut up; broken (sleep); vin c. d'eau, wine and water.

coupe-gorge [kupgɔrʒ], s.m.inv. death-trap.

coupe-papier [kuppapje], s.m.inv. paper-knife.

couper [kupe], v.tr. to cut. 1. se c. le, au, doigt, to cut one's finger; c. la tête à qn, to cut off s.o.'s head. 2. v.i. to cut across; c. au plus court, to take a short cut. 3. (a) to cut off; interrupt; P.T.T: c. la communication, to ring off; El: c. le courant, to switch off; (b) (at cards) to trump. s.m. -age.

couperosé [kuproze], a. blotchy (complexion).

couple [kupl]. 1. s.m. pair, (married) couple. 2. s.f. two, couple.

coupler [kuple], v.tr. to couple; El: to connect.

couplet [kuplɛ], s.m. verse (of song).

coupole [kupɔl], s.f. cupola, dome.

coupon [kupɔ̃], s.m. 1. cutting; remnant. 2. coupon.

coupon-réponse [kupɔ̃repɔ̃s], s.m. P.T.T: c.-r. international, international reply coupon. pl. coupons-réponse.

coupure [kupy:r], s.f. 1. cut. 2. (a) piece cut out; c. de journal, newspaper cutting; (b) (de courant) power cut.

cour [ku:r], s.f. 1. court; à la c., at court; faire la c., to court (a girl). 2. yard.

courage [kuraʒ], s.m. courage.

†courageu/x [kuraʒø], a. courageous, brave. adv. -sement.

couramment [kuramã], adv. 1. easily; fluently. 2. commonly.

courant [kurã]. 1. a. (a) running; (b) flowing; (c) Com: le cinq c., the fifth inst. 2. s.m. (a) current, stream; c.

d'air, draught; (b) course; dans le c. de l'année, in the course of the year; être au c. de qch., to know all about sth.

courbatur/e [kurbaty:r], s.f. stiffness; tiredness. a. -é, stiff.

courbe [kurb]. 1. a. curved. 2. s.f. curve, graph; c. de niveau, contour (line).

courber [kurbe]. 1. v.tr. to bend, curve. 2. v.i. to bend; to sag. se courber, to bend, stoop.

courge [kurʒ], s.f. gourd; vegetable marrow.

courgette [kurʒɛt], s.f. Cu: (young) marrow, courgette.

‡cour/ir [kurir]. 1. v.i. to run; (a) j'y cours, I'm going directly; (b) to race; (c) to be current; faire c. un bruit, to spread a rumour; par le temps qui court, nowadays. 2. v.tr. c. un risque, to run a risk. s. -eur, -euse.

couronne [kurɔn], s.f. 1. wreath. 2. crown; coronet.

couronn/er [kurɔne], v.tr. to crown. s.m. -ement, coronation.

courrier [kurje], s.m. 1. courier; messenger. 2. mail, post; par retour du c., by return of post.

courroie [kurwa], s.f. strap; (driving-) belt.

cours [ku:r], s.m. 1. course; flow; c. d'eau, river; stream; travail en c., work in progress; au c. de, during. 2. circulation, currency. 3. price; c. du change, rate of exchange. 4. (a) course (of lectures); class; (b) Sch: text book.

course [kurs], s.f. 1. race. 2. (a) excursion; (b) journey; (c) (business) errand; faire des courses, to go shopping. 3. path, course.

court[1] [ku:r]. 1. a. short; à c., hard up. 2. adv. short; tout c., simply.

court[2], s.m. (tennis) court.

court-circuit [kursirkɥi], s.m. El: short circuit. pl. courts-circuits.

courtier [kurtje], s.m. Com: broker; agent, salesman.

courtis/er [kurtize], v.tr. to court. s.m. -an, courtier.

courtois [kurtwa], a. courteous, polite. adv. -ement.

courtoisie [kurtwazi], s.f. courtesy.

couru [kury], a. popular; sought after.

cousin[1], -ine [kuzɛ̃, -in], s. cousin.

cousin[2], s.m. gnat, midge.

coussin [kusɛ̃], s.m. cushion.

coussinet [kusinɛ], s.m. 1. pad. 2. Techn: bearing.

coût [ku], s.m. cost.

couteau [kuto], s.m. knife.

coutellerie [kutɛlri], s.f. cutlery.

coût/er [kute], v.i. to cost; coûte que coûte, at all costs. a. †-eux, costly.

coutil [kuti], *s.m.* drill; (mattress) ticking.

coutume [kutym], *s.f.* custom, habit; comme de c., às usual.

coutur/e [kutyːr], *s.f.* 1. sewing, needlework. 2. seam (in dress). s. -ier, -ière, dressmaker.

couvée [kuve], *s.f.* 1. clutch (of eggs). 2. brood (of chicks).

couvent [kuvã], *s.m.* (a) convent; (b) monastery.

couver [kuve]. 1. *v.tr.* (a) to sit on (eggs); to hatch; (b) to brood over the fire. 2. *v.i.* to smoulder.

couvercle [kuverkl], *s.m.* lid, cover.

couvert [kuveːr]. 1. *a.* covered; overcast. 2. *s.m.* (a) cover(ing), shelter; (b) place (at table); mettre le c., to lay the table.

couverture [kuvertyːr], *s.f.* 1. covering, cover; blanket. 2. roofing.

couvre-feu [kuvrəfø], *s.m.inv.* curfew.

couvre-lit [kuvrəli], *s.m.* bedspread, counterpane. *pl. couvre-lits.*

couvre-pied(s) [kuvrəpje], *s.m.* bedspread; quilt. *pl. couvre-pieds.*

‡couvrir [kuvriːr], *v.tr.* 1. to cover (de, with). 2. c. une maison, to roof a house.

se couvrir, (of weather) to become overcast.

cover-girl [kœvərgəl], *s.f.* F: cover-girl. *pl. cover-girls.*

cowboy [kauboi], *s.m.* F: cowboy.

crabe [kraːb], *s.m.* crab.

crach/er [krafe]. 1. *v.i.* to spit; to splutter; El: to spark. 2. *v.tr.* c. des injures, to hurl abuse. *s.m.* -at, spittle. *s.m.* -ement, spitting. *s.m.* -eur. *s.m.* -in, fine drizzle.

craie [krɛ], *s.f.* chalk.

‡craindre [krɛ̃ːdr], *v.tr.* to fear, dread; il est à c., it is to be feared; craint l'humidité, to be kept dry.

craint/e [krɛ̃t], *s.f.* fear, dread; awe. *a.* †-if, timid. *adv.* -ivement.

cramoisi [kramwazi], *a.* & *s.m.* crimson.

crampe [krãːp], *s.f.* cramp.

cramponner (se) [səkrãpɔne], *v.pr.* to hold on; to clutch.

cran [krã], *s.m.* 1. notch; cog; c. d'arrêt, safety catch. 2. F: pluck.

crâne [kraːn]. 1. *s.m.* skull. 2. *a.* (a) F: plucky; (b) jaunty. *adv.* -ment.

crapaud [krapo], *s.m.* toad.

†crapuleu/x [krapylø], *a.* debauched, dissolute. *adv.* -sement.

craqu/er [krake], *v.i.* to crack; to crunch; to creak. *s.m.* -ement.

crasse [kras]. 1. *a.f.* gross, crass. 2. *s.f.* dirt, squalor.

cratère [krateːr], *s.m.* crater.

cravache [kravaʃ], *s.f.* riding-whip.

cravate [kravat], *s.f.* (a) (neck-)tie; (b) scarf.

†crayeux [krɛjø], *a.* chalky.

crayon [krɛjɔ̃], *s.m.* pencil; c. pastel, crayon; c. à bille, ball-point pen.

créance [kreãːs], *s.f.* 1. belief, credit. 2. lettre de c., letter of credit. 3. debt.

créancier, -ière [kreãsje, -jɛːr], *s.* creditor.

crécelle [kresɛl], *s.f.* (hand-)rattle; voix de c., rasping voice.

crèche [krɛʃ], *s.f.* 1. manger, crib. 2. day-nursery, crèche.

crédibilité [kredibilite], *s.f.* credibility.

crédit [kredi], *s.m.* 1. repute, prestige. 2. credit.

créditeur, -trice [kreditœːr, -tris], *s.*

credo [kredo], *s.m.inv.* creed.

crédule [kredyl], *a.* credulous.

crédulité [kredylite], *s.f.* credulity.

cré/er [kree], *v.tr.* to create. *a.* & *s.* -ateur, -atrice. *s.f.* -ation. *s.f.* -ature.

crémaillère [kremajɛːr], *s.f.* 1. pothanger; pendre la c., to give a house-warming party. 2. chemin de fer à c., rack-railway.

créma/tion [kremasjɔ̃], *s.f.* cremation. *a.* & *s.m.* -toire. *s.m.* -torium, *pl.* -toria.

crème [krɛm], *s.f.* (a) cream: *a.inv.* cream(-coloured); (b) custard.

crém/erie [krɛmri], *s.f.* 1. dairy, milk-shop. 2. small restaurant. *s.* -ier, -ière, dairyman, -woman.

†crémeux [kremø], *a.* creamy.

créneaux [kreno], *s.m.pl.* battlements.

crénelé [krenle], *a.* toothed, notched.

créole [kreɔl], *a.* & *s.* creole.

créosoter [kreɔzɔte], *v.tr.* to creosote.

crêpe [krɛːp]. 1. *s.f.* pancake. 2. *s.m.* crepe; c. satin, satin crêpe; c. de caoutchouc, crepe-rubber.

crépi [krepi], *a.* & *s.m.* rough-cast(ing).

crép/ir [krepiːr], *v.tr.* to rough-cast (wall). *s.m.* -issage.

crépit/er [krepite], *v.i.* to crackle; to patter; to sputter. *s.m.* -ement.

crépu [krepy], *a.* crisp, fuzzy (hair).

crépuscul/e [krepyskyl], *s.m.* twilight; dusk. *a.* -aire, twilight.

cresson [kresɔ̃], *s.m.* cress; c. de fontaine, watercress. *s.m.* -nière, watercress bed.

crête [krɛːt], *s.f.* 1. comb, crest. 2. crest; ridge; El: puissance de c., peak power.

crétin [kretɛ̃], *s.m.* (a) cretin; idiot; (b) F: idiot, dead loss.

creuser [krøze], *v.tr.* 1. to hollow (out). 2. to excavate.

creuset [krøze], *s.m.* crucible, melting-pot.

†creux [krø]. 1. *a.* hollow; voix creuse, deep voice. 2. *s.m.* hollow; trough (of wave).

crevasse [krəvas], *s.f.* crack (in skin); crevice (in wall); crevasse.

‡crev/er [krəve]. 1. v.i. (a) to burst, split; (b) (of animals, P: of people) to die; c. de faim, to be starving. 2. v.tr. to burst; to puncture (tyre); c. un œil à qn, to put out s.o.'s eye. s.f. -aison, puncture.

crevette [krəvet], s.f. shrimp; prawn.

cri [kri], s.m. (a) cry; chirp; cri perçant, shriek; squeal; (b) shout, call; pousser des cris, to shout out.

criailler [kriaje], v.i. 1. to cry out, bawl. 2. to whine, complain.

criard [kriaːr], a. (a) squalling, peevish; (b) shrill; couleur criarde, loud colour.

crible [kribl], s.m. sieve, riddle.

cribler [krible], v.tr. 1. to sift. 2. to riddle (de, with); criblé de dettes, head over ears in debt.

cric [krik], s.m. (lifting) jack.

criée [krie], s.f. auction.

crier [krie], v.i. (a) to cry; to call out; to shout; (b) to squeak; to chirp; (c) to creak.

crim/e [krim], s.m. crime. a., & s. -inel, -inelle, criminal.

crin [krɛ̃], s.m. horsehair. s.f. -ière, mane.

crique [krik], s.f. creek, cove.

criquet [krike], s.m. (a) locust; (b) cricket.

crise [kriːz], s.f. 1. crisis; (a) slump; (b) shortage (of housing, etc.). 2. attack; une c. de larmes, a fit of crying.

crisp/er [krispe], v.tr. to contract, clench. a. F: -ant, aggravating. s.f. -ation, wincing; (nervous) twitching.

criss/er [krise], v.tr. & i. to grate. s.m. -ement.

†cristal [kristal], s.m. 1. crystal. 2. c. taillé, cut glass.

cristallis/er [kristalize], v.tr. & i. to crystallize.

critique [kritik]. 1. a. critical. 2. s.m. critic. 3. s.f. criticism; review; censure.

critiqu/er [kritike], v.tr. to criticize. a. -able, open to criticism.

croass/er [kroase], v.i. to caw; to croak. s.m. -ement.

croc [kro], s.m. 1. (a) hook; (b) pawl, catch. 2. fang.

crochet [krɔʃe], s.m. 1. hook; dentelle au c., crochet-work. 2. c. de serrurier, skeleton key; F: vivre aux crochets de qn, to sponge on s.o. 3. sudden turn (in road).

crochu [krɔʃy], a. hooked.

crocodile [krɔkɔdil], s.m. crocodile.

‡croire [krwaːr]. 1. v.tr. to believe; je (le) crois bien! I should think so! n'en croyez rien! I don't believe it!

croyez-m'en, take my word for it. 2. v.i. (a) c. à qch., to believe in sth.; c'est à ne pas y c., it is beyond all belief; (b) c. en qn, to believe in, have faith in, s.o.

croisade [krwazad], s.f. crusade.

croisé [krwaze]. 1. a. crossed; mots croisés, crossword. 2. s.m. crusader.

croisée [krwaze], s.f. casement-window.

crois/er [krwaze]. 1. v.tr. to cross; to fold (the arms); to pass (s.o.); leurs regards se croisèrent, their eyes met. 2. to interbreed, to cross (animals, plants). 3. v.i. to cruise. s.m. -ement, crossing.

croiseur [krwazœːr], s.m. Nau: cruiser.

croisière [krwazjeːr], s.f. cruise.

croissance [krwasɑ̃ːs], s.f. growth.

croissant [krwasɑ̃], s.m. 1. crescent. 2. Cu: croissant.

‡croître [krwaːtr], v.i. to grow, increase (in size, volume); les jours croissent, the days are lengthening.

croix [krwa], s.f. cross; la Sainte C., the Holy Rood; la C. de guerre = the Military Cross; en (forme de) c., cross-shaped, cross-wise.

croquant [krɔkɑ̃], a. crisp.

croque-mort [krɔkmɔːr], s.m. (undertaker's) mute. pl. croque-morts.

croquer [krɔke], v.tr. (a) to crunch, munch; chocolat à c., eating chocolate; (b) to sketch.

croquette [krɔket], s.f. Cu: rissole, croquette.

croquis [krɔki], s.m. sketch.

crosse [krɔs], s.f. 1. (hockey-)stick; (golf-)club. 2. (a) crook; (b) butt (of rifle).

crotale [krɔtal], s.m. rattlesnake.

crotte [krɔt], s.f. 1. dung. 2. mud, dirt.

crotter [krɔte], v.tr. to dirty, soil.

croul/er [krule], v.i. to collapse. a. & s.m. -ant, (i) a. ramshackle; (ii) s.m. F: back number.

croupe [krup], s.f. 1. monter en c., to ride pillion. 2. ridge (of hill).

croupier [krupje], s.m. croupier.

croupir [krupiːr], v.i. 1. to wallow. 2. (of water) to stagnate.

croustillant [krustijɑ̃], a. crisp.

croûte [krut], s.f. 1. crust; (cheese-)rind; F: casser la c., to have a snack. 2. scab. 3. daub.

croûton [krutɔ̃], s.m. (a) crusty end (of loaf); (b) Cu: crouton.

croy/ance [krwajɑ̃ːs], s.f. belief (à, in). a. & s. -ant, (i) believing; (ii) believer.

cr/u[1] [kry], a. raw; crude. adv. -ûment, roughly.

cru², *s.m.* locality in which vines are grown; le c., of the district; les grands crus, the great wines.

cruauté [kryote], *s.f.* cruelty (envers, to).

cruche [kryʃ], *s.f.* pitcher, jug.

cruci/fier [krysifje], *v.tr.* to crucify. *s.m.* -**fix**, crucifix. *s.f.* -**fixion**.

crudité [krydite], *s.f.* crudity; manger des crudités, to eat raw fruit and vegetables.

crue [kry], *s.f.* rising (of river); flood.

†cru/el [kryɛl], *a.* cruel (envers, to). *adv.* -**ellement**.

crustacés [krystase], *s.m.pl.* shellfish.

crypte [kript], *s.f.* crypt.

cub/e [kyb]. 1. *s.m.* cube. 2. *a.* cubic. *a.* -**ique**. *s.m.* -**isme**. *s.m. & f.* -**iste**.

‡cueill/ir [kœjiːr], *v.tr.* to pick, gather. *s.f.* -**ette**, picking (of fruit, flowers).

cuiller, cuillère [kɥijɛːr], *s.f.* spoon.

cuillerée [kɥijre], *s.f.* spoonful.

cuir [kɥiːr], *s.m.* 1. hide. 2. leather.

cuirasse [kɥiras], *s.f.* 1. breast-plate. 2. armour (of warship).

cuirassé [kɥirase]. 1. *a.* armoured. 2. *s.m.* battleship.

‡cuire [kɥiːr]. 1. *v.tr.* (faire) c., to cook. 2. *v.i. a.* (of food) to cook; (b) to burn, smart; les yeux me cuisent, my eyes are smarting; il vous en cuira, you'll regret it.

cuisin/e [kɥizin], *s.f.* 1. kitchen. 2. (a) cookery; faire la c., to do the cooking. *s.* -**ier**, -**ière**, cook. *s.f.* -**ière**, cooking-stove, cooker.

cuisiner [kɥizine], *v.tr.* to cook (meat, etc.); *F:* c. les comptes, to cook the accounts, *F:* the books: c. un détenu, to grill a prisoner.

cuisse [kɥis], *s.f.* thigh; (chicken) leg.

cuivre [kɥiːvr], *s.m.* copper; c. jaune, brass; *Mus:* les cuivres, the brass.

cuivré [kɥivre], *a.* 1. copper-coloured. 2. sons cuivrés, brassy tones.

cul [ky], *s.m. P:* backside, behind (of pers.).

culasse [kylas], *s.f.* 1. breech (of gun). 2. *Aut: etc:* (detachable) cylinder-head.

culbute [kylbyt], *s.f.* (a) somersault; (b) tumble.

culbuteur [kylbytœːr], *s.m.* 1. *El:* interrupteur à c., tumbler switch. 2. *Aut: etc:* moteur à culbuteurs, overhead valve engine. 3. tripper device; tipping device (for truck).

culinaire [kylinɛːr], *a.* culinary.

culminant [kylminɑ̃], *a.* point c., highest point; height, climax.

culot [kylo], *s.m. P:* avoir du c., to have plenty of cheek.

culotte [kylɔt], *s.f.* breeches; (boy's) shorts; (woman's) panties.

culpabilité [kylpabilite], *s.f.* guilt-(iness.)

culte [kylt], *s.m.* 1. worship. 2. cult.

cultiv/er [kyltive], *v.tr.* to cultivate; to farm (land). *s.m.* -**ateur**, farmer.

culture [kyltyːr], *s.f.* 1. (a) cultivation; (b) *pl.* land under cultivation. 2. culture; c. physique, physical training. *a.* †-**el**, cultural.

cupidité [kypidite], *s.f.* cupidity, greed.

curateur, -trice [kyratœːr, -tris], *s.* trustee, administrator; guardian.

cure [kyːr], *s.f.* 1. care. 2. (course of) treatment; cure.

curé [kyre], *s.m.* parish priest.

cure-dents [kyrdɑ̃], *s.m.inv.* toothpick.

cure-pipe [kyrpip], *s.m.* pipe-cleaner. *pl.* cure-pipes.

curer [kyre], *v.tr.* (a) to pick (teeth); to clean (nails); (b) to clean out, dredge (drain, river).

†curieu/x [kyrjø], *a.* curious; (a) interested; (a) inquisitive (about); (b) odd. *adv.* -**sement**.

curiosit/e [kyrjozite], *s.f.* curiosity. 1. (a) interest; (b) inquisitiveness; (c) oddness. 2. curio.

cuv/e [kyːv], *s.f.* vat, tun. *s.f.* -**ette**, wash-basin; (w.c.) pan.

cyanure [sjanyːr], *s.m.* cyanide.

cyclable [siklabl], *a.* piste c., cycle track.

cycl/e [sikl], *s.m.* 1. cycle (of events). 2. bicycle. *s.m.* -**isme**. *s.m. & f.* -**iste**.

cyclomoteur [siklomɔtœːr], *s.m.* moped.

cyclone [siklon], *s.m.* cyclone.

cygne [siɲ], *s.m.* swan.

cylind/re [silɛ̃ːdr], *s.m.* cylinder. *a.* -**rique**, cylindrical.

cylindrée [silɛ̃dre], *s.f.* cubic capacity (of engine).

cymbale [sɛ̃bal], *s.f.* cymbal.

cynique [sinik]. 1. *a.* shameless; cynical. 2. *s.m.* cynic. *adv.* -**ment**.

cynisme [sinism], *s.m.* shamelessness; cynicism.

cyprès [siprɛ], *s.m.* cypress.

cytise [sitiːz], *s.m.* laburnum.

D

D, d [de], *s.m.* (the letter) D, d.
dac, d'ac [dak], *int.* F: O.K.
dactylo [daktilo], *s.f.* typist.
dada [dada], *s.m.* hobby.
dahlia [dalja], *s.m.* dahlia.
daigner [deɲe], *v.tr.* to deign, condescend; elle n'a même pas daigné me voir, she wouldn't even see me.
daim [dɛ̃], *s.m.* (*a*) (fallow) deer; buck; (*b*) buckskin; suede.
daine [dal], *s.f.* (*a*) flag(stone); (*b*) (stone) slab.
daltonisme [daltonism], *s.m.* colour-blindness.
dame¹ [dam], *s.f.* 1. (*a*) lady; (*b*) married woman; P: votre d., your missus. 2. (*a*) jeu de dames (game of) draughts, U.S.: checkers; (*b*) king (at draughts); queen (at cards and chess).
dame², *int.* F: d. oui! rather!
damier [damje], *s.m.* draught-board, U.S.: checker board.
damner [dane], *v.tr.* to damn.
dandiner [dãdine], *v.tr.* to dandle (baby). se dandiner, to -waddle.
danger [dãʒe], *s.m.* danger, peril; à l'abri du d., out of harm's way; pas de d.! not likely!
dangereu/x [dãʒrø], *a.* dangerous (pour, to). **-sement**, *adv.* -sement.
danois, -oise [danwa, -wa:z], 1. *a.* Danish; (chien) d., Great Dane. 2. *s.* Dane. 3. *s.m. Ling:* Danish.
dans [dã], *prep.* 1. (*of place*) (*a*) in; (*b*) within; d. un rayon de dix kilomètres, within a radius of ten kilometres; (*c*) into; mettre qch. d. une boîte, to put sth. into a box; (*d*) out of; boire qch. d. un verre, to drink sth. out of a glass. 2. (*of time*) in; within; during; d. le temps, long ago; payer d. dix jours, to pay within ten days. 3. (*a*) être d. le commerce, to be in trade; (*b*) être d. la nécessité de, to be under the necessity of; F: d. ce but, with this object in mind.
danse [dã:s], *s.f.* dance, dancing; d. de Saint-Guy, St. Vitus's dance.
danser [dãse], *v.i.* to dance.
danseur, -euse [dãsœr, -øːz], *s.* 1. dancer. 2. partner (at dance).
dard [dar], *s.m.* sting (of insect); forked tongue.
dare-dare [dardaːr], *adv.* post-haste.
date [dat], *s.f.* date; sans d., undated.
dater [date], 1. *v.tr.* to date (letter). 2. *v.i.* à d. de ce jour, from to-day; qui date, (i) *Hist:* epoch-making; (ii) *Cl:* old-fashioned.
datte [dat], *s.f. Bot:* date.
dattier [datje], *s.m.* date-palm.
dauphin [dofɛ̃], *s.m.* 1. dolphin. 2. dauphin.

davantage [davãtaːʒ], *adv.* more.
de [də], (*before vowels & h mute* d'; *contracts to* du, des, *with* le, les). I. *prep.* 1. (*a*) from; il vient de Paris, he comes from Paris; (*b*) (*time*) il part de nuit, he leaves by night; (*c*) (*agent*) accompagné de ses amis, accompanied by his friends; (*d*) (*manner*) d'une voix douce, in a gentle voice; (*e*) (*cause*) sauter de joie, to leap for joy; (*f*) (*measure*) âgé de 16 ans, 16 years old. 2. (*a*) of; le livre de David, David's book; les rues de Paris, the Paris streets; (*b*) (*material*) un pont de fer, an iron bridge; (*c*) (*distinguishing mark*) le professeur de français, the French master; (*d*) (*partitive*) un verre de vin, a glass of wine; pas de vin, no wine; quelque chose de bon, something good. II. (*link word*) 1. indigne de vivre, unfit to live. 2. un drôle de garçon, a funny chap; trois hommes de tués, three men killed. III. (*partitive article; pl. of* un, une) sans faute, without making any mistakes; avez-vous du pain? have you any bread? vous êtes des lâches, you are cowards.
dé¹ [de], *s.m. Sp:* die; jeter des dés, to throw the dice.
dé², *s.m.* thimble.
débâcle [debaːkl], *s.f.* downfall; collapse.
déballer [debale], *v.tr.* to unpack.
débarbouiller (se) [sədebarbuje], *v.pr.* to wash one's face.
débarcadère [debarkadɛːr], *s.m.* landing-stage, wharf.
débarquement [debarkəmã], *s.m.* unloading; landing, disembarkation.
débarquer [debarke]. 1. *v.tr.* to unload; to disembark, land. 2. *v.i.* to land, disembark; to alight.
débarras [debara], *s.m.* riddance; (chambre de) d., lumber-room.
débarrass/er [debarase], *v.tr.* to clear (table, etc.); to relieve s.o. of qch., to relieve s.o. of sth.; d. le plancher, (i) to clear the floor; (ii) F: to clear out. **-ement**.
se débarrasser de qch., to get rid of sth.
débat [deba], *s.m.* 1. debate. 2. dispute.
‡débattre [debatr], *v.tr.* to debate, discuss. se débattre, to struggle.
débauche [deboʃ], *s.f.* debauch(ery).
débauché [deboʃe], *a.* debauched.
débilité [debilite], *s.f.* debility, weakness.
débit¹ [debi], *s.m.* 1. (*a*) (retail) sale; (*b*) (retail) shop; d. de tabac, tobacconist's; d. de boissons = public house. 2. output; (of river). 3. avoir le d. facile, F: to have the gift of the gab.
débit², *s.m.* debit.

débitant, -ante [debitɑ̃, -ɑ̃:t], s. retail dealer; retailer; d. de tabac, tobacconist.

débiter [debite], v.tr. **1.** to retail. **2.** F: d. des histoires, to spin yarns.

débiter², v.tr. to debit.

débiteur, -trice [debitœːr, -tris], s. debtor.

‡**déblayer** [debleje], v.tr. **1.** to clear away. **2.** to clear (ground).

déblo/quer [debloke], v.tr. to free, to release. s.m. -cage.

déboire [debwaːr], s.m. disappointment.

déboiser [debwaze], v.tr. to deforest, clear (land). s.m. -ement.

débonnaire [debɔnɛːr], a. good-natured.

déborder [debɔrde], v.tr. & i. **1.** to overflow; débordé de travail, snowed under with work. **2.** to project, protrude.

débouché [debuʃe], s.m. **1.** outlet. **2.** opening; chance of success.

déboucher¹ [debuʃe], v.tr. **1.** to clear. **2.** to uncork.

déboucher², v.i. to emerge, issue.

débours [debuːr], s.m.pl. disbursement; out-of-pocket expenses.

débourser [deburse], v.tr. to spend. s.m. -ement.

debout [dabu], adv. **1.** (a) upright, on end; standing; "tenir d.", 'to be kept upright'; se tenir d., to stand; "places d. seulement," 'standing room only'; F: ça ne tient pas d., that doesn't hold water; histoire à dormir d., boring story; (b) être d., to be up; allons, d.! come on, get up! **2.** vent d., headwind.

déboutonner [debutɔne], v.tr. to unbutton.

débraillé [debraje], a. (pers.) untidy.

‡**débray/er** [debreje], v.tr. Aut: to declutch. s.m. -age.

débris [debri], s.m.pl. remains, debris.

débrouillard, -arde [debrujaːr, -ard], a. & s. resourceful (person).

débrouiller [debruje], v.tr. to unravel; to straighten out.
　　se débrouiller, to extricate oneself (from difficulties); to manage.

début [deby], s.m. **1.** first appearance. **2.** beginning, start, outset.

débutant, -ante [debytɑ̃, -ɑ̃:t], s. beginner.

débuter [debyte], v.i. **1.** to make one's first appearance. **2.** to begin.

‡**décacheter** [dekaʃte], v.tr. to unseal, open.

décade [dekad], s.f. decade.

décadence [dekadɑ̃:s], s.f. decadence, decline.

décadent [dekadɑ̃], a. decadent; in decay.

décalaminer [dekalamine], v.tr. Aut: to decarbonize, F: decoke. s.m. -age.

décamper [dekɑ̃pe], v.i. F: to clear out, beat it.

décanter [dekɑ̃te], v.tr. to decant.

décapiter [dekapite], v.tr. to decapitate, behead.

décapotable [dekapɔtabl], a. Aut: convertible.

décapsul/er [dekapsyle], v.tr. to open (a bottle); to take off a crown cork from (a bottle). s.m. -ateur, bottle opener.

‡**décéder** [desede], v.i. to die.

‡**déceler** [desle], v.tr. to disclose; to reveal.

décembre [desɑ̃br], s.m. December.

décence [desɑ̃:s], s.f. (a) decency; (b) propriety.

déc/ent [desɑ̃], a. (a) decent; modest; (b) proper, seemly. adv. -emment.

décentraliser [desɑ̃tralize], v.tr. to decentralize. s.f. -ation.

déception [desɛpsjɔ̃], s.f. disappointment.

décerner [desɛrne], v.tr. to award (prize, etc.).

décès [desɛ], s.m. decease, death.

décevant [desvɑ̃], a. **1.** deceptive. **2.** disappointing.

‡**décevoir** [desəvwaːr], v.tr. **1.** to deceive, delude. **2.** to disappoint.

déchaîn/er [deʃɛne], v.tr. to let loose; to unchain. s.m. -ement.
　　se déchaîner, to break out.

décharge [deʃarʒ], s.f. **1.** (a) unloading; (b) discharge. **2.** (a) relief; (b) témoin à d., witness for the defence; (c) release. **3.** outlet.

‡**décharg/er** [deʃarʒe], v.tr. **1.** to unload; to fire (gun). **2.** to lighten (ship, etc.) of its load; to acquit (s.o. of a charge). **3.** to empty (reservoir). s.m. -ement.

décharné [deʃarne], a. emaciated; bony; gaunt.

déchausser (se) [deʃoʃe], v.pr. to take off one's shoes.

déchéance [deʃeɑ̃:s], s.f. **1.** downfall; lapse; forfeiture.

déchet [deʃɛ], s.m. usu. pl. waste, refuse.

déchiffrer [deʃifre], v.tr. to decipher; to read (music).

déchiquet/er [deʃikte], v.tr. to cut into shreds. a. -é, jagged shape.

déchirant [deʃirɑ̃], a. heart-rending.

déchirer [deʃire], v.tr. to tear (up, open).

déchu [deʃy], a. fallen; lapsed (policy).

décidé [deside], a. **1.** settled. **2.** resolute; determined. **3.** decided. adv. -ment.

décider [deside], v.tr. **1.** to decide, settle. **2.** to persuade, induce.
　　se décider, to make up one's mind.

‡**décimal** [desimal], a. decimal.

décimale [desimal], s.f. decimal.

décimer [desime], v.tr. to decimate.

‡**décis/if** [desizif], a. **1.** decisive; conclusive. **2.** peremptory. adv. -ivement.

décision [desizjɔ̃], s.f. decision.

déclamation [deklamasjɔ̃], s.f. **1.** oratory. **2.** (a) declamation; (b) ranting.

déclamer [deklame], *v.tr.* **1.** to declaim. **2.** to rant.

déclaration [deklarasjɔ̃], *s.f.* declaration; proclamation; notification; **d. sous serment,** affidavit.

déclarer [deklare], *v.tr.* **1.** to declare, make known. **2.** to announce, make public.

déclench/er [deklɑ̃ʃe], *v.tr.* **1.** to unlatch (door). **2.** to release, disconnect (mechanism). **3.** to set (machine) in motion. *s.m.* -ement.

déclic [deklik], *s.m.* *(a)* pawl, catch; trigger; *(b)* click.

déclin [deklɛ̃], *s.m.* decline; waning (of moon); falling-off.

déclinaison [deklinɛzɔ̃], *s.f.* declension.

décliner [dekline]. **1.** *v.i. (of moon)* to wane. **2.** *v.tr.* to decline, refuse.

déclivité [deklivite], *s.f.* declivity, slope.

décoiffer (se) [sedekwafe], *v.pr.* **1.** to take off one's hat. **2.** to get one's hair in a mess.

décoller [dekɔle]. **1.** *v.tr.* to unstick. **2.** *vi. (of aircraft)* to take off.

décolleté [dekɔlte], *a.* low-necked.

décoloration [dekɔlɔrasjɔ̃], *s.f.* discolouration.

se décolorer, *(of features)* to become distorted.

décombres [dekɔ̃br], *s.m.pl.* rubbish, debris; ruins.

décommander [dekɔmɑ̃de], *v.tr.* to countermand; to cancel.

décompos/er [dekɔ̃poze], *v.tr.* to decompose. *s.f.* -ition.

déconcerter [dekɔ̃sɛrte], *v.tr.* **1.** to upset. **2.** to disconcert.

déconseiller [dekɔ̃sɛje], *v.tr.* to advise (s.o.) against (sth.).

décontenancer [dekɔ̃tnɑ̃se], *v.tr.* to put out of countenance.

déconvenue [dekɔ̃vny], *s.f.* disappointment; mortification.

décor [dekɔr], *s.m.* **1.** decor. **2.** *Th:* scenery. *Aut: F:* rentrer dans le d., to run off the road (into sth.).

décor/er [dekɔre], *v.tr.* to decorate. **2.** -ateur, (house) decorator. *s.f.* -ation.

décorum [dekɔrɔm], *s.m.* decorum.

découper [dekupe], *v.tr.* **1.** to cut up; to carve; **couteau à d.,** carving-knife. **2.** to cut out; **scie à d.,** fret-saw.

se découper, to stand out, show up (sur, against).

découpure [dekupyr], *s.f.* **1.** *(a)* cutting out; *(b)* fretwork. **2.** *(newspaper)* cutting. **3.** indentation (in coastline).

‡décourag/er [dekuraʒe], *v.tr.* **1.** to discourage, dishearten. **2.** to discountenance. *s.m.* -ement.

se décourager, to become disheartened, to lose heart.

décousu [dekuzy], *a.* disconnected, disjointed.

découvert [dekuvɛr]. **1.** *a. (a)* uncovered; *(b)* open; exposed. **2.** *à. d.,* uncovered, unprotected; *Fin:* overdrawn.

découverte [dekuvɛrt], *s.f.* discovery.

‡découvrir [dekuvriːr], *v.tr.* **1.** *(a)* to uncover; *(b)* to disclose. **2.** to perceive. **3.** to discover; to detect.

décrépit [dekrepi], *a.* decrepit, senile; dilapidated.

décret [dekrɛ], *s.m.* decree; order.

‡décréter [dekrete], *v.tr.* to decree.

‡décrire [dekriːr], *v.tr.* to describe.

décrocher [dekrɔʃe], *v.tr.* to unhook; to take down.

‡décroître [dekrwaːtr, -wɑ-], *v.i.* to decrease, diminish, decline.

décrotter [dekrɔte], *v.tr.* to clean (boots).

dédaigner [dedɛɲe], *v.tr.* to scorn, disdain.

†dédaign/eux [dedɛɲø], *a.* disdainful. *adv.* -eusement.

dédain [dedɛ̃], *s.m.* disdain, scorn.

dedans [dədɑ̃]. **1.** *adv.* inside; within; in (it); **donner d.,** to fall into the trap; **en d.,** inside; within. **2.** *s.m.* inside, interior; **au d.,** inside, within.

dédicace [dedikas], *s.f.* dedication.

dédier [dedje], *v.tr.* to dedicate.

‡dédommag/er [dedɔmaʒe], *v.tr.* to compensate (s.o.); to make amends to (s.o.); **se faire d.,** to receive compensation. *s.m.* -ement, compensation.

dédouan/er [dedwane], *v.tr.* to clear (goods) through the customs. *s.m.* -ement. *s.m.* -age.

déduction [dedyksjɔ̃], *s.f.* deduction.

‡déduire [dedɥiːr], *v.tr.* **1.** to deduce, infer. **2.** to deduct.

déesse [deɛs], *s.f.* goddess.

défaillance [defajɑ̃s], *s.f. (a)* failing; *(b)* fainting fit.

‡défaillir [defajiːr], *v.i. (a)* to become feeble, to lose strength; *(b)* to fail (in one's duty); *(c)* to faint.

‡défaire [defɛr], *v.tr.* **1.** to demolish, destroy. **2.** to undo, untie. **3.** to defeat.

se défaire. 1. to come undone. **2.** to get rid of (sth.); *F:* **se d. de qn,** to kill s.o., to bump s.o. off.

défait [defɛ], *a. (a)* discomposed; *(b)* dishevelled; *(c)* defeated.

défaite [defɛt], *s.f.* defeat.

défaut [defo], *s.m.* **1.** absence, (total) lack (of sth.); **à d. de qch.,** for lack of sth. **2.** *(a)* fault, shortcoming; *(b)* defect, flaw; **prendre qn en d.,** to catch s.o. out.

défaveur [defavœːr], *s.f.* disfavour, discredit.

défavoriser [defavɔrize], *v.tr.* to be unfair to (s.o.).

défection [defɛksjɔ̃], *s.f.* defection (from a cause).

†défectueux [defɛktɥø], *a.* defective, faulty.

défectuosité [defɛktɥozite], *s.f.* defect, flaw.

défendable [defɑ̃dabl], *a.* defensible.

défendeur, -eresse [defɑ̃dœːr, -ɛrɛs], *s. Jur.* defendant.

défendre [defɑ̃ːdr], *v.tr.* 1. (*a*) to defend; to uphold; (*b*) to protect. 2. to forbid. **se défendre.** 1. to defend oneself. 2. **se d. de,** to refrain from.

défense [defɑ̃ːs], *s.f.* 1. defence; **sans d.,** defenceless. 2. tusk (of elephant). 3. prohibition: "**d. d'entrer, de fumer,**" 'no admittance,' 'no smoking.'

défenseur [defɑ̃sœːr], *s.m.* (*a*) protector, defender; (*b*) supporter, upholder.

défensif, -ive [defɑ̃sif, -iv]. 1. *a.* defensive. 2. *s.f.* defensive, defensive.

déférence [deferɑ̃ːs], *s.f.* deference, respect.

‡déférer [defere], *v.i.* to defer (to s.o.).

déferler [defɛrle], *v.i.* (of waves) to break.

défi [defi], *s.m.* (*a*) challenge; (*b*) defiance.

défiance [defjɑ̃ːs], *s.f.* 1. mistrust, distrust. 2. **d. de soi-même,** diffidence.

défiant [defjɑ̃], *a.* mistrustful, distrustful.

déficit [defisit], *s.m.* deficit; shortage.

défier [defje], *v.tr.* (*a*) to challenge; (*b*) to defy; (*c*) to brave. **se défier de,** to distrust.

défigurer [defigyre], *v.tr.* to disfigure.

défilé [defile], *s.m.* 1. defile, gorge. 2. procession; march past; parade; *Av:* **d.** (**d'avions**), fly-past.

défiler [defile], *v.i.* (*a*) to march past; (*b*) to walk in procession.

défini [defini], *a.* definite.

définir [definiːr], *v.tr.* to define. **se définir,** to become distinct.

†définitif, -ive [definitif, -iv], *a.* definitive; final; permanent; **en définitive,** finally. *adv.* -**ivement**.

définition [definisjɔ̃], *s.f.* definition; **par d.,** by that very fact.

déflation [deflasjɔ̃], *s.f.* deflation.

‡défoncer [defɔ̃se], *v.tr.* 1. to stave in; to smash in. 2. to break up.

déformation [deformasjɔ̃], *s.f.* 1. (*a*) deformation; **d. professionnelle,** occupational bias; (*b*) distortion. 2. warping.

déformer [deforme], *v.tr.* to deform; to put out of shape; to distort. 2. to warp.

défraîchi [defreʃi], *a.* (shop-)soiled; faded.

†défrayer [defreje], *v.tr.* **d. qn,** to pay s.o.'s expenses.

défrich/er [defriʃe], *v.tr.* to clear, reclaim (land for cultivation); to break (new ground). *s.m.* -**age.** *s.m.* -**ement.**

défunt, -unte [defœ̃, -œ̃ːt], *a. & s.* deceased.

dégagé [degaʒe], *a.* (*a*) free, untrammelled; (*b*) free and easy.

‡dégag/er [degaʒe], *v.tr.* 1. to redeem (pledge). 2. (*a*) to disengage; to release; (*b*) to clear (road, etc.); **dégagez, s'il vous plaît!** gangway,

please! 3. to give off (smell). *s.m.* -**ement.**

se dégager. 1. to get free (from), clear (of.). 2. (of gas, etc.) to escape. 3. to emerge.

dégarn/ir [degarniːr], *v.tr.* to dismantle; to strip (bed). *s.m.* -**issement.**

se dégarnir. 1. to become bald; (of tree) to lose its leaves. 2. (of room) to empty. 3. to run, short, out of money.

dégâts [dega], *s.m.pl.* damage.

dégel [deʒɛl], *s.m.* thaw.

‡dégeler [deʒle], *v.tr. & i.* to thaw.

dégénération [deʒenerasjɔ̃], *s.f.* degeneration, degeneracy.

dégénéré [deʒenere], *a. & s.* degenerate.

‡dégénérer [deʒenere], *v.i.* to degenerate.

dégiv/rer [deʒivre], *v.tr.* to de-ice. *s.m.* -**age.**

dégonfl/er [degɔ̃fle], *v.tr.* to deflate (tyre). 2. to reduce (swelling). 3. *P:* to debunk (hero). *s.m.* -**ement.**

se dégonfler, to collapse, to go flat.

dégorger [degɔrʒe], *v.tr.* to disgorge. 2. *v.i.* to overflow.

dégourd/ir [degurdiːr], *v.tr.* to remove the stiffness from; to revive; *F:* to lick (s.o.) into shape. *s.m.* -**issement.**

se dégourdir, to lose one's stiff feeling; to stretch one's limbs; *F:* (of pers.) to improve (in manners).

dégoût [degu], *s.m.* disgust, distaste, dislike. *a.* -**ant,** disgusting, nasty.

dégoûté [degute], *a.* 1. disgusted (de, with); sick (of). 2. squeamish.

dégoûter [degute], *v.tr.* to disgust. **se dégoûter,** to take a dislike (de, to).

dégradant [degradɑ̃], *a.* degrading, lowering.

dégradation [degradasjɔ̃], *s.f.* 1. degradation. 2. *usu. pl.* damage; wear and tear.

dégrader [degrade], *v.tr.* 1. to degrade (s.o.). 2. to damage (sth.). **se dégrader,** to lower oneself.

degré [dəgre], *s.m.* step; degree.

†dégressif [degresif], *a.* decreasing (tariff).

dégringol/er [degrɛ̃gole], *v.i. F:* (*a*) to tumble down; (*b*) to collapse. *s.f.* -**ade.**

déguenillé [degnije], *a.* ragged, tattered.

déguerpir [degɛrpiːr], *v.i. F:* to get out, clear out.

déguis/er [degize], *v.tr.* to disguise; **parler sans rien d.,** to speak openly. *s.m.* -**ement.**

déguster [degyste], *v.tr.* to taste; to sip; to appreciate (meal).

dehors [dəɔːr]. 1. *adv.* (*a*) out, outside; "**ne pas se pencher d.**" 'do not lean out of the window!' (*b*) **en d.,** (on the) outside; outwards. 2. *s.m.* (*a*) outside, exterior; (*b*) *pl.* (outward) appearance.

déité [deite], *s.f.* deity.

déjà [deʒa], *adv.* 1. already; il est d. parti, he has already left. 2. before; je l'ai d. vu, I have seen him before.

déjeuner [deʒœne], *v.i.* (*a*) to (have) breakfast; (*b*) to (have) lunch.

déjeuner², *s.m.* 1. lunch; (petit) d., breakfast. 2. breakfast cup and saucer.

delà [d(ə)la]. 1. *prep.* beyond. 2. *adv.* au d., beyond; n'allez pas au d. de 100 francs, don't pay more than 100 francs. *s.m.* l'au-d., the next world.

délabr/er [delabre], *v.tr.* to wreck; to ruin. *-ement.*
se délabrer, to fall into decay; to become dilapidated.

délacer [delase], *v.tr.* to unlace, undo.

délai [dele], *s.m.* 1. delay. 2. respite, time allowed; à court d., at short notice.

délaisser [delese], *v.tr.* to desert, abandon.

délass/er [delase], *v.tr.* to rest, refresh. *s.m. -ement.*
se délasser, to relax.

délayer [deleje], *v.tr.* to add water to; to thin (paint); to water (liquid); F: d. un discours, to pad a speech.

Delco [dɛlko], *s.m. Aut: R.t.m:* distributor.

délectable [delɛktabl], *a.* delightful, pleasant.

délégation [delegasjɔ̃], *s.f.* delegation.

délégué, -ée [delege], *a.* & *s.* (*a*) delegate; (*b*) deputy.

déléguer [delege], *v.tr.* to delegate.

délibération [deliberasjɔ̃], *s.f.* 1. deliberation, discussion. 2. reflection. 3. resolution, decision.

délibéré [delibere], *a.* deliberate. *adv. -ment.*

délibérer [delibere]. 1. *v.i.* (*a*) to deliberate; (*b*) to reflect. 2. *v.tr.* to discuss; c'est une affaire délibérée, the matter is settled, decided.

délicat [delika], *a.* 1. discerning (person); tactful (behaviour). 2. sensitive (delicate health). 3. difficult, tricky (job). 4. scrupulous; fussy (about one's food). *adv. -ement.*

délicatesse [delikates], *s.f.* 1. delicacy; discernment; tactfulness; avec d., tactfully. 2. fragility, delicate state (of health). 3. difficulty, awkwardness (of situation).

délici/eux [delisjø], *a.* delicious, delightful. *adv. -eusement.*

délier [delje], *v.tr.* to untie, undo.

délimiter [delimite], *v.tr.* to demarcate (territory); to define (powers).

délinquance [delɛ̃kɑ̃s], *s.f.* delinquency; d. juvénile, juvenile delinquency.

délinquant, -ante [delɛ̃kɑ̃, -ɑ̃:t], *s.* offender, delinquent.

délire [deli:r], *s.m.* delirium.

délirer [delire], *v.i.* to be delirious; to rave.

délit [deli], *s.m.* misdemeanour, offence.

délivr/er [delivre], *v.tr.* 1. to deliver; to rescue. 2. to deliver, hand over. *s.f. -ance.*

déloger [deloʒe]. 1. *v.i.* to go off. 2. *v.tr.* to eject; to drive out; to dislodge.

déloyal [delwajal], *a.* false; unfaithful; dishonest; unfair; foul (play).

déloyauté [delwajote], *s.f.* disloyalty; treachery.

delta [delta], *s.m.* delta.

déluge [dely:ʒ], *s.m.* (*a*) deluge, flood; torrent (of abuse); cela remonte au d., it's as old as the hills; (*b*) downpour (of rain).

demain [dəmɛ̃], *adv.* & *s.m.* tomorrow.

demande [d(ə)mɑ̃d], *s.f.* 1. (*a*) request, application; F: il faut faire une d., you must fill in a form; (*b*) l'offre et la d., supply and demand; (*c*) petition (for divorce). 2. question.

demander [d(ə)mɑ̃de], *v.tr.* 1. to ask (for); on vous demande, somebody wants to see you; d. qch. à qn, to ask s.o. for sth. 2. to desire, need, require. 3. to ask, enquire.
se demander, to wonder.

démaquillant [demakijɑ̃], *s.m.* cleansing cream, make-up remover.

démang/er [demɑ̃ʒe], *v.i.* to itch. *s.f. -eaison, itching.*

démarcation [demarkasjɔ̃], *s.f.* demarcation; ligne de d., dividing line.

démarche [demarʃ], *s.f.* 1. gait, walk. 2. step; proceeding.

démarr/er [demare]. 1. *v.tr.* to unmoor (ship); to start (car). 2. *v.i.* (*of vehicle*) to start; (*of ship*) to get under way; (*of pers.*) to drive off. *s.m. -age.* *s.m. -eur. Aut:* self-starter.

démasquer [demaske], *v.tr.* to unmask; to expose.

démêl/er [demele], *v.tr.* to disentangle; to comb out (hair); to clear up (misunderstanding).
se démêler, to extricate oneself.

déménag/er [demenaʒe], *v.tr.* & *i.* to move (house); F: il déménage, he's taken leave of his senses; F: allez! déménagez! scram! *s.m. -ement.*

déménageur [demenaʒœr], *s.m.* furniture remover.

démence [demɑ̃s], *s.f.* insanity, madness.

démener (se) [sədemne], *v.pr.* 1. to struggle. 2. to bestir oneself.

démenti [demɑ̃ti], *s.m.* denial, contradiction.

démentir [demɑ̃ti:r], *v.tr.* 1. to contradict; to deny. 2. to belie.
se démentir, to contradict oneself; to go back on one's word.

démesuré [demzyre], *a.* inordinate; beyond measure; unbounded. *adv. -ment.*

démettre (se) [sədemɛtr], *v.pr.* to retire; to resign (office).

demeure [dəmœ:r], *s.f.* (place of) residence, dwelling place.

demeurer [dəmœre], v.i. 1. to remain; to stay. 2. to live, reside.

demi, -ie [dəmi]. 1. a. (a) half; deux heures et demie, (i) two and a half hours, (ii) half-past two; (b) semi-; **d.-cercle**, semicircle; (c) **d.-cuit**, half-cooked. 2. s.m. (a) un d., a large glass of beer; (b) Sp: les demis, the half-backs; (c) à d. mort, half dead; faire les choses à d., to do things by halves. 3. s.f. demie, half-hour; il est la demie, it's half-past.

NOTE. In all the following compounds DEMI is inv.; the second component takes the plural. For phonetics consult the second component.

demi-cercle, s.m. semicircle.
demi-douzaine, s.f. half-dozen.
demi-finale, s.f. Sp: semi-final.
demi-heure, s.f. une d.-h., half an hour.
demi-mot (à), adv.phr. entendre à d.-m., to take a hint.
demi-pension, s.f. half-board.
demi-place, s.f. half-fare; half-price.
demi-sec, a. & s.m. medium dry (wine).
demi-sœur, s.f. stepsister.
démission [demisjɔ̃], s.f. resignation (from job).
demi-tarif, s.m. half price.
demi-voix (à), adv.phr. in an undertone; under one's breath.
démobiliser [demɔbilize], v.tr. to demobilize. s.f. -ation.
démocrate [demɔkrat], s.m. & f. democrat.
démocratie [demɔkrasi], s.f. democracy.
démocratique [demɔkratik], a. democratic.
démodé [demɔde], a. old-fashioned; obsolete, out of date.
demoiselle [dəmwazɛl], s.f. 1. (a) spinster; (b) d. d'honneur, bridesmaid. 2. young lady. 3. dragon-fly.
démolir [demɔlir], v.tr. to demolish, pull down; to ruin (reputation). s.f. -ition, demolition.
démon [demɔ̃], s.m. demon, devil, fiend.
démonstrateur [demɔ̃stratœr], s.m. demonstrator.
†**démonstratif** [demɔ̃stratif], a. demonstrative.
démonstration [demɔ̃strasjɔ̃], s.f. demonstration.
démonté [demɔ̃te], a. 1. dismounted. 2. stormy (sea). 3. (of pers.) flustered. 4. dismantled.
démonte-pneu [demɔ̃tpnø], s.m. tyre lever. pl. démonte-pneus.
démonter [demɔ̃te], v.tr. 1. to unhorse; se laisser d., to get upset. 2. to dismantle; to remove (tyre).
　se démonter. (a) (of mechanism) to come apart; (b) F: il ne se démonte pas pour si peu, he's not so easily put out.

démontrer [demɔ̃tre], v.tr. to demonstrate.
démoraliser [demɔralize], v.tr. to demoralize. s.f. -ation.
démuni [demyni], a. unprovided (de, with).
démunir (se) [sədemynir], v.pr. se d. de qch., to part with sth.
dénaturé [denatyre], a. unnatural; hardhearted; perverted.
dénaturer [denatyre], v.tr. to misrepresent, distort.
dénégation [denegasjɔ̃], s.f. denial.
dénicher [denife], v.tr. F: to find, discover.
dénier [denje], v.tr. to deny.
dénigrer [denigre], v.tr. to disparage, run down. s.m. -ement.
dénombrement [denɔ̃brəmã], s.m. enumeration, counting; census.
dénombrer [denɔ̃bre], v.tr. to count; to take a census of.
dénominateur [denɔminatœr], s.m. denominator.
dénomination [denɔminasjɔ̃], s.f. denomination, name.
‡**dénoncer** [denɔ̃se], v.tr. 1. to declare. 2. (a) to denounce; (b) to expose. s.f. -iation.
dénonciateur, -trice [denɔ̃sjatœr, -tris]. 1. s. informer. 2. a. tell-tale (look).
dénoter [denɔte], v.tr. to denote; show.
dénouer [denwe], v.tr. to unknit; to undo.
denrée [dãre], s.f. commodity; usu.pl. produce; denrées alimentaires, food (stuffs).
dense [dãːs], a. dense; crowded.
densité [dãsite], s.f. denseness; density.
dent [dã], s.f. 1. tooth; coup de d., bite; manger à belles dents, to eat heartily; être sur les dents, to be on edge. 2. tooth (of saw); cog; prong.
denté [dãte], a. cogged, toothed.
dentelé [dãtle], a. notched, indented; serrated.
dentelle [dãtɛl], s.f. lace.
dentelure [dãtlyːr], s.f. indentation.
dentier [dãtje], s.m. set of false teeth, denture.
dentifrice [dãtifris], s.m. toothpaste.
dentiste [dãtist], s.m. & f. dentist.
denture [dãtyːr], s.f. 1. set of (natural) teeth. 2. teeth, cogs, gearing.
dénucléariser [denyklearize], v.tr. to free (zone) from nuclear weapons. s.f. -ation.
dénudé [denyde], a. bare, denuded; bald.
dénuder [denyde], v.tr. to denude, lay bare, strip.
dénué [denye], a. without, short of; d. d'argent, without money; d. de raison, senseless; d. d'intelligence, unintelligent, devoid of intelligence.
dénuement [denymã], s.m. destitution; d. d'idées, lack of ideas.

dépann/er [depane], *v.tr.* to do emergency repairs to (car, etc.); to help (s.o.) out. *s.m.* -age, breakdown service. *s.m.* -eur, breakdown mechanic. *s.f.* -euse, breakdown lorry.

départ [depar], *s.m.* departure, starting; point de d., starting point; prix d. usine, price ex works.

département [departəmã], *s.m.* department.

dépasser [depase], *v.tr.* 1. (a) to pass beyond; d. le but, to overshoot the mark; F: cela me dépasse, it's beyond me; (b) to overtake. 2. to exceed.

dépaysé [depe(j)ize], *a.* out of one's element; at a loss.

‡dépecer [depəse], *v.tr.* to cut up; to carve.

dépêche [depɛ(:)ʃ], *s.f.* (a) despatch; (b) telegram.

dépêcher [depeʃe], *v.tr.* to dispatch. se dépêcher, to hurry; dépêchez-vous! hurry up!

dépendance [depãdã:s], *s.f.* 1. dependence. 2. (a) dependency; (b) pl. outbuildings.

dépend/re [depã:dr], *v.i.* to depend (de, on). *a.* -ant, dependent.

dépens [depã], *s.m.pl.* cost, expenses; au d. de, at the expense of.

dépense [depã:s], *s.f.* expenditure, outlay, expense.

dépenser [depãse], *v.tr.* to spend.

dépérir [deperi:r], *v.i.* to waste away; to wither, decay.

dépeupler [depœple], *v.tr.* to depopulate.

dépister [depiste], *v.tr.* 1. to track down. 2. to outwit (s.o.); to put (s.o.) off the scent.

dépit [depi], *s.m.* resentment; en d. de, in spite of.

déplacé [deplase], *a.* out of place, ill-timed; personnes déplacées, displaced persons.

‡déplac/er [deplase], *v.tr.* 1. to displace; to transfer. 2. to take the place of (s.o.). *s.m.* -ement. (a) to move about; to travel; (b) to get out of place. se déplacer, to move about; to travel; (b) to get out of place.

‡déplaire [deplɛ:r], *v.ind.tr.* to displease.

déplaisant [deplɛzã], *a.* unpleasant.

déplier [deplije], *v.tr.* to unfold, spread out. se déplier, to open out.

déplorable [deplɔrabl], *a.* deplorable.

déplorer [deplore], *v.tr.* to deplore, lament; to regret.

déployer [deplwaje], *v.tr.* 1. to unfold; Mil: to deploy (troops). 2. to display.

dépopulation [depɔpylasjɔ̃], *s.f.* depopulation.

déport/er [depɔrte], *v.tr.* to deport. *s.f.* -ation.

déposer [depoze], *v.tr.* 1. to deposit. 2. (a) to register (trade-mark); (b) to lodge (a complaint). 3. to depose.

déposition [depozisjɔ̃], *s.f.* deposition; statement (of witness).

dépôt [depo], *s.m.* 1. (a) depositing; (b) deposit; d. en banque, bank deposit; marchandises en d., (i) goods in *i* cond; (ii) goods on consignment. 2. depository, depot, store. 3. deposit, sediment.

dépouille [depu:j], *s.f.* 1. skin, hide; d. mortelle, mortal remains. 2. *pl.* spoils, booty.

dépouiller [depuje], *v.tr.* 1. to skin (eel). 2. to deprive (of, de); to despoil; d. un câble, to strip a cable. 3. to analyse, go through; Pol: le scrutin, to count the votes. se dépouiller. (of reptile) to cast its skin; (of tree) to shed its leaves.

dépourvu [depurvy], *a.* destitute, devoid (de, of); pays d. d'arbres, treeless country; pris au d., caught unawares.

dépravé [deprave], *a.* depraved.

dépréci/er [depresje], *v.tr.* 1. to depreciate. 2. to undervalue. 3. to disparage. *s.f.* -ation, depreciation.

dépression [depresjɔ̃], *s.f.* 1. hollow, dip. 2. d. économique, economic depression. 3. Meteor: depression. 4. depression; dejection.

déprimer [deprime], *v.tr.* to depress.

depuis [depɥi], *prep.* 1. (time) since; d. quand êtes-vous ici? how long have you been here? 2 (b) *adv.* since (in time); afterwards, later; (c) d. que + *ind.*, since.... 2. (time, place) from; d. le matin jusqu'au soir, from morning till night.

députation [depytasjɔ̃], *s.f.* deputation; delegation.

député [depyte], *s.m.* delegate; member of Parliament.

députer [depyte], *v.tr.* to depute; to appoint as deputy.

déraciner [derasine], *v.tr.* 1. to uproot. 2. to eradicate.

dérailler [deraje], *v.i.* (of train) to become derailed; il déraille, he's talking nonsense; F:

déraisonn/er [derezɔne], *v.i.* to talk nonsense. *a.* -able, unreasonable; foolish.

dérangé [derãʒe], *a.* (of machine) out of order; (of mind) unhinged; (of stomach) upset.

‡dérang/er [derãʒe], *v.tr.* (a) to disarrange; (b) to disturb, trouble; si cela ne vous dérange pas, if it's no trouble to you; (c) to upset (plans). *s.m.* -ement. se déranger. 1. to move; ne vous dérangez pas, please don't move, don't trouble. 2. (of mind) to become deranged.

déraper [derape], *v.tr.* & *i.* Aut: to skid.

déréglé [deregle], *a.* 1. out of order. 2. lawless; wild (life); immoderate.

‡dérégler [deregle], *v.tr.* to upset, disarrange, disorder.

dérider [deride], *v.tr.* to smoothe; to cheer (s.o.) up.

dérision [derizjɔ̃], *s.f.* derision, mockery.

dérisoire [derizwaːr], *a.* ridiculous, laughable.

dérive [deriːv], *s.f.* leeway, drift.

dériv/er[1] [derive]. 1. *v.tr.* to divert (stream). 2. *v.i.* to be derived (from). *s.f.* -ation, derivation.

dériver[2], *v.i.* to drift.

†**dernier/re** [dɛrnje], *a. & s.* 1. last, latest; au d. moment, at the last moment; dans ces derniers temps, latterly; le mois d., last month. 2. (*a*) utmost, highest; de la dernière importance, of the utmost importance; (*b*) lowest; worst; le d. des derniers, the lowest of the low. *adv.* -èrement.

dérobé [derɔbe], *a.* hidden, concealed; à la dérobée, stealthily, secretly.

dérober [derɔbe], *v.tr.* 1. (*a*) to steal; (*b*) d. qn au danger, to save s.o. from danger. 2. to hide, conceal.
se dérober. 1. to escape, steal away, slip away (à, from); se d. aux coups, to dodge the blows. 2. le sol se déroba, the ground gave way.

dérouler [derule], *v.tr.* to unroll; to unwind.
se dérouler, to unfold; le paysage se déroule devant nous, the landscape spreads out in front of us; les événements qui se déroulent, the events which are taking place.

déroute [derut], *s.f.* rout.

dérouter [derute], *v.tr.* 1. (*a*) to lead astray; to put off; (*b*) to divert (traffic). 2. to confuse, baffle.

derrière [dɛrjɛːr]. 1. *prep.* behind. 2. *adv.* (*a*) behind, at the back; pattes de d., hind legs; attaquer qn par d., to attack s.o. from the rear; (*b*) aft. 3. *s.m.* (*a*) back, rear (of building); (*b*) F: behind, backside, bottom.

des [de, dɛ] = de les.

dès [dɛ], *prep.* since, from; as early as; dès le matin, first thing in the morning; *conj.phr.* dès que, as soon as; *adv.phr.* dès lors, ever since (then).

désabuser [dezabyze], *v.tr.* to disabuse, undeceive (s.o., about).

désaccord [dezakɔːr], *s.m.* 1. (*a*) disagreement; (*b*) clash. 2. discord; en d., out of tune.

désagréable [dezagreabl], *a.* disagreeable, unpleasant. *adv.* -ment.

‡**désagrég/er** [dezagreʒe], *v.tr.* to disintegrate. *s.f.* -ation.
se désagréger, to break up.

désagrément [dezagremɑ̃], *s.m.* source of annoyance; nuisance.

‡**désaltérer** (se) [sədezaltere], *v.pr.* to quench (one's thirst).

désappoint/er [dezapwɛte], *v.tr.* to disappoint. *s.m.* -ement.

désapprobation [dezaprɔbasjɔ̃], *s.f.* disapproval.

désapprouver [dezapruve], *v.tr.* to disapprove of, object to.

désarmé [dezarme], *a.* 1. disarmed. 2. unarmed, defenceless.

désarm/er [dezarme], *v.tr. & i.* to disarm. *s.m.* -ement.

désassocier [dezasɔsje], *v.tr.* to dissociate.

désastre [dezastr], *s.m.* disaster, calamity.

†**désastr/eux** [dezastrø], *a.* disastrous. *adv.* -eusement.

désavantage [dezavɑ̃taːʒ], *s.m.* disadvantage, drawback.

†**désavantag/eux** [dezavɑ̃taʒø], *a.* disadvantageous, unfavourable. *adv.* -eusement.

désavouer [dezavwe], *v.tr.* to repudiate, deny; to disown.
se désavouer, to go back on one's word.

descendre [desɑ̃ːdr, de-]. I. *v.i.* (aux. être) 1. to descend, come down, go down; (*b*) to come, go, downstairs; est-ce qu'il va d. dîner? is he coming down to dinner? 2. (*a*) to get out of car, train); "tout le monde descend!" 'all change!' (*b*) d. à un hôtel, to stay at an hotel. 3. la forêt descend jusqu'à la vallée, the forest stretches down to the valley. 4. (*of family*) to be descended (from). II. *v.tr.* (aux. avoir) 1. (*a*) to bring, take, down; d. les bagages, to bring down the luggage; (*b*) to shoot down (pheasant, man); (*c*) to put down (passengers); (*d*) d. la rue, to go down the street.

descente [desɑ̃ːt, de-], *s.f.* 1. (*a*) descent (from height); (ski) run; (*b*) d. de police, police raid; d. sur les lieux, visit to the scene (of a crime). 2. letting down, lowering; la D. de croix, the Descent from the Cross. 3. (*a*) d. dangereuse, dangerous hill; (*b*) d. de lit, bathmat; d. de lit, (bedside) rug.

†**descriptif** [deskriptif], *a.* descriptive.

description [deskripsjɔ̃], *s.f.* description.

déséquilibrer [dezekilibre], *v.tr.* to unbalance.

désert [dezer]. 1. *a.* deserted, uninhabited; lonely (spot); île déserte, desert island. 2. *s.m.* desert.

désert/er [dezerte], *v.tr.* to desert. *s.m.* -eur. *s.f.* -ion.

désespéré [dezɛspere], *a.* desperate, hopeless. *adv.* -ment.

‡**désespér/er** [dezɛspere]. 1. *v.i.* to despair; to lose hope. 2. *v.tr.* to drive to despair. *a.* -ant, heartbreaking.
se désespérer, to be in despair.

désespoir [dezɛspwaːr], *s.m.* despair.

déshabiller [dezabije], *v.tr.* to undress (s.o.).
se déshabiller, to undress.

déshériter [dezerite], *v.tr.* to disinherit.

déshonneur [dezɔnœːr], *s.m.* dishonour, disgrace.

déshonorer [dezɔnɔre], *v.tr.* to dishonour, disgrace.

désign/er [dezine], *v.tr.* 1. to show, indicate. 2. (*a*) to fix (date); (*b*) to appoint (s.o. to job). *s.f.* -**ation**.

désillusion [dezilyzjɔ̃], *s.f.* disillusion.

désillusionner [dezilyzjɔne], *v.tr.* to disillusion.

désinfect/er [dezɛ̃fɛkte], *v.tr.* to disinfect. *s.f.* -**ion**. *s.m.* -**ant**.

désintéressé [dezɛ̃terese], *a.* (*a*) disinterested; (*b*) unselfish.

désintéress/er (se) [sədezɛ̃terese], *v.pr.* se d. de qch., to take (i) no further interest, (ii) no part, in sth.; to let things slide. *s.m.* -**ement**.

désinvolture [dezɛ̃vɔltyr], *s.f.* unselfconsciousness; free and easy manner; avec d., in an off-hand manner.

désir [dezir], *s.m.* desire (de, for); wish.

désirable [dezirabl], *a.* desirable; peu d., undesirable.

désirer [dezire], *v.tr.* to desire, want; cela laisse à d., it leaves sth. to be desired; *Com:* madame désire? what can I show you, madam?

désister (se) [sədeziste], *v.pr.* to desist (from); to withdraw (candidature).

désobéir [dezɔbeir], *v.ind.tr.* d. à, to disobey.

désobéissance [dezɔbeisɑ̃s], *s.f.* disobedience.

désobéissant [dezɔbeisɑ̃], *a.* disobedient.

désoblige/ant [dezɔbliʒɑ̃], *a.* (*a*) disobliging; (*b*) disagreeable, ungracious.

‡**désobliger** [dezɔbliʒe], *v.tr.* 1. to be disobliging to (s.o.). 2. to offend.

désœuvré [dezœvre], *a.* unoccupied, idle, at a loose end.

désœuvrement [dezœvrəmɑ̃], *s.m.* idleness.

désolant [dezɔlɑ̃], *a.* distressing, sad.

désolation [dezɔlasjɔ̃], *s.f.* desolation.

désolé [dezɔle], *a.* 1. desolate (region). 2. je suis désolé d'apprendre . . ., I am very sorry to hear . . .

désoler [dezɔle], *v.tr.* 1. to devastate (country). 2. to distress (s.o.). se désoler, to grieve.

désordonné [dezɔrdɔne], *a.* 1. disordered; untidy. 2. disorderly.

désordre [dezɔrdr], *s.m.* 1. disorder, confusion. 2. disorderliness. 3. *pl.* disturbances, riots.

désorganis/er [dezɔrganize], *v.tr.* to disorganize. *s.f.* -**ation**.

désorienté [dezɔrjɑ̃te], *a.* puzzled; at a loss; (all) at sea.

désormais [dezɔrmɛ], *adv.* from now on; in future.

despote [dɛspɔt], *s.m.* despot. *a.* -**ique**, despotic. *s.m.* -**isme**, despotism.

‡**dessécher** [deseʃe], *v.tr.* to dry (up); to wither.

dessein [desɛ̃], *s.m.* 1. design, plan. 2. intention, purpose; à d., on purpose.

desserrer [desere], *v.tr.* to loosen (screw).

dessert [deser], *s.m.* dessert.

‡**desservir**[1] [deservir], *v.tr.* (*of railway*) to serve (district).

‡**desservir**[2], *v.tr.* 1. to clear (the table). 2. to do (s.o.) a bad turn.

dessin [desɛ̃], *s.m.* 1. (*a*) drawing, sketching; (*b*) drawing, sketch; d. animé, animated cartoon. 2. design. 3. draughtsmanship.

dessinateur, -trice [desinatœr, -tris], *s.* 1. designer; dress-designer. 2. draughtsman, -woman.

dessiner [desine], *v.tr.* 1. to draw, sketch. 2. to design.
se dessiner, to stand out; to be outlined; to take shape.

dessous [dəsu]. 1. *adv.* under(neath), below; vêtements de d., underwear; en d., underneath; down(wards). 2. *s.m.* lower part, bottom; avoir le d., to get the worst of it; les d. de la politique, the shady side of politics.

dessus [dəsy]. 1. *adv.* above, over; (up)on; en d., on top; above. 2. *s.m.* (*a*) top, upper part; d. de lit, bedspread; (*b*) avoir le d., to have the upper hand.

destin [destɛ̃], *s.m.* fate, destiny.

destinataire [destinater], *s.m. & f.* addressee; consignee.

destination [destinasjɔ̃], *s.f.* destination; trains à d. de Paris, trains for Paris.

destinée [destine], *s.f.* destiny.

destiner [destine], *v.tr.* to destine; to intend (sth. for s.o.).

†**destructif** [destryktif], *a.* destructive.

destruction [destryksjɔ̃], *s.f.* destruction.

désuétude [desɥetyd], *s.f.* disuse; mot tombé en d., obsolete word.

désunir [dezynir], *v.tr.* to disunite, divide.

détaché [detaʃe], *a.* 1. (*a*) loose; pièces détachées, spare parts; (*b*) isolated. 2. detached, unconcerned.

détachement [detaʃmɑ̃], *s.m.* 1. detaching, cutting off. 2. indifference (de, to).

détacher[1] [detaʃe], *v.tr.* to detach; (*a*) to unfasten; (*b*) to separate; to cut off.
se détacher. 1. to come undone. 2. to break off. 3. to stand out (against a background).

détach/er[2], *v.tr.* to remove stains (from sth.). *s.m.* -**age**. *s.m.* -**eur**, *s.m.* -**ant**, stain remover.

détail [detaj], *s.m.* 1. *Com:* retail. 2. detail.

détaill/er [detaje], *v.tr.* 1. (*a*) to divide up; (*b*) to retail. 2. to relate in detail. *s.* -**ant**, -**ante**, retailer.

détaler [detale], *v.i. F:* to beat it, scram.

détective [detektiv], *s.m.* detective; private enquiry agent.

détendre [detɑ̃dr], *v.tr.* to slacken, relax.

‡**détenir** [detniːr], *v.tr.* 1. to keep. 2. (*a*) to detain; (*b*) to withhold, keep back.

détente [detɑ̃ːt], *s.f.* 1. relaxation, slackening; easing (of situation). 2. trigger.

détention [detɑ̃sjɔ̃], *s.f.* detention; imprisonment.

détenu, -e [detny], *s.* prisoner.

détergent [detɛrʒɑ̃], *s.m.* detergent.

détériorer [deterjore], *v.tr.* to make worse. *s.f.* -ation.
se détériorer, to deteriorate; to spoil.

détermination [determinasjɔ̃], *s.f.* determination.

détermin/er [detɛrmine], *v.tr.* 1. to settle. 2. to cause; to bring about. 3. to resolve (de, to). *a.* -é, determined.

déterrer [detere], *v.tr.* to unearth, dig up.

détest/er [detɛste], *v.tr.* to detest, hate. *a.* -able. *s.f.* -ation.

déton/er [detone], *v.i.* to detonate, explode. *s.f.* -ation. *s.m.* -ateur, detonator; fog signal.

détour [detuːr], *s.m.* detour, deviation; sans détour(s), plainly, frankly.

détourn/er [deturne], *v.tr.* 1. (*a*) to divert; to turn aside; (*b*) to turn away, avert. 2. to misappropriate.

détraqu/er [detrake], *v.tr.* to put (machine) out of order; se d.l'estomac, to upset one's stomach. *s.m.* -ement.
se détraquer, (*of machine*) to get out of order.

détremper [detrɑ̃pe], *v.tr.* to moisten, soak.

détresse [detrɛs], *s.f.* distress.

détriment [detrimɑ̃], *s.m.* detriment, loss.

détroit [detrwa], *s.m. Geog:* strait(s).

détromper [detrɔ̃pe], *v.tr.* to undeceive.

‡**détruire** [detrɥiːr], *v.tr.* 1. to demolish. 2. to destroy, ruin.

dette [dɛt], *s.f.* debt.

deuil [dœːj], *s.m.* mourning.

deux [dø], *num.a.inv. & s.m.* two; Charles D., Charles the Second; d. fois, twice; tous (les) d., both.

deuxième [døzjɛm], *num.a. & s.* second; au d. (étage), on the second, *U.S:* third, floor. *adv.* -ment.

deux-points [døpwɛ̃], *s.m.* colon.

dévaliser [devalize], *v.tr.* to rob (s.o.); to burgle (house).

dévalu/er [devalɥe], *v.tr.* to devalue (currency). *s.f.* -ation, devaluation.

‡**devanc/er** [d(ə)vɑ̃se], *v.tr.* 1. to precede. 2. to outstrip. 3. to forestall. *s.m.* -ement. *s.* -ier, -ière, predecessor.

devant [d(ə)vɑ̃]. 1. *prep.* before, in front of. 2. *adv.* before, in front. 3. *s.m.* front (part); prendre les devants, to go on ahead.

devanture [d(ə)vɑ̃tyːr], *s.f.* (*a*) front(age); (*b*) d. de magasin, shop-front.

dévastation [devastasjɔ̃], *s.f.* devastation, destruction.

déveine [devɛn], *s.f. F:* (run of) ill-luck.

développ/er [devlope], *v.tr.* to develop. *s.m.* -ement.

‡**devenir** [dəvniːr], *v.pred.* (*a*) to become; qu'est-il devenu? what has become of him? (*b*) to grow into; (*c*) d. vieux, to grow old.

déverser [devɛrse], *v.tr.* to pour (water); to dump (material).

déviation [devjasjɔ̃], *s.f.* deviation; diversion (of road).

dévier [devje], *v.i.* to deviate; route déviée, diversion; faire d., to deflect.

deviner [d(ə)vine], *v.tr.* to guess.

devinette [d(ə)vinɛt], *s.f.* riddle.

devis [dəvi], *s.m.* estimate (of work to be done).

‡**dévisager** [deviza3e], *v.tr.* to stare at.

devise [dəviːz], *s.f.* 1. (*a*) motto; (*b*) slogan. 2. *pl.* currency.

dévoiler [devwale], *v.tr.* 1. to unveil. 2. to reveal, disclose.

‡**devoir** [dəvwaːr]. I. *v.tr.* 1. (*duty*) should, ought; je ne savais pas ce que je devais faire, I didn't know what I ought to do; vous devriez lire ce livre, you should read this book. 2. (*compulsion*) must, have to; tous les hommes doivent mourir, all men must die. 3. (*future idea*) am to; je dois partir demain, I am to start tomorrow; je devais venir, mais . . . , I was to have come, but . . . 4. (*opinion expressed*) must; vous devez avoir faim, you must be hungry. 5. to owe; vous me devez cent francs, you owe me a hundred francs. II. *s.m.* (*a*) duty; (*b*) *Sch:* exercise; homework, prep.

dévorer [devore], *v.tr.* to devour; to consume.

dévot, -ote [devo, -ɔt]. 1. *a.* devout, religious. 2. *s.* devout person; *Pej:* bigot.

dévotion [devosjɔ̃], *s.f.* devotion; piety.

dévoué [devwe], *a.* devoted, loyal.

dévouement [devumɑ̃], *s.m.* self-sacrifice; devotion (to duty).

dextérité [dɛksterite], *s.f.* dexterity, skill (à, in).

diabète [djabɛt], *s.m.* diabetes.

diable [djabl], *s.m.* devil; un bruit de tous les diables, a hell of a din.

diabolique [djabɔlik], *a.* diabolical, fiendish.

diacre [djakr], *s.m. Ecc:* deacon.

diadème [djadɛm], *s.m.* diadem.

diagnostic [djagnɔstik], *s.m.* diagnosis.

diagnostiquer [djagnɔstike], *v.tr.* to diagnose.

†**diagonal, -ale** [djagonal], 1. *a.* diagonal. 2. *s.f.* diagonale, diagonal (line). *adv.* -ement.

diagramme [djagram], *s.m.* diagram.

dialecte [djalɛkt], *s.m.* dialect.

dialogue [djalɔg], *s.m.* dialogue.

diamant [djamɑ̃], *s.m.* diamond.

diamètre [djamɛtr], *s.m.* diameter.

diane [djan], s.f. Mil: reveille.

diapason [djapazɔ̃], s.m. 1. diapason, pitch. 2. tuning-fork.

diaphragme [djafragm], s.m. diaphragm.

diarrhée [djare], s.f. diarrhoea.

dicta/teur [diktatœr], s.m. dictator. *a.* †**-torial**, dictatorial. *s.f.* **-ture.** dictatorship.

dictée [dikte], s.f. dictation.

dicter [dikte], v.tr. to dictate.

diction [diksjɔ̃], s.f. diction; elocution.

dictionnaire [diksjɔnɛːr], s.m. dictionary.

dicton [diktɔ̃], s.m. (common) saying.

dièse [djɛːz], s.m. Mus: sharp.

diète [djɛt], s.f. diet.

diététicien, -ienne [djetetisjɛ̃, -jɛn], s. dietician.

†**dieu** [djø]. **1.** s.m. (a) D., God; (b) (pagan) god; l'argent est son d., he worships money; (c) D. merci! thank goodness! D. sait que... , heaven knows that... **2.** int. F: mon D.! good heavens!

diffam/er [difame], v.tr. to slander, libel. *a.* **-atoire.** *s.f.* **-ation.** *s.* **-ateur, -atrice.**

différence [diferɑ̃ːs], s.f. difference.

différencier [diferɑ̃sje], v.tr. to differentiate.

différend [diferɑ̃], s.m. difference, dispute.

différent [diferɑ̃], a. different.

‡**différer** [difere]. **1.** v.tr. to defer; to put off. **2.** v.i. to differ.

difficile [difisil], a. difficult. adv. **-ment,** with difficulty.

difficulté [difikylte], s.f. difficulty.

difforme [difɔrm], a. deformed, misshapen.

difformité [difɔrmite], s.f. deformity.

diffuser [difyze], v.tr. 1. to diffuse (light). 2. to broadcast (news).

diffusion [difyzjɔ̃], s.f. 1. diffusion (of light). 2. Rad: broadcasting. 3. verbosity.

‡**digérer** [diʒere], v.tr. to digest.

digestible [diʒɛstibl], a. digestible.

†**digestif** [diʒɛstif], a. digestive; tube d., alimentary canal.

digestion [diʒɛstjɔ̃], s.f. digestion.

†**digital** [diʒital], a. empreinte digitale, finger-print.

digne [diɲ], a. 1. deserving, worthy (de, of). 2. dignified. adv. **-ment.**

dignitaire [diɲitɛːr], s.m. dignitary.

dignité [diɲite], s.f. dignity.

digression [digresjɔ̃], s.f. digression.

digue [dig], s.f. (a) dam; (b) breakwater; sea-wall.

dilapid/er [dilapide], v.tr. 1. to squander, waste (fortune). 2. to misappropriate (funds). s.f. **-ation.**

dilat/er [dilate], v.tr. to dilate, expand. s.f. **-ation.**

dilemme [dilɛm], s.m. dilemma.

diligence [diliʒɑ̃ːs], s.f. 1. (a) diligence; (b) haste, dispatch. 2. (stage-)coach.

dilig/ent [diliʒɑ̃], a. diligent, industrious. adv. **-emment.**

dilu/er [dilɥe], v.tr. to dilute (de, with). s.f. **-tion.**

dimanche [dimɑ̃ːʃ], s.m. Sunday.

dimension [dimɑ̃sjɔ̃], s.f. dimension, size.

diminué [diminɥe], a. 1. Mus: diminished (interval). 2. bas d., fully-fashioned stocking. 3. tapering (column). 4. s.m. un d. physique, a physically-handicapped person.

diminu/er [diminɥe], v.tr. & i. to lessen; to diminish; to grow less; (of prices) to fall. s.f. **-tion.**

†**diminutif** [diminytif], a. & s.m. diminutive.

dinde [dɛ̃ːd], s.f. turkey(-hen).

dindon [dɛ̃dɔ̃], s.m. turkey(-cock).

dîner [dine]. **I.** v.i. to dine, have dinner. **II.** s.m. dinner; dinner party; Fr.C: salle à d., dining room.

dîneur, -euse [dinœr, -øːz], s. diner.

diocèse [djosɛːz], s.m. Ecc: diocese.

diphtérie [difteri], s.f. diphtheria.

diphtongue [diftɔ̃ːg], s.f. diphthong.

diplomate [diplɔmat], s.m. diplomat(ist).

diplomatie [diplɔmasi], s.f. diplomacy.

diplomatique [diplɔmatik], a. diplomatic.

diplôme [diploːm], s.m. diploma.

‡**dire** [diːr]. **I.** v.tr. 1. to say, tell; (a) qu'en dira-t-on? what will people say? je vous l'avais bien dit! didn't I tell you so? comme on dit, as the saying goes; à vrai d., to tell the truth; vous l'avez dit, exactly! F: you've said it! cela va sans d., that goes without saying; il n'y a pas à d., there is no denying it; dites donc, I say! (b) il ne se le fit pas d. deux fois, he didn't wait to be told twice; (c) faire d. qch. à qn, to make s.o. tell sth. 2. d. à qn de faire qch., to tell s.o. to do sth. 3. (a) to express; ce nom ne me dit rien, this name means nothing to me; (b) to suit; to appeal to. 4. (a) vouloir d., to mean; (b) qu'est-ce à d.? what does this mean? **II.** s.m. statement, assertion.

direct [dirɛkt], a. direct, straight; train d., through train; T.V: émission en d., live broadcast. adv. **-ement.**

directeur, -trice [dirɛktœːr, -tris], **1.** s. director, manager, manageress; headmaster, -mistress; editor (of paper); head (of firm); d. général, general manager; d. gérant, managing director. **2.** a. directing, controlling.

direction [dirɛksjɔ̃], s.f. 1. (a) guidance; management (of firm); leadership (of party); (b) board of directors. 2. direction, course; train d. de, train for; P.N: d. de la gare, to the station. 3. pl. directions, instructions.

‡**diriger** [diriʒe], v.tr. 1. to direct, control, manage; to conduct (orchestra); économie dirigée, planned economy. 2. (a) to direct; to guide; (b) to aim, point (sur, at).
se **diriger**, to make one's way.

dirigisme [diriʒism], *s.m.* Pol: planning.

discern/er [diserne], *v.tr.* to discern, distinguish; to discriminate. *s.m.* -ement. *a.* -able.

disciple [disipl], *s.m.* disciple, follower.

discipline [disiplin], *s.f.* discipline.

discipliner [disipline], *v.tr.* to discipline.

discontinuer [diskɔ̃tinɥe], *v.tr.* to discontinue.

discordant [diskɔrdɑ̃], *a.* discordant (sound); clashing (colours).

discorde [diskɔrd], *s.f.* discord, dissension.

discothèque [diskɔtɛk], *s.f.* Rec: record library.

discours [diskur], *s.m.* 1. talk. 2. speech, address. 3. *Gram:* parties du d., parts of speech.

discourtois [diskurtwa], *a.* discourteous.

discrédit [diskredi], *s.m.* discredit; disrepute.

discréditer [diskredite], *v.tr.* to disparage, to run down; to discredit.

†**disc/ret** [diskrɛ], *a.* (*a*) discreet; (*b*) quiet, unobtrusive. *adv.* -rètement.

discrétion [diskresjɔ̃], *s.f.* discretion.

discrimin/er [diskrimine], *v.tr.* to discriminate. *s.f.* -ation.

discussion [diskysjɔ̃], *s.f.* discussion, debate.

discutable [diskytabl], *a.* debatable.

discuter [diskyte], *v.tr.* (*a*) to discuss, debate; (*b*) to question, dispute.

disgrâce [dizgrɑs], *s.f.* disfavour, disgrace.

disgracié [dizgrasje], *a.* out of favour.

†**disgracieux** [dizgrasjø], *a.* 1. uncouth. 2. ungracious. 3. unsightly.

dislocation [dislokasjɔ̃], *s.f.* dislocation.

disloquer [disloke], *v.tr.* to dislocate; to put (machine) out of order.

‡**disparaître** [disparɛtr], *v.i.* to disappear.

disparate [disparat], *a.* 1. (*a*) dissimilar; (*b*) ill-matched. 2. *s.f.* incongruity.

disparition [disparisjɔ̃], *s.f.* disappearance.

disparu [dispary], *a.* 1. missing. 2. extinct.

dispensaire [dispɑ̃sɛr], *s.m.* dispensary; out-patients' department.

dispense [dispɑ̃s], *s.f.* (*a*) exemption; (*b*) *Ecc:* dispensation.

dispens/er [dispɑ̃se], *v.tr.* 1. to exempt. 2. to dispense, distribute. *s.f.* -ation.

dispers/er [disperse], *v.tr.* to disperse, scatter. *s.f.* -ion.

disponibilité [disponibilite], *s.f.* 1. availability. 2. available time, funds.

disponible [disponibl], *a.* available.

dispos [dispo], *a.* fit, well, in good form.

disposer [dispoze]. 1. *v.tr.* to dispose, arrange. 2. *v.ind.tr* les moyens dont je dispose, the means at my disposal.

dispositif [dispozitif], *s.m.* apparatus, device; d. de sûreté, safety device.

disposition [dispozisjɔ̃], *s.f.* disposition. 1. arrangement; lie (of the land). 2. (*a*) state (of mind). 3. *pl.* arrangements. 4. disposal; fonds à ma d., funds at my disposal.

disproportionné [disproporsjone], *a.* disproportionate; out of proportion.

dispute [dispyt], *s.f.* quarrel.

disputer [dispyte], *v.tr.* (*a*) to dispute, contest (sth.); (*b*) d. un match, to play a match; (*c*) F: d. qn, to tell s.o. off. se disputer, to quarrel.

disquaire [diskɛr], *s.m.* record dealer.

disqualifi/er [diskalifje], *v.tr.* Sp: to disqualify. *s.f.* -cation.

disque [disk], *s.m.* 1. Sp: discus. 2. (*a*) disc (of moon, etc.); (*b*) d. d'embrayage, clutch plate; (*c*) Rec: record, disc; (*d*) d. intervertébral, (intervertebral) disc.

‡**dissatisf/aire** [disatisfɛr], *v.tr.* to dissatisfy. *s.f.* -action.

dissection [disseksjɔ̃], *s.f.* dissection.

dissemblance [dis(s)ɑ̃blɑ̃s], *s.f.* dissimilarity.

dissémin/er [dis(s)emine], *v.tr.* to scatter (seeds); to spread (germs, ideas). *s.f.* -ation.

dissension [dis(s)ɑ̃sjɔ̃], *s.f.* dissension, discord.

dissentiment [dis(s)ɑ̃timɑ̃], *s.m.* disagreement.

‡**disséquer** [dis(s)eke], *v.tr.* to dissect.

dissertation [disertasjɔ̃], *s.f.* (*a*) dissertation; (*b*) *Sch:* essay.

dissidence [dis(s)idɑ̃s], *s.f.* dissidence.

dissimilarité [dis(s)imilarite], *s.f.* dissimilarity.

dissimul/er [dis(s)imyle], *v.tr.* to dissimulate, conceal; *abs.* to dissemble. *s.f.* -ation.
se dissimuler, to hide, to be hidden.

dissipation [disipasjɔ̃], *s.f.* 1. (*a*) dissipation, dispersal; (*b*) wasting (of time); squandering (of money). 2. (*a*) dissipation, dissolute living; (*b*) inattention; fooling.

dissiper [disipe], *v.tr.* (*a*) to disperse, scatter (clouds); to clear up (misunderstanding); (*b*) to waste (time); to squander (money).
se dissiper, (of suspicions) to disappear; (of fog) to lift, clear; (of storm) to blow over.

dissolu [dis(s)ɔly], *a.* dissolute.

dissolution [dis(s)ɔlysjɔ̃], *s.f.* 1. dissolution, disintegration. 2. (*a*) dissolving; (*b*) solution. 3. dissolution (of parliament). 4. dissoluteness.

dissolvant [dis(s)ɔlvɑ̃], *a. & s.m.* (dis)solvent; d. (pour ongles), (nail varnish) remover.

dissonance [dissɔnɑ̃s], *s.f.* 1. dissonance. 2. *Mus:* discord.

dissonant [dissɔnɑ̃], *a.* discordant.

‡**dissoudre** [dis(s)udr], v.tr. **1.** to dissolve. **2.** to disintegrate.
　se dissoudre. 1. to dissolve. **2.** to break up.

dissuader [dis(s)qade], v.t.r. to dissuade.
dissuasion [dis(s)qazjɔ̃], s.f. dissuasion; arme de d., deterrent.

dissymétrie [dis(s)imetri], s.f. asymmetry.

distance [distãs], s.f. distance.

‡**distancer** [distãse], v.tr. to outdistance.

distant [distã], a. **1.** distant. **2.** standoffish.

distendre [distã:dr], v.tr. to distend.

distension [distãsjɔ̃], s.f. distension.

distill/er [distile], v.tr. to distil. s.f. -ation. s.f. -erie.

distinct [distɛ̃(:kt)], a. distinct. adv. -ement.

†**distinctif** [distɛ̃ktif], a. distinctive.

distinction [distɛ̃ksjɔ̃], s.f. distinction. **1.** faire une d. entre deux choses, to make a distinction between two things; sans d., indiscriminately. **2.** (a) distinction, honour; (b) decoration. **3.** distinction, eminence.

distingué [distɛ̃ge], a. **1.** distinguished, noted. **2.** (a) distinguished, polished; (b) smart (clothes). **3.** (in letter) veuillez agréer mes sentiments distingués, yours faithfully.

distinguer [distɛ̃ge], v.tr. to distinguish.
　se distinguer. 1. to distinguish oneself. **2.** to be noticeable, conspicuous.

distorsion [distɔrsjɔ̃], s.f. distortion.

distraction [distraksjɔ̃], s.f. **1.** absentmindedness. **2.** amusement, diversion.

‡**distraire** [distrɛr], v.tr. **1.** to distract. **2.** to divert, amuse.
　se distraire, to amuse oneself.

distrait [distrɛ], a. absent-minded. adv. -ement.

distribuer [distribɥe], v.tr. to distribute.

distributeur, -trice [distribɥtœ:r, -tris], s. **1.** distributor. **2.** s.m. (a) vending machine; d. d'essence, petrol pump; (b) Aut: distributor.

distribution [distribɥsjɔ̃], s.f. distribution. Sch: d. de prix, speech-day; d. d'eau, water supply.

dit [di], a. (a) settled, fixed; (b) (so-) called.

divaguer [divage], v.i. (a) to digress; (b) to ramble (in delirium).

divan [divã], s.m. divan; couch.

divergence [divɛrʒã:s], s.f. divergence; differences (of opinion).

divergent [divɛrʒã], a. divergent.

diverger [divɛrʒe], v.i. to diverge.

divers [divɛr], a. pl. (a) diverse, varied; faits d., news items; (b) indef. adj. various, sundry. adv. -ement.

diversifier [divɛrsifje], v.tr. to diversify, vary.

diversion [divɛrsjɔ̃], s.f. diversion; change.

diversité [divɛrsite], s.f. diversity.

divertir [divɛrti:r], v.tr. to entertain, amuse. a. -issant. s.m. -issement.

dividende [dividã:d], s.m. dividend.

divin [divɛ̃], a. divine; holy; sacred.

divinité [divinite], s.f. divinity.

divis/er [divize], v.tr. to divide. a. -ible. s.f. -ion. s.m. -eur, divisor.

divorce [divɔrs], s.m. divorce.

divulguer [divylge], v.tr. to divulge, reveal.

dix [dis, diz], num.a. & s.m.inv. **1.** ten. **2.** le dix mai, the tenth of May.

dix-huit [dizɥit], num.a. & s.m.inv. **1.** eighteen. **2.** le dix-huit mai, the eighteenth of May.

dix-huitième [dizɥitjɛm], num.a. & s. eighteenth.

dixième [dizjɛm], num.a. & s. tenth.

dix-neuf [diznœf)], num.a. & s.m.inv. **1.** nineteen. **2.** le dix-neuf mai, the nineteenth of May.

dix-neuvième [diznœvjɛm], num.a. & s. nineteenth.

dix-sept [disset], num.a. & s.m.inv. **1.** seventeen. **2.** le dix-sept mai, the seventeenth of May.

dix-septième [dissetjɛm], num.a. & s. seventeenth.

dizaine [dizɛn], s.f. (about) ten.

docile [dɔsil], a. docile. adv. -ment.

docilité [dɔsilite], s.f. docility.

dock [dɔk], s.m. Nau: dock; dockyard.

docker [dɔkɛr], s.m. docker.

docteur [dɔktœr], s.m. doctor.

doctoresse [dɔktɔrɛs], s.f. F: woman doctor.

doctrine [dɔktrin], s.f. doctrine.

document [dɔkymã], s.m. document.

documentaire [dɔkymãtɛ:r], a. documentary. s.m. documentary film.

documenter [dɔkymãte], v.tr. d. qn, to provide s.o. with information.
　se documenter, to collect material (for book, etc.).

dogmatique [dɔgmatik], a. dogmatic.

dogme [dɔgm], s.m. dogma.

dogue [dɔg], s.m. mastiff.

doigt [dwa], s.m. finger; (a) donner sur les doigts à qn, to rap s.o. over the knuckles; (b) être à deux doigts de, to be within an ace of; (c) d. de pied, toe.

domaine [dɔmɛn], s.m. **1.** domain; (real) estate, property. **2.** field, scope.

dôme [do:m], s.m. **1.** dome, cupola. **2.** d. du palais, roof of the mouth.

domestique [dɔmɛstik]. **I.** a. domestic. **2.** s.m. & f. (domestic) servant.

domicile [dɔmisil], s.m. residence; Jur: domicile; à d., at one's private house; franco à d., carriage paid.

domicilié [dɔmisilje], a. resident, domiciled.

domin/er [dɔmine]. **1.** v.i. to rule. **2.** v.tr. to dominate; (a) to rule; (b) to tower above. a. -ant. s.f. -ation.

†dominical [dɔminikal], a. l'oraison dominicale, the Lord's prayer.

domino [dɔmino], s.m. domino.

dommage [dɔmaːʒ], s.m. 1. (a) damage, injury; (b) quel d.! what a pity! 2. pl. (a) damage (to property); (b) Jur: dommages-intérêts, damages.

dompter [dɔ̃te], v.tr. to tame; to subdue; to master.

dompteur, -euse [dɔ̃tœːr, -øːz], s. tamer.

don [dɔ̃], s.m. gift.

donation [dɔnasjɔ̃], s.f. donation, gift.

donc [dɔ̃ːk], 1. conj. therefore, consequently. 2. adv. [dɔ̃] mais taisez-vous d.! do be quiet! pensez d.! just think!

donjon [dɔ̃ʒɔ̃], s.m. keep (of castle).

données [dɔne], s.f.pl. data.

donner [dɔne], v.tr. to give. 1. d. des conseils, to give advice; je vous le donne en vingt, I give you three guesses; F: c'est donné, it's dirt cheap; s'en d., to have a good time; d. les cartes, to deal (the cards). 2. (a) to provide, furnish; (of crops) to yield; cela donne à penser, this gives food for thought; (b) d. faim à qn, to make s.o. hungry. 3. to attribute; elle se donne trente ans, she claims to be thirty; d. raison à qn, to agree with s.o. 4. (a) to look out (sur, on); fenêtre qui donne sur la mer, window overlooking the sea; (b) d. de la tête contre, to knock one's head against; d. dans le piège, to fall into the trap; (c) to give (way).

dont [dɔ̃], rel.pron. (a) from, by, with, whom, which; la femme dont il est amoureux, the woman with whom he is in love; (b) of, about, whom, which; le livre dont je parlais, the book about which I was speaking; (c) whose, of whom, of which; Madame Martin, dont le fils est médecin, Mrs Martin, whose son is a doctor.

dorer [dɔre], v.tr. to gild.

dorloter [dɔrlɔte], v.tr. to fondle; to pamper.

‡dorm/ir [dɔrmiːr], v.i. 1. to sleep; to be asleep. d. sur les deux oreilles, to sleep soundly. 2. to be dormant. a. -ant. s. -eur, -euse.

dortoir [dɔrtwaːr], s.m. dormitory.

dorure [dɔryːr], s.f. gilding. 2. gilt.

doryphore [dɔrifɔːr], s.m. Colorado beetle.

dos [do], s.m. back; F: avoir qn sur le d., to be saddled with s.o.; P: j'en ai plein le d., I'm fed up with it.

dose [doːz], s.f. dose.

dossier [dosje], s.m. 1. back (of seat). 2. (a) documents, file; (b) record, dossier.

dot [dɔt], s.f. dowry.

doter [dɔte], v.tr. (a) to give a dowry to; (b) to endow.

douairière [dwɛrjɛːr], a. & s.f. dowager.

douane [dwan], s.f. customs; visite de la d., customs examination.

†douanier [dwanje]. 1. a. union douanière, customs union. 2. s.m. customs officer.

double [dubl]. 1. a. double, twofold. 2. adv. double; voir d., to see double. 3. s.m. (a) double; (b) duplicate. adv. -ment.

doubler [duble]. 1. v.tr. (a) to double; to understudy; Aut: défense de d., no overtaking; (b) to line (coat); (c) to dub (film). 2. v.i. to double.

doublure [dublyːr], s.f. 1. lining. 2. Th: understudy.

douceur [dusœːr], s.f. 1. (a) sweetness; (b) pl. sweet things, sweets. 2. softness. 3. pleasantness. 4. gentleness.

douche [duʃ], s.f. shower(bath).

doué [dwe], a. gifted.

douleur [dulœːr], s.f. suffering. 1. pain, ache. 2. sorrow, grief.

†doulour/eux [dulurø], a. painful. 1. aching; sore. 2. sad, distressing. adv. -eusement.

doute [dut], s.m. doubt, misgiving; sans d., no doubt, probably; sans aucun d., without (any) doubt.

douter [dute], v.i. to doubt; d. de, to mistrust.
　se douter de, to suspect.

†dout/eux [dutø], a. doubtful, uncertain. adv. -eusement.

†dou/x [du], a. (a) sweet; smooth, soft; eau douce, (i) fresh, (ii) soft, water; (b) pleasant; (c) gentle. adv. -cement.

douzaine [duzɛn], s.f. dozen.

douze [duːz], num.a.inv. & s.m.inv. twelve; le d. mai, the twelfth of May.

douzième [duzjɛm], num.a. & s. twelfth.

doyen [dwajɛ̃], s. (a) dean; (b) doyen of diplomatic corps.

dragée [draʒe], s.f. sugar(ed) almond.

dragon [dragɔ̃], s.m. 1. dragon. 2. Mil: dragoon.

drague [drag], s.f. dredger.

draguer [drage], v.tr. to dredge.

dragueur [dragœːr], a. & s.m. dredger; d. de mines, mine-sweeper.

dramatique [dramatik], a. dramatic. adv. -ment.

dramatiser [dramatize], v.tr. to dramatize.

dramaturge [dramatyrʒ], s.m. & f. dramatist.

drame [dram], s.m. 1. (a) (literary genre) drama; (b) play. 2. drama, sensational event.

drap [dra], s.m. 1. cloth. 2. d. (de lit), sheet; dans de beaux draps, in a fine mess; in a bad way.

drapeau [drapo], s.m. flag; Mil: colour.

draper [drape], v.tr. to drape.

draperie [drapri], s.f. drapery.

drapier [drapje], s.m. draper, clothier.

dresser [drɛse], v.tr. 1. to draw up. 2. to erect. 3. to adjust. 4. to train.
　se dresser. (a) to stand up; (b) to sit up; to become all attention.

dressoir [dreswa:r], *s.m.* sideboard; dresser.

drogue [drɔg], *s.f.* drug.

droguerie [drɔgri], *s.f.* = hardware shop.

droit[1], -e [drwa], *a.* 1. straight. 2. (*a*) direct, straight; (*b*) *adv.* allez tout à, keep straight on. 3. straightforward. 4. (*a*) right; (*b*) *s.f.* droite, right hand; *Aut:* tenir la droite, to keep to, to drive on, the right.

droit[2], *s.m.* 1. right; droits civils, civil rights; à bon d., with good reason. 2. charge, fee; droits d'auteur, royalties. 3. law; faire son d., to study, read, law.

droiture [drwaty:r], *s.f.* uprightness, rectitude.

drôle [dro:l], *a.* funny, odd; un d. de garçon, a funny chap, *F:* a queer fish; quelle d. d'idée! what a funny idea! *F:* la d. de guerre, the phoney war (1939–40). *adv.* -ment.

dromadaire [drɔmade:r], *s.m.* dromedary.

dru [dry]. 1. *a.* thick, close-set. 2. *adv.* tomber dru, to fall thick and fast.

du [dy] = de le.

†**dû** [dy]. 1. *a.* due (à) owing (to). 2. *s.m.* due; à chacun son dû, give the devil his due. *adv.* -ment.

duc [dyk], *s.m.* duke.

†**ducal** [dykal], *a.* ducal.

duché [dyʃe], *s.m.* duchy, dukedom.

duchesse [dyʃɛs], *s.f.* duchess.

duel [dɥɛl], *s.m.* duel, encounter.

duelliste [dɥelist], *s.m.* duellist.

dune [dyn], *s.f.* dune, sand-hill; down.

duo [dyo], *s.m.* duet.

dupe [dyp], *s.f.* dupe.

duper [dype], *v.tr.* to dupe, to fool (s.o.).

duperie [dypri], *s.f.* dupery, deception.

dupeur, -euse [dypœr, -øːz], *s.* (*a*) trickster, swindler; (*b*) hoaxer.

duplicateur [dyplikatœːr], *s.m.* duplicator.

duplication [dyplikasjɔ̃], *s.f.* duplication.

duplicité [dyplisite], *s.f.* duplicity, deceit.

dur [dyr], *a.* 1. hard; tough; œufs durs, hard-boiled eggs. 2. hard, difficult; la vie est dure, (i) to be hard to kill; (ii) to have a hard time of it; *adv.* travailler d., to work hard. 3. avoir l'oreille dure, to be hard of hearing. 4. hard, harsh. *adv.* -ement.

durabilité [dyrabilite], *s.f.* durability.

durant [dyrɑ̃], *prep.* during.

durc/ir [dyrsiːr]. 1. *v.tr.* to harden. 2. *v.i. & pr.* to grow hard. *s.m.* -issement.

durée [dyre], *s.f.* 1. lasting quality; wear. 2. duration.

dur/er [dyre], *v.i.* to last, endure. *a.* -able.

dureté [dyrte], *s.f.* 1. hardness; toughness. 2. difficulty. 3. harshness.

duvet [dyvɛ], *s.m.* down; d. du cygne, swansdown.

dynamique [dinamik]. 1. *a.* dynamic. 2. *s.f.* dynamics.

dynamite [dinamit], *s.f.* dynamite.

dynamo [dinamo], *s.f.* dynamo.

dynastie [dinasti], *s.f.* dynasty.

dysenterie [disɑ̃tri], *s.f.* dysentery.

dyspepsie [dispɛpsi], *s.f.* dyspepsia.

E

E, e [ə], *s.m.* (the letter) E, e.

eau [o], *s.f.* water. 1. e. douce, (i) fresh, (ii) soft, water; ville d'e., watering place; spa. 2. (*a*) cours d'e., stream; jet d'e., fountain; pièce d'e., lake, pond; tomber à l'e., (i) to fall into the water; (ii) (*of plan*) to fall through; (*b*) e. de pluie, rainwater; le temps est à l'e., it's rainy; (*c*) service des eaux, (town) water supply; château d'e., water tower; chambre avec e. courante, room with running water. 3. e. de Cologne, eau de cologne; e. de toilette, toilet water. 4. *Atom.Ph:* e. lourde, heavy water.

eau-de-vie [odvi], *s.f.* spirits; brandy. *pl.* eaux-de-vie.

eau-forte [ofort], *s.f.* 1. nitric acid. 2. etching. *pl.* eaux-fortes.

ébah/ir [ebaiːr], *v.tr.* to astound, flabbergast. *s.m.* -issement.

ébaucher [eboʃe], *v.tr.* to sketch out, outline; é. un sourire, to give a faint smile.

ébène [ebɛn], *s.f.* ebony.

ébéniste [ebenist], *s.m.* cabinet-maker.

éblou/ir [ebluiːr], *v.tr.* to dazzle. *s.m.* -issement.

éboulement [ebulmɑ̃], *s.m.* 1. caving in, collapsing. 2. landslide.

ébouler (s') [sebule], *v.pr.* to crumble, cave in.

éboulis [ebuli], *s.m.* mass of debris; (mountain) scree.

ébouriffer [eburife], *v.tr.* to dishevel, ruffle.

ébranl/er [ebrɑ̃le], *v.tr.* to shake; to set in motion. *s.m.* -ement.

s'ébranler, to start moving, get under way; (*of bells*) to start ringing.

‡**ébrécher** [ebreʃe], *v.tr.* to notch; to chip (plate).

ébullition [ebɥlisjɔ̃], *s.f.* 1. boiling; 2. turmoil.

écaille [ekaːj], *s.f.* 1. scale (of fish); flake, splinter (of wood). 2. shell (of oyster); é. (de tortue), tortoiseshell.

écailler [ekaje], *v.tr.* to scale (fish); to open (oyster); to flake off (paint).

écarlate [ekarlat], s.f. & a. scarlet.

écarquiller [ekarkije], v.tr. to open (the eyes) wide.

écart¹ [ekar], s.m. **1.** deviation; faire un é., to step aside; to shy. **2.** se tenir à l'é., to stand aside.

écart², s.m. (at cards): discard.

écart/er [ekarte], v.tr. **1.** to separate, part. **2.** to move aside. **3.** to divert (suspicion). s.m. -ement.
    s'écarter. 1. to move aside. **2.** to deviate, stray (de, from); maison écartée du chemin, house standing back from the road; s'é. du sujet, to wander from the subject.

ecclésiastique [eklezjastik]. **1.** a. ecclesiastical. **2.** s.m. ecclesiastic, clergyman.

écervelé [eservəle], a. scatter-brained.

échafaud [eʃafo], s.m. **1.** scaffolding. **2.** scaffold.

échafaudage [eʃafodaːʒ], s.m. **1.** scaffolding. **2.** pile.

échalote [eʃalɔt], s.f. shallot.

échancrure [eʃɑ̃kryːr], s.f. notch; indentation.

échange [eʃɑ̃ːʒ], s.m. exchange.

‡échanger [eʃɑ̃ʒe], v.tr. to exchange.

échantillon [eʃɑ̃tijɔ̃], s.m. sample.

échappée [eʃape], s.f. space, interval; vista.

échapper [eʃape], v.i. to escape; (a) é. à toute définition, to baffle definition; son nom m'échappe, his name has slipped my memory; (b) laisser é. une larme, to let fall a tear; laisser é. l'occasion, to miss the opportunity.
    s'échapper. to escape.

écharpe [eʃarp], s.f. (a) sash; (b) (arm-) sling; (c) scarf.

échauder [eʃode], v.tr. to scald.

échauff/er [eʃofe], v.tr. (a) to (over)heat; (b) to warm; (c) to excite, inflame. s.m. -ement.
    s'échauffer. (a) to become overheated; ne vous échauffez pas, don't get excited; (b) to warm (up); (c) (of engine) to run hot.

échéance [eʃeɑ̃s], s.f. date (of payment).

échec [eʃɛk], s.m. **1.** (a) check; é. et mat, checkmate; (b) failure. **2.** pl. chess.

échelle [eʃɛl], s.f. **1.** ladder. **2.** scale (of map).

échelon [eʃlɔ̃], s.m. **1.** rung (of ladder). **2.** Mil: echelon (formation). **3.** grade, stage.

échelonner [eʃlɔne], v.tr. to space out; to stagger (holidays).

échevelé [eʃəvle], a. dishevelled; disorderly.

échine [eʃin], s.f. spine, backbone.

échiquier [eʃikje], s.m. chessboard.

écho [eko], s.m. echo.

‡échoir [eʃwaːr], v.i. **1.** to fall (to the lot of s.o.); le cas échéant, in case of need. **2.** to fall due.

échouer [eʃwe], v.i. (a) to run aground; (b) to fail; to fall through.

éclabouss/er [eklabuse], v.tr. to splash, (be)spatter. s.m. -ement. s.f. -ure.

éclair [eklɛr], s.m. **1.** flash of lightning; pl. lightning. **2.** flash. **3.** Cu: éclair.

éclairage [eklɛraːʒ], s.m. lighting; illumination.

éclaircie [eklɛrsi], s.f. **1.** break, opening, rift (in clouds). **2.** clearing (in forest).

éclairc/ir [eklɛrsiːr], v.tr. **1.** to clear (sky). **2.** to solve, explain. **3.** to thin (liquid); to thin out (plants). s.m. -issement.
    s'éclaircir. (a) to clear (up); (b) to become clearer.

éclairer [eklɛre]. **1.** v.tr. (a) to light, illuminate; (b) to enlighten. **2.** v. impers. il éclaire, it is lightening.

éclaireur, -euse [eklɛrœːr, -øːz], s. (a) s.m. Mil: scout; (b) (boy) scout; (girl) guide.

éclat [ekla], s.m. **1.** splinter; voler en éclats, to fly into pieces. **2.** burst (of laughter); rire aux éclats, to laugh heartily. **3.** (a) flash (of light); (b) brightness; brilliancy.

éclatant, -ante [eklatɑ̃, -ɑ̃ːt], a. **2.** loud, blaring (sound). **2.** dazzling; vivid; brilliant.

éclat/er [eklate]. **1.** v.tr. to burst. **2.** v.i. to burst, explode; to fly (into pieces). **3.** é. de rire, to burst out laughing. **3.** v.i. to sparkle. s.m. -ement.

éclipse [eklips], s.f. eclipse.

éclipser [eklipse], v.tr. to eclipse.
    s'éclipser. to disappear, vanish.

‡éclore [eklɔːr], v.i. **1.** (of eggs) to hatch (out). **2.** (of flowers) to open.

éclopé [eklɔpe], a. footsore; lame, crippled.

écluse [eklyːz], s.f. (canal) lock.

éclusier [eklyzje], s.m. lock-keeper.

écœur/er [ekœre], v.tr. **1.** to disgust, sicken, nauseate. **2.** to dishearten. s.m. -ement, disgust. a. -ant, disgusting.

école [ekɔl], s.f. school; é. maternelle, kindergarten; é. primaire, primary school; é. libre, independent school; é. mixte, co-educational school; é. militaire, military academy; é. d'équitation, riding school.

écolier, -ière [ekɔlje, -jɛːr], s. schoolboy, -girl.

économe [ekɔnɔm]. **1.** s.m. & f. bursar; steward. **2.** a. economical, thrifty.

économie [ekɔnɔmi], s.f. **1.** economy; é. politique, political economy. **2.** economy, thrift.

économique [ekɔnɔmik], a. **1.** economic; sciences économiques, economics. **2.** economical.

économiser [ekɔnɔmize], v.tr. to economize, save.

écorce [ekɔrs], s.f. bark; rind, peel; l'é. terrestre, the earth's crust.

écorch/er [ekɔrʃe], v.tr. 1. to skin. 2. to graze (skin). s.f. -ure, graze.

écossais, -aise [ekɔsε, -εːz], 1. a. Scottish, Scots, Scotch. 2. s. Scot; Scotsman, -woman. 3. s.m. Scots (dialect). 4. a. & s.m. check; tartan.

écosser [ekɔse], v.tr. to shell (peas).

écot [eko], s.m. 1. share, quota. 2. score, bill, reckoning.

écoulement [ekulmɑ̃], s.m. 1. (a) (out)-flow, discharge of liquid); trou d'é., plug hole (of sink); (b) waste pipe (of bath); (c) dispersal (of crowd). 2. Com: sale, disposal, turnover (of goods).

s'écouler. (a) (of liquid) to flow out, run out; (b) (of time) to pass, elapse.

écourter [ekurte], v.tr. to shorten.

écoute [ekut], s.f. 1. se tenir aux écoutes, to keep one's ears open. 2. Rad: reception; listening in; station d'é., monitoring station; ne quittez pas l'é., Rad: don't switch off! P.T.T: hold the line, please.

écouter [ekute], v.tr. 1. (a) to listen to; (b) abs. to listen in. 2. to pay attention to.

écran [ekrɑ̃], s.m. screen; Phot: filter; F: le petit é., television.

écras/er [ekrɑze], v.tr. to crush; to squash; se faire é., to get run over; écrasé de travail, overwhelmed with work. s.m. -ement.

s'écraser, to crumple up; to collapse.

écrevisse [ekrəvis], s.f. (fresh-water) crayfish.

écrier (s') [ekrije], v.pr. (a) to cry (out); (b) to exclaim.

écrin [ekrɛ̃], s.m. (jewel-)case.

‡écrire [ekriːr], v.tr. to write; machine à é., typewriter; é. à la machine, to type.

écrit [ekri], 1. a. written (word). 2. s.m. (a) writing; je vais vous le donner par é., I'll put it down in writing; (b) written document; pl. works (of author); (c) Sch: written examination.

écriteau [ekrito], s.m. placard, bill, notice, sign.

écriture [ekrityːr], s.f. 1. (hand)writing; é. à la machine, typing. 2. pl. papers, documents; (in book-keeping) entry, item. 3. l'é. sainte, Holy Scripture.

écrivain [ekrivɛ̃], s.m. author, writer.

écrou [ekru], s.m. (screw-)nut.

écroul/er (s') [ekrule], v.pr. to collapse; (of plans) to fall through. s.m. -ement.

écueil [ekœːj], s.m. reef.

écume [ekym], s.f. (a) froth; foam; (b) scum.

écumer [ekyme], 1. v.tr. to skim. 2. v.i. to foam, froth.

écureuil [ekyrœj], s.m. squirrel.

écurie [ekyri], s.f. stable.

écuyer, -ère [ekɥije, -εːr]. 1. s.m. equerry. 2. s. rider.

eczéma [εgzema], s.m. eczema.

édifice [edifis], s.m. building, edifice.

édifi/er [edifje], v.tr. 1. to erect; to build. 2. to edify. s.f. -cation.

édit [edi], s.m. edict.

éditer [edite], v.tr. 1. to edit (text). 2. to publish.

éditeur, -trice [editœːr, -tris], s. 1. editor (of text). 2. publisher.

édition [edisjɔ̃], s.f. 1. edition. 2. publishing.

†éditorial [editorjal]. 1. a. editorial. 2. s.m. leading article, leader.

éditorialiste [editorjalist], s.m. & f. (a) leader writer; (b) Rad: programme editor.

édredon [edredɔ̃], s.m. eiderdown.

éducation [edykasjɔ̃], s.f. (a) education; (b) training (of animals); (c) upbringing, breeding.

‡effac/er [efase], v.tr. to efface, obliterate. s.m. -ement.

s'effacer. 1. to become obliterated; to fade. 2. to stand aside; to take a back seat.

effar/er [efare], v.tr. to frighten, scare. s.m. -ement.

s'effarer, to be frightened (de, at, by); to take fright (de, at).

effarouch/er [efaruʃe], v.tr. to startle. s.m. -ement.

s'effaroucher, to be startled (de, at, by); to take fright (de, at).

†effectif [efektif]. 1. a. effective. 2. s.m. effectives; complement; (total) staff.

effectivement [efektivmɑ̃], adv. 1. effectively. 2. actually. 3. (in answer) that is so.

effectuer [efektɥe], v.tr. to effect, carry out.

efféminé [efemine], a. effeminate.

effervescence [efεrvessɑ̃ːs], s.f. effervescence.

effervescent [efεrvessɑ̃], a. effervescent.

effet [efε], s.m. 1. effect, result; à cet e., to this end. 2. en e., as a matter of fact; indeed. 3. impression. 4. pl. possessions.

efficace [efikas], a. efficacious, effective.

efficacité [efikasite], s.f. effectiveness; efficiency.

effigie [efiʒi], s.f. effigy.

effilé [efile], a. slender; tapering; streamlined.

effleurer [eflœre], v.tr. to touch lightly; to graze (surface).

effondr/er (s') [efɔ̃dre], to fall in; to break down; to collapse; to subside; (of prices) to slump. s.m. -ement.

‡efforcer (s') [eforse], v.pr. s'e. de faire qch., to make an effort to do sth.

effort [efɔːr], s.m. 1. effort, exertion. 2. strain, stress.

effrayant [efrejɑ̃], a. frightful, terrifying, dreadful, appalling.

‡**effrayer** [efreje], *v.tr.* to frighten, scare. s'**effrayer**, to take fright.

effréné [efrene], *a.* unbridled; frantic.

effriter (s') [sefrite], *v.pr.* to crumble (away).

effroi [efrwa], *s.m.* fright, terror, fear.

effronté [efrɔ̃te], *a.* shameless; impudent. *adv.* -ment.

effronterie [efrɔ̃tri], *s.f.* effrontery, insolence, *F:* cheek.

effroyable [efrwajabl], *a.* frightful, dreadful. *adv.* -ment.

effusion [ef(f)yzjɔ̃], *s.f.* effusion, outpouring; e. de sang, bloodshed.

†**égal** [egal], *a.* 1. (a) equal; (b)·level, even. 2. cela m'est é., it's all the same to me; fair enough! si cela vous est é., if you don't mind.

également [egalmɑ̃], *adv.* 1. equally, alike. 2. also, as well.

égaler [egale], *v.tr.* to equal, be equal to; deux et deux égalent quatre, two and two make four.

égaliser [egalize], *v.tr.* 1. to equalize. 2. to level.

égalité [egalite], *s.f.* 1. equality; (at tennis) deuce. 2. evenness, regularity.

égard [egar], *s.m.* consideration, respect; (a) avoir é. à, to allow for (sth.); to give full consideration to (sth.); eu é. à ..., in consideration of ... ; à l'é. de, with respect to; (b) il est plein d'égards pour moi, he can't do enough for me.

égaré [egare], *a.* 1. stray, lost; out-of-the-way. 2. distraught.

égarer [egare], *v.tr.* 1. (a) to mislead; (b) to mislay (sth.). 2. to confuse (s.o.). *s.m.* -ement.

s'**égarer**. 1. to lose one's way; to get on the wrong track; colis qui s'est égaré, parcel that has gone astray. 2. son esprit s'égare, his mind's losing its grip.

‡**égayer** (s') [segeje], *v.tr.* to enliven; to cheer up; to brighten (up).

églantine [eglɑ̃tin], *s.f.* wild rose.

église [egliːz], *s.f.* church.

égoïsme [egɔism], *s.m.* selfishness.

égoïste [egɔist]. 1. *s.m. & f.* selfish person; egoist. 2. *a.* selfish.

†**égorger** [egɔrʒe], *v.tr.* 1. to cut the throat of. 2. to massacre, slaughter.

égout [egu], *s.m.* sewer; drain.

égoutter [egute], *v.tr. & t.* to drain. *s.m.* -ement.

s'**égoutter**, to drain, drip.

égratigner [egratiɲe], *v.tr.* to scratch. *s.f.* -ure, scratch.

égyptien, -ienne [eʒipsjɛ̃, -jɛn], *a. & s.* Egyptian.

eh [e], *int.* hey! eh bien! well!

éjectable [eʒektabl], *a. Av:* siège é., ejector seat.

éjection [eʒeksjɔ̃], *s.f.* ejection.

élabor/er [elabɔre], *v.tr.* to elaborate; to work out (plan). *s.f.* -ation.

élan¹ [elɑ̃], *s.m.* 1. (a) spring, dash; (b) impetus. 2. burst, outburst.

élan², *s.m.* elk, moose.

élancé [elɑ̃se], *a.* tall and slim; slender; aux formes élancées, streamlined.

élancer [elɑ̃se], *v.i.* to throb.

s'**élancer**. 1. to spring; to rush (sur, at). 2. to shoot up.

élarg/ir [elarʒir], *v.tr.* 1. to widen (b) to extend (ideas). 2. to release (prisoner). *s.m.* -issement.

s'**élargir**. (a) to widen out; (b) to grow, extend.

élasticité [elastisite], *s.f.* elasticity.

élastique [elastik], *a. & s.m.* e'lastic.

électeur, -trice [elektœːr, -tris], *s.* elector, voter; mes électeurs, my constituents.

élection [eleksjɔ̃], *s.f.* 1. election. 2. preference; mon pays d'é., the country of my choice.

†**électoral** [elektɔral], *a.* electoral; faire une tournée électorale, to canvass.

électricien [elektrisjɛ̃], *s.m.* electrician; ingénieur é., electrical engineer.

électricité [elektrisite], *s.f.* electricity.

électrifi/er [elektrifje], *v.tr.* to electrify. *s.f.* -cation.

électrique [elektrik], *a.* electric; electrical (industry).

électriser [elektrize], *v.tr.* to electrify.

électrocution [elektrɔkysjɔ̃], *s.f.* electrocution.

électrode [elektrɔd], *s.f.* electrode.

†**électroménager** [elektrɔmenaʒe], *a.* appareils électroménagers, electric household appliances.

électron [elektrɔ̃], *s.m. Ph:* electron.

électronique [elektrɔnik]. 1. *a.* electronic. 2. *s.f.* electronics.

élégance [elegɑ̃s], *s.f.* elegance.

élég/ant [elegɑ̃], *a.* elegant; well-dressed. *adv.* -amment.

élégie [eleʒi], *s.f.* elegy.

élément [elemɑ̃], *s.m.* 1. element. 2. mobilier par éléments, unit furniture. 3. *pl.* rudiments; data.

élémentaire [elemɑ̃tɛːr], *a.* elementary.

éléphant [elefɑ̃], *s.m.* elephant.

élevage [elvaːʒ], *s.m.* 1. stock farming. 2. stock farm; ranch; (in Austr.) (sheep) station.

élévation [elevasjɔ̃], *s.f.* 1. elevation, lifting; *Ecc:* elevation. 2. rise (in temperature). 3. height, altitude. 4. elevation, vertical section.

élève [elɛːv], *s.m. & f.* pupil; student.

élevé [elve], *a.* 1. high; noble, lofty. 2. bien é., well-bred; well brought up; mal é., ill-mannered, rude.

‡**élever** [elve], *v.tr.* 1. to elevate; to raise. 2. to bring up, rear; to breed. *s.* -eur, -euse, (stock) breeder.

s'**élever**. 1. to rise (up); to amount. 2. to raise oneself.

éligible [eliʒibl], *a.* eligible.

élimin/er [elimine], *v.tr.* to eliminate. *s.f.* -ation.

‡**élire** [elir], *v.tr.* to elect; to choose.

élite [elit], *s.f.* élite; personnel d'é., picked personnel.

elle, elles [εl], *s.f. pers. pron. f.* 1. (*subject*) she, it; they. 2. (*object, after prep.*) her, it; them.

elle-même, elles-mêmes [εlmε:m], *pers. pron. f.* herself, itself; themselves.

élocution [elɔkysjɔ̃], *s.f.* elocution.

éloge [elɔ:ʒ], *s.m.* 1. eulogy. 2. praise.

éloigné [elwaɲe], *a.* far; distant; remote.

éloignement [elwaɲmɑ̃], *s.m.* 1. removal; postponement. 2. (*a*) absence; (*b*) distance, remoteness; (*c*) estrangement.

éloigner [elwaɲe], *v.tr.* (*a*) to remove; (*b*) to postpone, put off.
s'éloigner, to move off, away.

éloquence [elɔkɑ̃:s], *s.f.* eloquence.

éloqu/ent [elɔkɑ̃], *a.* eloquent. *adv.* -ement.

élu [ely], *a.* chosen; successful; elected.

élucidation [elysidasjɔ̃], *s.f.* elucidation.

élucider [elyside], *v.tr.* to elucidate, clear up (mystery).

éluder [elyde], *v.tr.* to elude, evade.

émaciation [emasjasjɔ̃], *s.f.* emaciation.

émacié [emasje], *a.* emaciated; wasted (away).

†**émail** [ema:j], *s.m.* enamel.

émailler [emaje], *v.tr.* to enamel.

émancip/er [emɑ̃sipe], *v.tr.* to emancipate. *s.f.* -ation.

emball/er [ɑ̃bale], *v.tr.* 1. to pack; to wrap up. 2. *abs. Sp:* to spurt. *s.m.* -age. *s.m.* -ement.
s'emballer. (*a*) (*of horse*) to bolt; (*b*) (*of engine*) to race; (*c*) to be carried away (by excitement).

embarcadère [ɑ̃barkadε:r], *s.m.* landing-stage; wharf, quay.

embarcation [ɑ̃barkasjɔ̃], *s.f.* (ship's) boat.

embargo [ɑ̃bargo], *s.m.* embargo.

embarqu/er [ɑ̃barke]. 1. *v.tr.* to embark; to ship; to hoist in (boat); *Av:* to enplane (passengers). 2. *v.i. & pr.* to embark; *Av:* to enplane. *s.m.* -ement.

embarras [ɑ̃bara], *s.m.* 1. obstacle. 2. difficulty, trouble. 3. embarrassment.

embarrassant [ɑ̃barasɑ̃], *a.* 1. cumbersome. 2. embarrassing, awkward.

embarrasser [ɑ̃barase], *v.tr.* to embarrass. 1. to hamper; to obstruct. 2. to trouble, inconvenience.

embaucher [ɑ̃boʃe], *v.tr.* to engage (workers).

embaumer [ɑ̃bome], *v.tr.* 1. to embalm. 2. to perfume, scent.

embell/ir [ɑ̃beli:r]. 1. *v.tr.* to embellish. 2. *v.i.* to improve in looks. *s.m.* -issement.

embêtant [ɑ̃betɑ̃], *a. F:* annoying, tiresome; que c'est e.! what a bore!

embêter [ɑ̃bete], *v.tr. F:* to annoy, plague (s.o.).

emblée (d') [dɑ̃ble], *adv.phr.* straight off.

emblématique [ɑ̃blematik], *a.* emblematic(al).

emblème [ɑ̃blε:m], *s.m.* 1. (*a*) emblem, device; (*b*) badge, crest. 2. symbol, sign.

emboîter [ɑ̃bwate], *v.tr.* to pack in boxes; to fit (things) together; **e. le pas à qn,** to fall into step with s.o.

embonpoint [ɑ̃bɔ̃pwɛ̃], *s.m.* stoutness.

embouchure [ɑ̃buʃy:r], *s.f.* 1. mouthpiece. 2. opening (of bag); mouth (of river).

embourber (s') [sɑ̃burbe], *v.pr.* to stick in the mud; to flounder.

embouteillage [ɑ̃buteja:ʒ], *s.m.* 1. bottling. 2. blocking, bottling up. 3. traffic jam.

embouteiller [ɑ̃buteje], *v.tr.* 1. to bottle. 2. to block up, bottle up.

embranchement [ɑ̃brɑ̃ʃmɑ̃], *s.m.* 1. branching (off). 2. branch; branch-line, -road.

embras/er [ɑ̃braze], *v.tr.* to set fire to (sth.); to set (sth.) ablaze. *s.m.* -ement.
s'embraser, to catch fire.

embrass/er [ɑ̃brase], *v.tr.* 1. (*a*) to embrace (s.o.); to kiss (s.o.); (*b*) to adopt (career). 2. to include. *s.m.* -ement.

embrasure [ɑ̃brazy:r], *s.f.* embrasure; window-recess.

‡**embray/er** [ɑ̃breje], *v.tr. E:* to connect, couple, engage; *abs. Aut:* to let in the clutch. *s.m.* -age, clutch.

embrouill/er [ɑ̃bruje], *v.tr.* 1. to tangle. 2. to confuse, muddle. *s.m.* -ement.
s'embrouiller, to get muddled.

embrun [ɑ̃brœ̃], *s.m.* spray, spindrift.

embryon [ɑ̃briɔ̃], *s.m.* embryo.

embuscade [ɑ̃byskad], *s.f.* ambush.

émeraude [emro:d], *s.f. & a.inv.* emerald.

‡**émerger** [emerʒe], *v.i.* 1. to emerge. 2. to come into view.

émeri [emri], *s.m.* emery.

émerveill/er [emervεje], *v.tr.* to amaze; to fill with admiration. *s.m.* -ement.
s'émerveiller, to be filled with admiration (de, at).

émétique [emetik], *s.m.* emetic.

†**émetteur** [emetœ:r], *s.m.* 1. transmitter. 2. *a.* poste é., broadcasting station.

‡**émettre** [emεtr], *v.tr.* 1. (*a*) to emit; to give off; (*b*) to broadcast. 2. to issue.

émeu [emø], *s.m.* emu.

émeute [emø:t], *s.f.* riot.

émietter [emjete], *v.tr.* to crumble.

émigrant, -ante [emigrɑ̃, -ɑ̃:t], *a.* emigrating; migratory. *s.* emigrant.

émigration [emigrasjɔ̃], *s.f.* emigration.

émigré, -ée [emigre], *s.* émigré.

émigrer [emigre], *v.i.* 1. to migrate. 2. to emigrate.

éminence [eminɑ̃:s], *s.f.* eminence.

émin/ent [eminɑ̃], *a.* eminent; distinguished. *adv.* -emment, eminently.

émissaire [emiseːr], *s.m.* emissary; *a.* bouc é., scapegoat.

émission [emisjɔ̃], *s.f.* 1. (*a*) emission; (*b*) Rad: broadcast. 2. issue (of bank notes).

emmagasiner [ɑ̃magazine], *v.tr.* to store.

emmêler [ɑ̃mɛle], *v.tr.* (*a*) to tangle; (*b*) to mix up; to muddle.

†emménag/er [ɑ̃menaʒe], *v.tr. & i.* to move in (to a new house). *s.m.* -ement.

†emmener [ɑ̃mne], *v.tr.* to take (s.o.) away, out.

emmitoufler [ɑ̃mitufle], *v.tr.* to muffle (s.o.) up.

émoi [emwa], *s.m.* emotion, agitation.

émotion [emosjɔ̃], *s.f.* emotion; excitement.

émotionner (s') [semosjɔne], *v.pr.* to become excited, agitated.

émousser [emuse], *v.tr.* (*a*) to blunt; to take the edge off; (*b*) to dull, deaden (senses) to take the edge off (appetite).

émouvant, *a.* moving; (*a*) touching; (*b*) stirring, thrilling.

†émouvoir [emuvwaːr], *v.tr.* to move; (*a*) to stir up; (*b*) to affect, touch.
　　s'émouvoir. 1. to get excited. 2. to be touched.

empailler [ɑ̃paje], *v.tr.* to stuff (animal).

†empaqueter [ɑ̃pakte], *v.tr.* to pack up.

emparer (s') [sɑ̃pare], *v.pr.s'e. de qch.*, to take possession of sth., to seize (sth.).

empêch/er [ɑ̃peʃe], *v.tr.* to prevent, hinder. *s.m.* -ement.
　　s'empêcher, to refrain (de, from).

empereur [ɑ̃prœːr], *s.m.* emperor.

empeser [ɑ̃pəze], *v.tr.* to starch.

empester [ɑ̃peste], *v.tr.* to make (place) stink.

empêtr/er [ɑ̃petre], *v.tr.* to entangle. *s.m.* -ement.

emphase [ɑ̃faːz], *s.f.* pomposity.

emphatique [ɑ̃fatik], *a.* pompous.

†empiéter [ɑ̃pjete], *v.i.* to encroach. *s.m.* -ètement.

empiler [ɑ̃pile], *v.tr.* to stack, to pile (up).

empire [ɑ̃piːr], *s.m.* 1. dominion; sway; (*b*) control. 2. empire.

empirer [ɑ̃pire]. 1. *v.tr.* to make worse. 2. *v.i.* to grow worse.

emplacement [ɑ̃plasmɑ̃], *s.m.* (*a*) site; (*b*) location; (*c*) place, spot.

emplâtre [ɑ̃plɑːtr], *s.m.* 1. Med: plaster. 2. F: c'est un e., he's completely spineless.

emplette [ɑ̃plɛt], *s.f.* purchase; aller faire ses emplettes, to go shopping.

emploi [ɑ̃plwa], *s.m.* 1. use; Sch: e. du temps, timetable. 2. employment, post.

employé, -ée [ɑ̃plwaje], *s.* employee; assistant.

†employer [ɑ̃plwaje], *v.tr.* 1. to employ, use. 2. to employ (s.o.).

empocher [ɑ̃pɔʃe], *v.tr.* F: to pocket (money); e. un coup, to be hit.

empoigner [ɑ̃pwaɲe], *v.tr.* 1. to grasp, seize. 2. F: to catch, arrest (criminal). 3. to thrill, grip.

empoisonn/er [ɑ̃pwazɔne], *v.tr.* 1. to poison; to infect (air); *abs.* to stink. 2. F: to bore (s.o.) stiff; to pester (s.o.). *s.m.* -ement. *s.* -eur, -euse, poisoner.
　　s'empoisonner, to take poison.

emporté [ɑ̃pɔrte], *a.* quick-tempered.

emportement [ɑ̃pɔrtmɑ̃], *s.m.* fit (of anger).

emporter [ɑ̃pɔrte], *v.tr.* 1. to take away. 2. (*a*) to carry away; (*b*) to take (by assault). 3. l'e. sur qn, to get the better of s.o.
　　s'emporter, to lose one's temper.

s'empourprer [sɑ̃purpre], *v.pr.* 1. (of pers.) to flush. 2. to turn crimson.

empreinte [ɑ̃prɛ̃t], *s.f.* impression; (im)print; e. digitale, fingerprint.

empressé, -ée [ɑ̃prese], *a.* eager, zealous. *s.* 2. busybody.

empressement [ɑ̃presmɑ̃], *s.m.* eagerness, readiness, alacrity.

empresser (s') [sɑ̃prese], *v.pr.* 1. to hurry (to do sth.). 2. s'e. auprès de qn, to dance attendance on s.o.

emprisonn/er [ɑ̃prizɔne], *v.tr.* to imprison. *s.m.* -ement.

emprunt [ɑ̃prœ̃], *s.m.* borrowing; loan; nom d'e., assumed name.

emprunt/er [ɑ̃prœ̃te], *v.tr.* to borrow. *s.* -eur, -euse.

ému [emy], *a.* moved, touched; upset.

émulation [emylasjɔ̃], *s.f.* rivalry.

en[1] [ɑ̃], *prep.* 1. (*place*) in(to); en ville, in town; venir en avion, to come by air; (*with f. names of countries*) être, aller, en France, to be in, go to, France; (*b*) (*with pron.*) un homme en qui j'ai confiance, a man whom I trust; (*c*) en votre honneur, in your honour. 2. (*time*) en été, in summer; né en 1945, born in 1945; d'aujourd'hui en huit, today week. 3. (*a*) (*state*) en réparation, under repair; en congé, on leave; (*b*) (*material*) montre en or, gold watch; (*c*) in(to): traduire une lettre en français, to translate a letter into French; (*d*) de mal en pis, from bad to worse. 4. prendre la chose en philosophe, to take the thing philosophically.

en[2] (*unstressed adv. & pron.*) I. *adv.* 1. from there; de Londres? oui, j'en arrive, from London? yes, I've just come from there. 2. on that account; s'en trouver mieux, to feel better for it. II. *pron. inv.* 1. (*a*) of him, her, it, them; qu'en pensez-vous? what do you think about it? (*b*) (*quantity*) combien en voulez-vous? how many do you want? prenez-en dix, take ten. 2. some, any; j'en ai, I have some; je n'en ai pas, I have none. 3. (*indeterminate use*) si le cœur vous en dit, if you feel like it.

enamourer (s') [sănamure], *v.pr.* to fall in love (de, with).

encadrement [ăkadrəmă], *s.m.* 1. framing. 2. framework; frame; setting.

encadrer [ăkadre], *v.tr.* to frame.

encaissé [ăkese], *a.* deeply embanked (river); sunken (road).

encaisse/er [ăkese], *v.tr.* (a) to pack (goods) in cases; (b) to encash, collect (bill); *F*: e. des coups, to take (heavy) blows; *F*: je ne peux pas l'e., I can't stand him. *s.m.* -ement.

encan [ăkă], *s.m.* (public) auction.

en-cas [ăka], *s.m.inv.* 1. qch. en réserve comme e., sth. to fall back on. 2. (emergency) snack.

encastrer [ăkastre], *v.tr.* to embed, fit in.

enceinte[1] [ăsĕt], *s.f.* enclosure.

enceinte[2], *a.f.* pregnant.

encens [ăsă], *s.m.* incense.

encercler [ăserkle], *v.tr.* to encircle.

enchaîn/er [ăʃene], *v.tr.* 1. to chain up. 2. to link (up), connect. *s.m.* -ement.

enchanté [ăʃăte], *a.* 1. enchanted. 2. delighted (de, with); (on being introduced to s.o.) how do you do?

enchant/er [ăʃăte], *v.tr.* 1. to enchant. 2. to charm, delight. *s.m.* -ement.

enchère [ăʃeːr], *s.f.* bid(ding); mettre aux enchères, to put up for auction.

enchérir [ăʃeriːr], *v.i.* (a) to increase in price; (b) e. sur qn, to outbid s.o.

enchevêtr/er [ăʃvetre], *v.tr.* to mix up, confuse, tangle. *s.m.* -ement.

enclin [ăklĕ], *a.* inclined, disposed.

enclos [ăklo], *s.m.* enclosure; paddock.

encoignure [ăkoɲyːr], *s.f.* corner, angle.

encolure [ăkolyːr], *s.f.* 1. gagner par une e., to win by a neck. 2. size in collars.

encombrant [ăkŏbră], *a.* cumbersome.

encombr/er [ăkŏbre], *v.tr.* to encumber; to congest (streets). *s.m.* -ement.

encontre (à l') [ăkŏtr], *adv.phr.* à l'e. de, against; in opposition to.

encore [ăkoːr], *adv.* 1. (a) still; hier e., only yesterday; (b) yet; (c) more, again; e. une tasse de café, another cup of coffee. 2. moreover, furthermore. 3. (a) e. si, if even, if only; (b) e. qu'il. e. (bien) que, (al)though; even though.

‡encourag/er [ăkuraʒe], *v.tr.* to encourage. *s.m.* -ement.

‡encourir [ăkuriːr], *v.tr.* to incur.

s'encrasser [săkrase], *v.pr.* to get dirty, greasy; to get clogged up; to soot up.

encre [ăːkr], *s.f.* ink; e. de Chine, Indian ink.

encrier [ăkrie], *s.m.* inkpot; inkstand.

encyclopédie [ăsiklopedi], *s.f.* encyclopedia.

endetter (s') [sădete], *v.pr.* to get into debt.

endigu/er [ădige], *v.tr.* to dam up; to embank, to dyke. *s.m.* -ement.

endimanché [ădimăʃe], *a.* dressed in one's Sunday best.

endolori [ădolori], *s.* painful, sore; tender.

‡endommager [ădomaʒe], *v.tr.* to damage.

endormi [ădormi], *a.* 1. (a) asleep; (b) sleepy; (c) dormant. 2. numb.

endormir [ădormiːr], *v.tr.* 1. (a) to send to sleep; (b) *F*: to bore (s.o.); (c) to anaesthetize. 2. to benumb (limb). 3. to allay (suspicions).

s'endormir, to fall asleep.

endosser [ădose], *v.tr.* 1. to put on (coat); to take on. 2. to endorse.

endroit [ădrwa], *s.m.* 1. place, spot. 2. side, aspect. 3. right side (of material).

‡enduire [ăduiːr], *v.tr.* to smear, coat.

enduit [ădui], *s.m.* coat, coating (of sth.).

endurc/ir [ădyrsiːr], *v.tr.* to harden. *s.m.* -issement.

endur/er [ădyre], *v.tr.* to endure, bear. *s.f.* -ance. *a.* -able. *a.* -ant, patient.

énergie [enerʒi], *s.f.* 1. energy; force, vigour. 2. (fuel and) power; é. atomique, atomic energy.

énergique [enerʒik], *a.* (a) energetic; (b) strong, drastic. *adv.* -ment.

énerv/er [ănerve], *v.tr.* 1. to enervate. é. qn, to get on s.o.'s nerves. *s.m.* -ement.

enfance [ăfăːs], *s.f.* childhood; première e., infancy; seconde e., dotage, second childhood.

enfant [ăfă], *s.m. & f.* child; boy; girl.

enfant/er [ăfăte], *v.tr.* to give birth to. *s.m.* -ement.

enfantillage [ăfătijaːʒ], *s.m.* childishness.

enfantin [ăfătĕ], *a.* 1. infantile. 2. childish.

enfer [ăfeːr], *s.m.* hell; aller un train d'e., to go hell for leather; un bruit d'e., a hell of a noise.

enfermer [ăferme], *v.tr.* 1. to shut up; sentir l'enfermé, to smell stuffy. 2. to shut in; to enclose.

enfiler [ăfile], *v.tr.* 1. to thread; to string (beads). 2. to go along (a street). 3. to slip on (clothes).

enfin [ăfĕ]. 1. *adv.* (a) finally, lastly; (b) in fact, in short; (c) at last. 2. *int.* (a) at last! (b) (well) well!!

enflamm/er [ăflăme], *v.tr.* to inflame; to set on fire; to excite, stir up (s.o.).

s'enflammer, to catch fire; to become inflamed; to flare up.

enfl/er [ăfle], *v.tr., i.* to swell. *s.f.* -ure.

enfoncé [ăfŏse], *a.* 1. smashed (in). 2. sunken (cavity).

enfonc/er [ăfŏse], *v.tr.* (a) to drive (in) (nail); (b) to break (open) (door). *s.m.* -ement.

s'enfoncer, to penetrate (into sth.).

enfourcher [ăfurʃe], *v.tr.* to mount (horse, bicycle).

enfourchure [ăfurʃyːr], *s.f.* fork, crotch.

‡enfreindre [ăfrĕːdr], *v.tr.* to break (the law).

‡enfuir (s') [ãfɥir], v.pr. 1. to flee, fly; to run away. 2. (of liquid) to run out.

enfumé [ãfyme], a. (a) smoky; (b) smoke-blackened.

‡engag/er [ãgaʒe], v.tr. 1. to pawn; to pledge (one's word). 2. to engage (worker). 3. (a) to catch, entangle; (b) to engage (gears); to fit (key in lock). 4. to begin. 5. to urge (s.o. to do sth.). s.m. -ement. a. -eant, engaging, prepossessing.
s'engager. 1. to undertake (to do sth.). 2. to enlist. 3. (a) (of rope) to foul; (b) s'e. dans, to enter; (c) to begin.

engelure [ãʒlyːr], s.f. chilblain.

engendrer [ãʒãdre], v.tr. 1. to father (child). 2. to bring about.

engin [ãʒɛ̃], s.m. 1. engine, machine; device. 2. missile; e. téléguidé, guided missile.

englout/ir [ãglutiːr], v.tr. 1. to swallow; to engulf; to swallow up. s.m. -issement.

‡engorger [ãgɔrʒe], v.tr. to choke (up); to block (up).

engouffrer [ãgufre], v.tr. to engulf, swallow up.
s'engourdir [ãgurdiːr], v.pr. 1. to grow numb; (of foot) to go to sleep. 2. (of mind) to become dull, sluggish. s.m. -issement.

engrais [ãgrɛ], s.m. manure, fertiliser.

engraiss/er [ãgrese]. 1. v.tr. to fatten (animals). 2. v.i. to grow stout. s.m. -ement.

engrenage [ãgrənaːʒ], s.m. gears; gearing.

engueul/er [ãgœle], v.tr. P: to abuse, slang (s.o.) to tell (s.o.) where he gets off. s.f. -ade, telling-off.

enhardir [ãardiːr], v.tr. to embolden.
s'enhardir, to pluck up courage.

énigmatique [enigmatik], a. enigmatic.

énigme [enigm], s.f. enigma, riddle.

enivr/er [ãnivre], v.tr. to intoxicate. a. -ant. s.m. -ement.

enjambée [ãʒãbe], s.f. stride.

enjamber [ãʒãbe], v.tr. to step over; to span.

†enjeu [ãʒø], s.m. Sp: stake.

enjôler [ãʒole], v.tr. to coax, wheedle.

enjoliv/er [ãʒolive], v.tr. to embellish, beautify.

enjoliveur [ãʒolivœːr], s.m. Aut: wheel disc; hub cap.

enjoué [ãʒwe], a. playful, sprightly.

enjouement [ãʒumã], s.m. playfulness.

enlacer [ãlase], v.tr. 1. (a) to entwine; (b) to clasp (s.o.) in one's arms.

enlaidir [ãlediːr]. 1. v.tr. to make ugly; to disfigure. 2. v.i. to grow ugly.

enlèvement [ãlɛvmã], s.m. 1. removal. 2. carrying off. 3. storming.

†enlever [ãlve], v.tr. 1. (a) to remove; to take away; (b) e. qch. à qn, to take

sth. from s.o. 2. to carry off; to kidnap. 3. to raise; to lift (lid).
s'enlever, to come off; to wear off.

enliser (s') [ãlize], v.pr. to get bogged down.

enneigement [ãnɛʒmã], s.m. snowfall; bulletin d'e., snow report.

ennemi [ɛnmi]. 1. s. enemy. 2. a. hostile.

ennui [ãnɥi], s.m. 1. worry, anxiety. 2. boredom.

ennuy/er [ãnɥije], v.tr. 1. (a) to annoy; (b) to bother (s.o.). 2. to bore (s.o.). a. -eux, boring. a. -ant, annoying.
s'ennuyer, to be bored.

‡énonc/er [enõse], v.tr. 1. to state (opinion). 2. to articulate (word). s.f. -iation.

enorgueillir (s') [ãnɔrgœjiːr], v.pr. to pride oneself (de, on).

énorme [enɔrm], a. enormous, huge. adv. -ément.

énormité [enɔrmite], s.f. (a) enormity; (b) vastness, enormousness.

‡enquérir (s') [ãkeriːr], v.pr. to inquire (de, after); s'e. du prix, to ask the price.

enquête [ãkɛːt], s.f. inquiry, investigation.

enraciné [ãrasine], a. deep-rooted.

enraciner [ãrasine], v.tr. to establish.
s'enraciner, to take root.

enragé [ãraʒe], a. (a) mad; (b) keen; outand-out.

‡enrager [ãraʒe]. 1. v.tr. to enrage (s.o.). 2. v.i. to fume; to be furious.

enregistr/er [ãr(ə)ʒistre], v.tr. 1. to register. 2. to record (music). s.m. -ement.

enrhumer (s') [ãryme], v.pr. to catch cold.

enrichir [ãriʃiːr], v.tr. to enrich.
s'enrichir, to grow rich.

enrôl/er [ãrole], v.tr. 1. to enrol. s.m. -ement.

enroué [ãrwe], a. hoarse, husky.

enrouement [ãrumã], s.m. hoarseness.

enrouler [ãrule], v.tr. to roll up; to wrap up.

ensanglanté [ãsãglãte], a. covered with blood.

enseigne [ãsɛɲ], s.f. (a) sign, token; (b) sign(board); (c) Mil: ensign.

enseignement [ãsɛɲmã], s.m. 1. teaching. 2. education, instruction.

enseigner [ãsɛɲe], v.tr. 1. to show; to point out. 2. to teach.

ensemble [ãsãbl]. 1. adv. together; le tout e., the general effect. 2. s.m. (a) whole; vue d'e., general view; (b) unity; (c) Cl: ensemble.

ensevelir [ãsəvliːr], v.tr. to bury.

ensoleillé [ãsɔleje], a. sunny.

ensuite [ãsɥit], adv. after(wards), then.

†ensuivre (s') [ãsɥivr], v.pr. il s'ensuit que . . ., it follows that . . ., et tout ce qui s'ensuit, and what not.

entaille [ãtaːj], s.f. (a) notch, nick; groove; (b) gash, slash.

entamer [ãtame], *v.tr.* 1. to cut into. 2. to begin; to broach (subject).

entasser [ãtase], *v.tr.* (a) to accumulate; to heap (up); (b) to pack, crowd, together.
  s'entasser. (a) to accumulate; (b) to crowd together.

entendre [ãtã:dr], *v.tr.* 1. to intend, mean. 2. (a) to hear; e. dire qch. à qn, to hear s.o. say sth.; (b) to listen to. 3. to understand; c'est entendu, agreed; bien entendu! of course!
  s'entendre. 1. to agree. 2. to be skilled (à, in).

entente [ãtã:t], *s.f.* 1. (a) understanding; (b) à double e., with a double meaning. 2. agreement.

entérite [ãterit], *s.f.* enteritis.

enterrement [ãtermã], *s.m.* burial; funeral.

enterrer [ãtere], *v.tr.* to bury.

en-tête [ãtɛt], *s.m.* (a) heading; papier à e., headed notepaper; (b) headline. *pl.* en-têtes.

entêté [ãtete], *a.* obstinate, pig-headed.

entêtement [ãtetmã], *s.m.* obstinacy.

entêter (s') [ãtete], *v.pr.* to be obstinate, stubborn.

enthousiasme [ãtuzjasm], *s.m.* enthusiasm.

enthousiasmer (s') [sãtuzjasme], *v.pr.* to be enthusiastic, to enthuse (pour, de, over).

enthousiaste [ãtuzjast]. 1. *s.m. & f.* enthusiast. 2. *a.* enthusiastic.

enti/er [ãtje], *a.* 1. entire, whole. 2. †complete, full. 3. *adv.phr.* en e., entirely, in full. *adv.* -èrement.

entonner [ãtone], *v.tr.* 1. to intone. 2. to strike up (a song).

entonnoir [ãtɔnwa:r], *s.m.* funnel.

entorse [ãtɔrs], *s.f.* sprain, wrench.

entour [ãtu:r], *s.m.* à l'e., around, round about; à l'e. de, round.

entourage [ãtura:ʒ], *s.m.* 1. surroundings. 2. set; circle; environment.

entourer [ãture], *v.tr.* to surround (de, with).

entracte [ãtrakt], *s.m.* 1. *Th:* interval. 2. interlude.

entraide [ãtre(:)d], *s.f.* (no *pl.*) mutual aid.

entrailles [ãtra:j], *s.f.pl.* 1. entrails. 2. être sans e., to be ruthless.

entrain [ãtrɛ̃], *s.m.* liveliness, briskness, *F:* go.

entraîn/er [ãtrene], *v.tr.* 1. to carry along; to carry away. 2. to entail, involve. 3. *Sp:* to train, coach. *s.m.* -ement.

entraver [ãtrave], *v.tr.* 1. to shackle. 2. to hinder; to hold up (traffic).

entre [ã:tr], *prep.* 1. between; e. deux âges, middle-aged. 2. (a) among(st); (b) e. les mains de, in(to) the hands of; (c) l'un d'e. eux, one of them.

entrebâillé [ãtrəbaje], *a.* ajar, half-open.

entre-choquer (s') [sãtrəʃɔke], *v.pr.* (a) to collide; (b) to knock against one another.

entrecôte [ãtrəko:t], *s.f. Cu:* steak (cut from ribs), entrecote steak; e. minute, minute, thin grilled, steak.

entrecouper [ãtrəkupe], *v.tr.* 1. to intersect. 2. to interrupt.

entrée [ãtre], *s.f.* 1. entry, entering. 2. admission. *P.N:* e. interdite, no admittance; *Com:* e. libre, walk-round store. 3. way in; entrance. 4. *Cu:* entrée.

entrefaite [ãtrəfɛt], *s.f.* sur ces entrefaites, meanwhile.

†entrelac/er [ãtrəlase], *v.tr.* to interlace, intertwine, interweave. *s.m.* -ement.

entremets [ãtrəmɛ], *s.m. Cu:* entremets, side dish. 2. sweet (course).

entrepôt [ãtrəpo], *s.m.* warehouse, store.

entreprenant [ãtrəprənã], *a.* enterprising.

†entreprendre [ãtrəprã:dr], *v.tr.* to undertake.

entrepreneur [ãtrəprənœr], *s.* contractor; builder; e. de pompes funèbres, undertaker.

entreprise [ãtrəpri:z], *s.f.* undertaking; firm.

entrer [ãtre], *v.i.* (aux. être) 1. to enter; to go in; to come in. *P.N:* défense d'e., no admittance. 2. to enter into, take part in. 3. *v.tr.* to bring in; e. qch. en fraude, to smuggle sth. in.

entresol [ãtrəsɔl], *s.m.* mezzanine (floor).

†entretenir [ãtrətni:r], *v.tr.* 1. to maintain. 2. to talk (de, about).
  s'entretenir. 1. to talk, converse. 2. *Sp:* to keep fit.

entretien [ãtrətjɛ̃], *s.m.* 1. maintenance; servicing (of car); produits d'e., (household) cleaning materials. 2. support. 3. conversation; interview.

†entrevoir [ãtrəvwa:r], *v.tr.* to catch a glimpse of; laisser e., to hint at (sth.).

entrevue [ãtrəvy], *s.f.* interview.

entrouvert [ãtruver], *a.* half-open.

†entrouvrir [ãtruvri:r], *v.tr.* to half-open.

†énumér/er [enymere], *v.tr.* to enumerate. *s.f.* -ation.

envah/ir [ãvai:r], *v.tr.* to invade. *s.m.* -issement.

enveloppe [ãvlɔp], *s.f.* 1. envelope, cover(ing); wrapper. 2. exterior.

envelopp/er [ãvlɔpe], *v.tr.* to envelop; (a) to wrap up; (b) to cover. *s.m.* -ement.

envenimer [ãvnime], *v.tr.* 1. to poison. 2. to aggravate; to embitter.

envers¹ [ãvɛ:r], *s.m.* wrong side, reverse; à l'e., inside out; wrong way up.

envers², *prep.* towards.

envie [ãvi], *s.f.* 1. desire, longing; avoir e. de, to want. 2. envy. 3. birthmark.

†envieu/x [ãvjø], *a.* envious. *adv.* -sement.

environ [ãvirɔ̃]. 1. *adv.* about. 2. *s.m.pl.* surroundings, neighbourhood.

environn/er [āvirɔne], v.tr. to surround. s.m. -ement.

‡envisager [āvizaʒe], v.tr. to look (s.o.) in the face, envisage; (a) to look (s.o.) in the face; (b) to consider.

envoi [āvwa], s.m. 1. sending, dispatch. 2. consignment, parcel.

envol [āvɔl], s.m. (a) flight; (b) Av: take-off.

envoler (s') [sāvɔle], v.pr. (a) to fly away; to take flight; (b) Av: to take off.

envoyé [āvwaje], s.m. envoy; messenger.

‡envoyer [āvwaje], v.tr. to send; e. chercher qn, to send for s.o.; e. promener qn, to send s.o. packing.

épagneul, -eule [epaɲœl], s. spaniel.

épais [epɛ], a. thick.

épaisseur [epɛsœr], s.f. 1. thickness; depth. 2. density, thickness.

épanch/er [epāʃe], v.tr. to pour out; to shed (blood). s.m. -ement.
s'épancher, to unbosom oneself.

épandre [epādr], v.tr. to spread; to shed (light).

épanou/ir (s') [sepanwi:r], v.pr. (a) to open out, bloom. 2. (of face) to light up. s.m. -issement.

épargne [eparɲ], s.f. saving(s); economy; caisse d'é., savings bank.

épargner [eparɲe], v.tr. to save (time, money); to economize; to be sparing with.

éparpiller [eparpije], v.tr. to scatter.

épatant [epatā], a. F: wonderful; great; slap-up.

épater [epate], v.tr. F: to surprise, flabbergast; to bowl (s.o.) over.
s'épater. F: il ne s'épate de rien, nothing surprises him.

épaule [epo:l], s.f. shoulder.

épaulette [epolɛt], s.f. (a) shoulder-strap; (b) epaulette.

épave [epa:v], s.f. wreck; pl. wreckage.

épée [epe], s.f. sword.

‡épeler [eple], v.tr. to spell.

éperdu [eperdy], a. distracted, bewildered. adv. -ment.

éperon [eprɔ̃], s.m. spur.

éperonner [eprɔne], v.tr. to spur.

éphémère [efemɛ:r]. 1. a. ephemeral; short-lived. 2. s.m. mayfly.

épi [epi], s.m. ear (of grain).

épice [epis], s.f. spice; pain d'é., gingerbread.

épicé [epise], a. highly spiced; hot (seasoning).

‡épicer [epise], v.tr. to spice.

épicerie [episri], s.f. 1. spices. 2. (a) groceries; (b) grocer's shop.

épicier, -ière [episje, -jɛr], s. grocer.

épidémie [epidemi], s.f. epidemic.

épiderme [epidɛrm], s.m. epidermis.

épier [epje], v.tr. 1. to watch; to spy upon. 2. to be on the look-out for.

épilepsie [epilɛpsi], s.f. epilepsy.

épileptique [epileptik], a. & s. epileptic.

épilogue [epilɔg], s.m. epilogue.

épinard [epina:r], s.m. (usu. pl.) spinach.

épine [epin], s.f. 1. thorn-bush. 2. thorn, prickle. 3. é. dorsale, spine, backbone.

†épineux [epinø], a. thorny, prickly.

épingle [epɛ̃:gl], s.f. pin; coups d'é., pin-pricks.

épingler [epɛ̃gle], v.tr. to pin.

épisode [epizɔd], s.m. episode.

épitaphe [epitaf], s.f. epitaph.

épithète [epitɛt], s.f. epithet.

épître [epi:tr], s.f. epistle.

éplucher [eplyʃe], v.tr. to peel (potatoes).

épluchures [eplyʃy:r], s.f.pl. peelings.

éponge [epɔ̃:ʒ], s.f. sponge.

‡éponger [epɔ̃ʒe], v.tr. to mop (up); s'é. le front, to mop one's brow.

époque [epɔk], s.f. 1. epoch, era, age; meubles d'é., antique furniture. 2. à l'é. de, at the time of.

épouser [epuze], v.tr. 1. to marry. 2. to take up (a cause).

‡épousseter [epuste], v.tr. to dust.

épouvantable [epuvātabl], a. dreadful, frightful.

épouvantail [epuvāta:j], s.m. scarecrow.

épouvante [epuvā:t], s.f. terror, fright; film d'é., horror film.

épouvanter [epuvāte], v.tr. to terrify.
s'épouvanter, to take fright.

époux, -ouse [epu, -uz], s. husband, f. wife.

‡éprendre (s') [seprā:dr], v.pr. to fall in love with (s.o.); to take a fancy to (sth.).

épreuve [eprœv], s.f. 1. (a) proof, test; à l'é. de, proof against; (b) Sp: event. 2. trial, ordeal. 3. (a) proof (of book); (b) Phot: print.

épris [epri], a. in love (de, with).

éprouver [epruve], v.tr. 1. to test, try. 2. to feel, experience.

éprouvette [epruvɛt], s.f. test-tube.

épuis/er [epɥize], v.tr. to exhaust. s.m. -ement. a. -é, (i) exhausted; (ii) out of print.
s'épuiser, to become exhausted.

équateur [ekwatœr], s.m. equator; sous l'é., at the equator.

†équatorial [ekwatɔrjal], a. equatorial.

équestre [ekɛstr], a. equestrian.

équilibre [ekilibr], s.m. balance; stability.

équilibrer [ekilibre], v.tr. to balance.

équinoxe [ekinɔks], s.m. equinox.

équipage [ekipa:ʒ], s.m. crew.

équipe [ekip], s.f. team; Ind: shift.

équip/er [ekipe], v.tr. to equip; to fit out. s.m. -ement.

équitable [ekitabl], a. equitable, fair. adv. -ment.

équitation [ekitasjɔ̃], s.f. riding, horsemanship, école d'é., riding school.

équité [ekite], s.f. equity, fairness.

équivalent [ekivalā], a. & s.m. equivalent.

équivoque [ekivɔk]. 1. a. (a) equivocal, ambiguous; (b) questionable, dubious. 2. s.f. ambiguity.

érable [erabl], s.m. maple (tree).

érafl/er [erɑfle], v.tr. to scratch, graze. s.f. -ure.

ère [ɛ:r], s.f. era; epoch; en l'an 66 de notre è., in 66 A.D.

éreintant [erɛ̃tɑ̃], a. F: back-breaking (work).

éreinté [erɛ̃te], a. F: dead beat, all in.

éreinter [erɛ̃te], v.tr. F: 1. to exhaust. 2. to pull (s.o.'s work) to pieces.

‡ériger [eriʒe], v.tr. 1. to erect (statue). 2. to establish (tribunal).

ermitage [ɛrmita:ʒ], s.m. hermitage.

ermite [ɛrmit], s.m. hermit.

éroder [erɔde], v.tr. to erode.

érosion [erozjɔ̃], s.f. erosion; wearing away.

errer [ere], v.i. 1. to roam, wander. 2. to err; to be mistaken.

erreur [erœ:r], s.f. error; mistake.

erroné [erɔne], a. erroneous, mistaken.

érudit, -ite [erydi, -it]. 1. a. erudite, scholarly. 2. s. scholar.

érudition [erydisjɔ̃], s.f. erudition, scholarship.

éruption [erypsjɔ̃], s.f. eruption.

ès [ɛs] = en les; Sch: licencié ès lettres = B.A.; M.A.

escabeau [ɛskabo], s.m. (small) step-ladder.

escadre [ɛska:dr], s.f. Nau: squadron; Av: wing; chef d'e., Nau: Commodore; Squadron Commander; Av: Wing Commander.

escadrille [ɛskadri:j], s.f. Nau: flotilla; Av: flight.

escadron [ɛskadrɔ̃], s.m. Mil: squadron; Av: squadron, group.

escalade [ɛskalad], s.f. 1. scaling, climbing; Jur: cat burglary. 2. Pol: escalation.

escalader [ɛskalade], v.tr. to scale, climb.

escale [ɛskal], s.f. Nau: port of call; Av: intermediate landing; faire e., to put in, touch down, at; vol sans e., non-stop flight.

escalier [ɛskalje], s.m. staircase; stairs; e. roulant, escalator.

escalope [ɛskalɔp], s.f. fillet, escalope (of veal).

escamotable [ɛskamɔtabl], a. folding (table); Av: retractable (undercarriage).

escamoter [ɛskamɔte], v.tr. 1. (of conjuror) to vanish (card); to skip, to scamp (job); Av: to retract (undercarriage). 2. F: to steal, pinch.

escamoteur [ɛskamɔtœ:r], s.m. 1. conjuror. 2. sneak thief.

escapade [ɛskapad], s.f. escapade; prank.

escargot [ɛskargo], s.m. snail.

escarpé [ɛskarpe], a. steep (slope); sheer (cliff).

escarpement [ɛskarpmɑ̃], s.m. steep slope; escarpment.

esclavage [ɛsklava:ʒ], s.m. slavery.

esclave [ɛskla:v], s.m. & f. slave.

escompte [ɛskɔ̃:t], s.m. discount.

escompter [ɛskɔ̃te], v.tr. to discount (bill); to anticipate, allow for.

escorte [ɛskɔrt], s.f. escort; convoy.

escorter [ɛskɔrte], v.tr. to escort; to convoy.

escouade [ɛskwad], s.f. squad, gang.

escrime [ɛskrim], s.f. fencing.

escroc [ɛskro], s.m. swindler, crook.

escroquerie [ɛskrɔkri], s.f. swindling; fraud.

espace [ɛspas], s.m. space.

espacer [ɛspase], v.tr. to space (out).

espadrille [ɛspadri:j], s.f. (rope-soled) sandal.

espagnol, -ole [ɛspaɲɔl]. 1. a. Spanish. 2. s. Spaniard. 3. s.m. Ling: Spanish.

espèce [ɛspɛs], s.f. (a) kind, sort; Biol: species; P: e. d'idiot! you fool! what a fool! (b) pl. Fin: specie, cash, coin.

‡espér/er [ɛspere], v.tr. to hope.-s.f. -ance.

espiègle [ɛspjɛgl], a. & s. mischievous.

espion, -onne [ɛspjɔ̃, -ɔn], s. spy.

espionn/er [ɛspjɔne], v.tr. to spy (up)on; abs. to spy. s.m. -age.

espoir [ɛspwa:r], s.m. hope.

esprit [ɛspri], s.m. 1. (a) spirit; le Saint-E., l'E. Saint, the Holy Ghost, Spirit; (b) ghost, phantom; (c) spirit. 2. (a) mind; (b) wit. 3. spirit, feeling.

†Esquimau, -aude [ɛskimo, -o:d]. 1. s. & a. Eskimo. 2. s.m. F: choc ice.

esquinter [ɛskɛ̃te], v.tr. F: 1. to exhaust (s.o.), to tire (s.o.) out. 2. to damage, ruin, wreck.

esquisse [ɛskis], s.f. sketch; outline.

esquisser [ɛskise], v.tr. to sketch, outline.

esquiver [ɛskive], v.tr. to avoid, evade, dodge.

s'esquiver, to slip away; F: to make oneself scarce.

essai [esɛ], s.m. 1. trial, test(ing); à l'e., on approval; Av: pilote d'e., test pilot. 2. (a) attempt(ing), try; coup d'e., first attempt; (b) Lit: essay; (c) Sp: try (at rugger).

essaim [esɛ̃], s.m. swarm (of bees).

essaimer [eseme], v.i. (of bees) to swarm.

‡essayer [eseje], v.tr. 1. (a) to test, try; (b) to try on (garment); (c) to assay (ore). 2. e. de faire qch., to try to do sth.

essence [esɑ̃:s], s.f. 1. (a) petrol, U.S: gasoline; (b) essence, extract. 2. spirit; gist.

†essentiel [esɑ̃sjɛl], a. & s.m. essential. adv. -ellement.

essieu [esjø], s.m. axle.

essor [esɔ:r], s.m. (rising) flight (of bird); rapid development (of industry).

essorer [esɔre], v.tr. to dry (clothes).

essoreuse [esɔrø:z], s.f. centrifugal dryer; spin dryer.

essouffl/er (s') [esufle], v.pr. to get out of breath. s.m. -ement.

essuie-glace [esɥiglas], s.m. Aut: windscreen, U.S: windshield, wiper. pl. essuie-glaces.

essuie-main(s) [esчiɛ̃mɛ̃], *s.m.inv.* towel.

†**essuyer** [esчije], *v.tr.* to wipe; to wipe up.

est [ɛst], *s.m.* east.

estampe [ɛstɑ̃:p], *s.f.* print, engraving.

esthétique [ɛstetik], *a.* aesthetic.

estimation [ɛstimasjɔ̃], *s.f.* (a) estimation, valuing, appraising; (b) estimate, valuation.

estime [ɛstim], *s.f.* esteem, regard.

estimer [ɛstime], *v.tr.* 1. to estimate. 2. (a) to consider; (b) to have a high opinion of (s.o., sth.).

estivant, -ante [ɛstivɑ̃, -ɑ̃:t], *s.* summer visitor, holiday-maker.

estomac [ɛstɔma], *s.m.* stomach.

estrade [ɛstrad], *s.f.* platform, stage.

estragon [ɛstragɔ̃], *s.m.* tarragon.

estropier [ɛstrɔpje], *v.tr.* to cripple, maim.

estuaire [ɛstчɛr], *s.m.* estuary.

esturgeon [ɛstyrʒɔ̃], *s.m.* sturgeon.

et [e], *conj.* and; et...et..., both... and...

étable [etabl], *s.f.* cowshed; cattle-shed.

établi [etabli], *s.m.* (work-)bench.

établ/ir [etabliːr], *v.tr.* 1. (a) to establish (business); to set up (agency); to lay down (rule); to fix (price); (b) to establish (fact). 2. to work out (plan). -**issement**.

   s'**établir**. 1. to settle (in a place). 2. to set up in business. 3. (of custom) to become established.

étage [etaːʒ], *s.m.* 1. storey, floor; à deux étages, two-storeyed, U.S: three-storied. 2. (a) menton à deux étages, double chin; (b) de bas é., low, fourth-rate.

étagère [etaʒɛr], *s.f.* rack; (set of) shelves.

étain [etɛ̃], *s.m.* 1. tin. 2. pewter.

étalage [etalaʒ], *s.m.* (a) display, show; (b) window dressing.

étaler [etale], *v.tr.* (a) to display (goods); (b) to spread out; (c) to display, show off; (d) to stagger (payments).

étalon¹ [etalɔ̃], *s.m.* stallion.

étalon² [etalɔ̃], *s.m.* standard (of weights); l'é. or, the gold standard.

étamine [etamin], *s.f.* stamen.

étampe [etɑ̃:p], *s.f.* 1. stamp, die. 2. Tls: punch.

étanche [etɑ̃:ʃ], *a.* watertight; air-tight.

étancher [etɑ̃ʃe], *v.tr.* 1. to staunch (blood); to stop (a leak); (b) to quench (one's thirst). 2. to make (container) air-tight, watertight.

étang [etɑ̃], *s.m.* pond, pool.

étape [etap], *s.f.* stage (of journey); faire é., to stop; à par, petites étapes, by easy stages.

état [eta], *s.m.* 1. state, condition. 2. (a) statement, return; (b) to take into account; (c) é. civil, (i) civil status; (ii) = registry office. 3. State, nation; homme d'É., statesman.

étatisé [etatize], *a.* state-controlled.

étatisme [etatism], *s.m.* state control; State socialism.

état-major [etamaʒɔːr], *s.m.* (a) (general) staff; carte d'é.-m., ordnance survey map; (b) headquarters. *pl.* états-majors.

†**étau** [eto], *s.m.* Tls: vice.

†**étayer** [eteje], *v.tr.* to shore up, prop (up).

été [ete], *s.m.* summer.

‡**éteindre** [etɛ̃dr], *v.tr.* to extinguish; to put out (fire); to turn off (gas); to switch off (light).

   s'**éteindre**. 1. (of fire, light) to go out; (of colour) to fade; (of sound) to die away. 2. to become extinct, to die out.

éteint [etɛ̃], *a.* (a) extinguished; le feu est é., the fire is out; (b) extinct; (c) faint (voice).

étendard [etɑ̃daːr], *s.m.* colours, standard.

étendre [etɑ̃:dr], *v.tr.* 1. to spread, stretch; to hang out (washing). 2. to extend (knowledge).

   s'**étendre**. 1. to stretch oneself out; to enlarge (on a subject). 2. (a) to extend, stretch; (b) to spread.

étendu, -ue [etɑ̃dy]. 1. *a.* (a) extensive; (b) outstretched. 2. *s.f.* étendue, extent; stretch, expanse (of country).

†**étern/el** [etɛrnɛl], *a.* eternal. *adv.* -**ellement**.

éternité [etɛrnite], *s.f.* eternity.

éternu/er [etɛrnчe], *v.i.* to sneeze. *s.m.* -**ement**.

éther [etɛr], *s.m.* ether.

‡**étincel/er** [etɛ̃sle], *v.i.* 1. to throw out sparks. 2. to sparkle. *s.m.* -**lement**.

étincelle [etɛ̃sɛl], *s.f.* spark.

†**étiquet/er** [etikte], *v.tr.* to label; to ticket (goods).

étiquette [etikɛt], *s.f.* 1. label, ticket. 2. etiquette.

étirer [etire], *v.tr.* to stretch; to draw out; é. le fil, to draw wire.

   s'**étirer**, to stretch oneself, one's limbs.

étoffe [etɔf], *s.f.* material; fabric; il a l'é. d'un bon chef, he has the makings of a good leader.

étoile [etwal], *s.f.* star. 1. coucher à la belle é., to sleep in the open. 2. asterisk. 3. (film) star.

étoilé [etwale], *a.* starry, starlit; la Bannière étoilée, the Star-spangled Banner.

étonn/ant [etɔnɑ̃], *a.* astonishing, surprising. *adv.* -**amment**.

étonn/er [etone], *v.tr.* to astonish, surprise. *s.m.* -**ement**.

   s'**étonner**, to be astonished, surprised, to wonder (de, at).

étouffant [etufɑ̃], *a.* suffocating, stuffy, sultry.

étouffer [etufe]. 1. *v.tr.* (a) to suffocate, smother; (b) to stifle; to suppress. 2. *v.i. & pr.* to suffocate, choke.

étourderie [eturd(ə)ri], s.f. 1. thought-lessness. 2. thoughtless action.

étourdi [eturdi], a. thoughtless; foolish. adv. -ment.

étourdir [eturdiːr], v.tr. 1. to stun, daze. 2. to deaden.

étourdissement [eturdismɑ̃], s.m. giddiness, dizziness.

étourneau [eturno], s.m. starling.

étrange [etrɑ̃ːʒ], a. strange, peculiar, queer. adv. -ment.

étranger, -ère [etrɑ̃ʒe, -ɛːr]. 1. (a) a. foreign; (b) s. foreigner, alien; (c) s.m. à l'é., abroad. 2. (a) a. strange; (b) s. stranger. 3. a. extraneous.

étrangeté [etrɑ̃ʒte], s.f. strangeness, oddness.

étrangler [etrɑ̃gle]. 1. (a) v.tr. to strangle; (b) v.i. é. de colère, to choke with rage. 2. v.tr. to constrict, compress. s.m. -ement.

étrave [etraːv], s.f. Nau: stem.

être [ɛːtr]. I. v.i. & pred. 1. to be; to exist; cela étant, that being so; Ecc: ainsi soit-il, amen. 2. (a) il est chef de gare, he is a stationmaster; il est le chef de gare, he is the stationmaster; (b) l'homme est mortel, man is mortal; nous étions trois, there were three of us; (c) nous sommes le dix, to-day is the tenth; il est midi, it is twelve o'clock; (d) où en sommes-nous? how far have we got? c'en est trop! this is too much! il n'en est rien! nothing of the kind! 3. (a) é. à qn, to belong to s.o.; (b) c'est à vous de jouer, it is your turn to play. 4. (aux. use) il est arrivé, he has arrived. 5. (passive aux.) il fut puni par son père, he was punished by his father. 6. (= ALLER) j'avais été à Paris, I had been to Paris. II. s.m. 1. being, existence. 2. being, individual; ê. humain, human being.

‡étreindre [etrɛ̃ːdr], v.tr. to embrace, hug; to grasp, grip. s.f. -te.

étrenne [etren], s.f. (usu. pl.) New-Year's gift.

étrenner [etrene], v.tr. to christen (object); to use, wear (sth.) for the first time.

étrier [etrie], s.m. stirrup.

étroit [etrwa], a. 1. narrow; confined. 2. tight; tight(-fitting). 3. être à l'é., (i) to be cramped for room; (ii) to be hard up. adv. -ement.

étude [etyd], s.f. 1. (a) study; (b) research. 2. office (of solicitor, etc.).

étudiant, -ante [etydjɑ̃, -ɑ̃ːt], s. student.

étudier [etydje], v.tr. to study.

étui [etɥi], s.m. case, box; é. à lunettes, spectacle case.

eucalyptus [økaliptys], s.m. eucalyptus.

eucharistie [økaristi], s.f. Ecc: the Eucharist.

euphémisme [øfemism], s.m. euphemism.

Euratom [øratɔm], Pr.n.f. Euratom.

européen, -enne [ørɔpeɛ̃, -ɛn], a. & s. European.

Eurovision [ørɔvizjɔ̃], Pr.n.f. Eurovision.

euthanasie [øtanazi], s.f. euthanasia.

eux [ø], pers.pron.m.pl. (a) they; (b) them.

eux-mêmes [ømɛːm], pers.pron.m.pl. themselves.

évacuer [evakɥe], v.tr. to evacuate. s.f. -ation.

évader (s') [sevade], v.pr. to escape.

évaluer [evalɥe], v.tr. to value, appraise; to estimate. s.f. -ation.

évangile [evɑ̃ʒil], s.m. gospel.

évanouir (s') [sevanwiːr], v.pr. 1. to vanish, disappear. 2. to faint. s.m. -issement.

évaporer (s') [sevapɔre], to evaporate. s.f. -ation.

†évasif [evazif], a. evasive. adv. -ivement.

évasion [evazjɔ̃], s.f. 1. escape. 2. quibble, evasion. 3. escapism.

évêché [eveʃe], s.m. 1. bishopric, diocese, see. 2. bishop's palace.

éveil [evɛj], s.m. 1. (a) awakening; (b) en é., on the alert. 2. warning.

éveillé [eveje], a. 1. awake. 2. wide-awake; alert.

éveiller [eveje], v.tr. to wake (s.o.) up. s'éveiller, to wake (up).

événement [evenmɑ̃], s.m. event; incident.

éventail [evɑ̃taːj], s.m. fan.

éventrer [evɑ̃tre], v.tr. to rip open.

éventualité [evɑ̃tɥalite], s.f. possibility, eventuality.

†éventuel [evɑ̃tɥel]. 1. a. possible. 2. s.m. eventuality, contingency. adv. -lement.

évêque [evɛːk], s.m. bishop.

éviction [eviksjɔ̃], s.f. eviction.

évidence [evidɑ̃ːs], s.f. (a) obviousness, clearness; (b) être en é., to be (clearly) visible.

évident [evidɑ̃], a. evident, obvious. adv. -emment.

évier [evje], s.m. (kitchen) sink.

‡évincer [evɛ̃se], v.tr. 1. to evict. 2. to supplant.

évitement [evitmɑ̃], s.m. 1. (a) shunting (of train); gare d'é., siding; (b) route d'é., bypass. 2. passing-place; loop.

éviter [evite], v.tr. to avoid.

évoluer [evolɥe], v.i. to evolve, develop.

évolution [evolysjɔ̃], s.f. evolution.

évoquer [evoke], v.tr. to evoke; to call to mind.

exact [ɛgzakt], a. exact; (a) accurate, correct; (b) strict; (c) punctual. adv. -ement.

exaction [ɛgzaksjɔ̃], s.f. exaction.

exactitude [ɛgzaktityd], s.f. (a) exactness, accuracy, exactitude; (b) punctuality.

‡exagérer [ɛgzaʒere], v.tr. to exaggerate. s.f. -ation.

exalté, -ée [ɛgzalte]. 1. a. (a) impassioned; (b) hot-headed; (c) uplifted. 2. s. fanatic.

exalt/er [ɛgzalte], v.tr. 1. to exalt. 2. to excite, inflame. s.f. -ation.

s'**exalter**, to grow enthusiastic; to enthuse.

examen [ɛgzamɛ̃], s.m. examination.

examinateur, -trice [ɛgzaminatœɛr, -tris], s. examiner; Ind: inspector.

examiner [ɛgzamine], v.tr. to examine.

‡**exaspér/er** [ɛgzaspere], v.t. to exasperate. s.f. -ation.

excédent¹ [ɛksedɑ̃], a. 1. surplus (money); excess(ive) (luggage). 2. (of pers.) tiresome, exasperating.

excédent², s.m. excess, surplus.

‡**excéder** [ɛksede], v.tr. 1. to exceed, go beyond. 2. to tire (s.o.) out; to exasperate (s.o.).

excellence [ɛksɛlɑ̃:s], s.f. 1. excellence; par e., pre-eminently. 2. votre E., your Excellency.

excellent [ɛksɛlɑ̃], a. excellent.

exceller [ɛksɛle], v.i. to excel.

excentricité [ɛksɑ̃trisite], s.f. eccentricity.

excentrique [ɛksɑ̃trik], a. eccentric; odd.

excepté [ɛksɛpte], prep. except.

except/er [ɛksɛpte], v.tr. to except, exclude. s.f. -ion. a. -ionnel, exceptional. adv. ionnellement.

excès [ɛksɛ], s.m. (a) excess; (b) pl. excesses.

‡**excess/if** [ɛksɛsif], a. excessive; undue. adv. -ivement.

excitation [ɛksitasjɔ̃], s.f. 1. excitation; incitement. 2. excitement.

excit/er [ɛksite], v.tr. to excite. a. -ant. s.m. -ant, stimulant. s.f. -abilité. a. -able.

exclamation [ɛksklamasjɔ̃], s.f. exclamation.

exclamer (s') [sɛksklame], v.pr. (a) to exclaim; (b) to protest loudly.

‡**exclu/re** [ɛksklyːr], v.tr. to exclude, leave out. s.f. -sion.

‡**exclus/if** [ɛksklyzif], a. exclusive, sole. adv. -ivement.

excommuni/er [ɛkskɔmynje], v.tr. to excommunicate. s.f. -cation.

excrément [ɛkskremɑ̃], s.m. excrement.

excrétion [ɛkskresjɔ̃], s.f. excretion.

excroissance [ɛkskrwasɑ̃:s], s.f. excrescence.

excursion [ɛkskyrsjɔ̃], s.f. excursion; tour.

excursionniste [ɛkskyrsjɔnist], s.m. & f. tourist; tripper.

excuse [ɛkskyz], s.f. 1. excuse. 2. pl. apology.

excus/er [ɛkskyze], v.tr. to excuse (s.o.). a. -able. adv. -ablement.

s'**excuser**, to apologize.

exécrable [ɛgzekrabl], a. execrable, abominable. adv. -ment.

‡**exécrer** [ɛgzekre], v.tr. to loathe, detest.

exécutant, -ante [ɛgzekytɑ̃, -ɑ̃:t], s. Mus: performer.

exécuter [ɛgzekyte], v.tr. 1. to execute; to carry out. 2. to execute; to put to death.

s'**exécuter**, to comply; to pay up.

exécuteur, -trice [ɛgzekytœɛr, -tris], s. executor, executrix.

‡**exécutif** [ɛgzekytif], a. executive.

exécution [ɛgzekysjɔ̃], s.f. 1. execution, performance. 2. e. capitale, execution.

exemplaire¹ [ɛgzɑ̃plɛːr], a. exemplary.

exemplaire², s.m. (a) specimen (of work); (b) copy (of book).

exemple [ɛgzɑ̃pl], s.m. 1. example. 2. lesson, warning. 3. par e., for example, for instance; int. par e.! the ideal! good heavens!

exempt [ɛgzɑ̃], a. exempt, free; e. de droits, duty free.

exempt/er [ɛgzɑ̃te], v.tr. to exempt, excuse. s.f. -ion.

‡**exerc/er** [ɛgzɛrse], v.tr. to exercise. 1. to 'train. 2. to make use of. 3. to practise.

exercice [ɛgzɛrsis], s.m. exercise. 1. (a) prendre de l'e., to take exercise; (b) drill. 2. practice; use; avocat en e., practising barrister. 3. Com: (a) year's trading; (b) balance sheet.

exhaler [ɛgzale], v.tr. to exhale, emit. s.f. -aison.

exhausser [ɛgzose], v.tr. to raise, to increase the height of.

exhiber [ɛgzibe], v.tr. to show, produce; Pej: to show off (knowledge, etc.).

exhorter [ɛgzɔrte], v.tr. to exhort, urge.

exhumer [ɛgzyme], v.tr. to exhume; to unearth, bring to light.

exigeant [ɛgziʒɑ̃], a. exacting; hard to please.

‡**exig/er** [ɛgziʒe], v.tr. 1. to exact; to insist upon. 2. to require, call for. s.f. -ence.

‡**exigu** [ɛgzigy], a. tiny; scanty (resources); inadequate (means).

exiguïté [ɛgzigɥite], s.f. insufficiency; slenderness (of resources).

exil [ɛgzil], s.m. exile, banishment.

exilé, ée [ɛgzile], s. exile.

exiler [ɛgzile], v.tr. to exile, banish.

existant [ɛgzistɑ̃], a. (a) existing, existent; (b) extant.

existence [ɛgzistɑ̃:s], s.f. existence.

exister [ɛgziste], v.i. to exist, be; to live.

exode [ɛgzɔd], s.m. exodus; e. rural, rural depopulation.

‡**exonér/er** [ɛgzɔnere], v.tr. to exonerate. s.f. -ation.

exorbitant [ɛgzɔrbitɑ̃], a. exorbitant.

exotique [ɛgzɔtik], a. exotic.

‡**expansif** [ɛkspɑ̃sif], a. expansive.

expansion [ɛkspɑ̃sjɔ̃], s.f. expansion.

patri/er [ɛkspatrie], v.tr. to expatriate. s.f. -ation.

expédient [ɛkspedjɑ̃]. 1. a. expedient. 2. s.m. expedient, device; vivre d'expédients, to live by one's wits.

expédier [ɛkspedje], v.tr. to dispatch, send.

expéditeur, -trice [ɛkspeditœːr, -tris], s. sender.

expédition [ɛkspedisjɔ̃], s.f. 1. expedition. 2. Com: (a) forwarding; (b) consignment.

expérience [ɛksperjãːs], s.f. 1. experience. 2. experiment, test.

expérimental [ɛksperimãtal], a. experimental.

expérimenté [ɛksperimãte], a. experienced.

expérimenter [ɛksperimãte], v.tr. to test, try; abs. to make an experiment.

expert, -erte [ɛkspɛr, -ɛrt], a. & s.m. expert. adv. -ement.

expi/er [ɛkspje], v.tr. to expiate, atone for. s.f. -ation.

expir/er [ɛkspire], v.tr. & i. to expire. s.f. -ation.

†explétif [ɛkspletif], a. expletive.

explicable [ɛksplikabl], a. explicable.

†explicatif [ɛksplikatif], a. explanatory.

explication [ɛksplikasjɔ̃], s.f. explanation.

explicite [ɛksplisit], a. explicit, clear, plain. adv. -ment.

expliquer [ɛksplike], v.tr. (a) to explain; (b) to account for.

exploit [ɛksplwa], s.m. exploit; achievement.

exploit/er [ɛksplwate], v.tr. to exploit. s.f. -ation.

explor/er [ɛksplɔre], v.tr. to explore. s.f. -ation. s. -ateur, -atrice, explorer.

exploser [ɛksploze], v.i. to explode.

†explosif [ɛksplozif], a. & s.m. explosive.

explosion [ɛksplozjɔ̃], s.f. explosion.

exportateur, -trice [ɛksportatœːr, -tris], s. exporter.

export/er [ɛksporte], v.tr. to export. s.f. -ation, export.

exposé [ɛkspoze], 1. a. (a) in an exposed position; (b) liable. 2. s.m. statement.

exposer, v.tr. 1. to exhibit, show. 2. to expose.

exposition, s.f. 1. (a) exhibition; (b) exposure.

†exprès¹ [ɛksprɛ], a. express, explicit.

exprès², adv. intentionally.

express [ɛksprɛs], a. & s.m. 1. express (train). 2. a. F: café e., espresso coffee.

†expressif [ɛkspresif], a. expressive.

expression [ɛkspresjɔ̃], s.f. expression.

expresso [ɛkspreso], a. & s.m. (café e., espresso coffee.

exprimer [ɛksprime], v.tr. to express.

expropri/er [ɛksproprje], v.tr. to expropriate. s.f. -iation.

expuls/er [ɛkspylse], v.tr. to expel; to eject.

expulsion [ɛkspylsjɔ̃], s.f. expulsion; eviction.

exquis [ɛkski], a. exquisite.

extase [ɛkstaːz], s.f. ecstasy; trance.

extasier (s') [sɛkstazje], v.pr. to go into ecstasies.

extatique [ɛkstatik], a. ecstatic.

extension [ɛkstãsjɔ̃], s.f. extension.

exténu/er [ɛkstenɥe], v.tr. to exhaust. s.f. -ation.

s'exténuer, to work oneself to death.

extérieur [ɛksterjœːr]. 1. a. (a) exterior, external; (b) foreign (trade). 2. s.m. exterior. adv. -ement.

extermin/er [ɛkstɛrmine], v.tr. to exterminate. s.f. -ation.

externat [ɛkstɛrna], s.m. day-school.

externe [ɛkstɛrn]. 1. a. external, outer. 2. s. day-pupil.

extincteur [ɛkstɛ̃ktœːr], s.m. fire-extinguisher.

extinction [ɛkstɛ̃ksjɔ̃], s.f. 1. extinction. 2. (a) dying out; (b) loss (of voice).

extirper [ɛkstirpe], v.tr. to eradicate, to root out.

extorquer [ɛkstɔrke], v.tr. to extort.

extorsion [ɛkstɔrsjɔ̃], s.f. extortion.

extra [ɛkstra]. 1. s.m. extra. 2. a.inv. F: extra-special, first-rate.

extraction [ɛkstraksjɔ̃], s.f. extraction. 1. extracting. 2. descent, lineage.

extrader [ɛkstrade], v.tr. to extradite.

extradition [ɛkstradisjɔ̃], s.f. extradition.

extra-fin [ɛkstrafɛ̃], a. superfine.

extra-fort [ɛkstrafɔːr]. 1. a. extra-strong. 2. s.m. bias binding.

†extraire [ɛkstrɛːr], v.tr. to extract.

extrait [ɛkstrɛ], s.m. extract; e. de naissance = birth certificate.

extraordinaire [ɛkstr(a)ɔrdinɛːr], a. extraordinary. adv. -ment.

extra-scolaire [ɛkstraskɔlɛːr], a. activités extra-scolaires, out-of-school activities.

extravagance [ɛkstravagãːs], s.f. extravagance; absurdity.

extravag/ant [ɛkstravagã], a. extravagant. adv. -amment.

extrême [ɛkstrɛm]. 1. a. extreme; (a) farthest; (b) intense, excessive. 2. s.m. extreme limit. adv. -ment.

extrême-onction [ɛkstrɛmɔ̃ksjɔ̃], s.f. Ecc: extreme unction.

Extrême-Orient (l') [lɛkstrɛmɔrjã], s.m. the Far East.

extrémiste [ɛkstremist], a. & s. extremist.

extrémité [ɛkstremite], s.f. (a) extremity, end; tip; (b) extremity, extreme.

exubérance [ɛgzyberãːs], s.f. exuberance.

exubérant [ɛgzyberã], a. exuberant.

exult/er [ɛgzylte], v.i. to exult, rejoice. s.f. -ation.

ex-voto [ɛksvɔto], s.m.inv. ex-voto.

F

F, f [ɛf], *s.f.* (the letter) F, f.

fable [faːbl], *s.f.* (*a*) fable; (*b*) story, tale.

fabricant, -ante [fabrikã, -ãːt], *s.* maker, manufacturer.

fabrique [fabrik], *s.f.* **1. marque de f.**, trademark. **2.** factory, works.

fabri/quer [fabrike], *v.tr.* **1.** to manufacture; **qu'est-ce que vous fabriquez?** (i) what are you making? (ii) *F:* what are you up to? **2.** *-cation.*

†fabuleux [fabylø], *a.* fabulous.

façade [fasad], *s.f.* façade, front(age).

face [fas], *s.f.* **1.** face; **perdre la f.**, to lose face. **2.** head side (of coin); *Rec:* side (of record). **3. faire f. à qn, qch.**, to face s.o., sth.; to cope with sth.; **vue de f.**, front view. **4.** *prep.phr.* **f. à,** facing; **en f. de,** opposite.

facétie [fasesi], *s.f.* joke.

†facétieu/x [fasesjø], *a.* a facetious. *adv. -sement.*

fâche [ʃaʃe], *s.f.* **1.** sorry. **2.** angry.

fâcher [ʃaʃe], *v.tr.* **1.** to grieve. **2.** to anger.

   se fâcher, to get angry.

†fâcheux [ʃaʃø], *a.* troublesome, tiresome.

facile [fasil], *a.* **1.** easy. **2.** facile, ready, quick. *adv. -ment.*

facilité [fasilite], *s.f.* **1.** easiness; **avec f.**, with ease. **2.** aptitude, talent, facility.

faciliter [fasilite], *v.tr.* to facilitate; to make (sth.) easier.

façon [fasɔ̃], *s.f.* **1.** (*a*) making; workmanship; cut (of coat); **tailleur à f.**, bespoke tailor; (*b*) **cuir f. porc,** imitation pigskin. **2.** manner, way (of speaking, etc.); (*b*) **sans f.,** without ceremony; (*c*) **de cette f.,** in this way; **en aucune f.,** by no means. **3.** *conj. phr.* **de f. à,** so as to.

façonner [fasɔne], *v.tr.* to work, shape; to make (up) (dress).

facsimilé [faksimile], *s.m.* facsimile.

facteur [faktœːr], *s.m.* **1.** postman. **2.** *Mth:* factor.

factice [faktis], *a.* artificial, imitation; dummy (packet).

faction [faksjɔ̃], *s.f.* **1.** sentry-duty, guard. **2.** faction.

facture [faktyːr], *s.f.* invoice; bill.

†facultatif [fakyltatif], *a.* optional; **arrêt f.**, request stop.

faculté [fakylte], *s.f.* (*a*) option, right; (*b*) faculty; (*c*) *pl.* resources.

fade [fad], *a.* insipid, flavourless, tasteless.

fading [fediŋ], *s.m. Rad:* fading, fade-out.

fadeur [fadœːr], *s.f.* insipidity.

fagot [fago], *s.m.* faggot.

faible [fɛbl], *a.* **1.** *a.* (*a*) feeble, weak; (*b*) light; faint. **2.** *s.m.* weakness, failing. *adv. -ment.*

faiblesse [fɛbles], *s.f.* **1.** (*a*) feebleness, weakness; (*b*) smallness (of sum). **2.** failing.

faiblir [fɛbliːr], *v.i.* to grow weak.

faïence [fajãːs], *s.f.* crockery; earthenware.

failli [faji], *a.* bankrupt.

faillible [fajibl], *a.* fallible.

‡faillir [fajiːr], *v.i.* **1.** to fail. **2. j'ai failli manquer le train,** I nearly missed the train.

faillite [fajit], *s.f.* failure, insolvency; **faire f.**, to go bankrupt.

faim [fɛ̃], *s.f.* hunger; **avoir f.**, to be hungry; **manger à sa f.**, to eat one's fill.

fainéant, -ante [feneã, -ãːt], **1.** *a.* idle, lazy. **2.** *s.* idler.

‡faire [fɛːr], *v.tr.* **I.** to make. **1.** (*a*) **f. un chèque,** to write a cheque; **vêtements tout faits,** ready-made clothes; (*b*) **f. la guerre,** to wage war. **2.** (*a*) **f. sa fortune,** to make one's fortune; (*b*) **f. des provisions,** to lay in provisions; (*c*) *P:* **tu es fait, mon vieux!** you've had it, chum! **II.** to do. **1.** (*a*) **que f.?** what can I, we, do? **faire de l'hypertension,** to have high blood pressure; **c'est bien fait,** (i) it's well done; (ii) it serves you right. **2.** (*to perform, practise*) **f. son devoir,** to do one's duty; **toute réflexion faite,** all things considered; **f. du sport,** to go in for sport. **3. f. une promenade,** to go for (i) a walk, (ii) a drive. **4. combien cela fait-il?** how much does that come to? **5.** to matter; **si cela ne vous fait rien,** if you don't mind; **cela ne fait rien,** (i) it doesn't matter; (ii) never mind. **III. 1. f. la chambre,** to clean the bedroom. **2. il ne fait pas quarante ans,** he doesn't look forty. **3. f. l'imbécile,** to play the fool. **IV. 1. en faire:** **n'en faites rien,** don't do any such thing; **c'en est fait de lui,** it's all up with him. **2. y faire:** **qu'y f.?** how can it be helped? **V.** *impers.* **quel temps fait-il?** what's the weather like? **VI. 1. il ne fait que lire,** he does nothing but read. **2. je ne fais que d'arriver,** I've only just arrived. **VII.** (*with infin.*) **le soleil fait fondre la neige,** the sun makes the snow melt; **faites-le entrer,** show him in; **un bruit se fit entendre,** a noise was heard. **2.** (*a*) **se f. photographier,** to have one's photograph taken; (*b*) **se f. une robe,** to have a dress made. **3. f. qch. à qn,** to get s.o. to do sth.

   se faire. 1. (*a*) to develop, mature; **ce fromage se fera,** this cheese will ripen; (*b*) to become; **se f. soldat,** to become a soldier; (*c*) **se f. à qch,** to get used to, adapt oneself, to sth. **2.** *impers.* **il se fait tard,** it's getting late.

faire-part [fɛrpaːr], *s.m.inv.* f.-p. de naissance, décès, announcement of birth, death; f.-p. de mariage=wedding invitation.

faisan [fəzã], *s.* pheasant.

faisceau [fɛso], *s.m.* 1. bundle. 2. beam, searchlight; f. hertzien, radio beam; T.V.: f. cathodique explorateur, scanning electron beam; f. electronique, electron beam; f. de lumière, pencil of rays.

fait [fɛ], *s.m.* (*a*) act, deed; (*b*) fact; être au f. de la question, to know how things stand; en f., as a matter of fact; en f. de, as regards; f. occurrence.

fait-divers [fɛdivɛːr], *s.m.* news item; faits-divers, news in brief.

faite [fɛːt], *s.m.* 1. ridge (of roof). 2. top, summit.

faitout [fɛtu], *s.m.* stewpan.

falaise [falɛːz], *s.f.* cliff.

†fallacieux [falasjø], *a.* deceptive, misleading.

‡falloir [falwaːr], *v.impers.* 1. to be wanting, necessary; s'en f., to be lacking, wanting; tant s'en faut, far from it; peu s'en faut, very nearly; comme il faut, proper(ly). 2. to be necessary; il nous faut le voir, we must see him.

falsifi/er [falsifje], *v.tr.* to falsify; to tamper with (document). *s.f.* -cation.

†fameu/x [famø], *a.* 1. famous. 2. F: first-rate. *adv.* -sement.

†familial [familjal]. 1. *a.* family (life); *Com:* pot f., family-size jar. 2. *s.f.* *Aut:* familiale, seven-seater saloon, estate car.

familiariser (se) [səfamiljarize], *v.pr.* to make oneself familiar (with sth.); to get to know (sth.).

familiarité [familjarite], *s.f.* familiarity.

†famili/er [familje], *a.* 1. domestic. 2. familiar; expression familière, colloquialism. *adv.* -èrement.

famille [famiːj], *s.f.* family; household; en f., as a family party; dîner en f., to dine at home (informally).

famine [famin], *s.f.* famine, starvation.

fanatique [fanatik]. 1. *a.* fanatic(al). 2. *s.* fanatic.

fanatisme [fanatism], *s.m.* fanaticism.

faner (se) [səfane], *v.pr.* to wither, fade.

fanfare [fɑ̃faːr], *s.f.* 1. (*a*) flourish (of trumpets); (*b*) fanfare. 2. brass band.

fange [fɑ̃ːʒ], *s.f.* mud, filth.

fantaisie [fɑ̃tɛzi], *s.f.* 1. (*a*) imagination; (*b*) fantasia. 2. fancy, whim.

fantasque [fɑ̃task], *a.* odd, whimsical.

fantastique [fɑ̃tastik], *a.* fantastic; fanciful.

fantoche [fɑ̃tɔʃ], *s.m.* marionette, puppet; gouvernement f., puppet government.

fantôme [fɑ̃toːm], *s.m.* phantom, ghost; gouvernement f., shadow government.

faon [fɑ̃], *s.m.* Z: fawn.

farce [fars], *s.f.* 1. *Cu:* stuffing. 2. (*a*) *Th:* farce; (*b*) practical joke.

farceur, -euse [farsœːr, -øːz], *s.* practical joker.

farcir [farsiːr], *v.tr.* to stuff (poultry).

fard [faːr], *s.m.* make-up.

fardeau [fardo], *s.m.* burden, load.

farder (se) [səfarde], *v.pr.* to make up.

farine [farin], *s.f.* flour.

farouche [faruʃ], *a.* 1. fierce, savage. 2. (*a*) shy, timid; (*b*) unsociable.

fart [fart], *s.m.* wax (for skis).

farter [farte], *v.tr.* to wax (skis). *s.m.* -age.

fascicule [fasikyl], *s.m.* fascicule; part.

fasciner (se) [fasine], *v.tr.* to fascinate. *s.f.* -ation.

fascisme [faʃ(s)ism], *s.m.* fascism.

fasciste [faʃ(s)ist], *s.m.* & *f.* fascist.

faste [fast], *s.m.* ostentation, display.

†fastidieu/x [fastidjø], *a.* dull, tedious. *adv.* -sement.

†fatal [fatal], *a.* 1. fatal; mortal. 2. fated, inevitable. *adv.* -ement.

fatalisme [fatalism], *s.m.* fatalism.

fataliste [fatalist], *s.* fatalist.

fatalité [fatalite], *s.f.* 1. fate, fatality. 2. mischance, calamity. 3. death, casualty.

fatigant [fatigɑ̃], *a.* 1. tiring, fatiguing. 2. tiresome, tedious.

fatigue [fatig], *s.f.* (*a*) fatigue, weariness; (*b*) (metal) fatigue.

fatiguer [fatige]. 1. *v.tr.* (*a*) to tire (s.o.); (*b*) to overdrive (machine). 2. *v.i.* (of engine, etc.) to labour. se fatiguer, to get tired.

fatuité [fatɥite], *s.f.* self-satisfaction.

faubourg [fobuːr], *s.m.* suburb.

faucher [foʃe], *v.tr.* (*a*) to mow, cut, reap (field); (*b*) P: to steal, pinch (sth.).

faucheur, -euse [foʃœːr, -øːz], *s.* 1. mower, reaper. 2. *s.f.* faucheuse, mowing-machine.

faucille [fosiːj], *s.f.* sickle.

faucon [fokɔ̃], *s.m.* falcon, hawk.

faufiler (se) [səfofile], *v.pr.* to thread one's way; to slip, sneak (in, out, of a place).

faune [foːn], *s.f.* fauna, animal life.

fauss/er [fose], *v.tr.* (*a*) to falsify; to alter (facts); f. parole, to break one's word; f. compagnie (to a lock). *s.m.* -aire, forger.

fausseté [foste], *s.f.* 1. falseness, falsity. 2. falsehood, untruth.

faute [foːt], *s.f.* 1. lack, want; faire f., to be lacking; sans f., without fail; f. d'argent, for lack of money; f. de mieux, for want of something better. 2. (*a*) fault, mistake; f. d'orthographe, spelling mistake; f. d'impression, misprint; (*b*) transgression, offence; (*c*) *Sp:* foul; (*at tennis*) fault.

fauteuil [fotœːj], *s.m.* armchair; f. d'orchestre, orchestra stall; *Jur:* f. électrique, electric chair.

†**fautif** [fotif], *a*. 1. faulty, incorrect. 2. at fault.

fauve [fo:v]. 1. *a*. fawn-coloured; tawny. 2. *s.m.* **les** (grands) **fauves**, big game.

fauvette [fovɛt], *s.f.* warbler.

†**faux**[1] [fo], *a*. false. 1. untrue. 2. not genuine; **fausse monnaie**, counterfeit coin(age); **fausse clef**, skeleton key; **fausses côtes**, floating ribs; **f. bonhomme**, shifty customer. 3. wrong, mistaken; **fausse date**, wrong date; **faire un f. pas**, to blunder; *adv.* **chanter f.**, to sing out of tune; *adv.phr.* **à f.**, wrongly; (*of wheel*) **tourner à f.**, to run out of true. *adv.* **-sement**.

faux[2], *s.f.* scythe.

faux-filet [fofilɛ], *s.m. Cu:* sirloin. *pl. faux-filets.*

faux-monnayeur [fomonɛjœːr], *s.m.* counterfeiter. *pl. faux-monnayeurs.*

faveur [favœːr], *s.f.* favour; billet de f., complimentary ticket.

favorable [favɔrabl], *a*. favourable. *adv.* **-ment**.

†**favori, -ite** [favɔri, -it]. 1. *a. & s.* favourite. 2. *s.m.pl.* (side-)whiskers.

favoriser [favɔrize], *v.tr.* to favour.

fécond [fekɔ̃], *a*. prolific, fruitful, fertile.

fécondité [fekɔ̃dite], *s.f.* 1. fruitfulness. 2. fertility.

†**fédéral** [federal], *a*. federal. *s.m.* **-isme**. *s.* **-iste**.

fédération [federasjɔ̃], *s.f.* federation.

fée [fe], *s.f.* fairy.

feeder [fidœːr], *s.m.* (gas) pipeline.

†**feindre** [fɛ̃:dr], *v.tr.* to feign, sham; to pretend. *s.* **-te**.

fêler [fele], *v.tr.* to crack.

félicitations [felisitasjɔ̃], *s.f.pl.* congratulations.

félicité [felisite], *s.f.* bliss, happiness.

féliciter [felisite], *v.tr.* to congratulate.

félin [felɛ̃], *a.* feline.

fêlure [felyːr], *s.f.* crack; split.

femelle [fəmɛl], *s.f. & a.* female (animal).

féminin [feminɛ̃], *a.* feminine; **le sexe f.**, the female sex; *s.m.* feminine gender.

femme [fam], *s.f.* 1. woman; **f. médecin**, woman doctor. 2. wife. 3. **f. de chambre**, housemaid; chamber-maid; *Nau:* stewardess, **f. de ménage**, charwoman.

fémur [femyːr], *s.m. Anat:* femur.

fendre [fɑ̃:dr], *v.tr.* to split.

fenêtre [f(ə)nɛtr], *s.f.* window.

fente [fɑ̃t], *s.f.* (*a*) crack, crevice; (*b*) slot.

†**féodal** [feɔdal], *a.* feudal.

fer [fɛːr], *s.m.* iron; **f. forgé**, wrought iron; **fil de f.**, wire; **f. à repasser**, (laundry) iron; **f. à cheval**, horseshoe.

fer-blanc [fɛrblɑ̃], *s.m.* tin(plate).

férié [ferje], *a.* **jour f.**, (public) holiday.

ferme[1] [fɛrm]. 1. *a.* firm, steady. 2. *adv.* firmly; hard; **tenir f.**, to stand fast. *adv.* **-ment**.

ferme[2], *s.f.* farm.

fermé [fɛrme], *a.* 1. closed. 2. inscrutable.

ferment/er [fɛrmɑ̃te], *v.i.* to ferment. *s.f.* **-ation**.

fermer [fɛrme]. 1. *v.tr.* (*a*) to close, shut; **f. à clef**, to lock (door); *P:* **ferme-la!** shut up! (*b*) **f. la marche**, to bring up the rear. 2. *v.i.* to close, shut. **se fermer**, to close, shut.

fermeté [fɛrməte], *s.f.* firmness.

fermeture [fɛrmətyːr], *s.f.* closing, shutting. *R.t.m:* **f. éclair**, zip fastener.

fermier [fɛrmje], *s.m.* farmer; (*f. -ière* [fɛrmjɛːr]) (woman) farmer, farmer's wife.

féroce [ferɔs], *a.* ferocious, savage. *adv.* **-ement**. *s.f.* **-ité**, ferocity.

ferraille [fɛrɑːj], *s.f.* scrap iron.

ferré [fɛre], *a.* mounted with iron; **souliers ferrés**, hobnailed shoes; *Rail:* **voie ferrée**, permanent way; railway line.

ferrer [fɛre], *v.tr.* to shoe (a horse).

ferroviaire [fɛrɔvjɛːr], *a.* **trafic f.**, railway, *U.S:* railroad, traffic.

†**ferrugineux** [fɛrryʒinø], *a.* ferruginous.

ferry-boat [feribot], *s.m.* train ferry. *pl. ferry-boats.*

fertile [fɛrtil], *a.* fertile.

fertilis/er [fɛrtilize], *v.tr.* to fertilize. *s.f.* **-ation**.

fertilité [fɛrtilite], *s.f.* fertility.

fervent, -ente [fɛrvɑ̃, -ɑ̃ːt]. 1. *a.* fervent; enthusiastic. 2. *s.* enthusiast.

ferveur [fɛrvœːr], *s.f.* fervour; enthusiasm; **avec f.**, earnestly; enthusiastically.

fesser [fese], *v.tr. F:* to spank (s.o.).

festin [fɛstɛ̃], *s.m.* feast, banquet.

fête [fɛːt], *s.f.* 1. feast, festival; **f. légale**, public holiday; **f. (de qn)**, (s.o.'s) name-day; saint's day; **f. mobile**, movable feast. 2. fête; fair; *Av:* **f. d'aviation**, air display, show. 3. festivity; **air de f.**, festive air; **troubler la f.**, to spoil the party.

fête-Dieu [fɛtdjø], *s.f. Ecc:* Corpus Christi.

fêter [fɛte], *v.tr.* to celebrate (an event); to entertain (s.o.).

fétiche [fetiʃ], *s.m.* fetish; mascot.

fétide [fetid], *a.* fetid, stinking.

†**feu**[1] [fø], *s.m.* 1. (*a*) fire; light (for pipe); visage en feu, flushed face; (*b*) heat, ardour. 2. faire du feu, to light a fire; **f. d'artifice**, fireworks. 3. **armes à feu**, firearms; **faire feu**, to fire. 4. light; *Av:* **f. de balisage**, boundary light; *Av:* **feux de bord**, *Nau:* **feux de route**, navigation lights; **tous feux éteints**, without lights; *Aut:* **feux de position, de stationnement**, side, parking, lights; **f. arrière**, rear light; **feux de circulation**, *F:* **f. rouge**, traffic lights; *F:* **donner le f. vert à qn**, to give s.o. the green light, the go-ahead.

feu², *a.* late, deceased.

feuillage [fœjɑːʒ], *s.m.* foliage.

feuille [fœːj], *s.f.* 1. leaf. 2. sheet (of paper).

feuilleter [fœjte], *v.tr.* to flick over the pages of (book).

feuilleton [fœjtɔ̃], *s.m.* serial story.

feutre [føːtr], *s.m.* 1. felt. 2. felt hat.

fève [fɛːv], *s.f.* broad bean.

février [fevrie], *s.m.* February.

fiançailles [fjɑ̃saːj], *s.f.pl.* engagement.

fiancé, -ée [fjɑ̃se], *s.* fiancé(e).

fiancer (se) [safjɑ̃se], *v.pr.* to become engaged.

fiasco [fjasko], *s.m.inv.* fiasco.

fibre [fibr], *s.f.* fibre.

†**fibreux** [fibrø], *a.* fibrous, stringy.

ficeler [fisle], *v.tr.* to tie up.

ficelle [fisɛl], *s.f.* string, twine.

fiche [fiʃ], *s.f.* (*a*) slip (of paper); (hotel) registration form; *Ind:* f. de contrôle, docket; (*b*) card, ticket; (*c*) index card.

ficher [fiʃe], *v.tr.* 1. to drive in (stake). 2. *P:* (*p.p.* **fichu**; *the inf. is usu.* **fiche**) (*a*) f. qn à la porte, to throw s.o. out; (*b*) **fichez-moi la paix!** shut up!

fichier [fiʃje], *s.m.* card-index.

†**fictif** [fiktif], *a.* fictitious, imaginary.

fiction [fiksjɔ̃], *s.f.* fiction; invention.

fidèle [fidɛl], *a.* faithful, loyal; **copie f.,** exact copy; *Ecc:* **les fidèles,** (i) the faithful; (ii) the congregation. *adv.* **-ment.**

fidélité [fidelite], *s.f.* fidelity; allegiance.

†**fier/er¹** [fje:r], *a.* 1. proud. 2. haughty. *adv.* **-èrement.**

fier² (se) [safje], *v.pr.* to trust; **fiez-vous à moi,** leave it to me.

fierté [fjɛrte], *s.f.* pride.

fièvre [fjɛːvr], *s.f.* fever; **avoir la f.,** to have a temperature.

†**fiévreux/euse** [fjevrø], *a.* feverish. *adv.* **-eusement.**

‡**figer** [fiʒe], *v.tr.* to coagulate; congeal; **figé sur place,** rooted to the spot.
   se figer, to coagulate; to clot; **sourire figé,** set smile.

figue [fig], *s.f.* fig; **f. de Barbarie,** prickly pear.

figuier [figje], *s.m.* fig-tree.

†**figurat/if** [figyratif], *a.* figurative. *adv.* **-ivement.**

figure [figyːr], *s.f.* 1. figure, form. 2. (*a*) face, countenance; (*b*) appearance.

figuré [figyre], *a.* figurative.

figurer [figyre], *v.tr.* to represent. *v.i.* to appear, figure.
   se figurer, to imagine.

fil [fil], *s.m.* 1. (*a*) thread; (*b*) wire. 2. grain (of wood). 3. **fil de l'eau,** current. 4. (cutting) edge.

filament [filamɑ̃], *s.m.* filament; fibre.

file [fil], *s.f.* file; line.

filer [file]. I. *v.tr.* 1. to spin. 2. to shadow. II. *v.i.* to slip by; *F:* to make tracks, to clear off; *F:* **filez!** scram! **le temps file,** time flies.

filet¹ [filɛ], *s.m.* 1. small thread; thin streak. 2. *Cu:* fillet.

filet², *s.m.* net; f. de pêche, fishing net; f. (à provisions), string bag; *Rail:* f. (à bagages), luggage rack.

filial, -ale [filjal]. 1. *a.* filial. 2. *s.f.* filiale, branch; subsidiary (company).

filigrane [filigran], *s.m.* 1. filigree (work). 2. watermark.

fille [fiːj], *s.f.* 1. daughter. 2. girl; **jeune f.,** girl; **nom de jeune f.,** maiden name; **vieille f.,** old maid, spinster.

fillette [fijɛt], *s.f.* little girl.

filleul, -eule [fijœl], *s.* godchild; godson, god-daughter.

film [film], *s.m.* film; film fixe (d'enseignement), film strip.

filmer [filme], *v.tr.* to film (scene).

filmothèque [filmɔtɛk], *s.f.* film library.

filon [filɔ̃], *s.m.* vein, seam, lode.

filou [filu], *s.m.* pickpocket; thief; swindler.

filtre [filtr], *s.m.* filter, percolator; *a.* **bout f.,** filter tip (of cigarette).

filtrer [filtre]. 1. *v.tr.* to filter, strain. 2. *v.i. & pr.* to filter, percolate.

fin¹ [fɛ̃], *s.f.* 1. end, conclusion; expiration (of contract); 1. **prématurée,** untimely death; **f. de semaine,** week-end. 2. aim, object; **la f. justifie les moyens,** the end justifies the means.

fin², fine [fɛ̃, fin], *a.* 1. **au f. fond de la campagne,** in the depths of the country. 2. (*a*) fine, choice; *s.f.* **une fine,** a liqueur brandy; (*b*) subtle, shrewd; **avoir l'oreille fine,** to be quick of hearing; (*c*) fine, small, slender; *adv.* **café moulu f.,** finely ground coffee. *adv.* **-ment.**

†**final, -ale** [final]. 1. *a.* final. 2. *s.f. Sp:* finale, final. *adv.* **-ement.**

finaliste [finalist], *s.m. & f. Sp:* finalist.

finance [finɑ̃ːs], *s.f.* finance.

†**financer** [finɑ̃se], *v.tr.* to finance.

†**financier** [finɑ̃sje]. 1. *a.* financial. 2. *s.m.* financier.

finesse [finɛs], *s.f.* 1. fineness, good quality; delicacy. 2. (*a*) shrewdness; (*b*) cunning. 3. fineness (of dust).

fini [fini], *a.* 1. finished, ended; *F:* **il est f.,** he's done for. 2. (*a*) accomplished (actor, etc.); (*b*) *s.m.* finish. 3. finite (space, tense).

finir [finir]. *v.tr.* to finish, end. 2. *v.i.* to come to an end, to finish; **en f. avec qch.,** to have done with sth.

finish [finiʃ], *s.m. Sp:* finish.

finlandais, -aise [fɛ̃lɑ̃dɛ, -ɛːz], **finnois, -oise** [finwa, -waːz]. 1. *a.* Finnish. 2. *s.* Finn. *s.m. Ling:* Finnish.

firmament [firmamɑ̃], *s.m.* firmament.

fisc (le) [ləfisk], *s.m.* (*a*) the Treasury, the Exchequer; (*b*) the Inland Revenue.

†**fiscal** [fiskal], *a.* fiscal.

fission [fisjɔ̃], *s.f.* splitting, fission; f. de l'atome, nuclear fission.

fissure [fis(s)y:r], *s.f.* fissure, cleft.

fixe [fiks], *a.* 1. fixed, firm. 2. fixed, settled; *P.N*: arrêt f., all buses stop here. *adv. -ement. s.f. -ité.*

fixer [fikse], *v.tr.* 1. to fix; to make firm, fast; to stare at. 2. to fix, determine; to assess (damages).

flacon [flakɔ̃], *s.m.* bottle; flask.

flagrant [flagrɑ̃], *a.* flagrant, glaring; pris en f. délit, caught in the act.

flair [flɛːr], *s.m.* (a) (of dog) sense of smell; (b) flair.

flairer [flɛre], *v.tr.* (a) to scent, smell (out); (b) to smell.

flamand, -ande [flamɑ̃, ũːd]. 1. *a.* Flemish. 2. *s.* Fleming. 3. *s.m. Ling:* Flemish.

flamant [flamɑ̃], *s.m.* flamingo.

flambant [flɑ̃bɑ̃], *a.* blazing, flaming; *adv.* f. neuf, brand-new.

flambeau [flɑ̃bo], *s.m.* torch.

flamber [flɑ̃be]. 1. *v.i.* to flame, blaze. 2. *v.tr.* to singe.

flamboyant [flɑ̃bwajɑ̃], *a.* 1. flaming; fiery; *A. & A:* gothique f., late Gothic. 2. flamboyant.

‡flamboyer [flɑ̃bwaje], *v.i.* to blaze.

flamme [flɑ̃m], *s.f.* flame.

flan [flɑ̃], *s.m. Cu:* baked egg custard.

flanc [flɑ̃], *s.m.* flank, side.

flanelle [flanɛl], *s.f.* flannel; f. de coton, flannelette.

flân/er [flane], *v.i.* to stroll; to hang about, around. *s.f. -erie, s. -eur, -euse.*

flanquer [flɑ̃ke], *v.tr. F:* to throw, chuck; f. qn à la porte, to chuck s.o. out.

flaque [flak], *s.f.* 1. puddle, pool. 2. f. de neige, patch of snow.

flash [flaʃ], *s.m.F:* 1. *Phot:* flash. 2. news flash. *pl. flashes.*

flatt/er [flate], *v.tr.* 1. to stroke, caress. 2. to delight. 3. to flatter. 4. to delude.
     se flatter, to flatter oneself, delude oneself. *s.f. -erie. a. & s. -eur, -euse.*

flatulence [flatylɑ̃ːs], *s.f.* flatulence, *F:* wind.

†fléau [fleo], *s.m.* plague, pest, curse, calamity.

flèche [flɛʃ], *s.f.* 1. arrow. 2. spire.

fléch/ir [fleʃiːr]. 1. *v.tr.* (a) to bend; (b) to move to pity. 2. *v.i.* to give way. *s.m. -issement.*

flegmatique [flɛgmatik], *a.* phlegmatic.

flegme [flɛgm], *s.m.* phlegm.

flétan [fletɑ̃], *s.m.* halibut.

flétrir [fletriːr], *v.tr.* to fade; to wither.

fleur [flœːr], *s.f.* 1. flower; blossom, bloom. 2. à f. d'eau, at water-level; yeux à f. de tête, prominent eyes. *s. -iste,* florist.

fleurir [flœriːr], *v.i.* (a) to flower, bloom; (b) to flourish, prosper.

fleuve [flœːv], *s.m.* (large) river.

flexib/le [flɛksibl], *a.* flexible, pliable. *a. -ilité.*

flic [flik], *s.m. P:* policeman, cop.

flirter [flœrte], *v.i.* to flirt.

flocon [flokɔ̃], *s.m.* flake.

‡floconneux [flokonø], *a.* fleecy, fluffy.

†floral [floral], *a.* floral.

flore [floːr], *s.f.* flora.

florissant [florisɑ̃], *a.* flourishing.

flot [flo], *s.m.* 1. (a) wave; (b) flood (of tears); (c) flots, in torrents, in crowds. 2. à f., afloat.

flotte [flot], *s.f.* fleet.

flotter [flote], *v.i.* (a) to float; (b) to waver.

flottille [flotiːj], *s.f.* flotilla.

flou [flu], *a.* woolly (outline); hazy.

fluctu/er [flyktɥe], *v.i.* to fluctuate. *s.f. -ation.*

fluide [flɥid], *a. & s.m.* fluid.

flûte [flyːt], *s.f.* 1. flute. 2. long thin loaf (of bread).

flux [fly], *s.m.* flow; flux.

fluxion [flyksjɔ̃], *s.f.* inflammation.

foi [fwa], *s.f.* faith; ma f.! (yes) indeed!

foie [fwa], *s.m.* liver.

foin [fwɛ̃], *s.m.* hay.

foire [fwaːr], *s.f.* fair.

fois [fwa], *s.f.* time, occasion; une f., once; deux f., twice; à la f., at one and the same time.

foisonner [fwazone], *v.i.* to abound (de, in).

folie [fɔli], *s.f.* 1. madness. 2. folly; piece of folly.

follement [fɔlmɑ̃], *adv.* 1. madly; foolishly, unwisely. 2. extravagantly.

fomenter [fɔmɑ̃te], *v.tr.* to foment; to stir up (trouble).

foncé [fɔ̃se], *a.* dark (colour).

†foncer [fɔ̃se], *v.i.* to rush, swoop down.

†foncier [fɔ̃sje], *a.* 1. propriété foncière, real estate; impôt f., land tax. 2. fundamental.

fonction [fɔ̃ksjɔ̃], *s.f.* function; office; faire f. de, to act as.

fonctionnaire [fɔ̃ksjɔnɛːr], *s.m.* civil servant.

fonctionn/er [fɔ̃ksjɔne], *v.i.* 1. to function. 2. to act, work. *s.m. -ement.*

fond [fɔ̃], *s.m.* 1. bottom; *adv.phr.* à f., thoroughly. 2. foundation; au f., fundamentally. 3. back, far end; background (of picture).

†fondamental [fɔ̃damɑ̃tal], *a.* fundamental; basic; primary.

fondé [fɔ̃de], *a.* founded, justified.

fond/er [fɔ̃de], *v.tr.* to found, set up (business); to lay the foundations of (building); to base, build (one's hopes) (sur, on). *s.f. -ation. s.m. -ement. s. -ateur, -atrice,* founder.

fondre [fɔ̃dr]. (a) *v.tr.* to smelt (ore); (b) *v.tr. & i.* to melt; to dissolve.

fondrière [fɔ̃drjɛːr], *s.f.* (a) bog, quagmire; (b) muddy hole; *Fr.C:* f. de mousse, muskeg.

fonds [fɔ̃], *s.m.* 1. (*a*) f. de commerce, business, capital; (*b*) stock (in-trade). 2. (*a*) funds; ready money; (*b*) *pl. Fin:* stocks, securities.

fontaine [fɔ̃tɛn], *s.f.* 1. spring, source, well. 2. fountain.

fonte [fɔ̃t], *s.f.* 1. (*a*) melting (of snow); (*b*) smelting (of ore); (*c*) casting. 2. cast iron.

fonts [fɔ̃], *s.m.pl. Ecc:* font.

football [futbol], *s.m.* (association) football, *F:* soccer. *s.m.* -eur.

forage [fɔraːʒ], *s.m.* drilling, boring (of well).

forain [fɔrɛ̃], *a.* marchand f., *s.* forain stall keeper (at fair, etc.); fête foraine, fun fair.

forçat [fɔrsa], *s.m.* convict.

force [fɔrs], *s.f.* 1. (*a*) strength, force; être à bout de forces, to be exhausted; (*b*) force, violence; compulsion; à toute f., at all costs. 2. (*a*) force, power; f. motrice, motive power; (*b*) les forces armées, the armed forces. 3. *a.inv.* many. 4. à f. de, by dint of.

forcément [fɔrsemɑ̃], *adv.* inevitably.

forcené [fɔrsəne], *a.* frantic, frenzied, mad.

‡**forcer** [fɔrse], *v.tr.* to force. 1. to compel. 2. (*a*) to break open; to force (lock); (*o*) to str:in (heart, etc.); to force (flowers).

forer [fɔre], *v.tr.* to drill, bore.

foret [fɔrɛ], *s.m. Tls:* drill.

forêt [fɔrɛ], *s.f.* forest.

forfait[1] [fɔrfɛ], *s.m.* crime, outrage.

forfait[2], *s.m.* contract; acheter à f., to buy outright.

forfait[3], *s.m. Sp:* déclarer f. (pour un cheval), to scratch (a horse).

forge [fɔrʒ], *s.f.* 1. smithy, forge. 2. *pl.* ironworks.

‡**forger** [fɔrʒe], *v.tr.* to forge.

forgeron [fɔrʒərɔ̃], *s.m.* (black)smith.

formaliser [fɔrmalize], *a.* formal, stiff.

formalité [fɔrmalite], *s.f.* formality; ceremony.

format [fɔrma], *s.m.* format; size.

formation [fɔrmasjɔ̃], *s.f.* formation.

forme [fɔrm], *s.f.* 1. form, shape. 2. form; method of procedure; pour la f., for form's sake. 3. last; mould; chapeau haut de f., top hat.

†**formel** [fɔrmɛl], *a.* formal, strict; explicit; categorical. *adv.* -lement.

former [fɔrme], *v.tr.* to form.

formidable [fɔrmidabl], *a.* (*a*) fearsome, formidable; (*b*) *F:* wonderful, terrific.

formule [fɔrmyl], *s.f.* 1. formula. 2. (printed) form.

formuler [fɔrmyle], *v.tr.* to formulate.

fort [fɔːr]. I. *a.* 1. strong; forte mer, heavy sea; d'une voix forte, in a loud voice; c'est plus f. que moi! I can't help it! 2. large; stout. II. *adv.* 1. strongly. 2. very; much. III. *s.m.* 1. strong point; le f. de l'hiver, the depth of

winter. 2. fort, stronghold. *adv.* -ement. *s.f.* -eresse, fortress.

fortification, *s.f.* fortification.

fortifi/er [fɔrtifje], *v.tr.* to strengthen; to fortify (town); to confirm (suspicions). *s.f.* -cation. *s.m.* -ant, tonic.

fortuit [fɔrtɥi], *a.* fortuitous; accidental; chance (meeting). *adv.* -ement.

fortune [fɔrtyn], *s.f.* 1. fortune, chance, luck. 2. fortune, riches.

fosse [fos], *s.f.* 1. pit, hole; *Aut:* inspection pit. 2. grave.

fossé [fose], *s.m.* ditch, trench.

fossette [fosɛt], *s.f.* dimple.

fossile [fosil], *a.* & *s.m.* fossil.

fossoyeur [foswajœːr], *s.m.* grave-digger.

†**fou, folle** [fu, fɔl]. 1. *a.* (*a*) mad, insane; (*b*) foolish; (*c*) prodigious; succès fou, tremendous success. 2. *s.* (*a*) lunatic; (*b*) fool. 3. *s.m. Chess:* bishop.

foudre [fudr], *s.f.* thunderbolt, lightning.

‡**foudro/yer** [fudrwaje], *v.tr* to strike down; to crush; to overwhelm. *s.m.* -iement.

fouet [fwɛ], *s.m.* whip, lash.

fouetter [fwɛte], *v.tr.* to whip; to flog; to beat.

fougère [fuʒɛːr], *s.f.* fern; bracken.

†**fougueux** [fugø], *a.* spirited; impetuous.

fouille [fuːj], *s.f.* 1. *usu.pl.* excavation(s). 2. searching (of a suspect).

fouiller [fuje]. 1. *v.tr.* (*a*) to dig, excavate; (*b*) to search. 2. *v.i.* to rummage.

fouine [fwin], *s.f.* (stone-)marten.

foule [ful], *s.f.* crowd.

foul/er [fule], *v.tr.* 1. to crush; to trample. 2. to sprain, wrench. *s.f.* -ure, sprain.

four [fuːr], *s.m.* 1. (*a*) oven; (*b*) *Cu:* petits fours, petits fours. 2. kiln, furnace. 3. *F: Th:* faire f., to be a flop.

fourche [furʃ], *s.f.* (pitch)fork; (garden) fork.

fourcher [furʃe], *v.i.* to fork, branch, divide.

fourchette [furʃɛt], *s.f.* (table) fork.

fourchu [furʃy], *a.* forked; pied f., cloven hoof.

fourgon [furgɔ̃], *s.m.* van, wag(g)on.

fourmi [furmi], *s.f.* ant; avoir des fourmis, to have pins and needles.

fourmilière [furmiljɛːr], *s.f.* ant-hill.

fourmill/er [furmije], *v.i.* 1. to swarm. 2. le pied me fourmille, I've got pins and needles in my foot. *s.m.* -ement.

fourneau [furno], *s.m.* (*a*) furnace; bowl (of pipe); (*b*) stove, cooker; (*c*) haut f., blast furnace.

fourn/ir [furniːr], *v.tr.* to supply, furnish, provide; magasin bien fourni, well-stocked shop. *s.* -isseur, -isseuse, supplier.

fourniture [furnityːr], *s.f.* 1. supplying, providing. 2. *pl.* supplies.

fourré [fure], *s.m.* thicket.

fourreau [furo], *s.m.* (*a*) sheath, cover, case; *Cl:* sheath (dress); (*b*) *E:* sleeve.

fourr/er [fure], *v.tr.* **1.** to cover, line with fur. **2.** F: to stuff, cram; f. son nez partout, to poke one's nose into everything. *s.m.* -eur, furrier.

fourrure [furyr], *s.f.* **1.** fur, skin; coat (of animal). **2.** *Aut:* f. de frein, brake lining.

‡fourvoyer [furvwaje], *v.tr.* to mislead. se fourvoyer, to lose one's way, to go astray.

fox [foks], *s.m.* fox terrier.

foyer [fwaje], *s.m.* **1.** fire(place), hearth, grate. **2.** source of heat; focus (of infection). **3.** *(a)* hearth, home; *(b) Th:* f. du public, foyer. **4.** focus; verres à double f., bifocal lenses.

fracas [fraka], *s.m.* din; crash.

fraction [fraksjɔ̃], *s.f.* fraction.

fracture [fraktyr], *s.f.* **1.** breaking open. **2.** fracture.

fracturer [fraktyre], *v.tr.* **1.** to break open. **2.** to fracture.

fragil/e [fraʒil], *a.* **1.** fragile; brittle. **2.** frail. *s.f.* -ité.

fragment [fragmɑ̃], *s.m.* fragment.

†fr/ais¹ [frɛ], *a.* fresh; *(a)* cool; *(b)* new, recent. *adv.* -aîchement; *s.f.* -aîcheur, coolness; freshness.

frais², *sm.pl.* expenses, cost.

fraise [frɛːz], *s.f.* strawberry.

fraisier [frɛzje], *s.m.* strawberry plant.

framboise [frɑ̃bwaz], *s.f.* raspberry.

framboisier [frɑ̃bwazje], *s.m.* raspberry cane.

franc¹ [frɑ̃], *s.m.* franc.

†fran/c², *a.* **1.** free. **2.** *(a)* frank; open; *(b)* real, downright. *adv.* -chement.

français, -aise [frɑ̃sɛ, -ɛːz], *a.* **1.** French. **2.** *s.* Frenchman, -woman; les F., the French. **3.** *s.m. Ling:* French.

franchir [frɑ̃ʃir], *v.tr.* *(a)* to jump (over); to get over; *(b)* to cross; f. le mur du son, to break (through) the sound barrier.

franchise [frɑ̃ʃiːz], *s.f.* **1.** freedom; (diplomatic) immunity. **2.** exemption; en f. = O.H.M.S. **3.** frankness.

franc-maçon [frɑ̃masɔ̃], *s.m.* freemason. *pl.* francs-maçons.

franc-maçonnerie [frɑ̃masɔnri], *s.f.* freemasonry.

franco [frɑ̃ko], *adv.* free, carriage-free.

franc-parler [frɑ̃parle], *s.m.* plain speaking.

frange [frɑ̃ːʒ], *s.f.* fringe.

frapper [frape], *v.tr.* **1.** *(a)* to strike, hit; on frappe, there's a knock; f. du pied, to stamp; *(b)* to strike (coin). **2.** to chill (wine); servir frappé, to be served chilled.

†fraternel [fraternel], *a.* fraternal. *adv.* -lement.

fraternis/er [fraternize], *v.i.* to fraternize. *s.f.* -ation.

fraternité [fraternite], *s.f.* fraternity, brotherhood.

fraude [froːd], *s.f.* **1.** fraud, deception; smuggling. **2.** fraudulence, deceit; false pretences.

fraud/er [frode]. **1.** *v.tr.* to defraud, cheat, swindle. **2.** *v.i.* to cheat. *s.* -eur, -euse.

†frauduleu/x [frodylø], *a.* fraudulent. *adv.* -sement.

‡frayer [freje], *v.tr.* to clear (path, way).

frayeur [frɛjœːr], *s.f.* fright; fear, dread.

fredonner [frədɔne], *v.tr.* to hum (tune).

frégate [fregat], *s.f.* frigate; capitaine de f., commander.

frein [frɛ̃], *s.m.* **1.** (horse's) bit; mettre un f. à, to curb. **2.** brake; f. à disque, disc brake.

freiner [frene], *v.tr.* to brake; to slow down (production).

frêle [frɛːl], *a.* frail, weak.

frelon [frəlɔ̃], *s.m.* hornet.

frém/ir [fremir], *v.i.* **1.** to quiver. **2.** to tremble, shake, shudder. *s.m.* -issement.

frêne [frɛːn], *s.m.* ash(-tree).

frénésie [frenezi], *s.f.* frenzy, madness.

frénétique [frenetik], *a.* frantic, frenzied. *adv.* -ment.

fréqu/ent [frekɑ̃], *a.* frequent. *adv.* -emment. *s.f.* -ence.

fréquenter [frekɑ̃te], *v.tr.* *(a)* to frequent; to attend (school); *(b)* to associate with.

frère [frɛːr], *s.m.* brother.

fresque [frɛsk], *s.f.* fresco.

fret [frɛ], *s.m.* **1.** freightage. **2.** chartering. **3.** cargo; freight.

friable [friabl], *a.* friable, crumbly.

friand [friɑ̃], *a.* *(a)* fond (of delicacies); *(b)* morceau f., tasty morsel. *s.f.* -ise.

friche [friʃ], *s.f.* waste, fallow, land.

fricot [friko], *s.m.* made-up dish; stew.

friction [friksjɔ̃], *s.f.* friction.

frictionner [friksjɔne], *v.tr.* to rub (down); to massage.

Frigidaire [friʒideːr], *Pr.n.m. R.t.m:* refrigerator, Frigidaire.

frigo [frigo], *s.m.* F: fridge, frig, refrigerator.

frigorifi/er [frigɔrifje], *v.tr.* to refrigerate; to chill. *s.f.* -cation. *a.* -que.

frileusement [friløzmɑ̃], *adv.* cosily, snugly; huddled up.

†frileux [frilø], *a.* sensitive to cold; chilly.

frimas [frima], *s.m.* (hoar-)frost; rime.

friper [fripe], *v.tr.* to crumple (dress).

frip/erie [fripri], *s.f.* **(a)** secondhand clothes; *(b)* rubbish, frippery. *s.* -ier, -ière, secondhand clothes dealer.

fripon [fripɔ̃], *s.m.* swindler; rascal.

‡frire [friːr], *v.tr.* & *i.* to fry.

frise [friːz], *s.f. A. & A:* frieze.

friser [frize], *v.tr.* **1.** to curl, wave. **2.** to touch, skim. f. la cinquantaine, to be nearly fifty.

frisson [fris5], s.m. (a) shiver; (b) shudder (c) thrill.

frissonn/er [frisone], v.i. (a) to shiver; (b) to be thrilled; (c) to quiver. s.m. -ement.

frit, frite [fri, frit], a. fried; **pommes de terre frites,** s.f.pl. **frites,** chips, French fried potatoes.

frivol(e) [frivol], a. frivolous, shallow. s.f. -ité.

froid [frwa]. I. a 1. cold; **il fait f.,** it is cold; **j'ai f.,** I am cold. 2. cold, unresponsive; frigid. II. s.m. cold; coldness. adv. -ement. s.f. -eur, coldness.

froiss/er [frwase], v.tr. 1. to crumple. 2. to give offence to (s.o.), to hurt (s.o.'s) feelings. s.m. -ement.
se froisser, to take offence.

frôl/er [frole], v.tr. to touch lightly; to brush, rub. s.m. -ement.

fromage [fromaːʒ], s.m. cheese.

froment [fromɑ̃], s.m. wheat.

‡**fronc/er** [frɔ̃se], v.tr. 1. **f. les sourcils,** to knit one's brows; to frown. 2. to gather (material). s.m. -ement.

fronde [frɔ̃ːd], s.f. (a) sling; (b) (toy) catapult.

front [frɔ̃], s.m. 1. forehead. 2. face, front (of building); **Mil:** **le f.,** the front (line); **faire f. à,** to face. 3. **de f.,** abreast.

frontière [frɔ̃tjɛːr], s.f. frontier; border.

frontispice [frɔ̃tispis], s.m. frontispiece.

frottement [frotmɑ̃], s.m. rubbing; friction.

frotter [frote], v.tr. to rub.

fructifier [fryktifje], v.i. to bear fruit; **Fin:** to bear interest.

†**fructu/eux** [fryktuø], a. fruitful; profitable. adv. -eusement.

†**frugal** [frygal], a. frugal. adv. -ement. s.f. -ité.

fruit [frɥi], s.m. fruit.

fruitier, -ière [frɥitje, -jɛːr], 1. a. **arbre f.,** fruit tree. 2. s. fruiterer, greengrocer.

fruste [fryst], a. a worn; rough; unpolished (manner).

frustr/er [frystre], v.tr. 1. to frustrate. 2. to defraud. s.f. -ation.

fuel(-oil) [fiul(wal)], s.m. fuel-oil.

fugitif, -ive [fyʒitif, -iːv]. 1. s. fugitive. 2. a. fleeting, transitory; passing (desire).

‡**fuir** [fɥiːr]. 1. v.i. (a) to flee, run away; (b) to recede; (c) to leak. 2. v.tr. to shun.

fuite [fɥit], s.f. 1. flight, running away. 2. leak; leakage; **la f. des cerveaux,** the brain drain.

fumée [fyme], s.f. (a) smoke; (b) steam.

fumer [fyme]. 1. v.i. (a) to smoke; (b) to steam; to fume. 2. v.tr. to smoke.

fumeur, -euse [fymœːr, -øːz], s. smoker.

fumeux [fymø], a. smoky, smoking.

fumier [fymje], s.m. 1. manure, dung. 2. dunghill; manure heap.

fumiste [fymist], s.m. **F:** (pers.) humbug.

funèbre [fynɛbr], a. 1. funeral; **marche f.,** dead-march. 2. funereal, gloomy.

funérailles [fyneraːj], s.f.pl. funeral.

funeste [fynɛst], a. deadly, fatal.

funiculaire [fynikylɛːr], s.m. funicular railway.

fur [fyːr], s.m. used in **au f. et à mesure,** (in proportion) as; progressively.

furet [fyre], s.m. ferret.

†**fureter** [fyrte], v.i. to ferret, pry about.

fureur [fyrœːr], s.f. 1. fury, rage. 2. passion.

furibond [fyribɔ̃], a. furious; full of fury.

furie [fyri], s.f. fury, rage.

‡**furieu/x** [fyrjø], a. furious; in a passion. adv. -sement.

furoncle [fyrɔ̃kl], s.m. **Med:** boil.

†**furti/f** [fyrtif], a. furtive, stealthy. adv. -vement.

fuseau [fyzo], s.m. 1. spindle. 2. **f. horaire,** time zone. 3. taper; pl. **Cl:** (i) skiing trousers; (ii) drainpipe trousers.

fusée [fyze], s.f. (a) rocket; **f. éclairante,** flare; **avion (à) f.,** rocket-propelled aircraft; (b) fuse.

fuselage [fyzlaːʒ], s.m. **Av:** fuselage.

fuselé [fyzle], a. tapering, streamlined.

fusible [fyzibl], s.m. **El.E:** fuse.

fusil [fyzi], s.m. gun; rifle.

fusillade [fyzijad], s.f. fusillade.

fusiller [fyzije], v.tr. to shoot.

fusion [fyzjɔ̃], s.f. 1. fusion. 2. dissolving, melting. 3. **Com:** merger.

fût [fy], s.m. 1. (a) shaft (of column); (b) bole. 2. cask, barrel.

futile [fytil], a. futile, trifling. adv. -ment.

futilité [fytilite], s.f. futility.

futur [fytyːr], a. future.

fuyant [fɥijɑ̃], a. 1. fleeing (animal); fleeting (moment). 2. receding (forehead). 3. shifty (eyes).

fuyard, -arde [fɥijaːr, -ard], s. fugitive, runaway.

G

G, g [ʒe], *s.m.* (the letter) G, g.
gabardine [gabardin], *s.f.* 1. gabardine. 2. raincoat.
gâcher [gaʃe], *v.tr.* to spoil; to bungle.
gâchette [gaʃɛt], *s.f.* trigger; *F:* avoir la g. facile, to be trigger-happy.
gâchis [gaʃi], *s.m.* muddle, mess.
gaffe [gaf], *s.f.* 1. boat-hook. 2. blunder, gaffe; faire une g., to put one's foot in it.
gage [gaːʒ], *s.m.* 1. pledge, security; mettre en g., to pawn. 2. token, sign. 3. forfeit. 4. *pl.* wages, pay.
‡gager [gaʒe], *v.tr.* to wager, bet; g. -eure, bet.
gagnant, -ante [gaɲɑ̃, -ɑ̃ːt]. 1. *a.* winning. 2. *s.* winner.
gagne-pain [gaɲpɛ̃], *s.m.inv.* bread-winner.
gagner [gaɲe], *v.tr.* 1. (*a*) to earn; (*b*) to gain. 2. to win, gain. 3. to reach; arrive at. 4. to overtake.
gai [ge, gɛ], *a.* gay; merry; cheerful. *adv.* -ement.
gaieté [gete], *s.f.* gaiety, mirth; de g. de cœur, of one's own free will.
gaillard [gajaːr]. 1. *a.* (*a*) vigorous; (*b*) merry. 2. *s.m.* grand g., (great) strapping fellow. 3. *s.m. Nau:* g. d'avant, forecastle; g. d'arrière, quarter-deck.
gain [gɛ̃], *s.m.* (*a*) gain, profit; (*b*) earnings.
gaine [gɛn], *s.f.* sheath, casing; *Cl:* girdle, roll-on.
gal/ant [galɑ̃]. 1. *a.* (*a*) gay, elegant; (*b*) gallant. 2. *s.m.* ladies' man. *adv.* -amment.
galanterie [galɑ̃tri], *s.f.* politeness.
galantine [galɑ̃tin], *s.f. Cu:* galantine.
galaxie [galaksi], *s.f.* galaxy.
gale [gal], *s.f. Med:* scabies; *Vet:* mange.
galère [galɛːr], *s.f.* galley.
galerie [galri], *s.f.* 1. (*a*) gallery; g. de portraits, portrait gallery; (*b*) arcade. 2. *Th:* balcony; gallery. 3. *Aut:* roof rack. 4. *Fr.C:* porch.
galet [galɛ], *s.m.* (*a*) pebble; (*b*) *pl.* shingle.
galette [galɛt], *s.f.* girdle-cake; g. des Rois, twelfth-night cake.
†galeux [galø], *a.* mangy; brebis galeuse, black sheep.
galimatias [galimatja], *s.m.* gibberish.
gallicisme [galisism], *s.m. Ling:* Gallicism.
gallois, -oise [galwa, -waːz]. 1. *a.* Welsh. 2. *s.* Welshman, -woman; les G., the Welsh. 3. *s.m. Ling:* Welsh.
gallo-romain [galloromɛ̃], *a.* Gallo-Roman.
gallup [galœp], *s.m.* Gallup poll.
galoche [galɔʃ], *s.f.* (*a*) clog; (*b*) over-shoe.

galon [galɔ̃], *s.m.* 1. braid. 2. *pl. Mil:* stripes; gold braid.
galop [galo], *s.m.* gallop.
galoper [galɔpe], *v.i. & tr.* to gallop.
galopin [galɔpɛ̃], *s.* urchin; young scamp.
galvaniser [galvanize], *v.tr.* to galvanize.
gambade [gɑ̃bad], *s.f.* leap, gambol.
gambader [gɑ̃bade], *v.i.* to leap; to gambol.
gamelle [gamɛl], *s.f. Mil:* mess-tin, -kettle.
gamin, -ine [gamɛ̃, -in], *s.* child, young-ster.
gamme [gam], *s.f.* 1. scale, gamut. 2. range, series.
gang [gɑ̃ɡ], *s.m. F:* (*a*) gang; (*b*) racket.
gangrène [gɑ̃grɛn], *s.f.* gangrene.
gangster [gɑ̃gstɛːr], *s.m. F:* gangster; hooligan.
gant [gɑ̃], *s.m.* glove; g. de toilette = (face-)flannel.
ganter [gɑ̃te], *v.tr.* to glove; g. du sept, to take sevens in gloves.
garage [garaːʒ], *s.m.* 1. parking, garaging; storing; *Rail:* voie de g., siding. 2. garage.
garagiste [garaʒist], *s.m.* garage proprietor; garage mechanic.
garant [garɑ̃], *s.* (*a*) guarantor, surety; (*b*) authority, guarantee.
garantie [garɑ̃ti], *s.f.* guarantee.
garantir [garɑ̃tiːr], *v.tr.* 1. to warrant, guarantee. 2. to shelter, protect.
garçon [garsɔ̃], *s.m.* 1. (*a*) boy; (*b*) son. 2. young man; g. d'honneur, best man. 3. bachelor. 4. waiter; steward. *s.f.* -nière, bachelor's flat.
garde¹ [gard], *s.m.* 1. (*a*) keeper; (*b*) watchman. 2. *Mil:* guardsman.
garde², *s.f.* 1. (*a*) guardianship, care, custody; avoir qch. en g., to have charge of sth.; (*b*) protection; (*c*) keeping. 2. (*a*) watch(ing); (*b*) care, guard; être sur ses gardes, to be on one's guard; *Mil:* g. à vous! attention! 3. (*a*) prendre g. à, to beware of; (*b*) prendre g. à, de, faire qch., to be careful to do sth.; (*c*) prenez g. de tomber, mind you don't fall. 4. *Mil:* guard; (*a*) être de g., to be on guard, on duty; (*b*) la g., the Guards.

For compounds of garde-, consult the second component for phonetics.

garde-barrière, *s.m. & f.* gatekeeper (at level-crossing). *pl. gardes-barrière(s).*
garde-bébé, *s.m. & f.* babysitter. *pl. gardes-bébés.*
garde-boue, *s.m.inv.* mudguard.
garde-but, *s.m. Sp:* goalkeeper. *pl. garde-buts.*
garde-chasse, *s.m.* gamekeeper. *pl. gardes-chasse(s).*

garde-côte, s.m. coastguard(sman). pl. gardes-côte(s).

garde-feu, s.m.inv. (a) fender; (b) fireguard.

garde-fou, s.m. 1. parapet. 2. railing (of bridge). pl. garde-fous.

garde-malade, s.m. & f. nurse. pl. gardes-malades.

garde-manger, s.m.inv. larder.

garder [garde], v.tr. to keep. 1. to guard, protect. 2. (a) to retain; (b) to preserve. 3. to remain in (a place). 4. to observe, respect.
   se garder. 1. to protect oneself; garde-toi! look out for yourself! 2. se g. de, to beware of.

garde-robe, s.f. (a) wardrobe; (b) clothes. pl. garde-robes.

gardien, -ienne [gardjɛ̃, -jɛn], s. guardian, keeper; caretaker; (prison) warder.

gare¹ [gar], int. look out!

gare² [gar], s.f. (railway) station.

garenne [garɛn], s.f. (rabbit-)warren.

garer [gare], v.tr. (a) to shunt (train); (b) (i) to park, (ii) to garage (car).

gargouille [garguːj], s.f. (a) (water-)spout; (b) gargoyle.

garnement [garnəmã], s.m. scamp, rogue.

garni [garni], a. furnished; plat g., meat or fish served with vegetables.

garnir [garnir], v.tr. 1. to furnish, provide (de, with). 2. to trim (hat). 3. to lag (boiler); to pack (piston); to line (brake).

garnison [garnizɔ̃], s.f. garrison.

garniture [garnityːr], s.f. 1. fittings. 2. trimming(s); lagging (of boiler); ring (of piston); (brake) lining.

garrotter [garɔte], v.tr. to tie up (prisoner); to strangle (s.o.).

gars [gɑ], s.m. young fellow; lad, boy.

gascon, -onne [gaskɔ̃, -ɔn], a. & s. Gascon.

gas-oil [gazwal, gazoil], s.m. diesel oil.

gaspiller [gaspije], v.tr. to squander; to waste.

gastrite [gastrit], s.f. gastritis.

gastronomi/e [gastronɔmi], s.f. gastronomy. **-que.**

gâteau [gɑto], s.m. cake; (open) tart. a. F: papa g., (i) indulgent father; (ii) sugar daddy.

gâter [gɑte], v.tr. to spoil.
   se gâter, to spoil, deteriorate.

gauche [goːʃ], a. 1. awkward, clumsy. 2. left. 3. adv.phr. à g., to the left. adv. -ment.

gaucherie [goʃri], s.f. awkwardness.

gaufre [goːfr], s.f. 1. honeycomb. 2. waffle.

gaufrette [gofrɛt], s.f. wafer biscuit.

gaulois, -oise [golwa, -waz]. 1. a. Gallic; esprit g., (broad) Gallic humour. 2. s. les G., the Gauls.

gaver [gave], v.tr. to cram.

gaz [gɑz], s.m. gas.

gaze [gɑːz], s.f. gauze.

gazelle [gazɛl], s.f. gazelle.

†gazeux [gazø], a. 1. gaseous. 2. aerated; fizzy.

gazoduc [gazodyk], s.m. gas pipeline.

gazon [gazɔ̃], s.m. (a) turf; (b) lawn, green.

gazouill/er [gazuje], v.i. to twitter; to babble; to prattle. s.m. -ement.

geai [ʒɛ], s.m. jay.

géant, -ante [ʒeɑ̃, -ɑ̃ːt]. 1. s. giant, f. giantess. 2. a. gigantic; Com: giant (size).

†geindre [ʒɛ̃dr], v.i. to whine, whimper.

gel [ʒɛl], s.m. frost, freezing.

gélatine [ʒelatin], s.f. gelatine.

†gélatineux [ʒelatinø], a. gelatinous.

gelé [ʒ(ə)le], a. 1. frozen. 2. frost-bitten.

gelée [ʒ(ə)le], s.f. 1. frost. 2. jelly.

†geler [ʒ(ə)le], v.tr. & i. to freeze; impers. il gèle, it is freezing.
   se geler, to freeze, solidify.

gémir [ʒemir], v.i. to groan, moan; to wail. s.m. -issement.

gemme [ʒɛm]. (a) s.f. gem; precious stone; (b) a. sel g., rock-salt.

gênant [ʒɛnɑ̃], a. 1. cumbersome; in the way. 2. embarrassing, awkward.

gencive [ʒɑ̃siv], s.f. Anat: gum.

gendarme [ʒɑ̃darm], s.m. gendarme.

gendarmerie [ʒɑ̃darməri], s.f. 1. = the constabulary. 2. = police headquarters.

gendre [ʒɑ̃dr], s.m. son-in-law.

gêne [ʒɛːn], s.f. 1. discomfort; sans g., free and easy. 2. want; être dans la g., to be hard up.

gêné [ʒene], a. embarrassed; ill at ease.

généalogie [ʒenealɔʒi], s.f. genealogy; pedigree.

généalogique [ʒenealɔʒik], a. genealogical; arbre g., family tree; pedigree.

gêner [ʒene], v.tr. 1. to constrict. 2. to hinder; to be in (s.o.'s) way. 3. to inconvenience.
   se gêner, to put oneself out.

général, -ale [ʒeneral]. 1. a. general; répétition générale, s.f. générale, dress-rehearsal. 2. s.m. general. 3. s.f. (a) the general's wife; (b) Mil: alarm call. adv. -ement.

généraliser [ʒeneralize], v.tr. to generalize.

généralité [ʒeneralite], s.f. generality.

générateur, -trice [ʒeneratœːr, -tris]. 1. a. generating. 2. s. generator.

‡génér/er [ʒenere], v.tr. to generate. s.f. -ation.

†généreux [ʒenerø], a. liberal, generous. adv. -sement.

générosité [ʒenerozite], s.f. generosity.

genèse [ʒ(ə)nɛz], s.f. genesis, origin.

genêt [ʒ(ə)nɛ], s.m. (plant) broom.

génétique [ʒenetik], s.f. genetics.

genévrier [ʒ(ə)nevrie], s.m. juniper(-tree).

génie [ʒeni], *s.m.* **1.** (*a*) genius; (*b*) genie. **2.** (*a*) g. civil, (civil) engineering; (*b*) *Mil:* le g., the engineer corps, the sappers.

genièvre [ʒənjɛːvr], *s.m.* juniper-berry; juniper-bush.

génois, -oise [ʒenwa, -waːz], *a.* & *s.* Genoese.

†**genou** [ʒ(ə)nu], *s.m.* knee; à genoux, kneeling.

genre [ʒãːr], *s.m.* **1.** genus; kind; le g. humain, mankind. **2.** kind, manner, sort. **3.** (artistic) style. **4.** gender.

gens [ʃã], *s.m.pl.* people, folk.

†**gentil** [ʃãti], *a.* (*a*) pleasing, nice; (*b*) sois g., be a good boy; (*to adult*) be an angel.

gentilhomme [ʃãtijɔm], *s.m.* gentleman. *pl.* gentilshommes [ʃãtizɔm].

gentillesse [ʃãtijɛs], *s.f.* (*a*) graciousness; kindness; (*b*) auriez-vous la g. de, would you be so kind as to.

gentiment [ʃãtimã], *adv.* nicely; prettily.

géographie [ʒeɔgrafi], *s.f.* geography.

géographique [ʒeɔgrafik], *a.* geographic(al).

geôlier [ʒolje], *s.m.* gaoler, jailer.

géologie [ʒeɔlɔʒi], *s.f.* geology.

géologique [ʒeɔlɔʒik], *a.* geological.

géologue [ʒeɔlɔg], *s.m.* geologist.

géométrie [ʒeɔmetri], *s.f.* geometry.

géométrique [ʒeɔmetrik], *a.* geometric(al).

géranium [ʒeranjɔm], *s.m.* geranium.

gérant, -ante [ʒerã, -ãːt], *s.* manager, *f.* manageress; director.

gerbe [ʒɛrb], *s.f.* sheaf (of corn); g. de fleurs, sheaf of flowers; shower (of sparks); spray (of water).

gerçure [ʒɛrsyːr], *s.f.* crack, cleft; chap.

gérer [ʒere], *v.tr.* to manage.

germain [ʒɛrmɛ̃], *a.* frère g., full brother; cousin g., first cousin.

germe [ʒɛrm], *s.m.* germ.

germ/er [ʒɛrme], *v.i.* to germinate; to shoot. *s.f.* -ination.

gésier [ʒezje], *s.m.* gizzard.

†**gésir** [ʒeziːr], *v.i.* to lie; *used in* ci-gît, here lies.

geste [ʒɛst], *s.m.* gesture, movement; wave (of the hand).

gesticul/er [ʒɛstikyle], *v.i.* to gesticulate. *s.f.* -ation.

gestion [ʒɛstjɔ̃], *s.f.* management; administration.

geyser [ʒezɛːr], *s.m. Geog:* geyser.

gibecière [ʒipsjɛːr], *s.f.* game-bag.

gibet [ʒibɛ], *s.m.* gibbet, gallows.

giboulée [ʒibule], *s.f.* sudden shower.

gicler [ʒikle], *v.i.* to squirt out.

gicleur [ʒiklœːr], *s.m.* (spray) nozzle; jet.

gifle [ʒifl], *s.f.* slap in the face; box on the ear.

gifler [ʒifle], *v.tr.* to slap, smack (s.o.'s) face; to box (s.o.'s) ears.

gigantesque [ʒigãtɛsk], *a.* gigantic, huge.

gigot [ʒigo], *s.m.* leg of mutton.

gilet [ʒile], *s.m.* waistcoat, vest; g. de corps, singlet.

gin [dʒin, ʒin], *s.m.* gin.

gingembre [ʒɛ̃ʒãːbr], *s.m.* ginger.

girafe [ʒiraf], *s.f.* giraffe.

giration [ʒirasjɔ̃], *s.f.* gyration.

giratoire [ʒiratwaːr], *a.* gyratory; sens g., roundabout.

girl [gœrl], *s.f.* chorus girl.

girofle [ʒirɔfl], *s.m.* (clou de) g., clove.

giroflée [ʒirɔfle], *s.f.* g. des jardins, stock; g. des murailles, wallflower.

girouette [ʒirwɛt], *s.f.* weathercock; weather vane.

gisement [ʒizmã], *s.m.* layer; deposit.

gîte [ʒit], *s.m.* lodging (place); (animal's) lair.

givre [ʒiːvr], *s.m.* hoar-frost.

glace [glas], *s.f.* **1.** ice. **2.** (*a*) (plate-) glass; (*b*) (looking-)glass, mirror; (*c*) window. **3.** ice(-cream).

glacer [glase], *v.tr.* **1.** to freeze; to ice **2.** to glaze.

†**glacial** [glasjal], *a.* icy; frosty; frigid.

glacier [glasje], *s.m.* glacier.

glaçon [glasɔ̃], *s.m.* (*a*) block of ice; (*b*) icicle; (*c*) ice cube.

glaïeul [glajœl], *s.m.* gladiolus.

gland [glã], *s.m.* **1.** acorn. **2.** tassel.

glande [glãːd], *s.f.* gland.

glan/er [glane], *v.tr.* to glean. *s.* -eur, -euse.

glas [glã], *s.m.* knell.

glissade [glisad], *s.f.* **1.** slip; *Av:* g. sur la queue, tail dive. **2.** slide.

gliss/er [glise], *v.i.* **i.** **1.** to slip. **2.** to slide. **3.** to glide. **II.** *v.tr.* to slip (sth. into sth.). *s.m.* -ement. *s.f.* -ière, groove, slide. se glisser, to creep, steal (dans, into).

†**global** [glɔbal], *a.* total, inclusive.

globe [glɔb], *s.m.* **1.** globe, sphere. **2.** g. de l'œil, eyeball.

globulaire [glɔbylɛːr], *a.* globular.

globule [glɔbyl], *s.m.* globule.

gloire [glwaːr], *s.f.* **1.** glory. **2.** pride.

†**glorieu/x** [glɔrjø], *a.* **1.** glorious. **2.** proud. **3.** *s.m.* boaster. *adv.* -sement.

glorifier [glɔrifje], *v.tr.* to praise, glorify. se glorifier, to boast.

glossaire [glɔsɛːr], *s.m.* glossary.

glouss/er [gluse], *v.i.* to cluck; to gobble; to chuckle. *s.m.* -ement.

glouton, -onne [glutɔ̃, -ɔn], **1.** *a.* greedy, gluttonous. **2.** *s.* glutton. *adv.* -nement.

gloutonnerie [glutɔnri], *s.f.* gluttony.

gluant [glyã], *a.* sticky, gummy.

glucose [glykoːz], *s.m.* glucose.

glycérine [gliserin], *s.f.* glycerine.

glycine [glisin], *s.f.* wistaria.

gnome [gnoːm], *s.m.* gnome.

gnou [gnu], *s.m.* gnu.

goal [goːl], *s.m. F: Sp:* **1.** goal. **2.** (*also* goal-keeper [goːlkipœr]) goal-keeper.

gobelet [gɔblɛ], *s.m.* goblet, cup.

gober [gɔbe], *v.tr.* to swallow, gulp down; g. des mouches, to stand gaping.

goémon [gɔemɔ̃], *s.m.* seaweed.

goitre [gwatr], *s.m.* goitre.

golf [gɔlf], *s.m.* golf; (terrain de) g., golf course, links.

golfe [gɔlf], *s.m.* gulf, bay.

gomme [gɔm], *s.f.* 1. gum; g. arabique, gum-arabic. 2. g. (à effacer), (india)-rubber, *U.S:* eraser.

†gommeux [gɔmø], *a.* gummy, sticky.

gond [gɔ̃], *s.m.* hinge-pin (of door).

gondole [gɔ̃dɔl], *s.f.* gondola.

gondoler [gɔ̃dɔle], *v.i.* to warp; to buckle.

gonfl/er [gɔ̃fle]. 1. *v.tr.* (a) to inflate; to pump up; to puff out; (b) to swell. 2. *v.i. & pr.* to swell. *s.m.* -ement. *s.m.* -age.

gorge [gɔrʒ], *s.f.* 1. throat. 2. *Geog:* gorge.

gorgée [gɔrʒe], *s.f.* mouthful, draught.

‡gorger [gɔrʒe], *v.tr.* to stuff, gorge.

gorille [gɔrij], *s.m.* gorilla.

gosier [gozje], *s.m.* throat; gullet.

gosse [gɔs], *s.m. & f:* youngster, kid.

gothique [gɔtik], *a. & s.m.* Gothic.

goudron [gudrɔ̃], *s.m.* tar.

goudronner [gudrɔne], *v.tr.* to tar.

gouffre [gufr], *s.m.* gulf, pit, abyss; whirlpool.

goulet [gulɛ], *s.m.* narrow part, neck (of object); gully (in mountains).

goulot [gulo], *s.m.* neck (of bottle).

goul/u [guly], *a.* greedy. *adv.* -ûment.

goupille [gupij], *s.f.* (linch)pin.

goupillon [gupijɔ̃], *s.m.* sprinkler (for holy water).

gourde [gurd], *s.f.* 1. gourd. 2. water-bottle; flask.

gourmand [gurmã], -ande [gurmã, -ãd]. 1. *a.* greedy. 2. *s.* gourmand, glutton.

gourmandise [gurmãdiːz], *s.f.* 1. greediness. 2. *pl.* sweetmeats, dainties.

gourmet [gurmɛ], *s.m.* gourmet, epicure.

gousse [gus], *s.f.* pod, shell, husk; g. d'ail, clove of garlic.

gousset [gusɛ], *s.m.* (a) gusset; (b) waist-coat pocket.

goût [gu], *s.m.* 1. (sense of) taste. 2. flavour, taste. 3. les gens de g., people of taste.

goûter [gute]. I. *v.tr.* 1. to taste. 2. to enjoy. 3. g. à qch., to take a little of sth. II. *s.m.* = (afternoon) tea.

goutt/e [gut], *s.f.* 1. drop (of liquid). 2. spot, speck, fleck. 3. small quantity, sip; *F:* nip, spot (of brandy, etc.). 4. je n'y vois g., I can't see a thing. 5. gout. *a.* †-eux, gouty.

gouttière [gutjɛr], *s.f.* 1. gutter. 2. rain-pipe.

gouvernail [guverna:j], *s.m.* rudder, helm.

gouvernante [guvernã:t], *s.f.* house-keeper.

gouvernement [guvernəmã], *s.m.* government.

gouverner [guverne], *v.tr.* 1. to steer. 2. to govern, rule.

gouverneur [guvernœːr], *s.m.* governor.

grâce [graːs], *s.f.* 1. grace, charm; de bonne g., willingly. 2. favour; de g.! for pity's sake! 3. pardon. 4. thanks; (a) *pl.* action de grâces, thanksgiving; (b) *prep.phr.* g. à, thanks to.

†gracieu/x [grasjø], *a.* 1. graceful. 2. gracious. *adv.* -sement.

grade [grad], *s.m.* 1. rank; dignity, grade. 2. (university) degree.

gradé [grade], *s.m. Mil:* non-commissioned officer, N.C.O.

gradin [gradɛ̃], *s.m.* step, tier.

graduation [graduasjɔ̃], *s.f.* 1. graduation. 2. scale.

gradué [gradue], *a.* (a) graduated; (b) graded, progressive.

†graduel [graduɛl], *a.* gradual. *adv.* -lement.

grain¹ [grɛ̃], *s.m.* 1. (a) grain; (b) corn. 2. bean (of coffee); g. de raisin, grape; g. de beauté, mole. 3. particle. 4. bead. 5. grain, texture.

grain², *s.m.* squall; gust of wind.

graine [grɛn], *s.f.* seed; monter en g., to run to seed.

graisse [grɛs], *s.f.* grease, fat; g. de rôti, dripping.

graiss/er [grɛse], *v.tr.* to grease, oil, lubricate. *s.m.* -age.

†graisseux [grɛsø], *a.* (a) greasy, oily; (b) fatty.

grammaire [gra(m)mɛːr], *s.f.* grammar.

grammatical [gra(m)matikal], *a.* grammatical. *adv.* -ement.

gramme [gram], *s.m.* gram(me).

grand [grɑ̃], *a.* 1. (a) tall; large, big; (b) chief, main; g. ressort, mainspring; (c) grown up; (d) *adv.* voir, faire, g., to see, do, things on a large scale. 2. large, many; le g. public, the general public; en grande partie, to a great extent. 3. il fait g. jour, it is broad daylight; il est g. temps, it is high time. 4. *s.m.* les grands, the great (ones). *adv.* -ement.

For the phonetics of compound words beginning grand- please consult the second component. To form the plural add s to the second component, unless otherwise indicated.

grand-chose, *indef.pron.m.* (*usu.* with *neg.*) much.

grandeur [grɑ̃dœːr], *s.f.* 1. (a) size; height; (b) extent; scale. 2. greatness.

grandiose [grɑ̃djoːz], *a.* grand, imposing.

grandir [grɑ̃diːr], *v.i.* 1. to grow up; to increase.

grandissement [grɑ̃dismã], *s.m.* (a) growth, increase; (b) magnification.

grand-maman, *s.f.* granny.

grand-mère, s.f. grandmother.
grand-messe, s.f. high mass.
grand-oncle, s.m. great-uncle. pl. grands-oncles.
grand-papa, s.m. grandpa, grandad.
grand-père, s.m. grandfather. pl. grands-pères.
grand-route, s.f. highway, high road.
grand-rue, s.f. high street, main street.
grands-parents, s.m.pl. grandparents.
grand-tante, s.f. great-aunt.
grange [grɑ̃:ʒ], s.f. barn.
granit [grani(t)], s.m. granite.
granulaire [granylɛːr], a. granular.
†**granuleux** [granylø] a. granular.
graphique [grafik]. 1. a. graphic. 2. s.m. diagram, graph. -ment.
graphite [grafit], s.m. graphite, plumbago.
grappe [grap], s.f. cluster, bunch (of grapes).
†**gras** [grɑ], a. 1. fat; fatty; (b) rich (food); régime g., meat diet; (c) s.m. fat (of meat). 2. fat, stout. 3. greasy; oily.
gratification [gratifikasjɔ̃], s.f. gratuity; tip; bonus.
gratis [gratis], adv. gratis.
gratitude [gratityd], s.f. gratitude.
gratte [grat], s.f. F: pickings, perks, rake-off.
gratte-ciel [gratsjɛl], s.m.inv. skyscraper.
gratt/er [grate], v.tr. 1. to scrape; scratch. 2. to erase. s.m. -ement.
grattoir [gratwaːr], s.m. scraper.
gratuit [gratɥi], a. (a) free; (b) insulte gratuite, gratuitous insult. adv. -ement, free of charge.
grave [graːv], a. 1. a. grave; solemn; sober; (b) important. 2. deep (voice). 3. Gram: accent a, grave accent. adv. -ment.
graver [grave], v.tr. 1. to cut, engrave. 2. to record (music, etc.).
graveur [gravœːr], s.m. engraver; carver.
gravier [gravje], s.m. gravel, grit.
gravillon [gravijɔ̃], s.m. fine gravel; P.N: gravillons, loose chippings.
gravir [graviːr], v.tr. to climb; to ascend.
gravité [gravite], s.f. gravity.
graviter [gravite], v.i. to gravitate.
gravure [gravyːr], s.f. 1. engraving; g. sur bois, woodcut; g. à l'eau-forte, etching. 2. picture. 3. Rec: recording.
gré [gre], s.m. 1. liking, taste. 2. will, pleasure; de mon plein gré, of my own accord; bon gré mal gré, willy-nilly.
grec, grecque [grɛk]. 1. a. Greek; Grecian. 2. s. Greek. 3. s.m. Ling: Greek.
greffe [grɛf], s.f. 1. graft, slip. 2. grafting. 3. Med: g. (de cœur), (heart) transplant.
greffer [grefe], v.tr. to graft.
greffier [grefje], s.m. 1. clerk (of the court). 2. registrar.

grêle[1] [grɛ(ː)l], a. slender, thin; high-pitched.
grêle[2], s.f. hail.
grêler [grele], v.impers. il grêle, it's hailing.
grêlon [grelɔ̃], s.m. hail-stone.
grelot [grəlo], s.m. (small round) bell; sleigh bell.
grelotter [grəlɔte], v.i. to tremble, shiver.
grenade [grənad], s.f. 1. pomegranate. 2. grenade, bomb.
grenat [grəna], s.m. garnet.
grenier [grənje], s.m. 1. granary. 2. attic.
grenouille [grənuːj], s.f. frog.
grès [grɛ], s.m. 1. sandstone. 2. poterie de g., earthenware.
grésil [grezi], s.m. frozen pellets of snow.
grésill/er [grezije], v.i. (a) to crackle; to sizzle; (b) to chirp. s.m. -ement.
grève [grɛːv], s.f. 1. strand; beach. 2. strike; g. perlée, go-slow strike; g. de zèle, working to rule; g. de solidarité, sympathy strike.
gréviste [grevist], s.m. & f. striker.
grief [gri(j)ɛf], s.m. grievance.
grièvement [gri(j)ɛvmɑ̃], adv. severely, grievously.
griffe [grif], s.f. claw; talon.
griffonner [grifone], v.tr. to scrawl, scribble.
gril [gri], s.m. grid(iron), grill.
grillade [grijad], s.f. grill; grilled steak.
grillage [grijaːʒ], s.m. grating.
grille [grij], s.f. (a) (iron) bars; (b) iron gate; (c) railings; (d) (fire)-grate.
grille-pain [grijpɛ̃], s.m.inv. toaster.
griller [grije], v.tr. 1. to grill; to toast. 2. to scorch.
grillon [grijɔ̃], s.m. Z: cricket.
grimace [grimas], s.f. grimace.
grimacer [grimase], v.i. to grimace.
grimp/er [grɛ̃pe], v.i. & tr. to climb (up). s. -eur, -euse.
‡**grinc/er** [grɛ̃se], v.i. to grate; to grind; to creak. s.m. -ement.
‡**grincheux** [grɛ̃ʃø], a. grumpy, cross.
gris [gri], a. 1. (a) grey; (b) grey-haired. 2. F: (slightly) intoxicated, tipsy.
grisâtre [grizaːtr], a. greyish.
griser [grize], v.tr. F: to make (s.o.) tipsy. se griser, F: to get tipsy.
griserie [grizri], s.f. 1. tipsiness. 2. intoxication, exhilaration.
grive [griːv], s.f. thrush.
grogn/er [grɔɲe], v.i. 1. (a) to grunt; (b) to growl. 2. to grumble. s.m. -ement.
groin [grwɛ̃], s.m. snout (of pig).
‡**grommeler** [grɔmle], v.i. to grumble.
grond/er [grɔ̃de], 1. v.i. (a) to growl; (b) to rumble. 2. v.tr. to scold. s.m. -ement. s. -eur, -euse.

gros, grosse [gro, gro:s]. 1. a. (a) big, stout; g. mot, coarse expression; g. temps, heavy weather; avoir le cœur g., to be sad at heart; (b) adv. gagner g., to earn a great deal. 2. s.m. (a) bulk, chief part; le plus g. est fait, the hardest part (of the job) is done; (b) en g., roughly; (on the whole); (c) wholesale (trade); négociant en g., wholesaler. 3. s.f. grosse, gross, twelve dozen.

groseille [grozej], s.f. 1. (red, white) currant. 2. g. à maquereau, gooseberry.

groseillier [grozeje], s.m. 1. currant-bush. 2. g. à maquereau, gooseberry-bush.

grossesse [groses], s.f. pregnancy.

grosseur [grosœ:r], s.f. size, bulk, volume; Med: swelling, tumour.

†**grossi/er** [grosje], a. (a) coarse, rough; (b) faute grossière, glaring blunder; (c) rude (envers, to). adv. -èrement.

grossièreté [grosjerte], s.f. (a) coarseness; (b) rudeness; (c) grossness (of mistake).

gross/ir [grosi:r]. 1. v.tr. to enlarge, swell; to magnify. 2. v.i. to increase, swell. a. -issant. s.m. -issement.

grossiste [grosist], s.m. wholesaler.

grotesque [grotesk], a. ludicrous, absurd.

grotte [grot], s.f. grotto.

grouill/er [gruje], v.i. to crawl, swarm (de, with). s.m. -ement.
se grouiller, P: to hurry; grouille-toi! get a move on!

groupe [grup], s.m. group (of people, things); clump (of trees); party (of people).

group/er [grupe], v.tr. to group. s.m. -ement.
se grouper, to gather.

grue [gry], s.f. 1. Z: crane; faire le pied de g., to cool one's heels. 2. F: (a) grande g., great gawk of a woman; (b) tart. 3. (hoisting) crane.

gué [ge], s.m. ford.

guenille [gənij], s.f. en guenilles, in rags.

guenon [gən5], s.f. she-monkey.

guêpe [ge(:)p], s.f. wasp.

guêpier [gepje], s.m. wasps' nest; tomber dans un g., to bring a hornets' nest about one's ears.

guère [ge:r], adv. (with neg.) hardly; not much, not many; je ne l'aime g., I don't care much for him, it; il n'y a g. six ans, hardly six years ago.

guéridon [gerid5], s.m. pedestal table.

guérilla [gerija], s.f. band of guerrillas; guerre de guérillas, guerrilla warfare.

guérir [geri:r]. 1. v.tr. to cure, heal. 2. v.i. (a) to recover, be cured; (b) to heal.

guérison [geriz5], s.f. 1. recovery. 2. (a) cure; (b) healing.

guérisseur, -euse [gerisœ:r, -ø:z], s. (a) healer; (b) quack (doctor); (c) faith healer.

guérite [gerit], s.f. sentry-box.

guerre [ge:r], s.f. 1. war, warfare; g. sur mer, naval warfare; g. froide, cold war. 2. strife, feud; adv.phr. de g. lasse, for the sake of peace.

†**guerrier** [gerje], 1. a. warlike. 2. s.m. warrior.

guet [ge], s.m. watch(ing); look-out.

guet-apens [getapã], s.m. ambush, snare. pl. guets-apens.

guetter [gete], v.tr. to be on the look-out for.

gueule [gœl], s.f. 1. mouth (of animal); P: ta g.! shut up! F: avoir la g. de bois, to have a hangover. 2. mouth; muzzle (of gun).

gueuler [gœle], v.i. & tr. P: to bawl, shout.

gueuleton [gœlt5], s.m. P: blow-out, tuck in.

gueux, -euse [gø, -ø:z], s. beggar; tramp.

gui [gi], s.m. mistletoe.

guichet [giʃe], s.m. 1. (a) wicket (gate); (b) grating (in door). 2. booking-office; Th: box office; (in post office) position.

guide[1] [gid], s.m. 1. (a) guide; conductor; (b) s.f. (girl) guide. 2. guide (-book).

guide[2], s.f. rein.

guider [gide], v.tr. to guide, direct, lead.

guidon [gid5], s.m. handle-bar.

guigne [giɲ], s.f. bad luck.

guignol [giɲol], s.m. (a) Punch; (b) Punch and Judy show.

guillemets [gijme], s.m.pl. inverted commas, quotation marks.

guillotine [gijotin], s.f. 1. guillotine. 2. fenêtre à g., sash window.

guillotiner [gijotine], v.tr. to guillotine.

guindé [gɛde], a. stiff, stilted; starchy (person).

guirlande [girlɑ̃:d], s.f. garland, wreath.

guise [gi:z], s.f. 1. manner, way, fashion; faire à sa g., to do as one pleases; en g. de, by way of.

guitare [gita:r], s.f. guitar.

†**guttural** [gytyral], a. guttural.

gymkhana [ʒimkana], s.m. gymkhana.

gymnase [ʒimna:z], s.m. gymnasium.

gymnaste [ʒimnast], s.m. gymnast.

gymnastique [ʒimnastik]. 1. a. gymnastic. 2. s.f. gymnastics.

gynécologie [ʒinekoloʒi], s.f. gynaecology.

gynécologue [ʒinekolog], s. gynaecologist.

gyroscope [ʒiroskop], s.m. gyroscope.

gyrostabilisateur [ʒirostabilizatœ:r], s.m. Av: gyrostabilizer.

gyrostat [ʒirosta], s.m. gyrostat.

H

Words beginning with an 'aspirate' h are shown by an asterisk.

H, h [aʃ], *s.m. & f.* (the letter) H, h.

habile [abil], *a.* clever, skilful; artful. *adv.* -ment.

habileté [abilte], *s.f.* ability, skill; (*b*) cleverness, smartness.

habillement [abijmɑ̃], *s.m.* 1. dressing. 2. clothes, clothing, dress.

habiller [abije], *v.tr. a* (*a*) to dress (s.o.); (*b*) to provide (s.o.) with clothes. s'habiller, to dress.

habit [abi], *s.m.* 1. dress, costume; *pl.* clothes. 2. (*a*) coat; (*b*) en h., in evening dress; (*c*) (monk's nun's) habit.

habitable [abitabl], *a.* habitable.

habitant [abitɑ̃], *s.* (*a*) inhabitant; resident; (*b*) occupier; (*c*) inmate.

habitat [abita], *s.m.* habitat.

habitation [abitasjɔ̃], *s.f.* 1. habitation; le problème de l'h., the housing problem. 2. residence, dwelling; h. à loyer modéré (H.L.M.) = council house, flat.

habit/er [abite], *v.tr.* (*a*) to inhabit, to live in; (*b*) to occupy. 2. *v.i.* to live, reside (à, at). *s.f.* -ation.

habitude [abityd], *s.f.* (*a*) habit, custom; d'h., usually; (*b*) knack; je n'en ai plus l'h., I'm out of practice.

habitué, -ée [abitɥe], *s.* regular attendant, regular customer; habitué(e).

†**habituel** [abitɥɛl], *a.* usual; habitual. *adv.* -lement.

habituer [abitɥe], *v.tr.* to accustom (qn à qch., s.o. to sth.). s'habituer, to get accustomed (à, to).

*****hache** [aʃ], *s.f.* axe.

*****haché** [aʃe], *a.* staccato, jerky.

*****hache-légumes** [aʃlegym], *s.m. inv.* vegetable cutter, mincer.

*****hacher** [aʃe], *v.tr.* to chop (up); to mince.

*****hachette** [aʃɛt], *s.f.* hatchet.

*****hache-viande** [aʃvjɑ̃d], *s.m.inv.* mincer.

*****hachis** [aʃi], *s.m. Cu:* mince.

haddock [adɔk], *s.m.* smoked haddock.

*****hagard** [agaːr], *a.* haggard, wild.

*****haie** [ɛ], *s.f.* (*a*) hedge; (*b*) line, row (of trees, troops).

*****haillon** [ajɔ̃], *s.m.* rag.

haine [ɛːn], *s.f.* hatred; detestation.

†*****haineux** [ɛnø], *a.* full of hatred.

‡*****haïr** [aiːr], *v.tr.* to hate, detest.

haïssable [aisabl], *a.* hateful, destestable.

halage [alaːʒ], *s.m.* towing; chemin de h., towpath.

hâle [ɑːl], *s.m.* tan; sunburn.

haleine [alɛn], *s.f.* breath; politique de h., long-term policy.

*****haler** [ale], *v.tr.* to tow; to haul.

*****hâler** [ɑle], *v.tr.* (*of sun*) to tan (s.o.). se hâler, to get sunburnt.

‡*****hal/eter** [alte], *v.i.* to pant; to gasp. *s.m.* -ètement.

*****ha ll** [al, ɔl], *s.m.* 1. (large) entrance hall; (hotel) lounge. 2. *Ind:* shop, room; h. de montage, assembly shop.

*****halle** [al], *s.f.* (covered) market.

*****hallier** [alje], *s.m.* thicket, copse.

hallucination [al(l)ysinasjɔ̃], *s.f.* hallucination.

*****halo** [alo], *s.m.* 1. *Meteor:* halo. 2. *Phot:* halation.

*****halte** [alt], *s.f.* 1. stop, halt. 2. stopping-place, resting-place.

*****hamac** [amak], *s.m.* hammock.

*****hameau** [amo], *s.m.* hamlet.

hameçon [amsɔ̃], *s.m.* (fish-)hook.

*****hamster** [amstɛːr], *s.m. Z:* hamster.

*****hanche** [ɑ̃ʃ], *s.f.* 1. hip. 2. haunch.

*****handicap** [ɑ̃dikap], *s.m. Sp:* handicap.

*****handicaper** [ɑ̃dikapə], *v.tr. Sp:* to handicap.

*****hangar** [ɑ̃gaːr], *s.m.* 1. shed; lean-to; h. à bateaux, boat-house. 2. *Av:* hangar.

*****hanneton** [antɔ̃], *s.m.* cockchafer, may-bug.

*****hanter** [ɑ̃te], *v.tr.* to haunt.

*****hantise** [ɑ̃tiːz], *s.f.* obsession.

*****happer** [ap(p)e], *v.tr.* to snap up; to catch.

*****harangue** [arɑ̃ːg], *s.f.* harangue; speech.

*****haranguer** [arɑ̃ge], *v.tr.* (*a*) to harangue; (*b*) *F:* to lecture (s.o.).

haras [ara], *s.m.* 1. stud farm. 2. stud.

*****harasser** [arase], *v.tr.* (*a*) to tire (out), exhaust; (*b*) to harass, worry.

‡*****harceler** [arsəle], *v.tr.* to harass, torment, worry; *Av:* to buzz (aircraft).

*****hardes** [ard], *s.f.pl.* (worn) clothes.

*****hardi** [ardi], *a.* bold, audacious; daring; rash; impudent. *adv.* -ment.

*****hardiesse** [ardjɛs], *s.f.* boldness, daring; impudence.

harem [arɛm], *s.m.* harem.

*****hareng** [arɑ̃], *s.m.* herring; h. bouffi, bloater; h. saur, red herring; serrés comme des harengs, packed like sardines.

†*****hargneux** [arɲø], *a.* snarling; peevish.

*****haricot** [ariko], *s.m.* h. (blanc), haricot bean; haricots verts, French beans; h. d'Espagne, scarlet runner.

harmonie [armɔni], *s.f.* harmony; agreement.

†**harmonieu/x** [armɔnjø], *a.* harmonious. *adv.* -sement.

harmoniser [armɔnize], *v.tr.* to harmonize; to match (colours). s'harmoniser, to harmonize, agree (avec, with); (*of colours*) to tone (avec, with).

*****harnach/er** [arnaʃe], *v.tr.* to harness. *s.m.* -ement.

*harnais [arnɛ], *s.m.* harness.
*harpe/e [arp], *s.f.* harp. s. -iste.
*harpon [arpɔ̃], *s.m.* harpoon; pêche au h., spear fishing.
*harponner [arpɔne], *v.tr.* to harpoon; to anchor (aerial).
*hasard [azaːr], *s.m.* (a) chance, luck, accident; coup de h., stroke of luck; fluke; au h., at random; (b) risk, danger.
*hasarder [azarde], *v.tr.* to risk, venture. se hasarder, to take, run, risks.
†*hasardeux [azardø], *a.* 1. hazardous, risky. 2. daring, foolhardy.
*hâte [ɑːt], *s.f.* haste, hurry; à la h., hastily.
*hâter [ɑte], *v.tr.* to hasten; to hurry (sth.) on.
  se hâter, to hasten, hurry.
†*hâtif [ɑtif], *a.* (a) forward, early; premature; (b) hasty, hurried. adv. -vement.
*hausse [oːs], *s.f.* rise, rising; Fin: jouer à la h., to speculate on a rising market.
*hauss/er [ose]. 1. *v.tr.* to raise, lift; h. les épaules, to shrug. 2. *v.i.* to rise. *s.m.* -ement.
*haut [o]. I. *a.* 1. high; (a) tall; lofty; (b) important; la haute finance, high finance; (c) raised; voix haute, (i) loud voice; (ii) high voice; lire à haute voix, to read aloud; (d) haute trahison, high treason. 2. upper, higher; le plus h. étage, the top floor. II. *adv.* high (up), above, up; h. les mains! hands up! parler h., to speak loudly. III. *s.m.* 1. height; le mur a deux mètres de h., the wall is six foot high. 2. top, upper part; h. de la table, head of the table. 3. de h. en bas, (i) downwards; (ii) from top to bottom; en h., (i) above; (ii) upstairs. adv. -ement.
*hautain [otɛ̃], *a.* haughty.
*hautbois [obwa], *s.m.* oboe.
*haut-de-forme [odfɔrm], *s.m.* top hat.
*hauteur [otœːr], *s.f.* 1. height, elevation; altitude; Av: prendre de la h., to climb; à la h. de, abreast of, level with; equal to (the occasion). 2. haughtiness. 3. high place; hilltop.
*haut-fond [ofɔ̃], *s.m.* shoal, shallow. pl. hauts-fonds.
*haut-fourneau [ofurno], *s.m.* Ind: blast furnace. pl. hauts-fourneaux.
*haut-le-corps [olkɔːr], *s.m.inv.* sudden start, jump.
*haut-parleur [oparlœːr], *s.m.* loud-speaker; amplifier. pl. haut-parleurs.
*havre [ɑ̃vr], *s.m.* harbour, port.
*havresac [ɑvrəsak], *s.m.* knapsack; (workman's) tool bag.
hebdomadaire [ɛbdɔmadɛːr], *a.* & *s.m.* weekly (paper).
‡héberger [ebɛrʒe], *v.tr.* to harbour; to lodge, shelter; to put (s.o.) up.

‡héb/éter [ebete], *v.tr.* to dull; to daze. s.m. -étement.
hébraïque [ebraik], *a.* Hebraic, Hebrew.
hébreu [ebrø], *a.* & *s.m.* (hébraïque is used for the f.) Hebrew.
*hein [ɛ̃], *int.* eh? what?
*hélas [elas], *int.* alas!
*héler [ele], *v.tr.* to hail, call.
hélice [elis], *s.f.* propeller, (air-)screw.
hélicoptère [elikɔptɛːr], *s.m.* helicopter.
héligare [eligaːr], *s.f.* helicopter station.
héliport [elipɔːr], *s.m.* heliport.
helvétique [ɛlvetik], *a.* Swiss.
*hem [ɛm], *int.* (a)hem! hm!
hématite [ematit], *s.f.* haematite.
hémisphère [emisfɛːr], *s.m.* hemisphere.
hémisphérique [emisferik], *a.* hemi-spheric(al).
hémoglobine [emɔglɔbin], *s.f.* haemo-globin.
hémophilie [emɔfili], *s.f.* Med: haemo-philia.
hémorragie [emɔraʒi], *s.f.* haemorrhage.
hémorroïdes [emɔroid], *s.f.pl.* Med: haemorrhoids, F: piles.
*henné [ɛn(n)e], *s.m.* henna.
*henn/ir [enniːr], *v.i.* to whinny; to neigh. s.m. -issement.
héraldique [eraldik]. I. *a.* heraldic. 2. s.f. heraldry.
*héraut [ero], *s.m.* herald.
herbacé [ɛrbase], *a.* herbaceous.
herbage [ɛrbaːʒ], *s.m.* grassland; pasture.
*herbe [ɛrb], *s.f.* 1. herb, plant; Cu: fines herbes, culinary herbs; chives; mauvaise h., weed. 2. grass. 3. en h., (i) unripe (corn, etc.); (ii) (diplomat, etc.) in embryo, in the making. *a.* †-ux, grassy.
herbicide [ɛrbisid], *s.m.* weed-killer.
herbivore [ɛrbivɔːr]. 1. *a.* herbivorous, grass-eating. 2. *s.m.* herbivore.
herboriste [ɛrbɔrist], *s.m.* & *f.* herbalist.
†herculéen [ɛrkyleɛ̃], *a.* herculean.
héréditaire [eredite:r], *a.* hereditary.
hérédité [eredite], *s.f.* heredity.
hérésie [erezi], *s.f.* heresy.
hérétique [eretik]. 1. *a.* heretical. 2. *s.* heretic.
*hériss/er [erise], *v.tr.* to bristle (up); (of bird) to ruffle (feathers).
  se hérisser, to bristle (up); (of hair) to stand on end; to get one's back up.
*hérisson [erisɔ̃], *s.m.* hedgehog.
héritage [eritaːʒ], *s.m.* inheritance, heri-tage.
*hériter [erite]. 1. *v.i.* h. de, to inherit. 2. *v.tr.* to inherit (sth.).
héritier, -ière [eritje, -jɛːr], *s.* heir, *f.* heiress.
hermétique [ɛrmetik], *a.* hermetically sealed. adv. -vement.
hermine [ɛrmin], *s.f.* stoat; ermine.
hernie [ɛrni], *s.f.* 1. hernia, rupture; h. discale, slipped disc. 2. Aut: bulge, swelling (in tyre).
héroïne[1] [erɔin], *s.f.* heroine.

héroïne², *s.f.* heroin.

héroïque [erɔik], *a.* heroic. *adv.* -ment.

héroïsme [erɔism], *s.m.* heroism.

*héron [erɔ̃], *s.m.* heron.

*héros [ero], *s.m.* hero.

†hertzien [ertsjɛ̃], *a.* El: hertzian; faisceau h., radio link.

hésit/er [ezite], *v.i.* 1. to hesitate, waver. 2. to falter. *s.f.* -ation. *a.* -ant.

*hêtre [ɛ(:)tr], *s.m.* beech.

heure [œːr], *s.f.* hour. 1. (*a*) la dernière h., stop-press news; heures supplémentaires, overtime; (*b*) quelle h. est-il? what's the time? cinq heures, five o'clock; (*c*) l. d'éclairage, lighting-up time; Fr.C: h. avancée, summer time; être à l'h., to be punctual; (*d*) pour l'h., for the present. 2. *adv.phrs.* de bonne h., early; tout à l'heure, (*i*) just now; (*ii*) directly. 3. *int.* à la bonne h.! well done!

†heureu/x [œrœ, ørø], *a.* 1. happy. 2. (*a*) successful; (*b*) lucky. 3. favourable, fortunate. 4. felicitous, apt (phrase). *adv.* -sement.

*heurt [œr], *s.m.* shock, knock, bump.

*heurter [œrte], *v.tr. & i.* 1. to knock (against) into. 2. to shock, offend (s.o.'s feelings).
se heurter. 1. se h. à, contre, qn, to run into s.o.; se h. à une difficulté, to come up against a difficulty. 2. to collide.

hexagone [egzagɔn], 1. *a.* hexagonal. 2. *s.m.* hexagon.

hiberner [iberne], *v.i.* to hibernate.

†*hibou [ibu], *s.m.* owl.

†*hideu/x [idø], *a.* hideous. *adv.* -sement.

hier [iɛːr, jɛr], *adv.* yesterday; h. soir, last night.

*hiérarchie [jerarʃi], *s.f.* hierarchy.

hiéroglyphe [jerɔglif], *s.m.* (*a*) hieroglyph; (*b*) pl. hieroglyphics.

hi-fi [ifi], *a.* Rad: etc: F: hi-fi.

hilarité [ilarite], *s.f.* hilarity, mirth.

hindou, -e [ɛ̃du], *a. & s.* Hindu.

hippique [ip(p)ik], *a.* relating to horses; concours h., (*i*) horse-show; (*ii*) race meeting.

hippopotame [ip(p)ɔpɔtam], *s.m.* hippopotamus.

hirondelle [irɔ̃dɛl], *s.f.* 1. swallow. 2. F: = speed cop.

hirsute [irsyt], *a.* hirsute, hairy.

*hisser [ise], *v.tr.* to hoist (up). pull up.

histoire [istwaːr], *s.f.* 1. (*a*) history; (*b*) h. naturelle, natural history. 2. story, tale. 3. lie, story. 4. faire des histoires, to make a fuss.

historien, -ienne [istɔrjɛ̃, -jɛn], *s.* historian.

historique [istɔrik], *a.* historic(al). *adv.* -ment.

hiver [iveːr], *s.m.* winter; en h., in winter.

†hivernal [ivernal], *a.* winter (cold); wintry (weather).

hiverner [iverne], *v.i.* to winter.

*hoch/er [ɔʃe], *v.tr. & i.* h. (de) la tête, (i) to shake one's head; (ii) to nod; (iii) to toss the head. *s.m.* -ement.

*hockey [ɔkɛ], *s.m.* Sp: hockey, Fr.C: (ice) hockey; h. sur glace, ice hockey.

*holà [ɔla], *int.* 1. hallo! 2. stop!

*holding [ɔldiŋ], *s.m.* Fin: holding company.

*hollandais, -aise [ɔlɑ̃dɛ, -ɛːz]. 1. *a.* Dutch. 2. *s.* Dutchman, -woman; les H., the Dutch. 3. *s.m.* Ling: Dutch.

*homard [ɔmaːr], *s.m.* lobster.

homélie [ɔmeli], *s.f.* homily, sermon.

homéopathique [ɔmeɔpatik], *a.* homoeopathic.

homicide¹ [ɔmisid]. 1. *s.m. & f.* homicide. 2. *a.* homicidal.

homicide², *s.m.* homicide; h. involontaire, manslaughter.

hommage [ɔmaːʒ], *s.m.* 1. homage. 2. pl. respects. 3. tribute, token (of esteem).

homme [ɔm], *s.m.* man; mankind; l'abominable h. des neiges, the abominable snowman.

homme-grenouille [ɔmgrənuj], *s.m.* Nau: frogman. pl. hommes-grenouilles.

homme-sandwich [ɔmsɑ̃dvitʃ], *s.m.* sandwich-man. pl. hommes-sandwichs.

homogène [ɔmɔʒɛn], *a.* homogeneous.

homologue [ɔmɔlɔg]. 1. *a.* homologous. 2. *s.m.* homologue; opposite number.

homologué [ɔmɔlɔge], *a.* officially confirmed; prix homologués, authorized charges.

homologuer [ɔmɔlɔge], *v.tr.* Jur: to confirm, ratify; to grant probate of (will).

homonyme [ɔmɔnim]. 1. *a.* homonymous. 2. *s.m.* (*a*) homonym; (*b*) namesake.

†homosexu/el [ɔmɔsɛksɥɛl], *a.* homosexual. *s.f.* -alité.

*hongrois, -oise [ɔ̃grwa, -waːz]. 1. *a.* Hungarian. 2. *s.* Hungarian. 3. *s.m.* Ling: Hungarian.

honnête [ɔnɛ(:)t], *a.* 1. honest, honourable. 2. courteous, well-bred. 3. reasonable, fair. *adv.* -ment.

honnêteté [ɔnɛtte], *s.f.* 1. honesty, uprightness. 2. courtesy. 3. fairness.

honneur [ɔnœːr], *s.m.* 1. honour; piquer qn d'h., to put s.o. on his mettle. 2. faire h. au dîner, to do justice to the dinner; j'ai l'h. de vous faire savoir, I beg to inform you; jouer pour l'h., to play for love. 3. pl. rendre les derniers honneurs à qn, to pay the last tribute to s.o. 4. faire h. à sa signature, to honour one's signature. 5. pl. (at cards) honours.

honorab/le [ɔnɔrabl], *a.* (*a*) honourable; (*b*) respectable, reputable. *s.f.* -ilité. *adv.* -lement.

honoraire [ɔnɔrɛːr]. 1. *a.* honorary. 2. *s.m.pl.* fee(s)

honorer [ɔnɔre], *v.tr.* 1. (*a*) to honour; to respect; (*b*) to do honour to (s.o.); (*c*) to honour (one's obligations). 2. to do credit to (s.o.).

†**honte** [ɔ̃ːt], *s.f.* (*a*) shame; **faire h. à qn**, to put s.o. to shame; (*b*) **fausse h.**, bashfulness, self-consciousness.

†**honteu/x** [ɔ̃tø], *a.* 1. ashamed. 2. shameful, disgraceful. *adv.* **-sement**.

†**hôpital** [opital], *s.m.* hospital.

†**hoquet** [ɔkɛ], *s.m.* hiccup.

horaire [ɔrɛːr], 1. *a.* **signal h.**, time-signal. 2. *s.m.* timetable.

*†**horde** [ɔrd], *s.f.* horde.

horizon [ɔrizɔ̃], *s.m.* horizon.

†**horizontal** [ɔrizɔ̃tal], *a.* horizontal. *adv.* **-ement**.

horloge [ɔrlɔːʒ], *s.f.* clock.

horloger [ɔrlɔʒe], *s.m.* watchmaker.

horlogerie [ɔrlɔʒri], *s.f.* 1. clock-making; **mouvement d'h.**, clockwork. 2. watchmaker's shop.

hormone [ɔrmɔn], *s.f.* hormone.

hormonothérapie [ɔrmɔnoterapi], *s.f.* hormonotherapy, hormone treatment.

horoscope [ɔrɔskɔp], *s.m.* horoscope.

horreur [ɔr(r)œːr], *s.f.* horror.

horrible [ɔr(r)ibl], *a.* horrible. *adv.* **-ment**.

horripilant [ɔr(r)ipilɑ̃], *a.* F: maddening.

*****hors** [ɔːr], *prep.* 1. (*a*) out of, outside; longueur h. tout, over-all length; (*b*) except; tous h. un seul, all but one. 2. *prep.phr.* **h. de**, out of (outside; **être h. de soi**, to be beside oneself; **h. d'ici! get out!**

*****hors-bord** [ɔrbɔːr], *s.m.inv.* outboard motor.

*****hors-concours** [ɔrkɔ̃kuːr], *a., adv. & s.m.inv.* not competing, hors-concours.

*****hors-d'œuvre** [ɔrdœːvr], *s.m.inv.* Cu: hors-d'œuvre(s).

*****hors-jeu** [ɔrʒø], *a. & s.m.inv.* Sp: offside.

*****hors-texte** [ɔrtɛkst], *s.m.inv.* (inset) plate (in book).

hortensia [ɔrtɑ̃sja], *s.m.* hydrangea.

horticole [ɔrtikɔl], *a.* horticultural.

horticulture [ɔrtikyltyːr], *s.f.* horticulture; gardening.

hospice [ɔspis], *s.m.* 1. hospice. 2. (*a*) old people's home; (*b*) children's home.

†**hospitalier** [ɔspitalje], *a.* hospitable.

hospitalité [ɔspitalite], *s.f.* hospitality.

hospitalis/er [ɔspitalize], *v.tr.* to send (s.o.) to hospital. *s.f.* **-ation**.

hostie [ɔsti], *s.f.* (eucharistic) host.

hostile [ɔstil], *a.* hostile; unfriendly.

hostilité [ɔstilite], *s.f.* 1. hostility (contre, to); enmity. 2. *pl.* hostilities.

hôte, hôtesse [oːt, otɛs], *s.* 1. host, f. hostess; landlord, landlady; **hôtesse de l'air, air hostess**. 2. guest.

hôtel [otɛl, -ɔt], *s.m.* 1. public building; **h. de ville**, town hall. 2. (*a*) hotel; (*b*) **h. meublé**, residential hotel (providing rooms but not meals).

hôtellerie [otɛlri], *s.f.* hostelry, inn.

hôtel/ier, -ière [otalje, -jɛːr], (*a*) *a.* **l'industrie hôtelière**, the hotel trade; (*b*) **hotel keeper**.

*****houblon** [ublɔ̃], *s.m.* hop(s).

*****houe** [u], *s.f.* hoe.

*****houer** [ue], *v.tr.* to hoe.

*****houille** [uj], *s.f.* 1. coal. 2. **h. blanche**, water-power.

*****houillère** [ujɛːr], *s.f.* coal-mine.

*****houle** [ul], *s.f.* swell, surge (of sea). *a.* †**-ux**.

*****houppe** [up], *s.f.* (*a*) tuft; pompon; powder-puff; (*b*) tassel.

*****hourra** [ura], *int.* & *s.m.* hurrah(!)

*****houspiller** [uspije], *v.tr.* to hustle; to jostle; to handle roughly.

*****housse** [us], *s.f.* (*a*) loose cover; (*b*) dust sheet.

*****houx** [u], *s.m.* holly.

*****hublot** [yblo], *s.m.* Nau: porthole.

*****huche** [yʃ], *s.f.* (bread) bin.

*****huer** [ye, ɥe], 1. *v.i.* (*a*) to shout, halloo; (*b*) (*of owl*) to hoot. 2. *v.tr.* to boo.

huile [ɥil], *s.f.* oil; **h. comestible**, edible oil; **h. de lin**, linseed oil; **h. minérale**, mineral oil; F: **les huiles**, the big shots.

huiler [ɥile], *v.tr.* to oil; to lubricate.

†**huileux** [ɥilø], *a.* oily, greasy.

huis [ɥi], *s.m.* Jur: **à h. clos**, in camera.

huissier [ɥisje], *s.m.* bailiff.

*****huit** [ɥit], *num.a.* & *s.m.inv.* eight; **h. jours, a week; d'aujourd'hui en h.**, today week.

*****huitaine** [ɥitɛn], *s.f.* week.

*****huitante** [ɥitɑ̃t], *num.a.inv.* (*Swiss, Belgian, use*) eighty.

*****huitantième** [ɥitɑ̃tjɛm], *num.a.* (*Swiss, Belgian, use*) eightieth.

*****huitième** [ɥitjɛm], 1. *num.a.* & *s.* eighth. 2. *s.f.* eighth (part).

huitre [ɥitr], *s.f.* oyster.

humain [ymɛ̃], *a.* 1. human. 2. humane. *adv.* **-ement**.

humanitaire [ymanitɛːr], *a.* & *s.* humanitarian.

humanité [ymanite], *s.f.* humanity.

humble [œ̃ːbl], *a.* humble, lowly. *adv.* **-ment**.

humecter [ymɛkte], *v.tr.* to damp, moisten.

*****humer** [yme], *v.tr.* to suck in, up.

humérus [ymerys], *s.m. Anat:* humerus.

humeur [ymœːr], *s.f.* (*a*) humour, mood; (*b*) temper; **avec h.**, testily.

humide [ymid], *a.* damp, moist; **temps h. et froid**, raw weather.

humidificateur [ymidifikatœːr], *s.m. Ind:* humidor; H: humidifier.

humidité [ymidite], *s.f.* humidity, damp(ness), moisture; "**craint l'h.**," 'to be kept dry.'

humili/er [ymilje], *v.tr.* to humiliate. *s.f.* **-ation**. *a.* **-ant**.

humilité [ymilite], *s.f.* humility.

humoriste [ymɔrist], *s.m.* & *f.* humorist.

humoristique [ymɔristik], a. humorous.

humour [ymur], s.m. humour.

humus [ymys], s.m. humus.

*hurl/er [yrle]. 1. v.i. to howl; to roar. 2. v.tr. to bawl out. s.m. -ement.

*hutte [yt], s.f. hut, shed, shanty.

hybride [ibrid], a. & s.m. hybrid.

hydrate [idrat], s.m. hydrate.

hydraulique [idrolik]. 1. a. hydraulic; énergie h., hydroelectric power. 2. s.f. (a) hydraulics; (b) hydraulic engineering.

hydravion [idravjɔ̃], s.m. seaplane.

hydroélectrique [idroelektrik], a. hydro-electric.

hydrogène [idrɔʒɛn], s.m. hydrogen.

hydrophile [idrɔfil], a. absorbent (cotton wool).

hydropisie [idrɔpizi], s.f. dropsy.

hyène [jɛn], s.f. hyena.

hygiène [iʒjɛn], s.f. hygiene.

hygiénique [iʒjenik], a. hygienic; sanitary; papier h., toilet paper; serviette h., sanitary towel.

hymne [imn]. 1. s.m. patriotic song. 2. s.f. hymn.

hyperfréquence [iperfrekɑ̃s], s.f. microwave.

hypergol [ipergɔl], s.m. hypergol.

hypermétropie [ipermetrɔpi], s.f. hypermetropia, long-sightedness.

hypertension [ipertɑ̃sjɔ̃], s.f. hypertension, high blood-pressure.

hypnotiser [ipnotize], v.tr. to hypnotize.

hypnotisme [ipnotism], s.m. hypnotism.

hypocrisie [ipɔkrizi], s.f. hypocrisy.

hypocrite [ipɔkrit]. 1. a. hypocritical. 2. s.m. & f. hypocrite. adv. -ment.

hypotension [ipotɑ̃sjɔ̃], s.f. hypotension, low blood-pressure.

hypothécaire [ipotekɛ:r], s.m. & f. mortgagee.

hypothèque [ipotɛk], s.f. mortgage.

‡hypothéquer [ipoteke], v.tr. to mortgage.

hypothèse [ipotɛːz], s.f. hypothesis.

hypothétique [ipotetik], a. hypothetical.

hystérie [isteri], s.f. hysteria.

hystérique [isterik], a. hysterical.

I

I, i [i], s.m. 1. (the letter) I, i. 2. i grec, (the letter) Y, y.

ibérique [iberik], a. Geog: la péninsule i., the Iberian peninsula.

iceberg [isberg], s.m. iceberg.

ici [isi], adv. 1. here; i.-bas, here below, on earth; passez par i., this way; P.T.T: i. Dupont, Dupont speaking. 2. now; jusqu'i., up to now; d'i. peu, before long.

†idéal [ideal], a. & s.m. ideal. adv. -ement. -ism. a. & s.m. & f. -iste.

idée [ide], s.f. 1. idea; (a) notion; quelle i.! the idea! i. fixe, obsession; (b) view, opinion; (c) whim, fancy. 2. mind; cela m'est sorti de l'i., it went clean out of my mind.

identifi/er [idɑ̃tifje], v.tr. to identify. s.f. -cation.

identique [idɑ̃tik], a. identical (à, with). adv. -ment.

identité [idɑ̃tite], s.f. identity.

idiomatique [idjomatik], a. idiomatic. ●

idiome [idjom], s.m. language.

idiot, -ote [idjo, -ɔt]. 1. a. idiotic. 2. s. idiot. adv. -ement.

idiotie [idjɔsi], s.f. idiocy.

idiotisme [idjɔtizm], s.m. idiom; idiomatic expression.

idol/e [idɔl], s.f. idol, image. a. -âtre. s.f. -âtrie.

idyllique [idilik], a. idyllic.

if [if], s.m. yew (tree).

ignare [iɲaːr], a. ignorant.

ignifuge [iɲifyʒ]. 1. a. fire-proof. 2. s.m. fire-proof(ing) material.

‡ignifuger [iɲifyʒe], v.tr. to fire-proof.

ignoble [iɲɔbl], a. disgraceful; sordid; vile. adv. -ment.

ignomin/ie [iɲɔmini], s.f. ignominy, shame; disgrace. a. †-ieux. adv. -ieusement.

ignorance [iɲɔrɑ̃s], s.f. ignorance.

ignorant, -ante, [iɲɔrɑ̃, -ɑ̃ːt]. 1. a. ignorant, uninstructed. 2. s. ignoramus, dunce.

ignoré [iɲɔre], a. unknown.

ignorer [iɲɔre], v.tr. not to know; to be ignorant, unaware, of (sth.).

il, ils [il]. 1. pers.pron.nom.m. he, it; they. 2. inv. it, there; (a) il est six heures, it's six o'clock; (b) (with impers. vbs.) il faut partir, we must start; il y a, there is; there are.

île [il], s.f. island.

†illégal [illegal], a. illegal, unlawful. adv. -ement.

illégalité [illegalite], s.f. illegality.

illégitime [illeʒitim], a. illegitimate; unlawful. adv. -ment.

illégitimité [illeʒitimite], s.f. illegitimacy; unlawfulness.

illettré [illetre], a. illiterate; uneducated.

illicite [illisit], a. illicit, unlawful. adv. -ment.

illimité [illimite], a. unlimited, boundless.

illisible [illizibl], a. illegible, unreadable. adv. -ment.

illogique [illɔʒik], a. illogical; inconsequent. adv. -ment.

illumin/er [illymine], v.tr. 1. to light up. 2. to enlighten. s.f. -ation, illumination.

illus/ion [illyzjɔ̃], s.f. 1. illusion. 2. delusion. s.m. & f. -ionniste, conjurer. a. -oire, illusory.

illustrateur [illystratœ:r], s.m. illustrator.
illustration [illystrasjɔ̃], s.f. illustration.
illustre [illystr], a. illustrious, famous.
illustré [illystre], a. illustrated paper, magazine.
illustrer [illystre], v.tr. 1. to make famous. 2. to illustrate.
ilot [ilo], s.m. 1. islet, small island. 2. block (of houses).
image [ima:ʒ], s.f. 1. image. 2. picture.
imagé [imaʒe], a. vivid (style, etc.).
imagin/er [imaʒine], v.tr. to imagine. a. -able. a. -aire, imaginary. a. †-atif. s.f. -ation.
imbattable [ɛ̃batabl], a. unbeatable (record).
imbécile [ɛ̃besil]. 1. a. (a) imbecile; (b) silly, idiotic. 2. s.m. & f. idiot; fool.
imbécilité [ɛ̃besilite], s.f. (a) imbecility; (b) stupidity.
imberbe [ɛ̃berb], a. beardless; callow.
imbiber [ɛ̃bibe], v.tr. to soak.
s'imbiber, to absorb.
imbu [ɛ̃by], a. imbued, soaked; i. de préjugés, steeped in prejudice.
imbuvable [ɛ̃byvabl], a. undrinkable.
imit/er [imite], v.tr. to imitate. s. -ateur, -atrice. a. †-atif. s.f. -ation.
immaculé [immakyle], a. immaculate.
immangeable [i:mɑ̃ʒabl, ɛ̃m-], a. uneatable.
immanquable [ɛ̃mɑ̃kabl], a. inevitable. adv. -ment, for certain.
†immatériel [immaterjɛl], a. immaterial, unsubstantial; intangible (assets, etc.).
immatri/culer [immatrikyle], v.tr. to register, enroll (s.o., car, document); voiture immatriculée 809HC64, car with number (plate) 809HC64. s.f. -cule, registration number. s.f. -culation, registration.
immaturité [immatyrite], s.f. immaturity.
immédiat [immedja(t)], a. immediate. adv. -ement.
immen/se [immɑ̃:s], a. 1. immeasurable, boundless. 2. immense, vast, huge. s.f. -sité, immensity.
‡immer/ger [immerʒe], v.tr. to immerse, dip; to lay a (submarine) cable. s.f. -sion.
immérité [immerite], a. undeserved.
immesurable [ɛ̃mɔzyrabl], a. immeasurable.
immeuble [immœbl], s.m. (a) real estate; (b) block of flats; (business) premises.
immig/rer [immigre], v.i. to immigrate. a. & s. -rant. s.f. -ration. s. -ré, -rée, settler; immigrant.
immin/ence [imminɑ̃:s], s.f. imminence. a. -ent.
‡immiscer (s') [simmise], v.pr. to interfere.
immobile [imɔbil], a. 1. motionless, still. 2. immovable; firm.

†immobilier [imɔbilje], a. biens immobiliers, real estate; société, agence, immobilière, (i) building society; (ii) estate agency; agent i., estate agent.
immobilis/er [immɔbilize] v.tr. 1. to immobilize. 2. to tie up (capital). s.f. -ation.
immobilité [immɔbilite], s.f. immobility.
immodéré [immɔdere], a. immoderate. adv. -ment.
immonde [immɔ̃:d], a. filthy; vile.
immondices [immɔ̃dis], s.f.pl. dirt, refuse.
†immoral [immɔral], a. immoral. adv. -ement.
immoralité [immɔralite], s.f. immorality.
immort/el, -elle [immɔrtɛl]. 1. a. immortal. 2. s.f. immortelle, everlasting (flower). s.f. -alité, immortality.
immuable [immɥabl], a. immutable, unalterable; fixed, unchanging. adv. -ment.
immun/iser [immynize], v.tr. Med: to immunize (s.o., contre, from). s.m. -isant, protective serum. s.f. -isation. s.f. -ité, immunity.
impact [ɛ̃pakt], s.m. impact, shock.
impair [ɛ̃pɛ:r], a. odd, uneven; s.m. F: commettre un i., to drop a brick.
impardonnable [ɛ̃pardɔnabl], a. unpardonable.
imparfait [ɛ̃parfɛ], a. 1. unfinished, uncompleted. 2. imperfect, defective. 3. a. & s.m. Gram: imperfect (tense).
†impartial [ɛ̃parsjal], a. impartial, unprejudiced. adv. -ement.
impartialité [ɛ̃parsjalite], s.f. impartiality.
impasse [ɛ̃pɑ:s], s.f. 1. cul de sac; P.N: no through road. 2. deadlock, impasse.
impassi/bilité [ɛ̃pasibilite], s.f. impassibility. a. -ble, impassive. adv. -blement.
impati/enter [ɛ̃pasjɑ̃te], v.tr. to annoy, to irritate (s.o.). s.f. -ence. a. -ent. adv. -emment.
s'impatienter, to lose patience.
impayable [ɛ̃pejabl], a. priceless; F: killingly funny.
impecca/bilité [ɛ̃pekabilite], s.f. impeccability. a. -ble. adv. -blement.
impénétr/abilité [ɛ̃penetrabilite], s.f. 1. impenetrability. 2. inscrutability. a. -able.
impénitent [ɛ̃penitɑ̃], a. impenitent.
impensable [ɛ̃pɑ̃sabl], a. unthinkable.
imper [ɛ̃pɛr], s.m. Cl: F: mac.
†impérat/if [ɛ̃peratif], a. & s.m. imperative.
impératrice [ɛ̃peratris], s.f. empress.
imperceptible [ɛ̃persɛptibl], a. imperceptible. adv. -ment.
imperfection [ɛ̃perfɛksjɔ̃], s.f. imperfection; defect, flaw.
†impérial, -ale [ɛ̃perjal]. 1. a. imperial. 2. s.f. impériale, top (deck) (of bus).

†impérieu/x [ɛ̃perjø], *a.* 1. imperious, haughty. 2. imperative, pressing. *adv.* -sement.

impérissable [ɛ̃perisabl], *a.* imperishable.

imperméa/biliser [ɛ̃permeabilize], *v.tr.* to (water)proof (cloth, etc.). *s.f.* -bilité.

imperméable [ɛ̃permeabl]. 1. *a.* impervious; waterproof. 2. *s.m.* raincoat.

†impersonn/el [ɛ̃persɔnɛl], *a.* impersonal. *adv.* -ellement.

impertin/ence [ɛ̃pertinɑ̃ːs], *s.f.* impertinence. *a.* -ent. *adv.* -emment.

imperturb/abilité [ɛ̃pertyrbabilite], *s.f.* imperturbability. *a.* -able.

†impétueu/x [ɛ̃petɥø], *a.* impetuous. *adv.* -sement.

impétuosité [ɛ̃petɥozite], *s.f.* impetuosity.

impie [ɛ̃pi], *a.* impious; blasphemous.

impiété [ɛ̃pjete], *s.f.* impiety, godlessness.

impitoyable [ɛ̃pitwajabl], *a.* (*a*) pitiless; ruthless; (*b*) relentless. *adv.* -ment.

implac/abilité [ɛ̃plakabilite], *s.f.* implacability. *a.* -able, relentless. *adv.* -ablement.

implanter [ɛ̃plɑ̃te], *v.tr.* to implant. s'implanter, to take root; F: s'i. chez qn., to foist oneself on s.o.

implicite [ɛ̃plisit], *a.* implicit. *adv.* -ment.

impliquer [ɛ̃plike], *v.tr.* to implicate, involve.

implorer [ɛ̃plɔre], *v.tr.* to implore.

impoli [ɛ̃pɔli], *a.* impolite, rude. *adv.* -ment.

impolitesse [ɛ̃pɔlites], *s.f.* impoliteness; breach of good manners.

impolitique [ɛ̃pɔlitik], *a.* ill-advised. *adv.* -ment.

impopul/arité [ɛ̃pɔpylarite], *s.f.* unpopularity. *a.* -aire, unpopular.

import/er¹ [ɛ̃pɔrte], *v.tr.* to import (goods). *a.* & *s.* -ateur, -atrice, (i) importing (firm); (ii) importer. *s.f.* -ation.

importer², *v.i.* (*used only in third pers., participles and inf.*) to be of importance; to matter; n'importe, no matter, never mind; n'importe qui, quoi, anyone, anything.

importun, -une [ɛ̃pɔrtœ̃, -yn]. 1. *a.* importunate; tiresome; unwelcome. 2. *s.* nuisance.

importun/er [ɛ̃pɔrtyne], *v.tr.* to importune. *v.f.* -ité, importunity.

impos/er, -ée [ɛ̃poze]. 1. *a.* Com: prix i., fixed price. 2. *s.* tax-payer.

impos/er [ɛ̃poze]. I. *v.tr.* 1. to impose, prescribe; to set (task); to indicate (terms). 2. to tax. II. *v.i.* 1. (en) i., to inspire respect. 2. (en) i. à qn, to impose on s.o. *s.f.* -ition, imposition; tax(ation). *a.* -ant. *a.* -able, taxable.

s'imposer. 1. to assert oneself. 2. s'i. à qn, to foist oneself upon s.o. 3. to be indispensable; une visite au Louvre s'impose, we, you, simply must visit the Louvre.

imposs/ibilité [ɛ̃pɔsibilite], *s.f.* impossibility. *a.* -ible, impossible.

imposteur [ɛ̃pɔstœːr], *s.m.* impostor.

imposture [ɛ̃pɔstyːr], *s.f.* deception; swindle.

impôt [ɛ̃po], *s.m.* tax, duty.

impotent, -ente [ɛ̃pɔtɑ̃, -ɑ̃ːt]. 1. *a.* helpless; bedridden; crippled. 2. *s.* helpless invalid; cripple.

impraticable [ɛ̃pratikabl], *a.* impracticable, unworkable; chemin i., road unfit for traffic.

imprécation [ɛ̃prekasjɔ̃], *s.f.* curse.

imprécis [ɛ̃presi], *a.* vague, indefinite.

‡imprégn/er [ɛ̃pregne], *v.tr.* to impregnate (de, with). *s.f.* -ation. s'imprégner, to become saturated with, to soak up, to soak in.

imprenable [ɛ̃prənabl], *a.* impregnable; vue i., unspoilable view.

impression [ɛ̃presjɔ̃], *s.f.* 1. printing; faute d'i., misprint; i. en couleurs, colour print. 2. (mental) impression.

impressionn/er [ɛ̃presjɔne], *v.tr.* to impress. *a.* -able. *a.* -ant, impressive.

imprévisible [ɛ̃previzibl], *a.* unforeseeable.

imprévoy/ance [ɛ̃prevwajɑ̃ːs], *s.f.* (*a*) lack of foresight; (*b*) improvidence. *a.* -ant, improvident.

imprévu [ɛ̃prevy]. 1. *a.* unforeseen, unexpected (event). 2. *s.m.* en cas d'i., in case of an emergency; imprévus, unforeseen expenses.

imprimé [ɛ̃prime], *s.m.* printed paper; book; (official) form; P.T.T: imprimés, printed matter.

imprim/er [ɛ̃prime], *v.tr.* to print. *s.f.* -erie, printing works; press. *s.m.* -eur, printer.

improb/abilité [ɛ̃prɔbabilite], *s.f.* improbability. *a.* -able.

†improduct/if [ɛ̃prɔdyktif], *a.* unproductive. *adv.* -ivement.

impromptu [ɛ̃prɔ̃p(t)y]. 1. *adv.* impromptu. 2. *a.inv.* impromptu; extempore.

impropre [ɛ̃prɔpr], *a.* (*a*) incorrect, wrong; (*b*) unfit (à, for).

impropriété [ɛ̃prɔpriete], *s.f.* impropriety.

improvis/er [ɛ̃prɔvize], *v.tr.* to improvise; discours improvisé, impromptu speech. *s.f.* -ation, improvisation.

improviste (à l') [ɛ̃prɔvist], *adv.phr.* unexpectedly; unawares.

imprudence [ɛ̃prydɑ̃ːs], *s.f.* imprudence; F: cheek.

imprud/ent [ɛ̃prydɑ̃], *a.* imprudent, rash. *adv.* -emment.

impudence [ɛ̃pydɑ̃ːs], *s.f.* impudence; F: cheek.

impud/ent [ɛ̃pydɑ̃], a. impudent, F: cheeky; insolent.

impuiss/ance [ɛ̃pɥisɑ̃:s], s.f. impotence; powerlessness, helplessness. a. **-ant.**

†impulsif [ɛ̃pylsif], a. impulsive.

impulsion [ɛ̃pylsjɔ̃], s.f. 1. (a) E: El: impulse; **radar à impulsions**, pulse radar; (b) impetus, stimulus. 2. **sous l'i.** du moment, on the spur of the moment.

impuni/ [ɛ̃pyni], a. unpunished. adv. **-ément,** with impunity.

impunité [ɛ̃pynite], s.f. impunity.

impur [ɛ̃py:r], a. impure.

impureté [ɛ̃pyrte], s.f. impurity.

imput/er [ɛ̃pyte], v.tr. to impute, attribute; to charge (sth.) to s.o., to an account. a. **-able,** attributable (à, to). s.f. **-ation,** charge.

inabordable [inabɔrdabl], a. unapproachable, inaccessible; prohibitive (price).

inacceptable [inaksɛptabl], a. unacceptable.

inaccessib/le [inaksɛsibl], a. inaccessible, unapproachable; F: un-get-at-able (place, etc.); **i. à la pitié,** incapable of, proof against, pity. s.f. **-ilité.**

inaccoutumé [inakutyme], a. unaccustomed.

inachevé [inaʃve], a. unfinished.

inac/tion [inaksjɔ̃], s.f. inaction, idleness. a. **-tif,** idle. s.f. **-tivité,** inactivity.

inadaptation [inadaptasjɔ̃], s.f. maladjustment.

inadapté, -ée [inadapte], a. & s. maladjusted.

inadmis/ibilité [inadmisibilite], s.f. inadmissibility. a. **-ible.**

inadvertance [inadvɛrtɑ̃:s], s.f. 1. inadvertency; **par i.,** inadvertently. 2. oversight, mistake; carelessness.

inaliénable [inaljenabl], a. Jur: untransferable (property); indefeasible (right). adv. **-ment.**

inaltér/able [inaltérabl], a. (a) that does not deteriorate; **i. à l'air,** unaffected by air; (b) unfailing, unvarying (good humour).

inamovible [inamɔvibl], a. irremovable; untransferable (employee); (post) held for life.

inanimé [inanime], a. 1. inanimate, lifeless. 2. senseless, unconscious.

inanité [inanite], s.f. inanity, futility.

inapaisable [inapɛzabl], a. inappeasable.

inapaisé [inapɛze], a. unappeased.

inaperçu [inapɛrsy], a. (a) unseen; (b) unnoticed.

inapplicable [inaplikabl], a. inapplicable.

inappréciable [inapresjabl], a. 1. inappreciable. 2. inestimable, invaluable.

inapprécié [inapresje], a. unappreciated.

inapte [inapt], a. inapt; unfit (à, for); **les inaptes,** the unemployable.

inaptitude [inaptityd], s.f. inaptitude.

inarticulé [inartikyle], a. inarticulate.

inassouv/i [inasuvi], a. unappeased (hunger). a. **-issable,** insatiable.

inattaquable [inatakabl], a. unassailable (position, right); **i. aux acides,** acid-resisting, -proof.

inattendu [inatɑ̃dy], a. unexpected.

inatten/tion [inatɑ̃sjɔ̃], s.f. inattention (à, to), carelessness; **faute d'i.,** careless mistake. a. **†-tif.** adv. **-ivement.**

inaudible [inodibl], a. inaudible.

inaugur/er [inogyre], v.tr. to inaugurate. a. **†-al.** s.f. **-ation.**

inavoué [inavwe], a. unacknowledged, unconfessed.

incalculable [ɛ̃kalkylabl], a. incalculable.

incandescent [ɛ̃kɑ̃dɛssɑ̃], a. incandescent.

incapable [ɛ̃kapabl], a. 1. incapable, unfit. 2. unable.

incapacité [ɛ̃kapasite], s.f. incapacity, unfitness; **i. de travail,** industrial disablement.

‡incarcér/er [ɛ̃karsere], v.tr. to imprison. s.f. **-ation.**

incarné [ɛ̃karne], a. incarnate.

incendie [ɛ̃sɑ̃di], s.m. fire; **poste d'i.,** fire station; **i. volontaire,** arson.

incendi/er [ɛ̃sɑ̃dje], v.tr. to set (house, etc.) on fire. a. & s. **-aire,** incendiary.

incertain [ɛ̃sɛrtɛ̃], a. (a) uncertain, doubtful; (b) unreliable.

incertitude [ɛ̃sɛrtityd], s.f. (a) uncertainty, doubt; (b) indecision.

incessamment [ɛ̃sɛsamɑ̃], adv. 1. unceasingly, incessantly. 2. immediately.

incessant [ɛ̃sɛsɑ̃], a. unceasing, ceaseless.

incid/ent [ɛ̃sidɑ̃], s.m. incident; **arriver sans i.,** to arrive without mishap. adv. **-emment.**

‡incinér/er [ɛ̃sinere], v.tr. (a) to burn to ashes; (b) to cremate. s.m. **-ateur,** incinerator. s.f. **-ation.**

†incis/if [ɛ̃sizif], a. incisive, sharp, cutting. adv. **-ivement.**

incision [ɛ̃sizjɔ̃], s.f. incision.

incit/er [ɛ̃site], v.tr. to incite; to urge (on). s.f. **-ation,** incitement (à, to).

incivil [ɛ̃sivil], a. uncivil, rude. adv. **-ement.**

incivilité [ɛ̃sivilite], s.f. incivility, rudeness.

inclinaison [ɛ̃klinɛzɔ̃], s.f. incline; slant; slope; tilt; pitch (of roof).

inclination [ɛ̃klinasjɔ̃], s.f. inclination. 1. bending; bowing; nod (of head). 2. (a) propensity; (b) attachment; **mariage d'i.,** marrying for love.

incliner [ɛ̃kline]. 1. v.tr. to incline; (a) to slope; (b) to tip up; (c) to bend, bow; (d) to influence (s.o.). 2. v.i. (a) to lean, slope; (b) to feel inclined. **s'incliner.** 1. to slant, slope. 2. to yield (to s.o.); **j'ai dû m'i.,** I had to give in.

inclus [ɛ̃kly], a. (a) enclosed; (b) included.

inclus/ion [ɛ̃klyzjɔ̃], s.f. inclusion. a. **†-if.** adv. **-ivement.**

incohér/ence [ɛ̃kɔerɑ̃:s], s.f. incoherence. a. -ent.

incolore [ɛ̃kɔlɔːr], a. colourless.

incomber [ɛ̃kɔ̃be], v.i. (used only in the 3rd pers.) to be incumbent (à, on); impers. il nous incombe de, we must, should.

incombustible [ɛ̃kɔ̃bystibl], a. incombustible; fireproof.

incommod/e [ɛ̃kɔmɔd], a. inconvenient. adv. -ément.

incommoder [ɛ̃kɔmɔde], v.tr. to inconvenience, incommode; (of food, etc.) to upset (s.o.).

incomparable [ɛ̃kɔ̃parabl], a. incomparable. adv. -ment.

incompat/ibilité [ɛ̃kɔ̃patibilite], s.f. incompatibility. a. -ible. adv. -iblement.

incompét/ence [ɛ̃kɔ̃petɑ̃:s], s.f. incompetence. a. -ent, incompetent.

†incompl/et [ɛ̃kɔ̃plɛ], a. incomplete. adv. -ètement.

incompréhensible [ɛ̃kɔ̃preɑ̃sibl], a. incomprehensible. adv. -ment.

incompréhens/ion [ɛ̃kɔ̃preɑ̃sjɔ̃], s.f. lack of understanding, obtuseness. a. †-if.

incompris [ɛ̃kɔ̃pri], a. misunderstood.

inconcevable [ɛ̃kɔ̃s(ə)vabl], a. unthinkable, unimaginable. adv. -ment.

inconciliable [ɛ̃kɔ̃siljabl], a. irreconcilable, incompatible (avec, with).

†inconditionnel [ɛ̃kɔ̃disjɔnɛl], a. unconditional. adv. -ellement.

inconduite [ɛ̃kɔ̃dɥit], s.f. misconduct.

inconfort [ɛ̃kɔ̃fɔr], s.m. discomfort. a. -able, uncomfortable.

incongru [ɛ̃kɔ̃gry], a. 1. incongruous, foolish. 2. improper.

incongruité [ɛ̃kɔ̃gryite], s.f. (a) incongruity, absurdity; (b) impropriety; (c) foolish, tactless, remark, action.

inconnu, -ue [ɛ̃kɔny]. 1. a. & s.m. unknown. 2. s. unknown person.

inconsci/ence [ɛ̃kɔ̃sjɑ̃:s], s.f. unconsciousness. a. -ent. adv. -emment.

inconséqu/ence [ɛ̃kɔ̃sekɑ̃:s], s.f. inconsequence, inconsistency. a. -ent.

inconsist/ance [ɛ̃kɔ̃sistɑ̃:s], s.f. 1. insubstantiality. 2. inconsistency. a. -ant.

inconsolable [ɛ̃kɔ̃sɔlabl], a. inconsolable.

inconstance [ɛ̃kɔ̃stɑ̃:s], s.f. inconstancy, fickleness.

inconstant [ɛ̃kɔ̃stɑ̃], a. 1. inconstant; Sp: joueur i., erratic player. 2. changeable.

†inconstitutionnel [ɛ̃kɔ̃stitysjɔnɛl], a. unconstitutional. adv. -lement.

incontestable [ɛ̃kɔ̃tɛstabl], a. incontestable; beyond all question. adv. -ment.

inconvenant [ɛ̃kɔ̃vnɑ̃], a. improper, unseemly; indecent.

inconvénient [ɛ̃kɔ̃venjɑ̃], s.m. drawback; il n'y a pas d'i. there's no objection.

incorpor/er [ɛ̃kɔrpɔre], v.tr. to incorporate. s.f. -ation.

incorrect [ɛ̃kɔr(r)ɛkt], a. incorrect. adv. -ement.

incorrigible [ɛ̃kɔr(r)iʒibl], a. incorrigible; F: hopeless. adv. -ment.

incorruptible [ɛ̃kɔr(r)yptibl], a. incorruptible.

incrédibilité [ɛ̃kredibilite], s.f. incredibility.

incrédul/e [ɛ̃kredyl]. 1. a. incredulous. 2. s. unbeliever.

incrédulité [ɛ̃kredylite], s.f. incredulity.

increvable [ɛ̃krəvabl], a. puncture-proof (tyre); P: (of pers.) tireless.

incrimin/er [ɛ̃krimine], v.tr. to incriminate, accuse, indict (s.o.). s.f. -ation.

incroyable [ɛ̃krwajabl], a. incredible, unbelievable. adv. -ment.

incruster [ɛ̃kryste], v.tr. to encrust; Techn: to inlay (de, with). s'incruster. 1. (of boiler, etc.) to become furred up. 2. F: to dig oneself in; il s'incruste, he stays too long.

incuba/tion [ɛ̃kybasjɔ̃], s.f. incubation. s.m. -teur.

incul/per [ɛ̃kylpe], v.tr. to indict, charge. s.f. -pation, indictment, charge.

inculquer [ɛ̃kylke], v.tr. to inculcate, to instil.

inculte [ɛ̃kylt], a. uncultivated; waste (land); untutored (mind).

incurable [ɛ̃kyrabl], a. & s. incurable.

incursion [ɛ̃kyrsjɔ̃], s.f. inroad, incursion.

indéc/ence [ɛ̃desɑ̃:s], s.f. indecency. a. -ent. adv. -emment.

indéchiffrable [ɛ̃deʃifrabl], a. unintelligible; illegible.

indécis [ɛ̃desi], a. 1. unsettled; doubtful; vague. 2. undecided.

indéfendable [ɛ̃defɑ̃dabl], a. indefensible.

indéfini [ɛ̃defini], a. 1. indefinite. 2. undefined. adv. -ment, indefinitely. a. -ssable, undefinable.

indéfrichable [ɛ̃defriʃabl], a. waste (land).

indéfrisable [ɛ̃defrizabl], s.f. permanent wave.

indélicat [ɛ̃delika], a. 1. coarse; tactless; unscrupulous. adv. -ement.

indélicatesse [ɛ̃delikates], s.f. 1. tactlessness; unscrupulousness. 2. unscrupulous, dishonest, action.

indémaillable [ɛ̃demajabl], a. ladderproof (stocking).

indemne [ɛ̃dɛmn], a. (a) without loss; (b) undamaged; (c) uninjured.

indemnis/er [ɛ̃dɛmnize], v.tr. to compensate. s.f. -ation, compensation.

indemnité [ɛ̃dɛmnite], s.f. (a) indemnity, compensation; (b) penalty; (c) allowance, grant; i. de chômage, unemployment benefit; i. parlementaire = M.P.'s salary.

indéniable [ɛ̃denjabl], a. undeniable.

indépend/ance [ɛ̃depɑ̃dɑ̃:s], s.f. independence. a. -ant. adv. -amment.

indescriptible [ɛ̃deskriptibl], a. indescribable. adv. -ment.

indésirable [ɛ̃dezirabl], a. & s. undesirable.

indestructible [ɛ̃destryktibl], a. indestructible. adv. -ment.

indéterminé [ɛ̃determine], a. undetermined, indefinite.

index [ɛ̃deks], s.m.inv. 1. (a) forefinger; (b) pointer. 2. index (of book).

index/er [ɛ̃dekse], v.tr. to index. 2. to peg prices. s.f. -ation, pricepegging.

indicateur [ɛ̃dikatœr]. 1. (a) poteau i., signpost; lampe indicatrice, tell-tale lamp. 2. s.m. (a) timetable; directory; (b) indicator; gauge.

†indicatif [ɛ̃dikatif]. 1. a. indicative (de, of). 2. a. & s.m. Gram: indicative (mood). 3. s.m. Rad: P.T.T. etc. i. d'appel, call number; i. du poste, station signal; i. (musical), signature tune.

indication [ɛ̃dikasjɔ̃], s.f. 1. indication; (piece of) information; sign. 2. esp. pl. instruction(s).

indice [ɛ̃dis], s.m. 1. indication, sign; mark, token. 2. index.

indicible [ɛ̃disibl], a. inexpressible; unspeakable. adv. -ment.

indien, -ienne [ɛ̃djɛ̃, -jɛn]. 1. a. & s. Indian. 2. s.f. indienne, chintz.

indifférence [ɛ̃diferɑ̃:s], s.f. indifference. a. -ent. adv. -emment.

indig/ence [ɛ̃diʒɑ̃:s], s.f. poverty. a. -ent.

indigène [ɛ̃diʒɛn], a. & s. native.

indigeste [ɛ̃diʒɛst], a. indigestible; stodgy.

indigestion [ɛ̃diʒɛstjɔ̃], s.f. indigestion.

indigne [ɛ̃diɲ], a. unworthy. adv. -ment.

indign/er [ɛ̃diɲe], v.tr. to make indignant. s.f.-ation.

s'indigner, to be(come) indignant.

indignité [ɛ̃diɲite], s.f. 1. unworthiness. 2. indignity.

indiquer [ɛ̃dike], v.tr. to indicate; (a) to point to; (b) to show; (c) to name (a time, etc.).

indirect [ɛ̃dirɛkt], a. indirect; (b) circumstantial (evidence); (c) underhand (methods); (d) contributions indirectes, excise revenue. adv. -ement.

indiscipline [ɛ̃disiplin], a. undisciplined.

†indiscret [ɛ̃diskrɛ], a. indiscreet. adv. -ètement. s.f. -étion, indiscretion.

indiscutable [ɛ̃diskytabl], a. indisputable. adv. -ment.

indispensable [ɛ̃dispɑ̃sabl], a. indispensable.

indisposé [ɛ̃dispoze], a. 1. indisposed, unwell; off colour. 2. i. contre qn., ill-disposed towards s.o.

indispos/er [ɛ̃dispoze], v.tr. 1. (of food) to upset (s.o.). 2. to antagonize (s.o.). s.f. -ition, indisposition.

indistinct [ɛ̃distɛ̃(:kt)], a. indistinct. adv. -ement.

individu [ɛ̃dividy], s.m. 1. individual. 2. F: Pej: un i. louche, a shady customer.

individualité [ɛ̃dividɥalite], s.f. individuality.

†individu/el [ɛ̃dividɥɛl], a. individual; personal; private. adv. -ellement.

indivisible [ɛ̃divizibl], a. indivisible.

indol/ence [ɛ̃dɔlɑ̃:s], s.f. indolence. a. -ent. adv. -emment.

indomptable [ɛ̃dɔ̃tabl], a. unconquerable; untamable.

indompté [ɛ̃dɔ̃te], a. unconquered.

ind/u [ɛ̃dy], a. undue. adv. -ûment, unduly.

indubitable [ɛ̃dybitabl], a. beyond doubt, indubitable, unquestionable. adv. -ment.

induction [ɛ̃dyksjɔ̃], s.f. El: courant d'i., induced current; bobine d'i., induction coil.

indulg/ence [ɛ̃dylʒɑ̃:s], s.f. indulgence. a. -ent. adv. -emment.

†induire [ɛ̃dɥi:r], v.tr. 1. (usu. Pej:) to induce, tempt (s.o. to do sth.). 2. to infer, induce (conclusion).

induit [ɛ̃dɥi], s.m. El: (a) induced circuit; (b) armature (of large dynamo).

industrialis/er [ɛ̃dystrialize], v.tr. to industrialize. s.f. -ation, industrialization.

industrie [ɛ̃dystri], s.f. 1. (a) activity; industry; (b) ingenuity. 2. industry, trade.

industrie-clef [ɛ̃dystrikle], s.f. key industry. pl. industries-clefs.

†industriel [ɛ̃dystriɛl]. 1. a. industrial. 2. s.m. industrialist, manufacturer.

†industrieux [ɛ̃dystriø], a. busy, industrious. adv. -sement.

inébranlable [inebrɑ̃labl], a. (a) immovable, firm; (b) resolute.

inédit [inedi], a. unpublished (book); original; unprecedented.

ineffable [inefabl], a. ineffable, unutterable.

inefficace [inefikas], a. ineffectual; worthless.

†inégal [inegal], a. 1. unequal. 2. (a) uneven, rough (ground); (b) irregular. adv. -ement.

inégalé [inegale], a. unequalled.

inégalité [inegalite], s.f. 1. inequality, disparity. 2. unevenness.

inélég/ant [inelegɑ̃], a. inelegant. adv. -amment.

inéligible [ineliʒibl], a. ineligible.

inepte [inɛpt], a. inept, foolish. adv. -ment.

ineptie [inɛpsi], s.f. ineptitude, stupid remark.

inépuisable [inepɥizabl], a. inexhaustible.

inéquitable [inekitabl], a. inequitable, unfair. adv. -ment.

inerte [inɛrt], a. inert; sluggish; dull.

inertie [inɛrsi], s.f. inertia.

inespéré [inɛspere], a. unhoped-for.

inestimable [inɛstimabl], a. inestimable.

inévitable [inevitabl], a. 1. unavoidable. 2. inevitable. adv. -ment.

inexact [inɛgzakt], a. 1. inexact, inaccurate. 2. unpunctual; slack, lax. adv. -ement.

inexactitude [inɛgzaktityd], s.f. 1. inaccuracy, inexactitude; mistake. 2. unpunctuality; slackness.

inexcusable [inɛkskyzabl], a. inexcusable. adv. -ment.

inexistant [inɛgzistã], a. non-existent.

inexorable [inɛgzɔrabl], a. inexorable, unrelenting. adv. -ment.

inexpérimenté [inɛkspɛrimãte], a. 1. inexperienced; unskilled. 2. untested (process).

inexplicable [inɛksplikabl], a. inexplicable. adv. -ment.

inexploitable [inɛksplwatabl], a. unworkable (mine), uncultivable (land).

inexploité [inɛksplwate], a. unexploited; untapped (resources).

inexplorée [inɛksplore], a. unexplored.

inexprimable [inɛksprimabl], a. inexpressible. adv. -ment.

inextinguible [inɛkstɛ̃g(ɥ)ibl], a. inextinguishable, unquenchable (fire, thirst).

inextricable [inɛkstrikabl], a. inextricable.

infaillibilité [ɛ̃fajibilite], s.f. infallibility.

infaillible [ɛ̃fajibl], a. infallible. adv. -ment.

infaisable [ɛ̃fəzabl], a. unfeasible; c'est i., it can't be done.

infâme [ɛ̃faːm], a. infamous; unspeakable.

infamie [ɛ̃fami], s.f. 1. infamy, dishonour. 2. foul deed; shabby trick.

infanterie [ɛ̃fãtri], s.f. infantry.

infantile [ɛ̃fãtil], a. infantile; paralysie i., infantile paralysis; psychiatrie i., child psychiatry.

infantilisme [ɛ̃fãtilism], s.m. retarded development.

infarctus [ɛ̃farkty:s], s.m. Med: i. du myocarde, coronary thrombosis.

infatigable [ɛ̃fatigabl], a. indefatigable. adv. -ment.

infatuation [ɛ̃fatɥasjɔ̃], s.f. self importance.

infect [ɛ̃fɛkt], a. foul; odeur infecte, stench; F: temps i., filthy weather.

infect/er [ɛ̃fɛkte], v.tr. 1. to infect (de, with). 2. to pollute, taint. a. †-ieux. s.f. -ion.
s'infecter, to turn septic.

‡inférer [ɛ̃fere], v.tr. to infer (de, from).

inférieur, -e [ɛ̃ferjœːr], a. 1. inferior; lower. 2. i. à, inferior to; below. 3. s. inferior.

infériorité [ɛ̃ferjorite], s.f. inferiority; complexe d'i., inferiority complex.

†infernal [ɛ̃fɛrnal], a. infernal. adv. -ement.

infertile [ɛ̃fɛrtil], a. unfruitful, infertile, barren.

infester [ɛ̃fɛste], v.tr. to infest, overrun.

infidèle [ɛ̃fidɛl], 1. a. unfaithful; false. 2. s. infidel.

infidélité [ɛ̃fidelite], s.f. infidelity; unfaithfulness.

infiltrer (s') [sɛ̃filtre], v.pr. to percolate, seep (dans, into); to filter, soak in.

infime [ɛ̃fim], a. tiny, minute.

infini [ɛ̃fini], a. & s.m. infinite; adv.phr. à l'i., to infinity. adv. -ment. s.f. -té.

†infinitésimal [ɛ̃finitezimal], a. infinitesimal.

†infinitif [ɛ̃finitif], a. & s.m. Gram: infinitive (mood).

infirme [ɛ̃firm]. 1. a. (a) infirm; (b) disabled; (c) feeble. 2. s. cripple.

infirm/erie [ɛ̃firmɔri], s.f. hospital, infirmary; sick bay. s. -ier, -ière, nurse.

infirmité [ɛ̃firmite], s.f. infirmity.

inflamm/ation [ɛ̃flamasjɔ̃], s.f. inflammation. a. -able. a. -atoire.

inflation [ɛ̃flasjɔ̃], s.f. Pol: inflation. s.m. -nisme, inflationism.

inflexibilité [ɛ̃fleksibilite], s.f. inflexibility.

inflexible [ɛ̃flɛksibl], a. inflexible. adv. -ment.

‡infliger [ɛ̃fliʒe], v.tr. to inflict.

influenc/er [ɛ̃flyãse], v.tr. to influence. s.f. -ence. a. -ent, influential.

information [ɛ̃fɔrmasjɔ̃], s.f. (a) inquiry; Mil: service d'informations, intelligence service; (b) information; pl. Rad: news (bulletin).

informe [ɛ̃fɔrm], a. shapeless.

inform/er [ɛ̃fɔrme], 1. v.tr. to inform; mal informé, misinformed. 2. v.i. Jur: to investigate (a crime); i. contre qn., to inform against s.o. s. -ateur, -atrice, informant. a. †-atif.
s'informer, to make inquiries.

infortune [ɛ̃fɔrtyn], s.f. misfortune.

infortuné [ɛ̃fɔrtyne], a. unfortunate, unlucky.

infraction [ɛ̃fraksjɔ̃], s.f. 1. infringement; breach. 2. offence.

infranchissable [ɛ̃frãʃisabl], a. impassable; insuperable (difficulty).

infrasonore [ɛ̃frasonɔːr], a. infrasonic.

infréquent [ɛ̃frekã], a. infrequent, rare.

infroissable [ɛ̃frwasabl], a. Cl: etc: crease-resisting; uncrushable.

†infructueu/x [ɛ̃fryktɥø], a. (a) unfruitful; (b) fruitless, unavailing. adv. -sement, fruitlessly.

infuser [ɛ̃fyze], v.tr. to infuse; to instil (à, into).

infusion [ɛ̃fyzjɔ̃], s.f. infusion; decoction; i. de tilleul, lime tea.

ingénier (s') [sɛ̃ʒenje], v.pr. to exercise one's wits.

ingénieur [ɛ̃ʒenjœːr], s.m. (graduate) engineer; i. conseil, consulting engineer.

†ingénieu/x [ɛ̃ʒenjø], a. ingenious, clever. adv. -sement.

ingéniosité [ɛ̃ʒenjozite], s.f. ingenuity.

ingénu [ɛ̃ʒeny], a. ingenuous, artless. adv. -ment.

ingénuité [ɛ̃ʒenɥite], s.f. ingenuousness.

‡ingérer (s') [sɛ̃ʒere], v.pr. to meddle (dans, with).

ingouvernable [ɛ̃guvɛrnabl], a. ungovernable.

ingrat [ɛ̃gra], a. 1. ungrateful. 2. thankless. 3. unpleasing; l'âge i., the awkward age.

ingratitude [ɛ̃gratityd], s.f. 1. ingratitude. 2. thanklessness.

ingrédient [ɛ̃gredjɑ̃], s.m. ingredient.

inhabile [inabil], a. incompetent; clumsy; unskilled. adv. -ment.

inhabitable [inabitabl], a. uninhabitable.

inhabité [inabite], a. uninhabited.

inhabitué [inabitɥe], a. unaccustomed (à, to).

inhaler [inale], v.tr. to inhale.

inhérent [inerɑ̃], a. inherent (à, in).

†inhospitalier [inɔspitalje], a. inhospitable.

inhumain [inymɛ̃], a. inhuman; unfeeling.

inhumanité [inymanite], s.f. inhumanity.

inimaginable [inimaʒinabl], a. unimaginable.

inimitable [inimitabl], a. inimitable. adv. -ment.

inimitié [inimitje], s.f. enmity, hostility.

inintelligent [inɛ̃teliʒɑ̃], a. unintelligent. adv. -emment.

inintelligible [inɛ̃teliʒibl], a. unintelligible. adv. -ment.

ininterrompu [inɛ̃terɔ̃py], a. uninterrupted (progress); unbroken (sleep).

inique [inik], a. iniquitous. adv. -ment.

iniquité [inikite], s.f. iniquity.

†initial, -ale [inisjal], a. 1. a. initial; starting. 2. s.f. initiale, initial. adv. -ement.

initia/tion [inisjasjɔ̃], s.f. initiation (à, into). a. & s. -teur, -trice, initiator.

initiative [inisjativ], s.f. initiative; syndicat d'i., tourist bureau.

initier [inisje], v.tr. to initiate (à, in); être initié, F: to be in the know.
s'initier, to learn; s'i. aux détails d'un commerce, to get the hang of a business.

injecter [ɛ̃ʒɛkte], v.tr. to inject.
s'injecter, (of eyes) to become bloodshot.

injection [ɛ̃ʒɛksjɔ̃], s.f. injection; (a) E: moteur à i. (directe), (direct) injection engine; (b) grouting.

injonction [ɛ̃ʒɔ̃ksjɔ̃], s.f. injunction.

†injudicieu/x [ɛ̃ʒydisjø], a. injudicious. adv. -sement.

injure [ɛ̃ʒy:r], s.f. 1. wrong, injury. 2. insult; pl. abuse.

injuri/er [ɛ̃ʒyrje] v.tr. to abuse, to call (s.o.) names. a. †-eux, insulting, abusive.

injuste [ɛ̃ʒyst], a. unjust, unfair. adv. -ment.

injustice [ɛ̃ʒystis], s.f. injustice, unfairness (envers, towards).

injustifiable [ɛ̃ʒystifjabl], a. unjustifiable.

injustifié [ɛ̃ʒystifje], a. unjustified.

---

inlassable [ɛ̃lasabl], a. untiring; tireless. adv. -ment.

inné [inne], a. innate, inborn.

innoc/ence [inɔsɑ̃s], s.f. innocence. a. & s. -ent, -ente. adv. -emment.

innombrable [innɔ̃brabl], a. innumerable.

innova/tion [innɔvasjɔ̃], s.f. innovation. a. & s. -teur, -trice.

inoccupé [inɔkype], a. unoccupied. 1. idle. 2. vacant.

inocul/er [inɔkyle], v.tr. to inoculate. s.f. -ation.

inodore [inɔdɔ:r], a. odourless; scentless.

†inoffens/if [inɔfɑ̃sif], a. inoffensive. adv. -ivement.

inond/er [inɔ̃de], v.tr. to inundate; to flood (fields, etc.); to glut (market). s.f. -ation, flood.

inopérable [inɔperabl], a. Med: inoperable (tumour, patient).

inopiné [inɔpine], a. sudden, unexpected. adv. -ment.

inopportun [inɔpɔrtœ̃], a. inopportune; ill-timed.

inorganique [inɔrganik], a. inorganic.

inoubliable [inublijabl], a. unforgettable.

inouï [inui], a. unheard of; outrageous (behaviour).

inoxydable [inɔksidabl], a. rustproof; acier i., stainless steel.

inqualifiable [ɛ̃kalifjabl], a. beyond words; unspeakable (behaviour).

inquiet [ɛ̃kjɛ], a. (a) restless, fidgety; (b) anxious, uneasy.

†inquiét/er [ɛ̃kjete], v.tr. to worry (s.o.); to disturb (s.o.). a. -ant, upsetting (news). s.f. -ude, anxiety.
s'inquiéter, to worry.

insaisissable [ɛ̃sezisabl], a. elusive; imperceptible.

insatiable [ɛ̃sasjabl], a. insatiable. adv. -ment.

inscription [ɛ̃skripsjɔ̃], s.f. 1. registration, enrolment. 2. inscription; directions (on sign-post).

‡inscrire [ɛ̃skri:r], v.tr. 1. (a) to inscribe write down; (b) to register; (c) Ind: i. (un employé) à l'arrivée, à la sortie, to clock (an employee) in, out. 2. to engrave (epitaph).
s'inscrire, to put down one's name.

inscrutable [ɛ̃skrytabl], a. inscrutable. adv. -ment.

insect/e [ɛ̃sɛkt], s.m. insect. s.m. -icide, insecticide.

insécurité [ɛ̃sekyrite], s.f. insecurity.

insensé, -ée [ɛ̃sɑ̃se], a. (a) mad, insane; s. madman, -woman; (b) senseless, foolish.

insensibilis/er [ɛ̃sɑ̃sibilize], v.tr. Med: to anaesthetize. s.f. -ation.

insens/ibilité [ɛ̃sɑ̃sibilite], s.f. (a) insensitiveness; (b) callousness. a. -ible, imperceptible. adv. -iblement.

inséparable [ɛ̃separabl], a. inseparable.

‡insér/er [ɛ̃sere], v.tr. to insert. s.f. -tion.

†insidieu/x [ɛ̃sidjø], a. insidious. adv.
-sement.

insigne¹ [ɛ̃siɲ], a. 1. distinguished; remarkable. 2. Pej: notorious, out and
out (liar).

insigne² [ɛ̃siɲ], s.m. badge.

insignifi/ance [ɛ̃siɲifjɑ̃:s], s.f. insignificance. a. -ant, insignificant.

insinu/er [ɛ̃sinɥe], v.tr. to insinuate; to
hint at (sth.). a. -ant, insinuating. s.f.
-ation.

　　s'insinuer, to penetrate; to thread,
worm, one's way (through, into).

insipide [ɛ̃sipid], a. insipid.

insist/er [ɛ̃siste], v.i. to insist. s.f.
-ance, insistence.

insociable [ɛ̃sɔsjabl], a. unsociable.

insolation [ɛ̃sɔlasjɔ̃], s.f. (a) sunburn; (b)
a touch of the sun; (c) sun-bathing.

insol/ence [ɛ̃sɔlɑ̃:s], s.f. insolence, impertinence. a. -ent. adv. -emment.

insolite [ɛ̃sɔlit], a. unusual.

insoluble [ɛ̃sɔlybl], a. insoluble; situation
i., deadlock.

insolvable [ɛ̃sɔlvabl], a. insolvent.

insomnie [ɛ̃sɔmni], s.f. insomnia, sleep-
lessness.

insondable [ɛ̃sɔ̃dabl], a. unfathomable.

insonore [ɛ̃sɔnɔ:r], a. sound-proof.

insonoris/er [ɛ̃sɔnɔrize], v.tr. Cin: Rad:
etc: to sound-proof. s.f. -ation,
sound-proofing.

insouci/ance [ɛ̃susjɑ̃:s], s.f. (a) unconcern; (b) thoughtlessness, casualness.
a. -ant. adv. -amment. a. †-eux,
careless; casual.

insoupçonné [ɛ̃supsɔne], a. unsuspected
(de, of).

insoutenable [ɛ̃sutnabl], a. untenable.

inspec/ter [ɛ̃spekte], v.tr. to inspect. s.f.
-tion, inspection.

inspecteur, -trice [ɛ̃spektœ:r, -tris], s.
inspector; overseer; shopwalker; surveyor.

inspir/er [ɛ̃spire], v.tr. to inspire.
s.f. -ation, inspiration.

instabilité [ɛ̃stabilite], s.f. instability.

instable [ɛ̃stabl], a. unstable; shaky;
unsteady; unreliable.

install/er [ɛ̃stale], v.tr. (a) to install; (b)
to set up; to fit up, equip. s.f.
-ation, equipment, plant.

　　s'installer, to settle (down); to make
oneself at home; s'i. comme médecin,
to set up as a doctor.

instance [ɛ̃stɑ̃:s], s.f. (a) pl. requests,
entreaties; (b) Jur: action, suit;
tribunal d'i. = magistrate's court.

inst/ant¹ [ɛ̃stɑ̃], a. pressing, urgent. adv.
-amment.

instant² s.m. moment, instant.

instantané [ɛ̃stɑ̃tane], 1. a. instan-
taneous. 2. s.m. snapshot. adv.
-ment.

instaur/er [ɛ̃stɔre], v.tr. to found, to set
up. s. -ateur, -atrice, founder. s.f.
-ation, founding.

instiga/tion [ɛ̃stigasjɔ̃], s.f. instigation.
s. -teur, -trice, instigator.

instiller [ɛ̃stil(l)e], v.tr. to instil.

instinct [ɛ̃stɛ̃], s.m. instinct; d'i., in-
stinctively. a. †-if. adv. -ivement.

institu/er [ɛ̃stitɥe], v.tr. to institute,
found, instal. s.f. -tion.

institut [ɛ̃stity], s.m. institute.

institu/teur, -trice [ɛ̃stitytœ:r, -tris], s.
(primary school-)teacher.

instruc/tion [ɛ̃stryksjɔ̃], s.f. 1. instruction. 2. education. 3. juge d'i.,
examining magistrate. s.m. -teur. a.
†-tif. adv. -tivement.

‡instruire [ɛ̃strɥi:r], v.tr. 1. to inform.
2. to teach, instruct.

instruit [ɛ̃strɥi], a. educated; well-read.

instrument [ɛ̃strymɑ̃], s.m. instrument.

instrument/er [ɛ̃strymɑ̃te]. 1. v.i. Jur: to
order legal action (contre qn, against
s.o.). 2. v.tr. Mus: to score, orches-
trate (opera, etc.). a. †-al. s.f.
-ation, scoring. s.m. -iste, instru-
mentalist.

insu [ɛ̃sy], s.m. à l'i. de qn, without s.o.
knowing.

insubor/dination [ɛ̃sybɔrdinasjɔ̃], s.f.
insubordination. a. -donné, insubordinate.

insuccès [ɛ̃syksɛ], s.m. failure, miscarriage (of plan).

insuffis/ance [ɛ̃syfizɑ̃:s], s.f. insufficiency.
a. -ant. adv. -amment.

insulaire [ɛ̃sylɛ:r], 1. a. insular. 2. s.
islander.

insulte [ɛ̃sylt], s.f. insult.

insult/er [ɛ̃sylte], v.tr. to insult. a. -ant,
offensive.

insupportable [ɛ̃sypɔrtabl], a. unbearable
(pain, conduct); il est i.! he's the
limit!

insurgé [ɛ̃syrʒe], s. insurgent, rebel.

‡insurger (s') [ɛ̃syrʒe], v.pr. to revolt.

insurmontable [ɛ̃syrmɔ̃tabl], a. insurmountable.

insurrection [ɛ̃syr(r)ɛksjɔ̃], s.f. insurrection.

intact [ɛ̃takt], a. intact; untouched.

intangible [ɛ̃tɑ̃ʒibl], a. intangible.

intarissable [ɛ̃tarisabl], a. inexhaustible,
unfailing; endless (chatter).

†intégral [ɛ̃tegral], a. integral, whole.
adv. -ement, wholly, in full.

intégrité [ɛ̃tegrite], s.f. integrity.

intellect [ɛ̃telɛkt], s.m. intellect. a.
†-uel, intellectual. adv. -uellement.

intellig/ence [ɛ̃tel(l)iʒɑ̃:s], s.f. 1. understanding. 2. intelligence. 3. en bonne
i., on good terms. a. -ent, clever.
adv. -emment.

intelligible [ɛ̃telliʒibl], a. intelligible;
clear. adv. -ment.

intempér/ance [ɛ̃tɑ̃perɑ̃:s], s.f. intem-
perance. a. -ant, intemperate.

intempérie [ɛ̃tɑ̃peri], s.f. usu. pl. bad
weather.

intenable [ɛ̃tnabl], a. untenable.

intendant [ɛ̃tɑ̃dɑ̃], s.m. (a) steward, bailiff; (b) manager; (c) bursar.

intense [ɛ̃tɑ̃s], a. intense; severe; deep (colour); intensive (propaganda).

†intens/if [ɛ̃tɑ̃sif], a. intensive; El: courant i., heavy flow (of current). adv. -ivement.

intensifier [ɛ̃tɑ̃sifje], v.tr. to intensify.

intensité [ɛ̃tɑ̃site], s.f. intensity; force (of wind); depth (of colour); strength (of current).

intention [ɛ̃tɑ̃sjɔ̃], s.f. intention; (a) purpose, design; (b) will, wish; à l'i. de, for (the sake of).

intentionné [ɛ̃tɑ̃sjɔne], a. (used only in:-) bien-i., mal-i., well-, ill-, disposed (envers, towards).

†intention/nel [ɛ̃tɑ̃sjɔnɛl], a. intentional adv. -ellement.

interaction [ɛ̃tɛraksjɔ̃], s.f. reciprocal action.

interarmes [ɛ̃tɛrarm], a. inv. Mil: combined (staff, operations).

†interastral [ɛ̃tɛrastral], a. interstellar (space).

intercaler [ɛ̃tɛrkale], v.tr. to insert; El: to switch, cut, in (resistance).

†intercéder [ɛ̃tɛrsede], v.i. to intercede.

intercepter [ɛ̃tɛrsɛpte], v.tr. to intercept; to shut out (light).

interception [ɛ̃tɛrsɛpsjɔ̃], s.f. interception; Rad: i. des émissions, monitoring; Av: raid d'i., intruder raid.

interconnecter [ɛ̃tɛrkɔnɛkte], v.tr. El: to connect up (circuits).

†intercontinental [ɛ̃tɛrkɔ̃tinɑ̃tal], a. intercontinental; engin i., intercontinental ballistic missile.

interdiction [ɛ̃tɛrdiksjɔ̃], s.f. prohibition.

‡interdire [ɛ̃tɛrdir], v.tr. to forbid.

interdit [ɛ̃tɛrdi], a. disconcerted; taken aback.

intéressant [ɛ̃tɛresɑ̃], a. interesting; prix intéressants, attractive prices.

intéressé [ɛ̃tɛrese], a. 1. interested, concerned; le premier i., (the person) most directly affected. 2. selfish.

intéresser [ɛ̃tɛrese], v.tr. (a) to interest; (b) to give a financial interest; (c) to concern.

s'intéresser, to become interested; to take an interest.

intérêt [ɛ̃tɛre], s.m. interest. 1. share. 2. advantage; ligne d'i. local, branch-line. 3. porter i. à qn, to take an interest in s.o. 4. Fin: i. composé, compound interest.

intérieur [ɛ̃tɛrjœr], 1. a. (a) interior, inner (room); (b) inward (feelings); (c) domestic (administration); commerce i., home trade. 2. s.m. (a) interior (room), inside; à l'i., on the inside; (b) home, house; vie d'i., home life; femme d'i., domesticated woman; (c) Adm: le Ministère de l'I. = the Home Office; (d) Sp: i. gauche, inside left (player). adv. -ement.

intérim [ɛ̃terim], s.m. interim; faire l'i. (de qn), to deputize for s.o.; assurer l'i., to carry on (during s.o.'s absence).

interjection [ɛ̃tɛrʒɛksjɔ̃], s.f. interjection.

interlocuteur, -trice [ɛ̃tɛrlɔkytœr, -tris], s. speaker (in a conversation).

interloquer [ɛ̃tɛrlɔke], v.tr. to disconcert (s.o.).

intermède [ɛ̃tɛrmɛd], s.m. 1. medium, intermediary. 2. Th: interlude.

intermédiaire [ɛ̃tɛrmedjɛr], 1. a. intermediate. 2. s.m. agent; intermediary.

interminable [ɛ̃tɛrminabl], a. interminable. adv. -ment.

intermittent [ɛ̃tɛrmittɑ̃], a. intermittent; irregular (pulse); casual (worker).

internat [ɛ̃tɛrna], s.m. boarding-school.

†international [ɛ̃tɛrnasjɔnal], a. international.

interne [ɛ̃tɛrn]. 1. a. internal. 2. s. (a) boarder; (b) resident medical student.

intern/er [ɛ̃tɛrne], v.tr. to intern. s.m. -ement, internment.

interpeller [ɛ̃tɛrpɛl(l)e], v.tr. to call out to (s.o.); (of sentry) to challenge (s.o.); Pol: to heckle; Jur: to call on (s.o.) to answer.

interphone [ɛ̃tɛrfɔn], s.m. house telephone; intercom.

interplanétaire [ɛ̃tɛrplanetɛr], a. interplanetary; fusée i., space rocket.

interpoler [ɛ̃tɛrpɔle], v.tr. to interpolate.

interposer [ɛ̃tɛrpoze], v.tr. to interpose.

s'interposer, to intervene.

interprète [ɛ̃tɛrprɛt], s.m. & f. interpreter.

‡interprét/er [ɛ̃tɛrprete], v.tr. to interpret. s.f. -ation.

interroga/tion [ɛ̃tɛrɔgasjɔ̃], s.f. interrogation. & s. -teur, -trice, (i) interrogatory; (ii) questioner. a. †-tif. s.m. -toire, (cross-)examination.

interroger [ɛ̃tɛrɔʒe], v.tr. to interrogate.

‡interrompre [ɛ̃tɛrɔ̃pr], v.tr. (a) to interrupt; (b) to stop, suspend.

s'interrompre, to break off.

interrompu [ɛ̃tɛrɔ̃py], a. sommeil i., broken sleep; non i., unbroken, continuous.

interrup/tion [ɛ̃tɛrypsjɔ̃], s.f. (a) interruption; (b) stoppage, break(ing off); El: disconnection. s.m. -teur, El: switch.

intersection [ɛ̃tɛrsɛksjɔ̃], s.f. intersection.

interstice [ɛ̃tɛrstis], s.m. interstice; chink.

intervalle [ɛ̃tɛrval], s.m. interval; (a) gap (entre, between); (b) period of time); dans l'i., in the meantime.

†interven/ir [ɛ̃tɛrvənir], v.i. 1. to intervene. 2. to happen, occur. s.f. -tion, (a) intervention; (b) Med: operation.

interview/er [ɛ̃tɛrvju(v)e], v.tr. to interview (s.o.). s.m. -eur, interviewer.

intestin [ɛ̃tɛstɛ̃], s.m. intestine, bowel. a. †-al.

intime [ĕtim], *a.* intimate. *adv.* -ment.

intimid/er [ĕtimide], *v.tr.* to intimidate; to make (s.o.) shy. *a.* -ant, awe-inspiring. *s.f.* -ation.

intimité [ĕtimite], *s.f.* intimacy; (*a*) closeness; (*b*) privacy; dans l'i., in private (life).

intolérable [ĕtɔlɛrabl], *a.* intolerable. *adv.* -ment.

intoléer/ance [ĕtɔlɛrã:s], *s.f.* intolerance. *a.* -ant.

intoxiquer [ĕtɔksike], *v.tr. Med:* to poison; to cause (food, etc.) poisoning.

intraitable [ĕtrɛtabl], *a.* (*a*) intractable, unmanageable; (*b*) obstinate.

intramusculaire [ĕtramyskyle:r], *a. Med:* intramuscular (injection).

intransigeant [ĕträziʒã], *a.* uncompromising. 2. *s.* schemer, wire-puller.

†**intraveineux** [ĕtravenø], *a. Med:* intravenous (injection).

intrépid/e [ĕtrepid], *a.* intrepid, dauntless. *adv.* -ement. *s.f.* -ité, fearlessness.

intrigant [ĕtrigã]. 1. *a.* intriguing, scheming. 2. *s.* schemer, wire-puller.

intrigue [ĕtrig], *s.f.* 1. (*a*) intrigue; (*b*) (love-)affair. 2. plot (of play).

intriguer [ĕtrige]. 1. *v.tr.* to puzzle. *v.i.* to scheme, plot, intrigue.

introduc/tion [ĕtrɔdyksjɔ̃], *s.f.* introduction. *a.* -toire, introductory.

‡**introduire** [ĕtrɔdɥi:r], *v.tr.* to introduce; to bring in; to admit; to usher (s.o.) in. s'introduire, to get in, enter.

introuvable [ĕtruvabl], *a.* not to be found.

intrus [ĕtry], *s.* intruder; *F:* gate-crasher.

intrusion [ĕtryzjɔ̃], *s.f.* intrusion.

intui/tion [ĕtɥisjɔ̃], *s.f.* intuition. *a.* †-tif.

inusable [inyzabl], *a.* hard-wearing.

inusité [inyzite], *a.* not in common use.

inutile [inytil], *a.* (*a*) useless, unavailing; vain; (*b*) needless, unnecessary. *adv.* -ment.

invaincu [ĕvĕky], *a.* unconquered.

invalide [ĕvalid]. 1. *a.* (*a*) infirm; disabled; (*b*) invalid (document). 2. *s.* (*a*) *Med:* invalid; (*b*) *s.m. Mil:* disabled soldier; pensioner.

invariable [ĕvarjabl], *a.* invariable. *adv.* -ment.

invasion [ĕvazjɔ̃], *s.f.* invasion.

invective [ĕvɛkti:v], *s.f.* (*a*) invective; (*b*) *pl.* abuse.

invendable [ĕvãdabl], *a.* unsaleable.

inventaire [ĕvãte:r], *s.m.* inventory; *Com:* stock-list; faire, dresser l'i., (i) to draw up an inventory; (ii) to take stock.

inven/ter [ĕvãte], *v.tr.* to invent. *s.m.* -teur, inventor. *a.* †-tif, inventive. *s.f.* -tion, invention.

inventorier [ĕvãtɔrje], *v.tr.* to make an inventory; to take stock.

inverse [ĕvɛrs]. 1. *a.* inverse, opposite. 2. *s.m.* opposite, reverse. *adv.* -ment.

invers/er [ĕvɛrse], *v.tr.* to reverse (current, image, result). *s.m.* -eur, *El:* current reverser. *s.f.* -ion.

invertébré [ĕvertebre], *a.* invertebrate.

investiga/tion [ĕvɛstigasjɔ̃], *s.f.* investigation. *a.* & *s.* -teur, -trice, (i) investigating; (ii) investigator.

invest/ir [ĕvɛsti:r], *v.tr.* to invest (money). *s.m.* -issement.

invétéré [ĕvetere], *a.* inveterate.

invincible [ĕvĕsibl], *a.* invincible. *adv.* -ment.

inviolable [ĕvjɔlabl], *a.* inviolable; sacred. *adv.* -ment.

invisibilité [ĕvizibilite], *s.f.* invisibility.

invisible [ĕvizibl], *a.* invisible. *adv.* -ment.

invit/er [ĕvite], *v.tr.* 1. to invite. 2. to request. *s.f.* -ation.

invocation [ĕvɔkasjɔ̃], *s.f.* invocation.

involontaire [ĕvɔlɔ̃te:r], *a.* involuntary, unintentional. *adv.* -ment.

invoquer [ĕvɔke], *v.tr.* to invoke.

invraisembl/ance [ĕvrɛsãblã:s], *s.f.* unlikeliness, improbability. *a.* -able, improbable; histoire i., tall story.

invulnérable [ĕvylnerabl], *a.* invulnerable. *adv.* -ment.

iode [jɔd, iɔd], *s.m.* iodine.

iodure [jɔdy:r, iɔ-], *s.m.* iodide.

ion [jɔ̃], *s.m. Sc:* ion.

ionique [iɔnik], *a. Rad:* thermionic (valve); moteur-fusée i., ion rocket.

irascible [irasibl], *a.* irascible.

iris [iris], *s.m.* 1. iris (of eye). 2. *Bot:* iris, flag.

irlandais, -aise [irlãdɛ, -ɛ:z]. 1. *a.* Irish. 2. *s.* Irishman, -woman. 3. *s.m. Ling:* Irish, Erse.

iron/ie [irɔni], *s.f.* irony. *a.* -ique, ironical. *adv.* -iquement.

irradier [irradje], *v.i.* to (ir)radiate; (of pain) to spread.

†**irrationnel** [irrasjɔnɛl], *a.* irrational. *adv.* -lement.

irréalisable [irrealizabl], *a.* unrealizable.

irréconciliable [irrekɔ̃siljabl], *a.* irreconcilable. *adv.* -ment.

irrécouvrable [irrekuvrabl], *a.* irrecoverable.

irrécupérable [irrekyperabl], *a.* irreparable (loss, etc.).

†**irréel** [irreɛl], *a.* unreal.

irréfléchi [irreflɛʃi], *a.* 1. unconsidered, thoughtless. 2. hasty, rash.

irréflexion [irreflɛksjɔ̃], *s.f.* thoughtlessness.

irréfutable [irrefytabl], *a.* irrefutable.

irrégul/arité [irregylarite], *s.f.* irregularity; unpunctuality. *a.* †-ier, irregular. *adv.* -ièrement.

irrémédiable [irremedjabl], *a.* irremediable. *adv.* -ment.

irremplaçable [irrãplasabl], *a.* irreplaceable.

irréparable [irreparabl], *a.* irreparable. *adv.* -ment.

irréprochable [irreprɔʃabl], *a.* irreproachable. *adv.* -ment.

irrésistible [irrezistibl], *a.* irresistible. *adv.* -ment.

irrésolu [irrezɔly], *a.* irresolute, wavering. *adv.* -ment.

†irrespectueu/x [irrespektɥø], *a.* disrespectful. *adv.* -sement.

irrespon/sabilité [irrespɔ̃sabilite], *s.f.* irresponsibility. *a.* -sable, irresponsible.

irrévérenc/e [irreverɑ̃ːs], *s.f.* irreverence. *a.* †-ieux, irreverent. *adv.* -ieusement.

irrétrécissable [irretresisabl], *a.* unshrinkable.

irrévocable [irrevɔkabl], *a.* irrevocable. *adv.* -ment.

irrigation [irrigasjɔ̃], *s.f.* 1. irrigation. 2. *Med:* spraying, douching; i. du côlon, colonic irrigation.

irriguer [irrige], *v.tr.* 1. to irrigate. 2. to spray, to douche.

irrit/er [irrite], *v.tr.* to irritate. *s.f.* -abilité. *a.* -able. *adv.* -ablement. *s.f.* -ation.
  s'irriter. 1. to grow angry (contre, with). **2.** (*of sore*) to become inflamed.

irruption [irrypsjɔ̃], *s.f.* irruption; faire i. dans, to burst into.

isolant [izɔlɑ̃], *a.* **1.** (*a*) isolating; (*b*) insulating; bouteille isolante, vacuum flask; (*c*) sound-proof. **2.** *s.m.* insulator.

isolateur [izɔlatœːr], *s.m. El:* insulator.

isolement [izɔlmɑ̃], *s.m.* **1.** isolation, loneliness. **2.** *El:* insulation.

isoler [izɔle], *v.tr.* **1.** to isolate (de, from). **2.** to insulate.
  s'isoler, to live apart (from society).

isoloir [izɔlwaːr], *s.m. Adm:* polling-booth.

Isorel [izɔrɛl], *s.m. R.t.m:* hardboard.

israélien, -ienne, [israeljɛ̃, -jɛn], *a. & s.* Israeli.

issue [isy], *s.f.* **1.** issue, end. **2.** outlet; chemin sans i., dead end. **3.** *pl. Ind:* by-products.

isthme [ism], *s.m.* isthmus.

†italien, -ienne, [italjɛ̃, -jɛn], *a. & s.* Italian.

italique [italik], *a. & s.m.* italic; italics.

itinéraire [itinerɛːr], *s.m.* itinerary; route.

itinérant [itinerɑ̃], *a.* itinerant.

ivoire [ivwaːr], *s.m.* ivory.

ivre [iːvr], *a.* drunk; intoxicated.

ivresse [ivrɛs], *s.f.* (*a*) intoxication, drunkenness; (*b*) rapture.

ivrogne [ivrɔɲ], *s.m.* drunkard.

J

J, j [ʒi], *s.m.* (the letter) J, j. *Mil: etc:* le jour J, D-day.

jabot [ʒabo], *s.m.* **1.** crop (of bird). **2.** jabot, frills.

jacasser [ʒakase], *v.i.* to chatter, jabber.

jacinthe [ʒasɛ̃ːt], *s.f.* hyacinth; j. des bois, bluebell.

jade [ʒad], *s.m.* jade(stone).

jadis [ʒadis], *adv.* formerly, once; au temps j., once, long ago.

jaguar [ʒagwaːr], *s.m.* jaguar.

jaill/ir [ʒajiːr], *v.i.* to spring (up); to gush (forth); (*of sparks*) to fly. *s.m.* -issement.

jais [ʒɛ], *s.m.* jet.

jalonn/er [ʒalɔne], *v.tr.* to stake out; to blaze (a trail). *s.m.* -age. *s.m.* -ement.

jalouser [ʒaluze], *v.tr.* to envy (s.o.).

jalousie [ʒaluzi], *s.f.* **1.** jealousy. **2.** Venetian blind.

†jalou/x [ʒalu], *a.* jealous. *adv.* -sement.

jamais [ʒamɛ], *adv.* **1.** ever; à tout j., for ever and ever. **2.** (*with neg. expressed or understood*) never; j. de la vie! never! **3.** *s.m.* au grand j.! never, never!

jambe [ʒɑ̃ːb], *s.f.* leg; prendre ses jambes à son cou, to take to one's heels; n'avoir plus de jambes, to be tired out.

jambon [ʒɑ̃bɔ̃], *s.m.* ham.

jamboree [ʒɑ̃bori], *s.m.* (boy scouts') jamboree.

jante [ʒɑ̃ːt], *s.f.* rim (of wheel).

janvier [ʒɑ̃vje], *s.m.* January.

japonais, -aise [ʒapɔnɛ, -ɛːz], *a. & s.* Japanese.

japp/er [ʒape], *v.i.* to yelp, yap. *s.m.* -ement.

jaquette [ʒakɛt], *s.f.* (*a*) morning coat; (*b*) (woman's) jacket; (*c*) *Fr.C:* nightdress; (*d*) dust-jacket (of book).

jardin [ʒardɛ̃], *s.m.* garden; j. potager, kitchen garden; j. des plantes, botanical garden; *Sch:* j. d'enfants, kindergarten.

jardin/er [ʒardine], *v.i.* to garden. *s.m.* -age, gardening. *s.m.* -ier, gardener.

jarret [ʒarɛ], *s.m.* **1.** bend of the knee; hock (of horse, cow). **2.** *Cu:* knuckle (of veal); shin (of beef).

jarretelle [ʒartɛl], *s.f.* (stocking) suspender.

jarretière [ʒartjɛːr], *s.f.* garter.

jas/er [ʒaze], *v.i.* to chatter (de, about); to gossip. *a. & s.-eur, -euse.*

jasmin [ʒasmɛ̃], *s.m.* jasmine.

jauge [ʒoːʒ], *s.f.* gauge; *Nau:* tonnage; *Aut:* j. dipstick.

‡jaug/er [ʒoʒe], *v.tr.* to gauge. *s.m.* -eage. gauge.

jaun/e [ʒoːn]. 1. *a.* yellow; *Aut:* feu j., amber light. 2. *adv.* rire j., to give a sickly smile. 3. *s.m.* (a) yellow; (b) yolk (of egg); (c) *Ind:* blackleg. *a.* -âtre, yellowish. *s.f.* -isse, jaundice.

jaunir [ʒoniːr], 1. *v.tr.* to colour yellow. 2. *v.i.* to turn yellow, to fade.

Javel [ʒavɛl], *s.m.* eau de J., (potassium-chloride) disinfectant.

javellis/er [ʒavelize], *v.tr.* to chlorinate (water). *s.f.* -ation.

je [ʒ(ə)], (*before vowel* j'), *pers.pron.* I.

jeep [ʒip], *s.f.* *Aut:* jeep.

jerrican, jerrycan [ʒerikan], *s.m.* jerrican.

jésuite [ʒezɥit], *s.m.* Jesuit.

Jésus [ʒezy] *Pr.nm.* Jesus; J.-Christ, Jesus Christ; l'an 44 avant J.-C., the year 44 B.C.

jet [ʒɛ], *s.m.* 1. throw, cast. 2. jet, gush. 3. spout.

jetée [ʒəte], *s.f.* jetty, pier.

†jeter [ʒəte], *v.tr.* to throw, fling. se jeter, to jump; to fling oneself (on s.o., sth.).

jeton [ʒətɔ̃], *s.m.* *Sp:* counter, chip; (telephone) token, *U.S:* slug.

†jeu [ʒø], *s.m.* (a) play(ing); j. de mots, pun; les forces en j., the forces at work; (b) game; terrain de jeux, sports ground; (c) set (of tools, etc.); (*at cards*) (i) pack, *U.S:* deck; (ii) hand; (*e*) gaming, gambling; faites vos jeux, put down your stakes; (*e*) (*in machinery*) play.

jeudi [ʒødi], *s.m.* Thursday; j. saint, Maundy Thursday.

jeun (à) [aʒœ̃], *adj.phr.* fasting.

jeune [ʒœn], *a.* 1. young; youthful; j. homme, boy; j. fille, girl; jeunes gens, young people; (b) younger; junior.

jeûne [ʒøn], *s.m.* fast(ing).

jeûner [ʒøne], *v.i.* to fast.

jeunesse [ʒœnes], *s.f.* (a) youth; organismes de j., youth organizations; (b) youthfulness (of appearance).

joaill/erie [ʒɔajri], *s.f.* jewellery. *s.* -ier, -ière, jeweller.

joie [ʒwa], *s.f.* 1. joy; delight; gladness; feu de j., bonfire. 2. mirth, merriment.

‡joindre [ʒwɛ̃dr], *v.tr.* to join; to clasp; (a) to bring together; (b) to add; j. l'utile à l'agréable, to combine business with pleasure; (c) to get in touch (with s.o.). se joindre, to join.

joint [ʒwɛ̃]. 1. *a.* joined, united. 2. *s.m.* joint, join. *s.f.* *Anat:* -ure, joint.

joli [ʒɔli], *a.* pretty; nice. *adv.* -ment.

jonc [ʒɔ̃], *s.m.* *Bot:* rush.

jonch/er [ʒɔ̃ʃe], *v.tr.* to strew.

jonction [ʒɔ̃ksjɔ̃], *s.f.* junction, joining.

jongl/er [ʒɔ̃gle], *v.i.* to juggle. *s.f.* -erie. *s.* -eur.

joue [ʒu], *s.f.* cheek; coucher qn en j., to aim (a gun) at s.o.

jouer [ʒwe], *v.* to play. I. *v.i.* 1. j. aux cartes, au tennis, to play cards, tennis; j. du piano, to play the piano; j. des coudes, to elbow one's way. 2. to gamble. 3. faire j., to bring (sth.) into action; to release (spring). II. *v.tr.* 1. j. gros jeu, to play for high stakes. 2. to play (card, etc.); to act (a play).

jouet [ʒwɛ], *s.m.* toy.

joueur, -euse [ʒwœːr, -øz], *s.* 1. (a) player; être beau j., to be a good loser; (b) performer. 2. gambler, speculator.

joug [ʒu(g)], *s.m.* yoke.

jou/ir [ʒwiːr], *v.i.* j. (de), to enjoy. *s.f.* -issance, (a) enjoyment; (b) possession.

jour [ʒuːr], *s.m.* day. 1. (day)light; (a) il fait grand j., it's broad daylight; (b) mettre au j., to bring to light, to publish (a fact); (c) light. 2. aperture, opening; à j., open-work. 3. *Cu:* plat du j., to-day's special; de nos jours, nowadays; mettre à j., to bring up to date.

†journal [ʒurnal], *s.m.* 1. journal, diary; j. de bord, log book. 2. newspaper. *s.m.* -isme, journalism. *s.m. & f.* -iste. *a.* -istique.

†journalier [ʒurnalje]. 1. *a.* daily; everyday; (b) s.m. day-labourer; (b) *Aut:* (totalisateur) j., trip-recorder.

journée [ʒurne], *s.f.* 1. day(time); dans la j., in the course of the day. 2. femme de j., daily (help).

journellement [ʒurnɛlmɑ̃], *adv.* daily.

†jovial [ʒɔvjal], *a.* jovial, jolly, merry. *adv.* -ement. *s.f.* -ité.

†joyau [ʒwajo], *s.m.* jewel.

†joyeu/x [ʒwajø], *a.* joyful, cheerful; j. Noël! merry Christmas! *adv.* -sement.

jubilé [ʒybile], *s.m.* jubilee.

jubil/er [ʒybile], *v.i.* to exult.

jucher [ʒyʃe], *v.i.* to roost; to perch.

judiciaire [ʒydisjɛːr], *a.* judicial, legal (error, charges). *adv.* -ment.

†judicieu/x [ʒydisjø], *a.* judicious, discerning; peu j., injudicious. *adv.* -sement.

juge [ʒyːʒ], *s.m.* judge; j. d'instruction = examining magistrate; j. de paix = police-court magistrate.

jugé [ʒyʒe], *s.m.* au j., by guess-work.

‡jug/er [ʒyʒe], *v.tr.* 1. (a) to judge; to try (case, prisoner); to pass sentence on; (b) to pass judgment on, to criticize (book). 2. (a) to think, consider; (b) jugez de ma surprise, imagine my surprise. *s.m.* -ment.

jugeot(t)e [ʒyʒɔt], *s.f.* F: common sense; F: gumption.

jugulaire [ʒygylɛːr]. 1. *a. & s.f.* jugular (vein). 2. *s.f.* chin-strap.

juif, juive [ʒɥif, ʒɥiːv]. 1. *a.* Jewish. 2. *s.* Jew, Jewess; petit j., funny-bone.

juillet [ʒɥijɛ], *s.m.* July.

juin [ʒɥɛ̃], *s.m.* June.

jumeau, -elle [ʒymo, -ɛl]. **1.** *a.* & *s.* twin; **trois jumeaux**, triplets; **maisons jumelles**, semi-detached houses. **2.** *s.f.pl.* binoculars; **j. de théâtre**, opera-glasses.

‡**jumel/er** [ʒymle], *v.tr.* (*a*) to arrange in pairs; *Aut:* **pneus jumelés**, dual tyres; **textes jumelés**, bilingual texts; (*b*) to twin (towns). *s.m.* **-age**, twinning.

jument [ʒymɑ̃], *s.f.* mare.

jupe [ʒyp], *s.f.* skirt.

jupon [ʒypɔ̃], *s.m.* petticoat, underskirt.

juré, -ée [ʒyre], *s.* juror.

jurer [ʒyre], *v.tr.* **1.** to swear. **2.** *abs.* (*a*) to curse; (*b*) (*of colours*) to clash.

juridiction [ʒyridiksjɔ̃], *s.f.* jurisdiction. *a.* †**-nel.**

juridique [ʒyridik], *a.* judicial; legal. *adv.* **-ment.**

juron [ʒyrɔ̃], *s.m.* oath, *F:* swear-word.

jury [ʒyri], *s.m.* **1.** jury; **chef, membre, du j.**, foreman, member, of the jury. **2.** selection committee; board (of examiners).

jus [ʒy], *s.m.* **1.** juice. **2.** gravy. **3.** *P:* (*a*) water; (*b*) petrol; (*c*) electric current.

jusant [ʒyzɑ̃], *s.m.* ebb(-tide).

jusque [ʒysk(ə)], *prep.* **1.** as far as; up to; **jusqu'ici**, so far; **jusque-là**, thus far. **2.** till, until; **jusqu'à présent**, until now. **3.** *conj.phr.* **jusqu'à ce que**, till, until.

juste [ʒyst], *a.* **1.** just, right, fair. **2.** right, exact; **bien j.**, tight; scant. **3.** *adv.* (*a*) rightly; (*b*) exactly, precisely; (*c*) barely; *adv.phr.* **comme de j.**, as is only fair. *adv.* **-ment.**

justesse [ʒystɛs], *s.f.* exactness, accuracy; **arriver de j.**, to arrive just in time.

justice [ʒystis], *s.f.* **1.** justice; **en toute j.**, by rights. **2.** law, legal proceedings; **Palais de J.**, Law Courts.

justifi/er [ʒystifje], *v.tr.* to justify, vindicate. *a.* **-ablement.** *s.f.* **-cation. se justifier**, to clear oneself.

jute [ʒyt], *s.m.* *Tex:* jute.

†**juteux** [ʒytø], *a.* juicy.

juvénile [ʒyvenil], *a.* juvenile; youthful.

juxtapos/er [ʒykstapoze], *v.tr.* to place side by side. *s.f.* **-ition.**

K

K, k [kɑ], *s.m.* (the letter) K, k.

kaki [kaki]. **1.** *s.m.* & *a.inv.* khaki. **2.** *s.m. Bot:* persimmon.

kangourou [kɑ̃guru], *s.m.* kangaroo.

kaolin [kaolɛ̃], *s.m.* kaolin, china clay.

képi [kepi], *s.m.* kepi; peaked cap.

kermesse [kɛrmɛs], *s.f.* (*a*) (Flemish) village fair; (*b*) charity fête.

kérosène [kerozɛn], *s.m.* paraffin (oil), kerosene.

kidnapper [kidnape], *v.tr.* to kidnap.

kilo(gramme) [kilo(gram)], *s.m.* kilo-(gramme).

kilomètre [kilomɛtr], *s.m.* kilometre.

kilométrique [kilometrik], *a.* **borne k.** = milestone.

kilowatt [kilowat], *s.m.* kilowatt.

kiosque [kjɔsk], *s.m.* **1.** (*a*) kiosk; **k. à musique**, bandstand; (*b*) newspaper stall. **2.** conning-tower.

klaxon [klaksɔ̃], *s.m. Aut:* hooter, horn.

klaxonner [klaksɔne], *v.i. Aut:* to hoot.

kleptomane [klɛptɔman], *a.* & *s.* klepto-maniac. *s.f.* **-ie**, kleptomania.

knock-out [nɔkut], *a.inv. Sp:* **mettre (qn) k.-o.**, to knock (s.o.) out.

krach [krak], *s.m.* crash; failure (of bank, etc.).

L

L, l [ɛl], *s.f.* (the letter) L, l; **l mouillée**, liquid l.

la¹ [la], *def.art.* & *pron.f.* See LE¹,².

la² *s.m.inv. Mus:* (the note) A; **morceau en la**, piece in A.

là [la], *adv.* **1.** (*of place*) there. (*a*) **passer par là**, to go that way; (*b*) (*emphatic use*) **que dites-vous là?** what's that you're saying? **ce, cette,** *etc.***, . . . -là**, see CE¹ 1, CE² 2. **2.** (*of time*) then; **d'ici là**, between now and then. **3.** *int.* **oh là là!** heavens!

là-bas [labɑ], *adv.* (over) there.

laborantine [labɔrɑ̃tin], *s.f.* (woman) laboratory assistant.

laboratoire [labɔratwaːr], *s.m.* laboratory, *F:* lab.

†**laborieu/x** [labɔrjø], *a.* **1.** hard (work); laboured (style). **2.** hard-working. *adv.* **-sement.**

labour [labuːr], *s.m.* tilling; ploughing. *a.* **-able**, arable.

labour/er [labure], *v.tr.* to till; to plough. *s.m.* **-eur**, ploughman.

lac [lak], *s.m.* lake.

lacer [lase], *v.tr.* to lace (up).

‡**lacér/er** [lasere] *v.tr.* to lacerate, to tear. *s.f.* **-ation.**

lacet [lasɛ], *s.m.* **1.** lace (of shoe). **2.** hairpin bend (in road). **3.** noose, snare (for rabbits, etc.).

lâche [lɑːʃ], *a.* **1.** loose, slack; lax. **2.** cowardly; *s.m.* coward. *adv.* **-ment.**

lâch/er [lɑʃe], *v.tr.* to release; (*a*) to slacken; l. un coup de fusil, to fire a shot; *Aut*: l. le frein, to release the brake; (*b*) to let go; to release (bomb); to drop (parachutist); lâchezmoi, let me go; *F*: l. qn, to drop s.o.; (*c*) to set free. *s.* -eur, -euse, *F*: quitter.

lâcheté [lɑʃte], *s.f.* **1.** weakness, slackness. **2.** cowardice. **3.** despicableness.

lacrymogène [lakrimɔʒɛn], *a.* gaz l., tear gas.

lacté [lakte], *a.* milky; régime l., milk diet; la Voie lactée, the Milky Way.

lacune [lakyn], *s.f.* lacuna, gap; blank (in memory).

là-dedans [lad(ə)dɑ̃], *adv.* in there; within.

là-dehors [ladəɔːr], *adv.* outside.

là-dessous [latsu], *adv.* under there; underneath.

là-dessus [latsy], *adv.* on that; thereupon.

lagune [lagyn], *s.f.* lagoon.

là-haut [lao], *adv.* up there; upstairs.

laï/ciser [laisize], *v.tr.* to secularize (school, etc.). *s.f.* -cisation. *s.m.* -cisme. *s.f.* -cité.

laid [lɛ], *a.* (*a*) ugly; unsightly; (*of face*) plain; (*b*) mean, shabby (action). *adv.* -ement.

laideur [lɛdœr], *s.f.* **1.** ugliness; plainness. **2.** meanness.

lain/e [lɛn], *s.f.* wool. *s.m.* -age, woollen article, *pl.* woollen goods.

†**laineux** [lɛnø], *a.* fleecy; woolly.

laïque [laik], *a.* secular (education); lay (dress); école l. = state school.

laisse [lɛs], *s.f.* leash, lead.

laisser [lese], *v.tr.* **1.** to let, allow; laissez-le faire! leave it to him! 2. (*a*) to leave (sth., s.o., somewhere); l. là qn, to leave s.o. in the lurch; (*b*) laissez donc! please don't trouble.

laisser-aller [lɛseale], *s.m.inv.* slovenliness.

laisser-faire [lɛsefɛr], *s.m.inv.* non-interference, laissez-faire.

laissez-passer [lesepase], *s.m.inv.* pass, permit.

lait [lɛ], *s.m.* milk. **1.** vache à l., milch-cow; l. concentré, condensed milk; cochon de l., suck(l)ing pig. **2.** l. de chaux, limewash; l. de ciment, grout. *s.m.* -age, dairy produce. *s.f.* -erie, dairy. *a.* †-eux, milky.

laitier, -ière [lɛtje, -jɛːr]. **1.** *a.* l'industrie laitière, dairying; ferme laitière, dairy farm. **2.** *s.m.* milkman; dairyman; dairy-hand.

laiton [lɛtɔ̃], *s.m.* brass.

laitue [lety], *s.f.* lettuce; l. pommée, cabbage lettuce.

lambeau [lɑ̃bo], *s.m.* scrap, bit, shred of cloth, etc.).

lambris [lɑ̃bri], *s.m.* wainscoting; panelling.

lame [lam], *s.f.* **1.** (*a*) thin plate; (metal) strip; (spring)leaf; (*b*) blade (of razor, etc.). **2.** wave; l. de fond, ground swell.

lamentable [lamɑ̃tabl], *a.* lamentable, deplorable; plaintive (voice). *adv.* -ment.

lament/er (se) [səlamɑ̃te], *v.pr.* to lament; to wail; to bewail. *s.f.* -ation.

lamifié [lamifje], *s.m.* laminated plastic.

lamin/er [lamine], *v.tr.* to laminate, flat(ten), roll (metal, plastic, etc.); to calender, plate-glaze (paper). *s.m.* -age. *s.m.* -eur. *s.m.* -oir, rolling mill.

lampadaire [lɑ̃padɛːr], *s.m.* standard lamp.

lampe [lɑ̃ːp], *s.f.* **1.** lamp. **2.** (*a*) l. de poche, (electric) torch; *Aut*: l. de bord, dash-board light; (*b*) *Rad*: valve.

lampée [lɑ̃pe], *s.f.* *F*: draught, gulp.

lamper [lɑ̃pe], *v.tr. F*: to swig, toss off (a drink).

lampion [lɑ̃pjɔ̃], *s.m.* fairy-light; *Fr.C*: *Ecc*: votive light.

lance [lɑ̃ːs], *s.f.* **1.** (*a*) spear; (*b*) lance; (*c*) harpoon. **2.** l. à eau, water-hose nozzle.

lance-bombes [lɑ̃sbɔ̃ːb], *s.m.inv.* **1.** trench mortar. **2.** *Av*: bomb rack.

lance-fusée [lɑ̃sfyze], *s.m. Mil*: *etc*: rocket launcher. *pl.* lance-fusées.

†**lanc/er** [lɑ̃se], *v.tr.* **1.** to throw, fling. *Sp*: to pitch, to throw, to toss; *Fish*: to cast; l. une fusée, to launch a rocket. **2.** (*a*) to start, set (s.o., sth.) going; (*b*) to launch (ship, scheme). *s.m.* -ement.

se lancer, to rush; to launch out.

lanciner [lɑ̃sine], *v.i.* (*of pain*) to shoot; to throb.

landau [lɑ̃do], *s.m.* perambulator; *F*: pram.

lande [lɑ̃ːd], *s.f.* sandy moor; heath.

langage [lɑ̃gaːʒ], *s.m.* language; speech (of the individual); l. courant, every-day speech.

langoust/e [lɑ̃gust], *s.f.* spiny lobster; crayfish; *Com*: *pl.* scampi.

langue [lɑ̃ːg], *s.f.* **1.** tongue; tirer la l., to put out one's tongue; *F*: avoir la l. bien pendue, to have the gift of the gab. **2.** language, speech; l. maternelle, mother tongue; langues vivantes, modern languages.

languette [lɑ̃gɛt], *s.f.* tongue (of shoe).

langu/ir [lɑ̃giːr], *v.i.* to be listless; (*of business*) to be slack; (*of conversation*) to flag. *s.m.* -eur, listlessness. *a.* -issant, listless.

lanière [lanjɛːr], *s.f.* thin strap; thong.

lanterne [lɑ̃tɛrn], *s.f.* lantern.

laper [lape], *v.tr.* (*of dog, cat*) to lap (up).

lapin, -ine [lapɛ̃, -in], *s.* rabbit. *s.f.* -ière, rabbit-hutch, -warren.

laps [laps], *s.m.* space (of time).

laque [lak], *s.m.* lacquer; hair spray.

laquer [lake], *v.tr.* to lacquer.

larcin [larsɛ̃], *s.m.* petty theft.

lard [la:r], *s.m.* (a) fat (*esp.* of pig); (b) bacon.

large [larʒ]. 1. *a.* (a) broad, wide; (b) large, big, ample. 2. *s.m.* (a) open sea. au l. de Cherbourg, off Cherbourg; (b) breadth. *adv.* -ement. *s.m.* -esse, liberality. *s.f.* -eur, width.

larme [larm], *s.f.* tear.

†**larm/oyer** [larmwaje], *v.i.* 1. (*of the eyes*) to water. 2. to snivel. *a.* -oyant, tearful. *s.m.* -oiement.

larve [larv], *s.f.* larva; grub.

laryngite [larɛ̃ʒit], *s.f. Med:* laryngitis.

†**las** [lɑ, lɑːs], *a.* tired, weary.

laser [lazer], *s.m. Ph:* laser.

lass/er [lase], *v.tr.* to tire, weary; to exhaust (s.o.'s patience). *s.f.* -itude, weariness.

 se lasser, to grow weary; to tire.

lasso [laso], *s.m.* lasso.

latent [latɑ̃], *a.* latent; hidden.

latéral [lateral], *a.* lateral; rue latérale, side street. *adv.* -ement.

latin [latɛ̃], *a. & s.m.* Latin; F: l. de cuisine, dog Latin; j'y perds mon l., I can't make head or tail of it.

latitude [latityd], *s.f.* latitude.

latte [lat], *s.f.* lath, batten, slat.

laurier [lorje], *s.m.* (a) laurel; (b) Cu: feuille de l., bay leaf; (c) l. rose, oleander.

lavabo [lavabo], *s.m.* wash basin.

lavande [lavɑ̃d], *s.f.* lavender.

lave [la:v], *s.f.* lava.

lave-glace [lavglas], *s.m. Aut:* windscreen-washer. *pl.* lave-glaces.

lav/er [lave], *v.tr.* to wash; se l. les mains, to wash one's hands; l. la vaisselle, to wash up; se l. la tête, to wash one's hair; l. la tête à qn, to haul s.o. over the coals. *a.* -able, washable. *s.m.* -oir, washhouse.

 se laver, to wash (oneself).

lavette [lavet], *s.f.* (a) (dish-)mop; l. métallique, pot-scourer; (b) dishcloth.

†**laxatif** [laksatif], *a. & s.m.* laxative, aperient.

le[1], **la**, **les** [lə, la, le], *def.art* (le and la are elided to l' before a vowel or h 'mute'; le and les contract with à, de, into au, aux; du, des); the. 1. (*particularizing*) (a) il est arrivé le lundi, he arrived on Monday; (b) la France, France; (c) le colonel Chabot, Colonel Chabot; (d) (*with parts of the body*) elle ferma les yeux, she closed her eyes. 2. (*forming superlatives*) mon ami le plus intime, my closest friend; c'est elle qui travaille le mieux, she's the one who works best. 3. (*generalizing*) je préfère le café au thé, I prefer coffee to tea. 4. (*distributive*) cinq francs la

livre, five francs a pound. 5. (*rendered by indef. art. in Eng.*) (a) donner l'exemple, to set an example; (b) il n'a pas le sou, he hasn't a penny.

le[2], **la**, **les**, *pers.pron.* 1. (*replacing s.*) him, her, it, them. 2. *neut. pron.* le; (a) êtes-vous ma mère?—je le suis, are you a mother?—I am; (b) so; il me l'a dit, he told me so; (c) vous le devriez, you ought to (do so).

†**lécher** [leʃe], *v.tr.* to lick (up); se l. les doigts, to lick one's fingers; l. les bottes de qn, F: to suck up to s.o.; F: l. les vitrines, to go window-shopping.

leçon [ləsɔ̃], *s.f.* lesson.

lecteur, -trice [lɛktœːr, -tris], *s.* (a) reader; (b) foreign language assistant (at university).

lecture [lɛktyːr], *s.f.* reading.

ledit, ladite, pl. lesdits, lesdites [lədi, ladit, ledi, ledit], *a.* the aforesaid.

†**légal** [legal], *a.* legal; statutory. *adv.* -ement.

légal/iser [legalize], *v.tr.* to legalize. *s.f.* -ité.

légataire [legatɛːr], *s.m. & f. Jur:* legatee, heir.

légation [legasjɔ̃], *s.f.* legation.

légend/e [leʒɑ̃ːd], *s.f.* 1. legend. 2. (a) inscription (on coin); (b) caption (of illustration); (c) key (of map). *a.* -aire, legendary.

†**léger** [leʒe], *a.* 1. (a) light; avoir la main légère, to be quick with one's hands; (b) slight; gentle; faint. 2. *adv.phr.* à la légère, lightly. *adv.* -èrement. *s.f.* -èreté, lightness.

légion [leʒjɔ̃], *s.f.* legion; Hist: l. étrangère, Foreign Legion; L. d'honneur, Legion of Honour. l. -naire, soldier of the Foreign Legion.

législa/tion [leʒislasjɔ̃], *s.f.* legislation. *s.* -teur, -trice, legislator. *a.* †-tif. *s.f.* -ture.

légiste [leʒist], *s.m.* jurist; expert l., forensic scientist.

légitime [leʒitim], *a.* 1. legitimate; lawful. 2. justifiable; l. défense, self-defence. *adv.* -ment.

legs [le], *s.m.* legacy, bequest.

†**léguer** [lege], *v.tr.* to bequeath.

légume [legym], *s.m.* vegetable; F: l. grosse l., big shot.

lendemain [lɑ̃dmɛ̃], *s.m.* next day; le l. matin, the next morning.

lent [lɑ̃], *a.* slow. *adv.* -ement. *s.f.* -eur, slowness.

lentille [lɑ̃tij], *s.f.* 1. lentil. 2. lens.

léopard [leɔpaːr], *s.m.* leopard.

lèpre [lɛpr], *s.f.* leprosy.

lépreux, -euse [leprø, -øːz], *a.* 1. leprous. 2. *s.* leper.

lequel, laquelle, lesquels, lesquelles [ləkɛl, lakɛl, lekɛl], *pron.* (contracted with à, de, to auquel, auxquel(le)s, duquel, desquel(le)s). 1. *rel.pron.* who, whom; which. 2. *interr.pron.* which (one)?

lèse-majesté [lɛzamaʒɛste], *s.f.* high treason.

‡**léser** [leze], *v.tr.* (a) to wrong; injure (s.o.); (b) (of action) to prove injurious to (s.o., sth.).

lésin/er [lezine], *v.i.* to be stingy; to haggle (sur, over). *s.* -eur, -euse, haggler.

lessive [lesiːv], *s.f.* 1. detergent. 2. (household) washing; faire la l., to do the washing.

leste [lɛst], *a.* light; nimble, agile; *Pej:* unscrupulous. *adv.* -ment.

léthargie [letarʒi], *s.f.* lethargy, apathy. *a.* -ique, lethargic.

lettre [lɛtr], *s.f.* 1. letter; écrivez en toutes lettres, write out in full. 2. au pied de la l., literally. 3. (a) *P.T.T:* letter; l. recommandée, registered letter; (b) l. de change, bill of exchange. 4. *pl.* literature; homme de lettres, man of letters.

lettré [lɛtre], *s.* a. well-read (person). 2. *s.m.* scholar.

leucémie [løsemi], *s.f. Med:* leukaemia. *s.m.* debtor.

leur¹ [lœːr]. 1. *poss.a.* their. 2. le leur, la leur, les leurs; (a) *poss.pron.* theirs; (b) *s.m.* their own.

leur², *pers.pron.* See LUI¹.

leurrer [lœre], *v.tr.* to lure; to entice.

levain [ləvɛ̃], *s.m.* leaven.

levant [ləvɑ̃]. *a.* soleil l., rising sun. 2. *s.m.* East.

levé [ləve], *a.* 1. (a) raised; dessin à main levée, freehand drawing; (b) (of pers.) up; out of bed. 2. l. d'un terrain, plan, survey, of a piece of land.

levée [ləve], *s.f.* 1. (a) raising, lifting; (b) gathering; collection (of letters); la l. est faite, the box has been cleared. 2. (a) embankment, sea-wall; (b) cam, lifter; (c) (card-)trick.

‡**lever** [ləve]. I. *v.tr.* 1. (a) to raise, to lift (up). 2. to lift (root crops); to levy (tax); to collect (letters). 3. l. un plan, to get out a plan. 4. to make a survey. II. *v.i.* (of dough) to rise; (of plants) to shoot. II. *s.m.* 1. (a) rising; getting up; (b) l. du soleil, sunrise. 2. *Th:* l. de rideau, curtain-raiser.

se lever, (a) to stand up; (b) to get up; to rise.

levier [ləvje], *s.m.* 1. lever; *Aut:* l. des vitesses, gear lever. 2. crowbar.

lèvre [lɛːvr], *s.f.* lip; du bout des lèvres, 'in a forced manner; pincer les lèvres, to purse one's lips.

lévrier [levrije], *s.m.* greyhound.

levure [ləvyːr], *s.f.* yeast.

lézard [lezaːr], *s.m.* lizard.

lézarde [lezard], *a.* (of wall) cracked, full of cracks.

liaison [ljɛzɔ̃], *s.f.* 1. (a) joining, binding; bonding (of bricks, etc.); (b) *Ling:* liaison; (c) *Cu:* thickening (of sauce). 2. intimacy; close relationship; l. d'affaires, business connection.

liasse [ljas], *s.f.* bundle (of letters); wad (of banknotes); file.

libellule [libellyl], *s.f.* dragonfly.

†**libéral** [liberal], *a.* liberal. *adv.* -ement. *s.f.* -ité, liberality.

‡**libér/er** [libere], *v.tr.* to liberate, release; to set (s.o.) free. *s.* -ateur, -atrice. *s.f.* -ation.

liberté [libɛrte], *s.f.* 1. liberty, freedom; jour de l., day off. 2. prendre des libertés, to take liberties.

librair/e [librɛːr], *s.m.* & f. bookseller. *s.f.* -ie, bookshop.

libre [libr], *a.* 1. free. 2. clear (space); vacant (seat); (taxi sign) "l.," "for hire." *adv.* -ment.

libre-échange [libreʃɑ̃ːʒ], *s.m.* free trade. *s.m.* -iste, free-trader.

libre-service [librəsɛrvis], *s.m.inv.* self-service (shop, restaurant). *pl.* libres-services.

licence [lisɑ̃s], *s.f.* licence. 1. (a) leave, permission; *Adm:* l. d'importation, import licence; (b) *Sch:* passer sa l., to sit for one's degree. 2. abuse of liberty.

licencié, -iée [lisɑ̃sje], *s. Sch:* graduate.

licenci/er [lisɑ̃sje], *v.tr.* to disband; to lay off (workmen). *s.m.* -ement.

licite [lisit], *a.* lawful, permissible. *adv.* -ment.

lie [li], *s.f.* lees, dregs (of wine, etc.).

liège [ljɛːʒ], *s.m.* cork.

lien [ljɛ̃], *s.m.* tie, bond.

li/er [lje], *v.tr.* 1. (a) to bind, tie, tie up; (b) *Cu:* l. une sauce, to thicken a sauce. 2. l. conversation, to enter into conversation. *s.m.* -age.

se lier. 1. se l. (d'amitié) avec qn, to form a friendship with s.o. 2. to bind oneself (by oath).

lierre [ljɛːr], *s.m.* ivy.

†**lieu** [ljø], *s.m.* 1. place; (a) locality, spot; le l. du sinistre, the scene of the disaster; en (tout) premier l., firstly; en dernier l., finally; (b) *pl.* premises. 2. (a) avoir l., to take place; (b) grounds, cause; (c) au l. de, instead of. 3. lieux communs, platitudes.

lieutenant [ljøtnɑ̃], *s.m.* (a) *Mil: Nau:* lieutenant; *Av:* flying officer; (b) *Merchant Navy:* mate.

lieutenant-colonel [ljøtnɑ̃kɔlɔnɛl], *s.m. Mil:* lieutenant-colonel; *Av:* wing-commander. *pl.* lieutenants-colonels.

lièvre [ljɛːvr], *s.m.* hare.

liftier, -ière [liftje, -jɛːr], *s.* lift-attendant.

lignage [liɲaːʒ], *s.m.* lineage, descent.

ligne [liɲ], *s.f.* line. 1. (a) cord; (b) grandes lignes, broad outline; (c) hors l., out of the common. 2. (a) (railway) line; steamship line; airline; (b) *P.T.T:* l. téléphonique, telephone line; l. partagée, shared, *F:* party, line.

lignée [liɲe], *s.f.* issue; descendants.

ligoter [ligɔte], *v.tr.* to bind hand and foot; to lash (things) together.

ligue [lig], *s.f.* league, confederacy.
lilas [lilɑ], *s.m.* lilac.
limace [limas], *s.f.* slug.
limaçon [limasɔ̃], *s.m.* snail; escalier en l., spiral staircase.
limande [limɑ̃:d], *s.f. Fish:* dab.
lime [lim], *s.f.* file; l. à ongles, nail file.
limer [lime], *v.tr.* to file; to file down.
limier [limje], *s.m.* bloodhound.
limite [limit], *s.f.* 1. boundary; limit; l. d'âge, age limit; *Sp:* limites du jeu, boundary(-line). 2. cas l., borderline case; vitesse l., maximum speed; date l., deadline.
limit/er [limite], *v.tr.* 1. to mark the boundary of (county, etc.). 2. to limit; to restrict. *s.f.* -ation. *a.* -rophe, adjacent.
limon[1] [limɔ̃], *s.m.* mud, silt.
limon[2], *s.m. Bot:* sour lime.
limonade [limɔnad], *s.f.* (fizzy) lemonade.
limpide [lɛ̃pid], *a.* limpid, clear.
limpidité [lɛ̃pidite], *s.f.* limpidity.
lin [lɛ̃], *s.m.* 1. flax; graine de l., linseed; huile de l., linseed oil. 2. linen.
linge [lɛ̃:ʒ], *s.m.* 1. l. (de maison), household linen; l. (de corps), underwear. 2. essuyer avec un l., to wipe with a cloth.
lingerie [lɛ̃ʒri], *s.f.* underwear; lingerie.
lingot [lɛ̃go], *s.m.* ingot; or, argent, en lingots, bullion.
linguist/e [lɛ̃gɥist], *s.m. & f.* linguist. *a.* -ique, linguistic. *s.f.* -ique, linguistics.
lino [lino], *s.m. F:* (a) H: lino; (b) linocut; (c) linotype.
linoléum [linɔleɔm], *s.m.* linoleum.
linotte [linɔt], *s.f.* linnet; F: tête de l., feather-brained person.
lino/type [linɔtip], *s.f.* linotype (machine). *s.f.* -typie, linotype setting. *s.m. or f.* -typiste, linotype operator.
linteau [lɛ̃to], *s.m.* lintel.
lion, -onne [ljɔ̃, -ɔn], *s.* lion, f. lioness. *s.m.* -ceau, lion cub.
liquéfier [likefje], *v.tr.* to liquefy. *a.* -able.
liqueur [likœ:r], *s.f.* 1. liqueur. 2. *Ch:* l. titrée, standard solution.
liquide [likid]. 1. *a.* liquid; argent l., ready money. 2. *s.m.* (a) liquid; (b) drink.
liquid/er [likide], *v.tr.* 1. to liquidate. 2. to realize; to sell off. *s.f.* -ation.
lire [li:r], *v.tr.* to read; l. à haute voix, to read aloud.
lis [lis], *s.m.* lily.
liseron [lizrɔ̃], *s.m.* convolvulus, bindweed.
liseur, -euse [lizœ:r, -øːz], 1 (a) *s.m. & f.* (a great) reader. 2. *s.f.* (a) book cover; (b) bed-jacket.
lisib/le [lizibl], *a.* legible. *adv.* -lement. *s.f.* -ilité, legibility.
lisière [lizjɛ:r], *s.f.* 1. selvedge. 2. edge, border.
lisse [lis], *a.* smooth, polished; sleek.

liss/er [lise], *v.tr.* to smooth; to polish. *s.m.* -age.
liste [list], *s.f.* list; register.
lit [li], *s.m.* 1. bed; bedstead. 2. bed, layer (of sand, etc.); bed (of river). *s.f.* -erie, bedding.
litanie [litani], *s.f.* litany.
litige [liti:ʒ], *s.m. Jur:* litigation; lawsuit.
litre [litr], *s.m.* litre.
littéraire [literɛ:r], *a.* literary.
†**littéral** [literal], *a.* literal. *adv.* -ement.
†**littérature** [literaty:r], *s.f.* literature.
†**littoral** [litɔral], *s.m.* coastline.
liturgie [lityrʒi], *s.f.* liturgy.
livide [livid], *a.* livid; ghastly (pale).
livre[1] [li:vr], *s.f.* 1. pound (weight). 2. l. sterling, pound sterling.
livre[2], *s.m.* book; l. de classe, school book; l. de poche, paperback; tenue des livres, book-keeping.
livr/er [livre], *v.tr.* 1. (a) to deliver; to give up; livré à soi-même, left to oneself; l. un secret, to betray a secret; (b) l. bataille, to join battle. 2. to deliver (goods). *s.f.* -aison, delivery of (goods). *s.* -eur, -euse, delivery man, girl. se livrer, to give oneself up to justice, to drink (to despair).
livret [livre], *s.m.* 1. (savings bank, etc.) book. 2. libretto.
†**local** [lɔkal]. 1. *a.* local. 2. *s.m.* (a) premises, building; (b) *Sp:* les locaux, the home side. *adv.* -ement, *a.* -ité.
location [lɔkasjɔ̃], *s.f.* (a) hiring; (b) renting; letting; agent de l., house-agent; *Th:* bureau de l., box-office. *s.m. & f.* -taire, tenant.
lock-out [lɔk(a)ut], *s.m.inv.* Ind: lockout.
lock-outer [lɔk(a)ute], *v.tr. Ind:* to lock out.
locomotive [lɔkɔmɔti:v], *s.f.* locomotive, engine.
locution [lɔkysjɔ̃], *s.f.* expression, phrase.
loge [lɔ:ʒ], *s.f.* 1. hut; lodge. 2. *Th:* box.
logement [lɔʒmɑ̃], *s.m.* 1. lodging, housing. 2. accommodation; lodgings.
‡**loger** [lɔʒe]. 1. *v.i.* to lodge; l. en garni, to live in digs. 2. *v.tr.* (a) to lodge (s.o.), to put (s.o.) up; (b) to place, put; je ne sais où l. mes affaires, I don't know where to put my things.
logique [lɔʒik]. 1. *a.* logical, reasoned. 2. *s.f.* logic. *adv.* -ment.
loi [lwa], *s.f.* (a) law; faire la l., to lay down the law; (b) act (of Parliament); law; projet de l., bill.
loin [lwɛ̃], *adv.* 1. (a) far; plus l., farther (on); further; il ira l., he'll go far; (b) *s.m.* de l., (i) by far; (ii) from afar; au l., in the distance. 2. (of time) distant; de l. en l., at long intervals.
lointain [lwɛ̃tɛ̃], *a.* distant, remote (country, period). *s.m.* dans le l., in the distance.
loir [lwar], *s.m.* dormouse.

loisir [lwazi:r], s.m. leisure; **pendant mes loisirs**, in my spare time.

†long [l5]. 1. a. long; adv.phr. **à la longue**, in the long run. 2. s.m. length; (a) **de l. en large**, up and down; **le l. de**, along; alongside; (b) **regard qui en dit l.**, look which speaks volumes. adv. **-uement**, for a long time.

long-courrier [l5kurje], a. & s.m. ocean-going (ship); **avion l.-c.**, long-distance transport aircraft.

longe [l5ʒ], s.f. loin (of veal).

†longer [l5ʒe], v.tr. to go along(side); to skirt (forest); to hug (coast).

longitude [l5ʒityd], s.f. longitude.

longtemps [l5tɑ̃], adv. & s.m. a long time.

longueur [l5gœ:r], s.f. length.

longue-vue [l5gvy], s.f. telescope. pl. **longues-vues**.

lopin [lɔpɛ̃], s.m. plot (of ground).

loquace [lɔkwas], a. talkative, garrulous.

loquacité [lɔkwasite], s.f. loquacity, talkativeness.

loque [lɔk], s.f. rag; F: (of pers.) **être comme une l.**, to feel like a rag.

loquet [lɔkɛ], s.m. latch.

lors [lɔ:r], adv. (a) **depuis l.**, ever since then; **l. de**, at the time of; when.

lorsque [lɔrsk(ə)], conj. when.

lot [lo], s.m. 1. (a) share; lot; (b) prize. 2. lot, parcel (of goods).

loterie [lɔtri], s.f. (a) lottery; (b) raffle, draw.

lotion [losj5], s.f. lotion.

lotir [lɔti:r], v.tr. 1. to divide into lots; to parcel out (estate). 2. **bien loti**, well provided for.

lotissement [lɔtismɑ̃], s.m. 1. (a) allotment, dividing up; (b) development (of building land). 2. (a) building plot; (b) housing estate.

louable [lwabl], a. praiseworthy; commendable (de, for).

louage [lwa:ʒ], s.m. hiring, hire; **auto, avion, de l.**, hired car, charter aircraft.

louange [lwɑ̃:ʒ], s.f. praise.

louche¹ [luʃ], a. 1. squint-eyed. 2. (a) ambiguous; (b) shady, suspicious; s.m. **il y a du l.**, there's sth. fishy.

louche², s.f. (soup) ladle.

loucher [luʃe], v.i. to squint.

louer¹ [lue, lwe], v.tr. to hire; to rent; **maison à l.**, house to let; **l. une place**, to book a seat.

louer², v.tr. to praise, commend. **se louer**, to be pleased (de, with).

loufoque [lufɔk], a. P: mad, bats, crazy.

loup [lu], s.m. wolf; **à pas de l.**, stealthily; **un froid de l.**, bitter cold.

loupe [lup], s.f. magnifying-glass.

louper [lupe], v.tr. F: to bungle (work); **l. le train** (to fail (exam.); Th: **to fluff** (one's entrance); **c'est loupé**, you've had it.

lourd [lu:r], a. (a) heavy; ungainly; ponderous; Aut: **poids l.**, heavy lorry; (b) clumsy; dull; stupid; (c) **lourde**

bévue, gross blunder, F: clanger; (d) close, sultry (weather). adv. **-ement**. s.f. **-eur**, heaviness.

lourdaud [lurdo], a.s.f. (a) lout; (b) F: dimwit.

loutre [lutr], s.f. otter. Com: **l. d'Amérique**, nutria.

louve [lu:v], s.f. she-wolf. s.m. **-teau**, wolf-cub; (scouting) cub.

†louvoyer [luvwaje], v.i. Nau: to tack.

†loyal [lwajal], a. 1. honest, fair; **jeu l.**, fair play. 2. loyal, faithful. adv. **-ement**.

loyauté [lwajote], s.f. 1. honesty, uprightness; **manque de l.**, dishonesty, unfairness. 2. loyalty (**envers**, towards).

loyer [lwaje], s.m. rent(al).

lubie [lybi], s.f. whim, fad.

lubrifi/er [lybrifje], v.tr. to lubricate; to grease, oil. a. & s.m. **-ant**, lubricant. s.f. **-cation**, greasing.

lucarne [lykarn], s.f. (a) dormer-window; (b) skylight.

lucide [lysid], a. lucid, clear. adv. **-ment**.

lucidité [lysidite], s.f. lucidity, clearness.

†lucratif [lykratif], a. lucrative, profitable.

lueur [lɥœ:r], s.f. 1. gleam, glimmer; **la l. des étoiles**, starlight. 2. **l. momentanée**, flash of light.

luge [ly:ʒ], s.f. luge, toboggan.

†lug/er [lyʒe], v.i. Sp: to luge, to toboggan. s.m. **-eage**, tobogganing. s. **-eur, -euse**, tobogganer.

lugubre [lygy:br], a. lugubrious, gloomy. adv. **-ment**.

lui¹, pl. **leur** [lɥi, lœ(:)r], pers. pron. m & f: (to) him, her, it, them; (a) (unstressed) **je le lui donne**, I give it (to) him, (to) her; (b) (stressed in imp.) **montrez-le-leur**, show it to them.

lui², pl. **eux** [lɥi, ø], stressed pers.pron. m. (a) he, it, they; **c'est l.**, it is he, F: it's him; **l. et sa femme**, he and his wife; (b) him, her, them; **l., je le connais**, I know him; (of persons) **l.** (him(self), it(self), them(selves)).

lui-même [lɥimɛːm], pers.pron.m. himself, itself.

†luire [lɥi:r], v.i. to shine; to glimmer, to gleam.

luisant [lɥizɑ̃], a. shining, gleaming.

lumière [lymjɛ:r], s.f. light.

†lumineu/x [lyminø], a. luminous. adv. **-sement**.

lunaire [lynɛ:r], a. lunar.

lunch [lœːʃ], s.m. (a) snack; (b) buffet lunch.

lundi [lœ̃di], s.m. Monday.

lune [lyn], s.f. 1. moon; **clair de l.**, moonlight; **l. de miel**, honeymoon. 2. **en (forme de) l.**, crescent-shaped.

lunette [lynɛt], s.f. 1. **l. d'approche**, telescope; field-glass. 2. pl. **spectacles**.

lustre [lystr], s.m. 1. lustre, polish, gloss. 2. chandelier.

lutrin [lytrɛ̃], *s.m.* lectern; Fr.C: music stand.

lutte [lyt], *s.f.* 1. wrestling; l. libre, all-in wrestling. 2. (a) contest, struggle; l. contre la maladie, disease prevention; (b) strife.

lutt/er [lyte], *v.i.* 1. to wrestle. 2. to struggle, fight; to battle with. *s.* -eur, -euse, wrestler; fighter.

luxe [lyks], *s.m.* luxury; pros L, ostentation; édition de l., de luxe edition; train de l. = Pullman train.

†**luxueu/x** [lyksɥø], *a.* luxurious; rich. *adv.* -sement.

luxuri/ance [lyksyrjɑ̃:s], *s.f.* luxuriance (of vegetation, etc.). *a.* -ant.

luzerne [lyzɛrn], *s.f.* lucern(e).

lycée [lise], *s.m.* = grammar, high, school.

lycéen, -enne [liseɛ̃, -ɛn], *s.* pupil at a lycée.

lymph/e [lɛ̃:f], *s.f.* lymph. *a. & s.* -atique, lymphatic.

lyrique [lirik], *a.* lyric(al).

M

M, m [ɛm], *s.f.* (the letter) M, m.

ma [ma], *poss.a.f.* See MON.

macabre [makɑ:br], *a.* gruesome.

macaron [makarɔ̃], *s.m.* Cu: macaroon.

macédoine [masedwan], *s.f.* (a) m. de fruits, fruit salad; (b) medley.

†**macérer** [masere], *v.tr.* to macerate; to steep.

Mach [mak], *s.m.* Av: (nombre de) M., Mach (number).

mâcher [maʃe], *v.tr.* to chew, masticate.

machin [maʃɛ̃], *s.m.* gadget; Madame M., Mrs What's-her-name.

†**machinal** [maʃinal], *a.* mechanical. *adv.* -ement.

machine [maʃin], *s.f.* 1. machine; *pl.* machinery; (a) m. à coudre, à écrire, à laver, sewing-machine, typewriter, washing machine; écriture à la m., typing; (b) bicycle, motor-cycle; (c) gadget. 2. engine; (a) m. à vapeur, steam engine; (b) locomotive.

machine-outil [maʃinuti], *s.f.* machine-tool. *pl. machines-outils.*

machin/er [maʃine], *v.tr.* to scheme, plot. *s.f.* -ation, plot.

mâchoire [maʃwa:r], *s.f.* jaw.

mâchonn/er [maʃɔne], *v.tr.* 1. to chew; to munch. 2. to mumble. *s.m.* -ement.

maçon [masɔ̃], *s.m.* mason; bricklayer. *s.m.* -nage, mason's work. *s.f.* -nerie, masonry.

macul/er [makyle], *v.tr.* to stain, spot. *s.m.* -age.

†**madame** [madam], *s.f.* 1. (a) Mrs; (b) (pl. ces dames) the mistress; ces dames n'y sont pas, the ladies are not at home. 2. madam.

madeleine [madlɛn], *s.f.* sponge-cake.

†**mademoiselle** [madmwazɛl], *s.f.* 1. miss; Mesdemoiselles Martin, the Misses Martin. 2. (pl. ces demoiselles); que prendront ces demoiselles? what can I offer you, ladies?

madère [madɛ:r], *s.m.* madeira (wine).

madone [madɔn], *s.f.* madonna.

madrier [madrie], *s.m.* thick board, plank.

magasin [magazɛ̃], *s.m.* 1. (a) (large) shop; stores; (b) store, warehouse. 2. magazine (of rifle). *s.m.* -age, warehousing. *s.m.* -ier, warehouseman.

magicien [maʒisjɛ̃, -jɛn], *s.m.* magician.

mag/ie [maʒi], *s.f.* magic. *a.* -ique, magic. *adv.* -iquement.

magis/trat [maʒistra], *s.m.* magistrate; judge. *a.* †-tral, masterly. *adv.* -tralement.

magnanime [mananim], *a.* magnanimous.

magn/ésie [maɲezi], *s.f.* 1. magnesia. 2. sulfate de m., Epsom salts. *s.m.* -ésium, magnesium.

magné/tiser [maɲetize], *v.tr.* to magnetize. *a.* -tique, magnetic. *s.m.* -tisme, magnetism.

magnéto [maɲeto], *s.f.* magneto.

magnétophone [maɲetɔfɔn], *s.m.* R.t.m: tape recorder.

magnifi/er [maɲifje], *v.tr.* to magnify. *s.f.* -cence, magnificence. *a.* -que, magnificent. *adv.* -quement.

mai [mɛ], *s.m.* May.

maigre [mɛ:gr]. 1. *a.* thin; lean; m. repas, frugal meal; jour de m., day of abstinence. 2. *s.m.* lean. *adv.* -ment.

maigr/ir [megri:r], *v.i.* to grow thin, to lose weight. *s.m.* -eur, (i) leanness; (ii) meagreness.

mail [ma:j], *s.m.* avenue, promenade.

maille [mɑ:j], *s.f.* 1. (a) stitch (in knitting, etc.); (b) link (of chain). 2. mesh (of net).

maillet [mɑjɛ], *s.m.* mallet.

maillon [mɑjɔ̃], *s.m.* link (of a chain).

maillot [majo], *s.m.* Cl: (a) m. de corps, vest; (b) m. de bain, swimsuit; (c) Sp: jersey; singlet.

main [mɛ̃], *s.f.* 1. hand; (a) serrer la m. à (qn), to shake hands with (s.o.); donner un coup de m. à (qn), to lend (s.o.) a (helping) hand; en venir aux mains, to come to blows; haut les mains! hands up! à bas les mains! hands off! (b) en un tour de m., in a twinkling; se faire la m., to get one's hand in; avoir le coup de m., to have the knack; (c) gagner haut la m., to win hands down; (d) adv.phr. de longue m., for a long time (past). 2. hand(writing).

main-d'œuvre [mɛ̃dœ:vr], s.f. labour, manpower.

maintenant [mɛ̃tnɑ̃], adv. now.

‡**maintenir** [mɛ̃tni:r], v.tr. to maintain. 1. (a) to keep, hold, in position; to support; (b) to uphold, keep (the law, discipline).
se maintenir. 1. to last well. 2. to hold on; les prix se maintiennent, prices are keeping up.

maintien [mɛ̃tjɛ̃], s.m. 1. maintenance, keeping (of order). 2. bearing, carriage.

maire [mɛːr], s.m. mayor.

mairie [meri], s.f. town hall.

mais [mɛ]. 1. adv. m. oui! certainly! m. non! not at all! 2. conj. but.

maïs [mais], s.m. maize, U.S: corn; farine de m., cornflour.

maison [mɛzɔ̃], s.f. 1. house; (a) m. de commerce, business house; firm; (b) home; à la m., at home. 2. family; le fils de la m., the son of the house.

maître, -esse [mɛtr, mɛtres], s. 1. (a) master, f. mistress; (b) m. d'école, schoolmaster; coup de m., master stroke; (c) m. d'équipage, boatswain; m. d'hôtel, butler; head waiter; chief steward. 2. attrib. chief, principal; **maîtresse poutre**, main girder.

maîtrise [mɛtri:z], s.f. mastery; m. de soi, self-control.

maîtriser [mɛtrize], v.tr. to master.

majesté [maʒeste], s.f. 1. sa M., His, Her, Majesty. 2. (a) stateliness; (b) grandeur.

†**majestueux/x** [maʒestɥø], a. majestic. adv. -sement.

majeur [maʒœːr], a. (a) major, greater; en majeure partie, for the most part; (b) affaire majeure, important business; cas de force majeure, case of absolute necessity; (c) devenir m., to come of age.

major/er [maʒore], v.tr. to raise the price of (sth.). s.f. -ation, increase (in price).

major/ité [maʒorite], s.f. majority. a. -itaire; vote m., majority vote.

majuscule [maʒyskyl], a. & s.f. capital (letter).

†**mal¹** [mal], s.m. 1. evil; (a) hurt; harm; (b) prendre qch. en m., to take sth. amiss; (c) wrong(doing); evil. 2. (a) ailment; pain; m. de tête, headache; m. de mer, seasickness; faire (du) m. à qn, to hurt s.o.; (b) se donner du m., to take pains; avoir du m. à faire qch., to have difficulty in doing sth.

mal², adv. 1. (a) badly, ill; m. à l'aise, ill at ease; vous ne feriez pas m. de . . . it wouldn't be a bad plan to . . . (b) se porter m., to be ill; (c) pas m. (de

qch.), a fair amount (of sth.); pas m. de gens, a good many people. 2. (a) not right; (b) uncomfortable; badly off; on n'est pas m. ici, it's not bad here; (c) se trouver m., to faint.

malade [malad]. 1. a. ill, sick. 2. s. patient; invalid.

malad/ie [maladi], s.f. illness, sickness. a. †-if, sickly.

maladresse [maladres], s.f. 1. clumsiness, awkwardness; tactlessness. 2. blunder.

maladroit [maladrwa]. 1. a. (a) clumsy, awkward; (b) blundering. adv. -sement.

malais, -aise¹ [malɛ, -ɛːz], a. & s. Malay(an).

malaise² [malɛz], s.m. 1. uneasiness, discomfort. 2. indisposition.

malaisé [maleze], a. difficult. adv. -ment, with difficulty.

malavisé [malavize], a. ill-advised.

malchanc/e [malʃɑ̃ːs], s.f. bad luck. a. †-eux, unlucky.

malcommode [malkɔmɔd], a. inconvenient; F: (of pers.) difficult; il est bien m., he's very awkward.

mâle [mɑːl], a. & s.m. 1. male; cock (bird); dog (fox); bull (elephant). 2. manly; virile (courage, etc.).

malédiction [malediksjɔ̃], s.f. curse.

†**malencontreux** [malɑ̃kɔ̃trø], a. 1. unfortunate (event). 2. unlucky (person).

malentendu [malɑ̃tɑ̃dy], s.m. misunderstanding.

malfaisant [malfəzɑ̃], a. evil-minded, harmful.

malfaiteur, -trice [malfetœːr, -tris], s. criminal.

malfamé [malfame], a. of ill fame.

malgré [malgre], prep. in spite of.

malhabile [malabil], a. unskilful; clumsy. adv. -ment.

malheur [malœːr], s.m. 1. misfortune; calamity, accident. 2. bad luck; jouer de m., to be unlucky.

†**malheureu/x** [malœrø], a. (a) unfortunate, unhappy; badly off (pers.); le m.! poor man! m.! wretch! (b) unlucky. adv. -sement.

malhonnête [malɔnɛt], a. (a) dishonest; (b) rude. adv. -ment. s.f. -té, (a) dishonesty; (b) rudeness.

malice [malis], s.f. (a) malice; (b) mischievousness. 2. (a) smart remark; dire des malices, to tease; (b) trick; faire une m., to play a trick.

†**malicieu/x** [malisjø], a. (a) mischievous; (b) sly. adv. -sement.

maligne. See MALIN.

†**malin** [malɛ̃], a. 1. malignant, evil; s.m. le M., the Devil. 2. shrewd, cunning.

malingre [malɛ̃ːgr], a. sickly, puny.

mall/e [mal], s.f. trunk, box; Aut: boot, U.S: trunk; faire sa m., to pack. s.f. -ette, (small) (suit)case.

‡**malmener** [malməne], *v.tr.* to ill-treat.
malodorant [malɔdɔrɑ̃], *a.* evil-smelling, smelly.
malprop/reté [malprɔprəte], *s.f.* dirtiness; (b) indecency, dirt. *a.* -re, dirty. *adv.* -rement.
malsain [malsɛ̃], *a.* 1. unhealthy. 2. unwholesome.
malséant [malseɑ̃], *a.* unseemly; unbecoming.
maltraiter [maltrete], *v.tr.* to ill-treat.
malveill/ance [malvejɑ̃:s], *s.f.* malevolence; ill-will; *a.* -lant, spiteful.
maman [mamɑ̃, mãmã], *s.f.* mam(m)a, mummy.
mamelle [mamɛl], *s.f.* breast; udder.
mammifère [mammifɛ:r], *s.m.* mammal.
manche¹ [mɑ̃:ʃ], *s.f.* 1. (a) sleeve; (b) m. d'incendie, fire-hose. 2. *Sp:* (a) heat, round; (b) game, set. 3. la M., the English Channel.
manche², *s.m.* handle; m. à balai, (i) broomstick; (ii) *F: Av:* joy-stick.
manchette [mɑ̃ʃɛt], *s.f.* 1. cuff. 2. (newspaper) headline.
manchon [mɑ̃ʃɔ̃], *s.m.* (a) *E:* casing; sleeve; m. d'accouplement, couplingsleeve; bush(ing) (of bearing); (b) gas mantle.
manchot, -ote [mɑ̃ʃo, ɔt]. 1. *a. & s.* onearmed (person). 2. *s.m.* penguin.
mandarine [mɑ̃darin], *s.f.* tangerine.
mandat [mɑ̃da], *s.m.* 1. (a) mandate; territoire sous m., mandated territory; (b) *Jur:* proxy. 2. warrant. 3. money order.
mandataire [mɑ̃datɛ:r], *s.m. & f.* 1. (*pers.*) proxy. 2. *Jur:* authorized agent. 3. trustee.
mandat-poste [mɑ̃dapɔst], *s.m.* = postal, money, order. *pl. mandats-poste.*
mander [mɑ̃de], *v.tr.* 1. to instruct, to send word to s.o. (to do sth.). 2. to summon, to send for (s.o.).
manège [manɛ:ʒ], *s.m.* 1. (a) ridingschool; (b) roundabout. 2. trick; j'observais leur m., I was watching their little game.
manette [manɛt], *s.f.* handle, hand-lever.
‡**mang/er** [mɑ̃ʒe]. I. *v.tr.* 1. to eat; salle à m., dining-room; donner à m. à qn, aux poules, to feed s.o., the hens. 2. to squander. II. *s.m.* food. *a.* -eable, edible. *s.f.* -eaille, *F:* grub. *s.f.* -eoire, manger, trough. *s.* -eur, -euse, eater.
mange-tout [mɑ̃ʒtu], *s.m.* 1. spendthrift. 2. (a) sugar-pea; (b) French bean, *U.S:* string-bean.
maniaque [manjak], *s.* 1. maniac. *a.* faddist, *F:* fusspot.
manie [mani], *s.f.* mania; craze; fad.
mani/er [manje], *v.tr.* 1. to feel; to handle (tool, rope). 2. to handle (affair); to manage, control (horse, business); *a.* -able, manageable, handy (tool). *s.m.* -ement.

man/ière [manjɛ:r], *s.f.* 1. manner, way (of doing sth.); d'aucune m., under no circumstances; de (telle) m. que, so that. 2. *pl.* manners. *s.m.* -iérisme, mannerism.
maniéré [manjere], *a.* affected.
manifeste¹ [manifɛst], *a.* obvious, evident. *adv.* -ment.
manifeste², *s.m.* manifesto, proclamation; (ship's) manifest.
manifest/er [manifɛste], *v.tr.* 1. to reveal; to show, exhibit (confusion). 2. *Abs.* to demonstrate. *s.* -ant, -ante. *Pol:* demonstrator. *s.f.* -ation, *Pol:* demonstration.
　se manifester, to appear.
manipul/er [manipyle], *v.tr.* 1. to handle, operate (apparatus). 2. to manipulate, *F:* rig (a piece of business). *s.* -ateur, -atrice, manipulator. *s.f.* -ation.
manivelle [manivɛl], *s.f.* crank; *Aut:* starting-handle.
mannequin [mankɛ̃], *s.m.* 1. (a) lay figure; (b) dummy. 2. mannequin, model.
manœuvre [manœ:vr]. 1. *s.f.* (a) working, driving (of machine, etc.); (b) *Mil:* (tactical) exercise; (army) manœuvre(s); (c) *Rail:* shunting; (d) scheme, manœuvre, intrigue. 2. *s.m.* (unskilled) workman.
manœuvr/er [manœvre]. 1. *v.tr.* (a) to work, operate; (b) *Rail:* to shunt. 2. *v.i.* to scheme, manœuvre. *a.* -able, manageable, handy.
manque [mɑ̃:k], *s.m.* lack, want; deficiency, shortage.
manqué [mɑ̃ke], *a.* missed; unsuccessful (opportunity, attempt); coup m., miss, failure; garçon m., tomboy.
manqu/er [mɑ̃ke]. I. *v.i.* 1. (a) m. de, to lack, be short of; m. de courage, to lack courage; (b) il a manqué (de) tomber, he nearly fell; (c) *impers.* il s'en manque de beaucoup, far from it. 2. to fail; (a) to be wanting; les mots me manquent, words fail me; (b) to give way; le cœur lui manqua, his heart failed him; (c) to be missing; (d) m. à sa parole, to break one's word; *abs.* (of attempt) to fail; to miscarry. II. *v.tr.* to miss (aim, train, etc.). *s.m.* -ement, failure, omission.
mansarde [mɑ̃sard], *s.f.* attic, garret.
manteau [mɑ̃to], *s.m.* coat, wrap; m. de neige, de la nuit, mantle of snow, cover of darkness.
manucure [manyky:r], *s.m. & f.* manicurist.
†**manuel** [manɥɛl], 1. *a.* manual (work). 2. *s.m.* manual, handbook.
manufacture [manyfakty:r], *s.f.* factory; works.
manufactur/er [manyfaktyre], *v.tr.* to manufacture.
manuscrit [manyskri], *a. & s.m.* manuscript.

manutention [manytɑ̃sjɔ̃], s.f. 1. management, administration. 2. handling (of stores, materials).

mappemonde [mapmɔ̃ːd], s.f. map of the world in two hemispheres.

maquereau [makro], s.m. mackerel.

maquet/te [makɛt], s.f. miniature, scale, model; demonstration model. s.m. & f. -tiste, model maker.

maquill/er [makije], v.tr. to make up (s.o.'s face); to fake up (picture). s.m. -age, make-up.
se maquiller, to make up (one's face).

maquis [maki], s.m. 1. scrub, bush. 2. maquis, underground forces.

maraîch/er, -ère [marɛʃe, -ɛːr], s. market-gardener, U.S: truck farmer. s.m. -age, market gardening.

marais [marɛ], s.m. marsh; bog, fen.

maraud/er [marode], v.i. to maraud; to thieve; F: (of taxi) to cruise. s. -eur, -euse, petty thief.

marbre [marbr], s.m. marble.

marbré [marbre], a. marbled; mottled.

marc [maːr], s.m. 1. marc (spirit). 2. coffee-grounds.

marchand [marʃɑ̃], 1. s. dealer, merchant; tradesman; m. des quatre saisons, costermonger; m. en gros, en détail, wholesaler, retailer. 2. a. (a) saleable (article); (b) trading; ville marchande, commercial town; navire m., merchant ship.

marchand/er [marʃɑ̃de], v.tr. to haggle. s.m. -age. s. -eur, -euse. s.f. -ise, goods.

marche [marʃ], s.f. 1. step, stair. 2. (a) walking; ralentir sa m., to slacken one's pace; se mettre en m., to start off; (b) march (i) Mil: ordres de m., marching orders; (ii) Mus: march. 3. (a) mettre en m. un service, to start, to run, a service; (b) m. avant, arrière, forward gear, reverse. 4. (a) running, working (of machine, etc.); (b) course (of events, of time).

marché [marʃe], s.m. 1. (a) deal, bargain; par-dessus le m., into the bargain; (b) bon m., cheap(ness). 2. market; m. commun, common market.

marchepied [marʃəpje], s.m. footboard; running-board.

marcher [marʃe], v.i. 1. to tread. 2. (a) to walk, go; façon de m., gait; (b) to obey orders; il marchera, he'll do it; faire m. qn, to fool s.o.; (c) to march. 3. (a) (of trains, ships, etc.) to move, go; (b) (of machine) to work, run. s. -eur, -euse [marʃœːr, -øːz], s. walker.

mardi [mardi], s.m. Tuesday; m. gras, Shrove Tuesday.

mare [maːr], s.f. pool; pond.

marécag/e [mareka3], s.m. bog, swamp. a. †-eux, boggy.

†**maréchal** [mareʃal], s.m. (a) m. ferrant, shoeing-smith; (b) m. des logis, (cavalry) sergeant; (c) M. de France = field-marshal.

marée [mare], s.f. 1. tide. 2. fresh fish; train de m., fish-train.

margarine [margarin], s.f. margarine.

marge [mar3], s.f. (a) border (of ditch, road); (b) margin (of book).

mari [mari], s.m. husband.

mariage [marja3], s.m. marriage; wedding.

marié [marje], a. & s. married (person); le, la, marié(e), the bridegroom, the bride.

marier [marje], v.tr. 1. to marry (a couple) (a) (of priest) to marry (a couple); (b) to give (a daughter) in marriage. 2. to join, unite.
se marier, to get married; se m. avec qn, to marry s.o.

marin [marɛ̃], 1. a. marine (plant, engine). 2. s.m. sailor.

marine [marin], s.f. la m. marchande, the merchant service; la m. de guerre, the Navy.

marin/er [marine], v.tr. (a) to pickle; to salt; (b) Cu: to marinate, to souse. s.f. -ade, brine, marinade. s.m. -age.

†**marital** [marital], a. marital.

maritime [maritim], a. maritime; ville m., seaside town; commerce m., seaborne trade; agent m., shipping agent; gare m., harbour station.

marmelade [marməlad], s.f. stewed fruit.

marmite [marmit], s.f. (a) (cooking-)pot; pan; (b) dixie, camp-kettle.

marmot/ter [marmɔte], v.tr. to mumble, mutter. s.m. -age, -ement, mumbling. s. -eur, -euse, mumbler.

marocain, -aine [marɔkɛ̃, -ɛn], a. & s. Moroccan; crêpe m., marocain.

maroquin [marɔkɛ̃], s.m. Morocco (-leather); s.f. -erie, fancy-leather goods, shop.

marquant [markɑ̃], a. prominent, outstanding (incident, personality).

marque [mark], s.f. 1. mark; m. de fabrique, trade mark; m. déposée, registered trade mark; produits de m., branded goods. 2. Sp: score-board; score.

marqu/er [marke], 1. v.tr. to mark; (a) to put a mark on; (b) to record, note; Sp: to score; (c) to indicate. 2. v.i. to stand out. s. -eur, -euse, marker; scorer.

marquis [marki], s.m. marquis, marquess.

marquise [markiːz], s.f. 1. marchioness. 2. (a) awning; (b) glass porch.

marraine [marɛn], s.f. godmother.

marre [maːr], s.f. P: j'en ai m., I'm fed up with it.

mar/rer (se) [səmare], v.pr. P: to die (of laughing. a. -rant, screamingly funny; ce n'est pas m., it's no joke.

marron [marɔ̃], s.m. 1. (a) chestnut; (b) m. d'Inde, horse chestnut. 2. a. & s. (chestnut) brown. s.m. -nier, chestnut tree.

mars [mars], s.m. March; blé de m., spring wheat.

marseillais, -aise [marseje, -ɛːz], a. & s. 1. Geog: Marseillais, -aise. 2. la Marseillaise, the Marseillaise.

marsouin [marswɛ̃], s.m. porpoise.

marteau [marto], s.m. (a) hammer; (b) knocker.

‡marteler [martəle], v.tr. to hammer out (metal); cuivre martelé, hand-wrought copper.

†martial [marsjal], martial, warlike; loi martiale, martial law. adv. -ement.

martien, -ienne [marsjɛ̃, -jɛn]. 1. a. Martian. 2. s. spaceman.

martin-pêcheur [martɛ̃peʃœːr], s.m. king-fisher. pl. martins-pêcheurs.

martre [martr], s.f. marten; m. zibeline, sable; m. du Canada, mink.

martyr [martir], s. martyr.

martyre [martir], s.m. martyrdom.

martyriser [martirize], v.tr. to martyrize.

marx/isme [marksism], s.m. Pol: Marxism. a. & s. -iste, (i) Marxian; (ii) Marxist.

mascarade [maskarad], s.f. masquerade.

mascaret [maskarɛ], s.m. bore, tidal wave.

mascotte [maskɔt], s.f. mascot, charm.

masculin [maskylɛ̃], a. 1. male. 2. masculine.

masque [mask], s.m. mask.

masquer [maske], v.tr. to mask; to hide, screen. Aut: virage masqué, blind corner.

massacrante [masakrɑ̃t], a.f. (used in phr.) être d'une humeur m., to be in a bad, F: foul, temper.

massacre [masakr], s.m. (a) massacre; (b) (at a fair) jeu de m. = Aunt Sally.

massacr/er [masakre], v.tr. 1. to massacre. F: to bungle, spoil (work), to ruin (clothes). s.m. -eur, bungler.

massage [masaːʒ], s.m. massage.

masse [mas], s.f. 1. mass; m. de gens, crowd; en m., in a body. 2. El: mettre le courant à la m., to earth the current; Atom, Ph: m. critique, critical mass.

massepain [maspɛ̃], s.m. marzipan.

masser[1] [mase], v.tr. to mass.
se masser, to form a crowd.

masser[2], v.tr. to massage. s. -eur, -euse, masseur, masseuse.

†massi/f [masif]. 1. a. (a) massive; (b) solid (silver, gold). 2. s.m. (a) clump (of shrubs); (b) Geog: massif. adv. -ivement.

massue [masy], s.f. club, bludgeon; coup de m., staggering blow.

mastic [mastik], s.m. putty.

masti/quer [mastike], v.tr. to masticate, chew. s.f. -cation.

mat[1] [mat], a. mat(t), unpolished, dull; son m., dull sound; thud.

mat[2], s.m. (check)mate.

mât [mɑ], s.m. mast, pole.

match [matʃ], s.m. Sp: match; m. prévu, fixture.

matelas [matlɑ], s.m. mattress; m. pneumatique, inflatable mattress.

matelasser [matlase], v.tr. to pad, cushion (chair, etc.).

matelot [matlo], s.m. sailor, seaman.

mater [mate], v.tr. (a) to (check)mate; (b) m. qn, to master s.o.

matéria/liser [materjalize], v.tr. to materialize. s.f. -lisation. s. -liste.

matériau [materjo], s.m. Civ.E: building material.

matériaux [materjo], s.m.pl. materials.

†matériel [materjɛl]. 1. a. (a) material, physical (body); (b) materialistic. 2. s.m. plant, implements. Rail: m. roulant, rolling-stock; m. de camping, camping equipment. adv. -lement.

†maternel [matɛrnɛl], a. maternal; école maternelle, s.f. la maternelle, nursery school; langue maternelle, mother tongue. adv. -lement.

maternité [matɛrnite], s.f. 1. maternity. 2. maternity hospital.

mathématicien, -ienne [matematisjɛ̃, -jɛn] s. mathematician.

mathématique [matematik]. 1. a. mathematical. 2. s.f.pl. mathematics.

matière [matjɛːr], s.f. 1. material; matières premières, raw materials. 2. matter, substance; m. grasse, fat. 3. subject; table des matières, table of contents. 4. m. plastique, plastic.

matin [matɛ̃]. 1. s.m. morning; de grand m., early in the morning. 2. adv. se lever très m., to get up very early.

†matinal [matinal], a. (a) morning (breeze, etc.); (b) early. adv. -ement.

matinée [matine], s.f. 1. morning; dans la m., in the course of the morning; faire grasse m., to sleep late. 2. Th: matinee; afternoon performance.

matois [matwa], a. sly, cunning, crafty.

matou [matu], s.m. tom-cat.

matraque [matrak], s.f. bludgeon.

matri/culer [matrikyle], v.tr. 1. to enter (s.o.'s) name on a register, to enroll s.o. 2. to give a registration number to (car, etc.). s.m. -cule, registration number.

†matrimonial [matrimɔnjal], a. matrimonial.

matrone [matrɔn], s.f. matron (= married woman).

mâture [matyːr], s.f. Nau: masts.

maturité [matyrite], s.f. maturity, ripeness.

‡mau/dire [modiːr], v.tr. to curse. a. -dit (ac)cursed.

maugréer [mogree], *v.i.* to curse, fume; to grumble (contre, at).

mausolée [mozole], *s.m.* mausoleum.

maussade [mosad], *a.* (a) surly, sullen, *F:* grumpy; (b) dull, cheerless (weather).

mauvais [move], *a.* (a) evil; bad; wicked; (b) ill-natured; (c) nasty, unpleasant; m. pas, dangerous situation; *adv.* il fait m., the weather is bad; (b) le m. moment, the wrong moment.

mauve [mo:v], *a. & s.m.* mauve.

maximum [maksimom], *a. & s.m.* maximum.

mazout [mazut], *s.m.* fuel oil.

me [m(ə)], *pers.pron.* (before a vowel sound, m') (a) me; me voici, here I am; (b) (to) me; donnez-m'en, give me some; (c) myself.

méandre [meɑ̃:dr], *s.m.* meander.

mécanicien [mekanisjɛ̃], *s.m.* (a) mechanic; (b) engine-driver; engineer.

mécanique [mekanik]. 1. *a.* mechanical. 2. *s.f.* mechanics. *adv.* -ment.

mécani/ser [mekanize], *v.tr.* to mechanize. *s.f.* -sation, mechanization. s.m. -me, mechanism, works.

mécanographe [mekanograf], *s.m. & f.* computer-operator.

méchanceté [meʃɑ̃ste], *s.f.* 1. (a) wickedness; (b) unkindness, spitefulness. 2. spiteful, act, word.

méch/ant [meʃɑ̃], *a.* 1. (a) miserable, wretched (house, etc.); (b) unpleasant. 2. (a) wicked, evil; naughty; (b) spiteful, unkind. *adv.* -amment.

mèche [mɛʃ], *s.f.* 1. (a) wick; (b) fuse. 2. lock (of hair). 3. *Techn:* bit, drill.

mécompte [mekɔ̃:t], *s.m.* miscalculation, error.

‡mécon/naître [mekɔnɛ:tr], *v.tr.* to fail to recognize; not to appreciate (s.o.'s talent); to disregard; m. les faits, to ignore the facts. *a.* -naissable, unrecognizable.

méconnu [mekony], *a.* unrecognized; unappreciated; misunderstood.

mécontent [mekɔ̃tɑ̃], *a.* discontented, displeased. *s.* 2. malcontent.

mécontent/er [mekɔ̃tɑ̃te], *v.tr.* to displease, annoy (s.o.). *s.m.* -ement, displeasure.

mécréant, -ante [mekreɑ̃, -ɑ̃:t]. 1. *a.* misbelieving. 2. *s.* unbeliever.

médaill/e [medaj], *s.f.* medal. *s.m.* -on, medallion; locket.

médecin [medsɛ̃], *s.m.* doctor, physician; femme m., woman doctor; m. consultant, consultant.

médecine [medsin], *s.f.* 1. (*art of*) medicine; m. générale, general practice; m. légale, forensic medicine. 2. (dose) of medicine.

média/tion [medjasjɔ̃], *s.f.* mediation. s. -teur -trice, mediator.

†médical [medikal], *a.* medical.

médicament [medikamɑ̃], *s.m.* medicine.

†médicinal [medisinal], *a.* medicinal.

†médiéval [medjeval], *a.* medi(a)eval.

médiocre [medjokr], *a.* mediocre, second-rate. *adv.* -ment.

médiocrité [medjokrite], *s.f.* mediocrity.

‡mé/dire [medi:r], *v.i.* m. de qn, to speak ill of s.o.; to slander. *s.f.* -disance, slander. *a. & s.* -disant, -ante, (i) *a.* back-biting; (ii) *s.* slanderer.

médit/er [medite]. 1. *v.i.* to meditate, to muse. 2. *v.tr.* to contemplate (a journey, etc.); to have (an idea) in mind. *v.* †-atif: *s.f.* -ation.

†méditerranéen [mediteraneɛ̃], *a.* mediterranean (climate, etc.).

médium [medjom], *s.m.* medium.

méduse [medy:z], *s.f.* jellyfish.

méfait [mefɛ], *s.m.* misdeed.

méfi/ance [mefjɑ̃:s], *s.f.* distrust, mistrust. *a.* -ant, suspicious.

méfier (se) [səmefje], *v.pr.* se m. de qn, to distrust s.o.; *abs.* to be on one's guard.

mégarde (par) [parmegard], *adv.phr.* inadvertently; through carelessness.

mégère [meʒɛ:r], *s.f.* shrew, bad-tempered woman.

mégot [mego], *s.m. F:* fag-end (of cigarette); butt (of cigar).

meilleur [mejœ:r], *a.* 1. better. 2. le m., the better, the best.

mélancol/ie [melɑ̃koli], *s.f.* melancholy. *a.* -ique, melancholy. *adv.* -iquement.

mélange [melɑ̃:ʒ], *s.m.* mixture; blend.

‡mélanger [melɑ̃ʒe], *v.tr.* to mix; to blend.

mélasse [melas], *s.f.* molasses; treacle; m. raffinée, golden syrup.

mêlée [mele], *s.f.* scuffle; *Sp:* scrum.

mêl/er [mele], *v.tr.* (a) to mix, mingle, blend; (b) to confuse (matters); to tangle; (c) m. qn dans qch., to involve s.o. in sth.; m. les cartes, to shuffle the cards.

se mêler, to mix, mingle, blend; se m. de qch., to take a hand in sth.

mélod/ie [melodi], *s.f.* melody, tune. *a.* †-ieux, tuneful. *adv.* -ieusement.

mélodram/e [melodram], *s.m.* melodrama. *a.* -atique.

melon [məlɔ̃], *s.m.* 1. melon. 2. (chapeau) m. bowler (hat).

membrane [mɑ̃bran], *s.f.* 1. *Anat:* membrane. 2. *Rec:* diaphragm.

membre [mɑ̃:br], *s.m.* member; limb.

même [mɛm]. 1. *a.* (a) same; en m. temps, at the same time; at once; (b) (*following the noun*) very; c'est cela m., that's the very thing; (c) self; moi-même, myself; eux-mêmes, themselves. 2. *adv.* even. 3. de m., in the same way; likewise; tout de m., all the same; être à m. de faire qch., to be in a position to do sth.

mémoire[1] [memwa:r], *s.f.* (a) memory; (b) recollection, remembrance.

mémoire[2], *s.m.* 1. (a) memorial; (b) memoir, thesis. 2. account; bill (of costs). 3. *pl.* (autobiographical) memoirs.

mémorable [memɔrabl], *a.* memorable; eventful (year). *adv.* -ment.

mémorandum [memɔrɑ̃dɔm], *s.m.* 1. memorandum, note. 2. notebook.

‡**mena/cer** [mənase], *v.tr.* to threaten, menace. *a.* -çant, threatening (look, sky). *s.f.* -ce, threat.

ménage [mena:ʒ], *s.m.* 1. (a) housekeeping; (b) femme de m., daily (help); faire le m., to do the housework; (c) articles de m., household equipment. 2. household, family; (a) jeune m., young (married) couple; (b) faire bon, mauvais, m., to get on well, badly.

ménagement [menaʒmɑ̃], *s.m.* caution, care.

‡**ména/ger**[1] [menaʒe], *v.tr.* 1. to save; to be sparing of; m. sa santé, to take care of one's health; m. qn, to deal tactfully with s.o. 2. to contrive, arrange; m. une surprise à qn, to prepare a surprise for s.o. *s.m.* -ement, caution, care, consideration.

ménager[2], -ère [menaʒe, -ɛːr]. 1. *a.* (a) connected with the house; enseignement m., domestic science; salon des Arts Ménagers, = Ideal Home Exhibition; (b) housewifely (virtues, etc.); (c) thrifty. 2. *s.f.* (a) bonne ménagère, good housekeeper; (b) canteen of cutlery.

ménagerie [menaʒri], *s.f.* menagerie.

mend/ier [mɑ̃dje], *v.i. & tr.* to beg. *s.m.* -iant, beggar. *s.f.* -icité, begging.

menée [məne], *s.f.* intrigue; *pl.* (political) scheming.

‡**men/er** [m(ə)ne], *v.tr.* 1. to lead; to take. 2. to drive; to ride; to steer. 3. to manage, conduct (business, etc.). *s.* -eur, -euse, leader; ringleader.

menottes [mənɔt], *s.f. pl.* handcuffs.

mensonge [mɑ̃sɔ̃:ʒ], *s.m.* lie, falsehood. *a.* †-er, lying; deceitful.

menstruation [mɑ̃stryasjɔ̃], *s.f.* menstruation.

mensualité [mɑ̃sɥalite], *s.f.* monthly payment, instalment.

†**mensuel** [mɑ̃sɥɛl], *a.* monthly. *adv.* -lement.

mensuration [mɑ̃syrasjɔ̃], *s.f.* measurement; (of a man) measurements, (of a girl) F: vital statistics.

†**mental** [mɑ̃tal], *a.* mental. *adv.* -ement.

mentalité [mɑ̃talite], *s.f.* mentality.

ment/eur, -euse [mɑ̃tœːr, -øːz]. 1. *a.* (a) lying; (b) false, deceptive. 2. *s.* liar. *adv.* -eusement.

menthe [mɑ̃t], *s.f.* mint; m. anglaise, poivrée, peppermint.

mention [mɑ̃sjɔ̃], *s.f.* (a) mention; *Sch:* reçu avec m. = passed with distinction. (b) reference (at head of letter); (c) endorsement.

mentionner [mɑ̃sjɔne], *v.tr.* to mention.

‡**mentir** [mɑ̃tiːr], *v.i.* to lie; to tell lies.

menton [mɑ̃tɔ̃], *s.m.* chin.

menu [məny]. 1. *a.* (a) small; fine (gravel, etc.); slender; tiny; menue monnaie, small change; (b) trifling; petty; menus détails, minor details. 2. *adv.* small, fine; hacher menu, to mince (sth. up). 3. *s.m.* (a) par le m., in detail; (b) menu.

menuis/erie [mənɥizri], *s.f.* joinery, woodwork, carpentry. *s.m.* -ier, joiner, carpenter.

‡**mé/prendre (se)** [səmeprɑ̃ːdr], *v.pr.* to be mistaken, to make a mistake (sur, quant à, about). *s.f.* -prise, mistake.

mépris [mepri], *s.m.* contempt, scorn. *a.* -able, contemptible, despicable.

mépris/er [meprize], *v.tr.* to despise, scorn. *a.* -ant, contemptuous.

mer [mɛːr], *s.f.* (a) sea; la haute m., the high seas; au bord de la m., at the seaside; un homme à la m.! man overboard! (b) tide; la haute, high tide; basse m., low water.

mercantile [merkɑ̃til], *a.* mercantile; commercial.

mercenaire [mersənɛːr], *a. & s.m.* mercenary.

merc/erie [mersəri], *s.f.* haberdashery. *s.* -ier, -ière, haberdasher.

merci [mersi], *adv.* (a) thank you; (b) no, thank you.

mercredi [merkrədi], *s.m.* Wednesday.

mercure [merkyːr], *s.m.* mercury.

mère [mɛːr], *s.f.* 1. mother, F: la m. Martin, old Mrs Martin; *Ecc:* M. supérieure, Mother Superior. 2. *attrib.* (a) la reine m., the Queen Mother; (b) *Com:* maison m., parent establishment.

mère-patrie [mɛːrpatri], *s.f.* mother country. *pl.* mères-patries.

†**méridional** [meridjɔnal]. 1. *a.* south(ern). 2. *s.* southerner, southern Frenchman.

mérinos [merinɔs], *s.m.* merino (sheep).

mérite [merit], *s.m.* merit; (a) worth; (b) excellence, talent; homme de m., man of ability.

mérit/er [merite], *v.tr.* to deserve, merit. *a.* -oire, deserving.

merlan [merlɑ̃], *s.m.* whiting.

merle [merl], *s.m.* blackbird.

merluche [merlyʃ], *s.f.* 1. hake. 2. dried cod.

merveille [merveːj], *s.f.* marvel, wonder; à m., excellently.

†**merveilleu/x** [mervejø], *a.* marvellous, wonderful. *adv.* -sement.

mes. See **mon**.

mésalliance [mezaljɑ̃ːs], *s.f.* misalliance; faire une m., to marry beneath one.

mésaventure [mezavɑ̃tyːr], *s.f.* misadventure, mishap.

mésentente [mezɑ̃tɑ̃ːt], *s.f.* misunderstanding, disagreement.

mesquin [mɛskɛ̃], a. (a) mean, shabby (appearance); paltry, petty (excuse); (b) mean, stingy.

mesquinerie [mɛskinri], s.f. meanness; (a) pettiness; (b) niggardliness.

méson [mezɔ̃], s.m. Atom.Ph: meson.

mess [mɛs], s.m. Mil: mess.

message [mesaːʒ], s.m. message.

messag/er, -ère [mɛsaʒe, -ɛːr], s. 1. messenger. 2. s.m. carrier. s.f. -erie, carrying trade (esp. sea or rail).

messe [mɛs], s.f. Ecc: Mass.

mesure [məzyr], s.f. measure. 1. (a) measurement(s); adv.phr. à m., in proportion; à m. que, (in proportion) as. (b) prendre des mesures, to take action. 2. gauge, standard; garder la m., to keep within bounds; dépasser la m., to overdo it; être en m. de, to be in a position to. 3. Mus: (a) bar; (b) time.

mesuré [məzyre], a. measured (tread, etc.); temperate, restrained (language).

mesur/er [məzyre], v.tr. 1. to measure. 2. to calculate; to weigh (one's words, etc.). a. -able, measurable. s.m. -age.
se mesurer avec, contre, qn, to measure oneself against, to try conclusions with, s.o.

†metal [metal], s.m. metal. a. -lique, metallic. s.f. -lurgie, metallurgy. a. -lurgique, s.m. -lurgiste.

métamor/phoser [metamɔrfoze], v.tr. to metamorphose, transform. s.f. -phose, metamorphosis, transformation.
se métamorphoser, to change completely.

métaphor/e [metafɔːr], s.f. metaphor. a. -ique, metaphorical. adv. -iquement.

météor/e [meteɔːr], s.m. meteor. a. -ique, meteoric.

météo [meteo]. F: 1. s.f. (a) weather-report; (b) meteorological office. 2. s.m. meteorologist.

météoro/logie [meteɔrɔlɔʒi], s.f. meteorology. s.m. -logiste, -logue, meteorologist.

météoro/logique [meteɔrɔlɔʒik], a. meteorological; bulletin m., weather report; station, navire, m., weather centre, ship.

méthod/e [metɔd], s.f. method, system. a. -ique. adv. -iquement.

†méticuleu/x [metikyløː], a. meticulous. adv. -sement.

métier [metje], s.m. 1. trade, profession, business, craft; m. manuel, handicraft; gens de m., experts; terme de m., technical term. 2. m. à tisser, loom.

métis, -isse [meti, -is]. 1. a. half-bred; mongrel (dog, etc.); plante métisse, hybrid plant. 2. s. half-breed; mongrel. 3. toile métisse, cotton-linen mixture.

métrage [metraːʒ], s.m. 1. (a) measuring, measure(ment); (b) Cie.E: quantity surveying. 2. (metric) length; Cin: long m., full-length film; court m., short. 3. (metric) area, volume.

mètre¹ [mɛtr], s.m. Lit: metre.

mètre² [mɛtr], s.m. 1. metre. 2. (i) (metre) rule; (ii) tape measure.

métrique¹ [metrik], a.f. a metrical.

métrique², a. metric.

Métro (le) [ləmetro], s.m. the underground (railway), U.S: subway.

métropole [metrɔpɔl], s.f. (a) capital city; (b) parent state; (c) see of (archbishop).

mets [mɛ], s.m. food; dish (of food).

metteur [mɛtœːr], s.m. m. en scène, (i) Th: producer; (ii) Cin: director; Rad: m. en ondes, producer.

‡mettre [mɛtr], v.tr. 1. (a) to put, lay, place, set; m. la table, to lay the table; m. un enjeu, to lay a stake; m. le feu à qch., to set sth. on fire; (b) to put (clothes) on; qu'est-ce que je vais m.? what shall I wear? ne plus m., to leave off (a garment). 2. to set (going); m. une machine en marche, to start a machine working. 3. (a) to admit, grant; mettons cent francs, let's say a hundred francs; (b) mettez que je n'ai rien dit, consider that unsaid.
se mettre. 1. (a) to go, get; se m. au lit, to go to bed; (b) to begin, set about (sth.); se m. au travail, to set to work; se m. à rire, to start laughing; impers: il se mit à pleuvoir, it began to rain. 2. to dress; se m. simplement, to dress simply. 3. le temps se met au beau, the weather's turning out fine.

meuble [mœbl], s.m. piece of furniture; être dans ses meubles, to have a home of one's own.

meubler [mœble], v.tr. to furnish; to stock (farm, cellar) (de, with); non meublé, unfurnished; s.m. un meublé, furnished room.

meugl/er [mœgle], v.i. to low, moo. s.m. -ement.

meule [mœːl], s.f. 1. millstone; grindstone. 2. m. (de foin), hayrick, -stack.

meun/ier [mønje], s. miller. s.f. -erie, milling trade).

meurtre [mœrtr], s.m. murder.

meurtr/ier, -ère [mœrtrie, -ɛːr]. 1. a. murderous (war); deadly (weapon). 2. s. murderer, f. murderess. 3. s.f. meurtrière, loop-hole.

meurtr/ir [mœrtriːr], v.tr. to bruise. s.f. -issure, bruise.

meute [møt], s.f. (a) pack (of hounds); (b) F: mob (of pursuers); (c) (scouting): (cub) pack.

mexican, -aine [mɛksikɛ̃, -ɛn], a. & s. Mexican.

mi¹ [mi], s.m.inv. Mus: (the note) E; morceau en mi, piece in E.

mi², *adv.* half, mid, semi-; **la mi-avril**, mid-April; **à mi-hauteur**, half-way up.

miaou [mjau], *s.m.* miaow, mew.

miaul/er [mjole], *v.i.* to mew; to caterwaul. **s.m. -ement.**

mica [mika], *s.m.* mica.

mi-carême [mikarɛm], *s.f.* mid-Lent.

miche [miʃ], *s.f.* round loaf.

micheline [miʃlin], *s.f.* rail car.

mi-chemin (à), [amiʃmɛ̃], *adv.phr.* halfway.

mi-corps (à), [amikɔːr], *adv.phr.* to the waist; **portrait à m.-c.**, half-length portrait.

mi-côte (à), [amikoːt], *adv.phr.* half-way up, down, the hill.

micro [mikro], *s.m.* F: mike.

microbe [mikrɔb], *s.m.* microbe, germ.

microfilm [mikrofilm], *s.m.* microfilm.

microphone [mikrofɔn], *s.m.* microphone.

microphotograph/ie [mikrofotografi], *s.f.* 1. microphotography. 2. microphotograph. *a.* **-ique.**

microscop/e [mikrɔskɔp], *s.m.* microscope. *s.f.* **-ie**, microscopy. *a.* **-ique.**

microsillon [mikrɔsijɔ̃], *s.m.* long-playing record, L.P.

midi [midi], *s.m.* (*no pl.*) 1. midday, noon, twelve o'clock; **m. et demi**, half-past twelve. 2. south; **chambre au m.**, room facing south; **le M.** (de la France), the South of France.

mie [mi], *s.f.* crumb (of loaf).

miel [mjɛl], *s.m.* honey. *a.* †-**leux.** *adv.* -**euse ment**, blandly.

†**mien** [mjɛ̃], (*a*) *poss.pron.* **le mien, la mienne, les miens, les miennes, mine;** (*b*) *s.m.pl.* my own people.

miette [mjɛt], *s.f.* crumb; morsel; **mettre un vase en miettes**, to smash a vase to smithereens.

mieux [mjø], *adv.* 1. better; (*a*) **pour m. dire**, to be more exact; **de m. en m.** better and better; *adv.phr.* **faire qch. à qui m. m.**, to vie with one another in doing sth.; (*b*) (*with adj. function*) (i) **c'est on ne peut m.**, it couldn't be better; (ii) **vous serez m. dans ce fauteuil**, you'll be more comfortable in this chair; (iii) **il est m.**, he's (feeling) better; (*c*) **s. faute de m.**, for want of something better. 2. **le mieux**, (the) best; (*a*) **être le m. du monde avec qn**, to be on the best of terms with s.o.; (*b*) **s. faire de son m.**, to do one's best.

miève [mjɛːvr], *a. Pej:* finical, affected.

mignardise [miɲardiz], *s.f.* affectation.

mignon, -onne [miɲɔ̃, -ɔn], 1. *a.* dainty, tiny; adorable. 2. *s.* pet, darling.

migraine [migrɛn], *s.f. Med:* migraine.

migr/ation [migrasjɔ̃], *s.f.* migration. *a. & s.m.*† **-ateur**, (*i*) migratory; (*ii*) migrant.

mijoter [miʒɔte], 1. *v.tr.* to stew (sth.) slowly; F: **il se mijote qch.**, there's sth. in the wind. 2. *v.i.* to simmer.

mil [mil], *a.* (*used only in dates A.D.*) thousand; **l'an mil neuf cent trente**, 1930.

†**milieu** [miljø], *s.m.* 1. middle, midst; **au beau m.**, right in the middle. 2. surroundings, environment; social sphere; **les gens de mon m.**, people in my set. 3. middle course; mean; **le juste m.**, the happy medium.

militaire [militɛːr], 1. *a.* military. 2. *s.m.* soldier.

militar/iser [militarize], *v.tr.* to militarize. *s.f.* **-isation.** *s.m.* **-isme.** *s.m.* **-iste.**

millage [milaːʒ], *s.m. Fr.C:* mileage.

mille¹ [mil], *num.a.inv. & s.m.inv.* thousand.

mille², *s.m.* mile.

millésime [mil(l)ezim], *s.m.* (*a*) date (on coin); (*b*) *Ind:* year of manufacture; (*of wine*) year, vintage.

millet [mijɛ], *s.m.* millet.

milliard [miljaːr], *s.m.* one thousand million.

milliardaire [miljardɛːr], *a. & s.m.* multimillionaire.

millième [miljɛm], 1. *num.a. & s.* thousandth. 2. *s.m.* (one-)thousandth (part).

millier [milje], *s.m.* (about a) thousand.

million [miljɔ̃], *s.m.* million.

millionnaire [miljɔnɛːr], *a. & s.* millionaire.

mim/e [mim], *s.m.* 1. *Th:* mime. 2. mimic. *a. & s.f.* **-ique**, (i) mimic, (ii) mimicry.

mimer [mime], *v.tr.* 1. *Th:* to mime (a scene). 2. to mimic, to ape.

minable [minabl], *a.* seedy-looking; shabby; pitiable.

minaud/er [minode], *v.i.* to simper, smirk. *s.f.* **-erie**, simpering.

mince [mɛ̃ːs], *a.* thin; slender, slim.

minceur [mɛ̃sœːr], *s.f.* thinness; slimness.

mine¹ [min], *s.f.* 1. (*a*) mine; (*b*) *Mil: etc:* **champ de mines**, minefield. 2. lead (of pencil).

mine², *s.f.* appearance, look; (*a*) **avoir bonne m.**, to look well; (*b*) **faire bonne m.**, to be pleasant; **faire la m.**, to look sulky.

miner [mine], *v.tr.* to mine, undermine; **miné par l'envie**, consumed with envy. **rai** [minr̩], *s.m.* ore.

†**....éral** [mineral]. 1. *a.* mineral; **source minérale**, spa. 2. *s.m.* mineral.

minéralogie [mineralɔʒi], *s.f.* 1. mineralogy. 2. *Adm:* **numéro m.**, registration number (of a car).

mineur¹ [minœːr], *s.m.* miner.

mineur², -eure [minœːr]. 1. *a.* (*a*) minor, lesser; (*b*) under age. 2. *s.* minor.

miniatur/e [minjatyːr], *s.f.* miniature. *adv.phr.* **en m.**, on a small scale. *s.m. & f.* **-iste.**

†**minier** [minje], *a.* mining (industry).

minime [minim], *a.* small; trivial; trifling.

minimum [minimɔm], *a. & s.m.* minimum; **m. vital,** minimum living wage.

†**ministère** [minister], *s.m.* 1. agency. 2. ministry.

†**ministériel** [ministerjel], *a.* ministerial; **crise ministérielle,** cabinet crisis.

ministre [ministr], *s.m.* minister.

minor/ité [minorite], *s.f.* minority. *a.* **-itaire,** minority (party).

minuit [minɥi], *s.m.* midnight; **et demi,** half-past twelve at night).

minuscule [minyskyl], *a. (a)* small, minute, tiny; *(b) s.f.* small letter.

minute [minyt], *s.f.* 1. minute (of hour, degree). 2. *Adm:* minute, draft; record.

minuterie [minytri], *s.f. (a)* m. d'enregistrement, counting mechanism (of meter); *(b)* automatic time-switch (on staircase, cooker, etc.).

minutie [minysi], *s.f. (a)* minute detail; trifle; *(b)* meticulousness.

†**minutieu/x** [minysjø], *a.* scrupulously careful (person); minute, detailed (inspection). *adv.* **-sement.**

mioche [mjɔʃ], *s.m. & f. F:* small child; urchin.

mi-pente (à) [amipɑ̃t], *adv. phr.* halfway up, down, the slope.

miracle [mirakl], *s.m.* miracle.

†**miraculeu/x** [mirakylø], *a.* miraculous. *adv.* **-sement.**

mirage [miraʒ], *s.m.* mirage.

miroir [mirwar], *s.m.* mirror.

miroit/er [mirwate], *v.i.* to flash; to sparkle. *s.m.* **-ement,** flashing.

misanthrop/e [mizɑ̃trɔp]. 1. *s.m.* misanthrope. 2. *a.* misanthropic(al). *s.f.* **-ie,** misanthropy. *a.* **-ique.**

mise [mi:z], *s.f.* 1. *(a)* putting (of sth.) (in its) place; **m. en bouteilles,** bottling; **m. en plis,** setting (of hair); *(b)* **m. en marche,** starting (of engine); **m. en retraite,** pensioning (off); *Rad:* **m. en ondes,** production. 2. dress, way of dressing. 3. *(a)* stake, bet; *(b)* bid (at auction); *(c) Fin:* **m. (de fonds),** investment (of capital).

miser [mize], *v.i.* to lay a stake; to bet (on horse, etc.).

misérable [mizerabl]. 1. *a. (a)* miserable; wretched; *(b)* despicable. 2. *s. (a)* poor wretch; *(b)* scoundrel. *adv.* **-ment.**

misère [mizer], *s.f.* 1. *(a)* misery; *(b)* trouble, worry. 2. extreme poverty. 3. trifle; **cent francs? une m.!** a hundred francs? a mere nothing!

miséricord/e [mizerikɔrd], *s.f.* mercy. *a.* †**-ieux,** merciful.

missile [misil], *s.m.* guided missile.

mission [misjɔ̃], *s.f.* mission; *Mil:* **en m., on detached service;** *Ecc:* **missions étrangères,** foreign missions. *s.m.* **-naire,** missionary.

mite [mit], *s.f.* 1. mite. 2. clothes moth.

mité [mite], *a.* motheaten.

mi-temps [mitɑ̃], *s.f.* 1. *Sp:* **la m.-t.,** half time. 2. *adv.* **emploi à m.-t.,** part-time employment.

‡**mitig/er** [mitiʒe], *v.tr.* to mitigate (penalty). *s.f.* **-ation.**

mitrail/er [mitraje], *v.tr.* to machinegun. *s.f.* **-ette,** sub-machine-gun. *s.f.* **-euse,** machine-gun.

mi-voix (à) [amivwa], *adv.phr.* in an undertone, under one's breath.

mixe(u)r [miksœr], *s.m. H:* 1. mixer. 2. liquidizer.

mixte [mikst], *a.* mixed; **commission m.,** joint commission; **école m.,** co-educational school; **train m.,** composite train (goods and passengers).

mobil/e [mɔbil]. 1. *a. (a)* mobile, movable; *(b)* unstable, fickle (nature); *(c)* moving (target); changing (expression); **escalier m.,** escalator. 2. *s.m.* driving power; motive; **m. d'un crime,** motive of a crime. *s.f.* **-ité,** moveableness; changeableness.

mobilier [mɔbilje], *s.m.* furniture.

mobilis/er [mɔbilize], *v.tr.* to mobilize. *s.f.* **-able.** *s.f.* **-ation.**

mocassin [mɔkasɛ̃], *s.m.* moccasin; casual, informal, shoe.

mode¹ [mɔd], *s.f.* 1. fancy, fashion; **à la m. de,** after the style of. 2. *pl. (a)* fashions; *(b)* millinery.

mode² [mɔd], *s.m.* method, mode; **"m. d'emploi,"** "directions for use."

modèle [mɔdel]. 1. *s.m.* model; pattern; **m. déposé,** registered pattern. 2. *s.m.* (artist's) model. 3. *a.* **un mari m.,** a model husband.

‡**model/er** [mɔdle], *v.tr.* to model; to mould. *s.m.* **-age.** *s.m.* **-eur.**

‡**mo/dérer** [mɔdere], *v.tr.* 1. to moderate; to curb (impatience); to slacken (speed). 2. to reduce (price, penalty). *s.f.* **-dération.** *a.* **-déré,** moderate; temperate. *adv.* **-dérément.**
se modérer, to control oneself, to keep calm.

moderne [mɔdern], *a.* modern.

modern/iser [mɔdernize], *v.tr.* to modernize. *s.f.* **-isation.** *s.m.* **-isme.** *s.f.* **-ité,** up-to-dateness.

mo/destie [mɔdesti], *s.f.* modesty. *a.* **-deste,** unassuming. *adv.* **-destement.**

modifi/er [mɔdifje], *v.tr.* 1. to modify (statement); to alter, change (plan). 2. to qualify (verb). *s.f.* **-cation.**

modique [mɔdik], *a.* moderate, reasonable (cost); slender (income). *adv.* **-ment,** at a low price.

modiste [mɔdist], *s.f.* milliner.

modul/er [mɔdyle], *v.tr. El: Mus:* to modulate. *s.f.* **-ation.**

moelle [mwal], *s.f.* 1. marrow (of bone). 2. pith.

†**moelleu/x** [mwalø], *a.* 1. marrowy; pithy. 2. (*a*) soft, velvety; mellow (wine, voice); (*b*) *s.m.* softness; mellowness. *adv.* -**sement**.

mœurs [mœrs], *s.f.pl.* manners; customs; morals; habits.

moi [mwa]. 1. *stressed pers.pron.* (*a*) (*subject*) I; je veux bien, for my part, I am willing; (*b*) (*object*) me; à m.! help! ce livre est à m., this book is mine; (*c*) (*after imp.*) (i) (*object*) laissez-m. tranquille, leave me alone; (ii) (*indirect object*) donnez-le-m., give it (to) me. 2. *s.m.* ego, self.

moignon [mwaɲɔ̃], *s.m.* stump (of limb).

moi-même [mwamɛːm], *pers.pron.* myself.

moindre [mwɛ̃ːdr], *a.* 1. less(er). 2. le, la, m., the least.

moine [mwan], *s.m.* monk, friar.

moineau [mwano], *s.m.* sparrow.

moins [mwɛ̃]. 1. *adv.* (*a*) less; m. encore, still less; m. d'argent, less money; en m. de rien, in less than no time; *prep.phr.* à m. de, unless; à m. d'accidents, barring accidents; à m. que + *sub.*, unless; (*b*) le moins, least; pas le m. du monde, not in the least; *adv.phr.* du m., at least, at all events; au m., at least. 2. *prep.* minus, less; une heure m. cinq, five minutes to one.

moiré [mware], *a.* watered, moiré (silk).

mois [mwa], *s.m.* month.

moïse [mɔiːz], *s.m.* wicker cradle; m. de toile, carry-cot.

moisi [mwazi]. 1. *a.* mouldy; musty. 2. *s.m.* mould, mildew; sentir le m., to smell musty.

moisir [mwaziːr], *v.i.* & *pr.* to go mouldy. *s.f.* -issure, mould(iness).

moisson [mwasɔ̃], *s.f.* 1. (*a*) harvest(ing); (*b*) harvest time. 2. crop.

moissonn/er [mwasɔne], *v.tr.* to reap; to harvest. *s.* -eur, -euse, harvester.

moissonneuse-batteuse [mwasɔ̃øzbatøːz], *s.f.* combine-harvester. *pl.* moissonneuses-batteuses.

moite [mwat], *a.* moist; clammy (hand, etc.).

moiteur [mwatœːr], *s.f.* moistness.

moitié [mwatje]. 1. *s.f.* half; une bonne m., a good half; m.-m., fifty-fifty; *adv.phr.* à m., half; à m. cuit, half-cooked. 2. *adv.* m. l'un, m. l'autre, half and half.

môle [moːl], *s.m.* mole; breakwater.

molécul/e [mɔlekyl], *s.f.* molecule. *a.* -aire, molecular.

molest/er [mɔlɛste], *v.tr.* to molest. *s.f.* -ation.

mollement [mɔlmã], *adv.* (*a*) softly; (*b*) slackly, feebly.

mollesse [mɔlɛs], *s.f.* (*a*) softness (of cushion); flabbiness; (*b*) slackness, lifelessness; sans m., briskly.

mollet [mɔlɛ], *s.m.* calf (of leg).

moment [mɔmã], *s.m.* moment; à un m. donné, at a given time; au bon m., in

the nick of time; *conj.phr.* du m. que, seeing that. *a.* -ané, momentary (effort, etc.). *adv.* -anément.

momie [mɔmi], *s.f.* mummy.

mon, ma, mes [mɔ̃, ma, me], *poss.a.* (mon *is used for* ma *before f. words beginning with a vowel or h mute*), my.

monarchie [mɔnarʃi], *s.f.* monarchy.

monarque [mɔnark], *s.m.* monarch.

monastère [mɔnasteːr], *s.m.* monastery.

monceau [mɔ̃so], *s.m.* heap, pile.

mondain [mɔ̃dɛ̃], *a.* a mundane, worldly; *s.* socialite.

monde [mɔ̃ːd], *s.m.* 1. world; (*a*) le m. entier, the whole world; mettre qn, qch. au m., to give birth to s.o., sth.; pour rien au m., on no account; (*b*) society; le m. savant, the world of science; le beau m., (fashionable) society. 2. people; avoir du m. à dîner, to have people to dinner; tout le m., everybody.

mondial [mɔ̃djal], *a.* world-wide; guerre mondiale, global war; la (première, deuxième) guerre mondiale, World War (One, Two).

monégasque [mɔnegask], *a.* & *s.* (native) of Monaco.

monétaire [mɔnetɛːr], *a.* monetary; unité m., currency.

moniteur, -trice [mɔnitœːr, -tris], *s.* monitor; *Sp:* coach; *Aut:* driving instructor.

monnaie [mɔnɛ], *s.f.* 1. money; pièce de m., coin; la Monnaie, the Mint. 2. change; petite m., small change.

monnay/er [mɔneje], *v.tr.* to coin, mint. *s.m.* -age. *s.m.* -eur, (i) minter; (ii) counterfeiter.

monocoque [mɔnɔkɔk], *a.* avion m., monocoque *Aut:* monoshell.

monogramme [mɔnɔgram], *s.m.* monogram.

monolo/guer [mɔnɔlɔge], *v.i.* to soliloquize. *s.m* -gue, monologue. *s.m* -gueur, soliloquizer.

monopol/e [mɔnɔpɔl], *s.m.* monopoly. *v.tr.* -iser, to monopolize. *s.f.* -isation.

monorail [mɔnɔraːj], *a.* & *s.m.* monorail.

monosylla/be [mɔnɔsillab], *a.* & *s.m.* monosyllable. *a.* -bique, monosyllabic.

mono/tonie [mɔnɔtɔni], *s.f.* monotony. *a.* -tone, monotonous, dull.

†**monseigneur** [mɔ̃sɛɲœːr], *s.m.* 1. (*a*) his Highness; his Grace; (*of cardinal*) his Eminence; (*b*) your Highness; your Grace; your Eminence; my Lord (Bishop). 2. pince m. (*inv.*), (burglar's) jemmy.

†**monsieur** [m(ə)sjø], *s.m.* 1. Mr; *pl.* *Com:* Messrs; M. le Duc, (i) the Duke (of); (ii) his, your Grace; M. David Martin, Mr David Martin; (*on letter*) David Martin, Esq. 2. sir; bonsoir, messieurs, good evening, gentlemen. 3. gentleman.

monst/re [mɔ̃str]. 1. *s.m.* monster. 2. *a.* huge; colossal; monster. *a.* †-rueux, monstrous; shocking.

mont [mɔ̃], *s.m.* mount, mountain.

monta/gne [mɔ̃taɲ], *s.f.* mountain; montagnes russes, switchback, scenic railway, *s.* -gnard, *a.* mountain dweller. *a.* †-gneux, mountainous.

montant [mɔ̃tɑ̃]. 1. *a.* rising, ascending, (road, etc.); marée montante, flood-tide; col m., (i) high; (ii) stand-up, collar; train m., up train. 2. *s.m.* (*a*) upright, post, pillar; *Fb:* les montants, the goal-posts; (*b*) total amount of debt, account).

monté [mɔ̃te], *a.* 1. mounted. 2. worked up; excited; *F:* coup m., put-up job.

monte-charge [mɔ̃tʃarʒ], *s.m.inv.* goods-lift, *U.S:* elevator.

montée [mɔ̃te], *s.f.* 1. (*a*) rise, rising; tuyau de m., uptake pipe; (*b*) uphill pull, climb; vitesse en m., climbing speed. 2. gradient, slope (up).

monte-pente [mɔ̃tpɑ̃t], *s.m.inv.* ski-lift.

monte-plats [mɔ̃tpla], *s.m.inv.* service lift (in restaurant).

monter [mɔ̃te]. I. *v.i.* 1. (*a*) to go up (up), mount, ascend; to go upstairs; (*b*) to climb on, into (sth.). 2. (*a*) to rise, to go up; (*b*) to ascend; to climb. II. *v.tr.* 1. to mount. 2. (*a*) to raise, take, haul (sth.) up; se m. la tête, to get excited. 3. to set, mount (a jewel, etc.); to erect; to equip (work-shop, etc.).

　se monter. 1. to amount, to add up (à, to). 2. to equip oneself (en, with).

montre [mɔ̃tr], *s.f.* m.(-bracelet), (wrist) watch.

montrer [mɔ̃tre], *v.tr.* to show; to display; to point out.

　se montrer, to appear; (of sun) to come out.

monture [mɔ̃tyr], *s.f.* setting; mount (ing).

monument [mɔnymɑ̃], *s.m.* 1. monument; m. aux morts, War Memorial. 2. historic building. *a.* †-al.

moquer (se) [sǝmɔke], *v.pr.* se m. de, to make fun of; vous vous moquez, you're joking; c'est se m. du monde! it's the height of impertinence!

moqu/erie [mɔkri], *s.f.* mockery; deri-sion. *s.* -eur, -euse, (i) *a.* mock-ing; (ii) *s.* scoffer.

†moral [mɔral]. 1. *a.* (*a*) moral, ethical; (*b*) mental, intellectual. 2. *s.m.* (state of) mind; morale.

morale [mɔral], *s.f.* 1. (*a*) morals; (*b*) ethics. 2. moral (of story). *adv.* -ment.

mora/liser [mɔralize], *v.i.* to moralize, *s.m. & f.* -liste.

moralité [mɔralite], *s.f.* (*a*) morality; (*b*) morals; honesty.

morbide [mɔrbid], *a.* morbid.

morceau [mɔrso], *s.m.* morsel, piece; bit, scrap; lump (of sugar).

‡morc/eler [mɔrsəle], *v.tr.* to parcel out (an estate). *s.m.* -ellement.

mordant [mɔrdɑ̃]. 1. *a.* mordant, biting. 2. *s.m.* (*a*) bite (of saw); (*b*) mordancy, pungency.

mordre [mɔrdr], *v.tr. & ind.tr.* to bite.

mordu [mɔrdy], *a. F:* mad on sth. *s.* les mordus du football, football fans.

morfondre (se) [səmɔrfɔ̃dr], *v.pr.* to be bored to death.

morgue [mɔrg], *s.f.* 1. pride, arrogance. 2. mortuary, morgue.

moribond [mɔribɔ̃], *a.* dying, at death's door.

morne [mɔrn], *a.* dejected; gloomy (silence); dull (weather).

morose [mɔroz], *a.* morose, moody (person).

morphin/e [mɔrfin], *s.f.* morphia; mor-phine. *s.m. & f.* -omane, morphia addict.

mors [mɔr], *s.m.* 1. jaw (of vice). 2. bit of bridle).

morsure [mɔrsyr], *s.f.* bite.

mort¹, **morte** [mɔr, mɔrt]. 1. *a.* dead; stagnant (water); *Aut:* point m., neutral (gear). 2. *s.* dead person; Jour des Morts, All Souls' day. 3. *s.m.* dummy (at cards).

mort², *s.f.* death.

mortalité [mɔrtalite], *s.f.* mortality.

mortel, -elle [mɔrtel]. 1. *a.* (*a*) mortal; fatal (injury); (*b*) *F:* deadly dull. 2. *s.* mortal, human being. *adv.* -lement.

mortier [mɔrtje], *s.m.* mortar.

mortif/ier [mɔrtifje], *v.tr.* to mortify. *a.* -ant, mortifying. *s.f.* -cation, humilia-tion.

mortuaire [mɔrtɥɛr], *a.* mortuary; drap m., pall.

morue [mɔry], *s.f.* cod.

mosaïque [mɔzaik], *s.f.* mosaic.

mosquée [mɔske], *s.f.* mosque.

mot [mo], *s.m.* word; au bas m., at the lowest estimate; écrire un m. à qn, to drop s.o. a line; bon m., witty remark; m. à m., literal trans-lation.

motard [mɔtar], *s.m. F:* m. (de la route) = speed cop.

†moteur [mɔtœr]. 1. *a.* motive, driving (power, etc.); *E:* unité motrice, power unit; force motrice, driving force. 2. *s.m.* motor, engine; m. d'avion, aero-engine.

motif [mɔtif], *s.m.* (*a*) motive; incentive; reason; (*b*) motif, design, ornament; *Mus:* theme.

motion [mosjɔ̃], *s.f.* motion, proposal.

motiver [mɔtive], *v.tr.* to justify, warrant (action, etc.).

moto [mɔto], *s.f. F:* motorbike.

motocul/ture [mɔtokyltyr], *s.f.* mechan-ized farming. *s.m.* -teur, motor cultivator.

motocycl/ette [mɔtɔsiklɛt], *s.f.* motor-cycle. *s.m.* -iste.

motoris/er [mɔtɔrize], *v.tr.* to motorize. *s.f.* -ation, mechanization.

motte [mɔt], *s.f.* 1. mound. 2. clod, lump; sod, turf.

†mou [mu]. 1. *a.* soft; slack; weak, flabby. 2. *s.m.* slack (of rope).

mouchard [muʃaːr], *s.m.* informer; police pigeon.

mouche [muʃ], *s.f.* 1. fly; m. bleue, de la viande, bluebottle; prendre la m., to take offence; quelle m. vous pique? what's the matter with you? poids m., fly-weight (boxer). 2. (*a*) spot, speck; (*b*) bull's-eye (of target).

moucher (se) [(sə)muʃe], *v.pr.* to wipe, blow, one's nose.

moucheron [muʃrɔ̃], *s.m.* midge, gnat.

‡moucheter [muʃte], *v.tr.* to spot, speckle.

mouchoir [muʃwaːr], *s.m.* handkerchief.

‡moudre [mudr], *v.tr.* to grind.

moue [mu], *s.f.* pout; faire la m., to look sulky.

mouette [mwɛt], *s.f.* seagull.

mouillé [muje], *a.* 1. moist, damp, wet; *F:* poule mouillée, milksop, drip. 2. (*of ship*) at anchor.

mouill/er [muje], *v.tr.* 1. to wet, moisten. 2. (*a*) *Nau:* to anchor; (*b*) to lay (mine). 3. *Ling:* to palatalize (consonant). *s.m.* -age, (*a*) anchoring; (*b*) anchorage.

se mouiller, to get wet; (*of eyes*) to fill with tears.

moule¹ [mul], *s.m.* mould; matrix.

moule², *s.f.* mussel.

moul/er [mule], *v.tr.* to cast (statue); to mould; se m. sur qn., to model oneself on s.o. *s.m.* -age.

moulin [mulɛ̃], *s.m.* mill; m. à vent, windmill; m. à café, coffee mill.

moulu [muly], *a.* (*a*) ground, powdered; (*b*) *F:* dead beat.

moulure [mulyːr], *s.f.* (ornamental) moulding.

†mour/ir [muriːr], *v.i.* (aux. être) to die; il est mort hier, he died yesterday; s'ennuyer à m., to be bored to death; c'est à m. de rire, *F:* it's simply killing. *a. & s.* -ant, dying (person).

mousse¹ [mus], *s.f.* 1. moss. 2. froth, foam; lather; *Cu:* m. au chocolat, chocolate mousse.

mousse², *s.m.* ship's boy.

mousseline [muslin], *s.f.* muslin; m. de soie, chiffon.

mouss/er [muse], *v.i.* to froth; to lather; (*of wine*) to sparkle. *a.* †-eux.

moustache [mustaʃ], *s.f.* (*a*) moustache; (*b*) whiskers (of cat).

mousti/que [mustik], *s.m.* mosquito; (*b*) gnat. *s.f.* -quaire, mosquito-net.

moutard [mutar], *s.m.* *P:* urchin; brat.

moutard/e [mutard], *s.f.* mustard. *s.m.* -ier, mustard-pot.

mouton [mutɔ̃], *s.m.* 1. sheep. 2. mutton. 3. *pl.* white horses (on sea).

moutonn/er [mutɔne], *v.i.* (*of sea*) to break into white horses; to froth. *s.m.* -ement. *a.* †-eux, foam-flecked; fleecy (clouds).

mouvant [muvɑ̃], *a.* (*a*) unstable, moving, changeable; (*b*) sables mouvants, quicksand.

mouvement [muvmɑ̃], *s.m.* movement. 1. motion; faire un m., to move; se mettre en m., to start off; *E:* m. perpétuel, perpetual motion. 2. (*a*) change, modification; être dans le m., to be in the swim; m. de personnel, staff changes; (*b*) agitation; m. populaire, uprising of the people; (*c*) impulse; m. d'humeur, fit of temper. 3. traffic; mouvements des trains, train arrivals and departures. 4. action; movement (of clock, etc.).

mouvementé [muvmɑ̃te], *a.* 1. animated, lively. 2. terrain m., undulating ground.

‡mouvoir [muvwaːr], *v.tr.* to drive (machine); to propel (ship); mû par la colère, moved by anger.

se mouvoir, to move.

moyen¹, -enne [mwajɛ̃, -ɛn]. 1. *a.* (*a*) middle (age, classes); le m. âge [mwajɛnɑːʒ], the Middle Ages; (*b*) average, mean; le Français m., the average Frenchman; (*c*) medium (quality, etc.). 2. *s.f.* moyenne, average.

moyen², *s.m.* means; au m. de, by means of; y a-t-il m. de le faire? it is possible to do it?

moyennant [mwajɛnɑ̃], *prep.* on a (certain) condition; m. un prix convenu, for an agreed price.

†moyeu [mwajø], *s.m.* hub.

muable [mɥabl], *a.* changeable, mutable.

muer [mɥe], *v.i.* (*a*) to moult; 2. (*of voice*) to break.

muet, -ette [mɥe, -ɛt]. 1. *a.* dumb, mute; rester m., to remain silent. 2. *s.* dumb person.

muflier [myflje], *s.m.* *Bot:* antirrhinum, snapdragon.

mug/ir [myʒiːr], *v.i.* (*a*) (*of cow*) to low; to bellow; (*b*) (*of sea, wind*) to roar; to boom. *s.m.* -issement.

muguet [mygɛ], *s.m.* lily of the valley.

mulâtre [mylɑːtr], *a. & s.* mulatto.

mule¹ [myl], *s.f.* (she-)mule.

mule², *s.f.* mule, bedroom slipper.

mulet¹ [mylɛ], *s.m.* (he-)mule.

mulet², *s.m.* *Fish:* grey mullet.

mulot [mylo], *s.m.* fieldmouse.

multicolore [myltikɔlɔːr], *a.* multicoloured.

multiple [myltipl]. 1. *a.* multiple, manifold; maison à succursales multiples, chain store. 2. *s.m.* *Mth:* multiple.

multipli/er [myltiplie], *v.tr. & i.* to multiply (par, by). *s.f.* -cation. *s.f.* -cité, multiplicity. se **multiplier.** (*a*) to multiply; les crimes se multiplient, crime is on the increase; (*b*) to be here, there, and everywhere.

multitude [myltityd], *s.f.* multitude; crowd.

†municipal [mynisipal], *a.* municipal; conseil m., local council.

municipalité [mynisipalite], *s.f.* municipality; local council; town hall.

munir [myni:r], *v.tr.* to furnish, equip (de, with).

munitions [mynisjɔ̃], *s.f.pl.* stores, supplies; ammunition.

mur [my:r], *s.m.* wall; mettre qn au pied du m., to drive s.o. into a corner. *s.f.* -aille, high wall.

mûr [my:r], *a.* ripe; mellow; mature. *adv.* -ement, with consideration.

mûr/e [my:r], *s.f.* 1. mulberry. 2. m. (de ronce), blackberry. *s.m.* -ier, mulberry(tree).

murer [myre], *v.tr.* to wall in; to wall up.

mûrir [myri:r], *v.tr. & i.* to ripen, mature.

murmure [myrmy:r], *s.m.* murmur.

murmurer [myrmyre], *v.tr. & i.* (*a*) to murmur; (*b*) to grumble.

muscade [myskad], *s.f.* nutmeg.

mus/cle [myskl], *s.m.* muscle. *a.* -clé, brawny. *a.* †-culeux, muscular.

museau [myzo], *s.m.* muzzle, snout; F: joli petit m., nice little face; vilain m., ugly mug.

musée [myze], *s.m.* museum; art gallery.

‡mus/eler [myzle], *v.tr.* to muzzle. *s.m.* -ellement. *s.f.* -elière, muzzle.

muséum [myzeom], *s.m.* natural history museum.

†musical [myzikal], *a.* musical.

music-hall [myzikɔ:l], *s.m.* music hall; numéros de m.-h., variety turns.

musicien, -ienne [myzisjɛ̃, -jɛn], *s. 1. a.* musical. 2. *s.* musician; musical person.

musique [myzik], *s.f.* 1. music. 2. band; chef de m., bandmaster.

musulman, -ane [myzylmã, -an], *a. & s.* Moslem.

mutation [mytasjɔ̃], *s.f.* change, alteration; *Mus: Sc:* mutation.

mutil/er [mytile], *v.tr.* (*a*) to mutilate, main; *s.m.* **mutilé de guerre**, disabled ex-serviceman; (*b*) to deface. *s.f.* -ation.

mutiner (se) [səmytine], *v.pr.* to rise in revolt; to mutiny, to rebel.

mutisme [mytism], *s.m.* dumbness, muteness; stubborn silence.

mutualité [mytyalite], *s.f.* mutual insurance.

‡mutu/el [mytɥɛl], *a.* mutual; société de secours mutuels, friendly society. *adv.* -ellement.

my/ope [mjɔp], *a. & s.* short-sighted (person). *s.f.* -opie, short-sightedness.

myosotis [mjɔzɔtis], *s.m.* forget-me-not.

myriade [mirjad], *s.f.* myriad.

myrte [mirt], *s.m.* myrtle.

myrtille [mirti:j], *s.f.* bilberry.

mystère [mistɛ:r], *s.m.* mystery.

†mystérieu/x [misterjø], *a.* mysterious. *adv.* -sement.

mystifi/er [mistifje], *v.tr.* (*a*) to mystify; (*b*) to hoax (s.o.). *a. & s.* -cateur, -trice, (i *a.* mystifying; (ii *s.* hoaxer. *s.f.* -cation.

mystique [mistik], *a. & s.* mystic(al). *adv.* -ment, mystically.

myth/e [mit], *s.m.* myth, legend. *a.* -ique, mythical.

mytholo/gie [mitɔlɔʒi], *s.f.* mythology. *a.* -gique, mythological.

myxomatose [miksɔmato:z], *s.f. Vet:* myxomatosis.

N

N, n [ɛn], *s.f.* (the letter) N, n.

nacre [nakr], *s.f.* mother of pearl.

nacré [nakre], *a.* pearly (lustre).

nage [na:ʒ], *s.f.* 1. rowing, sculling. 2. swimming; être en n., to be bathed in perspiration.

nageoire [naʒwa:r], *s.f.* 1. to row; to scull. 2. flipper.

‡nag/er [naʒe], *v.i.* 1. to row; to scull. 2. (*a*) to swim; (*b*) to float; to bathe in (butter, blood); to be rolling in (money). *s.* -eur, -euse, (*a*) swimmer, (*b*) oarsman.

nsguère [nage:r], *adv.* not long ago.

†naï/f [naif], *a.* 1. naive. 2. simpleminded; F: green. *adv.* -vement. *s.* -veté.

nain, naine [nɛ̃, nɛn], *a. & s.* dwarf.

naissance [nɛsã:s], *s.f.* (*a*) birth; acte de n., birth certificate; (*b*) source, origin.

‡naître [nɛ:tr], *v.i.* (aux. être) (*a*) to be born; il est né en 1880, he was born in 1880; impers. il naît cent enfants par mois, a hundred children are born every month; (*b*) (of plan) to originate; faire n., to give rise to, to arouse (suspicion, etc.).

napalm [napalm], *s.m.* napalm.

naphte [naft], *s.m.* naphtha.

nappe [nap], *s.f.* 1. (table)cloth; n. d'autel, altar cloth. 2. sheet (of water, ice).

narcisse [narsis], *s.m. Bot:* narcissus.

narcotique [narkɔtik], *a. & s.m.* narcotic.

narine [narin], *s.f.* nostril.

narquois [narkwa], a. mocking, bantering.

narra/tion [narrasjɔ̃], s.f. 1. narrating, narration. 2. narrative. s. -teur, -trice, (story-)teller. a. †-tif.

†nasal [nazal], a. nasal. adv. -ement.

naseau [nazo], s.m. nostril (of horse, ox).

nasill/er [nazije], v.i. to speak through the nose. a. -ard, nasal.

†natal [natal], a. (rarely used in the pl.) native (country).

natalité [natalite], s.f. birth-rate.

natation [natasjɔ̃], s.f. swimming.

nation [nasjɔ̃], s.f. nation; les Nations Unies, the United Nations.

†national [nasjɔnal], a. national.

national/iser [nasjɔnalize], v.tr. to nationalize. s.f. -isation. s.m. -isme. a. & s.m. & f. -iste.

nationalité [nasjɔnalite], s.f. nationality.

natte [nat], s.f. 1. mat, matting (of straw, etc.). 2. plait, braid (of hair).

natural/iser [natyralize], v.tr. to naturalize. s.f. -isation.

naturaliste [natyralist], s. naturalist; taxidermist.

nature [natyr], s.f. nature. 1. n. morte, still li e. 2. (a) kind, character; la du sol, nature of the soil; (b) character, disposition; être timide de n., to be shy by nature. 3. a.inv. pommes n., plain boiled potatoes; (esp. in Switzerland) n., black coffee.

†naturel [natyrɛl]. 1. a. natural; (a) de grandeur naturelle, life-sized; (b) natural, unaffected (person). 2. s.m. nature, character, disposition. adv. -lement.

naufrage [nofraːʒ], s.m. (ship)wreck.

naufrag/é, -ée [nofraʒe]. 1. a. (ship) wrecked. 2. s. castaway.

nausé/e [noze], s.f. (a) nausea; (b) seasickness; avoir des nausées, to feel squeamish. a. -abond, nauseating, foul (smell).

nautique [notik], a. nautical; carte n., (sea) chart; ski n., water skiing.

†naval [naval], a. naval, nautical.

navet [navɛ], s.m. turnip.

navette [navɛt], s.f. shuttle; véhicule qui fait n., vehicle running a shuttle service.

navig/abilité [navigabilite], s.f. 1. navigability (of river, etc.). 2. seaworthiness; airworthiness. a. -able.

navigant [navigɑ̃], a. sailing; personnel n., seagoing personnel; Av: flying personnel; aircrew.

navig/uer [navige], v.i. to sail, navigate. s.m. -ateur, navigator. s.f. -ation, navigation.

navire [navir], s.m. ship, vessel.

navire-citerne [navirsitern], s.m. Nau: tanker. pl. navires-citernes.

navr/er [navre], v.tr. to grieve, upset (s.o.). a. -rant, heart-rending. a. -ré, heart-broken.

naz/i, -ie [nazi], a. & s. Nazi. s.m. -isme.

ne, n' [n(ə)] (usu. used with pas, jamais, que, etc. after vb.), neg.adv. not; je ne l'ai pas vu, I haven't seen him; n'importe, it doesn't matter; je n'ai qu'une sœur, I have only one sister; je ne sais que faire, I don't know what to do.

néanmoins [neɑ̃mwɛ̃], adv. nevertheless; yet; still.

néant [neɑ̃], s.m. (a) nothingness; réduire qch. à n., to annihilate sth, to wipe sth. out; (b) (when filling in form) none; nil.

†nébuleux [nebylø]. 1. a. (a) nebulous; (b) cloudy, hazy (sky).

nécessaire [nesesɛr]. 1. a. necessary. 2. s.m. (a) necessaries, the indispensable; je ferai le n., I'll take care of it; (b) outfit; n. de toilette, dressing-case. adv. -ment.

néces/siter [nesesite], v.tr. to necessitate, require, entail (sth). s.f. -sité, want. a. †-siteux, needy, in want.

nef [nɛf], s.f. nave (of church).

néfaste [nefast], a. luckless; ill-omened.

négatif, -ive [negatif, -iːv]. 1. a. negative. 2. s.m. Phot: negative. 3. s.f. dans la négative, in the negative.

négation [negasjɔ̃], s.f. negation, denial.

négligé [negliʒe]. 1. a. (a) neglected; (b) careless, slovenly (dress, etc.). 2. s.m. undress, deshabille.

‡néglig/er [negliʒe], v.tr. to neglect. a. -eable. s.f. -ence. a. -ent. adv. -emment.

négoc/e [negɔs], s.m. trade, business. s. -iant, (wholesale) merchant.

négoci/er [negɔsje], v.tr. to negotiate. a. -able. s.f. -ation. s. -ateur, -atrice, negociator.

nègre, négresse [nɛːgr, negrɛs], s. negro, f. negress.

neige [nɛːʒ], s.f. snow; n. fondue, sleet; slush; boule de n., snowball; Ind: n. carbonique, dry ice.

‡neig/er [neʒe], v.impers. to snow. a. †-eux, snowy, snow-covered.

nénuphar [nenyfar], s.m. waterlily.

néo-gallois, -oise [neogalwa, -waːz], a. New South Welshman, -woman.

néolithique [neɔlitik], a. neolithic.

néon [neɔ̃], s.m. neon.

néo-Zélandais, -aise [neozelɑ̃dɛ, -ɛːz], a. New Zealander.

nerf [nɛr, nɛrf, pl. always nɛːr], s.m. 1. Anat: nerve; crise de nerfs, attack of nerves. 2. F: energy, pep.

†nerveu/x [nɛrvø], a. 1. nervous (system, disease). 2. sinewy, wiry; vigorous. 3. highly-strung, F: nervy (pers.). adv. -sement.

nervosité [nɛrvozite], s.f. irritability.

n'est-ce pas? [nɛspa], *adv.phr.* (*a*) (*affirmative*) isn't it? etc.; il fait chaud, **n'est-ce pas?** it's hot, isn't it? il est là, **n'est-ce pas?** he's there, isn't he? (*b*) (*negative*) il ne comprend pas, **n'est-ce pas?** he doesn't understand, does he? non, **n'est-ce pas?** I shouldn't think so!

†net [nɛt], *a.* 1. clean, spotless. 2. (*a*) clear; distinct; (*b*) poids net, net weight. 3. *adv.* plainly, outright; s'arrêter n., to stop dead. *adv.* **-ement.**

netteté [nɛt(ə)te], *s.f.* 1. cleanness; cleanness. 2. clearness; distinctness.

†nettoy/er [nɛtwaje], *v.tr.* to clean; n. à sec, to dry-clean. *s.m.* **-age,** cleaning.

neuf¹ [nœf (*occ.* nœv *before vowel*)], *num.a.* & *s.m.inv.* nine; le n. mai, the ninth of May; Louis neuf, Louis the Ninth.

†neuf² [nœf]. 1. *a.* (*placed after noun*) new; F: quoi de n.? what's the news? 2. *s.m.* le vieux et le n., the old and the new; meublé de n., newly (re)furnished. 3. *adb.phr.* remettre à n., to renovate.

neurasthén/ie [nœrasteni], *s.f.* neurasthenia. *a.* **-ique,** neurasthenic.

neuro/logie [nœrɔlɔʒi], *s.f. Med:* neurology. *s.m.* **-logue,** neurologist.

neutralis/er [nøtralize], *v.tr.* to neutralize. *s.f.* **-ation.**

neutralité [nøtralite], *s.f.* neutrality.

neutre [nøtr]. 1. *a.* neuter. 2. *a.* & *s.m.* neutral (tint, nation).

neutron [nøtrɔ̃], *s.m. El:* neutron.

neuvième [nœvjɛm]. 1. *num.a.* & *s.* ninth. 2. *s.m.* ninth (part). *adv.* **-ment.**

†neveu [n(ə)vø], *s.m.* nephew.

névral/gie [nevralʒi], *s.f.* neuralgia. *a.* **-gique.**

névrite [nevrit], *s.f.* neuritis.

névros/e, -ée [nevroze], *a.* & *s.* neurotic (patient).

nez [ne], *s.m.* nose; nez à nez, face to face; (*of dogs*) scent; (*b*) n. à n., face to face; rire au n. de qn, to laugh in s.o.'s face.

ni [ni], *conj.* (*ne is either expressed or implied*) nor, or; (*a*) ni moi (non plus), neither do I; (*b*) il ne mange ni ne boit, he neither eats nor drinks; (*c*) ni . . . ni, neither . . . nor; ni l'un ni l'autre, neither (of them).

niais, -aise [njɛ, -ɛz]. 1. *a.* simple, foolish. 2. *s.* fool, idiot. *adv.* **-ement.**

niaiserie [njɛzri], *s.f.* 1. silliness, stupidity, foolishness. 2. dire des niaiseries, to talk nonsense.

niche [niʃ], *s.f.* 1. niche, nook, recess. 2. (dog) kennel.

niche², *s.f.* trick, prank.

nicher [niʃe], *v.i.* to (build a) nest; F: où niche-t-il? where does he hang out?

nickel [nikɛl], *s.m.* nickel. *s.m.* **-age.**

niçois, -oise [niswa, -waːz], *a.* & *s.* (native) of Nice.

nicotine [nikɔtin], *s.f.* nicotine.

nid [ni], *s.m.* 1. nest; *F:* n. de poule, pothole (in road). 2. *Mil:* nest (of machine guns); *Nau:* (submarine) pen.

nièce [njɛs], *s.f.* niece.

nier [nje], *v.tr.* to deny (fact); *abs.* l'accusé nie, the accused pleads not guilty; il n'y a pas à le n., there's no denying it.

nigaud, -aude [nigo, -oːd], (*a*) *s.* idiot. *F:* clot; (*b*) *a.* simple, *F:* clottish.

nimbe [nɛ̃ːb], *s.m.* nimbus, halo.

nipper (se) [sənipe], *v.pr. F:* to rig oneself out.

nippes [nip], *s.f.pl. F:* old clothes.

nitrate [nitrat], *s.m. Ch:* nitrate.

niveau [nivo], *s.m.* level. 1. (*instrument*) n. à balle d'air, spirit level. 2. (*a*) *Rail:* passage à n., level crossing; (*b*) n. de vie, standard of living.

‡nivel/er [nivle], *v.tr.* to level, to even up. *s.m.* **-lement,** surveying, levelling.

noble [nɔbl], *a.* & *s.* noble. *adv.* **-ment.**

noblesse [nɔblɛs], *s.f.* nobility.

noc/e [nɔs], *s.f.* 1. (*a*) wedding; (*b*) wedding reception; voyage de noces, honeymoon (trip); (*c*) épouser qn en secondes noces, to marry for the second time. 2. faire la n., to go on a binge. *s.m.* **-eur, -euse,** *F:* reveller.

†nocif [nɔsif], *a.* injurious, harmful (à, to).

noctambul/e [nɔktɑ̃byl], *s.* (*a*) sleepwalker; (*b*) night-prowler. *s.m.* **-isme,** sleep-walking.

nocturne [nɔktyrn]. 1. *a.* nocturnal. 2. *s.m. Mus:* nocturne.

Noël [nɔɛl], *s.m.* 1. Christmas. 2. un n., a carol.

nœud [nø], *s.m.* 1. (*a*) knot; (*b*) bow (of ribbon); (*c*) crux (of the matter). 2. knot (in timber); node (in stem). 3. *Nau:* knot.

noir, -e [nwaːr]. 1. *a.* black; (*a*) dark, swarthy; (*b*) dark; gloomy; il fait n., it is dark; bête noire, pet aversion; (*c*) dirty (hands); (*d*) base (ingratitude). 2. *s.* black (man, woman); negro, negress. 3. *s.m.* broyer du n., to be depressed. *a.* **-âtre,** darkish. *s.m.* **-aud,** swarthy.

noirc/ir [nwarsiːr]. 1. *v.i.* to become, turn, black; to darken. 2. *v.tr.* to blacken (one's face); n. du papier, scribble. *s.f.* **-eur,** blackness; darkness.

noiset/te [nwazɛt]. 1. *s.f.* hazel nut. 2. *a.inv.* nut-brown (colour). *s.m.* **-ier,** hazel (tree).

noix [nwa], *s.f.* 1. walnut. 2. nut; n. d'acajou, cashew nut.

nom [nɔ̃], *s.m.* 1. name; nom de famille, surname; n. de guerre, assumed, pen, name; n. de théâtre, stage name; faux n., alias; nom et prénoms, full name. 2. noun.

nomade [nɔmad]. 1. *a.* nomadic. 2. *s.* nomad; *pl.* gypsies.

nombre [nɔ̃:br], *s.m.* number; un (bon) n. de, a good many. . . .

nombr/er [nɔ̃bre], *v.tr.* to number, reckon. o. *-eux*, numerous.

nombril [nɔ̃bri], *s.m.* navel.

†**nominal** [nominal], *a.* nominal; *(a)* appel n., roll call; valeur nominale, face value. *adv.* -ement.

nomina/tion [nominasjɔ̃], *s.f.* 1. nomination. 2. appointment. *s.m.* -teur, nominator. *a. & s.m.* †-tif, nominative (case).

nommer [nome], *v.tr.* 1. to name; on le nomma Paul, they called him Paul. 2. to mention by name. 3. to appoint; à jour nommé, on the appointed day; être nommé au grade de . . ., to be promoted to the rank of . . .
se nommer, to be called, named.

non [nɔ̃], *adv. no;* not. 1. je pense que n., I think not; faire signe que n., to shake one's head. *s.m.inv.* les n. l'emportent, the noes have it. 2. n. loin de la ville, not far from the town. 3. *(in compound words)* non-, in-, un-.

nonagénaire [nonaʒenɛːr], *a. & s.* non-agenarian.

non-belligérance [nɔ̃belliʒerɑ̃:s], *s.f.* non-belligerancy.

nonchal/ance [nɔ̃ʃalɑ̃:s], *s.f.* nonchalance, listlessness, unconcern. *a.* -ant. *adv.* -amment.

non-combattant [nɔ̃kɔ̃batɑ̃], *a. & s.m.* non-combatant.

non-livraison [nɔ̃livrezɔ̃], *s.f.* non-delivery.

non-sens [nɔ̃sɑ̃:s], *s.m.inv.* meaningless sentence, action.

non-valable [nɔ̃valabl], *a.* 1. *Jur:* invalid (clause). 2. *(of ticket, passport)* not valid.

nord [nɔːr], *s.m.* (no pl.). 1. north; le grand N., the frozen North; *F:* perdre le n., to lose one's bearings. 2. *a.inv.* north, northern; le pôle n., the North Pole.

nord-africain, -aine [nɔrafrikɛ̃, -ɛn], *a. & s.* North African.

nord-américain, -aine [nɔramerikɛ̃, -ɛn], *a. & s.* North American.

nord-est [nɔr(d)ɛst], *s.m.* north-east; *(wind)* north-easter.

nord-ouest [nɔr(d)wɛst], *s.m.* north-west; *(wind)* north-wester.

†**normal** [normal]. 1. *a. (a)* normal; école normale = college of education; *(b)* standard (weight). 2. *s.f.* normale, normal. *adv.* -ement.

normand, -ande [normɑ̃, -ɑ̃:d], *a. & s.* Norman; *F:* réponse normande, non-committal answer.

norme [norm], *s.f.* norm, standard.

norvégien, -ienne [norveʒjɛ̃, -jɛn]. 1. *a. & s.* Norwegian. 2. *s.m. Ling:* Norwegian.

nostalg/ie [nostalʒi], *s.f.* home-sickness. *a.* -ique, homesick.

nota/bilité [notabilite], *s.f.* 1. notability. 2. person of note. *a. & s.m.* -ble. *adv.* -blement.

notaire [nɔtɛːr], *s.m.* lawyer; *U.S:* notary; *Scot:* notary public.

notamment [notamɑ̃], *adv.* (*a*) especially; (*b*) among others.

note [not], *s.f.* 1. note; memorandum, minute; n. d'avis, advice note; n. en bas de page, footnote. 2. *(a) Sch: etc:* mark; *(b) Mus:* note. 3. bill, account.

noter [note], *v.tr.* 1. to note; to take notice of. 2. to put down, jot down.

notice [notis], *s.f.* 1. note, account. 2. review (of book). 3. directions (for use).

notifi/er [nɔtifje], *v.tr.* to notify, to inform s.o. of sth. *s.f.* -cation.

notion [nosjɔ̃], *s.f.* notion, idea; quelques notions de chimie, a smattering of chemistry.

notoire [nɔtwaːr], *a.* well-known (fact); manifest (injustice). *adv.* -ment.

notoriété [nɔtɔrjete], *s.f.* notoriety (of fact); reputation (of pers.); avoir de la n., to be well-known.

notre, *pl.* nos [nɔtr, no], *poss.a.* our.

nôtre [noːtr]. 1. *poss.pron.* ours; our own. 2. *s.m.* our own (property, friends); est-il des nôtres? is he one of us?

nou/er [nwe, nue], *v.tr.* 1. to tie, knot. 2. n. conversation, to enter into conversation. *a.* †-eux, knotty, gnarled.

nouilles [nu:j], *s.f.pl.* 1. *Cu:* noodle(s). 2. *(in sg.) a. & s.f. P:* quelle nouille! what a drip (he, she, is)!

nourrice [nuris], *s.f.* (wet-)nurse.

nourr/ir [nurir], *v.tr.* to board (pupils); to nourish; to feed; to entertain (hope). *a.* -issant, nourishing. *s.f.* -iture, food.

nous [nu], *pers.pron.* 1. *(a) (subject)* we; *(b) (object)* us; to us; *(c) (reflexive)* ourselves; *(d) (reciprocal)* each other. 2. n. autres Anglais, we English; un ami à n., a friend of ours.

nous-mêmes [numɛm], *pers.pron.pl.* ourselves.

†**nouv/eau** [nuvo], *a.,* new; un nouvel époux, another husband; la nouvelle génération, the rising generation; le nouvel an, the new year; *s.m.* c'est du n., that's news to me; de n., again; à n., (all over) again. *adv.* -ellement, recently.

nouveau-né, -née [nuvone], *a. & s.* new-born child; *pl.* nouveau-né(e)s.

nouveauté [nuvote], *s.f.* 1. newness, novelty; de haute n., in the latest style. 2. change, innovation. 3. *pl.* fancy goods; marchand de nouveautés, draper.

nouvelle², *s.f.* 1. *(a)* (piece of) news; *(b) pl.* envoyez-moi de vos nouvelles, let me hear from you. 2. short story.

novembre [nɔvɑ̃:br], *s.m.* November.

novice [nɔvis], *s.m. & f.* novice.

‡noyau [nwajo], *s.m.* 1. stone (of fruit); kernel. 2. nucleus (of atom, etc.); *Pol:* n. communiste, communist cell.

noyeri [nwaje], *s.m.* walnut-(tree, -wood).

‡noyer², *v.tr.* to drown; yeux noyés de larmes, eyes filled with tears.
se noyer. (*a*) to drown oneself; (*b*) to be drowned.

nu [ny]. 1. *a.* (*a*) naked; bare; nûde;
Note: nu *before the noun it qualifies is invariable and hyphened, e.g.:* aller les pieds nus, aller au-pieds, to go bare-footed; (*b*) uncovered, plain; la vérité nue, the naked truth. 2. mettre qch. à nu, to lay bare, expose, strip, sth.

nuage [nɥaːʒ], *s.m.* (*a*) cloud; (*b*) mist (before the eyes); (*c*) shadow, gloom. *a.* †-eux, cloudy, overcast (sky).

nuance [nɥɑ̃ːs], *s.f.* shade, nuance.

nucléaire [nykleːr], *a.* nuclear; réaction, fission, n., nuclear reaction, fission.

nucléon [nykleɔ̃], *s.m. Atom. Ph:* nucleon.

nud/iste [nydist], *s.m. & f.* nudist. *s.m.* -isme.

nudité [nydite], *s.f.* nudity, nakedness.

nues [ny], *s.f.pl.* tomber des n., (i) to arrive unexpectedly; (ii) to be thunder-struck.

‡nuire [nɥiːr], *v.ind.tr.* to do harm to s.o., sth.

nuisible [nɥizibl], *a.* hurtful, harmful.

nuit [nɥi], *s.f.* night; (*a*) cette n., (i) to-night; (ii) last night; (*b*) de n., by night; (*c*) darkness; il se fait n., it is growing dark; à la n. tombante, at nightfall; à (la) n. close, after dark.

‡nul [nyl]. 1. (with ne *expressed or understood*) (*a*) indef. *a.* no; not one; n. espoir, no hope; sans nulle vanité, without any conceit; (*b*) indef.pron. no one; nobody; n. ne le sait, no one knows. 2. *a.* (*a*) worthless; homme n., nonentity; (*b*) null and void; partie nulle, drawn game. *adv.* -lement.

nullifier [nylifje], *v.tr.* to nullify.

nullité [nyllite], *s.f.* 1. nullity, invalidity. 2. incompetence; incapacity.

‡numéral [nymeral], *a. & s.m.* numeral.

numérique [nymerik], *a.* numerical. *adv.* -ment.

numéro [nymero], *s.m.* number.

numéroter [nymerɔte], *v.tr.* to number.

‡nuptial [nypsjal], *a.* messe nuptiale, nuptial mass; marche nuptiale, wedding march.

nuque [nyk], *s.f.* nape of the neck.

nutri/tion [nytrisjɔ̃], *s.f.* nutrition. *a.* †-tif, nourishing. *s.m. & f.* -tionniste, dietitian.

nymphe [nɛ̃ːf], *s.f.* 1. nymph. 2. *Z:* pupa, chrysalis.

O

O, o [o], *s.m.* (the letter) O, o.

oasis [oazi(ː)s], *s.f.* oasis.

obé/ir [obeiːr], *v.ind.tr.* to obey; o. à qn, to obey s.o.; se faire o., to enforce obedience. *s.f.* -issance, obedience. *a.* -issant, obedient.

obélisque [obelisk], *s.m.* obelisk.

obèse [obɛːz], *a.* obese, fat.

obésité [obezite], *s.f.* obesity, corpulence.

objec/ter [ɔbʒɛkte], *v.tr.* to raise (sth.) as an objection. *s.f.* -tion, objection.

†objectif [ɔbʒɛktif]. 1. *a.* objective, unbiassed. 2. *s.m.* aim, object(ive), end. 3. *s.m. Phot:* lens.

objet [ɔbʒɛ], *s.m.* 1. (*a*) object, thing; o. de luxe, luxury article; (*b*) *Gram:* o. direct, direct object. 2. subject (of an enquiry, etc.). 3. object, aim, purpose (of action).

obligation [ɔbligasjɔ̃], *s.f.* 1. (moral) obligation; duty. 2. bond, debenture; o. au porteur, bearer-bond. 3. obligation, favour.

obligatoire [ɔbligatwaːr], *a.* obligatory, compulsory, binding; arrêt o. (de l'autobus), all buses stop here. *adv.* -ment.

obligé [ɔbliʒe], *a.* (*a*) obliged, compelled; (de faire qch., to do sth.); (*b*) grateful (de, for).

oblig/er [ɔbliʒe], *v.tr.* 1. to oblige, compel. 2. o. qn, to do s.o. a favour. *s.f.* -eance, kindness. *a.* -eant, obliging, kind. *adv.* -eamment.
s'obliger à faire qch., to make a point of doing sth.

oblique [ɔblik], *a.* (*a*) oblique (line); slanting (stitch); (*b*) underhand, devious (behaviour). *adv.* -ment.

‡oblitér/er [ɔblitere], *v.tr.* to obliterate; to cancel (stamp). *s.f.* -ation.

†oblong [ɔblɔ̃], *a.* oblong.

obscène [ɔpsɛ(ː)n], *a.* obscene; lewd.

obscénité [ɔpsenite], *s.f.* obscenity.

obscur [ɔpskyːr], *a.* 1. dark; un écrivain o., an abstruse writer. 2. obscure; humble; un o. écrivain, an unknown writer. *adv.* -ément. *s.f.* -ité, obscurity; darkness.

obscur/cir [ɔpskyrsiːr], *v.tr.* to obscure; to darken, cloud; to dim (sight). *s.m.* -cissement, darkening.
s'obscurcir, to grow dark; to become dim.

‡obséder [ɔpsede], v.tr. (a) to beset; (b) to obsess; obsédé d'une idée, obsessed by an idea.

obsèques [ɔpsɛk], s.f.pl. funeral.

†obséquieux [ɔpsekjø], a. obsequious.

observateur, -trice [ɔpsɛrvatœːr, -tris]. 1. s. observer; Mil: spotter. 2. a. observant, observing.

observ/er [ɔpsɛrve], v.tr. to observe; (a) to keep (to), to comply with (rules, laws); (b) to watch; (c) to notice. s.f. -ance, observance (of laws). s.f. -ation, observation; remark. s.m. -atoire, observatory.

obsession [ɔpsɛsjɔ̃], s.f. obsession.

obstacle [ɔpstakl], s.m. obstacle, hindrance; Sp: hurdle, jump.

obstination [ɔpstinasjɔ̃], s.f. obstinacy, stubbornness.

obstiné [ɔpstine], a. stubborn, obstinate. adv. -ment.

obstiner (s') [sɔpstine], v.pr. to persist (à, in).

obstruct/ion [ɔpstryksjɔ̃], s.f. obstruction. a. †-if, obstructive.

obstruer [ɔpstrye], v.tr. to obstruct, block (street, view); to choke (pipe).

‡obtenir [ɔptəniːr], v.tr. to obtain, get; to gain, procure.

obturateur [ɔptyratœːr], s.m. obturator; E: stop-valve; thrɔttle; o. de joint, gasket; Phot: shutter.

obtur/er [ɔptyre], v.tr. to seal (aperture); to stop (tooth). s.f. -ation, stopping (in tooth).

obtus [ɔpty], a. 1. blunt(ed) (object). 2. obtuse (person). 3. obtuse (angle).

obus [ɔby(ːs)], s.m. Mil: shell.

occasion [ɔkazjɔ̃], s.f. 1. (a) opportunity, occasion, chance; (b) bargain; d'o., secondhand; une voiture d'o., a used car. 2. occasion; pour l'o., for this particular case. 3. reason, cause, motive. a. †-nel, occasional; rencontre o., chance meeting. adv. -nellement.

occasionner [ɔkazjone], v.tr. to cause; to give rise to (sth.).

occident [ɔksidɑ̃], s.m. west. a. †-al, western.

occulte [ɔkylt], a. occult; hidden (cause).

occuper [ɔkype], a. busy; engaged; P.T.T: ligne occupée, line engaged.

occup/er [ɔkype], v.tr. to occupy. 1. (a) to live in (house); (b) Mil: to hold (fort); (c) to fill (one's time, a post). 2. to give occupation to (s.o.). s.f. -ant, occupier, occupant. s.f. -ation, business, employment.

s'occuper. 1. to keep oneself busy. 2. je m'en occuperai, I shall see to it.

occurrence [ɔkyr(r)ɑ̃ːs], s.f. occurrence, event; en l'o., in the circumstances.

océan [ɔseɑ̃], s.m. ocean. a. -ique.

ocre [ɔkr], s.f. ochre.

octane [ɔktan], s.m. Ch: octane; indice d'o., octane number.

octave [ɔktaːv], s.f. Mus: octave.

octobre [ɔktɔbr], s.m. October.

octogénaire [ɔktɔʒeneːr], a. & s. octogenarian.

octogon/e [ɔktɔgon], s.m. octagon. a. †-al.

‡octroyer [ɔktrwaje] v.tr. to grant, concede.

oculaire [ɔkyleːr]. 1. a. ocular; témoin o. eyewitness. 2. s.m. Opt: eyepiece.

oculiste [ɔkylist], s.m. oculist.

ode [ɔd], s.f. ode.

odeur [ɔdœːr], s.f. odour, smell; bonne o., pleasant smell; mauvaise o., bad smell, stench.

†odieu/x [ɔdjø], a. odious; hateful (person, action). adv. -sement.

odorant [ɔdorɑ̃], a. sweet-smelling.

odorat [ɔdora], s.m. (sense of) smell.

†œil [œːj], s.m. 1. eye; il a les yeux [lezjø] bleus, he has blue eyes; F: risquer un o., to peep out; ouvrir de grands yeux, to open one's eyes wide; cela saute aux yeux, it is obvious; coûter les yeux de la tête, to cost the earth. 2. sight, look, eye; chercher qn des yeux, to look about for s.o.; à vue d'œil, visibly; coup d'œil, glance; avoir l'o., to be observant. 3. (a) eye (of needle, etc.); (b) Rad: o. cathodique, magic eye.

œillet [œje], s.m. 1. eyelet. 2. Bot: carnation; o. de poète, sweet william; o. d'Inde, French marigold.

œuf [œf], s.m. (a) egg; o. mollet, soft-boiled egg; o. sur le plat, fried egg; (b) pl. roe.

œuvre [œːvr], s.f. 1. (a) work, working, mettre qn à l'o., to set s.o. to work; (b) o. de bienfaisance, charitable institution. 2. work, production; les œuvres de Molière, Molière's works.

offensant [ɔfɑ̃sɑ̃], a. offensive, insulting.

offense [ɔfɑ̃ːs], s.f. offence, insult. 2. Ecc: pardonne-nous nos offenses, forgive us our trespasses.

offenser [ɔfɑ̃se], v.tr. 1. to offend (s.o.). 2. to shock (s.o.'s feelings).

s'offenser, to take offence (de, at).

offens/if, -ive [ɔfɑ̃sif, iːv]. 1. a. offensive (war, weapon). 2. s.f. l'offensive, the offensive. adv. -ivement.

offertoire [ɔfɛrtwaːr], s.m. Ecc: offertory.

office [ɔfis]. 1. s.m. (a) office, functions; faire o. de secrétaire, to act as secretary; adv.phr. d'o. (i) officially; (ii) automatically; (b) service, help; (c) (divine) service; (d) bureau, office. 2. s.f. (butler's) pantry.

†offici/el [ɔfisjɛl], a. official (statement); formal (call). adv. -ellement.

officier[1] [ɔfisje], v.i. to officiate.

officier[2], s.m. officer.

†officieu/x, -euse [ɔfisjø, -øːz]. 1. a. (a) over-obliging; (b) unofficial, semi-official; (c) kindly-meant (advice, etc.). 2. s. busybody. adv. -sement.

offrande [ɔfrɑ̃ːd], s.f. Ecc: offering.

offre [ɔfr], *s.f.* offer, proposal; tender (for contract); (*at auction sale*) bid.

†**offrir** [ɔfriːr], *v.tr.* to offer; to give; c'est pour o., it's for a present; o. un cocktail, to give a cocktail party. **s'offrir.** 1. to offer oneself; to volunteer (for a service). 2. to present itself; le spectacle qui s'offrit à ma vue, the sight that met my eyes.

offusquer [ɔfyske], *v.tr.* to offend, shock. **s'offusquer**, to take offence (de, at).

ogive [ɔʒiːv], *s.f.* 1. A. & A: voûte d'ogives, ribbed vault. 2. nose cone (of rocket).

ogre, ogresse [ɔgr, ɔgrɛs], *s.* ogre; ogress.

ohé [oe], *int.* hi! hullo!

oie [wa], *s.f.* goose.

oignon [ɔɲɔ̃], *s.m.* 1. (a) onion; (b) bulb. 2. bunion.

oiseau [wazo], *s.m.* bird; oiseaux de basse-cour, poultry; *P:* drôle d'o., queer customer.

oiseu/x [wazø], *a.* idle, lazy; trifling.

ois/if, -ive [wazif, -iːv], 1. *a.* idle. 2. *s.* idler. *adv.* -**ivement.** -**ivité,** idleness.

oison [wazɔ̃], *s.m.* gosling.

oléagineux [ɔleaʒinø], *a.* 1. oily. 2. oil-producing (seeds, nuts).

oliv/e [ɔliːv], *s.f.* (a) olive; huile d'o., olive oil; (b) *a.inv.* olive green. *s.m.* -**ier,** olive-tree. *a.* -**aie,** olive grove.

olympiade [ɔlɛ̃pjad], *s.f. Sp:* Olympiad.

olympique [ɔlɛ̃pik], *a.* Olympic; les jeux olympiques, the Olympic games.

ombrage [ɔ̃braːʒ], *s.m.* shade (of trees, etc.).

†**ombrager** [ɔ̃braʒe], *v.tr.* (a) to shade; (b) to overshadow.

†**ombrageu/x** [ɔ̃braʒø], *a.* 1. shy, skittish (horse). 2. easily offended, touchy. *adv.* -**sement.**

ombre [ɔ̃br], *s.f.* 1. shadow. 2. shade. 3. darkness; à l'o. de la nuit, under cover of darkness. 4. ghost; l'o. d'une chance, the ghost, shadow, of a chance.

ombrelle [ɔ̃brɛl], *s.f.* parasol, sunshade.

omelette [ɔmlɛt], *s.f.* omelette.

†**omettre** [ɔmɛtr], *v.tr.* to omit; to leave out; o. de faire qch., to fail to do sth.

omission [ɔmisjɔ̃], *s.f.* omission, oversight.

omnibus [ɔmnibyːs], *a.inv.* train o., *s.m.* omnibus, slow train; des règles o., blanket rules.

omnipotent [ɔmnipɔtɑ̃], *a.* omnipotent.

omnipraticien, -ienne [ɔmnipratisjɛ̃, -jɛn], *s. Med:* general practitioner, *F:* G.P.

omnivore [ɔmnivɔːr], *a.* omnivorous.

omoplate [ɔmɔplat], *s.f.* shoulder-blade.

on [ɔ̃], *indef.pron.* (*often l'on, esp. after a vowel sound*) one; people, they, we, etc.; on dit, it is said; on frappe, somebody's knocking at the door.

oncle [ɔ̃kl], *s.m.* uncle.

onction [ɔ̃ksjɔ̃], *s.f. Ecc:* unction; l'extrême unction.

†**onctueux** [ɔ̃ktɥø], *a.* unctuous, greasy, oily (to the touch, in manner).

onde [ɔ̃ːd], *s.f.* 1. wave. 2. *Ph:* o. sonore, sound wave; *Rad:* longueur d'o., wave-length.

ondée [ɔ̃de], *s.f.* heavy shower.

on-dit [ɔ̃di], *s.m.inv.* rumour, hearsay.

ondoyant [ɔ̃dwajɑ̃], *a.* undulating, waving (corn).

ondul/er [ɔ̃dyle], 1. *v.i.* to undulate, ripple. 2. *v.tr.* se faire o., to have one's hair waved. *s.f.* -**ation,** (hair-)wave. *a.* †-**eux,** wavy.

onéreux [ɔnerø], *a.* burdensome (tax); heavy (expense); à titre o., subject to payment.

ongle [ɔ̃ːgl], *s.m.* (finger-)nail; claw; coup d'o., scratch.

onze [ɔ̃ːz], *num.* & *inv.* & *s.m.inv.* (*the e of le, de, is not elided before onze and its derivatives*) eleven; le o. avril, the eleventh of April; Louis o., Louis the Eleventh.

onzième [ɔ̃zjɛm], 1. *num.* & *a.* eleventh. 2. *s.m.* eleventh (part).

opal/e [ɔpal], *s.f.* opal. *a.* -**escent.** *a.* -**in,** opaline.

opaque [ɔpak], *a.* opaque.

opéra [ɔpera], *s.m.* 1. opera. 2. opera-house.

opérateur, -trice [ɔperatœːr, -tris], *s.* (machine-)operator.

opération [ɔperasjɔ̃], *s.f.* 1. operation; working; process. 2. (military, surgical) operation. 3. transaction.

†**opér/er** [ɔpere], *v.tr.* to operate. 1. to bring about; o. un miracle, to work a miracle. 2. (*a*) to carry out, perform; (*b*) o. un malade, un abcès, to operate on a patient, an abscess; se faire o., to undergo an operation. 3. *abs.* (*of remedy*) to work, act. *a.* †-**atif,** operative (clause).

s'opérer, to take place, to come about.

opérette [ɔperɛt], *s.f.* operetta; musical comedy.

ophtalmolo/gie [ɔftalmɔlɔʒi], *s.f.* ophthalmology. *s.m.* -**giste,** oculist.

opiner [ɔpine], *v.i.* to be of opinion (que, that).

opiniâtre [ɔpinjɑtr], *a.* obstinate. *s.f.* -**té,** obstinacy. *adv.* -**ment.**

opinion [ɔpinjɔ̃], *s.f.* opinion (de, of; sur, about); view.

opium [ɔpjɔm], *s.m.* opium.

oppor/tunité [ɔpɔrtynite], *s.f.* 1. (a) opportuneness, timeliness; (b) expediency, advisability. 2. opportunity. *a.* -**tun,** timely; expedient.

opposé [ɔpoze], 1. *a.* opposed, opposing; opposite. 2. *s.m.* contrary.

opposer [ɔpoze], *v.tr.* 1. to oppose; o. une équipe à une autre, to match one team against another; o. une vigoureuse résistance, to offer a vigorous resistance. 2. to compare; to contrast (à, with).
    s'opposer à qch., to oppose (sth.), to be opposed to (sth.).

opposition [ɔpozisjɔ̃], *s.f.* 1. opposition; *Pol:* le parti de l'o., the opposition; *Com:* frapper d'o., to stop payment of (cheque, etc.). 2. contrast.

oppres/ser [ɔprese], *v.tr.* to oppress; to weigh down; to lie heavy on (the chest, conscience). *s.m.* -seur. *a.* †-sif. *adv.* -sivement. *s.f.* -sion.

opprim/er [ɔprime], *v.tr.* to oppress, crush (a people). *a.* -ant, oppressive (tyrant).

opter [ɔpte], *v.i.* o. pour qch., to decide in favour of sth., to choose sth.

opticien [ɔptisjɛ̃], *s.m.* optician.

optim/isme [ɔptimism], *s.m.* optimism. *a. & s.* -iste, (i) *a.* optimistic; (ii) *s.* optimist.

option [ɔpsjɔ̃], *s.f.* option, choice (entre, between); demander une o., to ask for an option.

optique [ɔptik]. 1. *a.* optical. 2. *s.f.* optics.

opul/ence [ɔpylɑ̃s], *s.f.* opulence, affluence, wealth. *a.* -ent, rich.

opuscule [ɔpyskyl], *s.m.* pamphlet, tract.

or¹ [ɔːr], *s.m.* 1. gold; or en barres, bullion; *F:* c'est en or, it's a piece of cake; affaire d'or, excellent bargain. 2. gold (colour); cheveux d'or, golden hair.

or², *conj.* now; or donc, well then.

oracle [ɔraːkl], *s.m.* oracle.

orage [ɔraːʒ], *s.m.* (thunder)storm.

†orageu/x [ɔraʒø], *a.* stormy (weather, discussion); threatening (sky). *adv.* -sement.

oraison [ɔrɛzɔ̃], *s.f.* 1. o. funèbre, funeral oration. 2. prayer.

†oral [ɔral]. 1. *a.* oral (examination); verbal (deposition); épreuve o., oral examination. *adv.* -ement, by word of mouth.

orangeade [ɔrɑ̃ʒad], *s.f.* orangeade.

oran/ge [ɔrɑ̃ːʒ], *s.f.* 1. orange. 2. *a.inv.* rubans o., orange(-coloured) ribbons. *s.m.* -ger, orange-tree. *s.f.* -geraie, orange-grove. *s.f.* -gerie, orangery.

orateur [ɔratœːr], *s.m.* orator, speaker.

oratoire [ɔratwaːr]. 1. *a.* oratorical; l'art o., the art of public speaking. 2. *s.m.* chapel (for private worship); Pères de l'O., Oratorians.

oratorio [ɔratorjo], *s.m. Mus:* oratorio.

orbite [ɔrbit], *s.f.* 1. orbit; mettre un satellite en o., to put a satellite into orbit. 2. Anat: (eye-)socket. 3. Pol: l'o. de la Russie, des U.S.A., the Russian, the American, orbit.

orches/tre [ɔrkɛstr], *s.m.* orchestra; chef d'o., (i) conductor, (ii) bandmaster. *a.* †-tral. *s.f.* -tration.

orchidée [ɔrkide], *s.f.* orchid.

ordinaire [ɔrdinɛːr]. 1. *a.* ordinary, usual, common; peu o., unusual, uncommon; vin o., table wine. 2. *s.m.* (a) custom, usual practice; d'o., usually; (b) ordinary, standard; au-dessus de l'o., above the common run. *adv.* -ment.

ordinateur [ɔrdinatœːr], *s.m.* computer.

ordonnance [ɔrdonɑ̃s], *s.f.* 1. order, (general) arrangement. 2. (a) o. de police, police regulation; (b) judge's order. 3. officier d'o., aide-de-camp. 4. *Med:* prescription.

ordonné [ɔrdone], *a.* orderly; tidy.

ordonner [ɔrdone], *v.tr.* 1. to arrange. 2. to order, command; to prescribe.

ordre [ɔrdr], *s.m.* order. 1. numéro d'o., serial number; avec o., methodically; sans o., untidy, untidily; homme d'o., methodical man. 2. o. public, law and order; le service d'o. = the police. 3. o. du jour, (i) agenda (of meeting); (ii) *Mil:* general orders; questions à l'o. du jour, (i) items on the agenda; (ii) questions of the day. 4. (a) order; class; de premier o., first-rate; (b) decoration; order. 5. (a) command; warrant; (b) billet à o., promissory note.

ordur/e [ɔrdyːr], *s.f.* 1. dirt, filth. 2. *pl.* refuse; ordures ménagères, household refuse. *a.* †-ier, filthy (book, language).

oreille [ɔrɛːj], *s.f.* ear. 1. baisser l'o., to be crestfallen. 2. souffler à l'o. de, to whisper to; faire la sourde o., to turn a deaf ear. *s.m.* -er, pillow. *s.m.pl.* -ons, mumps.

orfèvre [ɔrfɛːvr], *s.m.* goldsmith; gold and silver. *s.f.* -rie, gold, silver, plate.

organe [ɔrgan], *s.m.* 1. organ (of sight, etc.); les organes d'une machine, the parts of a machine. 2. (a) l'o. d'un parti, a (political) party newspaper; (b) agent, means, medium; par un nouvel o., through another agency.

organique [ɔrganik], *a.* organic. *adv.* -ment, organically.

organis/er [ɔrganize], *v.tr.* to organize. *s.-ateur, -atrice, organizer. *s.f.* -ation, organization.
    s'organiser, to get into working order; to get settled.

organisme [ɔrganism], *s.m.* 1. organism; Anat: system; un o. de fer, an iron constitution. 2. un o. comme l'O.N.U., a body such as U.N.O.

organiste [ɔrganist], *s.m. & f. Mus:* organist.

orge [ɔrʒ]. 1. *s.f.* barley. 2. *s.m.* o. perlé, pearl barley.

orgue [ɔrg], s.m. 1. (also Ecc: s.f.pl. orgues) Mus: organ. 2. o. de salon, harmonium; o. de cinéma, theatre organ; o. de barbarie, barrel-organ.

orgueil [ɔrgœːj], s.m. pride. a. †-leux, arrogant. adv. -leusement.

orient [ɔrjɑ̃], s.m. Orient, East; Pol: le proche, le moyen, l'extrême O., the Near, Middle, Far East. a. †-al, eastern.

orientation [ɔrjɑ̃tasjɔ̃], s.f. 1. table d'o., panoramic table; sens de l'o., sense of direction; Sch: o. professionnelle, vocational guidance; Rad: positioning (of aerial). 2. o. d'une maison, aspect of a house; l'o. de la politique, the trend of politics.

orienter [ɔrjɑ̃te], v.tr. 1. to orientate; (a) terrasse orientée au sud, terrace facing south; (b) Rad: antenne orientée, directional aerial; (c) to direct, guide (s.o.). 2. to take the bearings of (spot).

s'orienter, to take one's bearings; s'o. vers la politique, to prepare for (a career in) politics; s'o. vers le communisme, to move towards communism.

orifice [ɔrifis], s.m. aperture, opening.

originaire [ɔriʒinɛːr], a. originating (de, from, in); native (de, of). adv. -ment, originally; at the beginning.

†**original** [ɔriʒinal], a. 1. original (text); (in typing) top copy. 2. (a) novel, fresh; (b) odd; c'est un o., he's a character. adv. -ement.

originalité [ɔriʒinalite], s.f. (a) originality; (b) eccentricity, oddity.

origine [ɔriʒin], s.f. origin; vins d'o., vintage wines.

originel [ɔriʒinɛl], a. primordial, original. adv. -ement.

orme [ɔrm], s.m. elm(tree). s.m. -eau (young) elm.

orné [ɔrne], a. ornate.

ornement [ɔrnəmɑ̃], s.m. ornament, adornment, embellishment; sans o., unadorned.

ornement/er [ɔrnəmɑ̃te], v.tr. to ornament. a. †-al. s.f. -ation.

orner [ɔrne], v.tr. to ornament, adorn; orné de rubis, set with rubies.

ornière [ɔrnjɛːr], s.f. rut.

ornithol/ogie [ɔrnitɔlɔʒi], s.f. ornithology. a. -ique. s.m. or f. -giste.

orphelin, -ine [ɔrfəlɛ̃, -in], s. orphan. s.m. orphanage.

orteil [ɔrtɛj], s.m. toe.

orthodox/e [ɔrtɔdɔks], a. orthodox. s.f. -ie.

orthographe [ɔrtɔgraf], s.f. spelling; faute d'o., spelling mistake.

orthographier [ɔrtɔgrafje], v.tr. to spell.

orthopéd/ie [ɔrtɔpedi], s.f. orthopædics. a. -ique. s.m. -iste.

ortie [ɔrti], s.f. nettle; o. brûlante, stinging nettle.

os [ɔs; pl. o], s.m. bone; trempé jusqu' aux os, wet through. a. †-seux, bony.

oscill/er [ɔsile], v.i. to oscillate. 1. (of pendulum) to swing; to rock. 2. to waver; (of market) to fluctuate. a. -ant. s.f. -ation, a. -atoire, oscillatory.

osé [oze], a. (a) bold, daring; (b) risqué.

oseille [ozɛj], s.f. sorrel.

oser [oze], v.tr.a. to dare, venture.

osier [ozje], s.m. osier, water-willow; panier d'o., wicker basket.

ossature [ɔsatyːr], s.f. 1. frame, skeleton (of man, animal). 2. frame(work) (of car, plane); skeleton (of building).

ossements [ɔsmɑ̃], s.m.pl. bones, remains (of dead men, animals).

ostensible [ɔstɑ̃sibl], a. patent to all, open. adv. -ment.

ostentation [ɔstɑ̃tasjɔ̃], s.f. ostentation, show.

ostréicul/ture [ɔstreikyltyːr], s.f. oyster-farming. s.m. -teur, oyster-farmer.

otage [ɔtaːʒ], s.m. hostage (de, for); surety.

otarie [ɔtari], s.f. sea-lion.

ôter [ote], v.tr. to remove, take away; (a) ô. le couvert, to clear the table; (b) son pardessus, to take off one's overcoat; (b) il me l'a ôté des mains, he snatched it out of my hands.

ou [u], conj. or; either him or me, ou lui ou moi.

où [u], adv. 1. (interrogative) where? d'où? whence? where from?; d'où vient que? how does it happen that? jusqu'où? how far? 2. (relative) (a) where; n'importe où, anywhere; partout où il va, wherever he goes; (b) when; du temps où on était jeune, when we were young; (c) in which, at which; la maison où il demeure, the house he lives in. 3. où que vous soyez, wherever you may be.

ouate [wat], s.f. (l'ouate or la ouate) (a) wadding; (b) cotton-wool.

ouater [wate], v.tr. to pad; to quilt.

oubli [ubli], s.m. 1. (a) forgetfulness; (b) oblivion; tomber dans l'o., to be forgotten. 2. oversight.

oublier [ublie], v.tr. (a) to forget; (b) to overlook, neglect (duty, interests).

s'oublier. 1. to be unselfish. 2. to forget one's manners.

†**oublieux** [ublie], a. forgetful (de, of).

ouest [wɛst]. 1. s.m. (de l'o.) west. 2. a.inv. western, west.

oui [wi, ui], yes. 1. adv. je crois que oui, I think so; faire sugne que oui, to nod assent. 2. s.m.inv. vingt o. et trente non, twenty ayes and thirty noes.

ouï-dire [widiːr], s.m.inv. hearsay.

ouïe [wi], s.f. 1. (sense of) hearing; avoir l'o. fine, to be sharp of hearing. 2. pl. gills (of fish).

ouragan [uragɑ̃], s.m. hurricane; entrer en o., to burst in(to a room).

ourler [urle], v.tr. 1. to hem. 2. to lap joint (metal edges).

ourlet [urlɛ], s.m. 1. hem. 2. edge (of crater); rim (of ear). 3. lap-joint (in metal).

ours [urs], s. bear. s.m. -on, bear-cub.

oursin [ursɛ̃], s.m. sea-urchin.

outil [uti], s.m. tool, implement.

outillage [utijaːʒ], s.m. (a) set of tools; (b) gear, plant.

outiller [utije], v.tr. to equip, supply (man) with tools, (factory) with plant.

outrage [utraːʒ], s.m. outrage; flagrant insult; Jur: outrages (à magistrat), contempt of court.

‡outrag/er [utraʒe], v.tr. 1. to insult. 2. to outrage (nature, the law). a. -eant, outrageous. a. †-eux. adv. -eusement.

outrance [utrãːs], s.f. à o., to the bitter end; guerre à o., war to the knife.

outre [uːtr]. 1. prep. (a) beyond; o. mesure, beyond measure, inordinately; (b) in addition to; o. cela, besides, moreover. 2. adv. (a) passer o., to proceed further; passer o. à une objection, to overrule an objection; (b) en o., besides, moreover.

outré [utre], a. (a) exaggerated, overdone (praise); d'une activité outrée, hyperactive; (b) o. de colère, beside oneself with rage.

outre-Atlantique [utratlãtik], adv. phr. on the other side of the Atlantic.

outre-Manche [utrəmãːʃ], adv. phr. across the Channel.

outremer [utrəmeːr], s.m. ultramarine (blue).

outre-mer [utrəmeːr], adv.phr. overseas.

outrer [utre], v.tr. 1. to carry (sth.) to excess; to overdo. 2. to provoke (s.o.) beyond measure.

ouvert [uvɛr], a. open; le gaz est o., the gas is on; plaie ouverte, gaping wound; (b) ville ouverte, open town; (c) o. la nuit, open all night; (d) caractère o., frank nature. adv. -ement, frankly.

ouverture [uvɛrtyːr], s.f. 1. (a) opening (of door, etc.); o. d'hostilités, outbreak of hostilities; (b) faire des ouvertures, to make overtures (to s.o.); (c) Mus: overture; (d) heures d'o., business hours; visiting hours. 2. (a) opening; gap; break; les ouvertures (d'une maison), the doors and windows; (b) span (of arch); El: o. d'induit, armature gap. 3. (parachute) opening. 4. o. d'esprit, broadmindedness.

ouvrable [uvrabl], a. jour o., working day.

ouvrage [uvraːʒ], s.m. 1. (a) work; (b) workmanship. 2. piece of work; product; book; o. en prose, prose work.

ouvre-boîtes [uvrəbwat], s.m.inv. tin-opener, can-opener.

ouvre-bouteille(s) [uvrəbutɛj], s.m. bottle opener. pl. ouvre-bouteilles.

ouvreuse [uvrøːz], s.f. Cin: usherette.

ouvrier, -ère [uvrie, -ɛːr], s. 1. (a) worker; workman, -woman; craftsman, mechanic, operative; (b) mère ouvrière, forewoman; (c) être l'o. de sa fortune, to be a self-made man. 2. a. les classes ouvrières, the working classes; le parti o., the labour party; conflits ouvriers, industrial disputes.

‡ouvrir [uvriːr]. 1. v.tr. to open; (a) to turn on (a tap, the gas); to switch on (electricity); (b) to open up (canal, mine); (c) to begin. 2. v.i. to open. s'ouvrir, to open; to unbosom oneself (to s.o.).

ovale [ɔval], a. & s.m. oval.

oxyde [ɔksid], s.m. oxide; o. de carbone, carbon monoxide.

s'oxyder, to rust.

oxygène [ɔksiʒɛn], s.m. oxygen.

oxygéné [ɔksiʒene], a. eau oxygénée, peroxide of hydrogen.

ozone [ozɔn], s.m. ozone.

P

P, p [pe], s.m. (the letter) P, p.

pacifi/er [pasifje], v.tr. to pacify; to appease; a. & s. -cateur, -catrice, (i) a. peace-making; (ii) s. peace-maker. s.f. -cation.

pacifique [pasifik], a. (a) peaceable; (b) peaceful, quiet. adv. -ment.

paci/fisme [pasifism], s.m. Pol: pacifism. s.m. & f. -fiste.

pacte [pakt], s.m. pact, agreement.

pagaie [pagɛ], s.f. paddle (for canoe).

pagaïe, pagaille [pagaːj], s.f. disorder, muddle, clutter.

‡pagay/er [pageje], v.tr. & i. to paddle (a canoe). s. -eur, -euse, paddler.

page [paːʒ], s.f. page (of book); F: être à la p., to be (i) with it, (ii) in the know.

paie [pɛ], s.f. 1. pay, wages. 2. payment; jour de p., pay day.

paiement [pɛ(j)mã], s.m. payment.

païen, -ienne [pajɛ̃, -jɛn], a. & s. pagan, heathen.

paill/e [paːj], s.f. straw; (a) chaise de p., straw-bottomed chair; feu de p., flash in the pan; être sur la p., to be reduced to beggary; (b) a.inv. straw-coloured. s.f. -asse, straw mattress. s.m. -asson, (door-)mat.

paillette [pajɛt], s.f. (a) spangle; (b) (savon en) **paillettes**, soap-flakes.

pain [pɛ̃], s.m. 1. bread; p. frais, p. rassis, fresh, stale, bread. 2. loaf; petit p., roll.

pair [pɛːr]. 1. a. (a) equal; de p. (avec), on a par (with); (b) even (number). 2. s.m. (a) equal; (b) peer (of the realm). 3. s.m. a. Fin: par; (b) étudiant(e) au p., au pair student. s.f. -esse, peeress. s.f. -ie, peerage.

paire [pɛːr], s.f. pair (of gloves); brace (of birds); yoke (of oxen).

paisible [pezibl], a. peaceful, quiet. adv. -ment.

‡**paitre** [pɛːtr], v.i. (of animals) to graze.

paix [pɛ], s.f. peace.

palace [palas], s.m. de luxe hotel.

palais¹ [palɛ], s.m. 1. palace. 2. p. de justice, law-courts; gens du p., lawyers.

palais², s.m. (a) palate (of mouth); (b) (sense of) taste.

pâle [pɑl], a. pale (face); faint (light).

paletot [palto], s.m. overcoat.

palette [palɛt], s.f. 1. (table-tennis) bat. 2. paddle. 3. (painter's) palette.

pâleur [palœːr], s.f. pallor, paleness.

palier [palje], s.m. 1. (a) landing (of stairs); (b) stage, degree; taxes imposées par paliers, graduated taxation. 2. Aut: level run; vitesse en p., speed on the flat.

pâlir [palir], v.i. to become pale; to grow dim; to fade.

palissad/e [palisad], s.f. fence; paling; (street) hoarding. v.tr. -er, to fence in; to enclose.

palli/er [palje], v.tr. to palliate; to mitigate. a. & s.m. †-atif, palliative.

palmarès [palmarɛs], s.m. Sch: honours' list.

palmé [palme], a. webbed (foot).

palm/ier [palmje], s.m. palm-tree; huile de p., palm-oil. s.f. -eraie, palm-grove & s.m. -iste, palm-tree.

palombe [palɔ̃ːb], s.f. ring-dove, wood-pigeon.

palourde [palurd], s.f. clam.

palpable [palpabl], a. palpable. 1. tangible. 2. obvious, plain (truth, error).

palper [palpe], v.tr. to feel; to finger (an object).

palpi/ter [palpite], v.i. to palpitate; (a) to quiver; (b) to throb; (c) to thrill. a. -tant, F: thrilling. s.f. -tation.

paludisme [palydism], s.m. Med: malaria.

pamplemousse [pɑ̃pləmus], s.m. grape-fruit.

pan [pɑ̃], s.m. 1. skirt, flap; tail (of garment). 2. p. de mur, part, section, of wall.

panache [panaʃ], s.m. (a) plume; p. de fumée, wreath of smoke; (b) swagger; (c) faire p., (i) to take the header (off horse, cycle); (ii) (of car, aircraft) to turn over.

panais [panɛ], s.m. parsnip.

panama [panama], s.m. panama hat.

pancarte [pɑ̃kart], s.f. placard, bill; (show-)card.

paner [pane], v.tr. to fry (meat, fish) in breadcrumbs.

panier [panje], s.m. basket; p. à salade, (i) salad shaker; (ii) F: Black Maria.

pani/que [panik]. 1. a. panic. 2. s.f. panic, scare; stampede. s.m. F: **-quard**, scaremonger.

panne [pan], s.f. (mechanical) break-down; (electrical, etc.) failure; avoir une p. sèche, to run out of petrol; rester en p., to break down.

panneau [pano], s.m. 1. panel. 2. (advertisement) hoarding; (road) sign.

panoram/a [panorama], s.m. panorama. a. -ique.

pans/er [pɑ̃se], v.tr. 1. to dress (wound). 2. to groom (horse). s.m. -age, grooming (of horse). s.m. -ement, dressing (of wound).

pantalon [pɑ̃talɔ̃], s.m. (pair of) trousers; slacks.

panthère [pɑ̃tɛːr], s.f. panther.

pantin [pɑ̃tɛ̃], s.m. puppet.

pantomime [pɑ̃tɔmim], s.f. pantomime; mime.

pantoufl/e [pɑ̃tufl], s.f. slipper. s.m. F: **-ard**, stay-at-home type.

paon [pɑ̃], s.m. peacock.

papa [papa], s.m. F: papa, dad(dy); bon p., grandad; Aut: marcher à la p., to potter along.

†**papal** [papal], a. papal.

pape [pap], s.m. Ecc: Pope.

pape/rasse [papras], s.f. (usu. pl.) old archives; official papers; F: bumf. s.f. **-rasserie**, collection of old papers; F: red tape.

papet/erie [paptri], s.f. stationer's shop. s. **-ier, -ière**, stationer.

papier [papje], s.m. 1. p. à lettres, notepaper. 2. document, paper.

papillon [papijɔ̃], s.m. 1. butterfly; p. de nuit, moth; Sp: (nage) p., butterfly (stroke). 2. inset (in book); Techn: wing-nut.

papillot/er [papijote], v.i. to blink; (of light) to twinkle; Cin: to flicker. s.m. -ement, dazzle, flicker.

paquebot [pakbo], s.m. Nau: liner.

pâquerette [pakrɛt], s.f. Bot: daisy.

Pâques [pɑːk], s.m. Easter; (but s.f. pl. in) faire ses pâques, to take the Sacrament at Easter; P. fleuries, Palm Sunday.

paquet [pakɛ], s.m. 1. parcel, packet. 2. p. de mer, heavy sea.

par [par], prep. 1. (a) (of place) by; through; regarder p. la fenêtre, to look out of the window; p. tout le pays, all over the country; p. ici, this way; (b) (of time) p. le passé, in the past; p. le froid qu'il fait, in this cold weather. 2. (a) (agent) faire qch. p. soi-même, to do sth. unaided; je l'ai appris p. les Martin, I heard of it through, from, the Martins; (b) (means, instrument) réussir p. l'intrigue, to succeed through intrigue; (c) p. trop aimable, far too kind. 3. (motive) p. pitié! for pity's sake! 4. (distributive) trois fois p. jour, three times a day.

‡parach/ever [paraʃve], v.tr. to finish (sth.) off; to perfect. s.m. -èvement.

parachut/e [paraʃyt], s.m. parachute. s.m. & f. -iste. s.m. -age, drop.

parade [parad], s.f. parade, F: window-dressing; faire p. de, to show off.

parader [parade], v.i. to parade, make a display.

paradis [paradi], s.m. Paradise.

paradox/e [paradɔks], s.m. paradox. a. †-al, paradoxical. adv. -alement.

paraffine [parafin], s.f. Com: paraffin wax; Med: huile de p., liquid paraffin.

paragraphe [paragraf], s.m. paragraph.

‡paraître [parɛːtr], v.i. to appear. 1. (a) to come in sight; (b) to be published; vient de p., just published. 2. to be visible, apparent; cette tache paraît à peine, the stain hardly shows. 3. to seem, to look; il paraît triste, he seems sad; elle paraît son âge, she looks her age; impers: à ce qu'il paraît, as it would appear.

parallèle [paralɛl]. I. a. & s.f. parallel. 2. s.m. (a) parallel, comparison; (b) parallel (of latitude). adv. -ment.

paraly/ser [paralize], v.tr. (a) to paralyse; (b) to incapacitate, to cripple. a. †-sateur, paralysing (agent, etc.). s.f. -sie, paralysis. a. & s. Med: †-tique, paralytic.

paraneige [paranɛːʒ], s.m. snow-shield (over mountain road, railway).

parapet [parapɛ], s.m. parapet.

paraphraser [parafroze], v.tr. (a) to paraphrase; (b) to expand, add to (story, speech).

parapluie [paraplɥi], s.m. umbrella.

parasit/e [parazit]. 1. s.m. parasite; hanger-on. 2. a. parasitic (plant, etc.); Rad: bruits parasites, s.m.pl. parasites, interference. a. -ique, parasitic(al).

parasol [parasɔl], s.m. sunshade, beach umbrella.

paratonnerre [paratɔnɛːr], s.m. lightning-conductor.

paravent [paravɑ̃], s.m. (draught)-screen.

parc [park], s.m. 1. park. 2. p. à voitures, car park, U.S: parking lot; p. d'attractions, fun-fair; p. à enfants, playpen; p. à moutons, sheepfold; p. à huîtres, oyster-bed. 3. fleet (of buses, etc.). s.m. -age, parking.

parcelle [parsɛl], s.f. small fragment; particle; plot, patch (of land).

parceller [parsɛle], v.tr. to portion out (inheritance); to divide (land) into lots.

parce que [pars(ə)kə], conj.phr. because.

parchemin [parʃəmɛ̃], s.m. parchment; papier p., parchment paper.

par-ci par-là [parsi parla], adv. here and there.

parcimon/ie [parsimoni], s.f. stinginess. a. †-ieux, stingy, niggardly. adv. -ieusement.

‡parcourir [parkuriːr], v.tr. 1. to travel through, wander over; p. plusieurs kilomètres, to cover a (distance of) several kilometres. 2. to glance through (a book, etc.).

parcours [parkur], s.m. 1. (a) distance covered; (b) route of bus; course (of river). 2. run, trip.

par-dessous [pardəsu], prep. & adv. under, beneath, underneath.

par-dessus [pardəsy], prep. & adv. over (the top of); p.-d. le marché, into the bargain.

pardessus [pardəsy], s.m. overcoat.

pardon [pardɔ̃], s.m. forgiveness; p. de vous avoir retenu, I'm sorry to have kept you.

pardonn/er [pardɔne], v.tr. to pardon, forgive; pardonnez-moi, excuse me. a. -able, forgivable.

pare-boue [parbu], s.m.inv. mudguard.

pare-brise [parbriːz], s.m.inv. Aut: wind-screen, U.S: windshield.

pare-choc(s) [parʃɔk], s.m.inv. Aut: bumper, U.S: fender.

pareil, -eille [parɛj]. 1. a. (a) like, alike; similar; (b) same, identical; (c) such; like that; en p. cas, in such cases. 2. s. (a) like; mes pareils, my equals; (b) fellow, match; il n'a pas son p., there's no one like him. 3. s.f. la pareille, the like; rendre la pareille à qn, to give s.o. tit for tat.

pareillement [parɛjmɑ̃], adv. 1. in a similar manner. 2. also; likewise; à vous p., the same to you!

parent, -ente [parɑ̃, -ɑ̃ːt], s. 1. s.m.pl. parents. 2. s.m. & f. relation.

parenté [parɑ̃te], s.f. 1. relationship. 2. coll: family, relations.

parenthèse [parɑ̃tɛːz], s.f. 1. bracket; entre parenthèses, in brackets; soit dit par p., by the way.

parer¹ [pare], v.tr. 1. to prepare; to trim (meat, castings). 2. to ornament, embellish (de, with).
se parer, to dress oneself (up).

parer². 1. v.tr. to avoid, ward off (a blow, etc.). 2. v.ind.tr. p. à, to provide, guard, against, to avert (trouble, accident).

pare-soleil [parsɔlɛj], s.m. Aut: sun visor (on windscreen).

paresse [parɛs], s.f. (a) laziness, idleness; (b) sluggishness.

†paresseu/x [paresø]. 1. (a) lazy, idle; (b) sluggish. 2. s. lazy person; F: lazy-bones. adv. -sement, lazily.

parfait [parfɛ]. **1.** *a.* perfect; (a) faultless; (c'est) p.!, excellent!; (b) thorough; *F:* un p. imbécile, a complete idiot. **2.** *s.m. Gram:* perfect (tense). *adv.* -ement.

parfois [parfwa], *adv.* sometimes, at times.

parfum [parfœ̃], *s.m.* **1.** perfume; scent. **2.** flavour; p. vanille, vanilla-flavoured.

parfum/er [parfyme], *v.tr.* to scent; *Cu:* to flavour (with). *s.f.* -erie, perfumery (shop).

pari [pari], *s.m.* **1.** bet, wager. **2.** betting; p. mutuel = the tote.

parier [parje], *v.tr.* to bet, to wager, to lay; p. sur un cheval, to back a horse; p. gros, to bet heavily.

parisien, -ienne [parizjɛ̃, -jɛn], *a. & s.* Parisian.

parjure [parʒyːr]. **1.** *s.m.* perjury. **2.** *s.* perjurer.

parjurer (se) [səparʒyre], *v.pr.* to commit perjury.

parking [parkiŋ], *s.m.* car park, *U.S:* parking lot.

parlant [parlɑ̃], *a.* speaking; talking; portrait p., speaking likeness; *P.T.T:* l'horloge parlante = 'Tim.'

parlement [parləmɑ̃], *s.m.* parliament; legislative assembly. *a.* -aire, parliamentary.

parlementer [parləmɑ̃te], *v.i.* to parley; to discuss terms (avec, with).

parler [parle]. **I.** *v.i.* to speak, talk; entendre p. de qn, qch., to hear of, about, s.o., sth.; faire p. de soi, to get talked about. **II.** *v.tr.* speech, language; (way of) speaking; notre p. régional, our dialect.

parleur, -euse [parlœːr, -øːz], *s.* talker, speaker.

parmi [parmi], *prep.* among(st).

paro/dier [parɔdje], *v.tr.* to parody. *s.f.* -die, parody; skit (de, on).

paroi [parwa], *s.f.* (a) partition-wall; (b) wall (of rock); (rock) face.

paroiss/e [parwas], *s.f.* parish. *a.* †-ial, parochial, parish (hall).

paroissien, -ienne [parwasjɛ̃, -jɛn], *s.* **1.** parishioner. **2.** *s.m.* prayer-book.

parole [parɔl], *s.f.* **1.** word; remark. **2.** promise, word; manque de p., breach of faith. **3.** speech, speaking; (a) delivery; avoir la p. facile, to be a ready speaker; (b) prendre la p., to begin to speak; to take the floor.

paroxysme [parɔksism], *s.m.* paroxysm (of rage, laughter, etc.).

parpaing [parpɛ̃], *s.m.* parpen; breeze block.

parquer [parke], *v.tr.* to pen, to fold (cattle, sheep); to park (cars, etc.).

parquet [parkɛ], *s.m.* floor, flooring.

parrain [parɛ̃], *s.m.* godfather; sponsor. *s.m.* -age, sponsorship.

‡**parsemer** [parsəme], *v.tr.* to strew, sprinkle (de, with).

part [paːr], *s.f.* **1.** share, portion; pour ma p., as for me; prendre qch. en bonne p., to take sth. in good part. **2.** share, participation; faire p. de qch. à qn, to inform s.o. of sth. **3.** nulle p., nowhere; autre p., somewhere else; de p. en p., through and through; d'une p., on the one hand; d'autre p., on the other hand; dites-lui de ma p., tell him from me; *P.T.T:* c'est de la p. de qui? who's speaking? **4.** à p., apart, separately.

partage [partaːʒ], *s.m.* **1.** division; faire le p. de qch., to share out sth.; p. d'un pays, partition of a country. **2.** share, portion; avoir qch. en p., to receive sth. as one's share.

‡**partager** [partaʒe], *v.tr.* **1.** to divide; to share sth. **2.** to share (sth. with s.o.). se partager, to divide; (of river) to branch; (of road) to fork.

partance [partɑ̃ːs], *s.f.* navire, avion, en p., ship, plane, about to sail, take off.

partant [partɑ̃]. **1.** *a.* departing. **2.** *s.m.s.pl Sp:* les partants, the starters.

partenaire [partənɛːr], *s.m.* partner.

parterre [partɛːr], *s.m.* **1.** flower-bed. **2.** *Th:* pit.

parti [parti], *s.m.* **1.** (political, etc.) party; prendre p. pour, contre, qn, to side with, against, s.o. **2.** (marriageable person) un bon p., a good match. **3.** decision, choice; prendre (un) p., to make up one's mind; p. pris, prejudice. **4.** advantage; tirer p. de qch., to turn sth. to account.

†**partial** [parsjal], *a.* partial; biased. *adv.* -ement.

partialité [parsjalite], *s.f.* partiality; bias; unfairness.

participe [partisip], *s.m.* participle.

particip/er [partisipe], *v.i.* to participate (à, in); to (have a) share in; to take a hand in. *s.* -ant, -ante, participator. *s.f.* -ation.

particular/iser [partikylarize], *v.tr.* to specify (details); to give particulars (of sth.). *s.f.* -ité, detail; peculiarity. se particulariser, to make oneself conspicuous.

particule [partikyl], *s.f.* particle; p. nobiliaire = de (before name).

particul/ier, -ière [partikylje, -jɛr]. **1.** *a.* (a) particular, special; (b) peculiar, characteristic; (c) unusual; (d) private (room, lesson). **2.** *s.* (simple) p., private person. **3.** *s.m.* en p., particularly; recevoir qn en p., to receive s.o. privately. *adv.* -ièrement.

partie [parti], *s.f.* **1.** part (of a whole); *Gram: pl.* parts (of speech); les parties du corps, the parts of the body; en grande p., to a great extent. **2.** (a) p. de plaisir, picnic, outing; (b) game, match.

†**partiel** [parsjɛl], *a.* partial, incomplete. *adv.* -lement.

‡**partir**, *v.i.* (*aux:* être) (*a*) to depart, leave; to start, to go away; nous **voilà partis!**, now we're off!; (*b*) (*of button, etc.*) to come off; (*of rope*) to part, to give way; (*of gun*) to go off; p. **d'un éclat de rire**, to burst out laughing; (*c*) to emanate, spring (from); **il est parti de rien**, the rose from nothing; (*d*) **à p. d'aujourd'hui**, from today.

partisan [partizɑ̃], *s.m.* 1. partisan supporter. 2. guer(r)illa (soldier).

partition [partisjɔ̃], *s.f. Mus:* score.

partout [partu], *adv.* everywhere; on all sides.

parure [paryːr], *s.f.* (*a*) dress, finery; (*b*) ornament; set of jewellery.

‡**parvenir** [parvəniːr], *v.i.* (*aux:* être) 1. to arrive; **p. à un endroit**, to reach a place. 2. (*a*) to attain, reach; to succeed; (*b*) *abs.* to succeed in life.

parvenu [parvəny], *s.* parvenu, upstart; **les parvenus**, the newly rich.

pas¹ [pɑ], *s.m.* 1. step, pace, stride; (*a*) **allonger le p.**, to step out; **faux p.**, (i) slip, (ii) (social) blunder; **avoir le p. sur qn**, to have precedence of s.o.; (*b*) **au p.**, at a walking pace. 2. foot-print. 3. step (of stair); **le p. de la porte**, the doorstep. 4. (mountain) pass, strait; **mauvais p.**, tight corner.

pas², *neg.adv.* not; **je ne sais p.**, I don't know; **p. du tout!**, not at all!

passable [pɑsabl], *a.* tolerable; so-so. *adv.* -**ment**.

passage [pɑsaːʒ], *s.m.* passage. 1. crossing; going past; **droit de p.**, (i) right of way; (ii) toll; **p. interdit**, no thoroughfare. 2. (*a*) way, way through; **p. souterrain**, subway; (*b*) **p. à niveau**, level crossing; **p. clouté**, pedestrian crossing.

passag/er, -**ère** [pɑsaːʒe, -ɛːr]. 1. *a.* fleeting, transitory. 2. *s.* passenger (by sea or air). *adv.* -**èrement**.

passant, -**ante** [pɑsɑ̃, -ɑ̃t], *s.* passer-by.

passe [pɑːs], *s.f.* 1. permit; pass. 2. **être en mauvaise p.**, to be in a tight corner.

passé [pɑse]. 1. *a.* (*a*) past; gone by; **la semaine passée**, last week; (*b*) faded. 2. *s.m.* past; **oublions le p.**, let bygones be bygones; *Gram:* **verbe au p.**, verb in the past tense.

passe-partout [pɑspartu], *s.m.inv.* 1. master-key. 2. crosscut saw.

passe-passe [pɑspɑs], *s.m.* (*no pl.*) (*a*) **tour de p.-p.**, conjuring trick; (*b*) fraud.

passeport [pɑspɔːr], *s.m.* passport.

passer [pɑse]. I. *v.i.* 1. (*aux.* avoir *or* être) to pass; to go past; to proceed; **p. sur un pont**, to cross a bridge; **faire p. le plat**, to hand round the dish; **par où est-il passé?** which way did he go? **en passant**, by the way; **son chemin**, to go one's way; (**faire**) **p. le café**, to filter the coffee. 2. (*aux.*

avoir) to undergo, pass through (sorrow, sickness). 3. (*aux.* avoir) (*a*) to pass away, off; **la douleur a passé**, the pain has gone; (*b*) to elapse, go by. 4. (*aux.* avoir *or* être) to die. 5. *pred.* (*a*) (*aux.* avoir *or* être) to become; **p. capitaine**, to be promoted captain; (*b*) (*aux.* avoir) to pass for; **p. pour riche**, to be considered rich. II. *v.tr.* 1. to pass, cross (bridge, sea). 2. (*a*) to carry across; to ferry (goods, etc.) over; (*b*) **p. qch. à qn**, to hand, to pass sth. to s.o.; **je vous passe sa secrétaire**, I'll put you through to his secretary; *Cin:* to show (film). 3. to pass, spend (time). 4. to go beyond, exceed; **cela passe mes capacités**, that's beyond my powers. 5. (*a*) to pass over; to excuse (fault); (*b*) to omit, leave out. 6. (*a*) **p. une loi**, to pass a law; (*b*) **p. un examen**, (i) to sit for, (ii) to get through, an exam.

se passer. 1. to happen; to take place. 2. **se p. de qch.**, to do without sth.

passerelle [pɑsrɛl], *s.f.* 1. foot-bridge. 2. *Nau:* bridge; *Av:* steps.

passe-temps [pɑstɑ̃], *s.m.inv.* pastime.

passeur [pɑsœːr], *s.m.* ferryman.

passible [pɑsibl], *a.* liable (de, to, for).

‡**pass/if** [pɑsif]. 1. *a.* passive (obedience, voice). 2. *s.m.* liabilities. *adv.* -**ivement**.

passion [pɑsjɔ̃], *s.f.* 1. Passion (of Christ). 2. **p. pour la musique**, passion for music; **parler sans p.**, to speak dispassionately.

passionné, -**ée** [pɑsjɔne], *a.* passionate; ardent; *s.* enthusiast, *F:* fan. *adv.* -**ment**.

‡**passionnel** [pɑsjɔnɛl], *a.* **crime p.**, crime due to jealousy.

passionner [pɑsjɔne], *v.tr.* to impassion; to interest (s.o.) greatly; **le sport le passionne**, *F:* he's mad keen on sport, games; **livre qui passionne**, book that thrills you.

se passionner de, pour, qch., to become enthusiastic about sth.

passoire [pɑswaːr], *s.f. Cu:* strainer, colander.

pastel [pastɛl], *s.m.* pastel.

pasteur [pastœːr], *s.m.* 1. shepherd. 2. *Ecc:* (protestant) minister, pastor.

pasteuris/er [pastœrize], *v.tr.* to pasteurize (milk). *s.f.* -**ation**.

pastille [pastiːj], *s.f.* lozenge; **p. de chocolat**, chocolate drop.

pataug/er [patoʒe], *v.i.* (*a*) to flounder (in the mud); (*b*) to paddle (in sea).

pâte [pɑːt], *s.f.* (*a*) paste; dough; **p. brisée**, short pastry; **pâtes** (**alimentaires**), noodles, spaghetti, etc.; (*b*) **p. dentifrice**, toothpaste.

pâté [pɑte], *s.m.* 1. *Cu:* pâté; **p. de foie**, liver pâté; **p. en croûte**, meat pie. 2. block (of houses). 3. (ink-)blot.

patente [patã:t], *s.f.* licence (to exercise a trade).

patère [pate:r], *s.f.* hat-, coat-peg.

‡paternel/el [paternɛl], *a.* paternal. *adv.* **-ellement.**

paternité [paternite], *s.f.* paternity.

‡pâteux [pɑtø], *a.* (*a*) pasty, doughy; coated (tongue); (*b*) thick (voice); muddy (ink).

pathétique [patetik]. 1. *a.* pathetic, touching. 2. *s.m.* pathos. *adv.* **-ment.**

patholo/gie [patɔlɔʒi], *s.f.* pathology. **-gique.** *s.m.* **-giste.**

patience [pasjã:s], *s.f.* patience, long-suffering.

pati/ent, -ente [pasjã, -ã:t]. 1. *a.* patient. 2. *s.* (surgical) patient. *adv.* **-emment.**

patienter [pasjãte], *v.i.* to wait (patiently).

patin [patɛ̃], *s.m.* (*a*) skate; p. à roulettes, roller skate; (*b*) runner (of sledge); (*c*) brake-block.

patin/er [patine], *v.i.* to skate; (of wheel) to skid. *s.m.* **-age,** skating. *s.* **-eur, -euse,** skater.

pâtisse/rie [pɑtisri], *s.f.* 1. pastry, (fancy) cake. 2. tea-rooms. *s.* **-ier, -ière,** pastrycook.

patraque [patrak], *a. F:* se sentir p., to feel seedy, off colour.

patois [patwa], *s.m.* patois.

patriar/che [patriarʃ], *s.m.* patriarch. *a.* **†-cal.** **-calement.**

patrie [patri], *s.f.* fatherland; one's birthplace; mère p., mother country.

patrimoine [patrimwan], *s.m.* heritage.

patriot/e [patriɔt], *s.* patriot. *a.* **-ique.** *adv.* **-iquement.** *s.m.* **-isme.**

patron, -onne [patrɔ̃, -ɔn], *s.* 1. patron (saint). 2. (*a*) master, mistress (of house); employer; owner (of firm), proprietor; (*b*) skipper (of small vessel). 3. *s.m.* pattern (for dress); model. *a. -ne.* **-age.**

patrouil/e [patruj], *s.f.* patrol. *v.i.* **-er,** to patrol. *s.m.* **-eur,** patrol boat.

patte [pat], *s.f.* 1. paw; foot (of bird); leg (of insect). 2. clamp, clip, fastening. 3. tab, strap.

patte-d'oie [patdwa], *s.f.* 1. crossroads. 2. crow's-foot (wrinkle). *pl.* **pattes-d'oie.**

pâtur/e [pɑty:r], *s.f.* food, feed, fodder. *v.i.* **-er,** to graze. *s.m.* **-age,** pasture.

paume [po:m], *s.f.* palm (of hand).

paupière [popjɛ:r], *s.f.* eyelid.

pause [po:z], *s.f.* 1. pause; *Fb:* half time; *Ind:* p. café = tea break. 2. *Mus:* rest.

pauvre [po:vr]. 1. *a.* poor; (*a*) needy, in want; (*b*) unfortunate; (*c*) mean, shabby. 2. *s.* poor person; pauper. *adv.* **-ment.** *s.f.* **-té** poverty.

pavé [pave], *s.m.* 1. paving-stone. 2. (*a*) pavement; (*b*) paved road.

pav/er [pave], *v.tr.* to pave. *s.m.* **-age,** paving; pavement.

pavillon [pavijɔ̃], *s.m.* 1. pavilion; detached building; p. de banlieue, suburban house; p. de jardin, summer-house. 2. flag, colours.

pavois/er [pavwaze], *v.tr.* to deck with flags. *s.m.* **-ement.**

pavot [pavo], *s.m.* poppy.

paye [pɛj], *s.f.* pay, wages.

‡payer [peje], *v.tr.* to pay; (*a*) p. qn., to pay s.o.; trop payé, trop peu payé, overpaid, underpaid; p. d'audace, to take the risk; p. d'effronterie, to put a bold face on it; (*b*) to pay, settle (debt); p. la note, to foot the bill; congés payés, holidays with pay; (*c*) to pay for sth.; p. un dîner à qn., to stand s.o. a dinner; se p. une glace, to treat oneself to an ice; se p. la tête de qn., to make fun of s.o.; port payé, carriage paid.

pays [pe(j)i], *s.m.* country; (*a*) land; les p. chauds, the tropics; (*b*) region, district; vin du p., local wine; (*c*) native land; home; avoir le mal du p., to be homesick.

paysag/e [peiza:ʒ], *s.m.* 1. landscape; scenery. 2. landscape (painting). *s.m.* **-iste,** landscape-painter; -gardener.

paysan, -anne [peizɑ̃, -an], *s. & a.* country(man, -woman).

péag/e [pea:ʒ], *s.m.* toll. *s.* **-er, -ère,** toll-collector.

peau [po], *s.f.* 1. skin. 2. pelt, fur; hide; leather. 3. peel, skin (of fruit); skin (of boiled milk).

pêch/e[1] [pɛ:ʃ], *s.f.* peach. *s.m.* **-er[1],** peach tree.

pêche[2], *s.f.* 1. fishing. 2. catch (of fish). 3. fishery.

péché [peʃe], *s.m.* sin.

‡pécher [peʃe], *v.i.* to sin.

pêcher[2] [peʃe], *v.tr.* 1. to fish for (trout, compliments). 2. p. une truite, to catch a trout.

pêcheur, pécheresse [peʃœ:r, peʃrɛs], *s.* sinner.

pêcheur, -euse [peʃœ:r, -ø:z]. 1. *s.* fisherman, -woman. 2. *a.* fishing (boat).

pédale [pedal], *s.f.* pedal; treadle; frein à p., footbrake; p. d'embrayage, clutch pedal; *Mus:* petite, grande, p., soft, loud, pedal.

pédaler [pedale], *v.i.* to pedal; to cycle.

pédant, -ante [pedã, -ã:t]. 1. *s.* pedant. 2. *a.* pedantic, -ism, pedantry.

pédia/trie [pedjatri], *s.f. Med:* pediatrics. *s.m.* or *f.* **-tre,** pediatrician.

pédicure [pediky:r], *s.m. & f.* chiropodist.

peigne [pɛɲ], *s.m.* comb.

peign/er [peɲe], *v.tr.* to comb (out); mal peigné, slatternly (person); tousled (hair). *s.m.* **-oir,** dressing-gown. se peigner, to comb one's hair.

‡peindre [pɛ̃:dr], *v.tr.* to paint; papier peint, wallpaper.

peine [pɛn], *s.f.* **1.** punishment, penalty. **2.** (*a*) sorrow, affliction; faire de la p. à qn., to distress s.o.; (*b*) être dans la p., to be in trouble, want. **3.** pains, trouble; se donner de la p., to take trouble (over doing sth.). **4.** difficulty; à grand-p., with (great) difficulty. **5.** à p., hardly, scarcely.

peiner [pɛne], **1.** *v.tr.* to pain, distress (s.o.). **2.** *v.i.* to toil, labour.

peintre [pɛ̃tr], *s.m.* painter. **1.** (artiste-) p., artist; une femme p., a woman artist. **2.** p. en bâtiment(s), house-painter, decorator.

peinture [pɛ̃tyːr], *s.f.* **1.** painting. **2.** paint, colour; prenez garde à la p.!, wet paint.

pêle-mêle [pɛlmɛl], **1.** *adv.* pell-mell. **2.** *s.m.inv.* jumble, medley, confusion.

‡peler [p(ə)le], *v.tr. & i.* to peel; to skin (fruit); campagne pelée, bare country-side.

pèlerin [pɛlrɛ̃], *s.* pilgrim. *s.m.* -age.

pelle [pɛl], *s.f.* **1.** shovel, scoop; dustpan; (child's) spade. **2.** blade (of oar).

pelle/terie [pɛltri], *s.f.* coll: fur-skins, pelts. **1.** fur-trade. *s.* -tier, -tière, furrier.

pellicule [pel(l)ikyl], *s.f.* **1.** (*a*) thin skin; film (of ice, oil); (*b*) Phot: film. **2.** pl. dandruff.

pelote [plɔt], *s.f.* **1.** ball (of wool); avoir les nerfs en p., to be nervy, on edge. **2.** Sp: p. basque, pelota.

peloton [plɔtɔ̃], *s.m.* **1.** group (of people); Sp: le p., the ruck (of runners in a race). **2.** squad, party.

pelouse [pluːz], *s.f.* lawn.

peluche [plyʃ], *s.f.* plush; ours en p., teddy-bear.

pelure [plyːr], *s.f.* peel, skin; pairing; rind; p. d'oignon, dark rosé wine.

‡pénal [penal], *a.* a penal (code).

pénalis/er [penalize], *v.tr.* Sp: to penalize (a competitor, a player). *s.f.* -ation.

pénalité [penalite], *s.f.* Jur: Sp: penalty.

penaud [pəno], *a.* crestfallen; d'un air p., sheepishly.

penchant [pɑ̃ʃɑ̃], **1.** *a.* sloping, leaning (wall, tower). **2.** *s.m.* (*a*) slope; (*b*) leaning, tendency (to sth., s.o.); suivre son p., to follow one's bent; avoir un p. pour qn, to be (rather) fond of s.o.

pencher [pɑ̃ʃe], *v.tr. & i.* to bend, lean (forward, over).
se pencher, to bend, lean; se p. (en), (au), dehors, to lean out.

pendant [pɑ̃dɑ̃]. **I.** *a.* **1.** hanging, pendent; joues pendantes, baggy cheeks. **2.** pending (lawsuit); in suspense. **II.** *s.m.* **1.** pendant; p. d'oreille, drop earring. **2.** match, fellow. **III.** **1.** *prep.* during; p. l'été, during the summer; p. trois jours, for three days;

conj. phr. p. que, while, whilst. **2.** *adv.* during; je lis p. le repas, I read during my meal.

penderie [pɑ̃dri], *s.f.* (hanging) wardrobe.

pendre [pɑ̃dr], **1.** *v.tr.* (*a*) to hang (sth.) up; to hang (on the gallows). **2.** *v.i.* to hang (down), to sag.

pendu [pɑ̃dy], **1.** *a.* hanged; hung; hanging. **2.** *s.m.* hanged man.

pendule [pɑ̃dyl], **1.** *s.m.* pendulum. **2.** *s.f.* clock.

‡pénétr/er [penetre], *v.* to penetrate. **1.** *v.i.* to enter. **2.** *v.tr.* to penetrate; to pierce; to fathom; p. la pensée de qn., to see through s.o. *a.* -able. *a.* -ant, penetrating, sharp (wind, glance). *s.f.* -ation, shrewdness.

pénible [penibl], *a.* **1.** laborious, toilsome. **2.** painful, distressing, sad. *adv.* -ment.

péniche [peniʃ], *s.f.* barge, canal boat; Mil: p. de débarquement, landing craft.

pénicilline [penisilin], *s.f.* penicillin.

péninsul/e [penɛ̃syl], *s.f.* peninsula. *a.* -aire, peninsular.

pénit/ence [penitɑ̃ːs], *s.f.* **1.** penitence, repentance. **2.** penance; il est en p., he's in disgrace. *s.m.* -encier, reformatory (prison). *a. & s.* -ent, penitent.

pénombre [penɔ̃br], *s.f.* half-light.

pensée[1] [pɑ̃se], *s.f.* thought.

pensée[2], *s.f.* Bot: pansy.

pens/er [pɑ̃se], *v.* to think. **1.** *v.ind.tr.* p. à qn, qch., to think of s.o., sth.; vous n'y pensez pas! you don't mean it! **2.** *v.i.* manière de p., attitude of mind; je pense comme vous, I agree with you; pensez donc! just fancy! **3.** *v.tr.* (*a*) je le pensais bien, I thought as much; (*b*) to expect (to do sth.); je pense le voir, I expect to see him; j'ai pensé mourir, I nearly died. *s.* -eur, -euse, thinker. *a.* †-if, thoughtful. *adv.* -ivement.

pension [pɑ̃sjɔ̃], *s.f.* **1.** pension, allowance; p. viagère, life annuity. **2.** (*a*) être en p. chez qn, to board with s.o.; (*b*) p. de famille, residential hotel. **3.** (private) boarding-school. *s.m. & f.* -naire, pensioner; boarder. *s.m.* -nat, boarding-school.

pensionner [pɑ̃sjɔne], *v.tr.* to pension.

pente [pɑ̃ːt], *s.f.* slope, gradient.

Pentecôte [pɑ̃tkoːt], *s.f.* Whitsun(tide).

pénurie [penyri], *s.f.* scarcity, shortage; lack; (*b*) poverty.

pépi/er [pepje], *v.i.* (of birds) to cheep, to chirp. *s.m.* -ement.

pépin[1] [pepɛ̃], *s.m.* pip; stone; F: avoir un p., to have a spot of bother.

pépin[2], *s.m.* F: umbrella, F: brolly.

pépin/ière [pepinjɛːr], *s.f.* seed-bed; nursery. *s.m.* -iériste, nursery gardener.

perçant [pɛrsɑ̃], *a.* piercing (eyes, sound); shrill (voice); biting (wind).

percée [pɛrse], s.f. (a) glade; vista; (b) opening (in wall); (c) faire une p., to break through.

perce-neige [pɛrsənɛːʒ], s.m.inv. snow-drop.

perce-oreille [pɛrsɔrɛːj], s.m. earwig. pl. perce-oreilles.

perceptible [pɛrsɛptibl], a. 1. perceptible (à, by, to); discernible. 2. collectable (tax). adv. -ment, perceptibly.

†**perceptif** [pɛrsɛptif], a. perceptive.

percep/tion [pɛrsɛpsjɔ̃], s.f. 1. perception. 2. collection, receipt (of taxes, etc.). s.m. -teur, tax-collector.

‡**per/cer** [pɛrse]. 1. v.tr. (a) to pierce, to go through; p. un abcès, to lance an abscess; (b) to perforate; to make an opening in; p. un tonneau, to tap a cask; (c) to bore (tunnel, etc.). 2. v.i. to pierce; to come through. s.m. -çage. s.m. -cement. s.f. -ceuse, drill, drilling machine.

‡**percevoir** [pɛrsəvwaːr], v.tr. 1. to perceive, discern. 2. to collect (taxes).

perche [pɛrʃ], s.f. (thin) pole; Sp: saut à la p., pole-vaulting.

perch/er [pɛrʃe], v.i. to perch, roost. s.m. -oir, (bird's) perch.

se percher, to alight, perch.

percolateur [pɛrkɔlatœːr], s.m. percolator.

percussion [pɛrkysjɔ̃], s.f. percussion, impact, Mus: instruments à, de, p., percussion instruments.

percut/er [pɛrkyte], v.tr. to strike sth.; la voiture percuta un arbre, the car hit a tree. a. -ant, percussive, percussion. s.m. -eur, striker (of gun, fuse).

perdant, -ante [pɛrdɑ̃, -ãːt], a. losing. 2. s. loser.

perdre [pɛrdr], v.tr. 1. to lose; p. la partie, to lose the game; p. son temps, to waste one's time. 2. Abs: (a) le fût perd, the cask is leaking; (b) p. sur ses concurrents, to fall behind.

se perdre, to be lost; to vanish, disappear; to leak away, to escape.

perdr/ix [pɛrdri], s.f. partridge. s.m. -eau, young partridge.

perdu [pɛrdy], a. 1. ruined; âme perdue, lost soul. 2. lost; heures perdues, spare time; emballage p., non-returnable packing. 3. à corps p., recklessly.

père [pɛr], s.m. 1. father; M. Martin p., Mr Martin senior; F: le p. Martin, old (Mr) Martin. 2. Ecc: le Saint P., the Holy Father, the Pope; le P. Martin, Father Martin.

péremptoire [perɑ̃ptwaːr], a. peremptory (tone). adv. -ment.

perfection [pɛrfɛksjɔ̃], s.f. perfection; à la p., perfectly.

perfectionn/er [pɛrfɛksjɔne], v.tr. 1. to perfect. 2. to improve (machine, method). s.m. -ement, perfecting, improvement.

se perfectionner dans qch., to improve one's knowledge of sth.

perfide [pɛrfid], a. treacherous; perfidious. adv. -ment.

perfor/er [pɛrfɔre], v.tr. to perforate; to bore (through); to drill; to punch; carte perforée, punch card. s.m. -ateur, drill, punch. s.f. -ation. s.f. -euse, perforating machine.

péricliter [periklite], v.i. (of undertaking) to be in danger; ses affaires périclitent, his business is in a bad way.

péril [peril], s.m. peril, danger; risk.

†**périlleu/x** [perijø], a. perilous. adv. -sement.

périmé [perime], a. out-of-date; lapsed (ticket, passport).

périod/e [perjɔd], s.f. period. a. & s.m. -ique, periodical. adv. -iquement.

péripéties [peripesi], s.f. pl. ups and downs (of life); adventures.

pér/ir [periːr], v.i. to perish. a. -issable, perishable.

périscope [periskɔp], s.m. periscope.

péritonite [peritɔnit], s.f. Med: peritonitis.

perle [pɛrl], s.f. 1. pearl. 2. bead.

permanence [pɛrmanɑ̃ːs], s.f. 1. permanence; assemblée en p., permanent assembly. 2. (office, etc.) always open to the public; p. de police, police station open night and day; p. de trois employés, staff of three always on duty.

permanent [pɛrmanɑ̃]. 1. a. permanent; spectacle p., continuous performance. 2. s.f. permanente, permanent wave.

‡**permettre** [pɛrmɛtr], v.tr. to permit, allow; permettez!, excuse me!; vous permettez?, may I?

permis [pɛrmi]. 1. a. allowed, permissible. 2. s.m. permit; licence; p. de conduire, driving-licence; p. de circulation, car licence.

permission [pɛrmisjɔ̃], s.f. (a) permission, leave; (b) Mil: etc: leave of absence. s.m. -naire, soldier (etc.) on leave.

†**pernicieu/x** [pɛrnisjø], a. pernicious, injurious (action, influence). adv. -sement.

pérorer [perɔre], v.i. F: to hold forth, speechify.

perpendiculaire [pɛrpɑ̃dikylɛːr], a. & s. perpendicular. adv. -ment.

‡**perpétr/er** [pɛrpetre], v.tr. to perpetrate (crime, etc.). s.f. -ation.

perpét/uer [pɛrpetɥe], v.tr. to perpetuate. s.f. -uation. a. †-uel, perpetual, for life. adv. -uellement.

se perpétuer, to endure; to become established.

perpétuité [pɛrpetɥite], s.f. endlessness; à p., for ever; (penal servitude) for life.

perplexe [pɛrplɛks], a. perplexed, puzzled.

perplexité [pɛrplɛksite], s.f. perplexity.

perquisition [pɛrkizisjɔ̃], *s.f.* thorough search, inquiry; search-warrant.

perquisitionner [pɛkizisjɔne], *v.i.* p. chez qn, (*of police*) to search s.o.'s house.

perron [pɛrɔ̃], *s.m.* (flight of) steps.

perroquet [pɛrɔke], *s.m.* parrot.

perruche [pɛryʃ], *s.f.* (*a*) parakeet; (*b*) hen-parrot; (*c*) p. inséparable, budgerigar.

perruque [pɛryk], *s.f.* wig.

persécu/ter [pɛrsekyte], *v.tr.* (*a*) to persecute; (*b*) to pester (s.o.). *s.* -teur, -trice, persecutor. *s.f.* -tion.

‡persévér/er [pɛrsevere], *v.i.* to persevere (dans, in); to carry on. *s.f.* -ance. *a.* -ant, persevering.

persil [pɛrsi], *s.m.* parsley.

persist/er [pɛrsiste], *v.i.* to persist. *s.f.* -ance, persistence. *a.* -ant, persistent.

personnage [pɛrsɔnaʒ], *s.m.* (*a*) personage; être un p., to be somebody; (*b*) character (in play).

personnalité [pɛrsɔnalite], *s.f.* personality. 1. individuality. 2. personage; c'est une p., he's an important man.

personne [pɛrsɔn]. 1. *s.f.* person; (*a*) individual; une tierce p., a third party; les grandes personnes, the grown-ups; (*b*) own self; en p., in person; personally. (*c*) Gram.: (first, second, etc.) person. 2. *pron.indef.m. inv.* (*a*) anyone; (*with vaguely implied negation*) il s'y connaît comme p., nobody's better at it than he is; (*b*) (*with ne expressed or understood*) no one, nobody; je n'ai vu p., I didn't see anyone; p. n'était là, nobody was there.

†personnel [pɛrsɔnel]. 1. *a.* personal. 2. *s.m.* personnel, staff. *adv.* -lement.

personnifi/er [pɛrsɔnifje], *v.tr.* to personify. *s.f.* -cation.

†perspectif, -ive [pɛrspɛktif, -i:v]. 1. *a.* perspective. 2. *s.f.* perspective, outlook, view; prospect.

perspi/cacité [pɛrspikasite], *s.f.* shrewdness. *a.* -cace, shrewd.

persuader [pɛrsɥade], *v.tr.* to persuade; convince (s.o.) (de, of).

persua/sion [pɛrsɥazjɔ̃], *s.f.* 1. persuasion. 2. conviction, belief. *a.* †-if.

perte [pɛrt], *s.f.* 1. ruin, destruction. 2. loss; vendre à p., to sell at a loss; p. de temps, waste of time. 3. loss, leakage; El: p. de charge, drop in voltage.

pertin/ent [pɛrtinã], *a.* pertinent; relevant (à, to). *adv.* -emment.

perturbation [pɛrtyrbasjɔ̃], *s.f.* (*a*) agitation (of mind); (*b*) disturbance; Meteo: depression; Rad: (*usu. pl.*) atmospherics.

pervers [pɛrvɛːr], *a.* perverse, depraved. *adv.* -ement.

pervers/ion [pɛrvɛrsjɔ̃], *s.f* perversion. *s.f.* -ité.

pervertir [pɛrvɛrtiːr], *v.tr.* to pervert, to corrupt.

pesage [pəzaːʒ], *s.m.* 1. bureau de p., weigh-house. 2. Sp: (*a*) weighing in; (*b*) (members') enclosure.

pes/ant [pəzã], *a.* heavy, weighty. *adv.* -amment.

pesanteur [pəzãtœr], *s.f.* 1. weight; Ph: gravity. 2. (*a*) heaviness; (*b*) dullness (of mind).

pèse-bébé [pɛzbebe], *s.m.* baby-scales. *pl.* pèse-bébés.

pèse-lettre(s) [pɛzlɛtr], *s.m.* letter-scales. *pl.* pèse-lettres.

pèse-personne [pɛzpɛrsɔn], *s.m.* bathroom scales. *pl.* pèse-personnes.

‡peser [pəze]. 1. *v.tr.* to weigh (parcel; one's words); to ponder (advice). 2. *v.i.* to weigh; to be heavy; to press hard on (sth.).

pessim/isme [pesimism], *s.m.* pessimism. *a.* & *s.* -iste, (i) pessimistic; (ii) pessimist.

peste [pɛst], *s.f.* plague, pestilence; F: (*of child*) nuisance.

pétale [petal], *s.m.* petal.

pétanque [petãːk], *s.f.* (game of) bowls.

pétard [petaːr], *s.m.* firecracker; P: faire du p., to kick up a row.

pétill/er [petije], *v.i.* to crackle; (*of champagne*) to sparkle, bubble; pétillant d'esprit, sparkling with wit. *s.m.* -ement.

petit, -ite [pəti, -it], *a.* 1. small, little; en p., in miniature; p. à p., bit by bit. 2. insignificant, petty; p. négociant, small tradesman; petite propriété, smallholding. 3. mean, ungenerous; petites âmes, small-minded people. 4. *s.* little boy, girl; pauvre petit(e), poor little thing. 5. *s.m.pl.* young (of animals).

petite-fille [pə(ə)titfij], *s.f.* granddaughter. *pl.* petites-filles.

petitesse [pətites], *s.f.*; (*a*) smallness; (*b*) meanness, pettiness; faire des petitesses, to do mean things.

petit-fils [pə(ə)tifis], *s.m.* grandson. *pl.* petits-fils.

pétition [petisjɔ̃], *s.f.* petition.

pétitionn/er [petisjɔne], *v.i.* to petition. *s.m.* & *f.* -aire, petitioner.

petits-enfants [pə(ə)tizãfã], *s.m.pl.* grandchildren.

pétrifier [petrifje], *v.tr.* to petrify; pétrifié de peur, paralysed with fear.

pétrin [petrɛ̃], *s.m.* kneading-trough; F: être dans le p., to be in the soup.

pétr/ir [petriːr], *v.tr.* to knead (dough); to mould (s.o.'s character). *s.m.* -issage. *s.* -isseur, -isseuse, kneader.

pétrole [petrɔl] *s.m.* petroleum; p. brut, crude oil; p. lampant, paraffin oil, *U.S:* kerosene.

†pétrolier [petrɔlje]. 1. *a.* l'industrie pétrolière, the (mineral-)oil industry. 2. *s.m.* (oil) tanker.

pétrolifère [petrolifɛːr] a. gisement p., oilfield.

peu [pø]. 1. adv. (a) little; p. ou point, little or none; quelque p. surpris, somewhat surprised; p. de chose, little; not much; (b) few; p. de gens, few people; (c) p. very; un-; non-; p. intelligent, unintelligent; p. honnête, dishonest. 2. s.m. (a) little, bit; un p. de vin, a little wine; écoutez un p., just listen; (b) sous p., before long; depuis p., lately.

peuple [pœpl], s.m. people. 1. nation; le p. français, the French people. 2. the masses; les gens du p., the people.

peupl/er [pœple], v.tr. to people, populate (country); to stock (fish-pond); to plant (wood). s.m. -ement.

peuplier [pøplie], s.m. poplar.

peur [pœr], s.f. fear, fright; avoir p., to be afraid.

†peureu/x [pœrø], a. timorous; timid. adv. -sement.

peut-être [pøtɛːtr], adv. perhaps, possibly.

phare [faːr], s.m. 1. lighthouse; Av: beacon. 2. headlight.

pharisien [farizjɛ̃], s.m. Pharisee, hypocrite.

pharmac/ie [farmasi], s.f. (a) pharmacy, dispensing; (b) chemist's shop; (c) medicine chest. s. -ien, -ienne, chemist.

phase [faːz], s.f. phase.

phénol [fenɔl], s.m. carbolic acid.

phéno/mène [fenɔmɛn], s.m. (a) phenomenon; (b) freak of nature. a. †-ménal, amazing. adv. -ménalement.

philanthrop/e [filɑ̃trɔp], s.m. philanthropist. s.f. -ie, philanthropy. a. -ique, philanthropic(al).

philatél/ie [filateli], s.f. stamp-collecting. s.m. & f. -iste, stamp-collector.

philosoph/e [filozɔf]. 1. s.m. & f. philosopher. 2. a. philosophical. s.f. -ie, philosophy. a. -ique, philosophic. adv. -iquement.

phobie [fɔbi]. 1. s.f. phobia, morbid fear. 2. as suffix: claustrophobie, claustrophobia.

phonétique [fonetik], a. phonetic; s.f. phonetics. adv. -ment.

phonique [fɔnik], a. acoustic; P.T.T: appel p., buzzer.

phonograph/e [fɔnɔgraf], s.m. gramophone, record-player. s.f. -ie, sound-recording.

phonothèque [fɔnɔtɛk], s.f. record library.

phoque [fɔk], s.m. Z: seal.

phosphate [fɔsfat], s.m. phosphate; p. de chaux, calcium phosphate.

photo [foto], s.f. F: photo; Sp: décision par p., photo-finish.

photocop/ier [fɔtɔkɔpje], v.tr. to photostat. s.f. -ie, photocopy, photostat.

photograph/e [fɔtɔgraf], s.m. photographer. s.f. -ie, (i) photography;

(ii) photograph. a. -ique. adv. -iquement. v.tr. -ier, to photograph.

phrase [fraːz], s.f. sentence; phrase.

physiolog/ie [fizjɔlɔʒi], s.f. physiology. a. -ique, physiological. adv. -iquement.

physionomie [fizjɔnɔmi], s.f. physionomy; face; appearance; il manque de p., his face lacks character.

physiothéra/pie [fizjɔterapi], s.f. Med: physiotherapy. s.m. & f. -piste, physiotherapist.

physique [fizik]. 1. a. physical; bodily (pain); culture p., physical culture. 2. s.f. physics. 3. s.m. physique. adv. -ment.

pianiste [pjanist], s.m. & f. pianist.

piano [pjano], s.m. piano; p. à queue, grand piano.

pic¹ [pik], s.m. 1. pick, pickaxe; p. pneumatique, pneumatic drill. 2. (mountain) peak. adv.phr. à pic, perpendicular(ly), sheer; precipitous.

pic², s.m. woodpecker; pic-vert [pivɛr], green woodpecker.

pie [pi]. 1. s.f. magpie. 2. a. inv. piebald.

pièce [pjɛs], s.f. 1. piece; (a) p. de gibier, head of game; p. d'eau, sheet of water; vin en p., wine in the cask; F: donner une p. à qn., to give s.o. a tip; (b) Th: p. de théâtre, play. 2. (a) piece; part; pièces détachées, (i) spare parts; (ii) component parts; (b) room (in a house); (c) patch (on a garment). 3. fragment, bit; mettre qch. en pièces, to break sth. to pieces.

pied [pje], s.m. 1. (a) foot; mettre p. à terre, to alight; to step ashore; coup de p., kick; aller à p., to walk; (b) footing; le p. me manqua, I lost my footing; tenir p., to stand firm. 2. (a) foot (of stocking, bed); base (of wall); (b) leg (of chair); stem, foot (of glass); (c) p. de céleri, head of celery; (d) stand, rest. 3. foot (measure).

pied-à-terre [pjetatɛr], s.m.inv. pied-à-terre.

pied-de-poule [pjedpul], s.m. Cl: broken check (design).

†piédestal [pjedɛstal], s.m. pedestal.

pied-noir [pjenwaːr], s.m. Algerian (of European descent); pl. pieds-noirs.

piège [pjɛʒ], s.m. trap, snare; tendre un p., to set a trap (à, for).

pierr/e [pjɛr], s.f. (a) stone; p. de taille, ashlar; p. à huile, hone; p. précieuse, gem; (b) Med: calculus. s.f. -aille, road metal, rubble. s.f.pl. -eries, precious stones. a. †-eux, stony.

piété [pjete], s.f. piety.

piétin/er [pjetine]. 1. v.tr. to trample on (sth.). 2. v.i. p. de rage, to dance with rage; p. (sur place), to mark time; cette affaire piétine, this business is hanging fire. s.m. -ement.

piéton [pjetɔ̃], s.m. pedestrian.

piètre [pjɛtr], *a.* wretched, poor (meal, etc.); paltry (excuse).

†pieu [pjø], *s.m.* stake; post; *Civ.E:* pile.

†pieu/x [pjø], *a.* pious, devout. *adv.* **-sement.**

pigeon, -onne [piʒɔ̃, -ɔn], *s.* pigeon.

pignon [piɲɔ̃], *s.m.* 1. gable, gable-end. 2. *El:* pinion.

pile¹ [pil], *s.f.* 1. pile; heap. 2. pier (of bridge). 3. *El:* battery; p. de rechange, refill (for torch); *Atom. Ph:* p. atomique, atomic pile; p. couveuse, breeder reactor.

pile², *s.f.* p. ou face, heads or tails; *F:* s'arrêter p., to stop dead; ça tombe p., it's just right.

piler [pile], *v.tr.* to pound; to crush, to grind.

pilier [pilje], *s.m.* pillar, column, post.

pill/er [pije], *v.tr.* to pillage, sack. *s.m.* **-age,** looting. *a. & s.* **-ard, -arde** (i) *a.* pilfering; (ii) *s.* looter.

pilotage [pilotaʒ], *s.m. Nau: Av:* pilotage, piloting; *Av:* école de p., flying school.

pilote [pilot], *s.m. Nau: Av:* pilot; p. de ligne, airline pilot; p. d'essai, test pilot.

piloter [pilote], *v.tr.* to pilot (ship, aircraft); p. qn dans Londres, to show s.o. round London.

pilule [pilyl], *s.f.* pill.

piment [pimɑ̃], *s.m. Cu:* red pepper.

pimpant [pɛ̃pɑ̃], *a.* smart, spruce.

pin [pɛ̃], *s.m.* pine(-tree); p. d'Écosse, Scotch fir.

pince [pɛ̃s], *s.f.* 1. pincers, pliers; *Surg:* forceps; p. à sucre, sugar tongs; p. à linge, clothes peg; p. -monseigneur, (burglar's) jemmy. 2. claw (of lobster, etc.). 3. *Cl:* pleat, dart.

pincé [pɛ̃se], *a.* affected, supercilious; sourire p., wry smile.

pinceau [pɛ̃so], *s.m.* (artist's) paintbrush.

†pincer [pɛ̃se], *v.tr.* 1. to pinch, nip. 2. to grip, hold fast.

pincettes [pɛ̃sɛt], *s.f.pl.* (a) tweezers; (b) (fire-)tongs.

pinède [pinɛd], *s.f.* pine-grove.

pingouin [pɛ̃gwɛ̃], *s.m.* auk. P: royal, king penguin.

pin/gre [pɛ̃gr], *F:* 1. *a.* stingy. 2. *s.m.* skinflint.

pinson [pɛ̃sɔ̃], *s.m. Orn:* finch; p. vulgaire, chaffinch.

pintade [pɛ̃tad], *s.f.* guinea-fowl.

pioche [pjɔʃ], *s.f.* pickaxe, pick.

pioch/er [pjɔʃe], (a) *v.tr.* to dig (with a pick); (b) *v.tr. & i. Sch: F:* to grind, swot at (sth.); p. son anglais, to swot up one's English. *s.m.* **-age.**

piolet [pjɔlɛ], *s.m.* ice-axe.

pion [pjɔ̃], *s.m.* 1. *Sch: F: Pej:* master on duty, in charge of prep. 2. *(games)* (a) pawn; (b) draughtsman.

pionnier [pjɔnje], *s.m.* pioneer.

pipe [pip], *s.f.* pipe; p. de bruyère, briar p.

piquant [pikɑ̃]. 1. *a.* pungent (smell); piquant (story). 2. *s.m.* prickle, quill; spike.

pique¹ [pik], *s.m.* (at cards) spade(s).

pique², *s.f.* pique, ill-feeling; par p., out of spite.

piqué [pike], *a.* 1. quilted; padded. 2. worm-eaten, damp-spotted; p. de mouches, fly-blown; *F:* être p., to be mad, nuts. 3. sour (wine). 4. *Av:* descente piquée, nose-dive; attaquer en p., to dive-bomb.

pique-nique [piknik], *s.m.* picnic. *pl.* **pique-niques.**

piqu/er [pike], *v.tr.* 1. (a) to prick, sting; (of gnat, etc.) to bite; (b) to nettle, pique (s.o.). 2. to stick, insert (sth. into sth.). 3. p. une tête, to take a header. *s.m.* **-age.** se piquer. 1. to prick oneself. 2. to take offence. 3. se p. de, to pride oneself on (sth., doing sth.).

piquet [pikɛ], *s.m.* 1. peg, stake, post. 2. picket; p. de grève, strike picket.

piqûre [pikyːr], *s.f.* 1. (a) prick, sting; bite (of insect); (b) (hypodermic) injection. 2. small hole; pit (in metal).

pirate [pirat], *s.m.* (a) pirate; (b) plagiarist.

pire [piːr], *a.* 1. worse. 2. le p., the worst.

pis¹ [pi], *s.m.* udder (of cow).

pis², *adv.* (chiefly in certain set phrases; usu. form is plus mal). 1. (comparative) worse; aller de mal en p., to go from bad to worse. 2. (superlative) le p., (the) worst.

pis-aller [pizale], *s.m.inv.* last resource; makeshift.

piscine [pis(s)in], *s.f.* swimming-bath, pool.

pissenlit [pisɑ̃li], *s.m.* dandelion.

pistache [pistaʃ], *s.f.* pistachio(-nut).

piste [pist], *s.f.* 1. (a) running track, race-track; course de p., track-racing; tour de p., lap; *Adm:* route à double p., dual carriageway; (b) *Av:* p. d'envol, runway; p. d'atterrissage, landing strip; (c) *Cin:* p. sonore, sound track. 2. track, trail; scent; fausse p., wrong track.

pistolet [pistolɛ], *s.m.* pistol.

piston [pistɔ̃], *s.m. E:* piston; *F:* avoir du p., to have friends at court.

pitié [pitje], *s.f.* pity, compassion; faire p., to arouse pity.

pitoyable [pitwajabl], *a.* (a) pitiable; (b) paltry, despicable (excuse, etc.). *adv.* **-ment.**

pittoresque [pitorɛsk], *a.* picturesque; quaint.

pivert [piveːr], *s.m.* green woodpecker.

pivoine [pivwan], *s.f.* peony.

pivot [pivo], *s.m.* pivot, pin, axis; swivel.
pivot/er [pivote], *v.i.* to pivot; to turn; to swivel, revolve. *s.m.* **-ement**.
placard [plakaːr], *s.m.* **1.** (wall-)cupboard. **2.** poster, bill, placard.
placarder [plakarde], *v.tr.* to put up (a bill on a wall).
place/r [plas], *s.f.* place. **1.** (*a*) position; **rester sur p.**, F: to stay put; remettre **qch. en p.**, to put sth. away; (*b*) stead; **à votre p.**, if I were you; (*c*) **faire p. à qn**, to make room for s.o.; **p. aux dames!**, ladies first! **2.** (*a*) seat; (*b*) situation office; job; **perdre sa p.**, to lose one's place. **3.** locality, spot; (public) square; **sur p.**, on the spot. *s.m.* **-ier**, door-to-door salesman.
placement [plasmã], *s.m.* **1.** (*a*) bureau de p., employment bureau; (*b*) sale, disposal (of goods). **2.** investment; **faire un p.**, to invest money.
‡placer [plase], *v.tr.* to place. **1.** (*a*) to put, set (in a certain place); (*b*) to find a situation for (s.o.); (*c*) to invest. **2.** to sell, dispose of (goods).
se placer. 1. to take one's place. **2.** to obtain a job.
placide [plasid], *a.* placid; calm. *adv.* **-ment**.
plafond [plafõ], *s.m.* ceiling; Av: ceiling, maximum flying height; Aut: maximum speed.
plafon/ner [plafone], **1.** *v.tr.* to ceil (room). **2.** *v.i.* Av: to fly at the ceiling; Aut: to go at full speed; Pol: les prix **plafonnent à . . .**, prices have reached the ceiling of . . . . *s.m.* **-nage**, ceiling-work. *s.m.* **-neur**, ceiling-plasterer. *s.m.* **-nier**, ceiling light; Aut: roof light.
plage [plaːʒ], *s.f.* **1.** (*a*) beach, shore; (*b*) seaside resort.
plagi/at [plaʒja], *s.m.* plagiarism. *a.* & *s.m.* **-aire**, plagiarist.
plaid/er [plɛde], *v.tr.* to plead; Jur: p. **coupable**, to plead guilty. *s.* **-eur**, **-euse**, litigant.
plaie [plɛ], *s.f.* wound, sore; **p. sociale**, social evil.
plaignant [plɛɲã], *s.* Jur: plaintiff.
‡plaindre [plɛ̃dr], *v.tr.* to pity.
se plaindre, to complain.
plaine [plɛn], *s.f.* plain.
plaint/e [plɛ̃t], *s.f.* **1.** moan, groan. **2.** complaint. *a.* †**-if**, plaintive. *adv.* **-ivement**.
‡plaire [plɛːr], *v.ind.tr.* **p. à qn**, to please s.o.; **cet homme me plaît**, I like this man; *impers.* **s'il vous plaît**, (if you) please; **plaît-il?**, I beg your pardon?
se plaire, to be pleased, happy.
plais/ant [plɛzã], **1.** *a.* (*a*) funny, amusing; (*b*) (*always before the noun*) ridiculous. **2.** *s.m.* mauvais plaisant, practical joker. *adv.* **-amment**.
plaisant/er [plɛzãte], *v.i.* to joke, jest. *s.f.* **-erie**, joke, joking.

plaisir [plɛziːr], *s.m.* pleasure. **1.** delight; **faire p. à qn**, to please s.o.; **à p.**, ad lib. **2.** (*usu. pl.*) amusement, enjoyment.
plan¹ [plã]. **1.** *a.* even, level, flat. **2.** *s.m.* (*a*) plane; (*b*) premier p., (*of picture*) foreground; Th: down-stage.
plan², *s.m.* plan; (*a*) drawing; draft; blueprint; (*b*) scheme, project, design; **p. d'études**, curriculum.
planche [plãːʃ], *s.f.* **1.** (*a*) board, plank; (*b*) shelf. **2.** (printed) plate, engraving.
plancher [plãʃe], *s.m.* floor.
plan/er [plane], *v.i.* (*a*) (of bird) to soar; to hover; (*b*) Av: to glide. *s.m.* Av: **-eur**, glider.
planète [planɛt], *s.f.* planet.
planifi/er [planifje], *v.i.* Adm: to plan. *s.f.* **-cation**, planning.
plant [plã], *s.m.* seedling.
plantation [plãtasjõ], *s.f.* plantation.
plante¹ [plãt], *s.f.* sole (of the foot).
plante², *s.f.* plant; p. potagère, herb; vegetable; **p. à fleurs**, flowering plant.
plant/er [plãte], *v.tr.* **1.** to plant, set, (seeds) to fix set (up); **p. un pieu**, to drive a stake; **p. une tente**, to pitch a tent; F: **p. là qn**, to leave s.o. in the lurch. *s.m.* **-eur**, planter.
se planter, to (take one's) stand (firmly).
planton [plãtõ], *s.m.* Mil: orderly.
‡plantureu/x [plãtyrø], *a.* copious; lavish (meal); luxuriant (countryside). *adv.* **-sement**.
plaque [plak], *s.f.* **1.** plate; sheet (of metal); slab (of stone); **p. de neige**, thick layer of snow. **2.** (ornamental) plaque; **p. de porte**, door-plate. **3.** badge; Aut: p. matricule, number plate.
plaqué [plake], *a.* & *s.m.* **1.** (métal) plated metal; electro-plate; F: c'est **du p.**, it's cheap stuff. **2.** (bois) p., veneered wood.
plaquer [plake], *v.tr.* **1.** (*a*) to veneer (wood); to plate (metal); Fb: to tackle (opponent). **2.** Mus: to strike (and hold) a chord. **3.** P: to forsake, F: to chuck (s.o.); **tout p.**, to chuck everything up.
se plaquer, to lie flat, to flatten oneself (contre, against) (ground, wall).
plastic [plastik], *s.m.* plastic (explosive).
plastique [plastik]. **1.** *a.* plastic; *s.f.* art of modelling. **3.** *a.* Ind: matière **p.**, *s.m.* plastique, plastic.
plat [pla]. **1.** *a.* (*a*) flat, level; mer plate, smooth sea; calme **p.**, dead calm; (*b*) dull, tame; style, vin, p., commonplace style; flat wine; (*c*) tomber à p., to fall flat; **pneu à p.**, flat tyre; être à p., to be exhausted. **2.** *s.m.* (*a*) flat (part); blade; Sp: le p., flat racing; (*b*) dish; (*c*) Cu: course. *adv.* **-ement**.
platane [platan], *s.m.* plane tree.

plateau [plato], *s.m.* 1. (*a*) tray; (*b*) pan, scale (of balance). 2. *Geog:* plateau. 3. *E:* disc, plate; *Aut:* p. d'embrayage, clutch plate; p. tourne-disques, (gramophone) turn-table.

plate-bande [platbɑ̃d], *s.f.* flower-bed. *pl. plates-bandes.*

plate-forme [platform], *s.f.* platform; footplate. *pl. plates-formes.*

platine [platin], *s.m.* platinum.

platitude [platityd], *s.f.* 1. flatness, dullness. 2. platitude.

plâtre [plɑːtr], *s.m.* (*a*) plaster; p. de moulage, plaster of Paris; (*b*) *pl.* plaster-work (in house).

plâtr/er [platre], *v.tr.* to plaster. *s.m.* **-as**, (plaster) debris, rubbish. *a. s.m.* **-ier**, plasterer.

plausible [plozibl], *a.* plausible. *adv.* **-ment.**

plébiscite [plebissit], *s.m.* plebiscite, referendum.

plein [plɛ̃]. 1. *a.* full (de, of) (*a*) filled; bouteille pleine, full bottle; pleine bouteille, bottleful; (*b*) complete, entire; pleine lune, full moon; p. pouvoir, full power; (*c*) solid; (*d*) en p. visage, full in the face; en p. air, in the open. 2. *s.m.* (*a*) faire le p. (d'essence), to fill up with petrol; (*b*) la saison bat son p., the season is in full swing; (*c*) en p. dans le centre, right in the middle. *adv.* **-ement.**

plein-emploi [plɛ̃nɑ̃plwa], *s.m.* full employment.

plénipotentiaire [plenipotɑ̃sjɛːr], *a. &s.m.* (*a*) plenipotentiary; (*b*) authorized (agent).

pleur/er [plœre]. 1. *v.tr.* to weep, mourn, for (s.o., sth.). 2. *v.i.* (*a*) to weep, to cry (sur, over; pour, for); p. de joie, to weep for joy; (*b*) (*of the eyes*) to water, to run.

pleurnicher [plœrniʃe], *v.i.* to whine, snivel, grizzle. *s.* **-ard, -arde,** *s.* **-eur, -euse,** whiner, sniveller. *a.* †**-eux,** tearful, whining.

‡**pleuvoir** [plœvwaːr], *v.* to rain; *v.impers.* il pleut à verse, it's pouring (with rain).

pli [pli], *s.m.* 1. (*a*) *Cl:* fold; pleat; tuck; mise en plis, (hair-)set; *Geog:* fold; (*b*) crease (in trousers, etc.). 2. cover, envelope; sous p. séparé, under separate cover.

plie [pli], *s.f.* plaice.

pli/er [plie]. 1. *v.tr.* (*a*) to fold (up); to strike (tent); (*b*) to bend. 2. *v.i.* (*a*) to bend; (*b*) to submit, yield. *a.* **-able,** flexible. *a. & s.m.* **-ant,** (i) *a.* folding; (ii) *s.* folding chair.

pliss/er [plise]. 1. *v.tr.* to pleat; (*b*) to crease, crumple; to crinkle; p. les yeux, to screw up one's eyes. 2. *v.i. & pr.* to crease, crumple, pucker. *s.m.* **-age.** *s.m.* **-ement.**

plomb [plɔ̃], *s.m.* 1. lead. 2. shot; petit p., bird-shot. 3. fil à p., plumb-line; à

p., vertical(ly). 4. *El:* p. (de sûreté), fuse, cut-out.

plomb/ier [plɔ̃bje], *s.m.* plumber. *s.f.* **-erie,** plumbing.

plongée [plɔ̃ʒe], *s.f.* (*a*) plunge, dive; (*b*) submersion (of submarine).

‡**plong/er** [plɔ̃ʒe]. 1. *v.i.* to plunge; (*a*) to dive; (*b*) (of submarine) to submerge). 2. *v.tr.* to plunge, immerse (s.o., sth., in liquid). *s.m.* **-eoir,** diving-board. *a. & s.m.* **-eur,** (i) *a.* diving; (ii) *s.* diver. se plonger, to immerse oneself (dans, in).

‡**ploy/er** [plwaje]. 1. *v.tr.* to bend (the knee). 2. *v.i.* to bow (under burden). *a.* **-able,** pliable, flexible.

pluie [plɥi], *s.f.* rain; temps de p., wet weather.

plum/e [plym], *s.f.* 1. feather. 2. (pen) nib; dessin à la p., pen-and-ink drawing. *s.m.* **-age,** plumage. *s.m.* **-eau,** feather-duster.

plumer [plyme], *v.tr.* to pluck (poultry); to fleece (s.o.).

plupart (la) [laplypaːr], *s.f.* most; the greater part, number; la p. des hommes, most men; la p. du temps, most of the time, generally; pour la p., for the most part, generally.

†**pluriel** [plyrjɛl], *a. & s.m.* plural.

plus [ply]. 1. *adv.* (*a*) more; deux fois p. grand, twice as large; p. de dix hommes, more than ten men; p. loin, farther on; p. tôt, sooner; (*b*) (le) p. most; (*c*) (*with neg. expressed or understood*) ne . . . p., no more, no longer; il n'est p., he's dead; p. de doute, there is no more doubt about it; (*d*) non p., (not) either; ni moi non p., neither do I; (*e*) (*often* [plys]) also, in addition; (*f*) de p., more; de p. en p., more and more; en p., in addition. 2. *s.m.* (at) most; sans p., (just that and) nothing more; (*b*) most; (tout) au p., at (the very) most; (*c*) *Mth:* plus.

plusieurs [plyzjœːr], *a. & pron.pl.* several.

plus-value [plyvaly], *s.f.* increase in value, appreciation (of land, etc.); excess yield, surplus. *pl. plus-values.*

plutôt [plyto], *adv.* (*a*) rather, sooner; (*b*) rather; on the whole; il faisait p. froid, the weather was cold if anything.

†**pluvieux** [plyvjø], *a.* rainy; wet.

pneu [pnø], *s.m.* tyre.

pneumatique [pnømatik], *a.* pneumatic; air (pump, etc.); canot p., rubber dinghy.

pneumonie [pnømoni], *s.f.* pneumonia.

poche [pɔʃ], *s.f.* 1. pocket. 2. bag, pouch; paper bag; p. d'air, air-pocket.

pocher [pɔʃe], *v.tr.* to poach (eggs); œil poché, black eye.

pochette [pɔʃet], *s.f.* (*a*) hand-bag; (*b*) packet (of paper, etc.); (*c*) *Rec:* sleeve (of record).

poêle¹ [pwal], *s.f.* frying-pan.

poêle², *s.m.* stove; p. à feu continu, slow combustion stove.

poème [pɔɛːm], *s.m.* poem; F: c'est un p., it's priceless.

poésie [poezi], *s.f.* 1. poetry. 2. poem.

poète [pɔɛt], *s.m.* poet; femme p., woman poet.

poétique [poetik], *a.* poetical. *adv.* -ment.

poids [pwa], *s.m.* weight. 1. (a) vendre au p., to sell by weight; (b) importance; gens de p., people of consequence. 2. load, burden; *Av: etc:* p. utile, pay-load; p. mort, dead weight.

poignant [pwaɲɑ̃], *a.* poignant; spectacle p., (i) agonizing; (ii) thrilling, sight.

poignard [pwaɲaːr], *s.m.* dagger.

poignée [pwaɲe], *s.f.* 1. (a) handful; (b) p. de main, handshake. 2. handle (of door, etc.).

poignet [pwaɲɛ], *s.m.* 1. wrist. 2. cuff.

poil [pwal], *s.m.* 1. (a) (of animal) hair; fur, coat; à p. long, shaggy; (b) nap, pile. 2. (of pers.) hair (on the body); F: il a du p., he's got guts!; F: se mettre à p., to strip (naked).

poilu [pwaly], 1. *a.* hairy, shaggy. 2. *s.m.* French soldier (1914–18).

poinçon [pwɛ̃sɔ̃], *s.m.* 1. bradawl. 2. (a) punch; (b) p. de contrôle, hall-mark.

poinçonn/er [pwɛ̃sɔne], *v.tr.* to punch, clip. *s.m.* -age. *s.m.* -eur. *s.f.* -euse, ticket-punch.

‡**poindre** [pwɛ̃ːdr], *v.i.* (of day) to dawn, break; (of plants) to sprout.

poing [pwɛ̃], *s.m.* fist; serrer les poings, to clench one's fists; coup de p., punch; dormir à poings fermés, to sleep soundly.

point¹ [pwɛ̃], *s.m.* 1. hole (in strap). 2. stitch. 3. point; (a) (in time) le p. du jour, daybreak; à p. nommé, in the nick of time; (b) (in space) p. de départ, starting point; p. de vue, (i) point of view; (ii) viewpoint, view; mettre (qch.) au p., to focus, adjust (sth.); to tune (engine); to perfect (invention). 4. (a) point, dot; full stop, *U.S:* period; deux points, colon; p.-virgule, semicolon; p. d'exclamation, exclamation mark; (b) point; score; (c) mark; (d) speck, spot. 5. (a) point, degree; à ce p., so much so; (b) en bon p., in good condition; (c) à p., in the right condition; (cooked) to a turn. 6. point, particular: le p. capital, the main point; p. de droit, point of law.

point², *adv.* p. (du tout), not (at all).

pointe [pwɛ̃t], *s.f.* 1. (a) point; head (of lance); toe (of shoe); coup de p., thrust; p. d'asperge, asparagus tip; sur la p. des pieds, on tiptoe; (b) heures de p., rush hours; (b) p. du jour, daybreak; p. d'ironie, touch of irony; p. de vanille, dash of vanilla. 2. foreland, headland; spit. 3. nail.

pointer [pwɛ̃te], *v.tr.* 1. to check, tick off (names on list); *Ind:* p. à l'arrivée, au départ, to clock in, out. 2. to point, train (gun, etc.).

‡**pointilleux** [pwɛ̃tijø], *a.* 1. touchy (person). 2. particular; fastidious.

pointu [pwɛ̃ty], *a.* sharp-pointed; oreilles pointues, prick ears.

pointure [pwɛ̃tyːr], *s.f.* size in shoes, etc.).

poir/e [pwaːr], *s.f.* 1. pear. 2. *El:* pear-switch. 3. *P:* (a) face, mug; (b) quelle p.!, what a fool! *s.m.* -ier, pear tree.

poireau [pwaro], *s.m.* leek.

pois [pwa], *s.m.* 1. p. de senteur, sweet pea; petits p., green peas. 2. tissu à p., spotted, polka dot, material.

poison [pwazɔ̃], *s.m.* poison.

‡**poisseux** [pwasø], *a.* sticky.

poisson [pwasɔ̃], *s.m.* fish; p. d'eau douce, de mer, fresh-water, sea, fish; p. d'avril, April fool hoax. *s.f.* -nerie, fish shop. *s.* -nier, -nière, fishmonger, fishwife.

poitrine [pwatrin], *s.f.* breast, chest; bosom; tour de p., chest measurement.

poivre [pwavr], *s.m.* pepper.

poivr/er [pwavre], *v.tr.* to pepper (food); *F:* p. l'addition, *F:* to stick it on (the bill); cuisine, récit, poivré, peppery cooking, spicy tale. *s.m.* -ier, pepper-pot. *s.m.* -on, sweet pepper.

polaire [pɔlɛːr], *a.* polar; l'étoile p., the pole-star.

pôle [poːl], *s.m. Geog: El:* pole.

poli [pɔli], 1. *a.* (a) polished; bright; glossy; (b) polite. 2. *s.m.* polish, gloss. *adv.* -ment, politely.

police¹ [pɔlis], *s.f.* 1. faire la p., to keep order. 2. police; appeler P. Secours = to dial 999; P. judiciaire, *F: P.J.* = C.I.D.

police², *s.f.* (insurance) policy.

‡**policier** [pɔlisje], 1. *a.* ordonnance policière, police regulation; roman p., detective novel. 2. *s.m.* policeman; detective.

poliomyélite [pɔljɔmjelit], *s.f. F:* polio [pɔljo], *s.f. Med:* poliomyelitis, *F:* polio.

pol/ir [pɔliːr], *v.tr.* to polish. *s.m.* -issage. *s.f.* -issoire, (shoe-)shining brush.

polisson, -onne [pɔlisɔ̃, -ɔn], *s.* naughty child; scamp. *a.* smutty, mischievousness.

politesse [pɔlites], *s.f.* politeness; good manners.

politicien, -ienne [pɔlitisjɛ̃, -jɛn], *s. usu. Pej:* politician.

politique [pɔlitik], 1. *a.* (a) political; (b) politic, prudent. 2. *s.f.* (a) policy; (b) politics. *adv.* -ment.

pollu/er [pɔlɥe], *v.tr.* to pollute. *s.f.* -tion, pollution.

poltron, -onne [pɔltrɔ̃, -ɔn], 1. *a.* timid. 2. *s.* coward, *F:* funk. *s.f.* -nerie, timidity, *F:* funk.

polyarthrite [pɔliartrit], *s.f. Med:* p. chronique évolutive, rheumatoid arthritis.

poly/copier [pɔlikɔpje], *v.tr.* to stencil; to duplicate. *s.f.* -copie, (duplicated) copy.

polyculture [pɔlikyltyːr], *s.f.* mixed farming.

polyéthylène [pɔlietilɛn], *s.m.* polyethylene.

polyglotte [pɔliglɔt], *a. & s.* polyglot.

polytechnique [pɔlitɛknik], *a.* polytechnic.

polythène [pɔlitɛn], *s.m.I.R.t.m.* polythene.

pommade [pɔmad], *s.f.* pomade, ointment.

pomm/e [pɔm], *s.f.* 1. (a) apple; p. sauvage, crab-apple; (b) p. de terre, potato; bifteck aux pommes frites, steak and chips; pommes chips, potato crisps; (c) p. de pin, pine-cone. 2. knob (on furniture, etc.). *s.f.* -eraie, apple-orchard. *s.f.* -ette, cheek-bone. *s.m.* -ier, apple tree.

pommelé [pɔm(ə)le], *a.* dappled, mottled.

pompe[1] [pɔ̃ːp], *s.f.* pomp, ceremony, display; entrepreneur de pompes funèbres, undertaker; *U.S:* mortician.

pompe[2], *s.f.* pump; p. à incendie, fire-engine; *Aut:* p. à air, à essence, air-pump, petrol pump.

pomper [pɔ̃pe], *v.tr.* to pump.

†pompeu/x [pɔ̃pø], *a.* pompous. *adv.* -sement.

pompiste [pɔ̃pist], *s.m.* petrol pump attendant.

pompier [pɔ̃pje], *s.m.* fireman.

ponce [pɔ̃ːs], *s.f.* (pierre) p., pumice-stone.

ponctualité [pɔ̃ktɥalite], *s.f.* punctuality.

ponctuel [pɔ̃ktɥɛl], *a.* punctual (dans, en, in). *adv.* -lement.

ponctu/er [pɔ̃ktɥe], *v.tr.* to punctuate. *s.f.* -ation.

pond/re [pɔ̃ːdr], *v.tr.* to lay (eggs). *s.f.* -euse, laying hen.

poney [pɔnɛ], *s.m.* pony.

pont [pɔ̃], *s.m.* 1. bridge; p. tournant, swing-bridge; *Av:* p. aérien, airlift; *Adm:* les ponts et chaussées = government department responsible for roads. 2. deck (of ship). 3. *E:* live axle.

pontif/e [pɔ̃tif], *s.m.* pontiff; le souverain P., the Pope. *a.* †-ical. *adv.* -icalement.

pont-levis [pɔ̃ləvi], *s.m.* drawbridge. *pl.* ponts-levis.

populace [pɔpylas], *s.f.* rabble, riff-raff.

populaire [pɔpylɛːr], *a.* popular; (a) of, for the people; places populaires, cheap seats; expression p., (i) uneducated, (ii) slangy, expression; (b) se rendre p., to make oneself popular. *adv.* -ment.

populari/ser [pɔpylarize], *v.tr.* to popularize (idea, person). *s.f.* -isation. *s.f.* -ité.

popul/ation [pɔpylasjɔ̃], *s.f.* population. *a.* †-eux, populous, densely populated.

porc [pɔːr], *s.m.* 1. pig; *U.S:* hog. 2. pork.

porcelaine [pɔrsəlɛn], *s.f.* porcelain, china.

porche [pɔrʃ], *s.m.* porch.

porcherie [pɔrʃəri], *s.f.* piggery; pigsty.

por/e [pɔːr], *s.m.* pore. *a.* †-eux, porous.

port[1] [pɔːr], *s.m.* harbour, port; arriver à bon p., to arrive safely; droits de p., harbour dues.

port[2], *s.m.* 1. (act of) carrying. 2. cost of transport; postage; en p. dû, carriage forward; p. payé, carriage paid. 3. bearing, carriage (of pers.). *a.* -able, portable; wearable. *s.m.* -age, conveyance, transport.

†portail [pɔrtaːj], *s.m.* portal (of church).

portant [pɔrtɑ̃], *a.* être bien p., to be in good health.

†portatif [pɔrtatif], *a.* portable; *P.N:* glaces portatives, ices to take away; peu p., unwieldy.

porte [pɔrt], *s.f.* 1. gate(way), entrance; p. cochère, carriage entrance; (skiing) gate, pair of flags; *Techn:* p. de visite, inspection-door, manhole door. 2. door; p. d'entrée, front door; p. de service, back door. 3. eye (of hook and eye).

porte-avions [pɔrtavjɔ̃], *s.m.inv.* aircraft carrier.

porte-bagages [pɔrtbaga:ʒ], *s.m.inv.* luggage-rack; luggage grid (on bicycle); *Aut:* roof rack.

porte-bébé [pɔrtbebe], *s.m.inv.* 1. baby-carrier (for bicycle, etc.). 2. carry-cot.

porte-billets [pɔrt(ə)bijɛ], *s.m.inv.* note case, *U.S:* billfold.

porte-bonheur [pɔrtbɔnœːr], *s.m.inv.* lucky charm, mascot.

porte-clefs [pɔrtəkle], *s.m.inv.* key-ring.

porte-couteau [pɔrtkuto], *s.m.inv.* knife rest.

portée [pɔrte], *s.f.* 1. (a) litter, brood (of animals, birds); (b) *Mus:* stave. 2. (a) reach (of one's arm); range; scope; à p. de la main, within reach; à p. de voix, within call; (b) bearing, full significance; affirmation d'une grande p., weighty statement.

porte-fenêtre [pɔrtfənɛːtr], *s.f.* French window; *pl.* portes-fenêtres.

portefeuille [pɔrtəfœːj], *s.m.* 1. portfolio; ministre sans p., minister without portfolio. 2. pocket-book; note-case, wallet, *U.S:* billfold.

portemanteau [pɔrtmɑ̃to], *s.m.* coat(-and-hat)-rack, -stand.

porte(-)mine [pɔrtmin], *s.m.inv.* propelling pencil.

porte-monnaie [pɔrtmɔnɛ], *s.m.inv.* purse.

porte-parole [pɔrtparɔl], *s.m.inv.* spokesman.

porter [pɔrte]. 1. *v.tr.* to carry; (*a*) to bear, support (burden); (*b*) to wear (garment, etc.); (*c*) to carry, convey, take (sth. somewhere); (*d*) to inscribe, enter; p. un nom sur une liste, to enter a name on a list; (*e*) to produce; p. des fruits, to bear fruit; (*f*) p. témoignage, to bear witness. 2. *v.i.* to rest, bear; (*b*) to hit, reach (a mark); style qui porte, telling style.
se **porter** bien, mal, to be well, unwell.

porte-serviette(s) [pɔrtsɛrvjɛt], *s.m.inv.* towel-rail.

porteur, -euse [pɔrtœːr, -øːz], *s.* 1. porter, carrier, bearer (of news, etc.). *Com:* p. d'un chèque, payee of a cheque; payable au p., payable to bearer; *Med:* (germ-)carrier. 2. *s.m. Rail: etc:* porter.

porte-voix [pɔrtvwa], *s.m.inv.* megaphone.

portier, -ière[1] [pɔrtje, -jɛːr], *s.* porter, janitor.

portière[2], *s.f.* door (of car etc.).

portion [pɔrsjɔ̃], *s.f.* portion, share, part; helping (of food).

porto [pɔrto], *s.m.* port (drunk as an apéritif).

portrait [pɔrtrɛ], *s.m.* portrait, likeness. *s.m.* -iste, portrait-painter.

portugais, -aise [pɔrtygɛ, -ɛːz], *a.* & *s.* Portuguese.

pose [poːz], *s.f.* 1. placing; p. d'un tapis, laying of a carpet. 2. (*a*) pose, posture; (*b*) posing; affectation. 3. *Phot:* exposure.

posé [poze], *a.* staid, grave; steady; voix posée, calm voice. *adv.* -ment.

poser [poze]. 1. *v.i.* (*a*) to rest, lie (on sth.); (*b*) to pose; to sit (for a portrait); (*c*) to pose; to put on side. 2. *v.tr.* to place, put (sth. somewhere); to lay (sth.) down.
se **poser**, (*of bird, aircraft*) to settle, alight.

poseur, -euse [pozœːr, -øːz], *a.* & *s.* affected (person).

‡**posit/if** [pozitif], *a.* (*a*) positive, actual; c'est p., that's so; (*b*) matter-of-fact (person), practical (mind). *adv.* -ivement.

position [pozisjɔ̃], *s.f.* position. 1. (*a*) situation, site; (*b*) posture; (*c*) circumstances; p. sociale, social status. 2. post, job.

posologie [pozɔlɔʒi], *s.f. Med:* dosage.

‡**posséder** [posede], *v.tr.* to be in possession of (sth.); (*a*) to possess, own; (*b*) to be master of (a subject); (*c*) to curb, control (one's tongue).
se **posséder**, to contain oneself.

possess/ion [posesjɔ̃], *s.f.* 1. possession; être en p. de qch., to own sth. 2. property; *pl.* possessions. *s.m.* -eur, owner; occupier. *a.* †-if, possessive.

possib/le [posibl]. 1. *a.* possible; pas p.! not really! 2. *s.m.* dans la mesure du p., as far as possible; faire tout son p. pour . . ., to try one's hardest to . . . . *s.f.* -ilité, possibility.

post/e[1] [post], *s.f.* (*a*) les Postes et Télécommunications, the postal services; mettre une lettre à la p., to post a letter; (*b*) (bureau de) p., post office. *a.* †-al.

poste[2] [post], *s.m.* 1. (*a*) post, station; (*b*) p. d'incendie, fire-station; p. de police, police station; (*c*) p. de T.S.F., de télévision, radio, television, set; p. récepteur, receiving set; *P.T.T:* p. 35, extension 35. 2. post, appointment.

poster [poste], *v.tr.* to post, mail (letter).

poster (se) [saposte], *v.pr.* to take up position, one's stand.

postérieur [posterjœːr], 1. *a.* posterior; (*of time*) later; partie postérieure, back (part). 2. *s.m.* posterior, backside. *adv.* -ement, at a later date.

postérité [posterite], *s.f.* posterity; descendants.

posthume [postym], *a.* posthumous.

postiche [postiʃ]. 1. *a.* false; imitation (hair, etc.). 2. *s.m.* wig.

postscolaire [postskolɛːr], *a. Sch:* continuation (class).

postsynchronis/er [postsɛ̃krɔnize], *v.tr. Cin:* to post-synchronize (sound-track to film). *s.f.* -ation.

posture [postyr], *s.f.* posture, attitude; position.

pot [po], *s.m.* 1. pot, jug, can, jar; vase. 2. *Aut:* p. d'échappement, silencer, *U.S:* muffler.

potable [potabl], *a.* drinkable; eau p., drinking water.

potage [potaːʒ], *s.m.* soup.

‡**potager** [potaʒe], *a. Cu:* herbes potagères, herbs; jardin p., kitchen-garden.

pot-au-feu [potofø], *s.m.inv.* 1. stock-pot. 2. boiled beef with vegetables.

pot-de-vin [podvɛ̃], *s.m.* 1. gratuity. 2. bribe; *pl.* pots-de-vin.

poteau [poto], *s.m.* post, pole, stake; p. télégraphique, telegraph pole; *Sp:* p. de départ, d'arrivée, starting-, winning-post.

potelé [potle], *a.* plump (and dimpled).

potence [potɑ̃ːs], *s.f.* gallows.

potenti/el [potɑ̃sjɛl]. 1. *a.* potential. 2. *s.m.* (*a*) potentialities; (*b*) *El:* potential. *adv.* -ellement.

poterie [potri], *s.f.* pottery.

potiron [potirɔ̃], *s.m.* pumpkin.

‡**pou** [pu], *s.m.* louse.

poubelle [pubɛl], *s.f.* dustbin, *U.S:* garbage can.

pouce [puːs], *s.m.* 1. (*a*) thumb; manger sur le p., to take a snack; (*b*) big toe. 2. inch.

poudre [pu:dr], s.f. 1. powder; **café en p.**, instant coffee. 2. explosive (gunpowder, etc.).

poudr/er [pudre], v.tr. to powder; to dust on (flour, etc.). s.f. -erie, (gun)powder factory. a. †-eux, dusty. s.m. -ier, (powder) compact. s.f. -ière, powder-magazine.

pouf [puf]. 1. int. (a) plop!; (b) phew! 2. s.m. H: pouf(fe), hassock.

pouff/er [pufe], v.i. **p. (de rire)**, to burst out laughing. s.m. -ement.

poulain [pulɛ̃], s.m. colt, foal; Sp: trainee.

poul/e [pul], s.f. 1. hen; fowl; **lait de p.**, egg-flip; **chair de p.**, goose-flesh. 2. (a) (at games) pool; (b) sweepstake. s.f. -arde, fattened pullet. s.m. -et, chicken. s.m. -ailler, (a) hen house; (b) Th: gallery.

poulie [puli], s.f. pulley.

pouls [pu], s.m. pulse.

poumon [pumɔ̃], s.m. lung; **p. d'acier**, iron lung.

poupe [pup], s.f. Nau: stern; **avoir le vent en p.**, (i) to have the wind aft; (ii) to be doing well.

poupée [pupe] s.f. doll.

poupon, -onne [pupɔ̃, -ɔn], s. F: baby. s.f.-nière, day-nursery.

pour [pu:r]. I. prep. for. 1. (a) instead of; **agir p. qn**, to act on s.o.'s behalf; (b) laisser **qn p. mort**, to leave s.o. for dead; (c) (direction) **le train p. Paris**, the Paris train; (d) (time) **p. toujours**, for ever; **p. quinze jours**, for a fortnight; (e) (purpose) **p. affaires**, on business; **c'est p. cela qu'il est venu**, that's why he came; (f) because of; **p. moi**, for me, on my account; (g) **parler p. qn**, to speak in favour of s.o.; adv. moi, **je suis p.**, I'm in favour of it; (h) with regard to; **p. moi**, for my part; (i) **dix p. cent**, ten per cent. 2. **p. plus inf.** (a) (in order) to; **il faut manger p. vivre**, one must eat to live; (b) because of; **je sais p. l'avoir vu**, I know because I saw it, him. 3. (a) **p. que plus sub.**, in order that; (b) **p. peu que plus sub.**, if only, if ever. II. s.m. **le p. et le contre**, the pros and cons.

pourboire [purbwa:r], s.m. tip.

pourcentage [pursɑ̃ta:ʒ], s.m. percentage; rate (per cent); commission.

pourchasser [purʃase], v.tr. to pursue (obstinately).

pourparlers [purparle], s.m.pl. negotiations (avec, with).

pourpre [purpr], a. & s.m. crimson.

pourquoi [purkwa], adv. & conj. why? **p. faire?** what for? **p. pas? p. non?** why not?

pourr/ir [puri:r]. 1. v.i. to rot, decay; **to go bad.** 2. v.tr. to rot. s.m. -issement. s.f. -iture, rot(tenness). **se pourrir**, to go bad.

poursuite [pursɥit], s.f. 1. pursuit. 2. usu. pl. Jur: lawsuit, action; prosecution.

‡poursuivre [pursɥi:vr], v.tr. 1. to pursue; to chase (s.o.). 2. Jur: to prosecute (s.o.). 3. to continue, proceed with (work, etc.).

pourtant [purtɑ̃], adv. nevertheless, however.

‡pourvoir [purvwa:r], v. to provide. 1. v.ind.tr. **p. aux frais**, to defray the cost. 2. v.tr. (a) to supply, equip (s.o., de, with, sth.); (b) to equip, fit (de, with).

pourvu que [purvykə], conj.phr. provided (that); so long as.

pousse [pus], s.f. 1. growth (of leaves, hair). 2. young shoot.

poussée [puse], s.f. 1. Techn: thrust; **centre de p.**, centre of pressure; **force de p.**, upward thrust. 2. pushing, pressure (of crowd). 3. push, shove; Fb: **p. irrégulière**, foul. 4. growth (of pimples); rising (of sap, temperature).

pouss/er [puse]. 1. v.tr. (a) to push, shove, thrust; (b) to drive, impel; (c) to push on; **p. la vente**, to push sales; (d) to put forth, shoot out (leaves, roots); (e) to utter (a cry). 2. v.i. (a) to push; (b) to grow; **les enfants poussent**, the children are shooting up. s.f. -ette, (child's) push-chair.

pouss/ière [pusjɛ:r], s.f. dust. †-iéreux, dusty.

†poussif [pusif], a. a wheezy, short-winded.

poussin [pusɛ̃], s.m. a chick; (b) Cu: spring chicken.

poutre [putr], s.f. 1. beam. 2. girder.

‡pouvoir [puvwa:r]. I. v.tr. 1. to be able; **'can'**; **on n'y peut rien**, it can't be helped; **n'en plus p.**, to be exhausted; v.pr. **si cela se peut**, if possible. 2. 'may'; to be allowed; **puis-je entrer?** may I come in? 3. to be possible, probable; **cela se peut (bien)**, it may be (so). II. s.m. power. 1. force, means; **en dehors de mon p.**, beyond my power. 2. influence; **être au p. de qn**, to be in s.o.'s power. 3. (a) authority; competency; power; (b) **au p.**, in power. 4. power of attorney; procuration.

prairie [preri], s.f. meadow.

praticab/le [pratikabl], a. practicable. s.f. -ilité.

praticien [pratisjɛ̃], s.m. (legal, medical) practitioner

pratique¹ [pratik], a. practical. adv. -ment.

pratique², s.f. 1. practice; application (of theory). 2. practice, experience.

pratiquer [pratike], v.tr. 1. to practise; to use; to do, to carry out; Com: **les cours pratiqués**, the ruling prices. 2. **p. une ouverture**, to make an opening.

pré [pre], s.m. meadow.

préalable [prealabl]. 1. *a.* (*a*) previous; (*b*) preliminary (agreement). 2. *s.m.* au p., to begin with.

précaire [preke:r], *a.* precarious. *adv.* -ment.

précaution [prekosjɔ̃], *s.f.* 1. precaution. 2. caution; wariness; care; avec p., cautiously.

précédence [presedɑ̃:s], *s.f.* precedence (de, of); priority.

précéd/ent [presedɑ̃]. 1. *a.* preceding, previous, former. 2. *s.m.* precedent. *adv.* -emment.

‡**précéder** [presede], *v.tr.* to precede.

précepteur, -**trice** [preseptœ:r, -tris], *s.* tutor; (private) teacher; *f.* governess.

prêcher [prɛʃe], *v.tr.* to preach; p. d'exemple, to practise what one preaches.

†**précieu/x** [presjø], *a.* (*a*) precious; (*b*) valuable; (*c*) affected (manner, etc.). *adv.* -sement.

précipice [presipis], *s.m.* precipice.

précipit/er [presipite], *v.tr.* 1. to precipitate; to hurl down; to rush (s.o., dans, into, sth.). 2. to hurry, hasten (departure, etc.). *s.f.* -ation, violent hurry. *adv.* -amment.
se **précipiter**, to dash, to rush.

précis [presi]. 1. *a.* precise, exact, definite. 2. *s.m.* abstract, summary. *adv.* -ément, exactly.

préciser [presize], *v.tr.* (*a*) to specify; to state precisely; p. les détails, to go further into detail; (*b*) abs. to be precise.
se **préciser**, to become clear; (*of danger*) to take shape.

précision [presizjɔ̃], *s.f.* 1. precision, exactness, accuracy; instruments de p., precision instruments. 2. *pl.* demander des précisions sur qch., to ask for full particulars about sth.

précoce [prekɔs], *a.* precocious; forward.

précombustion [prekɔ̃bystjɔ̃], *s.f.* precombustion; moteur diesel à chambre de p., precombustion engine.

préconditionné [prekɔ̃disjɔne], *a.* Com: packaged.

précontraint [prekɔ̃trɛ̃], *a.* béton p., prestressed concrete.

précurseur [prekyrsœ:r]. 1. *s.m.* forerunner. 2. *a.m.* precursory (sign).

prédécesseur [predesesœ:r], *s.m.* predecessor.

prédicateur [predikatœ:r], *s.m.* preacher.

prédilection [predileksjɔ̃], *s.f.* partiality, fondness (pour, for).

‡**prédire** [predi:r], *v.tr.* to predict, foretell. *s.f.* -diction, forecast.

prédispos/er [predispoze], *v.tr.* to predispose (à, to); to prejudice (s.o. against s.o.). *s.f.* -ition.

prédomin/er [predɔmine], *v.i.* to predominate; to have the upper hand (sur, over). *a.* -ance. *a.* -ant.

prééminence [preeminɑ̃:s], *s.f.* preeminence. *a.* -ent.

préfabriqué [prefabrike], *a.* prefabricated.

préface [prefas], *s.f.* preface, foreword.

préfecture [prefɛkty:r], *s.f.* Fr: Adm: prefecture.

préférable [preferabl], *a.* preferable (à, to); better. *adv.* -ment.

‡**préfér/er** [prefere], *v.tr.* to prefer; to like better; à. & *s.* -é, favourite. *s.f.* -ence, preference. *a.* †-entiel, preferential.

préfet [prefɛ], *s.m.* Fr. Adm: prefect.

préfixe [prefiks], *s.m.* prefix; code letter, number.

préhist/oire [preistwa:r], *s.f.* prehistory. *s.* -orien, -orienne, prehistorian. *a.* -orique, prehistoric.

préjudice [preʒydis], *s.m.* prejudice, detriment; (moral injury); wrong; porter p. à qn, to inflict injury on s.o.

préjudic/ier [preʒydisje], *v.i.* to be detrimental (à, to). *a.* -iable, prejudicial, injurious.

préjugé [preʒyʒe], *s.m.* prejudice, bias; sans préjugés, unprejudiced.

‡**préjuger** [preʒyʒe], *v.tr.* to prejudge.

‡**prélever** [prelve], *v.tr.* to deduct in advance; p. un échantillon, to take a sample.

préliminaire [prelimine:r]. 1. *a.* preliminary. 2. *s.m.pl.* preliminaries.

prélude [prelyd], *s.m.* prelude (de, à, to).

prématuré [prematyre], *a.* premature. *adv.* -ment.

prémédit/er [premedite], *v.tr.* to premeditate; insulte prémédité, deliberate insult. *s.f.* -ation.

†**prem/ier** [prəmje], *a.* first. 1. (*a*) le p. janvier, January the first; du p. coup, at the first attempt; le p. venu, anyone; Aut: première (vitesse), bottom, first, (gear); (*b*) matières premières, raw materials. 2. au p., on the first floor. 3. p. ministre, Prime Minister; Rail: etc: première (classe), first (class); Th: p. rôle, lead. 4. Sch: (classe de) première = sixth form. 5. *s.f.* première, (*a*) forewoman; (*b*) Th: first night. *adv.* -ièrement, first(ly).

premier-né, -**née** [prəmjene], *a.* & *s.* first-born.

prémonition [premɔnisjɔ̃], *s.f.* premonition.

prémunir (se) [səpremyni:r], *v.pr.* to provide oneself (de, with, contre, against).

‡**prendre** [prɑ̃:dr]. I. *v.tr.* to take. 1. to take (up); to take hold of; (*a*) je sais comment le p., I know how to manage him; p. qch. sur la table, dans un tiroir, to take sth. from the table, out of a drawer; (*b*) p. des pensionnaires, to take boarders; p. qn au sérieux,

to take s.o. seriously; (c) p. qch. à qn, to take sth. from s.o.; (d) à tout p., everything considered. 2. to take, capture; p. un poisson, to catch a fish; se faire p., to get caught; qu'est-ce qui lui prend? what's up with him? 3. (a) p. des voyageurs, to take up passengers; (b) to take, rent (a room); (c) p. qn pour exemple, to take s.o. as an example; (d) p. une personne pour une autre, to (mis)take one person for another; (e) p. un bain, to take a bath; (f) p. une maladie, to catch an illness; (g) p. de l'âge, to be getting on in years. 4. p. le train, to take the train; p. le large, to take to the open sea; Aut: p. un virage, to take a corner; obs. p. à gauche, bear, fork, left. II. v.i. 1. (a) to set; (b) to freeze; (c) to jam. 2. to catch (in the pan).

se prendre. 1. (a) to catch, to be caught; (b) se p. d'amitié pour qn, to take a liking to s.o. 2. s'en p. à qn, to blame s.o. 3. il sait comment s'y p., he knows how to set about it.

preneur, -euse [prənœːr, -øːz], s. taker, purchaser.

prénom [prenɔ̃], s.m. Christian, U.S: given, name.

préoccup/er [preɔkype], v.tr. to pre-occupy, engross (s.o.); sa santé me préoccupe, I'm anxious about his, her, health. s.a. -ant, disquieting. s.f. -ation.

préparateur, -trice [preparatœːr, -tris], s. (laboratory) assistant; demonstrator; p. en pharmacie, chemist's assistant.

prépar/er [prepare], v.tr. to prepare; to get ready; p. un examen, to read for an exam. s.m.pl. -atifs, preparations. s.f. -ation, preparation, preparing. a. -atoire [preparatwaːr], preparing. se préparer. 1. to prepare. 2. to get ready.

prépondér/ance [prepɔ̃derɑ̃ːs], s.f. pre-ponderance. a. -ant.

préposé [prepoze], s. Adm: official; traffic warden; p. des postes, postman.

préposition [prepozisjɔ̃], s.f. Gram: preposition.

près [prɛ]. 1. adv. near. 2. adv.phr: à peu p., nearly, about; au plus p., to the nearest point; de p., near; from close to. 3. prep.phr: p. de qn, near, close to s.o.; p. de là, nearby; p. de partir, about to start.

présage [prezaːʒ], s.m. foreboding; mauvais p., bad omen.

presbyte [prɛzbit], a. long-sighted.

presbytère [prɛzbitɛːr], s.m. presbytery.

‡prescr/ire [prɛskriːr], v.tr. to prescribe. s.f. -iption.

présélection [preselɛksjɔ̃], s.f. 1. pre-selection (for special training). 2. short-listing (for job). 3. Aut: boîte de vitesse à p., preselector gears.

présence [prezɑ̃ːs], s.f. (a) presence; faire acte de p., F: to show up; Ind: feuille de p., time sheet; (b) p. d'esprit, presence of mind.

présent [prezɑ̃], a. present; à p., (just) now.

présent/er [prezɑ̃te], v.tr. 1. to present; to offer. 2. to introduce. a. -able. s.f. -ation. s.m. -oir, Com: display unit.

se présenter. 1. to offer; to arise. 2. to present oneself.

préserv/er [prezɛrve], v.tr. to preserve, to protect (de, from). a. & s.m. †-atif. s.f. -ation, protection.

présid/er [prezide], v.tr. & i. to preside (over). s.f. -ence, presidency; chairmanship. s. -ent. a. †-entiel, presidential (chair, etc.).

présomp/tion [prezɔ̃psjɔ̃], s.f. presumption. a. †-tif, (heir) presumptive. a. †-tueux, presumptuous. adv. -tueusement.

presque [prɛsk], adv. 1. almost, nearly. 2. (with negative) scarcely, hardly; p. jamais, hardly ever.

presqu'île [prɛskil], s.f. peninsula.

pressant [presɑ̃], a. pressing, urgent.

presse [prɛːs], s.f. 1. press, pressing-machine; livre sous p., book in the press. 2. press, newspapers. 3. crowd.

pressé [prese], a. 1. crowded; compressed; citron p., fresh lemon drink. 2. in a hurry.

presse-citron [pressitrɔ̃], s.m.inv. lemon-squeezer.

presse-fruits [presfrɥi], s.m.inv. juice extractor.

‡pressent/ir [presɑ̃tiːr], v.tr. to have a presentiment (of sth.). s.m. -iment.

presse-papiers [prespapje], s.m.inv. paper-weight.

presse-purée [prespyre], s.m.inv. potato-, vegetable-masher.

press/er [prese], v.tr. to press. 1. to squeeze (lemon, etc.). 2. to hurry, push on; p. le pas, to quicken one's pace; abs. l'affaire presse, the matter is urgent. s.m. -oir, wine-, oil-press.

se presser. 1. to crowd. 2. to hurry.

pressing [presiŋ], s.m. F: dry-cleaner's; dry-cleaning.

pression [presjɔ̃], s.f. (a) pressure; vérificateur de p., tyre pressure gauge; (b) El: tension; (c) Med: p. artérielle, blood pressure.

preste [prɛst], a. quick; alert; avoir la main p., to be quick with one's hands. adv. -ment.

pressuriser [presyrize], v.tr. Av: etc: to pressurize.

prestidigita/tion [prɛstidiʒitasjɔ̃], s.f. conjuring. s.m. -teur, conjurer.

prestige [prɛstiːʒ], s.m. prestige; high reputation. a. †-ieux, marvellous.

présumer [prezyme], v.tr. to presume.

prêt[1] [prɛ], a. ready, prepared.
prêt[2], s.m. loan; advance.
prétendant, -ante [pretɑ̃dɑ̃, -ã:t], s. 1. applicant, candidate; claimant. 2. s.m. suitor.
préten/dre [pretɑ̃:dr], v.tr. 1. to claim (as a right); to require. 2. to maintain, assert (a right, sth. as a fact). 3. To aspire (to rank, honours).
prétendu [pretɑ̃dy], a. alleged, would-be; self-styled.
préten/tion [pretɑ̃sjɔ̃], s.f. (a) pretension, claim (à, to); (b) homme sans prétentions, unassuming man. a. †-tieux, showy. adv. -tieusement.
prêt/er [prete], v.tr. 1. to lend (sth. to s.o.); p. sur gages, to lend against security; p. la main à qn, to lend s.o. a hand; p. attention, to pay attention. 2. to attribute; p. de généreux sentiments à qn, to credit s.o. with generous feelings. 3. v.ind.tr. privilège qui prête aux abus, privilege that gives rise to abuses. s. -eur, -euse, lender. se prêter, to lend oneself (à, to), to fall in with (a plan); si le temps s'y prête, weather permitting.
prétexte [pretɛkst], s.m. pretext, excuse; sous aucun p., not on any account.
prêtre [prɛːtr], s.m. priest.
preuve [prœːv], s.f. proof, evidence.
préven/ance [prevnɑ̃:s], s.f. attention, kindness. a. -ant, kind, attentive; prepossessing.
‡prévenir [prevniːr], v.tr. 1. (a) to anticipate (s.o.'s wishes); (b) to prevent illness, danger. 2. to predispose (s.o. in favour of s.o.). 3. to inform, forewarn (s.o. of sth.).
‡préventif [prevɑ̃tif], a. 1. preventive (medicine). 2. Jur: detention préventive, detention awaiting trial.
prévention [prevɑ̃sjɔ̃], s.f. 1. prejudice, bias (en faveur de, for; contre, against). 2. Adm: la p. routière, road safety (i) squad, (ii) measures.
prévenu, -ue [prevny], a. 1. prejudiced, biassed. 2. s. Jur: the accused.
prévis/ion [previzjɔ̃], s.f. forecast; anticipation; p. du temps, weather forecast(ing); p. budgétaire, (budget) estimates; selon toute p., in all likelihood. a. -ible, foreseeable.
‡prévoir [prevwaːr], v.tr. 1. to foresee, forecast. 2. to provide for (sth.); vitesse prévue, designed speed.
prévoy/ance [prevwajɑ̃:s], s.f. foresight, precaution; société de p., provident society. a. -ant, provident; far-sighted.
prier [prie], v.tr. 1. to pray. 2. to ask, beg; je vous en prie!, please, do! je vous prie de . . ., please. . . .
prière [priɛːr], s.f. 1. prayer. 2. request; p. de ne pas fumer, please do not smoke.
primaire [primɛːr], a. primary (education); El: courant p., inducing current.

prime [prim], s.f. 1. premium. 2. bonus; p. de vie chère, cost of living bonus.
primer [prime], v.tr. to give a prize, bonus (to s.o., sth.); taureau primé, prize bull; industrie primée, subsidized industry.
†prime-sautier [primsotje], a. impulsive.
primeurs [primœːr], s.f.pl. early fruit and vegetables.
primevère [primvɛːr], s.f. primula; p. (à grandes fleurs), primrose; p (commune), cowslip.
†primit/if [primitif], a. 1. primitive (times); primary (colours). 2. la question primitive, the original question. adv. -ivement, originally.
prince [prɛ̃s], s.m. prince.
princesse [prɛ̃sɛs], s.f. princess; F: aux frais de la p., at the expense of the State, the firm, F: on the house.
†principal [prɛ̃sipal], a. 1. principal, chief; associé p., senior partner. 2. s.m. (a) principal; headmaster; (b) main point (of discussion, etc.); (c) Com: principal, capital sum. adv. -ement.
principauté [prɛ̃sipote], s.f. principality.
principe [prɛ̃sip], s.m. principle; en p., usually, as a rule; in theory.
printemps [prɛ̃tɑ̃], s.m. spring.
priorit/é [priorite], s.f. priority; route à p., major road; P.N: p. à droite, give way. a. & s. -aire, (i) priority; (ii) priority-holder.
pris [pri], a. (a) engaged, occupied; (b) p. de colère, in a rage.
prise [priz], s.f. 1. hold, grasp, grip; (a) lâcher p., to let go; (b) être aux prises avec qn, to be at grips with s.o.; (c) Aut: etc: engagement (of gears, etc.); en p. (directe), in top gear. 2. congealing, setting (of wax, cement). 3. taking, capture; la p. de la Bastille, the fall of the Bastille; (a) Cin: p. de vues, photography; Cin: p. de son, recording. 4. (thing taken) p. de minerai, ore sample; Med: p. de sang, blood sample; El: p. (de courant), (wall-) plug, point.
priser [prize], v.tr. (a) to value (goods); (b) to prize, value (a possession).
prism/e [prism], s.m. prism. a. -atique, prismatic.
prison [prizɔ̃], s.f. prison. s. -nier, -nière, prisoner.
privé [prive], a. private (life, person, etc.).
priv/er [prive], v.tr. to deprive. s.f. -ation, privation; hardship. se priver, to deny oneself (of sth.).
privilège [privilɛ:ʒ], s.m. (a) privilege; prerogative; (b) licence, grant; p. d'une banque, bank charter.
privilégié [privilɛʒje], a. (a) privileged; (b) Fin: licensed, chartered (bank); preference (share).

prix [pri], *s.m.* 1. (*a*) value, worth, cost; à tout p., at all costs; (*b*) price; p. courant, market price; p. de revient, cost price; un p. d'ami, special terms; (repas à) p. fixe, table-d'hôte (meal); c'est hors de p., the price is prohibitive; n'avoir pas de p., to be priceless; (*c*) charge; fare. 2. reward, prize.

probab/le [probabl], *a.* probable. *adv.* -lement. *s.f.* -ilité, probability.

probité [probite], *s.f.* probity, integrity.

prob/lème [problɛm], *s.m.* problem. *a.* -lématique, problematical.

procédé [prosede], *s.m.* 1. proceeding, dealing, conduct. 2. process; method (of working).

‡procéd/er [prosede], *v.i.* 1. (*a*) to proceed; to initiate (an enquiry). (*b*) Jur: to take proceedings (contre, against, s.o.); (*c*) to act. 2. to proceed (de, from). *s.f.* -ure, procedure; proceedings.

procès [prosɛ], *s.m.* lawsuit; trial.

procession [prosesjɔ̃], *s.f.* procession.

procès-verbal [prosɛvɛrbal], *s.m.* 1. report; minute. 2. policeman's report; F: j'ai attrapé un p.-v., I've been had up; *pl.* procès-verbaux.

prochain [prɔʃɛ̃]. 1. *a.* (*a*) nearest; (*b*) next; (*c*) near at hand; dans un avenir p., before long. 2. *s.m.* neighbour, fellow-creature. *adv.* -ement, soon.

proche [prɔʃ]. 1. *adv.* near; de p. en p., by degrees; p. de mourir, near death. 2. *a.* near, neighbouring (town, house); ses proches (parents), his close relations.

proclam/er [prɔklame], *v.tr.* to proclaim; Pol: p. le résultat du scrutin, to declare the poll. *s.f.* -ation.

procuration [prɔkyrasjɔ̃], *s.f.* Com: Jur: proxy, power of attorney.

procurer [prɔkyre], *v.tr.* to procure (à, for); se p. de l'argent, to raise, obtain, money.

procureur [prɔkyrœːr], *s.m.* P. de la République = public prosecutor.

prodige [prɔdiʒ], *s.m.* prodigy, marvel; faire des prodiges, to work wonders; *attrib.* enfant p., infant prodigy.

‡prodigieu/x [prɔdiʒjø], *a.* prodigious. *adv.* -sement.

prodigue [prɔdig]. 1. *a.* prodigal, lavish (de, of). 2. *s.* spendthrift.

prodig/uer [prɔdige], *v.tr.* 1. to be lavish (of sth.). 2. to waste, squander. *adv.* -alement, lavishly. *s.f.* -alité, extravagance.

product/eur, -trice [prɔdyktœːr, -tris]. 1. *a.* productive (de, of); producing. 2. *s.* producer. *a. †-if. s.f.* -ivité.

production [prɔdyksjɔ̃], *s.f.* 1. production; (*a*) exhibiting; (*b*) producing; generation; output. 2. yield; output.

‡produire [prɔdɥiːr], *v.tr.* to produce. se produire, to occur, happen.

produit [prɔdɥi], *s.m.* (*a*) product; produits agricoles, farm produce; produits chimiques, chemicals; (*b*) proceeds (of sale); takings.

profane [prɔfan]. 1. *a.* profane; sacrilegious. 2. *s.* uninitiated person; layman; F: outsider.

profan/er [prɔfane], *v.tr.* to profane; to desecrate; to violate. *s.f.* -ation, desecration.

‡proférer [prɔfere], *v.tr.* to utter (a word, an oath).

profes/ser [prɔfese], *v.tr.* to teach; to exercise, carry on (a profession). *s.f.* -sion. *a.* †-sionnel, professional. *adv.* -sionnellement.

professeur [prɔfesœːr], *s.m.* professor; schoolmaster, -mistress.

professionnalisme [prɔfesjɔnalism], *s.m.* Sp: professionalism.

profil [prɔfil], *s.m.* 1. profile, side-face. 2. Ind: p. en long, en travers, longitudinal, cross-, section.

‡profit [prɔfi], *s.m.* profit, benefit.

profit/er [prɔfite], *v.i.* 1. (*a*) p. de qch., to take advantage of sth.; (*b*) to make a profit. 2. (of child, animal) to thrive. *a.* -able. *adv.* -ablement. *s.m.* -eur, F: profiteer.

profond [prɔfɔ̃]. 1. *a.* (*a*) deep; (*b*) profound. 2. *s.m.* creuser p., to dig deep. 3. *s.m.* au plus p. de la nuit, at dead of night. *adv.* -ément.

profondeur [prɔfɔ̃dœːr], *s.f.* depth.

profusion [prɔfyzjɔ̃], *s.f.* profusion; abundance; lavishness.

progéniture [prɔʒenityːr], *s.f.* offspring.

program/mation [prɔgramasjɔ̃], *s.f.* (of computers) programming. *s.* -mateur, -trice, (computer) programmer.

programme [prɔgram], *s.m.* programme; Pol: platform (of party); Sch: syllabus; p. d'études, curriculum.

progrès [prɔgrɛ], *s.m.* progress.

progress/er [prɔgrese], *v.i.* to progress; to improve. *a.* †-if. *adv.* -ivement.

prohib/er [prɔibe], *v.tr.* to prohibit, forbid. *a.* †-itif, prohibitory (law); prohibitive (price). *s.f.* -ition.

proie [prwa], *s.f.* prey.

projecteur [prɔʒɛktœːr], *s.m.* (*a*) searchlight; (*b*) floodlight; (*c*) Cin: etc: projector.

projectile [prɔʒɛktil], *s.m.* projectile; missile.

projection [prɔʒɛksjɔ̃], *s.f.* 1. projection. 2. conférence avec projections, lecture with films, slides.

projet [prɔʒɛ], *s.m.* project, plan; p. de contrat, draft agreement; p. de loi, (draft) bill.

‡projeter [prɔʒte], *v.tr.* to project. 1. to throw. 2. to plan, contemplate (journey). se projeter, to stand out.

prolét/ariser [proletarize], *v.tr.* to proletarianize. *s.m. coll:* -ariat, the proletariat. *a. & s.* -aire, *a.* †-arien, proletarian.

prolifique [prolifik], *a.* prolific.

prologue [prolog], *s.m.* prologue (de, to).

prolong/er [prolɔʒe], *v.tr.* to prolong; to extend; to spin out (lecture, etc.). *s.f.* -ation, prolongation; *pl. Sp:* extra time. *s.m.* -ement, extension.
  se prolonger, to be prolonged; to continue, extend.

promenade [promnad], *s.f.* 1. (a) walking; (b) stroll; outing; p. à cheval, ride; p. en voiture, drive. 2. (*place*) promenade, walk.

‡**promen/er** [promne], *v.tr.* 1. to take (s.o., dog) for a walk. 2. p. sa main sur qch., to pass one's hand over sth. *s.-eur*, -euse, walker; hiker.
  se promener, to walk; to go for a walk, for a drive, etc.; *F:* envoyer p. qn, to send s.o. packing.

promesse [promes], *s.f.* promise.

‡**promett/re** [prometr], *v.tr.* to promise (s.o. sth.); *F:* je vous promets qu'on s'est amusé! you bet we had a good time! *abs: F:* ça promet! that looks good! *a.* †-eur, promising, attractive.

promontoire [promɔ̃twaːr], *s.m.* headland, cape.

promotion [promosjɔ̃], *s.f.* promotion; *Sch:* class, year.

prompt [prɔ̃], *a.* prompt, ready. *adv.* -ement. *s.f.* -itude.

promu [promy], *a.* promoted, raised (à, to).

pronom [pronɔ̃], *s.m.* pronoun.

prononcé [pronɔ̃se], *a.* pronounced, decided; nez p., large nose; accent p., marked accent.

‡**pronon/cer** [pronɔ̃se], *v.tr.* to pronounce; (a) sans p. un mot, without a word; j'entendis p. mon nom, I heard my name (mentioned); (b) p. un discours, to make a speech; *F:* abs. p. pour qn, to decide in favour of s.o. *s.f.* -iation, pronunciation.
  se prononcer, to express one's opinion; to make a decision.

pronostic [pronostik], *s.m.* forecast.

pronostiquer [pronostike], *v.tr.* to forecast.

propagande [propagɑ̃ːd], *s.f.* propaganda; publicity; *Com:* faire de la p., to advertise.

‡**propag/er** [propaʒe], *v.tr.* to propagate; to spread (abroad). *s.f.* -ation. *s.-ateur*, -atrice, spreader (of news, disease).
  se propager, (of disease) to spread; (of living creatures) to reproduce.

propane [propan], *s.m.* propane (gas).

propension [propɑ̃sjɔ̃], *s.f.* propensity.

propergol [propergol], *s.m.* (rocket) propellant.

prophète, prophétesse [profɛːt, profetes], *s.* prophet, *f.* prophetess.

prophé/tiser [profetize], *v.tr.* (a) to prophesy; (b) to foretell. *s.f.* -tie [-si], prophecy. *a.* -tique, prophetic.

prophylactique [profilaktik], *a.* prophylactic.

propice [propis], *a.* propitious; favourable.

propitiation [propisjasjɔ̃], *s.f.* propitiation.

proportion [proporsjɔ̃], *s.f.* 1. proportion, ratio. 2. *pl.* size; salle de vastes proportions, enormous room.

proportionné [proporsjone], *a.* 1. bien p., well-proportioned (body); fully-fashioned (stockings). 2. proportionate, suited (à, to).

‡**proportion/el** [proporsjonɛl], *a.* proportional (à, to). *adv.* -ellement.

propos [propo], *s.m.* 1. purpose. 2. subject matter; à ce p., in this connection; à p., to the point; in the nick of time; by the way. 3. remark; *pl.* talk.

propos/er [propoze], *v.tr.* to propose. *s.f.* -ition, proposal, proposition.
  se proposer. 1. to come forward. 2. to have (sth.) in view.

propre [propr], *a.* (a) proper (meaning, etc.); aller en p. personne, to go in person; (b) peculiar (sable, à, to); une façon de marcher à lui p., his special way of walking; (c) own; mes propres yeux, my own eyes; (d) appropriate; fit for anything; p. à rien, good for nothing; (e) clean, neat. *adv.* -ment.

propreté [proprəte], *s.f.* cleanliness; neatness.

proprié/té [propriete], *s.f.* 1. (a) ownership; p. littéraire, copyright; p. industrielle, patent rights; (b) property, estate. 2. property, characteristic. 3. propriety, correctness (of language). *s.-taire*, owner; landlord, landlady.

propul/seur [propylsœːr], *s.m.* propeller; propellant; p. à hélice, screw propeller; avion à p. atomique, nuclear aircraft. *a.* †-sif, propelling.

propulsion [propylsjɔ̃], *s.f.* propulsion; à p. mécanique, mechanically propelled.

prosaïque [prozaik], *a.* prosaic. *adv.* -ment.

‡**pros/crire** [proskriːr], *v.tr.* to outlaw, banish; to ostracize (s.o. from a society); *F:* to taboo (a practice). *s.f.* -cription, outlawry; *F:* tabooing. *a. & s.* -crit, (i) *a.* banned; (ii) *s.* outlaw.

prose [proːz], *s.f.* prose.

prospect/er [prospekte], *v.tr.* 1. *Min:* to prospect. 2. *Com:* to canvass. *s.m.* -eur, prospector; canvasser. *a.* †-if, prospective. *s.f.* -ion, prospecting; canvassing.

prospectus [prɔspɛktyːs], s.m. 1. prospectus. 2. handbill.

prospère [prɔspɛːr], a. prosperous, thriving, flourishing.

‡**prospér/er** [prɔspere], v.i. to prosper, thrive. s.f. -ité, prosperity.

prosterner (se) [sɛprɔstɛrne], v.pr. (a) to prostrate oneself (devant, before); (b) to bow down; to grovel.

prostituée [prɔstitɥe], s.f. prostitute.

prostration [prɔstrasjɔ̃], s.f. 1. prostration. 2. exhaustion; p. nerveuse, nervous breakdown.

protec/teur, -trice [prɔtɛktœːr, -tris]. 1. s. (a) protector; (b) patron. 2. a. (a) protecting, protective; (b) patronizing (tone, etc.). s.f. -tion, protection; patronage. s.m. -torat, protectorate.

‡**protég/er** [prɔteʒe], v.tr. 1. to shelter, guard (contre, against). 2. to be a patron of (the arts, etc.). s. -é, -ée, protégé(e).

protéine [prɔtein], s.f. Ch: protein.

protestant [prɔtɛstɑ̃], a. & s. protestant. s.m. -isme.

protest/er [prɔtɛste]. 1. v.tr. to protest, affirm. 2. v.i. (a) p. de son innocence, to protest one's innocence; (b) p. contre qch., to protest against sth. s.f. -ation, protest(ation).

prothèse [prɔtɛːz], s.f. artificial limb, false teeth, etc.

protocole [prɔtɔkɔl], s.m. protocol; correct procedure, formalities.

proton [prɔtɔ̃], s.m. Atom. Ph: proton.

protoplasme [prɔtɔplasm], s.m. Biol: protoplasm.

prototype [prɔtɔtip], s.m. prototype.

protubér/ance [prɔtyberɑ̃s], s.f. protuberance; knob. a. -ant.

prouesse [prues], s.f. 1. valour. 2. (sportive, etc.), achievement (in sport, etc.).

prouver [pruve], v.tr. to prove.

provenance [prɔvnɑ̃s], s.f. source, origin; train en p. de Lille, train from Lille.

†**provençal** [prɔvɑ̃sal], a. & s. Provençal.

‡**provenir** [prɔvniːr], v.i. to proceed, result, come (de, from); to originate (de, in).

proverbe [prɔvɛrb], s.m. proverb. a. †-ial.

providen/ce [prɔvidɑ̃s], s.f. providence. a. †-tiel, providential. adv. -tiellement.

provinc/e [prɔvɛ̃s], s.f. province. a. †-ial, countrified; provincial.

proviseur [prɔvizœːr], s.m. headmaster (of a lycée).

provision [prɔvizjɔ̃], s.f. 1. provision, store, supply. 2. funds, reserve; chèque sans p., bouncing, dud cheque.

provisoire [prɔvizwaːr], a. provisional; acting (manager, etc.); temporary. adv. -ment.

provo/quer [prɔvɔke], v.tr. 1. to provoke. 2. to instigate, induce; to urge, to incite s.o. to crime. 3. to cause (an explosion); to give rise to (comments). a. -cant, provocative, tantalizing. s.f. -cation, provocation; incitement.

proximité [prɔksimite], s.f. proximity; à p., close by; p. du sang, near relationship.

prude [pryd]. 1. a. prudish. 2. s.f. prude.

prud/ence [prydɑ̃s], s.f. prudence, carefulness. a. -ent. adv. -emment.

prun/e [pryn], s.f. plum; p. de damas, damson; p.-pruneau plum-coloured. s.m. -ier, plum tree.

pruneau [pryno], s.m. prune.

prunelle [prynɛl], s.f. 1. sloe. 2. pupil (of the eye). s.m. -ier, blackthorn.

psalmodier [psalmɔdje], v.i. to intone, to chant.

psaume [psoːm], s.m. psalm. s.m. -tier, psalter.

pseudonyme [psødɔnim]. 1. a. pseudonymous. 2. s.m. pseudonym; nom de plume.

psychana/lyser [psikanalize], v.tr. to psychoanalyse. s.f. -lyse, psychoanalysis. s.m. or s.f. -lyste, psychoanalyst. a. -lytique, psychoanalytic.

psychia/trie [psikjatri], s.f. psychiatry. s.m. or s.f. -tre, psychiatrist. a. -trique, psychiatric.

psycholo/gie [psikɔlɔʒi], s.f. psychology. a. -gique, psychological. s. -gue, psychologist. adv. -giquement.

psychonévrose [psikɔnevroːz], s.f. psychoneurosis.

psychothérapie [psikɔterapi], s.f. psychotherapy.

puant [pɥɑ̃], a. stinking, evil-smelling.

puanteur [pɥɑ̃tœːr], s.f. stench; stink.

†**publ/ic** [pyblik]. 1. a. public (service, etc.). 2. s.m. public, people; le grand p., the general public. adv. -iquement.

publi/er [pyblie], v.tr. to publish. s.f. -cation, publication. s.f. -icité, publicity, advertising. a. -icitaire, advertising (campaign, etc.).

puc/e [pys], s.f. flea; p. à l'oreille, to be uneasy. s.m. -eron, green-fly.

pudeur [pydœːr], s.f. sense of decency.

pudibond [pydibɔ̃], a. prudish.

pudique [pydik], a. modest; chaste. adv. -ment.

puer [pɥe], v.i. to stink, smell; p. l'ail, to smell of garlic.

puéricul/ture [pɥerikyltyːr], s.f. child welfare; p. prénatale, ante-natal care. s.f. -trice, nursery nurse.

puéril [pɥeril], a. puerile, childish. s.m. -ement.

puis [pɥi], adv. (a) then, afterwards, next; (b) besides; et p. après? (i) what next? (ii) P: what about it?

puiser [pɥize], *v.tr.* to draw (water) (à, dans, from); to derive, to take (an idea) (chez qn, from s.o.).

puisque [pɥisk(ə)], *conj.* (puisqu' *before an initial vowel*) since, as.

puiss/ance [pɥisɑ̃ːs], *s.f.* power; force; power (of engine). -**ant**, *a.* -**ant**, powerful.

puits [pɥi], *s.m.* 1. well, hole. 2. shaft, pit (of mine).

pull(-**over**) [pul(ovœːr)], *s.m. Cl:* pullover.

pulluler [pylyle], *v.i.* (a) to multiply rapidly; (b) to swarm.

pulpe [pylp], *s.f.* pulp.

pulp/er [pylpe], *v.tr.* to pulp. *a.* †-**eux**, pulpy.

pulsation [pylsasjɔ̃], *s.f.* pulsation. 1. throbbing. 2. throb; (heart-)beat.

pulvéris/er [pylverize], *v.tr.* (a) to pulverize, to grind (sth.) to powder; (b) to spray (liquid). *s.m.* -**ateur**, (a) pulverizer; (b) spray(er). *s.f.* -**ation**, (a) crushing; (b) spraying.

punaise [pynɛːz], *s.f.* 1. bug. 2. drawing pin.

pun/ir [pyniːr], *v.tr.* to punish; to avenge. *a.* -**issable**; *a.* †-**itif**, punitive. *s.f.* -**ition**, punishment.

pupille[1] [pypij], *s.m. & f.* ward; p. de la Nation, war orphan.

pupille[2], *s.f.* pupil (of the eye).

pupitre [pypiːtr], *s.m.* desk; p. à musique, music-stand.

pur [pyːr], *a.* pure. 1. or p., pure gold; la pure vérité, plain truth; pur hasard, mere chance. 2. ciel pur, clear sky. *adv.* -**ement**.

purée [pyre], *s.f.* (a) purée; to purée; de pommes de terre, mashed potatoes; (b) *F:* être dans la p., to be in the soup.

pureté [pyrte], *s.f.* purity; pureness.

†**purgatif** [pyrgatif], *a.* & *s.m. Med:* purgative.

purgatoire [pyrgatwaːr], *s.m.* purgatory.

purge [pyrʒ], *s.f.* 1. purge. 2. paying off, redemption (of mortgage).

‡**purger** [pyrʒe], *v.tr.* (a) to purge, cleanse, clear (out); (b) to redeem, pay off (mortgage); to clear oneself (of debt, etc.); (c) *E:* to drain (cylinder); to bleed (pipe).

se purger, to take a laxative.

purifi/er [pyrifje], *v.tr.* to purify, cleanse; to refine (metal). *s.* -**cateur**, -**catrice**, cleanser. *s.f.* -**cation**, purification.

pur-sang [pyrsɑ̃], *s.m.inv.* thoroughbred (horse, dog).

†**putat/if** [pytatif], *a.* supposed, presumed. *adv.* -**ivement**.

putré/fier [pytrefje], *v.tr.* to putrefy. *s.f.* -**faction**.

se putréfier, *F:* to go bad.

pyjama [piʒama], *s.m.* pyjamas, *U.S:* pajamas; un p., a pair of pyjamas.

pyramide [piramid], *s.f.* pyramid.

python [pitɔ̃], *s.m.* python.

Q

Q, q [ky], *s.m.* (the letter) Q, q. qu' = que *before vowel and h mute.*

Quadragésime [kwadraʒezim], *s.f. Ecc:* Quadragesima (Sunday).

quadrangulaire [kwadrɑ̃gylɛːr], *a.* quadrangular.

quadrilat/ère [kwadrilateːr], *s.m.* quadrilateral. *a.* †-**éral**.

quadrillé [kadrije], *a.* squared, cross-ruled; chequered; carte quadrillée, squared map.

†**quadrimoteur** [kwadrimotœːr], *a.* & *s.m. Av:* four-engined (aircraft).

quadriréacteur [kwadrireaktœːr], *s.m. Av:* four-engined jet aircraft.

quadrisyllabique [kwadrisilabik], *a.* four-syllabled.

quadrupède [kwadryped], *s.m.* 1. *a.* four-footed. 2. *s.m.* quadruped.

quadruple [kwadrypl], *a.* & *s.m.* quadruple, fourfold.

quadruplés, -ées [kwadryple], *s.pl.* quadruplets, *F:* quads.

quai [ke], *s.m.* (a) quay, wharf, pier; (b) embankment; (c) platform; le train est à q., the train is in. *P.N:* accès aux quais, to the trains.

†**qualificatif** [kalifikatif], *a.* qualifying.

qualifié [kalifje], *a.* qualified; ouvrier q., skilled worker.

qualifi/er [kalifje], *v.tr.* to style, term, qualify. *s.f.* -**cation**.

se qualifier. 1. to style oneself. 2. to qualify.

qualité [kalite], *s.f.* 1. de bonne q., of good quality. 2. characteristics, property (of sth.). 3. qualifications, occupation.

quand [kɑ̃], *conj.* & *adv.* when; q. je le verrai, when I see him; q. viendra-t-il? when will he come? q. même, all the same.

quant [kɑ̃], *adv.* q. à, as for.

quantité [kɑ̃tite], *s.f.* quantity.

quarantaine [karɑ̃tɛn], *s.f.* 1. (about) forty. 2. quarantine.

quarante [karɑ̃ːt], *num.a.inv.* & *s.m.inv.* forty.

quarantième [karɑ̃tjɛm], *num.a.* & *s.m.* fortieth.

quart [kaːr], *s.m.* 1. quarter; *Com:* remise du q., discount of 25%; deux heures et q., a quarter past two. 2. *Nau:* watch; être de q., to be on watch.

quartier [kartje], *s.m.* **1.** quarter. **2.** part, portion. **3.** (*a*) district (of town); (*b*) q. général, headquarters.

quartz [kwarts], *s.m.* quartz.

quasi [kazi], *adv.* quasi, almost.

quatorze [katɔrz], *num.a.inv. & s.m.inv.* fourteen.

quatorzième [katɔrzjɛm], *num.a. & s.* fourteenth.

quatre [katr], *num.a.inv. & s.m.inv.* four.

quatre-vingt-dix [katrəvɛ̃dis], *num.a. & s.m.* ninety.

quatre-vingt-dixième [katrəvɛ̃dizjɛm], *num.a. & s.* ninetieth.

quatre-vingtième [katrəvɛ̃tjɛm], *num.a. & s.* eightieth.

quatre-vingts [katrəvɛ̃], *num.a. & s.m.* eighty; quatre-vingt-un, eighty-one; quatre-vingt-onze, ninety-one.

quatrième [katrjɛm], **1.** *num.a. & s.* fourth. **2.** *s.m.* fourth (floor).

quatuor [kwatɥɔːr], *s.m.* quartet.

que[1] [k(ə)], *rel.pron.* that; whom; which; what.

que[2], *interr.pron.neut.* what? **1.** what? **2.** (= COMME) qu'il est beau! how handsome he is! (= COMBIEN) que de gens! what a lot of people!

que[3], *conj.* that. **1.** je veux qu'il vienne, I want him to come; je pense q. non, I think not. **2.** (*a*) (*imperative*) qu'elle entre! let her come in! (*b*) qu'il pleuve ou qu'il neige, whether it rains or snows. **3.** (*in comparisons*) plus grand, aussi grand, que son frère, taller than, as tall as, his brother. **4.** (*a*) ne . . que, only; je n'ai que 100 francs, I've only 100 francs; (*b*) ne . . pas que, not only; il n'y a pas que lui qui le sache, he's not the only one who knows it.

quel, quelle [kɛl], *a. & pron.* what, which. **1.** q. que soit le résultat, whatever the result may be. **2.** (*interrogative*) q. livre lisez-vous? which book are you reading? q. homme? which man? **3.** (*exclamatory*) q. homme! what a man!

quelconque [kɛlkɔ̃ːk], *a.* **1.** any (whatever). **2.** répondre d'une façon q., to make some sort of a reply. **3.** *F:* son travail est q., his work isn't up to much.

quelque [kɛlk(ə)]. **1.** *a.* (*a*) some, any; (*b*) some, a few; il y a q. temps, some time ago; (*c*) q. . . . qui, que, whatever. **2.** *adv.* (*a*) some, about; q. mille francs, about a thousand francs; (*b*) q. grandes que soient ses fautes, however great his faults may be.

quelque chose [kɛlkəʃoːz], *indef.pron. m.inv.* something, anything.

quelquefois [kɛlkəfwa], *adv.* sometimes; now and then.

quelque part [kɛlkəpaːr], *adv.* somewhere.

quelqu'un, -qu'une [kɛlkœ̃, -kyn], *indef. pron.* **1.** *m. & f.* one (or other);

quelques -un(e)s d'entre nous, a few of us. **2.** *pron.m.* someone; anyone.

querelle [kərɛl], *s.f.* quarrel, dispute.

quereller [kərɛle], *v.tr.* to quarrel with. *a. F:* quarrelsome.

se quereller, to quarrel, wrangle.

qu'est-ce que [kɛskə], *interr.pron.* what? qu'est-ce que c'est que ça? what's that?

qu'est-ce qui [kɛski], *interr.pron.* (*subject*) what?

question [kɛstjɔ̃], *s.f.* question.

questionnaire [kɛstjɔnɛːr], *s.m.* questionnaire.

questionner [kɛstjɔne], *v.tr.* to question.

quête [kɛt], *s.f.* **1.** quest, search. **2.** faire la q., to take up the collection.

quêter [kɛte], *v.tr.* to collect (alms).

queue [kø], *s.f.* **1.** tail. **2.** handle (of pan); pin (of brooch); pigtail. **3.** queue; faire (la) q., to queue up. **4.** (billiard) cue.

qui[1] [ki], *rel.pron.* **1.** who, that, which. **2.** (*object*) whom; which. **3.** (*after prep.*) whom. **4.** (*a*) qui que, whoever, whomever; (*b*) qui que ce soit, anyone (whatever).

qui[2], *interr.pron.m.sg.* who? whom?

quiconque [kikɔ̃k], *indef.pron.m.sg.* **1.** whoever; anyone who. **2.** anybody.

qui est-ce que [kiɛskə], *interr.pron.* whom?

qui est-ce qui [kiɛski], *interr.pron.* who?

quille [kij], *s.f.* ninepin; skittle.

quille[2], *s.f.* keel.

quincaillerie [kɛ̃kɑjri], *s.f.* hardware, ironmongery.

quincaillier [kɛ̃kɑje], *s.m.* ironmonger.

quinine [kinin], *s.f.* quinine.

quinte [kɛ̃t], *s.f.* q. de toux, fit of coughing.

quintuplés, -ées [kɛ̃typle], *s.pl.* quintuplets, *F:* quins.

quinzaine [kɛ̃zɛn], *s.f.* **1.** (about) fifteen. **2.** fortnight.

quinze [kɛ̃ːz], *num.a.inv. & s.m.inv.* **1.** fifteen. **2.** q. jours, a fortnight.

quinzième [kɛ̃zjɛm], *num.a. & s.* fifteenth.

quiproquo [kiprɔko], *s.m.* mistake; misunderstanding.

quittance [kitɑ̃s], *s.f.* receipt, discharge.

quitte [kit], *a.* free, quit, rid (de, of).

quitter [kite], *v.tr.* to leave (place, pers.); q. ses vêtements, to take off one's clothes.

qui-vive [kiviːv], (*a*) *int.* who goes there? (*b*) *s.m.* être sur le q.-v., to be on the alert.

quoi [kwa], *rel.pron.* what. **1.** ce à q. je m'attendais, what I was expecting. **2.** il a de quoi vivre, he has enough to live on. **3.** q. qui, q. que, whatever; q. qu'il en soit, be that as it may; q. que ce soit, anything (whatever).

quoi[2] *interr.pron.* what? à q. bon? what's the use?

quoique [kwak(ə)], *conj.* (al)though; **quoiqu'il soit pauvre**, although he is poor.

quote-part [kɔtpaːr], *s.f.* share, quota, portion. *pl.* **quotes-parts**.

†**quotidien** [kɔtidjɛ̃]. **1.** *a.* daily, every-day. **2.** *s.m.* daily (paper).

quotient [kɔsjɑ̃], *s.m.* **1.** *Mth:* quotient. **2. q. intellectuel**, intelligence quotient, I.Q.

R

R, r [ɛːr], *s.f.* (the letter) R, r.

rabais [rabɛ], *s.m.* discount; reduction.

rabaisser [rabɛse], *v.tr.* to lower; to reduce (price).

†**rabattre** [rabatr], *v.tr.* **1.** to lower. **2.** to reduce; take down. **3.** to beat back.

rabbin [rabɛ̃], *s.m.* rabbi.

rabot [rabo], *s.m.* (*tool*) plane. *v.tr.* **-er**, to plane (wood).

rabougri [rabugri], *a.* stunted.

rabrouer [rabrue], *v.tr.* to scold, snub.

raccommoder [rakɔmɔde], *v.tr.* **1.** to mend, repair. **2.** to make up (quarrel). *s.m.* **-age**.

raccorder [rakɔrde], *v.tr.* to join, connect.

raccourci [rakursi]. **1.** *a.* shortened; short. **2.** *s.m.* (*a*) abridgement; (*b*) short cut.

raccourcir [rakursiːr]. **1.** *v.tr.* (*a*) to shorten; (*b*) to abridge; to cut short **2.** *v.i.* & *pr.* to grow shorter; to shrink. *s.m.* **-issement**.

raccrocher [rakrɔʃe], *v.tr.* to hang up again; *P.T.T:* to ring off.

race [ras], *s.f.* race; breed.

rachat [raʃa], *s.m.* repurchase; **offre de r.**, takeover bid.

racheter [raʃte], *v.tr.* (*a*) to buy back; (*b*) to redeem.

racine [rasin], *s.f.* root.

racisme [rasism], *s.m.* racialism. *a.* & *s.* **-iste**, racialist.

racler [rakle], *v.tr.* to scrape.

raconter [rakɔ̃te], *v.tr.* to tell, relate. *s.* **-eur, -euse**, (story) teller.

radar [radar], *s.m.* radar.

rade [rad], *s.f. Nau:* roadstead, roads.

radeau [rado], *s.m.* raft.

radiateur [radjatœːr], *s.m.* radiator.

radiation [radjasjɔ̃], *s.f.* radiation.

†**radical** [radikal], *a.* & *s.m.* radical. *adv.* **-ement**.

†**radieux** [radjø], *a.* radiant; beaming.

radio [radjo]. **1.** *s.m.* radio. **2.** *s.f.* radio (set).

†**radioactif** [radjoaktif], *a.* radio-active. *s.f.* **-ivité**.

radioalignement [radjoalinmã], *s.m. Nau: Av:* radio beacon route.

radiobalise [radjobaliz], *s.f.* radio beacon.

radiobalisage [radjobalizaːʒ], *s.m.* radio beacon navigation.

radiodiffuser [radjodifyze], *v.tr.* to broadcast. *s.f.* **-ion**.

radioémission [radjoemisjɔ̃], *s.f.* **1.** broadcasting. **2.** broadcast.

radiogénique [radjoʒenik], *a.* **voix r.**, good broadcasting voice.

radiogoniomètre [radjogonjɔmɛtr], *s.m.* radiogoniometer, direction finder.

radiogramme [radjogram], *s.m.* radiogram (= radio message).

radiographie [radjografi], *s.f.* radiography.

radioguidage [radjogidaːʒ], *s.m. Av: Nau:* radio direction.

radiojournal [radjoʒurnal], *s.m. Rad:* news bulletin.

radiolo/gie [radjolɔʒi], *s.f.* radiology. *s.* **-gue**, radiologist.

radionavigation [radjonavigasjɔ̃], *s.f.* navigation by radar, radio beacons, etc.

radio-reportage [radjorəpɔrtaːʒ], *s.m. Rad:* broadcasting of news); running commentary. *pl.* **radio-reportages**.

radiosonde [radjosɔ̃d], *s.f.* radiosonde.

radis [radi], *s.m.* radish.

radium [radjɔm], *s.m.* radium.

radotage [radotaːʒ], *s.m.* drivel; dotage.

radoter [radote], *v.i.* to (talk) drivel. *s.* **-eur, -euse**, dotard.

radoucir [radusiːr], *v.tr.* to calm, soften. *s.m.* **-issement**.
 se radoucir. 1. to grow softer. **2.** to grow milder.

rafale [rafal], *s.f.* squall; gust (of wind).

raffiner [rafine], *v.tr.* to refine. *s.m.* **-ement**. *s.m.* **-age**.
 se raffiner, to become refined.

raffinerie [rafinri], *s.f.* refinery.

raffoler [rafɔle], *v.i.* **r. de qch.**, to be excessively fond of. *F:* to adore, sth.

rafraîchir [rafrɛʃiːr], *v.tr.* **1.** to cool, refresh; to air (room). *a.* **-issant. 2.** to freshen up.
 se rafraîchir. 1. (*of weather*) to grow cooler. **2.** to refresh oneself; to have a (cool) drink.

rafraîchissement [rafrɛʃismɑ̃], *s.m.* **1.** (*a*) cooling; (*b*) freshening up. **2.** *pl.* refreshments, (cold) drinks.

rage [raːʒ], *s.f.* **1.** rabies. **2.** rage, fury.

†**rager** [raʒe], *v.i.* to (be in a) rage. *a.* **-eant**, maddening. *a.* & *s.* **-eur, -euse**, violent-tempered (person).

ragoût [ragu], *s.m.* stew, ragout.

raid [rɛd], *s.m. Mil:* raid; *Sp:* endurance test.

raide [rɛd]. **1.** *a.* (*a*) Stiff; tight; (*b*) stiff; unbending; (*c*) steep; abrupt; (*d*) ça, c'est un peu r., that's a bit thick! **2.** *adv.* tomber r. mort, to drop dead.

raideur [rɛdœːr], *s.f.* **1.** stiffness. **2.** steepness.

raidir [rɛdiːr], *v.tr.* to stiffen; to tighten. se raidir, to stiffen, to grow stiff.

raie¹ [rɛ], *s.f.* **1.** line, stroke. **2.** stripe, streak. **3.** parting (of the hair).

raie² [rɛ], *s.f.* ray, skate.

raifort [rɛfɔːr], *s.m.* horse-radish.

rail [rɑːj], *s.m.* rail.

railler [rɑje], *v.tr.* to jeer at, make fun of (s.o.). *s.f.* -erie. jeering *a.* & *s.* -eur, -euse, (i) *a.* mocking; (ii) *s.* scoffer, jeerer.

rainure [rɛnyːr], *s.f.* groove, furrow.

raisin [rɛzɛ̃], *s.m.* le r., du r., grapes; grappe de r., bunch of grapes; r. sec, raisin; r. de Smyrne, sultana; r. de Corinthe, (dried) currant.

raison [rɛzɔ̃], *s.f.* **1.** reason, motive; r. d'être, reason, justification. **2.** parler r., to talk sense; il n'a plus sa r., his mind is unhinged. **3.** avoir r., to be right; comme de r., as one might expect. **4.** satisfaction; avoir r. de qn, to get the better of s.o. **5.** r. sociale, name, style (of firm). **6.** *Mth:* ratio.

raisonnable [rɛzɔnabl], *a.* reasonable. *adv.* -ment.

raisonn/er [rɛzɔne]. **1.** *v.i.* to reason; to argue. **2.** *v.tr.* to reason with. *s.m.* -ement. *a.* & *s.* -eur, -euse.

rajeun/ir [raʒœniːr]. **1.** *v.tr.* to rejuvenate. **2.** *v.i.* to grow young again. *s.m.* -issement.

rajust/er [raʒyste], *v.tr.* to readjust. *s.m.* -ement.

râle [rɑːl], *s.m.* rattle (in the throat); death-rattle.

ralent/ir [ralɑ̃tiːr], *v.tr.* & *i.* to slacken, slow down; *P.N:* r.! slow! *s.m.* -issement, slowing down.

râler [rɑle], *v.i.* to be at one's last gasp.

ralli/er [ralje], *v.tr.* **1.** (*a*) to rally, assemble; (*b*) to rejoin (ship). **2.** to win (s.o.) over. *s.m.* -ement.

rallonge [ralɔ̃ʒ], *s.f.* extension; leaf (of table).

‡**rallonger** [ralɔ̃ʒe], *v.tr.* to lengthen.

rallumer [ralyme], *v.tr.* to relight.

rallye [rali], *s.m.* (car) rally.

ramassage [ramasaːʒ], *s.m.* collecting, picking up; r. scolaire, school bus service.

ramasser [ramase], *v.tr.* **1.** to gather together. **2.** to collect, gather. **3.** to pick up. se ramasser. **1.** to collect, gather (into a crowd). **2.** to pick oneself up.

rame¹ [ram], *s.f.* oar, scull.

rame², *s.f.* **1.** ream (of paper). **2.** r. (de métro), (underground) train.

rameau [ramo], *s.m.* **1.** (*a*) (small) branch; bough; (*b*) le dimanche des Rameaux, Palm Sunday. **2.** branch, subdivision.

‡**ramener** [ramne], *v.tr.* to bring back.

ramer [rame], *v.i.* to row.

ramier [ramje], *s.m.* wood pigeon.

ramifi/er (se) [səramifje], *v.pr.* to branch out. *s.f.* -cation, ramification.

ramoll/ir [ramɔliːr], *v.tr.* to soften. *s.m.* -issement.

ramon/er [ramɔne], *v.tr.* to sweep (chimney). *s.m.* -eur, sweep.

rampant [rɑ̃pɑ̃], *a.* (*a*) creeping; crawling; (*b*) grovelling, cringing.

rampe [rɑ̃p], *s.f.* **1.** slope, rise, incline. **2.** banisters. **3.** *Th:* footlights.

ramper [rɑ̃pe], *v.i.* to creep, crawl.

rancart [rɑ̃kaːr], *s.m.* mettre au r., to discard.

rance [rɑ̃s], *a.* rancid, rank.

rancœur [rɑ̃kœːr], *s.f.* rancour; bitterness.

rançon [rɑ̃sɔ̃], *s.f.* ransom.

rançonner [rɑ̃sɔne], *v.tr.* to ransom.

rancune [rɑ̃kyn], *s.f.* spite, malice; resentment. *a.* †-ier, spiteful.

randonnée [rɑ̃dɔne], *s.f.* outing, trip.

rang [rɑ̃], *s.m.* **1.** (*a*) row, line; (*b*) sortir du r., to rise from the ranks. **2.** rank; (social) status.

rangé [rɑ̃ʒe], *a.* **1.** orderly, tidy. **2.** steady (pers.).

rangée [rɑ̃ʒe], *s.f.* row, line.

‡**ranger** [rɑ̃ʒe], *v.tr.* **1.** to arrange; to draw up. **2.** to put away. **3.** to arrange, tidy. se ranger. **1.** to draw up, line up. **2.** to get out of the way. **3.** to settle down.

ranimer [ranime], *v.tr.* to revive; to put new life into (s.o.). se ranimer, to revive; (*of fire*) to burn up.

rapace [rapas], *a.* rapacious; les rapaces, birds of prey.

rapacité [rapasite], *s.f.* rapacity.

rapatrier [rapatrie], *v.tr.* to repatriate. *s.m.* -ement, repatriation.

râpe [rɑːp], *s.f.* rasp; (cheese) grater.

râpé [rɑpe], *a.* threadbare.

râper [rɑpe], *v.tr.* to rasp; to grate.

rapetisser [raptise]. **1.** *v.tr.* to make smaller. **2.** *v.i.* & *pr.* to shorten; to shrink.

rapide [rapid]. **1.** *a.* (*a*) rapid, fast; (*b*) steep. **2.** *s.m.* (*a*) rapid (in river); (*b*) express (train). *adv.* -ment.

rapidité [rapidite], *s.f.* rapidity, swiftness.

‡**rapiécer** [rapjese], *v.tr.* to patch (garment).

rappel [rapɛl], *s.m.* **1.** recall. **2.** repeal (of decree). **3.** r. arrière, back-spacer (of typewriter). **4.** injection de r., booster injection.

‡**rappeler** [raple], *v.tr.* 1. (*a*) to recall; to call back; (*b*) r. à l'ordre, to call to order. 2. to call back to mind. 3. *v.i.* (*mountaineering*) to rope down.
se rappeler, to recall, remember.

rapport [rapɔr], *s.m.* I. 1. return, yield, profit; maison de r., block of flats. 2. report; account. II. 1. relation, connection; en r., in keeping; par r. à, in comparison with. 2. proportion, ratio. 3. relations, intercourse; **mettre qn en r. avec qn,** to put s.o. in touch with s.o.

rapporter [raporte], *v.tr.* 1. to bring back. 2. to bring in, yield; cela ne rapporte rien, it doesn't pay. 3. to report (fact).
se rapporter. 1. to refer (à, to). 2. s'en r. à qn, to rely on s.o.

rapporteur [raportœ:r], *s.m.* 1. reporter, recorder. 2. *Mth:* protractor.

rapproché [raproʃe], *a.* near.

rapproch/er [raproʃe], *v.tr.* (*a*) to bring (objects) nearer; (*b*) to bring (persons) together. *s.m.* -ement.
se rapprocher, to draw near(er) (de, to).

rapt [rapt], *s.m. Jur:* abduction (of a minor).

raquette [raket], *s.f.* 1. *Sp:* racket. 2. snow-shoe.

rar/e [rɑ:r], *a.* 1. rare; uncommon. 2. thin, scanty (hair, etc.). *adv.* -ement. *s.f.* -eté.

ras [rɑ]. 1. *a.* (*a*) close-cropped; à poil ras, short-haired (dog); (*b*) rase campagne, open country; faire table rase, to make a clean sweep. 2. *s.m.* au ras de, flush with.

rase-mottes [razmɔt], *s.m.inv. Av:* F: vol en r.-m., hedge-hopping.

ras/er [raze], *v.tr.* 1. to shave. 2. to raze to the ground. 3. to graze, skim (over) *a.* -ant, F: boring. *s.* -eur, -euse, F: bore.
se raser, to shave.

rasoir [razwa:r], *s.m.* razor; F: quel r.! what a bore!

rassasier [rasazje], *v.tr.* 1. to satisfy. 2. to sate, satiate.
se rassasier, to eat one's fill.

rassembl/er [rasãble], *v.tr.* 1. to assemble; to gather together. *s.m.* -ement.
se rassembler, to assemble.

‡**rasseoir** [raswa:r], *v.tr.* to settle, compose (one's ideas).
se rasseoir, to sit down again.

‡**rasséréner (se),** [saserene] *v.pr.* (*of weather*) to clear up; (*of pers.*) to brighten up.

rassis [rasi], *a.* (*a*) staid, sedate; (*b*) pain r., stale bread.

rassurer [rasyre], *v.tr.* to reassure, cheer.
se rassurer, to feel reassured.

rat [ra], *s.m.* rat.

ratatiner (se) [səratatine], *v.pr.* to shrivel (up).

rate [rat], *s.f. Anat:* spleen.

raté, -ée [rate]. 1. *s. (pers.)* failure. 2. *s.m.* misfire.

râteau [rato, rɑ-], *s.m.* rake.

râtelier [ratəlje, rɑ-], *s.m.* 1. rack. 2. (*a*) row of teeth; (*b*) set of false teeth.

rater [rate]. 1. *v.i.* (*a*) to misfire; (*b*) to fail; to miscarry. 2. *v.tr.* to miss (shot, F: the train).

ratière [ratje:r], *s.f.* rat-trap.

ratification [ratifikasjɔ̃], *s.f.* ratification.

ratifier [ratifje], *v.tr.* to ratify; to approve.

ration [rasjɔ̃], *s.f.* ration(s), allowance.

‡**rationnel** [rasjonel], *a.* rational. *adv.* -lement.

ration/er [rasjone], *v.tr.* to ration. *s.m.* -ement.

ratisser [ratise], *v.tr.* to rake.

rattacher [rataʃe], *v.tr.* 1. to refasten, to connect, link (up), bind.
se rattacher, to be connected.

rattraper [ratrape], *v.tr.* 1. to recapture. 2. to catch up.
se rattraper, to recoup (oneself).

rauque [ro:k], *a.* hoarse, raucous, harsh.

ravage [rava:ʒ], *s.m.* (*usu. pl.*) havoc, devastation.

ravi [ravi], *a.* 1. entranced. 2. delighted.

ravin [ravɛ̃], *s.m.* ravine, gully.

raviser (se) [səravize], *v.pr.* to change one's mind.

ravissant [ravisã], *a.* delightful, lovely.

ravitaill/er [ravitaje], *v.tr.* to supply with provisions; to feed. *s.m.* -ment, (i) supplying; (ii) supplies.

raviver [ravive], *v.tr.* 1. to revive. 2. to brighten up.

‡**rayer** [reje], *v.tr.* 1. (*a*) to scratch; to score; (*b*) to rule, line; (*c*) to stripe. 2. to strike out; to delete.

rayon [rejɔ̃] *s.m.* 1. ray; beam. 2. radius. 3. spoke.

rayon² [rejɔ̃], *s.m.* 1. r. de miel, honeycomb. 2. (*a*) shelf; (*b*) department (in shop).

rayonne [rejon], *s.f.* rayon.

rayonnement [rejonmã], *s.m.* (*a*) radiation; (*b*) radiance.

rayonner [rejone], *v.i.* (*a*) to radiate; (*b*) to beam, shine.

rayure [rejy:r], *s.f.* 1. (*a*) stripe, streak; (*b*) scratch; (*c*) groove. 2. erasure.

raz [rɑ], *s.m.* strong current; race.

réacteur [reaktœ:r], *s.m.* 1. reactor; choke. 2. *Av:* jet engine. 3. r. atomique, atomic reactor.

réaction [reaksjɔ̃], *s.f.* reaction; avion à r., jet aircraft.

réactionnaire [reaksjone:r], *a. & s.* reactionary.

réadaptation [readaptasjɔ̃], *s.f.* 1. rehabilitation. 2. readjustment.

réagir [reaʒi:r], *v.i.* to react.

réalisation [realizasjɔ̃], *s.f.* realization; carrying out (of plan); selling out of shares; *Com:* r. du stock, clearance sale; *Cin: Rad:* production.

réaliser [realize], *v.tr.* 1. to carry out (plan). 2. to realize (assets). 3. F: to realize (that . . .).
se réaliser, to come true; to materialize.

réalis/te [realist]. 1. *a.* realistic. 2. *s.* realist. *s.m.* -isme, realism.

réalité [realite], *s.f.* reality.

réapparition [reaparisjɔ̃], *s.f.* reappearance.

rearm/er [rearme], *v.tr.* to rearm. *s.m.* -ement.

†rébarbatif [rebarbatif], *a.* grim, forbidding.

rebâtir [rəbɑtiːr], *v.tr.* to rebuild.

rebelle [rəbɛl]. 1. *a.* rebellious; stubborn, obstinate. 2. *s.m. & f.* rebel.

rebell/er (se) [sərəbɛle], *v.pr.* to rebel. *s.f.* -ion.

rebondi [rəbɔ̃di], *a.* chubby; plump.

rebond/ir [rəbɔ̃diːr], *v.i.* to rebound; to bounce. *s.m.* -issement.

rebord [rəbɔːr], *s.m.* edge, border.

rebours [rəbuːr], *s.m.* à r., against the grain, the wrong way.

rebrousser [rəbruse], *v.tr.* r. chemin, to turn back; to retrace one's steps.

rebuffade [rəbyfad], *s.f.* rebuff; snub.

rebut [rəby], *s.m.* papier de r., waste paper; mettre au r., to throw away.

rebuter [rəbyte], *v.tr.* to rebuff. 2. to discourage.

récapitul/er [rekapityle], *v.tr.* to recapitulate; to sum up. *s.f.* -ation.

†réceler [ros(ə)le], *v.tr.* to conceal.

receveur, -euse [rəsləːr, -øːz]. *s.* receiver, F: receiver.

recensement [rəsɑ̃smɑ̃], *s.m.* (a) census; (b) counting (of votes).

réce/nt [resɑ̃], *a.* recent, late. *adv.* -mment.

récépissé [resepise], *s.m.* receipt.

†récepteur [reseptœːr]. 1. *a.* receiving. 2. *s.m.* receiver (of telephone).

réception [resɛpsjɔ̃], *s.f.* 1. (a) receipt (of letter); (b) taking delivery (of goods). 2. (a) welcome; (b) reception, party. 3. (hotel) reception desk.

recette [rəsɛt], *s.f.* 1. receipts, returns; takings. 2. Cu: recipe.

receveur, -euse [rəsəvœːr, -øːz], *s.* 1. receiver. 2. (a) r. des postes, postmaster; (b) conductor (of bus).

‡recevoir [rəsəvwaːr], *v.tr.* 1. (a) to receive; (b) être reçu, to pass (exam.). 2. to accept, admit (excuse).

rechange [rəʃɑ̃ːʒ], *s.m.* replacement; linge de r., change of linen, underwear; pièces de r., spare parts.

réchapper [reʃape], *v.i.* to escape (de, from).

‡recharg/er [rəʃarʒe], *v.tr.* to reload; to recharge (battery). *s.m.* -ement.

réchauffer [reʃofe], *v.tr.* to reheat.
se réchauffer, to warm oneself.

rêche [rɛʃ], *a.* harsh, rough.

recherche [rəʃɛrʃ], *s.f.* (a) search; (b) research; (c) searching.

recherché [rəʃɛrʃe], *a.* 1. choice, select. 2. studied, strained.

rechercher [rəʃɛrʃe], *v.tr.* (a) to search for, inquire into; (b) to seek (favour).

rechute [rəʃyt], *s.f.* relapse; set-back.

récidiv/e [residiːv], *s.f.* relapse (into crime). *s.* -iste, habitual criminal, F: old lag.

récif [resif], *s.m.* reef.

récipient [resipjɑ̃], *s.m.* container, receptacle.

réciprocité [resiprosite], *s.f.* reciprocity.

réciproque [resiprɔk], *a.* reciprocal, mutual. *adv.* -ment.

récit [resi], *s.m.* narrative; account.

récit/er [resite], *v.tr.* to recite. *s.f.* -ation.

réclamation [reklamasjɔ̃], *s.f.* (a) complaint; protest; (b) claim, demand.

réclame [reklam], *s.f.* (a) advertising; publicity; (b) advertisement.

réclamer [reklame]. 1. *v.i.* to complain. 2. *v.tr.* (a) to claim; (b) to beg for; (c) to call for (care, etc.).

reclass/er [rəklase], *v.tr.* to reclassify, rearrange, redistribute. *s.m.* -ement.

reclus, -use [rəkly, -yːz], *s.* recluse.

recoin [rəkwɛ̃], *s.m.* nook, nosey.

récolte [rekɔlt], *s.f.* harvest.

récolter [rekɔlte], *v.tr.* to harvest.

recommandable [rəkɔmɑ̃dabl], *a.* 1. to be recommended; respectable. 2. advisable.

recommand/er [rəkɔmɑ̃de], *v.tr.* 1. to recommend. 2. to advise. 3. to register (letter). *s.f.* -ation.

‡recommencer [rəkɔmɑ̃se]. 1. *v.tr.* to begin again. 2. *v.i.* to do sth. again; to make a fresh start.

récompense [rekɔ̃pɑ̃ːs], *s.f.* recompense, reward.

récompenser [rekɔ̃pɑ̃se], *v.tr.* to reward, recompense.

réconcili/er [rekɔ̃silje], *v.tr.* to reconcile. *a.* -able. *s.f.* -ation.
se réconcilier, to make it up (with s.o.).

‡reconduire [rəkɔ̃dɥiːr], *v.tr.* to see (s.o.) home; to take (s.o.) back.

réconfortant [rekɔ̃fɔrtɑ̃], *a.* comforting.

reconnaissable [rəkɔnɛsabl], *a.* recognizable.

reconnaissance [rəkɔnɛsɑ̃ːs], *s.f.* 1. recognition. 2. acknowledgment. 3. Mil: etc: reconnaissance. 4. gratitude.

reconnaissant [rəkɔnɛsɑ̃], *a.* (a) grateful; (b) thankful.

‡reconnaître [rəkɔnɛtr], *v.tr.* 1. to recognize. 2. to acknowledge, admit (mistake). 3. to reconnoitre.

reconstitu/er [rəkɔ̃stitɥe], *v.tr.* to reconstitute. *s.f.* -tion.

reconstruction [rəkɔ̃stryksjɔ̃], *s.f.* reconstruction.

‡**reconstruire** [rəkɔ̃strɥiːr], *v.tr.* to reconstruct, rebuild.

record [rəkɔːr], *s.m.* 1. *Sp:* record. 2. *Ind:* peak output; chiffre r., record figure.

‡**recourir** [rəkuriːr], *v.i.* to have recourse (à qch., to sth.).

recours [rəkuːr], *s.m.* recourse, resource.

recouvrer [rəkuvre], *v.tr.* to recover (sth.).

‡**recouvrir** [rəkuvriːr], *v.tr.* 1. to recover. 2. to cover (over).

récréation [rekreasjɔ̃], *s.f.* recreation; amusement.

récriminer [rekrimine], *v.i.* to recriminate. *s.f.* -ation.

recrue [rəkry], *s.f.* recruit.

recrut/er [rəkryte], *v.tr.* to recruit. *s.m.* -ement.

rectangle [rɛktɑ̃ːgl]. 1. *a.* right-angled. 2. *s.m.* rectangle.

rectangulaire [rɛktɑ̃gylɛːr], *a.* rectangular.

rectifi/er [rɛktifje], *v.tr.* to rectify. *s.f.* -cation.

rectitude [rɛktityd], *s.f.* rectitude.

reçu [rəsy], (a) *a.* received, accepted; (b) *s.m.* receipt.

‡**recueillir** [rəkœjiːr], *v.tr.* 1. to collect, gather. 2. to take in; to shelter (s.o. in need).

    se recueillir, to collect one's thoughts.

recul [rəkyl], *s.m.* backward movement; kick (of rifle); *Aut:* phare de r., reversing light.

recul/er [rəkyle]. 1. *v.i.* to move back; to recoil; ne r. devant rien, to shrink from nothing. 2. *v.tr.* (a) to move back; (b) to postpone. *s.m.* -ement.

    se reculer, to draw back.

reculons (à) [arəkylɔ̃], *adv.phr.* backwards.

‡**récupér/er** [rekypere], *v.tr.* to recover; to salvage; to make up (lost time). *s.f.* -ation.

récurrence [rekyrrɑ̃ːs], *s.f.* recurrence.

récurrent [rekyrrɑ̃], *a.* recurrent.

rédacteur, -trice [redaktœːr, -tris], *s.* 1. drafter (of document). 2. member of staff (of newspaper); r. en chef, editor.

rédaction [redaksjɔ̃], *s.f.* 1. (a) drafting; (b) editing; (c) *Sch:* essay. 2. editorial staff.

rédemption [redɑ̃psjɔ̃], *s.f.* redemption.

redevable [rədvabl], *a.* indebted (de qch. à qn, to s.o. for sth.).

‡**rédiger** [rediʒe], *v.tr.* 1. to draw up, draft; to write. 2. to edit.

redire [rədiːr], *v.tr.* 1. to tell, say, again; to repeat. 2. trouver à r. à qch., to take exception to sth.

redoubl/er [rəduble], *v.tr.* & *i.* to redouble, increase; *Sch:* r. une classe, to stay down.

redout/er [rədute], *v.tr.* to dread, fear. *a.* -able.

redress/er [rədrese], *v.tr.* 1. (a) to straighten (out); (b) to redress; to rectify. *s.m.* -ement. *s.m.* -eur, *El:* rectifier.

    se redresser, to draw oneself up.

réduction [redyksjɔ̃], *s.f.* reduction.

‡**réduire** [redɥiːr], *v.tr.* to reduce.

réduit [redɥi], *s.m.* retreat; nook.

‡**réel** [reel], *a.* a real, actual. *adv.* -lement.

‡**réélire** [reeliːr], *v.tr.* to re-elect.

refaire [rəfɛːr], *v.tr.* to remake; to do again.

réfectoire [refɛktwaːr], *s.m.* refectory, dining-hall.

référence [referɑ̃ːs], *s.f.* reference.

‡**référer (se)** [(sə)refere], *v.pr.* se r. à qch., à qn, to refer to sth., to s.o.; to ask s.o.'s opinion.

refermer [rəfɛrme], *v.tr.* to shut (door) again.

réfléchi [refleʃi], *a.* reflective, thoughtful.

réfléchir [refleʃiːr]. 1. *v.tr.* to reflect (light). 2. *v.i.* to reflect, think (sur, à, qch., about sth.); cela donne à r., it makes one think.

réflecteur [reflɛktœːr], *s.m.* reflector.

reflet [rəflɛ], *s.m.* reflection.

refléter [rəflete], *v.tr.* to reflect.

réflexe [reflɛks], *a.* & *s.m.* reflex.

réflexion [reflɛksjɔ̃], *s.f.* reflection.

refluer [rəflye], *v.i.* to flow back; (of tide) to ebb.

reflux [rəfly], *s.m.* ebb(-tide).

réformateur, -trice [reformatœːr], *s.* reformer.

réformation [reformasjɔ̃], *s.f.* reformation.

réforme [rəfɔrm], *s.f.* 1. reformation, reform. 2. *Mil:* invaliding out.

réformé [rəfɔrme], (a) *a.* *Ecc:* protestant; (b) *s.m. Mil:* man invalided out of the services.

reformer [rəfɔrme], *v.tr.* to re-form.

réformer [rəfɔrme], *v.tr.* 1. to reform, amend. 2. (a) *Mil:* to invalid out; (b) *Ind:* to scrap (machinery).

    se réformer, to reform, to turn over a new leaf.

refouler [rəfule], *v.tr.* to force back.

réfractaire [refraktɛːr], *a.* refractory.

réfraction [refraksjɔ̃], *s.f. Ph:* refraction; *Cin:* film à r., 3 D(imensional) film.

refrain [rəfrɛ̃], *s.m.* refrain; chorus.

‡**refréner** [rəfrene], *v.tr.* to curb, bridle.

réfrigérateur [refriʒeratœːr], *s.m.* refrigerator.

réfrigération [refriʒerasjɔ̃], *s.f.* refrigeration.

refroid/ir [rəfrwadiːr]. 1. *v.tr.* to cool, chill. 2. *v.i.* & *pr.* to grow cold. *s.m.* -issement.

refuge [rəfyːʒ], *s.m.* refuge; shelter; (on road) lay-by.

réfugié, -ée [refyʒje], *s.* refugee.

réfugier (se), [sərefyʒje], *v.pr.* to take refuge.

refus [rəfy], *s.m.* refusal.

refuser [rəfyze], *v.tr.* 1. to refuse. 2. to reject.
se refuser, to refuse; to object.

réfut/er [refyte], *v.tr.* to refute (theory). *s.f.* -ation.

regagner [rəgɑɲe], *v.tr.* to regain, get back (sth.); r. son domicile, to return home.

‡regal [regal], *s.m.* feast.

régaler [regale], *v.tr.* to entertain (friends).
se régaler, to feast (de, on); F: on s'est bien régalé(s), we did ourselves well, proud.

regard [rəgaːr], *s.m.* look, glance, gaze; chercher qn du r., to look round for s.o.

regarder [rəgarde], *v.tr.* 1. (a) to regard, consider (sth.); (b) cela ne vous regarde pas, that's no business of yours. 2. to look at (s.o., sth.); puis-je r.? may I have a look?

régate [regat], *s.f.* regatta.

régence [reʒɑːs], *s.f.* regency.

régent [reʒɑ̃], *s. regent.

régie [reʒi], *s.f.* 1. *Jur:* administration. 2. r. des impôts indirects, excise (administration); r. française des tabacs, French State tobacco company.

regimber [rəʒɛ̃be], *v.i.* to kick; to jib.

régime [reʒim], *s.m.* 1. regime. 2. diet. 3. *Gram:* object. 4. bunch (of dates, bananas).

régiment [reʒimɑ̃], *s.m.* regiment.

régimentaire [reʒimɑ̃tɛːr], *a.* regimental.

région [reʒjɔ̃], *s.f.* region. *a.* -al.

régir [reʒiːr], *v.tr.* to govern, rule.

régisseur [reʒisœːr], *s.m.* steward; *Th:* stage-manager.

registre [rəʒistr], *s.m.* register.

réglable [reglabl], *a.* adjustable.

réglage [reglaːʒ], *s.m.* (a) regulating, adjusting; (b) *Rad:* tuning.

règle [rɛgl], *s.f.* 1. ruler; r. à calcul, slide rule. 2. rule; en r., in order. 3. *pl. Med:* menses, monthly period.

règlement [rɛgləmɑ̃], *s.m.* 1. settlement, adjustment. 2. regulation(s).

réglementaire [rɛgləmɑ̃tɛːr], *a.* regular, statutory, prescribed.

réglement/er [rɛgləmɑ̃te], *v.tr.* to regulate. *s.f.* -ation.

‡régler [regle], *v.tr.* 1. to rule. 2. to regulate. 3. (a) to settle (question); (b) to set (affairs) in order.

réglisse [reglis], *s.f.* liquorice.

règne [rɛɲ], *s.m.* 1. reign. 2. (vegetable, animal) kingdom.

régner [reɲe], *v.i.* to reign, rule.

‡regorger [rəgɔrʒe], *v.i.* to overflow, run over; to be crowded (de, with).

regret [rəgrɛ], *s.m.* regret; à r., reluctantly.

regrett/er [rəgrete], *v.tr.* to regret. *a.* -able.

régulariser [regylarize], *v.tr.* to regularize.

régularité [regylarite], *s.f.* (a) regularity; (b) steadiness; épreuve de r., reliability trial; (c) equability.

‡réguli/er [regylje], *a.* (a) regular; (b) steady; (c) equable. *adv.* -èrement.

rehausser [rəose], *v.tr.* 1. to raise. 2. to heighten (colour); to accentuate (a detail).

réimprimer [reɛ̃prime], *v.tr.* to reprint.

rein [rɛ̃], *s.m.* 1. kidney. 2. *pl.* back; se casser les reins, to break one's back.

reine [rɛn], *s.f.* queen; la R. mère, the Queen Mother.

reine-claude [rɛnkloːd], *s.f.* greengage. *pl.* reines-claude.

‡réintégr/er [reɛ̃tegre], *v.tr.* 1. to reinstate. 2. to return to. *s.f.* -ation.

‡réitér/er [reitere], *v.tr.* to reiterate. *s.f.* -ation.

rejeter [rəʒ(ə)te], *v.tr.* 1. to throw back. 2. to transfer. 3. to reject.

rejeton [rəʒtɔ̃], *s.m.* 1. shoot, sucker. 2. descendant, offspring.

rejoindre [rəʒwɛ̃dr], *v.tr.* to rejoin, reunite.

réjoui [reʒwi], *a.* jolly, cheerful.

‡réjou/ir [reʒwiːr], *v.tr.* to delight, gladden. *s.f.* -issance.
se réjouir. 1. to be delighted, glad (to see s.o., etc.). 2. to enjoy oneself.

relâche [rəlaːʃ]. 1. *s.m.* relaxation; respite; *Th:* (on bills) no performance. 2. *s.f. Nau:* (a) call; (b) port of call.

relâch/er [rəlaʃe]. 1. *v.tr.* (a) to loosen, slacken; (b) to relax (discipline). 2. *v.tr.* to release (prisoner). *s.m.* -ement.

relais [rəlɛ], *s.m.* relay; shift; r. gastronomique, restaurant with a reputation for good cooking.

‡relancer [rəlɑ̃se], *v.tr.* 1. to throw back. 2. r. lè moteur, to restart the engine.

relater [rəlate], *v.tr.* to relate, state (facts).

relati/f [rəlatif], *a.* relative. *adv.* -vement.

relation [rəlasjɔ̃], *s.f.* relation. 1. être en r. avec qn, to be in touch with s.o. 2. account, narrative, statement.

relayer [rəlɛje], *v.tr.* to relay, to take turns with (s.o.).

‡reléguer [rəlege], *v.tr.* to relegate; r. qch. au grenier, to banish sth. to the attic.

relent [rəlɑ̃], *s.m.* musty smell, taste.

relevé [rəlve], *a.* exalted. 2. *s.m.* summary.

rel/ever [rəlve]. I. *v.tr.* 1. (a) to raise, lift; (b) to pick up. 2. to call attention to. 3. to bring into relief; to heighten. 4. to relieve (sentry). 5. (com: to make out (account); to read (meter); *Sch:* to take in (the marks). II. *v.i.* 1. to have only just recovered (from illness). 2. r. de qn, to come under the authority of s.o. *s.m.* -èvement.

se relever. 1. to rise to one's feet. 2. (of trade, etc.) to revive. 3. to recover (from illness).

relief [rəljɛf], *s.m. Geog: etc:* relief.

relier [rəlje], *v.tr.* (*a*) to connect, join; (*b*) to bind (book).

relieur [rəljœːr], *s.m.* (book)binder.

religieu/x, -euse [rəliʒjø, -øːz]. 1. *a.* religious. 2. *s.m.* monk; *f.* nun. 3. *s.f. Cu:* (type of) eclair. *adv.* -sement.

religion [rəliʒjɔ̃], *s.f.* religion.

reliquaire [rəlikɛːr], *s.m.* reliquary, shrine.

relique [rəlik], *s.f.* relic (of saint).

†relire [rəliːr], *v.tr.* to read again.

reliure [rəljyːr], *s.f.* (book)binding.

†relui/re [rəluiːr], *v.i.* to shine; to glitter. *a.* -sant.

remanier [rəmanje], *v.tr.* to alter, adapt.

remarier (se) [rəmarje], *v.pr.* to remarry.

remarquable [rəmarkabl], *a.* remarkable. *adv.* -ment.

remarque [rəmark], *s.f.* remark.

remarquer [rəmarke], *v.tr.* (*a*) to remark, notice, observe; faire r., to point out; (*b*) se faire r., to attract attention.

rembarquer [rɑ̃barke], *v.tr. & i.* to re-embark.

remblai [rɑ̃blɛ], *s.m.* embankment, bank.

rembourrer [rɑ̃bure], *v.tr.* to stuff, pad.

rembours/er [rɑ̃burse], *v.tr.* to repay. *s.m.* -ement.

re．nbrunir [rɑ̃bryniːr], *v.tr.* to cast a gloom over.

remède [rəmɛd], *s.m.* remedy, cure.

remédi/er [rəmedje], *v.ind.tr.* r. à qch., to cure sth., to put sth. right. *a.* -able.

remembr/er [rəmɑ̃bre], *v.tr.* to regroup (farm land). *s.m.* -ement.

remerciement [rəmɛrsimɑ̃], *s.m.* thanks.

remercier [rəmɛrsje], *v.tr.* 1. to thank (de, for). 2. to dismiss.

†remettre [rəmɛtr], *v.tr.* 1. to put back; (*a*) to put on again; r. un os, to set a bone; (*b*) to calm, compose (s.o.'s mind); (*c*) to remember (sth.). 2. to send (application); to hand over (sth. to s.o.). 3. to forgive. 4. to postpone. **se remettre.** 1. se r. au lit, au travail, to go back to bed, to start work again; le temps se remet (au beau), it's clearing up. 2. to recover; pull oneself together. 3. s'en r. à (qn), to leave it to (s.o.).

réminiscence [reminissɑ̃ːs], *s.f.* reminiscence.

remise [rəmiːz], *s.f.* 1. putting back (of sth. in its place). 2. (*a*) delivery (of parcel); (*b*) remission (of penalty). 3. *Com:* discount. 4. shed, garage.

rémission [remisjɔ̃], *s.f.* remission.

remonte-pentes [rəmɔ̃tpɑ̃ːt], *s.m.inv.* ski lift.

remonter [rəmɔ̃te]. 1. *v.i.* (aux. -être) (*a*) to go up (again); (*b*) to go back. 2. *v.tr.* (aux. avoir) (*a*) to go, climb, up (hill, etc.) again; (*b*) to take, carry up; to pull up; (*c*) to wind (up) (watch).

remontrance [rəmɔ̃trɑ̃ːs], *s.f.* remonstrance.

remords [rəmɔːr], *s.m.* remorse.

remorque [rəmɔrk], *s.f.* 1. towing. 2. tow-line. 3. *Aut:* trailer.

remorquer [rəmɔrke], *v.tr.* to tow; to haul.

remorqueur [rəmɔrkœːr], *s.m.* tug.

remous [rəmu], *s.m.* eddy; wash (of ship); *Av:* slip stream.

rempart [rɑ̃paːr], *s.m.* rampart.

remplaçant, -ante [rɑ̃plasɑ̃, -ɑ̃ːt], *s.* substitute; locum tenens.

†remplac/er [rɑ̃plase], *v.tr.* to replace (s.o., sth.); to deputize for (s.o.) *s.m.* -ement.

remplir [rɑ̃pliːr], *v.tr.* 1. to fill up; to refill; to take up (time). 2. to fill in (form). 3. to carry out (instructions); *Th:* r. un rôle, to play a part.

remporter [rɑ̃pɔrte], *v.tr.* 1. to take back or away. 2. to carry off; to win.

remue-ménage [rəmymenaːʒ], *s.m.inv.* stir, bustle, confusion.

remuer [rəmɥe]. 1. *v.tr.* to move; to shift; to stir (coffee, etc.) 2. *v.i.* to move; (of child) to fidget.

†rémuner/er [remynere], *v.tr.* (*a*) to reward (s.o.); (*b*) to pay for (services). *s.f.* -ation, *s.* †-ateur.

renaissance [rənɛssɑ̃ːs], *s.f.* (*a*) rebirth; (*b*) Renaissance.

†renaître [rənɛːtr], *v.i.* (*a*) to be born again; (*b*) (of plants) to reappear, grow again.

renard, -arde [rənaːr, -ard], *s.* fox, *f.* vixen.

renchér/ir [rɑ̃ʃeriːr], *v.i.* (*a*) (of goods) to get dearer; (of pers.) r. sur qn, (i) to outbid s.o.; (ii) to go one better than s.o. *s.m.* -issement.

rencontre [rɑ̃kɔ̃ːtr], *s.f.* (*a*) meeting, encounter; aller à la r. de qn, to go to meet s.o.; connaissance de r., chance acquaintance; (*b*) collision.

rencontrer [rɑ̃kɔ̃tre], *v.tr.* to meet (s.o.). **se rencontrer.** 1. (*a*) to meet; (*b*) to collide. 2. (of ideas) to agree.

rendement [rɑ̃dmɑ̃], *s.m.* (*a*) produce, yield; return, profit; (*b*) output; (*c*) efficiency (of a machine).

rendez-vous [rɑ̃devu], *s.m.inv.* rendez-vous. 1. appointment. 2. resort, meeting place.

†rendormir (se) [rɑ̃dɔrmiːr], *v.pr.* to go to sleep again.

rendre [rɑ̃dr], *v.tr.* 1. (*a*) to give back, return (sth.); to repay (money); (*b*) r. hommage à qn, to pay homage to s.o.; (*c*) to produce, yield; terre qui ne rend pas, unproductive land; (*d*) to work; le moteur rend bien, the engine

works well. 2. to deliver (goods). 3. (a) r. un jugement, to deliver judgement; (b) F: to be sick, to vomit. 4. Mil: to surrender (town); r. les armes, to lay down arms; to admit defeat. 5. se r. ridicule, to make oneself ridiculous.
se rendre. 1. to go (to a place). 2. to surrender; to yield.

rendu [rɑ̃dy], a. exhausted, worn out.

rêne [rɛn], s.f. rein.

renégat [renega], s. renegade, turncoat.

renfermé [rɑ̃fɛrme]. 1. a. uncommunicative. 2. odeur de r., smell; sentir le r., to smell stuffy.

renfermer [rɑ̃fɛrme], v.tr. 1. to shut (sth.) up again. 2. to shut, lock (s.o., sth.) up. 3. to contain, include (ideas, etc.).

renfl/er [rɑ̃fle], v.tr. & i. to swell (out). s.m. -ement.

renflouer [rɑ̃flue], v.tr. to refloat (ship); to set (business) on its feet again.

‡renforcer [rɑ̃fɔrse], v.tr. to reinforce; to strengthen.

renfort [rɑ̃fɔːr], s.m. reinforcement(s); El: batterie de r., booster battery.

renfrogner (se) [sərɑ̃frɔɲe], v.pr. to scowl.

reni/er [rɑnje], v.tr. to disown (son, friend); to abjure (one's faith). s.m. -ement.

renifl/er [rɑnifle], v.i. to sniff. s.m. -ement.

renne [rɛn], s.m. reindeer.

renom [rɑnɔ̃], s.m. renommée [rɑnɔme], s.f. renown, fame.

‡renonc/er [rɑnɔ̃se], v.i. r. à (faire) qch., to give up (the idea of doing) sth. s.m. -ement. s.f. -iation.

‡renouvel/er [r(ə)nuvle], v.tr. to renew. s.m. -lement.
se renouveler. 1. to be renewed. 2. to recur, to happen again.

rénovation [renovasjɔ̃], s.f. renovation, restoration.

renseignement [rɑ̃sɛɲmɑ̃], s.m. (piece of) information; prendre des renseignements sur qch., to inquire about sth. P.N: renseignements, inquiries.

renseigner [rɑ̃sɛɲe], v.tr. r. qn sur qch., to give s.o. information about sth.; vous a mal renseigné, you have been misinformed.
se renseigner, to make inquiries (sur, about).

rente [rɑ̃ːt], s.f. 1. annuity. 2. pl. (unearned) income.

rentier, -ière [rɑ̃tje, -jɛːr], s. (a) Fin: stockholder, fundholder; (b) annuitant. 2. person of independent means.

rentrant, -ante [rɑ̃trɑ̃, -ɑ̃ːt]. 1. a. Av: retractable (undercarriage). 2. s. Sp: new player.

rentrée [rɑ̃tre], s.f. 1. (a) return, homecoming; (b) re-opening (of school, parliament); la r. (des classes), the beginning of term. 2. bringing in (of harvest).

rentrer [rɑ̃tre]. I. v.i. (aux. être) (a) to come, go, in again; r. au port, to return to port; Th: Macbeth rentre, re-enter Macbeth; (b) to return home; (c) Fin: faire r. ses fonds, to call in one's money. II. v.tr. (aux. avoir) to take, bring, (sth.) in; to put (sth.) away; Av: to retract (the undercarriage).

renverse [rɑ̃vɛrs], s.f. tomber à la r., to fall backwards.

renvers/er [rɑ̃vɛrse], v.tr. (a) to reverse, invert; r. les rôles, to turn the tables on s.o.; (b) to turn upside down; (c) to knock over; to overturn, upset; to spill (liquid); (d) to overthrow (government). s.m. -ement.
se renverser, to fall over; to overturn; to capsize.

renvoi [rɑ̃vwa], s.m. 1. return, sending back (of goods). 2. dismissal. 3. postponement. 4. (cross) reference.

‡renvoyer [rɑ̃vwaje], v.tr. 1. to send back; to return; 2. (a) to send away; (b) to dismiss. 3. to put off, postpone. 4. to refer.

réorganis/er [reorganize], v.tr. to reorganize. s.f. -ation.

réouverture [reuvɛrtyːr], s.f. reopening.

repaire [rəpɛːr], s.m. den; lair; haunt.

répandre [repɑ̃ːdr], v.tr. 1. to pour out; to spill, shed. 2. to spread (news, etc.); to give off (smell).
se répandre. (a) (of liquid) to spill; to run over; (b) (of smell, etc.) to spread (of rumour) to gain ground.

répandu [repɑ̃dy], a. wide-spread, prevalent.

reparaître [rəparɛːtr], v.i. to reappear.

réparateur, -trice [reparatœːr, -tris]. 1. a. repairing, restoring. 2. s. repairer.

répar/er [repare], v.tr. 1. to repair, mend. 2. to make amends for; to rectify (mistake). s.f. -ation.

reparler [rəparle], v.i. to speak again; nous en reparlerons, we'll talk about it later.

repartie [rəparti], s.f. retort, rejoinder; repartee.

‡repartir [rəpartiːr], v.i. 1. (aux. être) to set out again. 2. (aux. avoir) to retort, reply.

‡répartir [repartiːr], v.tr. to distribute, share out. s.f. -ition.

repas [rəpɑ], s.m. meal.

repasser [rəpase]. 1. v.i. to pass, go, by, again. 2. v.tr. (a) pass by, cross over (sth.) again; repassez-moi cette lettre, let me see that letter again; (b) to sharpen (tool); (c) to iron (clothes); fer à r., iron.

repêcher [rəpɛʃe], v.tr. to fish out (again).

‡repentir (se) [sərəpɑ̃tiːr], v.pr. se r. de, to repent.

répercussion [repɛrkysjɔ̃], s.f. repercussion; reverberation.

répercuter [reperkyte], *v.tr.* to reverberate.

repère [rəpɛːr], *s.m.* point de r., landmark.

‡**repérer** [rəpere], *v.tr.* to locate; to spot.

répertoire [repertwaːr], *s.m.* 1. index, list, catalogue; r. d'adresses, (i) directory; (ii) address book. 2. *Th:* repertoire.

‡**répéter** [repete], *v.tr.* (a) to repeat; (b) *Th:* to rehearse. *s.f.* -ition.
se répéter. 1. to repeat oneself. 2. to recur.

répétiteur, -trice [repetitœːr, -tris], *s.* (a) assistant-master, -mistress (in charge of preparation, etc.); (b) private tutor.

repiquer [rəpike], *v.tr.* to prick, pierce, (sth.) again; to plant out (seedlings); plant à r., bedding plant.

répit [repi], *s.m.* respite; breathing-space.

‡**replacer** [rəplase], *v.tr.* to put (sth.) back in its place; to reinvest (money).

repli [rəpli], *s.m.* 1. fold, crease. 2. coil (of serpent).

replier [rəplie], *v.tr.* to fold up (again).
se replier. (a) to fold up, turn back; (b) to wind, turn.

réplique [replik], *s.f.* 1. retort, rejoinder. 2. *Th:* cue. 3. replica.

répliquer [replike], *v.i.* to retort; to answer back.

répondant [repɔ̃dɑ̃], *s.m.* 1. *Ecc:* server (at mass). 2. *Jur:* guarantor.

répondre [repɔ̃ːdr]. 1. *v.tr.* to answer; *Ecc:* r. la messe, to serve the responses (at mass). 2. *v.i.* r. à une question, to answer a question; r. à un besoin, to answer a purpose, meet a need. 3. *v.i.* r. de qn, de qch. to be answerable, responsible, for s.o, sth.

répons [repɔ̃], *s.m. Ecc:* response.

réponse [repɔ̃ːs], *s.f.* answer, reply; response (to appeal, stimulus).

reportage [rəpɔrtaːʒ], *s.m.* (newspaper) report(ing); running commentary (on match, etc.).

reporter[1] [rəpɔrte], *v.tr.* to take back, (*in book-keeping*) to carry forward.
se reporter à qch, to refer to sth.

reporter[2] [rəpɔrtɛːr], *s.m.* reporter.

repos [rəpo], *s.m.* 1. (a) rest, repose; (b) pause. 2. peace, tranquillity.

reposer [rəpoze], *v.tr. & i.* to rest (sur, on).
se reposer, to rest.

repouss/er [rəpuse], *v.tr.* (a) to push back, repulse; to reject; (b) to repel. *a.* -ant, repulsive, repellent.

répréhensible [repreɑ̃sibl], *a.* reprehensible.

‡**reprendre** [rəprɑ̃ːdr]. 1. *v.tr.* (a) to recapture (town); (b) to take some more, a second helping; (c) *Com:* nos articles ne sont ni repris ni échangés, our goods cannot be returned or exchanged; (d) to go back to (one's work); (e) r. qn, to reprove s.o., *F:* to tell s.o. off. 2. *v.i.* to start again; (*of patient*) to recover; (*of business*) to improve.
se reprendre. 1. to recover oneself, pull oneself together. 2. to correct oneself.

représailles [rəprezaːj], *s.f.pl.* reprisals.

représentant, -ante [rəprezɑ̃tɑ̃, -ɑ̃ːt], *s.* representative; agent.

représent/er [rəprezɑ̃te], *v.tr.* to represent. 2. *Th:* (a) to perform (play); (b) to act (part). *a.* †-atif. *s.f.* -ation.

répression [represjɔ̃], *s.f.* repression.

réprimande [reprimɑ̃ːd], *s.f.* reprimand.

réprimander [reprimɑ̃de], *v.tr.* to reprimand.

réprimer [reprime], *v.tr.* to repress.

repris [rəpri]. 1. *s.m.* r. de justice, old offender. 2. *a. Com:* emballage non r., non-returnable packing.

reprise [rəpriːz], *s.f.* 1. retaking, recapture. 2. (a) resumption, renewal; (b) à plusieurs reprises, on several occasions. 3. darn. 4. *Aut:* pick-up.

repriser [rəprize], *v.tr.* to mend, darn.

réprobation [reprobasjɔ̃], *s.f.* reprobation.

reproche [rəprɔʃ], *s.m.* reproach.

reprocher [rəprɔʃe], *v.tr.* 1. to reproach. 2. r. un succès à qn, to grudge s.o. his success.

†**reproducteur** [rəprodyktœːr]. 1. *a.* reproductive (organ). 2. *s.m.* animal kept for breeding purposes; r. d'élite, pedigree sire.

reproduction [rəprodyksjɔ̃], *s.f.* 1. reproduction. 2. copy.

‡**reproduire** [rəprodɥiːr], *v.tr.* to reproduce; to copy.
se reproduire. 1. to recur; to happen again. 2. to reproduce, breed.

reptile [reptil], *s.m.* reptile.

repu [rəpy], *a.* satiated; full.

républicain, -aine [repyblikɛ̃, -ɛn], *a. & s.* republican.

république [repyblik], *s.f.* republic.

répudi/er [repydje], *v.tr.* 1. to repudiate. 2. to renounce. *s.f.* -ation.

répugnance [repyɲɑ̃ːs], *s.f.* 1. repugnance. 2. reluctance.

répugnant [repyɲɑ̃], *a.* repugnant.

répugner [repyɲe], *v.i.* 1. to feel repugnance; to feel reluctant. 2. il me répugne de, I am reluctant to.

répulsion [repylsjɔ̃], *s.f.* repulsion.

réputation [repytasjɔ̃], *s.f.* reputation, fame.

réputé [repyte], *a.* well-known; of note.

requiem [rekɥiem], *s.m.inv. Ecc:* (messe de) r., requiem (mass).

requête [rəkɛt], *s.f.* request, petition.

requin [rəkɛ̃], *s.m.* shark.

réquisition [rekizisjɔ̃], *s.f.* requisition.

réquisitionner [rekizisjɔne], *v.tr.* to requisition.

réseau [rezo], *s.m.* network (of roads, etc.); r. fluvial, river system; r. électrique, (electricity) grid.

réserve [rezɛrv], *s.f.* 1. (a) reservation; (b) reserve. 2. reserve, caution.

réserv/er [rezɛrve], *v.tr.* to reserve. *s.f.* -ation. *s.m.* -iste.
  se réserver, to hold back, wait.

réservoir [rezɛrvwaːr], *s.m.* 1. reservoir. 2. tank.

résidence [rezidãːs], *s.f.* residence.

†résidentiel [rezidãsjɛl], *a.* residential.

résider [rezide], *v.i.* 1. to reside, dwell, live. 2. toute la difficulté réside en ceci, the whole difficulty lies in this.

résidu [rezidy], *s.m.* residue; résidus urbains, town refuse.

résign/er [rezine], *v.tr.* to resign. *s.f.* -ation.

résine [rezin], *s.f.* resin.

†résineux [rezinø], *a.* resinous.

résistance [rezistãːs], *s.f.* resistance. 1. opposition. 2. (a) strength; (b) endurance.

résistant [rezistã], *a.* resistant; strong.

résister [reziste], *v.ind.tr.* to resist.

résolu [rezɔly], *a.* resolute; determined. *adv.* -ment.

résolution [rezɔlysjɔ̃], *s.f.* 1. solution (of problem); termination (of agreement). 2. resolution.

résonance [rezɔnãːs], *s.f.* resonance.

résonner [rezɔne], *v.i.* to resound.

‡résoudre [rezuːdr], *v.tr.* to solve (difficulty, problem); to settle (question).
  se résoudre, to make up one's mind.

respect [rɛspɛ], *s.m.* respect.

respectable [rɛspɛktabl], *a.* respectable.

respect/er [rɛspɛkte], *v.tr.* to respect. *s.f.* -abilité.

†respectif [rɛspɛktif], *a.* respective. *adv.* -ivement.

†respectueu/x [rɛspɛktɥø], *a.* respectful; dutiful. *adv.* -sement.

respiration [rɛspirasjɔ̃], *s.f.* respiration, breathing.

respirer [rɛspire], *v.i. & tr.* to breathe.

resplendissant [rɛsplãdisã], *a.* resplendent, dazzling.

responsabilité [rɛspɔ̃sabilite], *s.f.* responsibility; liability.

responsable [rɛspɔ̃sabl], *a.* responsible, answerable.

ressac [rəsak], *s.m.* 1. undertow. 2. surf.

ressaisir [rəseziːr], *v.tr.* to recapture.
  se ressaisir, to recover, to pull oneself together.

ressemblance [rəsãblãːs], *s.f.* resemblance, likeness.

ressemblant [rəsãblã], *a.* like, alike.

ressembler [rəsãble], *v.ind.tr.* r. à (qn, qch.), to resemble, to be like (s.o., sth.).
  se ressembler, to be (a)like.

ressentiment [rəsãtimã], *s.m.* resentment.

‡ressent/ir [rəsãtiːr], *v.tr.* (a) to feel; (b) to resent; (c) to feel, experience.
  se ressentir de, to feel the effects of.

resserrer [rəsɛre], *v.tr.* 1. to contract, close up. 2. to tighten. *s.m.* -ement.
  se resserrer, to contract, shrink.

ressort [rəsɔːr], *s.m.* 1. (a) elasticity; (b) spring. 2. en dernier r., in the last resort.

‡ressortir [rəsɔrtiːr], *v.i.* 1. (aux. être) (a) to come, go, out again; (b) *v.tr.* to bring out again. 2. (aux. être) (a) to stand out; (b) to be evident; (b) to result, follow (de, from). 3. (aux. avoir) to belong to; to be under the jurisdiction of.

ressource [rəsurs], *s.f.* resource. 1. resourcefulness. 2. expedient, shift. 3. *pl.* resources, means.

ressusciter [resysite], *v.tr. & i.* to resuscitate; to come to life (again).

restant [rɛstã], *a.* (a) remaining, left; (b) poste restante, poste restante.

restaurant [rɛstɔrã], *s.m.* restaurant.

restaurateur [rɛstɔratœːr], *s.m.* restaurant owner.

restauration [rɛstɔrasjɔ̃], *s.f.* restoration.

restaurer [rɛstɔre], *v.tr.* to restore.
  se restaurer, to take refreshment.

reste [rɛst], *s.m.* 1. rest, remainder; et le r., and so on; de r., over and above; au r., du r., besides, moreover. 2. *pl.* remains.

rester [rɛste], *v.i.* (aux. être). 1. to remain, to be left; il me reste cinq francs, I have five francs left. 2. to stay, remain (behind); r. au lit, to stay in bed; r. calme, to keep calm. 3. to stay (for a time); r. à Paris, to stay in Paris.

restitu/er [rɛstitɥe], *v.tr.* to restore; to give back. *s.f.* -tion.

‡restreindre [rɛstrɛ̃ːdr], *v.tr.* to restrict; to limit.
  se restreindre, to cut down expenses; to limit oneself (à, to).

restreint [rɛstrɛ̃], *a.* restricted, limited.

†restrictif [rɛstriktif], *a.* restrictive.

restriction [rɛstriksjɔ̃], *s.f.* restriction, limitation; r. mentale, mental reservation.

résultat [rezylta], *s.m.* result, outcome.

résulter [rezylte], *v.i.* (used only in third pers.) to result, follow; il en résulte que, it follows that, consequently . . .

résumé [rezyme], *s.m.* summary, résumé.

résumer [rezyme], *v.tr.* to summarize; to sum up.

résurrection [rezyrɛksjɔ̃], *s.f.* resurrection.

rétabl/ir [retabliːr], *v.tr.* to re-establish. *s.m.* -issement.
  se rétablir. 1. (a) to recover, get well again; (b) l'ordre se rétablit, order is being restored. 2. to re-establish oneself.

retard [rəta:r], s.m. delay, slowness; en r., late.

retardataire [rətardatɛ:r], s. (a) late-comer; (b) laggard.

retarder [rətarde]. 1. v.tr. to delay (s.o., sth.); to put back (clock). 2. v.i. to be late; (of clock) to be slow.

‡**retenir** [rətni:r], v.tr. 1. (a) to hold (back); to detain; (b) to hold in position, to secure. 2. (a) to retain, hold back (money); r. par cœur, to remember by heart; (b) to reserve (seat). 3. to restrain (anger, etc.). se retenir, to hold oneself in; to refrain (from doing sth.).

retentir [rətɑ̃ti:r], v.i. to resound, echo. a. -issant. s.m. -issement.

retenue [rətny], s.f. 1. deduction. 2. Sch: detention. 3. reserve, discretion.

réticence [retisɑ̃:s], s.f. reticence, reserve.

‡**rétif** [retif], a. restive, stubborn.

retiré [rətire], a. retired, remote.

retirer [rətire], v.tr. to pull out; to withdraw; to take off. se retirer, to retire, withdraw.

retomber [rətɔ̃be], v.i. (aux. usu. être) 1. to fall (down) again. 2. to fall (back).

retour [rətu:r], s.m. 1. (a) twisting, winding; (b) reversal (of fortune); (c) recurrence. 2. return; être de r., to be back (home); par r. du courrier, by return of post; Cin: r. en arrière, flash-back; Aut: avoir des retours, to backfire.

retourner [rəturne]. 1. v.tr. (a) to turn inside out; (b) to turn over; (c) to turn round. 2. v.tr. to return. 3. v.i. to go back. se retourner, to turn (round); to turn over.

rétracter [retrakte], v.tr. to draw in (claws); to withdraw; to go back on (opinion). se rétracter. 1. to shrink. 2. to eat one's words.

retrait [rətrɛ], s.m. 1. withdrawal. 2. recess; en r., set back.

retraite [rətrɛt], s.f. 1. retreat, withdrawal. 2. Mil: tattoo. 3. retirement; r. de vieillesse, old-age pension. 4. (a) retreat; maison de r., old people's home; (b) refuge; lair.

retranch/er [rətrɑ̃ʃe], v.tr. 1. to cut off. 2. to entrench. s.m. -ement.

rétréc/ir [retresi:r], v.i. & pr. to contract; to grow narrow; to shrink. s.m. -issement.

rétribuer [retribɥe], v.tr. to pay (employee, etc.).

rétribution [retribysjɔ̃], s.f. remuneration; salary.

†**rétroactif** [retroaktif], a. retroactive, retrospective.

rétrograde [retrograd], a. retrograde, backward, reversed (motion).

†**rétrospectif** [retrospɛktif], a. retrospective.

retrousser [rətruse], v.tr. to turn up, roll up; nez retroussé, snub nose.

retrouver [rətruve], v.tr. to find (again).

rétroviseur [retrovizœ:r], s.m. Aut: driving mirror.

réunion [reynjɔ̃], s.f. 1. reunion. 2. assembly, meeting.

réunir [reyni:r], v.tr. to (re)unite; to join (things) together; r. le comité, to call a committee meeting. se réunir, to meet.

réussi [reysi], a. successful.

réussir [reysi:r]. 1. v.i. to succeed. 2. v.tr. to make a success of.

réussite [reysit], s.f. 1. success. 2. (card game) patience.

revanche [rəvɑ̃:ʃ], s.f. 1. revenge; jouer la r., to play the return game. 2. requital; en r., on the other hand.

rêve [rɛ:v], s.m. dream.

réveil [revɛj], s.m. 1. (a) waking, awakening; (b) Mil: reveille. 2. alarm (clock).

réveille-matin [revɛjmatɛ̃], s.m.inv. alarm (clock).

réveiller [revɛje], v.tr. to wake (s.o.) up. 2. to awaken (memories). se réveiller, to wake (up).

réveillon [revɛjɔ̃], s.m. midnight supper.

réveillonner [revɛjone], v.i. to go to a midnight supper; to see the New Year in.

†**révélateur** [revelatœ:r]. 1. a revealing, tell-tale. 2. s.m. Phot: developer.

révélation [revelasjɔ̃], s.f. revelation.

‡**révéler** [revele], v.tr. (a) to reveal, disclose; (b) to show; to betray (faults). se révéler, to be revealed, to come to light.

revenant [rəvnɑ̃], s.m. ghost.

revendi/quer [rəvɑ̃dike], v.tr. to claim. s.f. -cation.

revendre [rəvɑ̃:dr], v.tr. to resell.

‡**revenir** [rəvni:r], v.i. 1. to return; to come back; to go back on (a promise). 2. son visage ne me revient pas, I don't like his looks. 3. je n'en reviens pas! I can't get over it! r. à soi, to recover consciousness. 4. en r. à qch., to come back to sth. 5. (a) to cost; (b) cela revient au même, it comes to the same thing.

revenu [rəvny], s.m. income; revenue.

rêver [rɛve], v.i. & tr. to dream.

réverbération [revɛrberasjɔ̃], s.f. reverberation.

réverbère [revɛrbɛ:r], s.m. street lamp.

révérence [reverɑ̃:s], s.f. 1. reverence. 2. bow; curtsey.

révérend [reverɑ̃], a. Ecc: reverend.

révérer [revere], v.tr. to revere.

rêverie [rɛvri], s.f. reverie; dreaming.

revers [rəvɛ:r], s.m. (a) reverse; wrong side; other side; (b) facing, lapel.

réversible [revɛrsibl], a. reversible.

réversion [reversjɔ̃], s.f. reversion.

revêtement [rəvetmɑ̃], s.m. facing, coating.

‡revêtir [rəvetiːr], v.tr. 1. to reclothe. 2. to clothe, dress. 3. to put on (coat).
se revêtir de, to put on; to assume.

†rêveur [revœːr], a. dreamy.

revient [rəvjɛ̃], s.m. prix de r., cost price.

revirement [rəvirmɑ̃], s.m. sudden change.

réviser [revize], v.tr. to revise; to overhaul (machinery).

réviseur [revizœːr], s.m. reviser; auditor; proof-reader.

révision [revizjɔ̃], s.f. revision; proofreading; inspection, overhaul(ing) (of machinery).

‡revivre [rəviːvr], v.i. to live again; to revive.

révocation [revokasjɔ̃], s.f. 1. revocation, repeal (of edict). 2. removal, dismissal (of official).

‡revoir [rəvwaːr], v.tr. 1. to see again; s.m.inv. au r., goodbye. 2. to revise.

révoltant [revoltɑ̃], a. revolting; shocking.

révolte [revolt], s.f. revolt, rebellion.

révolter [revolte], v.tr. to shock, disgust.
se révolter, to revolt, rebel.

révolution [revolysjɔ̃], s.f. revolution.

révolutionnaire [revolysjonɛːr], a. & s. revolutionary; (b) s. revolutionist.

révolutionner [revolysjone], v.tr. to revolutionize.

revolver [revolvɛːr], s.m. revolver.

révoquer [revoke], v.tr. 1. to revoke; to countermand. 2. to dismiss.

revue [rəvy], s.f. 1. review. 2. (a) magazine; (b) Th: revue.

rez-de-chaussée [redʒose], s.m.inv. (a) ground level; (b) ground-floor.

rhabiller (se) [sərabije], v.pr. (a) to dress (oneself) again; (b) to buy a new outfit.

rhéostat [reosta], s.m. El: rheostat.

rhésus [resys], s.m. rhesus.

rhinocéros [rinoseros], s.m. rhinoceros.

rhizome [rizoːm], s.m. rhizome.

rhododendron [rododɛ̃drɔ̃], s.m. rhododendron.

rhubarbe [rybarb], s.f. rhubarb.

rhum [rɔm], s.m. rum.

rhumatisme [rymatism], s.m. rheumatism.

rhume [rym], s.m. Med: cold.

riant [rjɑ̃], a. 1. smiling. 2. cheerful.

rican/er [rikane], v.i. to laugh unpleasantly, to sneer. s.m. -ement.

riche [riʃ], a. 1. rich, wealthy, well-off. 2. valuable. adv. -ment.

richesse [riʃɛs], s.f. 1. wealth; riches. 2. richness.

ricin [risɛ̃], s.m. huile de r., castor oil.

ricocher [rikoʃe], v.i. (a) to glance off; (b) to ricochet.

ricochet [rikoʃɛ], s.m. (a) rebound; (b) ricochet.

ride [rid], s.f. 1. wrinkle. 2. ripple (on water).

rideau [rido], s.m. screen; curtain; le r. de fer, the iron curtain.

rider [ride], v.tr. 1. (a) to wrinkle, line; (b) to corrugate. 2. to ripple.

ridicule [ridikyl]. 1. a. ridiculous, ludicrous. 2. s.m. (a) absurdity; (b) ridicule.

ridiculiser [ridikylize], v.tr. to ridicule.

rien [rjɛ̃]. 1. indef.pron. m. 1. anything. 2. nothing, not anything; cela ne fait r., that doesn't matter; il n'en est r.! nothing of the kind! en moins de r., in less than no time; (c) r. que, nothing but, only, merely. II. s.m. 1. trifle. 2. just a little.

†rieur [rjœːr], a. laughing; fond of laughter.

rigide [riʒid], a. rigid; tense; fixed. adv. -ment.

rigidité [riʒidite], s.f. rigidity; tenseness.

rigole [rigol], s.f. drain, gutter, channel.

rigol/er [rigole], v.i. F: to laugh (heartily); to have a good time. a. -o, F: funny; queer.

†rigoureu/x [rigurø], a. rigorous. 1. severe, harsh. 2. strict. adv. -sement.

rigueur [rigœːr], s.f. 1. rigour, harshness, severity. 2. strictness; de r., compulsory, obligatory; à la r., if need be.

rime [rim], s.f. rhyme.

rimer [rime], v.i. to rhyme.

‡rincer [rɛ̃se], v.tr. to rinse.

riposte [ripost], s.f. riposte; retort.

riposter [ripost], v.i. to retort.

‡rire [riːr]. I. v.i. 1. to laugh; il n'y a pas de quoi r., it's no laughing matter. 2. to joke; pour r., for fun. 3. to smile (à, on). II. s.m. (a) laughter; (b) un r., a laugh.

ris[1] [ri], s.m. reef (in sail).

ris[2], s.m. r. de veau, sweetbread.

risée [rize], s.f. a derision, jeer; (b) laughing-stock, butt.

risible [rizibl], a. ludicrous, laughable.

risque [risk], s.m. risk.

risqué [riske], a. (a) risky; (b) risqué (story).

risquer [riske], v.tr. to risk (one's life).
se risquer, to take a risk.

ristourne [risturn], s.f. refund, rebate; Com: discount.

rite [rit], s.m. rite.

†rituel [rityel], a. & s.m. ritual.

rivage [rivaːʒ], s.m. bank; shore.

†rival, -ale [rival], a. & s. rival.

rivaliser [rivalize], v.i. r. avec, (i) to rival; (ii) to compete with.

rivalité [rivalite], s.f. rivalry.

rive [riːv], s.f. bank; shore.

river [rive], v.tr. to rivet.

riverain [rivrɛ̃], a. riverside (property, etc.); P.N: Aut: interdit sauf aux riverains, residents' cars only.

rivet [rive], s.m. rivet.

†riveter [rivte], v.tr. to rivet.
rivière [rivjɛːr], s.f. river, stream.
rixe [riks], s.f. brawl, scuffle, fight.
riz [ri], s.m. rice.
rizière [rizjɛːr], s.f. rice-plantation.
robe [rɔb], s.f. 1. (a) dress; (b) r. de chambre, dressing-gown; (c) robe, gown (of lawyer, etc.). 2. coat (of horse).
robinet [rɔbinɛ], s.m. (stop-)cock; tap.
robot [rɔbo], s.m. robot; Jur: portrait r., identikit portrait.
robuste [rɔbyst], a. robust; strong.
robustesse [rɔbystes], s.f. robustness.
roc [rɔk], s.m. rock.
rocailleux [rɔkajø], a. rocky, stony.
roche [rɔʃ], s.f. rock, boulder.
rocher [rɔʃe], s.m. rock; crag.
†rocheux [rɔʃø], a. rocky, stony; les (montagnes) Rocheuses, the Rocky Mountains, the Rockies.
rodage [rɔdaːʒ], s.m. grinding; Aut: en r., running in.
rôder [rode], v.i. to prowl; to loiter.
rôdeur, -euse [rodœːr, -øːz], 1. a. prowling. 2. s. prowler.
rognon [rɔɲɔ̃], s.m. Cu: kidney.
roi [rwa], s.m. king.
roitelet [rwatlɛ], s.m. (gold-crested) wren.
rôle [roːl], s.m. 1. roll; list; register; à tour de r., in turn, in rotation. 2. Th: part, rôle.
romain, -aine [rɔmɛ̃, -ɛn], 1. a. & s. Roman. 2. s.f. cos lettuce. 3. s.m. Roman (type).
roman[1] [rɔmɑ̃], s.m. novel.
roman[2], a. & s.m. 1. Ling: Romance. 2. A. & A: romanesque, Norman.
romancier, -ière [rɔmɑ̃sje, -jɛːr], s. novelist.
romand [rɔmɑ̃], a. Suisse romande, French Switzerland.
romanesque [rɔmanɛsk], a. romantic.
romant[i]que [rɔmɑ̃tik], a. romantic. s.m. isme, romanticism.
romarin [rɔmarɛ̃], s.m. rosemary.
rompre [rɔ̃ːpr], 1. v.tr. to break; (a) to break in two; (b) to burst; se r. la tête, to rack one's brains; (c) r. le silence, to break the silence; (d) to break in. 2. v.i. to break.
se rompre, to break; to snap.
rompu [rɔ̃py], a. (a) broken; r. de fatigue, worn out; (b) broken in.
ronce [rɔ̃s], s.f. 1. bramble, blackberry-bush. 2. thorns.
rond, ronde [rɔ̃, rɔ̃ːd]. I. 1. a. (a) round, plump (figure); adv. tourner r., to run true; (b) compte r., round sum, even money. 2. s.m. (a) round, ring, circle; (b) disc; E: washer. II. 1. s.f. (policeman's) beat; faire la ronde, to go the rounds. 2. à la ronde, around. adv. -ement.
rondelle [rɔ̃dɛl], s.f. 1. disc; slice (of sausage). 2. (a) ring; (b) washer; (c) Fr.C: (ice-hockey) puck.

rondeur [rɔ̃dœːr], s.f. 1. roundness, rotundity. 2. outspokenness.
rond-point [rɔ̃pwɛ̃], s.m. roundabout, U.S: traffic circle. pl. ronds-points.
ronfler [rɔ̃fle], v.i. 1. to snore. 2. (of fire, etc.) to roar. s.m. -ement.
†ronger [rɔ̃ʒe], v.tr. 1. to gnaw. 2. to corrode; to eat away.
†rongeur [rɔ̃ʒœːr], 1. a. rodent, gnawing. 2. s.m. rodent.
ronronner [rɔ̃rɔne], v.i. (a) to purr; (b) to hum. s.m. -ement.
rosace [rozas], s.f. rose(-window).
rosaire [rozɛːr], s.m. rosary.
rosâtre [rozɑːtr], a. pinkish.
rosbif [rɔsbif], s.m. roast beef.
rose [roːz]. 1. s.f. rose; r. sauvage, dog rose; r. trémière, hollyhock. 2. a. & s.m. pink; voir tout en r., to see everything through rose-coloured spectacles. 3. s.f. r. des vents, compass-card.
rosé [roze], a. rosy; vin r., s.m. F: rosé, rose wine.
roseau [rozo], s.m. reed.
rosée [roze], s.f. dew.
rosette [rozɛt], s.f. rosette.
rosier [rozje], s.m. rose tree, rose bush.
rosiériste [rozjerist], s.m. rosarian, rose-grower.
rosser [rɔse], v.tr. to give (s.o.) a beating, a thrashing.
rossignol [rɔsiɲɔl], s.m. 1. nightingale. 2. skeleton key.
rot [ro], s.m. F: belch.
†rotatif [rɔtatif], a. rotary.
rotation [rɔtasjɔ̃], s.f. rotation.
roter [rɔte], v.i. F: belch.
rôti [roti], s.m. roast (meat).
rôtie [roti], s.f. round of toast.
rôtir [rotiːr], 1. v.tr. to roast; to toast. 2. v.i. to roast.
rôtisserie [rotisri], s.f. grill room.
rotondité [rɔtɔ̃dite], s.f. rotundity.
rotule [rɔtyl], s.f. knee-cap.
rouage [rwaːʒ], s.m. wheels; works.
roucouler [rukule], v.i. to coo. s.m. -ement.
roue [ru], s.f. wheel.
rouer [rwe], v.tr. r. qn de coups, to thrash s.o. soundly.
rouge [ruːʒ]. 1. a. red. 2. s.m. (a) red; (b) rouge; (bâton de) r., lipstick.
rougeâtre [ruʒɑːtr], a. reddish.
rouge-gorge [ruʒgɔrʒ], s.m. robin. pl. rouges-gorges.
rougeole [ruʒɔl], s.f. measles.
rougeur [ruʒœːr], s.f. 1. redness. 2. blush, flush.
rougir [ruʒiːr], 1. v.tr. (a) to redden; (b) to flush. 2. v.i. (a) to redden, to turn red; (b) to blush; to flush; r. de qch., to be ashamed of sth.
rouille [ruːj], s.f. rust.
rouiller [ruje], v.tr. to rust.
se rouiller, to rust (up).

roulant [rulɑ̃], a. rolling; sliding (door); escalier r., escalator; Rail: matériel r., rolling stock.

rouleau [rulo], s.m. 1. roller. 2. roll (of paper); spool (of film); coil (of rope); être au bout de son r., (i) to be at the end of one's tether; (ii) to be (stony) broke.

roulement [rulmɑ̃], s.m. 1. rolling; Aut: bande de r., tread (of tyre). 2. rumbling (of thunder). 3. bearing; r. à billes, ball-bearing. 4. (a) Com: r. de fonds, circulation of capital; (b) par r., in rotation.

roul/er [rule]. 1. v.tr. (a) to roll (along, up); (b) to roll (the lawn). 2. v.i. (a) to roll; Au: r. sur le sol, to taxi; r. par le monde, to knock about the world; to roll, rumble; (c) voiture qui roule bien, car that runs well; voiture qui a très peu roulé, car with a very small mileage.
se rouler. (a) to roll (over and over); (b) to roll up.

roulette [rulɛt], s.f. 1. caster; roller. 2. (game of) roulette.

roulis [ruli], s.m. rolling.

roulotte [rulɔt], s.f. caravan, U.S: trailer.

roumain, -aine [rumɛ̃, -ɛn], a. & s. R(o)umanian.

roupie [rupi], s.f. rupee.

roussâtre [rusɑːtr], a. reddish.

rousse [rus]. See ROUX.

rousseur [rusœːr], s.f. redness; tache de r., freckle.

roussir [rusiːr]. 1. v.tr. (a) to redden; (b) to scorch. 2. v.i. (a) to turn brown; (b) to scorch.

route [rut], s.f. 1. road; r. nationale, main road; r. départementale, secondary road. 2. route, way; se mettre en r., to set out. 3. mettre en r., to start (work, engine).

rout/er [rute], v.tr. P.T.T: to sort (letters). s.m. -age.

†routier [rutje], (a) a. carte routière, road map; transports routiers, road transport; gare routière, bus, coach, station; (b) s.m. (i) lorry driver, U.S: truckman; (ii) (scouting) rover; (c) s.m. Aut: heavy transport vehicle.

routine [rutin], s.f. routine.

routinier [rutinje], a. routine (duties).

‡rouvrir [ruvriːr], v.tr. & i. to reopen.

roux, rousse [ru, rus]. 1. (a) a. (russet-) red; red; (b) s. red-haired person. 2. s.m. russet.

†royal [rwajal], royal, regal, kingly.

royalement [rwajalmɑ̃], adv. royally; s'amuser r., to enjoy oneself enormously.

royaliste [rwajalist], a. & s. royalist.

royaume [rwajoːm], s.m. kingdom.

royauté [rwajote], s.f. royalty; kingship.

ruban [rybɑ̃], s.m. 1. ribbon; r. magnétique, magnetic tape. 2. metal strip; r. d'acier, steel band. 3. Ind: r. transporteur, belt conveyor.

rubéole [rybeɔl], s.f. German measles.

rubis [rybi], s.m. ruby; (of watch) montée sur r., jewelled.

rubrique [rybrik], s.f. (a) rubric; (b) heading.

ruche [ryʃ], s.f. (bee-)hive.

rude [ryd], a. 1. (a) unpolished; (b) rough; harsh; rugged. 2. (a) hard, arduous; (b) gruff, brusque. 3. hearty (appetite). adv. -ment.

rudesse [rydɛs], s.f. 1. uncouthness. 2. roughness. 3. (a) severity; (b) bluntness.

rudiment [rydimɑ̃], s.m. rudiment.

rudimentaire [rydimɑ̃tɛːr], a. rudimentary.

‡rudoyer [rydwaje], v.tr. to treat roughly.

rue [ry], s.f. street.

ruée [rɥe], s.f. rush; la r. vers l'or, the gold rush.

ruelle [rɥɛl], s.f. lane; alley.

ruer [rɥe], v.i. to kick, to lash out.
se ruer sur qn, sur qch., to hurl, fling, oneself at s.o., sth.

rugby [rygbi], s.m. Sp: rugby football, rugger.

rug/ir [ryʒiːr], v.i. to roar; to howl. s.m. -issement.

rugueux [rygø], a. rugged, rough.

ruine [rɥin], s.f. ruin, downfall; pl. ruins.

ruiner [rɥine], v.tr. to ruin, destroy.

ruineux [rɥinø], a. ruinous.

‡ruisseau [rɥiso], s.m. brook; stream.

ruissel/er [rɥisle], v.i. 1. to stream (down), run (down). 2. to run, drip, trickle. s.m. -lement.

rumeur [rymœːr], s.f. 1. (a) murmur; (b) din, clamour. 2. rumour, report.

rumin/er [rymine], v.tr. & i. to ruminate. s.f. -ation.

rupestre [rypɛstr], a. dessins rupestres, cave drawings.

rupture [ryptyr], s.f. breaking; rupture; r. de contrat, breach of contract.

†rural [ryral], a. rural; facteur r., country postman.

ruse [ryz], s.f. ruse, trick, dodge.

rusé [ryze], a. & s. artful, crafty, sly.

russe [rus], a. & s. Russian.

rustique [rystik], a. rustic.

rustre [rystr]. 1. a. boorish. 2. s.m. boor, lout.

rythme [ritm], s.m. rhythm.

rythmique [ritmik], a. rhythmic.

S

S, s [ɛs], *s.f.* (The letter) S, s.

sa [sa], *a.poss.f.* See SON¹.

sabbat [saba], *s.m.* (Jewish) Sabbath; *F:* faire un s. de tous les diables, to make the devil of a row.

sabl/e [sɑ:bl], *s.m.* sand. **-ière,** sandpit.

†sablonneux [sablonø], *a.* sandy.

sabord [sabɔr], *s.m. Nau:* port(hole).

saborder [sabɔrde], *v.tr.* to scuttle (ship).

sabot [sabo], *s.m.* 1. clog, sabot. 2. hoof (of horse). 3. s. de frein, brake shoe.

sabotage [sabota:ʒ], *s.m.* sabotage.

saboter [sabɔte], *v.tr.* to botch; to sabotage.

sabotteur [sabɔtœr], *s.m.* saboteur.

sabre [sabr], *s.m.* 1. sack; bag; s. de couchage, sleeping bag; *Av:* s. à vent, wind cone.

sac², *s.m.* sacking, pillage.

saccadé [sakade], *a.* jerky, abrupt.

‡saccager [sakaʒe], *v.tr.* to sack, pillage.

saccharine [sakkarin], *s.f.* saccharine.

sachet [saʃɛ], *s.m.* sachet.

sacoche [sakɔʃ], *s.f.* satchel, wallet; (cyclist's) saddle bag.

sacre [sakr], *s.m.* coronation.

sacré [sakre], *a.* 1. sacred, holy. 2. *F:* damned.

sacrement [sakrəmɑ̃], *s.m.* sacrament.

sacrer [sakre]. 1. *v.tr.* to anoint, crown (king); to consecrate (bishop). 2. *v.i.* to swear.

sacrifice [sakrifis], *s.m.* sacrifice.

sacrifier [sakrifje], *v.tr.* to sacrifice.

sacrilège [sakrilɛ:ʒ]. 1. *s.m.* sacrilege. 2. *a.* sacrilegious.

sacristain [sakristɛ̃], *s.m.* sacristan, sexton.

sacristie [sakristi], *s.f.* sacristy, vestry.

sadisme [sadism], *s.m.* sadism.

safran [safrɑ̃], *s.m.* saffron.

sagacité [sagasite], *s.f.* sagacity, shrewdness.

sage [sa:ʒ], *a.* 1. wise. 2. judicious. 3. well-behaved; good (child). *adv.* **-ment.**

sage-femme [saʒfam], *s.f.* midwife. *pl.* **sages-femmes.**

sagesse [saʒɛs], *s.f.* 1. (a) wisdom; (b) prudence. 2. good behaviour.

saignant [sɛɲɑ̃], *a.* 1. bleeding. 2. *Cu:* red, rare (meat).

saigner [sɛɲe], *v.i. & tr.* to bleed.

saillant [sajɑ̃]. 1. *a.* projecting. 2. *s.m. Mil:* salient.

saillie [saji], *s.f.* 1. sally; flash of wit. 2. projection.

sain [sɛ̃], *a.* healthy; sound; sane. *adv.* **-ement.**

saindoux [sɛ̃du], *s.m.* lard.

saint, sainte [sɛ̃, sɛ̃:t]. 1. *a.* (a) holy; (b) saintly; (c) consecrated (ground). 2. *s.* saint; la S.-Michel, Michaelmas; le S.-Siège, the Holy See; la S.-Sylvestre, New Year's Eve.

Saint-Esprit (le) [sɛ̃tɛspri]. *Pr.n.m.* the Holy Ghost, Spirit.

sainteté [sɛ̃tte], *s.f.* holiness, saintliness; sanctity.

sais/ir [sɛzir], *v.tr.* to seize; (a) to grasp; to take hold of; (b) to perceive; je n'ai pas saisi son nom, I didn't get his name. *s.m.* **-issement.**

se saisir de, to lay hands on (sth.).

saisissant [sezisɑ̃], *a.* striking; thrilling.

saison [sezɔ̃], *s.f.* season; de s., in season; hors de s., out of season; ill-timed (remark).

salade [salad], *s.f.* salad.

salaire [salɛr], *s.m.* wage(s); pay.

sale [sal], *a.* dirty; (a) unclean; soiled; (b) offensive, nasty.

saler [sale], *v.tr.* to salt; *F:* to overcharge, fleece (customers).

saleté [salte], *s.f.* 1. (a) dirtiness; (b) dirt, filth. 2. nastiness.

salière [saljɛr], *s.f.* salt-cellar.

salir [salir], *v.tr.* to dirty, soil.

salive [saliːv], *s.f.* saliva.

salle [sal], *s.f.* 1. hall; (large) room; s. de séjour, living room; s. à manger, dining room. 2. *Th:* house.

salon [salɔ̃], *s.m.* (a) drawing-room; (b) s. de thé, tearoom(s); s. de coiffure, hairdresser's (shop); (c) s. de peinture, art exhibition; s. de l'automobile, motor show.

salubr/e [salybr], *a.* healthy; wholesome. *s.f.* **-ité.**

saluer [salɥe], *v.tr.* to salute; to greet; to hail.

salut [saly], *s.m.* 1. (a) safety; (b) salvation; l'Armée du S., the Salvation Army. 2. (a) bow, greeting; (b) salute.

salutaire [salytɛr], *a.* a salutary, wholesome, beneficial.

salutation [salytasjɔ̃], *s.f.* salutation, greeting.

salve [salv], *s.f.* salvo.

samedi [samdi], *s.m.* Saturday.

sanatorium [sanatɔrjɔm], *s.m.* sanatorium.

sanctifier [sɑ̃ktifje], *v.tr.* to sanctify.

sanction [sɑ̃ksjɔ̃], *s.f.* 1. sanction, assent. 2. penalty, sanction.

sanctionner [sɑ̃ksjɔne], *v.tr.* to sanction. 1. to approve. 2. to penalize.

sanctuaire [sɑ̃ktɥɛr], *s.m.* sanctuary.

sandale [sɑ̃dal], *s.f.* sandal.

sandwich [sɑ̃dwitʃ], *s.m.* sandwich.

sang [sɑ̃], *s.m.* 1. blood. 2. blood, race; relationship.

sang-froid [sɑ̃frwa], *s.m. no pl.* coolness, composure.

sanglant [sɑ̃glɑ̃], *a.* bloody; bloodstained.

sangle [sɑ̃gl], *s.f.* strap, band, webbing.

sanglier [sɑ̃glie], *s.m.* wild boar.

sanglot [sɑ̃glo], *s.m.* sob.

sangloter [sãglɔte], *v.i.* to sob.

sanguin, -ine [sãgɛ̃, -in]. 1. *a.* Anat: vaisseaux sanguins, blood vessels; groupe s., blood group. 2. *s.f.* blood orange.

sanguinaire [sãginɛːr], *a.* bloodthirsty (*pers.*); bloody (fight).

sanitaire [sanitɛːr], *a.* sanitary.

sans [sã], *prep.* 1. without; s. faute, without fail; s. que vous le sachiez, without your knowing it. 2. but for; s. cela, s. quoi, otherwise, else.

sans-façon [sãfasɔ̃]. 1. *s.m.* homeliness. 2. *a.inv.* homely; without ceremony.

sans-fil [sãfil], *s.inv.* 1. *s.f.* wireless. 2. *s.m.* wireless message.

sans-gêne [sãʒɛn]. 1. *s.m.* off-handedness. 2. *a.inv.* unceremonious.

santé [sãte], *s.f.* health; well-being; à votre s.! good health! cheers!

saper [sape], *v.tr.* to sap, undermine.

sapeur [sapœːr], *s.m.* sapper.

sapeur-pompier [sapœrpɔ̃pje], *s.m.* fireman; *pl.* the fire brigade.

sapin [sapɛ̃], *s.m.* (a) fir(-tree); (b) bois de s., deal.

sarcasme [sarkasm], *s.m.* sarcasm.

sarcastique [sarkastik], *a.* sarcastic.

sarcler [sarkle], *v.tr.* to weed; to hoe.

sarcophage [sarkɔfaːʒ], *s.m.* sarcophagus.

sarde [sard], *a. & s.* Sardinian.

sardine [sardin], *s.f.* sardine.

sarment [sarmã], *s.m.* vine-shoot.

Satan [satã]. *Pr.n.m.* Satan.

satanique [satanik], *a.* satanic; fiendish.

satellite [satellit], *s.m.* satellite; s. artificiel, artificial satellite, sputnik; s. habité, biosatellite; *a.* pays s., satellite (country).

satiété [sasjete], *s.f.* satiety; surfeit.

satin [satɛ̃], *s.m.* satin.

satire [satiːr], *s.f.* satire. *a.* -ique, satirical.

satisfaction [satisfaksjɔ̃], *s.f.* 1. satisfaction. 2. reparation, amends.

‡**satisfaire** [satisfɛːr], *v.* to satisfy. 1. *v.tr.* (a) to content; (b) to make amends to. 2. *v.ind.tr.* s. à., to satisfy (honour); to carry out (duty); to comply with (rule).

satisfaisant [satisfəzã], *a.* satisfying, satisfactory; peu s., unsatisfactory.

satur/er [satyre], *v.tr.* to saturate. *s.f.* -ation.

sauc/e [soːs], *s.f.* sauce. *s.f.* -ière, sauce boat.

saucisse [sosis], *s.f.* sausage (for cooking).

saucisson [sosisɔ̃], *s.m.* (cooked) sausage.

†**sauf¹** [sof], *a.* safe, unhurt.

sauf², *prep.* except (for); s. de rares exceptions, with very few exceptions.

sauge [soːʒ], *s.f.* Bot: sage.

saule [soːl], *s.m.* willow.

saumâtre [somɑːtr], *a.* brackish, briny.

saumon [somɔ̃], *s.m.* 1. salmon. 2. ingot.

saumure [somyːr], *s.f.* brine; pickle.

saupoudrer [sopudre], *v.tr.* to sprinkle, powder.

saur [soːr], *a.m.* hareng s., red herring.

saut [so], *s.m.* 1. leap, jump, vault; j'ai fait un s. chez lui, I slipped round to his house; s. périlleux, somersault. 2. (water)fall.

saute [soːt], *s.f.* jump (in price, etc.); s. de vent, shift, change of wind.

sauté [sote], *a.* pommes (de terre) sautées, sauté potatoes.

saute-mouton [sotmutɔ̃], *s.m.* leap-frog.

saut/er [sote]. 1. *v.i.* (a) to jump, leap, skip; s. au cou de qn, to fling one's arms round s.o.'s neck; s. sur une offre, to jump at an offer; (b) to explode; to blow up; to fly off; (c) (of wind) to shift. 2. *v.tr.* to jump (over) (sth.); to skip (pages in reading).

sauterelle [sotrɛl], *s.f.* grasshopper; locust.

sauvage [sovaːʒ]. 1. *a.* (a) savage; wild, untamed; (b) unsociable; shy. 2. *s.* (a) savage; (b) unsociable person. *adv.* -ment. *s.f.* -rie, unsociability.

sauvegarde [sovgard], *s.f.* safeguard.

sauvegarder [sovgarde], *v.tr.* to safeguard, protect.

sauve-qui-peut [sovkipø], *s.m.inv.* stampede.

sauv/er [sove], *v.tr.* to save, rescue. se sauver. 1. to escape. 2. to run away.

sauvetage [sovtaːʒ], *s.m.* (a) life-saving; rescue; canot de s., lifeboat; échelle de s., fire-escape; (b) salvage.

sauveur [sovœːr], *s.m.* preserver, deliverer; Ecc: Notre S., our Saviour.

sav/ant [savã]. 1. *a.* (a) learned, scholarly; (b) skilful. 2. *s.m.* scientist; scholar. *adv.* -amment.

saveur [savœːr], *s.f.* taste, flavour.

‡**savoir** [savwaːr]. I. *v.tr.* to know. 1. to be aware of; sans le s., unconsciously; pas que je sache, not that I am aware of. 2. (a) c'est à s., that remains to be seen; (b) faire s. qch. à qn, to inform s.o. of sth.; (c) (à) s., namely. 3. to know how; to be able; il ne sait pas nager, he can't swim. 4. un je sais tout, a know-all. II. *s.m.* knowledge learning.

savoir-faire [savwarfɛːr], *s.m.* ability; tact; savoir-faire.

savoir-vivre [savwarviːvr], *s.m.* good breeding; etiquette.

savon [savɔ̃], *s.m.* (a) soap; s. de Marseille, household soap; (b) F: passer un s. à qn, to give s.o. a good dressing down. *a.* †-neux, soapy. *s.f.* -nette, cake of soap.

savonner [savɔne], *v.tr.* to soap; to lather.

savour/er [savure], *v.tr.* to relish, enjoy. *a.* †-eux, tasty.

†**scabreux** [skabrø], *a.* 1. difficult, risky. 2. indelicate; improper.

scandale [skɑ̃dal], *s.m.* scandal.

†**scandal/eux** [skɑ̃dalø], *a.* scandalous. *adv.* -eusement.

scandaliser [skɑ̃dalize], *v.tr.* to scandalize.

scandinave [skɑ̃dinav], *a.* & *s.* Scandinavian.

scaphandrier [skafɑ̃drje], *s.m.* diver (in diving suit).

scarabée [skarabe], *s.m.* 1. beetle. 2. scarab.

scarlatine [skarlatin], *s.f.* scarlatina, scarlet fever.

sceau [so], *s.m.* seal.

scélérat [selera], *s.* scoundrel.

scellé [sele]. 1. *a.* sealed; under seal. 2. *s.m.* seal.

sceller [sele], *v.tr.* (a) to seal; to seal up; (b) to ratify, confirm.

scénar/io [senarjo], *s.m. Th:* scenario; *Cin:* film script. s. -iste, scenario, script, writer.

scène [sɛn], *s.f.* 1. stage; entrer en s., to come on; metteur en s., producer. 2. (a) *Th:* scene; (b) scene of action; (c) *F:* scene, row.

scénique [senik], *a.* scenic; theatrical.

scepticisme [septisism], *s.m.* scepticism.

sceptique [septik]. 1. *a.* sceptical. 2. *s.* sceptic.

sceptre [septr], *s.m.* sceptre.

schisme [ʃism], *s.m.* schism.

sciatique [sjatik]. 1. *a.* sciatic. 2. *s.f.* sciatica.

scie [si], *s.f.* (tool) saw.

science [sjɑ̃:s], *s.f.* 1. knowledge, learning; skill. 2. science.

scientifique [sjɑ̃tifik], *a.* scientific. *adv.* -ment.

scier [sje], *v.tr.* 1. to saw. 2. to saw off.

scierie [siri], *s.f.* saw-mill.

scintillation [sɛ̃tijasjɔ̃], *s.f.* scintillation.

scintiller [sɛ̃tije], *v.i.* to scintillate; to twinkle.

scission [sisjɔ̃], *s.f.* scission, split.

sciure [sjy:r], *s.f.* s. de bois, sawdust.

scolaire [skɔlɛːr], *a.* scholastic; année s., school year.

scorpion [skɔrpjɔ̃], *s.m.* scorpion.

scrupule [skrypyl], *s.m.* scruple.

†**scrupuleu/x** [skrypylø], *a.* scrupulous. *adv.* -sement.

scruter [skryte], *v.tr.* to scrutinize; to scan.

scrutin [skrytɛ̃], *s.m.* poll; dépouiller le s., to count the votes.

sculpter [skylte], *v.tr.* to carve.

sculpteur [skyltœːr], *s.m.* sculptor.

sculpture [skylty:r], *s.f.* sculpture; s. sur bois, wood-carving.

se [s(ə)], *pers.pron.* (before vowel sound s') 1. (a) oneself; himself, herself, itself, themselves; (b) each other, one another. 2. (passive) cet article se vend partout, this article is sold everywhere.

séance [seɑ̃ːs], *s.f.* 1. sitting; session. 2. performance; seance.

séant [seɑ̃]. 1. *s.m.* sur son s., sitting (up). 2. *a.* becoming; fitting.

seau [so], *s.m.* pail, bucket; s. à charbon, coal-scuttle.

†**sec** [sɛk], *a.* 1. (a) dry; (b) dried; (c) perte sèche, dead loss. 2. (a) spare; lean; (b) sharp, curt; (c) barren, dry. 3. *adv.phr.* à sec, (i) dry; dried up; (ii) *F:* hard up.

sécession [sesesjɔ̃], *s.f.* secession.

sèche [sɛʃ]. See SEC. *adv.* ment, curtly.

‡**sécher** [seʃe], *v.tr.* 1. to dry (up); *Sch: F:* to cut (a lecture). 2. *v.i.* to dry; *F:* to be stumped.

sécheresse [seʃrɛs], *s.f.* 1. (a) dryness; (b) drought. 2. curtness.

second, -onde [səgɔ̃, -5:d]. 1. *a.* second. 2. *s.m.* (a) second floor; (b) principal assistant; second (in command). 3. *s.f.* seconde; (a) second (class); (b) second (of time).

secondaire [səgɔ̃dɛːr], *a.* secondary.

seconder [səgɔ̃de], *v.tr.* 1. to second, back up. 2. to forward, promote (s.o.'s interests).

secouer [səkwe], *v.tr.* 1. (a) to shake; (b) to shake up, rouse. 2. to shake off. se **secouer**. (a) to shake oneself; (b) to bestir oneself.

secourir [səkuri:r], *v.tr.* to help, aid.

secours [s(ə)ku:r], *s.m.* help, aid; sortie de s., emergency exit; roue de s., spare wheel.

secousse [s(ə)kus], *s.f.* shake; jolt, jerk.

†**secr/et** [səkrɛ]. 1. *a.* secret; hidden. 2. *s.m.* (a) secret; (b) secrecy; privacy; le s. de la confession, the seal of confession. *adv.* -ètement.

secrétaire [sokretɛːr]. 1. *s.m.* & *f.* secretary. 2. *s.m.* secretary bird. 3. *s.m.* writing desk.

secte [sɛkt], *s.f.* sect.

secteur [sɛktœːr], *s.m.* sector.

section [sɛksjɔ̃], *s.f.* 1. section. 2. stage (on bus route).

séculaire [sekylɛːr], *a.* century-old; time-honoured (custom).

†**séculier** [sekylje]. 1. *a.* (a) secular; (b) lay. 2. *s.* layman.

sécurité [sekyrite], *s.f.* 1. security. 2. safety.

†**sédatif** [sedatif], *a.* & *s.m.* sedative.

sédentaire [sedɑ̃tɛːr], *a.* sedentary.

sédiment [sedimɑ̃], *s.m.* sediment, deposit. *a.* -aire, sedimentary.

†**séditieux** [sedisjø], *a.* seditious.

sédition [sedisjɔ̃], *s.f.* sedition; mutiny.

séducteur, -trice [sedyktœːr, -tris]. 1. *s.* (a) tempter; (b) s. seducer. 2. *a.* (a) tempting; (b) seductive.

séduction [sedyksjɔ̃], *s.f.* seduction.

‡**séduire** [sedɥiːr], *v.tr.* 1. to seduce. 2. to fascinate, captivate. *a.* -isant.

segment [sɛgmɑ̃], *s.m.* segment.

ségrégation [segregasjɔ̃], *s.f.* segregation.

seiche [sɛʃ], *s.f.* cuttlefish.

seigle [sɛgl], *s.m.* rye.

seigneur [sɛɲœːr], *s.m.* lord; nobleman; *Ecc:* Notre S., our Lord.

sein [sɛ̃], *s.m.* breast, bosom.

seize [sɛːz], *num.a.inv.* & *s.m.inv.* sixteen.

seizième [sɛzjɛm], *num.a.* & *s.* sixteenth.

séjour [seʒuːr], *s.m.* 1. stay (in a place). 2. residence.

séjourner [seʒurne], *v.i.* to stay, stop (in a place).

sel [sɛl], *s.m.* salt.

sélection [selɛksjɔ̃], *s.f.* selection, choice.

sélectivité [selɛktivite], *s.f.* selectivity.

sell/e [sɛl], *s.f.* saddle. *s.m.* -ier, saddler.

selon [s(ə)lɔ̃], *prep.* according to; s. moi, in my opinion; c'est s., it all depends.

Seltz [sɛls], *s.m.* eau de S., soda-water.

semaine [s(ə)mɛn], *s.f.* (a) week; (b) working week; (c) week's pay.

sémaphore [semafoːr], *s.m.* semaphore.

semblable [sɑ̃blabl]. 1. *a.* (a) alike; similar; like; (b) such; en s. occasion, on such occasion. 2. *s.* like; nos semblables, our fellow-men. *adv.* -ment.

semblant [sɑ̃blɑ̃], *s.m.* semblance, appearance; faire s. de faire qch., to pretend to do sth.

sembler [sɑ̃ble], *v.i.* (a) to seem, appear; (b) *impers.* à ce qu'il me semble, as it strikes me.

semelle [s(ə)mɛl], *s.f.* sole (of shoe).

semence [s(ə)mɑ̃:s], *s.f.* 1. seed. 2. (tin)tacks.

‡sem/er [s(ə)me], *v.tr.* 1. to sow. 2. to spread, scatter. *s.* -eur, -euse.

semestr/e [s(ə)mɛstr], *s.m.* half-year. *a.* -iel.

semi-circulaire [səmisirkylɛːr], *a.* semicircular.

séminaire [seminɛːr], *s.m.* seminary.

semis [səmi], *s.m.* 1. sowing. 2. seedlings.

sémitique [semitik], *a.* Semitic.

semonce [səmɔ̃:s], *s.f.* reprimand, scolding.

semoule [s(ə)mul], *s.f.* semolina.

sénat [sena], *s.m.* senate.

sénateur [senatœːr], *s.m.* senator.

sénil/e [senil], *a.* senile. *s.f.* -ité.

sens [sɑ̃:s], *s.m.* 1. sense; judgment; meaning. 2. direction, way; rue à s. unique, one-way street; s. interdit, no entry; s. dessus dessous, topsyturvy.

sensation [sɑ̃sasjɔ̃], *s.f.* sensation. *a.* †-nel.

sensé [sɑ̃se], *a.* sensible, judicious.

sensib/le [sɑ̃sibl]. *a.* 1. (a) sensitive, susceptible; (b) sympathetic; (c) sensitive, tender. 2. perceptible. *adv.* -lement. *s.f.* -ilité.

†sensuel [sɑ̃sɥɛl], *a.* sensual. *s.f.* -alité.

sentence [sɑ̃tɑ̃:s], *s.f.* sentence; judgment.

†sentencieux [sɑ̃tɑ̃sjø], *a.* sententious.

senteur [sɑ̃tœːr], *s.f.* scent, perfume.

sentier [sɑ̃tje], *s.m.* (foot)path.

sentiment [sɑ̃timɑ̃], *s.m.* 1. feeling; (a) sensation; (b) sense, consciousness. 2. opinion.

†sentimental [sɑ̃timɑ̃tal], *a.* sentimental. *s.f.* -ité.

sentinelle [sɑ̃tinɛl], *s.f.* sentry.

sentir [sɑ̃tiːr]. 1. *v.tr.* (a) to feel; (b) to be conscious; (c) to smell. 2. *v.i.* (a) to taste of, smell of; (b) to smell. se sentir, to feel; je me sens fatigué(e), I feel tired.

sépale [sepal], *s.m.* sepal.

séparé [separe], *a.* 1. separate, different. 2. separated, apart.

sépar/er [separe], *v.tr.* to separate. *adv.* -ément. *a.* -able. *s.f.* -ation. se séparer. 1. to separate, part. 2. to divide. 3. to break up.

sépia [sepja], *s.f.* sepia.

sept [sɛt], *num.a.inv.* & *s.m.inv.* seven.

septembre [sɛptɑ̃br], *s.m.* September.

septième [sɛtjɛm]. 1. *num.a.* & *s.* seventh. 2. *s.m.* seventh (part).

septique [sɛptik], *a.* septic.

septuagénaire [sɛptɥaʒenɛːr], *a.* & *s.* septuagenarian.

sépulcr/e [sepylkr], *s.m.* sepulchre. *a.* -al.

séquence [sekɑ̃:s], *s.f.* sequence.

séquestr/er [sekɛstre], *v.tr.* to sequestrate; to lay an embargo on (ship). *s.f.* -ation.

séraphin [serafɛ̃], *s.m.* seraph.

séraphique [serafik], *a.* seraphic, angelic.

serein [sərɛ̃], *a.* serene, calm.

sérénade [serenad], *s.f.* serenade.

sérénité [serenite], *s.f.* serenity, calmness.

serf, serve [sɛrf, sɛrv], *s.* serf.

serge [sɛrʒ], *s.m.* serge.

sergent [sɛrʒɑ̃], *s.m.* sergeant; s. de ville, policeman.

série [seri], *s.f.* series; succession; fabrication en s., mass production; hors s., specially manufactured; fin de s., *Com:* oddment, remnant; (of book) remainder.

†sérieu/x [serjø]. 1. *a.* serious; (a) grave; (b) serious-minded; (c) earnest; (d) important. 2. *s.m.* seriousness, gravity. *adv.* -sement.

serin [s(ə)rɛ̃], *s.m.* canary.

seringue [s(ə)rɛ̃g], *s.f.* syringe.

seringuer [s(ə)rɛ̃ge], *v.tr.* (a) to syringe (b) to squirt.

serment [sɛrmɑ̃], *s.m.* (solemn) oath; faire un faux s., to commit perjury.

sermon [sɛrmɔ̃], *s.m.* sermon; *F:* talking-to, lecture.

sermonner [sɛrmɔne], *v.tr.* *F:* to give (s.o.)‖a talking-to.

serpent [sɛrpɑ̃], *s.m.* serpent, snake.

serpenter [sɛrpɑ̃te], *v.i.* to wind, meander.

serpentin [sɛrpɑ̃tɛ̃], *s.m.* (paper) streamer.

serpillière [sɛrpijɛːr], s.f. 1. packing cloth. 2. floor cloth.

serre [sɛːr], s.f. 1. greenhouse; s. chaude, hothouse. 2. (a) grip; (b) claw, talon.

serré [sɛre], a. tight; compact.

serr/er [sere], v.tr. 1. to put away, stow away. 2. to press, squeeze, clasp. 3. to tighten; to clench. 4. to close, close up. s.m. -ement. se serrer. 1. to keep close together; to crowd. 2. to become tighter.

serrur/e [seryːr], s.f. lock; trou de la s., keyhole. s.m. -ier, locksmith.

servant, -ante [sɛrvɑ̃, -ɑ̃ːt]. 1. a. serving. 2. s.m. Ecc: server; altar boy. 3. s.f. servante, maid, servant.

serveur, -euse [sɛrvœːr, -øːz], s. barman, barmaid; waitress.

serviable [sɛrvjabl], a. obliging.

service [sɛrvis], s.m. 1. (a) service; porte de s., tradesmen's entrance; Mil: en activité de s., on the active list; (b) department; chef de s., head of department; entreprise de s. public, public utility undertaking. 2. (a) duty; officier de s., orderly officer; (b) (in hotel) s. compris, service included; (in shop) libre s., self service. 3. service, good turn. 4. Rail: premier s., first lunch, dinner; s. de table, dinner service.

serviette [sɛrvjɛt], s.f. 1. (a) (table-) napkin; (b) towel; s. hygiénique, sanitary towel. 2. brief case.

servil/e [sɛrvil], a. servile. s.f. -ité, servility.

‡**serv/ir** [sɛrviːr], v. to serve. 1. v.i. (a) to be useful, to be in use; (b) s. de, to be used as. 2. v.tr. (a) to serve, wait on; madame est servie, dinner is served, madam; (b) to serve, dish up (dinner); servez-vous, help yourself; (c) to help (s.o.); (d) s. la messe, to serve at mass; (e) (at tennis) to serve. s.m. -iteur, servant. s.f. -itude. se servir de qch., to use sth.

ses [se, sɛ]. See SON[1].

servofrein [sɛrvofrɛ̃], s.m. servo-brake.

session [sesjɔ̃], s.f. session, sitting.

seuil [sœːj], s.m. threshold; doorstep.

seul [sœl], a. 1. (preceding noun) (a) only, single; pas un s., not a single one; (b) mere, bare. 2. (following noun) un homme s., a man by himself; dames seules, ladies only; je l'ai fait tout s., I did it (by) myself. 3. un homme peut le faire, only a man can do it. adv. -ement.

sève [sɛːv], s.f. sap.

sévère [sevɛːr], a. severe. 1. stern. 2. strict. adv. -ment.

sévérité [severite], s.f. severity; sternness.

sexagénaire [sɛksaʒenɛːr], a. & s. sexagenarian.

sex/e [sɛks], s.m. sex. a. †-uel. s.m. -ualisme.

seyant [sɛjɑ̃], a. becoming (dress, etc.).

shampooing [ʃɑ̃pwɛ̃], s.m. shampoo.

short [ʃɔrt], s.m. Cl: shorts.

si [si]. I. (s' before il, ils) 1. if. 2. whether. 3. what if; suppose. II. adv. 1. so; so much; (a) such; (b) (c) si bien que, with the result that. 2. (answering neg. question) yes.

siamois, -oise [sjamwa, -waːz], a. & s. Siamese; frères s., sœurs siamoises, Siamese twins.

sibérien, -ienne [siberjɛ̃, -jɛn], a. & s. Siberian.

sibilant [sibilɑ̃], a. sibilant, hissing.

sicilien, -ienne [sisiljɛ̃, -jɛn], a. & s. Sicilian.

sidérurg/ie [sideryrʒi], s.f. iron and steel industry. a. -ique.

siècle [sjɛkl], s.m. 1. century. 2. age, period (of time).

siège [sjɛːʒ], s.m. 1. seat, centre. 2. siege. 3. seat, chair.

‡**siéger** [sjeʒe], v.i. (of parliament, etc.) to sit.

sien, sienne [sjɛ̃, sjɛn]. 1. poss.a. his, hers, its, one's. 2. poss.pron. le sien, la sienne, les siens, les siennes, (a) his, hers, its, one's; (b) s.pl. his own, her own, one's own.

sieste [sjɛst], s.f. siesta, nap.

siffl/er [sifle]. 1. v.i. to whistle; to hiss; to whizz. 2. v.tr. (a) to whistle; (b) to whistle for; (c) to hiss. s.m. -ement. s.m. -et, whistle. s. -eur, -euse, whistler.

†**signal** [sinal], s.m. signal.

signal/er [sinale], v.tr. 1. (a) to make (sth.) conspicuous; (b) to report. 2. to signal. 3. to give a description of. s.m. -ement, description. s.m. -eur, signaller. se signaler, to distinguish oneself (par, by).

signalisation [sinalizasjɔ̃], s.f. 1. signalling. 2. s. routière, road signs.

signataire [sinatɛːr], s.m. & f. signatory, subscriber.

signature [sinatyːr], s.f. 1. signing. 2. signature.

signe [sin], s.m. sign. 1. indication; mark. 2. symbol. 3. gesture.

signer [sine], v.tr. to sign. se signer, to cross oneself.

signifi/er [sinifje], v.tr. to mean, signify. s.f. -cation. a. †-catif, significant.

silence [silɑ̃ːs], s.m. silence.

†**silencieu/x** [silɑ̃sjø], a. silent; (a) taciturn; (b) noiseless; (c) still, peaceful. adv. -ement.

silex [silɛks], s.m. flint.

silhouette [silwɛt], s.f. silhouette.

sillage [sijaːʒ], s.m. (a) wake, wash; (b) slipstream.

sillon [sijɔ̃], s.m. 1. (a) furrow; (b) line, wrinkle. 2. track; wake (of ship); streak (of light). 3. Rec: s. sonore, sound groove.

sillonner [sijɔne], v.tr. (a) to furrow; (b) to streak.

silo [silo], s.m. Agr: silo.

similaire [similɛːr], a. similar; like.

similarité [similarite], s.f. similarity, likeness.

similitude [similityd], s.f. resemblance, likeness; similarity; Gram: simile.

simple [sɛ̃pl], a. 1. simple. 2. (a) ordinary, common; s. soldat, private; (b) plain; (c) easy. 3. (a) simpleminded; (b) half-witted. adv. -ment.

simplicité [sɛ̃plisite], s.f. 1. simplicity; plainness. 2. artlessness, simpleness.

simplifier [sɛ̃plifje], v.tr. to simplify. s.f. -cation.

simuler [simyle], v.tr. to simulate, pretend. s.f. -ation.

simultané [simyltane], a. simultaneous. adv. -ment.

sincère [sɛ̃sɛːr], a. sincere. 1. frank, candid. 2. genuine. adv. -ment.

sincérité [sɛ̃serite], s.f. (a) sincerity, frankness, candour; (b) genuineness.

sinécure [sinekyːr], s.f. sinecure.

singe [sɛ̃ːʒ], s.m. monkey, ape.

†**singer** [sɛ̃ʒe], v.tr. to ape, mimic.

singulariser (se) [sɛ̃gylarize], v.pr. to make oneself conspicuous.

singularité [sɛ̃gylarite], s.f. singularity. 1. peculiarity. 2. oddness.

†**singulier** [sɛ̃gylje], 1. a. peculiar, odd. 2. s.m. Gram: au s., in the singular. s.m.

sinistre [sinistr], 1. a. sinister, ominous. 2. s.m. disaster, catastrophe.

sinistré, -ée [sinistre], 1. a. damaged, ruined (house, etc.); (person) who has suffered a disaster. 2. s. victim of a disaster.

sinon [sinɔ̃], conj. otherwise, else, if not.

†**sinueux** [sinɥø], a. sinuous; winding.

sinuosité [sinɥozite], s.f. (a) sinuosity, winding; (b) bend (of river).

siphon [sifɔ̃], s.m. siphon.

sirène [siren], s.f. 1. siren, mermaid. 2. siren, hooter.

sirop [siro], s.m. syrup.

situation [sitɥasjɔ̃], s.f. situation.

situer [sitɥe], v.tr. to place, situate, locate.

six [si, sis, siz], num.a.inv. & s.m. six.

sixième [sizjem]. 1. num.a. & s. sixth. 2. s.m. sixth (part).

ski [ski], s.m. 1. ski. 2. skiing; s. nautique, water skiing.

slave [slaːv]. 1. a. Slav, Slavonic. 2. s. Slav.

slip [slip], s.m. 1. Cl: (for men) slip; (for women) briefs. 2. Nau: slipway.

smoking [smɔkiŋ], s.m. dinner-jacket, U.S: tuxedo.

snob [snɔb]. (a) s.m. follower of fashion; (b) a.inv. ça fait très s., that's very smart.

snober [snɔbe], v.tr. to snub, to coldshoulder.

sobr/e [sɔbr], a. temperate, abstemious (pers.); sober, quiet (style). adv. -ement. s.f. -iété.

sobriquet [sɔbrikɛ], s.m. nickname.

sociab/le [sɔsjabl], a. sociable. s.f. -ilité.

social [sɔsjal], a. social; Com: raison sociale, name of firm; capital s., registered capital.

socialisme [sɔsjalism], s.m. socialism.

socialiste [sɔsjalist]. 1. a. socialistic; socialist. 2. s. socialist.

société [sɔsjete], s.f. 1. society; aimer la s., to like company. 2. Com: company, U.S: corporation.

socle [sɔkl], s.m. base, pedestal, plinth.

sœur [sœːr], s.f. (a) sister; (b) nun.

soi [swa], pers.pron. (often followed by -même) oneself; himself, herself, itself, etc.; être chez s., to be at home.

soi-disant [swadizɑ̃]. 1. a.inv. so-called. 2. adv. supposedly.

soie [swa], s.f. silk; papier de s., tissue paper. s.f. -rie, silk goods.

soif [swaf], s.f. thirst; avoir s., to be thirsty.

soigné [swaɲe], a. carefully done; repas s., carefully cooked meal.

soigner [swaɲe], v.tr. to look after, take care of, attend to.

†**soigneux** [swaɲø], a. careful; painstaking; tidy. adv. -sement.

soi-même [swamɛm], pers.pron. oneself.

soin [swɛ̃], s.m. care; (a) aux (bons) soins de, care of; (b) attention, trouble; avoir s. de faire qch., to take care to do sth.

soir [swaːr], s.m. (a) evening; dix heures du s., ten p.m.; (b) afternoon.

soirée [sware], s.f. 1. (duration of) evening. 2. (a) (evening) party; (b) représentation de s., evening performance.

soit. 1. [swat] s.! all right! 2. [swa] conj. s. l'un s. l'autre, either one or the other; s. lundi ou mardi, (either) Monday or Tuesday.

soixante [swasɑ̃ːt], num.a.inv. about sixty; avoir passé la s., to be in the sixties.

soixante [swasɑ̃ːt], num.a.inv. & s.m.inv. sixty.

soixante-dix [swasɑ̃tdis], num.a.inv. & s.m.inv. seventy.

soixante-dixième [swasɑ̃tdizjɛm], num.a. & s. seventieth.

soixantième [swasɑ̃tjɛm], num.a. & s. sixtieth.

sol [sɔl], s.m. ground, earth; soil.

solaire [sɔlɛːr], a. solar; cadran s., sundial.

soldat [sɔlda], s.m. soldier; Av: aircraftman.

solde [sɔld], s.f. Mil: pay.

solde² [sɔld], s.m. 1. Com: balance; pour s., in settlement. 2. vente de soldes, clearance sale.

sole [sɔl], s.f. Fish: sole.

soleil [sɔlɛːj], s.m. 1. sun. 2. sunshine; **coup de s.**, (i) touch of sunstroke; (ii) sunburn; **bains de s.**, sunbathing. 3. sunflower. 4. catherine wheel.

†**solennel** [sɔlanɛl], a. solemn. adv. -**ement**.

solennité [sɔlanite], s.f. solemnity.

solidarité [sɔlidarite], s.f. 1. joint responsibility. 2. grève de s., sympathetic strike.

solide [sɔlid], s.m. 1. a. (a) solid; (b) sound, solvent. 2. s.m. solid. adv. -**ment**.

solidifier [sɔlidifje], v.tr. to solidify.

solidité [sɔlidite], s.f. solidity; strength.

soliste [sɔlist], s.m. & f. soloist.

solitaire [sɔlitɛːr], 1. a. solitary, lonely. 2. s.m. (a) recluse; (b) solitaire (diamond).

solitude [sɔlityd], s.f. solitude, loneliness.

solive [sɔliːv], s.f. joist, beam.

sollicit/er [sɔllisite], v.tr. to solicit, beg for (favour), s.-**ation**.

sollicitude [sɔllisityd], s.f. (a) solicitude; care; (b) anxiety, concern.

solo [sɔlo], s.m. solo.

solstice [sɔlstis], s.m. solstice.

solub/le [sɔlybl], a. soluble. s.f. -ilité.

solution [sɔlysjɔ̃], s.f. solution.

solvab/le [sɔlvabl], a. solvent (financially). s.f. -ilité, solvency.

sombre [sɔ̃ːbr], a. dark, sombre, gloomy.

sombrer [sɔ̃bre], v.i. to founder; to sink.

sommaire [sɔmmɛːr], a. & s.m. summary. adv. -**ment**.

somme[1] [sɔm], s.f. bête de s., beast of burden.

somme[2], s.f. sum, amount; **s. toute**, altogether; **en s.**, in short.

somme[3], s.m. nap; short sleep.

sommeil [sɔmɛːj], s.m. 1. sleep; sleepiness; **avoir s.**, to be sleepy.

sommeiller [sɔmeje], v.i. to doze; to sleep lightly.

sommer [sɔme], v.tr. to summon (s.o.); to call on (s.o. to do sth.).

sommet [sɔmɛ], s.m. top, summit; Pol: conférence au s., summit meeting.

sommier [sɔmje], s.m. spring mattress.

somnambule [sɔmnɑ̃byl], s. sleepwalker.

somnol/er [sɔmnɔle], v.i. to drowse, doze. a. -**ent**. s.f. -**ence**.

†**somptueu/x** [sɔ̃ptɥø], a. sumptuous. adv. -**sement**.

son[1], sa, ses [sɔ̃, sa, sɛ], poss.a. his, her, its, one's.

son[2], s.m. sound; mur du s., sound barrier.

son[3], s.m. bran; tache de s., freckle.

sonate [sɔnat], s.f. sonata.

sondage [sɔ̃daːʒ], s.m. (a) Nau: sounding; Min: boring; (b) Med: probing; (c) s. Gallup, Gallup poll; enquête par s., sample survey.

sonde [sɔ̃ːd], s.f. (a) Nau: sounding line; Meteor: sounding; Min: borer; (b) Med: sound, probe.

sonder [sɔ̃de], v.tr. (a) Nau: to sound, take soundings; (b) Med: to probe; (c) to examine, investigate.

songe [sɔ̃ːʒ], s.m. dream.

†**songer** [sɔ̃ʒe], v.i. 1. (a) to dream; (b) to daydream; 2. (a) s. à qch., to think of sth.; (b) to imagine.

songeur, -euse [sɔ̃ʒœːr, -øːz]. 1. s. dreamer. 2. a. dreamy.

sonique [sɔnik], a. sonic; mur s., sound barrier; détonation s., supersonic bang.

sonnant [sɔnɑ̃], a. 1. striking; à dix heures sonnantes, on the stroke of ten. 2. espèces sonnantes, hard cash.

sonner [sɔne]. 1. v.i. to sound; to strike; to ring. 2. v.tr. to sound; to ring.

sonnerie [sɔnri], s.f. 1. ringing. 2. s. électrique, electric bell. 3. (trumpet-, bugle-) call.

sonnette [sɔnɛt], s.f. 1. (a) (small) bell; (b) (door) bell. 2. serpent à sonnettes, rattlesnake.

sonore [sɔnɔːr], a. sonorous; resounding; onde s., sound wave.

soporifique [sɔporifik], a. & s.m. soporific.

soprano [sɔprano], s.m. & f. soprano.

sorbet [sɔrbɛ], s.m. sorbet; water-ice.

sorc/ier, -ière [sɔrsje, -jɛːr], s. sorcerer, sorceress; wizard, f. witch; vieille sorcière, old hag. s.f. -**ellerie**, witchcraft.

sordide [sɔrdid], a. sordid; squalid.

sort [sɔːr], s.m. 1. lot; destiny, fate. 2. chance, fortune; tirer au s., to draw lots; Sp: to toss, spin the coin.

sorte [sɔrt], s.f. 1. manner, way; en s. que, so that. 2. sort, kind.

sortie [sɔrti], s.f. 1. going out, coming out, departure; à la s. des élèves, when the children come out of school. 2. trip, excursion. 3. Mil: sortie. 4. exit; way out.

sortilège [sɔrtilɛːʒ], s.m. spell, charm.

†**sortir** [sɔrtiːr]. I. v.i. (conj. with être) 1. (a) to go out, come out; Th: Macbeth sort, exit 'Macbeth'; Sch: est-ce que je peux s.? may I be excused? (b) s. en courant, to run out; (c) je sors de table, I've just finished my meal; abs. il sort à 6 heures, he finishes work at six. 2. s. d'une difficulté, to get out of a difficulty. 3. to descend, come from (good stock, etc.). 4. to stand out, project. II. v.tr. (conj. with avoir) to take out (child, book from library, etc.); to publish (book). III. s.m. au s. du théâtre, on coming out of the theatre; au s. de l'hiver, at the end of winter.

sosie [sɔzi], s.m. (s.o.'s) double.

sot, sotte [so, sɔt]. **1.** *a.* silly, stupid, foolish. **2.** *s.* fool, idiot, F: ass. *adv.* -**tement.**

sottise [sɔtiːz], *s.f.* **1.** stupidity, foolishness. **2.** piece of stupidity.

sou [su], *s.m.* = penny; être sans le s., to be penniless, F: broke; F: être près de ses sous, to be miserly, mean.

soubresaut [subraso], *s.m.* sudden start.

souche [suʃ], *s.f.* **1.** stump (of tree). **2.** counterfoil, stub (of cheque).

souci[1] [susi], *s.m.* marigold.

souci[2], *s.m.* care. **1.** solicitude. **2.** anxiety, worry.

soucier (se) [səsusje], *v.pr.* to concern oneself (de about); care (de, for); to mind.

†soucieux [susjø], *a.* (*a*) anxious, concerned; (*b*) full of care; worried.

soucoupe [sukup], *s.f.* saucer; s. volante, flying saucer.

soudain [sudɛ̃]. **1.** *a.* sudden, unexpected. **2.** *adv.* suddenly; all of a sudden. *adv.* -**ement.** *s.f.* -**eté.**

soude [sud], *s.f.* soda.

souder [sude], *v.tr.* to weld; to solder. **se souder,** (of bone) to knit.

souffle [sufl], *s.m.* breath. **1.** puff; blast. **2.** respiration, breathing.

souffl/er [sufle]. **1.** *v.i.* (*a*) to blow; (*b*) to pant. **2.** *v.tr.* (*a*) to blow; to blow out (a candle); (*b*) to breathe, utter (a sound); (*c*) *Th:* to prompt. *s.* -**eur, -euse,** prompter.

soufflet [sufle], *s.m.* **1.** (pair of) bellows. **2.** (*a*) box on the ear, slap; (*b*) affront.

souffrance [sufrɑ̃ːs], *s.f.* **1.** en s., in suspense, in abeyance; colis en s., parcels awaiting delivery, to be called for. **2.** suffering, pain.

souffrant [sufrɑ̃], *a.* unwell, indisposed.

†souffrir [sufriːr], *v.* to suffer. **1.** *v.tr.* (*a*) to endure; (*b*) to permit, allow. **2.** *v.i.* to feel pain; (*of thing*) to suffer (from); to be damaged (by).

soufre [sufr], *s.m.* sulphur.

souhait [swɛ], *s.m.* wish, desire; à s., to one's liking.

souhait/er [swɛte], *v.tr.* to wish, desire. *a.* -**able,** desirable.

souiller [suje], *v.tr.* **1.** to soil, dirty. **2.** to pollute. **3.** to tarnish, sully.

souillure [sujyːr], *s.f.* **1.** spot; stain. **2.** blot, blemish.

soûl [su], *a.* F: drunk, tipsy.

†soulag/er [sulaʒe], *v.tr.* to ease (pressure); to relieve (pain). *s.m.* -**ement,** relief.

　se soulager, to relieve one's feelings.

†soul/ever [sulve], *v.tr.* **1.** to raise; to lift (up). **2.** to rouse, stir up. *s.m.* -**èvement.**

　se soulever, to rise; to revolt.

soulier [sulje], *s.m.* shoe.

souligner [suliɲe], *v.tr.* (*a*) to underline; (*b*) to emphasize.

‡soumettre [sumɛtr], *v.tr.* **1.** to subdue. **2.** to submit, refer (question, etc.).

　se soumettre, to submit, yield, give in.

soumis [sumi], *a.* obedient.

soumission [sumisjɔ̃], *s.f.* (*a*) submission; (*b*) obedience.

soupape [supap], *s.f.* valve; s. de sûreté, safety valve.

soupçon [supsɔ̃], *s.m.* **1.** suspicion. **2.** small quantity, soupçon.

soupçonner [supsɔne], *v.tr.* to suspect.

†soupçonneux [supsɔnø], *a.* suspicious.

soupe [sup], *s.f.* soup.

soupente [supɑ̃ːt], *s.f.* loft, garret.

souper [supe]. **I.** *v.i.* to have supper. **II.** *s.m.* supper.

†soupeser [supze], *v.tr.* to feel, try, the weight of.

soupière [supjɛːr], *s.f.* soup tureen.

soupir [supiːr], *s.m.* sigh.

soupirer [supire], *v.i.* to sigh.

souple [supl], *a.* supple, pliant; flexible; versatile (mind). *s.f.* -**esse,** suppleness.

source [surs], *s.f.* **1.** spring; source (of river); eau de s., spring water. **2.** source, origin.

sourcil [sursi], *s.m.* eyebrow.

sourciller [sursije], *v.i.* **1.** to frown. **2.** to wince; sans s., without turning a hair.

sourd, -e [surr, surd]. **1.** *a.* (*a*) deaf; (*b*) dull, muffled (sound). **2.** *s.* deaf person. *adv.* -**ement.**

souricière [surisjɛːr], *s.f.* mousetrap.

souri/re [suriːr]. **I.** *v.i.* to smile. **II.** *s.m.* smile. *a.* -**ant,** smiling.

souris [suri], *s.f.* mouse.

sournois [surnwa], *a.* artful, sly, crafty. *adv.* -**ement.**

sous [su], *prep.* under(neath), beneath, below; s. les tropiques, in the tropics.

NOTE. Compound nouns and adjectives of which the first element is **sous** add a final **s** in the plural unless otherwise indicated.

sous-bois [subwa], *s.m. inv.* undergrowth.

souscription [suskripsjɔ̃], *s.f.* subscription.

‡souscrire [suskriːr], *v.tr.* to subscribe.

sous-entendre [suzɑ̃tɑ̃ːdr], *v.tr.* to imply.

sous-estimer [suzɛstime], *v.tr.* to underestimate.

sous-locataire [sulɔkatɛːr], *s.m. & f.* subtenant.

sous-marin [sumarɛ̃]. **1.** *a.* submarine; submerged. **2.** *s.m.* submarine.

sous-officier [suzɔfisje], *s.m.* non-commissioned officer; *Nau:* petty officer.

sous-produit [suprɔdɥi], *s.m.* by-product.

soussigné [susiɲe], *a. & s.* undersigned.

sous-sol [susɔl], *s.m.* basement.

sous-titre [sutitr], *s.m.* sub-title.

soustraction [sustraksjɔ̃], s.f. (a) removal, abstraction; (b) subtraction.

‡soustraire [sustrɛːr], v.tr. 1. to take away, steal. 2. Mth: to subtract.
se soustraire à, to avoid, get out of (sth.).

sous-vêtement [suvɛtmɑ̃], s.m. undergarment; pl. underwear.

soutane [sutan], s.f. cassock.

soute [sut], s.f. store-room; bunker.

soutenable [sutnabl], a. tenable.

‡soutenir [sutniːr], v.tr. to support; to maintain; to back (s.o.) up; to sustain (shock); to withstand, hold out against (attack).
se soutenir. 1. to hold up, keep up. 2. to last, continue.

soutenu [sutny], a. sustained.

souterrain [suterɛ̃], s.m. 1. a. underground, subterranean. 2. s.m. subway.

soutien [sutjɛ̃], s.m. support, prop; s. de famille, breadwinner.

soutien-gorge [sutjɛ̃gɔrʒ], s.m.inv. Cl: brassière.

soutirer [sutire], v.tr. to draw off; to tap.

souvenir [suvniːr], s.m. 1. remembrance, recollection. 2. memento; souvenir.

souvenir (se) v.pr. se s. de qch., to remember sth.

souvent [suvɑ̃], adv. often.

souverain, -aine [suvrɛ̃, -ɛn]. 1. a. sovereign; supreme. 2. s. sovereign.
s.f. -eté.

sovi/et [sɔvjɛt], s.m. Soviet. a. & s. -étique, Soviet.

soyeux [swajø], a. silky.

†spacieux [spasjø], a. spacious, roomy.

spasme [spasm], s.m. spasm.

spatule [spatyl], s.f. spatula.

†spécial [spesjal], a. special. adv. -ement.

spécial/iser [spesjalize], v.tr. to specialize. s. -iste. s.f. -ité.

spécif/ier [spesifje], v.tr. to specify. a. -ique, specific. adv. -iquement. s.f. -ication, specification.

spécimen [spesimɛn], s.m. specimen.

spectacle [spektakl], s.m. 1. spectacle, sight. 2. play, entertainment, show. 3. show, display.

spectateur, -trice [spektatœːr, -tris], s. spectator, onlooker, bystander.

spectral [spektral], a. spectral; couleurs spectrales, colours of the spectrum.

spectre [spektr], s.m. 1. spectre, ghost. 2. spectrum.

spéculateur, -trice [spekylatœːr, -tris], s. speculator.

†spéculatif [spekylatif], a. speculative. s.f. -ion.

spéculer [spekyle], v.i. to speculate.

spéléolo/gie [speleɔlɔʒi], s.f. spel(a)eology, potholing. s. -gue.

sperme [spɛrm], s.m. sperm, semen.

sphère [sfɛːr], s.f. sphere.

sphérique [sferik], a. spherical.

sphinx [sfɛ̃ks], s.m. sphinx.

†spinal [spinal], a. spinal.

spirale [spiral], s.f. spiral.

spiritisme [spiritism], s.m. spiritualism.

†spirituel [spiritɥɛl], a. 1. spiritual. 2. witty. adv. -lement.

†spiritueux [spiritɥø]. 1. a. alcoholic. 2. s.m.pl. spirits.

splendeur [splɑ̃dœːr], s.f. splendour.

splendide [splɑ̃did], a. splendid.

†spongieux [spɔ̃ʒjø], a. spongy.

spontané [spɔ̃tane], a. spontaneous. adv. -ment. s.f. -ité, spontaneity.

sporadique [spɔradik], a. sporadic. adv. -ment.

spore [spɔːr], s.f. spore.

sport [spɔːr], s.m. sports; games; costume s., clothes for casual wear; Aut: voiture s., sports model.

sportif, -ive [spɔrtif, -iːv], a. & s. 1. a. sporting; (of) sport; réunion sportive, athletic meeting. 2. s. person keen on sports.

square [skwaːr], s.m. (public) square.

squelette [skəlɛt], s.m. skeleton.

stabilis/er [stabilize], v.tr. to stabilize. s.f. -ation. s.m. -ateur, stabilizer.

stabilité [stabilite], s.f. stability.

stable [stabl], a. stable; firm, steady.

stade [stad], s.m. stadium, sportsground.

stagnant [stagnɑ̃], a. stagnant.

stagnation [stagnasjɔ̃], s.f. stagnation.

stalactite [stalaktit], s.f. stalactite.

stalagmite [stalagmit], s.f. stalagmite.

stalle [stal], s.f. stall (in cathedral); (numbered) seat (in theatre); stalles d'orchestre, orchestra stalls.

stance [stɑ̃s], s.f. stanza.

stand [stɑ̃d], s.m. 1. stand (on racecourse). 2. shooting gallery; rifle range.

standard [stɑ̃daːr], s.m. 1. P.T.T: switchboard. 2. s. de vie, standard of living; modèle s., standard model. s. -iste, switchboard operator. s.f. -isation, standardization.

standardiser [stɑ̃dardize], v.tr. to standardize.

standing [stɑ̃diŋ], s.m. standing; appartement de grand s., luxury flat.

star [staːr], s.f. Cin: star.

station [stasjɔ̃], s.f. 1. (a) (action of) standing; (b) position. 2. pause, (short) halt. 3. (a) s. de métro, underground station; s. de taxis, taxi rank; (b) s. balnéaire, seaside resort.

stationnaire [stasjɔnɛːr], a. stationary.

stationnement [stasjɔnmɑ̃], s.m. stopping; s. interdit, no parking.

stationner [stasjɔne], v.i. 1. to stop; to take up one's position. 2. Aut: to park.

station-service [stasjɔ̃sɛrvis], s.f. Aut: service station. pl. stations-service.

statique [statik]. 1. a. static. 2. s.f. statics.

statisticien, -ienne [statistisjɛ̃, -jɛn], s.m. & f. statistician.

statistique [statistik]. 1. a. statistical. 2. s.f. statistics.

statue [staty], s.f. statue.

stature [statyr], s.f. stature, height.

statut [staty], s.m. statute; regulation.

statutaire [statytɛːr], a. statutory.

stellaire [stelɛːr], a. stellar.

sténo [steno], s.f. F: 1. shorthand typist. 2. shorthand typing.

sténodactylo [stenodaktilo], s.f. 1. shorthand-typist. 2. shorthand typing.

sténographie [stenografi], s.f. shorthand.

sténographier [stenografje], v.tr. to write down in shorthand.

sténotyp/ie [stenotipi], s.f. stenotypy. s. -iste, stenotypist.

stéréoscope [stereoskɔp], s.m. stereoscope. a. -ique, stereoscopic.

stéréotyper [stereotipe], v.tr. to stereotype.

stérile [steril], a. sterile; barren; unprofitable.

stéril/iser [sterilize], v.tr. to sterilize. s.f. -sation.

stéthoscope [stetoskɔp], s.m. stethoscope.

stigmate [stigmat], s.m. stigma.

stigmatiser [stigmatize], v.tr. to stigmatize.

stimulant [stimylɑ̃]. 1. a. stimulating. 2. s.m. (a) stimulant; (b) stimulus.

stimul/er [stimyle], v.tr. to stimulate. s.f. -ation.

stipul/er [stipyle], v.tr. to stipulate. s.f. -ation.

stock [stɔk], s.m. stock (of goods).

stoïcien, -ienne [stɔisjɛ̃, -jɛn]. 1. a. stoical. 2. s. stoic.

stoïcisme [stɔisism], s.m. stoicism.

stoïque [stɔik]. 1. a. stoical. 2. s. stoic. adv. -ment.

stop [stɔp], int. stop!

stopper [stɔpe], v.i. & tr. to stop.

store [stɔːr], s.m. (window) blind.

strabisme [strabism], s.m. squinting.

strapontin [strapɔ̃tɛ̃], s.m. folding seat.

stratagème [strataʒɛm], s.m. stratagem.

stratégie [strateʒi], s.f. strategy.

stratégique [strateʒik], a. strategic(al). adv. -ment.

stratégiste [strateʒist], s.m. strategist.

strict [strikt], a. strict; severe. adv. -ement.

strident [stridɑ̃], a. strident, harsh.

strier [strie], v.tr. 1. to score, scratch. 2. to streak.

strophe [strɔf], s.f. stanza, verse.

†structural [stryktyral], a. structural.

structure [stryktyːr], s.f. structure.

strychnine [striknin], s.f. strychnine.

†studieu/x [stydjø], a. studious. adv. -sement.

studio [stydjo], s.m. 1. studio. 2. one-roomed flat.

stupéfaction [stypefaksjɔ̃], s.f. stupefaction.

stupéfait [stypefɛ], a. stupefied, amazed.

stupéfiant [stypefjɑ̃]. 1. a. amazing. 2. s.m. narcotic; drug.

stupéfier [stypefje], v.tr. to a‹tound, amaze; to stupefy.

stupeur [stypœːr], s.f. stupor.

stupid/e [stypid], a. stupid. adv. -ement. s.f. -ité.

style [stil], s.m. style.

stylo [stilo], s.m. fountain pen; s. à bille, ball(-point) pen.

suaire [sɥɛːr], s.m. winding-sheet; shroud.

suav/e [sɥaːv], a. (a) sweet, pleasant; (b) suave. adv. -ement. s.f. -ité.

subalterne [sybaltɛrn]. 1. a. subordinate. 2. s.m. underling, subaltern.

subdivis/er [sybdivize], v.tr. to subdivide. s.f. -ion.

subir [sybiːr], v.tr. to undergo; to suffer.

subit [sybi], a. sudden, unexpected. adv. -ement.

†subjonctif [sybʒɔ̃ktif], a. & s.m. subjunctive.

subjug/uer [sybʒyge], v.tr. to subjugate. s.f. -ation.

sublime [syblime], a. sublime; lofty, exalted.

‡submerger [sybmɛrʒe], v.tr. 1. to submerge. 2. to overwhelm.

submersion [sybmɛrsjɔ̃], s.f. submersion.

subordonner [sybɔrdɔne], v.tr. to subordinate.

subreptice [sybrɛptis], a. surreptitious. adv. -ment.

subséquent [sypsekɑ̃], a. subsequent.

subsidence [sypsidɑ̃s], s.f. subsidence.

subsidiaire [sypsidjɛːr], a. a subsidiary.

subsister [sybziste], v.i. to subsist.

substance [sypstɑ̃s], s.f. substance.

†substantiel [sybstɑ̃sjɛl], a. substantial. adv. -lement.

†substantif [sybstɑ̃tif], a. & s.m. noun.

substituer [sybstitɥe], v.tr. to substitute.

substitut [sybstity], s.m. assistant; deputy.

substitution [sybstitysjɔ̃], s.f. substitution.

subterfuge [sypterfyːʒ], s.m. subterfuge.

subtil [syptil], a. a subtle. adv. -ement. s.f. -ité.

suburbain [sybyrbɛ̃], a. suburban.

‡subvenir [sybvaniːr], v.ind.tr. s. à, to provide for.

subvention [sybvɑ̃sjɔ̃], s.f. subsidy.

subventionner [sybvɑ̃sjɔne], v.tr. to subsidize.

subversif [sybvɛrsif], a. a subversive.

suc [syk], s.m. juice; sap.

succéder [syksede], v.ind.tr. s. à, to succeed, follow; to inherit.

succès [syksɛ], s.m. 1. result. 2. success.

successeur [syksesœːr], s.m. successor.

†success/if [syksesif], a. successive. adv. -ivement.

succession [syksesjɔ̃], s.f. succession.

succion [syksjɔ̃], s.f. suction; sucking.

succomber [sykɔ̃be], v.i. to succumb.

succul/ent [sykylū], a. succulent, juicy. s.f. -ence.

succursale [sykyrsal], s.f. branch (of firm, etc.).

‡sucer [syse], v.tr. to suck.

sucre [sykr], s.m. sugar; s. d'érable, maple sugar.

sucrer [sykre], v.tr. to sugar; to sweeten.

sucrerie [sykrəri], s.f. 1. sugar mill. 2. pl. sweetmeats, sweets.

sucrier [sykrie], s.m. sugar-basin.

sud [syd], s.m. & a.inv. south.

sud-est [sydest], 1. s.m. south-east. 2. a.inv. south-easterly; south-eastern.

sud-ouest [sydwest], 1. s.m. south-west. 2. a.inv. south-westerly; south-western.

suédois, -oise [sɥedwa, -waːz]. 1. a. Swedish. 2. s. Swede. 3. s.m. Ling: Swedish.

suer [sɥe], v.i. to sweat; to perspire.

sueur [sɥœːr], s.f. sweat, perspiration.

‡suffire [syfiːr], v.i. (a) to suffice; to be sufficient; (b) s. à, to be equal to; il ne peut pas s. à tout, he can't cope with everything.

suffisance [syfizɑ̃ːs], s.f. 1. sufficiency, adequacy. 2. self-conceit.

suffis/ant [syfizɑ̃], a. 1. sufficient, adequate. 2. self-satisfied, conceited. adv. -amment.

suffixe [syfiks], s.m. suffix.

suffocant [syfɔkɑ̃], a. suffocating, stifling.

suffocation [syfɔkasjɔ̃], s.f. suffocation.

suffoquer [syfɔke]. 1. v.tr. to suffocate, stifle. 2. v.i. to choke (de, with).

suffrage [syfraːʒ], s.m. suffrage, vote.

‡suggérer [sygʒere], v.tr. to suggest.

†suggestif [sygʒestif], a. suggestive.

suggestion [sygʒestjɔ̃], s.f. suggestion.

suicide [sɥisid], s.m. suicide.

suicid/er (se) [səsɥiside], v.pr. to commit suicide. s. -é, -ée, (pers.) suicide.

suie [sɥi], s.f. soot.

suif [sɥif], s.m. tallow.

suinter [sɥɛ̃te], v.i. to ooze, seep.

suisse [sɥis]. 1. a. Swiss. 2. s.m. (a) Swiss; (b) Ecc: verger; (c) petit s., (small) cream cheese; (d) Fr.C: chipmunk.

Suissesse [sɥises], s.f. Swiss (woman).

suite [sɥit], s.f. 1. (a) continuation; effect; à la s. de, following; de s., in succession; tout de s., at once, immediately; dans la s., subsequently; (b) sequel; (c) coherence. 2. suite; retinue. 3. series. 4. consequence; par s. de, in consequence of.

suivant [sɥivɑ̃]. 1. prep. according to. 2. a. next, following.

suivi [sɥivi], a. connected; close.

‡suivre [sɥiːvr], v.tr. to follow; (on letter) prière de faire s., please forward; à s., to be continued; s. son chemin, to go on one's way; s. une profession, to practise a profession; s. un cours de français, to take a course in French.

sujet [syʒɛ], s.m. 1. subject. 2. individual; mauvais s., bad lot.

sulfate [sylfat], s.m. sulphate.

sulfure [sylfyːr], s.m. sulphide.

sulfurique [sylfyrik], a. sulphuric.

sultan [syltɑ̃], s.m. sultan.

super [syper], s.m. F: Aut: high-grade petrol.

superbe [sypɛrb], 1. a. superb; stately; magnificent. adv. -ment.

supercarburant [syperkarbyrɑ̃], s.m. high-grade petrol.

supercherie [syperʃeri], s.f. deceit; swindle.

superficie [syperfisi], s.f. area.

†superficiel [syperfisjɛl], a. superficial. adv. -lement.

superflu [syperfly]. 1. a. superfluous. 2. s.m. superfluity. s.f. -ité, superfluity.

supérieur, -eure [syperjœːr]. 1. a. (a) upper (storey, etc.); (b) superior; (c) higher. 2. s. superior.

super-impôt [syperɛ̃po], s.m. surtax. pl. super-impôts.

supériorité [syperjorite], s.f. superiority.

†superlatif [syperlatif], a. & s.m. superlative.

supermarché [sypermarʃe], s.m. supermarket.

superproduction [syperprɔdyksjɔ̃], s.f. Cin: spectacular.

supersonique [sypersɔnik], a. supersonic.

superstit/ion [syperstisjɔ̃], s.f. superstition. a. -ieux, superstitious.

supplanter [syplɑ̃te], v.tr. to supplant; to supersede.

suppléant [sypleɑ̃]. 1. s. substitute; deputy. 2. a. acting, temporary.

suppléer [syplee]. 1. v.tr. to supply, make up; (b) to take the place of, act as deputy for (s.o.). 2. v.i. s. à qch., to make up for sth.

supplément [syplemɑ̃], s.m. (a) supplement; (b) extra payment; excess fare.

supplémentaire [syplemɑ̃tɛːr], a. supplementary; heures supplémentaires, overtime.

suppliant [syplijɑ̃]. 1. a. supplicating, pleading. 2. s. supplicant.

supplication [syplikasjɔ̃], s.f. supplication.

supplice [syplis], s.m. (a) torture; (b) torment, anguish.

supplier [syplie], v.tr. to beseech, implore.

support [sypɔːr], s.m. 1. support, prop, stay. 2. rest; stand.

support/er [sypɔrte], v.tr. 1. to support; to prop up. 2. (a) to endure; (b) to tolerate. a. -able.

supposé [sypoze], a. supposed, alleged; false, fictitious.

supposer [sypoze], v.tr. 1. to suppose, assume, imagine. 2. to imply.

supposition [sypozisjɔ̃], s.f. supposition.

suppression [sypresjɔ̃], s.f. suppression.

supprimer [syprime], v.tr. to suppress.

suprématie [sypremasi], *s.f.* supremacy.

suprême [syprɛːm], *a.* supreme. *adv.* -ment.

sur [syr], *prep.* on, upon; page s. page, page after page; l'emporter sur qn, to get the better of s.o.; il est s. son départ, he is about to leave; un jour s. quatre, one day out of four; s. quoi, whereupon, and then; huit mètres s. six, eight metres by six.

sur², *a.* sour; tart.

sûr [syːr], *a.* sure. 1. (*a*) safe, secure; (*b*) trustworthy. 2. certain; à coup sûr, for certain. *adv.* -ement.

surabond/ance [syrabɔ̃dɑ̃ːs], *s.f.* superabundance. *a.* -ant.

suranné [syrane], *a.* antiquated, out of date.

surcharge [syrʃarʒ], *s.f.* 1. overloading. 2. (*a*) overload; (*b*) excess weight. 3. additional charge.

‡surcharger [syrʃarʒe], *v.tr.* (*a*) to overload; (*b*) to overcharge.

surchauffer [syrʃofe], *v.tr.* to overheat.

surcompresseur [syrkɔ̃prescœːr], *s.m.* Aut: supercharger.

surcroît [syrkrwa], *s.m.* addition, increase.

surdité [syrdite], *s.f.* deafness.

sureau [syro], *s.m.* elder (tree).

sûreté [syrte], *s.f.* 1. safety, security; la S., the Criminal Investigation Department. 2. sureness. 3. security, guarantee.

surestimer [syrestime], *v.tr.* to overestimate.

surface [syrfas], *s.f.* surface.

surgir [syrʒiːr], *v.i.* to rise; to loom (up).

surhomme [syrɔm], *s.m.* superman.

surhumain [syrymɛ̃], *a.* superhuman.

sur-le-champ [syrləʃɑ̃], *adv.* at once.

surlendemain [syrlɑ̃dmɛ̃], *s.m.* next day but one.

‡surmener [syrmøne], *v.tr.* to overwork.

surmonter [syrmɔ̃te], *v.tr.* to surmount; to overcome (difficulty).

‡surnager [syrnaʒe], *v.i.* (*a*) to float on the surface; (*b*) to remain afloat.

†surnaturel [syrnatyrel], *a.* supernatural.

surnom [syrnɔ̃], *s.m.* nickname.

surpasser [syrpase], *v.tr.* 1. to surpass. 2. to go beyond; to outdo.

surpeuplé [syrpœple], *a.* over-populated.

surplis [syrpli], *s.m.* surplice.

surplomber [syrplɔ̃be], *v.i. & tr.* to overhang.

surplus [syrply], *s.m.* surplus, excess.

surprenant [syrprønɑ̃], *a.* surprising, astonishing.

‡surprendre [syrprɑ̃ːdr], *v.tr.* to surprise.

surpris [syrpri], *a.* surprised.

surprise [syrpriːz], *s.f.* surprise.

sursaut [syrso], *s.m.* start, jump.

sursauter [syrsote], *v.i.* to start; to jump.

sursis [syrsi], *s.m.* respite; reprieve.

surtout [syrtu], *adv.* particularly, especially, principally, above all.

surveillant [syrvejɑ̃], *s.* supervisor, superintendent, overseer; inspector; Sch: s. (d'examen), invigilator.

surveill/er [syrveje], *v.tr.* to supervise, superintend; to watch over. *s.f.* -ance, supervision.

‡survenir [syrvøniːr], *v.i.* (*aux.* être) to supervene, happen; to arise.

survivant, -ante [syrvivɑ̃, -ɑ̃ːt]. 1. *a.* surviving. 2. *s.* survivor.

‡surviv/re [syrviːvr], *v.ind.tr.* to survive. *s.f.* -ance, survival.

survoler [syrvole], *v.tr.* to fly over.

suscept/ible [syseptibl], *a.* susceptible; (*a*) sensitive; (*b*) touchy. *s.f.* -ibilité.

susciter [sysite], *v.tr.* (*a*) to raise up; (*b*) to create; to give rise to.

suspect [syspe(kt)]. 1. *a.* suspicious, doubtful, suspect. 2. *s.m.* suspect.

suspecter [syspekte], *v.tr.* to suspect.

suspendre [syspɑ̃ːdr], *v.tr.* to suspend.

suspendu [syspɑ̃dy], *a.* suspended; hanging.

suspens (en) [ɑ̃syspɑ̃], *adv.phr.* in suspense.

suspension [syspɑ̃sjɔ̃], *s.f.* suspension.

suspicion [syspisjɔ̃], *s.f.* suspicion.

svelte [svelt], *a.* slender, slim.

sycomore [sikɔmɔːr], *s.m.* sycamore.

syllab/e [sillab], *s.f.* syllable. *a.* -ique.

sylphe [silf], *s.m.* sylphide [silfid], *s.f.* sylph.

sylviculture [silvikyltyːr], *s.f.* forestry.

symbol/e [sɛ̃bɔl], *s.m.* symbol. *a.* -ique. *adv.* -iquement.

symbolis/er [sɛ̃bɔlize], *v.tr.* to symbolize. *s.m.* -me.

symétrie [simetri], *s.f.* symmetry.

symétrique [simetrik], *a.* symmetrical. *adv.* -ment.

sympath/ie [sɛ̃pati], *s.f.* sympathy; instinctive attraction; liking.

sympathique [sɛ̃patik], *a.* 1. sympathetic. 2. likeable, attractive, congenial. *adv.* -ment.

sympathiser [sɛ̃patize], *v.i.* to sympathize.

symphonie [sɛ̃fɔni], *s.f.* symphony.

symptôme [sɛ̃ptoːm], *s.m.* symptom.

synchroniser [sɛ̃krɔnize], *v.tr.* to synchronize.

s...cope [sɛ̃kɔp], *s.f.* 1. syncope. 2. synd(ing). 2. syncopation.

s...dic/at [sɛ̃dika], *s.m.* syndicate; s. (ouvrier), trade union; s. -aliste, trade unionist. *s.m.* -isme, trade unionism.

synonyme [sinɔnim]. 1. *a.* synonymous (de, with). 2. *s.m.* synonym.

synthétique [sɛ̃tetik], *a.* synthetic.

systématique [sistematik], *a.* systematic.

système [sistem], *s.m.* system.

T

T, t [te], *s.m.* (the letter) T t.; t euphonique forms a link between *v.* endings in -a, -e and the prons. il, elle, on: va-t-il? ira-t-elle?

ta [ta], *poss.a.f.* see TON¹.

tabac [taba]. 1. *s.m.* tobacco. 2. *a.inv.* snuff-coloured.

table [tabl], *s.f.* 1. table; t. ronde, round-table conference. 2. (*a*) slab; tablet; (*b*) list, catalogue.

tableau [tablo], *s.m.* 1. board; *Sch:* t. noir, blackboard; *El:* t. de distribution, switchboard; *Aut:* t. de bord, dashboard. 2. picture, painting. 3. list, table; t. de service, duty roster; *Aut:* t. de graissage, lubrication chart.

tablette [tablet], *s.f.* 1. (*a*) shelf; (*b*) flat slab. 2. slab (of chocolate); tablet, lozenge.

tablier [tablie], *s.m.* apron; t. d'enfant, pinafore.

tabou [tabu], *s.m. & a.* taboo.

tabouret [tabure], *s.m.* (high) stool; footstool.

tache [taʃ], *s.f.* stain, spot; blob (of colour); blemish, bruise (on fruit); blot (on one's record); t. de rousseur, freckle.

tâche [taːʃ], *s.f.* task; ouvrier à la t., piece-worker.

tacher [taʃe], *v.tr.* to stain, spot; to tarnish.

tâcher [taʃe], *v.i.* to try, endeavour.

tacheté [taʃte], *a.* spotted; speckled.

tacite [tasit], *a.* tacit; implied. *adv.* -ment.

taciturne [tasityrn], *a.* taciturn.

tacot [tako], *s.m. F:* old car, jalopy.

tact [takt], *s.m.* tact.

tacticien [taktisjɛ̃], *s.m.* tactician.

tactique [taktik]. 1. *a.* tactical. 2. *s.f.* tactics.

taffetas [tafta], *s.m.* taffeta.

taie [tɛ], *s.f.* t. d'oreiller, pillow-case.

taille [taj, taːj], *s.f.* 1. cutting (of diamonds); *Agr:* pruning, trimming; t. de cheveux, hair-cutting. 2. cut (of garment). 3. edge (on knive, etc.). 4. (*a*) height (of pers.); (*b*) figure, waist; tour de t., waist measurement.

taille-crayons [tajkrɛjɔ̃], *s.m.inv.* pencil-sharpener.

taille-légumes [tajlegym], *s.m.inv.* vegetable slicer.

tailler [taje], *v.tr.* (*a*) to cut; to hew (stone); to trim (hedge); (*b*) t. un vêtement, to cut out a garment; complet bien taillé, well-cut suit.

tailleur, -euse [tajœr, -øːz], *s.* 1. (*a*) cutter; hewer; (*b*) tailor, tailoress. 2. *s.m.* tailor-made costume.

taillis [taji], *s.m.* copse; brushwood.

‡taire [tɛːr], *v.tr.* to say nothing about (sth.), to hush (sth.) up.
se taire, to be silent; tais-toi! taisez-vous! be quiet!

talc [talk], *s.m.* talc; French chalk; (poudre de) t., talcum powder.

talent [talɑ̃], *s.m.* talent, faculty, gift.

taloche [talɔʃ], *s.f. F:* cuff (on the head); flanquer une t. à qn, to clout s.o.

talon [talɔ̃], *s.m.* 1. heel. 2. (*a*) fag-end, remnant; (*b*) t. de souche, counterfoil (of cheque).

talonn/er [talɔne], *v.tr.* (*a*) to follow closely; (*b*) to spur on, urge. *s.m.* -ement. *s.m.* -eur, *Fb:* hooker.

tambour [tɑ̃buːr], *s.m.* 1. drum; t. de basque, tambourine. 2. drummer. 3. revolving door. 4. *El:* (cable) drum; *Aut:* t. de frein, brake drum.

tamis [tami], *s.m.* sieve, sifter; strainer.

tamiser [tamize], *v.tr.* to sift; to strain; to filter (air).

tampon [tɑ̃pɔ̃], *s.m.* 1. plug. 2. (*a*) (inking-)pad; (*b*) rubber stamp. 3. buffer.

‡tancer [tɑ̃se], *v.tr.* to rate, scold (s.o.).

tandis que [tɑ̃di(s)kə], *conj.phr.* (*a*) whereas; (*b*) while, whilst.

tangente [tɑ̃ʒɑ̃ːt], *s.f.* tangent.

tangible [tɑ̃ʒibl], *a.* tangible.

tango [tɑ̃go], *s.m.* tango.

tang/uer [tɑ̃ge], *v.i.* (of ship) to pitch. *s.m.* -age, pitching.

tanière [tanjɛːr], *s.f./den,* lair; (fox's)earth.

tanker [tɑ̃kœːr], *s.m. Nau:* (oil-)tanker.

tann/er [tane], *v.tr.* to tan. *s.m.* -eur, tanner. *s.f.* -erie, tannery.

tant [tɑ̃], *adv.* 1. (*a*) so much; pour t. faire, *F:* t. qu'à faire, j'aimerais autant . . , while I'm about it, I'd just as soon . . . ; t. s'en faut, far from it; t. soit peu, a little, somewhat; (*b*) so many; so many; (*c*) so; to such a degree; en t. que, in so far as; (*d*) however; (*e*) t. mieux, so much the better; I'm very glad; t. pis! so much the worse; what a pity! 2. (*a*) as much, as well (as); (*b*) as long, as far (as).

tante [tɑ̃ːt], *s.f.* aunt.

tantôt [tɑ̃to], *adv.* 1. soon, presently; à t., goodbye for now; see you later. 2. just now. 3. t. triste, t. gai, now sad, now gay.

taon [tɑ̃], *s.m.* horsefly.

tapag/e [tapaːʒ], *s.m.* din, uproar; row. *a. & s.* -eur, -euse, noisy, rowdy (person). *adv.* -eusement.

tape [tap], *s.f.* tap, rap, pat, slap.

tape-à-l'œil [tapalœːj], *s.m.inv. F:* flashy display.

tap/er [tape], *v.tr. F:* to tap, strike, hit; t. une lettre, to type a letter; t. sur le piano, to strum; t. sur les nerfs (à qn), to get on s.o.'s nerves; la soleil tape, *F:* ça tape, it's pretty hot; *F:* t. qn de dix francs, to touch s.o. for ten francs. *s.f.* -ette, carpet-beater; fly-swat. *s.* -eur, -euse, cadger.

tapioca [tapjɔka], *s.m.* tapioca.

tapis [tapi], *s.m.* 1. cloth, cover; t. de table, table cover. 2. carpet. 3. *Ind:* t. roulant, conveyor belt.

tapiss/er [tapise], *v.tr.* to paper (room). 2. (*with*, with) to hang. *s.f.* -erie, tapestry; wallpaper. *s.m.* -ier, upholsterer.

taquin [takɛ̃]. 1. *a.* (given to) teasing. 2. *s.* tease. *s.f.* -erie, teasing.

taquin/er [takine], *v.tr.* to tease; to worry.

tard [ta:r], *adv.* late.

tarder [tarde], *v.i.* 1. to delay. 2. *impers.* il lui tarde, he is longing (de, to).

†tard/if [tardif], *a.* tardy; belated; backward. *adv.* -ivement.

tare [ta:r], *s.f.* 1. (physical, moral) defect, blemish. 2. tare; allowance for weight.

tarif [tarif], *s.m.* (a) tariff, price-list; (b) scale of charges. *a.* -aire, tariff (laws).

tarif-album [tarifalbɔm], *s.m.* trade catalogue. *pl.* tarifs-albums.

tar/ir [tari:r]. 1. *v.tr.* (a) to dry up (spring, tears); (b) to exhaust. 2. *v.i.* to dry up, run dry. *a.* -issable. *s.m.* -issement.

tartare [tarta:r], *a.* & *s.* tartar; *Cu:* sauce t., tartare sauce.

tarte [tart], *s.f.* (open) tart; flan.

tartelette [tart(ə)let], *s.f.* (small) tart.

tartine [tartin], *s.f.* slice of bread and butter, or bread and jam.

tas [tɑ], *s.m.* heap, pile; lot; t. de foin, haycock; piquer dans le t., to help oneself.

tasse [tɑs], *s.f.* cup.

tasser [tɑse], *v.tr.* to compress, squeeze, together; to pack.
     se **tasser**. 1. (of foundations) to settle; to sink. 2. to crowd together.

tâter [tate], *v.tr.* to feel, touch; to finger (sth.); t. le terrain, to throw out feelers.
     se **tâter**, to think it over; to hesitate.

tâtonn/er [tatɔne], *v.i.* to grope. *s.m.* -ement.

tâtons (à) [atatɔ̃], *adv.phr.* gropingly.

tatou/er [tatwe], *v.tr.* to tattoo. *s.m.* -age, tattooing.

taudis [todi], *s.m.* miserable room; hovel; slum.

taul/e [to:l], *s.f. P:* prison, jug.

taup/e [to:p], *s.f.* mole. *s.f.* -inière, molehill.

taur/eau [tɔro], *s.m.* bull. *s.f.* -omachie, (art of) bull-fighting.

taux [to], *s.m.* rate; established price; scale; t. du change, d'intérêt, rate of exchange, of interest.

taxe [taks], *s.f.* 1. controlled price; fixed rate (of wages); t. postale, postage; t. supplémentaire, surcharge. 2. tax, duty.

tax/er [takse], *v.tr.* 1. to regulate, fix (prices, rates). 2. to impose a tax on (luxuries, etc.). 3. to accuse (s.o. of sth.). *s.f.* -ation. *a.* -able.

taxi [taksi], *s.m.* taxi(-cab).

taxiphone [taksifɔn], *s.m. P.T.T:* public call-box.

tchèque [tʃɛk], *a.* & *s.* Czech.

te, **t'** *before a vowel,* [t(ə)], *pers.pron. sg.* (a) you; (b) (to) you; (c) (*with pr. vb.*) yourself.

technic/ien, -ienne [tɛknisjɛ̃, -jɛn], *s.* technician. *s.f.* -ité, technicality.

technique [tɛknik]. 1. *a.* technical. 2. *s.f.* technique. *adv.* -ment.

techno/logie [tɛknɔlɔʒi], *s.f.* technology. *a.* -logique, technological. *s.m.* -logue, technologist.

‡teindre [tɛ̃:dr], *v.tr.* 1. to dye. 2. to stain, tinge.

teint [tɛ̃], *s.m.* 1. dye, colour; *Com:* grand t., fast dye. 2. complexion, colour.

teinte [tɛ̃:t], *s.f.* (a) tint, shade, hue; (b) tinge, touch (of irony, etc.).

teinter [tɛ̃te], *v.tr.* to tint.

teintur/e [tɛ̃ty:r], *s.f.* 1. dyeing. 2. (a) dye; (b) colour, tinge. *s.f.* -erie, dyeing and cleaning business. *s.* -ier, -ière, dyer and cleaner.

tel, telle [tɛl], *a.* 1. such; (a) un t. homme, such a man; (b) en t. lieu, in such and such a place; (c) sa bonté est telle que . . , such is his (her) kindness that . . 2. like; as; (a) un homme t. que lui, a man like him; voir les choses telles qu'elles sont, to look facts in the face; t. quel, just as it (he) is; j'achète la maison telle quelle, I'll buy the house as it stands. 3. *pron.* such a one; t. qui, he who, many a one who . . . *s:* Monsieur un t., Mr So-and-so. *adv.* -lement, in such a manner; to such a degree; so.

télé [tele], *s.f. T.V: F:* the 'telly.'

télécommande [telekɔmɑ̃:d], *s.f.* remote control.

télécommunication [telekɔmynikasjɔ̃], *s.f.* telecommunication.

télégramme [telegram], *s.m.* telegram.

télégraphe [telegraf], *s.m.* telegraph.

télégraph/ier [telegrafje], *v.tr.* & *i.* to wire, to cable. *s.f.* -ie, telegraphy. *a.* -ique, telegraphic. *s.* -iste, telegraphist.

téléguid/er [telegide], *v.tr.* to radio-control; missile téléguidé, guided missile. *s.m.* -age, radio-control.

téléimprimeur [teleɛ̃primœ:r], *s.m.* teleprinter.

télépath/ie [telepati], *s.f.* telepathy. *a.* -ique, telepathic.

téléphone [telefɔn], *s.m.* telephone; coup de t., phone call.

téléphon/er [telefɔne], *v.tr.* & *i.* to telephone; F: to phone, to ring (s.o.) up. *s.f.* -ie, telephony. *a.* -ique, cabine t., telephone box. *s.* -iste, telephonist.

télescop/e [teleskɔp], *s.m.* (reflecting) telescope. *a.* -ique, telescopic.

téléski [teleski], *s.m.* ski-lift.

téléspectateur, -**trice** [telespɛktatœːr, -tris], *s.* (tele)viewer.

télévision [televizjɔ̃], *s.f.* television (set).

téméraire [temerɛːr], *a.* rash, reckless. *adv.* -**ment**.

témérité [temerite], *s.f.* rashness; daring deed.

témoigner [temwaɲe], **1.** *v.i.* to testify. **2.** to bear witness; to give evidence. **2.** *v.tr. or ind. tr.* t. (de) qch., to testify to sth. *s.m.* -**age**, testimony; evidence.

témoin [temwɛ̃], *s.m.* **1.** witness; second (in duel). **2.** *Ind:* échantillon t., check sample; lampe t., telltale (lamp); appartement t., show flat.

tempe [tɑ̃p], *s.f. Anat:* temple.

tempérament [tɑ̃peramɑ̃], *s.m.* **1.** (a) constitution, temperament; (b) t. violent, placide, violent, placid, temper. **2.** *Com:* vente à t., hire-purchase.

tempér/ance [tɑ̃perɑ̃ːs], *s.f.* temperance. *a.* -**ant**, temperate.

température [tɑ̃peratyr], *s.f.* temperature.

‡**tempérer** [tɑ̃pere], *v.tr.* to temper (sun's heat, etc.). *a.* -**éré**; temperate, moderate (climate, speech).

tempête [tɑ̃pɛt], *s.f.* storm; t. de neige, blizzard.

temple [tɑ̃pl], *s.m.* **1.** temple. **2.** (protestant) church, chapel.

temporaire [tɑ̃pɔrɛːr], *a.* temporary. *adv.* -**ment**.

temporis/er [tɑ̃pɔrize], *v.i.* to temporize. *s.* -**ateur**, -**atrice**, procrastinator. *s.f.* -**ation**, procrastination, calculated delay.

temps [tɑ̃], *s.m.* **1.** time (a) vous avez bien le t., you have plenty of time; de t. en t., from time to time; à plein t., full-time (employment); (b) while, period; entre t., meanwhile; t. d'arrêt, pause; (c) age, times; par le t. qui court, nowadays; être de son t., to be up to date; (d) hour; il n'est plus t., it is too late; en t. utile, in due time. **2.** weather; par tous les temps, in all weathers; prévision du t., weather forecast. **3.** *Gram:* tense. **4.** *Mus:* beat; time.

tenace [tɔnas], *a.* tenacious; retentive.

ténacité [tenasite], *s.f.* tenacity.

tenaille [tɔnɑːj], *s.f.* pincers; tongs.

tendance [tɑ̃dɑ̃ːs], *s.f.* tendency, trend.

tendon [tɑ̃dɔ̃], *s.m.* tendon, sinew.

tendre[1] [tɑ̃ːdr], *a.* tender; (a) soft, delicate (colour); early (age); (b) fond, affectionate.

tendre[2]. **1.** *v.tr.* (a) to stretch, tighten (cord, belt); (b) to lay (carpet); to hang (wallpaper); (c) to stretch out, hold out (one's hand). **2.** *v.i.* to tend, lead (à qch.). se tendre, to become taut, strained.

tendresse [tɑ̃drɛs], *s.f.* tenderness; love.

tendu [tɑ̃dy], *a.* tense, taut, tight.

ténèbres [tenɛːbr], *s.f.pl.* darkness; gloom.

†**ténébreux** [tenebrø], *a.* gloomy, dark.

teneur [tɔnœːr], *s.f.* **1.** tenor, purport (of document). **2.** amount; t. en eau, degree of humidity.

‡**tenir** [tɔniːr]. **I.** *v.tr.* **1.** to hold; (a) t. serré qch., to hold sth. tight; je tiens mon homme, I've got my man; auto qui tient bien la route, car that holds the road well; tiens! tiens! (look) here! (b) to contain; (c) t. de, to have, derive, from; t. qch. de mains sûres, to have sth. on good authority; (d) to keep, stock. **2.** to keep (a shop); to run (a school); le marché se tient le samedi, market day's on Saturday. **3.** to hold (opinion); to maintain; to keep (promise). **4.** to hold back, restrain; control (s.o.). **5.** to occupy, take up (space). **II.** *v.i.* **1.** to hold; to adhere; to remain; ne pas t. en place, to be restless. **2.** (a) t. (bon), to hold out, to stand fast; (b) to last; couleur qui tient bien, fast colour. **3.** t. pour, to be in favour of (s.o., sth.). **4.** t. à qch., (a) to value, prize (sth.); (b) t. à faire qch., to be set on doing sth.; je n'y tiens pas, I'm not keen on it; (c) to depend on, result from, sth.; to be due to sth.; à quoi cela tient-il? what's the reason for it? **5.** t. de qn, to take after s.o.

se tenir. **1.** (a) to keep, be, remain, stand, sit; se t. chez soi, to stay at home; tenez-vous droit, (i) sit up straight, (ii) stand up straight; (b) se t. à, to hold on to. **2.** to contain oneself. **3.** s'en t. à qch., to be content with sth.; savoir à quoi s'en t., to know where one stands.

tennis [tenis], *s.m.* **1.** (lawn) tennis. **2.** tennis court.

tenor [tenɔːr], *s.m.* tenor; *F: Pol: etc:* star performer.

tension [tɑ̃sjɔ̃], *s.f.* tension. **1.** stretching, tightening (of muscles, etc.). **2.** *Ph:* pressure; *Med:* t. artérielle, blood pressure; *El:* t. du courant, voltage; haute t., high voltage, tension.

tente [tɑ̃ːt], *s.f.* (a) tent; (b) awning.

tent/er [tɑ̃te], *v.tr.* **1.** to tempt s.o.; t. la chance, to try one's luck. **2.** to attempt, try (to do sth.). *a. & s.* -**ateur**, -**atrice**, (i) tempting; (ii) tempter, temptress. *s.f.* -**ation**, temptation. *s.f.* -**ative**, attempt.

tenture [tɑ̃tyːr], *s.f.* (a) hangings; *Fr.C:* curtain, *U.S:* drape; (b) (papier-)t., wallpaper.

tenu [tɔny], *a.* (a) bien t., well-kept; (b) être t. de, à, faire qch., to be obliged to do sth.

tenue [tɔny], *s.f.* **1.** (a) session; (b) keeping, managing (of shop, etc.); t. des livres, book-keeping. **2.** bearing, behaviour; avoir de la t., to have good manners. **3.** dress; en grande t., in full dress.

térébenthine [terebãtin], *s.f.* turpentine.

terme[1] [term], *s.m.* 1. term, end, limit (of life, journey). 2. (appointed) time; accouchement avant t., premature childbirth. 3. (a) quarter; term; (b) quarter's rent.

terme[2], *s.m.* 1. term, expression; t. de métier, technical term. 2. *pl.* wording; terms. 3. *pl.* (friendly, etc.) terms.

termin/er [termine], *v.tr.* 1. to terminate. 2. to end, finish; to conclude. *s.f.* -aison, termination, ending. se terminer, to come to an end.

terminus [terminys], *s.m.* (railway) terminus; (air) terminal.

terne [tern], *a.* dull, lustreless; lifeless, colourless.

ternir [ternir], *v.tr.* to tarnish, dull, dim.

terrain [terɛ̃], *s.m.* ground; (a) piece of ground, plot of land; t. à bâtir, building site; (b) (football) field; (golf) course.

terrasse [terɑs], *s.f.* (a) terrace; bank; (b) pavement (in front of a café).

terrass/er [terɑse], *v.tr.* 1. to embark. 2. (a) to lay (s.o.) low; to throw (wrestler); (b) to dismay, crush (s.o.). *s.m.* -ement, embankment. *s.m.* -ier, navvy.

terr/e [tɛːr], *s.f.* 1. earth; (a) the world; (b) ground, land; attaquer par t. et par mer, to attack by land and sea. 2. soil, land; t. grasse, rich soil. 3. estate, property. 4. loam, clay; t. cuite, terra-cotta; t. végétale, loam. *a.* -estre, terrestrial, earthly.

terre-neuve [tɛrnœ:v], *s.m.inv.* Newfoundland (dog).

terreur [terœːr], *s.f.* terror; dread.

†**terreux** [terø], *a.* (a) earthy (taste, smell); (b) grubby (hands); (c) dull (colour); sickly (face).

terrible [teribl], *a.* terrible, dreadful. *adv.* -ment.

terrier[1] [terje], *s.m.* burrow, hole; earth (of fox).

terrier[2], *a.m. & s.m.* terrier.

terrifier [ter(r)ifje], *v.tr.* to terrify.

terrine [terin], *s.f.* 1. (earthenware) pot. 2. *Cu:* pâté.

terri/toire [teritwaːr], *s.m.* territory. *a.* †-torial, territorial.

terror/iser [ter(r)orize], *v.tr.* to terrorize. *s.m.* -iste.

tertre [tɛrtr], *s.m.* hillock, mound, knoll.

test [test], *s.m. Psy:* test; t. d'intelligence pratique, aptitude test; t. professionel, occupational test.

testa/ment[1] [testamã], *s.m.* will, testament. *s.* -teur, -trice, testator, testatrix.

testament[2], *s.m.* l'ancien, le nouveau T., the Old, the New, Testament.

têtard [tɛtaːr], *s.m.* tadpole.

tête [tɛt], *s.f.* head. 1. (a) tenir t. à qn, to stand up to s.o.; j'en ai par-dessus la t., F: I'm fed up; mal de t., headache; se laver la t., to wash one's hair; (b) face, appearance; F: faire une t., to look glum; il a une sale t., he's a nasty-looking customer. 2. headpiece, brains; une femme de t., a capable woman; mauvaise tête, unruly boy, workman; en faire à sa t., to have one's way. 3. (a) leader; (b) summit, top; *Aut:* soupapes en t., overhead valves; (c) front (place); être à la t. de la classe, to be top of the form; *Rail:* t. de ligne, terminus.

tête-à-tête [tetatɛt], *s.m.inv.* tête-à-tête.

têtu [tety], *a.* stubborn, obstinate.

teuton, -onne [tøtõ, -ɔn]. 1. *a.* Teuton(ic). 2. *s.* Teuton.

texte [tekst], *s.m.* (a) text; gravure hors t., full-page engraving; plate; (b) letterpress (to illustration).

textile [tekstil], *a. & s.m.* textile.

thé [te], *s.m.* 1. tea. 2. tea-party. *s.f.* -ière, tea-pot.

théâtre [teɑːtr], *s.m.* 1. theatre. 2. stage. 3. (a) dramatic art; pièce de t., play; coup de t., dramatic turn (to events); (b) plays, dramatic works; le t. anglais, English drama. *a.* †-al, theatrical. *adv.* -alement.

thème [tem], *s.m.* (a) theme, subject; (b) *Sch:* prose; t. latin, Latin prose.

théolo/gie [teɔlɔʒi], *s.f.* theology. *s.m.* -ien, theologian. *a.* -ique, theological.

théorème [teɔrem], *s.m.* theorem.

théor/ie [teɔri], *s.f.* theory. *a.* -ique, theoretic(al). *adv.* -iquement.

théor/iser [teɔrize], *v.tr. & i.* to theorize. *s.m. & f.* -iste, theorist.

thérapie [terapi], *s.f. Med:* therapy; t. rééducative, occupational therapy.

†**thermal** [termal], *a.* thermal; eaux thermales, hot springs; station thermale, spa.

thermomètre [termɔmetr], *s.m.* thermometer.

thermonucléaire [termɔnykleɛːr], *a. Atom.Ph:* thermonuclear.

thermostat [termɔsta], *s.m.* thermostat. *a.* -ique, thermostatic (control, etc.).

thermothérapie [termɔterapi], *s.f. Med:* heat treatment.

thèse [tɛːz], *s.f.* 1. proposition, argument; pièce à t., problem play. 2. *Sch:* thesis.

thon [tõ], *s.m.* tunny(-fish). *s.m.* -ier, tunny-fishing boat.

thorax [tɔraks], *s.m. Anat:* thorax, chest.

thym [tɛ̃], *s.m.* thyme.

tic [tik], *s.m.* (a) tic; nervous twitch(ing); (b) (unconscious) mannerism.

ticket [tike], *s.m.* numbered slip, check; ticket.

tiède [tjɛd], *a.* tepid; (luke)warm.

tiédeur [tjedœːr], *s.f.* lukewarmness.

tien, tienne [tjɛ̃, tjɛn]. **1**. *poss.a.* yours. **2**. le tien, la tienne, les tiens, les tiennes; (*a*) *poss.pron.* yours; (*b*) *s.m.* (i) your own (property, etc.); yours; (ii) *pl.* your own (friends, etc.).

tiens [tjɛ̃], *int.* **1**. hullo! **2**. t., t.! indeed? well, well!

tiers, t. *f.* **tierce** [tjɛr, tjɛrs], *s.* (*a*) third (part); (*b*) third person, third party.

tige [tiːʒ], *s.f.* **1**. stem, stalk. **2**. (*a*) shaft; shank; (*b*) rod (of piston, etc.).

tigre, tigresse [tigr, tigrɛs], *s.* tiger, tigress.

tigré [tigre], *a.* striped; speckled; chat t., tabby cat; lis t., tiger lily.

tilleul [tijœl], *s.m.* lime tree.

timbale [tɛ̃bal], *s.f.* **1**. kettle-drum. **2**. metal drinking-cup. **3**. pie-mould.

timbre [tɛ̃br], *s.m.* **1**. (*a*) t. électrique, electric bell; *F*: avoir le t. fêlé, to have a screw loose; (*b*) stamp (on document); postmark; rubber, (date, etc.) stamp. **2**. stamp (on document); postmark; rubber, (date, etc.) stamp. **2**. stamp (on document); timbre (of voice, instrument).

timbre(-poste) [tɛ̃brəpɔst], *s.m.* postage stamp. *pl.* timbres-poste.

timbre-quittance [tɛ̃brəkitɑ̃ːs], *s.m.* receipt stamp. *pl.* timbres-quittance.

timbr/er [tɛ̃bre], *v.tr.* to stamp. *s.m.* -age.

timide [timid], *a.* timid; (*a*) timorous; (*b*) shy; diffident (envers, with). *adv.* -ment.

timidité [timidite], *s.f.* timidity; shyness.

tint/er [tɛ̃te]. **1**. *v.tr.* to ring. **2**. *v.i.* to ring; to tinkle; to clink. *s.m.* -ement.

tir [tiːr], *s.m.* **1**. shooting; gunnery. **2**. fire, firing. **3**. rifle-range.

tirade [tirad], *s.f.* tirade.

tiraill/er [tiraje], *v.tr.* **1**. to pull (s.o., sth.) about; *Fr.C:* to scuffle. **2**. *abs.* to shoot (aimlessly), to pot at (sth., s.o.). *s.m.* -eur, skirmisher.

tire [tiːr], *s.f.*: voleur à la t., pickpocket.

tiré [tire], *a.* worn-out, haggard; il avait les traits tirés, his face was drawn.

tire-bouchon [tirbuʃɔ̃], *s.m.* corkscrew. *pl.* tire-bouchons.

tir/er [tire]. **I**. *v.tr.* **1**. to pull out; stretch. **2**. to pull, tug, draw. **3**. to pull off, draw off (boots); t. son chapeau à qn, to raise one's hat to s.o.; t. de l'eau, to draw water. **4**. to take out, extract. **5**. (*a*) to draw; (*b*) to print (off) proofs, photos; (*c*) *Com:* to draw (bill of exchange). **6**. to shoot, fire. **II**. *v.i.* **1**. to pull. **2**. to incline (to); to verge (on).

tiret [tire], *s.m.* (*punctuation*) dash. *s.m.* -age.

tireur, -euse [tirœːr, øːz], *s.* **1**. (*a*) shooter; marksman; (*b*) fencer.

tiroir [tirwaːr], *s.m.* drawer.

tisane [tizan], *s.f.* infusion (of herbs).

tisonn/er [tizɔne], *v.tr.* to poke, stir (the fire). *s.m.* -ier, poker.

tiss/er [tise], *v.tr.* to weave. *s.m.* -age. *s.* -eur, -euse. *s.* -erand, -ande, weaver.

tissu [tisy], *s.m.* (*a*) tissue; (*b*) fabric, material.

tissu-éponge [tisypɔ̃ːʒ], *s.m.* towelling. *pl.* tissus-éponges.

titre [titr], *s.m.* **1**. (official) title, form of address. **2**. (*a*) diploma, certificate; (*b*) title-deed; (*c*) bond, certificate; *pl.* securities. **3**. title, right; à t. de . . , (i) by right of . . , (ii) by way of . . , à t. d'essai, on approval. **4**. title (of book); (chapter) heading; les gros titres, big headlines.

titré [titre], *a.* **1**. titled (person). **2**. qualified (teacher).

titub/er [titybe], *v.i.* to reel; to stagger.

titulaire [titylɛːr]. **1**. *a.* titular (bishop). **2**. *s.* holder (of certificate); bearer (of passport).

toast [tost], *s.m.* **1**. toast; health. **2**. t. beurré, buttered toast.

toboggan [tɔbɔgɑ̃], *s.m.* toboggan.

toc [tɔk], *s.m. F:* sham, fake (gold, etc.); bijoux en t., imitation jewellery.

tocsin [tɔksɛ̃], *s.m.* tocsin; alarm-bell.

toi [twa], *pers.pron.* you (subject or object); ce livre est à t., this book is yours, belongs to you.

toile [twal], *s.f.* **1**. (*a*) linen; t. à chemises, shirting; t. à matelas, ticking; (*b*) cloth; t. cirée, oilcloth; (*c*) canvas. **2**. oil painting. **3**. *Nau:* sail.

toilette [twalɛt], *s.f.* **1**. dressing table. **2**. toilet; faire sa t., to wash (and dress); cabinet de t., dressing room (with wash-basin, etc.). **3**. lavatory; (*in restaurant*) cloakroom; ladies' room. **4**. (woman's) dress; aimer la t., to be fond of clothes.

toi-même [twamɛm], *pers.pron.* yourself.

toison [twazɔ̃], *s.f.* fleece.

toit [twa], *s.m.* roof. *s.f.* -ure, roofing.

tôl/e [toːl], *s.f.* sheet-metal; t. ondulée, corrugated iron. *s.f.* -erie, rolling mills. *s.m.* -ier, sheet-iron merchant.

tolérable [tɔlerabl], *a.* bearable, tolerable; permissible. *adv.* -ment.

‡**tolér/er** [tɔlere], *v.tr.* **1**. to tolerate, wink at (abuses). **2**. *Med:* to tolerate (drug). *s.f.* -ance. *a.* -ant.

tomate [tɔmat], *s.f.* tomato.

tombe [tɔ̃ːb], *s.f.* tomb, grave.

tombeau [tɔ̃bo], *s.m.* tomb; monument.

tombée [tɔ̃be], *s.f.* fall (of rain, night, etc.).

tomber [tɔ̃be], *v.i.* (*aux. usu.* être). **1**. to fall; laisser t., to drop (s.o.), (sth.). **2**. to abate, subside. **3**. t. sur, to come across, (s.o.); vous tombez bien, you've come at the right moment. **4**. to fall, hang down; cheveux qui tombent, hair falling (i) down, (ii) out. **5**. t. amoureux, to fall in love (de, with); t. malade, to fall ill, dead.

tombereau [tɔ̃bro], *s.m.* tip-cart.

tome [toːm, tɔm], *s.m.* volume; tome.

ton[1], ta, tes [tɔ̃, ta, te], *poss.a.* (ton *is used instead of* ta *before f. words beginning with a vowel or h 'mute'; for use of* ton *as opposed to* votre, *see* TU) your; ton ami(e), your friend.

ton[2], *s.m.* 1. (a) intonation; (b) manners; le bon ton, good form. 2. *Mus:* (a) pitch; (b) key. 3. tone, tint.

tondeur, -euse [tɔ̃dœr, -øːz]. 1. *s.* (a) shearer; (b) *f.* tondeuse; (a) clippers; (b) lawn mower.

tond/re [tɔ̃dr], *v.tr.* to shear; to clip; to mow.

tonifi/er [tɔnifje], *v.tr.* to tone up, to invigorate. *s.f.* -cation, toning up.

tonique [tɔnik]. 1. *a. Med:* tonic. 2. *a. Ling:* tonic (accent, note).

tonnage [tɔnaːʒ], *s.m.* tonnage, (i) of a ship; (ii) of a port.

tonne [tɔn], *s.f.* 1. tun. 2. ton.

tonneau [tɔno], *s.m.* cask, barrel.

tonner [tɔne], *v.i.* to thunder; il tonne, it's thundering.

tonnerre [tɔnɛːr], *s.m.* thunder; coup de t. thunder-clap; *F:* c'est du t! it's terrific!

tonte [tɔ̃t], *s.f.* (a) sheep-shearing; (b) clip.

top [tɔp], *s.m. Rad:* les tops, the pips.

topaze [tɔpaːz], *s.f.* topaz.

topinambour [tɔpinãbuːr], *s.m.* Jerusalem artichoke.

topograph/ie [tɔpɔgrafi], *s.f.* topography. *a.* **-ique**, topographical.

toqué [tɔke], *a. F:* crazy, cracked; être t. de qn, to be infatuated with s.o.; *F:* to be gone on s.o.

torche [tɔrʃ], *s.f.* torch.

torchon [tɔrʃɔ̃], *s.m.* dishcloth; duster.

tordant [tɔrdã], *a. F:* screamingly funny (story, joke).

tord/re [tɔrdr], *v.tr.* to twist; to wring (clothes, one's hands).
   se tordre, to writhe, twist; *F:* se t. (de rire), to split one's sides (with laughter).

toréador [tɔreadɔr], *s.m.* bullfighter.

tornade [tɔrnad], *s.f.* tornado.

torpeur [tɔrpœːr], *s.f.* torpor.

torpille [tɔrpij], *s.f.* torpedo.

torpill/er [tɔrpije], *v.tr.* to torpedo (ship). *s.m.* -age. *s.m.* -eur, destroyer.

torrent [tɔr(ã)ɑ̃], *s.m.* torrent; mountain stream. *a.* †-iel, torrential. *adv.* -iellement.

torride [tɔrrid], *a.* torrid (zone); scorching (heat).

torsion [tɔrsjɔ̃], *s.f.* torsion; *Aut:* barre de t., torsion bar.

tort [tɔːr], *s.m.* wrong. 1. error, fault; à t., wrongly. 2. injury, harm.

torticolis [tɔrtikɔli], *s.m.* crick in the neck.

tortill/er [tɔrtije], *v.tr.* to twist; twirl; twiddle (sth.). *s.m.* -ement.
   se tortiller. 1. to wriggle, twist. 2. to squirm.

tortue [tɔrty], *s.f.* tortoise; turtle.

†**tortueu/x** [tɔrtɥø], *a.* tortuous; winding (road); underhand (conduct). *adv.* -sement.

torture [tɔrtyr], *s.f.* torture.

torturer [tɔrtyre], *v.tr.* to torture.

tôt [to], *adv.* (a) soon; au plus t., at the earliest; t. ou tard, sooner or later; (b) venez t., come early.

†**total** [tɔtal]. 1. *a.* total, complete, whole. 2. *s.m.* whole, total. *adv.* -ement.

totalisateur [tɔtalizatœr], *s.m.* adding machine; *Sp:* totalizator, *F:* tote.

totalitaire [tɔtalitɛr], *a.* totalitarian.

totalité [tɔtalite], *s.f.* totality, whole.

toubib [tubib], *s.m. F:* doctor.

touchant [tuʃã]. 1. *a.* touching, moving (speech). 2. *prep.* touching, concerning, about.

touche [tuʃ], *s.f.* 1. (a) touch, touching; (b) *Sp:* ligne de t., touch-line. 2. key (of typewriter, piano). 3. *El:* contact.

toucher [tuʃe]. I. *v.tr.* to touch. 1. *v.tr.* (a) to hit (target); to cash (a cheque); t. son salaire, to get one's pay; *F:* je n'ai pas pu le t., I couldn't get hold of him; (b) to move, affect; (c) to concern, affect (s.o.). 2. (a) *v.tr.* to touch on; to allude to (a subject); (b) *v.ind.tr.* to meddle, interfere (à, with). 3. *v.i.* t. à, to be near, to border on (sth.). II. *s.m.* touch, feel (of sth.).
   se toucher, to touch, adjoin.

touff/e [tuf], *s.f.* tuft; wisp; clump (of trees). *a.* -u, bushy; thick.

toujours [tuʒuːr], *adv.* 1. always, ever; un ami de t., a lifelong friend. 2. still; cherchez t., go on looking. 3. nevertheless, all the same.

toupet [tupɛ], *s.m.* 1. (a) tuft of hair; (b) forelock. 2. *F:* cheek, impudence.

toupie [tupi], *s.f.* (toy) top; *F:* ronfler comme une t., to snore like a pig; vieille t., old frump.

tour[1] [tuːr], *s.f.* 1. tower; *Av:* t. de contrôle, control tower. 2. castle, rook (at chess).

tour[2], *s.m.* 1. lathe. 2. (a) circumference, circuit; *Sp:* lap; t. de poitrine, chest, bust, measurement; (b) turn (of phrase); shape (of face). 3. (a) round, turn; 2.000 tours à la minute, 2.000 revolutions a minute; donner un t. de clef, to lock (the door); (b) stroll; (c) trip, tour. 4. t. à t., in turn. 5. trick, feat.

tourbe [turb], *s.f.* peat, turf.

tourbillon [turbijɔ̃], *s.m.* 1. whirlwind; swirl. 2. (a) whirlpool; (b) eddy.

tourbillonn/er [turbijɔne], *v.i.* to whirl (round); to eddy, swirl. *s.m.* -ement.

tourelle [turɛl], *s.f.* turret.

tour/isme [turism], *s.m.* 1. tourist trade. 2. touring; bureau de t., travel agency; *Aut:* voiture de t., private car. *s.m.* -iste. *a.* -istique.

tourment [turmã], *s.m.* (*a*) torment, torture; (*b*) anguish, pain.

tourmenter [turmãte], *v.tr.* 1. to torment. 2. to worry; to pester, tease (s.o.). se tourmenter, to fret, worry.

tournant [turnã]. 1. *a.* turning; revolving; pont t., swing bridge. 2. *s.m.* turning, bend of road).

tourne-disques [turnədisk], *s.m.inv.* record-player.

tournedos [turnədo], *s.m. Cu:* tournedos steak.

tournée [turne], *s.f.* 1. round; tour (of official); *Com:* notre représentant est en t., our traveller is out. 2. F: payer une t., to stand a round (of drinks).

tourner [turne], *v.* to turn. 1. *v.tr.* (*a*) to revolve, turn round; t. la tête, to turn one's head; *Cin:* t. un film, to shoot a film; (*b*) to change, convert; t. qn en ridicule, to hold s.o. up to ridicule; (*c*) to turn over (page); (*d*) to get round; to evade (a difficulty, the law). 2. *v.i.* (*a*) to revolve; to go round; (*b*) tournez à gauche, turn to the left; (*c*) to turn out, result; mal t., to go to the bad; (*d*) (*of fruit, etc.*) to colour, ripen. se tourner, to turn (round); se t. vers qn, to turn towards s.o.

tournesol [turnəsɔl], *s.m.* sunflower.

tournevis [turnəvis], *s.m.* screwdriver.

tourniquet [turnike], *s.m.* 1. turnstile. 2. (*a*) catherine-wheel; (*b*) garden sprinkler. 3. *Med:* tourniquet.

tournoi [turnwa], *s.m.* (chess, bridge) tournament; (whist) drive.

‡**tourno/yer** [turnwaje], *v.i.* to whirl; to eddy. *s.m.* -iement, whirling. 2. dizziness.

tournure [turnyːr], *s.f.* 1. turn, course (of events). 2. shape, figure, appearance; t. d'esprit, turn of mind.

tourte [turt], *s.f.* (covered) tart.

tourterelle [turtərel], *s.f.* turtle-dove.

Toussaint [la [latusɛ̃]] *Pr.n.f.* All Saints' day; la veille de la T., Hallowe'en.

tousser [tuse], *v.i.* to cough.

tout, toute, *pl.* **tous, toutes** [tu, tut, tu, tut] (*when* tous *is a pron. it is pronounced* [tuːs]) all. I. *a.* 1. (*noun undetermined*) any, every, all; repas à toute heure, meals served at any time. 2. à toute vitesse, at full speed. 3. the whole; all. 4. **tous (les) deux,** both. II. *pron.* 1. all, everything; il mange de t., he eats anything; c'est t. dire, I needn't say more. 2. pl. tous à la fois, all together. III. *s.m.* le t., the whole; pas du t., not at all. IV. *adv.* (*intensive*) (*before a f. adj. beginning with a consonant or h 'aspirate',* tout *becomes* toute). 1. quite, entirely; t. fait, ready-made; t. à fait, quite; elle est toute petite, she's quite small. 2. t. en parlant, while speaking. 3. être t. oreilles, to be all ears.

tout-à-l'égout [tutalegu], *s.m.inv.* main drainage.

toutefois [tutfwa], *adv.* yet, however.

toutou [tutu], *s.m.* (*child's word*) doggie.

tout-puissant [tupɥisɑ̃], *a.* almighty, omnipotent.

toux [tu], *s.f.* cough.

toxico/mane [tɔksikɔman], *s.m. & f.* drug addict. *s.f.* -manie, drug-habit.

trac [trak], *s.m.* F: funk (stage-)fright; avoir le t., to have the wind up.

tracas [traka], *s.m.* worry, trouble, bother.

tracass/er [trakase], *v.tr.* to worry, bother. *s.f.* -erie, worry, fuss. se tracasser, to worry.

trace [tras], *s.f.* 1. trace. 2. (*a*) track, spoor; (foot-)print, (wheel-)track; (*b*) weal, scar.

‡**tracer** [trase], *v.tr.* to trace; to plot (curve); to map out (road); to draw (line); to outline (plan).

tract [trakt], *s.m.* tract; leaflet.

tracteur [traktœːr], *s.m.* tractor.

traction [traksjɔ̃], *s.f.* traction; (*a*) pulling; (*b*) draught; *Aut:* t. avant, front-wheel drive.

tradition [tradisjɔ̃], *s.f.* tradition. *a.* †-nel, traditional. *adv.* -nellement.

traduc/tion [tradyksjɔ̃], *s.f.* 1. translating. 2. translation. *s.* -teur, -trice, translator.

‡**traduire** [tradɥiːr], *v.tr.* (*a*) to translate; (*b*) to interpret, explain.

trafic [trafik], *s.m.* traffic. 1. (*a*) trade; (*b*) Pej: illicit trading. 2. t. ferroviaire, railway traffic.

trafi/quer [trafike], *v.i.* to traffic, trade; Pej: to sell (one's conscience, etc.). *s.m.* -quant, Pej: trafficker.

tragéd/ie [traʒedi], *s.f.* tragedy. *s.* -ien, -ienne, tragedian.

tragique [traʒik], *a.* tragic. *adv.* -ment.

trah/ir [traiːr], *v.tr.* to betray; to reveal; F: to give away. *s.f.* -ison, treachery, treason.

train [trɛ̃], *s.m.* 1. (*a*) train, string, line (of vehicles, etc.); set (of wheels, etc.); *Aut:* t. avant, arrière, front, rear, axle (assembly); (*b*) Rail: train. 2. (*a*) movement; pace; à fond de t., at full speed; (*b*) mettre (qch.) en t., to set (sth.) going; en t. de faire qch., (busy) doing sth. 3. être en t., to be in good form.

traînée [trɛne], *s.f.* trail (of smoke, etc.); train (of gunpowder).

train/er [trɛne]. 1. *v.tr.* to drag, pull, draw (sth.) along; to spin out (speech); to drawl. 2. *v.i.* (*a*) to lag behind; (*b*) to linger, to dawdle; (*c*) laisser t. ses affaires, to leave one's belongings lying about. *s.m.* -ard, straggler. *s.m.* -eau, sledge. se traîner, to crawl (along).

train-train [trɛ̃trɛ̃], *s.m.* round, routine; le t.-t. de la vie, the daily grind.

‡**traire** [trɛːr], *v.tr.* to milk (a cow).

trait [trɛ], *s.m.* **1.** pulling; tout d'un t., at one stretch; cheval de t., cart horse. **2.** (a) armes de t., missile weapons; (b) arrow, dart; partir comme un t., to be off like a shot; (c) beam, flash (of light); t. d'esprit, witticism. **3.** draught, gulp. **4.** (a) stroke, line; dash; (b) t. d'union, hyphen. **5.** (a) feature (of face); (b) trait (of character). **6.** act, deed (of kindness, etc.); t. de génie, stroke of genius.

traite [trɛt], *s.f.* **1.** stretch (of road); stage (of journey). **2.** (banker's) draft, bill of exchange). **3.** milking.

traité [trɛte], *s.m.* **1.** treatise. **2.** treaty.

traitement [trɛtmã], *s.m.* treatment; (a) t. brutal, rough handling; Med: premier t., first aid; (b) processing (of raw material). **2.** salary; pay.

trait/er [trɛte], *v.tr.* **1.** (a) to treat; t. qn de lâche, to call s.o. a coward; (c) to treat (patient); (d) Ind: to process. **2.** (a) to negotiate (business); (b) to discuss, deal with (subject). **3.** *v.i.* (a) to treat (de, for) (peace, etc.); (b) (of book) to deal (de, with) (a subject). *a.* **-able**, manageable, docile. *s.m.* **-eur**, caterer.

trait/re, traîtresse [trɛːtr, trɛtrɛs]. **1.** *a.* treacherous. **2.** *s.* traitor, traitress. *adv.* **-reusement** *a.* **-rise**, treachery.

trajet [traʒɛ], *s.m.* journey by rail, etc.); t. de mer, passage, crossing.

trame [tram], *s.f.* **1.** woof, weft. **2.** T.V: frame.

tram(way) [tram(wɛ)], *s.m.* tram(car).

tranchant [trɑ̃ʃɑ̃]. **1.** *a.* (a) cutting, sharp (knife); (b) trenchant (words, tone). **2.** *s.m.* (cutting) edge of tool, etc.).

tranche [trɑ̃ʃ], *s.f.* **1.** (a) slice; rasher, (b) block, portion (of lottery, prizes, etc.). **2.** slab. **3.** edge (of coin); cut edge (of book).

tranchée [trɑ̃ʃe], *s.f.* trench; cutting.

trancher [trɑ̃ʃe], *v.tr.* (a) to slice; to cut; (b) to cut short (discussion); to settle (question) out of hand; (c) to decide.

tranquille [trɑ̃kil], *a.* tranquil; (a) calm, still; (b) quiet; (c) undisturbed. *adv.* **-ment**.

tranquill/iser [trɑ̃kilize], *v.tr.* to tranquillize; to soothe. *s.m.* **-ité**, quiet; peace. *s.m.* **-isant**, Med: tranquillizer. se tranquilliser, to calm down.

transaction [trɑ̃zaksjɔ̃], *s.f.* transaction; *pl.* dealings; proceedings (of a society, etc.).

transat [trɑ̃zat], *s.m. F:* deck chair.

transatlantique [trɑ̃zatlɑ̃tik]. **1.** *a.* transatlantic. **2.** *s.m.* (Atlantic) liner.

transbord/er [trɑ̃zbɔrde], *v.tr.* to tranship (cargo, passengers). *s.m.* **-eur**, aerial ferry.

‡**transcr/ire** [trɑ̃skriːr], *v.tr.* to transcribe. *s.m.* **-ipteur**, transcriber. *s.f.* **-iption**, (i) transcription; (ii) copy.

‡**transfér/er** [trɑ̃sfere], *v.tr.* to transfer. *a.* **-able**.

transfigurer [trɑ̃sfigyre], *v.tr.* to transfigure.

transform/er [trɑ̃sfɔrme], *v.tr.* to change (en, into); to make over (a dress); Fb: to convert (a try). *a.* **-able**. *s.f.* **-ation**. *s.m.* **-ateur**, transformer. se transformer, to change, turn (en, into).

transgress/er [trɑ̃sgrese], *v.tr.* to transgress, infringe (the law). *s.m.* **-eur**. *s.f.* **-ion**.

transi [trɑ̃si], *a.* perished with cold.

‡**transiger** [trɑ̃ziʒe], *v.i.* to compromise; ne pas t., to be adamant.

transistor [trɑ̃zistɔr], *s.m. Rad:* transistor (set).

transit [trɑ̃zit], *s.m.* **1.** maison de t., forwarding agency. **2.** Rail: through traffic. *a.* **-aire**.

transiter [trɑ̃zite]. **1.** *v.tr.* to forward (goods). **2.** *v.i.* (of goods) to be in transit.

†**transitif** [trɑ̃zitif], *a.* transitive.

trans/ition [trɑ̃zisjɔ̃], *s.f.* transition; sans t., abruptly. *a.* **-itoire**, transitory, temporary. *adv.* **-itoirement**.

‡**transmett/re** [trɑ̃smɛtr], *v.tr.* to transmit; to pass on, convey. *s.m.* **-eur**, transmitter.

transmiss/ion [trɑ̃smisjɔ̃], *s.f.* (a) **1.** transmission; passing on (of order); Rad: t. en direct, live broadcast; t. en différé, recorded broadcast; (b) E: la t., transmission gear; arbre de t., driving shaft. **2.** Adm: t. des pouvoirs, handing over. *a.* **-ible**, transferable.

‡**transpar/aître** [trɑ̃sparɛtr], *v.i.* to show through. *s.f.* **-ence**, transparency. *a.* **-ent**, transparent.

‡**transperc/er** [trɑ̃sperse], *v.tr.* to transfix; to stab (s.o., sth.) through.

transpir/er [trɑ̃spire], *v.i.* **1.** (aux. avoir) to perspire. **2.** (aux. avoir or être) to transpire; (of news) to leak out. *s.f.* **-ation**, perspiration, sweat.

transplanter [trɑ̃splɑ̃te], *v.tr.* to transplant.

transport [trɑ̃spɔr], *s.m.* **1.** transport; frais de t., freight charges. **2.** rapture.

transporter [trɑ̃spɔrte], *v.tr.* to transport.

transpos/er [trɑ̃spoze], *v.tr.* to transpose. *s.f.* **-ition**.

†**transversal** [trɑ̃sversal], *a.* transverse, transversal.

trapp/e [trap], *s.f.* **1.** trap. **2.** trap-door. *s.m.* **-eur**, trapper.

trapu [trapy], *a.* thick-set, squat, stocky (man, horse).

traqu/er [trake], *v.tr.* to hunt down. *s.m.* **-eur**, tracker.

†travail [trava:j], s.m. work. 1. (a) labour; t. de tête, brainwork; t. manuel, manual labour; t. en série, mass production; (b) working, operation; (c) employment. 2. (a) piece of work; (b) Adm: travaux publics, public works.

travaill/er [travaje], 1. v.tr to work; shape. 2. v.i. to work, labour. a. & s. -eur, -euse, (i) a. industrious; (ii) s. worker. a. & s.m. Pol: -iste, Labour (party, member).

travelling [travəliŋ], s.m. Cin: (camera) dolly.

travers [traver], s.m. 1. (breadth) en t. de, across; à t qch., au t. de qch., through sth. 2. de t., askew, crooked.

traverse [travers], s.f. 1. (chemin de) t. cross-road, short cut. 2. Rail: sleeper; cross-bar, cross-piece.

traversée [traverse], s.f. 1. passage, crossing (by sea). 2. Rail: voie de voie, cross-over.

traverser [traverse], v.tr. 1. to cross; to go through. 2. to traverse, thwart.

traversin [travεrsɛ̃], s.m. bolster.

travest/ir [travesti:r], v.tr. 1. to disguise; bal travesti, fancy-dress ball. 2. to parody. s.m. -issement, disguise; travesty (of truth, etc.).

trébucher [trebyʃe], v.i. to stumble.

trèfle [trefl], s.m. 1. trefoil, clover. 2. (at cards) clubs.

treillis [treji], s.m. 1. trellis(-work); lattice; t. métallique, wire netting. 2. (coarse) canvas; sacking; Cl: jeu de t., dungarees, denims.

treize [trε:z], num.a.inv. & s.m.inv. thirteen.

treizième [trεzjεm], num.a. & s. thirteenth. adv. -ment.

tréma [trema], s.m. diaeresis.

tremble [trɑ̃:bl], s.m. Bot: aspen.

tremblement [trɑ̃bləmɑ̃], s.m. 1. trembling. 2. tremor; t. de terre, earthquake.

trembler [trɑ̃:ble], v.i. to tremble, shake; to quake; (of light) to flicker; (of voice) to quaver.

trempe [trɑ̃:p], s.f. 1. Ind: tempering, hardening (of steel). 2. (a) temper (of steel); (b) quality; les hommes de sa t., men of his stamp.

tremper [trɑ̃pe], 1. v.tr. (a) to soak; to drench; trempé comme une soupe, soaked to the skin; (b) to temper, harden (steel). 2. v.i. to soak, to steep.

tremplin [trɑ̃plɛ̃], s.m. spring-board, diving-board.

trentaine [trɑ̃tεn], s.f. (about) thirty.

trente [trɑ̃:t], num.a.inv. & s.m.inv. thirty.

trentième [trɑ̃tjεm], num.a. & s. thirtieth.

trépidation [trepidasjɔ̃], s.f. tremor; vibration; agitation.

trépider [trepide], v.i. to vibrate.

trépied [trepje], s.m. (a) tripod; (b) trivet.

trépigner [trepiɲe], v.i. t. de colère, to dance with rage.

très [trε], adv. very, most; (very) much.

trésor [trezɔ:r], s.m. 1. treasure; F: mon t., darling. 2. pl. riches; le T. (public), the (French) treasury. s.f. -erie, treasury; treasurership. s. -ier, -ière, treasurer; paymaster, -mistress.

‡tressaill/ir [tresaji:r], v.i. to start; to give a start; to wince (with pain); to shudder (from fear); faire t. qn., to startle s.o. s.m. -ement.

tresse [tres], s.f. plait (of hair).

tresser [trese], v.tr. to plait (hair, straw).

tréteau [treto], s.m. trestle, support.

treuil [trœj], s.m. winch, windlass.

trève [trε:v], s.f. (a) truce; (b) respite.

tri [tri], s.m. sorting (out); classifying. s.m. -age, sorting.

triang/le [triɑ̃:gl], s.m. triangle. a. -ulaire.

tribord [tribɔ:r], s.m. Nau: starboard.

tribu [triby], s.f. tribe.

tribulation [tribylasjɔ̃], s.f. trouble.

†tribunal [tribynal], s.m. tribunal; Jur: the bench; (law-)court.

tribune [tribyn], s.f. 1. (speaker's) platform. 2. (a) gallery; (b) Sp: grandstand.

tributaire [tribytε:r], a. & s.m. Geog: tributary (river).

trich/er [triʃe], v.i. & tr. to cheat. s.f. -erie. s. -eur, -euse, cheat.

tricolore [trikɔlɔ:r], a. tricolour(ed).

tricot [triko], s.m. 1. knitting; knitted wear; jersey-fabric. 2. (a) jumper; F: woolly; (b) (under) vest.

tricot/er [trikɔte], v.tr. to knit. s. -eur, -euse, knitter.

tri/er [trie], v.tr. (a) to sort; (b) to pick out (the best). s. -eur, -euse, sorter.

trigonométrie [trigɔnɔmetri], s.f. trigonometry.

trimestr/e [trimεstr], s.m. 1. quarter; three months; Sch: term. 2. quarter's pay, rent; term's fees. a. †-riel, quarterly.

tringle [trε̃:gl], s.f. rod.

trinité [trinite], s.f. trinity.

trinquer [trε̃ke], v.i. to clink glasses (before drinking); t. avec qn, to have a drink with s.o.

†triomphal [triɔ̃fal], a. triumphal. adv. -ement.

triomphe [triɔ̃:f], s.m. triumph; arc de t., triumphal arch.

triomph/er [triɔ̃fe], v.i. 1. to triumph; t. d'une difficulté, to overcome a difficulty. 2. to exult; to gloat (de, over). a. & s. -ateur, -atrice, (i) triumphing; (ii) triumpher.

tripes [trip], s.f.pl. Cu: tripe.

triple [tripl], a. & s.m. treble, triple. adv. -ement.

tripot/er [tripɔte], F: **1.** *v.i.* (a) to mess around; (b) to engage in shady business; **t. dans la caisse,** to tamper with the cash. **2.** (a) to finger, to meddle with, sth.; to paw (s.o.); (b) to deal dishonestly with (money, etc.). *s.m.* **-age.** *s.* **-eur, -euse.**

triste [trist], *a. sad.* **1.** (a) sorrowful, melancholy; (b) dreary. **2.** unfortunate, painful (news, duty). *adv.* **-ment.**

tristesse [tristes], *s.f.* (a) sadness; melancholy; (b) dullness, dreariness.

†**trivial** [trivjal], *a.* vulgar, low, coarse. *adv.* **-ment.** *s.f.* **-ité,** vulgarity, coarseness.

troc [trɔk], *s.m.* exchange; barter.

troène [trɔɛn], *s.m.* privet.

trognon [trɔɲɔ̃], *s.m.* core (of apple), stump (of cabbage).

trois [trwa], *num.a.inv. & s.m.* three. *num. a. & s.* **-ième,** third.

trombe [trɔ̃b], *s.f.* **1.** waterspout. **2.** whirlwind; **entrer, sortir, en t.,** to burst in, out.

trombone [trɔ̃bɔn], *s.m.* trombone; F: wire paper-clip.

trompe [trɔ̃p], *s.f.* **1.** trump, horn. **2.** proboscis; (elephant's) trunk.

tromp/er [trɔ̃pe], *v.tr.* to deceive. **1.** (a) to cheat; (b) to betray, be unfaithful to (wife, husband). **2.** (a) to mislead, disappoint s.o.; (b) to outwit s.o.; (c) to while away (the time). *s.f.* **-erie,** fraud; illusion. *a. & s.* **-eur, -euse,** (i) deceitful, deceptive; (ii) deceiver. *adv.* **-eusement.**

se tromper, to be mistaken; to be wrong.

trompette [trɔ̃pɛt], **1.** *s.f.* trumpet. **2.** *s.m.* trumpeter.

tronc [trɔ̃], *s.m.* **1.** trunk (of tree). **2.** collecting-box (in church). **3.** *Mth:* frustrum (of cone).

tronçon [trɔ̃sɔ̃], *s.m.* (broken) piece, stump.

tronçonn/er [trɔ̃sɔne], *v.tr.* to cut (wood, etc.) into lengths; to cut up. *s.m.* **-ement.** *s.f.* **-euse,** motor (chain) saw.

trône [troːn], *s.m.* throne.

tronquer [trɔ̃ke], *v.tr.* to curtail, cut down.

trop [tro]. **1.** *adv.* too; (a) **t. fatigué,** overtired; (b) too much; **t. travailler,** to overwork; **t. répéter** (qch.), to say (sth.) too often; **je ne sais t. que dire,** I hardly know what to say. **2.** too much, too many; **être de t.,** to be in the way.

trophée [trɔfe], *s.m.* trophy.

tropi/que [trɔpik], *s.m. Geog:* tropic (of Cancer, Capricorn); *pl.* the Tropics. *a.* †**-cal.**

troposphère [trɔposfɛr], *s.f. Meteo:* troposphere.

trop-plein [troplɛ̃], *s.m.* overflow (of bath, dam).

troquer [trɔke], *v.tr.* to exchange, barter; F: swop (sth.).

trot [tro], *s.m.* trot.

trotte [trɔt], *s.f.* F: distance, run; c'est une bonne t., it's a fair step.

trott/er [trɔte], *v.i.* to trot; to scamper; F: être toujours à t., to be always on the go. *s.f.* **-inette,** (child's) scooter. *s.m.* **-oir,** pavement, kerb; *U.S:* sidewalk.

trou [tru], *s.m.* hole.

trouble [trubl]. **1.** *a.* **1.** turbid, cloudy; dim; murky. **2.** confused. **II.** *s.m.* (a) confusion, disorder; (b) agitation, perturbation; *pl.* public disturbance.

troubl/er [truble], *v.tr.* **1.** to make (liquid, etc.) thick, muddy. **2.** to disturb (silence, the peace). **3.** to perturb; (a) to confuse; (b) to agitate, excite.

se troubler. 1. (of sky) to cloud over. **2.** to falter; to get confused.

trouée [true], *s.f.* gap, opening, breach.

trouer [true], *v.tr.* to make a hole in (wall, etc.).

trouill/e [truːj], *s.f. P:* avoir la t., to be in a funk; flanquer la t. à qn, to put the wind up s.o. *s.m. P:* **-ard,** funk.

troupe [trup], *s.f.* **1.** (a) troop, band; gang; (b) *Th:* troupe; (c) herd, flock (of cows, geese). **2.** *pl.* troops, forces.

troupeau [trupo], *s.m.* herd, drove; flock; *P.N:* (passage de) troupeaux, cattle crossing.

trousse [trus], *s.f.* **1.** bundle, package. **2.** case, kit (of instruments).

trousseau [truso], *s.m.* **1.** bunch (esp. of keys). **2.** (a) outfit (esp. school outfit); (b) trousseau.

trouvaille [truvaːj], *s.f.* (lucky) find, windfall.

trouver [truve], *v.tr.* **1.** (a) to find; je lui trouve mauvaise mine, I think he's looking ill; (b) to discover, invent (process). **2.** to discover, hit upon, come across (by accident). **3.** to think; vous trouvez? you think so?

se trouver. 1. (a) to be; je me trouvais alors à Paris, I was in Paris then; (b) to feel; je me trouve mieux, I feel better. **2.** to happen; to turn out; cela se trouve bien, this comes at the right moment; *impers.* il se trouve que . . ., it happens that . . .

truc [tryk], *s.m.* **1.** (a) a knack; trouver le t., to find, learn, the knack; (b) trick, dodge. **2.** contraption, gadget.

truelle [tryɛl], *s.f.* **1.** trowel. **2.** t. à poisson, fish-slice.

truffe [tryf], *s.f.* (a) truffle; (b) bulbous nose; (c) dog's nose.

truite [tryit], *s.f. Z:* sow.

truite [tryit], *s.f.* trout.

truqu/er [tryke], *v.tr.* to fake, F: to cook (accounts). *s.* **-eur, -euse.**

tu [ty], *pers.pron.* (*form of address to relations, close friends, children, animals*) you; être à tu et à toi avec qn, to be on familiar terms with s.o.

tub/e [tyb], *s.m.* tube, pipe. *a.* -ulaire, tubular.

tubercule [tyberkyl], *s.m. Bot:* tuber.

tubercu/lose [tyberkylo:z], *s.f.* tuberculosis. *a.* †-eux, tubercular.

tu/er [tɥe], *v.tr.* to kill; se faire t., to get killed; tué à l'ennemi, killed in action. *a.* -ant, killing (work); boring, exasperating. *s.f.* -erie, slaughter. *s.m.* -eur, killer.
　se tuer. (*a*) to commit suicide; (*b*) to get killed.

tue-tête [tytɛt], *adv.phr.* at the top of one's voice.

tuile [tɥil], *s.f.* 1. (roofing) tile. 2. *F:* (piece of) bad luck; quelle t.! what a blow!

tulipe [tylip], *s.f. Bot:* tulip.

tumeur [tymœ:r], *s.f.* tumour.

tumulte [tymylt], *s.m.* tumult, uproar.

†tumultueu/x [tymyltɥø], *a.* tumultuous, noisy. *adv.* -sement.

tunique [tynik], *s.f.* tunic.

tunnel [tynɛl], *s.m.* tunnel.

turbine [tyrbin], *s.f.* turbine.

turboréacteur [tyrboreaktœ:r], *s.m. Av:* turbo-jet.

turbot [tyrbo], *s.m.* turbot.

turbotrain [tyrbotrɛ̃], *s.m.* turbotrain.

turbul/ence [tyrbylã:s], *s.f.* unruliness, boisterousness. *a.* -ent.

turc, f. turque [tyrk]. 1. *a.* Turkish. 2. *s.* (*a*) Turk; (*b*) *m. Ling:* Turkish.

turf [tyrf], *s.m.* 1. race-course. 2. le t., racing; the turf. *s.m.* -iste, race-goer.

turquoise [tyrkwa:z]. 1. *s.f.* turquoise. 2. *a.inv. & s.m.inv.* turquoise (blue).

tutelle [tytɛl], *s.f.* 1. guardianship. 2. *Pol:* trusteeship.

tuteur, -trice [tytœ:r, -tris], *s.* guardian.

‡tutoyer [tytwaje], *v.tr.* to address (s.o.) as tu and toi; to be on familiar terms with s.o. *s.m.* -oiement

tuyau [tɥijo], *s.m.* 1. *a* pipe; tube; t. flexible, rubber-tubing; t. d'incendie, fire-hose; t. d'orgue, organ-pipe; *Aut:* t. d'échappement, exhaust pipe; (*b*) stem (of pipe). 2. *F:* tip (at horse-racing).

tympan [tɛ̃pã], *s.m.* (*a*) drum (of ear); bruit à briser le t., ear-splitting noise; (*b*) *A: & A:* tympanum.

type [tip], *s.m.* type; *Com:* sample, pattern; model. 2. *F:* (*a*) character; drôle de t., queer customer; (*b*) chap; chic t., good sort.

typhoïde [tifɔid], *a. & s.f.* typhoid.

typhon [tifɔ̃], *s.m.* typhoon.

typique [tipik], *a.* typical. *adv.* -ment.

typographe [tipograf], *s.m.* printer.

typographie [tipografi], *s.f.* 1. typography. 2. printing-works.

tyran [tirã], *s.m.* tyrant.

tyran/niser [tiranize], *v.tr.* to tyrannize over (s.o.). *s.f.* -nie, tyranny. *a.* -nique, tyrannical. *adv.* -niquement.

U

U, u [y], *s.m.* (the letter) U, u.

ulcère [ylsɛ:r], *s.m.* ulcer.

ultérieur [ylterjœ:r], *a.* 1. ulterior. 2. subsequent; later.

ultimatum [yltimatɔm], *s.m.* ultimatum.

ultime [yltim], *a.* ultimate, final, last.

ultrasonique [yltrasɔnik], *a.* ultrasonic.

ultrasonore [yltrasɔnɔːr], *a.* supersonic.

†ultra-violet [yltravjɔlɛ], *a.* ultra-violet (rays).

un, une [œ̃, yn]. 1. *num. a. & s.* one; un à un, one by one; une heure, one o'clock; *F:* il était moins une, that was a close shave. 2. *indef.pron.* one; les uns disent, some say. 3. *indef.art.* (*pl.* des) a, an; pour une raison ou pour une autre, for some reason or other.

unanim/e [ynanim], *a.* unanimous. *adv.* -ement. *s.f.* -ité.

Unesco [ynɛsko], *s.f.* Unesco.

uni [yni], *a.* 1. united. 2. smooth, level, even. 3. plain (colour).

uniform/e [yniform], *a. & s.m.* uniform. *adv.* -ément.

uniformité [yniformite], *s.f.* uniformity.

†unilatéral [ynilateral], *a.* unilateral; one-sided; *P.N:* stationnement u., parking on one side only.

union [ynjɔ̃], *s.f.* 1. union. 2. unity.

unique [ynik], *a.* unique. *adv.* -ment.

unir [yni:r], *v.tr.* to unite, join. 2 to smooth, level.
　s'unir, to unite, join.

unisson [ynisɔ̃], *s.m.* unison.

unité [ynite], *s.f.* 1. unit. 2. unity.

univers [ynivɛr], *s.m.* universe.

universel [yniversɛl], *a.* universal; *Jur:* légataire u., (i) sole, (ii) residuary, legatee.

universitaire [yniversitɛ:r]. 1. *a.* university (study, etc.). 2. *s.m.* graduate teacher or professor.

université [yniversite], *s.f.* university.

uranium [yranjɔm], *s.m.* uranium.

urbain [yrbɛ̃], *a.* urban; town.

urbanisme [yrbanism], *s.m.* town planning.

urbanité [yrbanite], *s.f.* urbanity.

urgence [yrʒã:s], *s.f.* urgency.

urgent [yrʒã], *a.* urgent, pressing.

urine [yrin], *s.f.* urine.

urinoir [yrinwaːr], *s.m.* (public) urinal.

urne [yrn], *s.f.* urn; ballot-box.

usage [yzaːʒ], *s.m.* 1. (*a*) use, employment; (*b*) wear, service. 2. (*a*) usage; custom; (*b*) experience, practice.

usager, -ère [yzaʒe, -ɛːr], *s.* user (of sth.); les usagers de la route, road users.

usé [yze], *a.* worn (out).

user [yze]. 1. *v.ind.tr.* u. de, to make use of. 2. *v.tr.* (*a*) to use (up); (*b*) to wear (out).
s'user, to wear (away); to wear oneself out.

usine [yzin], *s.f.* works, factory.

usité [yzite], *a.* used; in use; current.

ustensile [ystãsil], *s.m.* utensil, implement.

†usuel [yzɥɛl], *a.* usual, habitual; le français u., everyday French.

usure[1] [yzyːr], *s.f.* usury.

usure[2], *s.f.* wear (and tear).

usurier [yzyrje], *s.* usurer.

usurpateur, -trice [yzyrpatœːr, -tris]. 1. *s.* usurper. 2. *a.* usurping.

usurper [yzyrpe], *v.tr.* to usurp. *s.f.* -ation.

utile [ytil], *a.* useful, serviceable.

utiliser [ytilize], *v.tr.* to utilize, to use.

utilité [ytilite], *s.f.* utility; use(fulness).

utopie [ytɔpi], *s.f.* utopia.

V

V, v [ve], *s.m.* (the letter) V, v.

vacance [vakãːs], *s.f.* 1. vacancy. 2. *pl.* vacation, holidays.

vacant [vakã], *a.* vacant; unoccupied.

vacarme [vakarm], *s.m.* uproar, din.

vaccin [vaksɛ̃], *s.m.* vaccine.

vaccin/er [vaksine], *v.tr.* to vaccinate. *s.f.* -ation.

vache [vaʃ], *s.f.* cow.

vacill/er [vasije, -ile], *v.i.* 1. (*a*) to be unsteady; (*b*) to flicker. 2. to waver. *a.* -ant. *s.f.* -ation.

va-et-vient [vaevjɛ̃], *s.m.inv.* coming and going.

vagabond, -onde [vagabɔ̃, -ɔ̃ːd]. 1. *a.* vagabond; roving. 2. *s.* tramp. *s.m.* -age.

vague[1] [vag], *s.f.* wave; v. de fond, tidal wave.

vague[2]. 1. *a.* vague, indefinite; dim. 2. *s.m.* vagueness. *adv.* -ment.

vague[3]. 1. *a.* regard v., vacant stare; terrains vagues, waste land. 2. *s.m.* empty space.

vaillance [vajãːs], *s.f.* valour, bravery.

vaill/ant [vajã], *a.* valiant, brave. *adv.* -amment.

vain [vɛ̃], *a.* 1. vain, ineffectual. 2. vain, conceited. *adv.* -ement.

‡vaincre [vɛ̃ːkr], *v.tr.* to vanquish, defeat. 2. to overcome, conquer.

vainqueur [vɛ̃kœːr]. 1. *s.m.* victor, conqueror. 2. *a.m.* conquering.

vaisselle [vɛsɛl], *s.f.* crockery; plates and dishes; laver la v., to wash up; eau de v., dish-water.

†val [val], *s.m.* le V. de Loire, the Loire valley.

valable [valabl], *a.* valid; available.

valet [valɛ], *s.m.* 1. (*at cards*) knave, jack. 2. v. de chambre, valet, manservant.

valeur [valœːr], *s.f.* 1. value, worth. 2. *Fin:* (*a*) asset; (*b*) *pl.* shares, securities. 3. valour.

valide [valid], *a.* 1. valid. 2. able-bodied.

validité [validite], *s.f.* validity.

valise [valiz], *s.f.* suitcase; la v. (diplomatique), the (diplomatic) bag.

vallée [vale], *s.f.* valley.

vallon [valɔ̃], *s.m.* small valley; glen.

‡valoir [valwaːr], *v.tr. & i.* (*a*) to be worth; cela ne vaut rien, that's no good; cela m. à v., sum on account; advance (on royalties); (*b*) to be equivalent to; (*c*) *impers:* il vaudrait mieux partir, it would be better to leave; (*d*) faire v. qch., to make the most of sth.

valse [vals], *s.f.* waltz.

valser [valse], *v.i.* to waltz.

valve [valv], *s.f.* valve.

vandalisme [vãdalism], *s.m.* vandalism.

vanille [vanij], *s.f.* vanilla.

vanité [vanite], *s.f.* vanity, conceit.

†vaniteux [vanitø], *a.* vain, conceited.

vanne [van], *s.f.* sluice(-gate), water-gate.

vanneau [vano], *s.m.* lapwing, peewit.

vanner [vane], *v.tr.* to winnow; *F:* je suis vanné, I'm exhausted.

vant/er [vãte], *v.tr.* to praise (s.o., sth.). *a. & s.* -ard, -arde, boastful, boaster. *s.f.* -ardise, boastfulness.
se vanter, to boast; se v. d'être . . ., to pride oneself on being. . . .

va-nu-pieds [vanypje], *s.m. &f.inv.* (barefoot) tramp, beggar.

vapeur [vapœːr]. 1. *s.f.* vapour; haze; steam. 2. *s.m.* steamer, steamship.

vaporisateur [vaporizatœːr], *s.m.* (*a*) atomizer; sprayer; (*b*) scent spray.

vaporiser [vaporize], *v.tr.* to spray (liquid).

varech [varɛk], *s.m.* seaweed.

vareuse [varøːz], *s.f.* (*a*) (sailor's) jersey; (*b*) pilot-coat.

variable [varjabl], *a.* (*a*) variable; (*b*) changeable.

variation [varjasjɔ̃], *s.f.* variation.

varicelle [varisɛl], *s.f.* chickenpox.

varier [varje], *v.tr. & i.* to vary.

variété [varjete], *s.f.* variety; diversity.

vase¹ [vɑːz], s.m. vase, vessel, receptacle.
vase², s.f. mud, silt, slime, ooze.
vaseline [vazlin], s.f. vaseline (R.t.m.).
†vaseux [vazø], a. muddy, slimy.
vasistas [vazistas], s.m. fanlight.
vaste [vast], a. vast, immense, spacious.
vaurien [vorjɛ̃], s. waster, rotter, bad lot.
vautour [votur], s.m. vulture.
vautrer (se) [sǝvotre], v.pr. to wallow.
veau [vo], s.m. 1. calf. 2. veal. 3. calf
   (skin).
vedette [vǝdɛt], s.f. 1. motor-launch. 2.
   (a) mots en v., words displayed in bold
   type; mettre en v., to highlight; (b) Th:
   Cin: star.
†végétal [veʒetal], 1. a. plant; vegetable.
   2. s.m. plant.
végétar/ien, -ienne [veʒetarjɛ̃, -jɛn], a. &
   s. vegetarian. s.m. -isme.
végétation [veʒetasjɔ̃], s.f. 1. vegetation. 2. pl. Med: adenoids.
végéter [veʒete], v.i. to vegetate.
véhém/ent [veemɑ̃], a. vehement, violent.
   s.f. -ence.
véhicule [veikyl], s.m. vehicle.
veille [vɛːj], s.f. 1. (a) sitting up (at
   night); (b) vigil; (c) look-out; (d)
   wakefulness. 2. eve; preceding day.
veillée [veje], s.f. 1. watching, vigil. 2.
   evening (spent in company).
veiller [veje]. 1. v.i. (a) to sit up, keep
   awake; (b) to watch; (c) v. sur, to look
   after; (d) v. à, to see to. 2. v.tr. to
   watch over.
veilleur, -euse [vejœːr, -øːz], s. 1.
   watcher. 2. s.f. (a) nightlight; (b)
   pilot light.
veine [vɛn], s.f. 1. Anat: vein. 2. (a)
   Geog: vein; lode; (b) humour, mood;
   (c) luck.
vélin [velɛ̃], s.m. vellum.
vélo [velo], s.m. bicycle.
vélocité [velɔsite], s.f. speed, velocity.
velours [v(ǝ)luːr], s.m. velvet.
velouté [v(ǝ)lute]. 1. a. velvety; downy.
   2. s.m. softness; bloom (of fruit).
velu [vǝly], a. hairy.
venaison [vǝnɛzɔ̃], s.f. venison.
†vénal [venal], a. venal.
vendable [vɑ̃dabl], a. saleable, marketable.
vendange [vɑ̃dãːʒ], s.f. grape harvest.
‡vendang/er [vɑ̃dãʒe], v.tr. & i. to gather
   (grapes). s.m. -eur, -euse, (grape)
   harvester.
vendetta [vɑ̃detta], s.f. vendetta.
vendeur, -euse [vɑ̃dœːr, -øːz], s. seller;
   salesman, saleswoman; vendor.
vendre [vɑ̃dr], v.tr. 1. to sell; à v., for
   sale. 2. to betray.
vendredi [vɑ̃drǝdi], s.m. Friday; le v.
   saint, Good Friday.
†vénéneux [venenø], a. poisonous
   (plant).
‡vénér/er [venere], v.tr. to venerate,
   reverence, revere. s.f. -ation. a. able.
†vénérien [venerjɛ̃], a. Med: venereal.

vengeance [vɑ̃ʒãːs], s.f. 1. revenge. 2.
   vengeance, retribution.
‡venger [vɑ̃ʒe], v.tr. to avenge.
   se venger, to have one's revenge.
vengeur, -eresse [vɑ̃ʒœːr, -ǝrɛs], 1. s.
   avenger. 2. a. avenging, vengeful.
†véniel [venjel], a. venial (sin).
†venimeux [vǝnimø], a. venomous;
   poisonous.
venin, [vǝnɛ̃], s.m. venom.
‡venir [v(ǝ)niːr], v.i. to come. 1. (a)
   faire v., to send for, fetch; (b) v. de
   faire qch., to have just done sth; il
   vient de sortir, he has just gone out. 2.
   d'où vient(-il) que? how is it that? 3.
   (a) to occur; l'idée me vient que...;
   *it comes to my mind that...; (b)
   v. à faire qch., to happen to do sth.
   4. (a) to attain, reach; (b) v. à bien, to
   succeed; (c) en v. aux mains, to come
   to blows.
vénitien, -ienne [venisjɛ̃, -jɛn], a. & s.
   Venetian.
vent [vɑ̃], s.m. 1. (a) wind; coup de v.,
   gust of wind; squall; côté du v.,
   weather side; (b) aire de v., point of
   the compass; (c) Med: flatulence,
   wind. 2. avoir v. de qch., to get
   wind of sth.
vente [vɑ̃t], s.f. sale; salle des ventes,
   auction room.
ventilateur [vɑ̃tilatœːr], s.m. ventilator.
ventil/er [vɑ̃tile], v.tr. to ventilate, air.
   s.f. -ation.
ventre [vɑ̃ːtr], s.m. (a) abdomen, belly;
   Av: atterrissage sur le v., belly landing; (b) stomach; n'avoir rien dans le
   v., to be starving; (c) prendre du v.,
   to put on weight.
ventriloque [vɑ̃trilɔk], s.m. & f. ventriloquist.
ventru [vɑ̃try], a. fat, F: pot-bellied.
venue [vǝny], s.f. coming, arrival.
vêpres [vɛːpr], s.f.pl. Ecc: vespers.
ver [vɛːr], s.m. 1. worm. 2. (a) grub,
   maggot; (b) v. luisant, glowworm;
   (c) v. à soie, silkworm.
véracité [verasite], s.f. veracity, truthfulness; truth (of a statement).
véranda [verɑ̃da], s.f. veranda.
†verbal [verbal], a. verbal. adv. -ement.
verbe [verb], s.m. verb.
†verb/eux [verbø], a. verbose, long-
   winded. s.f. -osité, verbosity.
verdâtre [verdɑːtr], a. greenish.
verdeur [verdœːr], s.f. greenness.
verdict [verdikt], s.m. verdict.
verdir [verdiːr], v.i. to become, turn,
   green.
verdoyant [verdwajɑ̃], a. verdant, green.
verdure [verdyːr], s.f. (a) greenness; (b)
   verdure.
†véreux [verø], a. 1. maggoty (fruit).
   2. F: dubious, dishonest, F: fishy.
verge [verʒ], s.f. (a) rod, cane; (b)
   shank (of anchor); (c) Bot: v. d'or,
   golden rod; (d) Anat: penis.

verger [verʒe], s.m. orchard.
verglas [vergla], s.m. glazed frost; silver thaw.
vergogne [vergɔŋ], s.f. sans v., shameless.
vergue [verg], s.f. Nau: yard.
véridique [veridik], a. true, authentic. adv. -ment.
vérifi/er [verifje], v.tr. 1. to verify; to check; to audit. 2. to verify, confirm. s.f. -cation.
véritable [veritabl], a. 1. true. 2. genuine.
vérité [verite], s.f. 1. truth; en v., really, actually. 2. fact, truth.
†vermeil [verme:j]. 1. a. vermilion, bright red. 2. s.m. silver-gilt.
vermicelle [vermisɛl], s.m. vermicelli.
vermillon [vermijɔ̃], s.m. vermilion.
vermine [vermin], s.f. vermin.
vermoulu [vermuly], a. worm-eaten.
vermouth(h) [vermut], s.m. vermouth.
verni [verni], a. varnished; cuir v., patent leather.
vernir [verni:r], v.tr. to varnish; to polish.
vernis [verni], s.m. varnish, polish; v. (à ongles), nail varnish.
vérole [verɔl], s.f. petite v., smallpox.
verre [veːr], s.m. 1. glass; papier de v., sandpaper. 2. porter des verres, to wear glasses; verres de contact, contact lenses. 3. (a) v. à vin, wine glass; (b) glassful; v. de vin, glass of wine.
verrerie [ver(ə)ri], s.f. glassware.
verrou [veru], s.m. bolt, bar.
verrouiller [veruje], v.tr. to bolt (door).
verrue [very], s.f. verruca; wart.
vers¹ [veːr], s.m. verse, line (of poetry); faire des vers, to write poetry.
vers², prep. 1. (of place) toward(s), to. 2. (of time) toward(s); about.
versant [versɑ̃], s.m. slope, side (of mountain).
versatile [versatil], a. changeable, inconstant.
versatilité [versatilite], s.f. inconstancy.
verse [vers], s.f. à v., in torrents.
versé [verse], a. versed, experienced (dans, in).
verser [verse], v.tr. (a) to overturn; (b) to pour (out); (c) to shed (tears); (d) to pay (in) money.
version [versjɔ̃], s.f. version; account; Sch: unseen, translation.
verso [verso], s.m. voir au v., see overleaf.
vert [veːr]. 1. a. (a) green; (b) unripe (fruit); (c) sharp; severe (reprimand). 2. s.m. green.
vert-de-gris [verdəgri], s.m. verdigris.
†vertébral [vertebral], a. vertebral.
†vertical [vertikal], a. vertical; upright. adv. -ement.
vertige [vertiʒ], s.m. dizziness, giddiness.
†vertigineux [vertiʒinø], a. vertiginous (height); breath-taking (speed).

vertu [verty], s.f. 1. virtue. 2. quality, property; en v. de, by virtue of.
†vertueux [vertyø], a. virtuous.
verve [verv], s.f. animation, verve.
vessie [vesi], s.f. bladder.
veste [vest], s.f. (short) jacket.
vestiaire [vestjɛːr], s.m. (a) cloakroom; F: mon v., s'il vous plaît, my things, coat, please; (b) hat and coat rack.
vestibule [vestibyl], s.m. (entrance) hall.
vestige [vesti:ʒ], s.m. vestige; mark, trace.
veston [vestɔ̃], s.m. (man's) jacket; complet v., lounge suit.
vêtement [vɛtmɑ̃], s.m. garment, pl. clothes, clothing.
vétéran [veterɑ̃], s.m. veteran.
vétérinaire [veterinɛːr]. 1. a. veterinary. 2. s.m. veterinary surgeon, F: vet.
vétille [veti:j], s.f. trifle; mere nothing.
‡vêtir [veti:r], v.tr. to clothe; to dress. se vêtir, to dress.
veto [veto], s.m. veto.
vétusté [vetyste], s.f. decay, decrepitude.
veuf, veuve [vœf, vœːv]. 1. a. (a) widowed. 2. s. widower; f. widow.
vex/er [vekse], v.tr. to annoy, offend (s.o.). s.f. -ation. a. -atoire. a. -ant.
viabilité [viabilite], s.f. viability; practicability (of road).
viaduc [vjadyk], s.m. viaduct.
viager [vjaʒe], a. for life; rente viagère, (life) annuity.
viande [vjɑ̃:d], s.f. meat.
vibrant [vibrɑ̃], a. 1. vibrating, vibrant. 2. (a) resonant; (b) stirring.
vibr/er [vibre], v.i. to vibrate. s.f. -ation. a. -atoire.
vicaire [vikɛːr], s.m. curate of (parish); (assistant) priest.
vice [vis], s.m. 1. vice. 2. fault, defect.
vice-amiral [visamiral], s.m. vice-admiral. pl. vice-amiraux.
vice-roi [vis(ə)rwa], s.m. viceroy. pl. vice-rois.
vicier [visje], v.tr. to vitiate, corrupt, taint.
†vicieux [visjø], a. vicious.
vicinal [visinal], a. chemin v., local road.
vicomte [vikɔ̃t], s.m. viscount.
vicomtesse [vikɔ̃tes], s.f. viscountess.
victime [viktim], s.f. victim.
victoire [viktwaːr], s.f. victory.
†victorieu/x [viktɔrjø], a. victorious (de, over). adv. -sement.
victuailles [viktɥaj], s.f.pl. food.
vidange [vidɑ̃:ʒ], s.f. emptying, draining; Aut: faire la v., to drain the sump (and replace the oil).
vide [vid]. 1. a. empty; blank; void. 2. s.m. (a) empty space; void; (b) vacuum; (c) emptiness.
vide-ordures [vidordyːr], s.m.inv. rubbish shoot.
vider [vide], v.tr. 1. to empty; to clear out (room); videz vos verres! drink up! 2. to clean (fish); to draw (fowl).

vie [vi], s.f. life. 1. être en v., to be alive; il y va de la v., it's a case of life and death. 2. lifetime. 3. existence, mode of life; changer de v., to mend one's ways. 4. living, livelihood; coût de la v., cost of living.

vieillard [vjɛjaːr], s.m. old man.

vieillesse [vjɛjɛs], s.f. (old) age.

vieillir [vjejiːr]. 1. v.i. to grow old; (b) to age. 2. v.tr. to age (s.o.); to make (s.o.) look older.

vierge [vjɛrʒ]. 1. s.f. virgin, maiden; la (Sainte) V., the Blessed Virgin (Mary). 2. a. virgin; page v., blank page.

†vieux, vieil, f. vieille [vjø, vjɛ(ː)j], a. 1. old; (a) se faire v., to be getting old; s. un v., une vieille, an old man, an old woman; (b) of long standing. 2. old, ancient; stale (news); v. papiers, waste paper; a.phr.inv. v. jeu, old-fashioned.

†vif [vif]. 1. a. (a) alive, living; de vive voix, by word of mouth; eau vive, running water; (b) lively, animated; fast; (c) sharp (retort); (d) keen, quick (wit); (e) bright (colour). 2. s.m. living flesh; quick.

vigilance [viʒilɑ̃ːs], s.f. vigilance.

vigilant [viʒilɑ̃], a. vigilant, watchful.

vigne [viɲ], s.f. 1. (a) vine; (b) vineyard. 2. v. vierge, Virginia creeper.

vigneron [viɲrɔ̃], s. vine-grower.

vignette [viɲɛt], s.f. vignette.

vignoble [viɲɔbl], s.m. vineyard.

†vigoureux/x [viɡurø], a. vigorous; strong. a. -sement.

vigueur [viɡœːr], s.f. 1. vigour, strength. 2. (of law, etc.) entrer en v., to come into force.

vil [vil], a. 1. cheap, low-priced. 2. low(ly); base. 3. vile, base.

vilain, -aine [vilɛ̃, -ɛn]. 1. a. & s. naughty (child). 2. a. ugly; unpleasant; bad (weather); un v. tour, a nasty, dirty, trick. adv. -ement.

villa [villa], s.f. villa.

village [vilaʒ], s.m. village.

villageois, -oise [vilaʒwa, -waːz]. 1. s. villager. 2. a. rustic, country.

ville [vil], s.f. town; v. d'eau(x), spa; tenue de v., (i) town, city, clothes; (ii) (on invitations) lounge suit; hôtel de v., town hall.

villégiature [vil(l)eʒjatyːr], s.f. (a) stay in the country; en v., on holiday; (b) summer resort.

villégiaturiste [vileʒjatyrist], s.m. & f. holiday-maker.

vin [vɛ̃], s.m. wine; les grands vins, vintage wines; v. de Bordeaux, claret, v. de Bourgogne, Burgundy; v. du Rhin, hock.

vinaigre [vinɛːgr], s.m. vinegar.

†vindicatif/if [vɛ̃dikatif], a. vindictive, spiteful. adv. -ivement.

vingt [vɛ̃], num.a.inv. & s.m.inv. twenty.

vingtaine [vɛ̃tɛn], s.f. (about) twenty.

vingtième [vɛ̃tjɛm]. 1. num.a. & s. twentieth. 2. s.m. twentieth (part).

vinicole [vinikɔl], a. wine (industry); vine-growing (area).

viol [vjɔl], s.m. rape.

violacé [vjɔlase], a. purplish-blue.

violation [vjɔlasjɔ̃], s.f. violation, breach (of law, etc.).

violence [vjɔlɑ̃ːs], s.f. violence; force.

viol/ent [vjɔlɑ̃], a. violent. adv. -emment.

violer [vjɔle], v.tr. to violate; to rape (woman).

violet [vjɔlɛ], a. violet; purple.

violette [vjɔlɛt], s.f. violet.

violon [vjɔlɔ̃], s.m. 1. (a) violin; (b) violin (player). 2. P: (prison) cells.

violoncelle [vjɔlɔ̃sɛl], s.m. (violon)cello.

violoniste [vjɔlɔnist], s.m. & f. violinist.

vipère [vipɛːr], s.f. viper, adder.

virage [viraːʒ], s.m. 1. turning; tacking. 2. (sharp) turn, corner, bend.

virement [virmɑ̃], s.m. 1. Nau: tacking and veering. 2. (bank) transfer.

virer [vire]. 1. v.i. to turn; (a) to take a corner; (b) to slew round; (c) Nau: v. de bord, to tack. 2. v.tr. (a) to turn (sth.) over; (b) to transfer (money to an account).

virginité [virʒinite], s.f. virginity.

virgule [virɡyl], s.f. (a) comma; (b) = (decimal) point.

viril [viril], a. virile; male; manly.

virilité [virilite], s.f. virility, manliness.

†virtuel [virtɥɛl], a. virtual. adv. -lement.

virtuose [virtyoːz], s.m. & f. virtuoso.

virulence [virylɑ̃ːs], s.f. virulence.

virulent [virylɑ̃], a. virulent.

vis [vis], s.f. screw.

visa [viza], s.m. visa.

visage [vizaːʒ], s.m. face.

vis-à-vis [vizavi]. 1. adv.phr. opposite. 2. prep.phr. v.-à-v. de: (a) opposite, facing; (b) with respect to, in relation to. 3. s.m. person opposite; partner (at cards).

visée [vize], s.f. 1. aim; ligne de v., line of sight. 2. pl. aims, designs.

viser [vize]. 1. v.i. to aim. 2. v.tr. (a) to aim, take aim, at; to address (the ball); (b) to have in view; (c) to allude to.

viseur [vizœːr], s.m. Phot: viewfinder; Av: v. de lancement, bomb sight.

visibilité [vizibilite], s.f. visibility; Av: pilotage sans v., blind flying.

visible [vizibl], a. 1. (a) visible, perceptible; (b) evident. 2. (a) ready to receive visitors; free, visible; (b) (of building) open to the public. adv. -ment.

visière [vizjɛːr], s.f. (a) visor (of helmet); (b) peak of (cap); (c) eyeshade.

vision [vizjɔ̃], s.f. vision.

visionnaire [vizjɔnɛːr], a. & s. visionary.

visite [vizit], *s.f.* visit. **1.** (*a*) (social) call; (*b*) caller, visitor. **2.** inspection; survey; v. de la douane, customs examination.

visiter [vizite], *v.tr.* **1.** to visit. **2.** to examine, inspect.

visiteur, -euse [vizitœːr, -øːz], *s.* visitor; inspector.

vison [vizɔ̃], *s.m.* mink.

†**visqueux** [viskø], *a.* viscous, sticky.

visser [vise], *v.tr.* to screw (on, downwards, up).

†**visuel** [vizɥɛl], *a.* visual; champ v., field of vision.

†**vital** [vital], *a.* vital.

vitalité [vitalite], *s.f.* vitality.

vitamine [vitamin], *s.f.* vitamin.

vite [vit], *adv.* quickly; au plus v., as quickly as possible.

vitesse [vites], *s.f.* speed, rapidity; velocity; rate; *Aut:* gear; indicateur de v., speedometer; boîte de vitesses, gearbox.

viticole [vitikɔl], *a.* vine growing (area); wine (industry).

viticult/ure [vitikyltyːr], *s.f.* vine growing. *s.m.* -eur.

†**vitrail** [vitraːj], *s.m.* stained glass window.

vitre [vitr], *s.f.* (window)pane.

vitr/er [vitre], *v.tr.* to glaze. *s.m.* -ier, glazier.

vitrine [vitrin], *s.f.* **1.** shop window. **2.** case; glass cabinet.

vitriol [vitriɔl], *s.m.* vitriol.

vitupération [vityperasjɔ̃], *s.f.* vituperation.

vivace [vivas], *a.* (*a*) long-lived; (*b*) *Bot:* hardy; perennial.

vivacité [vivasite], *s.f.* **1.** hastiness. **2.** (*a*) acuteness; intensity; (*b*) vividness, brilliancy. **3.** vivacity; liveliness.

vivant [vivɑ̃]. **1.** *a.* (*a*) alive, living; langue vivante, modern language; (*b*) lively, animated; (*c*) vivid, live. **2.** *s.m.* living being. **3.** *s.m.* de son v., during his lifetime.

vivement [vivmɑ̃], *adv.* **1.** briskly; sharply. **2.** keenly, deeply.

vivifier [vivifje], *v.tr.* to invigorate.

‡**vivre** [viːvr]. **I.** *v.i.* to live. **1.** vive le roi! long live the King! qui vive? who goes there? **2.** savoir v., to know how to behave. **3.** avoir de quoi v., to have enough to live on. **II.** *vivres, s.m.pl.* provisions.

vocabulaire [vɔkabylɛːr], *s.m.* vocabulary.

†**vocal** [vɔkal], *a.* vocal. *adv.* -ement.

vocation [vɔkasjɔ̃], *s.f.* vocation.

‡**vociférer** [vɔsifere], *v.i.* & *tr.* to vociferate; to shout (insults).

†**vœu** [vø], *s.m.* **1.** vow. **2.** wish.

vogue [vɔg], *s.f.* fashion, vogue.

voici [vwasi], *prep.* here is, are.

voie [vwa], *s.f.* **1.** (*a*) way, road, track; par v. de terre, by land; overland; (*b*) v. ferrée, railway track; v. de garage, siding; mettre sur une v. de garage, to shelve; (*c*) *Anat:* passage, duct. **2.** way; en bonne v., going well.

voilà [vwala], *prep.* there is, are; en v. assez! that's enough (of that)! en v. une idée! what an idea! v. tout, that's all.

voile [vwal]. **I.** *s.f.* sail. **II.** *s.m.* (*a*) veil; (*b*) voile.

voiler [vwale], *v.tr.* (*a*) to veil; (*b*) to obscure; to muffle. se voiler, to cloud over.

voilier [vwalje], *s.m.* sailing ship.

‡**voir** [vwaːr], *v.tr.* to see. **1.** to set eyes on; to sight; à le v., to judge by his looks; faites v.! let me see it! **2.** (*a*) v. venir qn, to see s.o. coming; (*b*) v. faire qch, to see s.o. do sth. **3.** (*a*) to visit. **4.** (*a*) to understand; (*b*) to perceive; cela se voit, that's obvious. **5.** *int.* voyons! (i) let's see; (ii) come! come! **6.** être bien vu, to be well thought of (de, by).

voisin, -ine [vwazɛ̃, -in]. **1.** *a.* neighbouring, adjoining. **2.** *s.* neighbour.

voisinage [vwazinaːʒ], *s.m.* proximity, vicinity. **2.** neighbourhood.

voiture [vwatyːr], *s.f.* (*a*) (horse-drawn) carriage; (*b*) car, *U.S:* automobile; (*c*) *Rail:* coach, *U.S:* car; "en v.!" take your seats! (*d*) v. d'enfant, perambulator.

voix [vwa], *s.f.* **1.** voice. **2.** d'une commune v., by common consent; mettre aux v., to put to the vote.

vol¹ [vɔl], *s.m.* **1.** (*a*) flying, flight; au v., on the wing; à v. d'oiseau, as the crow flies; vue à v. d'oiseau, bird's-eye view; (*b*) *Av:* heures de v., flying hours; v. à voile, gliding; v. en piqué, dive. **2.** flock, flight (of birds, etc.).

vol², *s.m.* theft; vol à l'étalage, shop-lifting.

volaille [vɔlaj], *s.f.* poultry; *Cu:* foies de v., chicken livers.

volant [vɔlɑ̃]. **I.** *a.* **1.** flying; fluttering. **2.** loose; movable. **II.** *s.m.* **1.** fly-wheel. **2.** steering-wheel.

volatil [vɔlatil], *a.* volatile.

volatiliser [vɔlatilize], *v.tr.* to volatilize; se v., to vanish into thin air.

vol-au-vent [vɔlovɑ̃], *s.m.inv. Cu:* vol-au-vent.

volcan [vɔlkɑ̃], *s.m.* volcano.

volcanique [vɔlkanik], *a.* volcanic.

volée [vɔle], *s.f.* **1.** flight (of bird); prendre sa v., to take wing. **2.** flock, flight. **3.** (*a*) volley; shower (of missiles, etc.); (*b*) sonner à toute v., to set all the bells ringing.

voler¹ [vɔle], *v.i.* to fly.

voler², *v.tr.* **1.** to steal. **2.** to rob (s.o.).

volet [vɔlɛ], *s.m.* shutter.

voleter [vɔlte], v.i. to flutter.

voleur, -euse [vɔlœːr, øːz], s. thief, robber, burglar; au v.! stop thief!

volière [vɔljɛːr], s.f. aviary.

volontaire [vɔlɔ̃tɛːr], a. 1. voluntary. 2. s.m. volunteer. 3. self-willed. adv. -ment.

volonté [vɔlɔ̃te], s.f. 1. will; manque de v., spinelessness; en faire à sa v., to have one's own way. 2. wishes, desires (of s.o.); dernières volontés, (last) will (and testament).

volontiers [vɔlɔ̃tje], adv. (a) willingly, gladly; (b) readily.

volt [vɔlt], s.m. El: volt.

voltage [vɔltaːʒ], s.m. El: voltage.

volubilis [vɔlybilis], s.m. convolvulus.

volubilité [vɔlybilite], s.f. volubility.

volume [vɔlym], s.m. volume.

†volumineux [vɔlyminø], a. voluminous.

volupté [vɔlypte], s.f. (sensual) pleasure.

†voluptueu/x [vɔlyptɥø], a. voluptuous. adv. -sement.

volute [vɔlyt], s.f. volute; scroll; wreath (of smoke).

vom/ir [vɔmiːr], v.tr. to vomit. s.m. -issement.

vorac/e [vɔras], a. voracious. adv. -ement. s.f. -ité, voraciousness.

vote [vɔt], s.m. (a) vote; (b) voting, poll; droit de v., franchise.

vot/er [vɔte], v.i. & tr. to vote. s. -ant, -ante, voter.

†votif [vɔtif], a. votive.

votre [vɔtr], s, poss.a. your.

vôtre [voːtr], poss.pron. yours; your own; F: à la v.! here's to you! cheers!

vouer [vwe], v.tr. to vow, dedicate.

‡vouloir [vulwaːr], v.tr. 1. to will; to be determined on. 2. (a) to want, to wish (for); faites comme vous voudrez, do as you please; je ne le veux pas! I will not have it! que voulez-vous! well, (that's how it is)! (b) en v. à qn, to bear s.o. a grudge; ne m'en veuillez pas, don't be angry with me. 3. (a) to will, require, demand; (b) to want, wish; que voulez-vous qu'il fasse? what do you expect me to do? (c) to try to (do sth.); (d) to mean, intend. (e) v. bien faire qch., to consent, be willing to do sth.; veuillez vous asseoir, please sit down; (f) (intensive) voulez-vous bien vous taire! be quiet, will you! 4. to be convinced, to insist.

voulu [vuly], a. 1. required, requisite. 2. deliberate, intentional.

vous [vu], pers.pron. sg. & pl. 1. (a) you; (b) you, to you; (c) yourself; (d) vous vous connaissez, you know one another. 2. c'est à vous de jouer, it's your turn (to play).

vous-même(s) [vumɛm], pers.pron. yourself; yourselves.

voûte [vut], s.f. vault, arch.

voûté [vute], a. (a) vaulted, arched; (b) stooping, bent.

voûter [vute], v.tr. to arch, vault. se voûter, to become bent, round-shouldered.

voyage [vwajaːʒ], s.m. journey, voyage; v. d'agrément, pleasure trip; il est en v., he is travelling; compagnon de v., travelling companion; fellow passenger.

voyager [vwajaʒe], v.i. to travel; to make a journey; Com: v. pour une maison d'éditions, to travel in books.

voyageur, -euse [vwajaʒœːr, -øːz]. 1. s. traveller; passenger. 2. (a) a. travelling; (b) pigeon v., carrier pigeon.

voyant [vwajɑ̃], a. gaudy, loud; showy.

voyelle [vwajɛl], s.f. vowel.

vrac [vrak], s.m. en v., in bulk.

vrai [vrɛ]. 1. a. (a) true, truthful; (b) true, real, genuine; (c) downright (liar, etc.). 2. adv. truly, really, indeed; à v. dire, as a matter of fact. 3. s.m. truth.

vraiment [vrɛmɑ̃], adv. really, truly; v.? indeed? is that so?

vraisemblable [vrɛsɑ̃blabl], a. probable, likely. adv. -ment.

vraisemblance [vrɛsɑ̃blɑ̃ːs], s.f. probability, likelihood.

vrille [vriːj], s.f. 1. Bot: tendril. 2. gimlet. 3. Av: tailspin.

vromb/ir [vrɔ̃biːr], v.i. to buzz; to hum. s.m. -issement.

vu [vy]. 1. s.m. au vu de tous, openly. 2. prep. considering, seeing.

vue [vy], s.f. 1. sight; à perte de vue, as far as the eye can see. 2. view.

vulgaire [vylgɛːr]. 1. a. vulgar; (a) common; (b) low, coarse. 2. s.m. le v., the common people.

vulgariser [vylgarize], v.tr. to popularize. se vulgariser, to grow vulgar.

vulgarité [vylgarite], s.f. vulgarity.

vulnérabilité [vylnerabilite], s.f. vulnerability.

vulnérable [vylnerabl], a. vulnerable.

W

W, w [dubləve], *s.m.* (the letter) W, w.
wagon [vagɔ̃], *s.m. Rail:* (passenger) carriage; coach; (goods) wagon; w. détaché, slip coach; monter en w., to get into the train.

NOTE. In the following compounds both nouns add s in the plural.

wagon-citerne [vagɔ̃sitern], *s.m.* tank car.
wagon-lit [vagɔ̃li], *s.m.* sleeping car, sleeper.
wagon-poste [vagɔ̃pɔst], *s.m.* mail van.

wagon-restaurant [vagɔ̃rɛstɔrɑ̃], *s.m.* dining car.
walkover [wɔlkɔvœ:r], *s.m. Sp:* walkover.
wallon, -onne, [valɔ̃, -ɔn] *a. & s.* Walloon.
water [water], *s.m. usu. pl. F:* lavatory, toilet.
wattman [watman], *s.m.* (tram, electric train) driver.
W.C. [dubləvese, vese], *s.m. usu. pl.* lavatory, W.C.
week-end [wikɛnd], *s.m.* weekend. *pl. week-ends.*
whisky [wiski], *s.m.* whisky.
wolfram [vɔlfram], *s.m.* wolfram.

X

X, x, [iks], *s.m.* (the letter) X, x; rayons X, X rays.

xylophone [ksilɔfɔn], *s.m.* xylophone.

Y

Y, y¹ [igrɛk], *s.m.* (the letter) Y, y, **y²** [i]. 1. *adv.* there; here; madame y est-elle? is Mrs X at home? pendant que vous y êtes, while you are about it. 2. *pron.inv.* by it; at it; to it; to him; to her, etc.; pendant que j'y pense, by the way, while I think of it; je m'y attendais, I expected as much. 3. ça y est [saje], (i) that's done! (ii)

well, I was sure that would happen! 4. vas-y [vazi], (i) go there; (ii) get on with it!
yacht [jak(t), jɔt], *s.m.* yacht. *s.m.* -eur. *s.m.* -ing.
yeux. See ŒIL.
yougoslave [jugoslaːv], *a. & s.* Yugoslav.
youyou [juju], *s.m.* dinghy.

Z

Z, z [zɛd], *s.m.* (the letter) Z, z.
zèbre [zɛbr], *s.m.* zebra.
zébré [zebre], *a.* striped (de, with).
zèle [zɛːl], *s.m.* zeal, enthusiasm.
zélé, -ée [zele], *a. & s.* zealous (person); enthusiast.
zénith [zenit], *s.m.* zenith.
zéro [zero], *s.m.* 1. nought; (*in telephone numbers*) O [ou]; (*at tennis*) trois à z., three love. 2. starting point, zero; partir de z., to start from scratch.
zeste [zɛst], *s.m.* zest (of orange); z. confit, candied peel.
‡zézayer [zezeje], *v.i. & tr.* to lisp. *s.m.* -iement.
zibeline [ziblin], *s.f.* sable.
zigzag [zigzag], *s.m.* zigzag; éclair en z., forked lightning.

zigzaguer [zigzage], *v.i.* to zigzag.
zinc [zɛ̃g], *s.m.* 1. zinc. 2. *F:* (*in café*) counter, bar.
zodiaque [zɔdjak], *s.m.* zodiac.
zona [zɔna], *s.m. Med:* shingles.
zone [zoːn], *s.f.* zone; sphere (of influence); z. verte, green belt; z. sterling, sterling area; *Aut:* z. bleu = pink zone; z. quadrillée, box junction.
zoo [zo, zoo], *s.m. F:* zoo.
zoologie [zɔɔlɔʒi], *s.f.* zoology.
zoologique [zɔɔlɔʒik], *a.* zoological; jardin z., zoological garden(s), zoo.
zoologiste [zɔɔlɔʒist], *s.m.* zoologist.
zouave [zwaːv], *s.m.* zouave.
zoulou [zulu], *a. & s.* Zulu.
zut [zyt], *int. P:* (a) blast (it)! (b) rats! shut up!

PART II
ENGLISH-FRENCH: ANGLAIS-FRANÇAIS

NOTES GRAMMATICALES

I. PLURIEL des NOMS.

(1) **Règle générale.** La plupart des noms forment leur pluriel en -s: *ex.* cat, cats; table, tables.

(2) Les noms qui se terminent en -s, -sh, -ch, ou -x forment leur pluriel en -es: *ex.* glass, glasses; brush, brushes; church, churches; box, boxes. *A noter:* cloth; *pl.* cloths (tissus) et clothes (vêtements). Ces noms ne sont pas indiqués comme irréguliers dans le dictionnaire.

(3) La plupart des noms qui se terminent en -o forment leur pluriel en -s. Cependant un certain nombre se terminent au pluriel en -oes: banjo, banjoes; buffalo, buffaloes; cargo, cargoes; domino, dominoes; echo, echoes; flamingo, flamingoes; go, goes; hero, heroes; no, noes; potato, potatoes; tomato, tomatoes; volcano, volcanoes.

(4) Les noms qui se terminent en -y forment leur pluriel en -ies, sauf si l'y est précédé par une voyelle; dans ce dernier cas le pluriel est en -s: *ex.* army, armies; fly, flies; story, stories; boy, boys; storey, storeys; valley valleys.

(5) Les noms qui se terminent en -f forment normalement leur pluriel en -s; mais certains noms (et leur composés) qui se terminent en -f ou -fe forment leur pluriel en -ves: calf calves; half, halves; leaf, leaves; loaf, loaves; self, selves; sheaf, sheaves; shelf, shelves; wolf, wolves; knife, knives; life, lives; wife, wives. Hoof, scarf, turf et wharf forment leur pluriel ou en -s ou en -ves.

(6) **Pluriels irréguliers**

(a) pluriel en -en: child, children; man, men; woman, women; ox, oxen. Les noms composés qui dérivent de child, man, woman, forment leur pluriel en -en: *ex.* grandchild, grandchildren; gentleman, gentlemen; policewoman, policewomen. *A noter:* German, Germans.

(b) six autres noms sont à signaler à cause du changement de voyelle au pluriel: dormouse, dormice; foot, feet; goose, geese; louse, lice; mouse, mice; tooth, teeth.

(c) Les noms suivants sont invariables au pluriel: deer; fruit; gross; grouse; salmon; sheep; trout; Chinese; Japanese; Portuguese; Swiss. Le pluriel de fish est généralement fish, mais on voit parfois fishes.

3

au pluriel s'ils sont précédés par un nombre: dozen; hundred; hundred-weight; million; stone; thousand; *ex.* he weighs ten stone; two dozen eggs; *mais* dozens of people.

(d) **Certain noms d'origine étrangère** conservent au pluriel la terminaison de la langue étrangère.

(i) (*latin*) axis, axes; larva, larvae; radius, radii; stimulus, stimuli; stratum, strata.

A noter: formula, *pl.* formulas ou formulae; appendix, *pl.* appendices ou appendixes; medium, *pl.* media (= *moyens de communication, ex.* mass media), mais mediums (= *médiums*).

(ii) (*grec*) analysis, analyses; basis, bases; crisis, crises; criterion, criteria; oasis, oases; phenomenon, phenomena; thesis, theses.

(iii) (*francais*) bureau, bureaux; plateau, plateaux.

(iv) (*hébreu*) cherub, cherubs, *Ecc:* cherubim; seraph, seraphs, *Ecc:* seraphim.

(7) **Noms composés.** Le pluriel d'un nom composé, écrit en un seul mot, en deux mots ou avec un trait d'union, est généralement indiqué par un -s final: *ex.* housewife, housewives; ticket collector, ticket collectors; forget-me-not, forget-me-nots. Mais dans certains mots, notamment les composés de man ou de woman dans les mots où le premier élément man, woman, est suivi par un autre nom, chaque élément prend l'indication du pluriel: *ex.* manservant, menservants; woman doctor, women doctors.

Pour quelques noms composés où le nom qui constitue le premier élément est suivi d'un adjectif ou d'un adverbe qualificatif, l'-s du pluriel s'ajoute au premier élément: *ex:* father-in-law, fathers-in-law, mother-in-law, mothers-in-law, etc.: governor-general, governors-general; court-martial, courts-martial; commander-in-chief, commanders-in-chief. Il est néanmoins à noter que ces mots-ci suivent la règle générale pour la formation du possessif, en ajoutant un 's à la fin du mot: *ex.* his father-in-law's house.

II. CONJUGAISON DES VERBES.

(1) **Verbes réguliers**

Pour former le passé ou le participe passé d'un verbe régulier, on ajoute -ed à l'infinitif: *ex.* walk, walked. Si l'infinitif se termine en -e, on ajoute simplement un -d: *ex.* dance, danced. Si l'infinitif se termine en -y, le passé et le participe passé se terminent en -ied: *ex.* marry, married; try, tried. Le participe présent se termine en -ing; mais quand l'infinitif se termine en -e, l'e ne figure pas au participe présent: *ex.* dance, dancing; *exception:* singe, singeing (pour éviter la confusion avec sing, singing). Pour les verbes qui se terminent en -ie, le participe présent se termine en -ying, *ex.* die, dying; lie, lying.

(2) **Les verbes monosyllabiques** dont l'infinitif se termine par une

Notes Grammaticales

seule consonne, ceux dont l'infinitif termine par une voyelle + 1, ou ceux dont l'accent tonique tombe sur la dernière syllabe doublent la consonne finale au passé et au participe passé: *ex.* hop, hopped; step, stepped; travel, travelled. Ces verbes sont indiqués dans le dictionnaire par le signe ‡ mais ne figurent pas dans la liste des verbes irréguliers.

(3) **Verbes irréguliers.** Les principaux verbes irréguliers sont indiqués ci-dessous par ordre alphabétique. L'infinitif est suivi du passé et du participe passé.

A noter: (a) **To be:** *présent:* I am, he is; we, you, they, are: *passé:* I, he, was, we, you, they, were; *participe passé:* been; *participe présent:* being.

(b) *Verbes auxiliaires de mode* (*verbes défectifs*). Ces verbes n'ont ni infinitif ni participe passé et tous sauf ought sont suivis de l'infinitif (présent ou passé selon le temps employé) sans to. (i) can, *passé* could (*pour l'infinitif employer* to be able *et pour le participe passé* been able). (ii) may, *passé* might. (iii) must (*suivi de l'infinitif présent ou passé*); *pas de passé.* (iv) **ought** (*suivi de l'infinitif présent ou passé*); *pas de passé.* (v) shall, *passé* should. (vi) will, *passé* would.

BEAR, bore, born(e). **BEAT,** beat, beaten. **BECOME,** became, become. **BEGIN,** began, begun. **BET,** bet *ou* betted, bet. **BID,** bid, bid. **BIND,** bound, bound. **BITE,** bit, bitten. **BLEED,** bled, bled. **BLESS,** blessed, blessed *ou* blest. **BLOW,** blew, blown. **BREAK,** broke, broken. **BREED,** bred, bred. **BRING,** brought, brought. **BROADCAST,** broadcast, broadcast. **BUILD,** built, built. **BURN,** burnt (*occ.* burned), burnt. **BURST,** burst, burst. **BUY,** bought, bought. **CAST,** cast, cast. **CATCH,** caught, caught. **CHOOSE,** chose, chosen. **CLING,** clung, clung. **COME,** came, come. **COST,** cost, cost. **CREEP,** crept, crept. **CUT,** cut, cut. **DIG,** dug, dug. **DO,** did, done (*prés.* he does). **DRAW,** drew, drawn. **DREAM,** dreamed *ou* dreamt, dreamed *ou* dreamt. **DRINK,** drank, drunk. **DRIVE,** drove, driven. **EAT,** ate [et], eaten. **FALL,** fell, fallen. **FEED,** fed, fed. **FEEL,** felt, felt. **FIGHT,** fought, fought. **FIND,** found, found. **FLING,** flung, flung. **FLY,** flew, flown. **FORBID,** forbade, forbidden. **FORGET,** forgot, forgotten. **FORGIVE,** forgave, forgiven. **FREEZE,** froze, frozen. **GET,** got, got (*U.S.:* gotten). **GIVE,** gave, given. **GRIND,** ground, ground. **GO,** went, gone (*prés.* he goes). **GROW,** grew, grown. **HANG,** hung, hung (hanged, hanged *dans le sens de mourir pendu*). **HAVE,** had, had (*prés.* he has). **HEAR,** heard, heard. **HIDE,** hid, hidden. **HIT,** hit, hit. **HOLD,** held, held. **HURT,** hurt, hurt. **KEEP,** kept, kept. **KNEEL,** knelt, knelt. **KNOW,** knew, known. **LAY,** laid, laid. **LEAD,** led, led. **LEAP,** leapt, leapt. **LEARN,** learnt, learnt. **LEAVE,** left, left. **LEND,**

lent, lent. **LET**, let, let. **LIE**, lay, lain. **LIGHT**, lit *ou* lighted, lit *ou* lighted. **LOSE**, lost, lost. **MAKE**, made, made. **MEAN**, meant, meant. **MEET**, met, met. **MISLAY**, mislaid, mislaid. **MISLEAD**, misled, misled. **MISTAKE**, mistook, mistaken. **MOW**, mowed, mown. **OVERCOME**, overcame, overcome. **OVERHEAR**, overheard, overheard. **PAY**, paid, paid. **PICNIC**, picnicked, picnicked. **PUT**, put, put. **READ**, read [red], read [red]. **RENDEZVOUS**, *noter prononciation* rendezvoused [rɔndivu:d], rendezvousing [rɔndivu:iŋ]. **RIDE**, rode, ridden. **RING**, rang, rung. **RISE**, rose, risen. **RUN**, ran, run. **SAY**, said, said. **SAW**, sawed, sawn. **SEE**, saw, seen. **SEEK**, sought, sought. **SELL**, sold, sold. **SEND**, sent, sent. **SET**, set, set. **SEW**, sewed, sewn. **SHAKE**, shook, shaken. **SHED**, shed, shed. **SHINE**, shone, shone. **SHOOT**, shot, shot. **SHOW**, showed, shown. **SHRINK**, shrank, shrunk. **SHUT**, shut, shut. **SING**, sang, sung. **SINK**, sank, sunk. **SIT**, sat, sat. **SKI**, ski'd, ski'd, *pres. part.* skiing. **SLEEP**, slept, slept. **SLIDE**, slid, slid. **SLING**, slung, slung. **SLINK**, slunk, slunk. **SLIT**, slit, slit. **SMELL**, smelt, *ou* smelled, smelt. **SOW**, sowed, sown. **SPELL**, spelt *ou* spelled, spelt *ou* spelled. **SPEND**, spent, spent. **SPILL**, spilt *ou* spilled, spilt *ou* spilled. **SPIN**, spun, spun. **SPIT**, spat, spat. **SPLIT**, split, split. **SPOIL**, spoilt, *ou* spoiled, spoilt *ou* spoiled. **SPEAK**, spoke, spoken. **SPREAD**, spread, spread. **SPRING**, sprang, sprung. **STAND**, stood, stood. **STEAL**, stole, stolen. **STICK**, stuck, stuck. **STING**, stung, stung. **STINK**, stank, stunk. **STRIDE**, strode, stridden. **STRIKE**, struck, struck *ou* stricken. **STRIVE**, strove, striven. **SWEAR**, swore, sworn. **SWEEP**, swept, swept. **SWELL**, swelled, swollen. **SWIM**, swam, swum. **SWING**, swung, swung. **TAKE**, took, taken. **TEACH**, taught, taught. **TEAR**, tore, torn. **TELL**, told, told. **THINK**, thought, thought. **THRIVE**, throve *ou* thrived, thrived. **THROW**, threw, thrown. **THRUST**, thrust, thrust. **TREAD**, trod, trodden. **UNDERGO**, underwent, undergone. **UNDERSTAND**, understood, understood. **WAKE**, woke, woken. **WEAR**, wore, worn. **WEAVE**, weaved, weaved *ou* woven. **WEEP**, wept, wept. **WIN**, won, won. **WIND** [waind], wound [waund], wound [waund]. **WITHDRAW**, withdrew, withdrawn. **WITHSTAND**, withstood, withstood. **WRING**, wrung, wrung. **WRITE**, wrote, written.

6

PRONONCIATION

Un tableau des signes phonétiques employés pour les mots anglais est donné ci-dessous; nous attirons toutefois l'attention de l'usager sur les points suivants:

(a) L'accent tonique est indiqué par un accent précédant la syllabe accentuée, *p. ex.* sugar ['ʃugər], impossible [im'posibl]. Il est à noter que certains mots, surtout des composés, peuvent avoir deux accents toniques.

(b) Les caractères mis entre parenthèses, *p. ex.* nation ['nei(ə)n] signifient que le mot peut se prononcer aussi bien avec que sans le son correspondant à cette lettre.

(c) Le son [r] ne s'entend généralement pas devant une consonne ou devant une pause; on emploie le caractère italique [*r*] à la fin des mots tels que better, four, here, pour indiquer que le son [*r*] peut se faire entendre dans ces mots dans le cas, et uniquement dans le cas, où le mot suivant dans la phrase commence par une voyelle sans qu'il y ait de pause, *p. ex.* here and now ['hiərənd 'nau].

(d) Les mots tels que which, why, what ont été écrits avec l'[h] entre parenthèses, à savoir [(h)witʃ], [(h)wai], [(h)wɔt]; l'[h] peut se faire entendre, mais on prononce souvent ces mots sans [h], surtout en parlant vite.

Les consonnes suivantes ont été omises du tableau, parce que le signe phonétique correspond à la lettre utilisée dans le mot écrit:

b, d, h, l, m, n, p, t, v.

TABLEAU DES SIGNES PHONÉTIQUES

VOYELLES

[iː]	bee, fever, sea, police	[ɔi]	boil, toy, oyster, loyal
[iə]	beer, appear, real	[ou]	low, soap, rope, no, diploma
[i]	bit, added, physics	[u]	put, wool, would, full
[e]	bet, menace, leopard, said, bury	[uː]	shoe, prove, too, true, truth
[ei]	date, day, nail	[uə]	poor, surely, tourist
[ɛə]	bear, bareness, heir, airy, therefore	[ʌ]	cut, sun, son, some, cover, rough
[æ]	bat, add	[əː]	burn, learn, herb, whirl
[ai]	aisle, height, life, fly, type	[ə]	china, annoy, treachery, photograph
[ɑː]	art, cart, ask	[(ə)]	nation, ocean, reason, sudden
[au]	fowl, house, bough	[jə]	opinion, pillion
[ɔ]	lot, wasp, what	[ju]	huge, duke, beauty
[ɔː]	all, haul, short, saw		

CONSONNES

[f]	fat, laugh, ruffle, rough, elephant	[ks]	except, exercise, expect, axe, accident
[s]	sat, scene, mouse, psychology	[kʃ]	action, eviction
[θ]	thatch, ether, faith, breath	[g]	go, ghost, guard, again, egg, peg, rogue
[z]	zinc, buzz, houses, usual		
[ð]	that, the, mother, breathe	[gz]	exist, exact
[ʃ]	sham, dish, pressure, ocean, nation, machine	[x]	loch
[tʃ]	chat, search, church, thatch, rich	[ŋ]	bang, sing, link, anchor
[ʒ]	pleasure, vision	[ŋg]	anger, finger, English
[dʒ]	rage, edge, pigeon, jet, digit, spinach, judge	[r]	rat, arise, barring
		[*r*]	sailor, martyr, finger, here
k]	act, cat, ache, kitten, technique	[j]	yacht, yet

7

A

A, a¹ [ei], s. 1. (la lettre) A, a m; A1, de première qualité; (house number) 51a, 51 bis. 2. Mus: la m. 3. A. bomb, bombe f A.

a², before vowel usu. an [stressed ei, æn, unstressed ə, ən], indef. art. 1. (a) un, une; a man, un homme; an apple, une pomme; an M.P. [ən'em'piː] = un député. 2. (def. art. in Fr.) to have a big mouth, avoir la bouche grande; to have a taste for sth., avoir le goût de qch. 3. five francs a kilo, cinq francs le kilo; three times a week, trois fois par semaine. 4. it gives me an appetite, cela me donne de l'appétit. 5. (a) (= a certain) in a sense, dans un certain sens; (b) to eat two at a time, manger deux à la fois; to come in two at a time, entrer deux par deux; (c) (= a single) not a word, pas un seul mot. 6. (art. omitted in Fr.) he is a doctor, il est médecin; (apposition) Caen, a town in Normandy, Caen, ville de Normandie; what a man! quel homme!

aback [ə'bæk], adv. taken a., déconcerté, interdit.

abandon [ə'bændən], v.tr. abandonner; renoncer à (un projet).

abase [ə'beis], v.tr. abaisser, humilier.

abash [ə'bæʃ], v.tr. décontenancer.

abate [ə'beit], v.i. (of storm, fear) se calmer, s'apaiser; (of flood) baisser.

abbess [æbes, -is], s. abbesse f.

abbey [æbi], s. abbaye f; a. (church), (église) abbatiale (f).

abbot [æbət], s. abbé m.

abbreviate [ə'briːvieit], v.tr. abréger.

abbreviation [ə'briːvi'eiʃ(ə)n], s. abréviation f.

abdicate [æbdikeit], v.tr. & i. abdiquer. abdi'cation, s. abdication f.

abduct [æb'dʌkt], v.tr. enlever (qn). ab'duction, s. enlèvement m.

aberration [æbə'reiʃ(ə)n], s. aberration f.

†abet [ə'bet], v.tr. encourager.

abeyance [ə'be(i)əns], s. suspension f; in a., en suspens.

abhor [əb'hɔːr], v.tr. avoir (qn, qch.) en horreur.

abide [ə'baid], v.i. to a. by, rester fidèle à (une promesse).

†ability [ə'biliti], s. 1. capacité f (de faire qch.); to the best of my a., de mon mieux. 2. habileté f; a man of great a., un homme très doué.

abject [æbdʒekt], a. 1. abject. 2. bas, vil. -ly, adv. abjectement.

ablaze [ə'bleiz], adv. en feu, en flammes.

able [eibl], a. 1. (a) capable, habile; (b) to be a. to do sth., (i) savoir, être capable de, (ii) pouvoir, être à même de, faire qch. 2. a work, (i) œuvre de talent; (ii) travail bien fait. 'able-'bodied, a. fort, robuste. 'ably, adv. habilement.

abnormal [əb'nɔːməl], a. anormal. -ly, adv. anormalement.

aboard [ə'bɔːd]. 1. adv. à bord. 2. prep. à bord de.

abolish [ə'bɔliʃ], v.tr. abolir, supprimer. abo'lition, s. abolition f.

abominable [ə'bɔminəbl], a. abominable. -ly, adv. abominablement.

abomination [əbɔmi'neiʃ(ə)n], s. abomination f.

aborigine [æbə'ridʒini:], s. aborigène m.

abortion [ə'bɔːʃ(ə)n], s. 1. avortement m. 2. F: œuvre mal venue. a'bortive, a. avorté, manqué.

abound [ə'baund], v.i. abonder (in, with, en).

about [ə'baut], adv. & prep. 1. (a) autour (de); (b) de côté et d'autre. 2. Mil: a. turn! demi-tour! 3. environ, presque; that's a. right, c'est à peu près cela; a three o'clock, vers trois heures. 4. au sujet de; what is it all a.? de quoi s'agit-il? to speak a. sth., parler de qch. 5. (a) a. to, sur le point de; (b) while you are a. it, pendant que vous y êtes.

above [ə'bʌv], adv. & prep. 1. au-dessus (de); (a) from a., d'en haut; (b) the Seine above Paris, la Seine en amont de Paris; (c) supérieur à; a. all, surtout. 2. as a., comme ci-dessus. a'bove-board, a. franc.

abreast [ə'brest], adv. (a) de front; (b) to walk a., marcher côte à côte; a. of the times, de son temps, à la page.

abridge [ə'bridʒ], v.tr. abréger; abridged edition, édition réduite.

abroad [ə'brɔːd], adv. 1. à l'étranger. 2. (of news) to get a., se répandre.

abrupt [ə'brʌpt], a. brusque. -ly, adv. 1. brusquement. 2. à pic. a'bruptness, s. brusquerie f.

abscess [æbses], s. abcès m.

abscond [əb'skɔnd], v.i. s'enfuir; décamper.

absence [æbs(ə)ns], s. 1. absence f. 2. in the a. of sth., faute de qch. 3. a. of mind, distraction f.

absent. I. a. [æbs(ə)nt] absent. II. v.pr. [æb'sent], to a. oneself, s'absenter. absen'tee, s. absent m. absen'teeism, s. absentéisme m. 'absent-'minded, a. distrait. -ly, adv. distraitement. 'absent-'mindedness, s. distraction f.

absolute [æbsəl(j)uːt], a. (a) absolu; (b) an a. scandal, un véritable scandale. -ly, adv. absolument.

absolution [æbsə'l(j)uːʃ(ə)n], s. absolution f.

absolve [əb'zɔlv], v.tr. absoudre.

absorb [əb'sɔːb], v.tr. absorber. ab'sorber, s. Aut: shock a., amortisseur m.

abstain [əbs'tein], v.i. s'abstenir.

abstemious [əbs'ti:miəs], *a.* sobre, tempérant. **-ly,** *adv.* sobrement; frugalement. **ab'stemiousness,** *s.* sobriété *f;* abstinence *f.*

abstention [əbs'tenʃ(ə)n], *s.* abstention *f.*

abstinence ['æbstinəns], *s.* abstinence *f.*

abstract. I. *a.* & *s.* ['æbstrækt] abstrait *(m).* II. *s.* ['æbstrækt], résumé *m,* abrégé *m.* III. *v.tr.* [æb'strækt], soustraire (from, à). **ab'straction,** *s.* 1. soustraction *f.* 2. idée abstraite. **ab'stracted,** *a.* distrait; rêveur. **-ly,** *adv.* distraitement.

abstruse [əbs'truːs], *a.* abstrus.

absurd [əb'sə:d], *a.* absurde. **-ly,** *adv.* absurdement. **ab'surdity,** *s.* absurdité *f.*

abundant [ə'bʌndənt], *a.* abondant; copieux. **-ly,** *adv.* abondamment; copieusement. **a'bundance,** *s.* abondance *f.*

abuse. I. *s.* [ə'bjuːs]. 1. abus *m.* 2. insultes *fpl,* injures *fpl.* II. *v.tr.* [ə'bjuːz] 1. abuser (de son autorité). 2. injurier (qn). **a'busive,** *a.* injurieux; (homme) grossier.

abyss [ə'bis], *s.* abîme *m,* gouffre *m.*

acacia [ə'keiʃə], *s.* acacia *m.*

academic [ækə'demik], *a.* académique. **aca'demical,** *a.* universitaire. **a'cademy** *s.* académie *f.*

accede [æk'siːd], *v.i.* accéder (au trône).

accelerate [æk'seləreit], *v.tr.* accélérer. **acceler'ation,** *s.* accélération *f.* **ac'celerator,** *s.* accélérateur *m.*

accent ['æksənt], *s.* accent *m.*

accentuate [æk'sentjueit], *v.tr.* accentuer. **accentu'ation,** *s.* accentuation *f.*

accept [ək'sept], *v.tr.* & *ind.tr.* accepter: agréer; admettre. **ac'ceptable,** *a.* acceptable, agréable. **ac'ceptance,** *s.* acceptation *f;* accueil *m* favorable; réception *f* (d'un article commandé). **accep'tation,** *s.* acception *f,* signification *f* (d'un mot).

access ['æksəs], *s.* accès *m;* abord *m;* easy of a., abordable. **ac'cessible,** *a.* accessible; (of *pers.*) accueillant.

†**accessory** [æk'sesəri]. 1. *a.* accessoire, subsidiaire. 2. *s.* accessoire *m* (d'une machine, etc.). 3. *s.* complice *mf.*

accident ['æksid(ə)nt], *s.* accident *m;* by a., accidentellement. **acci'dental** *(a)* *a.* accidentel, fortuit; *(b) s. Mus:* accident *m.* **-ally,** *adv.* accidentellement.

acclaim [ə'kleim], *v.tr.* acclamer.

acclimatize [ə'klaimətaiz], *v.tr.* acclimater. **ac'climatization,** *s.* acclimatation *f.*

accommodate [ə'kɔmədeit], *v.tr.* 1. *(a)* accommoder; *(b)* ajuster, adapter (qch. à qch.). 2. loger, recevoir (qn). **ac'commodating,** *a.* complaisant, peu difficile. **accommo'dation,** *s.* logement *m;* we have no sleeping a., nous n'avons pas de chambres.

accompany [ə'kʌmp(ə)ni], *v.tr.* accompagner. **ac'companiment,** *s.* accompagnement *m.*

accomplice [ə'kɔmplis], *s.* complice *mf.*

accomplish [ə'kɔmpliʃ], *v.tr.* accomplir (qch.). **ac'complished,** *a.* (musicien, fait) accompli; (homme) doué. **ac'complishment,** *s.* 1. accomplissement *m* (d'une tâche). 2. *usu.pl.* talents *m* d'agrément.

accord [ə'kɔːd], *s.* 1. accord *m,* consentement *m.* 2. of one's own a., de son plein gré. **ac'cordance,** *s.* accord *m;* in a. with your instructions, conformément à vos ordres. **ac'cording,** *adv.* 1. *conj.phr.* a. as, selon que. 2. *prep.phr.* a. to, selon, d'après; a. to age, par rang d'âge. **-ly,** *adv.* en conséquence, donc.

accordion [ə'kɔːdiən], *s.* accordéon *m.*

accost [ə'kɔst], *v.tr.* accoster, aborder.

account [ə'kaunt]. I. *s.* 1. *(a)* compte *m,* note *f;* a sum on a., un acompte; bank a., compte en banque; the accounts *(of a firm),* la comptabilité; *(b)* to keep the accounts, tenir les livres; *(b)* expense a.; *(c)* to turn to a., tirer parti de; *(d)* to call s.o. to a., demander une explication à qn. 2. *(a)* to take sth. into a., tenir compte de qch.; *(b)* on a. of (s.o., sth.), à cause de (qn, qch.); to no a., dans aucun cas. 3. récit *m;* by all accounts, au dire de tout le monde; **ac'count book,** *s.* livre *m* de comptes. II. *v.tr.* & *ind.tr.* to a. for (sth.), justifier (qch.); être responsable (d'une perte, etc.); I can't a. for it, je ne me l'explique pas. **ac'countable,** *a.* responsable (for, de; to, envers). **ac'countancy,** *s.* comptabilité *f.* **ac'counting,** *s.* comptabilité *f.* **ac'countant,** *s.* comptable *m;* chartered a. = expert *m* comptable.

accredit [ə'kredit], *v.tr.* accréditer.

accrue [ə'kruː], *v.i.* 1. provenir, dériver. 2. Fin: (of *interest)* s'accumuler.

accumulate [ə'kjuːmjuleit]. 1. *v.tr.* accumuler. 2. *v.i.* s'accumuler. **accumu'lation,** *s.* accumulation *f.* **ac'cumulator,** *s. El:* accumulateur *m, F:* accu *m.*

accurate ['ækjurit], *a.* exact, juste, précis. **-ly,** *adv.* exactement, avec précision. **'accuracy,** *s.* exactitude *f.*

accuse [ə'kjuːz], *v.tr.* accuser. **accu'sation,** *s.* accusation *f.* **ac'cused,** *s. Jur:* the a., l'inculpé(e).

accustom [ə'kʌstəm], *v.tr.* accoutumer, habituer. **a'ccustomed,** *a.* to be a. to sth., to doing sth., être accoutumé à qch., être habitué à faire qch.; to get a. to sth., to doing sth., s'habituer à qch., à faire qch.

ace [eis], *s.* 1. *(at cards, etc.)* as *m.* 2. *Av: etc:* as *m;* a: driver, as du volant.

acetate ['æsiteit], *s. Ch:* acétate *m;* cellulose a., acétocellulose *f.*

acetic [ə'siːtik], *a. Ch:* acétique.

acetylene [ə'setiliːn], s. acétylène m.

ache [eik]. I. s. mal m, douleur f. II. v.i. my head, back, aches, j'ai mal à la tête, au dos.

achieve [ə'tʃiːv], v.tr. 1. accomplir; réaliser. 2. atteindre (un but). a'chievement, s. 1. accomplissement m, réalisation f. 2. exploit m, chose f accomplie.

acid ['æsid]. 1. a. (a) acide; (b) aigre. 2. s. acide m. a'cidity, s. acidité f.

acknowledge [ək'nɔlidʒ], v.tr. 1. reconnaître, avouer (qch.). 2. répondre à (un salut); accuser réception d'(une lettre). ac'knowledge(e)ment, s. reconnaissance f; aveu m (d'une faute); accusé m de réception d'(une lettre).

acorn ['eikɔːn], s. gland m.

acoustic [ə'kuːstik]. 1. a. acoustique. 2. s.pl. acoustics, acoustique f.

acquaint [ə'kweint], v.tr. to be acquainted with s.o., connaître qn. ac'quaintance s. connaissance f.

acquiesce [ækwi'es], v.i. acquiescer (in, à); donner son assentiment (in, à). acqui'escence, s. assentiment m.

acquire [ə'kwaiər], v.tr. acquérir; to a. a habit, prendre une habitude. acquisition [ækwi'ziʃ(ə)n], s. acquisition f. ac'quisitive, a. âpre au gain.

‡acquit [ə'kwit], v.tr. acquitter. -'quittal, s. acquittement m; accomplissement m (d'un devoir).

acrid ['ækrid], a. âcre. -ly, adv. avec âcreté. a'cridity, s. âcreté f.

acrimonious [ækri'mouniəs], a. acrimonieux. -ly, adv. avec acrimonie. acrobat ['ækrobæt], s. acrobate mf. acro'batic, a. acrobatique.

across [ə'krɔs], adv. & prep. en travers (de). 1. (a) to walk a., traverser; to run a., traverser en courant; (b) to come a. s.o., rencontrer qn. 2. (a) the distance a., la distance en largeur; (b) de l'autre côté de (la rue).

act [ækt]. I. s. 1. acte m; a. of parliament, loi f. 2. action f; to catch s.o. in the a., prendre qn sur le fait. II. v. 1. v.tr. jouer (une pièce); remplir (un rôle); faire l'imbécile. 2. v.i. (a) agir; to a. for the best, faire pour le mieux; to a. for s.o., agir au nom de qn; to a. as secretary to s.o., servir de secrétaire à qn; (b) Th: Cin: jouer. 'acting. I. a. suppléant; intérimaire; provisoire. II. s. jeu m (d'un acteur); he likes a., il aime faire du théâtre; it's only a.! c'est de la comédie. 'action, s. 1. action f; to take a., agir; out of a., détraqué; hors de service. 2. Jur: a. at law, procès m. 3. Mil: combat m, engagement m; killed in a., tué à l'ennemi. 'actionable, a. Jur: poursuivable.

active ['æktiv], a. 1. actif; agile, alerte. 2. Mil: on a. service, en campagne. ac'tivity, s. activité f.

actor ['æktər], s. acteur m.

actress ['æktris], s. actrice f.

actual ['æktju(ə)l], a. 1. réel, véritable. 2. actuel, présent. -ally, adv. réellement, véritablement; he a. said . . ., il est allé (même) jusqu'à dire.

acute [ə'kjuːt], a. 1. (angle, accent) aigu. 2. (of pain) aigu, intense. 3. (of hearing) fin. a'cute-angled, a. (triangle) acutangle. a'cuteness, s. intensité f (d'une douleur); finesse f (de l'ouïe); acuité f (de la vision); perspicacité f (de l'esprit).

ad [æd], s. F: (in newspaper) annonce f.

adapt [ə'dæpt], v.tr. adapter, ajuster. adapta'bility, s. faculté f d'adaptation. a'daptable, a. adaptable, ajustable. adap'tation, s. adaptation f. a'dapter, s. 1. adapteur m. 2. El: raccord m (de lampe); Rec: centreur m (de tourne-disques).

add [æd], v.tr. 1. ajouter (to, à). 2. Mth: additionner, totaliser. 'adding machine, s. machine f à calculer.

adder ['ædər], s. vipère f.

addict ['ædikt], s. drug a., toxicomane mf; F: Sp: etc: fanatique mf. a'diction, s. manie f (pathologique); drug a., toxicomanie f.

addition [ə'diʃ(ə)n], s. addition f; in a., en outre, de plus. a'dditional, a. supplémentaire, additif. 'additive, s. additif m.

addled ['æd(ə)ld], a. (œuf) pourri; F: (cerveau) troublé, brouillé.

address [ə'dres]. I. s. 1. adresse f; a. book, carnet d'adresses. 2. discours m. II. v.tr. 1. mettre, écrire l'adresse (sur une lettre). 2. parler, s'adresser (à qn, à un auditoire). 3. (at golf) viser (la balle). addres'see, s. destinataire mf. ad'dressograph, s. R.t.m: machine f à imprimer les adresses.

adenoids ['ædinɔidz], s.pl. Med: végétations f (adénoïdes).

adept [ə'dept], a. [ə'dept] expert, habile. 2. s. ['ædept], expert m.

adequate ['ædikwət], a. suffisant. -ly, adv. suffisamment.

adhere [əd'hiər], v.i. adhérer. ad'herence, s. 1. (of thing) adhérence f (to, à). 2. (of pers.) attachement m (to, à). ad'herent, a. & s. adhérent, -ente.

adhesion [əd'hiːʒ(ə)n], s. 1. adhésion f (to, à). 2. Med: adhérence f. ad'hesive, a. & s. adhésif (m).

adjacent [ə'dʒeis(ə)nt], a. adjacent, attenant.

adjective ['ædʒiktiv], s. adjectif m. adjec'tival, a. adjectif.

adjoining [ə'dʒɔiniŋ], a. contigu, -uë; avoisinant.

adjourn [ə'dʒəːn], v.tr. & i. ajourner, différer, remettre (qch.); (of meeting) s'ajourner. a'djournment, s. ajournement m; suspension f; remise f (d'une affaire).

adjudicate [ə'dʒu:dikeit], *v.tr. & i.* juger, décider (une affaire); décerner (un prix). **adjudi'cation**, *s.* jugement *m*, décision *f*. a'**djudicator**, *s.* arbitre *m*; (*in competitions*) membre *m* du jury.

adjunct [ˈædʒʌŋkt], *s.* accessoire *m*.

adjust [əˈdʒʌst], *v.tr.* (a) arranger; ajuster; to a. oneself, s'adapter; (b) régler (un instrument). a'**djustable**, *a.* ajustable; réglable. a'**djustment**, *s.* ajustement *m*; réglage *m*; adaptation *f*.

ad lib [æd'lib], *adv.phr.* à volonté; à discrétion.

administer [ədˈministər], administrer (un pays); gérer (des affaires). admini'**stration**, *s.* administration *f*, gestion *f*; *coll.* l'administration, les pouvoirs publics. ad'**ministrative**, *a.* administratif. ad'**ministrator**, *s.* administrateur *m*; gestionnaire *m*.

admiral [ˈædmərəl], *s.* amiral *m*.

admire [ədˈmaiər], *v.tr.* admirer. 'ad**mirable**, *a.* admirable. admi'**ration**, *s.* admiration *f*. ad'**mirer**, *s.* admirateur, -trice.

admission [ədˈmiʃ(ə)n], *s.* (a) admission *f*; a. free, entrée libre; (b) confession *f*; aveu *m*.

‡**admit** [ədˈmit], *v.tr.* (a) admettre laisser, entrer (qn); a. bearer, laisser passer; (b) admettre, reconnaître (qch.). ad'**mittance**, *s.* entrée *f* (to, dans); accès *m* (à qch., auprès de qn); no ad., entrée interdite. ad'**mittedly**, *adv.* de l'aveu général.

ado [əˈdu:], *s. used in:* without (any) more a., sans plus de façons, d'histoires.

adolescence [ædəˈles(ə)ns], *s.* adolescence *f*. ado'**lescent**, *a. & s.* adolescent, -ente.

adopt [əˈdɔpt], *v.tr.* adopter. a'**dopted**, *a.* adopté; (fils) adoptif. a'**doption**, *s.* adoption *f*.

adore [əˈdɔːr], *v.tr.* adorer (qn, qch.). a'**dorable**, *a.* adorable. ado'**ration**, *s.* adoration *f*.

adorn [əˈdɔːn], *v.tr.* orner, embellir, (with, de).

adrift [əˈdrift], *adv.* à la dérive; to cut oneself a. from s.o., rompre avec qn.

adult [ˈædʌlt], *a. & s.* adulte (*mf*).

adulterate [əˈdʌltəreit], *v.tr.* adultérer. adulte'**ration**, *s.* adultération *f*.

adulterer [əˈdʌltərər], *s.* adultère *mf*. a'**dultery**, *s.* adultère *m*.

advance [ədˈvɑːns]. I. *s.* 1. (*a*) marche *f* en avant; *Mil. etc:* a. guard, avant-garde *f*; (*b*) to pay in a., payer d'avance. 2. avancement *m*, progrès *m*. 3. *F:* (*of woman*) to make advances, provoquer, aguicher (un homme). 4. *Fin:* avance (de fonds); *s. on securities*, prêt *m* sur titres; (*at auction sale*) any a.? qui dit mieux? II. *v.* 1. *v.tr.* avancer (qch.); faire progresser (qch.), *Aut:* to a. the ignition, mettre de l'avance à l'allumage. 2. *v.i.* s'avancer

(towards, vers); the work is advancing, le travail fait des progrès. ad'**vanced**, *a.* avancé. ad'**vancement**, *s.* avancement *m*; progrès *m*.

advantage [ədˈvɑːntidʒ], *s.* avantage *m*; to take a. of sth., s.o., profiter de qch.; exploiter qn; to turn sth. to a., tirer parti de qch.; to show sth. off to a., faire valoir qch. advan'**tageous**, *a.* avantageux; profitable. **-ly**, *adv.* avantageusement.

advent [ˈædvənt], *s.* 1. *Ecc:* Avent *m.* 2. arrivée *f*, venue *f*.

adventure [ədˈventʃər], *s.* aventure *f*. ad'**venturer**, *s.* aventurier *m*.

adverb [ˈædvəːb], *s.* adverbe *m*.

†**adversary** [ˈædvəs(ə)ri], *s.* adversaire *mf*.

adverse [ˈædvəːs], *a.* adverse; hostile; défavorable. **-ly**, *adv.* to influence a., exercer une influence défavorable (sur).

advertise [ˈædvətaiz], *v.tr. & i.* faire de la réclame, de la publicité (pour). ad'**vertisement**, *s.* publicité *f*; annonce *f*; (*on wall*) affiche *f*. ad'**vertiser**, *s.* auteur *m* d'une annonce, annonceur *m*. 'ad**vertising**, *s.* publicité *f*; réclame *f*.

advice [ədˈvais], *s.* (*no pl.*) conseil(s) *m(pl)* avis *m*.

advise [ədˈvaiz], *v.tr.* conseiller (qn); recommander (qch.). ad'**visable**, *a.* (démarche) recommandable, indiquée. ad'**visedly**, *adv.* à dessein. ad'**viser**, *s.* conseiller *m*. ad'**visory**, *a.* consultatif.

advocate [ˈædvəkeit], *v.tr.* préconiser, recommander; plaider en faveur de (qch.).

aerial [ˈɛəriəl]. 1. *a.* aérien. 2. *s. Rad:* antenne *f*.

aero [ˈɛərou-], *prefix*, aérien, de l'air; *used in:* 'aero**drome**, *s.* aérodrome *m*. 'aero**dynamics**, *s.pl.* aérodynamique *f*. 'aero **engine**, *s.* moteur *m* d'avion. 'aero**foil**, *s. Av:* plan *m* à profil d'aile; voilure *f*. 'aero**naut**, *s.* aéronaute *m*. 'aero**nautics**, *s.pl.* aéronautique *f*. 'aero**plane**, *s.* avion *m*. 'aero**sol**, *m.* aérosol *m.* 'aero**train**, *s.* aérotrain *m*.

affable [ˈæfəbl], *a.* affable, courtois. **-bly**, *adv.* avec affabilité. affa'**bility**, *s.* affabilité *f*, courtoisie *f*.

affect[1] [əˈfekt], *v.tr.* affecter (une manière); simuler (la stupidité, etc.). af'**fected**, *a.* maniéré. **-ly**, *adv.* avec affectation. affec'**tation**, *s.*, af'**fectedness**, *s.* affectation *f*.

affect[2], *v.tr.* atteindre, toucher; attaquer. af'**fected**, *a.* (*a*) atteint (d'une maladie); (*b*) ému, touché. af'**fection**, *s.* affection *f*, attachement *m*. af'**fectionate**, *a.* affectueux. **-ly**, *adv.* affectueusement.

affidavit [æfiˈdeivit], *s.* déclaration *f* sous serment.

†**affinity** [əˈfiniti], *s.* affinité *f*.

affirm [ə'fə:m], v.tr. affirmer, soutenir. affir'mation, s. affirmation f, assertion f. a'ffirmative. I. a. affirmatif. 2. s. the answer is in the a., la réponse est oui.

afflict [ə'flikt], v.tr. affliger; tourmenter. a'ffliction, s. affliction f; calamité f.

affluence ['æfluəns], s. abondance f, richesse f. 'affluent, a. riche.

afford [ə'fɔ:d], v.tr. (usu. with 'can') (a) avoir les moyens, être en mesure (de faire qch.); (b) I can a. to wait, je peux attendre.

afforestation [əfɔris'teiʃ(ə)n], s. boisement m, afforestation f.

afloat [ə'flout], adv. & pred.a. à flot; sur l'eau; (of pers.) to keep a., surnager.

afoot [ə'fut], adv. a plan is a. to ..., on envisage un projet pour ...; there's something a., il se prépare quelque chose.

afraid [ə'freid], pred.a. pris de peur; to be a., avoir peur; craindre.

afresh [ə'freʃ], adv. de nouveau, à nouveau.

African ['æfrikən], a. & s. africain, -aine.

Africanization [æfrikənai'zeiʃ(ə)n], s. africanisation f.

Afro-Asian [æfrou'eiʃn], a. & s. afro-asiatique (mf).

aft [ɑ:ft], adv. Nau: sur, à, vers, l'arrière.

after ['ɑ:ftər]. I. adv. après; plus tard; you speak first, I shall speak a., parlez d'abord, je parlerai ensuite. II. prep. après. 1. to close the door a. s.o., fermer la porte sur qn; F: the police are a. you, la police est à vos trousses; F: what's he a.? (i) qu'est-ce qu'il a en tête? (ii) qu'est-ce qu'il cherche? 2. (time) on and a. the 15th, à partir du quinze; a. hours, après le travail, les heures de service, la fermeture; the day a., le lendemain; the day a. to-morrow, après-demain; a. all, enfin. 3. a man a. my own heart, un homme qui a les mêmes idées que moi. III. conj. après. 'after-effects, s.pl.; 'aftermath, s. suites fpl, répercussion f (d'un évènement). after'noon, s. après-midi m inv. good a.! bonjour! 'afters, s.pl. Cu: F: dessert m ou fromage m. 'afterthought, s. réflexion f après coup. 'afterwards, adv. après, plus tard, ensuite.

again [ə'gen], adv. 1. (a) de nouveau, encore; don't do it a.! ne recommencez pas!; a. and a., à plusieurs reprises; now and a., de temps en temps; (b) to send sth. back a., renvoyer qch. 2. (a) de plus, d'ailleurs; (b) (then) a., d'autre part.

against [ə'genst], prep. 1. (a) contre; a. one's will, à contre-cœur; a. the rules, contraire aux règlements; leaning against

the wall, appuyé contre le mur; to go a. nature, aller à l'encontre de la nature. 2. to show up a. a background, se détacher sur un fond. 3. as a., comparé à.

agate ['ægət], s. agate f.

age [eidʒ]. I. s. 1. âge m; (a) what a. are you? quel âge avez-vous? to be under a., être mineur; to come of a., atteindre sa majorité; (b) (old) a., vieillesse f, âge, époque f; the Middle Ages, le moyen âge; the atomic a., l'ère atomique. II. v.i. & tr. vieillir. aged, a. 1. [eidʒd] âgé, vieux. 2. [eidʒd] âgé de.

agency ['eidʒənsi], s. 1. through the a. of sth., s.o., par l'action f de qch., par l'intermédiaire m de qn. 2. agence f, bureau m; travel a., agence de voyages.

agent ['eidʒənt], s. agent m.

agglomeration [əglomə'reiʃ(ə)n], s. agglomération f.

aggravate ['ægrəveit], v.tr. 1. aggraver (une faute, etc.). 2. F: agacer, exaspérer (qn). 'aggravating, a. F: exaspérant, agaçant. aggra'vation, s. F: agacement m, exaspération f.

aggregate ['ægrigeit], s. ensemble m, total m.

aggression [ə'greʃ(ə)n], s. agression f. ag'gressive, a. agressif. -ly, adv. d'une manière, d'un ton, agressif.

aghast [ə'gɑ:st], pred.a. consterné (at, de); sidéré.

aggrieved [ə'gri:vd], a. chagriné, blessé.

agile ['ædʒail], a. agile, leste. a'gility, s. agilité f.

agitate ['ædʒiteit], v.tr. agiter, remuer (qch.); abs. to a. for sth., faire de l'agitation en faveur de qch. 'agitated, a. agité, ému, troublé. agi'tation, s. agitation f. 'agitator, s. agitateur m.

ago [ə'gou], adv. ten years, a long time, a., il y a dix ans, longtemps; how long a. is it since ...? combien de temps y a-t-il que ...?

agonizing ['ægənaiziŋ], a. (douleur) atroce; (spectacle) navrant; (cri) déchirant.

†agony ['ægəni], s. angoisse f.

agree [ə'gri:], v.i. & tr. 1. consentir; admettre; to a. to do sth., accepter de faire qch. 2. (a) être d'accord; tomber d'accord; I don't a. with this theory, je n'accepte pas cette théorie. 3. (a) Gram: s'accorder; (b) (of climate, etc.) to a. with s.o., convenir à qn; (of food) not to a. with s.o., ne pas réussir à qn. a'greeable, a. agréable; (of pers.) aimable, -bly, adv. agréablement. a'greement, s. 1. convention f, contrat m. 2. to be in a. with s.o., être d'accord avec qn. 3. Gram: accord m.

agriculture ['ægrikʌltʃər], s. agriculture f. agri'cultural, a. agricole.

aground [ə'graund], adv. Nau: échoué; au sec; to run a., échouer, s'échouer.

ahead [ə'hed], adv. En avant de qn; to be two hours a. of s.o., en avant de qn; to be two hours a. of s.o., avoir deux heures d'avance sur qn; he's going a., il fait du progrès; to look a., penser à l'avenir; there's fog a., il y a du brouillard plus loin; Nau: full speed a.! en avant toute!

aid [eid]. I. v.tr. aider, assister. II. s. (a) aide f, assistance f, appui m; in a. of, au profit de; collection in a. of . . ., quête f en faveur de . . .; (b) hearing a., appareil auditif; audio-visual aids, aides audiovisuelles.

aide-de-camp ['eid(d)ə'kɔŋ], s. officier m d'ordonnance.

ailment ['eilmənt], s. mal m; maladie (légère). 'ailing, a. souffrant; malade; he's always a., il a une petite santé.

aim [eim]. I. v. 1. v.tr. to a. a stone, a blow, at s.o., lancer une pierre, porter un coup, à qn; to a. a gun at s.o., viser qn; measure aimed against our industry, mesure dirigée contre notre industrie. 2. v.ind.tr. what are you aiming at? quel but poursuivez vous? II. s. 1. to miss one's a., manquer son but; to take a. at, viser. 2. but, objet m. aimless, a. sans but, sans objet. -ly, adv. sans but.

air [eər]. I. v.tr. 1. aérer (une pièce); chauffer (le linge). 2. to a. grievances, exposer des griefs. 2. to a. one's knowledge, faire parade de son savoir. 'airing, s. ventilation f (d'une pièce); a cupboard, chauffe-linge m. II. s. 1. (a) air m; to travel by a., voyager par avion; there's something in the a., il se prépare quelque chose; (b) attrib. a. raid, attaque aérienne; the Fleet A. Arm = l'Aéronautique navale; the Royal A. Force = l'Armée de l'air; (c) Rad: to put on the a., parler à la radio. 2. Mus: air. 3. air, apparence f; to put on airs, faire l'important. 'airbase, s. base f d'aviation. 'airborne, a. aéroporté. 'air conditioning, s. climatisation f, conditionnement m (de l'air). 'air-cooled, a. refroidi par air; (moteur) à refroidissement par air, †aircraftman, s. soldat m (de l'Armée de l'air). 'aircrew, s. équipage m d'avion. 'airdrome, s. U.S: aérodrome m. 'air-duct, s. 1. canal aérien (d'un poisson). 2. Ind: porte-vent m. 'airfield, s. champ m d'aviation. 'air hostess, s. Av: hôtesse f de l'air. 'airless, a. 1. (of room) renfermé. 2. (of weather) sans vent. 'air letter, s. aérogramme m. 'airlift, s. pont m aérien. 'airline, s. service m de transports aériens. 'airliner, s. avion m de ligne. 'airmail 1. s. service postal aérien; by a., par avion. 2. v.tr. envoyer par avion. 'airman, s. aviateur m. 'Air Marshal, s. Général

m de corps d'armée aérien. 'air mechanic, s. mécanicien m d'avion. 'airplane, s. U.S: avion m. 'air pocket, s. Av: trou m d'air. 'airport, s. aéroport m. 'air-sickness, s. mal m de l'air, d'avion. 'air sock, s. Av: manche f à air. 'airstrip, s. Av: terrain m d'atterrissage. 'air terminal, s. aérogare f. 'airtight, a. étanche (à l'air). 'air-to-air, a. (engin) air-air. 'air-to-ground, a. (engin) air-sol. 'airway, s. (a) aéroroute f. (b) radio-alignement m. 'airwoman, s. aviatrice f. 'airworthy, a. Av: muni d'un certificat de navigabilité. 'airy, a. 1. bien aéré; ouvert à l'air. 2. (of promise) vain; en l'air. -ily, adv. légèrement.

aisle [ail], s. nef latérale (d'une église); passage m (entre bancs).

ajar [ə'dʒɑːr], adv. & pred.a. (of door) entrebâillé.

alabaster [ælə'bɑːstər], s. albâtre m.

alacrity [ə'lækriti], s. empressement m, alacrité f.

alarm [ə'lɑːm]. I. v.tr. (a) alarmer; (b) alerter. II. s. 1. alarme f, alerte f. 2. avertisseur m; a. (clock), réveille-matin m inv. 'alarmist, s. alarmiste mf. a'larming, a. alarmant.

alas [ə'læs], int. hélas!

albatross ['ælbətrɔs], s. albatros m.

†albino [æl'biːnou], s. albinos mf.

album ['ælbəm], s. album m.

alcohol ['ælkəhɔl], s. alcool m. alco'holic, a. & s. alcoolique (mf).

alcove ['ælkouv], s. 1. alcôve f. 2. niche f.

alder ['ɔːldər], s. aune m.

†alderman ['ɔːldəmən], s. = conseiller m municipal.

ale [eil], s. bière anglaise (légère); pale a., bière blonde.

Alec(k) ['ælik]. Pr.n. F: a smart A., un combinard.

alert [ə'ləːt]. 1. a. (a) alerte, vigilant; (b) actif, vif. 2. s. alerte f; to be on the a., être sur le qui-vive. -ly, adv. d'une manière alerte. a'lertness, s. 1. vigilance f; promptitude f. 2. vivacité f.

algebra ['ældʒibrə], s. algèbre f.

Algerian [æl'dʒiəriən], a. & s. Algérien, -ienne.

alias ['eiliæs]. 1. adv. autrement dit. 2. s. nom m d'emprunt.

alibi ['ælibai], s. alibi m.

alien ['eiliən], a. & s. étranger, -ère.

alienate ['eiliəneit], v.tr. aliéner (des biens); éloigner (qn).

alight¹ [ə'lait], v.i. 1. Adm: descendre (d'un train, etc.). 2. (of bird) se poser; Av: atterrir, (on sea) amerrir.

alight² [ə'lait], pred.a. allumé; en feu.

alignment [ə'lainmənt], s. alignement m.

alike [ə'laik]. 1. pred. a. semblable, pareil; you are all a.! vous vous ressemblez tous! 2. adv. pareillement; de même.

alimentary [æli'mentəri], *a.* alimentaire; *Anat:* a. canal, tube digestif.

alimony ['æliməni], *s.* pension *f* alimentaire.

alive [ə'laiv], *a.* 1. (*a*) vivant, en vie; dead or a., mort ou vif; to be buried a., être enterré vif; to keep the conversation a., entretenir la conversation. 2. to be a. to the danger, se rendre compte du danger. 3. he's very much a., (i) il est très remuant; (ii) il a l'esprit très éveillé. 4. the street was a. with people, la rue fourmillait de monde.

alkali ['ælkəlai], *s.* alcali *m*.

alkaline ['ælkəlain], *a.* alcalin.

all [ɔːl]. I. *a., pron. & adv.* 1. tout; a. men, tous les hommes; a. the others, tous les autres; a. his life, toute sa vie; is that a. the luggage you're taking? c'est tout ce que vous emportez de bagages? you're not as ill as a. that, vous n'êtes pas si malade que ça; a. of us, nous tous; *Sp:* five a., cinq à cinq; (*at tennis*) fifteen a., quinze à quinze; (*that*) I did, tout ce que j'ai fait; is that a.? (i) est-ce tout? (ii) *iron:* is that a.? 2. once for a., une fois pour toutes; for a. I know, autant que je sache; most of a., surtout; not at a., pas du tout; taking it a. in a., à tout prendre; he thinks he's a. in a. to the business, il s'imagine indispensable; *P:* damn a., que dalle. 3. *adv.* tout; she's a. ears, elle est tout oreilles; his hands are a. paint, ses mains sont couvertes de peinture; a. at once, (i) (*suddenly*) tout à coup; (ii) (*at one time*) tout d'un coup; *F:* he's not a. there, il est un peu simple d'esprit. II. *s.* tout *m*, totalité *f*; to stake one's a., risquer le tout pour le tout. **'all 'clear**, *s.* (signal *m* de) fin *f* d'alerte.

allege [ə'ledʒ], *v.tr.* alléguer, prétendre (that, que + *ind.*). **alle'gation**, *s.* allégation *f*. **al'leged**, *a.* prétendu.

allegiance [ə'liːdʒ(ə)ns], *s.* fidélité *f* (to, à).

†**allergy** ['ælədʒi], *s. Med:* allergie *f*. **al'lergic**, *a.* allergique; I'm a. to fish, le poisson ne me réussit pas.

alleviate [ə'liːvieit], *v.tr.* alléger, soulager. **allevi'ation**, *s.* soulagement *m*.

†**alley** ['æli], *s.* allée *f*; ruelle *f*, passage *m*.

alliance [ə'laiəns], *s.* alliance *f*; to enter into an a., s'allier.

allied ['ælaid], *a.* allié.

alligator ['æligeitər], *s.* alligator *m*.

all-'in, *a. El:* a.-in agreement, forfait mixte; *Ins:* a.-i. policy, police tous risques; *F:* to feel a.-i., être à plat. **all-'night**, *a.* a.-n. service, permanence de nuit; *Mil:* a.-n. pass, permission de la nuit.

allocate ['æləkeit], *v.tr.* allouer, assigner. **allo'cation**, *s.* allocation *f*.

‡**allot** [ə'lɔt], *v.tr.* 1. attribuer, assigner (qch. à qn). 2. répartir, distribuer.

al'lotment, *s.* 1. attribution *f*; distribution *f*; lotissement *m*. 2. (*a*) portion *f*, lot *m*; (*b*) *pl.* jardins ouvriers.

'all-'out, *a.* (effort) maximum.

allow [ə'lau], *v.tr.* 1. admettre. 2. permettre, souffrir; to a. s.o. to do sth., permettre à qn de faire qch. 3. (*a*) accorder (qch.) à (qn); (*b*) *Ind:tr.* to a. for sth., tenir compte de qch. **a'llowance**, *s.* 1. pension *f* alimentaire; rente *f*; argent *m* de poche (d'un enfant); family allowances, allocations familiales. 2. *Com:* remise *f*, rabais *m*. 3. to make a. for sth., tenir compte de qch.

alloy ['æloi], *s.* alliage *m*.

'all-'purpose, *a.* universel; à tout faire. **'all-'round**, *a.* (homme) universel; (amélioration) totale. **'all-time**, *a.* a.-t. high, low, record *m* le plus élevé, record de médiocrité.

allude [ə'l(j)uːd], *v.ind.tr.* faire allusion (to, à).

allure [ə'l(j)uər], *v.tr.* attirer, séduire. **al'luring**, *a.* attrayant, séduisant.

allusion [ə'l(j)uːʒ(ə)n], *s.* allusion *f*.

ally. I. †*s.* ['ælai] allié, -iée. II. *v.i.* [ə'lai] s'allier (with, avec).

almanac ['ɔːlmənæk], *s.* almanach *m*.

almighty [ɔːl'maiti], *a.* tout-puissant; *s.* the A., le Tout-Puissant; *F:* an a. din, un bruit de tous les diables.

almond ['aːmənd], *s.* 1. amande *f*; burnt a., praline *f*. 2. a. (tree), amandier *m*.

almoner ['aːmənər], *s.* aumônier *f*.

almost ['ɔːlmoust], *adv.* presque; à peu près; he a. fell, il a failli tomber.

alms [aːmz], *s.sg. or pl.* aumône *f*.

alone [ə'loun], *pred.a.* 1. seul; I want to speak to you a., je voudrais vous parler seul à seul. 2. to leave s.o., sth., a., laisser qn, qch., tranquille; ne pas se mêler de qch.

along [ə'lɔŋ]. 1. *prep.* le long de; to walk along the riverside, longer la rivière. 2. *adv.* to move a., avancer; come a.! venez donc! I knew that all a., je le savais dès le commencement. **a'longside**, *adv. & prep.* le long de; *Nau:* to come a., aborder à quai.

aloof [ə'luːf], *adv. & pred.a.*, à l'écart, éloigné. **a'loofness**, *s.* réserve *f*.

aloud [ə'laud], *adv.* à haute voix; (tout) haut.

alphabet ['ælfəbet], *s.* alphabet *m*. **alpha'betical**, *a.* alphabétique. **-ally**, *adv.* par ordre alphabétique.

alpine ['ælpain], *a.* (club) alpin; (paysage) alpestre; (plantes) alpines.

already [ɔːl'redi], *adv.* déjà.

Alsatian [æl'seiʃ(ə)n]. 1. *a. & s. Geog:* Alsacien, -ienne. 2. (*dog*) berger allemand.

also ['ɔːlsou], *adv.* aussi; également.

altar ['ɔːltər], *a.* autel *m*.

alter ['ɔːltər]. 1. *v.tr.* modifier; changer de (plans); fausser (les faits). 2. *v.i.* he has greatly altered, il a bien changé. alter'ation, *s.* changement *m.*, modification *f.*

alternate. I. *a.* [ɔːl'təːnit]. alternatif; alterné. -ly, *adv.* alternativement; tour à tour. II. *v.i.* ['ɔːltəneit] alterner; se succéder. 'alternating, *a.* alternant; alterné; El: (courant) alternatif.

alternative [ɔːl'təːnətiv]. 1. *a.* alternatif. 2. *s.* alternative *f.*; choix *m.* (to, avec l'alternative de. . . .

although [ɔːl'ðou], *conj.* quoique, bien que (+ *sub.*)

altitude [ˈæltitjuːd], *s.* altitude *f.*, élévation *f.*

altogether [ɔːltəˈgeðər], *adv.* (a) (wholly) entièrement, tout à fait; (b) (on the whole) somme toute; (c) how much a.? combien en tout?

aluminium [æljuˈminjəm], *s. U.S:* aluminum [əˈluːminəm], *s.* aluminium *m.*

always [ˈɔːlweiz], *adv.* toujours.

a.m. [ˈeiˈem]. avant midi; du matin.

amalgamate [əˈmælgəmeit]. 1. *v.tr.* amalgamer. 2. *v.i.* fusionner; s'amalgamer. amalgam'ation, *s.* 1. amalgamation *f.* 2. fusion *f.*

amateur [ˈæmətəːr], *s.* amateur *m.*

amaze [əˈmeiz], *v.tr.* confondre, stupéfier. a'mazed, a confondu, stupéfait. a'mazement, *s.* stupéfaction *f.* a'mazing, *a.* stupéfiant; renversant. -ly, *adv.* étonnamment.

ambassador [æmˈbæsədər], *s.* ambassadeur *m.*; (woman) a., ambassadrice *f.*

amber [ˈæmbər], *s.* ambre *m.*; a. light, feu jaune.

ambiguous [æmˈbigjuəs], *a.* 1. ambigu; équivoque. 2. incertain. -ly, *adv.* avec ambiguïté. ambiguity, *s.* ambiguïté *f.*

ambition [æmˈbiʃ(ə)n], *s.* ambition *f.* am'bitious, *a.* ambitieux. -ly, *adv.* ambitieusement.

amble [ˈæmbl], *v.i.* to a. (along), marcher d'un pas tranquille.

ambulance [ˈæmbjuləns], *s.* ambulance *f.*

ambush [ˈæmbuʃ]. I. *s.* embuscade *f*; in a., à l'affût. II. *v.tr.* attirer (qn) dans un piège.

ameliorate [əˈmiːliəreit], *v.tr.* améliorer. amelior'ation, *s.* amélioration *f.*

amen [ˈɑːˈmen], *int.* amen.

amenable [əˈmiːnəbl], *a.* soumis; docile; a. to reason, raisonnable.

amend [əˈmend]. 1. *v.tr.* amender; corriger. 2. *v.i.* s'amender, se corriger. a'mendment, *s.* (a) modification *f*; rectification *f*; (b) Pol: amendement *m.* a'mends, *s.pl.* to make a. for an injury, réparer un tort.

†**amenity** [əˈmiːniti], *s.* 1. aménité *f.* 2. *pl.* the amenities of life, les agréments *m* de l'existence.

American [əˈmerikən], *a.* & *s.* américain, -aine.

amethyst [ˈæmiθist], *s.* améthyste *f.*

amiable [ˈeimjəbl], *a.* aimable (to, envers). -bly, *adv.* aimablement. amia'bility, *s.* amabilité *f.*

amicable [ˈæmikəbl], *a.* amical. -bly, *adv.* amicalement.

amiss [əˈmis], *adv.* & *pred.a.* 1. mal; to take sth. a., prendre qch. en mauvaise part. 2. that doesn't come a., cela n'arrive pas mal à propos.

ammonia [əˈmounjə], *s.* ammoniaque *f.*

ammunition [æmjuˈniʃ(ə)n], *s.* munitions *fpl.*

amnesty [ˈæmnisti], *s.* amnistie *f.*

among [əˈmʌŋ], *prep.* parmi, entre; au milieu de.

amorous [ˈæmərəs], *a.* amoureux.

amount [əˈmaunt]. I. *s.* 1. somme *f*, montant *m.*, total *m.* 2. quantité *f.* II. *v.i.* (of money) s'élever, (se) monter (to, à). 2. that amounts to the same thing, cela revient au même; *F:* he'll never a. to much, il ne fera jamais grand-chose.

amphibian [æmˈfibiən], *s.* 1. *Z:* amphibie *m.* 2. *Mil:* (véhicule) amphibie. am'phibious, *a.* amphibie.

amphitheatre [ˈæmfiˈθiətər], *s.* amphithéâtre *m.*

ample [ˈæmpl], *a.* ample. -ply, *adv.* amplement.

amplify [ˈæmplifai], *v.tr.* amplifier. 'amplifier, *s.* amplificateur *m.*

amputate [ˈæmpjuteit], *v.tr.* amputer. ampu'tation, *s.* amputation *f.*

amulet [ˈæmjulit], *s.* amulette *f.*

amuse [əˈmjuːz], *v.tr.* amuser, divertir. a'musement, *s.* amusement *m.*, divertissement *m*; a park, parc m d'attractions. a'musing, *a.* amusant, divertissant.

an. *See* a².

anaemia [əˈniːmiə], *s.* anémie *f.* a'naemic, *a.* anémique.

anaesthetic [ænisˈθetik], *a.* & *s.* anesthésique (*m*). a'naesthetist, *s.* anesthésiste *m.*

analogous [əˈnæləgəs], *a.* analogue. 'analogy, *s.* analogie *f.*

analyse [ˈænəlaiz], *v.tr.* analyser. analysis [əˈnælisis], *s.* analyse *f.* 'analyst, *s.* analyste *m.* ana'lytic, *a.* analytique.

anarchy [ˈænəki], *s.* anarchie *f.* 'anarchist, *s.* anarchiste *m.*

anathema [əˈnæθəmə], *s.* anathème *m.*

anatomy [əˈnætəmi], *s.* anatomie *f.* ana'tomical, *a.* anatomique.

ancestor [ˈænsestər], *s.* ancêtre *m.* an-'cestral, *a.* héréditaire; his a. castle, le château de ses ancêtres. 'ancestry, *s.* race *f*; ascendance *f*; coll. ancêtres *mpl.*; aïeux *mpl.*

anchor ['æŋkər]. I. s. ancre f. II. v. 1.
v.tr. ancrer (un navire). 2. v.i. jeter
l'ancre; mouiller. 'anchorage, s.
'anchoring, s. ancrage m, mouillage m.
'anchored, a. ancré, mouillé.

anchovy [æn'tʃovi, æn'tʃouvi], s. anchois
m.

ancient ['ein(ə)nt], a. ancien; antique.
s. the ancients, les anciens.

and [ænd, ənd], conj. et. 1. (a) to walk
two and two, marcher deux à deux; (b)
better and better, de mieux en mieux.
2. wait and see, attendez voir; try and
help me, tâchez de m'aider.

anecdote ['ænikdout], s. anecdote f.

anemone [ə'nemǝni], s. anémone f.

angel ['eindʒǝl], s. ange m. F: you're an
a., tu es chic, tu es un amour. an'gelic,
a. angélique; F: be a., sois chic.

anger ['æŋgǝr], s. colère f; emportement
m.

angle¹ ['æŋgl], s. (a) angle m; (b) coin m.

angle², v.i. pêcher à la ligne; to a. for
compliments, quêter des compliments. 'angler, s. pêcheur m à la ligne.
'angling, s. pêche f à la ligne.

Anglican ['æŋglikən], a. & s. Ecc:
anglican, -ane.

anglicism ['æŋglisizm], s. anglicisme m.

Anglo-Saxon ['æŋglou'sæks(ə)n], a. & s.
anglo-saxon, -onne.

angora [æŋ'gɔːrə], s. angora (m) inv.

angry ['æŋgri], a. fâché, irrité (with s.o.,
about sth., contre qn, de qch.); to get
a., se fâcher; to make s.o. a., fâcher,
exaspérer, qn. -ily, adv. avec colère,
avec colère.

anguish ['æŋgwiʃ], s. angoisse f; douleur f.

angular ['æŋgjulǝr], a. anguleux (of pers.)
décharné.

animal ['ænim(ə)l], a. & s. animal (m).

animate ['ænimeit], v.tr. (a) animer (b)
encourager, stimuler. 'animated, a.
animé; Cin: a. cartoons, dessins
animés. ani'mation, s. animation f;
vivacité f.

animosity ['æni'mositi], s. animosité f.

anion ['ænaiǝn], s. Ph: anion m.

aniseed ['ænisiːd], s. (graine f d')anis m.

ankle ['æŋkl], s. cheville f.

annex ['ɔ'neks], v.tr. annexer. annex'a-
tion, s. annexion f. 'annexe, s. annexe
f (d'un hôtel, etc.).

annihilate [ə'naiəleit], v.tr. anéantir;
supprimer. annihil'ation, s. anéan-
tissement m; annihilation f.

anniversary [æni'vǝːs(ǝ)ri], s. anniversaire m.

annotate ['ænǝteit], v.tr. annoter. anno-
'tation, s. annotation f.

announce [ə'nauns], v.tr. annoncer.
an'nouncement, s. annonce f. an-
'nouncer, s. Rad: T.V: speaker m,
speakerine f.

annoy [ə'nɔi], v.tr. 1. contrarier. 2.
gêner, ennuyer. an'noyance, s. 1.
chagrin m. 2. désagrément m, ennui

m. an'noyed, a. contrarié, ennuyé.
an'noying, a. contrariant, ennuyeux,
ennuyant.

annual ['ænju(ǝ)l]. 1. a. annuel. 2. s. (a)
plante annuelle; (b) annuaire m. -ally,
adv. tous les ans.

†annuity [ə'njuiti], s. rente (annuelle);
life a., rente viagère.

‡annul [ə'nʌl], v.tr. annuler; abroger
(une loi); dissoudre (un mariage).
an'nulment, s. annulation f; dissolution f (d'un mariage).

anode ['ænoud], s. El: anode f.

anoint [ə'nɔint], v.tr. oindre; sacrer.

†anomaly [ə'nɔmǝli], s. anomalie f.
a'nomalous, a. anormal.

anonymous [ə'nɔniməs], a. anonyme.
-ly, adv. anonymement. anon'ymity, s.
anonymat m.

anorak ['ænəræk], s. anorak m.

another [ə'nʌðǝr], a. & pron. 1. (additional) encore (un(e)); a. cup of tea,
encore une tasse de thé; without a.
word, sans un mot de plus. 2.
(different) un(e) autre; that's a.
matter, c'est tout autre chose; a.
dress, (i) une autre robe; (ii) une
nouvelle robe; F: tell me a.! va conter
ça ailleurs! 3. (reciprocal) near one a.,
l'un près de l'autre; love one a.,
aimez-vous les uns les autres; to help
one a., s'entr'aider.

answer ['ɑːnsǝr]. I. s. 1. réponse f;
réplique f. 2. solution f. II. v.tr. & i.
répondre; to a. s.o., a letter, répondre
à qn, à une lettre; to a. for s.o., (i)
(= instead of) répondre pour qn; (ii)
se porter garant de qn; to a. back,
répliquer; don't a. back, pas de
répliques; to a. the door, aller ouvrir
(la porte); to a. to a description, répondre à un signalement; to a. the purpose, remplir le but; he has a lot to a.
for, il est responsable de bien des
choses.

ant [ænt], s. fourmi f. 'anthill, s. fourmilière f.

antagonize [æn'tægǝnaiz], v.tr. éveiller
l'antagonisme, l'hostilité (de qn).
an'tagonism, s. antagonisme m, opposition f. an'tagonist, s. antagoniste mf,
adversaire mf. antago'nistic, a. opposé
(to, à), hostile.

antarctic [ænt'ɑːktik], a. antarctique.

antecedent [ænti'siːd(ǝ)nt], s. antécédent
m.

antedate ['ænti'deit], v.tr. antidater (un
document); précéder (un événement).

antelope ['æntiloup], s. antilope f.

antenatal ['ænti'neit(ǝ)l], a. prénatal.

anthem ['ænθǝm], s. 1. motet m. 2.
national a., hymne national.

anthology [æn'θɔlǝdʒi], s. anthologie f.

anthracite ['ænθrǝsait], s. anthracite
m.

anthropology [ænθrǝ'pɔlǝdʒi], s. anthropologie f.

anti- ['ænti], *prefix.* contre. **'anti-aircraft**, *a.* (canon) anti-aérien, contre-avion(s). **'anti-'atomic**, *a.* antiatomique. **antibi'otic**, *a. & s.* antibiotique (*m*).

anticipate [æn'tisipeit], *v.tr.* savourer (un plaisir) d'avance; aller au-devant (des désirs de qn); envisager (une difficulté). **antici'pation**, *s.* anticipation *f*.

antics ['æntiks], *s.pl.* bouffonneries *fpl*, cabrioles *fpl*.

'anti'climax, *s.* retour *m* à l'ordinaire, au terre à terre. **'anti'clockwise**, *a. & adv.* dans le sens inverse des aiguilles d'une montre. **'anticonsti'tutional**, *a.* anticonstitutionnel. **'anti'cyclone**, *s.* anticyclone *m*. **'anti-'dazzle**, *a.* antiaveuglant. **'antidote**, *s.* antidote *m*, contre-poison *m*. **'anti'fading**, *a. Rad: T.V:* antifading *m*. **'anti-G** (suit), *s. Av:* vêtement *m* anti-g. **'anti-'knock**, *a. Aut:* (produit) antidétonant. **'anti-'nuclear**, *a.* antinucléaire.

antipathy [æn'tipəθi], *s.* antipathie *f* (to, pour).

antipodes [æn'tipədi:z], *s.pl. Geog:* the a., les antipodes *m*.

†**antiquary** ['æntikwəri], *s.* étudiant, -ante, amateur *m*, d'antiquités; *anti'quarian*, *a.* ancien; *s.* bookseller, libraire *m* qui vend des vieilles éditions.

antique [æn'ti:k]. 1. *a.* antique; a. furniture, meubles d'époque. 2. *s.* objet *m* antique; a. dealer, antiquaire *m*; a. shop, magasin d'antiquités. **'antiquated**, *a.* vieilli; démodé. **an'tiquity**, *s.* l'antiquité (grecque, etc.).

anti'septic, *a. & s.* antiseptique (*m*). **'anti-'skid**, *a. Aut:* antidérapant. **'anti'social**, *a.* antisocial. **'anti'theft**, *a.* antivol *inv*.

†**antithesis** [æn'tiθisis], *s.* 1. antithèse *f* (to, of, de). 2. opposé *m*, contraire *m* (de).

antler ['æntlər], *s.* andouiller *m*.

anus ['einəs], *s. Anat:* anus *m*.

anvil ['ænvil], *s.* enclume *f*.

anxiety [æŋ'zaiəti], *s.* (*a*) inquiétude *f*; anxiété *f*; (*b*) sollicitude *f*.

anxious ['æŋ(k)ʃəs], *a.* 1. (*a*) inquiet; soucieux; (*b*) inquiétant. 2. désireux; I'm a. that he should come, je tiens beaucoup à ce qu'il vienne. **-ly**, *adv.* 1. avec inquiétude. 2. avec sollicitude. 3. avec impatience.

any ['eni]. I. *a. & pron.* 1. du, de la, des; en; have you a. milk? avez-vous du lait? have you a. (of them)? en avez-vous? if a. of them should see him, si aucun d'entre eux le voyait. 2. not a., ne . . . aucun, nul; I can't find a., je n'en trouve pas. '3. n'importe lequel; quelconque; come a. day, venez n'importe quel jour; a. other man, tout autre (homme); take a. two cards, prenez deux cartes quelconques; at a.

hour of the day, à toute heure de la journée. II. *adv.* to go a. further, je ne peux pas aller plus loin; will you have a. more tea? voulez-vous encore du thé?

anybody, **anyone** ['enibɔdi, 'eniwʌn], *s. & pron.* 1. quelqu'un; personne. 2. not a., ne . . . personne. 3. n'importe qui; tout le monde; le premier venu; quiconque. a. but him, tout autre que lui.

anyhow ['enihau]. 1. *adv.* tant bien que mal. 2. *conj.* en tout cas, de toute façon.

anything ['eniθiŋ], *pron. & s.* 1. quelque chose; rien; if a. should happen, s'il arrivait quelque malheur; is there a. more pleasant? est-il rien de plus agréable? 2. not a. . . ., ne . . . rien; hardly a., presque rien. 3. n'importe quoi; tout; he eats a., il mange de tout; he's a. but mad, il n'est rien moins que fou; *F:* (*intensive*) it's raining like a., il pleut tant qu'il peut.

anyway ['eniwei], *conj.* en tout cas.

anywhere ['eniwɛər], *adv.* 1. n'importe où; quelque part; a. else, partout ailleurs. 2. not a., nulle part.

aorta [ei'ɔːtə], *s. Anat:* aorte *f*.

apart [ə'pɑːt], *adv.* 1. à part; a class a., un genre à part. 2. to come a., se détacher, se défaire; to take a machine a., démonter une machine; you can't tell them a., on ne peut pas les distinguer l'un de l'autre. 3. lines ten centimetres a., lignes espacées de dix centimètres; a. from the fact that . . ., outre que . . .; joking a., plaisanterie à part; sans blague.

apartheid [ə'pɑːteit], *s.* (*In S. Africa*) ségrégation *f*.

apartment [ə'pɑːtmənt], *s.* (*a*) salle *f*; pièce *f*; (*b*) *pl.* logement *m*; to let furnished apartments, louer en meublé. *c) U.S.:* appartement *m*.

apathy ['æpəθi], *s.* apathie *f*, nonchalance *f*. **apa'thetic**, *a.* apathique, indifférent, **-ally**, *adv.* apathiquement, nonchalamment.

ape [eip]. I. *s.* singe *m*. II. *v.tr.* singer, imiter, mimer.

aperient [ə'piəriənt], *a. & s.* laxatif (*m*).

aperitif [ə'peritif], *s.* apéritif *m*.

aperture ['æpətjuər], *s.* ouverture *f*, orifice *m*.

apex ['eipeks], *s.* sommet *m*; point culminant.

apiary ['eipiəri], *s.* rucher *m*.

apiece [ə'piːs], *adv.* chacun; la) pièce; a franc a., un franc la pièce.

apologetic [əpɔlə'dʒetik], *a.* d'excuse; he was a. about it, il s'en excusa. **-ally**, *adv.* en s'excusant.

apologize [ə'pɔlədʒaiz], *v.i.* s'excuser. †**a'pology**, *s.* excuses *fpl*.

apostle [ə'pɔsl], *s.* apôtre *m*.

apostrophe [ə'pɔstrəfi], *s.* apostrophe *f*.

‡appal [ə'pɔːl], v.tr. consterner; épouvanter. ap'palling, a. épouvantable, effroyable; F: an a. din, un bruit de tous les diables.

apparatus [æpə'reitəs], s. appareil m.

apparent [ə'pær(ə)nt], a. apparent, évident. -ly, adv. apparemment; évidemment.

apparition [æpə'riʃ(ə)n], s. 1. apparition f. 2. fantôme m, revenant m.

appeal [ə'piːl]. I. s. appel m. II. v.i. faire appel (à qn). 1. to a. for help, demander secours (à qn); (of thing) attirer (qn); it doesn't a. to me, cela ne me dit rien. ap'pealing, a. (ton) suppliant, émouvant; (personnalité) sympathique. -ly, adv. d'un ton, d'un regard, suppliant.

appear [ə'piər], v.i. 1. paraître, se paraître; se montrer. 2. se présenter; comparaître (devant un tribunal). 3. (= seem) paraître, sembler; so it would a., il paraît que oui. ap'pearance, s. 1. apparition f; entrée f. 2. apparence f, air m; at first a., à première vue; for the sake of appearances, pour sauver les apparences; pour la forme.

appease [ə'piːz], v.tr. apaiser. ap'peasement, s. apaisement m; policy of a., politique f d'apaisement, de conciliation.

append [ə'pend], v.tr. attacher; joindre; ajouter.

†appendix [ə'pendiks], s. appendice m. appendi'citis, s. appendicite f.

appetite ['æpitait], s. appétit m. 'appetizer, s. (a) apéritif; (b) amuse-gueule m; (c) a walk is a good a., une promenade vous ouvre l'appétit. 'appetizing, a. appétissant; alléchant.

applaud [ə'plɔːd], v.tr. applaudir. ap'plause, s. applaudissements mpl.

apple ['æpl], s. pomme f; eating a., pomme à couteau; a. core, trognon m de pomme; a. green, vert pomme inv; a. pie, tart, tourte f, tarte f aux pommes; in a. pie order, en ordre parfait; a. pie bed, lit m en portefeuille; a. sauce, stewed a., compote f de pommes; a. tree, pommier m.

appliance [ə'plaiəns], s. appareil m; dispositif m; pl. accessoires m (d'une machine).

apply [ə'plai], v.tr. & i. 1. appliquer (sth. to sth., qch. sur qch.); to a. the brake, freiner; to a. one's mind to sth., s'appliquer à qch. 2. s'adresser (to qn pour obtenir qch.); to a. for a job, poser sa candidature à un emploi. ap'plicable, a. applicable; approprié. 'applicant, s. candidat m. application, s. 1. application f (de qch. à, sur qch.). 2. assiduité f, application. 3. demande f, requête f.

appoint [ə'pɔint], v.tr. nommer (qn); fixer, désigner (l'heure). ap'pointed,

a. nommé; désigné; at the a. time, à l'heure indiquée; well a. house, maison bien installée. ap'pointment, s. 1. rendez-vous m. 2. nomination f (à un emploi); (b) emploi m.

appreciate [ə'priːʃieit], v.tr. 1. apprécier. 2. Fin: hausser la valeur de (qch.). ap'preciable, a. appréciable; sensible. -bly, adv. sensiblement. appreci'ation, s. 1. appréciation f. 2. critique f (d'un livre, etc.). ap'preciative, a. (jugement) élogieux; (of pers.) reconnaissant; a. of music, qui apprécie la musique. -ly, adv. favorablement; avec satisfaction; avec reconnaissance.

apprehension [æpri'henʃ(ə)n], s. appréhension f, crainte f. appre'hensive, a. timide, craintif.

apprentice [ə'prentis], s. apprenti, -ie.

approach [ə'proutʃ]. I. s. 1. approche f; abord m; his a. to the problem, la façon dont il aborde le problème. 2. voie f d'accès; approches (d'une ville). II. v. 1. v.i. (s')approcher. 2. v.tr. s'approcher de (qn, qch.); aborder, approcher (qn); to be easy to a., avoir l'abord facile. ap'proachable, a. accessible, approchable; (of pers.) abordable.

appropriate [ə'prouprieit]. I. v.tr. s'approprier (qch.); s'emparer de (qch.). II. a. [ə'proupriit] 1. propre, convenable; à propos. -ly, adv. convenablement; à propos. ap'propriateness, s. convenance f; justesse f; à-propos m; applicabilité f.

approve [ə'pruːv]. 1. v.tr. approuver, ratifier (une décision). 2. v.ind.tr. to a. of sth., approuver qch. ap'proval, s. approbation f, agrément m; Com: on a., à l'essai.

approximate [ə'prɔksimit], a. approximatif. -ly, adv. approximativement.

apricot ['eiprikɔt], s. abricot m; a. tree, abricotier m.

April ['eipril], s. avril m.

apron ['eiprən], s. tablier m; Av: aire f de manœuvre; F: to be tied to one's mother's a. strings, être pendu(e) aux jupons de sa mère.

apse [æps], s. abside f.

apt [æpt], a. (a) (mot) juste; (expression) heureuse; (b) (of pers.) a. to do sth., enclin, porté, à faire qch.; we are a. to believe that . . ., on croit facilement que . . .; (of thing) a. to go wrong, sujet à, susceptible de, se détraquer; (c) (élève) intelligent. -ly, adv. avec justesse; avec à-propos. 'aptitude, s. aptitude f. 'aptness, s. (a) justesse f (d'une observation); (b) tendance f à faire qch.

aqualung ['ækwəlʌŋ], s. scaphandre m autonome.

aquarium [ə'kwɛəriəm], s. aquarium m.

aquatic [ə'kwætik], a. aquatique.

aqueduct ['ækwidʌkt], s. aqueduc m.

aquiline ['ækwilain], a. aquilin.

Arab ['ærəb], a. & s. arabe (mf).

Arabian [ə'reibiən], a. arabe, d'Arabie.

Arabic ['ærəbik]. 1. a. (gomme) arabique; (langue) arabe. S. Ling: l'arabe m.

arable ['ærəbl], a. arable, labourable.

arbitrate ['ɑːbitreit]. 1. v.tr. arbitrer, juger. 2. v.i. arbitrer. 'arbitrary, a. arbitraire. -ily, adv. arbitrairement. arbi'tration, s. arbitrage m. 'arbitrator, s. arbitre m.

arc [ɑːk], s. arc m.

arcade [ɑː'keid], s. arcade f.

arch [ɑːtʃ]. I. v.tr. arquer (le dos). II. s. (a) arc m; rounded a., arc en plein cintre; (b) arche f (d'un pont). 'archway, s. passage m voûté; portail m.

archaeology [ɑːki'ɔlədʒi], s. archéologie f. archae'ologist, s. archéologue mf.

archaic [ɑː'keiik], a. archaïque.

archangel [ɑːk'eindʒ(ə)l], s. archange m.

archbishop ['ɑːtʃ'biʃəp], s. archevêque m.

archery ['ɑːtʃəri], s. tir m à l'arc.

†archipelago [ɑːki'peləgou], s. archipel m.

architect ['ɑːkitekt], s. architecte m. 'architecture, s. architecture f.

archives ['ɑːkaivz], s.pl. archives f.

ardent ['ɑːdənt], a. ardent. -ly, adv. ardemment.

ardour ['ɑːdər], s. ardeur f.

arduous ['ɑːdjuəs], a. pénible, difficile.

area ['ɛəriə], s. 1. aire f, superficie f; surface f. 2. région f; postal a., zone f postale; sterling a., zone sterling.

arena [ə'riːnə], s. arène f.

argue ['ɑːgjuː], v.i. & tr. discuter, (se) disputer, raisonner; to a. against sth., plaider contre qch. 'argument, s. 1. argument m (for, against, en faveur de, contre); for the sake of a., à titre d'exemple. 2. discussion f, dispute f. argu'mentative, a. raisonneur, -euse.

arid ['ærid], a. aride.

†arise [ə'raiz], v.i. (a) (of storm) survenir; (of difficulty) se présenter; (b) problems that a. from . . ., problèmes qui proviennent, résultent, de . . .

aristocrat ['æristəkræt], s. aristocrate mf. aris'tocracy, s. aristocratie f. aristo'cratic, a. aristocratique.

arithmetic [ə'riθmətik], s. arithmétique f, calcul m.

ark [ɑːk], s. arche f.

arm¹ [ɑːm], s. bras m; a. in a., bras dessus, bras dessous; to put one's a. round s.o., prendre qn par la taille; to keep s.o. at arm's length, tenir qn à distance; to welcome s.o. with open arms, recevoir qn à bras ouverts. 'arm,chair, s. fauteuil m. 'armful, s. brassée f. 'armhole, s. Cl: emmanchure f. 'armlet, s. brassard m. 'arm,pit, s. aisselle f.

arm². I. v.tr. & i. (s')armer. II. s. 1. usu.pl. arme(s) f(pl); to be up in arms, se gendarmer (against, contre); the arms race, la course aux armements. 2. (coat of) arms, armoiries fpl; 'armaments, s.pl. armements mpl; matériel m de guerre. 'armed, a. armé (with, de); the a. forces, les forces armées. 'armistice, s. armistice m. 'armour, s. armure f. 'armoured, a. cuirassé; blindé; a. car, (i) automobile blindée; (ii) fourgon m bancaire blindé. 'armoury, s. armurerie f. 'army, s. armée f; the Salvation A., l'Armée du Salut.

aroma [ə'roumə], s. arôme m; bouquet m (d'un vin).

around [ə'raund]. 1. adv. autour, à l'entour. 2. prep. autour de.

arouse [ə'rauz], v.tr. 1. (a) réveiller, éveiller (qn); (b) stimuler (qn). 2. éveiller, susciter (un sentiment).

arrange [ə'reindʒ], v.tr. 1. ranger, disposer (des livres, etc.). 2. to a. to do sth., prendre des dispositions pour faire qch.; s'arranger, convenir, de faire qch. a'rrangement, s. 1. arrangement m, disposition f. (de qch.). 2. accord m, entente f (avec qn); price by a., prix à débattre.

array [ə'rei], s. étalage m.

arrears [ə'riəz], s.pl. arriéré m; rent in a., loyer arriéré.

arrest [ə'rest]. I. s. arrestation f. II. v.tr. arrêter (un malfaiteur, l'attention de qn).

arrive [ə'raiv], v.i. arriver. ar'rival, s. 1. arrivée f; arrivage m (de marchandises); a new a., un nouveau venu.

arrogant ['ærəgənt], a. arrogant. -ly, adv. avec arrogance. 'arrogance, s. arrogance f.

arrow ['ærou], s. flèche f.

arsenal ['ɑːsənl], s. arsenal m.

arsenic ['ɑːsnik], s. arsenic m.

arson ['ɑːsn], s. incendie m volontaire.

art [ɑːt], s. 1. art m; the (fine) arts, les beaux-arts. 2. adresse f, habileté f artifice m. 'artful, a. rusé. 'artfulness, s. astuce f.

arteriosclerosis [ɑː'tiəriouskle'rousis], s. Med: artériosclérose f.

artery ['ɑːtəri], s. 1. Anat: artère f. 2. artère, grande route. ar'terial, a. 1. Anat: artériel. 2. a. road, grande route.

artesian [ɑː'tiːzjən], a. a. well, puits m artésien.

arthritis [ɑː'θraitis], s. Med: arthrite f.

artichoke ['ɑːtitʃouk], s. 1. artichaut m. 2. Jerusalem a., topinambour m.

article ['ɑːtikl], s. article m; objet m.

articulate [ɑː'tikjuleit]. I. v.tr. & i. articuler. II. a. articulé; distinct. -ly, adv. (parler) distinctement. arti-cu'lation, s. articulation f.

artificial [ɑːti'fiʃ(ə)l], a. 1. artificiel. 2. factice, simulé. **-ally**, adv. artificiellement.

artillery [ɑː'tiləri], s. artillerie f.

artisan [ɑːti'zæn], s. artisan m, ouvrier m.

artist ['ɑːtist], s. (a) artiste mf; (b) artiste-peintre mf; he's an a., il est peintre. **ar'tistic**, a. artistique. **-ally**, adv. avec art.

artiste [ɑː'tiːst], s. Th: artiste mf.

artless ['ɑːtlis], a. 1. naturel; sans artifice. 2. naïf. **-ly**, adv. 1. naturellement. 2. naïvement. **'artlessness**, s. 1. naturel m. 2. naïveté f.

arty ['ɑːti], a. F: qui affiche des goûts artistiques.

as [æz, (unstressed) əz], adv., conj. & rel. pron. 1. (a) as . . . as: you are as tall as I (am), F: as me, vous êtes aussi grand que moi; as pale as death, pâle comme un mort; by day as well as by night, le jour comme la nuit; (b) as for me, quant à moi; as from the 15th, à partir du quinze; as to that, quant à cela; (c) to consider s.o. as a friend, considérer qn comme un ami; to act as a father, agir en père; as a child he . . ., dans son enfance il . . .; (d) beasts of prey such as the lion, les bêtes fauves telles que, comme, le lion. 2. as if, as though, he didn't know, comme s'il ne le savait pas; leave it as it is, laissez-le tel qu'il est; do as you like, faites comme vous voudrez; as it is, les choses étant ainsi; as he, she, grew older, en vieillissant.

asbestos [æz'bestɔs], s. amiante m.

ascend [ə'send], v.tr. & i. monter. **As'cension**, s. Ecc: l'Ascension f. **as'cent**, s. ascension f (d'une montagne).

ascertain [æsə'tein], v.tr. s'informer, s'assurer, de; constater.

ascetic [ə'setik]. 1. a. ascétique. 2. s. ascète mf.

ascribe [ə'skraib], v.tr. attribuer, imputer (to, à).

asdic ['æzdik], s. Nau: asdic m.

ash[1] [æʃ], s. Bot: frêne m.

ash[2], s. cendre f; A. Wednesday, le mercredi des Cendres. **'ashcan**, s. U.S: boîte f aux ordures. **'ashpan**, s. cendrier m (de poêle); garde-cendres m inv. **'ashtray**, s. cendrier m (de fumeur).

ashamed [ə'ʃeimd], a. honteux, confus; to be a., avoir honte.

ashore [ə'ʃɔːr], adv. à terre.

Asian ['eiʃn, 'eiʒn], a. asiatique; A. flu, grippe f asiatique. 2. s. Asiate. **Asiatic** [eiʃi'ætik], a. & s. asiatique (mf); a. d'Asie.

aside [ə'said]. 1. adv. de côté; à l'écart; à part; to stand a., se ranger. 2. s. Th: aparté m.

asinine ['æsinain], a. F: stupide, sot.

ask [ɑːsk], v.tr. & i. demander. 1. to ask s.o. a question, poser une question à qn; F: a. me another! je n'ai pas la moindre idée! 2. to a. s.o. to do sth., demander à qn de faire qch. 3. to a. s.o. about, se renseigner sur qch. 4. (a) to a. for a., demander à avoir qch; (b) to a. for sth., demander qch.; to a. for sth. back, redemander un objet prêté. 5. to a. s.o. to lunch, inviter qn à déjeuner; to a. s.o. back, inviter qn pour lui rendre la politesse. **'asking**, s. it's yours for the a., il n'y a qu'à le demander.

askew [ə'skjuː], adv. de biais, en côté.

asleep [ə'sliːp], adv. & pred.a. endormi; to be a., dormir; to fall a., s'endormir.

asparagus [əs'pærəgəs], s. asperges fpl.

aspect ['æspekt], s. 1. exposition f, orientation f. 2. aspect m, air m; to see sth. in its true a., voir qch. sous son vrai jour.

aspen ['æspən], s. Bot: tremble m.

aspersion [ə'spəːʃ(ə)n], s. calomnie f; to cast aspersions on s.o., dénigrer qn.

asphalt ['æsfælt], s. asphalte m.

asphyxiate [æs'fiksieit], v.tr. asphyxier. **as'phyxia**, s. asphyxi'ation, s. asphyxie f.

aspire [ə'spaiər], v.i. aspirer. **aspirate**, a. & s. Ling: aspiré. **aspi'ration**, s. aspiration f. **as'piring**, a. ambitieux.

aspirin ['æspərin], s. aspirine f; an a., un comprimé d'aspirine.

ass [æs, ɑːs], s. 1. âne, f. ânesse. 2. F: sot, f. sotte; âne.

assailant [ə'seilənt], s. assaillant m.

assassinate [ə'sæsineit], v.tr. assassiner. **as'sassin**, s. assassin m. **assassi'nation**, s. assassinat m.

assault [ə'sɔːlt]. I. v.tr. assaillir. II. s. (a) Mil: assaut; (b) attaque f; Jur: a. and battery, voies fpl de fait; coups mpl et blessures fpl.

assemble [ə'sembl]. 1. v.tr. (a) assembler; (b) monter (une machine). 2. v.i. s'assembler; se rassembler. **as'sembly**, s. 1. assemblée f. 2. assemblement m, réunion f. 3. montage m (d'une machine); Ind: a. line, banc m, chaîne f, de montage; a. shop, atelier m d'assemblage.

assent [ə'sent]. I. v.tr. acquiescer, donner son assentiment (to, à). II. s. consentement m.

assert [ə'səːt], v.tr. 1. (a) revendiquer, faire valoir (ses droits); (b) to a. one-self, s'imposer. 2. affirmer, a'sser-tion, s. 1. revendication f (de ses droits). 2. affirmation f. **as'sertive**, a. 1. autoritaire. 2. (ton) péremptoire, cassant, a. **'assertiveness**, s. assurance f; ton m autoritaire.

assess [ə'ses], v.tr. estimer (l'importance de qch.); imposer, taxer (qn); to a. sth. (for taxation), évaluer qch. **as'sessment**, s. 1. évaluation (de dégâts); imposition f (d'une propriété); cotisation f (du contribuable); a. of damages, fixation f de dommages-intérêts. 2. (amount) cote f; taxe officielle. **as'sessor**, s. contrôleur m (des contributions directes).

asset ['æset], s. 1. possession f, avoir m; he's one of our assets, c'est une de nos valeurs. 2. pl. Fin: actif m, avoir m; Jur: personal assets, biens m meubles; real assets, biens immobiliers.

assiduous [ə'sidjuəs], a. assidu. **-ly,** adv. assidûment.

assign [ə'sain], v.tr. 1. assigner (qch. à qn). 2. céder, transférer (qch. à qn). **assig'nation,** s. distribution f (de biens); transfert m (de biens); rendezvous m (galant). **as'signment,** s. 1. allocation f; transfert m (de biens). 2. tâche f assignée.

assimilate [ə'simileit], v.tr. assimiler. **assimi'lation,** s. assimilation f.

assist [ə'sist]. 1. v.tr. aider (qn). 2. v.i. assister à (une cérémonie). **as'sistance,** s. aide f, secours m; Adm: national a. l'assistance publique. **as'sistant.** 1. a. auxiliaire, adjoint; a. manager, sous-directeur, -trice, sousgérant, -ante; Sch: a. master, mistress, professeur m (de lycée). 2. s. aide mf; (in shop) vendeur, -euse; (in office, etc.) employé, -ée, collaborateur, -trice.

assizes [ə'saiziz], s.pl. Jur: assises fpl.

associate. I. v.tr. & i. (s') associer (with, avec qn, qch.). II. s. associé, -ée; adjoint, -te; camarade mf. **associ'ation,** s. association f; a. football, football m.

assortment [ə'sɔːtmənt], s. assortiment m.

assume [ə'sjuːm], v.tr. 1. prendre sur soi, assumer (une responsabilité). 2. présumer, supposer (qch.); assuming (that) the story is true, en supposant que l'histoire soit vraie. **as'sumed,** a. supposé, feint; a. name, pseudonyme m. **as'sumption,** s. 1. Ecc: the A., l'Assomption f (de la Vierge). 2. supposition f.

assure [ə'ʃuər], v.tr. assurer. **as'surance,** s. 1. assurance f; promesse f; affirmation f. 2. life a., assurance sur la vie. 3. assurance, aplomb m. **as'sured.** 1. a. a success, succès assuré. 2. a. s. a. (person), assuré(e). **-ly,** adv. [ə'ʃuəridli], assurément, certainement.

aster ['æstər], s. Bot: aster m.

asterisk ['æstərisk], s. astérisque m.

astern [ə'stəːn], adv. Nau: (a) à l'arrière; (b) en arrière.

asteroid ['æstərɔid], s. astéroïde m.

asthma ['æsmə], s. asthme m. **asth'matic,** a. asthmatique.

astigmatism [ə'stigmətizm], s. astigmatisme m.

astonish [ə'stɔniʃ], v.tr. étonner, surprendre. **a'stonishing,** a. étonnant, surprenant. **-ly,** adv. étonnamment. **a'stonishment,** s. étonnement m, surprise f.

astound [ə'staund], v.tr. confondre; stupéfier. **a'stounding,** a. abasourdissant.

astray [ə'strei], adv. & pred.a. égaré; to go a., s'égarer; to lead s.o. a., dévoyer qn.

astride [ə'straid], adv., pred.a., & prep. à califourchon; à cheval sur (qch.).

astrology [ə'strɔlədʒi], s. astrologie f. **a'strologer,** s. astrologue m.

astronaut ['æstrənɔːt], s. astronaute mf. **astro'nautics,** s.pl. astronautique f.

astronomy [ə'strɔnəmi], s. astronomie f. **a'stronomer,** s. astronome m. **astro'nomical,** a. astronomique.

astrophysics ['æstrou'fiziks], s.pl. astrophysique f.

astute [ə'stjuːt], a. fin, avisé, pénétrant. **-ly,** adv. avec finesse; astucieusement. **a'stuteness,** s. finesse f, pénétration f.

asylum [ə'sailəm], s. asile m, refuge m.

at [æt], prep. à. 1. (a) at sea, en mer; (b) at the tailor's, chez le tailleur. 2. two at a time, deux à la fois; at night, la nuit. 3. at my request, sur ma demande. 4. (a) to look at, regarder; surprised at, étonné de; (b) to be at work, être au travail; while we are at it, pendant que nous y sommes.

atheism ['eiθiizm], s. athéisme m. **'atheist,** s. athée mf.

athlete ['æθliːt], s. athlète mf. **ath'letic,** a. athlétique. **ath'letics,** s.pl. sports m (athlétiques).

atlas ['ætləs], s. atlas m.

atmosphere ['ætməsfiər], s. atmosphère f. **atmos'pheric.** 1. a. atmosphérique. 2. s.pl. Rad: atmospherics, parasites m.

atoll ['ætɔl], s. atoll m.

atom ['ætəm], s. atome m; a. bomb, bombe f atomique. **a'tomic,** a. atomique; a. scientist, atomiste mf. **'atomize,** v.tr. atomiser, pulvériser. **'atomizer,** s. atomiseur m, vaporisateur m.

atone [ə'toun], v.ind.tr. to a. for, expier (une faute). **a'tonement,** s. expiation f, réparation f; Day of A., Fête f du Grand Pardon.

atrocious [ə'trouʃəs], a. 1. atroce. 2. exécrable. **-ly,** adv. 1. atrocement. 2. exécrablement. **a'trocity,** s. atrocité f.

attach [ə'tætʃ], v.tr. attacher, lier. 2. v.i. s'attacher. **a'ttached,** a. attaché, -ée (d'ambassade). **a'ttachment,** s. 1. accessoire m (d'un appareil). 2. attachement m, affection f.

attack [ə'tæk]. I. *v.tr.* attaquer (qn); s'attaquer à (qch.). II. *s.* attaque *f*; crise *f* (de nerfs); accès *m* (de fièvre).

attain [ə'tein], *v.tr.* atteindre, arriver à. a'ttainable, *a.* accessible, à la portée. a'ttainment, *s.* 1. réalisation *f*. 2. *usu.pl.* connaissance *f*; savoir *m*.

attempt [ə'tem(p)t]. I. *v.tr.* (a) essayer, tenter; (b) attempted murder, tentative *f* d'assassinat. II. *s.* tentative *f*, essai *m*; first a., coup *m* d'essai.

attend [ə'tend]. 1. *v.ind.tr.* to a. to (a) faire attention à (qch.); (b) écouter (qn); (c) s'occuper de qch., d'un client). 2. *v.tr.* to a. school, aller à l'école; to a. a meeting, assister à une réunion. a'ttendance, *s.* 1. (*in hotels, etc.*) service *m*. 2. présence *f*; there was a good a., l'assistance était nombreuse; school a., fréquentation *f* scolaire. a'ttendant, *s.* gardien,-ienne.

attention [ə'ten(ʃ)ən], *s.* 1. (a) attention *f*; pay a.! faites attention! to attract a., se faire remarquer; (b) soins *mpl.* 2. *Mil:* a.! garde à vous!

attentive [ə'tentiv], *a.* 1. attentif. 2. empressé (to, auprès de). -ly, *adv.* avec attention.

attenuate [ə'tenjueit], *v.tr.* atténuer; *Jur:* attenuating circumstances, circonstances *f* atténuantes.

attic ['ætik], *s.* mansarde *f*, grenier *m*.

attire [ə'taiər], *s.* vêtement *m*; costume *m*.

attitude ['ætitjuːd], *s.* attitude *f*, pose *f*.

attorney [ə'tə:ni], *s.* 1. *U.S:* = avoué *m*; District A. = procureur *m* de la République. 2. A. General, avocat *m* du gouvernement et chef du barreau. 3. *s.* power of a., procuration *f*, mandat *m*, pouvoirs *mpl*.

attract [ə'trækt], *v.tr.* attirer. a'ttraction, *s.* attraction *f*; attraits *mpl.* a'ttractive, *a.* attrayant, séduisant. -ly, *adv.* d'une manière attrayante. a'ttractiveness, *s.* charme *m*.

attribute. I. *v.tr.* [ə'tribjut] attribuer, imputer. II. *s.* ['ætribjuːt] attribut *m*, qualité *f*. attri'bution, *s.* attribution *f*.

auburn ['ɔːbən], *a.* châtain roux.

auction ['ɔːkʃən]. I. *s.* vente *f* aux enchères. II. *s.* vente *f* aux enchères. auction'eer, *s.* commissaire-priseur *m*.

audacity [ɔː'dæsiti], *s.* audace *f*. au'dacious [-deiʃ-], *a.* audacieux, hardi.

audible ['ɔːdibl], *a.* audible, intelligible. -ly, *adv.* distinctement. audi'bility, *s.* audibilité *f*. au'dition, *s. Th:* audition *f.* 'audience, *s.* assistance *f*, auditoire *m*.

audiovisual ['ɔːdiouvizju(ə)l], *a.* audiovisuel.

audit ['ɔːdit]. I. *v.tr.* vérifier (des comptes). II. *s.* vérification *f* (de comptes). 'auditor, *s.* expert *m* comptable.

augment [ɔːg'ment], *v.tr.* augmenter. aug'mentation, *s.* augmentation *f*.

August ['ɔːgəst], *s.* août *m*.

aunt [ɑːnt], *s.* tante *f.* 'auntie, 'aunty, *s. F:* ma tante, tantine *f*.

auspices ['ɔːspisiz], *s.pl.* auspices *m*. aus'picious, *a.* favorable, propice; de bon augure.

austere [ɔːs'tiər], *a.* austère. -ly, *adv.* avec austérité. aus'terity, *s.* austérité *f*; times of a., période *f* de restrictions.

Australian [ɔːs'treiljən], *a.* & *s.* australien,-ienne.

Austrian ['ɔːstriən], *a.* & *s.* autrichien, -ienne.

authentic [ɔː'θentik], *a.* authentique. au'thenticate, *v.tr.* 1. certifier. 2. vérifier. authen'ticity, *s.* authenticité *f*.

author ['ɔːθər], *s.* auteur *m*.

authorize ['ɔːθəraiz], *v.tr.* autoriser. au'thoritative, *a.* 1. (caractère) autoritaire; (ton) péremptoire. 2. (document) qui fait autorité; (renseignement) de bonne source. -ly, *adv.* 1. autoritairement. 2. avec autorité. au'thority, *s.* 1. autorité *f*. 2. autorisation *f* (de faire qch.). 3. on good a., de bonne source. 4. the authorities, l'administration *f*. authori'zation, *s.* autorisation *f.* 'authorized, *a.* autorisé; **a. prices,** prix homologués; **the A. Version (of the Bible),** la traduction anglaise de la Bible de 1611.

auto- ['ɔːtou], *prefix.* auto-. auto'biography, *s.* autobiographie *f.* 'autocrat, *s.* autocrate *m*. auto'cratic, *a.* autocratique. 'autograph, *s.* 1. *s.* autographe *m*. II. *v.tr.* écrire son autographe dans, signer, dédicacer (un livre). auto'matic, *a.* automatique; *a.* (pistol), automatique *m*. auto'mation, *s.* automation *f.* automatisation *f.* au'tomatize, *v.tr.* automatiser. au'tomaton, *s.* automate *m.* 'automobile, *s. U.S:* auto(mobile) *f*, voiture *f.* au'tonomous, *a.* autonome. au'tonomy, *s.* autonomie *f.* 'autopsy, *s.* autopsie *f*.

autumn ['ɔːtəm], *s.* automne *m*. au'tumnal, *a.* automnal, d'automne.

auxiliary [ɔːg'ziljəri], *a.* & *s.* auxiliaire (*mf*).

avail [ə'veil]. I. *v.tr.* & *i.* to a. oneself of sth., se servir de qch.; profiter de qch. II. *s.* avantage *m*; of no a., inutile(ment). availa'bility, *s.* disponibilité *f.* a'vailable, *a.* (a) disponible; (b) accessible.

avalanche ['ævəlɑːnʃ], *s.* avalanche *f*.

avarice ['ævəris], *s.* avarice *f*. ava'ricious, *a.* avare.

avenge [ə'ven(d)ʒ], *v.tr.* venger. a'venger, *s.* vengeur,-eresse.

avenue ['ævinjuː], *s.* (a) avenue *f*; (b) *U.S:* boulevard *m*; (c) chemin *m* d'accès.

average ['ævəridʒ]. 1. *s.* moyenne *f*; on an a., en moyenne. 2. *a.* moyen.

aversion [əˈvəːʃ(ə)n], s. 1. aversion f, répugnance f. 2. objet m d'aversion; pet a., bête noire.

avert [əˈvəːt], v.tr. détourner (les yeux, un coup).

aviary [ˈeiviəri], s. volière f.

aviation [eiviˈeiʃ(ə)n], s. aviation f. **'aviator**, s. aviateur, -trice. avi'onics, s.pl. avionique f.

avid [ˈævid], a. avide. a'vidity, s. avidité f.

avoid [əˈvɔid], v.tr. éviter. a'voidable, a. évitable.

avoirdupois [ævədəˈpɔiz], s. (a) poids m du commerce; (b) F: embonpoint m.

await [əˈweit], v.tr. attendre.

‡**awake** [əˈweik]. I. v.i. se réveiller. II. pred.a. éveillé; I was a., je ne dormais pas; wide a., bien éveillé. a'waken. I. v.tr. éveiller (la curiosité, les soupçons). 2. se réveiller. a'wakening, s. réveil m; a rude a., une amère désillusion.

award [əˈwɔːd]. I. v.tr. adjuger, décerner (un prix, etc.). II. s. prix m, récompense f.

aware [əˈwɛər], a. avisé, informé, instruit; to be a. of sth., savoir qch.; not that I am a. of, pas que je sache.

away [əˈwei], adv. loin; au loin. 1. (a) to go a., partir, s'en aller; (b) to run a., s'enfuir; to take s.o. a., emmener qn; to carry a., emporter. 2. (a) far a., dans le lointain; au loin; five paces

a., à cinq pas de là; (b) when he is a., lorsqu'il n'est pas là; Sp: a. match, match m à l'extérieur; a. (from work), absent.

awe [ɔː], s. crainte f, terreur f; respect m. 'awe-inspiring, a. terrifiant, impressionnant. 'awful, a. terrible; what a weather! quel chien de temps! an a. din, un bruit de tous les diables. -fully, adv. F: (intensive) très; a. funny, drôle comment tout.

awkward [ˈɔːkwəd], a. 1. gauche, maladroit. 2. embarrassé, gêné. 3. fâcheux, gênant. 4. incommode; he's an a. customer, c'est un homme difficile. -ly, adv. 1. gauchement. 2. d'une manière embarrassée. 'awkwardness, s. 1. gaucherie f, maladresse f; manque m de grâce. 2. embarras m. 3. inconvénient m (d'une situation).

awl [ɔːl], s. alène f, poinçon m, percoir m.

awning [ˈɔːniŋ], s. tente f, vélum m.

awry [əˈrai], adv. & a. de travers.

axe [æks]. I. s. hache f, cognée f; to have an a. to grind, agir dans un but intéressé. II. v.tr. Adm: F: réduire (les dépenses); mettre à pied (des fonctionnaires).

‡**axis** [ˈæksis], s. axe m; scan a., axe radioélectrique.

axle [ˈæksl], s. 1. essieu m. 2. arbre m, axe m (d'une roue, etc.).

azalea [əˈzeiljə], s. Bot: azalée f.

B

B, b [biː]. 1. (la lettre) B, b, m. 2. Mus: si m.

babble [ˈbæbl]. I. s. 1. babil m, babillage m. 2. bavardage m. II. v.i. (a) babiller; (b) bavarder, jaser; (c) murmurer.

baboon [bəˈbuːn], s. Z: babouin m.

baby [ˈbeibi], s. 1. bébé m; F: to hold the b., avoir l'affaire sur les bras; F: that's your b., débrouille-toi! 2. attrib. (a) d'enfant; F: b. face, visage poupard; (b) de petites dimensions; b. grand, piano m (à) demi-queue; crapaud m; (c) (young animal) b. gazelle, bébé gazelle. 'babyhood, s. première enfance. 'babyish, a. de bébé; puéril. 'baby-sit, v.i. garder les bébés. 'baby 'sitter, s. garde-bébé mf.

bachelor [ˈbætʃələr], s. 1. célibataire m, garçon m. 2. B. of Arts, of Science = licencié ès lettres, ès sciences.

back [bæk]. I. s. 1. dos m; to b. to b., dos à dos; adossé; to do sth. behind s.o.'s b., faire qch. à l'insu de qn; F: to put s.o.'s b. up, fâcher qn; (b) les reins m; to break one's b., se casser les reins, l'échine; to break the b. of the work, faire le plus dur du travail. 2. dos

(d'un couteau); verso m (d'une page); dossier m (d'une chaise); arrière m (d'une voiture); fond m (d'une armoire); he knows London like the b. of his hand, il connaît Londres comme (le fond de) sa poche. 3. Sp: arrière m; the backs, l'arrière-défense f. II. a. arrière; de derrière; b. door, porte de derrière, de service; F: to get in through the b. door, entrer par la petite porte; b. room, pièce f sur le derrière; F: b. room boy, savant m (qui travaille à l'arrière-plan); the b. streets of a town, les bas quartiers d'une ville; b. seat, siège m arrière; to take a b. seat, (i) s'asseoir sur un banc de derrière, (ii) s'effacer; passer au second plan; Aut: b. axle, pont m arrière; Pol: b. bench, banc pour les membres sans portefeuille. III. adv. 1. (place) (a) en arrière; stand b.! rangez-vous! (b) dans le sens contraire; to hit b., rendre coup pour coup; to call s.o. b., rappeler qn. 2. (time) a few years b., il y a quelques années; as far b. as 1900, déjà en 1900. IV. v.tr. & i. 1. v.i. reculer; Aut: faire marche arrière. 2. *v.tr.* soutenir (qn); financer (qn, *Th:* une pièce); parier, miser, sur (un cheval); mettre (une voiture) en marche arrière. 'back**ache,** *s.* douleurs *fpl* de reins. 'back'**bencher,** *s. Pol:* député *m* sans portefeuille. 'back**bite,** *v.tr. & i.* médire de (qn). 'back'**biter,** *s.* mauvaise langue. 'back**bone,** *s.* épine *f* dorsale, colonne *f* vertébrale; *F:* he's got no b., c'est un emplâtre. 'back 'down, *v.i.* rabattre de ses prétentions; en rabattre; se dédire. 'back**er,** *s.* partisan, -ane; *Com: Fin:* commanditaire *m*; *Sp:* parieur, -euse. back'**fire.** I. *v.i. Aut:* pétarader, avoir des retours. II. *s.* (*also* back**firing**) *Aut:* contre-allumage *m*; pétarades *fpl.* 'back**ground,** *s.* fond *m*, arrière-plan *m.* 'back**hand,** *s.* b. (stroke), coup *m* de revers. 'back**hander,** *s.* coup *m* du revers de la main; *F:* riposte inattendue, attaque *f* déloyale. 'back**ing,** *s.* 1. renforcement *m.* 2. *Sp:* paris *mpl* (sur un cheval). 3. *Aut:* marche *f* arrière. 'back**less,** *a.* (robe) sans dos; (banc) sans dossier. 'back**log,** *s.* arriéré *m* (de travail). 'back'**number,** *s.* (*a*) vieux numéro (d'un journal); (*b*) *F:* (*of pers.*) to be a b. n., être vieux jeu, *F:* un croulant. 'back '**out,** *v.i. Aut:* sortir en marche arrière; *F:* retirer sa promesse; se dédire. 'back**side,** *s. Anat:* *F:* derrière *m.* back'**stairs,** *s.* escalier *m* de service; *F:* b. influence, protections en haut lieu; *F:* b. gossip, propos d'antichambre. 'back '**up,** *v.tr.* soutenir (qn, qch.); prêter son appui (à qn). 'back**ward.** I. *a.* (mouvement) en arrière; (enfant) arriéré; b. in doing sth., lent à faire qch. II. *adv.* backward(s), en arrière; to fall b., tomber à la renverse. 'back**wardness,** *s.* lenteur *f* d'intelligence; hésitation *f*, lenteur *f* (à faire qch.). 'back**water,** *s.* eau arrêtée (par un bief); bras *m* de décharge (d'une rivière); to live in a b., vivre dans un bled. 'back**woods,** *s.pl.* forêts *fpl* vierges (de l'Amérique du Nord); to live in the b., vivre au bout du monde.

bacon ['beik(ə)n], *s.* lard *m*, bacon *m*; *F:* to save one's b., sauver sa peau.

bacteria [bak'tiəria], *s.pl.* bactéries *f.*

bad [bæd]. I. *a.* 1. mauvais; (*of food*) to go b., se gâter; in a b. way, en mauvais état; from b. to worse, de mal en pis; *F:* it's not b., ce n'est pas mal (du tout); he's not b. looking, il n'est pas mal; to be b.-tempered, être grincheux, de mauvaise humeur. 2. (*a*) (= *wicked*) méchant; *F:* he's a b. lot, c'est un vaurien; (*b*) (= *unpleasant*) b. smell, mauvaise odeur; a b. cold, un gros rhume; b. accident, grave accident; it's too b.! c'est trop fort! (*c*) b. leg, jambe malade. -**ly,** *adv.* (worse,

worst). 1. mal; things are going b., les choses vont mal. 2. b. wounded, gravement blessé. 3. to want sth. b., (i) avoir grand besoin, (ii) avoir grande envie, de qch. II. *s.* (*a*) mauvaise fortune; (*b*) (*of pers.*) to go to the b., mal tourner; (*c*) I'm 500 francs to the b., j'ai perdu 500 francs.

badge [bædʒ], *s.* 1. insigne *m*; plaque *f*; brassard *m.* 2. symbole *m.*

badger[1] ['bædʒər], *s. Z:* blaireau *m.*

badger[2], *v.tr.* harceler, importuner (qn).

baffle ['bæfl], *v.tr.* confondre, déconcerter (qn); dérouter (les soupçons).

bag [bæg], *s.* 1. 1. sac *m*; (diplomatic) b., valise *f* (diplomatique); *P:* there's bags of it, il y en a à gogo. 2. tear b., sac lacrymal; bags under the eyes, poches *f* sous les yeux. 3. to get a good b., faire bonne chasse; *F:* in the b., sûr et certain, dans le sac. 4. *pl. F:* pantalon *m.* II. *v.* 1. *v.i.* (*of garment*) bouffer. 2. *v.tr.* tuer (du gibier); *F:* empocher, s'emparer de (qch.); mettre la main sur (qch.). 'bag**gy,** *a.* (vêtement) trop ample.

baggage ['bægidʒ], *s.* bagages *mpl.*

bagpipes ['bægpaips], *s.pl.* cornemuse *f.*

bail[1] ['beil]. I. *s.* 1. *Jur:* cautionnement *m*; (*of pers.*) caution *f*, garant *m.* II. *v.tr. Jur:* to b. s.o. (out), se porter caution pour obtenir l'élargissement provisoire de qn. 'bail**iff,** *s.* 1. agent *m* de poursuites, huissier *m.* 2. intendant *m* (d'un domaine).

bail[2], *v.tr.* to b. out, vider (un canot).

bait [beit]. I. *s.* amorce *f*; appât *m.* II. *v.tr.* 1. harceler (un animal). 2. amorcer (un hameçon).

bake [beik], *v.tr. & i.* cuire, faire cuire (au four); baking powder, levure artificielle. 'bake**house,** *s.* boulangerie *f.* 'bake**r,** *s.* boulanger *m*; the b.'s wife, la boulangère; b.'s shop, boulangerie *f.* 'bake**ry,** *s.* boulangerie *f.*

balance ['bæləns]. I. *s.* 1. balance *f.* 2. équilibre *m*; to keep one's b., tenir en équilibre. 3. *Fin:* (*a*) b. in hand, solde *m* créditeur; (*b*) bilan *m*; on b. ..., à tout prendre; b. sheet, bilan *m* (d'inventaire). II. *v.* 1. *v.tr.* balancer, peser (les conséquences); équilibrer, faire contrepoids à (qch.); balancer, solder (un compte). 2. *v.i.* (*a*) (*of accounts*) se solder; (*b*) osciller, balancer; (*of pers.*) hésiter. 'bal**anced,** *a.* équilibré; compensé. 'bal**ancing.** I. *a.* 1. (mouvement) de bascule. 2. (ressort) compensateur. II. *s.* 1. balancement *m.* 2. mise *f* en équilibre; solde *m* des comptes. 3. ajustement *m*, compensation *f.*

†**balcony** ['bælkəni], *s.* balcon *m.*

bald [bɔ:ld], *a.* 1. chauve. 2. (style) plat; sec. -**ly,** *adv.* platement, sèchement. 'bald**ness,** *s.* calvitie *f.*

bale[1] ['beil], *s.* balle *f*, ballot *m.*

bale², *v.i.* to b. out, sauter en parachute.

balk [bɔːk]. **1.** *v.tr.* contrarier (qn); entraver (qn). **2.** *v.i.* *(of horse)* refuser; to b. at sth., reculer devant qch.

ball¹ [bɔːl], *s.* **1.** *(a)* boule *f*; balle *f* (de tennis); ballon *m* (de football); bille *f* (de billard); pelote *f* (de laine); *(b)* E: bille *f*; b. bearing, roulement m à billes; b. point pen, stylo m à bille. **2.** globe *m* (de l'œil). **'ballcock,** *s.* robinet m, soupape *f*, à flotteur.

ball², *s.* bal m. **'ballroom,** *s.* salle *f* de bal.

ballad ['bæləd], *s.* **1.** romance *f.* **2.** ballade *f.*

ballast ['bæləst], *s.* lest m.

ballet ['bælei], *s.* ballet m; b. dancer, danseur, -euse, d'opéra; ballerine *f.*

balloon [bə'luːn], *s.* ballon m.

ballot ['bælət]. **I.** *s.* scrutin m, vote m; b. box, urne *f* (de scrutin); b. paper, bulletin m de vote. **II.** *v.i.* voter au scrutin.

balmy ['bɑːmi], *a.* P: toqué, loufoque.

balustrade [,bæləs'treid], *s.* balustrade *f.*

bamboo [bæm'buː], *s.* bambou m.

ban [bæn]. **I.** *s.* *(a)* ban m, proscription *f*; *(b)* interdit m. **II.** ‡*v.tr.* interdire (qch.).

banal [bæ'nɑːl], *a.* banal; ordinaire. **ba'nality,** *s.* banalité *f.*

banana [bə'nɑːnə], *s.* banane *f*; b.(tree), bananier m.

band¹ [bænd], *s.* **1.** lien m; cercle m; elastic b., élastique m; Rad: frequence b, bande *f* de fréquence. **2.** E: bande *f*, courroie *f* (de transmission); Ind: moving b. production, travail m à la chaîne. **'bandage.** *I.* *s.* bandage m, bande *f.* **II.** *v.tr.* bander (une plaie).

band². *I.* *s.* **1.** bande *f*; troupe *f*; compagnie *f.* **2.** orchestre m; the regimental b., la musique du régiment; brass b., fanfare *f.* **II.** *v.i.* to b. together, (i) se réunir en bande; (ii) s'ameuter. **'bandmaster,** *s.* chef m de musique. **'bandsman,** *s.* musicien m. **'bandstand,** *s.* kiosque m à musique. **'band-wagon,** *s.* F: to jump on the b.-w., se mettre dans le mouvement; se ranger du bon côté.

bandit ['bændit], *s.* bandit m, brigand m.

bandy ['bændi], *v.tr.* (se) renvoyer (des paroles); échanger (des plaisanteries). **bandy²,** *a.* b. legs, jambes arquées, bancales.

bane [bein], *s.* fléau m, peste *f.*

bang [bæŋ]. **I.** *s.* coup (violent); détonation *f*; fracas m; supersonic b., double bang m. **II.** *v.i.* frapper avec bruit; heurter; *(of door)* claquer. **2.** *v.tr.* frapper (violemment); (faire) claquer (la porte). **'banging,** *s.* coups violents; claquement m.

banish ['bæniʃ], *v.tr.* bannir, exiler. **'banishment,** *s.* bannissement m, exil m.

banisters ['bænistəz], *s.pl.* balustres m; rampe *f.*

‡**banjo** ['bændʒou], *s.* banjo m.

bank¹ [bæŋk]. **I.** *s.* **1.** *(a)* talus m; remblai m; *(b)* banc m (de sable). **2.** berge *f*, rive *f.* **3.** Av: virage m incliné. **II.** *v.* **1.** *v.tr.* endiguer (une rivière); surhausser (un virage); couvrir (un feu); to b. up, remblayer (de la terre). **2.** *(of clouds, etc.)* s'entasser, s'amonceler.

bank². *s.* banque *f*; b. account, compte en banque; b. clerk, employé(e) de banque; b. holiday, jour férié; b. rate, taux m d'escompte. **II.** *v.tr.* & *i.* **1.** mettre, déposer, (de l'argent) en banque. **2.** to b. on sth., compter sur qch. **'banker,** *s.* banquier m. **'banking,** *s.* **1.** opérations *fpl* de banque. **2.** la banque. **'banknote,** *s.* billet m de banque. **'bankrupt,** *a.* & *s.* (commerçant) failli (m); to go b., faire faillite. **'bankruptcy,** *s.* faillite *f.*

bank³, *s.* clavier m (d'un orgue); rang m (d'une machine à écrire); Cin: b. of projectors, rampe *f* de projecteurs.

banner ['bænər], *s.* bannière *f*, étendard m.

banns [bænz], *s.pl.* bans m (de mariage).

banquet ['bæŋkwit], *s.* banquet m.

bantam ['bæntəm], *s.* bantam m; coq nain; b. weight (boxer), poids m coq.

baptize [bæp'taiz], *v.tr.* baptiser. **'baptism,** *s.* baptême *f.*

bar [bɑːr]. **I.** *s.* **1.** barre *f* (de fer); lingot m (d'or); *pl.* barreaux m (d'une cage); behind prison bars, sous les verrous. **2.** empêchement m, obstacle m; colour b., ségrégation *f* (raciale). **3.** Jur: barre (des accusés); barreau m (des avocats); to be called to the b., être reçu avocat. **4.** bar m, buvette *f*; comptoir m. **II.** ‡*v.tr.* barrer (le chemin). **2.** défendre, interdire (une action); F: ne pas supporter (qn, une habitude). **III.** *prep.* *(also barring)* excepté, sauf.

barbarian [bɑːˈbɛəriən], *s.* barbare *mf.* **barˈbaric,** *a.* barbare. **barˈbarity,** *s.* barbarie *f*, cruauté *f.* **ˈbarbarous,** *a.* barbare; cruel, inhumain.

barbecue ['bɑːbikjuː], *s.* barbecue m.

bare [bɛər]. **I.** *a.* nu; b. legs, jambes nues; b. countryside, pays nu, dénudé, pelé; El: b. wire, fil dénudé; to earn a b. living, gagner tout juste de quoi vivre; a b. thank you, un merci tout sec. **II.** *v.tr.* mettre à nu. **'bareback,** *adv.* to ride b., monter (un cheval) à nu, à poil. **'barefaced,** *a.* (mensonge) éhonté, cynique. **'barefoot,** *adv.* nu-pieds, pieds nus. **'bare'headed,** *a.* & *adv.* nu-tête, tête nue.

bargain ['bɑːgin]. **I.** s. **1.** (a) marché m, affaire f; (b) occasion f; **into the b.,** par-dessus le marché. **2. b. sale,** vente de soldes. **II.** v.i. (a) négocier (avec qn); (b) marchander.

barge [bɑːdʒ], s. chaland m, péniche f.

baritone ['bæritoun], s. baryton m.

bark¹ [bɑːk], s. écorce f (d'arbre).

bark². **I.** v.i. aboyer. **II.** s. aboiement m; **his bark's worse than his bark,** il fait plus de bruit que de mal. **'barking. I.** a. (chien) aboyeur. **2.** s. aboiement m.

barley ['bɑːli], s. orge f; **b. sugar,** sucre m d'orge.

barmaid ['bɑːmeid], s. serveuse f (de café).

†barman ['bɑːmən], s. garçon m de comptoir; barman, pl. barmen.

barn [bɑːn], s. grange f.

barnacle ['bɑːnəkl], s. bernache f.

barometer [bə'rɔmitər], s. baromètre m.

baron ['bærən], s. baron m. **'baroness,** s. baronne f. **'baronet,** s. baronnet m.

barrack ['bærək], s. **1.** usu.pl. caserne f; quartier m; **b. room,** chambrée f. **2.** Pej: **great b. of a place,** grand bâtiment m (laid).

barrage ['bærɑːʒ], s. **1.** barrage m (d'un fleuve). **2.** Mil: tir m de barrage; **b. balloon,** ballon m de protection.

barrel ['bærəl], s. **1.** tonneau m, barrique f, fût m. **2.** cylindre m; canon m (de fusil). **3. b. organ,** orgue m de Barbarie.

barren ['bærən], a. stérile; improductif. **'barrenness,** s. stérilité f.

barricade ['bærikeid]. **I.** s. barricade f. **II.** v.tr. barricader.

barrier ['bæriər], s. barrière f; obstacle m.

barrister ['bæristər], s. avocat m.

barrow ['bærou], s. baladeuse f; voiture f à bras; **b. boy,** marchand m des quatre-saisons.

barter ['bɑːtər]. **I.** s. échange m; troc m. **II.** v.tr. échanger; troquer.

base [beis]. **I.** s. **1.** base f; fondement m; (of apparatus) socle m, pied m; **submarine b.,** nid m de sous-marins. **II.** v.tr. baser, fonder (on, sur). **III.** a. (motif) bas, indigne; (métal) vil. **baseless,** a. sans base, sans fondement. **'basement,** s. sous-sol m.

baseball [beisbɔːl], s. Sp: U.S: base-ball m.

bash [bæʃ], v.tr. F: cogner; défoncer.

bashful ['bæʃf(u)l], a. (a) timide; (b) modeste, pudique. **-ly,** adv. (a) timidement; (b) pudiquement. **'bashfulness,** s. timidité f; fausse honte.

basin ['beisn], s. (a) H: bassin m; (small) bol m; (large) bassine f; (b) bassin (d'un fleuve).

†basis ['beisis], s. base f; fondement m. **basic,** a. fondamental. **b. pay,** salaire m de base; **b. English,** l'anglais m de base. **-ally,** a. fondamentalement.

bask [bɑːsk], v.i. se chauffer; prendre le soleil.

basket ['bɑːskit], s. corbeille f; panier m; **b. work,** vannerie f. **'basketball,** s. Sp: basket(-ball).

bass [beis], a. & s. basse f; **b. voice,** voix de basse.

bastard ['bæstəd, bɑː-], a. & s. (a) bâtard, -e; (b) s. P: salaud m. **'bastardy,** v.tr. abâtardir.

bat¹ [bæt], s. chauve-souris f, pl. chauves-souris.

bat². **1.** s. batte f (de cricket, etc.); **to do sth. off one's own b.,** faire qch. de sa propre initiative. **II.** v.l. **1.** v.i. (cricket, etc.) manier la batte; être au guichet. **2.** v.tr. F: **he never batted an eyelid,** il n'a pas sourcillé, bronché. **†'batsman** s. (at cricket) batteur m.

batch [bætʃ], s. fournée f (de pain); paquet m (de lettres).

bate [beit], v.tr. **with bated breath,** en baissant la voix.

bath [bɑːθ]. **I.** s. **1.** bain m; **to take a b.,** prendre un bain; **b. salts,** sels m pour le bain; **b. towel,** serviette f de bain. **2.** baignoire f. **II.** v. **1.** v.tr. baigner (un enfant). **2.** v.i. prendre un bain. **'bathmat,** s. descente f de bain. **'bathroom,** s. salle f de bain(s).

bathe [beið]. **I.** v.tr. & i. baigner; se baigner; laver, lotionner (une plaie). **II.** s. bain m (de mer); baignade f. **'bather,** s. baigneur, -euse. **'bathing,** s. (a) bains mpl (de mer); baignades fpl; **b. costume,** costume m, maillot m, de bain; **b. trunks,** slip m de bain; (b) lotion f (d'une plaie).

baton ['bæt(ə)n], s. bâton m.

battalion [bə'tæljən], s. bataillon m.

batter¹ ['bætər], s. pâte f lisse; pâte à frire.

batter², v.tr. battre. **'battered,** a. (chapeau) délabré; (visage) meurtri.

battery ['bætəri], s. **1.** Mil: batterie f. **2.** (a) El: pile f; (b) éleveuse f (à poulets), batterie. **3.** Jur: **assault and b.,** coups mpl et blessures fpl.

battle ['bætl], s. bataille f, combat m; **b. axe,** hache f d'armes; F: (of woman) (old) **b. axe,** virago f; Mil: **b. dress,** tenue f de campagne. **'battlefield,** s. champ m de bataille. **'battlements,** s.pl. créneaux m. **'battleship,** s. cuirassé m.

bauxite ['bɔːksait], s. bauxite f.

bawl [bɔːl], v.tr. & i. beugler; crier à tue-tête.

bay¹[bei], s. bay(tree), laurier m; **b. leaf,** feuille f de laurier.

bay². s. Geog: baie f.

bay³. s. enfoncement m; baie f; **b. window,** fenêtre f en saillie; Aut: parking **b.,** place f de stationnement; Com: **loading b.,** quai m de chargement.

bay⁴. **I.** v.i. (of hound) aboyer. **II.** s. (also baying) aboiement m; **to be at b.,** être aux abois.

bay⁵. a. & s. (cheval) bai (m).

bayonet ['beiənit], s. baïonnette f.

bazaar [bə'zɑːr], s. 1. bazar m (oriental). 2. vente f de charité; kermesse f.

‡be [stressed biː, unstressed bi(ː)], v.i. être. 1. (a) he is an Englishman, il est Anglais; (b) three and two are five, trois et deux font cinq. 2. (a) to be in danger, se trouver en danger; here I am, me voici; (b) how are you? comment allez-vous? (c) how much is that? combien cela coûte-t-il? (d) to-morrow is Friday, c'est demain vendredi. 3. (a) to be cold, avoir froid; (b) to be twenty, avoir vingt ans. 4. (a) that may be, cela se peut; (b) impers. there is, there are, il y a. 5. I have been into every room, j'ai visité toutes les pièces; has anyone been? est-il venu quelqu'un? 6. impers. (a) it is fine, il fait beau; (b) as one says; as it were, pour ainsi dire. 7. (a) (auxiliary use) I am, was, doing sth., je fais, faisais, qch.; (b) (passive) he was killed, il fut tué; he is to be pitied, il est à plaindre; what is to be done? que faire? (c) (future) I am to see him to-morrow, je dois le voir demain. 8. to be for s.o., tenir pour qn. 9. he is back.—is he? il est de retour.—vraiment? are you happy?—I am! êtes-vous content?—oui.

beach [biːtʃ], s. plage f, grève f, rivage m. **'beachwear,** s. vêtements mpl de plage.

beacon ['biːk(ə)n], s. balise f. 1. (b. (light), fanal m, phare m; Aut: Belisha, traffic, b., sphère m orange, indiquant un passage clouté.

bead [biːd], s. 1. to tell one's beads, dire son chapelet. 2. perle f; (string of) beads, collier m.

beak [biːk], s. 1. bec m (d'oiseau). 2. F: magistrat m.

beaker ['biːkər], s. gobelet m; coupe f.

beam [biːm]. I. s. 1. poutre f; solive f. 2. (a) rayon m; b. of delight, large sourire; (b) navigation, navigation f radiogoniométrique; wireless b., faisceau m hertzien; T.V: electron b., faisceau électronique; F: to be off b., dérailler. 3. (of ship) to be on her b. ends, être engagé; F: (of pers.) to be on one's b. ends, être à bout de ressources. II. v.i. rayonner. **'beaming,** a. rayonnant; radieux.

bean [biːn], s. 1. broad b., fève f; French beans, haricots m verts. 2. grain m (de café).

bear[1] ['beər], s. 1. ours m; she-b., ourse f; polar b., ours blanc. 2. baissier m (à la Bourse).

‡bear[2], v.tr. & i. 1. porter (un fardeau, une date); (b) supporter (la douleur); soutenir (un poids); F: I can't b. him, je ne peux pas le sentir; (c) Aut: etc: b. right, tournez à droite; (d) donner naissance à (un enfant); Fin: to b. interest, porter intérêt. **'bearable,** a.

supportable. **'bearer,** s. porteur, -euse; titulaire mf (d'un passeport); Fin: b. bond, titre m au porteur. **'bearing,** s. (a) E: (i) palier m, roulement m; (ii) coussinet; (b) orientation f; Nau: relèvement m. **bear 'out,** v.tr. confirmer. **bear 'up,** v.i. faire face (au malheur).

beard [biəd], s. barbe f. **'bearded,** a. barbu.

beast [biːst], s. bête f; (of pers.) what a b.! quel animal! quel abruti! **'beastliness,** s. bestialité f, brutalité f. 2. saleté f (d'esprit). **beastly.** 1. a. bestial, dégoûtant, infect. 2. adv. F: (intensive) terriblement, bigrement.

‡beat [biːt]. I. v.tr. & i. battre (qn, qch.); F: that beats everything, ça c'est le comble. II. s. 1. (a) battement m (du cœur); (b) Mus: mesure f, temps m. 2. ronde f (d'un agent de police). **beat 'back,** v.tr. repousser (qn); rabattre (les flammes). **beat 'down,** v.tr. (r)abattre (qch.); marchander avec (qn). **'beaten,** a. 1. the b. track, le chemin battu; house off the b. track, maison écartée. 2. (fer) battu, martelé. **'beating,** s. 1. battement m (du cœur). 2. (a) coups mpl; F: rossée f; (b) défaite f. **beat 'off,** v.tr. repousser (une attaque). **beat 'up,** v.tr. 1. battre, fouetter (des œufs, etc.). 2. F: rosser (qn).

beautiful ['bjuːtif(u)l], a. beau, magnifique. **'beautify,** v.tr. embellir. **'beauty,** s. beauté f.

beaver ['biːvər], s. castor m; F: eager b., fayot m.

because [bi'kɔ(ː)z]. 1. conj. parce que. 2. prep.phr. b. of, à cause de.

beck [bek], s. at s.o.'s b. and call, aux ordres de qn.

beckon ['bek(ə)n], v.tr. & i. faire signe; appeler de la main.

‡become [bi'kʌm], v.i. devenir; to b. a doctor, se faire médecin; to b. old, vieillir; to b. accustomed to sth., s'accoutumer à qch.; what's b. of him? qu'est-il devenu? **be'coming,** a. her dress is very b., sa robe lui va bien.

bed [bed], s. 1. lit m; to go to b., se coucher; to be in b., (i) être couché; (ii) (when ill) garder le lit. 2. lit (d'une rivière); banc m (d'huîtres); (flower) b., parterre m. **'bedclothes,** s.pl. couvertures f de (lit); literie f. **'bedding,** s. 1. literie f. 2. b. (out), dépotage m (de plantes). **'bedridden,** a. cloué au lit. **'bedroom,** s. chambre f (à coucher). **'bedside,** s. chevet m; bord m du lit; b. rug, descente f de lit; b. lamp, lampe f de chevet. **'bedspread,** s. couvre-lit m. **'bedstead,** s. bois m de lit. **'bedtime,** s. heure f du coucher.

bedlam ['bedləm], s. charivari m, tohubohu m.

bee [biː], s. abeille f; b. keeping, apiculture f; beehive, s. ruche f; beeline, s. ligne f droite; to make a b. for sth., aller droit vers qch.

beech [biːtʃ], s. hêtre m; copper b., hêtre rouge; b. nut, faîne f.

beef [biːf], s. bœuf m; roast b., rosbif m; b. tea, bouillon m. beefy, a: F: costaud. beef'steak, s. bifteck m.

beer [ˈbiər], s. bière f; F: to think no small b. of oneself, ne pas se moucher du pied.

beet [biːt], s. (also beetroot) betterave f; sugar beet, betterave à sucre.

beetle [ˈbiːtl], s. coléoptère m; scarabée m.

before [biˈfɔːr]. 1. adv. (a) (place) en avant; devant; (b) (time) auparavant; précédent; the day b., la veille; I have seen him b., je l'ai déjà vu. 2. prep. (a) (place) devant; b. my eyes, sous mes yeux; (b) (time) avant. 3. conj. avant que; avant de. be'forehand, adv. préalablement; d'avance.

befriend [biˈfrend], v.tr. secourir.

‡beg [beg], v.tr. & i. 1. mendier. 2. solliciter; supplier; I beg (of) you, je vous en prie! beggar, s. 1. mendiant, -ante. 2. F: individu m; poor b.! pauvre diable! 'begging, s. mendicité f.

‡begin [biˈgin], v.tr. & i. commencer; se mettre à (faire qch.); to b. with, tout d'abord; to b. again, recommencer. be'ginner, s. commençant, -ante, débutant, -ante; novice mf. be'ginning, s. commencement m; début m; origine f.

behalf [biˈhɑːf], s. 1. on b. of, au nom de (qn); de la part de (qn). 2. in favour of (qn).

behave [biˈheiv], v.i. se conduire, se comporter; to know how to b., savoir vivre; (to child) b. yourself! sois sage! be'haved, a, used in: well b., sage, poli; qui se conduit bien; badly b., qui se conduit mal. be'haviour, s. tenue f, maintien m, conduite f.

behead [biˈhed], v.tr. décapiter (qn).

behind [biˈhaind]. 1. adv. derrière; par derrière; (a) to remain b., rester en arrière; (b) en retard (dans son travail). 2. prep. (a) derrière; (b) en arrière de, en retard sur (qch.). 3. s.f: derrière m; to sit on one's b., ne rien faire. be'hindhand, adv. & pred.a, en arrière; en retard; attardé.

being [ˈbiːiŋ]. I. s. 1. existence f; to bring a plan into b., réaliser un projet. 2. être m (humain). II. a. for the time b., pour le moment.

belated [biˈleitid], a. 1. attardé. 2. tardif.

belch [bel(t)ʃ]. I. v.i. 1. v.i. éructer. 2. v.tr. vomir (des flammes). II. s. éructation f. 'belching, s. 1. éructations fpl. 2. vomissement m (de flammes).

belfry [ˈbelfri], s. beffroi m, clocher m.

Belgian [ˈbeldʒən], a. & s. belge (mf).

believe [biˈliːv]. 1. v.tr. croire; ajouter foi à; to make s.o. b., faire accroire à qn. 2. v.i. croire. 3. to make b., faire semblant. be'lief, s. croyance f; conviction f; foi f. be'lievable, a. croyable. be'liever, s. croyant, -ante.

belittle [biˈlitl], v.tr. rabaisser, déprécier.

bell [bel], s. cloche f; clochette f; sonnette f; timbre m; grelot m; b. tower, clocher m; electric b., sonnerie f (électrique); to ring the b., sonner; F: that rings a b., cela me rappelle, dit, quelque chose. 'bellboy, s., 'bellhop, s. U.S: groom m (d'hôtel), chasseur m. 'bellringer, s. carillonneur m.

belligerent [beˈlidʒər(ə)nt], a. & s. belligérant (m).

bellow [ˈbelou]. I. v.i. beugler, mugir; hurler. II. s. beuglement m, mugissement m; hurlement m.

bellows [ˈbelouz], s.pl. soufflet m (pour le feu).

‡belly [ˈbeli], s. ventre m. bellyache. I. s.f: mal de ventre m; colique f. II. v.i. P: ronchonner, rouspéter. 'bellyful, s. plein ventre; F: to have a b., en avoir plein le dos. 'bellyland, v. Av: F: atterrissage m sur le ventre.

belong [biˈlɔŋ], v.i. 1. appartenir (to, à). 2. to b. to a society, être membre d'une société; put it back where it belongs, remettez-le à sa place. be'longings, s.pl. affaires f, effets m.

below [biˈlou]. 1. adv. (a) en bas, (audessous); (b) ci-dessous. 2. prep. (a) au-dessous de; (b) sous.

belt [belt], s. 1. ceinture f; Av: Aut: seat b., ceinture de sécurité; F: to hit s.o. below the b., donner à qn un coup en traître. 2. El: courroie f (de transmission). 3. Adm: green b., zone verte, zone de verdure.

bench [ben(t)ʃ], s. 1. banc m; banquette f. 2. établi m (de menuisier).

‡bend [bend]. I. v.tr. & i. 1. courber; plier; baisser (la tête); arquer (le dos); F: to b. the elbow, lever le coude. 2. to b. (sth.) out of shape, forcer, fausser (qch.). II. s. 1. courbure f, courbe f; (of pipe) coude m; (of road) virage m; P.N: bends for 3 miles, virages sur 5 kilomètres; F: to be round the b., être fou, cinglé, dingo. 2. Med: F: the bends, mal m des caissons. bend 'down, v.i. se baisser.

beneath [biˈniːθ]. 1. adv. dessous, au-dessous. 2. prep. au-dessous de; sous; it is b. him, c'est indigne de lui.

benedictine [beniˈdiktin]. 1. a. & s. Ecc: Bénédictin, -e. 2. s. Cu: Bénédictine f.

benediction [beniˈdik(ʃ)ən], s. bénédiction f.

benefactor [ˈbenifæktər], s. bienfaiteur, -trice.

benefice [ˈbenifis], s. Ecc: bénéfice m.

beneficial [beni'fiʃ(ə)l], *a.* profitable, avantageux. **-ally,** *adv.* avantageusement.

†**beneficiary** [beni'fiʃəri], *s.* bénéficiaire *m.*

benefit ['benifit]. I. *s.* 1. avantage *m,* profit *m.* 2. *Adm:* indemnité *f,* allocation *f;* unemployment b., indemnité de chômage. II. *v.i.* to b. by sth., profiter de qch.

benevolence [bi'nevələns], *s.* bienveillance *f,* bonté *f.* be'nevolent, *a.* bienveillant.

benign [bi'nain], *a. Med:* (of tumour) bénin.

bent [bent]. I. *a.* 1. courbé, plié; b. back, dos voûté. 2. b. on doing sth., déterminé, résolu, à faire qch. II. *s.* penchant *m,* disposition *f* (for, pour).

bequeath [bi'kwi:ð], *v.tr.* léguer. be'quest, *s. legs m.*

bereavement [bi'ri:vmənt], *s.* perte *f* (d'un parent); deuil *m.*

beret ['berei], *s.* béret *m.*

†**berry** ['beri], *s. Bot:* baie *f.*

berth [bə:θ], *s.* 1. *Nau:* (a) (to give a ship a wide b., passer au large d'un navire; *F:* to give s.o. a wide b., éviter qn; (b) poste *m* de mouillage. 2. *Nau: Rail:* couchette *f.*

beryl ['beril], *s.* béryl *m.*

beside [bi'said], *prep.* 1. à côté, auprès, de. 2. (a) b. the point, en dehors du sujet; (b) b. oneself, hors de soi.

besides [bi'saidz]. 1. *adv.* (a) en outre, en plus; (b) d'ailleurs, 2. *prep.* en plus de.

besiege [bi'si:dʒ], *v.tr.* assiéger.

bespoke [bi'spouk], *a.* (vêtement) (fait) sur mesure.

best [best]. I. *a. & s.* (a) (le) meilleur, (la) meilleure; le mieux; b. man, garçon d'honneur; in one's b., endimanché; the b. of it, le plus beau de l'affaire; to do one's b., faire de son mieux; to get the b. of it, avoir le dessus; (b) *adv.phr.* at b., pour dire le mieux; to the b. of my belief, à ce que je crois. 2. *adv.* (le) mieux; as b. I could, de mon mieux; b. seller, s. (a) livre m à succès; (b) auteur m à gros tirages; (c) article m de grosse vente.

bestial ['bestjəl], *a.* bestial.

bet [bet]. I. *s.* pari *m,* gageure *f.* II. *v.tr.* parier. 'better[1], *s.* parieur *m.* 'betting, *s.* les paris *m;* b. shop = bureau *m* du pari mutuel.

betray [bi'trei], *v.tr.* trahir. be'trayal, *s.* trahison *f.*

better[2] ['betər]. I. *a., s. & adv.* meilleur, -e; I had hoped for b. things, j'avais espéré mieux. 2. *a. & s.* mieux; that's my b., voilà qui est mieux; so much the b., tant mieux; to get b., s'améliorer; guérir; to be b., aller mieux; to get the b. of s.o., l'emporter sur qn.

3. *adv.* (a) mieux; to think b. of it, se raviser; (b) b. known, plus connu. II. *v.tr.* to b. oneself, améliorer sa position.

between [bi'twi:n], *prep.* entre; b. now and Monday, d'ici (à) lundi; b. twenty and thirty, de vingt à trente; b. ourselves, entre nous.

beverage ['bevəridʒ], *s.* boisson *f.*

beware [bi'wɛər], *v.ind.tr.* (*used only in infin. & imperative*) se méfier (de qn, qch.); *P.N.:* b. of the trains! attention aux trains!

bewilder [bi'wildər], *v.tr.* désorienter, égarer; ahurir. be'wildered, *a.* désorienté; ahuri. be'wildering, *a.* déroutant. be'wilderment, *s.* désorientation *f;* ahurissement *m.*

beyond [bi'jɔnd]. 1. *adv.* au delà, par delà, plus loin. 2. *prep.* au delà de, par delà; it is b. me, cela me dépasse; b. doubt, hors de doute. 3. *s.* he lives at the back of b., il habite un trou perdu, en plein bled.

bias ['baiəs], *s.* 1. material cut on the b., tissu coupé en biais *m.* 2. parti pris; penchant *m* (pour qch.); vocational b., déformation *f* professionnelle. 'biased, *a.* partial.

bib [bib], *s.* bavette *f.*

Bible ['baibl], *s.* Bible *f.* 'biblical, *a.* biblique.

†**bibliography** [bibli'ɔgrəfi], *s.* bibliographie *f.*

bicarbonate [bai'ka:bənit], *s.* bicarbonate *m.*

bicker ['bikər], *v.i.* se chamailler.

bicycle ['baisikl], *s.* bicyclette *f,* vélo *m.*

†**bid** [bid]. I. *v.tr. & i.* (a) (*at auction sale*) faire une offre (pour qch.); (b) (*at cards*) demander, appeler (trois carreaux, etc.). II. *s.* (a) (*at auction sale*) enchère *f,* offre *f;* (b) (*at cards*) appel *m,* demande *f;* no b.! parole! 'bidder, *s.* enchérisseur *m.* 'bidding, *s.* 1. ordre *m.* 2. enchères *fpl,* mises *fpl.*

bier ['biər], *s.* civière *f.*

biff [bif]. I. *v.tr. P:* flanquer un gnon (à qn). II. *s. P:* gnon *m.*

bifocal [bai'fouk(ə)l], *a.* bifocal; (verres) à double foyer.

big [big]. 1.*a.* (*a*) grand; gros; to have b. ideas, voir grand; *F:* b. noise, gros bonnet *m;* (b) lourd (de conséquences). 2. *adv.* to talk b., faire l'important.

bigamy ['bigəmi], *s.* bigamie *f.* 'bigamist, *s.* bigame *mf.* 'bigamous, *a.* bigame.

bigot ['bigət], *s.* sectaire *mf;* fanatique *mf.* 'bigoted, *a.* fanatique. 'bigotry, *s.* bigoterie *f;* fanatisme *m.*

bigwig ['bigwig], *s. F:* gros bonnet *m,* grosse légume *f.*

bilberry ['bilbəri], *s. Bot:* airelle *f,* myrtille *f.*

bile [bail], *s.* bile *f.*

bilge [bildʒ], *s.* eau *f* de cale; *P:* to talk b., dire des bêtises.

bilingual [bai'lingw(ə)l], a. bilingue.

bilious ['biljəs], a. bilieux. **'biliousness,** s. attaque f de bile.

bill[1] [bil], s. bec m.

bill[2] [bil], s. 1. note f, mémoire m; addition f. 2. (a) U.S: billet m de banque; (b) Fin: b. of exchange, lettre f de change. 3. affiche f, placard m; P.N: stick no bills! défense d'afficher! 4. b. of fare, menu m. 5. projet m de loi. **'billfold,** s. U.S: portefeuille m.

billet ['bilit], I. v.tr. Mil: loger (des troupes). II. s. Mil: logement m.

billiard ['biljəd], s. 1. pl. billiards, (jeu m de) billard m. 2. b. ball, bille f de billard; b. table, billard m.

billion ['biljən], s. billion m, U.S: milliard m.

bin [bin], s. coffre m, huche f; wine b., casier m à bouteilles.

‡**bind** [baind], v.tr. attacher, lier. 1. bound hand and foot, pieds et poings liés. 2. bander (une blessure). 3. relier (un livre); paper bound, broché. 4. F: rendre obligatoire. **'binding.** I. a. 1. (agent) agglomérant. 2. (of promise, etc.) obligatoire; qui lie. 3. constipant. II. s. 1. agrégation f; fixation f. 2. reliure f (d'un livre).

biography [bai'ɔgrəfi], s. biographie f. bi'ographer, s. biographe m. bio'graphical, a. biographique.

biology [bai'ɔlədʒi], s. biologie f. bi'ologist, s. biologiste m f.

biophysics ['baiou'fiziks], s. biophysique f.

biosatellite ['baiou'sætəlait], s. satellite m habité.

biped ['baiped], a. & s. bipède (m).

birch [bəːtʃ], s. 1. bouleau m. 2. verge f (pour fouetter).

bird [bəːd], s. oiseau m; F: to give s.o. the b., (i) envoyer promener qn; (ii) Th: siffler qn. 2. P: (a) individu m, type m; (b) femme f.

birth [bəːθ], s. 1. naissance f; French by b., Français de naissance; b. certificate, acte m, extrait m, de naissance; b. control, limitation f, contrôle m, des naissances; b. rate, natalité f; (of animal) to give b. to, mettre bas. **'birthday,** s. anniversaire m (de naissance); F: to be in one's b. suit, être à poil. **'birthmark,** s. envie f; tache f de naissance. **'birthplace,** s. lieu m de naissance; maison f natale.

biscuit ['biskit], s. biscuit m; gâteau sec.

bisect [bai'sekt], v.tr. couper, diviser (en deux parties égales).

bishop ['biʃəp], s. 1. évêque m. 2. (chess) fou m. **'bishopric,** s. évêché m.

bismuth ['bizməθ], s. bismuth m.

bison ['baisən], s. bison m.

bit[1] [bit], s. 1. mors m. 2. mèche f (de vilebrequin).

bit[2], s. 1. (a) morceau m; (b) bout m, brin m; (c) threepenny b., pièce f de trois pence. 2. a b. (of), un peu (de); he's a b. of a liar, il est tant soit peu menteur; not a b. (of it)! n'en croyez rien!

bitch [bitʃ]. I. s. 1. chienne f. 2. P: (of woman) garce f. II. v.tr. P: gâcher, saboter (l'ouvrage).

‡**bite** [bait]. I. v.tr. 1. mordre; piquer. 2. bite off: to b. off more than one can chew, tenter qch. au-dessus de ses forces; F: to b. s.o.'s head off, rembarrer qn. II. s. 1. (a) coup m de dent; (b) Fish: touche f, piqûre f, morsure f. **'biting,** a. mordant; piquant; cinglant.

bitter ['bitər], a. 1. amer; (vent) piquant; implacable; b. experience, expérience cruelle; to go on to the b. end, aller jusqu'au bout. 2. s. (a) bière f blonde (anglaise) sous pression; (b) pl. bitter(s) m, amer(s) m. **-ly,** adv. amèrement. **'bitterness,** s. (a) amertume f; (b) rancune f, rancœur f.

bivouac ['bivuæk]. I. s. bivouac m. II. v.i. bivouaquer.

bizarre [bi'zɑːr], a. bizarre.

black [blæk]. I. a. 1. noir; b. and blue, tout meurtri; b. eye, œil poché; b. market, marché noir; b. pudding, boudin m. II. s. noir m; to put sth. down in b. and white, coucher qch. par écrit. III. v.tr. noircir; to b. sth. out, effacer, rayer, qch. **'blackbeetle,** s. blatte f, cafard m. **'blackberry,** s. mûre f (de ronce). **'blackbird,** s. merle m. **'blackboard,** s. tableau m noir. **'blacken,** v.tr. noircir (un mur, la réputation de qn). **'blackguard,** s. vaurien m. **'blackleg,** s. Ind: renard m, jaune m. **'blacklist,** v.tr. mettre (qn) sur la liste des suspects. **'blackmail.** I. s. chantage m. II. v.tr. soumettre (qn) à un chantage. **'blackmailer,** s. maître-chanteur m. **'blackness,** s. noirceur f; obscurité f. **'blacksmith,** s. forgeron m; maréchalferrant m.

bladder ['blædər], s. vessie f.

blade [bleid], s. 1. brin m (d'herbe). 2. lame f (de couteau). 3. pelle f, pale f (d'aviron); aile f, pale f (d'hélice).

blame [bleim]. I. s. 1. reproches mpl; condamnation f. 2. faute f, responsabilité f. II. v.tr. blâmer, condamner (qn); he is to blame, il y a de sa faute; you've only yourself to b., vous l'avez voulu! **'blameless,** a. innocent, irréprochable.

blanch [blɑːn(t)ʃ]. 1. v.tr. blanchir (des légumes); dérober (des amandes). 2. v.i. blêmir, pâlir.

blank [blæŋk]. I. a. 1. (papier) blanc; (page) vierge, blanche; b. verse, vers blancs, non rimés. 2. b. look, regard sans expression; to look b., avoir l'air déconcerté. **-ly,** adv. d'un air déconcerté. II. s. 1. (a) U.S: formulaire m, formule f; to fill out a b., remplir une formule; (b) to leave blanks, laisser des blancs; my mind is a b., j'ai la tête vide. 2. (in lottery) billet blanc.

blanket ['blæŋkit], s. couverture f (de lit); electric b., couverture chauffante; attrib. général; b. ordre, ordre d'une portée générale.

blare [blɛər], v.i. sonner; the radio is blaring away, la radio fonctionne à casser les oreilles.

blaspheme [blæs'fiːm], v.i. & tr. blasphémer. **'blasphemous**, a. (of pers.) blasphémateur; (of words) blasphématoire. **'blasphemy**, s. blasphème m.

blast [blɑːst]. I. s. 1. coup m de vent; rafale f. 2. (of furnace) in full b., en pleine activité. 3. (of explosion) souffle m; charge f d'explosif. II. v.tr. (a) faire sauter (à la dynamite, etc.); (b) (of lightning) foudroyer (un arbre); (c) int. F: b. (it, you)! zut! 'blast-furnace, s. haut-fourneau m. 'blasting, s. travail m aux explosifs. 'blast-off, s. mise f à feu (d'une fusée). 'blast-screen, s. Av: déflecteur m de souffle.

blatant ['bleit(ə)nt], a. 1. d'une vulgarité criarde. 2. (mensonge) flagrant.

blaze [bleiz]. I. s. 1. flamme(s) f, flambée f. 2. flamboiement m; éclat m. 3. pl. F: go to blazes! allez au diable! II. v.i. (of fire) flamber; (of sun) flamboyer. 'blazing, a. (a) en feu; enflammé; embrasé; (b) F: flambant.

blazer ['bleizər], s. Cl: blazer m.

bleach [bliːtʃ], v.tr. & i. blanchir; oxygéner (les cheveux).

bleak [bliːk], a. 1. (terrain) exposé au vent. 2. (vent) froid. 3. (sourire) pâle. 'bleakness, s. tristesse f; froidure f; aspect m morne.

bleat [bliːt], v.i. bêler; F: what's he bleating about? de quoi se plaint-il? 'bleating, s. (also bleat) bêlement m.

‡**bleed** [bliːd], v.tr. & i. saigner. 'bleeding. I. s. a. saignant. II. s. écoulement m de sang; saignement m.

blemish ['blemiʃ], s. 1. défaut m; imperfection f. 2. tache f, tare f.

blench [blen(t)ʃ], v.i. sourciller, broncher.

blend [blend]. I. v. 1. v.tr. mélanger; couper (des vins). 2. v.i. se mêler, se confondre; (of colours) s'allier, se marier. II. s. mélange m (de cafés, etc.). 'blending, s. mélange m.

‡**bless** [bles], v.tr. bénir; to be blessed with sth., jouir de qch.; well, I'm blest! par exemple! (when s.o. sneezes) b. you! à tes, tes, souhaits! blessed ['blesid], a. 1. Ecc: The B. Virgin, la Sainte Vierge; the B. Martyrs, les bienheureux martyrs. 2. P: the whole b. day, toute la sainte journée. 'blessing, s. (a) bénédiction f; (b) usu.pl. avantages m, bienfaits m (de la civilisation).

blight [blait]. I. s. 1. rouille f, brûlure f; (on cereals) charbon m; (on potatoes) brunissure f. 2. (insect) puceron m. 3. fléau m. II. v.tr. rouiller (le blé, etc.); flétrir (les espérances). 'blighter, s. P: bon m à rien; individu m, type m.

blind[1] [blaind]. I. a. 1. aveugle; b. in one eye, borgne; to turn a b. eye to sth., refuser de voir qch. 2. b. alley, cul-de-sac m, impasse f. -ly, adv. aveuglément; en aveugle. II. v.tr. aveugler. 'blindfold. I. v.tr. bander les yeux à, de (qn). II. a. & adv. 1. les yeux bandés. 2. (= recklessly) aveuglément. 'blindness, s. 1. cécité f. 2. (ignorance) aveuglement m.

blind[2], s. store m; venetian b., jalousie f.

blink [bliŋk], v.i. cligner les yeux; clignoter; to b. the facts, fermer les yeux sur la vérité.

bliss [blis], s. béatitude f, félicité f.

blister ['blistər]. I. s. ampoule f, bulle f; (in paint) boursouflure f. II. v.i. se couvrir d'ampoules; (of paint) (se) cloquer.

blitz [blits]. I. s. F: bombardement m aérien. II. v.tr. the house was blitzed, la maison a été détruite, endommagée, par un bombardement.

blizzard ['blizəd], s. tempête f de neige.

bloated ['bloutid], a. boursouflé, bouffi.

bloater ['bloutər], s. hareng m bouffi.

blob [blɔb], s. tache f; pâté m.

bloc [blɔk], s. Pol: bloc m.

block [blɔk]. I. s. 1. (a) bloc m (de marbre, etc.); Aut: engine b., bloc moteur; (b) P: tête f, caboche f. 2. (a) pâté m, îlot m (de maisons); b. of flats, immeuble m; (b) (in Austr.) lot m (de terrains); (c) Fin: tranche f (d'actions). 3. traffic b., encombrement m. 4. b. capitals, majuscules f d'imprimerie. II. v.tr. bloquer, obstruer. block'ade. I. s. blocus m. II. v.tr. bloquer (un port). 'blockhead, s. F: lourdaud m, sot m. 'block 'up, v.tr. boucher, bloquer (un trou); condamner (une porte); obstruer (un tuyau).

blond, blonde [blɔnd], a. & s. blond, -e.

blood [blʌd], s. sang m; it makes my b. boil, cela m'indigne; in cold b., de sang-froid; blue b., sang royal, aristocratique; b. horse, (cheval) pur-sang m; attrib. b. donor, donneur m, -euse, de sang; b. group, groupe m sanguin; b. orange, (orange) sanguine (f); b. pressure, tension f artérielle; to have high b. pressure, faire de l'hypertension; b. sports, la chasse; b. vessel, vaisseau sanguin. 'bloodcurdling, a. qui vous fige le sang. 'bloodhound, s. limier m. 'bloodless, a. 1. exsangue, anémié. 2. sans effusion de sang. 'bloodshed, s. carnage m. 'bloodshot, a. (oeil) injecté de sang. 'bloodstain, s. tache f de sang. 'bloodstained, a. taché de sang. 'bloodsucker, s. sangsue *f*; vampire *m*. 'bloodthirsty, *a*. sanguinaire; assoiffé de sang. 'bloody, *a*. 1. sanglant, taché de sang; (combat) sanguinaire. 2. *P*: *a*. (intensive) sacré; *a b*. liar, un sacré menteur; it's *b*. hot, il fait bigrement chaud. 'bloody-'minded, *a*. *P*: pas commode; he's *b.-m.*, c'est un mauvais coucheur.

bloom [bluːm]. I. *s*. 1. fleur *f*; in full *b*., épanoui; en pleine fleur. 2. velouté *m*, duvet *m* (d'une pêche, etc.). II. *v.i.* fleurir; être en fleur. 'blooming, *a*. (*a*) en fleur; (*b*) *F*: florissant.

blossom ['blɔsəm]. I. *s*. fleur. II. *v.i.* fleurir; to *b*. out, s'épanouir.

blot [blɔt]. I. *s*. tache *f*; (*of* ink) pâté *m*. II. *v.tr*. 1. tacher; (*of* ink) faire des pâtés sur (qch.). 2. sécher l'encre (d'une lettre). 'blotter, *s*. (bloc) buvard (*m*). 'blotting, *s*. 1. séchage (au papier buvard); *b*. paper, (papier) buvard (*m*).

blotchy ['blɔtʃi], *a*. (teint) couperosé; (peau) couverte de rougeurs.

blouse [blauz], *s. Cl*: corsage *m*.

‡blow[1] [blou], *v.tr. & i*. 1. souffler; it's blowing hard, il fait grand vent; to *b*. one's nose, se moucher; *F*: to *b*. one's own trumpet, chanter ses propres louanges; *El*: to *b*. a fuse, faire sauter les plombs. 'blow 'down, *v.tr*. (*of* wind) abattre, renverser (un arbre). 'blowfly, *s*. mouche *f* à viande. blow 'in. 1. *v.tr*. (*of* wind) enfoncer (une vitre). 2. *v.i. F*: (*of* pers.) entrer en passant. 'blowlamp, *s*. lampe *f* à souder, chalumeau *m*; brûloir *m* (de peintre en bâtiments). 'blow 'off. 1. *v.tr*. (*of* wind) emporter (un chapeau, etc.); to *b*. off steam, (i) (*of machine*) lâcher de la vapeur; (ii) *F*: (*of* pers.) épancher sa bile. 'blow 'out. 1. *v.tr*. (*of* wind) gonfler (les voiles). 2. *v.i*. (*of* candle) s'éteindre; (*of* paper) s'envoler (par la fenêtre). 'blow-out, *s. P*: gueuleton *m*. 'blow 'over, *v.i. & tr*. (se) renverser; (*of* storm) se calmer; (*of* scandal) rentrer dans l'oubli. blow 'up, *v.tr. & i*. (faire) sauter, éclater, exploser.

blow[2], *s*. coup *m*; to come to blows, en venir aux mains.

blubber[1] ['blʌbər], *s*. graisse *f* de baleine.

blubber[2], *v.i.* pleurnicher.

blue [bluː]. I. *a*. bleu; *Med*: *b*. baby, enfant bleu; out of the *b*., soudainement; *F*: you can talk till you're *b*. in the face, vous avez beau parler. II. *s*. (*a*) bleu *m*; (*b*) *H*: bleu (d'empois). III. *v.tr*. 1. (*a*) bleuir; teindre (qch.) au bleu; (*b*) *H*: passer (le linge) au bleu. 2. *F*: to *b*. one's money, gaspiller son argent. 'bluebell, *s*. jacinthe *f* des prés, des bois. 'bluebottle, *s*. mouche *f* à viande. 'blue-eyed, *a*. (*a*) aux yeux bleus; (*b*) *F*: innocent; mother's *b.-e*.

boy, le chou-chou de maman. 'blue-'pencil, *v.tr*. marquer au crayon bleu; censurer. 'blueprint, *s*. dessin négatif; photocalque *m*. 'bluestocking, *s.f*: bas-bleu *m*.

bluff[1] [blʌf]. I. *a*. brusque. II. *s*. cap *m* à pic; a-pic *m*.

bluff.[2] *s*. bluff *m*. II. *v.tr*. bluffer (qn); *abs*. faire du bluff.

blunder ['blʌndər]. I. *s*. bévue *f*, maladresse *f*, gaffe *f*. II. *v.i. & tr*. 1. faire une bévue, une maladresse. 2. se heurter (contre qn). 'blunderer, *s*. maladroit, -e; gaffeur, -euse. 'blundering, *a*. maladroit.

blunt [blʌnt]. I. *a*. 1. émoussé. 2. brusque, -ly, *adv*. brusquement, carrément. II. *v.tr*. émousser. 'bluntness, *s*. 1. manque *m* de tranchant. 2. brusquerie *f*, franchise *f*.

‡blur [blǝːr], *v.tr*: to *b*. out a secret, laisser échapper un secret.

blush [blʌʃ]. I. *s*. rougeur *f*. II. *v.i*. rougir. 'blushing, *a*. rougissant; timide.

boa ['bouə], *s*. boa *m*; *b*. constrictor, boa constrictor.

boar ['bɔːr], *s*. verrat *m*; wild *b*., sanglier *m*.

board [bɔːd]. I. *s*. 1. planche *f*; madrier *m*; *Aut: Av*: (fascia), tableau *m* de bord. 2. *b*. and lodging, pension *f* et chambre(s). 3. *b*. of enquiry, commission *f* d'enquête; *b*. of examiners, jury *m* (d'examen); *Com*: *b*. of directors, conseil *m* d'administration. 4. *Nau*: on *b*. a ship, à bord. II. *v*. 1. *v.i*. être en pension. 2. *v.tr*. monter à bord (d'un navire); monter dans (un train). 'boarder, *s*. pensionnaire *mf*; *Sch*: interne *mf*. 'boarding house, *s*. pension *f* de famille. 'boarding school, *s*. pensionnat *m*, internat *m*.

boast [boust]. I. *v*. 1. *v.i.* se vanter. 2. *v.tr*. être fier de posséder (qch.); the school boasts a fine library, l'école possède une belle bibliothèque. II. *s*. vanterie *f*. 'boaster, *s*. vantard *m*. 'boastful, *a*. vantard. 'boastfulness, *s*. 'boasting, *a*. vantardise *f*.

boat [bout], *s*. bateau *m*; canot *m*; barque *f*; navire *m*; we're all in the same *b*., nous sommes tous dans le même panier; *attrib*. *b*. builder, constructeur *m* de canots, de bateaux; *b*. race, course *f* de bateaux; *b*. train, train *m* du bateau. 'boathouse, *s*. hangar *m*, garage *m*, pour canots. 'boating, *s*. canotage *m*. 'boatswain [bousn], *s*. maître *m* d'équipage.

bob[1] [bɔb], *s*. 1. coiffure *f* à la Ninon, à la Jeanne d'Arc. 2. *U.S*: patin *m* (de traîneau); (*b*) *b*.(-sleigh), bob (-sleigh) *m*.

‡bob², *v.i.* (*a*) s'agiter; (*b*) to b. up, surgir brusquement; to b. up again, revenir à la surface.

bob³, *s.inv. F:* shilling *m.*

bobby ['bɔbi], *s. F:* agent *m* de police, flic *m.* 'bobby pin, *s. U.S:* pince *f* à cheveux.

bobbin ['bɔbin], *s.* bobine *f.*

bodice ['bɔdis], *s.* corsage *m* (d'une robe).

bodkin ['bɔdkin], *s.* (*a*) passe-lacet *m;* (*b*) poinçon *m.*

body ['bɔdi], *s.* 1. (*a*) corps *m;* (dead) b., cadavre *m;* (*b*) consistence *f.* 2. legislative b., corps législatif; public b., corporation *f;* large b. of people, foule *f* nombreuse. 3. corps (de document); nef *f* (d'église); *Aut:* carrosserie *f.* 'bodily. I. *a.* corporal, physique. 2. *adv.* en corps; ensemble. 'bodyguard, *s.* garde *f* du corps.

bog [bɔg]. I. *s.* fondrière *f;* marécage *m; F:* what a b.! quelle gaffe! II. *v.tr. usu. passive* to get bogged (down), s'embourber, s'enliser. 'boggy, *a.* marécageux.

bogey ['bɔugi], *s.* 1. spectre *m;* épouvantail *m.* 2. *Golf:* la normale du parcours.

boggle [bɔgl], *v.i.* rechigner, reculer (devant qch.).

bogus ['bɔugəs], *a.* faux; feint.

Bohemian [bou'hi:miən]. 1. *a. & s. Geog:* bohémien, -ienne. 2. *attrib.* b. life, vie de bohème.

boil¹ [bɔil], *s.* furoncle *m.*

boil². 1. *v.i.* bouillir. 2. *v.tr.* faire bouillir; faire cuire à l'eau; boiled egg, œuf à la coque. boil a'way, *v.i.* (*of liquid*) se réduire. boil 'down, *v.i.* se réduire, *F:* se borner, revenir (to, à). 'boiler, *s.* chaudière *f;* b. suit, bleus *mpl,* bleu *m* de chauffe. 'boiling. I. *s.* ébullition *f;* b. point, point d'ébullition. II. *a.* bouillant; *adv.* b. hot, tout bouillant. boil 'over, *v.i.* (*a*) (*of liquid*) se sauver; (*b*) bouiller (de colère).

boisterous ['bɔist(ə)rəs], *a.* bruyant, turbulent; violent. -ly, *adv.* bruyamment; tempêtueusement.

bold [bould], *a.* 1. hardi; audacieux; assuré, courageux. 2. impudent, effronté. -ly, *adv.* 1. hardiment. 2. effrontément. 'boldness, *s.* 1. hardiesse *f;* audace *f.* 2. effronterie *f.*

Bolshevik ['bɔlʃəvik], *a. & s.* bolchéviste (*mf*).

bolster ['boulstər]. I. *s.* traversin *m.* II. *v.tr.* to b. s.o. up, soutenir qn (qui a tort).

bolt [boult]. I. *s.* 1. (thunder) b., coup *m* de foudre; b. from the blue, événement *m* imprévu. 2. *F:* fuite *f.* 3. verrou *m;* (rifle) b., culasse *f* mobile. 4. *E:* boulon *m;* cheville *f;* nuts and bolts, boulonnerie *f.* II. *v.* 1. *v.i.* (*a*) *F:* décamper; (*of horse*) s'emballer. 2.

v.tr. F: gober (un repas). 3. *v.tr.* (*a*) verrouiller (une porte); mettre les verrous; (*b*) boulonner; cheviller. III. *adv.* b. upright, tout droit.

bomb [bɔm]. I. *s.* bombe *f;* atom b., bombe atomique; b. disposal, (i) désobusage *m,* (ii) déminage *m; Av:* b. rack, ratelier *m* à bombes. II. *v.tr.* bombarder (une ville). 'bombardment, *s.* bombardement *m.* 'bomber, *s.* avion *m* de bombardement. 'bombing, *s.* bombardement *m;* dive b., bombardement en piqué. 'bombshell. *s.* to be, come like, a b., consterner (qn); tomber des nues.

bombastic [bɔm'bæstik], *a.* emphatique, ampoulé.

bona fide ['bɔunə'faidi], *a. & adv.* de bonne foi; b. f. offer, offre sérieuse.

bond [bɔnd], *s.* 1. lien *m;* attache *f.* 2. (*a*) contrat *m;* obligation *f;* (*b*) bon *m;* bearer b., bon au porteur; premium bonds, bons à lots; (*c*) *Jur:* caution *f.* 3. *Com:* (of goods) to be in b., être à l'entrepôt.

bone [boun]. I. *s.* 1. os *m;* fish b., arête *f;* b. china, demi-porcelaine *f;* b. dry, absolument sec; b. idle, b. lazy, paresseux comme une couleuvre. 2. *pl.* (*of the dead*) ossements *m.* II. *v.tr.* 1. désosser (la viande); ôter les arêtes (du poisson). 2. *P:* voler, chiper (qch.). 'boneless, *a.* désossé; sans os; sans arêtes. 'bony, *a.* osseux. 2. décharné. 3. (*of meat*) plein d'os; (of fish) plein d'arêtes.

bonfire ['bɔnfaiər], *s.* feu *m* de joie.

bonnet ['bɔnit], *s.* 1. *Cl:* bonnet *m.* 2. *Aut:* capot *m.*

bonus ['bɔunəs], *s.* surpaye *f,* boni *m;* prime *f.*

boo [bu:]. 1. *int.* hou! 2. *v.tr. & i.* huer.

book [buk]. I. *s.* 1. (*a*) livre *m;* b. club, club *m* du livre; b. post, service postal des imprimés; 2. *knowledge,* connaissances *f;* livresques; school b., text b., livre de classe; (*b*) livret *m* (d'un opéra). 2. (*a*) registre *m;* account b., livre de comptes; to be in s.o.'s bad books, être mal vu de qn; (*b*) exercise b., cahier *m;* telephone b., annuaire *m* du téléphone; (*c*) betting b., livre de paris; to make a b., faire un livre; *F:* that suits my b., ça fait mon beurre; (*d*) b. matches, allumettes *f* en pochette. II. *v.tr.* inscrire, enregistrer (une commande); *Com:* shall I b. it for you? dois-je l'inscrire à votre compte? 2. retenir, réserver (une chambre, une place). 3. *Aut: F:* to be booked = avoir une contravention. 'bookable, *a.* qui peut être retenu, réservé. 'bookbinder, *s.* relieur *m.* 'bookbinding, *s.* reliure *f.* 'bookcase, *s.* bibliothèque *f.* 'bookie, *s. F:* book (maker) *m.* 'booking, *s.* 1. enregistrement *m,* inscription *f.* 2. réservation *f* (des places); b. clerk, employé(e) du guichet; b. office, guichet *m*. **'bookish,** *a.* 1. studieux. 2. pédantesque. **'book-keeping,** *s.* comptabilité *f*. **'booklover,** *s.* bibliophile *m*. **'bookmaker,** *s.* bookmaker *m*. **'bookseller,** *s.* libraire *mf*. **'bookshop,** **'bookstore,** *s.* librairie *f*, rayon *m*. **bookstall** *s.* bibliothèque *f* (de gare). **'bookworm,** *s.* F: liseur acharné; bouquineur *m*.

boom¹ [bu:m], *s.* 1. barrage *m* (à l'entrée d'une rade); chaîne *f* (de fermeture), barre *f*. 2. *Av:* longeron *m*.

boom², I. *s.* 1. grondement *m*, mugissement *m*; bourdonnement *m*. 2. *Com:* (a) hausse *f* rapide, boom *m*; (b) vague *f* de prospérité; (période *f* de) vogue *f*. II. *v.* 1. *v.i.* gronder, mugir; bourdonner. 2. *v.i. Com:* être en hausse; trade is booming, le commerce va très fort.

boor [buər], *s.* rustre *m*, rustaud *m*. **'boorish,** *a.* rustre, grossier.

boost [bu:st], I. *v.tr.* soulever (qn) par derrière; faire de la réclame pour (qch.). 2. *El:* survolter. II. *s.* 1. (a) to give s.o., sth., a b., (i) soulever qn par derrière; (ii) faire de la réclame pour qn, qch. **'booster,** *s.* 1. *El:* survolteur *m*. 2. (a) *Med:* b. dose, dose *f* de rappel; (b) *(rocket)* fusée *f* de lancement. **'boosting,** *s.* 1. réclame *f*. 2. *El:* survoltage *m*.

boot [bu:t], I. *s.* 1. botte *f*; bottine *f*; to get the (order of the) b., être congédié; b. polish, crème *f* à chaussures. 2. *Aut:* coffre *m*. II. *v.tr.* F: to b. s.o. out, flanquer qn à la porte. **boo'tee,** *s.* bottine *f* d'enfant. **'bootlace,** *s.* lacet *m*. **'bootmaker,** *s.* bottier *m*. **'bootboy** (b) cordonnier *m*, boots, *s.* (in hotel) garçon *m* d'étage.

booty [bu:ti], *s.* butin *m*.

booze [bu:z], I. *s.* F: boisson *f* (alcoolique). II. *v.i.* F: boire (beaucoup); faire la ribote. **'boozer,** *s.* F: 1. ivrogne *m*. 2. bistrot *m*.

boracic [bə'ræsik], *a.* borique; b. powder, poudre *f* boriquée.

border ['bɔːdər], I. *s.* 1. bord *m*; lisière *f*; marge *f*; frontière *f*. 2. (a) (= edging) bordure *f*; (b) grass b., cordon *m* de gazon; (c) b. line, ligne *f* de séparation, limites *fpl*, bornes *fpl* (d'une catégorie); b.-line case, cas *m* limite. II. *v.i.* to b. on (sth.), toucher à (qch.), être limitrophe (d'un autre pays); friser (la folie, etc.). **'bordering,** *a.* contigu; voisin (on, de); statement b. on falsehood, déclaration qui frise le mensonge.

bore¹ [bɔːr]. I. *v.tr. & i.* creuser (un puits); forer (un puits); to b. through, percer, perforer. II. *s.* calibre *m* (d'une arme à feu, etc.). **'borehole,** *s. Min:* trou *m* de sonde; trou de mine.

bore². I. *v.tr.* ennuyer, raser, assommer (qn); to be bored stiff, s'ennuyer à mourir; avoir le cafard. II. *s.* (of pers.) raseur, -euse; (of thing) ennui *m*, corvée *f*. **'boredom,** *s.* ennui *m*. **'boring,** *a.* ennuyeux; ennuyant; F: rasant.

bore³, *s.* mascaret *m*.

born [bɔːn]. 1. *p.p.* to be b., naître; b. in London, né(e) à Londres. 2. *a.* a Londoner b. and bred, un vrai Londonien de Londres; F: b. fool, parfait idiot. 3. *s.* her latest b., son dernier né, sa dernière née.

borough ['bʌrə], *s.* ville *f*.

borrow ['bɔrou], *v.tr.* emprunter (from, à). **'borrower,** *s.* emprunteur, -euse. **'borrowing,** *s.* emprunts *mpl*.

bosom ['buzəm], *s.* sein *m*; poitrine *f*.

boss¹ [bɔs]. I. *s. F:* (a) patron *m*; chef *m*; (b) *Ind:* contremaître *m*. II. *v.tr. F:* mener, diriger (qn). **'bossy,** *a. F:* autoritaire.

boss², *a. & s. P:* to make a b. (shot) of sth., louper qch. **'boss-eyed,** *a. F:* qui louche.

botany ['bɔtəni], *s.* botanique *f*. **botanical,** *a.* botanique. **'botanist,** *s.* botaniste *mf*.

both [bouθ]. 1. *a. & pron.* tous (les) deux, tous (les) deux; l'un(e) et l'autre; to hold sth. in b. hands, tenir qch. à deux mains; b. alike, l'un comme l'autre. 2. *adv.* b... and... et... et...

bother ['bɔðər]. I. *v.* 1. *v.tr.* gêner, ennuyer, tourmenter. 2. *v.i.* s'inquiéter (about, de). II. *s.* ennui *m*; F: embêtement *m*. **'bothered,** *a.* inquiet; embarrassé.

bottle ['bɔtl]. I. *s.* 1. bouteille *f*; flacon *m*; bocal *m*; b. opener, ouvre-bouteille *m*; décapsuleur *m*; b. party, réunion intime à laquelle chacun apporte à boire; b. rack, casier *m* à bouteilles. 2. feeding b., biberon *m*. 3. hot water b., bouillotte *f*. II. *v.tr.* mettre (du vin) en bouteilles; mettre (des fruits) en bocal. **'bottled,** *a.* (a) en bouteille; (b) F: ivre. **'bottling,** *s.* mise *f* en bouteille(s), en bocal. **'bottleneck,** *s.* 1. goulot *m* (de bouteille). 2. *Aut:* embouteillage *m*. **'bottle 'up,** *v.tr.* étouffer (ses sentiments).

bottom ['bɔtəm], *s.* 1. (a) bas *m*; (b) fond *m* (d'un puits, etc.); (of pers.) to be at the b. of sth., être l'instigateur de qch. 2. *Anat: F:* derrière *m*. **'bottomless,** *a.* sans fond; insondable.

bough [bau], *s.* branche *f*, rameau *m*.

boulder ['bouldər], *s.* grosse pierre *f*.

bounce [bauns]. I. *v.* 1. *v.i. & tr.* (faire) rebondir (une balle). 2. *v.tr. U.S: F:* flanquer (qn) à la porte. II. *s.* 1. rebond(issement) *m*. 2. (of pers.) vantardise *f*, épate *f*. **'bouncer,** *s. F:* 1. vantard *m*. 2. *U.S:* expulseur *m*,

videur *m*. **3.** chèque *m* sans provision.
'bouncing, *a.* **1.** rebondissant. **2.** b. baby, enfant *mf* plein(e) de vie et de santé. **3.** (chèque) sans provision.
bound [baund]. **I.** *s. usu. pl.* limite *f*, bornes *fpl*; *Sch:* out of bounds, (endroit) défendu aux élèves; to keep within bounds, rester dans la juste mesure. **II.** *a.* en partance pour; en route pour, allant à. **'boundary,** *s.* limite *f*; bornes *fpl*; frontière *f*.
bouquet [bu'kei, 'bukei], *s.* bouquet *m*.
bourbon ['buəbən], *s. U.S:* whisky *m* de maïs.
bout [baut], *s.* **1.** *Sp:* tour *m*; reprise *f*. **2.** accès *m* (de fièvre); attaque *f* (de grippe).
boutique [bu'ti:k], *s.* (*a*) petit magasin de modes; (*b*) (*in store*) teenage b., rayon *m* des jeunes.
bow¹ [bou], *s.* **1.** arc *m*. **2.** archet *m* (de violon). **3.** nœud *m* (de ruban). **4.** b. window, fenêtre *f* en saillie (courbe). **'bow-legged,** *a.* bancal.
bow² [bau]. **I.** *s.* salut *m*; inclination *f* de tête. **II.** *v.* **1.** *v.i.* s'incliner; baisser la tête. **2.** *v.tr.* incliner, baisser (la tête); fléchir (le genou).
bow³ [bau], *s.* **1.** *Nau:* avant *m*, nez *m*; to cross the bows of a ship, couper la route à un navire. **2.** *Av:* nez *m*.
bowels ['bauəlz], *s.pl.* intestins *m*, entrailles *f*; the b. of the earth, les entrailles de la terre.
bowl¹ [boul], *s.* bol *m*; coupe *f* (de cristal); (= *basin*) bassin *m*, cuvette *f*.
bowl². **I.** *v.tr.* rouler (un cerceau); lancer, rouler (la boule); (*at cricket*) (i) servir (la balle); (ii) renverser le guichet (à qn). **II.** *s.* boule *f*; (*game of*) bowls, (i) (jeu de) boules; pétanque *f*; (ii) *U.S:* (jeu de) quilles *f*. **'bowler¹,** *s.* **1.** joueur, -euse, de boules, de pétanque. **2.** (*at cricket*) serveur *m*, lanceur *m*. **'bowling,** *s.* **1.** (*a*) jeu *m* de boules, de pétanque; b. green, (terrain pour) jeu de boules; (*b*) *U.S:* jeu de quilles; b. alley, bowling *m*.
bowler² ['boulər], *s.* b. (hat), (chapeau) melon *m*.
box¹ [bɔks], *s. Bot:* buis *m*.
box², *s.* **1.** boîte *f*; (*large wooden*) caisse *f*, coffre *m*; (*of cardboard*) carton *m*; letter b., boîte aux lettres. **2.** *Th:* loge *f*; (*in stable*) stalle *f*, box *m*; *Jur:* witness b. = barre *f* des témoins. **'box office,** *s. Th:* bureau *m* de location; guichet *m*. **'boxroom,** *s.* chambre *f* de débarras.
box³. **I.** *s.* b. on the ear, gifle *f*, claque *f*. **II.** *v.* **1.** *v.tr.* to b. s.o.'s ears, gifler qn. **2.** *v.i. Sp:* boxer; faire de la boxe. **'boxer¹,** *s.* boxeur *m*, pugiliste *m*. **'boxing,** *s.* la boxe; b. gloves, gants *m* de boxe; b. match, match *m* de boxe; B. Day, le lendemain de Noël.
boxer², ['bɔksər], *s.* (chien) boxer *m*.

†**boy** [bɔi], *s.* (*a*) garçon *m*; *F:* the old b., (i) le paternel; (ii) le patron; (*b*) élève *m*; an old b., un ancien élève; (*c*) *P:* b. (friend), flirt *m*, amoureux *m*; (*d*) fils *m*; (*e*) (i) domestique *m* indigène; (ii) (the grocer's b., le garçon épicier. **'boyhood,** *s.* enfance *f* (d'un garçon). **'boyish,** *a.* enfantin.
boycott ['bɔikɔt]. **I.** *v.tr.* boycotter. **II.** *s.* mise *f* en interdit. **'boycotting,** *s.* boycottage *m*.
bra [brɑ:], *s. F:* soutien-gorge *m inv.*
brace [breis]. **I.** *s.* **1.** attache *f*, lien *m*; croisillon *m*; (dental) b., rectificateur *m* dentaire. **2.** *pl. Cl:* bretelles *fpl*. **3.** *inv.* couple *f* (de perdrix). **4.** b. (and bit), vilebrequin *m*. **II.** *v.tr.* **1.** ancrer (une construction); armer (une poutre). **2.** fortifier (le corps); to b. s.o. up, remonter qn. **'bracing,** *a.* (air, etc.) fortifiant.
bracelet ['breislit], *s.* bracelet *m*.
bracken ['bræk(ə)n], *s.* fougère *f*.
bracket ['brækit], *s.* **1.** (*a*) support *m*; console *f*; corbeau *m*; (*b*) parenthèse *f*; (*brace*) accolade *f*; (*c*) the middle-income b., la tranche des salariés moyens. **II.** *v.tr.* (*a*) mettre (des mots) entre parenthèses; (*b*) réunir (des mots) par une accolade; (*c*) *F:* faire un rapport entre (des personnes, des choses).
brackish ['brækiʃ], *a.* saumâtre.
bradawl ['brædɔ:l], *s.* poinçon *m*.
‡**brag** [bræg], *v.i.* se vanter. **'bragging,** *s.* vantardise *f*.
braid [breid], *s.* galon *m*, ganse *f*.
braille [breil], *s.* braille *m*.
brain [brein]. **I.** *s.* **1.** cerveau *m*; electronic b., cerveau électronique; to have sth. on the b., avoir l'obsession d'une idée. **2.** *pl.* cervelle *f*; calves' brains, cervelle de veau; to rack one's brains, se creuser la cervelle; he has brains, il est intelligent; b. child, idée *f*, conception *f*, originale; b. drain, fuite *f* des cerveaux. **II.** *v.tr. F:* assommer (qn). **'brainless,** *a. F:* intelligence. **-brainless,** *a.* stupide. **'brainwash,** *v.tr. F:* faire un lavage de crâne, de cerveau, à (qn). **'brainwashing,** *s. F:* lavage *m* de crâne, de cerveau. **'brainy,** *a. F:* intelligent; débrouillard. **'brainwave,** *s.* inspiration *f*, trouvaille *f*.
braise [breiz], *v.tr.* braiser; **braised** beef, bœuf en daube.
brake¹ [breik]. **I.** *s.* frein *m*; hand b., frein à main; disc b., frein à disque; b. fluid, liquide pour freins (hydrauliques); b. lining, fourrure *f* de frein. **II.** *v.tr.* appliquer le frein sur (les roues); *abs.* freiner. **'braking,** *s.* freinage *m*; b. distance, distance *f* d'arrêt.
brake², *s. Aut:* shooting b., break *m* de chasse, canadienne *f*.

bramble ['bræmbl], *s.* ronce *f.*
bran [bræn], *s.* son *m.*
branch [brɑːn(t)ʃ]. **I.** *s.* **1.** branche *f.* rameau *m* (d'un arbre). **2.** (*a*) ramification *f;* bras *m* (d'un fleuve); (*b*) *Rail:* embranchement *m;* b. line, ligne *f* d'intérêt local; (*c*) *Com:* succursale *f,* filiale *f.* **II.** *v.* **1.** *v.i.* to b. out, se ramifier; (*of road, etc.*) (se) bifurquer. **2.** *v.tr. El:* brancher (un circuit); dériver (le courant).
brand [brænd]. **I.** *s.* **1.** brandon *m,* tison *m.* **2.** (*a*) fer chaud; (*b*) marque *f* (faite avec un fer chaud). **3.** *Com:* marque *f* (de fabrique). **II.** *v.tr.* **1.** marquer (au fer chaud). **2.** to be branded as a liar, être noté comme menteur. '**branded**, *a.* (*a*) marqué à chaud; (*b*) b. goods, produits de marque; b. petrol = super(carburant) *m.* '**brand 'new**, *a.* tout (flambant) neuf.
brandish ['brændiʃ], *v.tr.* brandir.
brandy ['brændi], *s.* eau-de-vie *f;* cognac *m;* liqueur b., fine champagne *f;* b. and soda, fine *f* à l'eau.
brass [brɑːs], *s.* **1.** cuivre *m* jaune; laiton *m; F:* b. hat, officier *m* d'état-major; *F:* top b., les grosses légumes, les gros bonnets. **2.** (*a*) *H:* les cuivres, robinets, etc.; (*b*) *Mus:* the b., les cuivres; b. band, fanfare *f;* (*c*) (*in churches*) brasses, plaques *f* (mortuaires en cuivre. **3.** *F:* argent *m,* fric *m.* **4.** *attrib.* (*a*) *F:* to get down to b. tacks, en venir aux faits; (*b*) *P:* to part b. rags, se brouiller, rompre.
brassière ['bræsiɛər], *s.* soutien-gorge *m inv;* strapless b., bustier *m.*
brat [bræt], *s. F:* marmot *m,* mioche *mf.*
bravado [brə'vɑːdou], *s.* bravade *f.*
brave [breiv]. **I.** *a.* courageux, brave. **-ly**, *adv.* courageusement. **II.** *v.tr.* braver, défier. '**bravery**, *s.* courage *m.*
bravo [brɑː'vou], *int.* bravo!
brawl [brɔːl]. **I.** *s.* rixe *f,* bagarre *f.* **II.** *v.i.* brailler, se chamailler.
brawn [brɔːn], *s.* **1.** muscles *mpl.* **2.** *Cu:* fromage *m* de tête.
bray [brei], *v.i.* braire.
brazen ['breizn]. **I.** *a.* effronté, impudent; b. lie, mensonge cynique. **II.** *v.tr.* to b. it out, payer d'effronterie; crâner.
Brazilian [brə'ziljən], *a. & s.* brésilien, -ienne.
breach [briːtʃ], *s.* **1.** infraction *f;* b. of the law, violation *f* de la loi; b. of the peace, attentat *m* contre l'ordre public; b. of trust, abus *m* de confiance; b. of promise, violation *f* de promesse de mariage. **2.** brèche *f* (dans un mur). **3.** brouille *f* (entre amis).
bread [bred], *s.* (*a*) pain *m;* a loaf of b., un pain; b. and butter, pain beurré; to earn one's b., gagner sa croûte; b. and milk, panade *f* au lait; (*b*) *attrib.* b. basket, (i) corbeille *f* à

pain; (ii) *P:* estomac *m;* b. bin, boîte *f* à pain; b. knife, couteau *m,* scie *f* à pain; b. sauce, sauce *f* à la mie de pain. '**breadcrumbs**, *s.pl. Cu:* chapelure *f.* '**breadwinner**, *s.* gagne-pain *m inv;* soutien *m* de famille.
breadth [bredθ], *s.* largeur *f.*
break [breik]. **I.** *s.* rupture *f;* (*a*) brisure *f,* fracture *f;* brèche *f;* b. in the voice, (i) altération *f* de la voix, (ii) mue *f* (à la puberté); b. (in a journey), arrêt *m; without a b.,* sans interruption; b. of continuity, solution *f* de continuité; (*b*) rupture, brouille *f;* (*c*) to make a bad b., faire une bourde, une gaffe. **2.** (*a*) repos *m,* répit *m;* (*b*) intervalle *m.* **3.** b. of day, point *m* du jour. **II.** *v.tr.* **1.** (*a*) casser, briser, rompre; to b. one's journey, interrompre son voyage; to b. the sound barrier, franchir le mur du son; *abs.* to b. even, joindre les deux bouts; (*b*) to b. gaol, s'évader de prison; (*c*) briser, crever (le cœur à qn); (*d*) to b. a fall, amortir une chute; (*e*) (*of losses*) ruiner (qn); (*of sniper*) briser (qn); to b. the bank, faire sauter la banque; (*f*) violer, enfreindre (la loi); to b. one's word, manquer de parole. **2.** *v.i.* (*a*) casser, se rompre, se briser; (*of wave*) déferler; (*b*) to b. with s.o., rompre avec qn; (*c*) (*of day*) poindre; (*d*) (*of voice*) muer, (*with emotion*) s'altérer; (*e*) (*of storm*) éclater. '**breakable**, *a.* cassant, fragile. '**breakage**, *s.* casse *f.* '**break a'way.** **1.** *v.tr.* détacher. **2.** *v.i.* se détacher; s'échapper. '**break 'down.** **1.** *v.tr.* abattre, démolir; vaincre. **2.** *v.i.* (*a*) échouer; (*b*) rester en panne. '**breakdown**, *s.* **1.** rupture *f* (de négociations); arrêt complet (dans un service); répartition *f* (de la population par âge etc.). **2.** *Aut: etc:* panne *f;* b. lorry, dépanneuse *f.* '**breaker**, *s.* camion-grue *m.* '**breaker**, *s.* brisant *m,* vague déferlante. **break 'in.** **1.** *v.tr.* enfoncer; défoncer (une porte). **2.** *v.i.* (*a*) to b. in upon, interrompre (qn); *abs.* intervenir; (*b*) s'introduire par effraction. **break 'loose**, *v.i.* **1.** s'évader, s'échapper. **2.** se déchaîner. **break 'off.** **1.** *v.tr.* (*a*) casser, rompre; (*b*) interrompre, abandonner (son travail). **2.** *v.i.* (*a*) se détacher; (*b*) discontinuer, cesser. **break 'open**, *v.tr.* enfoncer, forcer (un coffre-fort). **break 'out**, *v.i.* **1.** (*of war, etc.*) éclater. **2.** (*a*) s'échapper, s'évader. **break 'through**, *v.tr.* percer; enfoncer; *abs.* se frayer un passage. **break 'up.** **1.** *v.tr.* mettre en morceaux; démolir; disperser. **2.** *v.i.* (*a*) (*of empire*) se démembrer; (*of crowd*) se disperser; (*b*) se séparer; (*c*) *Sch:* entrer en vacances; (*d*) (*of weather*) se gâter. '**breakwater**, *s.* brise-lames *m inv.*

breakfast ['brekfəst]. I. s. (petit) déjeuner m; wedding b., repas m de noces; b. cup (and saucer), déjeuner m. II. v.i. déjeuner (le matin).

breast [brest], s. 1. sein m. 2. poitrine f; poitrail m (de cheval); Cu: blanc m (de volaille); b. pocket, poche f de poitrine; (swimming) b. stroke, brasse f.

breath [breθ], s. haleine f, souffle m, respiration f; to draw b., respirer; to gasp for b., haleter; to waste one's b., perdre ses paroles; out of b., essoufflé; under one's b., à mi-voix. 'breath-alyser, s. Aut: b. test, alcotest m. 'breathless, a. hors d'haleine, essoufflé. -ly, adv. en haletant.

breathe [briːð]. I. v.i. respirer, souffler. 2. v.tr. to b. (in) the air, aspirer l'air; to b. a sigh, laisser échapper un soupir; to b. one's last, rendre le dernier soupir. 'breather, s. F: moment m de repos. 'breathing, s. respiration f, souffle m; b. apparatus, appareil m respiratoire; b. space, le temps de souffler; répit m.

breeches ['britʃiz], s. (pair of) b., culotte f, pantalon m.

breed [briːd]. I. ‡v. 1. v.tr. (a) produire, engendrer (des vices, etc.); (b) élever (du bétail). 2. v.i. multiplier, se reproduire. II. s. race f; lignée f. bred, a. (used in compounds) country-b., élevé à la campagne; well-b., bien élevé. 'breeder, s. 1. Agr: éleveur m. 2. Atom Ph: b. reactor, réacteur (auto-)régénérateur. 'breeding, s. 1. (a) reproduction f; (b) élevage m. 2. éducation f; (good) b., savoir-vivre m.

breeze [briːz]. I. s. brise f. II. v.i. F: to b. in, out, entrer, sortir, en coup de vent. 'breezy, a. 1. venteux. 2. (of pers.) jovial, désinvolte. 'breeziness, s. cordialité bruyante; verve f (d'un discours).

breeze-block ['briːzblɔk], s. Civ.E: parpaing m.

breviary ['briːviəri], s. bréviaire m.

brevity ['breviti], s. brièveté f.

brew [bruː]. 1. v.tr. brasser (la bière); abs. brasser, faire de la bière. 2. v.i. (of tea) s'infuser; (of storm) couver; se préparer; there's sth. brewing, il se trame qch. 'brewer, s. brasseur m. 'brewery, s. brasserie f.

briar ['braiər], s. (a) églantier m; (b) pl. ronces f.

bribe [braib]. I. s. paiement m illicite. II. v.tr. corrompre, acheter (qn); suborner (un témoin). 'bribery, s. corruption f.

brick [brik], s. (a) brique f; to drop a b., faire une bourde, une gaffe; F: he came down on me like a ton of bricks, il m'est tombé dessus; red b. university, université de fondation relativement récente; (b) (toy) box of bricks,

boîte f de constructions. 'bricklayer, s. maçon m. 'brick-'red, a. rouge brique inv.

bride [braid], s.f., bridegroom ['braidgrum], s.m. nouvelle mariée, nouveau marié. 'bridal, a. nuptial. 'brides-maid, s.f. demoiselle f d'honneur.

bridge[1] [bridʒ]. I. s. 1. pont m. 2. Nau: passerelle f (de commandement). 3. dos m, arête f (du nez). II. v.tr. jeter un pont sur (un fleuve); to b. a gap, combler une lacune.

bridge[2], s. (game) bridge m; to play b., bridger.

bridle ['braidl]. I. s. (a) bride f; (b) frein m; b. path, piste f cavalière. II. v. 1. v.tr. brider (un cheval). 2. v.i. se rengorger; prendre la mouche.

brief [briːf]. I. a. bref, court; in b., bref, en deux mots. -ly, adv. brièvement; en peu de mots. II. s. 1. Ecc: bref m. 2. (a) Jur: dossier m; b. case, serviette f (en cuir); (b) F: I don't hold much b. for him, je n'ai guère confiance en lui. 3. Cl: pl. slip m. III. v.tr. 1. confier une cause à (un avocat). 2. donner une mission à (qn); fournir des directives à (qn); Av: F: briefer. 'briefing, s. 1. constitution f du dossier. 2. instructions fpl, directives fpl; Av: briefing m. 'briefness, s. brièveté f; concision f.

brigade [bri'geid], s. Mil: brigade f. briga'dier, s. général m de brigade.

brigand ['brigənd], s. brigand m, bandit m.

bright [brait], a. 1. (a) lumineux; (b) vif, éclatant. 2. (of pers.) (a) vif, animé; (b) éveillé; a b. idea, une idée lumineuse. -ly, adv. brillamment; avec éclat. 'brighten, v. 1. v.tr. faire briller, égayer (qch.). 2. v.i. (of face, weather) s'éclaircir; (of pers.) to b. up, s'animer. 'brightness, s. éclat m; clarté f; vivacité f; intelligence f (d'un enfant).

brilliant ['briljənt]. I. a. (a) brillant, éclatant; (b) (of pers.) très doué, brillant; b. idea, idée lumineuse. -ly, adv. brillamment. II. s. (diamond) brillant m. 'brilliance, s. éclat m, brillant m.

brim [brim]. I. s. bord m. II. ‡v.i. to b. over, déborder. 'brimful, a. débordant.

brine [brain], s. eau f salée; saumure f.

‡bring [brin], v.tr. (a) amener (qn); apporter (qch.); (b) to b. luck, porter bonheur (à); (c) to b. an action against s.o., intenter un procès à qn; to b. oneself to do sth., se résoudre à faire qch. bring a'bout, v.tr. (a) amener, causer; (b) effectuer, accomplir. bring a'long, v.tr. amener (qn); apporter (qch.). bring a'way, v.tr. emmener (qn); emporter (qch.). bring 'back, v.tr. rapporter (qch.); ramener (qn). 'bring 'down, v.tr. 1. abattre; faire tomber; Th: to b. d. the

house, faire crouler la salle. 2. (a) faire descendre (qn); (b) descendre (une valise). 3. faire baisser (le prix). **bring 'forward**, v.tr. avancer; Com: reporter (une somme). **bring 'in**, v.tr. 1. faire entrer (qn); servir (le dîner). 2. Fin: to b. in interest, rapporter. 3. Jur: rendre (un verdict). **bring 'off**, v.tr. réussir, conduire à bien. **bring 'out**, v.tr. 1. sortir. 2. faire ressortir. 3. publier. **bring 'over**, v.tr. transporter, amener. **bring 'round**, v.tr. 1. (a) rappeler (qn) à la vie; (b) remettre (qn) de bonne humeur. 2. (ramener (qch.). **bring 'to**, v.tr. faire reprendre connaissance à (qn). **bring to'gether**, v.tr. réunir; mettre en contact. **bring 'up**, v.tr. 1. monter (qch.). 2. élever (un enfant). 3. vomir (qch.). 4. mettre (un sujet) sur le tapis. **bringing 'up**, s. éducation f.

brink [brink], s. bord; on the b. of ruin, à deux doigts de la ruine; to be on the b. of tears, avoir peine à retenir ses larmes.

brisk [brisk], a. vif, actif, alerte. -ly, adv. vivement; avec entrain. **brisk-ness**, s. vivacité f, animation f, entrain m; fraîcheur f (de l'air).

bristle ['brisl]. I. s. soie f (de porc); poil m raide. II. v.i. (of animal) se hérisser; F: (of pers.) se rebiffer, se hérisser. **bristly**, a. couvert de poils raides.

British ['britiʃ], a. britannique; anglais. s.pl. the B., les Anglais m. **Britisher**, s. U.S: Austr: Anglais,-aise. **Briton**, s. 1. (ancient) B., Breton, -onne (de la Grande Bretagne). 2. Anglais, -aise.

brittle [britl], a. fragile, cassant.

broach [broutʃ], v.tr. entamer (un fût).

broad [brɔːd], a. large; in b. daylight, en plein jour; it's as b. as it's long, cela revient au même; b. humour, grosse gaieté. -ly, adv. largement; b. speaking, généralement parlant. **broad-brimmed**, a. à larges bords. **broad-cast**. I. to.tr. 1. semer (la grain) à la volée; diffuser (une nouvelle). 2. Rad: radiodiffuser. II. s. (radio)émission f. III. adv. à tout vent, à la volée. IV. a. radiodiffusé. **broadcasting**, s. radiodiffusion f. **broadcaster**, s. radiodiffuseur m; speaker, m; speak-erine. **broaden**, v.tr. & i. (s')élargir. **broad-minded**, a. to be b.-m., avoir l'esprit large. **broad-mindedness**, s. largeur f d'esprit; tolérance f. **broad-shouldered**, a. large d'épaules.

brocade [brou'keid], s. brocart m.

brogue[1] [broug], s. soulier m de golf.

brogue[2], s. (a) accent m de terroir; (b) accent irlandais.

broil [brɔil], v.tr. & i. griller. **broiler**, s. poulet m (à rôtir). **broiling**, a. F: (of sun) ardent, brûlant.

broke [brouk], a. F: sans le sou, fauché, à sec.

broken ['broukn], a. (a) cassé, brisé, rompu; (b) interrompu; (c) in a b. voice, d'une voix entrecoupée; (d) b. down, cassé; en panne. **broken-hearted**, a. au cœur brisé.

broker ['broukər], s. courtier m (de commerce). **brokerage**, s. (frais mpl. de) courtage m.

bromide ['broumaid], s. Ch: bromure m.

bronchitis [brɔŋ'kaitis], s. bronchite f.

bronze [brɔnz]. I. s. bronze m. 2. attrib. de, en, bronze.

brooch [broutʃ], s. broche f.

brood [bruːd]. I. s. couvée f (de poussins); F: enfants mpl, marmaille f. II. v.i. 1. (of hen) couver. 2. broyer du noir. **brooding**, a. (poule) couveuse.

brook [bruk], s. ruisseau m.

broom [bruːm, brum], s. 1. Bot: genêt m. 2. H: balai m.

broth [brɔθ], s. bouillon m, potage m.

brother ['brʌðər], s. frère m. **brother-hood**, s. confraternité f; Ecc: fraternité f; U.S: syndicat m (ouvrier). **brother-in-law**, s. beau-frère m.

brow [brau], s. front m. **browbeat**, v.tr. intimider, rudoyer (qn).

brown [braun]. I. a. (a) brun, marron; (b) bruni (par le soleil). II. s. brun m, marron m. III. v. 1. v.tr. brunir; Cu: rissoler; faire dorer. 2. v.i. se brunir; Cu: roussir. **brown 'off**, v.tr. F: to be browned off, être découragé, avoir le cafard.

brownie ['brauni], s. (Guide movement) Jeannette f.

browse [brauz], v.tr. & i. brouter.

bruise [bruːz]. I. s. meurtrissure f, contusion f. II. v.tr. meurtrir.

brunette [bruː'net], a. & s. brune (f.).

brunt [brʌnt], s. choc m; to bear the b., payer de sa personne; to bear the b. of the expenses, faire la plupart des frais.

brush[1] [brʌʃ]. I. s. 1. brosse f. 2. (a) brosse f; (b) (paint-)b., pinceau m; (c) queue f. 3. coup m de brosse. 4. rencontre m (avec l'ennemi). II. v. 1. v.tr. brosser (qch.); se brosser (les cheveux); frôler (une surface). 2. v.tr. to b. past, against, s.o., sth., frôler qn en passant. **brush a'side**, v.tr. écarter (qch.). **brush a'way**, v.tr. enlever (qch.) (d'un coup de brosse); écarter (une difficulté). **brush 'down**, v.tr. donner un coup de brosse à (qn, qch.). **brush 'up**, v.tr. to b. up one's French, dérouiller son français. **brushwood**, s. broussailles fpl.

brusque [bruː(ə)sk], a. brusque; rude, bourru. -ly, adv. d'une manière brusque. **brusqueness**, s. brusquerie f.

brute [bruːt], s. brute f; you b.! espèce d'animal! F: a b. of a job, un métier, un travail, de chien. **brutal**, a. brutal. -ly, adv. brutalement. **bru'tality**, s. brutalité f. **'brutalize**, v.tr. abrutir.

bubble ['bʌbl]. I. s. bulle f. II. v.i. bouillonner; pétiller; to b. over, déborder.

buck [bʌk]. I. s. (a) daim m; chevreuil m; (b) mâle m (du lapin, etc.). II. v. F: to b. s.o. up, stimuler, qn.

bucket ['bʌkit], s. seau m. bucketful, s. plein seau.

buckle ['bʌkl]. I. s. boucle f. II. v. 1. v.tr. boucler. 2. v.i. se déformer, gauchir.

buckram ['bʌkrəm], s. bougran m.

bud [bʌd], s. 1. bourgeon m; to come into b., bourgeonner. 2. bouton m (de fleur). 3. taste b., papille f gustative. 'budding, a. (a) qui bourgeonne; (b) b. artist, artiste en herbe.

Buddhist ['budist], s. & a. bouddhiste mf. 2. a. bouddhique.

budge [bʌdʒ], v.i. bouger.

budget ['bʌdʒit]. I. s. budget m. II. v.i. budgétiser; inscrire (qch.) au budget.

buff [bʌf], a. & s. jaune clair inv.; F: in the b., tout nu, à poil.

†buffalo ['bʌfəlou], s. buffle m.

buffer ['bʌfər], s. Rail: tampon m.

buffet ['bʌfei], s. buffet m.; (on menu) cold b., viandes froides.

buffeted ['bʌfitid], a. secoué.

buffoon [bʌ'fu:n], s. bouffon m. buffoonery, s. bouffonneries fpl.

bug [bʌg]. I. s. (a) punaise f; (b) U.S: insecte m; (c) microbe m. II. †v.tr. F: installer un microphone clandestin dans.

bugle ['bju:gl], s. clairon m.

‡build [bild]. I. v.tr. bâtir; construire. II. s. carrure f, taille f. 'builder, s. entrepreneur m (en bâtiments). 'building, s. 1. construction f; b. land, terrain m à bâtir. 2. bâtiment m; immeuble m; public b., édifice m public; b. society, société f immobilière.

bulb [bʌlb], s. 1. Bot: bulbe m, oignon m. 2. ampoule f; lampe f.

Bulgarian [bʌl'geəriən], a. & s. bulgare (mf).

bulge [bʌldʒ]. I. s. bombement m, ventre m. II. v.tr. & i. bomber; faire saillie. 'bulging, a. bombé; ballonnant; protubérant.

bulk [bʌlk], s. 1. grandeur f, grosseur f, volume m. 2. masse f, plupart f. 'bulky, a. volumineux, encombrant; gros.

bull [bul], s. 1. (a) taureau m; (b) b. elephant, éléphant mâle. 2. Fin: spéculateur m à la hausse. 'bulldog, s. bouledogue m. 'bulldozer, s. bulldozer m, bélier m mécanique. 'bullfight, s. corrida f; course f de taureaux. 'bullfighter, s. toréador m. 'bullfinch, s. bouvreuil m. 'bullfrog, s. grenouille f taureau, Fr.C: ouaouaron m. 'bullock, s. bœuf m. 'bullring, s. arène f (pour les courses de taureaux). 'bullseye, s. noir m, mouche f (d'une cible).

bullet ['bulit], s. balle f (de fusil, etc.).

bulletin ['bulitin], s. bulletin m.

bully ['buli]. I. †s. tyran m. II. v.tr. intimider, malmener. 'bullying. I. a. brutal. II. s. intimidation f, brutalité f.

bumble-bee ['bʌmblbi:], s. bourdon m.

bump [bʌmp]. I. s. 1. choc (sourd); heurt m; cahot m. 2. bosse f. II. v. 1. v.tr. cogner, frapper. 2. v.i. se cogner, se heurter, buter (into, against, contre); to b. into s.o., rencontrer qn par hasard. 'bump 'off, v.tr. P: assassiner, supprimer (qn). 'bumpy, a. (chemin, etc.) cahoteux, défoncé.

bumper ['bʌmpər], s. 1. rasade f; b. crop, récolte magnifique. 2. Aut: pare-choc m inv.; Rail: U.S: tampon m.

bumptious ['bʌm(p)ʃəs], a. présomptueux, suffisant. 'bumptiousness, s. suffisance f.

bun [bʌn], s. petit pain au lait.

bunch [bʌnʃ], s. bouquet m (de fleurs); grappe f (de raisins); trousseau m (de clefs); the best of the b., le meilleur de la bande.

bundle ['bʌndl], s. paquet m; liasse f (de papiers); fagot m (de bois).

bung [bʌŋ], s. bondon m (de fût); tampon m. II. v.tr. to b. up, bondonner (un fût); boucher (un trou); F: my nose is all bunged up, j'ai le nez bouché.

bungalow ['bʌŋgəlou], s. maison f sans étage, bungalow m.

bungle ['bʌŋgl], v.tr. bousiller, gâcher. 'bungler, s. bousilleur, -euse; gâcheur, -euse; maladroit, -oite. 'bungling. I. a. maladroit. II. s. bousillage m; maladresse f.

bunion ['bʌnjən], s. Med: oignon m.

bunk[1] ['bʌŋk], s. couchette f.

bunk[2], s. & v.i. F: to do a b., to b., filer, décamper.

bunker ['bʌŋkər], s. 1. soute f. 2. (golf) bunker m.

bunkum ['bʌŋkəm], s. F: blague f, bêtises fpl.

bunting ['bʌntiŋ], s. coll: drapeaux m, pavillons m.

buoy [bɔi]. I. s. bouée f; balise flottante. II. v.tr. to b. up, soutenir (qch., qn). 'buoyancy, s. 1. flottabilité f (d'un object). 2. entrain m. 'buoyant, a. 1. flottable, léger. 2. (of pers.) plein d'entrain.

burden ['bə:dn]. I. s. fardeau m, charge f; beast of b., bête de somme. II. v.tr. charger, alourdir (qn with sth., qn de qch.).

bureau ['bjuərou], s. bureau m.

bureaucrat ['bjuərəkræt], s. bureaucrate m. bureau'cratic, a. bureaucratique.

burgle ['bə:gl], v.tr. cambrioler. 'burglar, s. cambrioleur m. 'burglary, s. cambriolage m.

†**Burgundy** ['bɔːgəndi], s. (vin m de) bourgogne m.

burial ['beriəl], s. enterrement m.

burlesque [bɔːlesk], a. & s. burlesque (m).

burly ['bɔːli], a. solidement bâti.

Burmese [bɔːmiːz], a. & s. birman, -ane.

‡**burn** [bɔːn]. I. v.tr. & i. brûler. II. s. brûlure f. 'burner, s. (of gas cooker) brûleur m; Bunsen b., bec m Bunsen. 'burn 'out, v.tr. (a) (also burn down) their house was burnt out, leur maison a été réduite en cendres; (b) El: brûler (une bobine); griller (une lampe). 'burnt, a. brûlé; carbonisé; b. taste, goût de brûlé. burn 'up. 1. v.tr. brûler, consumer. 2. v.i. (of fire) se ranimer, flamber.

burp [bɔːp], v.i. U.S: F: éructer, roter.

burrow ['bʌrou]. I. s. terrier m (de lapin). II. v.i. (a) (of rabbit) (i) fouir la terre; (ii) se terrer; (b) (of pers.) fouiller (dans un tiroir, etc.).

bursar ['bɔːsər], s. Sch: économe m. 'bursary, s. Sch: 1. économat m. 2. bourse f (d'études).

‡**burst** [bɔːst]. I. v. 1. v.i. (a) éclater, faire explosion; (of boiler) sauter; (of tyre) crever; (b) to b. into pieces, voler en éclats; (b) to b. into tears, se mettre à pleurer; (c) I was bursting to tell him, je mourais d'envie de le lui dire. 2. v.tr. faire éclater (qch.); crever (un ballon, un pneu). II. s. éclatement m, explosion f; jaillissement m (de flamme); coup m (de tonnerre); éclat m (de rire); salve f (d'applaudissements); poussée f (d'activité). 'burst 'in, v.i. faire irruption, entrer en coup de vent. burst 'open. 1. v.tr. enfoncer (une porte). 2. v.i. s'ouvrir tout d'un coup. burst 'out, v.i. s'écrier, s'exclamer; to b. out laughing, éclater de rire.

‡**bury** ['beri], v.tr. enterrer; ensevelir.

‡**bus** [bʌs], s. autobus m; car m; double decker b., autobus à impériale; to miss the b., (i) manquer, rater, l'autobus; (ii) F: laisser échapper l'occasion. 'busman, s. (i) conducteur m, (ii) receveur m, d'autobus; to take a b.'s holiday, faire du métier en guise de congé.

bush [buʃ], s. 1. (a) buisson m; (b) fourré m, taillis m. 2. brousse f.

business ['biznis], s. 1. affaire f, besogne f, occupation f; it is my b. to, c'est à moi de; it's none of your b., cela ne vous regarde pas. 2. (a) les affaires f; to mean b., avoir des intentions sérieuses. attrib. b. hours, heures de travail, (of shop) d'ouverture; b. man, homme d'affaires; F: the b. end of a chisel, le tranchant d'un ciseau; (b) fonds m de commerce. 'business-like, a. 1. pratique. 2. sérieux.

bust [bʌst], s. buste m; poitrine f (de femme).

bustle ['bʌsl]. I. v.i. to b. (about), se remuer, s'activer, s'affairer. II. s. remue-ménage m. 'bustling, a. affairé; empressé.

busy ['bizi], a. affairé; occupé; b. day, jour chargé; b. street, rue mouvementée. 2. s. P: détective m. 'busily, adv. d'un air affairé. 'busybody, s. officieux, -euse.

but [bʌt]. 1. conj. mais; b. yet, b. all the same, néanmoins. 2. adv. ne . . . que; seulement; had I b. known! si j'avais su! 3. conj. or prep. (a) excepté; anything b., rien moins que; b. for, sans; b. for that, à part cela.

butcher ['butʃər]. I. s. boucher m. II. v.tr. 1. abattre (des bêtes de boucherie). 2. massacrer.

butler ['bʌtlər], s. maître m d'hôtel (d'une maison privée).

butt¹ [bʌt], s. barrique f, gros tonneau; water b., tonneau m (pour l'eau de pluie).

butt², s. bout m; crosse f (de fusil); b. end, extrémité inférieure; gros bout.

butt³, s. 1. Mil: the butts, le champ de tir. 2. but m, cible f; (of pers.) souffre-douleur m inv.

butt⁴, s. 1. coup m de tête, de corne. II. v.tr. & i. donner un coup de corne à (qn, qch.); to b. into sth., buter contre qch.; to b. in, intervenir.

butter ['bʌtər]. I. s. beurre m; b. bean, haricot m beurre; b. dish, beurrier m; b. knife, couteau m à beurre. II. v.tr. beurrer. 'butter-fingered, a. F: maladroit. 'butterscotch, s. caramel m au beurre.

buttercup ['bʌtəkʌp], s. bouton m d'or.

butterfly ['bʌtəflai], s. papillon m.

button ['bʌtn]. I. s. (a) bouton m; (b) buttons, chasseur m (d'hôtel). II. v.tr. to b. sth. (up), boutonner qch. 'buttonhole, s. boutonnière f.

buttress ['bʌtris]. I. s. contrefort m; flying b., arc-boutant m. II. v.tr. arc-bouter, étayer.

‡**buy** [bai], v.tr. acheter (from, à). buy 'back, v.tr. racheter. buy 'up, v.tr. rafler, accaparer. 'buyer, s. acheteur, -euse; Com: chef m de rayon.

buzz [bʌz]. I. s. bourdonnement m. II. v.i. bourdonner, vrombir; Av: F: harceler (un avion). 'buzzer, s. vibreur m, vibrateur m. 'buzzing, s. bourdonnement m.

buzzard ['bʌzəd], s. buse f, busard m.

by [bai]. I. prep. 1. (near) près de, à côté de; by the sea, au bord de la mer; by oneself, seul; à l'écart. 2. (a) by land and sea, par terre et par mer; punished by s.o., puni par qn; made by hand, fait à la main; three metres by two, trois mètres sur deux; I'll come by car, by train, je viendrai en auto, par le train; (b) what do you gain by doing that? que gagnez-vous à faire cela? 3. by right, de droit; by rights, de toute justice; three o'clock by my watch, trois heures d'après ma montre; to sell sth. by the kilo, vendre qch. au kilo. 4. one by one, un à un. 5. by day, de jour, le jour; by Monday, d'ici lundi; by three o'clock, avant trois heures; by now, déjà. 6. to know s.o. by sight, connaître qn de vue; grocer by trade, épicier de métier. II. adv. 1. près; taking it by and large, à tout prendre. 2. to put sth. by, mettre qch. de côté. III. a. & prefix. (also bye) secondaire; Pol: by-election, élection partielle. 'by(-)law, s. arrêté m municipal. 'bypass. I. s. route f d'évitement; déviation f. II. v.tr. contourner, éviter. 'by-product, s. Ind: sous-produit m; dérivé m. 'by-stander, s. spectateur, -trice. 'by(-) way, s. chemin m détourné; chemin vicinal.

bye [bai], s. 1. Sp: (in tournament) to have a b., être exempt (d'une épreuve). 2. (at cricket) balle f passée.

C

C, c [si:]. 1. (la lettre) C, c m. 2. Mus: ut m, do m.

cab [kæb], s. taxi m.

cabbage ['kæbidʒ], s. chou m; c. lettuce, laitue f pommée; c. white (butterfly), piéride f, papillon m blanc, du chou.

cabin ['kæbin], s. 1. cabane f, case f. 2. (a) Rail: poste m de conduite; (b) Nau: cabine f; (c) Av: carlingue f.

cabinet ['kæbinit], s. 1. meuble m à tiroirs; glass c., vitrine f; c. maker, ébéniste m. 2. Pol: cabinet m; c. minister, ministre m d'État.

cable ['keibl]. I. s. 1. câble m. 2. (also cablegram) câblogramme m. II. v.tr. & i. câbler.

caboodle [kə'bu:dl], s. P: the whole c., tout le bazar.

cackle ['kækl]. I. s. caquet m. II. v.i. caqueter.

cactus ['kæktəs], s. cactus m.

cad [kæd], s. goujat m, cuistre m.

cadaverous [kə'dævərəs], a. cadavéreux.

caddie ['kædi], s. (golf) caddie m.

†caddy ['kædi], s. boîte f à thé.

cadet [kə'det], s. élève m d'une école militaire.

cadge [kædʒ], v.tr. & i. (a) mendier; to c. sth. from s.o., taper de qn. 'cadger, s. (a) mendiant m; (b) chineur m.

café ['kafei], s. café-restaurant m. cafe'teria, s. cafétéria f.

cage [keidʒ], s. 1. cage f. 2. cabine f (d'ascenseur). 'cagey, a. F: prudent, circonspect.

cajole [kə'dʒoul], v.tr. cajoler; enjôler.

cake [keik]. I. s. 1. gâteau m; c. shop, pâtisserie f; F: that takes the c.! c'est la fin des haricots! F: it's a piece of c., c'est donné. 2. pain m (de savon); cattle c., tourteau m. II. v.i. former une croûte; (of blood) se cailler; caked with mud, plaqué de boue.

†calamity [kə'læmiti], s. 1. calamité f, malheur m. 2. désastre m.

calcium ['kælsiəm], s. calcium m.

calculate ['kælkjuleit], v.tr. & i. calculer; abs. faire un calcul. 'calculated, a. (of rudeness, etc.) délibéré, calculé. 'calculating, a. (of pers.) calculateur. II. s. (also calcu'lation) calcul m; estimation f.

calendar ['kælindər], s. calendrier m.

†calf¹ [ka:f], s. veau m.

†calf², s. mollet m (de la jambe).

calibre ['kælibər], s. calibre m.

call [kɔ:l]. I. s. 1. appel m; cri m. 2. within c., à portée de voix; telephone c., appel téléphonique; coup m de téléphone; Th: rappel (d'un acteur). 3. visite f; Nau: port of c., port d'escale; F: to pay a c., aller faire pipi. 4. demande f (d'argent). II. v. 1. v.tr. (a) appeler (qn); crier (qch.); (b) héler (un taxi); U.S: téléphoner à (qn); (c) réveiller (qn); (d) he is called Martin, il s'appelle Martin; to c. s.o. names, injurier qn. 2. v.i. has anyone called? est-il venu quelqu'un? (b) Rail: s'arrêter (à une gare); Nau: faire escale (à un port). 'call 'back. 1. v.tr. rappeler (qn). 2. v.i. repasser (chez qn). 'call-box, s. cabine f (téléphonique). 'call-boy, s. 1. Th: avertisseur m. 2. U.S: chasseur m (d'hôtel). 'caller, s. visiteur, -euse; P.T.T: demandeur, -euse. 'call for, v.ind.tr. (a) to c. for help, crier au secours; (b) venir prendre (qn); (c) demander (l'attention, etc.). 'call-girl, s. prostituée f (sur rendez-vous téléphonique). 'calling, s. vocation f; métier m. 'call on, v.i. 1. faire visite chez (qn). 2. faire appel à (qn). 'call out, v.i. appeler; appeler au secours. 'call up, v.tr. Mil: mobiliser. 'call-up, s. Mil: mobilisation f.

callous ['kæləs], a. insensible, endurci. -ly, adv. sans pitié, sans cœur.

calm [ka:m]. I. a. calme, tranquille. -ly, adv. tranquillement. II. s. (also 'calmness) calme m, tranquillité f.

III. v. 1. v.tr. calmer, apaiser; to c. s.o. down, pacifier qn. 2. v.i. to c. down, se calmer.

calorie ['kæləri], s. calorie f.

camber ['kæmbər], s. cambrure f (d'une poutre); bombement m (d'une route). 'cambered, a. arqué, courbé, cambré; bombé.

camel ['kæm(ə)l], s. chameau m; she-c., chamelle f.

cameo ['kæmiou], s. camée m.

camera ['kæm(ə)rə], s. appareil m (photographique).

camouflage ['kæmuflɑːʒ]. I. s. camouflage m. II. v.tr. camoufler.

camp [kæmp]. I. s. camp m; campement m; to bed, lit m de camp; c. stool, pliant m. II. v.i. camper. 'camping, s. camping m. c. site, ground, (terrain m de) camping.

campaign [kæm'pein]. I. s. campagne f. II. v.i. faire une campagne.

camphor ['kæmfər], s. camphre m. 'camphorated, a. camphré.

can¹ [kæn]. I. s. 1. bidon m. 2. boîte f (de conserves). II. ‡v.tr. mettre en boîte, conserver. 'canned, a. 1. (of food) en conserve. 2. P: ivre.

‡can², modal aux. v. 1. pouvoir; I cannot allow that, je ne saurais permettre cela; that cannot be, cela ne se peut pas; what c. it be? qu'est-ce que cela peut bien être? 2. savoir; I c. swim, je sais nager. 3. you c. but try, vous pouvez toujours essayer. 4. I c. see nothing, je ne vois rien.

Canadian [kə'neidjən], a. & s. canadien, -ienne.

canal [kə'næl], s. canal m; the Suez C., le Canal de Suez; Anat: the alimentary c., le canal alimentaire.

†canary [kə'nɛəri], s. serin m.

‡cancel ['kæns(ə)l], v.tr. annuler; supprimer (un train); oblitérer (un timbre); Mth: éliminer. **cancel'lation**, s. annulation f.

cancer ['kænsər], s. cancer m.

candid ['kændid], a. franc; sincere. **-ly,** adv. franchement, sincèrement.

candidate ['kændidit], s. candidat, -ate.

candle ['kændl], s. wax c., bougie f; tallow c., chandelle f; (in church) cierge m. 'Candlemas, s. Ecc: the Chandeleur f. 'candlestick, s. chandelier m; bougeoir m.

candour ['kændər], s. franchise f, sincérité f.

†candy ['kændi], s. U.S: bonbon m. 'candy-striped, a. pékiné.

cane [kein]. I. s. 1. canne f. 2. raspberry c., framboisier m. 3. c. sugar, sucre m de canne. II. v.tr. battre, frapper (qn) (à coups de canne). 'caning, s. Sch: correction f.

canine ['kænain], a. canin; de chien; c. tooth, canine f.

canister ['kænistər], s. boîte f (en fer blanc).

canker ['kæŋkər], s. chancre m.

cannibal ['kænibəl], s. & a. cannibale (mf); anthropophage (mf). 'cannibalism, s. cannibalisme m.

cannon ['kænən]. I. s. Mil: canon m. 2. (billiards) carambolage m. II. v.i. (at billiards) caramboler; to c. into s.o., heurter violemment qn.

canoe [kə'nuː], s. 1. périssoire f. 2. pirogue f.

canon¹ ['kænən], s. (a) canon m (de la messe); c. law, droit canon; (b) critère m.

canon², s. Ecc: chanoine m.

†canopy ['kænəpi], s. dais m; auvent m, marquise f.

cantankerous [kæn'tæŋk(ə)rəs], a. revêche, acariâtre.

cantata [kæn'tɑːtə], s. cantate f.

canteen [kæn'tiːn], s. 1. cantine f. 2. c. of cutlery, service m de table (en coffre).

canter ['kæntər]. I. s. petit galop; to win at a c., arriver bon premier. II. v.i. aller au petit galop.

canting ['kæntiŋ], a. hypocrite.

canvas ['kænvəs], s. toile f (à voiles); under c., sous la tente.

canvass ['kænvəs], v.tr. solliciter (des suffrages); abs. faire une tournée électorale; Com: faire la place. 'canvasser, s. Pol: agent m électoral; Com: placier m. 'canvassing, s. prospection f; sollicitation f (de suffrages); Com: démarchage m.

canyon ['kænjən], s. cañon m.

cap [kæp]. I. s. 1. casquette f; Sch: c. and gown, costume m académique. 2. Techn: chapeau m (de protection); capuchon m (de stylo). 3. amorce f, capsule f. II. ‡v.tr. 1. coiffer, couronner (qch. de qch.); capsuler (une bouteille). 2. F: surpasser; that caps it all! ça c'est le bouquet!

capable ['keipəbl], a. capable; compétent. **-ably,** adv. avec compétence. **capa'bility,** s. capacité f (pour faire qch.); faculté f (de faire qch.).

capacity [kə'pæsiti], s. 1. (a) contenance f; (b) rendement m; carrying c., charge f utile; seating c., nombre m de places assises; Th: house filled to c., salle comble. 2. capacité f; aptitude f. **ca'pacious,** a. vaste, spacieux.

cape¹ [keip], s. pèlerine f, cape f.

cape², s. cap m, promontoire m.

caper¹ ['keipər], s. Cu: câpre f.

caper², s. 1. cabriole f, gambade f. II. v.i. faire des cabrioles; gambader.

capital¹ ['kæpitl], s. A. & A: chapiteau m.

capital². I. a. 1. capital; c. letter, majuscule. 2. Jur: c. punishment, peine capitale. 3. of c. importance, de la plus haute importance. 4. excellent, F: fameux. **-ally,** adv. admirablement.

II. s. **1.** Fin: capital m, capitaux mpl, fonds mpl. **2.** Geog: capitale f. **3.** majuscule f. 'capitalism, s. capitalisme m. 'capitalist, s. capitaliste mf. capitali'zation, s. capitalisation f (des intérêts). 'capitalize, v.tr. capitaliser.

capitulate [kə'pitjuleit], v.i. capituler. capitu'lation, s. capitulation f.

capon ['keipən], s. chapon m, poulet m.

capricious [kə'priʃəs], a. capricieux. -ly, adv. capricieusement. ca'priciousness, s. humeur capricieuse, inégale.

capsize [kæp'saiz]. **1.** v.i. chavirer. **2.** v.tr. faire chavirer.

capstan ['kæpstən], s. cabestan m.

capsule ['kæpsju:l], s. capsule f.

captain ['kæptin]. **I.** s. (a) chef m, capitaine m; (b) Mil: Nau: capitaine; Mil.Av: group m, colonel m; Civil Av: (pilote) commandant m de bord, (as title) commandant. **II.** v.tr. commander (une compagnie); conduire (une expédition); Sp: diriger (une équipe).

captivate ['kæptiveit], v.tr. charmer, captiver, séduire.

captive ['kæptiv]. **1.** a. captif. **2.** s. captif, -ive, prisonnier, -ière. cap'tivity, s. captivité f. 'capture. **I.** s. capture f; prise f. **II.** v.tr. capturer; prendre; Com: to c. the market, accaparer la vente. **II.** s. capture f; prise f.

car [ka:r], s. auto(mobile) f, voiture f; Rail: U.S: voiture, wagon m; Rail: dining c., wagon-restaurant m; sleeping c., wagon-lit m; c. ferry, ferry-boat m; c. licence, permis m de circulation; c. sleeper, train m auto-couchette(s). 'carpark, s. parc m (à voitures), parking m.

carafe [kə'ra:f, -æf], s. carafe f.

caramel ['kærəmel], s. **1.** caramel m. **2.** bonbon m au caramel.

carat ['kærət], s. carat m.

caravan ['kærəvæn], s. caravane f, roulotte f.

caraway ['kærəwei], s. carvi m.

carbolic [ka:'bolik], a. phénique; c. acid, phénol m.

carbon ['ka:bən], s. **1.** Ch: carbone m. **2.** c. (paper), papier m carbone; c. copy, copie f, double m. 'carbonate [-ba:nit], s. carbonate m.

carbonic [ka:'bonik], a. carbonique; c. acid gas, anhydride m carbonique.

carboniferous [ka:bə'nifərəs], a. carbonifère.

carbonize ['ka:bənaiz], v.tr. carboniser.

carborundum [ka:bə'rʌndəm], s. carborundum m.

carbuncle ['ka:bʌŋkl], s. **1.** escarboucle f. **2.** Med: anthrax m; bourgeon m.

carburettor [ka:bju'retər], s. carburateur m.

carcass ['ka:kəs], s. cadavre m; corps m.

card [ka:d], s. carte f; billet m; it is on the cards, c'est bien possible; game of cards, partie f de cartes; c. table, table f de jeu; visiting c., carte de visite; identity c., carte d'identité; (post) c., carte (postale); Adm: passport control c., fiche f de voyageur. 'cardboard, s. carton m. 'card-index. **I.** s. (a) fichier m, classeur m; (b) catalogue m sur fiches. **II.** v.tr. mettre sur fiches. 'card-sharper, s. tricheur m.

cardigan ['ka:digən], s. gilet m (de tricot); cardigan m.

cardinal ['ka:dinl]. **1.** a. cardinal. **2.** s. (a) Ecc: cardinal m; (b) c. bird, cardinal.

cardiogram ['ka:diougræm], s. cardiogramme m. 'cardiograph, s. cardiographe m. cardi'ographer, s. cardiologue m. cardi'ology, s. cardiologie f.

care [kɛər]. **I.** s. **1.** souci m, inquiétude f. **2.** soin(s) mf(pl), attention f, ménagement m; take c.! faites attention! prenez garde! **3.** soin(s), charge f, tenue f; (on letter) c. of, c/o., aux bons soins de. **4.** cares of state, responsabilités f d'État. **II.** v.i. **1.** se soucier, s'inquiéter, se préoccuper; I don't c.! ça m'est égal! **2.** to c. for, soigner. **3.** to c. for s.o., aimer qn. 'carefree, a. libre de soucis; insouciant. 'careful, a. **1.** soigneux, attentif; be c.! prenez garde! faites attention! **2.** prudent, circonspect. -fully, a. **1.** soigneusement. **2.** prudemment. 'carefulness, s. **1.** soin m, attention f. **2.** prudence f. 'careless, a. **1.** insouciant; c. mistake, faute f d'inattention. **2.** négligent. -ly, adv. avec insouciance; négligemment; sans soin. 'carelessness, s. **1.** insouciance f; inattention f. **2.** négligence f. 'caretaker, s. concierge mf; gardien m.

career [kə'riər]. **I.** s. **1.** course f (précipitée). **2.** carrière f; Sch: careers master, mistress, orienteur, -euse, professionnel(le). **II.** v.i. courir rapidement, follement; to c. along, aller à toute vitesse.

caress [kə'res]. **I.** s. caresse f. **II.** v.tr. caresser.

†cargo ['ka:gou], s. cargaison f, cargo m.; c. boat, cargo m.

caricature ['kærikətjuər]. **I.** s. caricature f. **II.** v.tr. caricaturer. 'caricaturist, s. caricaturiste mf.

carnage ['ka:nidʒ], s. carnage m.

carnal ['ka:nl], a. **1.** charnel. **2.** mondain.

carnation [ka:'neiʃ(ə)n], s. œillet m.

carnival ['ka:niv(ə)l], s. carnaval m.

carnivorous [ka:'niv(ə)rəs], a. carnassier.

carol ['kær(ə)l], s. chant m; Christmas c., noël m.

†carp¹ [ka:p], s. Fish: carpe f.

carp², v.i. trouver à redire.

carpenter ['ka:pintər], s. charpentier m; menuisier m. 'carpentry, s. charpenterie f; grosse menuiserie f.

carpet[1] ['kɑːpit], s. tapis m; c. sweeper, balai m mécanique. II. v.tr. recouvrir d'un tapis.

carriage ['kærid3]. 1. 1. port m, transport m; c. free, franco. 2. port, maintien m. 3. (a) voiture f (à chevaux); (b) Rail: voiture, wagon m. 4. chariot m (d'une machine à écrire). 'carriageway, s. Aut: dual c., route f à double voie.

carrier ['kæriər]. 1. 1. (a) porteur, -euse; (b) camionneur m; (c) c. pigeon, pigeon m voyageur. 2. aircraft c., porte-avions m inv.

carrion ['kæriən], s. charogne f.

carrot ['kærət], s. carotte f.

carry ['kæri], 1. 1. porter; transporter. 2. to c. into effect, mettre à exécution. 3. to c. all before one, vaincre toutes les résistances; to c. one's point, imposer sa manière de voir. 4. adopter, faire adopter (une proposition). 5. abs. his voice carries well, sa voix porte bien. 'carry a'long, v.tr. emporter, entraîner. 'carry a'way, v.tr. emporter; emmener, enlever. 2. entraîner. 'carry-cot, s. porte-bébé m inv. carry forward, v.tr. (book-keeping) reporter. carry 'off, v.tr. 1. emporter; emmener, enlever. 2. remporter (le prix). carry 'on, v.tr. poursuivre; continuer; exercer; entretenir; soutenir. carry 'out, v.tr. mettre à exécution, effectuer. carry 'through, v.tr. mener à bonne fin.

cart[1] [kɑːt]. 1. s. charrette f. II. v.tr. charrier; F: to c. about, trimbaler (qn, qch.). 'carthorse, s. cheval m de trait.

carton ['kɑːtən], s. carton m.

cartoon [kɑː'tuːn], s. carton m; dessin m humoristique; Cin: dessin animé.

cartridge ['kɑːtrid3], s. cartouche f; c. paper, papier fort.

carve [kɑːv], v.tr. 1. sculpter, graver. 2. découper (la viande). 'carving, s. 1. sculpture f. 2. découpage m de la viande; c. knife, fork, couteau m, fourchette f à découper.

cascade [kæs'keid]. 1. s. chute f d'eau; cascade f. II. v.i. cascader.

case[1] [keis], s. 1. cas m; if that is the c., s'il en est ainsi; in any c., en tout cas. just in c., à tout hasard; in most cases, en général. 2. malade mf; blessé, -ée. 3. cause f, affaire f.

case[2], s. 1. caisse f; colis m. 2. mallette f; étui m (à lunettes, à cigarettes); écrin m (pour bijoux). 3. pillow c., taie f d'oreiller.

cash [kæʃ]. 1. s. no pl. espèces fpl; argent m comptant; hard c., espèces sonnantes.; c. with order, payable à la commande; c. on delivery, (C.O.D.), expédié contre remboursement; c. box, caisse f, cassette f; c. desk, caisse; c. register, caisse enregistreuse. II. v.tr. toucher (un chèque). ca'shier[1], s. caissier, -ière.

cashew[2] [kæ'ʃuː], s. Bot: acajou m à pommes; c. nut, noix f d'acajou.

cashier[2] [kə'ʃiər], v.tr. casser (un officier).

cashmere ['kæʃmiər], s. cachemire m.

casino [kə'siːnou], s. casino m.

cask [kɑːsk], s. barrique f, tonneau m.

casket ['kɑːskit], s. coffret m, cassette f.

casserole ['kæsəroul], s. cocotte f (en terre). 2. ragoût m en cocotte.

cassette [kæ'set], s. Phot: chargeur m.

cassock ['kæsək], s. soutane f.

cast [kɑːst]. 1. 1. (a) jet m; coup m (de dés); lancer m (du filet); (b) bas m de ligne. 2. moulage m. 3. Th: distribution f (des rôles). II. ‡v.tr. 1. jeter, lancer. 2. donner (un suffrage). 3. fondre (du métal); mouler (un cylindre); couler (une statue). III. a. coulé; c. iron, fonte f (de fer); c.-iron excuse, excuse f irréfutable. 'cast a'way, v.tr. a. jeter au loin; rejeter; (b) to be c.a., faire naufrage. 'castaway, s. naufragé, -ée. 'casting. 1. a. to give the c. vote, départager la voix. II. s. 1. (a) moulage m, fonte f; (b) Th: distribution f des rôles. 2. Ind: pièce f de fonte, pièce coulée. 'cast 'off, v.tr. rejeter; c.o. clothing, vêtements mpl de rebut; (knitting) to c.o. five stitches, fermer cinq mailles. 'cast 'on, v.tr. (knitting) monter (des mailles).

castanets [kæstə'nets], s. castagnettes fpl.

caste [kɑːst], s. caste f.

castle [kɑːsl]. 1. s. 1. château m (fort). 2. (at chess) tour f. II. v.tr. abs. (at chess) roquer.

castor, -er ['kɑːstər], s. 1. saupoudroir m. 2. roulette f (de fauteuil).

castor oil ['kɑːstər'ɔil], s. huile f de ricin.

casual ['kæʒju(ə)l], a. (a) fortuit, accidentel; (b) insouciant; Cl: c. clothes, costume m sport. -ally, adv. (a) en passant; (b) négligemment. 'casualness, s. indifférence f; insouciance f.

†casualty ['kæʒju(ə)lti], s. 1. accident m (de personne); c. ward, salle f des accidentés. 2. mort, -e; blessé, -ée.

cat [kæt], s. 1. (a) chat m, chatte f; tom c., matou m; to let the c. out of the bag, vendre la mèche; it's not big enough to swing a c. in, c'est grand comme un mouchoir de poche; it's enough to make a c. laugh, c'est à mourir de rire; (b) F: (of pers.) an old c., une vieille chipie. 2. the (great) cats, les grands félins. 3. attrib. c. burglar, monte-en-l'air m inv.; c. nap, sieste f; comme m. 'cat's-eye, s. (on roads) cataphote m (R.t.m.).

cataclysm ['kætəklizm], s. cataclysme m.

catacombs ['kætəkuːmz], s.pl. catacombes f.

catalogue ['kætələg]. 1. s. catalogue m, liste f. II. v.tr. cataloguer.

catapult ['kætəpʌlt]. I. s. 1. fronde f. 2.
Av: catapulte f (de lancement). II.
v.tr. lancer (un avion).

cataract ['kætərækt], s. cataracte f.

catarrh [kə'tɑ:r], s. catarrhe m.

catastrophe [kə'tæstrofi], s. catastrophe
f. cata'strophic, a. désastreux.

catch [kætʃ]. I. †v. 1. v.tr. (a) attraper,
prendre (qch.); ne pas manquer (le
train); (b) I didn't c. what you said, je
n'ai pas entendu ce que vous disiez.
2. v.i. (a) (of lock) s'engager; (b) (of
fire) prendre; (c) Cu: attacher,
brûler. s. prise f. 2. (on door)
loquet m. 3. (deception) attrape f.
'catching, a. (of illness) contagieux;
(of tune) entraînant. 'catch 'on, v.i.
F: (of fashion) prendre; (b) comprendre, F: piger. 'catch 'out, v.tr. F:
prendre (qn) sur le fait. 'catch 'up,
v.tr. rattraper (qn). 'catchword, s.
scie f, rengaine f.

catechism ['kætikizm], s. catéchisme m.

catechize ['kætikaiz], v.tr. 1. catéchiser.
2. interroger.

categorical [kætə'gorik(ə)l], a. catégorique. -ally, adv. catégoriquement.

category ['kætig(ə)ri], s. catégorie f.

cater ['keitər], v.i. to c. for, approvisionner (qn); pourvoir à (tous les
goûts). 'caterer, s. approvisionneur
m; pourvoyeur m; traiteur m.
'catering, s. approvisionnement m.

caterpillar ['kætəpilər], s. chenille f; c.
tractor, autochenille f.

caterwaul ['kætəwɔ:l], v.i. miauler.

cathedral [kə'θi:drəl], s. cathédrale f.

cathode ['kæθoud], s. cathode f; c. rays,
rayons m cathodiques.

catholic ['kæθ(ə)lik]. 1. a. (a) universel;
(b) tolérant. 2. a. & s. catholique
(mf). ca'tholicism, s. catholicisme m.

catkin ['kætkin], s. chaton m.

cattle ['kætl], s. coll. bétail m; bestiaux
mpl; P.N: c. crossing, passage m de
troupeaux.

catty ['kæti], a. F: méchant, rosse.

cauliflower ['koliflauər], s. chou-fleur m.

cause [kɔ:z]. I. s. 1. cause f. 2. raison f,
motif m, sujet m; with good c.,
et pour cause. II. v.tr. causer, occasionner.

causeway ['kɔ:zwei], s. (a) chaussée f;
(b) levée f, digue f.

caustic ['kɔ:stik], a. caustique. -ally,
adv. d'un ton mordant.

cauterize ['kɔ:təraiz], v.tr. cautériser.

caution ['kɔ:ʃ(ə)n]. I. s. 1. précaution
f, prudence f. 2. (a) avis m, avertissement m; (b) réprimande f. II. v.tr.
avertir (qn). 'cautious, a. circonspect,
prudent. -ly, adv. prudemment.

cavalry ['kævəlri], s. cavalerie f.

cave [keiv]. I. s. caverne f; antre m;
attrib. c. art, art rupestre. II. v.i. to
c. in, s'effondrer; F: (of pers.) céder.

cavern ['kævən], s. caverne f.

caviar ['kæviɑ:r], s. caviar m.

cavity ['kæviti], s. cavité f; creux m;
trou m.

caw [kɔ:], v.i. croasser.

cease [si:s], v.tr. & i. cesser; without
ceasing, sans arrêt. 'cease-fire, s. Mil:
cessez-le-feu m. 'ceaseless, a. incessant; sans arrêt. -ly, adv. sans cesse.

cedar ['si:dər], s. cèdre m.

cedilla [si'dilə], s. cédille f.

ceiling ['si:liŋ], s. plafond m.

celebrate ['selibreit], v.tr. célébrer; F:
fêter (un événement). 'celebrated, a.
célèbre; renommé. cele'bration, s.
célébration f. ce'lebrity, s. célébrité f;
renommée f.

celery ['seləri], s. céleri m.

celestial [si'lestiəl], a. céleste; Av: c.
navigation, navigation par visée f
astronomique.

celibate ['selibit], a. & s. célibataire (mf).
'celibacy, s. célibat m.

cell [sel], s. 1. cellule f. 2. El: élément
m (de pile). 3. communist c., noyau m
communiste.

cellar ['selər], s. cave f.

cello ['tʃelou], s. violoncelle m.

cellophane ['seləfein], s. R.t.m: cellophane f.

cellular ['seljulər], a. cellulaire.

cellulose ['seljulouz], s. cellulose f.

Celt [kelt], s. Celte mf. 'Celtic, a.
celtique; celte.

cement [si'ment]. I. s. ciment m. II.
v.tr. cimenter.

†cemetery ['semətri], s. cimetière m.

censer ['sensər], s. Ecc: encensoir m.

censor ['sensər]. I. s. censeur m. II. v.tr.
interdire (une pièce de théâtre);
passer (une lettre) par le contrôle.
'censorship, s. censure f.

censure ['senʃər]. I. s. censure f, blâme
m. II. v.tr. censurer.

census ['sensəs], s. recensement m.

cent [sent], s. 1. (a) cent m; (b) F: I
haven't a c., je n'ai pas le sou. 2. per
c., pour cent.

†centenary [sen'ti:nəri], a. & s. centenaire
(mf). cente'narian, s. centenaire m.

centigrade ['sentigreid], a. centigrade.

central ['sentr(ə)l], a. central. -ally, adv.
centralement; au centre. 'centralize,
v.tr. centraliser.

centre ['sentər], s. centre m; milieu m;
infant welfare c., consultation f de
nourrissons. 'centre-forward, s. Sp:
avant-centre m.

century ['sentʃəri], s. 1. siècle m. 2. (at
cricket) centaine f.

cereal ['siəriəl], a. & s. (usu.pl.) céréale
f; (breakfast) cereals, céréales en
flocons.

ceremony ['seriməni], s. cérémonie f;
to stand on c., faire des façons. cere-
'monial. 1. a. de cérémonie. 2. s.
cérémonial m. cere'monious, a. cérémonieux. -ly, adv. avec cérémonie.

cert [səːt], s. F: a dead c., une certitude (absolue); une affaire sûre; it's a c., c'est couru.

certain ['səːtin], a. certain; to know sth. for c., être bien sûr de qch.; to make c. of sth., (i) s'assurer de qch.; (ii) s'assurer qch. 1. (a) certainement, certes, (b) assurément; par- faitement. **'certainty**, s. certitude f; chose certaine.

certificate [se'tifikit], s. 1. certificat m; titre m (d'actions). 2. diplôme m. 3. birth c., acte m de naissance. 4. savings c., bon m d'épargne.

certify ['səːtifai], v.tr.&i. (a) certifier, dé- clarer; to c. a death, constater un décès; (b) authentiquer, légaliser (un document). **certi'fiable**, a. F: fou à lier. **'certified**, a. (aliéné) interdit.

certitude ['səːtitjuːd], s. certitude f.

cessation [se'seiʃ(ə)n], s. cessation f, arrêt m.

cesspool ['sespuːl], s. fosse f d'aisances.

chafe [tʃeif], v.tr. écorcher (la peau).

chaffinch ['tʃæfin(t)ʃ], s. pinson m.

chain [tʃein]. I. s. chaîne f; to pull the c., tirer la chasse d'eau; c. store, magasin m à succursales multiples. II. v.tr. attacher, retenir, par une chaîne.

chair [tʃɛːr], s. (a) chaise f, siège m; to take a c., s'asseoir; (b) to be in the c., présider; to take the c., prendre la présidence. **'chairman**, s. président, -ente.

chalice ['tʃælis], s. calice m.

chalk [tʃɔːk], s. craie f; coloured c., pastel m; French c., stéatite f. 'chalky, a. crayeux.

challenge ['tʃælin(d)ʒ]. I. s. (a) défi m; provocation f; (b) interpellation f. II. v.tr. 1. (a) défier; provoquer; (b) interpeller. 2. disputer (une affirma- tion). **'challenger**, s. Sp: challenger m.

chamber ['tʃeimbər], s. (a) audience c., salle f d'audience; B: music, musique f de chambre; (b) H: vase m de nuit; (c) C. of Commerce, chambre f de commerce. **'chambermaid**, s. femme f de chambre.

chamois ['ʃæmwɑː], s. chamois m; c. leather, (peau f de) chamois.

champagne [ʃæm'pein], s. (vin m de) champagne (m).

champion ['tʃæmpjən], s. champion, -onne. **'championship**, s. championnat m.

chance [tʃɑːns]. I. s. 1. chance f, hasard m, sort m; by c., par hasard; the chances are, il y a a fort à parier; on the off c., à tout hasard. 2. occasion f; to take one's c., risquer les chances. 3. to take a c., encourir un risque. 4. attrib. fortuit, accidentel. II. v. 1. v.i. to c. to do sth., faire qch. par hasard. 2. v.tr. to c. it, risquer le coup. 'chancy, a. chanceux, hasar- deux, risqué.

chancel ['tʃɑːnsəl], s. Ecc: 1. sanctuaire m. 2. chœur m.

chancellor ['tʃɑːnsələr], s. chancelier m.

change [tʃein(d)ʒ]. I. s. 1. changement m; revirement m; for a c., comme dis- traction f; pour changer. 2. c. of clothes, vêtements mpl de rechange. 3. monnaie f; small c., petite monnaie. II. v. 1. v.tr. changer; (a) modifier; (b) to c. one's clothes, changer de vêtements; (c) all c.! tout le monde descend! (d) échanger (qch. contre qch.). 2. v.i. (se) changer; se modifier. **'changeable**, a. changeant; variable; inconstant. **'changing**. I. a. changeant. II. s. changement m; Mil: relève f (de la garde); Sp: c. room, vestiaire m.

channel ['tʃænl], s. 1. (a) passe f, chenal m; (b) the (English) C., la Manche; the C. Islands, les îles Anglo-normandes. 2. canal m, conduit m. 3. voie f; Adm: official channels, la voie hiérarchique. 4. T.V: canal m.

chant [tʃɑːnt]. I. s. chant m. II. v.tr. psalmodier.

chaos ['keiɔs], s. chaos m. **cha'otic**, a. chaotique. **-ally**, adv. sans ordre.

chap¹ ['tʃæp], s. gerçure f, crevasse f.

chap², s. type m, individu m.

chapel ['tʃæpl], s. (a) chapelle f; (b) temple m (protestant).

chaperon ['ʃæpəroun]. I. s. chaperon m. II. v.tr. chaperonner.

chaplain ['tʃæplin], s. aumônier m.

chaplet ['tʃæplit], s. chapelet m.

chapter ['tʃæptər], s. chapitre m; Ecc: house, salle f du chapitre.

‡char¹ [tʃɑːr], s. carbonisée.

char², F: 1. s. femme f de ménage. II. ‡v.i. to go out charring, faire des ménages.

character ['kæriktər], s. 1. caractère m. 2. personnage m (de roman, etc.). **characte'ristic**. 1. a. caractéristique. 2. s. trait m, particularité f. **'charac- terize**, v.tr. caractériser. **'charac- terless**, a. dépourvu de caractère.

charcoal ['tʃɑːkoul], s. charbon m (de bois).

charge [tʃɑːdʒ]. I. s. 1. charge f (d'une cartouche, etc.). 2. frais mpl, prix m. 3. garde f, soin m; Adm: person in c., préposé m; Jur: to give s.o. in c., faire arrêter qn. 4. Jur: chef m d'accusation. 5. Mil: charge, attaque f. II. v.tr. & i. charger; c. it on the bill, portez-le sur la note. 'charger, s. chargeur m (d'accumulateur).

charity ['tʃæriti], s. 1. charité f. 2. aumônes fpl, bienfaisance f; c. bazaar, vente f de charité. 3. œuvre f de bienfaisance; fondation pieuse. **'char- itable**, a. (personne) charitable; (œuvre) de bienfaisance.

charm [tʃɑːm]. I. s. 1. charme m. 2. amulette f, fétiche m, porte-bonheur m.inv. II. v.tr. charmer, enchanter. **'charming**, a. charmant, ravissant.

chart [tʃɑːt]. I. s. 1. carte f (marine). 2. (a) diagramme m, graphique m; (b) (of computer) operating c., organigramme m. II. v.tr. Nau: dresser la carte (d'une côte, etc.).

charter ['tʃɑːtər]. I. s. 1. charte f (d'une ville); statuts m (d'une société); the Atlantic C., la Charte de l'Atlantique. 2. affrètement m; c. plane, avion-taxi m. II. v.tr. 1. instituer (une compagnie) par charte. 2. affréter (un navire, un avion).

†**charwoman** ['tʃɑːwʊmən], s. femme f de ménage.

chary ['tʃɛəri], a. circonspect, prudent.

chase [tʃeis]. I. v.tr. chasser; poursuivre. II. s. chasse f, poursuite f; wild goose c., poursuite vaine.

chasm ['kæz(ə)m], s. gouffre (béant); chasme m; vide m énorme.

chassis ['ʃæsi], s. châssis m.

chaste [tʃeist], a. chaste; pudique. 'chastity, s. chasteté f.

chastise [tʃæs'taiz], v.tr. châtier; corriger.

‡**chat** [tʃæt]. I. v.i. causer, bavarder. II. s. causerie f, causette f.

chatter ['tʃætər]. I. v.i. bavarder; caqueter; (of teeth) claquer. II. s. caquetage m; bavardage m.

chauffeur ['ʃoufər], f. chauffeuse [ʃou'fəːz], s. chauffeur, -euse (salarié(e)) d'automobile.

cheap [tʃiːp]. 1. a. (a) (à) bon marché; cheaper, (à) meilleur marché; (b) de peu de valeur. 2. adv. (à) bon marché. -ly, adv. (à) bon marché; he got off c., il en est quitte à bon compte. 'cheapen, v.tr. diminuer la valeur de (qch.). 'cheapness, s. bon marché m; médiocrité f (de qch.).

cheat [tʃiːt]. I. v.tr. 1. tromper, frauder (qn), voler (qn). 2. tricher. II. s. 1. trompeur, -euse; escroc m. 2. tricheur, -euse. 'cheating, s. 1. tromperie f. 2. tricherie f.

check[1] [tʃek]. I. v.tr. (a) (at chess) mettre (le roi) en échec; (b) faire échec (à qn, qch.); (c) réprimer (une passion); (d) vérifier (qch.). II. s. 1. (at chess) échec m. 2. contrôle m; (a) vérification f (d'un compte, etc.); c. sample, échantillon m témoin; (b) ticket m; bulletin m (de bagages); U.S: c. room, consigne f; (c) U.S: (P: in Eng.) addition f, note f; (d) P: to hand in one's checks, mourir. 3. U.S: chèque m. 'check 'in, v.i. 1. s'inscrire (à l'hôtel). 2. Ind: signer à l'arrivée. 'checking, s. 1. répression f. 2. contrôle m; vérification f. 'check 'out, v.tr. U.S: retirer (des bagages). 'check up, s. Med: examen médical (complet).

check[2], s. Tex: carreau m; tissu à carreaux. 'checkers, s. U.S: jeu m de dames.

checkmate ['tʃekmeit]. I. s. échec m et mat m. II. v.tr. faire échec et mat; contrecarrer (les projets de qn).

cheek [tʃiːk]. 1. s. 1. joue f; c. bone, pommette f. 2. F: toupet m, impudence f. II. v.tr. F: se payer la tête de (qn). 'cheeky, a. F: effronté.

cheer [tʃiər]. I. s. 1. hourra m; pl. acclamations f. II. v. 1. v.tr. (a) c. s.o. (up), égayer qn; (b) applaudir. 2. v.i. to c. up, reprendre sa gaieté; (b) applaudir. 'cheerful, a. gai; de bonne humeur. -fully, adv. allégrement; de bon cœur. 'cheerfulness, s. gaieté f; contentement m. 'cheering, s. acclamation f; applaudissements mpl. 'cheerless, a. morne, triste. 'cheery, a. joyeux, gai.

cheese [tʃiːz]. I. s. 1. fromage m. 2. biscuit, biscuit m non sucré; c. straws, allumettes f au fromage. II. v. P: c. it! en voilà assez! la ferme! to be cheesed off, avoir le cafard. 'cheeseparing, s. parcimonie f, lésine f.

chef [ʃef], s. chef m de cuisine.

chemical ['kemik(ə)l]. 1. a. chimique. 2. s.pl. produits m chimiques.

chemist ['kemist], s. 1. pharmacien m; chemist's shop, pharmacie f. 2. chimiste m.

chemistry ['kemistri], s. chimie f.

cheque [tʃek], s. chèque m; c. book, carnet m de chèques.

cherish ['tʃeriʃ], v.tr. 1. chérir. 2. caresser.

†**cherry** ['tʃeri]. 1. s. 1. cerise f; c. tree, cerisier m; c. orchard, cerisaie f. 2. a. cerise inv.

†**cherub** ['tʃerəb], s. chérubin m.

chess [tʃes], s. jeu m d'échecs; to play c., jouer aux échecs. 'chessboard, s. échiquier m. 'chessmen, s.pl. pièces f (du jeu d'échecs).

chest [tʃest], s. 1. coffre m; c. of drawers, commode f. 2. poitrine f.

chestnut ['tʃes(t)nʌt]. 1. s. (a) châtaigne f; marron m; (b) c. (tree), châtaignier m; marronnier m. 2. attrib. châtain; (cheval) alezan.

chew [tʃuː], v.tr. mâcher, mastiquer. 'chewing gum, s. chewing-gum m.

chick [tʃik], s. poussin m.

chicken ['tʃikin], s. poulet m; spring c., poussin m. 'chicken-pox, s. Med: varicelle f.

chicory ['tʃikəri], s. 1. chicorée f. 2. endive f.

chief [tʃiːf]. 1. s. chef m. 2. a. principal; premier; (en) chef. -ly, adv. surtout; principalement. 'chieftain, s. chef m (de clan).

chiffon ['ʃifon], s. Tex: mousseline f de soie.

chilblain ['tʃilblein], s. engelure f.

†**child** [tʃaild], s. enfant mf; from a c., dès son enfance; that's c.'s play, ça, c'est facile! 'childbirth, s. enfantement

m. 'childhood, *s.* enfance *f.* 'childish, d'enfant; d'enfant; *(of old pers.)* to grow c., retomber en enfance. -ly, *adv.* comme un enfant; puérilement.

chill [tʃil]. I. *s.* 1. *(a) Med:* coup *m* de froid; *(b)* frisson *m* (de crainte). 2. to take the c. off, tiédir (l'eau). II. *v.tr.* refroidir, glacer (qch.); réfrigérer (la viande); faire frissonner (qn). 'chilliness, *s.* froid *m*, froideur *f.* 'chilly, *a.* 1. *(of pers.)* frileux; to feel c., avoir froid; *(of weather)* frais. 2. *(of manner)* froid; glacial.

chime [tʃaim]. I. *s.* carillon *m.* II. *v.i.* & *tr.* carillonner.

chimney ['tʃimni], *s.* cheminée *f*; c. pot, pot *m* de cheminée; c. sweep, ramoneur *m.* 'chimneypiece, *s.* cheminée *f.*

chimpanzee [tʃimpæn'ziː], *s.* chimpanzé *m.*

chin [tʃin], *s.* menton *m.*

china ['tʃainə], *s. (a)* porcelaine *f*; faïence *f* fine; *(b)* vaisselle *f* (de porcelaine).

Chinese [tʃai'niːz], *a.* & *s.* Chinois, -e.

chink[1] [tʃiŋk], *s.* fente *f*, crevasse *f*; entrebâillement *m* (de la porte).

chink[2] I. *s.* tintement *m.* II. *v.tr.* & *i.* (faire) sonner; (faire) tinter.

chintz [tʃints], *s. Tex:* cretonne *f*, indienne *f.*

chip [tʃip]. I. *s.* 1. éclat *m*, copeau *m.* 2. brisure *f.* 3. chips, (pommes de terre) frites *(fpl).* 4. *(at cards, etc.)* jeton *m.* II. *v.tr.* 1. tailler par éclats. 2. ébrécher; écorner. 'chippings, *s.pl. P.N:* loose c., gravillons *m.*

chipmunk ['tʃipmʌŋk], *s. Z:* tamia *m* rayé.

chiropodist [ki'rɔpɔdist], *s.* pédicure *mf.* chi'ropody, *s.* chirurgie *f* pédicure.

chirp [tʃəːp], *v.i.* pépier, gazouiller.

chisel ['tʃizl]. I. *s.* ciseau *m.* II. *v.tr.* ciseler; *P:* rouler, carotter (qn).

chivalrous ['ʃivəlrəs], *a.* chevaleresque; courtois. 'chivalry, *s.* conduite *f* chevaleresque; courtoisie *f.*

chlorate ['klɔːreit], *s.* chlorate *m.*

chloride ['klɔːraid], *s.* chlorure *m.*

chlorine ['klɔːriːn], *s.* chlore *m.* 'chlorinated, *a.* chloré.

chloroform ['klɔrəfɔːm], *s.* chloroforme *m.*

chocolate ['tʃɔklit]. 1. *s.* chocolat *m.* 2. *a.* chocolat *inv.*

choice [tʃɔis]. 1. *s.* choix *m*; alternative *f.* II. *a.* choisi; de choix.

choir ['kwaiər], *s.* chœur *m.* 'choirboy, *s.* jeune choriste *m.* 'choirmaster, *s.* maître *m* de chapelle.

choke [tʃouk]. I. *v.tr.* & *i.* étouffer; suffoquer; obstruer (un tuyau). II. *s. Aut:* starter *m.* 'choking, *s.* étouffement *m.*

cholesterol [kɔ'lestərɔl], *s. Med:* cholestérol *m.*

‡choose [tʃuːz], *v.tr.* choisir; there's nothing to c. between them, l'un vaut l'autre.

chop [tʃɔp]. I. *v.tr.* couper, fendre. II. *s. Cu:* côtelette *f.* 'chop 'down, *v.tr.* abattre (un arbre). 'chop 'up, *v.tr.* couper en morceaux. 'chopper, *s.* couperet *m*, hachoir *m.* 'choppy, *a. Nau:* sea, mer hachée.

choral ['kɔːr(ə)l], *a.* 1. c. society, (société *f*) chorale *(f).* 2. chanté en chœur.

chord [kɔːd], *s. Mus:* accord *m.*

chore [tʃɔːr], *s.* corvée *f.*

chorus ['kɔːrəs], *s.* 1. chœur *m*; *Th:* c. girl, girl *f.*

chosen ['tʃouzn], *a.* choisi.

Christ [kraist], *Pr.n.* le Christ. christen ['krisn], *v.tr.* baptiser. 'christening ['kri-], *s.* baptême *m.* 'Christian ['kri-], *a.* & *s.* chretien, -ienne. Christi'anity [kri-], *s.* christianisme *m.* Christmas ['krisməs], *s.* Noël *m.*; C. card, carte *f* de Noël; C. Day, le jour de Noël; C. tree, arbre *m* de Noël.

chromium ['kroumiəm], *s.* chrome *m*; c. plated, chromé.

chronic ['krɔnik], *a. (a)* chronique; *(b)* constant, continuel.

chronicle ['krɔnikl], *s.* chronique *f.*

chronological [krɔnə'lɔdʒik(ə)l], *a.* chronologique.

chrysalis ['krisəlis], *s.* chrysalide *f.*

chrysanthemum [kri'sænθ(ə)məm], *s.* chrysanthème *m.*

chubby ['tʃʌbi], *a.* rond, joufflu.

chuck [tʃʌk], *v.tr. F: (a)* jeter (une pierre); *(b)* lâcher, plaquer (qn); *(c)* c. it! en voilà assez! *(d)* to c. one's weight about, faire l'important; *(e)* to c. s.o. out, flanquer qn à la porte; *(f)* to c. up one's job, démissionner. 'chucker-'out, *s. F:* expulseur *m*, videur *m.*

chuckle ['tʃʌkl]. I. *s.* rire sous cape. II. *s.* rire *m* étouffé.

chum [tʃʌm], *s.* camarade *mf.*

chump [tʃʌmp], *s.* 1. *Cu:* c. chop, côtelette *f* de gigot. 2. *F:* rigaud *m*, cruche *f.*

chunk [tʃʌŋk], *s.* gros morceau *m.*

church [tʃəːtʃ], *s.* église *f*; to go to c., aller à l'office; aller à la messe; c. hall, salle paroissiale. 'church'warden, *s.* marguillier *m.* 'churchyard, *s.* cimetière *m.*

churn [tʃəːn], *s.* 1. baratte *f.* 2. bidon *m* à lait.

cider ['saidər], *s.* cidre *m.*

cigar [si'gɑːr], *s.* cigare *m.*

cigarette [sigə'ret], *s.* cigarette *f.*

cinder ['sindər], *s.* 1. cendre *f.* 2. *pl.* escarbilles *fpl.* 3. c. track, piste *f* (en) cendrée.

cine-camera ['sini'kæmərə], *s.* caméra *f.*

cinema ['sinimə], *s.* cinéma *m.*

cinnamon ['sinəmən], *s.* cannelle *f.*

cipher ['saifər], *s.* 1. zéro *m.* 2. *(a)* chiffre *m*; *(b)* message chiffré.

circle ['səːkl]. I. s. 1. cercle *m*; *U.S*: traffic c., rond-point *m*. 2. *Th*: dress c., (premier) balcon *m*; upper c., seconde galerie *f*. 3. milieu *m*, coterie *f*. II. *v.tr. & i*. entourer (qch.) (with, de); tournoyer (autour de qch.); *Av*: décrire des cercles (au-dessus de qch.). **'circular**. 1. *a*. circulaire. 2. *s*. prospectus *m*.

circuit ['səːkit], *s*. 1. pourtour *m*. 2. (*a*) révolution *f* (du soleil); (*b*) *Jur*: tournée *f*. 3. *El*: circuit *m*; short c., court-circuit *m*.

circulate ['səːkjuleit], *v.tr. & i*. (faire) circuler. **circu'lation**, *s*. circulation *f* (du sang, de l'argent); tirage *m* (d'un journal).

circumcise ['səːkəmsaiz], *v.tr.* circoncire. **circum'cision**, *s*. circoncision *f*.

circumference [sə'kʌmfərəns], *s*. circonférence *f*.

circumflex ['səːkəmfleks], *a. & s*. c. (accent), accent *m* circonflexe.

circumstances ['səːkəmstənsiz], *s.pl.* circonstances *fpl*; under the c., puisqu'il en est ainsi; in no c., en aucun cas; that depends on c., c'est selon; if his c. allow, si ses moyens le permettent. **circum'stantial**, *a*. circonstanciel; c. evidence, preuves *f* indirectes.

circus ['səːkəs], *s*. cirque *m*.

cirrhosis [si'rousis], *s. Med*: cirrhose *f*.

Cistercian [sis'təːʃ(ə)n], *a. & s. Ecc*: cistercien, -ienne.

cistern ['sistən], *s*. réservoir *m* à eau; citerne *f*; *H*: (réservoir de) chasse *f* d'eau.

citadel ['sitədel], *s*. citadelle *f*.

cite [sait], *v.tr.* citer.

citizen ['sitiz(ə)n], *s*. citoyen, -enne.

citric ['sitrik], *a. Ch*: citrique.

citrus ['sitrəs], *a. c. fruit*, agrumes *mpl*.

†**city** ['siti], *s*(*a*) grande ville *f*; the C., la Cité de Londres; he's in the C., il est dans les affaires, *U.S*: ville épiscopale; c. hall, hôtel *m* de ville.

civic ['sivik]. 1. *a*. civique; c. centre, centre civique, social. 2. *s.pl. Sch*: civics, instruction civique.

civil ['siv(i)l], *a*. 1. civil; c. rights, droits civiques; c. war, guerre civile; life, dans le civil. 2. poli, courtois. **ci'vilian**, *a. & s*. civil (*m*). **ci'vility**, *s*. civilité *f*, politesse *f*. **'civilly**, *adv*. poliment.

civilize ['sivilaiz], *v.tr.* civiliser. **civili'zation**, *s*. civilisation *f*.

claim [kleim]. I. s. 1. demande *f*; réclamation *f*. 2. droit *m*, titre *m* (to sth., à qch.). 3. concession *f* (minière). II. *v.tr.* (*a*) réclamer (un droit); demander (de l'attention); (*b*) prétendre, affirmer (que . . .). **'claimant**, *s*. prétendant, -ante.

clamber ['klæmbər], *v.i.* grimper; to c. over a wall, escalader un mur.

clammy ['klæmi], *a*. (froid et) moite. **'clamminess**, *s*. moiteur *f* froide.

clamour ['klæmər]. I. s. clameur *f*; cris *mpl*. II. *v.i.* vociférer; to c. for sth., réclamer qch. à grands cris.

clamp [klæmp]. I. s. crampon *m*. II. *v.tr.* agrafer; brider; to c. down on an abuse, supprimer un abus.

clan [klæn], *s*. clan *m*. 2. (*a*) tribu *f*; (*b*) coterie *f*.

clandestine [klæn'destin], *a*. clandestin.

clang [klæŋ]. I. s. son *m* métallique. II. *v.i.* retentir, résonner. **'clanger**, *s. F*: to drop a c., faire une boulette.

clank [klæŋk]. I. s. bruit *m* métallique; cliquetis *m*. II. *v.i.* rendre un bruit métallique.

clap [klæp]. I. s. (*a*) battement *m*; applaudissement *m*; (*b*) c. of thunder, coup *m* de tonnerre. II. ‡*v.tr.* applaudir; to c. s.o. on the back, donner à qn une tape dans le dos. **'clapping**, *s*. applaudissements *mpl*.

claret ['klærət], *s*. (vin *m* de) Bordeaux *m*.

clarinet [klæri'net], *s*. clarinette *f*.

clarity ['klæriti], *s*. clarté *f*.

clash [klæʃ]. I. s. 1. fracas *m*; choc *m* (de verres). 2. conflit *m*. II. *v.i.* (*of opinions*) s'opposer; (*of interests*) se heurter; (*of colours*) jurer; the dates c., les deux réunions (etc.) tombent le même jour.

clasp [klɑːsp]. I. s. fermeture *f* (de collier); fermoir *m* (de porte-monnaie). II. *v.tr.* serrer, étreindre (qn).

class [klɑːs], *s*. 1. classe *f*; the middle c., la bourgeoisie. 2. *Sch*: (*a*) classe; (*b*) (*at university*) mention *f* obtenue. 3. sorte *f*, genre *m*. **classifi'cation** [klæ-], *s*. classification *f*. **'classify** [klæ-], *v.tr.* classer. **'classroom**, *s*. (salle *f* de) classe *f*

classic ['klæsik], *a. & s*. classique (*m*).

classical ['klæsik(ə)l], *a*. classique.

clatter ['klætər], *s*. bruit *m*, vacarme *m*.

clause [klɔːz], *s*. clause *f*, article *m*; *Gram*: membre *m* de phrase.

claw [klɔː]. I. s. griffe *f* (d'un chat); serre *f* (d'un aigle); pince *f* (d'un homard). II. *v*. 1. *v.tr.* griffer, égratigner. 2. *v.i.* to c. at sth., s'accrocher à qch.

clay [klei], *s*. argile *f*.

clean [kliːn]. I. *a*. propre, net; c. break, cassure *f* nette; c. hands, (i) mains propres, (ii) mains nettes; to come c., (i) (*of clothes*) devenir propre; (ii) *F*: avouer. **-ly**, *adv*. proprement, nettement. II. *adv. F*: tout à fait; I c. forgot j'ai complètement oublié. III. *v.tr.* to c. (up), nettoyer. **'cleaner**, *s*. 1. *Ind*: *etc*: nettoyeur, -euse; femme *f* de ménage; dry c., nettoyeur à sec. 2. vacuum c., aspirateur *m*. **'cleaning**, *s*. nettoyage *m*; dry c., nettoyage à sec. **'cleanness**, *s*. 1. propreté *f*. 2. netteté *f* (de contours). **'clean-shaven**, *a*. glabre, sans barbe (ni moustache).

cleanse [klenz], *v.tr.* 1. curer (un égout). 2. purifier (le sang). 'cleansing, *a.* c. cream, démaquillant *m*.

clear [kliər], *a.* 1. clair, limpide; net. 2. certain, évident. 3. lucide. 4. c. profit, bénéfice clair; three clear days, trois jours francs. 5. libre, dégagé; *Mil:* all c.! fin d'alerte. **-ly,** *adv.* clairement, nettement; évidemment. II. *a. or adv.* to keep c. off, éviter qch.; **stand c. of the door!** dégagez la porte! III. *v.tr.* 1. exonérer (un accusé); to c. oneself, se disculper. 2. désencombrer; déblayer; défricher; to c. (the table), desservir, enlever le couvert; **to c. the letter box,** lever les lettres. 3. **to c. a barrier,** franchir une barrière. 4. solder (des marchandises); liquider (un compte); virer (un chèque). 'clearance, *s.* 1. (at customs) dédouanage *f*, dédouanement *m*. 2. c. sale, (vente *f* de) soldes *f*. 'clear a'way, *v.tr.* enlever, ôter (qch.); *abs.* desservir. 'clear-cut, *a.* net. 'clearing, *s.* 1. enlèvement *m* (de débris); dégagement *m* (d'une voie). 2. (in forest) clairière *f*. 'clearness, *s.* clarté *f*; netteté *f* (d'une image). 'clear 'off, *v.tr. & i.* s'acquitter de (ses dettes); *F:* filer, décamper. 'clear 'out, *v.tr. & i.* nettoyer (une pièce); *F:* filer, décamper. 'clear 'up, *v.tr. & i.* éclaircir, élucider (un problème); (of weather) s'éclaircir; *abs.* remettre (une pièce) en ordre. 'clearway, *s.* route *f* à stationnement interdit.

clef [klef], *s. Mus:* clef *f*.

cleft [kleft], *s.* 1. fente *f*, fissure *f*, crevasse *f*. 2. *a. Med:* c. palate, palais *m* fendu.

clematis [kli'meitis], *s.* clématite *f*.

clench [klen(t)ʃ], *v.tr.* serrer (les dents); crisper (les mains).

clergy [klə:dʒi], *s.* 1. clergé *m*. 2. membres *m* du clergé. 'clergyman, *s. Ecc:* pasteur *m* (protestant).

clerical ['klerik(ə)l], *a.* 1. clérical, du clergé. 2. c. work, travail *m* de bureau; c. error, faute *f* de copiste.

clerk [klɑ:k, *U.S:* klə:k], *s.* employé, -ée *f* de bureau; clerc *m* (de notaire); *U.S:* vendeur, -euse *f* (de magasin).

clever ['klevər], *a.* 1. habile, adroit. 2. (*a*) intelligent; (*b*) ingénieux. **-ly,** *adv.* habilement. 'cleverness, *s.* 1. habileté *f*. 2. intelligence *f*; ingéniosité *f*.

click [klik], I. *s.* bruit sec; clic *m*; cliquetis *m*. II. *v.tr. & i.* 1. cliqueter; claquer. 2. *v.i. F:* that clicks! ça me rappelle quelque chose.

client ['klaiənt], *s.* client, -ente.

clientele [klaiən'tel, kliãtel], *s.* clientèle *f*.

cliff [klif], *s.* falaise *f*.

climate ['klaimət], *s.* climat *m*.

climax ['klaimæks], *s.* comble *m*.

climb [klaim]. I. *s.* 1. ascension *f*. 2. montée *f*, côte *f*. II. *v.tr. & i.* monter; faire l'ascension (d'une montagne); to c. over, franchir; *F:* to c. up the wall, être cinglé, dingo. 'climb 'down, *v.i.* 1. descendre. 2. *F:* en rabattre. 'climber, *s.* 1. alpiniste *mf*. 2. *F:* arriviste *mf*. 'climbing, *s.* escalade *f*; montée *f*; alpinisme *m*.

clinch [klin(t)ʃ], *v.tr.* (a) river; (b) conclure (un marché).

‡cling [kliŋ], *v.i.* (a) s'attacher, s'accrocher, se cramponner (to, à); (b) adhérer (to, à).

clinic ['klinik], *s.* clinique *f*. 'clinical, *a.* clinique; c. thermometer, thermomètre *m* médical.

clink¹ [kliŋk]. I. *s.* tintement *m*, choc *m*. II. *v.i. & tr.* (faire) tinter.

clink², *s. P:* prison *f*, taule *f*.

clip¹ [klip]. I. *s.* pince *f*, attache *f*. II. *v.tr.* pincer, serrer.

‡clip², *v.tr.* 1. tailler (une haie). 2. poinçonner (un billet).

clique [kli:k], *s.* coterie *f*.

cloak [klouk]. I. *s.* manteau *m*. II. *v.tr.* masquer (ses projets). 'cloakroom, *s.* 1. vestiaire *m*. 2. (*in hotel, etc.*) toilette *f*. 3. *Rail:* consigne *f*.

clock [klɔk], *s.* (a) (large) horloge *f*; (smaller) pendule *f*; it's one, two, o'clock, il est une heure, deux heures; **to work round the c.,** (i) *Ind:* faire trois équipes (dans les 24 heures); (ii) travailler d'arrache-pied; (b) compteur *m* kilométrique (d'un taxi). II. *v.i. Ind:* to c. in, out, pointer à l'arrivée, au départ. 'clockwise, *a. & adv.* dans le sens des aiguilles d'une montre. 'clockwork, *s.* mouvement *m* d'horlogerie; to go like c., aller comme sur des roulettes.

‡clog [klɔg]. I. *v.tr.* boucher, obstruer (un tuyau, etc.). II. *s.* galoche *f*.

cloister ['klɔistər], *s.* cloître *m*.

close¹ [klous]. I. *a.* 1. (a) bien fermé; clos; (b) renfermé; c. weather, temps lourd; (c) (secret) impénétrable; (d) c. season, chasse fermée. 2. c. connection, rapport étroit; c. friend, ami(e) intime; c. resemblance, ressemblance exacte. 3. peu communicatif. 4. avare, regardant. II. *adv.* 1. (also closely) étroitement. 2. près, de près; c. together, serrés. 3. c. at hand, c. by, tout près. 'close-'fitting, *a.* (vêtement) ajusté, collant. 'closeness, *s.* 1. proximité *f*. 2. manque *m* d'air; lourdeur *f* (du temps). 3. réserve *f* (de qn). 'close-up, *s. Cin:* (vue *f* de) premier plan.

close² [klous], *s.* clos *m*, enclos *m*.

close³ [klouz]. I. *v.* 1. *v.tr.* (a) fermer; (b) terminer, conclure. 2. *v.i.* (a) se fermer, se renfermer; (b) finir, se terminer; (c) conclure le marché (avec qn). II. s. fin f, conclusion f; to draw to a c., prendre fin. 'close 'down, v.tr. & i. fermer; Rad: terminer l'émission. 'closed, a. 1. fermé; P.N: road c., route barrée. 2. Ind: c. shop, entreprise fermée aux travailleurs non-syndiqués. 'closing. I. a. qui se ferme; dernier, final; the c. bid, la dernière enchère; Fin: c. prices, derniers cours. II. s. 1. fermeture f. 2. clôture (d'un compte, etc.). 'close 'up. I. v.tr. fermer (complètement). 2. v.i. se renfermer; serrer, se tasser.

clot [klɔt]. I. s. 1. caillot m (de sang); c. on the brain, embolie f cérébrale. 2. F: idiot, -ote, imbécile mf. II. v.i. ‡(of milk) se cailler; (of blood) se figer.

†cloth [klɔθ], s. 1. (a) drap m; (b) toile f. 2. (a) torchon m; (b) nappe f.

clothe [klouð], v.tr. (re)vêtir, habiller. 'clothes, s.pl. vêtements mpl; to put on, take off, one's c., s'habiller; se déshabiller; c. brush, brosse f à habits; c. line, corde f à (étendre le) linge; c. peg, pince f à linge. 'clothing, s. 1. vêtements mpl. 2. the c. trade, l'industrie du vêtement.

cloud [klaud]. I. s. nuage m; to be under a c., être l'objet de soupçons. II. v. 1. v.tr. couvrir, voiler. 2. v.i. se couvrir (de nuages); s'assombrir. 'cloudburst, s. trombe f; rafale f de pluie. 'cloudless, a. sans nuages. 'cloudy, a. (temps) couvert; (ciel) nuageux; (liquide) trouble.

clove¹ [klouv], s. clou m de girofle.

clove² [klouv], s. c. of garlic, gousse f d'ail.

cloven ['klouv(ə)n], a. c. hoofed, au pied fourchu.

clover ['klouvər], s. trèfle m.

clown [klaun], s. (a) bouffon m; (b) clown m.

club [klʌb]. I. s. 1. (a) massue f, gourdin m; (b) (golf) c., club m. 2. (at cards) trèfle m. 3. (a) cercle m; (b) association f; youth c., foyer m des jeunes; tennis c., club de tennis. 4. c. foot, pied bot m. II. ‡v.i. to c. together, se cotiser; mettre son argent en commun. 'clubhouse, s. Sp: pavillon m.

cluck [klʌk], v.i. (of hen) glousser.

clue [klu:], s. indication f, indice m; F: I haven't a c., je n'en sais rien. 'clueless, a. F: he's quite c., il ne sait jamais rien.

clump [klʌmp], s. groupe m (d'arbres); massif m (de fleurs).

clumsy ['klʌmzi], a. maladroit, gauche. -sily, adv. maladroitement, gauchement. 'clumsiness, s. maladresse f, gaucherie f.

cluster ['klʌstər], s. nœud m (de diamants); amas m (d'étoiles).

clutch¹ [klʌtʃ]. I. s. 1. to fall into s.o.'s clutches, tomber sous la patte de qn. 2. Aut: embrayage m; automatic c., autodébrayage m. II. v.tr. & ind.tr. to c. (at) sth., saisir qch.

clutch² [klʌtʃ], s. couvée f (d'œufs).

clutter ['klʌtər]. I. s. encombrement m; confusion f. II. v.tr. to c. up (a room), encombrer (une pièce).

coach [koutʃ]. I. s. 1. (a) carosse m; (b) (auto)car m; (c) Rail: voiture f, wagon m. 2. (a) professeur m qui donne des leçons particulières; (b) Sp: entraîneur m. II. v.tr. (a) donner des leçons particulières à (qn); (b) Sp: entraîner (qn).

coagulate [kou'ægjuleit], v.tr. & i. (se) coaguler, (se) figer. coagu'lation, s. coagulation f.

coal [koul], s. charbon m; houille f; c. merchant, marchand m de charbon. 'coalfield, s. bassin m houiller. †'coalman, s. livreur m de charbon. 'coalmine, s. mine f de houille. 'coalscuttle, s. seau m à charbon.

coalesce [kouə'les], v.i. s'unir; se fondre; Ch: se combiner; (of parties) fusionner.

coalition [kouə'liʃ(ə)n], s. coalition f.

coarse [kɔ:s], a. grossier; vulgaire. -ly, adv. grossièrement. 'coarseness, s. grossièreté f.

coast [koust]. I. s. côte f, rivage m. II. v.i. & tr. 1. Nau: suivre la côte. 2. descendre (une pente) en toboggan; (on bicycle) descendre en roue libre. 'coastal, a. côtier. 'coaster, s. 1. Nau: caboteur m. 2. F: dessous m de bouteille. 'coastline, s. littoral m.

coat [kout]. I. s. 1. (a) (for men) veste f; veston m; (b) (for women) manteau m. (c) c. of arms, armoiries fpl. 2. robe f (d'un chien); pelage m (d'un fauve). 3. couche f (de peinture). II. v.tr. enduire (qch.) (with, de); Cu: enrober (qch.) (de chocolat, etc.). 'coathanger, s. cintre m; porte-vêtements m inv.

coax [kouks], v.tr. cajoler, enjôler.

cobalt [koubɔ:lt], s. Ch: cobalt m.

cobber ['kɔbər], s. F: Austr: copain m.

cobble¹ ['kɔbl], s. c. (stone), galet m, caillou m (de chaussée).

cobble², v.tr. rapetasser. 'cobbler, s. cordonnier m (qui fait les raccommodages).

cobra ['kɔ:brə], s. cobra m.

cobweb ['kɔbweb], s. toile f d'araignée.

cocaine [kou'kein], s. cocaïne f.

cock¹ [kɔk]. I. s. 1. (a) coq m; (b) oiseau mâle. 2. (a) robinet m; (b) chien m (de fusil): at full c., au cran d'armé. II. v.tr. 1. to c. one's ears, (of animal) dresser les oreilles; (of pers.) dresser l'oreille. 2. armer (un fusil). 'cock-'sure, F: 'cocky, a. sûr de soi; suffisant.

cockade [kɔ'keid], s. cocarde f.

cockatoo [kɔkə'tu:], s. cacatoès m.

cockchafer ['kɔkt∫eifər], *s.* hanneton *m.*
cockerel ['kɔk(ə)r(ə)l], *s.* jeune coq *m.*
cock-eyed ['kɔkaid], *a. F:* 1. qui louche. 2. de travers.
cockle ['kɔkl], *s.* coque *f.*
cockney ['kɔkni], *a.* & *s.* londonien, -ienne (des quartiers populaires de l'est de Londres).
cockpit ['kɔkpit], *s. Av:* carlingue *f.*
cockroach ['kɔkrout∫], *s.* blatte *f.*
cocktail ['kɔkteil], *s.* cocktail *m;* c. party, cocktail; c. snack, amuse-gueule *m.*
cocoa ['koukou], *s.* cacao *m.*
coconut ['koukənʌt], *s.* noix *f* de coco; c. palm, cocotier *m.*
cocoon [kə'ku:n], *s.* cocon *m.*
cod [kɔd], *s.* morue *f;* cabillaud *m.*
coddle ['kɔdl], *v.tr.* gâter, choyer.
code [koud], *s.* 1. code *m.* 2. (*a*) c. word, mot *m* convenu; (*b*) chiffre *m;* to write a message in c., chiffrer un message.
codicil ['kɔdisil], *s.* codicille *m* (d'un testament).
codify ['koudifai], *v.tr.* codifier.
co-education ['kouedju'kei∫(ə)n], *s.* co-éducation *f.*
coefficient [koui'fi∫ənt], *s.* coefficient *m.*
coerce [kou'əːs], *v.tr.* forcer, contraindre. **co'ercion,** *s.* coercition *f;* contrainte *f.*
coffee ['kɔfi], *s.* café *m;* black c., café noir; white c., café au lait; café crème; instant c., café soluble; ground c., café moulu; c. cup, tasse *f* à café; c. pot, cafetière *f.*
coffin ['kɔfin], *s.* cercueil *m.*
cog [kɔg], *s. E:* dent *f.* '**cogwheel,** *s.* roue *f* dentée.
coherent [kou'hiər(ə)nt], *a.* cohérent. **-ly,** *adv.* avec cohérence. **co'herence,** *s.* suite *f* (logique); cohérence *f.*
cohesion [kou'hi:ʒ(ə)n], *s.* cohésion *f;* adhérence *f.*
coil [kɔil]. I. *s.* 1. rouleau *m.* 2. pli *m,* repli *m;* anneau *m* (d'un serpent); 3. enroulement *m,* bobine *f.* II. *v.* 1. *v.tr.* (en)rouler. 2. *v.i.* serpenter.
coin [kɔin]. I. *s.* pièce *f* de monnaie. II. *v.tr.* 1. to c. money, (i) frapper de la monnaie; (ii) faire des affaires d'or. 2. inventer (un mot nouveau). '**coinage,** *s.* (*a*) système monétaire; (*b*) monnaie(s) *f.*
coincide [kouin'said], *v.i.* coïncider. 2. s'accorder, être d'accord. **co'inci-dence,** *s.* coïncidence *f.*
coke [kouk], *s.* coke *m.*
colander ['kʌləndər], *s.* passoire *f.*
cold [kould]. I. *a.* froid; it is c., il fait froid; to grow c., se refroidir; c. storage, conservation *f* par le froid; to be c., to feel c., avoir froid. **-ly,** *adv.* froidement. II. *s.* 1. froid *m.* 2. rhume *m;* to have a c., être enrhumé; c. in the head, rhume de cerveau. '**cold-'blooded,** *a.* 1. à sang froid. 2. froid, insensible; délibéré. '**coldness,** *s.* froideur *f.*

collaborate [kə'læbəreit], *v.i.* collaborer. **collabo'ration,** *s.* collaboration *f.* **col-'laborator,** *s.* collaborateur, -trice.
collapse [kə'læps]. I. *s.* 1. écroulement *m,* effondrement *m.* 2. affaissement *m* subit. II. *v.i.* 1. s'affaisser; s'écrouler, s'effondrer. **col'lapsible,** *a.* pliant; démontable; escamotable.
collar ['kɔlər]. I. *s.* 1. (*a*) col *m;* collet *m* (de manteau); (*b*) faux col; size in collars, encolure *f.* 2. collier *m* (de chien). 3. *E:* anneau *m,* collier, collet. II. *v.tr. F:* pincer, mettre la main sur (qn, qch). '**collar-bone,** *s.* clavicule *f.*
collate [kɔ'leit], *v.tr.* collationner. **col-'lation,** *s.* collation *f.*
colleague ['kɔli:g], *s.* collègue *mf;* con-frère *m.*
collect [kə'lekt]. 1. *v.tr.* (*a*) rassembler; assembler; (*b*) collectionner; (*c*) percevoir, lever (les impôts); (*d*) rassembler (ses idées); (*e*) to c. oneself, se reprendre; to c. one's thoughts, se recueillir; (*e*) aller chercher (ses bagages, etc.). 2. *v.i.* (*of people*) s'assembler, se rassembler; (*of things*) s'amasser. **col'lected,** *a.* (*a*) recueilli; (*b*) (plein) de sang-froid. **-ly,** *adv.* (*a*) avec recueille-ment; (*b*) avec calme, avec sang-froid. **col'lection,** *s.* 1. rassemblement *m* (de gens); levée *f* (des lettres). 2. *Ecc: etc:* quête *f.* 3. amas *m,* assem-blage *m.* 4. collection *f* (de timbres, etc.). **col'lective,** *a.* collectif; c. farm, ferme collect.ve. **col'lector,** *s.* collectionneur, -euse; (*b*) (tax) c., percepteur *m* (des contributions directes); receveur *m* (des contribu-tions indirectes); ticket c., contrôleur *m.*
college ['kɔlidʒ], *s.* collège *m;* lycée *m;* technical c. = lycée technique; agri-cultural c. = institut *m* agronomique; military c., école *f* militaire; c. of edu-cation = école normale.
collide [kə'laid], *v.i.* se rencontrer, se heurter.
†**colliery** ['kɔljəri], *s.* houillère *f.*
collision [kə'liʒ(ə)n], *s.* collision *f;* abordage *m* (de navires).
colloquial [kə'loukwiəl], *a.* familier; de (la) conversation; c. French, le français parlé. **col'loquialism,** *s.* expression *f* familière.
collusion [kə'lju:ʒ(ə)n], *s.* collusion *f.*
colon ['koulən], *s.* deux-points *m.*
colonel ['kə:nl], *s.* colonel *m.*
†**colony** ['kɔləni], *s.* colonie *f.* **co'lonial,** *a.* & *s.* colonial (*m*). **co'lonialism,** *s.* colonialisme *m.* '**colonist,** *s.* colon *m.* **coloni'zation,** *s.* colonisation *f.* '**colon-ize,** *v.tr.* coloniser.
Colorado [kɔlə'ra:dou]. *Pr.n.* C. beetle, doryphore *m.*
colossal [kə'lɔs(ə)l], *a.* colossal.
colour ['kʌlər]. I. *s.* 1. couleur *f;* the c. problem, le (problème du) racisme; c. bar, ségrégation *f* raciale. 2. matière

f colorante; pigment *m*; water c., aquarelle *f.* 3. teint *m*, couleurs; to change c., changer de visage; F: to be off c., ne pas être dans son assiette. 4. *pl.* pavillon *m*; drapeau *m.* II. *v.tr.* colorer; colorier. 'colour-blind, *a.* daltonien. 'colour-blindness, *s.* daltonisme *m.* 'coloured, *a.* coloré; colorié; (personne) de couleur. 'colourful, *a.* coloré; F: (of pers.) original. 'colourless, *a.* (*a*) sans couleur; (*b*) terne, insipide.

colt [koult], *s.* poulain *m.*

column ['kɔləm], *s.* colonne *f.* 'columnist, *s.* journaliste *m.*

coma ['koumə], *s.* coma *m.*

comb [koum]. I. *s.* 1. peigne *m.* 2. crête *f* (de coq). II. *v.tr.* (se) peigner; to c. out, (i) démêler (les cheveux); (ii) (of police) ratisser (un quartier).

combat ['kɔmbæt]. I. *s.* combat *m.* 1. ‡*v.i.* & *tr.* combattre. 'combatant, *a.* & *s.* combattant (*m*).

combine. I. *v.* [kəm'bain]. 1. *v.tr.* combiner; allier (with, à). 2. *v.i.* (*a*) (of people) s'associer; (*b*) Ch: se combiner. II. *s.* ['kɔmbain]. 1. Fin: cartel *m*, trust *m.* 2. c. harvester, moisson-neuse-batteuse *f.* combi'nation, *s.* 1. combinaison *f.* 2. association *f.* 3. chiffre *m* (de la serrure d'un coffre-fort). com'bined, *a.* (*a*) (of effort) réuni; (*b*) Mil: c. operation, (i) opération interarmes, (ii) opération amphibie.

combustion [kəm'bʌstʃ(ə)n], *s.* combustion *f.*

‡come [kʌm], *v.i.* venir, arriver; c. to, and, see me soon, venez me voir bientôt; *F:* he had it coming to him, ça lui pendait au nez; *F:* to come to (one's senses), (i) reprendre connaissance; (ii) recouvrer sa raison. 2. that comes on page 20, cela se trouve à la page 20; how does the door c. to be open? comment se fait-il que la porte soit ouverte? 3. what will c. of it? qu'en adviendra-t-il? that's what comes of doing . . ., voilà ce qu'il en est de faire. . . . 4. (in shop) how much does c. to? combien cela fait-il? he'll never c. to much, il ne fera jamais grand-chose; come to that, à propos. . . . 5. it comes easy to him, cela lui est facile; to c. undone, se défaire. 'come a'cross. 1. *v.tr.* rencontrer (qn). 2. *v.i. F:* payer. come 'after, *v.tr.* suivre. 'come 'back, *v.i.* revenir. 'come-back, *s.* retour *m* (en vogue, au pouvoir). 'come 'by. 1. *v.i.* passer. 2. *v.tr.* obtenir (de l'argent). come 'down. 1. *v.i.* descendre; (of rain) tomber; (of prices) baisser; to c. d. in the world, déchoir; F: to c. d. handsomely, se montrer généreux; 'come-down, *s.* F: humiliation *f.* come 'forward, *v.i.* s'avancer. 'come

'in, *v.i.* entrer; (of tide) monter; *Sp:* to c. in first, arriver premier; to c. in useful, servir (à qn, à qch.). 'coming, I. *a.* qui vient, qui approche; a c. man, un homme d'avenir. II. *s.* a lot of c. and going, beaucoup de va-et-vient *m.* 'come 'off, *v.tr.* (*a*) to c. o. the gold standard, abandonner l'étalon or; *F:* c. o. it! en voilà assez! (*b*) (of button) se détacher; (of event) avoir lieu; (of attempt) réussir. come 'on, *v.i.* faire des progrès; *Th:* entrer en scène; c. on! dépêche-toi! allons-y! 'come 'out, *v.i.* (*a*) sortir; (*b*) se mettre en grève; (*c*) (of stars) paraître; (*d*) (of buds) éclore; *Phot:* you've c. o. well, vous êtes très réussi. come 'up, *v.i.* (*a*) monter; (of plant) sortir de terre; (*b*) he doesn't c. up to his brother, il n'égale pas son frère; to c. up to expectations, répondre à l'attente (de qn); to c. up against sth., se heurter à qch.; to c. up against s.o., entrer en conflit avec qn; (*c*) *F:* the table comes up well, la table revient bien à l'astiquage.

comedy ['kɔmədi], *s.* comédie *f.* co'median, *s.* comédien, -ienne *f.* comique *m.*

comet ['kɔmit], *s.* comète *f.*

comfort ['kʌmfət]. I. *s.* 1. consolation *f*; soulagement *m*; bien-être *m.* 3. confort *m*; aisance *f.* II. *v.tr.* consoler, soulager. 'comfortable, *a.* confortable; agréable; c. income, revenu suffisant; *-ably, adv.* confortablement; agréablement; to be c. off, avoir de quoi (vivre). 'comforting, *a.* réconfortant. 'comfortless, *a.* dépourvu de confort; triste.

comic ['kɔmik]. 1. *a.* (also 'comical) comique, risible. 2. *s.* (*a*) *Th:* comique *m*; (*b*) journal *m* de bandes illustrées.

command [kə'mɑːnd]. I. *s.* 1. ordre *m*, commandement *m.* 2. under the c. of, sous le commandement de; second in c., commandant *m* en second. 3. connaissance *f*, maîtrise *f* (d'une langue). II. *v.tr.* 1. ordonner, commander. 2. commander (un régiment). 3. to c. respect, inspirer le respect. comman'dant [kɔman'dænt], *s.* commandant *m.* com'mander *m*, *s.* Nau: capitaine *m* de frégate. com'manding, *a.* 1. (officier) commandant. 2. (ton) d'autorité, de commandement. com'mandment, *s.* commandement *m.* com'mando, *s.* Mil: commando *m.*

commemorate [kə'meməreit], *v.tr.* commémorer.

commence [kə'mens], *v.tr.* & *i.* commencer. co'mmencement, *s.* 1. commencement *m.* 2. Sch: U.S: collation *f* des grades universitaires.

commend [kə'mend], *v.tr.* 1. recommander, confier. 2. louer. com'mend**able**, *a.* louable. commen'dation, *s.* éloge *m*; approbation *f*.

commensurate [kə'mensərit], *a.* proportionné (with, à).

comment ['koment]. I. *s.* commentaire *m*; observation *f*. II. *v.i.* critiquer; faire des observations. 'commentary, *s.* commentaire *m* (running). c. (running), reportage *m* en direct. 'commentator, commentateur, -trice; *Rad: T.V:* radio-reporter *m*.

commerce ['komə:s], *s.* commerce *m*. co'mmercial. 1. *a.* commercial. c. **vehicle**, voiture *f* de livraison. 2. *s. T.V: F:* émission *f* publicitaire. co'mmercialize, *v.tr.* commercialiser.

commissar ['komisɑ:r], *s.* commissaire *m* (du peuple).

commissariat [komi'sɑriət], *s. Mil: etc:* intendance *f*.

commission [kə'miʃ(ə)n]. I. *s.* 1. commission *f*; *Mil:* to get a c., être nommé officier; Royal C., commission d'enquête (ordonnée par décret parlementaire). 2. to put a ship into c., armer un navire; *F:* (of car, etc.) out of c., en réparation. 3. *Com:* pourcentage *m*. II. *v.tr.* 1. nommer (un officier) à un commandement; commander (un tableau, etc.). 2. armer (un navire). commissio'naire, *s.* chasseur *m* (d'hôtel); portier *m*. co'mmissioner, *s.* commissionnaire *m*; c. for oaths, avoué *m* qui reçoit les déclarations sous serment.

‡**commit** [kə'mit], *v.tr.* 1. commettre, confier. 2. to c. to prison, envoyer aux assises. 3. to c. oneself, se compromettre. 4. commettre (un crime). co'mmitment, *s.* (*usu. pl.*) engagement(s) *m*. co'mmittal, *s.* mise *f* en terre (d'un cadavre); *Jur:* mise en prison.

committee [kə'miti], *s.* comité *m*, commission *f*, conseil *m*.

commodious [kə'moudiəs], *a.* spacieux.

commodity [kə'moditi], *s.* marchandise *f*, denrée *f*, article *m*.

commodore ['komədɔ:r], *s.* (*a*) *Nau:* chef *m* de division; commodore *m*; (*b*) air-c., général de brigade (aérienne); (*c*) capitaine *m* (d'un yacht-club).

common ['komən], *s.* 1. commun *n*. 2. (*a*) ordinaire; in c. use, d'usage courant; (*b*) de peu de valeur; the c. people, les gens du peuple. 3. vulgaire, trivial. -ly, *adv.* ordinairement. II. *s.* 1. terrain *m* communal; pré *m*. 2. to have sth. in c., avoir qch. en commun (avec qn); out of the c., extraordinaire. 'commoner, *s.* homme *m* du peuple; bourgeois *m*. 'commonplace. 1. *s.* banalité *f*. 2. *a.* banal. 'commons, *s.* 1. le peuple; the House

of C., la Chambre des Communes. 2. to be on short c., faire maigre chère. 'Commonwealth (the), *s.* le Commonwealth (britannique).

commotion [kə'mouʃ(ə)n], *s.* 1. confusion *f*, commotion *f*. 2. troubles *mpl*.

communal ['komjun(ə)l], *a.* communal.

communicate [kə'mju:nikeit], *v.tr. & i.* communiquer; *Ecc:* recevoir la communion, communier. co'mmunicant, *s. Ecc:* communiant, -ante. communi'cation, *s.* communication *f*; *Rail:* c. **cord**, corde *f* de signal d'alarme. co'mmunicative, *a.* communicatif. co'mmunion, *s. Ecc:* communion *f*.

communism ['komjunizm], *s.* communisme *m*. 'communist, *s.* communiste *mf*.

community [kə'mju:niti], *s.* 1. communauté *f*. 2. c. **centre**, centre *m*, salle *f*, de loisirs (d'une ville).

commute [kə'mju:t], *v.tr.* (*a*) *Jur:* commuer (une peine); (*b*) *abs.* faire un long trajet journalier (pour se rendre à son travail). co'mmuter, *s. Rail: etc:* abonné, -ée; personne qui fait un long trajet journalier.

companion [kəm'pænjən], *s.* compagnon *m*, compagne *f*. com'panionship, *s.* (*a*) compagnie *f*; (*b*) camaraderie *f*.

‡**company** ['kampəni], *s.* 1. compagnie *f*. to part c., se séparer (with, de). 2. assemblée *f*, compagnie. 3. *Com:* compagnie; société *f*; limited c., société à responsabilité limitée. 4. (*a*) *Th:* troupe *f*; (*b*) the ship's c., l'équipage *m*. 5. *Mil:* compagnie.

compare [kəm'pɛər]. 1. *v.tr.* comparer; compared with, en comparaison de. 2. *v.i.* être comparable (with, à); to c. favourably with, ne céder en rien à (qch.). comparable ['komp(ə)rəbl], *a.* comparable. com'parative, *a.* comparatif; relatif; he's a c. stranger, je ne le connais guère. -ly, *adv.* relativement. com'parison, *s.* comparaison *f*.

compartment [kəm'pɑːtmənt], *s.* compartiment *m*.

compass ['kampəs], *s.* 1. (a pair of) compasses, un compas. 2. boussole *f*; compas.

compassion [kəm'pæʃ(ə)n], *s.* compassion *f*. com'passionate, *a.* compatissant; *Mil:* c. **leave**, permission *f* exceptionnelle (pour raisons familiales).

compatible [kəm'pætibl], *a.* compatible. compati'bility, *s.* compatibilité *f*.

compatriot [kəm'pætriot], *s.* compatriote *mf*.

‡**compel** [kəm'pel], *v.tr.* contraindre obliger (qn à faire qch.).

compensate ['kɔmpənseit]. 1. v.tr. dédommager (qn de qch.). 2. v.i. to c. for sth., remplacer qch.; E: compenser (l'usure). **compen'sation**, s. compensation f; dédommagement m.

compère ['kɔmpɛːr]. I. s. Rad: etc: compère m. II. v.tr. être le compère (d'un programme).

compete [kəm'piːt], v.i. 1. faire concurrence (with, à). 2. concourir (pour un prix).

competent ['kɔmpitənt], a. 1. capable. 2. compétent. **'competence**, **'competency**, s. compétence f; capacité f.

competition [kɔmpə'tiʃ(ə)n], s. 1. rivalité f, concurrence f. 2. concours m. **com'petitive**, a. (esprit de) concurrence; c. prices, prix concurrentiels. **com'petitor**, s. concurrent, -ente.

compile [kəm'pail], v.tr. compiler. **com-pi'lation**, s. compilation f. **com'piler**, s. compilateur, -trice.

complacent [kəm'pleisənt], a. content de soi-même; suffisant. -ly, adv. avec satisfaction; avec suffisance. **com-'placency**, s. satisfaction f; suffisance f.

complain [kəm'plein], v.i. se plaindre. **com'plaint**, s. 1. grief m; plainte f. 2. maladie f, mal m.

complement. I. s. ['kɔmplimənt], 1. Nau: etc: effectif m. 2. complément m. II. v.tr. [kɔmpli'ment] compléter. **comple'mentary**, a. complémentaire.

complete [kəm'pliːt]. I. a. 1. complet, entier. -ly, adv. complètement. 2. achevé, accompli. II. v.tr. compléter, achever, accomplir. **com'pletion**, s. achèvement m; (of house) possession on c., prise f de possession dès la signature du contrat.

complex ['kɔmpleks], a. & s. complexe (m). **com'plexity**, s. complexité f.

complexion [kəm'plekʃ(ə)n], s. teint m.

complicate ['kɔmplikeit], v.tr. compliquer. **'complicated**, a. compliqué. **compli'cation**, s. complication f.

complicity [kəm'plisiti], s. complicité f.

compliment. I. s. ['kɔmplimənt] compliment m. II. v.tr. [kɔmpli'ment] complimenter, féliciter (qn (on, de). **compli'mentary**, a. flatteur; c. copy, exemplaire envoyé à titre gracieux.

comply [kəm'plai], v.i. se conformer (with, à); accéder (with, à).

component [kəm'pounənt]. 1. a. constituant. 2. s. composant m.

compose [kəm'pouz], v.tr. 1. composer. 2. c. yourself! calmez-vous! **com-'posed**, a. calme, tranquille. **com-'poser**, s. Mus: compositeur, -trice. **compo'sition**, s. 1. composition f, constitution f. 2. mélange m, composé m. 3. (a) Mus: composition; (b) Sch: dissertation f. **com'positor**, s. compositeur m, typographe m. **com-'posure**, s. calme m, sang-froid m.

compost ['kɔmpɔst], s. compost m; terreau m.

compound. I. a. (a) compound: Fin: c. interest, intérêts composés. II. s. (corps) composé m; Gram: mot m composé. III. v.tr. [kəm'paund], Jur: to c. a felony, pactiser avec un crime.

comprehension [kɔmpri'henʃ(ə)n], s. compréhension f. **compre'hensible**, a. compréhensible, intelligible. **com-pre'hensive**, a. compréhensif; c. school = centre m d'études secondaires. **compre'hensiveness**, s. étendue f, portée f.

compress. I. v.tr. [kəm'pres], comprimer; condenser; concentrer. II. s. ['kɔm-pres], compresse f. **com'pression**, s. compression f; concentration f (du style). **com'pressor**, s. compresseur m.

comprise [kəm'praiz], v.tr. comprendre, comporter, renfermer.

compromise ['kɔmprəmaiz]. I. s. compromis m. II. v.tr. & i. compromettre. **'compromising**, a. compromettant.

compulsion [kəm'pʌlʃ(ə)n], s. contrainte f, compulsion f. **com'pulsory**, a. obligatoire. -rily, adv. obligatoirement.

compunction [kəm'pʌŋ(k)ʃ(ə)n], s. componction f; remords m; without c., sans scrupule.

computer [kəm'pjuːtər], s. ordinateur m.

comrade ['kɔmreid], s. camarade mf.

concave ['kɔnkeiv], a. concave.

conceal [kən'siːl], v.tr. cacher; dissimuler. **con'cealed**, a. caché; masqué; c. lighting, éclairage indirect.

concede [kən'siːd], v.tr. concéder.

conceit [kən'siːt], s. vanité f, suffisance f. **con'ceited**, a. suffisant, vaniteux.

conceive [kən'siːv], v.tr. concevoir. **con-'ceivable**, a. concevable, imaginable. -ably, adv. imaginablement.

concentrate ['kɔnsəntreit]. I. v.tr. & i. (se) concentrer. II. s. concentré m; tomato c., concentré de tomate. **con-cen'tration**, s. concentration f; c. camp, camp m de concentration.

conception [kən'sep(ə)n], s. conception f; idée f.

concern [kən'səːn]. I. s. 1. intérêt m (in, dans); it's no c. of mine, cela ne me regarde pas. 2. souci m, anxiété f, inquiétude f. 3. (a) Com: entreprise f; (b) F: machin m, truc m. II. v.tr. 1. concerner, regarder, intéresser (qn, qch.). 2. to be concerned about s.o., sth., s'inquiéter, être inquiet, de qn, de qch.; as far as I am concerned, quant à moi.

concert ['kɔnsət], s. Mus: concert m. **con'certed**, a. c. action, action f d'ensemble.

concertina [kɔnsə'tiːnə], s. accordéon m hexagonal.

concerto [kən'tʃɛətəu], s. concerto m.

concession [kɔn'seʃ(ə)n], s. concession f.

conciliate [kən'silieit], v.tr. concilier, réconcilier. concili'ation, s. conciliation f.; c. board, conseil m d'arbitrage. con'ciliator, s. conciliateur, -trice. con'ciliatory, a. conciliant; conciliatoire.

concise [kən'sais], a. concis. -ly, adv. avec concision. con'ciseness, con'cision f.

conclude [kən'klu:d], v.tr. & i. conclure; arranger, régler; terminer. con'clusion, s. conclusion f.; fin f. con'clusive, a. concluant, décisif.

concoct [kən'kɔkt], v.tr. composer, confectionner (un plat); imaginer, combiner (un plan). con'coction, s. conception f (d'un plan); c. of lies, tissu m de mensonges; F: boisson f, plat m (de sa propre composition).

concord ['kɔnkɔːd], s. concorde f, harmonie f.

concrete ['kɔnkriːt]. I. a. concret. II. s. béton m; reinforced c., béton armé; c. mixer, bétonneuse f.

concurrent [kən'kʌr(ə)nt], a. concourant; simultané; coexistant. -ly, adv. concurremment; Jur: the two sentences to run c., avec confusion des deux peines.

concussion [kən'kʌʃ(ə)n], s. commotion f (cérébrale).

condemn [kən'dem], v.tr. condamner. condem'nation, s. condamnation f; censure f, blâme m.

condense [kən'dens], v.tr. condenser; concentrer (un produit). conden'sation, s. condensation f. con'densed, a. condensé; c. milk, lait concentré. con'denser, s. 1. E: condenseur m. 2. El: condensateur m.

condescend [kɔndi'send], v.i. condescendre (à faire qch.); se montrer condescendant (envers qn). conde-'scending, a. condescendant. -ly, adv. avec condescendance. conde'scension, s. condescendance f.

condiment ['kɔndimənt], s. condiment m; assaisonnement m.

condition [kən'diʃ(ə)n]. I. s. condition f. 1. on c. (that), à la condition (que). 2. état m, situation f; in c., en forme. II. v.tr. conditionner. con'ditional, a. & s. conditionnel (m). -ally, adv. sous certaines conditions.

condone [kən'doun], v.tr. pardonner.

conduce [kən'djuːs], v.i. contribuer, tendre (to, à). con'ducive, a. favorable (à qch.).

conduct. I. s. ['kɔndʌkt], conduite f. II. [kən'dʌkt]. 1. v.tr. conduire; conducted tours, excursions f accompagnées / vacances f en groupe. 2. mener, gérer (des affaires); diriger (un orchestre). 3. Ph: être conducteur de (la chaleur). con'duction, s. Ph: conduction f, transmission f (de la chaleur). con'ductor, s. 1. (a) chef m d'orchestre;

(b) (f. con'ductress) receveur, -euse (d'un autobus); (c) Rail: U.S: chef m de train. 2. conducteur m (de la chaleur, etc.).

confectionery [kən'fekʃən(ə)ri], s. confiserie f; pâtisserie f. con'fectioner, s. confiseur m; baker and c., boulanger-pâtissier m.

confederate [kən'fed(ə)rit], s. complice mf.

confederation [kənfedə'reiʃ(ə)n], s. confédération f.

‡confer [kən'fəːr]. 1. v.tr. conférer; accorder. 2. v.i. entrer en consultation (avec qn). 'conference, s. 1. entretien m, consultation f; press c., conférence f de presse. 2. congrès m.

confess [kən'fes], v.tr. 1. (a) confesser, avouer; (b) abs. faire des aveux. 2. Ecc: (a) se confesser; (b) confesser (un pénitent). con'fession, s. 1. confession f, aveu m. 2. Ecc: to make one's c., se confesser. con'fessor, s. confesseur m. con'fessional, s. 1. confession f, aveu m. 2. confesse f.

confide [kən'faid], v.tr. confier. 2. v.i. to c. in s.o., avouer (qch.) à qn en confidence. 'confidence, s. 1. (a) confiance f (en qn); (b) assurance f. 2. confidence f. 3. c. trick, vol m à l'américaine. 'confident, a. assuré; c. of success, sûr de réussir. -ly, adv. avec assurance. confi'dential, a. confidentiel; c. clerk, homme m de confiance. -ally, adv. à titre confidentiel.

confine [kən'fain], v.tr. (a) confiner à bed, alité; Mil: confined to barracks, consigné; (b) to c. oneself to doing sth., se borner à faire qch.; (c) confined space, espace restreint. con'finement, s. 1. emprisonnement m; réclusion f; in solitary c., au secret. 2. couches fpl.

confirm [kən'fəːm], v.tr. confirmer. confir'mation, s. confirmation f. con'firmed, a. (ivrogne, etc.) invétéré.

confiscate ['kɔnfiskeit], v.tr. confisquer. confis'cation, s. confiscation f.

conflagration [kɔnflə'greiʃ(ə)n], s. conflagration f; incendie f.

conflict. I. s. ['kɔnflikt], conflit m, lutte f. II. v.i. [kən'flikt] être en conflit, en contradiction. con'flicting, a. incompatible; c. evidence, témoignage discordant.

confluence ['kɔnfluəns], s. Geog: confluent m.

conform [kən'fɔːm], v.i. se conformer. con'formity, s. conformité f.

confront [kən'frʌnt], v.tr. affronter, faire face à (une épreuve, etc.).

confuse [kən'fjuːz], v.tr. 1. mêler, brouiller. 2. confondre (qch. avec qch.). 3. (a) embrouiller (qn); (b) troubler (qn). con'fused, a. (a) embrouillé; (b) bouleversé; (c) confus. con'fusing, a. dérouter. con'fusion, s. confusion f; désordre m.

congeal [kən'dʒiːl]. 1. v.tr. congeler. 2. v.i. se congeler; (a) (of oil, blood) se figer.

congenial [kən'dʒiːniəl], a. sympathique; aimable; agréable.

congenital [kən'dʒenitl], a. congénital; c. idiot, (i) idiot, -ote de naissance; (ii) F: parfait idiot.

conger ['kɔŋgər], s. c.(-eel), congre m.

congest [kən'dʒest], v.tr. encombrer, embouteiller. con'gested, a. (of street) encombré; c. area, région surpeuplée. con'gestion, s. 1. Med: congestion f. 2. encombrement m.

conglomeration [kənglɔmə'reiʃ(ə)n], s. conglomération f.

congratulate [kən'grætjuleit], v.tr. féliciter (qn de qch.). congratu'lation, s. félicitation f.

congregation [kɔŋgri'geiʃ(ə)n], s. (in church) assistance f.

congress ['kɔŋgres], s. (a) congrès m; (b) U.S: session f du Congrès.

conical ['kɔnikl], a. conique.

coniferous [kə'nifərəs], a. conifère.

conjecture [kən'dʒektʃər], s. conjecture f; v.tr. conjecturer.

conjugate ['kɔn(d)ʒugeit], v.tr. conjuguer. conju'gation, s. conjugaison f.

conjunction [kən'dʒʌŋ(k)ʃ(ə)n], s. conjonction f; in c. with s.o., de concert avec qn.

conjunctivitis [kən(d)ʒʌŋ(k)ti'vaitis], s. conjonctivite f.

conjure ['kʌndʒər], (a) v.tr. to c. up, évoquer (qch.); (b) v.i. faire des tours de passe-passe. 'conjuring, s. prestidigitation f. 'conjuror, s. prestidigitateur m.

conker ['kɔŋkər], s. F: marron m d'Inde.

connect [kə'nekt]. 1. v.tr. (re)lier; (ré)unir; joindre; associer (sth. with sth., qch. avec, à, qch.). 2. v.i. Rail: etc: faire correspondance. co'nnected, a. 1. suivi. 2. associé; apparenté. co'nnection, s. 1. rapport m, liaison f; connexion f. 2. Rail: etc: correspondance f. 3. raccord m; contact m.

connive [kə'naiv], v.i. to c. at sth., tolérer, fermer les yeux sur, qch.

connoisseur [kɔni'səːr], s. connaisseur m.

conquer ['kɔŋkər], v.tr. conquérir; vaincre. 'conqueror, s. conquérant m; vainqueur m. 'conquest, s. conquête f.

conscience ['kɔnʃəns], s. conscience f; c.-stricken, pris de remords. consci'entious, a. consciencieux; scrupuleux; c. objector, réfractaire m, objecteur m de conscience. -ly, adv. consciencieusement. consci'entiousness, s. conscience f; droiture f.

conscious ['kɔnʃəs], a. 1. (a) to be c. of sth., avoir conscience de qch.; to become c. of sth., s'apercevoir de qch.; (b) (mouvement) conscient. 2. to become c., reprendre connaissance. -ly, adv. consciemment. 'consciousness, s. 1. conscience f, sentiment m

(of, de). 2. to lose c., perdre connaissance; to regain c., revenir à soi.

conscript. I. v.tr. [kən'skript] enrôler, engager (des troupes). II. s. ['kɔnskript] conscrit m. con'scription, s. conscription f.

consecrate ['kɔnsikreit], v.tr. consacrer. conse'cration, s. consécration f.

consecutive [kən'sekjutiv], a. consécutif. -ly, adv. consécutivement.

consent [kən'sent]. I. v.i. consentir. II. s. consentement m, assentiment m; by common c., d'une commune voix.

consequence ['kɔnsikwens], s. 1. conséquence f; suites fpl. 2. importance f. conse'quential, a. (of pers.) suffisant; plein d'importance. 'consequently, adv. & conj. par conséquent.

conservatory [kən'səːvətri], a. & s. conservateur, -trice; on a c. estimate, au bas mot.

conservatory [kən'səːvətri], s. serre f.

consider [kən'sidər], v.tr. considérer (une question); all things considered, toute réflexion faite. 2. to c. s.o.'s feelings, ménager qn; to c. the expense, regarder à la dépense. 3. to c. oneself happy, s'estimer heureux; c. it done, tenez-le pour fait; considering the circumstances, vu les circonstances. con'siderable, a. considérable. -ably, adv. considérablement. con'siderate, a. prévenant, aimable, plein d'égards (pour, envers, qn). conside'ration, s. 1. considération f; taking all things into c., tout bien considéré; to treat s.o. with c., ménager qn. 2. (of pers.) importance f; money is no c., l'argent n'entre pas en ligne de compte.

consignment [kən'sainmənt], s. envoi m (de marchandises).

consist [kən'sist], v.i. consister (of, en, dans; in, à). con'sistency, s. 1. consistance f. 2. uniformité f. con'sistent, a. 1. (of pers.) logique. 2. compatible (with, avec). -ly, adv. 1. avec logique. 2. conformément.

console [kən'soul], v.tr. consoler. con-so'lation, s. consolation f.

consolidate [kən'sɔlideit], v.tr. consolider. consoli'dation, s. consolidation f.

consonant ['kɔnsənənt], s. consonne f.

consort ['kɔnsɔːt], s. prince m, prince m consort.

consortium [kən'sɔːtjəm], s. consortium m.

conspicuous [kən'spikjuəs], a. 1. visible; manifeste. 2. frappant, marquant; to make oneself c., se faire remarquer. -ly, adv. manifestement.

conspiracy [kən'spirəsi], s. conspiration f; conjuration f. con'spirator, s. conspirateur, -trice.

constable ['kʌnstəbl], s. agent m de police; gendarme m; con'stabulary, s. coll. la police.

constant ['kɔnst(ə)nt], *a.* (*a*) constant; (*b*) incessant, continuel; (*c*) fidèle, loyal. -ly, *adv.* constamment; continuellement. 'constancy, *s.* constance *f.*

constellation [kɔnstə'leiʃ(ə)n], *s.* constellation *f.*

consternation [kɔnstə'neiʃ(ə)n], *s.* consternation *f.*

constipate ['kɔnstipeit], *v.tr.* constiper. consti'pation, *s.* constipation *f.*

constituent [kən'stitjuənt], 1. *a.* constituant. 2. *s.* élément constitutif. 3. *s.pl.* électeurs *m.* con'stituency, *s.* circonscription *f* électorale.

constitute ['kɔnstitjut], *v.tr.* constituer. consti'tution, *s.* constitution *f.* consti'tutional, *a.* constitutionnel. -ally, *adv.* 1. constitutionnellement. 2. par tempérament.

constraint [kən'streint], *s.* contrainte *f.*

constrict [kən'strikt], *v.tr.* resserrer, étrangler. con'striction, *s.* resserrement *m;* étranglement *m.*

construct [kən'strakt], *v.tr.* construire, bâtir. con'struction, *s.* construction *f;* interprétation *f.* con'structive, *a.* constructif. con'structor, *s.* constructeur *m.*

consul ['kɔns(ə)l], *s.* consul *m.* 'consular, *a.* consulaire. 'consulate, *s.* consulat *m.*

consult [kən'salt], *v.tr. & i.* consulter. con'sultant, *s.* médecin, chirurgien, consultant; expert *m* en conseil. consul'tation, *s.* consultation *f.* con'sulting, *a.* consultation *f;* c. hours, room, heures, cabinet, de consultation.

consume [kən'sjuːm], *v.tr.* consommer. con'sumer, *s.* consommateur, -trice; c. goods, biens *m* de consommation.

consummate ['kɔnsəmeit], *v.tr.* consommer. consum'mation, *s.* 1. consommation *f.* 2. fin *f;* but *m.*

consumption [kən'sam(p)ʃ(ə)n], *s.* 1. consommation *f.* 2. *Med:* phtisie *f.*

contact ['kɔntækt], *s.* 1. contact *m;* c. lens, verre *m,* lentille *f,* de contact. II. *v.tr.* contacter (qn).

contagion [kən'teidʒ(ə)n], *s.* contagion *f.* con'tagious, *a.* contagieux.

contain [kən'tein], *v.tr.* contenir. con'tainer, *s.* récipient *m;* boîte *f.*

contaminate [kən'tæmineit], *v.tr.* contaminer. contami'nation, *s.* contamination *f.*

contemplate ['kɔntempleit], 1. *v.tr.* (*a*) contempler; (*b*) envisager; projeter. 2. *v.i.* méditer. contem'plation, *s.* (*a*) contemplation *f;* (*b*) méditation *f.* con'templative, *a.* contemplatif.

contemporary [kən'temp(ə)rəri], *a. & s.* contemporain, -aine.

contempt [kən'tempt], *s.* mépris *m;* dédain *m; Jur:* c. of court, (i) outrage *m* au tribunal; (ii) refus *m* de comparaître. con'temptible, *a.* méprisable. -ibly, *adv.* d'une manière méprisable. con'temptuous, *a.* dédaigneux; méprisant. -ly, *adv.* avec mépris.

content ['kɔntent], *s.* (*a*) contenu *m;* volume *m;* contenance *f* (d'un vase); (*b*) *pl.* contenu; (*of book*) table *f* des matières; (*c*) teneur *f* (en or).

content [kən'tent]. I. *a.* contenter, satisfaire. II. *a.* satisfait (with, de). III. *v.tr.* contenter, satisfaire. con'tented, *a.* content, satisfait. -ly, *adv.* 'content; con'tentedness, *s.,* con'tentment, *s.* contentement *m.*

contest. I. *v.tr.* [kən'test] contester; débattre; disputer. II. *s.* ['kɔntest] (*a*) combat *m,* lutte *f;* (*b*) concours *m.*

context ['kɔntekst], *s.* contexte *m.*

continent ['kɔntinənt], *s.* continent *m.* conti'nental, *a.* continental; de l'Europe; c. breakfast, café *m* complet.

†**contingency** [kən'tindʒənsi], *s.* éventualité *f;* cas *m* imprévu.

contingent [kən'tindʒənt], *s. Mil:* contingent *m.*

continue [kən'tinju], *v.tr. & i.* continuer; to be continued, à suivre. con'tinual, *a.* continuel. -ally, *adv.* continuellement; sans cesse. continu'ation, *s.* 1. continuation *f.* 2. prolongation *f;* suite *f* (d'une histoire). contin'uity, *s.* continuité *f; Cin:* scénario *m;* c. man, découpeur *m;* c. girl, scriptgirl *f.* con'tinuous, *a.* continu; *Cin:* c. performance, spectacle permanent. -ly, *adv.* sans interruption.

contortion [kən'tɔːʃ(ə)n], *s.* contorsion *f.*

contour ['kɔntuər], *s.* contour *m;* profil *m.*

contraband ['kɔntrəbænd], *s.* contrebande *f.*

contraceptive [kɔntrə'septiv], *a.* anticonceptionnel.

contract. I. *v.* [kən'trækt] *v.tr. & i.* 1. (se) contracter; (se) crisper. 2. (*a*) *v.tr.* contracter (une obligation, etc.); (*b*) *v.i.* to c. for work, entreprendre des travaux par forfait. II. *s.* ['kɔntrækt] 1. pacte *m;* contrat *m.* 2. entreprise *f;* adjudication *f.* con'traction, *s.* contraction *f.* con'tractor, *s.* entrepreneur *m.*

contradict [kɔntrə'dikt], *v.tr.* contredire. contra'diction, *s.* contradiction *f.* contra'dictory, *a.* contradictoire.

contralto [kən'træltou], *s.* contralto *m.*

contraption [kən'træpʃ(ə)n], *s. F:* dispositif *m,* machin *m,* truc *m.*

contrast. I. *s.* ['kɔntraːst] contraste *m.* II. *v.tr. & i.* contraster.

contravene [kɔntrə'viːn], *v.tr.* transgresser, enfreindre (la loi).

contribute [kən'tribju(ː)t], *v.tr. & i.* contribuer à (qch.); collaborer à (un journal); aider (au succès). contri'bution, *s.* 1. contribution *f;* cotisation *f.* 2. article *m* (écrit pour un journal). con'tributor, *s.* collaborateur, -trice. con'tributory, *a.* contribuant; contributif.

contrite ['kɔntrait], *a.* contrit, pénitent. con'trition, *s.* contrition *f.*

contrive [kən'traiv], v.tr. trouver moyen (de faire qch.). con'trivance, s. appareil m; dispositif m.

control [kən'troul]. I. s. (a) autorité f; (b) maîtrise f; everything's under c., tout est très en ordre; (c) gouverner f, manœuvre f; (d) gouverne f. II. v.tr. 1. diriger; régler; to c. the traffic, réglementer la circulation. 2. maîtriser, gouverner. con'troller, s. contrôleur, -euse.

controversial [kɔntrə'və:ʃ(ə)l], a. controversable; (of pers.) enclin à la controverse. con'troversy, s. controverse f.

contusion [kən'tju:ʒ(ə)n], s. contusion f.

conundrum [kə'nʌndrəm], s. énigme f.

conurbation [kɔnə:'beiʃ(ə)n], s. conurbation f.

convalesce [kɔnvə'les], v.i. relever de maladie. conva'lescence, s. convalescence f. conva'lescent, a. & s. convalescent, -ente.

convene [kən'vi:n]. 1. v.tr. convoquer, réunir. 2. v.i. s'assembler, se réunir.

convenience [kən'vi:njəns], s. 1. commodité f; convenance f. 2. public c., W.C. public. 3. pl. commodités, agréments m; all modern conveniences, tout le confort moderne. con'venient, a. commode; pratique; if it's c. to you, si cela ne vous dérange pas. -ly, adv. commodément; sans inconvénient.

convent ['kɔnvənt], s. couvent m (de femmes).

convention [kən'venʃ(ə)n], s. 1. convention f; accord m. 2. pl. convenances fpl, bienséances fpl. con'ventional, a. conventionnel; (arme, etc.) classique. -ally, adv. conventionnellement; normalement.

converge [kən'və:dʒ], v.i. & tr. (faire) converger. con'vergence, s. convergence f. con'vergent, a. convergent.

converse [kən'və:s], v.i. causer. conver'sation, s. conversation f.

convert I. v.tr. [kən'və:t] convertir. II. s. ['kɔnvə:t] converti, -ie. con'version, s. conversion f. con'verter, s. convertisseur m; adapteur m. conver'tibility, s. convertibilité f. con'vertible. 1. a. convertible, convertissable. 2. s. Aut: décapotable f.

convex ['kɔnveks], a. convexe.

convey [kən'vei], v.tr. 1. transporter, porter. 2. transmettre; communiquer. con'veyance, s. 1. transport m; transmission f. 2. véhicule m.

convict I. v.tr. [kən'vikt] convaincre; condamner. II. s. ['kɔnvikt] Jur: détenu, -ue. con'viction, s. 1. condamnation f. 2. conviction f.

convince [kən'vins], v.tr. convaincre. con'vincing, a. convaincant.

convolvulus [kən'vɔlvjuləs], s. volubilis m.

convoy ['kɔnvɔi]. I. s. convoi m. II. v.tr. convoyer, escorter.

convulse [kən'vʌls], v.tr. 1. bouleverser (qn). to be convulsed with laughter, se tordre de rire. convulsions, s.pl. 1. Med: convulsions fpl. 2. to be in c. (of laughter), se tordre de rire. con'vulsive, a. convulsif.

coo [ku:], v.i. roucouler. 'cooing, s. roucoulement m.

cook [kuk]. I. v.tr. & i. (faire) cuire; abs. faire la cuisine. II. s. cuisinier, -ière. 'cookbook, s. U.S: livre m de cuisine. 'cooker, s. 1. (stove) cuisinière f. 2. pomme f à cuire. 'cookery, s. cuisine f; c. book, livre m de cuisine. 'cookie, s. U.S: biscuit m; petit gâteau. 'cooking, s. cuisson f. 2. to do the c., faire la cuisine.

cool [ku:l]. I. a. frais; c. drink, boisson rafraîchissante; it's c., il fait frais; (of pers.) to keep c., garder son sang-froid; F: he's a c. customer, il ne se laisse pas démonter. 'coolly, adv. 1. fraîchement. 2. (agir) de sang-froid. 3. froidement. II. s. frais m; fraîcheur f. III. v.tr. & i. (se) rafraîchir; (se) refroidir. cool 'down, v.i. se rafraîchir; (after anger) se calmer. 'cooler, s. 1. rafraîchisseur m; refroidisseur m. 2. F: boisson rafraîchissante. 3. P: prison f, taule f. 'cooling. 1. a. rafraîchissant. 2. s. rafraîchissement m; refroidissement m. 'coolness, s. 1. fraîcheur f (de l'air). 2. sang-froid m; aplomb m. 3. froideur f (d'un accueil). 'cool 'off, v.i. (of enthusiasm) se refroidir.

coop [ku:p], s. cage f à poules.

co-operate [kou'ɔpəreit], v.i. coopérer. co-oper'ation, s. coopération f. co-'operative. 1. a. coopératif; c. stores, s. Ecc: chape f. co-op, société f coopérative de consommation. 2. s. coopérative f. (vinicole, etc).

co-opt [kou'ɔpt] v.tr. coopter.

co-ordination [kouə:di'neiʃ(ə)n], s. co-ordination f.

cop [kɔp]. I. s. F: (=policeman) flic m. 2. v.tr. P: attraper, pincer (qn).

cope¹ [koup], s. Ecc: chape f.

cope², v.i. tenir tête à qn; faire face (à une situation); F: I'll c., je me débrouillerai.

copious ['koupjəs], a. copieux. -ly, adv. copieusement.

copper ['kɔpər], s. 1. cuivre m (rouge); coppers = des sous. 2. H: lessiveuse f. 3. attrib. de cuivre, en cuivre; c. (coloured), cuivré. 4. F: flic m.

copse [kɔps], s. taillis m.

copy ['kɔpi]. I. v.tr. copier; imiter. II. †s. copie f; (typed) double m. 2. exemplaire m (d'un livre); numéro m (d'un journal). 'copying, s. transcription f; imitation f. 'copyright. I. s. copyright m. II. v.tr. déposer (un livre).

coquette [kɔ'ket], s. coquette f.

cord [kɔːd], s. (a) corde f; ficelle f; (b) the vocal cords, les cordes vocales; the spinal c., le cordon médullaire.

cordial ['kɔːdjəl], a. cordial. -ally, adv. cordialement. **cordi'ality**, s. cordialité f.

cordon ['kɔːdən], s. cordon m.

core [kɔːr]. I. s. cœur m (du bois); trognon m (d'une pomme); Min: etc. noyau m; s. sample, carotte f. II. v.tr. vider (une pomme).

cork [kɔːk]. I. s. 1. liège m; c. oak, chêne-liège m. 2. bouchon m. II. v.tr. boucher (une bouteille). '**corked**, a. (of wine) qui sent le bouchon. '**corkscrew**, s. tire-bouchon m.

corm [kɔːm], s. Bot: bulbe m.

corn¹ [kɔːn], s. coll. blé(s) m; céréales f; U.S: maïs m; c. salad, mâche f.

corn², s. cor m (au pied); to tread on s.o.'s corns, froisser qn.

cornea ['kɔːniə], s. cornée f (de l'œil).

corned ['kɔːnd], a. c. beef, bœuf m de conserve.

corner ['kɔːnər]. I. s. 1. coin m; angle m; c. cupboard, encoignure f. 2. tournant m, virage m; blind c., virage sans visibilité. 3. Com: monopole m. II. v.i. 1. accaparer (le marché). 2. abs. Aut: prendre un virage.

cornet ['kɔːnit], s. 1. Mus: cornet m à pistons. 2. Cu: cornet (de crème glacée).

cornflour ['kɔːnflauər], s. farine f de maïs.

cornflower ['kɔːnflauər], s. bluet m.

cornice ['kɔːnis], s. corniche f.

coronary ['kɔrənəri], a. Med: c. thrombosis, infarctus m du myocarde.

coronation [kɔrə'neiʃ(ə)n], s. couronnement m.

coronet ['kɔrənit], s. (a) petite couronne; (b) diadème m.

corporal¹ ['kɔːp(ə)r(ə)l], s. Mil: caporal m; brigadier m.

corporal², a. (châtiment) corporel.

corporation [kɔːpə'reiʃ(ə)n], s. 1. conseil m municipal. 2. F: bedaine f.

corps [kɔːr], s. corps m (diplomatique).

corpse [kɔːps], s. cadavre m.

corpulence ['kɔːpjuləns], s. corpulence f. '**corpulent**, a. corpulent.

corpus ['kɔːpəs], s. Ecc: C. Christi, la Fête-Dieu.

corpuscle ['kɔːpʌsl], s. corpuscule m.

correct [kə'rekt]. I. v.tr. 1. corriger. 2. rectifier (une erreur). 3. punir qn. II. a. 1. correct, exact. 2. conforme à l'usage. -ly, adv. correctement. co'rrection, s. 1. correction f (d'un devoir); rectification f (d'une erreur). 2. punition f. co'rrectness, s. correction f, convenance f; exactitude f, justesse f.

correspond [kɔris'pɔnd], v.i. correspondre (to, avec; with s.o., avec qn). corres'pondence, s. correspondance f. corres'pondent, s. correspondant m.

corres'ponding, a. correspondant. **-ly**, adv. également.

corridor ['kɔridɔːr], s. couloir m; corridor m.

corroborate [kə'rɔbəreit], v.tr. corroborer. corrobo'ration, s. corroboration f.

corrode [kə'roud], v.tr. & i. (se) corroder. co'rrosion, s. corrosion f. co'rrosive, a. & s. corrosif (m).

corrupt [kə'rʌpt]. I. v.tr. corrompre. II. a. corrompu. co'rruption, s. corruption f.

corset ['kɔːsit], s. corset m.

Corsican ['kɔːsik(ə)n], a. & s. corse (mf).

cortisone ['kɔːtizoun], s. cortisone f.

cos [kɔs], s. c. (lettuce), romaine f.

cosh [kɔʃ]. I. s. F: matraque f. II. v.tr. F: assommer (qn).

cosmetic [kɔz'metik], a. & s. cosmétique (m).

cosmonaut ['kɔzmounɔːt], s. cosmonaute m.

cosmopolitan [kɔzmə'pɔlit(ə)n], a. & s. cosmopolite (mf).

†cost [kɔst]. I. v. 1. v.i. coûter; whatever it costs, coûte que coûte. 2. v.tr. Com: établir le prix de revient (d'un article). II. s. 1. coût m; frais mpl; at all costs, à tout prix. 2. pl. Jur: frais d'instance. '**costing**, s. établissement m du prix de revient.

costermonger ['kɔstəmʌŋgər], s. marchand m des quatre saisons.

costume ['kɔstjuːm], s. costume m; (for women) (tailor-made) c., tailleur m; bathing c., maillot m de bain.

cosy ['kouzi], a. chaud, confortable.

cot [kɔt], s. lit m d'enfant.

cottage ['kɔtidʒ], s. 1. chaumière f. 2. villa f. petite maison f de campagne.

cotton ['kɔtn], s. 1. coton m; c. wool, ouate f. 2. fil m (à coudre). 3. c. mill, filature f de coton; c. plantation, cotonnerie f.

couch [kautʃ], s. canapé m, divan m.

cough [kɔf], s. 1. toux f; c. lozenge, pastille, pastille f pectorale. II. v.i. tousser. '**coughing**, s. fit of c., quinte f de toux.

council ['kauns(i)l], s. 1. conseil m; town c., conseil municipal; county c. = conseil départemental; c. house, flat = habitation f à loyer modéré (H.L.M.). 2. Ecc: concile m. '**councillor**, s. conseiller m municipal; county c. = conseiller général.

counsel ['kauns(ə)l], s. 1. délibération f; consultation f. 2. conseil m, avis m. 3. avocat m; conseil. '**counsellor**, s. conseiller m (d'ambassade).

count¹ [kaunt]. I. v. 1. v.tr. compter; calculer. 2. v.i. compter (sur qn). 3. avoir de l'importance. II. s. compte m; calcul m; dépouillement m (du scrutin); blood c., numération f globulaire; Techn: c. down, compte à rebours.

count², s. (*title*) comte m.

countenance ['kauntinəns]. I. s. visage m; to keep one's c., ne pas se laisser décontenancer. II. v.tr. approuver, sanctionner (qch.).

counter ['kauntər]. I. s. 1. E: compteur m. 2. fiche f; jeton m. 3. (*in shop*) comptoir m; (*in bank*) guichet m. II. a. contraire, opposé. III. adv. en sens inverse; à contre-sens. **counter'act**, v.tr. neutraliser. **'counter-at'tack**. I. s. contre-attaque f. II. v.tr. & i. contre-attaquer. **'counter'balance**, v.tr. compenser. **'countercharge**, s. Jur: contre-accusation f. **'counter-'espionage**, s. contre-espionnage m. **'counterfeit**. I. a. faux. III. v.tr. contrefaire (la monnaie). **'counterfoil**, s. souche f, talon m. **'counter'mand**, v.tr. contremander; révoquer (un ordre). **'counterpart**, s. contre-partie f; double m. **'counterpoise**, s. contrepoids m. **'countersign**, v.tr. contresigner.

countess ['kauntis], s. comtesse f.

counting, s. compte m; dépouillement m (du scrutin); c. house, comptabilité f. **'countless**, a. innombrable.

†**country** ['kʌntri], s. 1. pays m; région f; my native c., ma patrie. 2. campagne f; house in the c., maison f à la campagne; c. house, manoir m; gentilhommière f; château m.

†**county** ['kaunti], s. comté m (= département m); c. town, chef-lieu m de comté.

couple ['kʌpl]. I. s. couple m; to work in couples, se mettre à deux pour travailler; in a c. of minutes, dans un instant; the young c., les jeunes mariés. II. v.tr. coupler; associer. **'couplet**, s. distique m.

coupon ['ku:pɔn], s. coupon m.

courage ['kʌridʒ], s. courage m. **cou'rageous** [-rei-], a. courageux. **-ly**, courageusement.

courier ['kuriər], s. courrier m, messager m; (*of tourist party*) guide m.

course ['kɔːs], s. 1. (*a*) cours m; marche f; in c. of time, à la longue; in the ordinary c., normalement; in due c., en temps voulu, en temps utile; (*b*) of c., bien entendu; (*c*) as a matter of c., comme de juste. 2. (*a*) Med: traitement m, régime m; (*b*) Sch: cours; French c., (*book*) méthode f de français. 3. route f, direction f; c. of action, ligne f de conduite. 4. Cu: service m, plat m. 5. Sp: (*a*) champ m; terrain m; (*b*) piste f.

court ['kɔːt]. I. s. 1. cour f (royale). 2. Jur: tribunal m; c. of appeal, cour d'appel; assize court, (*building*) palais m de justice. 3. tennis c., tennis m. II. v.tr. 1. faire la cour à (une femme). 2. aller au-devant de (la mort). **courteous** ['kɔː-], a. courtois, poli. **-ly**,

adv. courtoisement, avec politesse.

courtesy ['kɔː-], s. courtoisie f; politesse f; F: Aut: c. cop, motard m.

'courtier, s. courtisan m. **court-'martial**. I. s. conseil m de guerre. II. v.tr. faire passer (qn) en conseil de guerre. **'courtship**, s. cour f (faite à une femme). **'courtyard**, s. cour f (de maison).

cousin ['kʌzn], s. cousin, -ine; first c., cousin(e) germain(e).

cove [kouv], s. anse f; petite baie.

covenant ['kʌvənənt]. I. s. 1. convention f, contrat m. 2. pacte m, traité m. II. v.tr. promettre, accorder (qch.) par contrat.

cover ['kʌvər]. I. s. 1. couverture f; loose c. (*of chair*), housse f; outer c., enveloppe f (de pneu). 2. P.T.T: under separate c., sous pli séparé. 3. to take c., se mettre à l'abri. 4. Com: Fin: couverture, provision f, marge f; full c., garantie f totale. 5. (*at restaurant*) couvert m. II. v.tr. 1. couvrir. 2. comprendre, englober. **'covering**. 1. a. c. letter, lettre d'explication (d'une autre, d'un document). II. s. couverture f; enveloppe f. **cover 'up**, v.tr. couvrir entièrement; dissimuler (la vérité).

covet ['kʌvit], v.tr. convoiter. **'covetous**, a. avide (de gain, etc.).

cow [kau]. I. s. 1. vache f. 2. Austr: P: it's, he's, a fair c., que c'est, qu'il est, moche. II. v.tr. intimider, dompter (qn). **'cowboy**, s. cowboy m. **'cowhand**, s. †cowman, s. **'cowherd**, s. †cowman, s. vacher m, bouvier m. **'cowshed**, s. étable f.

coward ['kauəd], s. & a. lâche (mf). **'cowardice**, s. lâcheté f. **'cowardly**, a. lâche; in a c. way, lâchement.

cower ['kauər], v.i. se blottir, se tapir; trembler (devant qn).

cowl [kaul], s. capuchon m; abat-vent m (de cheminée).

cowslip ['kauslip], s. primevère f, coucou m.

cox [kɔks], s. Nau: barreur m.

coxswain ['kɔksn], s. Nau: patron m (d'une chaloupe); timonier m.

coy [kɔi], a. timide, farouche. **-ly**, adv. timidement.

crab¹ [kræb], s. crabe m, cancre m; Nau: F: to catch a c., engager un aviron.

crab², s. c. (*apple*), pomme f sauvage.

crack [kræk]. I. s. 1. claquement m; détonation f; coup sec (de fusil); c. on the head, coup violent sur la tête. 2. fente f, fissure f; (*in pottery*) fêlure f; (*in pottery*) fêlure f. 3. a c. at s.o., une plaisanterie aux dépens de qn. II. a. d'élite; c. player, as m. III. v. 1. v.tr. (*a*) faire claquer (un fouet); (*b*) fêler (un verre); fracturer (un crâne); P: to c. a crib, cambrioler une maison. 2. v.i. (*a*) craquer; claquer; (*b*) se fêler; se fissurer; (of wall) se lézarder; (c) F: to get cracking, s'y mettre; (d) F: to c. down on s.o., laver la tête à qn. 'cracked, a. fêlé, fendu; F: (of pers.) timbré, toqué, loufoque. 'cracker, s. 1. (a) pétard m; (b) diablotin m. 2. U.S: biscuit m (sec). 'cracking, s. cracking m, craquage m (du pétrole); c. plant, cracking m, cracking m. F: c. up, F: v.tr. vanter, prôner (qn, qch.). 2. v.i. (of pers.) flancher, s'effondrer.

crackle ['krækl], s. 1. v.i. craqueter; pétiller; grésiller. II. s. craquement m; crépitement m. 'crackling, s. peau croquante (de porc rôti).

cradle ['kreidl], s. berceau m; c. song, berceuse f.

craft ['krɑːft], s. 1. ruse f; fourberie f. 2. métier m. 3. (inv.) bateau m, embarcation f. 'craftiness, s. ruse f, astuce f. †'craftsman, s. 1. artisan m; ouvrier m qualifié. 2. artiste m dans son métier. 'crafty, a. astucieux, rusé. -ily, adv. astucieusement.

crag [kræg], s. rocher m escarpé, à pic. †cram [kræm]. I. v.tr. (a) fourrer (qch. dans qch.); (b) gaver (une volaille); (c) Sch: chauffer (un candidat). 2. v.i: (a) se gorger de nourriture; (b) to c. for an exam, potasser un examen.

cramp [kræmp]. I. s. 1. Med: crampe f. 2. (a) happe f, agrafe f, crampon m; (b) serre-joint m. II. v.tr. 1. gêner; to c. s.o.'s style, priver qn de ses moyens. 2. (a) cramponner, agrafer (des pierres, etc.); (b) presser, serrer (à l'étau). 'crampon, s. crampon m à glace.

crane [krein]. I. s. grue f. II. v.tr. to c. one's neck, allonger le cou.

cranium ['kreiniəm], s. crâne m.

crank [kræŋk]. I. s. 1. manivelle f; c. case, carter m (du moteur). 2. (pers.) excentrique mf. II. v.tr. to c. up a car, faire démarrer une voiture à la manivelle. 'crankshaft, s. vilebrequin m.

crash [kræʃ]. I. s. 1. fracas m. 2. catastrophe f; Fin: krach m. 3. Aut: accident m; c. helmet, casque m protecteur; Av: to c. land, atterrir brutalement, F: casser du bois. II. v.i. (a) éclater, tomber, avec fracas; (b) Aut: to c. into a tree, tamponner un arbre; (c) Av: (of plane) s'écraser sur le sol; (of pilot) F: casser du bois. 'crash-proof, a. antichoc.

crate [kreit], s. caisse f à claire-voie, cageot m.

crater ['kreitər], s. cratère m.

crave [kreiv], v.tr. & i. to c. for sth., avoir un désir obsédant de qch. 'craving, s. désir m ardent, obsédant.

crawl [krɔːl]. I. v.i. 1. ramper; aller à quatre pattes; Aut: F: faire du sur-place. 2. to be crawling with vermin, grouiller de vermine. 3. (swimming)

crawler, faire du crawl. II. s. (swimming) crawl m. 'crawlers, s.pl. Cl: barboteuse f.

crayfish ['kreifiʃ], s. 1. (fresh-water) c., écrevisse f. 2. langouste f.

crayon ['kreiən], s. pastel m, crayon.

craze [kreiz], s. manie f, (craziness) folie f, démence f. 'crazy, a. fou, toqué. -ily, adv. follement.

creak [kriːk]. I. v.i. crier, grincer; craquer. II. s. (also creaking) grincement m; craquement m.

cream [kriːm], I. s. crème f. II. v.tr. (a) écrémer (du lait); (b) battre (du beurre et du sucre) en crème. 'creamy, a. crémeux.

crease [kriːs]. I. v.tr. & i. (a) plisser; (b) chiffonner, froisser. II. s. (faux) pli m; c. resisting, infroissable.

create [kriˈeit], v.tr. créer; produire; abs. P: rouspéter, faire une scène. creˈation, s. création f; creˈative, a. créateur. creˈator, s. créateur, -trice.

creature ['kriːtʃər], s. 1. créature f; être m. 2. animal m, bête f. 3. attrib: c. comforts, douceur f matérielle.

credentials [kriˈden(ʃ)əlz], s.pl. pièces f justificatives, d'identité.

credible ['kredibl], a. croyable; digne de foi.

credit ['kredit]. I. s. 1. croyance f, foi f. 2. crédit m, influence f. 3. mérite m; it does him c., cela lui fait honneur. 4. Com: Fin: (a) crédit; (b) avoir m. II. v.tr. 1. ajouter foi à; croire. 2. attribuer (qch., une qualité, à qn). 3. Com: Fin: créditer (with, de). 'creditable, a. (action) honorable. 'creditor, s. créancier, -ière.

credulous ['kredjuləs], a. crédule. creˈdulity, s. crédulité f.

creed [kriːd], s. Ecc: Pol: credo m.

creek [kriːk], s. crique f, anse f.

creep [kriːp]. I. v.i. 1. ramper; se traîner, se glisser. 2. (of plant, etc.) grimper. 3. (of rails) cheminer; (of tyres) glisser sur la jante. II. s. 1. cheminement m, glissement m. 2. F: personnage m déplaisant. 3. F: he, it, gives me the creeps, ça me met les nerfs en pelote. 'creeper, s. plante grimpante; Virginia c., vigne f vierge.

cremate [kriˈmeit], v.tr. incinérer (un mort). creˈmation, s. crémation f. creˈmatorium, s. crématorium m.

creosote ['kriːəsout], s. créosote f.

crepe [kreip], s. crêpe m; c. bandage, bande f velpeau.

crescent ['kres(ə)nt], s. (a) croissant m; (b) rue f en arc de cercle.

cress [kres], s. cresson m.

crest [krest], s. 1. crête f. 2. armoiries f.pl.

crestfallen ['krestfɔːl(ə)n], a. abattu, découragé.

crevasse [kriˈvæs], s. Geog: crevasse f.

crevice ['krevis], s. fente f; lézarde f; fissure f.

crew [kruː], s. **1.** équipage m; équipe f. **2.** Pej: bande f, troupe f.

crib [krib]. **I.** s. **1.** mangeoire f, râtelier m. **2.** lit m d'enfant; Ecc: crèche f. **3.** F: Sch: traduction f (d'auteur) (employée subrepticement). **II.** v.tr. F: Sch: copier (un devoir) (sur un camarade).

crick [krik]. **I.** s. c. in the neck, torticolis m; c. in the back, tour m de reins. **II.** v.tr. to c. one's neck, one's back, se donner le torticolis, un tour de reins.

cricket[1] ['krikit], s. grillon m, cricri m.

cricket[2], s. cricket m. **'cricketer**, s. joueur m de cricket.

crime [kraim], s. **(a)** crime m; **(b)** délit m. **'criminal. 1.** a. criminel; the C. Investigation Department = la Police judiciaire. **2.** s. criminel, -elle.

crimson ['krimz(ə)n], a. & s. cramoisi (m); pourpre (m).

cringe [krindʒ], v.i. s'humilier, ramper. **'cringing**, a. **1.** craintif. **2.** servile.

crinkle ['kriŋkl]. **1.** v.tr. froisser, chiffonner; crinkled paper, papier gaufré. **2.** v.i. se froisser.

cripple ['kripl]. **I.** s. a. estropié, -ée; boiteux, -euse; infirme mf. **II.** v.tr. **(a)** estropier (qn); crippled with rheumatism, perclus de rhumatismes; **(b)** paralyser (l'industrie, etc.).

†crisis ['kraisis], s. crise f.

crisp [krisp], a. **(a)** croquant, croustillant; **(b)** (ton) tranchant; **(c)** (air) vif. **'crispness**, s. **1.** qualité f croustillante. **2.** netteté f. **3.** froid m vif.

†criterion [krai'tiəriən], s. critère m.

critic ['kritik], s. **(a)** critique m; **(b)** censeur m; critiquer m. **'critical**, a. critique. **-ally**, adv. **1.** en critique. **2.** c. ill, dangereusement malade. **'criticism**, s. critique f. **'criticize**, v.tr. **1.** critiquer (qch.). **2.** censurer, blâmer (qn).

croak [krouk]. **I.** v.i. **1.** coasser; croasser. **2.** P: mourir. **II.** s. coassement m; croassement m. **'croaky**, a. (voix) enrouée, rauque.

crock [krok]. **I.** s. **1.** pot m de terre. 2. Aut: F: tacot m. **3.** F: (pers.) bonhomme m fini, claqué m. **II.** F: v.i. to c. (up), tomber malade; flancher. **'crockery**, s. faïence f, poterie f. **'crocky**, a. F: malade.

crocodile ['krokədail], s. crocodile m.

crocus ['kroukəs], s. crocus m.

†crony ['krouni], s. compère m, commère f; old u., vieux copain.

crook [kruk]. **I.** s. **1.** houlette f (de berger). **2.** F: escroc m. **II.** a. Austr: F: malade; souffrant. **'crooked**, a. **1.** tordu; tortueux; de travers. **2.** malhonnête.

croon [kruːn], v.tr. chantonner; fredonner. **'crooner**, s. chanteur, -euse, de charme.

crop [krop], s. **I.** récolte f, moisson f. **II.** †v.tr. (of animal) brouter l'herbe. **'cropper**, s. F: to come a c., (i) faire une chute; (ii) faire faillite; (iii) se heurter à un obstacle imprévu. **crop 'up**, v.i. F: surgir.

cross [kros]. **I.** s. **1.** croix f; the Red C., la Croix rouge. **2.** croisement m (de races); to be a c. between sth. and sth., être un mélange de qch. et de qch. **II.** v. **1.** v.tr. **(a)** croiser; **(b)** Ecc: to c. oneself, se signer; **(c)** barrer (un chèque); **(d)** traverser (la rue); passer (sur) (un pont). **2.** v.i. (of roads, etc.) se croiser; **(b)** passer (d'un lieu à un autre); to c. from Calais to Dover, faire la traversée de Calais à Douvres. **III.** a. & combined form (adj.) transversal; c. section, coupe f, section f transversale; tranche f (de la population); **(b)** contraire, opposé; c. purposes, malentendu m; c. reference, renvoi m (dans un livre). **2.** maussade, de mauvaise humeur; fâché. **-ly**, adv. avec mauvaise humeur. **'cross-breed**, s. race f croisée. **'cross-exami'nation**, s. contre-interrogatoire m. **'cross-ex'amine**, v.tr. contre-interroger. **'cross-eyed**, a. qui louche. **'crossing**, s. **1.** traversée f (de la mer); pedestrian c., passage m pour piétons. **2.** croisement m; intersection f; level c., passage à niveau. **3.** croisement (de races). **'cross-legged**, a. les jambes croisées. **'crossroads**, s.pl. carrefour m. **'crossword**, s. c. (puzzle), mots croisés.

crotchet ['krotʃit], s. Mus: noire f.

crotchety ['krotʃiti], a. capricieux; à l'humeur difficile.

crouch [krautʃ], v.i. se tapir, s'accroupir.

croupier ['kruːpiər], s. croupier m.

crow[1] [krou], s. Z: corneille f.

crow[2], v.i. (of cock) chanter; to c. over s.o., chanter victoire sur qn.

crowbar ['kroubɑːr], s. pince f (à levier).

crowd [kraud]. **I.** s. foule f; Cin: the figurants m. **II.** v. **1.** v.tr. serrer, (en)tasser; remplir; crowded hall, salle bondée. **2.** v.i. to c. (together), se presser en foule.

crown [kraun]. **I.** s. **1.** couronne f; c. prince, prince héritier. **2.** half a c., deux shillings et six pence. **3.** sommet m, haut m (de la tête); bombement m (d'un pont); Aut: to drive on the c. of the road, conduire sur l'axe de la chaussée. **4.** c. cork, capsule f (métallique) de bouteille; c. cork opener, décapsuleur m. **II.** v.tr. couronner.

crucial ['kruːʃl], a. décisif, critique.

crucify ['kruːsifaks], s. crucifix m. **cruci'fixion**, s. crucifixion f. **'crucify**, v.tr. crucifier.

crude [kruːd], a. (of metal) brut; (of colour) cru; (of manners) grossier. -**ly,** adv. crûment; grossièrement. '**crudeness,** s. crudity s. crudité f (d'expression); grossièreté f (de manières).

cruel [kruəl], a. cruel. -**ly,** adv. cruellement. '**cruelty,** s. cruauté f (to, envers); society for the prevention of c. to animals, société protectrice des animaux.

cruet ['kruit], s. H: huilier m.

cruise [kruːz]. I. s. croisière f. II. v.i. 1. Nau: croiser; Aut: Av: Nau: cruising speed, vitesse f de croisière, économique. 2. (of taxi) faire la maraude. '**cruiser,** s. Nau: croiseur m.

crumb [krʌm], s. miette f; (opposed to crust) mie f. '**crumble,** v.tr. & i. (s')émietter; (s')effriter.

crumpet ['krʌmpit], s. Cu: sorte de crêpe peu sucrée (servie rôtie et beurrée).

crumple ['krʌmpl], v.tr. friper, froisser.

crunch [krʌn(t)ʃ]. I. v. 1. v.tr. croquer; broyer. 2. v.i. (of snow) crisser, craquer. II. s. 1. coup m de dents. 2. bruit m de broiement.

crush [krʌʃ]. I. v.tr. écraser; accabler (qn); froisser (une robe); Min: etc: broyer, concasser. II. s. presse f, foule f. '**crushing,** a. écrasant. -**ly,** adv. d'un ton écrasant.

crust [krʌst], s. croûte f. '**crusty,** a. (pain) qui a une forte croûte; (biscuit) croustillant.

crustacean [krʌs'teiʃən], s. crustacé m.

crutch [krʌtʃ], s. béquille f.

crux [krʌks], s. nœud m (de la question).

†**cry** [krai]. I. v.tr. & i. 1. to c. (out), pousser des cris. 2. (= say) s'écrier. 3. pleurer. II. s. 1. cri m (de douleur). 2. to have a good c., donner libre cours à ses larmes. '**crying,** 1. a. c. injustice, injustice criante. 2. s. pleurs mpl, larmes fpl. '**cry 'off,** v.i. se dédire, se récuser.

crypt [kript], s. crypte f.

cryptic ['kriptik], a. secret, occulte; c. silence, silence énigmatique.

crystal ['kristl], s. cristal m. '**crystallize.** 1. v.tr. cristalliser; crystallized fruit, fruits confits. 2. v.i. (se) cristalliser. crystal'lography, s. cristallographie f.

cub [kʌb], s. petit m (d'un animal); (scouting) louveteau m.

cube [kjuːb], s. cube m. '**cubic,** a. cubique; c. metre, mètre cube; c. capacity, volume m; c. equation, équation f du troisième degré.

cubicle ['kjuːbikl], s. alcôve f (d'un dortoir); cabine f (d'une piscine).

cuckoo ['kuku], s. coucou m; c. clock, (pendule f à) coucou.

cucumber ['kjuːkʌmbər], s. concombre m.

cud [kʌd], s. to chew the c., ruminer.

cuddle ['kʌdl], v.tr. serrer (qn) doucement dans ses bras. 2. v.i. to c. up to s.o., se pelotonner contre qn.

cue[1] [kjuː], s. (a) Th: réplique f; (b) avis m, mot m, indication f; to take one's c. from s.o., s'ajuster, s'aligner, sur qn.

cue[2], s. queue f (de billard).

cuff[1] [kʌf], s. 1. poignet m; manchette f; F: off the c., (discours) impromptu. 2. U.S: revers m (de pantalon).

cuff[2] F: 1. s. taloche f, calotte f. II. v.tr. flanquer une taloche (à qn).

cul-de-sac ['kʌldəsæk], s. impasse f.

culinary ['kʌlinəri], a. culinaire.

culminate ['kʌlmineit], v.i. to c. in sth., aboutir à, se terminer en, qch. cul-mi'nation, s. point m culminant.

culpability [kʌlpə'biliti], s. culpabilité f. '**culpable,** a. coupable.

culprit ['kʌlprit], s. coupable mf.

cult [kʌlt], s. culte m (of, de).

cultivate ['kʌltiveit], v.tr. cultiver. culti'**vation,** s. culture f. '**cultivator,** s. cultivateur m; motoculteur m.

culture ['kʌltʃər], s. culture f. '**cultured,** a. (homme) cultivé.

cumbersome ['kʌmbəsəm], a. encombrant, gênant, incommode.

cumulative ['kjuːmjulətiv], a. cumulatif.

cunning ['kʌnin]. I. s. ruse f; finesse f; low c., astuce f. II. a. 1. rusé, malin, astucieux. 2. (a) (dispositif) ingénieux; (b) U.S: gentil, coquet.

cup [kʌp], s. 1. tasse f; c. of tea, tasse de thé; F: that's not my c. of tea, c'est pas mes oignons; F: that's another c. of tea, c'est une autre affaire. 2. Sp: coupe f. 3. bonnet m (de soutien-gorge). '**cupful,** s. pleine tasse, f.

cupboard ['kʌbəd], s. armoire f; placard m.

curate ['kjuərit], s. Ecc: vicaire m.

curator [kjuə'reitər], s. conservateur m (de musée).

curb [kəːb]. I. v.tr. réprimer, contenir (sa colère); mettre un frein à (ses passions). II. s. 1. gourmette f (d'un cheval). 2. bordure f (de trottoir); Aut: to hit the c., heurter le trottoir.

curdle ['kəːdl], v.i. (of milk) se cailler; (of blood) se figer.

cure [kjuər]. I. v.tr. 1. guérir. 2. saler, fumer (la viande); saler (les peaux). II. s. 1. guérison f. 2. (a) cure f; (b) remède m. '**curing,** s. salaison f.

curio ['kjuəriou], s. curiosité f; bibelot m.

curiosity [kjuəri'ositi], s. 1. curiosité f. 2. objet curieux, rareté f. '**curious,** a. curieux; singulier. -**ly,** adv. singulièrement.

curl [kəːl]. I. s. boucle f. II. v.tr. & i. boucler, friser. '**curl 'up,** v.i. se mettre en boule; se pelotonner. '**curly,** a. bouclé, frisé.

currant ['kʌrənt], s. 1. red c., groseille f (rouge); black c., cassis m. 2. raisin m de Corinthe.

currency ['kʌrənsi], s. unité f monétaire (d'un pays); monnaie f; hard c., devise f forte.

current ['kʌrənt]. I. s. courant m (d'eau, d'air, électrique). II. a. courant, en cours; in c. use, d'usage courant; c. events, actualités f. -ly, adv. couramment.

curriculum [kə'rikjuləm], s. Sch: programme m d'études.

†curry¹ [kʌri]. I. s. Cu: curry m. II. v.tr. apprêter (qch.) au curry.

curry² v.tr. I. étriller (un cheval). 2. corroyer (le cuir). 3. to c. favour with s.o., s'insinuer dans les bonnes grâces de qn.

curse [kəːs]. I. s. 1. malédiction f. 2. juron m. 3. fléau m. 4. F: to have the c., avoir ses règles. II. v. 1. v.tr. maudire. II. v.i. sacrer, jurer. cursed a. ['kəːsid] F: fichu.

cursory ['kəːsəri], a. rapide; superficiel.

curt [kəːt], a. brusque; sec. -ly, adv. sèchement. 'curtness, s. brusquerie f.

curtail [kəːˈteil], v.tr. écourter; diminuer (l'autorité de qn); restreindre (ses dépenses).

curtain ['kəːtən]. I. s. rideau m; Pol: iron c., rideau de fer. II. v.tr. garnir de rideaux.

curtsey ['kəːtsi]. I. s. révérence f. II. faire une révérence.

curve [kəːv]. I. s. courbe f. II. v.i. décrire une courbe. 'curvature, s. courbure f; c. of the spine, déviation f de la colonne vertébrale. 'curved, a. courbé, courbe.

cushion ['kuʃ(ə)n], s. coussin m.

cushy ['kuʃi], a. F: (emploi) facile et bien payé.

cussedness ['kʌsidnis], s. F: perversité f; out of sheer c., rien que pour embêter tout le monde.

custard ['kʌstəd], s. Cu: crème f (au lait); baked c., flan m.

custody ['kʌstədi], s. 1. garde f; in safe c., en lieu sûr. 2. emprisonnement m; to take s.o. into c., arrêter qn. cus'todian, s. gardien, -ienne; conservateur m (de musée).

custom ['kʌstəm], s. 1. coutume f, usage m, habitude f. 2. the customs, la douane; customs officer, douanier m. 3. Com: (a) (of shop) clientèle f; (b) patronage m (du client); (c) made, built, fait sur commande; Ind: hors série; (vêtements) faits sur mesure. 'customary, a. habituel. 'customer, s. client, -ente; F: a queer c., un drôle de type.

‡cut [kʌt]. I. v.tr. & i. 1. couper; tailler; to c. one's finger, se couper un doigt. 2. to c. a speech short, raccourcir un discours; to c. s.o. short, couper la parole à qn; F: c. it short! abrégez! 3. to c. s.o. (dead), faire semblant de ne

pas voir qn. 4. F: manquer exprès à (un rendez-vous); Sch: sécher (un cours). II. s. 1. coupe f. 2. réduction f (de salaires); El: coupure f (du courant). 3. (wound) coupure, balafre f. 4. short c., raccourci m. 5. Cu: c. off the joint, tranche f de rôti; cheap cuts, bas morceaux. III. a. 1. (cristal) taillé; Cl: well c., de bonne coupe; c. and dried, opinions toutes faites. 2. c. prices, prix de concurrence. cut 'down, v.tr. abattre (un arbre); rogner (les dépenses); restreindre (la production).

cute [kjuːt], a. F: 1. (of pers.) malin, rusé. 2. U.S: gentil, coquet.

cut 'in, v.i. 1. se mêler à la conversation. 2. Aut: couper la route à qn (après avoir doublé). 'cutlery, s. coutellerie f. 'cutlet, s. Cu: (a) côtelette f (de mouton); côte f (de veau); (b) croquette f (de viande). cut 'off. I. v.tr. couper (qch.). 2. interrompre (le courant); to c. s.o. off with a shilling, déshériter qn. 2. v.i. F: décamper, filer. cut 'out, v.tr. 1. couper (du bois mort); F: to c. s.o. out, supplanter qn. 2. découper (des images); tailler (un vêtement); to be c. o. for sth., avoir des dispositions pour qch. 3. supprimer (des détails). 'cutter, s. (pers.) coupeur m; tailleur m (de pierres); coupoir m; rotary c., roue f à couteaux. 3. Nau: canot m. 'cut-throat, s. 1. coupejarret m. 2. c. competition, concurrence acharnée. 'cutting. I. a. 1. c. edge, tranchant m (d'un objet). 2. (of remark) mordant. II. s. 1. coupure f (prise dans un journal). 2. (of plant) bouture f. 3. Rail: etc. tranchée f. cut 'up, v.tr. 1. découper (une volaille). 2. F: to be c. up about sth., être affligé de qch; (b) v.i. to c. up rough, se fâcher.

cyanide ['saiənaid], s. cyanure m.

cycle ['saikl]. I. s. 1. cycle m. 2. bicyclette f; c. track, piste f cyclable. II. v.i. faire de la bicyclette. 'cycling, s. cyclisme m. 'cyclist, s. cycliste mf.

cyclone ['saikloun], s. cyclone m.

cygnet ['signit], s. jeune cygne m.

cylinder ['silindər], s. cylindre m. cy'lindrical, a. cylindrique.

cynic ['sinik], s. censeur m caustique; railleur m; sceptique m. 'cynical, a. sarcastique; sceptique; désabusé. -ally, adv. d'un ton sceptique. 'cynicism, s. scepticisme railleur; désillusionnement m.

cypress ['saiprəs], s. cyprès m.

Cypriot ['sipriət], a. & s. cypriote (mf).

cyst [sist], s. Med: kyste m.

Czech [tʃek], a. & s. tchèque (mf).

D

D, d [di:], s. 1. (la lettre) D, d, m. 2. *Mus:* ré m.

‡**dab**[1] [dæb], v.tr. tapoter; (se) tamponner.

dab[2], s. Fish: limande f.

dabble ['dæbl], v.i. to d. in politics, se mêler de politique.

dachshund ['dækshund], s. teckel m.

dad, daddy [dæd, 'dædi], s. papa m. **daddy-long-legs**, s. tipule f.

daffodil ['dæfədil], s. narcisse m des bois; jonquille f.

daft [dɑ:ft], a. 1. écervelé. 2. toqué.

dagger ['dægər], s. poignard m, dague f; **at daggers drawn**, à couteaux tirés (with, avec).

dahlia ['deiljə], s. dahlia m.

†**daily** ['deili]. I. a. journalier, quotidien; **d. help**, s. F: daily, femme f de ménage; **d. (paper)**, quotidien m. II. adv. journellement, quotidiennement.

dainty ['deinti], a. 1. (of food) friand. 2. (of pers.) délicat, exquis. adv. -**ily**, délicatement. '**daintiness**, s. délicatesse f, raffinement m.

†**dairy** ['dɛəri], s. 1. laiterie f. 2. (shop) crémerie f. **dairy produce**, produits laitiers. 2. '**dairy-farming**, s. l'industrie laitière. '**dairyman**, s. Com: laitier m, crémier m.

dais ['deiis], s. estrade f.

†**daisy** ['deizi], s. pâquerette f; marguerite f.

dam [dæm]. I. s. barrage m. II. ‡v.tr. contenir, endiguer (un lac, etc.).

damage ['dæmidʒ]. I. s. 1. dommage(s) m (pl), dégâts mpl; avarie f. 2. préjudice m, tort m. 3. pl. dommages-intérêts m. II. v.tr. 1. endommager; avarier; abîmer. 2. nuire à (qn). '**damaged**, a. avarié, endommagé. '**damaging**, a. préjudiciable, nuisible.

damn [dæm]. I. s. juron m; gros mot; F: I don't care a d., je m'en fiche. 2. adv. P: bigrement; d. all, rien. 3. int: F: zut! II. v.tr. 1. (a) condamner (un livre); perdre (qn, un projet). 2. damner; (of God) réprouver. '**damnable**, a. odieux. -**ably**, adv. odieusement, F: bigrement (mauvais). **dam'nation**, s. damnation f (éternelle). '**damned**, a. 1. damné, réprouvé. 2. F: (a) **what a d. nuisance!** quel empoisonnement! (b) adv. it's d. hard, c'est bigrement difficile. '**damning**, a. qui porte condamnation f; **d. evidence**, preuves accablantes.

damp [dæmp]. I. s. humidité f. II. v.tr. 1. mouiller; humecter (le linge). 2. étouffer (le feu). 3. refroidir (le courage), décourager (qn). III. a. humide; (of skin) moite. '**damp-course**, s. couche f hydrofuge. '**dampness**, s. humidité f; (of skin)

moiteur f. '**damp-proof**, a. imperméable.

damson ['dæmz(ə)n], s. prune f de Damas.

dance [dɑ:ns]. I. s. 1. danse f. 2. bal m; soirée f dansante. II. v. 1. v.i. (a) danser. **to d. with s.o.**, faire danser qn; (b) **to d. with rage**, trépigner de colère. 2. v.tr. danser (une valse). '**dancer**, s. danseur, -euse. '**dancing**, s. la danse.

dandelion ['dændilaiən], s. pissenlit m.

Dane [dein], s. 1. danois, -oise. 2. Z: (Great) D., danois.

danger ['deindʒər], s. danger m, péril m. '**dangerous**, a. dangereux. -**ly**, adv. dangereusement.

dangle ['dæŋgl], v.i. pendre; with **dangling legs**, les jambes ballantes.

Danish ['deiniʃ]. 1. a. danois. 2. s. Ling: le danois.

dank [dæŋk], a. humide (et froid).

‡**dare** ['dɛər]. 1. modal aux. oser; I d. say, sans doute. 2. v.tr. (a) oser (faire qch.); how d. you! vous osez! (b) braver (le danger). (c) défier (qn à faire qch.). '**dare-devil**, s. casse-cou m inv. '**daring**. I. a. audacieux. II. s. audace f.

dark [dɑ:k]. I. a. 1. sombre; obscur, noir; it is d., il fait nuit. 2. (of colour) foncé. 3. (of pers.) brun; basané. 4. to keep sth. d., tenir qch. secret. II. s. ténèbres fpl, obscurité f. '**darken**. 1. v.tr. obscurcir; assombrir. 2. v.i. s'obscurcir. '**darkness**, s. 1. obscurité f, ténèbres fpl. 2. teinte f foncée.

darling ['dɑ:liŋ], s. & a. bien-aimé, -ée. my d.! mon chéri! ma chérie! a mother's d., un enfant gâté.

darn [dɑ:n], s. 1. reprise f. II. v.tr. repriser. '**darning**, s. reprise f; d. needle, aiguille f à repriser.

dart [dɑ:t]. I. s. (a) dard m, trait m; (b) (game of) darts, (jeu m de) fléchettes fpl; (c) Cl: pince f. II. v. 1. v.tr. darder (des rayons); lancer (un regard). 2. v.i. se précipiter, s'élancer, foncer (at, upon, sur).

dash [dæʃ]. I. s. 1. soupçon m, goutte f (de cognac). 2. (of colour, tache f de couleur). 3. trait m de plume; tiret m. 4. to make a d. at sth., se précipiter sur qch. 5. élan m, fougue f; F: to cut a d., faire de l'effet. II. v. 1. v.tr. to d. sth. to pieces, fracasser qch. 2. v.i. (a) se heurter (contre qch.); (b) to d. at s.o., sth., se précipiter sur qn, qch. '**dash a'long**, v.i. filer à fond de train. '**dash a'way**, v.i. s'éloigner en coup de vent. '**dashboard**, s. Aut: tableau m de bord.

data ['deitə], *s.pl.* données *f*.

date[1] [deit], *s.* datte *f*; d. (palm), dattier *m*.

date[2]. I. *s.* (*a*) date *f*; to be up to d., être à la page; to bring up to d., remettre au point, tenir à jour; out of d., démodé; (*b*) F: rendez-vous *m*. II. *v.* 1. *v.tr.* date (une lettre); F: prendre rendez-vous avec (qn). 2. *v.i.* to d. back, remonter (au Xe siècle, etc.); his style dates, son style commence à dater.

daub [dɔːb]. I. *s.* 1. barbouillage *m*. 2. (*picture*) croûte *f*. II. *v.tr.* barbouiller, enduire (with, de).

daughter ['dɔːtər], *s.* fille *f*. 'daughter-in-law, belle-fille *f*.

dawdle ['dɔːdl], *v.i.* flâner. 'dawdler, *s.* flâneur, -euse. 'dawdling, *s.* flânerie *f*.

dawn [dɔːn]. I. *s.* aube *f*, aurore *f*; at d., au point du jour. II. *v.i.* (*of day*) poindre, se lever.

day [dei], *s.* 1. jour *m*; it's a fine d., il fait beau aujourd'hui; (*working, etc., day*) journée *f*; all day (long), toute la journée; twice a day, deux fois par jour; the d. before sth., la veille de qch.; the d. after sth., le lendemain de qch.; from d. to d., de jour en jour; d. labourer, ouvrier *m* à la journée; d. nursery, pouponnière *f*, garderie *f* (d'enfants); Sch: d. boarder, demi-pensionnaire *mf*; Ind: d. shift, équipe *f* du jour. 2. (*a*) what d. of the month is it? c'est le combien aujourd'hui? d. off, jour de congé; (*b*) fête *f*; All Saints' D., la Toussaint; Michaelmas D., la Saint-Michel. 3. in our days, de nos jours. 'daybreak, *s.* aube *f*. 'daydream, *s.* rêv(ass)erie *f*. 'daylight, *s.* by d., de jour *m*; in broad d., en plein jour.

daze [deiz]. I. *s.* in a d., hébété, stupéfait. II. *v.tr.* (*of blow*) étourdir.

dazzle ['dæzl], *v.tr.* éblouir, aveugler. 'dazzling, *a.* éblouissant, aveuglant.

dead [ded]. I. *a.* 1. (*a*) mort; the d. man, woman, le mort, la morte; (*b*) (*of limb*) to go d., s'engourdir. 2. d. calm, calme plat; d. silence, silence de mort; d. on time, à la minute; d. loss, perte sèche. El: d. cell, pile à plat; d. period, période *f* d'inactivité. II. *s.* 1. *pl.* the d., les morts. 2. at d. of night, au milieu de la nuit. III. *adv.* (*a*) absolument; d. tired, éreinté, F: claqué; d. drunk, ivre mort; d. slow, au grand ralenti; (*b*) to stop d., s'arrêter net; d. against, (*a*) 'dead(-and)-'alive, a. (*endroit*) mort, triste. 'dead-'beat. I. *a.* F: épuisé, fourbu. 2. *s. U.S: P:* (*a*) clochard *m*; (*b*) filou *m*. 'deaden, *v.tr.* amortir (un coup); étouffer (un bruit); émousser (les sens). 'dead 'end, *s.* cul-de-sac *m*. 'deadline, *s.* date *f* limite. 'deadlock, *s.* impasse *f*; situation *f* inextricable. 'deadly. 1. *a.* mortel; d. hatred, haine

mortelle, implacable. 2. *adv.* mortellement; it was d. cold, il faisait un froid de loup. 'dead 'march, *s. Mus:* marche *f* funèbre. 'deadpan. *esp U.S: F:* (*a*). (*visage*) figé; (*b*) *s.* pince-sans-rire *m*. 'dead-weight, *s.* poids mort.

deaf [def], *a.* sourd; d. and dumb, sourd-muet; to turn a d. ear, faire la sourde oreille. 'deafen, *v.tr.* assourdir (qn); rendre (qn) sourd. 'deafening, *a.* assourdissant. 'deaf-'mute, *s.* sourd-muet, sourde-muette. 'deafness, *s.* surdité *f*.

deal[1] [diːl], *s. & adv.* a good d., beaucoup.

deal[2]. I. 1. *v.* 1. *v.tr.* (*a*) to d. out, distribuer; (*b*) donner, porter (un coup); (*c*) donner (les cartes). 2. *v.i.* to d. with (s.o., sth.), avoir affaire à (qn); traiter de, s'occuper de (qch.); conclure (une affaire); venir à bout (d'une difficulté); *Com:* to d. in timber, faire le commerce du bois; (*b*) (*at cards*) faire la donne, donner. II. *s.* 1. (*cards*) la donne; whose d. is it? à qui de donner? 2. *Com:* affaire *f*; marché *m*. 'dealer, *s.* 1. (*cards*) donneur *m*. 2. *Com:* négociant *m*; marchand, -ande. 'dealing, *s.* 1. d. (out), distribution *f*. 2. *pl.* relations *fpl* avec qn.

dean [diːn], *s.* doyen *m*.

dear [diər]. I. *a.* (*a*) cher; my d. fellow, mon cher; (*in letter*) D. Madam, D. Sir, Madame, Mademoiselle; D. Monsieur; (*b*) cher, coûteux. -ly, *adv.* cher, chèrement. II. *s.* cher, *f* chère. III. *adv.* (vendre, payer) cher. IV. *int.* d. me! mon Dieu! oh d.! (i) diable! (ii) hélas!

death [deθ], *s.* (*a*) mort *f*; he'll be the d. of me, (i) il me fera mourir; (ii) il me fait mourir (de rire); (*b*) *Adm:* décès *m*; d. rate, mortalité *f*; *P.N:* (*in newspaper*) deaths, nécrologie *f*; d. duty, droit *m* de succession; (*c*) at death's door, à l'article de la mort. 'deathbed, *s.* lit *m* de mort. 'death-blow, coup mortel, fatal. 'deathly, *adv.* mortellement. 'death-trap, *s.* casse-cou *m inv*; *Aut:* croisement *m* dangereux. 'death-warrant, *s.* arrêt *m* de mort.

‡**debar** [di'bɑːr], *v.tr.* to d. s.o. from sth., exclure qn de qch.; to d. s.o. from doing sth., défendre à qn de faire qch.

debase [di'beis], *v.tr.* 1. avilir, dégrader (qn). 2. déprécier (la monnaie).

debate [di'beit]. I. *s.* débat *m*, discussion *f*; conférence *f* contradictoire. II. *v.* 1. *v.tr.* débattre, discuter, agiter (une question). 2. *v.i.* discuter, disputer (with s.o. on sth., avec qn sur qch.). de'batable, *a.* contestable, discutable.

debauched [di'bɔːtʃt], *a.* débauché, corrompu.

debility [di'biliti], *s. Med:* affaiblissement *m*.

debit ['debit]. I. s. débit m, doit m; d. balance, solde m débiteur. II. v.tr. 1. débiter (un compte). 2. to d. s.o. with a sum, porter une somme au débit de qn.

debris ['debri:]. s. débris mpl; décombres mpl.

debt [det], s. dette f; créance f. bad debts, mauvaises créances. in d., endetté. **'debtor,** s. débiteur, -trice.

debunk [di'bʌŋk], v.tr. F: déboulonner (qn).

decadence ['dekəd(ə)ns], s. décadence f. **'decadent,** a. décadent.

decamp [di'kæmp], v.i. décamper, filer.

decant [di'kænt], v.tr. décanter. **de'canter,** s. carafe f.

decarbonize [di:'kɑ:bənaiz], v.tr. Aut: décarboniser, décalaminer (un cylindre). **decarboni'zation,** s. décalaminage m; décrassage m.

decay [di'kei]. I. s. 1. décadence f (d'une famille); délabrement m (d'une maison); sénile d, affaiblissement m sénile. to fall into d., tomber en ruine. 2. pourriture f. II. v.i. tomber en décadence; (of house) tomber en ruine; se délabrer; pourrir; (of teeth) se carier.

decease [di'si:s], s. Adm: décès m. **de'ceased.** I. a. décédé; David Martin, d, (le) feu David Martin. 2. s. défunt, défunte.

deceit [di'si:t], s. tromperie f, duperie f. **de'ceitful,** a. trompeur; faux. adv. **-fully,** avec duplicité.

deceive [di'si:v], v.tr. tromper, abuser.

December [di'sembər], s. décembre m.

decent ['di:snt], a. (a) bienséant, convenable; (b) décent, honnête, modeste; (c) passable, assez bon. adv. **-ly,** convenablement; assez bien. **'decency,** s. 1. décence f; bienséance f (de costume, etc.). 2. the decencies, common d., les convenances (sociales); le respect humain. 3. (sense of) d., pudeur f.

decentralize [di:'sentrəlaiz], v.tr. décentraliser. **decentrali'zation,** s. décentralisation f.

deception [di'sep[(ə)n], s. tromperie f; fraude f. **de'ceptive,** a. trompeur; décevant. **-ly,** adv. trompeusement.

decide [di'said]. 1. v.tr. (a) décider (une affaire); trancher (une question); (b) décider (de (qch.); (c) to d. to do sth., se décider à faire qch. 2. v.i. se décider (on, à); to d. on a day, fixer un jour. **de'cided,** a. (of opinion) arrêté; (of manner) décidé. **-ly,** adv. avec décision. **de'ciding,** a. décisif; the d. game, la belle.

decimal ['desim(ə)l]. 1. a. décimal; d. point = virgule f. 2. s. décimale f.

decipher [di'saifər], v.tr. déchiffrer.

decision [di'siʒ(ə)n], s. décision f. **de'cisive,** a. 1. décisif; (of experiment) concluant. 2. (ton) tranchant, net. **-ly,** adv. décisivement.

deck [dek], s. (a) Nau: pont m; (b) (of bus) top d., impériale f; (c) U.S: jeu m (de cartes). **'deck-chair,** s. transatlantique m. **'deck-hand,** F: transa(t)nt m.

declaim [di'kleim], v.i. & tr. déclamer.

declare [di'kleər], v.tr. & i. déclarer; have you anything to d.? avez-vous quelque chose à déclarer? abs. (at cards) annoncer son jeu. **decla'ration,** s. déclaration f; (at cards) annonce f.

decline [di'klain]. I. s. déclin m (du jour, d'un empire); baisse f (de prix). II. v. 1. v.tr. (a) refuser (qch.); décliner (un honneur); abs. s'excuser; (b) Gram: décliner (un nom). 2. v.i. décliner; baisser.

declutch [di'klʌtʃ], v.i. Aut: débrayer.

decode [di'koud], v.tr. transcrire en clair (une dépêche). **de'coding,** s. transcription f en clair.

decompose [di:kəm'pouz]. 1. v.tr. décomposer. 2. v.i. se décomposer; pourrir. **decompo'sition,** s. décomposition f; putréfaction f.

decontaminate [di:kən'tæmineit], v.tr. 1. désinfecter. 2. décontaminer. **'decontami'nation,** s. 1. désinfection f. 2. décontamination f.

decorate ['dekəreit], v.tr. décorer (with, de). **deco'ration,** s. 1. décoration f. 2. décor m (d'un appartement). 3. décoration, médaille f. **'decorative,** a. décoratif. **'decorator,** s. (house) d., peintre décorateur m (d'appartements); tapissier m.

decoy. I. s. ['di:koi] appât m, leurre m, piège m. II. v.tr. [di'koi] leurrer; to d. s.o. into a trap, attirer qn dans un piège.

decrease. I. s. diminution f, décroissance f; d. in speed, ralentissement m. II. v.tr. & i. diminuer. **de'creasing,** a. décroissant; (tarif) dégressif.

decree [di'kri:]. I. s. 1. décret m, édit m, arrêté m. 2. jugement m. II. v.tr. décréter, ordonner.

decrepitude [di'krepitju:d], s. décrépitude f. **de'crepit** a. (of pers.) décrépit, caduc, -uque; (of thing) vermoulu.

dedicate ['dedikeit], v.tr. consacrer (une église); dédier (un livre). **dedi'cation,** s. dédicace f (d'un livre).

deduce [di'dju:s], v.tr. déduire (from, de).

deduct [di'dʌkt], v.tr. déduire, retrancher (from, de); rabattre (qch. sur le prix). **de'duction,** s. déduction f; (of pay) retenue f.

deed [di:d], s. 1. action f. 2. Jur: acte m notarié. **'deed-box,** s. coffret m à documents.

deep [di:p]. I. a. 1. profond. 2. (of colour) foncé, sombre. 3. rusé, malin. II. adv. profondément; d. into the night, très avant dans la nuit. III. s. the ocean deeps, l'abysse m. **'deepen,** v. 1. v.tr. (a) approfondir, creuser;

(b) rendre plus intense. 2. *v.i.* devenir plus profond; s'approfondir. **'deepening**, *s.* approfondissement *m.* **'deep freeze.** I. *s.* *R.t.m:* congélateur *m*, quick-freezing *m.* II. *v.tr.* surgeler. **'deep 'fry,** *v.tr.* & *i.* (faire) cuire en pleine graisse. **'deeply,** *adv.* profondément; to go d. into sth., pénétrer fort avant dans qch. **'deepness,** *s.* 1. profondeur *f*; gravité *f* (d'un son). 2. astuce *f.* **'deep'rooted,** *a.* profondément enraciné. **'deep-'seated,** *a.* profond, enraciné.

deer ['diər], *s.* cerf *m*; fallow d., daim *m.* **'deerskin,** *s.* peau *f* de daim.

deface [di'feis], *v.tr.* défigurer; mutiler. **de'facement,** *s.* mutilation *f.*

defamatory [di'fæmətri], *a.* diffamatoire, diffamant.

default [di'fɔːlt]. I. *s.* 1. (a) manquement *m* (à un engagement); défaut *m*; *Jur:* contumace *f.* 2. *prep.phr:* in d. of, faute de. II. *v.i.* faire défaut; manquer à ses engagements. **de'faulter,** *s.* délinquant, -ante.

defeat [di'fiːt]. I. *s.* 1. défaite *f.* 2. renversement *m* (d'un projet); insuccès *m* (d'une entreprise). II. *v.tr.* 1. battre, vaincre (une armée). 2. renverser; faire échouer (un projet).

defect [di'fekt, 'diː-], *s.* défaut *m*; vice *m* (de construction). **de'fective,** *a.* défectueux.

defence [di'fens], *s.* défense *f*, protection *f*; *Jur:* witness for the d., témoin *m* à décharge. **de'fenceless,** *a.* sans défense. **de'fensive.** 1. *a.* défensif. 2. *s.* défensive *f.*

defend [di'fend], *v.tr.* 1. défendre, protéger (from, against, contre) 2. défendre, justifier (une opinion). **de'fendant,** *a.* & *s.* défendeur, -eresse; *Jur:* accusé, -ée. **de'fender,** *s.* défenseur *m.*

defer [di'fəːr], *v.tr.* ajourner. **de'ferment,** *s.* ajournement *m.*

deference ['def(ə)rns], *s.* déférence *f*; respect *m.* **defe'rential,** *a.* (air, ton) de déférence.

defiance [di'faiəns], *s.* défi *m.* **de'fiant,** *a.* (a) provocant; (air) de défi; (b) intraitable. **-ly,** *adv.* d'un air de défi.

†**deficiency** [di'fiʃənsi], *s.* 1. manque *m*, insuffisance *f.* 2. défaut *m*; imperfection *f.* 3. *Med:* carence *f* (in, of, de). **de'ficient,** *a.* insuffisant, incomplet; to be d. in sth., manquer de qch.

deficit ['defisit], *s.* *Com:* *Fin:* déficit *m.*

defile ['diːfail], *s.* *Geog:* défilé *m.*

define [di'fain], *v.tr.* 1. définir; to d. one's position, préciser son attitude. 2. déterminer; délimiter (un territoire). **'definite,** *a.* 1. défini; bien déterminé. d. answer, réponse catégorique; *Com:* d. order, commande ferme. 2. *Gram:* d. article, article défini; past d., passé

défini. **-ly,** *adv.* décidément. **defi'nition,** *s.* 1. définition *f.* 2. *Rad:* netteté *f* (du son, etc.).

deflate [di'fleit], *v.tr.* dégonfler. **de'flation,** *s.* *Fin:* déflation *f.*

deflect [di'flekt], *v.tr.* détourner; (faire) dévier.

deform [di'fɔːm], *v.tr.* déformer. **de'formed,** *a.* (of pers.) contrefait, difforme. **de'formity,** *s.* difformité *f.*

defraud [di'frɔːd], *v.tr.* 1. frauder (le fisc, etc.). 2. to d. s.o. of sth., escroquer qch. à qn.

defray [di'frei], *v.tr.* to d. s.o.'s expenses, défrayer qn; to d. the cost of sth., couvrir les frais de qch.

de-freeze [di'friːz], *v.tr.* décongeler. **de'freezing,** *s.* décongélation *f.*

defrost [di'frɔst], *v.tr.* dégivrer (un réfrigérateur). **de'froster,** *s.* dégivreur *m.*

deft [deft], *a.* adroit, habile. **-ly,** *adv.* adroitement. **'deftness,** *s.* adresse *f*, dextérité *f.*

defunct [di'fʌŋkt], *a.* défunt; décédé.

defy [di'fai], *v.tr.* défier qn; mettre qn au défi.

degenerate. I. *a.* & *s.* [di'dʒen(ə)rit], dégénéré, -ée. II. *v.i.* [di'dʒenəreit], dégénérer (from, de; into, en); s'abâtardir. **degene'ration,** *s.* dégénérescence *f*, dégénération *f*; abâtardissement *m.*

degrade [di'greid], *v.tr.* dégrader. **de'grading,** *a.* avilissant, dégradant. **degra'dation,** *s.* (a) dégradation *f*; (b) avilissement *m*, abrutissement *m.*

degree [di'griː], *s.* degré *m.* 1. (a) in some d., dans une certaine mesure; to a d., au plus haut degré; by slow degrees, petit à petit, lentement; (a) of humidity, teneur *f* en eau; (b) *Mth: Ph: etc:* degré (d'un cercle, de température). 2. *Sch:* grade *m* (universitaire); he has a d. = il a sa licence.

dehydrate [di'haidreit], *v.tr.* *Ch: Ind:* déshydrater. **dehy'dration,** *s.* déshydratation *f.*

de-ice [di'ais], *v.tr.* *Av: Aut:* dégivrer. **'de-icing,** *s.* dégivrage *m.* **'de-'icer,** *s.* dégivreur *m.*

deign [dein], *v.tr.* (usu. neg.) daigner (faire qch.).

dejected [di'dʒektid], *a.* abattu, déprimé. **-ly,** *adv.* d'un air découragé. **de'jection,** *s.* découragement *m.*

delay [di'lei]. I. *s.* 1. délai *m*, retard *m*; without further d., sans plus tarder. 2. retardement *m.* II. *v.* 1. *v.tr.* (a) retenir, retarder (qn). 2. *v.i.* (a) tarder (in doing sth., à faire qch.); (b) s'attarder. **de'layed,** *a. Phot:* d. action shutter, obturateur *m* à action différée; *Mil:* d. action bomb, bombe *f* à retardement.

delegate ['deligit]. I. *s.* délégué, -ée. II. ['deligeit], *v.tr.* déléguer. dele'gation, *s.* délégation *f.*

delete [di'li:t], *v.tr.* effacer, rayer (un mot). de'letion, *s.* 1. rature *f.*, suppression *f.* 2. passage supprimé.

deliberate. I. *a.* [di'lib(ə)rit] 1. prémédité, voulu; d. insolence, insolence calculée. 2. (of pers.) (a) réfléchi, avisé; (b) lent; d. tread, pas mesuré. -ly, *adv.* 1. à dessein; exprès. 2. (agir) sans hâte, délibérément. II. *v.tr.* & *i.* [di'libəreit] délibérer (on, de, sur). delibe'ration, *s.* 1. (a) délibération *f.*, réflexion *f.*; (b) the deliberations of an assemblée. 2. to act with d., agir posément, après réflexion.

†delicacy ['delikəsi], *s.* délicatesse *f.* 1. (a) finesse *f.* (d'un dessin); (b) d. (of feeling), pudeur *f.* 2. table delicacies, friandises *f.* 'delicate, *a.* délicat; d. feelings, sentiments raffinés; d. situation, situation *f.* difficile. -ly, *adv.* délicatement.

delicatessen ['delikə'tes(ə)n], *s.* plats cuisinés; charcuterie *f.*; d. shop, charcuterie *f.*

delicious [di'liʃəs], *a.* délicieux, exquis. -ly, *adv.* délicieusement.

delight [di'lait]. I. *s.* délices *fpl.* délice *m.* 2. joie *f.* II. *v.* 1. *v.tr.* enchanter, ravir, réjouir (qn). 2. *v.i.* to d. in sth., se délecter à (l'étude), dans (le péché). de'lighted, *a.* enchanté, ravi. de'lightful, *a.* délicieux, ravissant. -fully, *adv.* délicieusement; (chanter, etc.) à ravir.

delinquency [di'liŋkwənsi], *s.* 1. culpabilité *f.*; juvenile d., délinquance juvénile. 2. délit *m.*, faute *f.* de'linquent, *a.* & *s.* 1. délinquant, -ante, coupable (*mf*). 2. *U.S.:* d. taxes, impôts non payés.

delirious [di'liriəs], *a.* (malade) en délire; délirant; d. with joy, fou de joie. de'lirium, *s.* délire *m.*

deliver [di'livər], *v.tr.* 1. délivrer, sauver (s.o. from sth., qn de qch.). 2. to d. s.o., sth. (up, over) to s.o., livrer qn, qch., à qn; to d. up, restituer, rendre (to, à). 3. (a) remettre, livrer (un paquet); distribuer (des lettres); to d. a message, faire une commission; *Com:* delivered free, livraison franco; (b) (of dynamo, etc.) débiter, fournir (du courant). 4. porter, donner (un coup); lancer (une attaque). 5. (a) faire, prononcer (un discours); *Jur:* rendre (un jugement); de'liverance, *s.* délivrance *f* (from, de). de'livery, *s.* 1. *Med:* accouchement *m.* 2. livraison *f* (d'un paquet); distribution *f* (des lettres); *Com:* d. price, prix rendu; d. note, bulletin *m* de livraison; cash on d., payable à livraison.

delta ['deltə], *s.* 1. *Geog:* delta *m.* 2. *Ind:* d. metal, (métal *m*) delta *m.* *Av:* d. wing aircraft, avion *m* aux ailes (en) delta.

delude [di'lu:d], *v.tr.* 1. abuser, tromper (qn); to d. oneself, se faire illusion. 2. duper (qn); en faire accroire à (qn). de'lusion, *s.* illusion *f*; erreur *f*; to be under a d., se faire illusion.

deluge ['delju:dʒ]. I. *s.* déluge *m.* II. *v.tr.* inonder (with, de).

demand [di'mɑ:nd]. I. *s.* 1. demande *f*, réclamation *f*, revendication *f*. 2. *Com:* supply and d., l'offre *f* et la demande. 3. *pl.* I have many demands on my time, je suis très pris. II. *v.tr.* demander, réclamer (qch. à qn); exiger (qch. à qn).

demented [di'mentid], *a.* fou, *f.* folle.

demise [di'maiz], *s.* *Jur:* dispositif *m* antibuée.

demobilize [di:'moubilaiz], *F:* ‡**demob** [di:'mɔb], *v.tr.* *Mil:* démobiliser. de'mobilization, *F:* de'mob, *s.* démobilisation *f.*

democracy [di'mɔkrəsi], *s.* démocratie *f.* people's d., démocratie populaire. 'democrat, *s.* démocrate, *mf.* demo'cratic, *a.* démocratique. -ally, *adv.* démocratiquement.

demolish [di'mɔliʃ], *v.tr.* démolir. demo'lition, *s.* démolition *f.*

demon ['di:mən], *s.* démon *m*, diable *m.*

demonstrate ['demənstreit]. 1. *v.tr.* (a) démontrer (une vérité); (b) décrire, expliquer (un système); *Com:* faire la démonstration (d'une voiture, etc.). 2. *v.i.* *Pol:* manifester. demon'stration, *s.* 1. démonstration *f* (d'une vérité, d'un appareil). 2. *Pol:* manifestation *f.* de'monstrative, *a.* démonstratif. -ly, *adv.* avec effusion. 'demonstrator, *s.* 1. démonstrateur *m.* 2. *Pol:* manifestant *m.*

demoralize [di'mɔrəlaiz], *v.tr.* 1. dépraver, corrompre. 2. démoraliser. demorali'zation, *s.* démoralisation *f.*

‡demur [di'mə:r], *v.i.* faire des difficultés.

den [den], *s.* tanière *f*, repaire *m.*

denial [di'naiəl], *s.* 1. refus *m.* 2. démenti *m* (de la vérité de qch.).

denier ['deniei], *s.* a 15 d. stocking, un bas 15 deniers *mpl.*

denim ['denim], *s.* *Cl:* 1. serge *f* de coton. 2. *Mil:* *pl.* denims, treillis *mpl.*

denomination [dinɔmi'neiʃ(ə)n], *s.* 1. dénomination *f.* 2. *Ecc:* culte *m.* 3. catégorie *f.* de'nominator, *s.* *Mth:* common d., dénominateur commun.

denote [di'nout], *v.tr.* 1. dénoter. 2. signifier.

denounce [di'nauns], *v.tr.* 1. (a) dénoncer (qn à la justice); (b) démasquer (un imposteur). 2. s'élever contre (un abus).

dense [dens], *a.* 1. *Ph:* dense. 2. d. smoke, fumée épaisse; d. crowd, foule compacte. 3. stupide, bête. -ly, *adv.* d. wooded country, pays fortement boisé; d. populated, très peuplé. '**density**, *s.* 1. densité *f.* 2. stupidité *f.*

dent [dent]. I. *s.* marque *f* de coup; bosselure *f*; renfoncement *m.* II. *v.tr.* bosseler, bossuer (qch.).

dentist ['dentist], *s.* dentiste *m* f. '**dental**, *a.* dentaire; d. surgeon, chirurgien dentiste. '**dentistry**, *s.* art *m* dentaire. '**denture**, *s.* dentier *m* f; râtelier *m.*

denude [di'nju:d], *v.tr.* dénuder.

denunciation [dinʌnsi'eiʃ(ə)n], *s.* 1. dénonciation *f.* 2. condamnation *f.*

deny [di'nai], *v.tr.* 1. nier (un fait); démentir (une nouvelle). 2. refuser (de qch.). 3. to d. oneself, se priver (de qch.).

deodorizer [di:'ouдəraizər], *s.* désodorisant *m*, désodorisant *m.*

depart [di'pɑːt], *v.i.* 1. s'en aller, partir. 2. s'écarter (d'une règle). de'**parture**, *s.* 1. départ *m.* 2. a new d., une nouvelle tendance.

department [di'pɑːtmənt], *s.* 1. (a) *Adm:* département *m*; service *m*, bureau *m*; head of a d., chef *m* de service; (b) *Com:* rayon *m*; d. store, grand magasin. 2. *U.S:* State D. = Ministère des Affaires étrangères. de'part'mental, *a.* départemental.

depend [di'pend], *v.i.* 1. dépendre (on, de); that depends, *F:* c'est selon. 2. compter (sur qn); d. upon it, comptez là-dessus. de'**pendable**, *a.* (of pers.) digne de confiance; (of news) sûr, bien fondé. de'**pendants**, *spl.* charges *f* de famille. de'**pendence**, *s.* dépendance *f* (on s.o.). de'**pendency**, *s.* dépendance *f* (on, de); two children, deux enfants à charge; (2) *Gram:* d. clause, proposition subordonnée.

†**depilatory** [di'pilətəri], *a. & s.* dépilatoire (*m*).

deplete [di'pli:t], *v.tr.* épuiser (des provisions, etc.). de'**pletion**, *s.* épuisement *m.*

deplore [di'plɔːr], *v.i.* déplorer; regretter vivement. de'**plorable**, *a.* déplorable, lamentable. -ly, *adv.* lamentablement.

depopulate [di'pɒpjuleit], *v.tr.* dépeupler. depopu'lation, *s.* dépopulation *f*; rural d., exode *m* rural.

deport [di'pɔːt], *v.tr.* (a) expulser (un pays). depor'tation, *s.* (a) expulsion *f* (d'un étranger); (b) déportation (forcée, d'un peuple). 'depor'tee, *s.* déporté, -ée.

deportment [di'pɔːtmənt], *s.* (a) tenue *f*, maintien *m*; (b) conduite *f.*

depose [di'pouz], *v.tr.* déposer (un roi).

deposit [di'pɔzit]. I. *s.* 1. dépôt *m* (en banque). 2. to pay a d., donner des

arrhes *fpl.* 3. dépôt, sédiment *m*; *Aut:* etc: carbon d., calamine *f.* II. *v.tr.* 1. déposer (qch. sur qch.). 2. to d. money, consigner, déposer de l'argent. 3. (of liquid) déposer. de'positor, *s.* déposant, -ante (en banque). de'**pository**, *s.* dépôt *m*, entrepôt *m.*

depot ['depou, *U.S:* 'di:pou], *s.* (a) dépôt *m*; entrepôt *m*; (b) bus d., garage *m* d'autobus; goods d., dépôt de marchandises; (c) *U.S: Rail:* gare *f.*

deprave [di'preiv], *v.tr.* dépraver. de'**pravity**, *s.* dépravation *f.*

deprecate ['deprikeit], *v.tr.* désapprouver; déconseiller (une action). '**deprecating**, *a.* désapprobateur. 'depre'cation, *s.* désapprobation *f.*

depreciate [di'pri:ʃieit]. 1. *v.tr.* déprécier. 2. *v.i.* se déprécier; (of shares) baisser. depreci'ation, *s.* dépréciation *f.*

depress [di'pres], *v.tr.* 1. abaisser; baisser(qn); appuyer sur (la pédale). 2. décourager (qn, le commerce); attrister. de'**pressed**, *a.* triste, abattu; to feel d., *F:* avoir le cafard. de'**pressing**, *a.* attristant, déprimant. de'**pression**, *s.* 1. abaissement *m* (de qch.). 2. *Meteo:* dépression *f*, cyclone *m.* 3. creux *m* (de terrain). 4. crise *f* (économique); marasme *m* (des affaires). 5. découragement *m.*

deprive [di'praiv], *v.tr.* priver (qn de qch.).

depth [depθ], *s.* 1. (a) profondeur *f*; (b) fond *m*, hauteur *f* (de l'eau); to get out of one's d., (i) perdre pied; (ii) sortir de sa compétence; (c) épaisseur *f* (d'une couche). 2. (a) gravité *f* (d'un son); (b) intensité *f* (de coloris). 3. fond (d'une forêt); milieu *m* (de la nuit); in the d. of winter, au plus fort de l'hiver. 4. *pl.* the depths of despair, le plus profond désespoir. '**depth-charge**, *s. Nau:* grenade *f* sous-marine. '**depth-finder**, *s. Nau:* sonic d.-f., sondeur *m* sonore.

depute [di'pjuːt], *v.tr.* députer, déléguer (qn pour faire qch.). depu'tation, *s.* députation *f*, délégation *f.* '**deputize**, *v.i.* to d. for s.o., remplacer qn. †'**deputy**, *s.* substitut *m*; délégué *m*; d. chairman, vice-président *m*; d. mayor, (maire *m*) adjoint *m.*

derail [di'reil], *v.tr.* (faire) dérailler (un train). de'**railment**, *s.* déraillement *m.*

derange [di'reindʒ], *v.tr.* déranger. de'**rangement**, *s.* dérèglement *m.*

derelict ['derilikt]. 1. *a.* abandonné, à l'abandon. 2. *s.* navire abandonné; épave *f.*

deride [di'raid], *v.tr.* tourner en dérision; railler, se moquer de (qn). de'**rision**, *s.* dérision *f*; object of d., objet *m* de risée. de'**risive**, *a.* moqueur. -ly, *adv.* d'un air moqueur.

derive [di'raiv], v.tr. & i. 1. tirer (son origine) de qch.; devoir (son bonheur) à qch.; trouver (du plaisir) à qch.; income derived from investment, revenu provenant de placements. 2. to be derived, v.i. to derive, (pro-) venir (from, de). deri'vation, s. dérivation f. de'rivative, a. & s. Gram: Ch: Ind: dérivé (m); Mth: dérivée (f).

dermatology [dəːmə'tɔlədʒi], s. Med: dermatologie f. derma'tologist, s. dermatologiste mf, dermatologue mf.

derogatory [di'rɔgət(ə)ri], a. dérogeant, qui déroge (to, à).

derv [dəːv], s. gas-oil m, gaz-oil m.

descend [di'send], 1. v.i. (a) descendre (of rain) tomber; (b) s'abaisser; (c) (of property) passer (de qn à qn). 2. v.tr. descendre (l'escalier). de'scendant, s. descendant, -ante; pl. descendants, postérité f. de'scent, s. 1. descente f. 2. descendance f.

describe [dis'kraib], v.tr. 1. (a) décrire, dépeindre; (b) to d. s.o. as . . ., qualifier qn de . . . 2. décrire (une courbe). des'cription, s. 1. description f; signalement m; désignation f (de marchandises). 2. sorte f, espèce f. des'criptive, a. descriptif.

desert[1] [di'zəːt], s. (usu. pl.) mérite(s) m; to get one's deserts, avoir ce que l'on mérite.

desert[2] ['dezət], a. & s. désert (m).

desert[3] [di'zəːt], v.tr. (a) Mil: déserter; (b) abandonner, délaisser (qn). de-serted, a. (of place) désert; (of pers.) abandonné. de'serter, s. Mil: déserteur m. de'sertion, s. 1. abandon m, délaissement m. 2. Mil: désertion f; Pol: défection f.

deserve [di'zəːv], v.tr. mériter (qch.). de'servedly [di'zəːvidli], adv. à juste titre.

design [di'zain], I. s. 1. dessein m, intention f, projet m. 2. Ind: dessin m; étude f, avant-projet m (d'une machine, etc.). II. v.tr. préparer (un projet); créer (une robe); établir un plan; étudier, calculer. de'signing, I. a. intrigant. II. s. dessin m (d'une machine). designedly [di'zainidli], adv. à dessein. de'signer, s. Com: dessinateur, -trice; décorateur, -trice.

desire [di'zaiər], I. s. 1. désir m, souhait m; envie f. 2. at s.o.'s d., à la demande de qn. II. v.tr. désirer (qch.); avoir envie de (qch.). de'sirable, a. désirable; à désirer; souhaitable; avantageux.

desk [desk], s. 1. (school) pupitre m; (office) bureau m. 2. pay at the d.! payez à la caisse!

desolate I. a. ['desɔlit] 1. (lieu) désert. 2. affligé. II. ['desəleit], v.tr. 1. ravager (un pays). 2. affliger (qn). deso'lation, s. désolation f.

despair [dis'pɛər]. I. s. désespoir m. in d., au désespoir; to drive s.o. to d., désespérer qn. II. v.i. (a) désespérer (de faire qch.); (b) perdre espoir, (se) désespérer. des'pairing, a. déses-péré. -ly, adv. en désespéré.

desperate ['desp(ə)rit], a. 1. (of condition) désespéré. 2. (a) a d. man, un désespéré; (b) d. conflict, combat acharné. -iy, adv. 1. (lutter) avec acharnement. 2. d. ill, gravement malade. despe'ration, s. in d., au désespoir.

despise [dis'paiz], v.tr. (a) mépriser (qn); (b) dédaigner (qch.). des'picable, a. méprisable. -ably, adv. bassement.

despite [dis'pait], prep. en dépit de (qch.).

despondency [dis'pɔndənsi], s. abatte-ment m. des'pondent, a. découragé, déprimé. -ly, adv. d'un air découragé.

despot ['despɔt], s. tyran m, des'potic, a. 1. (pouvoir) despotique. 2. (of pers.) arbitraire, tyrannique. -ally, adv. despotiquement. 'despotism, s. des-potisme m.

dessert [di'zəːt], s. (a) dessert m; (b) entremets m sucré; d. spoon, cuiller f à dessert.

destination [desti'neiʃ(ə)n], s. destina-tion f.

destine ['destin], v.tr. destiner (for, à). 'destiny, s. destin m, destinée f; sort m.

destitute ['destitjut], a. 1. dépourvu, dénué (of, de). 2. indigent; sans ressources.

destroy [dis'trɔi], v.tr. détruire; anéantir; tuer (une bête). des'troying, a. destructeur. des'troyer, s. 1. des-tructeur, -trice. 2. Nau: destroyer m.

destruction [dis'trʌkʃ(ə)n], s. destruc-tion f. des'tructive, a. destructif; a d. child, un prise-tout inr. des'truc-tiveness, s. 1. pouvoir m destructeur. 2. penchant m à détruire.

desultory ['desəlt(ə)ri], a. décousu; sans suite; (conversation) à bâtons rompus.

detach [di'tætʃ], v.tr. détacher, séparer (from, de). de'tached, a. 1. détaché; d. house, maison séparée. 2. (of pers.) désintéressé; d. manner, manière désinvolte. de'tachable, a. détachable, amovible. de'tachment, s. 1. sépara-tion f (from, de); décollement m. 2. détachement m; indifférence f.

detail ['diːteil]. I. s. détail m, parti-cularité f. II. v.tr. détailler; raconter en détail; énumérer (les faits); affecter (qn) à un service.

detain [di'tein], v.tr. 1. détenir (qn en prison). 2. retenir (qn); empêcher (qn) de partir. detain'ee, s. Jur: détenu, -ue.

detect [di'tekt], v.tr. 1. découvrir (le coupable). 2. détecter; discerner. de'tection, s. 1. découverte f; to escape d., passer inaperçu. **Rad: etc:** détection *f.* de'tective, *s.* agent *m* de la Sûreté; private d., détective *m.* 2. story, roman policier. de'tector, *s.* **Mil:** mine d., détecteur *m* de mines.

detention [di'tenʃ(ə)n], *s.* 1. détention *f* (en prison). 2. retard *m* (inévitable); arrêt *m.*

‡deter [di'təːr], *v.tr.* détourner, décourager (qn de faire qch.).

detergent [di'təːdʒənt], *a. & s.* détersif (*m*), détergent (*m*); lessive *f.*

deteriorate [di'tiəriəreit], *v.i.* (*a*) (se) détériorer; (*b*) (*of race*) dégénérer. deterio'ration, *s.* détérioration *f*; dégénération *f.*

determine [di'təːmin], *v.tr. & i.* 1. (*a*) déterminer, fixer (une date, des conditions); (*b*) constater (un fait). 2. décider (qch.). 3. **Jur:** résoudre (un contrat). de'termined, *a.* (*of pers.*) déterminé, résolu. -ly, *adv.* résolument. determi'nation, *s.* (*of pers.*) détermination *f*, résolution *f.* 2. décision *f* (d'une affaire).

deterrent [di'terənt], *s.* **Mil: Pol:** arme *f* de dissuasion; to act as a d., exercer un effet préventif.

detest [di'test], *v.tr.* détester. de'testable, *a.* détestable.

detonate ['detəneit], *v.tr.* faire détoner, faire sauter (une mine). deto'nation, *s.* détonation *f*, explosion *f.* 'detonator, *s.* détonateur *m*; amorce *f.*

detour ['deituər], *s.* détour *m.*

detractor [di'træktər], *s.* détracteur -trice.

detriment ['detrimənt], *s.* détriment *m*; to the d. of . ., au préjudice de. detri'mental, *a.* nuisible (to, à). -ally, *adv.* nuisiblement.

deuce [djuːs], *s.* 1. (*of dice, cards*) deux *m.* 2. (*at tennis*) à deux; égalité *f* (à quarante).

deuterium [dju(ː)'tiəriəm], *s.* **Atom. Ph:** deutérium *m.*

devalue [diː'vælju], *v.tr.* dévaluer, dévaloriser (une monnaie). devalu'ation, *s.* dévaluation *f.*

devastate ['devəsteit], *v.tr.* dévaster, ravager. 'devastating, *a.* 1. (*of storm*) dévastateur (*argument*) accablant; **F:** (charme) fatal. -ly, *adv.* **F:** d. funny, d'un comique à se tordre. deva'station, *s.* dévastation *f.*

develop [di'veləp]. 1. *v.tr.* (*a*) développer, amplifier (ses pensées). (*b*) to d. a district, exploiter une région; (*a*) engendrer (de la chaleur); (*b*) contracter (une maladie); (*e*) **Phot:** développer. 2. *v.i. a*) se développer; (*b*) se manifester. de'veloping, *s.* 1. développement *m*; mise *f* en valeur (d'une région). 2. **Phot:** développement *m.* de'veloper, *s.* **Phot:** révélateur *m.* de'velopment, *s.* 1. développement *m* (des facultés);

retarded d., infantilisme *m.* 2. exploitation *f.* (d'une région). 3. déroulement *m* (des événements).

deviate ['diːvieit], *v.i.* dévier, s'écarter (from, de). devi'ation, *s.* déviation *f* (from, de); écart *m.*

device [di'vais], *s.* 1. (*a*) expédient *m*; (*b*) stratagème *m*, ruse *f.* 2. dispositif *m*, appareil *m*; **F:** truc *m.* 3. emblème *m*, devise *f.*

devil ['devl], *s.* diable *m*; démon *m*; to go to the d., se ruiner; to work like the d., travailler avec acharnement; how the d. . .? comment diable . . .? 'devilish, *a.* (*a* diabolique; (*b*) maudit, satané. -ly, *adv.* 1. diaboliquement. 2. **F:** bigrement. 'devilment, 'devilry, *s.* 1. méchanceté *f*; there's some d. afoot, il se trame qch. 2. to be full of d., avoir le diable au corps. 'devil-may-'care, *a.* (esprit) (i) téméraire, (ii) insouciant.

devious ['diːviəs], *a.* détourné, tortueux.

devise [di'vaiz], *v.tr.* combiner (un projet); imaginer, tramer (un complot).

devote [di'vout], *v.tr.* vouer, consacrer (du temps à qch.); to d. oneself to sth., se vouer à, s'adonner à (l'étude). de'voted, *a.* dévoué, attaché (to, à). -ly, *adv.* avec dévouement. de'votion, *s.* 1. dévotion *f* (à Dieu). 2. dévouement *m* (to à, pour qn); to d. to work, assiduité *f* au travail.

devour [di'vauər], *v.tr.* dévorer.

devout [di'vaut], *a.* 1. dévot, pieux. 2. (*of wish*) fervent, sincère. -ly, *adv.* 1. avec dévotion. 2. sincèrement.

dew [djuː], *s.* rosée *f.* 'dewdrop, *s.* (*a*) goutte *f* de rosée; (*b*) **F:** roupie *f.*

dexterity [deks'teriti], *s.* dextérité *f*; habileté *f.* 'dext(e)rous, *a.* adroit, habile. -ly, *adv.* avec dextérité; habilement.

diabetes [daiə'biːtiːz], *s.* **Med:** diabète *m.* dia'betic, *a. & s.* diabétique (*mf*).

diabolical [daiə'bolik(ə)l], *a.* diabolique. -ally, *adv.* diaboliquement.

diagnose ['daiəgnouz], *v.tr.* diagnostiquer. diag'nosis, *s.* diagnostic *m.*

diagonal [dai'ægənl]. 1. *a.* diagonal. 2. *s.* diagonale *f.* -ally, *adv.* diagonalement, en diagonale.

diagram ['daiəgræm], *s.* 1. diagramme *m*, tracé *m*, schéma *m.* 2. graphique *m* (de pression, etc.).

dial ['daiəl]. 1. *s.* cadran *m.* II. ‡*v.tr.* **P.T.T:** appeler (qn) à l'automatique; composer un numéro; to d. 999, appeler Police Secours. 'dialling, *s.* composition *f* du numéro; d. tone, tonalité *f* continue.

dialect ['daiəlekt], *s.* dialecte *m.*

dialogue ['daiəlog], *s.* dialogue *m.*

diameter [dai'æmitər], *s.* diamètre *m.* dia'metrical, *a.* diamétral. -ally, *adv.* diamétralement.

diamond ['daiəmənd], s. 1. diamant *m*; cutting d., diamant de vitrier. 2. (*at cards*) carreau *m*; Sp: U.S: terrain *m* de baseball, d.-shaped, en losange.

diaphragm ['daiəfræm], s. diaphragme *m*.

diarrhoea [daiə'ri:ə], s. diarrhée *f*.

†**diary** ['daiəri], s. 1. journal *m* (intime). 2. desk d., bloc *m* calendrier. 'diarist, s. auteur *m* d'un journal (particulier).

dice [dais], s.pl. dés *m* (à jouer).

dictaphone ['diktəfoun], s. R.t.m: dictaphone *m*.

dictate [dik'teit], s. 1. v.tr. dicter (une lettre, etc.). 2. v.i. faire la loi. dic'tation, s. dictée *f*. dic'tator, s. Pol: dictateur *m*. dicta'torial, a. 1. (pouvoir) dictatorial. 2. (ton) impérieux.

†**dictionary** ['dikʃ(ə)nri], s. dictionnaire *m*.

diddle ['didl], v.tr. 1. P: rouler, carotter (qn). 2. U.S: to d. (away) (time, etc.) flâner.

die[1] [dai], s. 1. (*minting*) coin *m*. 2. matrice *f*. 'die-casting, s. moulage *m* mécanique.

die[2], v.i. 1. mourir; (*of animals*) crever; to be dying, être à l'agonie. 2. to d. of laughing, mourir de rire; I'm dying of thirst, je meurs de soif; to be dying to do sth., brûler d'envie de faire qch. die a'way, o.i. (*of sound*) s'affaiblir; s'éteindre. die 'down, o.i. (*of fire*) baisser; (*of wind*) s'apaiser; se calmer. 'die'hard, s. réactionnaire endurci. die 'out, o.i. (*of custom*) disparaître; (*of race*) s'éteindre.

diesel ['di:z(ə)l], a. & s. d. (oil), gaz-oil *m*; d. (engine), (locomotive *f*) diesel; (in) (moteur *m*) diesel.

diet ['daiət], s. I. s. 1. nourriture *f*, régime *m*. II. v.tr. mettre (qn) au régime; to d. (oneself), se mettre au régime. 'die'tetics, s.pl. diététique *f*. 'die'tician, s. diététicien, -ienne.

differ ['difər], v.i. 1. différer (from, de); être différent. 2. to d. about sth., ne pas s'accorder sur qch.

difference ['difr(ə)ns], s. 1. différence *f*, écart *m* (between, entre); to see the d., saisir la nuance; with a slight d., à peu de chose près; it makes no d., cela ne fait rien. 2. to split the d., partager la différend. 3. dispute *f*; settle your differences, mettez-vous d'accord. 'different, a. 1. différent (from, de); that's quite a d. matter, ça, c'est une autre affaire. 2. divers, différent; at d. times, à diverses reprises. -ly, adv. 1. différemment. 2. diversement.

differentiate [difə'renʃieit], v.tr. différencier (sth. from sth., qch. de qch.).

difficult ['difikəlt], a. difficile, malaisé, pénible; (*of pers.*) peu commode; d. to get on with, difficile à vivre.

†**difficulty** ['difikəlti], s. 1. difficulté *f*. 2. obstacle *m*; I see no d., je ne vois pas d'inconvénient. 3. embarras *m*; (*money*) difficulties, soucis *mpl* d'argent.

diffidence ['difidəns], s. 1. manque *m* d'assurance; modestie excessive. 'diffident, a. qui manque d'assurance, hésitant. -ly, adv. timidement, en hésitant.

diffraction [di'frækʃ(ə)n], s. Ph: diffraction *f*.

diffuse. [di'fju:z]. 1. v.tr. répandre; diffuser. 2. (*of light*) se diffuser.

dig [dig]. I. s. 1. (*a*) to give s.o. a d. in the ribs, pousser qn du coude; (*b*) to have a d. at s.o., lancer un sarcasme à qn. 2. a(n archaeological) d., une fouille (d'intérêt archéologique). II. ‡v. 1. v.tr. (*a*) bêcher, retourner (la terre); (*b*) creuser (un trou). 2. enfoncer (qch. dans qch.). 3. v.i. (*a*) F: loger en garni; (*b*) faire des fouilles (archéologiques) 'digger, s. 1 bêcheur *m*; terrassier *m*; fouilleur *m* (de monuments); Austr: P: Australien *m*. 2. Agr: plantoir *m*; (potato-)d., arracheuse *f* (de pommes). dig 'in, 1. v.tr. enterrer (le fumier). 2. v.r. to d. oneself in (to a place), s'incruster. dig 'up, v.tr. déraciner (une plante); mettre à jour (un trésor); piocher (la terre); déterrer (un corps). 'digging, s. (*a*) bêchage *m*; excavation *f*; (*b*) fouilles *fpl.* digs, s.pl. F: logement *m*; to live in d., loger en garni.

digest. I. s. ['daidʒest] sommaire *m*, abrégé *m*. II. v.tr. [di'dʒest] 1. (*a*) mettre en ordre (des faits); (*b*) résumer (un compte rendu). 2. digérer (les aliments). di'gestible, a. digestible. di'gestion, s. digestion *f*; to spoil one's d., s'abîmer l'estomac. di'gestive, a. digestif.

dignify ['dignifai], v.tr. donner de la dignité à (qch.). 'dignified, a. plein de dignité; (air) digne. 'dignitary, s. dignitaire *m*. 'dignity, s. dignité *f*.

digress [dai'gres], v.i. faire une digression (from, de); s'écarter (du sujet). di'gression, s. digression *f*, écart *m*.

dike [daik], s. see DYKE.

dilapidated [di'læpideitid], a. délabré.

dilapidation [dilæpi'deiʃ(ə)n], s. délabrement *m*, dégradation *f* (d'une maison).

dilatory ['dilət(ə)ri], a. lent (à agir); (*of action*) tardif.

dilemma [di'lemə], s. embarras *m*.

diligence ['dilidʒəns], s. assiduité *f*, diligence *f*. 'diligent, a. assidu, diligent. -ly, adv. avec assiduité, diligemment.

dilute [dai'lju:t], v.tr. 1. diluer; arroser, couper (le vin). 2. atténuer (une doctrine). 3. délaver, délayer (une couleur).

dim [dim]. I. a. (of light) faible, pâle; (of memory) vague; F: to take a d. view of (sth.), avoir une piètre opinion de (qch.); he's a d. sort of chap, c'est un mou. **-ly**, adv. faiblement; vaguement; confusément. II. †v. 1. v.tr. (a) obscurcir; ternir (un miroir); (b) Aut: U.S: to d. the headlights, mettre les phares en code. 2. v.i. (of light) baisser; (of outlines) s'effacer. **'dim-wit**, s. F: idiot m, andouille f.

dimension [di'menʃ(ə)n], s. dimension f; Ind: cote f. d'mensional, a. two-, three-d., à deux, à trois, dimensions.

diminish [di'miniʃ]. I. v.tr. diminuer; amoindrir. 2. v.i. diminuer; aller en diminuant. **dim'nution**, s. diminution f; amoindrissement m. **di'minutive**, a. 1. a. & s. Gram: diminutif m. 2. a. tout petit; minuscule.

din [din], s. tapage m, vacarme m.

dine [dain], v.i. dîner; to d. out, dîner (i) en ville; (ii) chez des amis. **'diner**, s.1. dîneur, -euse. 2. Rail: (also 'dining car), wagon-restaurant m. **'dining-room**, s. salle f à manger. **di'nette**, s. coin-repas m (dans un studio, etc.).

dinghy ['diŋ(g)i], s. canot m, youyou m; rubber d., canot pneumatique.

dingy ['dindʒi], a. défraîchi; terne. **'dinginess**, s. propreté f douteuse.

dinner ['dinər], s. dîner m. public d., banquet m; to be at d., être à table; d. jacket, smoking m; d. party, dîner (prié) m; d. service, service m de table.

dint [dint], s. by d. of, à force de.

dip [dip]. 1. s. 1. immersion f (de qch. dans un liquide). 2. plongée f (du terrain). 3. F: baignade f. II. p. 1. v.tr. (a) plonger, tremper (qch. dans l'eau); F: to d. one's hand into one's pocket, débourser; (b) Aut: to d. the headlights, se mettre en code; (c) Nau: Av: abs. to d. (one's flag, one's wings), saluer. 2. v.i. (a) plonger (dans l'eau); (b) (of sun) baisser; (c) to d. into a book, feuilleter (un livre); d. puiser (dans sa bourse). **'dipping**, s. immersion f; Ind: dérochage m; décapage m. **'dipstick**, s. Aut: jauge f d'huile.

diphtheria [dif'θiəria], s. diphtérie f.

diploma [di'plouma], s. diplôme m.

diplomacy [di'ploumasi], s. diplomatie f. **'diplomat**, **di'plomatist**, s. diplomate m. **diplo'matic**, a. 1. diplomatique; the d. service, la diplomatie, F: la carrière. 2. adroit, prudent; d. answer, réponse f politique. **-ally**, adv. 1. diplomatiquement. 2. avec tact.

dippy ['dipi], a. P: cinglé, timbré, toqué.

dipsomania [dipsou'meinia], s. dipsomanie f. **'dipso'maniac**, **'dipso**, a. & s. dipsomane (mf).

dire ['daiər], a. désastreux, néfaste; d. necessity, nécessité f implacable; in d. distress, dans la dernière misère.

direct [dai'rekt, di-]. I. v.tr. 1. gérer, régir (une entreprise). 2. (a) attirer (l'attention de qn sur qch.); (b) to d. one's efforts to(wards) an end, orienter ses efforts vers un but. 3. could you d. me to the station? pourriez-vous m'indiquer le chemin de la gare? 4. to d. s.o. to do sth., ordonner à qn de faire qch.; as directed, selon les instructions. II. 1. a. (a) direct; d. cause, cause immédiate; d. taxation, contributions directes; Gram: d. object, complément direct; (of pers.) franc, f. franche; (c) (réponse) absolue, catégorique. 2. adv. (aller) directement, tout droit. **-ly**, 1. adv. (a) to go d. to the point, aller droit au fait; (b) absolument; d. opposite the church, juste en face de l'église; (c) (of time) tout de suite, tout à l'heure. 2. conj. aussitôt que, dès que. **di'rectness**, s. franchise f (d'une réponse).

direction [dai'rekʃ(ə)n, di-], s. 1. direction f, administration f (d'une société). 2. direction, sens m. 4. pl. instruction(s) f (pl); directions for use, mode f d'emploi.

director [dai'rektər, di-], s. (pers.) administrateur m, directeur m (d'une société); gérant m (d'une entreprise); Board of Directors, conseil m d'administration. Th: Cin: metteur m en scène. **di'rectorate**, s. (conseil m d')administration. **di'rectory**, s. 1. annuaire m (des téléphones). U.S: conseil m d'administration.

dirge [dəːdʒ], s. chant m funèbre.

dirt [dəːt], s. saleté f. 1. boue f, crotte f, ordure f; it's d. cheap, c'est pour trois fois rien. 2. malpropreté f. **'dirt-farmer**, s. U.S: exploitant m agricole. **'dirtiness**, s. 1. saleté f. 2. (of speech) grossièreté f (of action) bassesse f. **'dirt-track**, s. Sp: piste f en cendrée. **'dirty**, I. a. 1. sale, malpropre, crasseux; crotté. 2. d. weather, mauvais temps; Nau: gros temps. 3. a d. trick, un vilain tour; F: to do the d. on s.o., jouer un sale coup à qn. **-ily**, adv. salement. II. v. 1. v.tr. salir, encrasser (qch.); se salir (les mains). 2. v.i. to d. easily, se salir facilement.

disability [disə'biliti], s. (a) incapacité f; (b) physical d., infirmité f; (c) Adm: invalidité f.

disable [dis'eibl], v.tr. mettre hors de combat; estropier (qn). **dis'ablement**, s. 1. mise f hors de combat. 2. invalidité f; incapacité f de travail.

disadvantage [disəd'vɑːntidʒ], s. 1. désavantage m, inconvénient m. to be at a d., être pris au dépourvu. **dis-advan'tageous**, a. désavantageux, défavorable.

disagree [disə'gri:], v.i. 1. (a) être en désaccord, ne pas être en accord (with, avec); (b) donner tort (à qn). 2. (quarrel) se brouiller (with s.o., avec qn). 3. (of climate, etc.) ne pas convenir (à qn). dis'agreeable, a. (of pers., thing) désagréable; (incident) fâcheux. -ably, adv. désagréablement, fâcheusement. dis'agreement, s. 1. différence f (between, entre). 2. désaccord m (with s.o. about sth., avec qn sur qch.). 3. querelle f, brouille f.

disappear [disə'piər], v.i. disparaître. disa'ppearance, s. disparition f.

disappoint [disə'point], v.tr. (a) désappointer (qn); (b) décevoir, chagriner (qn); (c) tromper (les espérances, l'attente, de qn). disa'ppointing, a. décevant. disa'ppointment, s. déception f.

disapproval [disə'pru:v(ə)l], s. désapprobation f (of, de). disa'pprove, v.i. to d. of sth., désapprouver qch. disa'pproving, a. (regard) désapprobateur. -ly, adv. d'un air, d'un ton désapprobateur.

disarm [dis'ɑ:m], v.tr. & i. désarmer. dis'arming, a. (franchise, etc.) qui vous désarme. dis'armament, s. Pol: désarmement.

disarrange [disə'reindʒ], v.tr. déranger, mettre (qch.) en désordre. disa'rrangement, s. dérangement m; désordre m.

disaster [di'zɑ:stər], s. désastre m; (by fire, flood, etc.) sinistre m. dis'astrous, a. désastreux; funeste. -ly, adv. désastreusement.

disbelieve [disbi'li:v], 1. v.tr. ne pas croire (qch.). 2. v.i. ne pas croire (in sth. à qch.). disbe'lief, s. incrédulité f. disbe'liever, s. incrédule m, f.

disc [disk], s. (a) disque m; (b) rondelle f; Mus: disque (pour tourne-disque); Rad: d. jockey, présentateur m (de disques); Med: slipped d., hernie f discale; Aut: wheel d., enjoliveur m; d. brake, frein m à disque; d. clutch, embrayage à disques.

discard [dis'kɑ:d], v.tr. 1. (at bridge) se défausser d'une couleur). 2. mettre (qch.) de côté, se défaire de (qch.); abandonner, renoncer à (un projet).

discern [di'sərn], v.tr. distinguer, discerner. di'scerning, a. (of pers.) judicieux; (of intelligence) pénétrant; (of taste) sûr. di'scernment, s. discernement m.

discharge ['distʃɑ:dʒ]. I. s. 1. déchargement m. 2. (a) décharge f, déversement m (d'eau); débit m (d'une pompe); d. pipe, tuyau m de vidange; (b) El: décharge. 3. renvoi m (d'un employé). 4. Jur: mise f en liberté (d'un prisonnier); acquittement m (d'un accusé). 5. (a) paiement m (d'une dette); (b) quittance f. II. v. [dis'tʃɑ:dʒ] 1. v.tr. (a) décharger (un navire); (b) El: décharger; (c) congédier (un employé); (d) Jur: libérer; acquitter; (e) Med: (of wound) suppurer; (f) régler, solder (une dette). 2. v.i. se décharger.

disciple [di'saipl], s. disciple m.

discipline ['disiplin], s. discipline f.

disclose [dis'klouz], v.tr. révéler (qch.); divulguer (un secret). dis'closure, s. révélation f; divulgation f.

discolour [dis'kʌlər], v.tr.& i. décolorer; (b) ternir, délaver (un tissu). disco'u)ration, s. décoloration f.

discomfort [dis'kʌmfət], s. (a) manque m de confort; (b) malaise m, gêne f.

disconcert [diskən'sə:t], v.tr. déconcerter, interloquer. discon'certing, a. déconcertant, troublant.

disconnect [diskə'nekt], v.tr. 1. désunir, séparer, détacher (qch. de qch.); décrocher (des wagons). 2. El: débrancher (une prise); (of telephone) couper la communication. discon'nected, a. 1. (a) détaché, isolé; (b) El: débranché, coupé. 2. (of speech) décousu. -ly, adv. (parler) à bâtons rompus.

disconsolate [dis'kɔnsəlit], a. inconsolable; désolé. -ly, adv. tristement.

discontent [diskən'tent], s. mécontentement m. discon'tented, a. mécontent (with, de); peu satisfait. -ly, adv. avec mécontentement.

discontinue [diskən'tinju:]. 1. v.tr. discontinuer (qch.); cesser. 2. v.i. cesser.

discord ['diskɔ:d], s. 1. discorde f, désunion f. 2. Mus: dissonance f; accord dissonant. dis'cordant, a. 1. (of sound) discordant; Mus: dissonant. 2. (opinions) opposées.

discount ['diskaunt]. I. s. 1. remise f, ristourne f, rabais m. 2. escompte m. II. v.tr. [dis'kaunt] 1. Com: escompter (un effet). 2. (a) ne pas tenir compte de (qch.); (b) faire peu de cas de (l'avis de qn).

discourage [dis'kʌridʒ], v.tr. décourager (qn). dis'couraging, a. décourageant. -ly, adv. d'une manière décourageante. dis'couragement, s. découragement m.

discourteous [dis'kə:tiəs], a. impoli. dis'courtesy, s. impolitesse f.

discover [dis'kʌvər], v.tr. découvrir, trouver. dis'coverer, s. découvreur, -euse. †dis'covery, s. découverte f; voyage of d., voyage m d'exploration; F: (of a find) trouvaille f.

discredit [dis'kredit], v.tr. 1. ne pas croire (un bruit); mettre en doute (un bruit). 2. discréditer (une opinion); déconsidérer (qn). dis'creditable, a. peu digne. -ably, adv. de façon indigne, déshonorante.

discreet [dis'kri:t], a. 1. avisé, sage. 2. discret. -ly, adv. 1. avec réserve. 2. discrètement. dis'cretion, s. 1. discrétion f. 2. sagesse f, jugement m.

discrepancy [dis'krepənsi], s. désaccord m; divergence f (de témoignage).

discriminate [dis'krimineit]. 1. v.tr. distinguer (from, de, d'avec). 2. v.i. distinguer, discriminer (between, entre). 3. discriminating purchaser, acheteur avisé; Adm: discriminating tariff, tarif m différentiel. discrimi'nation, s. 1. discernement m. 2. jugement m, discrimination f. 3. distinction f (discriminatoire); préférence f; racial d., discrimination raciale.

discuss [dis'kʌs], v.tr. discuter, débattre (un problème); délibérer (d'une question); agiter (une question). dis'cussion, s. discussion f; oral d., débat m.

disdain [dis'dein]. I. s. dédain m (of, de). II. v.tr. dédaigner. dis'dainful, a. dédaigneux (of, de). -fully, adv. dédaigneusement.

disease [di'zi:z], s. maladie f; mal m. di'seased, a. 1. malade. 2. morbide.

disembark [disem'bɑːk], v.tr. & i. débarquer. disembar'kation, s. débarquement m.

disenchantment [disin'tʃɑːntmənt], s. désenchantement m; désillusion f.

disengage [disin'geidʒ]. 1. v.tr. dégager (qch. de qch.). 2. v.i. se dégager; se déclencher. disen'gaged, a. libre, inoccupé.

disentangle [disin'tæŋgl], v.tr. démêler.

disfavour [dis'feivər], s. défaveur f; to fall into d., tomber en disgrâce.

disfigure [dis'figər], v.tr. défigurer; enlaidir (un visage, le paysage). dis'figurement, s. défiguration f; enlaidissement m.

disgorge [dis'gɔːdʒ], v.tr. dégorger, rendre (des objets volés).

disgrace [dis'greis]. I. s. 1. disgrâce f. 2. honte f, déshonneur m. II. v.tr. disgracier (un ministre); déshonorer (qn). dis'graceful, a. honteux, déshonorant, scandaleux. -fully, adv. honteusement.

disgruntled [dis'grʌntld], a. contrarié, mécontent (at, de); maussade.

disguise [dis'gaiz]. I. s. 1. déguisement m. in d., déguisé. 2. feinte f; fausse apparence f. II. v.tr. 1. déguiser, travestir (qn). 2. déguiser (sa pensée); masquer (une odeur); dissimuler (ses sentiments).

disgust [dis'gʌst]. I. s. 1. dégoût m (at, towards, pour). 2. profond mécontentement; écœurement m. II. v.tr. dégoûter; écœurer (qn). dis'gusting, a. dégoûtant; répugnant; écœurant.

dish [diʃ]. I. v.tr. 1. to d. up, servir (le repas). 2. F: to d. s.o., rouler, enfoncer qn; he's dished! il est flambé! II. s. 1. plat m; vegetable d., légumier

m. 2. plat (de viande, etc.); mets m. 'dishcloth, s. torchon m. 'dishwater, s. eau f (de vaisselle); F: (thin soup, etc.) lavasse f.

dishearten [dis'hɑːtn], v.tr. décourager, abattre. dis'heartening, a. décourageant; (travail) ingrat.

dishevelled [di'ʃev(ə)ld], a. 1. échevelé. 2. aux vêtements chiffonnés.

dishonesty [dis'ɔnisti], s. improbité f; piece of d., malhonnêteté f. dis'honest, a. malhonnête. -ly, adv. malhonnêtement.

dishonour [dis'ɔnər]. I. s. déshonneur m. II. v.tr. déshonorer. dis'honourable, a. 1. (of pers.) sans honneur. 2. (of action) honteux, indigne. -ably, adv. d'une façon peu honorable.

disillusion [disi'lju:ʒ(ə)n]. I. s. désillusion f. II. v.tr. désillusionner, désabuser.

disinclination [disinkli'neiʃ(ə)n], s. répugnance f, aversion f (for, to, pour). disinclined [disin'klaind], a. peu disposé (à faire qch.).

disinfect [disin'fekt], v.tr. désinfecter. disin'fectant, a. & s. désinfectant (m). disin'fection, s. désinfection f.

disinherit [disin'herit], v.tr. déshériter.

disintegrate [dis'intigreit]. 1. v.tr. désagréger; effriter. 2. v.i. se désagréger. disinte'gration, s. désagrégation f.

disinterested [dis'intərestid], a. désintéressé. -ly, adv. avec désintéressement.

disjointed [dis'dʒɔintid], a. disjoint, (discours) sans suite.

disk [disk], s. see DISC.

dislike [dis'laik]. I. s. aversion f, répugnance f (to, of, for, pour); to take a d. to s.o., prendre qn en grippe. II. v.tr. ne pas aimer; détester; I don't d. him, il ne me déplaît pas.

dislocate ['dislokeit], v.tr. (a) désorganiser (les affaires); (b) luxer, déboîter (un membre). dislo'cation, s. (a) désorganisation f (des affaires); luxation f, déboîtement m.

dislodge [dis'lɔdʒ], v.tr. 1. déloger (qn). 2. détacher (une brique).

disloyal [dis'lɔiəl], a. infidèle f, déloyauté f. dis'loyal, a. infidèle; déloyal. -ally, adv. infidèlement, perfidement.

dismal ['dizml], a. sombre, triste; lugubre. -ally, adv. lugubrement, tristement.

dismantle [dis'mæntl], v.tr. démonter (une machine).

dismay [dis'mei]. I. s. consternation f. II. v.tr. consterner, épouvanter.

dismiss [dis'mis], v.tr. 1. congédier (qn); donner congé à (qn); destituer (un fonctionnaire). 2. (a) congédier (aimablement) (qn); (b) dissoudre (une assemblée). 3. bannir, chasser (des pensées tristes). 4. (a) écarter (une proposition); (b) acquitter (un inculpé). **dis'missal**, s. 1. congédiement m, renvoi m (d'un employé); destitution (d'un fonctionnaire); 2. acquittement m (d'un inculpé).

dismount [dis'maunt], v.i. mettre pied à terre.

disobey [diso'bei], v.tr. désobéir à (qn). **diso'bedience**, s. désobéissance f (à to s.o., à qn). **diso'bedient,** a. désobéissant.

disobliging [diso'blaidʒiŋ], a. désobligeant.

disorder [dis'ɔːdər]. I. v.tr. déranger; mettre le désordre dans (les affaires). II. s. 1. désordre m, confusion f. 2. (riots, etc.) désordre, tumulte m. **dis'orderliness** s. 1. désordre m. 2. turbulence f. **dis'orderly,** a. 1. désordonné; en désordre. 2. (of mob) turbulent. 3. (of pers.) désordonné, déréglé.

disorganize [dis'ɔːgənaiz], v.tr. désorganiser.

disown [dis'oun], v.tr. désavouer; renier.

disparage [dis'pæridʒ], v.tr. déprécier, dénigrer. **dis'paraging,** a. 1. dépréciateur; 2. peu flatteur. **-ly,** adv. to speak d. of s.o., parler de qn en termes peu flatteurs. **dis'paragement,** s. dénigrement m.

dispassionate [dis'pæʃənit], a. 1. sans passion; calme. 2. impartial. **-ly,** adv. 1. avec calme. 2. sans parti pris.

dispatch [dis'pætʃ]. I. v.tr. 1. expédier (un paquet); envoyer. 2. tuer; achever (une bête blessée). II. s. 1. expédition f; envoi m (de qn, qch.); Com: d. note, bulletin m d'expédition. 2. expédition f (d'une affaire); promptitude f, diligence f; with the utmost d., au plus vite. 3. d. box, boîte f à documents; d. case, serviette f (en cuir); Mil: d. rider, estafette f.

‡**dispel** [dis'pel], v.tr. chasser, dissiper (la crainte, etc.).

dispense [dis'pens]. 1. v.tr. (a) dispenser, distribuer (des aumônes); (b) administrer (la justice); (c) Med: préparer (des médicaments); exécuter (une ordonnance). 2. v.i. to d. with sth., se passer de qch. **dis'pensing,** s. Med: préparation f (des ordonnances); d. chemist, pharmacien, -ienne diplômé(e). **dis'pensary,** s. pharmacie f.

disperse [dis'pəːs]. 1. v.tr. disperser; dissiper (les nuages). 2. v.i. se disperser. **dis'persal, dis'persion,** s. dispersion f; diffusion f (de chaleur, etc.).

dispirited [di'spiritid], a. découragé, abattu. **-ly,** adv. d'un air découragé.

displace [dis'pleis], v.tr. 1. déplacer (qch.). 2. (a) destituer; (b) remplacer (by, par); évincer (qn). **dis'placement,** s. (a) déplacement m (de qch.); changement m de place; (b) Nau: déplacement d'un navire.

display [dis'plei]. I. s. 1. étalage m (de marchandises); manifestation f (de colère); air, fête f aéronautique; Com: d. window, vitrine f. 2. étalage (de luxe); affichage m (d'opinions). II. v.tr. 1. exposer (des marchandises); afficher (un avis). 2. manifester (du courage); révéler (son ignorance).

displease [dis'pliːz], v.tr. déplaire à (qn); contrarier, mécontenter (qn). **dis'pleasing,** a. déplaisant, désagréable (to, à). **dis'pleasure,** s. déplaisir m, mécontentement m.

dispose [dis'pouz], v.tr. & i. 1. (a) disposer, arranger (des objets); (b) to d. of sth., se défaire de qch.; to d. of a matter, régler une affaire. 2. Com: to d. of goods, écouler, placer, des marchandises; to be disposed of, à vendre. **dis'posed,** a. 1. to be well, ill, d. (towards s.o.), être bien, mal, intentionné (envers qn). 2. to d. sth., enclin, porté, à qch. **dis'posal,** s. 1. d. unit, broyeur m à ordures; to be at s.o.'s d., être à la disposition, au service, de qn. 2. cession f (de biens); for d., à vendre. **dispo'sition,** s. 1. disposition f. 2. caractère m, naturel m (de qn). 3. penchant m, tendance f (to, à).

dispossess [dispo'zes], v.tr. déposséder (qn) (of, de).

disproportionate [disprə'pɔːʃənit], a. disproportionné (to, à). **-ly,** adv. d'une façon disproportionnée.

disprove [dis'pruːv], v.tr. réfuter; démontrer la fausseté (d'un dire).

dispute [dis'pjuːt]. I. s. 1. contestation f, débat m. beyond d., incontestable. 2. querelle f, dispute f. II. v.i. 1. (a) débattre (qch. avec qn); (b) se disputer. 2. v.tr. débattre (une question); contester (une affirmation).

disqualify [dis'kwɔlifai], v.tr. 1. rendre incapable (for sth., de faire qch.). 2. retirer le permis de conduire (à qn). 3. Sp: disqualifier (un joueur). **disqualifi'cation,** s. 1. incapacité f (to act, à agir). 2. cause f d'incapacité (for, à). 3. Sp: disqualification f.

disquieting [dis'kwaiətiŋ], a. inquiétant.

disregard [disri'gɑːd], v.tr. ne tenir aucun compte de (qn, qch.); to d. a rule, désobéir à une règle.

disrepair [disri'pεər], s. délabrement m; in d., délabré.

disrepute [disri'pjuːt], s. to bring sth. into d., discréditer qch. **dis'reputable,** a. 1. (of action) honteux. 2. (of pers.) de mauvaise réputation; d. house, maison louche. 3. (of clothes) minable.

disrespect [disris'pekt], s. manque m d'égards, de respect (for, envers). **disres'pectful,** a. irrespectueux, irrévérencieux. **-fully,** adv. (parler) avec irrévérence.

dissatisfaction [dissætis'fækʃ(ə)n], s. mécontentement m (with, at, de). **dis'satisfied,** a. mécontent (with, at, de).

dissect [di'sekt], v.tr. disséquer. **dis'section,** s. 1. dissection f. 2. découpage m.

dissension [di'senʃ(ə)n], s. dissension f.

dissent [di'sent]. I. s. 1. dissentiment m; avis m contraire. 2. Ecc: dissidence f. II. v.i. 1. différer (de qn sur qch.). 2. Ecc: être dissident. **dis'senter,** s. Ecc: dissident, -ente.

dissertation [disə'teiʃ(ə)n], s. dissertation f.

dissimulate [di'simjuleit], v.tr. & i. dissimuler; cacher (un fait).

dissipate ['disipeit], 1. v.tr. dissiper (une fortune, ses efforts); dissipated man, débauché m. 2. v.i. se dissiper. **dissi'pation,** s. 1. dissipation f (de la brume); gaspillage m (d'une fortune). 2. vie désordonnée.

dissociate [di'souʃieit], v.tr. désassocier (from, de); to d. oneself from a question, se désintéresser d'une affaire.

dissolute ['disəlju:t], a. dissolu, débauché.

dissolve [di'zɔlv], 1. v.tr. dissoudre. 2. v.i. se dissoudre; fondre; Cin: dissolving view, fondu m.

dissuade [di'sweid], v.tr. dissuader (qn de faire qch.). **dis'suasion,** s. dissuasion f.

distance ['distəns], s. 1. (a) distance f, éloignement m. seen from a d., vu de loin; (b) in the d., dans le lointain; (c) at this d. of time, après cet intervalle (de temps). 2. distance, intervalle m; **'distant,** a. 1. (a) (endroit) éloigné, (pays) lointain; (b) likeness, faible ressemblance; (b) (in time) éloigné, reculé; d. memory, souvenir lointain. 2. (of pers.) réservé, froid. -ly, adv. 1. de loin. 2. avec réserve; froidement.

distaste [dis'teist], s. dégoût m (for, de); aversion f, répugnance f. **dis'tasteful,** a. désagréable (au goût); déplaisant, antipathique (to s.o., à qn).

distemper [dis'tempər], s. (for walls) détrempe f, badigeon m.

distend [dis'tend]. 1. v.tr. dilater, gonfler (un ballon, etc.). 2. v.i. (a) se dilater; (b) se distendre. **dis'tension, -tion,** s. dilatation f, distension f, gonflement m.

†distil [dis'til], v.tr. distiller (l'eau); raffiner (le pétrole). **dis'tillery,** s. distillerie f.

distinct [dis'tin(k)t], a. 1. distinct, différent (from, de). 2. d. memory, souvenir clair; d. promise, promesse formelle. 3. d. preference, préférence

marquée. **-ly,** adv. 1. distinctement, clairement. 2. décidément. **dis'tinctness,** s. clarté f, netteté f. **dis'tinction,** s. distinction f. **dis'tinctive,** a. distinctif.

distinguish [dis'tingwiʃ], 1. v.tr. (a) distinguer, discerner; (b) distinguer, différencier (from, de); (c) to d. oneself, se signaler. 2. v.i. faire une distinction (between, entre). **dis'tinguished,** a. (homme) distingué; d. writer, écrivain de distinction.

distort [dis'tɔ:t], v.tr. (a) tordre; décomposer, convulser (par la fureur); (b) fausser, dénaturer (la vérité, les faits); distorted ideas, idées biscornues; Rad: distorted sound, image, son déformé, image déformée. **dis'tortion,** s. déformation f.

distract [dis'trækt], v.tr. 1. distraire (l'attention de qn); brouiller (l'esprit). 2. affoler (qn). **dis'tracted,** a. 1. distrait, inattentif. 2. affolé, éperdu. **dis'traction,** s. 1. distraction f. 2. confusion f. 3. affolement m.

distress [dis'tres]. I. s. 1. détresse f. 2. misère f; gêne f. II. v.tr. 1. affliger, angoisser (qn). 2. épuiser, excéder. **dis'tressed,** a. 1. affligé, désolé. 2. economiquement faible; d. area, zone f de dépression économique.

distribute [dis'tribju:t], v.tr. distribuer, répartir. **distri'bution,** s. distribution f, répartition f. **dis'tributor,** s. (a) distributeur, -trice; (b) El: distributeur de courant. 3. Aut: distributeur d'allumage, F: delco m (R.t.m.); d. arm, rotor m du delco.

district ['distrikt], s. 1. région f, territoire m. 2. (a) Adm: electoral d., circonscription f électorale; Com: d. manager, directeur m régional; (b) quartier m (d'une ville); d. nurse, (infirmière) visiteuse.

distrust [dis'trast]. I. s. méfiance f, défiance f. II. v.tr. se méfier de qn. **dis'trustful,** a. défiant, méfiant. **-fully,** adv. avec méfiance.

disturb [dis'tə:b], v.tr. 1. déranger (qn); 2. inquiéter, troubler (qn). **disturbing,** a. perturbateur; d. news, nouvelle fâcheuse. **dis'turbance,** s. 1. dérangement m; Meteor: perturbation f atmosphérique; Rad: (bruit) parasite m. 2. bruit m, tapage m; émeute f.

disuse [dis'ju:s], s. désuétude f. **dis'used,** a. hors d'usage; (of church, etc.) désaffecté.

ditch [ditʃ]. I. s. fossé m. II. v.tr. Aut: to d. one's car, verser sa voiture dans le fossé. 2. v.i. Av: faire un amerrissage forcé. 3. v.tr. jeter (qch.).

dither ['diðər], v.i. F: 1. trembloter. 2. s'agiter sans but.

ditto ['ditou], *a.* & *s.* idem; de même.

divan [di'væn], *s.* divan *m.*

dive [daiv]. I. *s.* 1. (*a*) plongeon *m;* (*b*) plongée *f* (d'un sous-marin); (*c*) *Av:* piqué *m.* 2. *P:* gargote *f.* II. *v.i.* (*a*) plonger (into, dans); piquer une tête; (*b*) *Av:* to (nose-)d., piquer (du nez). 'diver, *s.* (*a*) plongeur *m;* (*b*) scaphandrier *m.* 'diving-board, *s.* plongeoir *m.* 'diving-suit, *s.* scaphandre *m.*

diverge [dai'və:dʒ], *v.i.* diverger, s'écarter. di'vergent, *a.* divergent.

diverse [dai'və:s], *a.* divers.

diversion [dai'və:ʃ(ə)n], *s.* 1. détournement *m;* déviation *f* (d'une route). 2. (*a*) diversion *f;* (*b*) divertissement *m.*

divide [di'vaid]. 1. *v.tr.* (*a*) diviser (qch. en parties); (*b*) (*share out*) partager, répartir (among, entre); (*c*) *Mth:* diviser; (*d*) séparer (from, de); (*e*) désunir (une famille). 2. *v.i.* (*a*) se diviser, se partager (into, en); (*of road*) se bifurquer. 'dividend, *s.* *Fin:* dividende *m.*

divine [di'vain], *a.* divin; *F:* admirable. -ly, *adv.* divinement; divinement.

divinity [di'viniti], *s.* 1. divinité *f,* dieu *m.* 2. théologie *f.*

division [di'viʒ(ə)n], *s.* 1. division *f,* partage *m* (into, en). 2. répartition *f.* 3. division, désunion *f.* 4. *Mth:* division. di'visible, *a.* divisible (by, par).

divorce [di'vɔ:s]. I. *s.* divorce *m.* II. *v.tr.* (*of husband or wife*) divorcer (d'avec qn). divor'cee, *s.* divorcé, -ée.

divulge [di'vʌldʒ], *v.tr.* divulguer, répandre (un secret).

dizziness ['dizinis], *s.* étourdissement *m,* vertige *m.* 'dizzy, *a.* 1. to feel d., avoir le vertige; to make s.o. d., étourdir qn. 2. *F:* (*of height, speed*) vertigineux. -ily, *adv.* vertigineusement.

‡do [du:]. I. *v.tr.* 1. (*perform*) faire (son devoir); what do you do (for a living)? quel est votre métier? to do good, faire le bien; the car was doing sixty, la voiture filait à soixante; it isn't done, cela ne se fait pas; what's to be done? que faire? what can I do for you? en quoi puis-je vous être utile? well done! bravo! à la bonne heure! *F:* that's done it! ça c'est le bouquet! *F:* nothing doing! rien à faire! 2. (*a*) faire (une chambre, les cheveux à qn); (*b*) cuire, faire cuire (la viande); done to a turn, cuit à point; (*d*) *F:* visiter; *F:* faire (un musée); (*e*) *F:* (*cheat*) escroquer (qn); to do s.o. out of sth., soutirer qch. à qn; (*f*) *F:* they do you well here, on mange bien ici. 3. how do you do? (i) comment allez-vous?

(ii) (*on being introduced*) enchanté (de faire votre connaissance). 4. (*to suffice*) that will do, c'est bien (comme cela); that won't do, cela ne fera pas l'affaire. II. *verb substitute,* he writes better than I do, il écrit mieux que moi. 2. may I read this letter?—please do, puis-je lire cette lettre?—je vous en prie; did you see him?—I did, l'avez-vous vu?—oui (je l'ai vu). 3. you like Paris? so do I, vous aimez Paris? moi aussi. III. *v.aux.* 1. (*emphasis*) he 'did go, il y est bien allé; why don't you work? *F:* I 'do (work)! pourquoi ne travaillez-vous pas?—mais si, je travaille! 'do shut up! voulez-vous bien vous taire! 2. (*usual form in questions and negative statements*) do you see him? le voyez-vous? don't do it! n'en faites rien! IV. (*with certain prepositions*) 1. to do well, badly, by s.o., bien, mal, agir envers qn. 2. *F:* to do for s.o., (i) faire le ménage de qn; (ii) tuer qn. 3. (*a*) to have to do with s.o., sth., avoir affaire à qn, avoir rapport à qch.; (*b*) what have I done with my bag? où ai-je mis mon sac? (*c*) how many can you do with? combien en désirez-vous? (*d*) to do without, se passer de (qch.). II. *s.* (*a*) *F:* it's a poor do! c'est plutôt minable! (*b*) *F:* réception *f;* soirée *f.* 'do a'gain, *v.tr.* refaire, recommencer (qch.). 'do a'way, *v.i.* to do away with, abolir, supprimer (un usage); détruire (qch.); *F:* tuer (qn). 'do 'out, *v.tr.* nettoyer (une pièce). 'do 'up, *v.tr.* 1. remettre (qch.) à neuf. 2. faire, ficeler (un paquet); boutonner, agrafer (un vêtement). 3. *F:* to be done up, n'en pouvoir plus.

docile ['dousail], *a.* docile.

dock[1] [dɔk], *v.tr.* diminuer, rogner (le salaire de qn).

dock[2]. I. *s.* (*a*) bassin *m* (d'un port); the docks, les docks *m;* (*b*) dry d., cale sèche; *Aut: Av:* to be in d., être en réparation. II. *v.i.* 1. *v.tr.* faire entrer (un navire) au bassin. 2. *v.i.* entrer au bassin. 'docker, *s.* docker *m.* 'docking, *s.* entrée *f* au bassin. 'dockyard, *s.* chantier *m* naval; naval d., arsenal *m* maritime.

dock[3], *s.* *Jur:* banc *m* des prévenus.

doctor ['dɔktər]. I. *s.* 1. *Sch:* docteur *m* (ès sciences, etc.). 2. médecin *m,* docteur *m;* woman d., (femme) docteur. II. *v.tr.* 1. (*a*) soigner (un malade); (*b*) doper (un cheval). 2. *F:* truquer (des comptes).

doctrine ['dɔktrin], *s.* doctrine *f.*

document ['dɔkjumənt], *s.* document *m.* docu'mentary, *a.* & *s.* documentaire (*m*).

dodderer ['dɔdərər], *s.* *F:* gâteux *m.*

dodge [dɔdʒ]. I. s. ruse f, artifice m; Sp: esquive f. II. v. 1. v.i. (a) se jeter de côté; (b) Sp: esquiver; (c) biaiser. 2. v.tr. esquiver (un coup); éviter (qn). **'dodgy**, a. F: d. situation, situation délicate.

doe [dou], s. Z: 1. daine f. 2. (rabbit) lapine f; (hare) hase f. **'doeskin**, s. peau m de daim.

dog [dɔg]. I. s. 1. chien m, chienne f; house d., chien de garde; sporting d., chien de chasse. 2. F: the dogs, courses f de lévriers. 2. E: chien, cliquet m, détente f. II. ‡v.tr. suivre (qn) à la piste; to d. s.o.'s footsteps, talonner qn. **'dog-collar**, s. 1. collier m de chien. 2. F: faux col m d'ecclésiastique. **'dog-house**, s. (a) U.S: niche f; (b) to be in the d.-h., être en défaveur (auprès de qn). **'dog-'tired**, a. F: éreinté.

dogged ['dɔgid], a. résolu, tenace. -ly, adv. avec ténacité; opiniâtrement.

dogmatic [dɔg'mætik], a. 1. dogmatique. 2. autoritaire, tranchant. -ally, adv. d'un ton autoritaire.

doing ['du(:)iŋ], s. 1. (a) that takes some d., ce n'est pas facile; (b) this is your d., c'est vous qui en êtes la cause. 2. pl. ce qu'on fait; (a) agissements mpl; (b) événements mpl; faits mpl.

dole [doul]. I. s. allocation f de chômage. II. v.tr. to d. sth. out, distribuer qch. (parcimonieusement).

doll [dɔl]. I. s. poupée f. II. v.tr. F: to d. oneself up, se pomponner.

dollar ['dɔlər], s. dollar m.

dome [doum], s. dôme m.

domestic [dɔ'mestik], a. 1. d. (servant), domestique mf, bonne f. 2. d. science, (i) les arts ménagers; (ii) enseignement ménager. 2. d. animal, animal m domestique. 3. (of pers.) casanier; (femme) d'intérieur. **do'mesticate**, v.tr. apprivoiser (un animal). **do'mesticated**, a. (of animal) apprivoisé; (of woman) bonne ménagère.

domicile ['dɔmisail], s. domicile m.

dominant ['dɔminənt]. 1. a. dominant. 2. s. Mus: dominante f.

dominate ['dɔmineit], v.tr. & i. dominer. **'dominating**, a. dominant. **domi'nation**, s. domination f.

domineer [dɔmi'niər], v.i. 1. se montrer autoritaire. 2. to d. over s.o., tyranniser (qn). **domi'neering**, a. autoritaire.

dominion [dɔ'minjən], s. the D. of Canada, le Dominion du Canada.

don [dɔn], s. = professeur m (d'université). **'donnish**, a. F: pédant.

donation [dɔ'neiʃ(ə)n], s. donation f, don m.

donkey ['dɔŋki], s. 1. âne, f. ânesse; baudet m; F: d. work, travail m de routine; d.'s years, très longtemps. 2. F: imbécile mf, âne m.

donor ['dounər], s. 1. donateur, -trice. 2. blood d., donneur, -euse, de sang.

doom ['du:m]. I. s. 1. destin m (funeste); sort (malheureux). 2. perte f, ruine f. 3. the day of d., le jugement dernier. II. v.tr. condamner (to, à); doomed man, homme perdu; doomed to failure, voué à l'échec.

door [dɔːr], s. 1. porte f; to turn s.o. out of doors, mettre qn à la porte; Com: d. to d. selling, porte à porte m. 2. portière f (de voiture). **'doormat**, s. paillasson m. **'doorstep**, s. 1. seuil m, pas m (de la porte). 2. F: grosse tartine. **'doorway**, s. (encadrement m de la) porte; in the d., sous la porte.

dope [doup], v.l. 1. radoter. 2. stupéfiant m, narcotique m; d. habit, toxicomanie f. 2. F: to get the d., se mettre au courant; se tuyauter. II. v.tr. administrer un narcotique à (qn); doper (un cheval); F: to d. (oneself), prendre des stupéfiants.

†dormitory ['dɔːmitri], s. dortoir m.

†dormouse ['dɔːmaus], s. loir m.

dose [dous], s. 1. dose f; dosage, posologie f (d'un médicament).

dot [dɔt]. I. s. point m. II. ‡v.tr. 1. mettre un point sur (un i). 2. pointiller; dotted line, ligne en pointillé.

dote [dout], v.i. 1. radoter. 2. to d. on s.o., aimer qn à la folie. **'dotage**, s. seconde enfance f; gâtisme m. **'dotard**, s. radoteur, -euse; F: gâteux, -euse.

double [dʌbl]. I. a. 1. double; with a d. meaning, à deux sens; d. bedroom, chambre à deux personnes; d. whisky, double whisky. 2. (of pers.) bent d., courbé en deux. 3. d. the number, deux fois autant; d. the length of, deux fois plus long que. -bly, adv. doublement. II. adv. to see d., voir double. III. s. 1. double m; deux fois autant. 2. (of pers.) double; F: sosie m. 3. at the d., au pas de course. 4. Sp: men's doubles, double messieurs. IV. v. 1. v.tr. (a) doubler (un nombre); Th: to d. parts, jouer deux rôles; (b) Nau: to d. a cape, doubler un cap; (c) (at bridge) contrer. 2. v.i. (se) doubler; to d. back, faire un brusque crochet. **'double-'barrelled**, a. (fusil) à deux coups; F: (nom) à rallonge. **'double-'breasted**, a. (gilet, etc.) croisé. **'double-'cross**, v.tr. F: tromper (qn). **'double-'decker**, s. 1. (autobus) à impériale. 2. F: (sandwich) double m. **'double-'faced**, a. 1. hypocrite. 2. (tissu) à double envers. **'double-'parking**, s. Aut: stationnement m en double file. **'double-'up**, v.i. se (re)plier; to d. up with laughter, se tordre de rire; to d. up with s.o., partager une chambre avec qn.

doubt [daut]. I. v. 1. v.tr. douter (de la parole de qn). 2. v.i. hésiter; douter. II. s. doute m; to be in d., être dans le doute; beyond a d., sans le moindre doute; no d., sans doute. '**doubtful**, *a.* 1. (*of thing*) douteux. 2. (*of pers.*) indécis, incertain. 3. d. society, compagnie *f* louche, équivoque; in d. taste, d'un goût douteux. -**fully**, *adv.* avec hésitation. '**doubtfulness**, *s.* 1. ambiguïté *f.* 2. incertitude *f.* 3. indécision *f.* '**doubtless**, *adv.* sans doute, probablement.

dough [dou], *s.* 1. pâte *f* (à pain). 2. *F:* fric *m.* '**doughnut**, *s.* beigne *m* (*Fr. C.*) (sorte de beignet).

dove [dʌv], *s.* colombe *f.*

dovetail ['dʌvteil]. 1. *v.tr. Techn:* assembler à queue-d'aronde. 2. *v.i.* se rejoindre, se raccorder.

dowdy ['daudi], *a.* sans élégance. '**dowdiness**, *s.* manque *m* d'élégance.

down[1] [daun], *s.* duvet *m.*

down[2]. I. *adv.* 1. (*direction*) vers le bas; to go d., descendre; to fall d., tomber par terre; cash d., argent comptant; d. with the traitors! à bas les traîtres! 2. (*position*) d. below, en bas; d. there, là, en bas; he isn't d. yet, il n'est pas encore descendu; d. with 'flu, grippé; *F:* d. under, aux antipodes; face d., face en dessous; your tyres are d., vos pneus sont dégonflés. 3. to be d. on s.o., en vouloir à qn; d. in the mouth, abattu; *F:* d. and out, ruiné; à bout de ressources; fichu. II. *prep.* her hair is hanging d. her back, les cheveux lui pendent dans le dos; to fall d. the stairs, tomber en bas de l'escalier; d. town, en ville. III. *a.* d. train, train montant; d. payment, acompte *m.* IV. *s. F:* to have a d. on s.o., avoir une dent contre qn. V. *v.tr.* to d. tools, (i) cesser de travailler; (ii) se mettre en grève. '**down-at-'heel**, *a.* (soulier) éculé; (*of pers.*) râpé. '**downcast**, *a.* abattu, déprimé. '**downfall**, *s.* chute *f*; écroulement *m.* '**downgrade**, *s.* to be on the d., sur le déclin. II. *v.tr.* réduire (qn) à une position inférieure. **down-hearted**, *a.* découragé. **down-hill**, *adv.* to go d., (i) descendre; (ii) être sur le déclin. '**downpour**, *s.* grosse averse. '**downright**. 1. *adv.* (*a*) tout à fait, complètement; (*b*) nettement, carrément. 2. *a.* (*langage*) direct, franc; absolu, véritable. **down-'stairs**. 1. *adv.* en bas, au rez-de-chaussée. 2. *a.* (pièces) d'en bas. '**down-stream**, *adv.* en aval. '**downtown**, *a. & s. U.S:* d. (sector), centre commercial (d'une ville). '**downward**, *a.* (mouvement) descendant. '**downwards**, *adv.* de haut en bas; en descendant; face d., face en dessous.

downs [daunz], *s.pl.* collines *f* crayeuses.

doze [douz]. I. *s.* petit somme. II. *v.i.* sommeiller.

†**dozen** ['dʌzn], *s.* douzaine *f*; half a d., une demi-douzaine; six d. bottles, six

douzaines de bouteilles; *F:* to talk nineteen to the d., avoir la langue bien pendue; *F:* dozens of people, beaucoup de gens.

drab [dræb], *a.* gris-brun; terne.

draft [drɑ:ft]. I. *s.* 1. *Mil:* détachement *m* (de troupes); *U.S:* conscription *f.* 2. *Com:* traite *f*; lettre *f* de change. 3. brouillon *m* (de lettre). II. *v.tr.* 1. détacher (des troupes); *U.S:* appeler (des soldats) sous les drapeaux. 2. affecter (qn) à un poste. 3. rédiger (un acte); faire le brouillon (d'une lettre).

‡**drag** [dræg]. I. *v.tr.* traîner, tirer; to d. (sth.) about, along, traîner qch.; to d. (s.o.) (along), entraîner (qn) (contre sa volonté); to d. (s.o.) away, emmener (qn) de force. 2. *v.i.* (*of pers.*) traîner, rester en arrière; (*of thing*) traîner à terre; (*of lawsuit, etc.*) traîner (en longueur); (*of conversation*) languir.

dragon ['drægən], *s.* dragon *m.* '**dragon-fly**, *s.* libellule *f.*

drain [drein]. I. *s.* 1. tranchée *f*, rigole *f.* 2. égout *m.* 3. tuyau *m* d'écoulement. II. *v.* 1. *v.tr.* (*a*) to d. water (away), évacuer les eaux; faire écouler l'eau; (*b*) vider (un verre, un fût); assécher, drainer (un terrain); vider (un étang); *Aut:* to d. the sump, vidanger le carter. 2. *v.i.* to d. (away), s'écouler. '**drainage**, *s.* système *m* d'égouts. '**draining**, *s.* assèchement *m*, drainage *m* (d'un terrain). 2. d. board, égouttoir *m* (d'évier). '**drain-pipe**, *s.* canalisation *f* d'écoulement.

drake [dreik], *s.* canard *m* mâle.

drama ['drɑ:mə], *s.* 1. drame *m.* 2. the d., le théâtre. dra'matic, *a.* dramatique. -**ally**, *adv.* dramatiquement. '**dramatist**, *s.* auteur *m* dramatique. '**dramatize**, *v.tr.* dramatiser; adapter (un roman) à la scène.

draper ['dreipər], *s.* marchand *m* de tissus, de nouveautés. '**drapery**, *s.* magasin *m* de tissus, de nouveautés; mercerie *f.*

drastic ['dræstik], *a.* to take d. measures, prendre des mesures énergiques. -**ally**, *adv.* énergiquement, rigoureusement.

draught [drɑ:ft], *s.* 1. traction *f*, tirage *m.* 2. *Fish:* coup *m* de filet; pêche *f.* 3. trait *m*, coup (de vin); at a d., d'un seul trait. 4. tirant *m* d'eau (d'un vaisseau). 5. *pl.* (jeu *m* de) dames *fpl.* d. board, damier *m.* 6. (*a*) (*in room*) courant *m* d'air; (*b*) (*of chimney*) tirage. 7. d. beer, bière *f* à la pression. '**draughty**, *a.* plein de courants d'air.

†**draughtsman** ['drɑ:ftsmən], *s.* 1. *Ind:* dessinateur *m.* 2. pion *m* (du jeu de dames).

draw [drɔː]. I. *s.* 1. (*a*) tirage *m*; (*b*) to be quick on the d., avoir la repartie facile. 2. tirage au sort; loterie *f*; tombola *f*. 3. clou *m* (de la fête). 4. *Sp:* partie nulle. ‡II. *v. t.* 1. *v.tr.* (*a*) tirer (un verrou); (i) fermer, (ii) ouvrir, les rideaux; (*b*) tirer, remorquer (une caravane); (*c*) (*take in*) aspirer (de l'air); (*d*) (*attract*) attirer (une foule); (*e*) tirer, retirer, ôter (qch. de qch.); to d. lots for sth., tirer qch. au sort; (*f*) arracher (un clou, une dent); (*g*) to d. water, puiser, tirer, de l'eau; (*h*) toucher (de l'argent); (i) vider (une volaille); (*j*) to d. a blank, *F:* revenir bredouille; (*k*) tracer (un plan); tirer (une ligne); dresser (une carte); dessiner (un paysage); (*l*) to d. a cheque, tirer un chèque; (*m*) *Sp:* to d. a game, faire match nul. 2. *v.i.* (*a*) to d. near (to s.o.), s'approcher (de qn); to d. to one side, se ranger; to d. into (a station), entrer (en gare); to d. to an end, toucher à sa fin; (*c*) (*of chimney*) tirer; (*of pump*) aspirer; (*d*) to let the tea d., laisser infuser le thé. '**draw a'side.** 1. *v.tr.* (*a*) détourner, écarter (qch.); (*b*) prendre qn à l'écart. 2. *v.i.* s'écarter, se ranger. '**draw 'back.** 1. *v.tr.* (*a*) tirer en arrière; retirer (sa main); (*b*) ouvrir (les rideaux). 2. *v.i.* se reculer; se retirer en arrière. '**drawback,** *s.* inconvénient *m*. '**draw 'down.** *v.tr.* faire descendre (qch.); baisser (les stores). **draw 'in.** 1. *v.tr.* (*a*) (*of cat*) rentrer (ses griffes); (*b*) aspirer (l'air). 2. *v.i.* the days are drawing in, les jours diminuent. '**drawer,** *s.* tiroir *m*; chest of drawers, commode *f*. '**drawing,** *s.* 1. tirage *m*, puisage (d'eau). 2. dessin *m*; freehand d., dessin à main levée; d.-board, planche *f* à dessin; d. paper, papier *m* à dessin; d. pin, punaise *f*. '**drawing-room,** *s.* salon *m*. **drawn,** *a.* 1. tiré; d. features, traits tirés, décomposés. 2. *Sp:* d. match, match nul. **draw 'out,** *v.tr.* 1. sortir retirer (qch. de qch.); arracher (un clou). 2. prolonger, tirer (une affaire) en longueur. **draw 'up.** 1. *v.tr.* (*a*) faire (re)monter (qch.); to d. oneself up, se (re)dresser; (*b*) to d. up a chair, approcher une chaise; (*c*) to d. up a document, dresser, rédiger un document. 2. *v.i.* s'approcher (de la table); (*of car*) stopper.

drawl [drɔːl]. I. *s.* voix traînante. II. *v.i.* parler d'une voix traînante.

dread [dred]. I. *s.* crainte *f*, épouvante *f*. '**dreadful,** *a.* 1. redoutable. 2. atroce, épouvantable. **-fully,** *adv.* terriblement, affreusement; *F:* I'm d. sorry, je regrette infiniment. II. *v.tr.* redouter, craindre.

‡**dream** [driːm]. I. *v.tr. & i.* 1. rêver. 2. rêvasser. 3. I never dreamt that . . ., je ne songeais guère que . . . II. *s.* rêve *m*; songe *m*. '**dreamer,** *s.* 1. rêveur, -euse. 2. (*esprit*) songeur. '**dreaming,** *s.* rêves *mpl*; songes *mpl*. '**dreamy,** *a.* rêveur, rêveur; songe-ar. **-ily,** *adv.* d'un air rêveur.

dreary ['driəri], *a.* triste, morne. '**dreariness,** *s.* tristesse *f*, aspect *m* morne (d'un paysage).

dredge [dredʒ], *v.tr. & i.* draguer.

dregs [dregz], *s.pl.* lie *f* (de vin, etc.).

drench [dren(t)ʃ], *v.tr.* tremper, mouiller. '**drenching,** *a.* (pluie) battante.

dress [dres]. I. *s.* 1. (*a*) habillement *m*; vêtements *mpl*; in full d., en grande tenue; (*b*) *Th:* d. circle, (premier) balcon; d. rehearsal, (répétition) générale *f.* 2. robe *f.* II. *v.tr.* 1. (*a*) habiller (qn); (*b*) s'habiller, faire sa toilette. 2. orner, parer (with, de); *Com:* to d. a window, faire l'étalage. 3. *Mil:* (s')aligner. 4. *Med:* panser (une blessure). 5. apprêter (une surface, un mets). '**dress 'down,** *v.tr. F:* chapitrer (qn). '**dresser,** *s.* 1. (*pers.*) *Th:* habilleur, -euse. 2. *H:* (*a*) buffet *m* de cuisine; (*b*) *U.S:* coiffeuse *f*. '**dressing,** *s.* 1. habillement *m*, toilette *f.* 2. *Cu:* (*a*) accommodage *m* (des mets); (*b*) salad d., (*genre*) sauce mayonnaise; French d., vinaigrette *f.* 3. *Med:* pansement *m*. 4. *attrib.* d. case, sac *m* (de voyage); d. gown, robe *f* de chambre; d. room, (i) cabinet *m* de toilette; (ii) *Th:* loge *f* (d'acteur); d. table, coiffeuse *f*. '**dressmaker,** *s.* couturier, -ière. '**dressmaking,** *s.* couture *f*; confection *f*. **dress 'up,** *v.i.* often *Pej:* se parer, *F:* s'attifer; se travestir. '**dressy,** *a.* often *Pej:* chic, élégant.

dribble ['dribl]. 1. *v.i.* baver. 2. *v.tr. Sp:* dribbler (le ballon). '**dribbling,** *s. Sp:* dribbling *m.* '**dribbler,** *s.* baveux, -euse. 2. *Sp:* dribbleur *m*.

driblet ['driblit], *s.* petite quantité *f*; to pay in driblets, payer petit à petit.

dried [draid], *a.* séché, desséché; d. fruit, fruits secs; d. eggs, œufs en poudre.

drift [drift]. I. *s.* 1. (*a*) mouvement *m*; (*b*) direction *f*, sens *m* (d'un courant). 2. *Av: Nau:* dérive *f.* 3. but *m*, tendance *f*, portée *f* (de questions, etc.). 4. amoncellement *m* (de neige), congère *f.* II. (*a*) *v.i.* flotter; French d., *Av:* déporter; (*b*) to let oneself d., se laisser aller; (*c*) (*of snow*) s'amonceler; (*d*) (*of events*) tendre (vers un but). '**drifter,** *s. Fish:* chalutier *m*.

drill [dril]. I. *s.* 1. *E:* foret *m*, mèche *f*. 2. *Mil:* exercice(s) *m(pl)*, manœuvre(s) *f(pl)*; *F:* what's the d.? qu'est-ce qu'on fait? II. *v.* 1. *v.tr. E:* forer; perforer. 2. *Mil:* instruire, faire manœuvrer (des soldats). 3. *v.i.* faire l'exercice; manœuvrer.

drink [driŋk]. I. s. 1. (a) food and d., le boire et le manger; (b) to give s.o. a d., donner à boire à qn; to have a d., se désaltérer; (c) consommation f; to have a d., F: boire un coup. 2. boisson f, breuvage m; soft d., boisson sans alcool; strong d., spiritueux mpl. 3. boisson; ivrognerie f; the d. question, le problème de l'alcoolisme. ‡II. v.tr. 1. boire; to d. the waters, prendre les eaux; d. your soup, mange ta soupe. 2. abs. boire, s'adonner à la boisson. 'drinkable, a. (a) buvable; (b) potable. 'drinker, s. buveur, -euse. 'drinking, s. ivrognerie f; alcoolisme m; d. trough, abreuvoir m; d. water, eau f potable. 'drink up, v.tr. achever de boire; vider (un verre).

‡drip [drip]. v.i. dégoutter; tomber goutte à goutte. 'drip-dry, a. Cl: (tissu m) qu'on ne repasse pas. 'dripping. I. a. ruisselant; (robinet) qui pleure. II. s. 1. égouttement m. 2. Cu: graisse f de rôti.

drive [draiv]. I. s. promenade f en voiture. 2. battue f du gibier. 3. E: (mouvement m de) propulsion f; Aut: left-hand d., conduite f à gauche; direct d., prise directe; front-wheel d., traction f avant. 4. Sp: (a) (golf) coup m de départ; (b) (tennis) drive m. 5. (of pers.) to have lots of d., être très dynamique. 6. (cards) bridge d., tournoi m de bridge. ‡II. v. 1. v.tr. (a) chasser (devant soi); conduire, mener (le bétail aux champs); to d. (game), rabattre (le gibier); (b) faire marcher (une machine); conduire (un cheval, une auto); can you d.? savez-vous conduire? (c) contraindre (qn à faire qch.); (d) enfoncer (un clou); percer (un tunnel); (e) to d. a bargain, conclure un marché. 2. v.i. (a) to let d. at s.o., décocher un coup à qn.; (b) (of snow) s'amonceler; (c) to d. (along the road), rouler (sur la route); to d. to London, se rendre en voiture à Londres; to d. on the right, circuler à droite. 'drive a'long, v.tr. chasser, pousser (qn). 2. v.i. rouler (en voiture). 'drive a'way. 1. v.tr. éloigner, repousser (qn). 2. v.i. Aut: s'en aller, démarrer. 'drive 'back. 1. v.tr. (a) refouler, faire reculer (qn); (b) reconduire (qn) en voiture. 2. v.i. rentrer, revenir, en voiture. 'drive 'down, v.i. se rendre en voiture (de Londres en province). 'drive-in, s. (a) Aut: piste f de ravitaillement; (b) U.S: cinéma m en plein air; (c) U.S: restoroute m (R.t.m.). 'drive 'on. 1. v.tr. pousser (qn). 2. v.i. Aut: continuer sa route. 'drive 'over, v.i. se rendre (à un endroit) en voiture. 'driver, s. Aut: conducteur, -trice. 'driving. I. a. 1. E: (force) motrice.

2. (pluie) battante. II. s. Aut: conduite f; d. school, auto-école f; d. test, examen m pour permis de conduire; d. wheel, (i) E: roue motrice; (ii) Aut: volant m.

drizzle ['drizl]. I. s. bruine f, crachin m. II. v.i. bruiner, crachiner.

drone [droun]. I. s. 1. (a) abeille f mâle; faux bourdon; (b) fainéant m. 2. (a) bourdonnement m; (b) ronronnement m, vrombissement m (d'un moteur).

droop [druːp], v.i. (se) pencher, languir.

drop [drop]. I. s. 1. goutte f. 2. chute f; d. in prices, baisse f de prix; El: d. in voltage, chute de tension; Av. Mil: parachutage m. ‡II. v. 1. v.i. (a) tomber goutte à goutte, dégoutter (from, de); (b) (of pers.) tomber, se laisser tomber; (c) (of prices) baisser; (of wind) se calmer. 2. v.tr. (a) laisser tomber, lâcher (qch.); larguer (une bombe); Fb: dropped goal, drop (-goal) m. 3. perdre (de l'argent) (over sth., sur qch.). 4. (set down) I'll d. you at your door, je vous déposerai chez vous en passant. 5. (a) omettre, supprimer (une syllabe); (b) ne pas prononcer (les h etc.). 6. baisser (les yeux, la voix). 7. (a) abandonner (un travail); renoncer à (une idée); (b) lâcher (un parachutiste); (c) F: d. it! en voilà assez! 'dropper, s. Med: compte-gouttes m inv. drop 'in, v.i. entrer en passant. drop 'off, tomber, se détacher; drop 'out, 1. v.tr. omettre, supprimer. 2. v.i. to d. out of a contest, se retirer, renoncer.

drought [draut], s. sécheresse f; disette f d'eau.

drown [draun], v.tr. 1. noyer; to be drowned, se noyer. 2. étouffer, couvrir (un son).

drowse [drauz], v.i. somnoler, s'assoupir. 'drowsiness, s. somnolence f. 'drowsy, a. assoupi, somnolent; to feel d., avoir sommeil. -ily, adv. à demi endormi.

drudge [drʌdʒ]. I. s. femme f, homme m, de peine. II. v.i. trimer, peiner. 'drudgery, s. travail m pénible, ingrat.

drug [drʌg]. I. s. 1. produit m pharmaceutique, drogue f. 2. narcotique m, stupéfiant m; d. addict, toxicomane mf; d. habit, toxicomanie f. 3. (of product) to be a d. on the market, être invendable. II. ‡v.tr. donner un narcotique à qn; to d. oneself, s'adonner aux stupéfiants. 'drugstore, s. U.S: magasin m où l'on vend des produits pharmaceutiques, des articles de toilette, etc., et où on sert des repas rapides.

drum [drʌm]. I. s. 1. tambour m; big d., grosse caisse; d. major, tambour major m. 2. Anat: tympan m. 3. tonneau m (en fer); tonnelet m.

II. ‡v. 1. v.i. battre du tambour; tambouriner. 2. v.tr. to d. sth. into s.o.'s head, enfoncer, fourrer, qch. dans la tête de qn. 'drummer, s. tambour m. 'drumstick, s. 1. baguette f de tambour. 2. Cu: pilon m (d'une volaille).

drunk [drʌŋk], a. (a) ivre, gris; to get d., s'enivrer; (b) enivré, grisé. 'drunkard, s. ivrogne, ivrognesse. 'drunken, a. d. state, état d'ivresse. -ly, adv. en ivrogne. 'drunkenness, s. 1. ivresse f. 2. ivrognerie f.

dry [drai]. I. a. 1. sec; (of well, etc.) à sec; d. land, terre ferme; to feel d., avoir soif. 2. aride; sans intérêt. 3. d. humour, esprit mordant. -ly, adv. sèchement. II. v. 1. v.tr. (faire) sécher (qch.); to d. one's eyes, s'essuyer les yeux. 2. v.i. sécher, se dessécher. 'dryer, s. 1. Ind: séchoir m; H: spin d., essoreuse f. 'drying, s. séchage m; dessèchement m; essorage m; spin d., essorage m. 'dryness, s. 1. sécheresse f, aridité f. 2. sévérité f (du ton); aridité (de l'esprit). dry 'off, v, dry 'out, v. 1. v.tr. faire sécher (qch.). 2. v.i. (of moisture) s'évaporer. dry 'up, v.i. 1. (of well) se dessécher, tarir. 2. F: se taire; P: d. up! la ferme! 3. F: essuyer la vaisselle.

dual ['dju(:)əl], a. double; d. carriage-way, route f à double chaussée.

dubious ['dju(:)biəs], a. 1. douteux; (a) incertain, vague; (b) équivoque, louche. 2. hésitant. -ly, adv. d'un air de doute.

duchess ['dʌtʃis], s. duchesse f.

duck¹ [dʌk], s. 1. (a) cane f; (b) canard m. wild d., canard sauvage; Sp: lame d., un pauvre type; Sp: to make a d., faire chou blanc. 'duckling, s. caneton m.

duck², 1. v.i. se baisser (subitement). 2. v.tr. (a) plonger (qn) dans l'eau; (b) baisser subitement (la tête). 'ducking, s. bain m forcé; to give s.o. a d., F: faire boire une tasse à qn.

dud [dʌd], a. & s. F: incapable; he's a d., (i) c'est un zéro; (ii) c'est un raté; d. cheque, chèque sans provision.

due [dju:]. I. a. 1. a. exigible; (of bill) échéant, échu; the balance d. to us, la solde qui nous revient; (b) dû, f. due; juste; (c) what is it d. to? à quoi cela tient-il? (d) the train is d. at two o'clock, le train arrive à deux heures. II. adv. d. north, droit vers le nord, plein nord. III. s. 1. dû m. 2. pl. droits mpl.

duel¹ ['dju(:)əl], s. duel m.

duet [dju(:)'et], s. duo m.

duke [dju:k], s. duc m.

dull [dʌl], a. 1. lent, lourd; à l'esprit épais; d. of sight, hearing, (avoir) la vue faible, l'oreille dure. 2. (bruit) sourd, mat. 3. triste, morne. 4.

ennuyeux. 5. (of colour) terne, mat. 6. (of weather) sombre. 'dully, adv. 1. tristement; ennuyeusement. 2. sans éclat; sourdement. 'dullness, s. 1. lenteur m de l'esprit. 2. matité f (d'un son). 3. ennui m, tristesse f. 4. stagnation f (du marché). 5. manque m d'éclat; bruit sourd.

duly ['dju:li], adv. 1. dûment; convenablement. 2. en temps voulu.

dumb [dʌm], a. 1. muet, f. muette; d. animals, les bêtes; to strike s.o. dumb, rendre qn muet. 2. F: sot. -ly, adv. sans mot dire; en silence. 'dumbness, s. 1. mutisme m; silence m. 2. F: sottise f; niaiserie f.

dummy ['dʌmi], s. 1. homme m de paille. 2. Com: (a) mannequin m; (b) factice m (pour vitrine); (c) (baby's) d., sucette f. 3. (at cards) mort m. 4. attrib: postiche; faux.

dump [dʌmp]. I. s. 1. tas m, amas m; rubbish d., décharge f publique. 2. dépôt m. 3. F: what a d! quel trou! II. v.tr. 1. décharger (un camion de matériau); déposer (qch.) (lourdement). 2. se défaire de (qch.); Com: to d. goods, faire du dumping.

‡dun [dʌn], v.tr. harceler (un débiteur).

dunce [dʌns], s. ignorant, -ante; âne m.

dune [dju:n], s. dune f.

dung [dʌŋ], s. fumier m. 'dunghill, s. tas m de fumier.

dungarees [dʌŋɡə'ri:z], s.pl. Cl: combinaison f; bleus mpl (de mécanicien).

dungeon ['dʌn(d)ʒ(ə)n], s. cachot m.

dupe [dju:p]. I. s. dupe f. II. v.tr. duper, tromper.

duplicate ['dju:plikeit]. I. a. & s. double (m); in d., en double exemplaire. II. v.tr. reproduire (un document) au duplicateur. 'duplicating, s. 1. duplication f. 2. reproduction f au duplicateur. dupli'cation, s. duplication f. 'duplicator, s. duplicateur m.

durable ['djuərəbl], a. durable; résistant; dura'bility, s. durabilité f; stabilité f.

duration [dju'reiʃ(ə)n], s. durée f; étendue f (de la vie).

during ['djuəriŋ], prep. pendant, durant; au cours de (l'année).

dusk [dʌsk]. I. s. crépuscule m, Fr.C: brunante f; it's getting d., la nuit tombe. 'dusky, a. (teint) bistré; noiraud.

dust [dʌst]. I. s. poussière f. II. v.tr. 1. saupoudrer (with, de). 2. épousseter (un meuble). 'dustbin, s. poubelle f. 'dustcart, s. voiture f de boueur. 'duster, s. chiffon m, torchon m; feather d., plumeau m. 'dust-jacket, s. (for book) jaquette f. 'dustman, s. boueur m, boueux m. 'dustpan, s. pelle f à main. 'dust-up, s. F: querelle f. 'dusty, a. poussiéreux.

Dutch [dʌtʃ]. 1. a. hollandais; de Hollande. 2. s. (a) the D., les Hollandais; (b) Ling: le hollandais. 3. adv. F: to go d., payer chacun son écot. †'Dutchman, s. Hollandais m.

†'duty ['djuːti], s. 1. obéissance f, respect m. 2. devoir m (to, envers). 3. fonction(s) f(pl); to do d. for s.o., remplacer qn. 4. service m; on d., de service. 5. droit m (de douane, etc.). 'dutiable, a. soumis aux droits de douane. 'dutiful, a. respectueux, soumis. -fully, adv. avec soumission. 'duty-free, a. exempt de droits (de douane).

dwarf [dwɔːf]. I. s. & a. nain, naine. II. v.tr. rabougrir (une plante); rapetisser (qch.) (par contraste).

dwindle ['dwindl], v.i. diminuer.

dye [dai]. 1. s. teinture f; fast d., grand teint. 2. matière f colorante, colorant m. II. v.tr. teindre. 'dyeing, s. 1. teinture f (d'un tissu). 2. (trade) la teinture. 'dyer, s. teinturier m.

dying ['daiiŋ]. 1. a. mourant, agonisant; F: moribond. 2. s. agonie f.

dyke [daik], s. digue f; levée f.

dynamic [dai'næmik], a. dynamique. II. s. dynamite f.
dynamite ['dainəmait]. I. s. dynamite f. II. v.tr. faire sauter (des roches) à la dynamite; dynamiter (un édifice).
dynamo ['dainəmou], s. dynamo f.
dysentery ['disəntri], s. dysenterie f.
dyspepsia [dis'pepsiə], s. dyspepsie f.
dys'peptic, a. & s. dyspepsique (mf), dyspeptique (mf).

E

E, e [iː], s. 1. (la lettre) E, e m. 2. Mus: mi m.

each [iːtʃ]. 1. a. chaque; e. day, chaque jour. 2. pron. (a) e. of us, chacun, -une, de nous; (b) e. other, l'un l'autre, les uns les autres.

eager ['iːgər], a. ardent, passionné, impatient. -ly, adv. ardemment, passionnément, avidement. 'eagerness, s. ardeur f; impatience f; vif désir.

eagle [iːgl], s. aigle mf.

ear¹ [iər], s. oreille f. F: to be up to the ears in work, être débordé de travail; F: to go off with a flea in one's e., partir l'oreille basse; Mus: to have an e., avoir l'oreille musicienne; to keep one's ears open, se tenir aux écoutes. 'earache, s. mal m, maux mpl, d'oreille(s). 'earmark, v.tr. to e. funds for a purpose, assigner, affecter, des fonds à un projet. 'earring, s. boucle f d'oreille. 'earshot, s. within e., à portée de voix. 'earwig, s. Z: perce-oreille m.

ear², s. épi m (de blé, de maïs).

earl [əːl], s. comte m.

early ['əːli]. I. a. 1. (a) matinal; to be an e. riser, se lever (de bon) matin, se lever tôt; (b) e. youth, première jeunesse; (of fruit, flowers) précoce, hâtif; e. death, mort prématurée. 3. prochain; at an e. date, prochainement, sous peu. II. adv. (a) de bonne heure, tôt; earlier, plus tôt; too e., trop tôt; de trop bonne heure; e. in the afternoon, au commencement de l'après-midi; as e. as the tenth century, dès le dixième siècle; as e. as possible, le plus tôt possible; (b) to die e., (i) mourir jeune; (ii) mourir prématurément.

earn [əːn], v.tr. 1. gagner (de l'argent). 2. mériter (des éloges). 'earnings, s.pl. 1. salaire m, gages mpl. 2. profits mpl, bénéfices mpl.

earnest ['əːnist]. 1. a. sérieux. 2. s. in e., sérieusement; pour de bon. -ly, adv. sérieusement. 'earnestness, s. gravité f, sérieux m (de ton).

earth [əːθ], s. 1. terre f; where on e. have you been? où diable êtes-vous? (a) le monde; (b) le sol; down to e., terre à terre, réaliste. 2. terrier m, tanière f (d'un renard); to run s.o. to e., dénicher qn. 3. El: e. (cable), câble m de terre; prise f de terre. 'earthen, a. de terre. 'earthenware, s. poterie f; faïence f. 'earthly, a. 1. terrestre. 2. for no e. reason, à propos de rien. 'earthquake, s. tremblement de terre; séisme m. 'earthworm, s. ver m de terre.

ease [iːz]. I. s. 1. tranquillité f; repos m, bien-être m, aise f. 2. to live a life of e., vivre (i) dans l'oisiveté, (ii) une vie de loisirs. 3. (a) aisance f (de manières); (b) simplicité f; facilité f; with e., facilement; aisément. II. v.tr. 1. (a) adoucir, calmer (la souffrance); soulager (un malade); (b) calmer (l'esprit). 2. débarrasser (qn de qch.). 3. détendre, relâcher (un cordage). 'ease off, up, v.tr. 1. Nau: filer (un cordage); soulager (un palan). 2. v.i. F: se relâcher; moins travailler; (b) ralentir.

easel [iːzl], s. chevalet m.

east [iːst]. I. s. est m, orient m, levant m. 2. adv. to the e., à l'est, à l'orient; (voyager) vers l'orient. 3. adj. (vent) d'est; (pays) de l'est. 'easterly. 1. a. e. wind, vent d'est. 2. adv. vers l'est. 'eastern, a. est, de l'est; oriental. 'eastwards, adv. à l'est, vers l'est.

Easter ['iːstər], s. Pâques m.

easy ['iːzi]. I. a. 1. (a) facile; to feel easier, se sentir mieux; (b) tranquille; sans inquiétude. 2. (a) (of manners, etc.) aisé, libre; (b) style, style facile; (b) Cl: e. fit, coupe f ample. 3. (a) e.

task, travail facile, aisé; that's e. to see, cela se voit; within e. reach of (sth.), à distance commode de (qch.); (b) (of pers.) facile, accommodant; (c) (to travel) by e. stages, (voyager) par petites étapes; Com: by e. payments, avec facilités de paiement. -lly, adv. 1. tranquillement, à son aise, paisiblement; to take life e., se laisser vivre. 2. (a) doucement, sans secousse; (b) avec confort. 3. facilement, avec facilité. II. adv. to take things e., prendre les choses en douceur; to go e. with s.o., ménager qn. 'easy 'chair, s. fauteuil m, bergère f. 'easy-going, a. (a) insouciant; (b) d'humeur facile, facile à vivre.

‡eat [iːt], v.tr. manger; to e. one's breakfast, dinner, supper, déjeuner, dîner, souper; fit to e., mangeable. 'eatable. 1. a. bon à manger. 2. s.pl. comestibles m. eat a'way, v.tr. ronger, éroder; (of acid) mordre, attaquer (un métal). 'eating, s. manger m; e. apple, pomme f à couteau. eat 'up, v.tr. 1. achever de manger, dévorer. 2. consumer (qch.) sans profit.

eaves [iːvz], s.pl. (of house) avant-toit m. ‡eavesdrop ['iːvzdrɔp], v.i. écouter aux portes. 'eavesdropper, s. écouteur, -euse, aux portes.

ebb [eb]. I. s. 1. jusant m, baisse f (de la marée); e. tide, marée descendante. 2. déclin m (de la fortune); to be at a low e., être très bas. II. v.i. 1. (of tide) baisser. 2. (of life, etc.) décliner, baisser; to e. away, s'écouler.

ebony ['ebəni], s. ébène f; bois m d'ébène.

eccentric [ek'sentrik], a. & s. excentrique (mf); original, -ale, -aux. eccen'tricity, s. excentricité f de caractère; bizarrerie f.

‡echo ['ekou]. I. s. écho m. II. 1. v.tr. répéter. 2. v.i. (a) faire écho; (b) retentir.

eclipse [i'klips], s. éclipse f (de la lune, etc.).

‡economy [i(:)'kɔnəmi], s. 1. économie f; Aut: e. run, concours m de consommation. 2. political e., économie politique; controlled e., économie dirigée. eco'nomical, a. (a) (of pers.) économe; (b) (of methods, etc.) économique. -ally, adv. économiquement; to use (sth.) e., ménager (qch.). eco'nomics, s. 1. l'économie politique. 2. rentabilité f, aspect financier d'une affaire). e'conomist, s. économiste m. e'conomize, v.tr. économiser, ménager; abs. faire des économies.

ecstasy ['ekstəsi], s. transport m (de joie); ravissement m.

eddy ['edi]. I. s. remous m; tourbillon m. II. v.i. faire des remous; tourbillonner, tournoyer.

edge [edʒ]. I. s. 1. fil m, tranchant m (d'une lame, etc.); to take the e. off (sth.), émousser (un couteau, l'appétit). 2. bord m, rebord m; tranche f (d'un livre); (of pers.) on e., énervé. 3. lisière f (d'un bois). II. v.tr. to e. one's way into a room, se faufiler, se glisser, dans une pièce; to e. away (from s.o., sth.), se reculer tout doucement (de qn, qch.). 'edgeways, adv. (vu) de côté; F: I can't get a word in e., impossible de placer un mot. 'edgy, a. F: (of pers.) énervé.

edible ['edibl], a. comestible; bon à manger.

edifice ['edifis], s. (grand) bâtiment m.

edit ['edit], v.tr. (a) annoter, éditer (un texte); (b) rédiger (un journal); diriger (une série de textes, etc.). 'editing, s. 1. annotation f (d'un texte). 2. rédaction f (d'un journal). 3. Cin: montage m. e'dition, s. édition f. 'editor, s. 1. éditeur m (d'un texte). 2. (a) directeur m (d'une série); (b) rédacteur m en chef (d'un journal); (c) Rad: programme m. édito'rial. 1. a. éditorialiste mf. edi'torial. 1. a. éditorial. 2. s. article m de fond; éditorial m.

educate ['edjukeit], v.tr. 1. (a) instruire (qn); (b) faire faire ses études à (un enfant). 2. former (qn, le goût de qn); educated man, homme cultivé. edu'cation, s. 1. éducation f. 2. enseignement m, instruction f; adult e., enseignement post-scolaire; university e., enseignement supérieur. edu'cational, a. (ouvrage) d'enseignement; e. film, film éducatif.

eel [iːl], s. anguille f.

eerie ['iəri], a. étrange, mystérieux.

effect [i'fekt], s. 1. effet m, influence f; résultat m, conséquence f; to take e., (i) faire (son) effet; (ii) (of regulations) entrer en vigueur; of no e., sans effet, inutile; to no e., en vain; words to that e., quelque chose d'approchant. 2. pl. personal effects, biens m (personnels); Th: stage effects, effets scéniques. e'ffective. 1. a. (a) efficace; effectif; (b) (tableau, etc.) qui fait de l'effet. 2. s.pl. Mil: effectifs m. -ly, adv. efficacement, utilement; (b) d'une façon frappante.

effeminate [i'feminit], a. efféminé.

effervesce [efə'ves], v.i. être, entrer, en effervescence; (of drinks) mousser. effer'vescence, s. effervescence f.

efficacious [efi'keiʃəs], a. efficace. -ly, adv. efficacement. effi'caciousness, 'efficacy, s. efficacité f.

efficiency [i'fiʃ(ə)nsi], s. 1. efficacité f (d'un remède). 2. rendement m (d'une machine); bon fonctionnement m (d'une entreprise). 3. capacité f, compétence f (d'une personne). e'fficient, a. (a) (travail) efficace; (b) qui fonctionne bien; (c) (pers.) capable, compétent. -ly, adv. d'une manière efficace, compétente.

effort ['efət], s. effort m; to make an e., s'efforcer (de faire qch.); he spares no e., il ne s'épargne pas. **'effortless,** a. (a) sans effort; (b) facile.

effusive [i'fju:ziv], a. démonstratif, expansif. -ly, adv. avec effusion.

egg[1] [eg], s. œuf m; boiled e., œuf à la coque; a bad e., (i) un œuf pourri; (ii) F: un vaurien. **'egg-cup,** s. coquetier m. **'eggshell,** s. coquille f d'œuf.

egg[2], v.tr. to e. s.o. on, inciter qn (à faire qch.).

egoism ['egəuizm], s. egoïsme m. **'egoist,** s. égoïste mf.

Egyptian [i'dʒipʃ(ə)n], a. & s. égyptien, -ienne. **Egyp'tology,** s. égyptologie f.

eiderdown ['aidədaun], s. édredon m.

eight [eit], num. a. & s. huit (m); to be e. (years old), avoir huit ans; page twenty-eight, page vingt-huit; it's e. o'clock, il est huit heures. **eigh'teen,** num. a. & s. dix-huit (m). **eigh-'teenth,** num. a. & s. (a) dix-huitième; (b) (on) the e. (of May), le dix-huit (mai). **eighth,** num. a. & s. (a) huitième; (b) (on) the e., le huit; (c) one-e., un huitième. **'eighty,** num. a. & s. quatre-vingts; e.-one, quatre-vingt-un.

either ['aiðər]. I. a. & pron. (a) l'un(e) et l'autre; e. side, de chaque côté; (b) l'un(e) ou l'autre; ni l'un(e) ni l'autre; e. of them, soit l'un(e), soit l'autre, n'importe lequel. II. conj. & adv. (a) e... or ..., ou ..., ou ... soit ... soit ...; (b) not ... e., ne ... non plus.

ejaculate [i'dʒækjuleit], v.tr. pousser, lancer (un cri, un juron). **ejacu'lation,** s. cri m, exclamation f.

eject [i'dʒekt], v.tr. 1. jeter, émettre (des flammes, etc.). 2. expulser, F: éjecter, sortir (un locataire). **e'jector,** s. Av: e. seat, siège m éjectable.

eke [i:k] v.tr. to eke out, augmenter (ses revenus); ménager (les vivres); allonger (la sauce).

elaborate [i'læb(ə)rit], a. compliqué; (travail) soigné, minutieux. -ly, adv. avec soin, minutieusement.

elapse [i'læps], v.i. (of time) s'écouler; (se) passer.

elastic [i'læstik], a. & s. élastique (m). **elas'ticity,** s. élasticité f; ressort m (de caractère); souplesse f (de corps).

elbow ['elbəu]. I. s. 1. coude m; to rest one's e. on sth., s'accouder sur qch. 2. coude, genou m (d'un tuyau). II. v.tr. e. il coudoyer (qn); pousser (qn) du coude; to e. one's way, se frayer un passage. **'elbow-grease,** s. F: put some e.-g. into it! mettez-y un peu de nerf! **'elbow-room,** s. to have e.-r., avoir ses coudées franches; être au large.

elder ['eldər], a. & s. aîné, -ée; plus âgé, -ée; to obey one's elders, obéir à ses aînés. **'elderly,** a. d'un certain âge. **'eldest,** a. aîné.

elect [i'lekt], v.tr. 1. choisir (de faire qch.); se décider (à faire qch.). 2. élire (qn député); the Mayor e., le futur maire. **e'lection,** s. élection f; parliamentary elections, élections législatives. **e'lector,** s. électeur, -trice, votant, -ante.

electricity [ilek'trisiti], s. électricité f. **e'lectric, e'lectrical,** a. électrique. **-ally,** adv. électriquement; e. driven, actionné par électromoteur. **elec'trician,** s. Ind: (monteur-)électricien m. **electrifi'cation,** s. 1. électrisation f (d'un corps). 2. électrification f (d'un chemin de fer). **e'lectrify,** v.tr. 1. électriser (un corps, son auditoire). 2. électrifier (un chemin de fer). **e'lectro'cardiogram,** s. électrocardiogramme m. **e'lectrocute,** v.tr. électrocuter. **elec'trolysis,** s. électrolyse f. **e'lectron,** s. électron m. **elec'tronic,** I. a. électronique. 2. s.pl. électronique f; e. specialist, électronicien, -ienne. **e'lectrotech'nology,** s. électrotechnique f. **e'lectro'therapy,** s. Med: électrothérapie f.

elegance ['eligəns], s. élégance f. **'elegant,** a. élégant. **-ly,** adv. élégamment.

element ['elimənt], s. 1. élément m; to be in, out of, one's e., (i) F: être à son affaire; (ii) être dépaysé. 2. (a) the personal e., le facteur humain; (b) partie f (d'un tout). 3. Ch: corps m simple. 4. pl. rudiments m (d'une science). **ele'mentary,** a. élémentaire.

elephant ['elifənt], s. éléphant m.

elevate ['eliveit], v.tr. élever (l'hostie, son style); hausser, élever (la voix). **'elevated,** a. 1. (rang) élevé; F: (être) un peu gris. 2. (overhead) surélevé. **ele'vation,** s. 1. élévation f (de l'hostie, etc.). 2. Ind: sectional e., coupe verticale; front e., façade f.

eleven [i'levn]. 1. num. a. & s. onze (m). 2. s. (cricket) équipe f de onze joueurs. 3. s.pl. F: elevenses, casse-croûte m (à onze heures du matin). **e'leventh,** num. a. & s. onzième; at the e. hour, au dernier moment; (on) the e., le onze (du mois).

elicit [i'lisit], v.tr. to e. the facts, tirer les faits au clair.

eligible ['elidʒibl], a. (a) to be e., être éligible à, avoir droit à (qch.); (b) e. for a job, admissible à un emploi.

eliminate [i'limineit], v.tr. éliminer. **e'liminating,** a. Sp: e. heats, épreuves éliminatoires.

elk [elk], s. élan m; Canadian e., orignal m.

elm [elm], s. orme m.

elocution [elə'kju:ʃ(ə)n], s. élocution f, diction f.

elongate ['i:lɔŋgeit], v.tr. allonger, étendre.

elope [i'loup], v.i. (of girl) s'enfuir (avec un jeune homme).

eloquence ['eləkwəns], s. éloquence f. 'éloquent, a. éloquent; to speak, regard m qui en dit long. -ly, adv. éloquemment.

else [els]. **1.** adv. autrement; come in or e. go out, entrez ou bien sortez. **2.** (a) a. or adv. (i) anyone e., toute autre personne; n'importe qui d'autre; (ii) (interrogative) did you see anyone e.? avez-vous vu encore qn? anything e., n'importe quoi d'autre; someone e., un autre, qn d'autre; something e., autre chose; nothing e., rien m d'autre; everything e., tout le reste; (b) adv. everywhere e., partout ailleurs; somewhere e., autre part, ailleurs; nowhere e., nulle part ailleurs. 'elsewhere, adv. ailleurs, autre part.

elucidate [i'lju:sideit], v.tr. élucider, éclaircir (un problème). eluci'dation, s. élucidation f.

elude [i'lju:d], v.tr. éluder (une question); tourner (la loi); échapper à (la poursuite). e'lusive, a. insaisissable, intangible; évasif. -ly, adv. évasivement.

emaciated [i'meiʃieitid], a. décharné, amaigri. emaci'ation, s. amaigrissement m.

emancipate [i'mænsipeit], v.tr. émanciper (qn); affranchir (un esclave). emanci'pation, s. émancipation f; affranchissement m.

embalm [im'ba:m], v.tr. embaumer.

embankment [im'bæŋkmənt], s. (a) digue f; (b) remblai m, talus m.

†**embargo** [im'ba:gou], s. embargo m; (of ship, goods) to be under an e., être séquestré.

embark [im'ba:k]. **1.** v.tr. embarquer. **2.** v.i. s'embarquer. embar'kation, s. embarquement m; e. card, carte f d'accès à bord.

embarrass [im'bærəs], v.tr. embarrasser, gêner (qn); déconcerter (qn). em'barrassment, s. embarras m, gêne f.

embassy ['embəsi], s. ambassade f.

embellish [im'beliʃ], v.tr. embellir, orner (qch.); enjoliver (un récit). em'bellishment, s. ornement m.

embers ['embəz], s.pl. braise f; cendres f ardentes.

embezzle [im'bezl], v.tr. détourner (des fonds). em'bezzlement, s. détournement m de fonds.

embittered [im'bitəd], a. aigri (by, par).

emblem ['embləm], s. emblème m, symbole m; insigne (sportif). emble'matic, a. emblématique.

embody [im'bɔdi], v.tr. **1.** incarner. **2.** réaliser, concrétiser (une idée).

personnifier (une qualité). **3.** Jur: incorporer. em'bodiment, s. incarnation f; personnification f; incorporation f.

embrace [im'breis]. **I.** s. étreinte f. **II.** v.tr. embrasser, étreindre (qn).

embroider [im'brɔidər], v.tr. broder. em'broidery, s. broderie f.

embryo ['embriou], s. embryon m.

emend [i'mend], v.tr. corriger (un texte).

emerald ['emərəld]. **1.** s. émeraude f. **2.** a. & s. e.(-green), émeraude f.

emerge [i'mə:dʒ], v.i. **1.** émerger (from, de); surgir. **2.** déboucher; sortir.

†**emergency** [i'mə:dʒənsi], s. circonstance f critique; cas urgent, imprévu; Med: an e., une urgence; in case of e., au besoin; e. exit, sortie f de secours.

emery ['eməri], s. émeri m; e. paper, cloth, papier m, toile f d'émeri.

emigrate ['emigreit], v.i. émigrer. 'emigrant, a. & s. émigrant, -ante. emi'gration, s. émigration f.

eminence ['eminəns], s. éminence f. Ecc: Your E., votre Éminence. 'eminent, a. éminent. -ly, adv. éminemment.

†**emit** [i'mit], v.tr. dégager, émettre (de la chaleur); répandre (une odeur); rendre (un son). e'mission, s. émission f; dégagement m (de chaleur, etc.).

emotion [i'mouʃ(ə)n], s. émotion f, trouble m; attendrissement m. e'motional, a. e. voice, voix émue; to be e., s'attendrir facilement.

emperor ['empərər], s. empereur m.

emphasize ['emfəsaiz], v.tr. accentuer, appuyer sur, souligner (un fait); faire ressortir (une qualité). 'emphasis, s. force f (énergie f d')accentuation f. em'phatic, a. (manière) énergique; (ton) autoritaire; (refus) net, positif. -ally, adv. énergiquement; (refuser) carrément.

empire ['empaiər], s. empire m.

employ [im'plɔi], v.tr. employer (qn, son temps); faire usage de (la force, etc.). em'ployee, s. employé, -ée; the firm's employees, le personnel de la maison. em'ployer, s. Ind: patron, -onne; maître, maîtresse; employers' union, syndicat patronal. em'ployment, s. emploi m, travail m; place f, situation f; e. agency, bureau m de placement.

empower [im'pauər], v.tr. autoriser (qn à faire qch.).

empress ['empris], s. impératrice f.

empty ['em(p)ti]. **I. 1.** v.tr. vider; décharger (un wagon); vidanger (un carter). **2.** v.i. (of river, etc.) se décharger, se déverser (into, dans); (of hall) se vider. **II. 1.** a. vide (of, de); (a) (immeuble) inoccupé; (estomac) creux; (b) e. words, vaines paroles. **2.** s.pl. Com: empties, f; caisses f, (les) bouteilles f vides. 'emptiness, s. vide m. empty-'handed, a. les mains vides.

enable [i'neibl], *v.tr.* to e. s.o. to do sth., rendre qn capable, mettre qn à même, de faire qch.

enamel [i'næməl], *s.* I. *s.* 1. émail *m*, pl. émaux. 2. vernis *m*; laque *f*; e. paint, peinture *f* au vernis. 3. fer *m* émaillé. II. *v.tr.* 1. émailler (la porcelaine). 2. ripoliner; vernir, vernisser; enamelled saucepan, casserole *f* en fer émaillé.

encampment [in'kæmpmənt], *s.* campement *m*.

enchant [in'tʃɑːnt], *v.tr.* 1. enchanter, ensorceler. 2. enchanter, charmer, ravir. **en'chanting**, *a.* enchanteur; ravissant, charmant, -ly, *adv.* à ravir. **en'chantment**, *s.* enchantement *m*; ravissement *m*.

encircle [in'səːkl], *v.tr.* ceindre, encercler; entourer (une armée).

enclose [in'klouz], *v.tr.* 1. enclore, clôturer (un champ) (with, de). 2. inclure, joindre, enclosed (herewith), ci-inclus. **en'closure**, *s.* 1. clôture *f*. 2. (*a*) enclos *m*, clos *m*; (*b*) (*horse racing*) le pesage. 3. Com: pièce *f* annexée, document *m* ci-joint.

encore [ɔŋ'kɔːr]. I. *s. & int.* bis *m*; rappel *m*. II. *v.tr.* bisser (un acteur); *abs.* crier bis.

encounter [in'kauntər], *v.* I. *s.* rencontre *f*. 2. combat *m*. II. *v.tr.* rencontrer (un obstacle); éprouver (des difficultés); affronter (l'ennemi).

encourage [in'kʌridʒ], *v.tr.* encourager. **en'couragement**, *s.* encouragement *m*. **en'couraging**, *a.* encourageant. -ly, *adv.* d'une manière encourageante.

encroach [in'kroutʃ], *v.i.* empiéter (on, sur) (une terre); to e. upon s.o.'s time, abuser du temps de qn. **en'croachment**, *s.* empiétement *m* (on, sur); usurpation *f* (des droits de qn).

encumber [in'kʌmbər], *v.tr.* encombrer (with, de); gêner (qn, le mouvement). **en'cumbrance**, *s.* embarras *m*, charge *f* (to s.o., à qn).

encyclopaedia [insaiklə'piːdiə], *s.* encyclopédie *f*.

end [end]. I. *s.* 1. bout *m*, extrémité *f*; fin *f*; *Fb*: to change ends, changer de camp; the e. house, la dernière maison; from e. to e., d'un bout à l'autre; two hours on e., deux heures de suite; *Aut*: big e., tête *f* de bielle. 2. limite *f*, borne *f*. 3. bout, fin (du mois); terme *m* (d'un procès); to make an e. of sth., en finir avec qch.; to achever qch.; mettre fin à qch.; to come to an e., prendre fin; in the e., à la longue; à la fin; enfin; to come to a bad e., mal finir. 4. fin, but *m*. II. *v.* 1. *v.tr.* finir, achever, terminer (un ouvrage); conclure (un discours). 2. *v.i.* finir, se terminer. **'ending**, *s.* 1. terminaison *f*, achèvement *m*. 2. fin *f* (d'un ouvrage); happy e.,

dénouement heureux. **'endless**, *a.* 1. (*a*) (voyage) sans fin; (*b*) sans bornes; infini. 2. (*in time*) éternel. -ly, *adv.* sans fin; éternellement; perpétuellement.

endanger [in'deindʒər], *v.tr.* mettre en danger; risquer (sa vie); compromettre (ses intérêts).

endear [in'diər], *v.tr.* rendre cher (to, à). **en'dearing**, *a.* 1. qui inspire l'affection. 2. (mot) tendre, affectueux. -ly, *adv.* tendrement, affectueusement. **en'dearments**, *s.pl.* caresses *f*; mots *m* tendres.

endeavour [in'devər]. I. *s.* effort *m*, tentative *f*. II. *v.i.* s'efforcer; essayer, tâcher (de faire qch.).

endorse [in'dɔːs], *v.tr.* 1. endosser (un chèque); viser (un passeport); Com: avaliser (un effet). 2. appuyer (une opinion); souscrire à (une décision). **en'dorsement**, *s.* 1. endossement *m* (d'un chèque); (on passport) mention *f* spéciale. 2. approbation *f*; adhésion *f* (à une opinion).

endow [in'dau], *v.tr.* doter (qn) (with, de); fonder (un lit d'hôpital). **en'dowment**, *s.* 1. (*a*) dotation *f*; (*b*) fondation *f* (léguée à une œuvre, etc.). 2. e. insurance, assurance *f* à terme fixe.

endure [in'djuər], *v.tr.* 1. supporter, endurer (le mal, les insultes). 2. *v.i.* durer, rester. **en'durance**, *s.* 1. (*a*) endurance *f*, résistance *f*; beyond e., insupportable; (*b*) e. test, (i) *E*: essai *m* de durée; (ii) *Sp*: épreuve *f* d'endurance. 2. patience *f*.

†**enemy** ['enəmi], *s.* ennemi, -ie.

energy ['enədʒi], *s.* énergie *f*, force *f*; atomic e., énergie atomique. **ener'getic**, *a.* énergique. **-ally**, *adv.* énergiquement. **'energize**, *v.tr.* donner de l'énergie à (qn); stimuler (qn); amorcer (une dynamo).

enervate ['enəveit], *v.tr.* affaiblir, énerver (le corps, la volonté).

enforce [in'fɔːs], *v.tr.* 1. faire valoir (un argument). 2. mettre en vigueur; to e. the law, appliquer la loi. 3. faire observer (un règlement). **en'forcement**, *s.* Jur: mise *f* en vigueur, application *f* (d'une loi).

engage [in'geidʒ], *v.tr. & i.* 1. engager (sa parole); s'engager (à faire qch.). 2. (*a*) embaucher (des ouvriers); (*b*) réserver (une chambre); louer (un taxi). 3. to e. s.o. in conversation, lier conversation avec qn. 4. *E:* (*a*) mettre en prise (un engrenage); (*b*) (*of cogwheel*) s'engrener (with, avec). **en'gaged**, *a.* 1. to become e., se fiancer. 2. (*of seat, taxi*) occupé, pris. **en'gagement**, *s.* 1. promesse *f*, obligation *f*. 2. poste *m*, situation *f* (de secrétaire, etc.). 3. fiançailles *fpl*. 4. *E:* embrayage *m*. **en'gaging**, *a.* attrayant, séduisant.

engine ['endʒin], s. 1. machine f, appareil m. 2. Rail: locomotive f; electric e., locomotrice f. 3. moteur m. 'engine-driver, s. mécanicien m. engi'neer, I. s. 1. ingénieur m. 2. Nau: mécanicien m. 3. Mil: soldat m du génie, the Engineers, le génie. II. v.tr. 1. construire (en qualité d'ingénieur). 2. machiner (un coup). engi'neering, s. technique f de l'ingénieur; l'industrie f mécanique; chemical e., chimie industrielle; electrical e., électrotechnique f; nuclear e., génie m atomique.

English ['iŋgliʃ]. 1. a. & s. anglais, -aise. 2. s. Ling: l'anglais m. †'Englishman, -†woman, s. Anglais m, -aise. 'English-speaking, a. anglophone, de langue anglaise.

engrave [in'greiv], v.tr. graver. en'graver, s. graveur m.

engross [in'grous], v.tr. absorber, occuper (qn, l'attention).

engulf [in'gʌlf], v.tr. engloutir, engouffrer.

enigma [i'nigmə], s. énigme f. enig'matic, a. énigmatique.

enjoy [in'dʒɔi], v.tr. 1. aimer, goûter; prendre plaisir à (qch.). 2. to e. oneself, s'amuser. 3. jouir de, posséder (la santé, la confiance de qn). en'joyable, a. agréable; (of food) savoureux. -ably, adv. agréablement; avec plaisir. en'joyment, s. 1. jouissance f (d'un droit, etc.). 2. plaisir m.

enlarge [in'lɑ:dʒ], v.tr. (a) agrandir; augmenter (sa fortune); élargir (un trou); (b) développer, amplifier (une idée). 2. v.i. to e. upon, s'étendre sur (un sujet). en'largement, s. agrandissement m.

enlighten [in'laitn], v.tr. éclairer (qn sur un sujet). en'lightened, a. éclairé.

enlist [in'list]. 1. v.tr. (a) enrôler (un soldat); to e. the services of s.o., s'assurer le concours de qn. 2. v.i. s'engager, s'enrôler. en'listed, a. Mil: U.S: e. man, simple soldat, marin, gradé. en'listment, s. engagement m, enrôlement m.

enliven [in'laiv(ə)n], v.tr. (a) animer (qn); stimuler (les affaires); (b) égayer (une fête).

enmity ['enmiti], s. inimitié f, hostilité f.

enormous [i'nɔ:məs], a. énorme (succès) fou. -ly, adv. énormément.

enough [i'nʌf], 1. a. & s. assez; e. money, assez d'argent; that's e., en voilà assez! more than e., plus qu'il n'en faut; he has e. to live on, il a de quoi vivre; it was e. to drive one crazy, c'était à vous rendre fou. 2. adv. (a) good e., assez bon; (b) you know well e., vous savez très bien; he sings well e., elle ne chante pas mal.

enquire [in'kwaiər], v.i. s'informer, se renseigner (de qch.); to e. for s.o.,

demander qn. †en'quiry, s. 1. enquête f. 2. demande f de renseignements; Enquiries, bureau m de renseignements.

enrage [in'reidʒ], v.tr. rendre (qn) furieux; faire rager (qn).

enrapture [in'ræptʃər], v.tr. ravir, enchanter (un auditoire).

enrich [in'ritʃ], v.tr. enrichir. en'richment, s. enrichissement m.

‡**enrol** [in'roul], v.tr. enrôler, encadrer (des recrues); embaucher (des ouvriers); immatriculer (des étudiants).

ensign ['ens(ə)n], s. Nau: 1. pavillon national; red e. = pavillon marchand. 2. U.S: lieutenant m.

enslave [in'sleiv], v.tr. asservir. en'slavement, s. asservissement m.

ensue [in'sju:], v.i. s'ensuivre; silence ensued, il se fit un silence.

ensure [in'ʃuər], v.tr. 1. assurer (contre le malheur); garantir. 2. assurer (le succès).

entail [in'teil], v.tr. amener, entraîner (des conséquences); occasionner (des dépenses).

entangle [in'tæŋgl], v.tr. 1. empêtrer; to get entangled, s'empêtrer. 2. emmêler; enchevêtrer; embrouiller. en'tanglement, s. embrouillement m, enchevêtrement m.

enter ['entər]. 1. v.i. entrer (into, through, dans, par); to e. into relations with s.o., entrer en relations avec qn. 2. v.tr. (a) entrer dans (une maison); s'engager sur (une route); (b) to e. the Army, the Navy, entrer au service; (c) to e. for a race, se faire inscrire pour une course.

enterprise ['entəpraiz], s. 1. entreprise f. 2. esprit m d'entreprise, hardiesse f. 'enterprising, a. entreprenant.

entertain [entə'tein], v.tr. 1. amuser, divertir (qn). 2. offrir un repas à (qn); abs. recevoir des amis. 3. accueillir (une proposition). 4. concevoir (des doutes); nourrir (un espoir). enter'taining, a. amusant, divertissant. enter'tainment, s. 1. (a) divertissement m (d'une foule, d'un auditoire); (b) Th: spectacle m. 2. hospitalité f; Adm: e. allowance, frais mpl de représentation.

enthusiasm [in'θju:ziæzm], s. enthousiasme m (for, about, pour). en'thuse, v.i. F: s'enthousiasmer, se passionner (de, pour). en'thusiast, s. enthousiaste mf; fervent(e). F: enragé(e) (du ski, etc.). enthusi'astic, a. enthousiaste. -ally, adv. avec enthousiasme.

entice [in'tais], v.tr. attirer, séduire; entraîner (qn à faire qch.). en'ticement, s. 1. séduction f. 2. attrait m, charme m. 3. appât m. en'ticing, a. (of offer) séduisant, attrayant.

entire [in'taiər], a. (a) entier, tout; the e. population, la population (tout) entière; (b) entier, complet; an e. success, un véritable succès. -ly, adv. entièrement, tout à fait. **en'tirety**, s. in its e., en entier, en totalité, intégralement.

entitle [in'taitl], v.tr. to e. s.o. to do sth., donner à qn le droit de faire qch. **en'titled**, a. to be e. to do sth., avoir droit à qch.; to be e. to do sth., être en droit de faire qch.

entrance[1] ['entrəns], s. 1. (a) entrée f. P.N: e. gate, barrière f; grille f d'entrée; (b) admission f, accès m; e. fee, (i) prix m d'entrée; (ii) droit m d'inscription. 2. main e., entrée principale; side e., porte f de service.

entrance[2] [in'trɑːns], v.tr. extasier, ravir (qn). **en'trancing**, a. enchanteur, ravissant.

entreat [in'triːt], v.tr. prier, supplier (qn de faire qch.). **en'treating**, a. (ton, regard) suppliant. -ly, adv. d'un air, d'un ton suppliant. **en'treaty**, s. prière f, supplication f.

entrust [in'trast], v.tr. charger qn (d'une tâche, etc.); confier (un secret, un enfant) à qn.

†entry ['entri], s. 1. (a) entrée f. P.N: no e., défense d'entrer; (one-way street) sens interdit; (b) début m (dans la politique, etc.). 2. Com: single, double, e., comptabilité f en partie simple, en partie double. 3. Sp: inscription (d'un concurrent).

entwine [in'twain]. 1. v.tr. (a) entrelacer; (b) enlacer (with, de). 2. v.i. s'entrelacer.

enumerate [i'njuːməreit], v.tr. énumérer. **enume'ration**, s. énumération f.

enunciate [i'nʌnsieit], v.tr. 1. énoncer, exprimer (une opinion). 2. prononcer, articuler (distinctement).

envelop [in'veləp], v.tr. envelopper. **'envelope** ['en-], s. enveloppe f.

environment [in'vaiərənmənt], s. milieu m, entourage m; environnement m, ambiance f.

envisage [in'vizidʒ], v.tr. envisager (une difficulté, un danger).

†envoy ['envɔi], s. envoyé, -ée (diplomatique).

envy ['envi]. I. s. envie f. II. v.tr. envier, porter envie à (qn). **'enviable**, a. enviable, digne d'envie. **'envious**, a. envieux. -ly, adv. avec envie.

epic ['epik]. 1. a. épique. 2. s. poème m épique; épopée f.

epicure ['epikjuər], s. gourmet m.

epidemic [epi'demik]. 1. a. épidémique. 2. s. épidémie f.

epigram ['epigræm], s. épigramme f.

episode ['episoud], s. épisode m.

epitaph ['epitɑːf], s. épitaphe f.

epithet ['epiθet], s. épithète f.

epoch ['iːpɔk], s. époque f, âge m. '**epoch-making**, a. historique; inoubliable.

equability [iːkwə'biliti], s. uniformité f (de climat); égalité f, régularité f (d'humeur). **'equable** ['ek-], a. uniforme, régulier; égal.

equal ['iːkwəl]. I. a. 1. égaler (in, en). II. a. 1. égal (to, with, à); (b) to be e. to the occasion, être à la hauteur de la situation; I don't feel e. to it, je ne m'en sens pas le courage. III. s. égal, -ale; pair m; to treat s.o. as an e., traiter qn d'égal à égal. -ally, adv. également, pareillement. **e'quality**, s. égalité f. **'equalize**. 1. v.tr. (a) égaliser; Fb: to e. (the score), marquer égalité de points; (b) compenser, équilibrer (des forces, etc.). 2. v.i. (a) s'égaliser; (b) s'équilibrer.

equanimity [ekwə'nimiti], s. tranquillité f d'esprit; équanimité f.

equation [i'kweiʒ(ə)n], s. Mth: equation f.

equator [i'kweitər], s. equateur m. **equa'torial**, a. équatorial.

equilibrium [iːkwi'libriəm], s. équilibre m; aplomb m.

equinox ['ekwinɔks], s. équinoxe m.

†equip [i'kwip], v.tr. 1. équiper, armer (un navire, etc.). 2. meubler, monter (une maison); outiller, monter (une usine); well equipped, (laboratoire) bien installé; (ménage) bien monté. **e'quipment**, s. équipement m; armement m (d'un navire); outillage m (d'une usine); camping m, matériel m de camping.

equity ['ekwiti], s. équité f, justice f. **'equitable**, a. équitable, juste. -ably, adv. avec justice, équitablement.

equivalent [i'kwivələnt], a. & s. équivalent (m).

equivocal [i'kwivək(ə)l], a. équivoque.

era ['iərə], s. ère f.

eradicate [i'rædikeit], v.tr. extirper (des préjugés); déraciner (une plante).

erase [i'reiz], v.tr. effacer; raturer, gommer (un mot); e'raser, s. gomme f (à effacer); e'rasure, s. rature f; grattage m.

erect [i'rekt]. I. a. droit, debout; with head e., la tête haute. II. v.tr. 1. dresser (un mât, etc.). 2. ériger, construire (un édifice); monter, installer (une machine). **e'rection**, s. 1. (a) dressage m; (b) construction f, érection f; montage m, installation f. 2. bâtisse f, édifice m.

erode [i'roud], v.tr. éroder; ronger (of acid) corroder. **e'rosion**, s. érosion f; usure f.

erotic [i'rɔtik], a. érotique.

errand ['er(ə)nd], s. commission f, course f; e. boy, garçon m de courses.

erratic [i'rætik], a. 1. irrégulier. 2. (of pers.) excentrique. -ally, adv. sans méthode; (travailler) à bâtons rompus.

error ['erər], s. 1. erreur f, faute f, méprise f; typing, e. faute de frappe. 2. to be in e., être dans l'erreur; avoir tort. e'roneous, a. erroné; faux. -ly, adv. à tort; par erreur.

erudite ['erudait], a. érudit, savant. eru'dition, s. érudition f.

erupt [i'rʌpt], v.i. (of volcano) faire éruption, s. éruption f.

escalate ['eskəleit], v.i. Pol: Mil: passer d'un conflit localisé à une guerre plus importante. esca'lation, s. Pol: Mil: escalade f.

escalator ['eskəleitər], s. escalier roulant.

escape [is'keip]. I. s. (a) fuite f, évasion f; to make one's e., s'échapper, se sauver; to have a narrow e., (l')échapper belle; (b) échappement m, fuite (de gaz, etc.); (c) (fire-)e., escalier m de secours. II. v. 1. v.i. s'échapper (from, out of, de); s'évader (de prison). 2. v.tr. échapper à (un danger); to notice, passer inaperçu. es'capade, s. escapade f, frasque f. es'capism, s. évasion f de la réalité.

escort. I. s. ['eskɔːt], escorte f. II. v.tr. [is'kɔːt] escorter; to e. s.o. home, reconduire qn.

especial [is'peʃ(ə)l], a. spécial; particulier. -ally, adv. surtout, particulièrement.

espionage [espiə'nɑːʒ], s. espionnage m.

esplanade [esplə'neid], s. esplanade f.

esquire [is'kwaiər], s. (abbr. Esq.) J. Martin, Esq. = Monsieur J. Martin.

essay ['esei], s. 1. essai m; effort m; tentative f. 2. essai; composition f (littéraire).

essence ['esəns], s. essence f; the e. of the matter, le fond de l'affaire; meat e., extrait m de viande. e'ssential. 1. a. (outil, produit) essentiel, indispensable. 2. s. usu.pl. l'essentiel m. -ally, adv. essentiellement.

establish [is'tæbliʃ], v.tr. 1. établir (un gouvernement); fonder (une maison de commerce); créer (une agence); to e. oneself (in business), s'établir. 2. établir, constater (un fait); established reputation, réputation solide. es'tablishment, s. 1. (a) constatation f (d'un fait); (b) établissement m, fondation f (d'une industrie); business e., maison f de commerce. 2. personnel m (d'une maison). 3. l'ordre établi.

estate [is'teit], s. 1. domaine m. 2. terre f, propriété f; housing e., cité f, lotissement m; e. agent, agent m immobilier. e. agency, agence f d'immobilière.

esteem [is'tiːm], s.1. estime f, consideration f. es'timable, a. estimable.

estimate ['estimit]. I. s. 1. appréciation f, évaluation f; at the lowest e., au plus mot. 2. devis m; to put in an e.,

soumissionner; e. of expenditure, chiffre prévu pour les dépenses. II. v.tr. estimer, évaluer (les frais); estimated cost, coût estimatif. esti-'mation, s. jugement m.

estuary ['estjuə(ə)ri], s. estuaire m.

etch [etʃ], v.tr. graver à l'eau-forte. 'etching, s. eau-forte f; 'etcher, s. aquafortiste mf.

eternity [i'tə:niti], s. éternité f. e'ternal, a. (a) éternel; (b) F: continuel; sans fin. -ally, adv. éternellement.

ether ['iːθər], s. éther m.

ethics ['eθiks], s.pl. éthique f, morale f. 'ethic(al), a. moral.

ethnology [eθ'nɔlədʒi], s. ethnologie f. eth'nologist, s. ethnologue mf.

etiquette ['etiket], s. (les) convenances f; protocole m.

etymology [eti'mɔlədʒi], s. étymologie f. etymo'logical, a. étymologique. -ally, adv. étymologiquement. ety'mologist, s. étymologiste mf.

euphemism ['juːfimizm], s. euphémisme m. euphe'mistic, a. euphémique. -ally, adv. par euphémisme.

European [juərə'piː(ə)n], a. & s. européen, -enne.

evacuate [i'vækjueit], v.tr. évacuer. evacu'ation, s. évacuation f.

evade [i'veid], v.tr. éviter (un danger); se soustraire à (un châtiment); tourner (une question); déjouer (la vigilance de qn).

evaporate [i'væpəreit]. 1. v.tr. faire évaporer (un liquide). 2. v.i. s'évaporer, se vaporiser. evapo'ration, s. évaporation f.

evasion [i'veiʒ(ə)n], s. 1. évitement m; dérobade f. 2. échappatoire f; fauxfuyant m; without e., sans détours. e'vasive, a. évasif. -ly, adv. (répondre) évasivement.

eve [iːv], s. veille f; Christmas E., la veille de Noël.

even ['iːv(ə)n], s. 1. a. (a) (of surface) uni; plan; égal; uniforme; (b) (of spacing, weights, etc.) égal. 2. (souffle) régulier; (allure) uniforme; (humeur) égale. 3. Sp: to be e., être manche à manche; to get e. with s.o., rendre la pareille à qn. 4. (a) (nombre) pair; odd or e., pair ou impair; (b) e. money, somme rond. 5. Com: of e. date, de même date. -ly, adv. 1. uniment. 2. régulièrement (diviser) également; e. matched, de force égale. II. v.tr. 1. aplanir, niveler, égaliser (une surface). 2. rendre égal. III. adv. même; (with comparative) encore; (with negative) seulement même; e. so, mais cependant, quand même. 'evenness, s. 1. égalité f; régularité f (de mouvement). 2. sérénité f (d'esprit); égalité f (d'humeur).

evening ['i:vniŋ], s. soir m; soirée f; **in the e.,** le soir, au soir; **at nine o'clock in the e.,** à neuf heures du soir; **the e. before,** la veille au soir; **the next e.,** le lendemain (au) soir; **every e.,** tous les soirs; **all the e.,** toute la soirée; **e. performance,** (représentation de) soirée. **'evening 'dress,** s. (man) tenue f de soirée; (woman) robe f du soir.

event [i'vent], s. 1. cas m. 2. (a) événement m; (b) issue f, résultat m; **at all events,** en tout cas. 3. Sp: (a) réunion f sportive; (b) (athletics) field events, épreuves fpl sur terrain; track events, courses fpl sur piste. **e'ventful,** a. plein d'événements; mouvementé; (jour) mémorable.

eventual [i'ventjuəl], a. 1. (profit, etc.) éventuel. 2. définitif; final. **-ally,** adv. finalement, en fin de compte. **even-tu'ality,** s. éventualité f.

ever ['evər], adv. 1. jamais; (a) he hardly e. smokes, il ne fume presque jamais; it's raining faster than e., il pleut de plus belle; (b) e. since (then), dès lors, depuis. 2. (a) toujours; "yours e.," 'bien cordialement à vous'; (b) for e., pour toujours; à jamais; à perpétuité; Scotland for e.! vive l'Écosse! he's for e. grumbling, il grogne sans cesse. 3. (intensive) (a) as soon as e. he comes home, aussitôt qu'il rentrera; worst, best, e., sans précédent; F: e. so long ago, il y a bien, bien longtemps; (b) what e. shall we do? qu'est-ce que nous allons bien faire? when e. will he come? quand donc viendra-t-il? why e. not? mais pourquoi pas? **'evergreen.** 1. a. toujours vert; (arbre) à feuilles persistantes. 2. s.pl. plantes f vertes. **ever'lasting,** a. (a) éternel; (b) (of object) solide, durable; (c) perpétuel; (plaintes) sans fin.

every ['evri], a. (a) chaque; tout; tous les . . .; e. day, chaque jour, tous les jours; (b) (intensive) I have e. reason to believe that . . ., j'ai toute raison de croire, que . . .; (c) e. one, chacun, chacune. **'everybody, 'everyone,** indef. pron. chacun; tout le monde; tous. **'every'day,** a. journalier, quotidien; e. occurrence, fait banal; in e. use, d'usage courant. **'everything,** indef. pron. tout; they sell e., on y vend de tout. **'everywhere,** adv. partout.

evict [i'vikt], v.tr. évincer, expulser (qn) (from, de). **e'viction,** s. éviction f, expulsion f.

evidence ['evid(ə)ns], s. 1. évidence f; a man much in e., un homme très en vue. 2. signe m, marque f (de l'intelligence, etc.). 3. (a) preuve f; (b) Jur: témoignage m; to give e., témoigner. **'evident,** a. évident. **-ly,** adv. évidemment, manifestement.

evil ['i:v(i)l]. 1. a. mauvais; e.-minded, mal intentionné, malveillant. 2. s. mal m.

evoke [i'vouk], v.tr. évoquer; provoquer (un sourire).

evolve [i'vɔlv]. 1. v.tr. développer (des projets); élaborer (une méthode). 2. v.i. (of race, species) se développer, évoluer. **evo'lution,** s. évolution f.

ewe [ju:], s. brebis f.

ex- [eks], prefix. ex-; ex-minister, ex-ministre; ex-schoolmaster, ancien professeur.

exact¹ [ig'zækt], a. exact; (a) e. details, détails précis; e. copy, copie textuelle (d'un document); (b) the e. word, le mot juste. **-ly,** adv. exactement; tout juste, justement; e.! parfaitement! **ex'actitude,** s. exactitude f. **ex'actness,** s. précision f.

exact² v.tr. (a) exiger (un impôt) (from, of, de); extorquer (des soins). **ex'acting,** a. (of pers.) exigeant; (of work) astreignant.

exaggerate [ig'zædʒəreit], v.tr. exagérer. **exagger'ation,** s. exagération f.

examine [ig'zæmin], v.tr. examiner; vérifier; Sch: faire passer un examen (à qn). **exami'nation,** F: **ex'am,** s. examen m; vérification f; visite f (médicale); competitive e., concours m. **exami'nee,** s. Sch: candidat, -ate. **ex'aminer,** s. 1. inspecteur, -trice. 2. examinateur, -trice.

example [ig'zɑːmpl], s. exemple m; précédent m; for e., par exemple.

exasperate [ig'zɑːspəreit], v.tr. exaspérer. **exaspe'ration,** s. exaspération f; to drive s.o. to e., pousser qn à bout.

excavate ['ekskəveit], v.tr. creuser (un tunnel), fouiller (la terre); abs. faire des fouilles. **exca'vation,** s. excavation f; fouille f.

exceed [ik'si:d], v.tr. excéder, dépasser (ses droits, etc.); Aut: to e. the speed limit, dépasser la vitesse légale. **ex'ceedingly,** adv. très, extrêmement, excessivement.

‡**excel** [ik'sel]. 1. v.i. exceller (in, at, sth., à qch.). 2. v.tr. surpasser (qn); to e. oneself, se surpasser. **'excellence,** s. excellence f. **'excellency,** s. Your E., (votre) Excellence. **'excellent,** a. excellent, parfait. **-ly,** adv. excellemment.

except [ik'sept]. I. v.tr. excepter, exclure (from, de). II. 1. prep. excepté; à l'exception de; sauf; he does nothing e., sleep, il ne fait rien sinon dormir. 2. conj. phrase: e. that, excepté que, sauf que. **ex'ception,** s. 1. exception f; with the e. of . . ., exception faite de . . . 2. objection f; to take e. to sth., (i) trouver à redire à qch.; (ii) se froisser de qch. **ex'ceptional,** a. exceptionnel. **-ally,** adv. exceptionnellement.

excess [ik'ses], s. 1. excès m. 2. excédent m (de poids, etc.); e. luggage, bagages mpl. en surpoids m; **e. fare**, supplément m. **ex'cessive**, a. excessif; immodéré; extrême. -ly, adv. excessivement; (manger) à l'excès.

exchange [iks'tʃeindʒ]. I. s. 1. échange m; (car etc., taken in) part e., reprise f. 2. Fin: rate of e., taux m de change. 3. (a) bourse f (des valeurs); (b) telephone e., central m (téléphonique). II. v.tr. échanger, troquer (qch. pour, contre, qch.).

exchequer [iks'tʃekər], s. (a) the E., (i) la trésorerie, le fisc; (ii) le trésor public; (b) the Chancellor of the E. . . . le Ministre des Finances.

excise [ek'saiz], s. contributions indirectes; the E. Office, la Régie.

excite [ik'sait], v.tr. 1. (a) provoquer, exciter (un sentiment); (b) Anat: stimuler (un nerf). 2. (a) exciter, enflammer (une passion); (b) surexciter, agiter (qn); don't get excited! ne vous énervez pas! **excita'bility**, s. 1. émotivité f; El: excitabilité f. **ex'citable**, a. (of nerves) surexcitable. **ex'citement**, s. agitation f, surexcitation f; the thirst for e., la soif des sensations fortes; what's all the e. about? qu'est-ce qui se passe? **ex'citing**, a. passionnant, émouvant, captivant; (roman) palpitant; Sp: (partie) mouvementée.

exclaim [eks'kleim], v.i. s'écrier, s'exclamer. **excla'mation**, s. exclamation f; e. mark, point m d'exclamation.

exclude [iks'klu:d], v.tr. (a) exclure (from, de); excluding, à l'exclusion de; (b) écarter (le doute). **ex'clusion**, s. 1. exclusion f (from, de). 2. refus m d'admission (from, à). **ex'clusive**, a. 1. (of rights) exclusif. 2. very e. club, cercle très fermé. 3. adv. price of the dinner, e. of wine, prix du dîner, vin non compris. -ly, adv. exclusivement.

excommunicate [ekskə'mjunikeit], v.tr. Ecc: excommunier.

excrescence [eks'kresns], s. excroissance f.

excrete [eks'kri:t], v.tr. excréter; (of plant) sécréter (un suc). **'excrement**, s. excrément m.

excruciating [iks'kru:ʃieitiŋ], a. (of pain) atroce, affreux; an e. joke, une plaisanterie atroce. -ly, adv. atrocement; F: it's so funny, c'est à se tordre.

excursion [iks'kə:ʃ(ə)n], s. excursion f; voyage m d'agrément; Aut: etc: randonnée f.

excuse. I. s. excuse f; prétexte m. II. v.tr. [-u:z] (a) excuser (qn); e. me! (i) excusez-moi! (ii) pardon!; (b) excuser, dispenser (qn de faire qch.). **ex'cusable** [-'ku:z-], a. excusable, pardonnable.

execrable ['eksikrəbl], a. exécrable, détestable. **-ably**, adv. détestablement.

execute ['eksikjut], v.tr. exécuter. **exe'cution**, s. exécution f. **exe'cutioner**, s. bourreau m. **ex'ecutive**. 1. a. exécutif. 2. s. (a) (pouvoir m) exécutif; (b) administrateur m; sales e., directeur m commercial. **ex'ecutor, -trix**, s. Jur: exécuteur, -trice, testamentaire.

exempt [ig'zem(p)t]. I. v.tr. exempter, dispenser, exonérer (qn de qch.). II. a. exempt, dispensé. **ex'emption**, s. exemption f; exonération f, dispense f (de qch.).

exercise ['eksəsaiz]. I. s. exercice m. II. v.tr. 1. exercer (un droit, l'esprit, etc.). 2. mettre à l'épreuve (la patience de qn).

exert [ig'zə:t], v.tr. 1. employer (la force); exercer (une influence). 2. to e. oneself to do sth., se donner du mal, s'efforcer à faire qch. **ex'ertion**, s. effort(s) m(pl).

exhaust [ig'zɔːst]. I. s. E: (a) échappement m (de la vapeur, des gaz); (b) gaz m d'échappement; (c) Aut: e. pipe, tuyau m d'échappement. II. v.tr. (a) aspirer (l'air); (b) épuiser, tarir (une source); (c) épuiser, éreinter, exténuer (qn). **ex'haustion**, s. épuisement m (du sol, de qn); to be in a state of e., être à bout de forces. **ex'haustive**, a. complet. **ex'haustively**, adv. à traiter un subject e., traiter un sujet à fond. -ly, adv. to treat a subject e., traiter un sujet à fond.

exhibit [ig'zibit]. I. s. 1. Jur: pièce f à conviction. 2. objet exposé (à une exposition). II. v.tr. 1. exhiber, montrer (un objet); exposer (des marchandises). 2. Jur: produire (une pièce à conviction). **exhi'bition**, s. exposition f; étalage m; démonstration f. **ex'hibitor**, s. (at show) exposant, -ante.

exhilarate [ig'ziləreit], v.tr. vivifier; mettre à la joie au cœur. **ex'hilarated**, a. ragaillardi. **ex'hilarating**, a. vivifiant, exhilarant; e. gaieté f; joie f de vivre.

exhume [eks'hju:m], v.tr. exhumer.

exile ['eksail]. I. s. 1. exil m, bannissement m. II. s. exilé e; banni, -ie. III. v.tr. exiler, bannir (from, de); to e. oneself, se dépayser.

exist [ig'zist], v.i. exister; to continue to e., subsister; we e. on very little, nous vivons de très peu. **ex'istence**, s. existence f; vie f. **ex'isting**, a. actuel, présent; in e. circumstances, dans les circonstances actuelles.

exit ['eksit]. I. s. sortie f. II. v.i. Th: sortir.

exodus ['eksədəs], s. exode m.

exonerate [ig'zɔnəreit], v.tr. 1. exonérer, dispenser (from, de). 2. to e. so. (from blame), disculper qn. **exone'ration**, s. exonération f, disculpation f.

exorbitant [ig'zɔːbit(ə)nt], *a.* exorbitant, extravagant.

exotic [eg'zɔtik], *a.* exotique.

expand [iks'pænd]. 1. *v.tr.* dilater (un gaz); développer (un abrégé); élargir (l'esprit); déployer (les ailes). 2. *v.i.* se dilater; se développer. **ex'panding,** *a.* 1. the e. universe, l'univers en expansion. 2. e. bracelet, bracelet *m* extensible. **ex'panse,** *s.* étendue *f* (de pays). **ex'pansion,** *s.* dilatation *f* (d'un gaz, d'un métal); développement *m* (d'un abrégé, de la poitrine). **ex'pansive,** *a.* 1. (of force) expansif. 2. (of pers.) démonstratif. 3. vaste, étendu.

expatriate [eks'pætrieit]. I. *v.tr.* expatrier (qn). II. *a. & s.* expatrié, -ée.

expect [iks'pekt], *v.tr.* 1. attendre (qn); s'attendre à (un événement); compter sur (l'arrivée de qn); **I** expected as much, je m'y attendais; **to e.** to do sth., compter faire qch.; *abs.* F: she's expecting, elle attend un bébé. **to e.** sth. from s.o., attendre, exiger, qch. de qn; **I e.** you to be punctual, je vous demanderai d'être à l'heure. 3. **I e.** so, je pense que oui. **ex'pectancy,** *s.* attente *f.* **ex'pectant,** *a.* qui attend; d'attente; e. mother, femme enceinte. **-ly,** *adv.* (regarder qn) avec l'air d'attendre qch. **expec'tation,** *s.* 1. attente *f,* espérance *f.* 2. *usu. pl. Jur:* expectative d'héritage, espérances.

expediency [iks'piːdiənsi], *s.* (a) convenance *f,* opportunité *f* (d'une mesure). (b) opportunisme *m.* **ex'pedient.** 1. *a.* convenable, opportun. 2. *s.* expédient *m,* moyen *m.*

expedition [ekspi'diʃ(ə)n], *s.* 1. (a) expédition *f* (au pôle sud, etc.); (b) excursion *f.* 2. célérité *f.*

‡expel [iks'pel], *v.tr.* expulser (un locataire); bannir (qn d'une société); renvoyer (un élève).

expendable [iks'pendəbl], *a.* non-récupérable.

expenditure [iks'penditʃər], *s.* dépense *f.*

expense [iks'pens], *s.* dépense *f;* frais *mpl; Com:* e. account, indemnité *f* pour frais professionnels; a laugh at s.o.'s e., un éclat de rire aux dépens de qn. **ex'pensive,** *a.* coûteux, cher; **to be e.,** coûter cher.

experience [iks'piəriəns]. I. *s.* expérience *f;* practical e., la pratique; a painful e., une rude épreuve. II. *v.tr.* éprouver; faire l'expérience de (qch.). **ex'perienced,** *a.* qui a de l'expérience; expérimenté.

experiment [iks'perimənt]. I. *s.* expérience *f;* essai *m.* II. *v.i.* expérimenter, faire une expérience (on, with, sur, avec). **experi'mental,** *a.* 1. expérimental. 2. *Ind:* the e. department, le service des essais. **-ally,** *adv.* expérimentalement.

expert ['ekspəːt]. I. *a.* habile, expert. II. *s.* expert *m;* spécialiste *mf.*

expire [iks'paiər], *v.i.* (a) expirer, mourir; (of hope) s'évanouir; (b) expirer, cesser, prendre fin; *Com:* expired bill, effet périmé. **expi'ration,** *s.* expiration *f;* cessation *f,* terme *m;* échéance *f.* **ex'piry,** *s.* expiration *f,* terminaison *f;* terme *m.*

explain [iks'plein] *v.tr.* expliquer, éclaircir; **to e.** oneself, se justifier; **to e.** sth. away, donner une explication satisfaisante de qch. (d'offensant). **expla'nation,** *s.* explication *f;* éclaircissement *m.* **ex'planatory,** *a.* explicatif.

explicable [iks'plikəbl], *a.* explicable.

explicit [iks'plisit], *a.* explicite; formel; catégorique. **-ly,** *adv.* explicitement; catégoriquement.

explode [iks'ploud]. 1. *v.tr.* (a) discréditer (une théorie); (b) faire éclater (un obus); faire sauter (une mine). 2. *v.i.* faire explosion; éclater, sauter.

exploit[1] ['eksplɔit], *s.* exploit *m.*

exploit[2] [iks'plɔit], *v.tr.* exploiter. **exploi'tation,** *s.* exploitation *f.*

explore [iks'plɔːr], *v.tr.* explorer. **explo'ration,** *s.* exploration *f;* voyage *f* de découverte. **ex'plorer,** *s.* explorateur, -trice.

explosion [iks'plouʒ(ə)n], *s.* explosion *f.* **ex'plosive,** *a. & s.* explosif (*m*).

export [eks'pɔːt], *v.tr.* exporter. **expor'tation,** *s.* exportation *f.* **ex'porter,** *s.* exportateur, -trice. **'exports,** *s.pl.* articles *m* d'exportation; exportations *f.*

expose [iks'pouz], *v.tr.* 1. exposer. 2. démasquer (qn); dévoiler (un secret). **ex'posed,** *a.* (a) e. position, endroit exposé; (b) (laid bare) à nu. **ex'posure,** *s.* 1. (a) exposition *f* (à l'air); to die of e., mourir de froid; (b) *Phot:* (temps *m* de) pose *f.* 2. dévoilement *m* (d'un crime; fear of e., crainte *f* d'un scandale. 3. exposition *f,* orientation *f* (d'un lieu).

expostulate [iks'postjuleit], *v.i.* faire des remontrances (with, à). **expostu'lation,** *s.* (often in pl.) remontrance *f.*

express[1] [iks'pres]. 1. *a.* (of order) exprès, formel; for this e. purpose, pour cela même. 2. *a. Rail:* e. (train), express *m;* rapide *m.* **-ly,** *adv.* 1. expressément, formellement. 2. e. to please you, à seule fin de vous plaire.

express[2], *v.tr.* exprimer. **ex'pression,** *s.* expression *f;* locution *f.* **ex'pressive,** *a.* expressif. **-ly,** *adv.* avec expression.

expulsion [iks'pʌlʃ(ə)n], *s.* expulsion *f.*

expurgate ['ekspəːgeit], *v.tr.* expurger.

exquisite ['ekskwizit], *a.* exquis; délicat. **-ly,** *adv.* d'une manière exquise.

†ex-serviceman ['eks'səːvismən], *s.* ancien combattant *m.*

extempore [eks'tempəri]. 1. adv. to speak e., parler d'abondance, impromptu. 2. a. improvisé, impromptu inv. **ex'temporize,** v.tr. & i. improviser.

extend [iks'tend], v.tr. (a) prolonger (une ligne, une période de temps); (b) étendre, porter plus loin (les limites); accroître (son pouvoir); agrandir (son pouvoir). **ex'tension,** s. 1. extension f; prolongement m; agrandissement m (d'une usine). 2. (r)allonge f (de table); P.T.T: e. 35, poste m, Fr. C: local m, 35; annexe f (d'un bâtiment). 3. prolongation f (de congé). **ex'tensive,** a. étendu, vaste, ample; e. researches, travaux approfondis. **-ly,** adv. to use sth. e., se servir beaucoup de qch.

extent [iks'tent], s. étendue f (d'un terrain); importance f (d'une avarie); to a certain e., dans une certaine mesure; to a slight e., quelque peu.

extenuating [eks'tenjueitiŋ], a. e. circumstance, circonstance atténuante.

exterior [iks'tiəriər]. 1. a. extérieur (to, à); en dehors (to, de). 2. s. extérieur m, dehors mpl.

exterminate [eks'tə:mineit], v.tr. exterminer.

external [eks'tə:nl], a. (a) externe; Med: for e. application, pour usage externe; (b) extérieur; du dehors. **-ally,** adv. extérieurement; à l'extérieur.

extinction [iks'tiŋ(k)ʃ(ə)n], s. extinction f. **ex'tinct.** a. (a) (of volcano) éteint; (b) (of species) disparu.

extinguish [iks'tiŋgwiʃ], v.tr. éteindre (le feu). **ex'tinguisher,** s. (appareil) extincteur m (d'incendie).

extort [iks'tɔ:t], v.tr. extorquer; arracher (from, out of, s.o., à qn). **ex'tortion,** s. extorsion f. **ex'tortionate,** a. (prix) exorbitant.

extra [ekstrə]. 1. a. (a) en sus, de plus; supplémentaire; e. charge, supplément m de prix. 2. adv. (a) plus que d'ordinaire; e. strong, extra-solide; (b) en plus; (vin) non-compris. 3. s. (a) supplément m; (b) Cin: figurant, -ante; (c) pl. frais m supplémentaires.

extract. I. s. [ekstrækt] extrait m; (a) meat e., concentré m de viande; (b) Sch: extracts, morceaux choisis. II. v.tr. [iks'trækt], extraire, tirer; arracher (une dent, un aveu). **ex'traction,** s. 1. extraction f, arrachement m. 2. to be of French e., être d'origine française.

extradition [ekstrə'diʃ(ə)n], s. extradition f.

extraordinary [iks'trɔ:dinri], a. extraordinaire. **-ily,** adv. extraordinairement.

extravagance [iks'trævəgəns], s. 1. extravagance f. 2. prodigalités fpl; folles dépenses; a piece of e., une dépense inutile. **ex'travagant,** a. 1. extravagant; e. praise, éloges outrés. 2. (of pers.) dépensier. 3. (of price) exorbitant. **-ly,** adv. 1. d'une façon extravagante. 2. excessivement; à l'excès.

extreme [iks'tri:m]. 1. a. extrême. 2. s. in the e., au dernier degré; to drive s.o. to extremes, pousser qn à bout. **-ly,** adv. extrêmement; au dernier point; to be e. witty, avoir énormément d'esprit.

†**extremity** [iks'tremiti], s. 1. extrémité f; point m extrême; bout m (d'une corde). 2. to be in great e., être dans une grande gêne.

extricate [ekstrikeit], v.tr. dégager; to e. oneself from difficulties, se débrouiller, se dépêtrer.

exuberance [ig'zju:b(ə)r(ə)ns], s. exubérance f. **ex'uberant,** a. exubérant.

eye [ai]. I. s. 1. œil m, pl. yeux; to have blue eyes, avoir les yeux bleus; to open one's eyes wide, ouvrir de grands yeux; to open s.o.'s eyes, éclairer qn; F: to keep one's eyes skinned, avoir l'œil (ouvert); to shut one's eyes to the truth, se refuser à l'évidence; (b) to catch the e., frapper l'œil; to set eyes on, apercevoir, voir; (c) to see e. to e. with s.o., voir les choses du même œil que qn; to make eyes at s.o., faire de l'œil à qn; (d) to give an e. to sth., veiller à qch.; (e) to be much in the public e., être très en vue; (f) private e., détective m privé. 2. chas m (d'une aiguille); trou m. II. v.tr. regarder, observer (qn, avec attention). **'eyeball,** s. globe m oculaire. **'eyebrow,** s. sourcil m. **'eyelash,** s. cil m. **'eyelid,** s. paupière f. **'eye-opener,** s. F: révélation f; surprise f. **'eyepiece,** s. (a) oculaire m (de télescope); (b) viseur m (de théodolite). **'eye-shade,** s. visière f. **'eyesight,** s. vue f; my e. is failing, ma vue baisse. **'eyesore,** s. qch. qui blesse la vue; that house is an e., cette maison est hideuse. **'eye-strain,** s. to suffer from e., avoir les yeux fatigués. **'eyewash,** s. 1. Med: collyre m. 2. F: that's all e., tout ça, c'est du boniment. **'eye-witness,** s. témoin m oculaire.

F

F, f [ef], s. 1. (la lettre) F, f, m or f. 2. Mus: fa m.

fable [feibl], s. fable f, conte m. **'fabulous,** a. 1. fabuleux, légendaire. 2. F: prodigieux; à f. price, un prix fou. -**ly,** adv. fabuleusement.

fabric [fæbrik], s. 1. (a) édifice m; (b) structure f. 2. tissu m; silk and woollen fabrics, soieries f et lainages m. **fabri'cation,** s. 1. invention f. 2. contrefaçon f.

face [feis], s. I. s. 1. figure f, visage m, face f; f. cream, crème f de beauté; to come f. to f. with s.o., se trouver nez à nez avec qn; to set one's f. against sth., s'opposer résolument à qch.; in the f. of danger, en présence du danger. 2. (a) mine f, physionomie f; to make faces, faire des grimaces; to keep a straight f., garder son sérieux; (b) F: audace f, front m; he had the f. to tell me so, il a eu le toupet de me le dire. 3. apparence f, aspect m; to save f., sauver les apparences; on the f. of things, à première vue. 4. surface f (de la terre). 5. face (d'une pièce de monnaie); façade f (d'un bâtiment); cadran m (de montre). II. v. 1. v.tr. affronter, faire face (à un danger); envisager (les faits). 2. (a) v.tr. se tenir devant (qn); donner sur (la rue); (b) v.i. the house faces north, la maison est exposée au nord. face 'up, v.i. to f. up to s.o., to the facts, affronter qn, envisager la situation. **'face-value,** s. valeur nominale. **'facing,** s. 1. surfaçage m. 2. (a) revers m (d'un habit); (b) revêtement m (d'un mur).

facet [fæsit], s. facette f (d'un diamant, etc.).

facetious [fe'siːʃəs], a. plaisant, farceur; (style) bouffon. -**ly,** adv. facétieusement.

facilitate [fə'siliteit], v.tr. faciliter. **fa'cility,** s. 1. facilité f (de parole, etc.); to give full facilities, donner toutes facilités; harbour facilities, installations portuaires; we have no facilities for that, nous ne sommes pas équipés pour cela.

fact [fækt], s. 1. fait m, action f. 2. to stick to facts, s'en tenir aux faits; it is a f. that, il est de fait que; to know for a f. that . . ., savoir pertinemment que . . .; the fact is, I have no money, c'est que je n'ai pas d'argent; in point of f., par le fait; as a matter of f., à vrai dire.

factor ['fæktər], s. 1. (pers.) agent m (dépositaire). 2. (a) Mth: prime f, diviseur premier; (b) E: etc: f. of safety, facteur m de sûreté. 3. the human f., l'élément humain.

†factory ['fækt(ə)ri], s. fabrique f, usine f; f. inspector, inspecteur m du travail.

†faculty ['fæk(ə)lti], s. (a) faculté f; (b) talent m.

fad [fæd], s. marotte f, dada m, manie f. **'faddy,** a. capricieux, maniaque.

fade [feid]. 1. v.i. (a) se faner, se flétrir; (of colour) passer; (of cloth) déteindre; guaranteed not to fade, garanti bon teint; (b) to f. away, s'évanouir. 2. v.tr. faner; Cin: enchaîner (deux scènes). **'fading,** s. 1. flétrissure f; décoloration f. 2. Rad: fading m; Cin: f. out, (fermeture f en) fondu m.

faggot ['fægət], s. fagot m.

Fahrenheit ['færənhait], a. (thermomètre) Fahrenheit.

fail [feil]. I. v.i. (a) manquer, faillir, faire défaut; to f. to do sth., négliger de faire qch.; (b) (of engine) rester en panne; (of sight, health, memory) baisser; (d) ne pas réussir; échouer; Sch: être refusé (à un examen); I f. to see why, je ne vois pas pourquoi; (e) Com: faire faillite. II. adv. phr. without f., (i) sans faute, (ii) à coup sûr. **'failing.** 1. s. (a) affaiblissement m, défaillance f (de forces); baisse f (de la vue, etc.); (b) échec m. 2. faible m, faiblesse f, défaut m. II. prep. à défaut (de); faute de (paiement). **'failure,** s. 1. (a) manque m, défaut m; (b) panne f (d'électricité, etc.). 2. (a) insuccès m; échec (à un examen); (b) Com: faillite f. 3. (of pers.) raté, -ée.

faint [feint]. I. s. évanouissement m, syncope f, défaillance f. II. a. 1. (a) faible, affaibli; f. voice, voix éteinte; (b) (of colour) pâle, délavé; (of sound, breeze) léger; (c) (of idea) vague. 2. to feel f., se sentir mal. -**ly,** adv. 1. faiblement. 2. légèrement. III. v.i. s'évanouir, défaillir; se trouver mal. **'faintness,** s. 1. (a) faiblesse f (de la voix); légèreté f (d'une brise). 2. malaise f.

fair¹ ['feər], s. foire f.

fair². I. a. 1. beau. 2. (of hair) blond. 3. juste, équitable; f. play, franc jeu. 4. passable; assez bon. 5. (of wind) propice; f. weather, beau temps. -**ly,** adv. 1. impartialement. 2. honnêtement, franchement. 3. passablement; assez (riche, habile, etc.). II. adv. (agir) loyalement, de bonne foi; to play f., jouer beau jeu. **'fair and 'square.** 1. a. it's all f. and s., c'est de bonne guerre. 2. adv. (a) au plein milieu; (b) loyalement. **'fairhaired,** a. aux cheveux blonds. **'fair-'minded,** a. impartial. **'fairness,** s. 1. couleur blonde (des cheveux); fraîcheur f (du teint). 2. honnêteté f, impartialité f; in all f., en toute justice. **'fair-'sized,** a. assez grand.

†**fairy** ['fɛəri]. 1. s. fée f. 2. a. féerique; de(s) fée(s). 'fairyland, s. (a) le royaume des fées; (b) féerie f. 'fairy-tale, s. 1. conte m de fées. 2. F: mensonge m, F: craque f.

faith [feiθ], s. 1. foi f; to have f. in s.o., avoir confiance f en qn; f. in God, croyance f en Dieu. 2. fidélité f à ses engagements; to act in good f., agir en bonne foi. 'faithful. a. 1. fidèle, loyal. 2. (of copy) exact. -fully, adv. 1. fidèlement; (letter-ending) (we remain) yours f., agréez nos meilleures salutations. 2. (traduire) exactement, fidèlement. 'faithfulness, s. fidélité f. 1. loyauté f (to, envers). 2. exactitude f. 'faithless. a. 1. infidèle; sans foi. 2. déloyal, perfide. 'faithlessness, s. 1. infidélité f (to, à). 2. déloyauté f.

fall [fɔːl]. I. s. 1. chute f (d'un corps) descente f (d'un marteau, etc.); Th: baisser m (du rideau); to have a f., faire une chute, tomber. *U.S:* the f., l'automne m. 3. (a) usu. pl. chute (d'eau), cascade f, cataracte f; (b) hauteur f de chute (d'un barrage). 4. (a) décrue f, baisse f (des eaux); (b) baisse (des prix). 5. perte f (d'une échelle); F: to f. on one's feet, avoir de la chance; to let sth. f., laisser tomber qch.; night is falling, (i) la nuit tombe, (ii) le jour baisse. 2. (of building, etc.) crouler, s'écrouler, s'effondrer. 3. (a) (of tide, barometer) baisser; (of wind, sea) se calmer, tomber; (of ground) aller en pente, descendre; his face fell, sa figure s'allongea. 4. (a) the shame falls upon . . ., le blâme retombe sur . . .; (b) (of pers.) to f. under suspicion, devenir suspect; (c) to f. into a habit, contracter une habitude. 6. to f. sick, tomber malade. 'fall 'back, v.i. tomber (i) en arrière, (ii) à la renverse. 'fall be'hind, v.i. rester en arrière. 'fall 'down, v.i. tomber à terre, par terre. 'fall for, v.i. F: 1. tomber amoureux (de qn). 2. to f. for a trick, s'y laisser prendre. 'fall 'in, v.i. 1. (a) (of roof) s'écrouler; (b) tomber à l'eau. 2. *Mil:* former les rangs. 'fall 'off, v.i. 1. his hat fell off, son chapeau tomba. 2. (of profits) diminuer; (of speed) ralentir. 'fall 'out, v.i. 1. tomber (dehors (de qch.). 2. se brouiller avec qn. 'fall-out, s. *Atom Ph:* retombée f. 'fall 'over, v.i. tomber à la renverse, se renverser. 'fall 'through, v.i. (of scheme) échouer, F: tomber à l'eau. 'fall 'to, v.i. F: se mettre au travail; (b) s'attaquer au repas.

†**fallacy** ['fæləsi], s. faux raisonnement m.

false [fɔːls], a. 1. faux, f. fausse. 2. perfide; trompeur; mensonger. 3. (of

hair, etc.) artificiel, postiche; (of coin) contrefait. -ly, adv. faussement, perfidement. 'falsehood, s. mensonge m. 'falseness, s. fausseté f. 'falsify, v.tr. falsifier. 'falsity, s. fausseté f.

falter ['fɔːltər], v.i. (a) (of voice) hésiter, trembler; (b) (of pers.) vaciller; (c) (of pers. or courage) défaillir.

fame [feim], s. renom m, renommée f. 'famous, a. célèbre.

familiar [fə'miljər], a. 1. familier, intime; you are too f., vous vous croyez tout permis; (of thg.) bien connu. -ly, adv. familièrement, intimement. famili'arity, s. intimité f; intimité f; connaissance f (with, de). fa'miliarize, v.tr. 1. rendre (qch.) familier. 2. to f. s.o. with sth., habituer qn à qch.

†**family** ['fæm(i)li], s. famille f; f. life, vie familiale; f. man, (i) père de famille; (ii) homme d'intérieur; *Com:* in f.-size jar, en pot familial; *Adm:* f. allowances, allocation f familiale.

famine ['fæmin], s. (a) famine f; (b) disette f. 'famished, a. affamé.

fan[1] [fæn]. I. s. 1. éventail m. 2. ventilateur m (rotatif). II. *v.tr.* éventer.

fan[2], s. *F:* passionné, -ée, enragé, -ée, fervent m (du sport, etc.); film f., cinéphile mf; football fans, les mordus du football.

fanatic [fə'nætik], a. & s. fanatique (mf). fa'natical, a. fanatique. -ally, adv. fanatiquement. fa'naticism, s. fanatisme m.

fancy ['fænsi]. I. †s. 1. imagination f, fantaisie f; (b) idée f. 2. (a) fantaisie, caprice m; as the f. takes me, comme ça me chante; (b) fantaisie, goût m; to take a f. to sth., prendre goût à qch.; s'éprendre, s'enticher, de qn. II. a. (a) (bouton m, etc.) de fantaisie; f. goods, nouveautés f; f. dress, travesti m; f. work, travaux mpl pour dames. III. *v.tr.* 1. (a) s'imaginer, se figurer (qch.); (b) croire, penser; he fancied he heard footsteps, il crut entendre des pas. 2. (a) to f. sth., se sentir attiré vers qch.; (b) F: to f. oneself, se gober, s'en croire. 'fanciful, a. (of pers.) capricieux, fantasque; (b) (projet) chimérique; (conte) imaginaire.

fang [fæŋ], s. (a) croc m (de loup); (b) crochet m (de vipère).

†**fantasy** ['fæntəzi], s. fantaisie f. fan'tastic, a. fantastique, bizarre; invraisemblable.

far [fɑːr]. I. adv. loin. 1. (a) how f. is it from . . . to . . .? combien y a-t-il de . . . à . . .? as f. as the eye can reach, à perte de vue; f. and wide, de tous côtés; partout; (b) to go so f. as to do sth., aller jusqu'à faire qch.; as f. as I know, autant que je sache; in so f. as, dans la mesure où; f. from it, tant s'en faut; by f., de beaucoup. 2. (of time) so f., jusqu'ici; not 'so f., pas encore; as f. back as 1900, déjà en 1900. 3. (with qualifying adj., adv. etc.) beaucoup, bien, fort; it's f. better, c'est beaucoup, bien, mieux; f. advanced, fort avancé. II. s. lointain, éloigné; in the f. distance, tout à fait au loin. 'far-away, a. lointain, éloigné. 'far-'fetched, a. (of example, etc.) forcé. 'far-'reaching, a. d'une grande portée. 'far-'seeing, a. prévoyant, perspicace. 'far-'sighted, a. prévoyant, perspicace.

farce [fɑːs], s. Th: farce f; farcical, a. risible, grotesque.

fare [fɛər], s. 1. (a) prix m du voyage, de la place, de la course (en taxi); single f., (prix du) billet simple; return f., aller (et) retour; fares, please! les places, s'il vous plaît! (b) voyageur, -euse; (in taxi) client m. 2. chère f, manger m; prison f., régime m de prison.

farewell ['fɛə'wel], s. to bid s.o. f., faire ses adieux à qn; attrib. a f. dinner, un dîner d'adieu.

farm [fɑːm]. I. s. ferme f. II. v.tr. (a) cultiver, exploiter (une propriété); (b) être fermier. 'farmer, s. fermier, -ière; cultivateur m; exploitant m; stock f., éleveur m. 'farm-hand, s. ouvrier m agricole. 'farming, s. exploitation f agricole; agriculture f; stock f., élevage m. 'farmyard, s. basse-cour f.

farther ['fɑːðər]. 1. adv. plus loin (than, que); f. off, plus éloigné; f. on, plus en avant; plus loin. 2. a. plus lointain, plus éloigné. 'farthest. 1. a. (a) f. off, le plus lointain, le plus éloigné; (b) (of way, etc.) le plus long. 2. adv. le plus loin.

fascinate ['fæsineit], v.tr. fasciner, charmer, séduire. 'fascinating, a. enchanteur, séduisant. fasci'nation, s. fascination f; charme m, attrait m.

fashion ['fæ∫(ə)n]. I. s. 1. façon f; manière f; after a f., tant bien que mal. 2. (of clothes, etc.) mode f, vogue f; in (the) f., à la mode; out of f., démodé; f. house, maison f de haute couture; f. book, journal m de modes; f. show, présentation f de collection; défilé m de mannequins. II. v.tr. façonner, former (une poterie); confectionner (une robe). 'fashionable, a. à la mode, élégant; a f. resort, un endroit mondain. -ably, adv. élégamment; à la mode.

fast[1] [fɑːst], v.i. jeûner; faire maigre.

fast[2]. I. a. 1. (a) ferme, fixe, solide; (b) (of colour) résistant; bon teint inv. 2. rapide, vite; f. train, express m. 3. (of clock) en avance. 4. (of pers.) dissipé; de mœurs légères. II.

adv. 1. ferme, solidement; to hold, stand, fast, tenir bon. 2. vite, rapidement; not so f.! pas si vite!

fasten ['fɑːsn]. I. v.tr. (a) attacher (to, on, à); (b) fixer, assurer (la porte, etc.); to f. (up) a garment, agrafer, boutonner un vêtement. 2. v.i. s'attacher, se fixer, se cramponner (à qch.); saisir (un prétexte). 'fastener, s. attache f. (of garment) agrafe f; (of purse, etc.) fermoir m; (of window, etc.) fermeture f. 'fastening, s. attache f; agrafage m, fermeture f.

fastidious [fəs'tidiəs], a. (of pers.) difficile; délicat. -ly, adv. d'un air de dégoût; dédaigneusement.

fat [fæt]. I. s. graisse f; Cu: frying f. (graisse de) friture f; fats, matières grasses. 2. gras m (de viande). II. a. gras; to get f., engraisser.

fate [feit], s. destin m, sort m. 'fatal, a. 1. f. disease, maladie mortelle; a f. mistake, une faute capitale. -ally, adv. 1. fatalement, inévitablement. 2. mortellement (blessé, etc.). fa'tality, s. accident mortel; sinistre m. 'fated, a. 1. (of occurrence) fatal, inévitable. 2. destiné, condamné (à faire qch.). 'fateful, a. (jour, etc.) décisif, fatal.

father ['fɑːðər], s. père m. 'father-in-law, s. beau-père m. 'fatherland, s. patrie f. 'fatherless, a. orphelin de père. 'fatherly, a. paternel.

fathom ['fæðəm], v.tr. approfondir, sonder (un mystère).

fatigue [fə'tiːg]. I. s. 1. fatigue f. 2. corvée f. II. v.tr. fatiguer, lasser (qn). fa'tiguing, a. fatigant, épuisant.

fatten ['fætn]. 1. v.tr. engraisser (des moutons, etc.). 2. v.i. engraisser; to f. on sth., s'engraisser de qch. 'fattening, s. engraissement m. 'fatty, a. (a) graisseux, oléagineux; f. foods, aliments gras; (b) (of tissue, etc.) adipeux.

fatuous ['fætjuəs], a. sot, imbécile, idiot. -ly, adv. sottement. 'fatuousness, s. sottise f, imbécillité f.

fault [fɔːlt], s. 1. défaut m; imperfection f; Ind: vice m de construction; scrupulous to a f., scrupuleux à l'excès; to find f. with s.o., trouver à redire contre qn. 2. faute f; to be in f., être fautif. 3. at f., en défaut. 'fault-finding, a. critiqueur, chicanier. 'faultless, a. sans défaut; impeccable, irréprochable. -ly, adv. parfaitement, irréprochablement; f. dressed, d'une mise impeccable. 'faulty, a. défectueux, imparfait; (of style) incorrect; (of reasoning) erroné, inexact.

favour ['feivər], s. 1. faveur f. 2. approbation f; bonnes grâces; to be in f. with s.o., jouir de la faveur de qn; to be out of f., (i) être mal en cour; (ii) n'être plus en vogue. 2. grâce f, bonté f; **to ask a f. of s.o.**, solliciter une faveur de qn; **as a f.**, à titre gracieux. 3. (a) partialité f, préférence f; (b) appui m, protection f. 4. prep. phr. **in f. of . . .**, en faveur de . . .; **to be in f. of sth.**, être partisan de qch. II. v.tr. favoriser. 1. approuver, préférer. 2. obliger (qn); accorder une grâce à (qn). 3. (a) avantager (qn); (b) faciliter (qch.). **'favourable**, a. favorable; (of weather) propice; (of terms) bon, avantageux. **-ably**, adv. favorablement, avantageusement. **'favourite**, a. & s. favori, -ite; préféré, -ée.

fawn[1] [fɔːn], v.ind.tr.; **to f. on s.o.**, (i) (of dog) caresser qn; (ii) (of pers.) ramper devant qn; aduler (qn). **'fawning**, a. (i) caressant; (ii) servile.

fawn[2]. 1. s. Z: faon m. 2. a. & s. (colour) fauve (m).

fear [fiər]. I. s. crainte f, peur f; deadly f., effroi m. II. v.tr. 1. craindre, avoir peur de, redouter (qn, qch.). 2. appréhender, craindre (un événement); s'inquiéter (au sujet de qn). **'fearful**, a. 1. affreux, effrayant. 2. peureux, craintif. **-fully**, adv. 1. affreusement, terriblement. 2. peureusement, craintivement. **'fearless**, a. intrépide, courageux **-ly**, adv. intrépidement; sans peur. **'fearlessness**, s. intrépidité f.

feasible ['fiːzibl], a. 1. faisable, possible, praticable. 2. vraisemblable, probable.

feast [fiːst]. I. s. 1. fête f. 2. festin m, banquet m. II. 1. v.i. faire festin; se régaler. 2. v.tr. régaler, fêter (qn).

feat [fiːt], s. 1. exploit m, haut fait m. 2. **tour m de force**.

feather ['feðər], s. plume f. **'feather-brained**, a. écervelé, étourdi.

feature ['fiːtʃər], s. 1. trait m (du visage); **the features**, la physionomie. 2. (a) trait, caractéristique f (d'un paysage, etc.); (b) spécialité f; Cin: **the f. film**, le grand film du programme.

February ['februəri], s. février m.

federation [fedə'reiʃ(ə)n], s. fédération f.

fee [fiː], s. (a) honoraires mpl; (b) school fees, frais mpl de scolarité; examination f., droit m d'examen.

feeble ['fiːbl], a. faible, infirme, débile. **-bly**, adv. faiblement. **'feeble-'minded**, a. d'esprit faible. **'feebleness**, s. faiblesse f.

feed [fiːd]. I. s. 1. (a) alimentation f (d'un animal); (b) nourriture f, pâture f; fourrage m; F: **to be off one's f.**, bouder sur la nourriture; (c) F: repas m, festin m. 2. Techn: gravity f., alimentation par (la) pesanteur; pressure f. (of oil), graissage m sous pression. II. v. 1. v.tr. (a) nourrir; donner à manger à (qn); allaiter (un enfant); (b) alimenter (une

machine, le feu). 2. v.i. manger; (of cattle, sheep) paître, brouter; **to f. on sth.**, s'alimenter, se nourrir de qch. **'feed-pipe**, s. E: tuyau m d'alimentation. **'feed 'up**, v.tr. engraisser (une bête); suralimenter (qn); F: **I'm fed up**, j'en ai plein le dos.

feel [fiːl]. I. s. 1. toucher m, tact m; **to know sth. by the f.**, reconnaître qch. au toucher. II. ‡p. 1. (a) v.tr. toucher, palper; tâter; manier; (b) v.tr. & i. **to f. (about) for sth.**, chercher qch. à tâtons; **to f. in one's pockets**, fouiller dans ses poches. 2. (a) v.tr. sentir (qch.); (b) v.tr. & i. (of pers.) sentir, éprouver (de la peine, etc.); **to f. the heat, the cold**, être sensible à la chaleur, au froid; **to f. for s.o.**, avoir de la pitié pour qn; (c) v.tr. avoir conscience de (qch.). 3. v.i. (of pers.) (a) **to f. cold**, avoir froid; **to f. ill**, se sentir malade; **to f. like crying**, avoir envie de pleurer; **I don't f. like it**, ça ne me dit rien; **I f. like a cup of tea**, je prendrais bien une tasse de thé. **'feeling**. I. a. 1. (of pers.) sensible. 2. ému. **-ly**, adv. **to speak f. of sth.**, parler (i) d'une voix émue, (ii) avec sympathie, (iii) avec chaleur, de qch. II. s. 1. toucher m, tact m. 2. sensation (douloureuse, etc.). 3. sentiment m; sensibilité f.

feign [fein], v.tr. feindre, simuler.

feint [feint], s. (boxing, etc.) feinte f.

fell [fel], v.tr. abattre (un arbre).

fellow ['feləu], s. 1. f. creature, semblable m; f. countryman, compatriote m; f. student, condisciple mf; Pol: f. traveller, communisant, -ante. 2. associé, -ée (d'une société savante). 3. F: homme m, F: type m; **a queer f.**, un drôle de type.

†felony ['feləni], s. crime m.

felt [felt], s. feutre m.

female ['fiːmeil]. 1. a. (a) (of pers.) féminin; de femme; (b) (of animals, etc.) femelle. 2. s. (a) femme f; (b) femelle f.

feminine ['feminin], a. féminin; s. Gram: **in the f.**, au féminin.

fence [fens], s. 1. clôture f, palissade f, barrière f. 2. F: receleur, -euse. II. v. 1. v.tr. clôturer (un terrain). 2. v.i. faire de l'escrime. **'fencing**, s. 1. clôture f, barrière f. 2. escrime f.

fend [fend]. 1. v.tr. **to f. off**, détourner, parer (un coup). 2. v.i. **to f. for oneself**, se débrouiller. **'fender**, s. 1. Aut: U.S: (i) pare-choc(s) m; (ii) aile f. 2. garde-feu m.

ferment [fə'ment], v.i. fermenter; (of wine) travailler. **fermen'tation**, s. fermentation f.

fern [fəːn], s. fougère f.

ferocity [fə'rositi], s. férocité f. **fe'rocious**, a. féroce. **-ly**, adv. férocement.

ferret] F:5 **[figure**

ferret ['ferit]. I. s. furet m. II. v. 1. v.i. chasser au furet; to f. about, fureter, fouiner, partout. 2. v.tr. to f. out (sth.), dénicher (qch.).

†ferry ['feri]. I. s. 1. bac m; to cross the f., passer le bac; f. dues, droits m de passage. 2. train, car, f., ferry-boat m. II. v.tr. to f. (s.o., a car) across, passer (qn, une voiture) en bac. 'ferry-boat, s. bac m.

fertility [fə'tiliti], s. fertilité f, fécondité f. 'fertile, a. fertile, fécond.

fertilize ['fə:tilaiz], v.tr. fertiliser (le sol), féconder (un œuf). fertili'zation, s. fertilisation f; fécondation f (d'un œuf). 'fertilizer, s. engrais m.

fervent ['fə:vənt], a. ardent, fervent. 'fervour, s. ardeur f, ferveur f, zèle m.

fester ['festər], v.i. (of wound) suppurer.

festive ['festiv], a. joyeux; (air) de fête. fes'tivity, s. fête f; festivity, s. réjouissances f, festivité f.

fetch [fetʃ], v.tr. 1. (a) aller chercher (qn, qch.); (b) apporter (qch.); amener (qn). 2. rapporter; it fetched a high price, cela se vendit cher. fetch 'back, v.tr. ramener; rapporter. fetch 'down, v.tr. faire descendre (qn); descendre (qch.). fetch 'in, v.tr. rentrer (la lessive, etc.).

fête [feit], s. fête f.

fetish ['fi:tiʃ, 'fe-], s. fétiche m.

fetter ['fetər], v.tr. enchaîner; entraver. 'fetters, s.pl. chaînes f, fers m.

feud [fju:d], s. blood f., vendetta f; family feuds, dissensions f domestiques.

feudal ['fju:d(ə)l], a. féodal.

fever ['fi:vər], s. fièvre f. 'feverish, a. (état) fiévreux, fébrile. -ly, adv. fiévreusement, fébrilement.

few [fju:], a. 1. he has f. friends, il a peu d'amis; a f. books, quelques livres; a f. more, encore quelques-uns. 2. (noun function) f. of them, peu d'entre eux; a f. of the survivors, quelques-uns (des survivants; F: there were quite a f., il y en avait pas mal. 'fewer, a. moins nombreux. 'fewest, a few f., le moins (de).

fiancé, f. -ée [fi'ã(n)sei], s. fiancé, -ée.

fiasco [fi'æskou], s. fiasco m.

fib [fib], s. F: petit mensonge m.

fibre ['faibər], s. fibre f; filament m; Com: glass f., laine f de verre. 'fibrous, a. fibreux; filamenteux.

fickle ['fikl], a. inconstant, volage. 'fickleness, s. inconstance f.

fiction ['fikʃ(ə)n], s. 1. fiction f. 2. (works of) f., romans m. fic'titious, a. fictif; f. being, être imaginaire.

fiddle ['fidl]. I. s. F: 1. violon m. (joueur m de) violon. 2. it's a f.! c'est une combine! II. v.i. F: 1. jouer du violon. 2. (a) tripoter, trifouiller; bricoler; (b) to f. the accounts, maquiller la comptabilité. 'fiddler, s.

F: 1. joueur m de violon. 2. he's an awful f.! c'est un fameux combinard! 'fiddling, a. F: futile, insignifiant.

fidelity [fi'deliti], s. fidélité f, loyauté f; Rec: high f., haute fidélité.

fidget ['fidʒit], v.i. 1. (a) remuer continuellement; (b) s'inquiéter, se tourmenter. 'fidgeting, s. nervosité f. 'fidgety, a. 1. remuant, agité. 2. nerveux, impatient.

field [fi:ld], s. 1. champ m; in the fields, aux champs; Mil: f. of battle, champ de bataille; f. service, service m en campagne. 2. Sp: terrain m; (horse racing) les coureurs mpl; f. events, épreuves f d'athlétisme; f. sports, (i) athlétisme m; (ii) la chasse et la pêche; to be first in the f., (i) être au premier rang; (ii) être le premier à faire qch. 3. (a) théâtre m, champ (d'opération); domaine m (d'une science); in the political f., sur le plan politique; (b) f. study, études f sur le terrain. 'field-glasses, s.pl. jumelles fpl. 'field-marshal, s. Mil: maréchal m. †'field-mouse, s. mulot m. 'field-officer, s. Mil: officier supérieur.

fiend [fi:nd], s. démon m, diable m; monstre m (de cruauté). 'fiendish, a. diabolique. -ly, adv. diaboliquement.

fierce [fiəs], a. féroce; (of battle) acharné; (of wind) violent; f. brake, frein brutal. -ly, adv. férocement; avec acharnement. 'fierceness, s. violence f (de qn); férocité f (d'une bête); acharnement m (de la bataille).

fiery ['faiəri], a. 1. ardent, brûlant, enflammé. 2. (of pers.) fougueux, emporté.

fifteen [fif'ti:n], num. a. & s. quinze (m); a Rugby f., une équipe de rugby. fif'teenth, num. a. & s. quinzième; the f. of August, le quinze août.

fifth [fifθ], num. a. & s. cinquième; Henry the Fifth, Henri Cinq. 'fifth-rate, a. de cinquième ordre.

†fifty ['fifti], num. a. & s. cinquante (m); to go f.-f. with s.o., se mettre de moitié avec qn; about f., une cinquantaine (de livres, etc.).

fig [fig], s. figue f; f. tree, figuier m.

fight [fait]. I. s. 1. combat m, bataille f; (b) assaut m; free f., mêlée générale. 2. (a) lutte f; (b) to show f., résister. II. v. 1. v.i. se battre; combattre; lutter; to f. back, livrer (une) bataille. 2. v.tr. se battre avec, contre, (qn); combattre (qn, un incendie). 'fighter, s. 1. combattant m; militant m. 2. Av: chasseur m; rocket f., chasseur-fusée m. 'fighting, s. combat m; Sp: boxe f.

figure ['figər]. I. s. 1. (of pers.) taille f, tournure f; to keep one's f., garder sa ligne. 2. (a) forme f humaine, silhouette f; (b) personnage m; the central f. (of the play, etc.) le pivot de l'action. 3. figure *f* (géométrique); illustration *f*, diagramme *m* (dans un livre). 4. chiffre *m*. 5. f. of speech, façon *f* de parler. II. *v.i.* his name figures on the list, son nom figure sur la liste. 'figurative, *a.* figuré, métaphorique. -ly, *adv.* au figuré.

filament ['filəmənt], *s.* filament *m.*

file[1] [fail]. I. *s.* lime *f*. II. *v.tr.* limer.

file[2]. I. *s.* 1. classeur *m*; fichier *m*. 2. liasse *f* (de papiers); dossier *m*. II. *v.tr.* 1. classer (des fiches etc.). 2. *Jur:* to f. a petition, enregistrer une requête. 'filing, *s.* classement *m*; f. clerk, archiviste *mf*; f. cabinet, classeur *m*.

file[3]. I. *s.* file *f*; in single f., en file indienne. II. *v.i.* défiler (devant qn, qch.).

filial ['filiəl], *a.* filial.

filibuster ['filibʌstər]. *Pol: U.S:* I. *s.* obstructionniste *m*. II. *v.i.* faire de l'obstruction.

fill [fil]. I. *s.* 1. to eat, drink, one's f., manger à sa faim, boire à sa soif. 2. charge *f*, plein *m*. II. *v.* 1. *v.tr.* (a) remplir, emplir (with, de); charger (un wagon); bourrer (sa pipe); (b) combler (une brèche); obturer, plomber (une dent); (c) occuper (un poste). 2. *v.i.* se remplir, s'emplir; the hall is beginning to fill, la salle commence à se garnir. 'fill 'in, *v.tr.* 1. remplir (un trou). 2. remplir (une formule); libeller (un chèque). 'filling. I. *a.* (of food, etc.) rassasiant. II. *s.* 1.(a)remplissage *m*; chargement *m* (d'un wagon); comblement *m* (d'un trou); obturation *f*, plombage *m* (d'une dent). *Aut:* f. station, poste *m* d'essence. 'fill 'out. 1. *v.tr.* enfler, gonfler (un ballon). 2. *v.i.* (a) s'enfler, se gonfler; (b) *U.S:* remplir (une formule). 'fill 'up. 1. *v.tr.* (a) combler (une mesure); *Aut:* to f. up with petrol, faire le plein d'essence; (b) boucher (un trou); (c) remplir (une formule). 2. *v.i.* se remplir, s'emplir se combler.

fillet ['filit]. I. *s. Cu:* filet *m.*

†filly ['fili], *s.* pouliche *f.*

film [film]. I. *s.* 1. pellicule *f* (d'huile, etc.); voile *m* (de brume). 2. *Phot: Cin:* (a) film *m*, bande *f*; (b) the films, le cinéma *f*; f. library, cinémathèque *f*; f. star, vedette *f* (de l'écran). II. *v.tr. Cin:* filmer, tourner (une scène).

filter ['filtər]. I. *s.* 1. filtre *m*; épurateur *m. Phot:* écran *m* coloré, filtre. II. *v.* 1. *v.tr.* filtrer (un liquide); épurer (l'air). 2. *v.i.* (of water) filtrer, s'infiltrer (through, à travers).

filth [filθ], *s.* ordure *f*; immondices *mpl.* 'filthiness, *s* saleté *f.* 'filthy, *a.* sale, immonde, dégoûtant.

fin [fin], *s.* nageoire *f*; aileron *m.*

final ['fain(ə)l], *a.* 1. final; (a) dernier; (b) (judgement, etc.) définitif, décisif; sans appel. 2. *s. Sp:* the finals, les (épreuves) finales. -ally, *adv.* finalement. 'finalize, *v.tr.* mettre (qch.) au point.

finale [fi'nɑːli], *s. Mus:* finale *m.*

finance [fai'næns]. I. *s.* finance *f.* II. *v.tr.* financer, commanditer (une entreprise). fi'nancial, *a.* financier; f. statement, bilan *m.; Adm:* f. year, année *f* budgétaire. fi'nancier *m.* 1. financier *m.* 2. bailleur *m* de fonds.

finch [fin(t)ʃ], *s.* pinson *m.*

find [faind]. I. *s.* 1. découverte *f.* 2. trouvaille *f.* II. ‡*v.tr.* 1. trouver; rencontrer, découvrir; to f. some difficulty, éprouver quelque difficulté (à faire qch.); I found myself crying, je me surpris à pleurer. 2. (a) (by searching) retrouver; to try to f. sth., chercher qch.; to f. a leak, localiser une fuite; I can't f. time, je n'ai pas le temps de . . .; (b) obtenir. 3. constater. 4. to f. s.o. guilty, déclarer qn coupable. 5. (a) fournir (l'argent, pour une entreprise); (b) wages £20, all found, gages £20, tout fourni. 'findings, *spl.* conclusions *fpl* (d'un procès-verbal). find 'out, *v.tr.* (a) deviner, découvrir (un secret); constater (une erreur); *abs.* to f. out about sth., se renseigner sur qch.; (b) to f. s.o. out, démasquer qn; trouver qn en défaut.

fine[1] [fain]. I. *s.* amende *f.* II. *v.tr.* frapper (qn) d'une amende.

fine[2], *a.* 1. (a) fin, pur; (b) fin, subtil. 2. beau; a f. man, woman, un bel homme, une belle femme; the f. arts, les beaux-arts *m.* 3. (a) of the finest quality, de premier choix; (b) excellent, magnifique; that's f.! voilà qui est parfait; (c) that's all very f., tout cela est bel et bon. 4. (of weather) beau. 5. (a) fin; to chop (meat) fine, hacher menu; (b) f. nib, plume pointue. 6. to cut it f., faire qch. tout juste, arriver de justesse. -ly, *adv.* 1. (a) finement; (b) délicatement, subtilement. 2. admirablement. 'finery, *s.* parure *f.*

finger ['fingər]. I. *s.* doigt *m*; first f., index *m.* II. *v.tr.* manier, tâter (qch.). 'fingerprint, *s.* empreinte *f* digitale.

finish ['finiʃ]. I. *v.tr. & i.* finir, (se) terminer. II. *s.* 1. *Sp:* arrivée *f*; to be in at the f., (i) *Sp:* assister à l'arrivée; (ii) voir la fin de l'aventure. 2. fini *m*, achevé *m*, finesse *f* de l'exécution (d'un travail); apprêt *m* (d'un drap). 'finished, *a.* 1. (article) fini, apprêté. 2. (of appearance) soigné.

finite ['fainait], *a. Gram:* fini.

fir [fəɾ], *s.* f. (tree), sapin *m*; f. plantation, sapinière *f*; f. cone, pomme *f* de pin.

fire [faiər]. I. s. 1. (a) feu m; to light a f., faire du feu; electric f., radiateur m électrique; (b) incendie m; f.! au feu! (c) attrib. f. alarm, avertisseur m d'incendie; f. brigade, (corps m de sapeurs-)pompiers mpl; f. engine, pompe f à incendie; f. escape, échelle f de sauvetage; escalier m de secours; f. insurance, assurance f (contre l'in-cendie; Can: f. ranger, guetteur m. 2. (of firearm) feu, tir m, coups mpl de feu. II. v. 1. v.tr. (a) incendier (une maison); stimuler (l'enthousiasme de qn); (b) cuire (de la poterie); (c) lancer (une torpille); tirer (un canon); abs. tirer (sur qn); to f. a question at s.o., poser à qn une question à brûle-pourpoint; (d) F: renvoyer (un employé). 2. v.i. (of shot) partir. 'firearm, s. arme f à feu. 'fireguard, s. 1. garde-feu m. 2. (pers.) U.S: guetteur m. 'firelight, s. in the f., à la lumière du feu. 'firelighter, s. allume-feu m. †'fireman, s. (sapeur-)pompier m. 'fireplace, s. cheminée f, foyer m. 'fireproof, a. (a) incombustible, ig-nifuge; (b) réfractaire; f. dish, plat m allant au four. 'fireside, s. foyer m; coin m du feu. 'firewood, s. bois m de chauffage. 'fireworks, s.pl. feu m d'artifice.

firm¹ [fəːm], s. maison f (de commerce).

firm², a. ferme. 1. compact; solide. (of friendship, etc.) constant; (of intention, character) résolu. 3. adv. to stand f., tenir bon. -ly, adv. 1. fermement, solidement; (tenir qch.) d'une main ferme. 2. (parler) d'un ton ferme. 'firmness, s. fermeté f; solidité f.

first [fəːst]. I. a. premier; (a) on the f. floor, au premier; U.S: au rez-de-chaussée; Charles the First, Charles premier; at f. sight, de prime abord; au premier abord; in the f. place, d'abord; head f., la tête la première; Th: f. night, première f; f. edition, édition originale; Aut: f. (gear), première (vitesse); (b) at f. hand, de première main. -ly, adv. premiè-rement; en premier lieu. II. s. (a) premier, (la) première; Sp. etc: to come in an easy f., arriver bon premier. 2. commencement m; at f., d'abord. III. adv. 1. premièrement. 1. commencement, d'abord; f. of all, en premier lieu. 2. pour la première fois. 3. plutôt; I'd die f., plutôt mourir. 4. he arrived f., il arriva le premier; you go f.! allez devant! ladies f.! place aux dames! 'first-'aid, s. soins mpl d'urgence; f.-a. post, poste m de (premiers) secours. 'first-'class, a. (wagon) de première classe; (mar-chandises) de premier choix; (travail) de premier ordre. 'first-'rate, a. ex-cellent; de première classe; f.-r. dinner, dîner soigné; f.-r. idea, fameuse idée.

fish [fiʃ]. I. s. poisson m; f. bone, arête f; F: a queer f., un drôle de type. II. v.i. pêcher (la truite, etc.); to go fishing, aller à la pêche. 'fishcake, s. croquette f de poisson. †'fisherman, s. pêcheur m. †'fishery, s. pêche f; high-seas f., la grande pêche. 'fish-hook, s. hameçon m. 'fishing, s. la pêche; f. boat, bateau m de pêche; f. line, ligne f (de pêche); f. rod, canne f à pêche; f. tackle, attirail m de pêche. 'fishmonger, s. marchand m de poisson. 'fishy, a. 1. (odeur, goût) de poisson. 2. F: a f. business, une affaire louche.

fission ['fiʃ(ə)n], s. Ph: fission f; nuclear f., fission nucléaire.

fissure ['fiʃər], s. fissure f, fente f, crevasse f.

fist [fist], s. poing m.

fit¹ [fit], s. 1. accès m, attaque f (de fièvre ou de folie); quinte f (de toux); fainting f., syncope f. 2. accès, mouvement m (de colère); crise f (de larmes); to be in fits of laughter, avoir le fou rire; to work by fits and starts, travailler par à-coups. 'fitful, a. irrégulier, capricieux.

fit². I. a. 1. bon, propre (for sth., à qch.); to think f., juger convenable; do as you think f., faites comme bon vous semblera. 2. capable; f. for nothing, propre à rien. 3. en bonne santé; to keep f., se maintenir en forme. II. s. ajustement m. III. †v. 1. v.tr. (a) (of clothes, etc.) aller à qn; être à la taille de qn; shoes that f. well, souliers qui chaussent bien; (b) adapter, ajuster (qch. à qch., une robe à qn); to f. parts together, monter, assembler, des pièces. 2. v.i. (a) s'ajuster, s'adapter, se raccorder; s'emboîter (sur qch.); (b) your dress fits well, votre robe (vous) va bien; to f. in, être en harmonie (avec qch.); your plans f. in with mine, vos projets cadrent avec les miens. fit 'out, v.tr. (a) équiper (qn, qch., de qch.); (b) fitted, a. ajusté, monté; (pardessus) à taille; (coffret à outils) garni; (b) to be f. for a job, être apte à occuper un poste. 'fitting. I. a. approprié (to, à); well-f. (dress), (robe) qui va bien. -ly, adv. conven-ablement. II. s. 1. (a) ajustage m, montage m (d'une machine, d'un pneu); (b) essayage m (d'une robe). 2. usu. pl. installations f; équipement m; brass fittings, garnitures f en cuivre. 'fitness, s. 1. aptitude f (for, à, pour). 2. (a) à-propos m, justesse f (d'une remarque); (b) bienséance f, con-venance f. 3. physical f., bonne forme. 'fitter, s. E: ajusteur m.

five [faiv], num. a. & s. cinq (m). 'fiver, s. F: billet m de cinq livres, U.S: de cinq dollars.

fix [fiks]. I. *s.* embarras *m*, difficulté *f*, mauvais pas. II. *v.tr.* fixer. 1. caler; assujettir (une poutre); assurer (une planche); fixer (qn du regard). 2. fixer (une limite, un jour); to f. on sth., se décider pour qch. '**fixed,** *a.* fixe, arrêté; f. wheel, roue calée; *Com*: f. prices, prix fixes; f. smile, sourire figé. '**fixture,** *s.* 1. appareil *m*, (etc.) fixe, inamovible. 2. *Sp*: engagement *m*; match (prévu); list of fixtures, programme *m*.

fizz [fiz], *v.i.* (*of champagne, etc.*) pétiller. '**fizzy,** *a.* (*of mineral water, etc.*) gazeux; (*of wine*) mousseux. **fizzle out,** *v.i.* F: (*of plan, etc.*) avorter.

flabbergast ['flæbəga:st], *v.tr.* F: abasourdir, ahurir (qn); I was flabbergasted, j'en suis resté abberlué.

flabbiness ['flæbinis], *s.* flaccidité *f*; mollesse *f.* '**flabby,** *a.* (*of muscles*) flasque; mou; (*of pers.*) mollasse, avachi.

flag[1] [flæg], *s.* (*a*) drapeau *m*; (*b*) Nau: pavillon *m.* '**flagship,** *s.* (navire *m*) amiral *m.* '**flagstaff,** *s.* mât *m* de drapeau.

‡**flag**[2], *v.i.* (*of pers.*) s'alanguir; (*of conversation*) traîner; (*of zeal*) se relâcher.

flagrant ['fleigrənt], *a.* (*of offence*) flagrant, énorme; a f. case, un cas notoire. -**ly,** *adv.* scandaleusement.

flagstone ['flægstoun], *s.* carreau *m*, dalle *f.*

flair ['flɛər], *s.* flair *m*, perspicacité *f.*

flake [fleik], *s.* (*a*) flocon *m* (de neige, etc.); (*b*) écaille *f*, éclat *m* (de métal).

flame [fleim]. I. *s.* flamme *f*; to burst into flames, s'enflammer brusquement. II. *v.i.* flamber, jeter des flammes. '**flaming,** *a.* 1. (feu) flambant, flamboyant; (maison, etc.) en flammes. 2. P: a f. liar, un sacré menteur.

flamingo [flə'miŋgou, flæm-], *s.* flamant *m.*

flan [flæn], *s.* Cu: tarte *f* aux fruits.

flange [flændʒ], *s.* collet *m*, collerette *f*; f. coupling, joint *m* à brides.

flank [flæŋk]. I. *s.* (*a*) flanc *m*; (*b*) Cu: flanchet *m* (de bœuf).

flannel ['flænl], *s.* flanelle *f*; face f. = gant *m* de toilette, Fr. C: débarbouillette *f.* **flannel'ette,** *s.* flanelle *f* de coton.

flap [flæp]. I. *s.* 1. battement *m*, coup *m* (léger, de l'aile). 2. (*a*) patte *f* (d'une enveloppe); (*b*) abattant *m* (de table); trappe *f* (de cave). 3. F: to get into a f., s'affoler. II. *v.* 1. *v.tr.* battre (des ailes); agiter (les bras). 2. *v.i.* (*of sail, shutter, etc.*) battre, claquer; F: (*of pers.*) s'affoler.

flare ['flɛər]. I. *s.* 1. (*a*) flamboiement *m*; (*b*) feu *m* de signal; Av: landing f., feu d'atterrissage. 2. évasement *m*, godet *m* (d'une jupe). II. *v.* 1. *v.i.* flamboyer. 2. *v.tr.* évaser (une jupe). '**flare-path,** *s.* Av: piste *f* balisée.

flare 'up, *v.i.* (*a*) s'enflammer, lancer des flammes; (*b*) (*of pers.*) s'emporter.

flash [flæʃ]. I. *s.* éclair *m*, Phot: flash *m*; news f., flash; Phot: f. bulb, ampoule *f* flash; in a f., en un rien de temps. II. *v.* 1. *v.i.* (*a*) jeter des éclairs; (*of jewels, etc.*) étinceler; (*b*) to f. past, passer comme un éclair. 2. *v.tr.* (*a*) faire étinceler (ses bijoux); (*b*) projeter (un rayon de lumière); (*c*) répandre (une nouvelle) par la radio. '**flash-back,** *s.* 1. retour *m* de flamme. 2. Cin: retour en arrière. '**flashing,** *a.* éclatant, flamboyant. '**flashy,** *a.* (*of dress, etc.*) voyant, éclatant.

flask [fla:sk], *s.* flacon *m.*

flat [flæt]. I. *a.* 1. plat; to fall f. on one's face, tomber à plat ventre; Aut: to go f. out, filer à toute allure; f. tyre, pneu à plat; *Sp*: f. racing, le plat; f. fish, poisson plat. 2. net, positif; f. refusal, refus catégorique. 3. monotone, ennuyeux; (style) fade, insipide; to feel f., se sentir à plat. 4. (taux) uniforme. 5. (son) sourd; to sing f., chanter faux. -**ly,** *adv.* nettement, carrément; (nier qch.) absolument. II. *s.* 1. plat *m* de la (main). 2. *Sp*: on the f., sur le plat. 3. appartement *m*; block of flats, immeuble *m.* 4. *Mus*: bémol *m.* III. *adv.* F: nettement; f. broke, sans le sou. '**flatlet,** *s.* studio *m.* '**flatness,** *s.* égalité *f* (d'une surface); manque *m* de relief; insipidité *f* (du style). '**flatten,** *v.tr. & i.* (s')aplatir; (s')aplanir.

flatter ['flætər], *v.tr.* flatter (qn). '**flatterer,** *s.* flatteur, -euse; flagorneur, -euse. '**flattering,** *a.* flatteur. -**ly,** *adv.* flatteusement. '**flattery,** *s.* flatterie *f*, adulation *f.*

flaunt [flɔ:nt], *v.tr.* (*of pers.*) faire étalage de (son luxe, etc.); s'afficher.

flavour ['fleivər]. I. *s.* saveur *f*, goût *m*, parfum *m* (d'une glace). II. *v.tr.* assaisonner, parfumer; to f. a sauce, relever une sauce. '**flavouring,** *s.* assaisonnement *m*; condiment *m.* '**flavourless,** *a.* sans saveur; insipide.

flaw [flɔ:], *s.* défaut *m*, imperfection *f.* '**flawless,** *a.* sans défaut; parfait; (technique) impeccable. -**ly,** *adv.* parfaitement.

flea [fli:], *s.* puce *f*; fleabite, s. 1. morsure *f* de puce. 2. vétille *f*, bagatelle *f.*

fleck [flek]. I. *s.* 1. petite tache, moucheture *f.* 2. particule *f* (de poussière, etc.). II. *v.tr.* tacheter (with, de).

fledgeling ['fledʒliŋ], *s.* oisillon *m.*

flee [fli:], *v.i.* fuir, s'enfuir; se sauver.

fleece [fli:s]. I. *s.* 1. toison *f.* 2. Com: molleton *m.* II. *v.tr.* tondre, écorcher, plumer (qn, un client). '**fleecy,** *a.* (*of wool*) floconneux; (*of cloud*) moutonné.

fleet [fli:t], *s.* flotte *f* (de navires); fishing f., flotille *f* de pêche; *Av:* air f., flotte aérienne.

Fleming ['flemiŋ], *s.* Flamand *m*, Flamande *f*. **'Flemish,** *a.* flamand; *s. Ling:* le flamand.

flesh [fleʃ], *s.* chair *f*; in the f., en chair et en os; his own f. and blood, les siens. **'fleshy,** *a.* charnu.

flex [fleks], *s. El: Techn:* câble *m*, fil *m* souple; flexible *m*.

flexibility [fleksi'biliti], *s.* flexibilité *f*, souplesse *f*. **'flexible,** *a.* flexible, souple, pliant.

flick [flik]. I. *s.* chiquenaude *f* (du doigt); petit coup. II. *v.tr.* effleurer; (*with finger*) donner une chiquenaude à (qch.).

flicker ['flikər]. I. *s.* tremblotement *m*; battement *m*, clignement *m* (de paupière). II. *v.i.* (*of flame*) trembloter, vaciller; (*of light*) clignoter; (*of instrument needle*) osciller.

flight [flait]. *s.* 1. (*a*) vol *m* (d'un oiseau, d'un avion); *Av:* f. "A" for Paris, ligne 'A' pour Paris; (*b*) course *f* (d'un projectile); (*c*) envol; f. of fancy, essor *m* de l'imagination. 2. volée *f* (d'oiseaux); *Av:* escadrille *f*. 3. f. of stairs, escalier *m*. 4. (*a*) bande *f*, vol *m* (d'oiseaux); *Av:* escadrille *f*. **'flight-deck,** *s. Av: Nau:* pont *m* d'envol. **'flight-lieutenant,** *s. Av:* capitaine *m* aviateur.

flight², *s.* fuite *f*.

flimsiness ['flimzinis], *s.* manque *m* de solidité; (*a*) légèreté *f*; (*b*) futilité *f* (d'une excuse). **'flimsy,** *a.* sans solidité; (tissu) léger.

flinch [flin(t)ʃ], *v.i.* 1. reculer, fléchir. 2. without flinching, sans broncher.

‡fling [fliŋ], *v.tr.* jeter (une pierre); lancer (une balle); to f. open the door, ouvrir brusquement la porte; to f. one's money away, gaspiller son argent; *F:* to f. s.o. out, flanquer qn à la porte.

flint [flint], *s.* silex *m*. 2. pierre *f* à briquet.

flippancy ['flipənsi], *s.* légèreté *f*, désinvolture *f*. **'flippant,** *a.* léger, désinvolte. **-ly,** *adv.* légèrement.

flirt [flə:t]. I. *s.* flirteur *m*; coquette *f*. II. *v.i.* flirter. **flir'tation,** *s.* flirt *m*.

‡flit [flit], *v.i.* 1. to f. away, partir. 2. to f. by, passer comme une ombre; to f. about, aller et venir sans bruit.

float [flout]. I. *s.* (*a*) flotteur, nageur; nager; (*b*) faire la planche. **'floating,** *a.* 1. flottant. à flot. 2. (*a*) libre, mobile; f. population, population flottante; (*b*) *Pol:* f. voter, voteur indécis; (*c*) *Com:* f. capital, fonds *mpl* de roulement.

flock [flɔk]. I. *s.* troupe *f* (d'animaux); troupeau *m* (de bétail, etc.). II. *v.i.* s'attrouper.

‡flog [flɔg], *v.tr.* fouetter; to f. oneself, s'éreinter.

flood [flʌd]. I. *s.* 1. flot *m*, flux *m* (de la marée). 2. (*a*) déluge *m*, inondation *f*; (*b*) crue *f* (d'une rivière). II. *v.* 1. *v.tr.* inonder, submerger. 2. *v.i.* (*of river*) déborder; être en crue. **'flooding,** *s.* 1. inondation *f*. 2. débordement *m*. **'floodlight,** *v.tr.* illuminer (un monument, etc.) par projecteurs. **'flood-lighting,** *s.* éclairage *m* diffusé; illumination *f* par projecteurs. **'flood-tide,** *s.* marée *f* montante.

floor [flɔ:r]. I. *s.* 1. plancher *m*, parquet *m*. 2. étage *m* (de maison). II. *v.tr.* 1. parqueter (une pièce). 2. (*a*) terrasser (un adversaire); *Sch:* coller (un candidat). **'floor-cloth,** *s.* serpillière *f*. **'floor-polish,** *s.* encaustique *f*; cire *f* à parquet. **'floorshow,** *s.* spectacle *m* de cabaret.

florid ['flɔrid], *a.* fleuri; orné à l'excès; to have a f. complexion, être haut en couleur.

florist ['flɔrist], *s.* fleuriste *mf*.

flotilla [flə'tilə], *s.* flotille *f*.

flounce [flauns], *v.i.* to f. in, out, entrer, sortir, dans un mouvement d'indignation.

flounder ['flaundər], *v.i.* patauger, barboter.

flour ['flauər], *s.* farine *f*.

flourish ['flʌriʃ]. I. *s.* 1. grand geste *m*. 2. trait *m* de plume; (*after signature*) paraphe. 3. fanfare *f* (de trompettes). II. 1. *v.i.* (*a*) (*of plant*) bien venir; (*b*) (*of pers., trade*) prospérer. 2. *v.tr.* brandir (un bâton, sa canne). **'flourishing,** *a.* florissant; (*commerce*) prospère.

flout [flaut], *v.tr.* se moquer de (l'autorité de qn).

flow [flou]. I. *s.* (*a*) écoulement *m*; (*b*) *El:* passage *m* (du courant); (*c*) courant *m*, arrivée *f* (d'air, d'essence, etc.); (*d*) flot *m*, flux *m* (de la marée). II. *v.i.* 1. couler, s'écouler; se déverser (dans la mer); (*b*) (*of tide*) monter; (*c*) (*of blood, el. current, etc.*) circuler. 2. dériver, découler (from, de). **flow 'in,** *v.i.* (*of people, money*) affluer.

flower ['flauər]. I. *s.* 1. fleur *f*; wild flowers, fleurs sauvages; bunch of flowers, bouquet *m*. 2. fine fleur, élite *f* (de l'armée, etc.). 3. fleuraison; in f., en fleur. II. *v.i.* fleurir. **'flower-bed,** *s.* parterre *m*; plate-bande *f*. **'flowered,** *a.* f. material, tissu *m* à fleurs, à ramages. **'flower garden,** *s.* jardin *m* d'agrément. **'flowering,** *a.* fleuri; en fleur. **'flowerpot,** *s.* pot *m* à fleurs. **'flower show,** *s.* exposition *f* horticole; floralies *fpl*.

fluctuate ['flʌktjueit], *v.i.* fluctuer, varier. **'fluctuating,** *a.* variable. **fluctu'ation,** *s.* variations *fpl*, fluctuation *f*.

fluency ['fluːənsi], s. facilité f (de parole). 'fluent, a. (of speech) coulant, facile. -ly, adv. (parler une langue) couramment.

fluff [flʌf], s. duvet m; peluches fpl. 'fluffy, a. (drap) pelucheux (poussin, etc.) duveteux; (of hair, cheveux flous.

fluid ['fluːid], a. & s. fluide (m).

fluke [fluːk], s. coup m de veine, de hasard; chance f.

flurry ['flʌri]. I. s. agitation f, émoi m. II. v.tr. agiter, effarer (qn); to get flurried, perdre la tête.

flush [flʌʃ]. I. s. 1. H: chasse f (d'eau). 2. élan m (d'émotion, etc.). 3. (a) éclat m (de la beauté); (b) rougeur f (au visage). II. 1. v.tr. to f. (out) a drain, donner une chasse à un égout; to f. the W.C., tirer la chasse d'eau. 2. v.i. (of pers.) rougir. flushed, a. (visage) (i) enfiévré, empourpré, (ii) allumé par la boisson; f. with success, grisé par le succès.

fluster ['flʌstər]. I. s. agitation f, trouble m. II. v.tr. agiter, bouleverser (qn).

flute [fluːt], s. Mus: flûte f.

flutter ['flʌtər]. I. s. 1. battement m (des ailes); palpitation f (du cœur); flottement m (d'un drapeau). 2. agitation f, émoi m. 3. F: petite spéculation (à la Bourse, aux cartes, etc.). II. 1. v.i. (of birds) voleter, battre des ailes; (of flag) flotter, s'agiter; (of heart) palpiter, battre. 2. v.tr. agiter (un chapeau); battre des ailes; troubler (qn).

†fly¹ [flai], s. mouche f. F: fishing, pêche f à la mouche; f. swatter, tapette f à mouches.

†fly² [flai]. I. v.i. 1. (of bird, plane) voler; to f. over Paris, survoler Paris; (b) (of flag) flotter; (c) (of pers.) courir (à toute vitesse); (of time) fuir; (d) to f. at s.o., s'élancer sur qn, (ii) invectiver qn; to f. into a rage, s'emporter; the door flew open, la porte s'ouvrit brusquement; (e) F: to let f. at s.o., (i) tirer sur qn, (ii) flanquer un coup à qn; (iii) s'en prendre à qn; (f) fuir, s'enfuir. 2. v.tr. (a) lancer, faire voler (un cerf-volant); (b) Av: piloter (un avion). 'fly away, v.i. 1. (of bird, etc.) s'envoler. 2. (of pers.) s'enfuir. 'flyer, s. aviateur, -trice. 'flying. I. a. 1. (oiseau) volant; f. hours, heures de vol m; Av: f. officer, lieutenant m; 2. (a) (course, etc.) rapide; Mil: f. column, colonne f mobile; (b) a f. visit, une visite courte, éclair; (c) Sp: f. start, départ lancé. II. s. vol m (d'un oiseau, d'un avion); aviation f; f. club, aéro-club m; f. buttress, arc-boutant m. 'fly-over, s. Civ. E: saut-de-mouton m. 'fly-past, s. défilé m aérien.

foal [foul], s. poulain m.

foam [foum]. I. s. écume f; (on beer) mousse f. II. v.i. (of sea) écumer; (of beer, etc.) mousser. 'foam(-)rubber, s. caoutchouc m mousse.

focus ['foukəs]. I. s. 1. foyer m (de lentille); f. f., au point. II. 1. concentrer, faire converger (des rayons) (on, sur). 2. mettre au point (un microscope, etc.). 'focusing, s. 1. concentration f, convergence f. 2. mise f au point (d'une jumelle, etc.).

fodder ['fodər], s. fourrage m.

fog [fog]. I. s. brouillard m; brume f. II. †v. v.tr. (a) embrumer (un endroit); brouiller (les idées); embrouiller (qn); Phot: voiler (un cliché). 2. v.i. Phot: se voiler. 'foggy, a. (a) brumeux; (b) voilé, confus. 'fog-horn, s. sirène f. 'fog-lamp, a. Aut: phare m antibrouillard.

foil¹ [foil], s. feuille f, clinquant m (d'étain, d'aluminium, etc.).

foil², v.tr. faire échouer; déjouer (un complot, etc.).

foil³, s. (fencing) fleuret m.

foist [foist], v.tr. refiler (sth. on s.o., qch. sur qn); to f. oneself on s.o., s'imposer chez qn.

fold [fould]. I. s. pli m, repli m (d'un tissu, etc.); battant m (d'une porte). II. v. 1. v.tr. (a) plier; to f. back, rabattre (un col, la couverture); (b) to f. sth. in sth., envelopper qch. de, dans, qch.; (c) to f. one's arms, (se) croiser les bras. 2. v.i. se (re)plier. 'folder, s. Com: etc: prospectus m, dépliant m; (for papers, etc.) chemise f. 'folding, a. pliant, rabattable; f. chair, chaise pliante; f. steps, escabeau m.

foliage ['fouliidʒ], s. feuillage m.

folk [fouk], s.pl. gens mf, personnes f; country f., campagnards; my f., les miens, ma famille. 'folklore, s. folklore m; traditions f populaires. 'folksong, s. chanson f traditionnelle.

follow ['folou], v.tr. suivre; (a) to f. s.o. about, suivre qn partout; (b) succéder à qn; (c) être le disciple, le partisan de (qn); poursuivre (l'ennemi); suivre, se conformer à (la mode, etc.); (f) exercer (une profession); embrasser (une carrière); (g) suivre, comprendre (une leçon, etc.). 2. v.i. (a) to f. (after), suivre; our method is as follows, notre méthode est la suivante; (b) s'ensuivre, résulter (from, de). 'follower, s. partisan m, disciple m. 'following. I. a. 1. qui suit. 2. (a) suivant; the f. day, le jour suivant, le lendemain; (b) the f. resolution, la résolution que voici. II. s. Pol: etc: suite f; parti m (d'un chef).

folly ['foli], s. folie f, sottise f.

foment [fou'ment], v.tr. fomenter (une plaie, la discorde).

fond [fɔ̃d], *a.* 1. affectueux, tendre. 2. to be f. of, aimer (qn); (friend) amateur *m* de (musique, etc.); f. of sweets, friand de sucreries. -ly, *adv.* tendrement, affectueusement. **'fondness,** *s.* 1 indulgence excessive (d'une mère, etc.). 2. affection *f*, tendresse *f* (for, pour, envers). 3. penchant *m*, goût *m* (for sth., pour qch.).

fondle ['fɔ̃dl], *v.tr.* caresser, câliner.

food [fud], *s.* 1. nourriture *f*; aliments *mpl*; vivres *mpl*; f. value, valeur *f* nutritive; f. poisoning, intoxication *f* alimentaire; the f.-processing industry, l'industrie *f* alimentaire. 2. f. and drink, le boire et le manger. **'foodstuffs,** *s.pl.* comestibles *m*.

fool [fuːl]. I. *s.* 1. imbécile *mf*; idiot, -ote; *sot, f.* sotte; to make a f. of oneself, se rendre ridicule; F: silly f! espèce d'idiot! 2. dupe *f*. II. *v.* 1. *v.i.* to be a fool; to f. around, flâner; gâcher son temps. 2. *v.tr.* duper (qn), F: se payer la tête de qn. **'foolery,** *s.* 1. sottise *f*, bêtise *f*. 2. bouffonnerie *f*. **'foolhardy,** *a.* téméraire, imprudent. **'fooling,** *s.* 1 bouffonnerie *f*. duperie *f* (de qn). **'foolish,** *a.* (a) étourdi; sot; bête; (b) absurde, ridicule; to look f., avoir l'air penaud. -ly, *adv.* sottement, bêtement. **foolishness,** *s.* étourderie *f*; sottise *f*, bêtise *f*. **'foolproof,** *a.* (mecanisme) indéréglable, indétraquable.

†foot [fut], *s.* 1. pied *m*; to keep one's feet, rester debout; tenir ferme; to set s.o. on his feet again, (i) (re)mettre qn sur pied, (ii) (r)établir qn; to find one's feet, se débrouiller; to put one's f. down, faire acte d'autorité; *Aut: F:* accélérer; *F:* to put one's f. in it, mettre les pieds dans le plat; *F:* to have cold feet, avoir la frousse; (b) marche *f*, allure *f*; to have a light, a heavy, f., avoir le pied léger, lourd; (c) *adv. phr.* on f., (i) à pied; (ii) sur pied, en train; under f., sous les pieds. 2. pied (de cheval, etc.); patte *f* (de chien, de chat, d'oiseau). 3. bas bout *m* (d'une table); pied (d'un lit; base *f* (de colonne, etc.); pied (de verre à vin); bas *m* (d'échelle, de page). 4. *(measurement:)* pied anglais (= 30 cm. 48). **'foot-brake,** *s.* frein *m* à pédale. **'football,** *s.* 1. ballon *m*. le football; Rugby f., le rugby. **'footballer,** *s.* footballeur *m*. **'footbridge,** *s.* passerelle *f*. **'foot-sure-f.,** au pied sûr. **'footfall,** *s.* (bruit *m* de) pas *m*. **'foothills,** *s.pl.* contreforts *m* (d'un massif). **'footing,** *s.* 1. (a) pose *f* des pieds; (b) to lose, miss, one's f., perdre pied; faire un faux mouvement. 2. (a) to gain a f., s'implanter, prendre pied; (b) to be on a good f. with s.o., être en bons termes avec qn. **'footlights,** *s.pl. Th:*

rampe *f*. **'footmark,** *s.* empreinte *f* de pied. **'footnote,** *s.* renvoi *m* en bas de page. **'footpath,** *s.* sentier *m*; (in street) trottoir *m*. **'footstep,** *s.* 1. pas *m*. 2. to walk in s.o.'s footsteps, suivre les traces de qn. **'footwear,** *s. Com:* chaussures, *fpl.*

for [fɔːr, fər]. I. *prep.* pour. 1. (a) (i) (representing) member f. Liverpool, député de Liverpool; (ii) (instead of) to act f. s.o., agir pour, au nom de, à la place de, qn; (b) to exchange sth, for sth. else, échanger qch. contre qch. d'autre; to sell sth. for ten francs, vendre qch. dix francs. 2. (a) what f.? pourquoi (faire)? for sale, à vendre; f. example, par exemple; (b) to jump f. joy, sauter de joie. 3. (a) trains for London, les trains pour, sur, direction de, Londres; (b) his feelings f. you, ses sentiments envers vous. 4. (of time, distance) pendant (un an); I've been here for three days, je suis ici depuis trois jours. 5. to care f. s.o., aimer qn; fit f. nothing, bon à rien. 6. (a) as f. him, quant à lui; f. all that, malgré tout; (c) but f. her, sans elle; (d) word f. word, mot à mot. 7. (introducing an infinitive clause) (a) it is easy for him to come, il lui est facile de venir; (b) it is not for me to decide, ce n'est pas à moi de le décider. II. *conj.* car.

forage ['fɔridʒ], *v.i.* 1. fourrager. 2. F: fouiller.

forbearance [fɔːr'bɛərəns], *s.* patience *f*. **for'bearing,** *a.* patient, endurant.

†forbid [fɔ'bid], *v.tr.* 1. défendre, interdire; smoking forbidden, défense de fumer; to f. s.o. to do sth., défendre à qn de faire qch. 2. empêcher (qch.). **for'bidding,** *a.* (visage) sinistre; (ciel) menaçant.

force [fɔːs], *s.* force *f*. 1. (a) violence *f*, contrainte *f*; by sheer f., de vive force; (b) influence *f*, autorité *f*. 2. (a) énergie *f*; intensité *f* (du vent, etc.); (b) Ph: E: force, effort *m*; f. of gravity, pesanteur *f*. 3. puissance *f*; force (militaire). 4. (of law, etc.) to come into f., entrer en vigueur. II. *v.tr.* forcer. 1. (a) she forced a smile, elle eut un sourire contraint; (b) to f. one's way, se frayer un chemin; pénétrer de force (dans une maison); (c) forcer (une plante); Aut: trop pousser (le moteur). 2. contraindre, obliger (qn à faire qch.). **'force back,** *v.tr.* repousser; faire reculer. **'forced,** *a.* forcé. 1. obligatoire, inévitable. 2. contraint; f. laugh, rire *m* jaune. **'forceful,** *a.* (of pers., speech) énergique. -fully, *adv.* avec force. **'forcible,** *a.* 1. (entrée) de force. 2. (langage) vigoureux. -ibly, *adv.* 1. par la force, de force. 2. énergiquement.

ford [fɔːd]. I. s. gué m. II. v.tr. passer à gué (une rivière).

fore [fɔːr]. I. a. antérieur; de devant. II. s. à vue d'œil; to the f., en évidence. III. int. attention! 'forearm, s. avant-bras m inv. 'forecast. I. s. prévision f; Sp: (pari) tiercé; betting f., pronostic m. II. v.tr. calculer, prévoir (les événements, le temps). fore'doomed, a. condamné d'avance; plan f. to failure, projet mort-né. 'forefather, s. ancêtre m; our forefathers, nos aïeux. 'forefinger, s. index m. †'fore-foot, s. pied m antérieur; patte f de devant. 'fore'going, a. précédent; déjà cité; the f., ce qui précède. 'foreground, s. Phot: etc. premier plan m. 'forehand, s. 1. (of horse) avant-main m. 2. (tennis) coup m droit. forehead ['fɔrid], s. front m. 'foreland, s. cap m; promontoire m. 'foreleg, s. 1. jambe f de devant; patte f de devant. †'foreman, s. contremaître m; chef m d'équipe. 'foremost. 1. a. premier; le plus avancé. 2. adv. first and f., tout d'abord. 'forerunner, s. précurseur m. †'fore'see, v.tr. prévoir, entrevoir (l'avenir, des difficultés). fore'seeable, a. prévisible. 'fore'shadow, v.tr. annoncer (un événement). 'foresight, s. prévoyance f; want of f., imprévoyance f. 'fore'stall, v.tr. anticiper, devancer (un événement). 'foretaste, s. avant-goût m. ‡fore'tell, v.tr. 1. (of pers.) prédire. 2. présager. 'forethought, s. 1. préméditation f. 2. prévoyance f. 'fore'warn, v.tr. prévenir, avertir (qn de qch.). †'forewoman, s. contremaîtresse f, F: première f. 'foreword, s. avant-propos m inv, préface f.

foreign ['fɔrin], a. étranger; f. trade, commerce extérieur; the F. Office = le Ministère des Affaires étrangères. 'foreigner, s. étranger, -ère.

forest ['fɔrist], s. forêt f; f. ranger, garde m forestier. 'forestry, s. sylviculture f.

forfeit ['fɔːfit]. I. v.tr. perdre (qch.) par confiscation; payer de (sa vie, son honneur). II. s. (a) (turf) forfait m; (b) f. clause, clause de dédit m; (c) (in game) gage m. 'forfeiture, s. perte f (de biens) par confiscation; perte (de l'honneur, etc.).

forge [fɔːdʒ]. I. s. forge f. II. v.tr. 1. forger (le fer). 2. contrefaire (une signature); abs. commettre un faux. 'forger, s. Jur: faussaire mf. 'forgery, s. Jur: 1. contrefaçon f; falsification f. 2. faux m.

‡**forget** [fə'get], v.tr. 1. oublier; f. about it! n'y pensez plus! 2. s'oublier, oublier; don't f. to (do sth.), ne manquez pas de (faire qch.); (b) négliger (son devoir, etc.). for'getful, a. 1. oublieux (of, de); he is very f., il a

a très mauvaise mémoire. 2. négligent. for'getfulness, s. 1. (a) manque (habituel) de mémoire; (b) (un moment d')oubli m. 2. négligence f. for'get-me-not, s. Bot: myosotis m.

‡**forgive** [fə'giv], v.tr. 1. pardonner (une injure, etc.). 2. pardonner à (qn). for'giveness, s. 1. pardon m. 2. indulgence f, clémence f. for'giving, a. indulgent; peu rancunier.

‡**forgo** [fɔː'gou], v.tr. renoncer à (qch.); s'abstenir de (qch.).

fork [fɔːk]. I. s. 1. (garden) f., fourche f; (table) f., fourchette f; bifurcation f (de routes); enfourchure f (de branches). II. v. 1. (of roads) (se) bifurquer; P.N: f. right for York, prenez à droite pour York. 2 v.tr. (a) remuer (le sol, le foin); (b) F: to f. out, up, payer, F: abouler (de l'argent).

forlorn [fə'lɔːn], a. abandonné; triste; f. hope, aventure désespérée.

form [fɔːm]. I. s. 1. (a) forme f, conformation f (d'un objet); (b) figure f, silhouette f; in the f. of a dog, sous la forme d'un chien. 2. (a) forme, formalité f; (b) les convenances f; l'étiquette f; it's good f., c'est de bon ton; it's bad f., cela ne se fait pas, ne se dit pas. 3. formule; a f. of speech, une façon de parler; to fill up a f., remplir une formule, un formulaire. 4. (a) Sp: forme, état m; condition f; (b) (of pers.) to be in good f., être en train. 5. Sch: classe f. 6. banc m, banquette f. II. v. 1. v.tr. former, faire, façonner. 2. v.i. prendre forme; se former. 'formroom, s. Sch: (salle f de) classe f.

formal ['fɔːm(ə)l], a. 1. formel, en règle; (of order) formel, positif; f. denial, démenti formel. 2. protocolaire, cérémonieux, cérémonial. -ally, adv. 1. formellement. 2. cérémonieusement. †for'mality, s. 1. formalité f.

former ['fɔːmər], a. 1. antérieur, précédent, ancien; my f. pupils, mes anciens élèves; in f. times, autrefois, jadis. 2. pron. the f., celui-là, celle-là, ceux-là, celles-là. -ly, adv. autrefois, jadis.

formidable ['fɔːmidəbl], a. formidable, redoutable.

†**formula** ['fɔːmjulə], s. formule f. 'formulate, v.tr. formuler.

‡**forsake** [fə'seik], v.tr. 1. abandonner (qn). 2. renoncer à (une habitude).

forte. 1. a., adv. & s. [fɔːt] Mus: forte (m inv). 2. s. [fɔːt] singing is not his f., le chant n'est pas son fort.

forth [fɔːθ], adv. and so f., et ainsi de suite. forth'coming, a. 1. (a) qui arrive; (b) prochain, à venir. 2. (livre) prêt à paraître.

fortify ['fɔːtifai], *v.tr.* 1. (*a*) renforcer, fortifier (un navire, etc.); (*b*) affermir (qn). 2. remonter (un vin) en alcool. **fortifi′cation,** *s.* fortification *f.*

†**fortitude** ['fɔːtitjuːd], *s.* force *f* d'âme; courage *m.*

fortnight ['fɔːtnait], *s.* quinzaine *f*, quinze jours *m.* -ly, 1. *a.* bimensuel. 2. *adv.* tous les quinze jours.

fortress ['fɔːtris], *s.* forteresse *f.*

fortune ['fɔːtʃən], *s.* fortune *f.* 1. (*a*) hasard *m*, chance *f*; (*b*) sort *m.* 2. (*a*) bonne chance; bonheur *m*; (*b*) richesse *f*, prospérité *f*; to make a f. faire fortune. 3. f. teller, diseur, -euse, de bonne aventure. **′fortunate,** *a.* heureux; propice; to be f., avoir de la chance. -ly, *adv.* heureusement; par bonheur.

†**forty** ['fɔːti], *num. a. & s.* quarante (*m*); about f., une quarantaine de; to be in the forties, avoir passé la quarantaine; the forties, les années quarante (1940–49).

forward[1] ['fɔːwəd]. I. *a.* 1. (*a*) de devant, d'avant; f. turret, tourelle *f* avant; (*b*) (mouvement) progressif, en avant. 2. (*of plant, child*) avancé, précoce. 3. effronté. II. *s. Sp:* (*pers:*) avant *m.* III. *adv.* (*also* **′forwards**). 1. to look f. to sth., attendre qch. avec plaisir. 2. (*a*) en avant; to move f., avancer; to go straight f., aller tout droit; to rush f., se précipiter (en avant); (*b*) (*position*) à l'avant; f.! en avant; (*c*) *Com:* (carried) f., à reporter; report *m.* 3. to come f., se proposer; to push oneself f., se mettre en avant. IV. *v.tr.* (*a*) expédier, envoyer (des marchandises); please f., prière de faire suivre. **′forwarding,** *s.* (*a*) expédition *f* (d'un colis); (*b*) transmission *f* (d'une lettre).

fossil ['fɔsl], *a. & s.* fossile (*m*).

foster ['fɔstər], *v.tr.* entretenir, nourrir (un enfant, une idée); développer, encourager (l'amitié, etc.). **′foster-child,** *s.* 1. nourrisson *m.* 2. enfant adopté(e).

foul[1] [faul]. I. *a.* 1. infect, nauséabond. 2. (*a*) to fall f. of s.o., se brouiller avec qn; (*b*) f. weather, sale temps. 3. f. play, (i) *Sp:* jeu déloyal; (ii) malveillance *f.* -lly, *adv.* 1. salement. 2. abominablement. II. *s. Sp:* faute *f*; coup *m* illicite. III. *v.* 1. *v.tr.* encrasser (un canon de fusil); *Nau:* engager (une ancre). 2. *v.i.* (*of gun barrel*) s'encrasser; *Nau:* (*of anchor*) s'engager.

found [faund], *v.tr.* (*a*) fonder (un édifice); créer, établir (une institution, etc.); to f. a family, faire souche; (*b*) baser, appuyer (son opinion) (on, sur). **foun′dation,** *s.* 1. fondation *f*; établissement *m.* 2. fondement *m* (d'un édifice); assise *f* (d'un mur). **′founder**[1], *s.* fondateur *m.*

founder[2] ['faundər], *v.i.* (*of wall, etc.*) s'effondrer, s'écrouler; (*of ship*) sombrer.

foundling ['faundliŋ], *s.* enfant trouvé(e).

†**foundry** ['faundri], *s. Ind:* fonderie *f.*

fountain ['fauntin], *s.* fontaine *f*; source *f*; f.-pen, stylo *m.*

four [fɔːr], *num. a. & s.* quatre (*m*); **on all fours,** à quatre pattes. **four-′engined,** *a. Av:* quadrimoteur; f.-e. jet (plane), quadriréacteur *m.* **four-′figure,** *attrib. a.* à quatre chiffres. **′fourfold.** 1. *a.* quadruple. 2. *adv.* quatre fois autant; au quadruple. **′four-′footed,** *a.* quadrupède; à quatre pattes. **′four-′seater,** *s. Aut:* voiture *f* à quatre places. **′fourth.** 1. *num. a. & s.* quatrième. 2. *s.* (*fractional*) quart *m.* -ly, *adv.* quatrièmement; en quatrième lieu.

fourteen [fɔː′tiːn], *num. a. & s.* quatorze (*m*). **′four′teenth,** *num. a. & s.* quatorzième; (*on the*) f. of March, le quatorze mars.

fowl [faul], *s.* 1. *coll:* oiseaux; **wild f.,** gibier *m* d'eau. 2. poule *f*, coq *m*; volaille *f.*

fox [fɔks], *s.* renard *m.* **′foxglove,** *s. Bot:* digitale (pourprée). **′fox-hound,** *s.* chien *m* courant. **′fox-hunting,** *s.* la chasse au renard. **fox ′terrier,** *s.* fox *m.*

fraction ['frækʃ(ə)n], *s.* 1. petite portion *f*; fragment *m.* 2. *Mth:* fraction *f.*

fractious ['frækʃəs], *a.* revêche, difficile (de caractère); (*b*) pleurnicheur.

fracture ['fræktʃər]. I. *s.* fracture *f.* II. *v.tr.* fracturer (un os).

fragility [frə′dʒiliti], *s.* fragilité *f*; (*of pers.*) délicatesse *f* (de santé). **′fragile,** *a.* fragile; faible (de santé).

fragment ['frægmənt], *s.* fragment *m*; morceau *m.*

fragrance ['freigrəns], *s.* parfum *m.* **′fragrant,** *a.* parfumé, odorant.

frail [freil], *a.* 1. fragile; frêle. 2. (*of health, etc.*) faible, délicat.

frame [freim]. I. *s.* 1. construction *f*; forme *f.* f. of mind, disposition *f* d'esprit. 2. (*a*) ossature *f* (d'un animal); (*b*) charpente *f* (d'un bâtiment); châssis *m* (d'une voiture). 3. cadre *m*, encadrement *m* (d'un tableau). II. *v.tr.* 1. former (ses pensées). 2. (*a*) projeter (un dessin); (*b*) articuler, prononcer (un mot); imaginer (une idée); se faire (une opinion). 3. encadrer (un tableau). **′frame-up,** *s. F:* coup monté. **′framework,** *s.* 1. charpente *f*, ossature *f*, carcasse *f*; (*b*) coffrage *m* (de travaux en béton); (*c*) cadre *m.*

franchise ['fræntʃaiz], *s. Pol:* droit *m* de vote.

frank [fræŋk], *a.* franc, sincère. -ly, *adv.* franchement, ouvertement. **′frank-ness,** *s.* franchise *f*, sincérité *f.*

frantic ['fræntik], *a.* frénétique, forcené; fou (de joie, de douleur). **-ally,** *adv.* frénétiquement.

fraternal [frə'tə:n(ə)l], *a.* fraternel. **-ally,** *adv.* fraternellement. **'fraternize,** *v.i.* fraterniser (with, avec).

fraud [frɔːd], *s.* 1. (*a*) fraude *f*; (*b*) supercherie *f*. 2. imposteur *m*. **'fraudulent,** *a.* frauduleux. **-ly,** *adv.* frauduleusement, en fraude.

fray[1] [frei], *s.* bagarre *f*, échauffourée *f*.

fray[2], *v.i.* (*of material*) s'érailler, s'effiler.

freak [friːk], *s.* 1. caprice *f*, fantaisie *f*, lubie *f*. 2. f. (*of nature*), phénomène *m*, curiosité *f*.

freckle ['frekl], *s.* tache *f* de rousseur, de son. **'freckled,** *a.* couvert de taches de rousseur.

free [friː]. I. *a. & adv.* 1. libre; en liberté; **f.** will, libre arbitre; **f. house,** débit *m* de boissons non lié à un fournisseur particulier. 2. (*un-occupied*) is this table free? est-ce que cette table est libre? *P.T.T.:* **f. line,** ligne dégagée. 3. to give s.o. a f. hand, donner carte blanche à qn; **he is not f. to act,** il a les mains liées. 4. exempt (de droits de douane); **you may bring in a bottle f.,** il y a tolérance d'une bouteille; **f. trade,** libre-échange *m*. 5. (*a*) **f. offer,** offre spontanée; **as a f. gift,** en pur don; **to be f. with one's money,** ne pas regarder à l'argent; (*b*) franc, ouvert; **f. and easy,** sans façons; désinvolte. 6. gratuit; franco; **admission f.,** entrée gratuite; **post f.,** franco de port. **-ly,** *adv.* 1. librement, volontairement. 2. (*par-ler*) franchement. II. *v.tr.* (*a*) affranchir, libérer; (*b*) débarrasser (from, of, de); dégager (un sentier). **'free-dom,** *s.* 1. liberté *f*, indépendance *f*; **f. of speech,** le franc-parler. 2. **f.** exemption *f*, immunité *f* (from, de); **f. of the city,** droit *m* de cité. **'free-hand,** *a. & adv.* à main levée. **'free-hold.** 1. *a.* tenu en propriété perpétuelle et libre. 2. *s.* propriété foncière libre. **'freelance,** *a. & s.* **f.** (*journalist*), journaliste indépendant. **'freemason,** *s.* franc-maçon *m.* **'free-masonry,** *s.* franc-maçonnerie *f.* **'free-style,** *s.* nage *f* libre.

‡freeze [friːz], *v. geler.* 1. *v.i.* (*a*) impers. **it's freezing,** il gèle; (*b*) (se) geler, se congeler, prendre; (*of pers.*) **to f.** mourir de froid. 2. *v.tr.* geler, congeler (qch.); glacer (le sang de qn); **to f. wages,** bloquer les salaires.

freight [freit], *s.* 1. (*a*) fret *m* (d'un navire); (*b*) transport *m* (de mar-chandises); **f. plane,** avion *m* de transport. 2. fret, cargaison *f.*

French [fren(t)ʃ]. I. *a. & (s*) français; **F. Canadian,** canadien (français); (*b*) **F. lesson,** leçon *f* de français; (*c*) (*of fashion, etc.*) à la française; *Cu:* **F.** dressing, vinaigrette *f*; **F. window,** porte-fenêtre *f.* II. *s.* 1. le français; **to speak F.,** parler français. 2. *pl.* **the F.,** les Français. **†'Frenchman,** *s.* Français *m.* **'French-speaking,** *a.* francophone; **F.-s.** Switzerland, la Suisse romande. **†'Frenchwoman,** *s.* Française *f.*

frequent. I. *a.* ['friːkwənt] 1. répandu. 2. fréquent; qui arrive souvent. 3. (*client, etc.*) habituel. II. *v.tr.* [fri'kwent] fréquenter (un endroit).

fresh [freʃ]. I. *a.* 1. (*a*) nouveau; **to put f.** courage into s.o., ranimer le courage de qn; (*b*) frais; récent. 2. (*a*) (beurre) frais, (légume) vert; (*b*) (air) frais, pur; (*c*) **f.** water, (i) (*newly drawn*) eau fraîche; (ii) (*not salt*) eau douce; **in the f. air,** en plein air. 3. (*a*) (teint) frais; (*b*) *F:* effronté. **-ly,** *adv.* (*a*) fraîchement; (*b*) nouvelle-ment; (*c*) vivement. II. *adv.* fraîche-ment, nouvellement; **f. shaven,** rasé de frais. **'freshen.** 1. *v.i.* (*of tem-perature*) (se) rafraîchir; (*of wind*) fraîchir. 2. *v.tr.* rafraîchir (la mé-moire, etc.). **'freshman,** *s. Sch:* étudiant, -ante, de première année. **'freshness,** *s.* 1. nouveauté *f* (d'un événement). 2. fraîcheur *f.* 3. (*of pers.*) (*a*) vigueur *f*; (*b*) *F:* effronterie *f*, *F:* toupet *m.*

‡fret [fret]. 1. *v.tr.* inquiéter, tracasser (qn). 2. *v.pr. & i.* se tourmenter. **'fretful,** *a.* irritable. **-fully,** *adv.* d'un ton, d'un air chagrin, inquiet.

friar ['fraiər], *s.* frère *m*, religieux *m.*

friction ['frik∫(ə)n], *s.* 1. *Med: etc:* friction *f.* 2. frottement *m.* 3. dé-saccord *m.*

Friday ['fraidi], *s.* vendredi *m*; **Good F.,** (le) vendredi saint.

fridge [fridʒ], *s. F:* réfrigérateur *m*, *F:* frigo *m.*

friend [frend], *s.* 1. ami *m*, amie *f*; **a f. of mine,** un(e) de mes ami(e)s; **to make friends with s.o.,** se lier (d'amitié) avec qn; **the Society of Friends,** les Quakers. **'friendless,** *a.* délaissé; sans amis. **'friendliness,** *s.* bienveillance *f*, bonté *f*, (to, towards, envers). **'friendly,** *a.* 1. (*sentiment*) amical; sym-pathique; **to be on f. terms with s.o.,** être en bons rapports avec qn. 2. (*of pers.*) bienveillant. 3. **f.** society, mutuelle *f.* **'friendship,** *s.* amitié *f.*

frieze [friːz], *s.* 1. frise *f.* 2. bordure *f.*

fright [frait], *s.* 1. peur *f*, effroi *m*; **to take f.,** s'effrayer (at, de). 2. *F:* (*of pers.*) épouvantail *m.* **'frighten,** *v.tr.* effrayer (qn); faire peur à (qn); **to f.** (away) thieves, the birds, faire dé-camper les voleurs; effaroucher les oiseaux. **'frightened,** *a.* (*of pers.*) apeuré; **easily f.,** peureux; **to be f.,** avoir peur. **'frightening,** *a.* effrayant.

'frightful, a. terrible, affreux, épouvantable. -fully, adv. terriblement, affreusement; F: I'm f. sorry, je regrette énormément. 'frightfulness, s. horreur f, atrocité f (d'un crime, etc.).

frigid ['fridʒid], a. glacial; froid; f. politeness, politesse glaciale.

frill [fril], s. Cl: volant m, ruche f.

fringe [frindʒ], s. 1. frange f. 2. (a) bordure; T.V: f. area, zone f limitrophe; F: f. benefits, la gratte f; (b) cheveux mpl à la chien.

frisk [frisk]. 1. v.i. s'ébattre; gambader. 2. v.tr. (a) (of dog) frétiller (de la queue); (b) U.S: fouiller (un suspect). 'frisky, a. vif, folâtre; fringant.

fritter¹ ['fritər], s. Cu: beignet m.

fritter², v.tr. to f. away, gaspiller (son argent, son temps).

†frivolity [fri'vɔliti], s. frivolité f. 'frivolous, a. frivole; (of claim, etc.) futile; (of pers.) évaporé. -ly, adv. frivolement.

frizzy ['frizi], a. (of hair) crépu.

frock [frɔk], s. robe f.

frog [frɔg], s. grenouille f. †frogman, s. homme-grenouille m; f.'s mask, masque m sous-marin.

frolic ['frɔlik]. 1. s. (a) ébats mpl, gambades fpl; (b) fredaine f. II. v.i. se divertir, folâtrer.

from [frɔm], prep. 1. de. to go f. home, partir de chez soi; f. . . . to . . ., de . . ., à . . .; depuis . . . jusqu'à . . .; wines f. two francs a bottle, vins à partir de deux francs la bouteille. 2. depuis, dès; f. his childhood, dès son enfance. 3. (a) de, à; to take sth. f. s.o., enlever qch. à qn; to dissuade s.o. f. doing sth., dissuader qn de faire qch.; (b) to shelter f. the rain, s'abriter contre la pluie. 4. (a) I had to worse, de mal en pis; (b) d'avec, de; to distinguish the good f. the bad, distinguer le bon d'avec le mauvais; (c) to drink f. the bottle, boire à même la bouteille 5. where are you f.? d'où êtes-vous? 6. (with adv., prep.) f. afar, de loin; I know him f. of old, je le connais de longue date.

front [frʌnt]. I. s. 1. front m; to put a bold f. on it, faire bonne contenance. 2. devant m; façade f (d'un bâtiment); plastron m (de chemise). 3. to come to the f., arriver au premier rang; Pol: popular f., front populaire. 4. adv.phr. in f., devant, en avant; in f. of, (i) en face de; (ii) devant. II. a. antérieur, de devant, d'avant, de face; f. door, porte f d'entrée; f. seat, (i) siège du premier rang; (ii) Aut: siège avant; Rail: f. carriage, voiture f de tête. 'frontage, s. 1. terrain m en bordure (d'une route, etc.). 2. (longueur f de) façade f; devanture f (d'un magasin).

frontier ['frʌntiər], s. frontière f.

frost [frɔst], s. gelée f, gel m; white f., gelée blanche; glazed f. (on road), verglas m; ten degrees of f., dix degrés de froid. 'frost-bite, s: Med: gelure f. 'frost-bitten, a. gelé; brûlé par le froid. 'frosted, a. 1. gelé. 2. (of glass) dépoli. 'frosty, a. 1. f. day, jour m de gelée; f. reception, accueil glacial. 2. couvert de givre.

froth [frɔθ]. I. s. écume f; mousse f (du savon, de la bière). II. v.i. écumer; mousser. 'frothy, a. écumeux, écumant; mousseux.

frown [fraun]. I. s. froncement m de sourcils; regard sévère. II. v.i. froncer les sourcils; to frown upon s.o., a suggestion, (i) regarder qn de travers; (ii) désapprouver une suggestion.

frozen ['frouz(ə)n], a. gelé, glacé; Com: f. meat, viande frigorifiée; f. foods, aliments congelés.

frugal ['frug(ə)l], a. 1. frugal; économe. 2. (repas) simple. -ally, adv. frugalement; sobrement; (manger) simplement.

fruit [frut], s. fruit m; f. tree, arbre m fruitier. 'fruiterer, s. (pers.) fruitier, -ière. fru'ition, s. réalisation f (d'un projet); to come to f., fructifier. 'fruitless, a. (of plant, work) stérile, infructueux; f. efforts, vains efforts. -ly, adv. vainement. 'fruity, a. 1. (a) (goût, etc.) de fruit; (b) (of oil, wine) fruité. 2. F: (scandale, etc.) corsé.

frump [frʌmp], s. F: vieille caricature f. 'frumpish, a. (of woman) (mal) fagotée.

frustrate [frʌs'treit], v.tr. (a) faire échouer (un projet); frustrer (l'espoir de qn); (b) contrecarrer (qn).

fry [frai]. 1. v.tr. (faire) frire (la viande, etc.); fried eggs, œufs sur le plat. 2. v.i. (of food) frire. 'frying-pan, s. poêle à frire; sauteuse f.

fuddle ['fʌdl], v.tr. F: (a) soûler, griser (qn); (b) brouiller les idées de (qn). 'fuddled, a. 1. F: soûl; gris; to get f., s'enivrer. 2. brouillé (dans ses idées).

fuel ['fjuəl], s. combustible m; Aut: carburant m.

fug [fʌg], s. F: atmosphère f étouffante et chaude.

fugitive ['fjuːdʒitiv], a. & s. fugitif, -ive.

‡fulfil [ful'fil], v.tr. (a) répondre à, remplir (l'attente de qn); (b) satisfaire (un désir); (c) accomplir (une tâche). ful'filment, s. 1. accomplissement m (d'un devoir); (b) satisfaction f (d'un désir); (c) exécution f (d'un projet).

full [ful]. I. a. 1. plein, rempli, comble; f. of holes, tout troué. 2. (of bus, etc.) plein, complet; to be f. up, avoir son plein; f. up! complet! 3. (of facts, etc.) ample, abondant, copieux; f. particulars, tous les détails. 4. complet, entier; f. meal, repas complet; to pay f. fare, payer place entière; f. stop, point m (final); f. weight, poids juste: in f. flower, en pleine fleur. 5. (of face) plein; (of figure) rond. **fully,** adv. pleinement, entièrement, (of stockings) f. fashioned, entièrement diminué; I'll write more f., j'écrirai plus longuement. II. s. 1. plein m (de la lune, etc.). 2. adv. phr. (a) in f., (nom, date) en toutes lettres; (to pay the f., complètement. III. adv. précisément, en plein; f. in the middle, au beau milieu; to work f. out, travailler à plein rendement. **full-back,** s. Sp: arrière m. **'fullness,** s. 1. plénitude f., totalité f (de qch.). 2. ampleur f (d'un vêtement); abondance f (de détails).

fumble ['fʌmbl], v.i. fouiller; tâtonner. **'fumbling,** a. maladroit, gauche.

fume [fju:m], s. 1. fumée f, vapeur f; factory fumes, fumée d'usine. II. v.i. F: (of pers.) rager.

fun [fʌn], s. amusement m, gaieté f., plaisanterie f; to make f. of s.o., se moquer de qn; for f., in f., pour rire. 'fun fair, s. (a) fête f foraine; (b) parc m d'attractions.

function ['fʌŋk)f(ə)n]. I. s. 1. fonction f, charge f; in his f. as a magistrate, en sa qualité de magistrat. 2. (a) soirée f; society f., réunion f mondaine; (b) cérémonie f publique. II. v.i. fonctionner, marcher; F: this gadget won't f., ce truc ne marche pas.

fund [fʌnd], s. 1. fonds m, caisse f; to start a f., lancer une souscription. 2. pl. to be in funds, être en fonds.

fundamental [fʌndə'ment(ə)l], a. fondamental; essentiel; f. question, question de fond; f. qualities of s.o., qualités foncières de qn. **-ally,** adv. fondamentalement; foncièrement.

funeral ['fju:n)ərəl], s. (a) enterrement m; funérailles fpl; obsèques fpl; F: that's your f.! ça c'est votre affaire! (b) attrib: f. procession, convoi m funèbre.

†**fungus** ['fʌŋgəs], s. Bot: champignon m; edible f., champignon comestible.

funicular [fju:'nikjulər], a. & s. funiculaire (m).

funk [fʌŋk]. I. s. F: 1. frousse f, trac m, trouille f. 2. froussard, -arde. II. v.tr. & i. F: to f. (it), caner, se dégonfler; to f. doing sth., avoir peur de faire qch.

funnel ['fʌnl], s. 1. entonnoir m; loading f., trémie f. 2. cheminée f (de locomotive ou de navire à vapeur).

funny ['fʌni], a. drôle. 1. comique, amusant, facétieux. 2. curieux, bizarre; a f. idea, une drôle d'idée. **-ily,** adv. drôlement 1. comiquement. 2. curieusement; f. enough . . ., chose curieuse . . . **'funny-bone,** s. F: le petit juif (à l'articulation du coude).

fur [fə:r], s. 1. (a) fourrure f, pelleterie f; f. coat, manteau m de fourrure; (b) poil m, pelage m (d'un animal); (c) pl. peaux fpl. 2. (in kettle, etc.) dépôt m.

furious ['fjuəriəs], a. furieux; (of look) furibond; (of rage) acharné; (of wind) violent. **-ly,** adv. furieusement; avec furie; (conduire) à une allure folle.

furl [fə:l], v.tr. serrer, ferler (une voile).

furnace ['fə:nis], s. 1. fourneau m, four m; (hot place) fournaise f. 2. (a) oil-fired f., brûleur m à mazout; (b) E: foyer m (de chaudière).

furnish ['fə:niʃ], v.tr. 1. fournir, pourvoir, munir (qn de qch.). 2. meubler, garnir (une maison, etc.); furnished flat, appartement meublé. **'furnishings,** s.pl. ameublement m (d'une maison). **'furniture,** s. meubles mpl, ameublement m, mobilier m; antique f., meubles d'époque.

furrow ['fʌrou], s. 1. Agr: sillon m. 2. cannelure f, rainure f. 3. (on face) ride f profonde. II. v.tr. 1. labourer (la terre), sillonner (les mers). 2. canneler (une planche), etc.).

further ['fə:ðər]. I. adv. 1. plus loin; f. off, plus éloigné. 2. (a) davantage, plus; without troubling f., sans plus se tracasser; (b) to go f. into sth., entrer plus avant dans qch.; (c) de plus, du reste. II. a. 1. plus lointain, plus éloigné. 2. nouveau, additionnel, supplémentaire; without f. ado, sans plus; upon f. consideration, (toute) réflexion faite; Com: f. orders, commandes ultérieures. III. v.tr. avancer, favoriser (les intérêts de qn, etc.). **'further'more,** adv. en outre, de plus.

furtive ['fə:tiv], a. furtif; sournois. **-ly,** adv. furtivement.

fury ['fjuəri], s. furie f, fureur f; to get into a f., s'emporter; (travailler avec) acharnement m.

furze [fə:z], s. ajonc m.

fuse [fju:z]. I. s. fusible m; plomb m; f. box, boîte f à fusibles; f. wire, (fil m) fusible m. II. v. 1. v.tr. (a) fondre (un métal, etc.). (b) fusionner, amalgamer (deux partis, etc.). 2. v.i. (of metals) (a) fondre; the light has fused, les plombs ont sauté; (b) s'amalgamer. **'fusion,** s. 1. fonte f (d'un métal, etc.); Atom. Ph: fusion f. 2. fusionnement m (de deux partis); Pol: fusion f (de deux partis).

fuselage ['fju:zələ:dʒ], s. Av: fuselage m.

fusillade [fju:zi'leid], s. Mil: fusillade f.

fuss [fʌs]. I. s. 1. bruit m exagéré; to make a f. about nothing, faire beaucoup de bruit pour rien. 2. embarras *mpl*; façons *fpl*; to make a f. of s.o., être aux petits soins pour qn. II. *v.* 1. *v.i.* tatillonner; faire des histoires; se tracasser; to f. round, faire l'affairé; s'affairer. 2. *v.tr.* tracasser, agiter (qn). 'fussiness, *s.* affairement *m.* 'fussy, *a.* (*of pers.*) tatillon; méticuleux. -ily, *adv.* (a) d'une manière tatillonne; (b) d'un air important.

fusty ['fʌsti], *a.* f. smell, odeur de renfermé.

futile ['fjuːtail], *a.* 1. futile, vain. 2. puéril. fu'tility, *s.* 1. futilité *f.* 2. puérilité *f.*

future ['fjuːtʃər]. 1. *a.* (*of life, etc.*) futur; (*of events*) à venir; (*of prospects*) d'avenir. 2. *s.* avenir *m*; in (the) f., à l'avenir; the near f., le proche avenir; *Gram*: (temps) futur *m.* futu'ristic, *a.* futuriste.

fuzzy ['fʌzi], *a.* (*of hair*) (i) bouffant, flou; (ii) crêpu, frisotté.

G

G, g [dʒiː], *s.* 1. (la lettre) G, g *m.* 2. *Mus:* sol *m.*

gab [gæb], *s.* to have the gift of the g., avoir la langue bien pendue.

gabble ['gæbl], *v.i.* (a) bredouiller; **don't g.!** ne parlez pas si vite! (b) caqueter, jacasser.

gable ['geibl], *s.* pignon *m.*

gadget ['gædʒit], *s.* F: dispositif *m*; chose *m*, machin *m*, truc *m.*

Gaelic ['geilik], *a. & s.* gaélique (*m*).

gaff [gæf], *s.* P: to blow the g., vendre la mèche.

gag [gæg]. I. *s.* bâillon *m.* II. ‡*v.tr.* bâillonner; *Th: F: abs.* enchaîner.

gaga ['gɑːgɑː], *a. F:* gâteux.

gaiety ['geiəti], *s.* gaieté *f.*

gaily ['geili], *adv.* gaiement, allégrement.

gain [gein]. I. *v.tr.* gagner; acquérir (une réputation); prendre (du poids); *abs.* (*of clock*) avancer. II. *s.* 1. gain *m*, profit *m.* 2. augmentation *f.*

gala ['gɑːlə], *s.* fête *f*, gala *m.*

galantine [gælən'tiːn], *s. Cu:* galantine *f.*

gale [geil], *s.* 1. coup *m* de vent; vent fort. 2. tempête *f.*

gall [gɔːl]. I. *s.* fiel *m*; g. bladder, vésicule *f* biliaire. II. *v.tr.* irriter, exaspérer; 'galling, *a.* irritant, exaspérant; (*of remark*) blessant.

gallant ['gælənt], *a.* 1. vaillant. 2. galant. -ly, *adv.* galamment. 'gallantry, *s.* 1. vaillance *f.* 2. galanterie *f.*

†gallery ['gæləri], *s.* 1. (a) galerie *f*; (b) *Th:* (troisième) galerie *f*; to play to the g., jouer pour la galerie. 2. art g., musée *m* (de peinture).

galley ['gæli], *s.* 1. *Nau:* (a) *Hist:* galère *f*; (b) yole *f* (d'amiral). 2. *Nau:* cuisine *f.* 3. (*of book*) g. (proof), épreuve *f* en placard.

gallop ['gæləp]. I. *v.i. & tr.* galoper. II. *s.* galop *m.*

gallows ['gæləuz], *s.* potence *f*, gibet *m.*

galore [gə'lɔːr], *adv.* F: en abondance, F: à gogo.

galvanize ['gælvənaiz], *v.tr.* galvaniser.

gamble ['gæmbl]. I. *s.* (a) jeu *m* de hasard; (b) spéculation *f*; affaire *f* de chance. II. *v.i.* jouer (de l'argent); to g. on the Stock Exchange, agioter; to g. on a rise in prices, jouer à la

hausse. 'gambling, *s.* le jeu. 'gambler, *s.* joueur, -euse; spéculateur, -trice.

game [geim]. I. *s.* 1. (a) amusement *m*, divertissement *m*; (b) jeu; (c) to play the g., jouer franc jeu; (d) partie *f*; match *m*; the deciding g., la belle. 2. gibier *m*; big g., (i) gros gibier; (ii) les grands fauves. II. *a.* g. arm, bras estropié; g. leg, jambe boiteuse. 'gamekeeper, *s.* garde-chasse *m.*

gamma ['gæmə], *s. Ph:* g. rays, rayons *m* gamma.

gammon ['gæmən], *s. Cu:* quartier *m* de lard fumé.

gamut ['gæmət], *s.* gamme *f.*

gander ['gændər], *s.* jars *m.*

gang [gæŋ]. I. *s.* (a) équipe *f* (d'ouvriers); (b) bande *f*, gang *m* (de voleurs, etc.); the whole g., toute la bande. II. *v.i. F:* to g. up with s.o., faire bande avec qn; to g. up on s.o., attaquer qn; to liguer contre qn. 'ganger, *s. Rail:* chef *m* d'équipe; *Civ. E:* chef cantonnier. 'gangster, *s.* bandit *m*; gangster *m.* 'gangway, *s.* 1. passage *m*; g. please! dégagez s'il vous plaît! 2. *Nau:* passerelle *f* de service.

gangrene ['gæŋgriːn], *s. Med:* gangrène *f.*

gaol [dʒeil], *s.* prison *f.*

gap [gæp], *s.* (a) trou *m*; trouée *f*; (b) interstice *m*; intervalle *m*; (c) trou, lacune *f*, vide *m.*

gape [geip], *v.i.* 1. (a) bâiller; (b) (*of thing*) s'ouvrir (tout grand). 2. rester bouche bée.

garage ['gærɑːʒ]. I. *s.* garage *m*; g. proprietor, garagiste *m.* II. *v.tr.* garer; remiser (une auto).

garbage ['gɑːbidʒ], *s. esp. U.S:* ordures *fpl* (ménagères); g. can, poubelle *f.*

garble ['gɑːbl], *v.tr.* tronquer; dénaturer.

garden ['gɑːdn]. I. *s.* (a) jardin *m*; kitchen g., potager *m*; g. of remembrance = cimetière *m* dans un crématorium; *F:* to lead s.o. up the g. path, duper qn; (b) *pl.* jardin public, parc; (c) *attrib.* g. party, réception *f* en plein air; g. produce, produits *m* maraîchers. II. *v.i.* jardiner. 'gardener, *s.* jardinier, -ière; landscape g., jardiniste *m.* 'gardening, *s.* jardinage *m*; horticulture *f.*

gargle ['gɑ:gl], v.i. se gargariser.

gargoyle ['gɑ:gɔil], s. gargouille f.

garland ['gɑ:lənd], s. guirlande f; couronne f (de fleurs).

garlic ['gɑ:lik], s. ail m.

garment ['gɑ:mənt], s. vêtement m.

garnish ['gɑ:niʃ], v.tr. garnir (un plat). **'garnishing,** s. garniture f.

garret ['gærət], s. mansarde f, soupente f.

garrison ['gærisn], s. garnison f.

garrulous ['gærələs], a. loquace, bavard.

garter ['gɑ:tər], s. jarretière f.

gas [gæs], s. **1.** gaz m; F: (at dentist's) to have g., se faire anesthésier; g. cooker, cuisinière f à gaz; g. fire, radiateur m à gaz; g. lighter, briquet m (à gaz); g. meter, compteur m à gaz. **2.** U.S: F: Aut: essence f. **gas'ometer,** s. gazomètre m. **'gasworks,** s. usine f à gaz.

gash [gæʃ], s. coupure f, entaille f.

gasket ['gæskit], s. E: joint m; Aut: obturateur m de joint.

gasoline ['gæsəlin], s. U.S: essence f.

gasp [gɑ:sp]. **I.** s. hoquet m, sursaut m (de surprise); to be at one's last g., agoniser. **II.** v.i. (a) avoir un hoquet (de surprise); (b) to g. for breath, haleter, suffoquer.

gastric ['gæstrik], a. gastrique; g. flu, grippe f intestinale; g. ulcer, ulcère m d'estomac. **gas'tritis,** s. gastrite f.

gate [geit], s. porte f; (wooden) barrière f. **'gatecrasher,** s. resquilleur, -euse. **'gateway,** s. porte f, entrée f.

gather ['gæðər]. **1.** v.tr. (a) assembler (une foule); rassembler (ses forces); cueillir (des fruits); (b) to g. speed, prendre de la vitesse; (c) conclure; I g. that . . ., je crois comprendre que. **2.** v.i. (a) se réunir; s'assembler; (b) (of clouds) s'amonceler; (of storm) se préparer; (c) abcéder. **'gathering,** s. (a) assemblée f; family g., réunion f de famille; (b) Med: abcès m; (c) fronces fpl (d'une robe).

gaudy ['gɔ:di], a. voyant, criard.

gauge [geidʒ]. **I.** s. jauge f; calibre m (d'un écrou); Rail: écartement m (de la voie); fine g. stockings, bas de fine jauge; Aut: petrol g., jauge d'essence; oil g., (indicateur m de) niveau m d'huile. **II.** v.tr. jauger, mesurer.

gaunt [gɔ:nt], a. maigre, décharné.

gauze [gɔ:z], s. gaze f.

gawky ['gɔ:ki], a. dégingandé, gauche.

gaze [geiz]. **I.** s. regard m fixe. **II.** v.i. regarder fixement.

gazelle [gə'zel], s. gazelle f.

gazeteer [gæzə'tiər], s. répertoire m géographique.

gear [giər], s. **1.** effets mpl. **2.** E: mécanisme m; transmission f; Aut: vitesse f; in g., en prise; in bottom, top, g., en première (vitesse), en prise (directe); g. box, boîte f de vitesses.

Geiger counter ['gaigəkauntər], s. Atom. Ph: compteur m de Geiger.

gelatine ['dʒelətin], s. gélatine f.

gem [dʒem], s. pierre f précieuse.

gender ['dʒendər], s. genre m.

gene [dʒi:n], s. Biol: gène m.

†genealogy [dʒi:ni'ælədʒi], s. généalogie f. **genea'logical,** a. généalogique.

general ['dʒenər(ə)l]. **I.** a. général; the g. public, le grand public; in g., en général. **-ally,** adv. généralement. **II.** s. général m (d'armée). **gene'rality,** s. généralité f. **generali'zation,** s. généralisation f. **'generalize,** v.tr. généraliser.

generate ['dʒenəreit], v.tr. générer, produire (de la chaleur, etc.). **gene'ration,** s. génération f. **'generator,** s. El.E: etc. générateur m.

generous ['dʒenərəs], a. généreux. **-ly,** adv. généreusement. **gene'rosity,** s. no pl. générosité f.

genial ['dʒi:njəl], a. plein de bonne humeur.

genius ['dʒi:niəs], s. génie m.

gentle ['dʒentl], a. doux. **-tly,** adv. doucement.

†gentleman ['dʒentlmən], s. (a) homme bien élevé, comme il faut; (b) monsieur m; (to audience) ladies and gentlemen! mesdames, mesdemoiselles, messieurs! P.N: (W.C. public) gentlemen, hommes, messieurs; gentlemen's hairdresser, coiffeur pour hommes.

genuine ['dʒenjuin], a. (a) authentique, véritable; (b) sincère. **-ly,** adv. (a) authentiquement; (b) franchement.

†geography [dʒi'ɔgrəfi], s. géographie f. **geo'graphical,** a. géographique. **ge'ographer,** s. géographe mf.

geology [dʒi'ɔlədʒi], s. géologie f. **geo'logical,** a. géologique. **ge'ologist,** s. géologue m.

†geometry [dʒi'ɔmitri], s. géométrie f. **geo'metrical,** a. géométrique.

geranium [dʒə'reinjəm], s. géranium m.

germ [dʒə:m], s. germe m; microbe m.

German ['dʒə:mən], a. & s. **1.** allemand, -ande. **2.** s. l'allemand m.

germinate ['dʒə:mineit], v.i. germer. **germi'nation,** s. germination f.

gesticulate [dʒes'tikjuleit], v.i. gesticuler. **gesticu'lation,** s. gesticulation f.

gesture ['dʒestʃər], s. geste m, signe m.

‡get [get], v. **1.** v.tr. (a) procurer, obtenir; to g. one's own way, faire valoir sa volonté; I'll see what I can g. for it, je verrai ce qu'on m'en donnera; (b) recevoir (un cadeau); attraper (une maladie); F: to g. ten years, attraper dix ans de prison; (c) F: I don't g. you, je ne comprends pas; you've got it! vous y êtes! what's got him? qu'est-ce qu'il a? (d) aller chercher (un médecin, son manteau); (e) to g. lunch (ready), préparer le déjeuner; F: that gets me down, cela me donne le cafard; (f) to g. sth. done, faire faire qch.; to g. the house painted, faire repeindre la maison; to g. one's work finished, finir son travail; (g) have got, (i) (= have) I haven't g. any, je n'en ai pas; he's g. measles, il a la rougeole; (ii) (= must) you've g. to do it, il faut absolument que vous le fassiez. 2. v.i. (a) deviner (riche, etc.); to g. angry, se mettre en colère; to g. killed, se faire tuer; to g. dressed, s'habiller; (b) aller, arriver; he'll g. here tomorrow, il arrivera demain; F: we're not getting anywhere, nous n'aboutissons à rien; to g. to know sth., apprendre qch.; when one gets to know him, quand on le connaît mieux. get a'cross, v.tr. F: he couldn't g. it across, il n'a pas réussi à se faire comprendre. get at, v.i. atteindre; to g. at the root of the trouble, trouver la racine du mal; difficult to g. at, peu accessible; F: what are you getting at? (i) où voulez-vous en venir? (ii) qu'est-ce que vous voulez insinuer? F: who are you getting at? à qui en avez-vous? get-'at-able, a. F: d'accès facile. get a'way, v.i. (a) partir; (b) s'échapper; (c) Aut: démarrer; (d) to g.a. with £1000, (of burglars) rafler £1000; to g.a. with sth., faire accepter la chose. 'get-away, s. (a) fuite f; (b) départ m; (c) démarrage m. get 'back, v.tr. retrouver (qch.); reprendre (ses forces); to g. one's money back, être remboursé; F: to g. one's own back, prendre sa revanche. get 'by, v.i. F: se débrouiller. get 'down. 1. v.i. descendre; to g. down to the facts, en venir aux faits. 2. v.tr. descendre (un livre, etc.). get 'in. 1. v.i. entrer, monter (en voiture, etc.); Pol: être élu; if the train gets in on time, si le train arrive à l'heure. 2. v.tr. to get in a man to repair sth., faire venir un ouvrier pour réparer qch.; to g. one's hand in, se faire la main. get 'into, v.i. monter dans (une voiture); to g.i. bad company, faire de mauvaises connaissances. get 'off. 1. v.i. (a) descendre (de l'autobus); P: I told him where he got off, je lui ai dit ses vérités; (b) to g.o. with a fine, en être quitte pour une amende; (c) F: (of girl) décrocher un mari; (d) partir. 2. v.tr. (a) expédier (un colis); to g. sth. off one's hands, se débarrasser de qch.; (b) faire acquitter (un prévenu). get 'on, v.i. faire des progrès; réussir (dans la vie); to be getting on for forty, friser la quarantaine; time is getting on, l'heure s'avance. get 'out. 1. v.tr.

prendre (qch. dans un tiroir); sortir (la voiture); emprunter (un livre à la bibliothèque). 2. v.i. to g.o. of s.o.'s way, céder le pas à qn; g.o. (of here)! fiche-moi le camp! to g.o. of a difficulty, venir à bout d'une difficulté. 'get-out, s. F: échappatoire f. get 'over, v.i. guérir (d'une maladie); he can't g. it, il n'en revient pas. get 'through, v.i.r. être reçu à (un examen); venir à bout de (un travail). get to'gether, v.i. se réunir, se rassembler. 'get-together, s. F: réunion f; rassemblement m. get 'up. 1. v.i. se lever. 2. v.tr. organiser (une fête); to g. up speed, donner de la vitesse. 'get-up, s. F: habillement m, toilette f.

geyser ['giːzər], s. 1. geyser m. 2. chauffe-bain m.

ghastly ['gɑːstli], a. (a) horrible, affreux; (b) blême.

gherkin ['gəːkin], s. Cu: cornichon m.

ghost [goust], s. fantôme m, revenant m; F: to g. story, histoire f de revenants. 'ghostly, a. spectral.

giant ['dʒaiənt], a. & s. géant (m). 'gian'tess, s. géante f. gi'gantic, a. géant, gigantesque.

gibe [dʒaib], s. raillerie f; sarcasme m.

giblets ['dʒiblits], s.pl. abattis m (de volaille).

giddy ['gidi], a. (a) étourdi; I feel g., la tête me tourne; (b) vertigineux. 'giddiness, s. étourdissement m; vertige m.

gift [gift], s. don m; cadeau m. 'gifted, a. (bien) doué.

giggle ['gigl], v.i. rire bêtement.

gild [gild], v.tr. dorer. 'gilding, s. dorure f. 'gilt. a. & s. doré (m); g.-edged, (i) (of book) doré sur tranche; (ii) Fin: (valeurs) de tout repos.

gills [gilz], s.pl. ouïes f, branchies f (de poisson); lames f, lamelles f (d'un champignon).

gimlet ['gimlit], s. vrille f; foret m.

gin [dʒin], s. gin m.

ginger ['dʒin(d)ʒər]. 1. s. gingembre m. 2. a. F: (of hair) roux. 'gingerbread, s. pain m d'épice.

†**gipsy** ['dʒipsi], s. bohémien, -ienne; nomade mf.

giraffe [dʒiˈrɑːf, -ˈræf], s. girafe f.

girder ['gəːdər], s. (a) solive f; (b) poutre f.

girdle [gəːdl], s. ceinture f; gaine f.

girl [gəːl], s. jeune fille f; little g., fillette f; girls' school, école f, lycée m, de filles; old g., (i) ancienne élève (d'un lycée, etc.); (ii) F: vieille fille; a French g., une jeune Française; chorus g., girl f. 'girlish, a. de petite fille, de jeune fille; (of boy) mou, efféminé.

gist [dʒist], s. fond m, essence f.

‡**give** [giv]. I. *v.* 1. *v.tr.* (*a*) donner (qch. à qn); to give s.o. sth. to eat, donner à manger à qn; how much did you g. for it? combien l'avez-vous payé? (*b*) to g. a toast, porter un toast; (*c*) to g. pleasure, faire, causer, du plaisir; (*d*) to g. way, céder; to g. way to s.o., céder la place, le pas, à qn; *P.N.*: g. way = priorité à droite; (*e*) *F*: to g. as good as one gets, rendre coup pour coup; *P*: to g. s.o. what for, arranger qn de la belle façon. 2. *v.i.* (*of elastic, etc.*) to g. way, céder. II. *s. F*: élasticité *f.* give a'way, *v.tr.* (*a*) donner; I'd rather g. it away, je préférerais en faire cadeau; (*b*) to g. a. the bride, conduire la mariée à l'autel; (*c*) to g. s.o. away, trahir, dénoncer, qn. 'give-away, *s. F*: révélation *f* involontaire. give 'back, *v.tr.* rendre, restituer (qch. à qn). give 'in, *v.i.* céder; se soumettre. 'given, *a.* 1. at a g. time, place, à une heure convenue; à un point donné; *U.S:* g. name, prénom *m.* 2. porté, enclin à; g. to drink, adonné à la boisson. give 'out. 1. *v.tr.* to g.o. a notice, lire une communication. 2. *v.i.* manquer; faire défaut; my brakes gave out, mes freins ont lâché. 'giver, *s.* donneur, -euse; donateur, -trice. give 'up, *v.tr* (*a*) abandonner (ses biens); to g. up one's seat, céder sa place (à qn); (*b*) renoncer à (un projet); to g. up. as a bad job, y renoncer; (*c*) to g. s.o. up for lost, considérer qn comme perdu; (*d*) to g. oneself up, se constituer prisonnier.

glacier [ˈglæsiər], *s.* glacier *m.* 'glacial, *a.* 1. *Geog:* glaciaire. 2. (vent, etc.) glacial.

glad [glæd], *a.* heureux; content. -ly, *adv.* avec plaisir; volontiers.

glamour [ˈglæmər], *s.* 1. enchantement *m,* charme *m.* 2. fascination *f;* éclat *m.* 'glamorize, *v.tr.* donner un prestige, une beauté, factice à (qch.). 'glamorous, *a.* enchanteur, charmeur.

glance [glɑːns]. I. *s.* regard *m;* coup d'œil; at a g., d'un coup d'œil. II. *v.i.* 1. jeter un regard (at, sur): to g. through (a book), parcourir, feuilleter (un livre). 2. to g. off, ricocher.

gland [glænd], *s.* glande *f.*

glare [gleər]. I. *s.* 1. éclat *m,* clarté *f;* éblouissement *m* (d'un phare, etc.). 2. regard *m* irrité. II. *v.i.* 1. briller d'un éclat éblouissant. 2. lancer un regard furieux. 'glaring, *a.* 1. éblouissant, aveuglant. 2. (*of injustice*) flagrant.

glass [glɑːs], *s.* 1. verre *m;* pane of g., vitre *f,* carreau *m;* cut g., cristal *m* taillé; stained g. window, vitrail *m;* safety g., verre de sûreté. 2. verre (à boire). 3. magnifying g., loupe *f;* looking g., glace *f,* miroir *m.* 4. *pl.* glasses, lunettes *fpl.* 5. the g. is falling, le baromètre baisse. 6. *attrib.* g. de, en, verre; g. door, porte vitrée. 'glassful, *s.* (plein) verre *m.* 'glassware, *s.* verrerie *f.* 'glassy, *a.* vitreux.

glaze [gleiz]. I. *v.tr.* vitrer. II. *s.* lustre *m;* glaçure *f;* vernis *m;* *Cu:* glace *f,* dorure *f.* 'glazed, *a.* vitré; vitrifié. 'glazier, *s.* vitrier *m.*

gleam [gliːm]. I. *s.* (*a*) lueur *f;* (*b*) reflet *m.* II. *v.i.* luire; (*of water*) miroiter.

glean [gliːn], *v.tr.* glaner.

glen [glen], *s.* vallée *f* étroite; vallon *m.*

glide [glaid], *v.i.* (*a*) (se) glisser, couler; (*b*) *Av:* (i) planer; (ii) faire du vol à voile. 'glider, *s. Av:* (*machine*) planeur *m.* 'gliding, *s.* (*a*) glissement *m;* (*b*) *Av:* vol *m* plané.

glimmer [ˈglimər]. I. *s.* faible lueur *f;* miroitement *m.* II. *v.i.* jeter une faible lueur; miroiter.

glimpse [glimps], *s.* vision *f* momentanée; to catch a g. of sth., entrevoir qch.

glint [glint], *s.* éclair *m;* reflet *m.*

glisten [ˈglisn], *v.i.* reluire, scintiller.

glitter [ˈglitər]. I. *s.* scintillement *m,* éclat *m;* brillant *m.* II. *v.i.* scintiller, étinceler.

gloat [glout], *v.i.* to g. over, savourer (un spectacle); se réjouir (méchamment) de (la nouvelle); triompher (du malheur de qn).

globe [gloub], *s.* 1. globe *m;* sphère *f.* 2. globe. 'global, *a.* 1. global. 2. mondial; g. warfare, guerre mondiale.

gloom [gluːm], *s.* 1. obscurité *f.* 2. assombrissement *m,* mélancolie *f.* 'gloomy, *a.* 1. sombre, obscur. 2. lugubre, morne, sombre.

glorious [ˈglɔːriəs], *a.* 1. glorieux. 2. resplendissant; magnifique; superbe; what g. weather! quel temps magnifique!

glory [ˈglɔːri], *s.* gloire *f.*

gloss [glɔs]. I. *s.* lustre *m,* vernis *m.* II. *v.tr.* to g. over the facts, farder les faits. 'glossy, *a.* lustré; g. paper, papier brillant; *Phot:* g. print, épreuve glacée.

†**glossary** [ˈglɔsəri], *s.* glossaire *m,* lexique *m.*

glove [glʌv], *s.* gant *m.* the g. counter, la ganterie; *Aut:* g. compartment, boîte *f* à gants.

glow [glou]. I. *s.* 1. lueur *f* rouge; incandescence *f.* 2. (*a*) sensation *f* de chaleur; (*b*) ardeur *f,* chaleur *f.* II. *v.i.* 1. rougeoyer. 2. rayonner. 'glowing, *a.* 1. rougeoyant. 2. embrasé. 3. rayonnant. 4. chaleureux. 'glow-worm, *s.* ver luisant.

glucose ['glu:kouz], s. glucose m.
glue [glu:]. I. s. colle (forte). II. v.tr. coller.
glum [glʌm], a. renfrogné, maussade.
glut [glʌt], s. surabondance f (d'une denrée); encombrement m (du marché).
glutinous ['glu:tinəs], a. glutineux.
glutton ['glʌtn], s. glouton, -onne; F: he's a g. for work, c'est un bourreau de travail. **'gluttonous**, a. glouton. **'gluttony**, s. gloutonnerie f.
glycerine ['glisərin, -in], s. glycérine f.
gnarled [nɑ:ld], a. noueux.
gnash [næʃ], v.tr. grincer (des dents).
gnat [næt], s. cousin m, moustique m.
gnaw [nɔː], v.tr. & i. ronger.
†go [gou]. I. v.i. aller. 1. (a) to come and go, aller et venir; to go for a walk, faire une promenade; to go to prison, être mis en prison; to go first! à vous d'abord; (b) to go to the head, monter à la tête; (c) to go hungry, souffrir de la faim; (d) to go one's own way, faire à sa guise. 2. (of machinery, etc.) marcher; it has just gone twelve, midi vient de sonner; to keep industry going, maintenir l'activité de l'industrie; (b) F: vendre goes like descendre, vendre se conjugue comme descendre. 3. (of time) passer; that goes without saying, cela va sans dire. 4. (a) partir; s'en aller; after I have gone, après mon départ; (b) disparaître; it has all gone, il n'y en a plus; El: a fuse went, un plomb a sauté; (at auction) going! going! gone! une fois! deux fois! adjugé! 5. (a) to go and see s.o., aller voir qn; (b) he is going to see about it, il va s'en occuper; (c) to go fishing, aller à la pêche. 6. (a) to go to war, se mettre en guerre. 7. Aut: cases that will go in the boot, des valises qui se casent dans le coffre; where does this book go? où est la place de ce livre? 8. contribuer (à qch.); to go to prove sth., servir à prouver qch. 9. s'étendre; the garden goes down to the river, le jardin s'étend jusqu'à la rivière. 10. to go mad, devenir fou; to go white, red, etc., blanchir, rougir, etc. 11. to let go, lâcher prise; let me go! lâchez-moi; to let oneself go, (i) se laisser aller; (ii) s'étendre (sur un sujet). †II. s. 1. to be always on the go, être toujours à trotter, à courir, à trimer. 2. F: entrain m. 3. coup m, essai m; it's your go, à vous de jouer. 4. F: that was a near go, nous l'avons échappé belle! no go! rien à faire. **go a'bout**, v.i. how to go at it, comment s'y prendre. **go a'cross**, v.i. traverser; franchir. **go-a'head**, a. F: entreprenant. **go a'way**, v.i. s'en aller, partir. **go 'back**, v.i. (a) retourner; (b) revenir (sur un sujet). **'go-**

between, s. intermédiaire mf. **go 'by**, v.i. 1. passer. 2. suivre; juger d'après (qch.). **go 'down**, v.i. 1. descendre. 2. (of sun) se coucher; (of ship) couler à fond; (of temperature) baisser; (of neighbourhood) déchoir. **'go for**, v.i. aller chercher (qn); F: attaquer (qn). **go 'forward**, v.i. avancer. **go in**, v.i. (a) entrer; (b) se présenter (à un examen). **go 'into**, v.i. 1. entrer dans. 2. examiner, étudier. **go 'off**, v.i. 1. (of gun) partir; to go off well, bien se passer; F: I've gone off sweets, je n'aime plus les bonbons. 2. to go off the rails, dérailler. **go 'on**, v.i. 1. (a) marcher; continuer sa route; (b) continuer; reprendre la parole. 2. se fonder sur (une hypothèse). **go 'out**, v.i. 1. sortir. 2. to go out of one's way, s'écarter de son chemin. 3. (of light) s'éteindre. 4. (of tide) baisser. **go 'over**, v.i. (a) traverser, passer; (b) examiner. **go 'round**, v.i. (a) faire un détour; (b) (of wheel) tourner; (of rumour) circuler. **go 'through**, v.i. 1. (a) (space) traverser; (b) remplir; subir, essuyer (une épreuve); (c) percer; (d) examiner en détail. 2. aller jusqu'au bout (with, de). **go 'under**, v.i. succomber, sombrer. **go 'up**, v.i. (a) monter; (b) to go up to s.o., aborder qn; (of prices) monter, hausser. **go 'with**, v.i. 1. (a) accompagner; (b) marcher avec. 2. s'accorder avec. **go with'out**, v.i. se passer de (qch.); (b) manquer de (qch.).

goal [goul], s. but m.
goat [gout], s. chèvre f; he-g., bouc m; F: he gets my g., il m'embête.
gobble ['gɔbl], v.tr. avaler (qch.) goulûment.
god [gɔd], s. God, Dieu m; (pagan) g., dieu; Th: F: the gods, le poulailler, le paradis. **†'godchild**, s. filleul, f. filleule. **'god-daughter**, s. filleule f. **'goddess**, s. déesse f. **'godfather**, s. parrain m. **'godless**, a. athée, impie. **'godmother**, s. marraine f. **'godparents**, fpl. le parrain et la marraine. **'godsend**, s. aubaine f. **'godson**, s. filleul m.
gold [gould], s. (a) or m; (b) couleur f de l'or. **'gold-digger**, s. 1. chercheur m d'or. 2. F: (woman) exploiteuse f d'hommes riches. **'golden**, a. d'or. **'goldfield**, s. champ m aurifère. **'goldfinch**, s. chardonneret m. **'goldfish**, s. poisson m rouge. **'goldmine**, s. mine f d'or. **'gold-'plated**, a. doublé d'or. **'goldsmith**, s. orfèvre m.
golf [gɔlf], s. golf m; g. club, (i) crosse f de golf; (ii) club m de golf; g. course, terrain m de golf. **'golfer**, s. golfeur, -euse.
gong [gɔŋ], s. gong m.

good [gud]. **I.** *a.* bon. **1.** (*a*) g. handwriting, belle écriture; (*b*) g. reason, raison valable; (*c*) that's a g. thing! tant mieux! à la bonne heure! very g.! très bien! (*d*) g. morning, afternoon! bonjour! g. evening! bonsoir! **2.** (*a*) g. man, homme de bien; (*b*) (*of child*) sage; (*c*) aimable. **3.** a g. while, pas mal de temps; a g. deal, beaucoup. **4.** it is as g. as new, c'est comme neuf. **II.** *s.* **1.** bien *m*; (*a*) that won't be much g., ça ne servira pas à grand-chose; (*b*) it is all to the g., c'est autant de gagné; (*c*) *adv.phr.* he is gone for g., il est parti pour de bon. **2.** *pl.* (*a*) biens, effets *m*; (*v*) by goods train, par régime ordinaire. **good'bye.** **1.** *s.* adieu *m.* **2.** *int.* au revoir! **good-'humoured,** *a.* de bonne humeur. **good-'looking,** *a.* beau. **good-'natured,** *a.* bon. **'goodness,** *s.* bonté *f*; thank g.! Dieu merci!

†**goose** [guːs], *s.* oie *f.*

†**gooseberry** ['guzb(ə)ri], *s.* groseille *f* à maquereau, groseille verte; g. bush, groseiller *m* à maquereau.

gorge [gɔːdʒ], *s. Geog:* gorge *f*, défilé *m.*

gorgeous ['gɔːdʒəs], *a.* magnifique, splendide.

gorilla [gə'rilə], *s.* gorille *m.*

gorse [gɔːs], *s.* ajonc(s) *m(pl).*

gosling ['gɔzliŋ], *s.* oison *m.*

gospel ['gɔsp(ə)l], *s.* évangile *m*; *F:* to take sth. for g., accepter qch. comme parole d'évangile.

gothic ['gɔθik], *a.* gothique.

gourmand ['guəmã(d)], *s.* gourmand, -ande.

gourmet ['guəmei], *s.* gourmet *m.*

gout [gaut], *s. Med:* goutte *f.*

govern ['gʌvən], *v.tr.* **1.** gouverner; administrer. **2.** maîtriser (ses passions). **'governess,** *s.* institutrice *f* (privée). **'government,** *s.* gouvernement *m.* **'governor,** *s.* gouverneur *m.*

gown [gaun], *s.* robe *f.*

grab [græb]. **I.** *s. Civ. E:* excavateur *m*, pelle *f* mécanique. **II.** ‡*v.tr.* saisir (qch.); se saisir de qch.

grace [greis], *s.* **1.** grâce *f.* **2.** bénédicité *m.* **'graceful,** *a.* gracieux. **-fully,** *adv.* avec grâce. **'gracefulness,** *s.* grâce *f*, élégance *f.* **'gracious,** *a.* gracieux.

grade [greid], *s.* **1.** grade *m*, rang *m*, degré *m*; *Sch: U.S:* classe *f*; g. school = école *f* primaire. **2.** (*a*) *U.S: Civ. E:* pente *f*, rampe *f*; (*b*) to make the g., réussir; (*c*) *U.S:* g. crossing, passage *m* à niveau.

gradient ['greidiənt], *s.* rampe *f*; pente *f.*

gradual ['grædju(ə)l], *a.* graduel, progressif. **-ally,** *adv.* graduellement; peu à peu.

graft [grɑːft]. **I.** *v.tr.* greffer. **II.** *s. F:* corruption *f*; gratte *f.* **'grafting,** *s.* greffe *f*; skin g., greffe épidermique.

grain [grein], *s.* **1.** grain *m.* **2.** fil *m* (du bois); against the g., à contre-fil; it goes against the grain, c'est à contre-cœur que je le fais.

grammar ['græmər], *s.* grammaire *f*; g. school = lycée *m*. **gram'matical,** *a.* grammatical. **-ally,** *adv.* grammaticalement.

gramophone ['græməfoun], *s.* phonographe *m.*

grand [grænd], *a.* **1.** grand, principal; g. piano, piano *m* à queue. **2.** *F:* excellent, épatant. †**grandchild,** *s.* petit-fils *m*, petite-fille *f*; *pl.* grandchildren, petits-enfants *m*. **'grand-daughter,** *s.* petite-fille *f.* **'grandeur,** *s.* grandeur *f.* **'grandfather,** *s.* grand-père *m.* **'grandmother,** *s.* grand-mère *f.* **'grandparents,** *s.pl.* grands-parents *mpl.* **'grandson,** *s.* petit-fils *m.* **'grandstand,** *s. Sp:* tribune *f.*

granite ['grænit], *s.* granit *m.*

grant [grɑːnt]. **I.** *s.* aide *f* pécuniaire; subvention *f*; (un privilège). **II.** *v.tr.* **1.** accorder (un privilège). **2.** to take sth. for granted, considérer qch. comme allant de soi. **'grant-aided,** *a.* subventionné.

granulated ['grænjuleitid], *a.* granulé; (sucre) cristallisé.

grape [greip], *s.* raisin *m*; dessert grapes, raisin(s) de table; g. harvest, vendange *f.* **'grapefruit,** *s.* pamplemousse *m.* **'grape-'hyacinth,** *s. Bot:* muscari *m.* **'grapevine,** *s.* **1.** *U.S:* vigne *f.* **2.** *F:* téléphone *m* arabe.

graph [græf], *s.* raisin *m*, courbe *f*; g. paper, papier *m* quadrillé. **'graphic,** *a.* **1.** *Mth:* graphique. **2.** pittoresque, vivant.

grapple ['græpl], *v.i.* en venir aux prises (avec qn).

grasp [grɑːsp]. **I.** (*a*) poigne *f*; (*b*) prise *f*, étreinte *f*; (*c*) compréhension *f.* **II.** *v.tr.* (*a*) saisir; empoigner; serrer; (*b*) s'emparer, se saisir, de (qch.); (*c*) comprendre. **'grasping,** *a.* âpre au gain.

grass [grɑːs], *s.* herbe *f*; *P:N:* keep off the g., défense de marcher sur le gazon. **'grasshopper,** *s.* sauterelle *f.* **'grassland,** *s.* pré *m*; prairie *f.* **grass-'widow, -'widower,** *s. F:* femme, homme, dont le mari, la femme, est absent(e). **'grassy,** *a.* herbeux.

grate [greit], *s.* foyer *m*, âtre *m.*

grate², **I.** *v.tr.* râper (du fromage); grincer (des dents). **2.** *v.i.* grincer, crisser; to g. on the nerves, taper sur les nerfs. **'grater,** *s.* râpe *f.* **'grating,** *s.* grille *f*, grillage *m.*

grateful ['greitf(u)l], *a.* reconnaissant. **-fully,** *adv.* avec reconnaissance. **'gratefulness,** *s.* reconnaissance *f.*

gratify ['grætifai], *v.tr.* **1.** faire plaisir, être agréable, à (qn). **2.** satisfaire (le désir de qn). **grati'fication,** *s.* satisfaction, *s.* **'gratifying,** *a.* agréable; flatteur.

gratis ['greitis]. **1.** *a.* gratis, gratuit. **2.** *adv.* gratis, gratuitement.

gratitude ['grætitju:d], *s.* gratitude *f*, reconnaissance *f* (de, envers).

gratuitous [grə'tju:ʲitəs], *a.* gratuit; g. insult, insulte injustifiée. **'gratuity,** *s.* **1.** *Mil*: prime *f* de démobilisation. **2.** *Adm*: P.N: no gratuities, défense de donner des pourboires.

grave¹ [greiv]. **I.** *s.* tombe *f*, tombeau *m*; F: to have one foot in the g., être au bord de la tombe. **II.** *a.* grave, sérieux. **-ly,** *adv.* gravement, sérieusement. **'gravity,** *s.* gravité *f*.

gravel ['græv(ə)l], *s.* gravier *m*.

†gravy ['greivi], *s.* jus *m* (de la viande); sauce *f* (au jus).

graze¹ [greiz], *v.i.* paître, brouter.

graze², **I.** *s.* écorchure *f*, éraflure *f*. **II.** *v.tr.* **1.** écorcher, érafler. **2.** effleurer, raser.

grease [gri:s]. **I.** *s.* graisse *f*; g. remover, dégraisseur *m*. **II.** *v.tr.* graisser. **'greasing,** *s.* graissage *m*, lubrification *f*. **'greasy,** *a.* graisseux; (chemin) gras, glissant.

great [greit], *a.* grand; greater London, l'agglomération londonienne; a g. many, beaucoup de (+ *pl.*); the g. majority, la plupart (of, de); to have no g. opinion of s.o., tenir qn en médiocre estime. **-ly,** *adv.* grandement; beaucoup; très. **'great-aunt,** grand-tante *f*. **'great-'grandfather,** **-'grandmother,** *s.* arrière-grand-père *m*; arrière-grand-mère *f*. **'greatness,** *s.* grandeur *f*. **'great-'uncle,** *s.* grandoncle *m*.

greed [gri:d], *s.* (*a*) avidité *f*, cupidité *f*; (*b*) gourmandise *f*. **'greedy,** *a.* (*a*) avide, cupide; (*b*) gourmand. **-ily,** *adv.* (*a*) avidement; (*b*) avec gourmandise.

Greek [gri:k]. **1.** *a.* & *s.* grec, grecque. **2.** *Ling*: le grec.

green [gri:n]. **1.** *a.* (*a*) vert; to turn g., blêmir; (*b*) F: naïf. **2.** *s.* (*a*) vert *m*; the village g., la pelouse communale, la place du village; (*b*) *pl.* F: greens, légumes *m* verts. **'greenback,** *s.* *U.S*: billet *m* de banque. **'greenery,** *s.* coll. verdure *f*; feuillage *m*. **greengage,** *s.* reine-claude *f*. **'greengrocer,** *s.* marchand, -ande, de légumes; fruitier, -ière. **'greenhouse,** *s.* serre *f* chaude.

greet [gri:t], *v.tr.* saluer, accueillir (qn). **'greeting,** *s.* salutation *f*; greetings card, carte *f* de vœux.

gregarious [gri'gɛəriəs], *a.* grégaire.

grenade [grə'neid], *s.* *Mil*: grenade *f*.

grey [grei], *a.* & *s.* gris (*m*): g. matter, matière grise (du cerveau); g.-haired, aux cheveux gris; grisonnant; (*of hair*) to go g., grisonner. **'greyhound,** *s.* lévrier *m*. **'greyness,** *s.* teinte *f* grise, grisaille *f*.

grid [grid], *s.* **1.** grille *f*, grillage *m*. **2.** réseau *m* électrique (national).

grief [gri:f], *s.* chagrin *m*, douleur *f*; to come to g., (i) (*of plan*) échouer; (ii) avoir un accident.

grieve [gri:v]. **1.** *v.tr.* chagriner, affliger. **2.** *v.i.* se chagriner, s'affliger. **'grievance,** *s.* **1.** grief *m*. **2.** injustice *f*.

grill [gril]. **I.** *s.* **1.** *Cu*: grillade *f*; g. room, grill-room *m*. **2.** (*appliance*) gril *m*. **II.** *v.tr.* griller.

grille [gril], *s.* grille *f*; *Aut*: radiator g., calandre *f*.

grim [grim], *a.* sinistre; sévère. **-ly,** *adv.* sévèrement; d'un air sinistre.

grimace [gri'meis], *s.* grimace *f*.

grime [graim], *s.* saleté *f*. **'grimy,** *a.* sale, encrassé.

grin [grin]. **I.** *s.* large sourire *m*. **II.** **‡***v.i.* sourire à belles dents.

‡grind [graind]. **1.** *v.tr.* (*a*) moudre; (*b*) to dust, réduire en poudre; (*b*) repasser (un outil) (sur la meule); (*c*) to g. one's teeth, grincer des dents. **2.** *v.i.* grincer, crisser. **'grindstone,** *s.* meule *f* à aiguiser.

grip [grip]. **I.** *s.* prise *f*; étreinte *f*; to come to grips, en venir aux mains. **2.** poignée *f*. **II.** **‡***v.tr.* saisir, empoigner.

gristle ['grisl], *s.* cartilage *m*, croquant *m*.

grit [grit]. **I.** *s.* grès *m*, sable *m*. **II.** **‡***v.tr.* to g. one's teeth, grincer des dents.

groan [groun]. **I.** *s.* gémissement *m*. **II.** *v.i.* gémir.

grocer ['grousər], *s.* épicier, -ière; g.'s shop, épicerie *f*, alimentation *f*. **'grocery,** *s.* épicerie *f*.

groin [groin], *s.* **1.** aine *f*. **2.** *A.* & *A*: arête *f* (de voûte).

groom [gru:m], *s.* valet *m* d'écurie.

groove [gru:v], *s.* **1.** rainure *f*. **2.** to get into a g., devenir routinier.

grope [group], *v.i.* tâtonner; to g. one's way, avancer à tâtons.

†gross¹ [grous], *s.* douze douzaines *f*, grosse *f*.

gross², *a.* **1.** grossier; g. **ignorance,** ignorance crasse. **2.** (*of amount*) brut; *Nau*: g. tonnage, jauge brute; g. profit, bénéfice brut. **-ly,** *adv.* grossièrement; g. exaggerated, exagéré outre mesure. **'grossness,** *s.* grossièreté *f*.

grotesque [grou'tesk], *a.* grotesque; absurde.

grotto ['grɔtou], *s.* grotte *f*.

ground¹ [graund], *a.* moulu; broyé, pilé.

ground². **I.** *s.* **1.** (*a*) sol *m*, terre *f*; g. floor, rez-de-chaussée *m*; (*b*) *Mil*: parade g., terrain *m* de manœuvres; *Av*: g. personnel, personnel *m* nonnavigant; (*c*) *pl.* parc *m*, jardin *m* (d'une maison). **2.** fond *m* (d'un tableau). **3.** raison *f*, cause *f*; on health grounds, pour raison de santé; grounds for divorce, motifs *m* de divorce. **4. coffee grounds,** marc *m*, fond *m*, du café. II. v. 1. v.tr. (a) fonder, baser, appuyer (on, in, sth., sur qch.); (b) *Av:* interdire de vol. **2.** v.i. (of ship) s'échouer (on, sur). **'groundless,** a. (soupçon) mal fondé, sans fondement. **'groundsheet,** s. tapis *m* de sol. **'groundsman,** s. préposé *m* à l'entretien d'un terrain de jeux.

group [gruːp]. **I.** s. groupe *m.* II. v. 1. v.tr. grouper. 2. v.i. se grouper.

†grouse[1] [graus], s. tétras *m*; (red) g., lagopède *m* rouge d'Écosse, grouse *m.*

grouse[2], v.i. *F:* ronchonner, bougonner.

grove [grouv], s. bocage *m*, bosquet *m.*

‡grovel ['grɔv(ə)l], v.i. ramper; se mettre à plat-ventre (devant qn).

‡grow [grou]. **1.** v.i. (a) (of plant) pousser; (of pers.) grandir; to g. up, grandir; (b) atteindre l'âge adulte; (b) devenir; to g. old, devenir vieux, vieillir; to g. alarmed, s'alarmer. **2.** v.tr. (a) cultiver (des roses, etc.); (b) laisser pousser (ses cheveux). **'growing,** a. croissant; grandissant; wheat-g. district, région *f* à blé. **'grown-'up,** a. & s. grand; adulte (*mf*). **growth,** s. 1. croissance *f.* 2. accroissement *m*; augmentation *f.* 3. *Med:* grosseur *f*; tumeur *f.*

growl [graul]. **I.** s. grognement *m*; grondement *m.* II. v.i. grogner.

grub [grʌb], s. 1. (a) larve *f*; (b) ver *m* (blanc). **2.** *P:* mangeaille *f.*

grubby ['grʌbi], a. *F:* sale, malpropre.

grudge [grʌdʒ]. **I.** s. rancune *f.* II. v.tr. donner, accorder (qch.) à contre-cœur. **'grudging,** a. (consentement) donné à contre-cœur. **-ly,** adv. à contre-cœur.

gruesome ['gruːsəm], a. macabre, affreux.

gruff [grʌf], a. bourru, revêche, rude.

grumble ['grʌmbl], v.i. & tr. grommeler, grogner, murmurer; trouver à redire (à qch.). **'grumbler,** s. grognon, -onne; mécontent, -ente. **'grumbling,** s. grognonnerie *f* (murmure *m* de) mécontentement.

grumpy ['grʌmpi], a. maussade, grincheux.

grunt [grʌnt]. **I.** s. grognement *m.* II. v.i. grogner.

guarantee [gærən'tiː]. **I.** s. garantie *f*; caution *f.* II. v.tr. garantir (qn, qch.); se porter garant pour (qn, qch.). **'guaranteed,** a. *Com:* avec garantie *f.*

guard [gɑːd]. **I.** s. 1. garde *f*; *Mil:* on g., en garde, en, de, faction; to be on one's g. against sth., se méfier de qch. 2. (a) chef *m* de train; (b) *U.S:* gardien *m* de prison. II. v. 1. v.tr. garder; protéger. 2. v.i. to g. against sth., se garder de qch. **'guarded,** a. (of speech) prudent, mesuré. **'guar-**

dian, s. 1. gardien, -ienne. 2. tuteur, -trice (d'un mineur). 3. g. angel, ange *m* gardien.

guer'rilla [gə'rilə], s. g. warfare, guerre *f* de guérillas.

guess [ges]. **I.** s. conjecture *f*; estimation *f.* II. v.tr. & i. deviner, conjecturer; to g. right, wrong, bien, mal, deviner. **2.** *U.S:* croire, penser; I g. you're right, il me semble que vous avez raison.

guest [gest], s. 1. invité, -ée; hôte, hôtesse. 2. g. pensionnaire *mf*; g. house, pension *f* de famille.

guide [gaid]. **I.** s. 1. (pers.) guide *m*; (girl) g., éclaireuse *f*; guide *f.* 2. (book) guide *m*; g. to photography, introduction *f* à la photographie. II. v.tr. guider, conduire, diriger. **'guidance,** s. direction *f*; *Sch:* vocational g., orientation *f* professionnelle. **'guided,** a. (of missile) téléguidé.

guillotine [gilə'tiːn], s. guillotine *f.* II. v.tr. guillotiner.

guilt [gilt], s. culpabilité *f.* **'guilty,** a. coupable; g. conscience, mauvaise conscience. **-ily,** adv. d'un air coupable.

guinea ['gini], s. vingt-et-un shillings; dress costing 10 guineas, robe qui coûte dix livres et dix shillings. **'guinea-fowl,** s.inv. pintade *f.* **'guinea-pig,** s. cobaye *m*, cochon *m* d'Inde; *F:* to be a g.-p., servir de cobaye.

guise [gaiz], s. apparence *f.*

guitar [gi'tɑːr], s. guitare *f.*

gulf [gʌlf], s. 1. golfe *m*; the G. Stream, le Courant du Golfe, the Gulf-Stream. **2.** gouffre *m*, abîme *m.*

gull [gʌl], s. mouette *f*, goéland *m.*

gullible ['gʌlibl], a. facile à duper.

†gully ['gʌli], s. (petit) ravin; couloir *m.*

gulp [gʌlp]. **I.** v.tr. to g. sth. down, avaler qch. à grosses bouchées; avaler (une boisson) à pleine gorge; to g. down a sob, ravaler un sanglot. II. s. coup *m* de gosier; at one g., d'un (seul) coup, d'un (seul) trait.

gum[1] [gʌm], s. gomme *f*; colle *f.*

gum[2], s. gencive *f.*

gun [gʌn], s. 1. canon *m.* 2. fusil *m.* **3.** (for paint) spray *m*, pistolet *m* (vaporisateur). **'gunfire,** s. cannonade *f.* **†'gunman,** s. *U.S:* voleur *m* armé. **'gunpowder,** s. poudre *f* (à canon). **'gunshot,** s. coup *m* de fusil, de canon; within g., à portée de fusil. gunwale ['gʌn(ə)l], s. *Nau:* plat-bord *m.*

gurgle ['gəːgl], v.i. glouglouter.

gush [gʌʃ]. **I.** v.i. jaillir, couler à flots. II. s. jaillissement *m*; effusion *f* (de larmes); jet *m*, flot *m* (de sang). **'gushing,** a. (of pers.) exubérant, expansif.

gust [gʌst], s. g. of wind, coup *m* de vent; rafale *f.* **'gusty,** a. (vent) à rafales; (journée) de grand vent.

gusto ['gʌstou], s. F: to do sth. with g., faire qch. (i) avec plaisir, (ii) avec entrain.

gut [gʌt]. I. s. 1. Anat: boyau m, intestin m. 2. F: to have guts, avoir du cran. II. v.tr. étriper (un animal); vider (un poisson); (of fire) to g. a house, détruire complètement l'intérieur d'une maison.

gutter [gʌtər], s. 1. gouttière f. 2. ruisseau m (de rue); caniveau m.

guttural ['gʌt(ə)rəl], a. guttural.

gym [dʒim], s. F: 1. gymnase m. 2. gymnastique f; g. shoe, chaussure f de gymnastique.

gymnasium [dʒim'neiziəm], s. gymnase m. gym'nastic, a. gymnaste mf. gym'nastics, s.pl. gymnastique f.

gynaecology [gaini'kɔlədʒi], s. gynécologie f. gynae'cologist, s. gynécologue m.

gyrate [dʒɑi'reit], v.i. tourner, tournoyer.

†gyro [dʒɑirou], s. Av: directional g., conservateur m de cap. 'gyro'compass, s. Nau: gyro-compas m. 'gyroplane, s. Av: giravion m. 'gyroscope, s. gyroscope m. 'gyro'stabilizer, s. Av: gyrostabilisateur m. 'gyrostat, s. gyrostat m.

H

H, h [eitʃ], s. 1. (la lettre) H, h mf; to drop one's h's, ne pas aspirer les h. 2. Mil: H bomb, bombe H.

haberdasher ['hæbədæʃəri], s. 1. mercerie f. 2. esp. U.S: chemiserie f.

habit ['hæbit], s. 1. habitude f, coutume f. 2. Cl: habit m (de religieuse); amazone f.

habitat ['hæbitæt], s. habitat m.

habitation [hæbi'teiʃ(ə)n], s. habitation f; fit for h., en état (d'être habité). 'habitable, a. habitable.

habitual [hə'bitjuəl], a. habituel, d'habitude. -ally, adv. habituellement, par habitude. ha'bituate, v.tr. habituer.

hack[1] [hæk], v.tr. & i. hacher; tailler (qch. en morceaux). 'hacking, s. h. cough, toux sèche et pénible.

hack[2], s. 1. cheval m de louage. 2. h. writer, écrivain m besogneux.

hackneyed ['hæknid], a. rebattu, usé.

haddock ['hædək], s. aiglefin m; smoked h., haddock m.

haemoglobin [hi:mou'gloubin], s. hémoglobine f.

haemophilia [hi:mou'filiə], s. Med: hémophilie f.

haemorrhage ['heməridʒ], s. hémorragie f.

hag [hæg], s. 1. F: old h., vieille rombière f. 2. h.-ridden, tourmenté.

haggard ['hægəd], a. (a) hâve; (b) hagard.

haggle ['hægl], v.i. marchander.

hail[1] [heil]. I. s. grêle f. II. v.i. & tr. it is hailing, il grêle. 'hailstone, s. grêlon m.

hail[2]. I. s. appel m; within h., à portée de voix. II. v.tr. (a) saluer; (b) héler. III. int. salut! Ecc: the H. Mary, la salutation angélique.

hair [hɛər], s. 1. cheveu m; coll. the h., les cheveux; to do one's h., se coiffer; to wash one's h., se laver la tête; h. drier, sèche-cheveux m; to split hairs, couper un cheveu en quatre. 2. (on body) poil m; (of animal) coll. poil, pelage m. 'hairbreadth, a. to have a h.

escape, l'échapper belle. 'hairbrush, s. brosse f à cheveux. 'haircut, s. taille f, coupe f de cheveux; to have a h., se faire couper les cheveux. 'hairdresser, s. coiffeur, -euse. 'hairdressing, s. coiffure f. 'hairless, a. sans cheveux; (of animal) sans poils. 'hairpin, s. épingle f à cheveux; h. bend, (virage m en) épingle à cheveux. 'hairspring, s. (ressort) spiral m (de montre). 'hairy, a. velu, poilu.

hake [heik], s. Fish: merluche f; colin m.

†half [hɑːf]. 1. s. (a) moitié f; to cut sth. in h., couper en deux; (b) demi m, demie f; three and a half, trois et demi; (c) Rail: return h., (billet m de) retour m. 2. a. demi; h. an hour, une demi-heure; at h. price, à moitié prix; (d) Sp: the first h., la première mi-temps. 3. adv. (a) à moitié; h. understand, comprendre à moitié; (b) h. past two, deux heures et demie; (c) h. as big, moitié aussi grand; h. as big again, plus grand de moitié. 'half-'baked, a. F: (of pers.) niais; (projet) qui ne tient pas debout; 'half-back, s. Sp: demi(-arrière) m. 'half-brother, s. demi-frère m. 'half-caste, a. & s. métis, -isse. 'half-holiday, s. demi-congé m. half-'open, a. entr'ouvert. halfpenny ['heipni], s. demi-penny m; three halfpence, un penny et demi; three halfpennies, trois pièces d'un demi-penny. 'half-shaft, s. Aut: demi-arbre m. 'half-'term, s. Sch: congé m de mi-trimestre. 'half-'timbered, a. (maison) en colombage. 'half-'way, adv. à moitié chemin. 'half-'wit, s. idiot, -ote. 'half-'yearly, a. & adv. tous les six mois.

halibut ['helibət], s. Fish: flétan m.

hall [hɔːl], s. 1. vestibule m; h. porter, concierge m. 2. dining h., réfectoire m; concert h., salle f de concert; music h., music-hall m. 3. Sch: h. (of residence) = cité f universitaire. 'hallmark, s. poinçon m (sur les objets d'orfèvrerie).

hallo [hə'lou], int. & s. (a) holà! ohé! (b) bonjour!

hallow ['hælou], v.tr. sanctifier; Ecc: hallowed be thy name, que ton nom soit sanctifié. 'Hallowe'en, s. veille f. de la Toussaint.

hallucination [həljuːsi'neif(ə)n], s. hallucination f.

†**halo** ['heilou], s. auréole f.

halt [hɔːlt]. I. s. halte f.; arrêt m. II. v.i. s'arrêter; h.! (i) Mil: halte! (ii) P.N: Aut: stop. 'halting, a. hésitant.

halter ['hɔːltər], s. licou m, longe f.

halve [haːv], v.tr. (a) diviser en deux; (b) réduire de moitié.

ham [hæm], s. jambon m. 'hamstring. I. s. tendon m du jarret. II. ‡v.tr. F: couper les moyens à (qn).

hamlet ['hæmlit], s. hameau m.

hammer ['hæmər]. I. s. marteau m. II. v.tr. marteler; battre.

hammock ['hæmɔk], s. hamac m.

hamper[1] ['hæmpər], s. manne f, banne f.

hamper[2], v.tr. embarrasser, gêner.

hamster ['hæmstər], s. Z: hamster m.

hand [hænd]. I. s. 1. main f; (a) on one's hands and knees, à quatre pattes; hands up! haut les mains! (b) to have a h. in sth., se mêler de qch.; (c) to have one's hands full, avoir fort à faire; on one's hands, à sa charge, sur les bras; Com: to change hands, changer de propriétaire. 2. adv.phrs. (a) (near) at h., sous la main; (b) hat in h., chapeau bas; revolver in h., revolver au poing; the matter in h., la chose en question; (c) work on h., travail en cours; (d) on the right h., du côté droit; on the one h., d'une part; (e) to come to h., arriver (à destination); to get out of h., perdre toute discipline; (f) h. in h., la main dans la main; (g) h. to h., (combat) corps m à corps; (h) from h. to mouth, (vivre) au jour le jour; to win hands down, gagner haut la main. 3. (a) ouvrier, -ière; manœuvre m; (b) Nau: all hands on deck! tout le monde sur le pont! to be lost with all hands, périr corps et biens. 4. (cards) jeu m. 5. aiguille f (de montre). 6. horse of 15 hands, cheval de 15 paumes. 7. attrib. h. luggage, bagages m à main. II. v.tr. passer, remettre (qch. à qn). 'handbag, s. sac m à main. 'handbook, s. guide m; manuel m. 'handcuff, v.tr. mettre les menottes à (qn). 'handcuffs, s.pl. menottes f. hand 'down, v.tr. 1. descendre (qch.). 2. transmettre (une tradition). 'handful, s. (a) poignée f. h. of people, quelques personnes; (b) (child) enfant mf terrible. handicap. I. s. Sp: handicap m; Aut: Sp: désavantage m. II. ‡v.tr. (a) Sp: handicaper; (b) to be handicapped, être désavantagé. hand 'in, v.tr. remettre (un paquet,

etc.). 'handiwork, s. ouvrage m, œuvre f. 'handkerchief, s. mouchoir m. 'handle. I. s. manche m (de couteau); poignée f (de porte); anse f (de seau); Aut: manivelle f; F: to fly off the h., sortir de ses gonds. II. v.tr. manier. 'handlebar, s. guidon m. 'handling, s. maniement m; rough h., traitement m brutal. hand 'made, a. fait, fabriqué, à la main. hand 'on, v.tr. transmettre. hand 'out, v.tr. distribuer. 'hand-out, s. F: communiqué m (à la presse). hand 'over, v.tr. remettre (qch. à qn). 'hand 'round, v.tr. passer (les gâteaux); faire circuler (la bouteille). 'handshake, s. poignée f de main.

handsome ['hænsəm], a. (of pers.) beau; (of action) gracieux, généreux; h. profit, de beaux bénéfices.

handwork, s. travail m à la main; travail manuel. 'handwriting, s. écriture f. 'handwritten, a. manuscrit; écrit à la main. 'handy, a. 1. maniable. 2. commode. 3. à portée de la main. †'handyman, s. homme m à tout faire.

‡**hang** [hæŋ]. I. v. 1. v.tr. (a) pendre, suspendre (qch.); (b) to h. (down) one's head, baisser la tête; (c) (of plan) to h. fire, traîner. 2. v.i. (a) pendre, être suspendu (from, à); (b) être pendu. II. s. F: to get the h. of sth., (i) saisir le sens de qch.; (ii) saisir le truc de qch. hang a'bout, a'round, v.i. rôder, flâner. hang 'back, v.i. 1. rester en arrière. 2. hésiter. hang 'down, v.i. pendre. 'hanger, s. coat h., cintre m; porte-vêtements m. 'hanger-'on, s. (pers.) dépendant m. 'hanging, s. 1. (a) suspension f; (b) pendaison f. 2. pl. tenture f. †'hangman, s. bourreau m. hang 'on, v.i. s'accrocher (à qch.); P.T.T: h. on! ne raccrochez pas! hang 'out. 1. v.tr. pendre au dehors; étendre (le linge). 2. v.i. F: habiter, nicher. 'hangover, s. P: gueule f de bois. hang 'up, v.tr. accrocher, pendre (un vêtement, un tableau); P.T.T: raccrocher (l'appareil).

hangar ['hæŋər], s. Av: hangar m.

hank [hæŋk], s. écheveau m (de laine).

hanker ['hæŋkər], v.i. to h. after sth., désirer ardemment qch. 'hankering, s. to have a h. for sth., soupirer après qch.

hanky-panky ['hæŋki'pæŋki], s. F: supercherie f; finasseries fpl.

haphazard ['hæp'hæzəd]. 1. a. fortuit. 2. adv. à l'aventure.

happen ['hæp(ə)n], v.i. 1. (a) arriver; se passer; se produire; whatever happens, quoi qu'il arrive; as it happens, justement; F: worse things h. at sea, il y a pire; (b) what's happened to him? (i) qu'est-ce qui lui est arrivé? (ii) qu'est-ce qu'il est devenu? if anything happened to you, si vous veniez à mourir. 2. if I h. to forget, s'il m'arrive d'oublier; the house happened to be empty, la maison se trouvait vide. 'happening, s. événement m.

happy ['hæpi], a. 1. heureux, bien aise, content. 2. h. thought! bonne inspiration! -ily, adv. heureusement. 'happiness, s. bonheur m, félicité f. 'happy-go-'lucky, a. sans souci; insouciant.

harass ['hærəs], v.tr. harasser, tracasser.

harbour ['hɑːbər]. I. s. port m; h. installations, installations portuaires. II. v.tr. héberger; receler (un criminel); to h. a grudge against s.o., garder rancune à qn.

hard [hɑːd]. I. a. 1. dur; to get h. durcir; h. currency, devise forte. 2. difficile; pénible; h. work, (i) travail difficile; (ii) travail assidu; (iii) travail ingrat; to be h. of hearing, être dur d'oreille. 3. dur, sévère (to, envers); h. lines! pas de chance! in fact, fait brutal; to try one's hardest, faire tout son possible. 4. h. frost, forte gelée; h. winter, hiver rigoureux. II. adv. 1. (a) fort; as h. as one can, de toutes ses forces; to think h., réfléchir profondément; it's raining h., il pleut à verse; (b) to be h. up, être à court (d'argent). 2. difficilement. 'hardboard, s. Isorel (R.t.m.). hard-'boiled, a. (œuf) dur; F: (of pers.) tenace; dur à cuire. 'harden, v.tr. & i. durcir. hard-'hearted, a. insensible, au cœur dur. 'hardly, adv. 1. (a) sévèrement; (b) péniblement. 2. à peine; ne ... guère; I h. know, je n'en sais trop rien; I need h. say, point besoin de dire; h. anyone, presque personne. 'hardness, s. 1. dureté f. 2. difficulté f. 3. sévérité f, rigueur f; dureté f. 'hardship, s. privation f, fatigue f; (dure) épreuve f. 'hardware, s. quincaillerie f. hard-'wearing, a. durable. 'hardwood, s. bois m dur. hard-'working, a. laborieux, assidu. 'hardy, a. 1. hardi; audacieux. 2. robuste; endurci; Bot: vivace; (plante) de pleine terre.

hare [heər]. I. s. lièvre m; jugged h., civet m de lièvre. 2. Belgian h., léporide m. II. v.i. F: to h. off, se sauver à toutes jambes. 'hare-lip, s. bec-de-lièvre m.

haricot ['hærikou], s. (bean), haricot m blanc; Cu: h. mutton, haricot de mouton.

hark [hɑːk], v.i. to h. back to sth., revenir à un sujet.

harm [hɑːm]. I. s. mal m, tort m; out of harm's way, à l'abri du danger. II. v.tr. faire du mal à, nuire à (qn). 'harmful, a. malfaisant, pernicieux;

nuisible. 'harmless, a. (animal) in-offensif; (homme) sans malice; (passe-temps) innocent.

harmony ['hɑːməni], s. harmonie f. har'monious, a. harmonieux; mélo-dieux. 'harmonize. 1. v.tr. harmo-niser. 2. v.i. s'harmoniser; s'accorder.

harness ['hɑːnis]. I. s. harnais m. II. v.tr. 1. (a) harnacher; (b) atteler. 2. aménager (une chute d'eau).

harp [hɑːp]. I. s. harpe f. II. v.i. jouer de la harpe; F: he's always harping on it, c'est toujours la même ritournelle.

harpoon [hɑː'puːn]. I. s. harpon m. II. v.tr. harponner.

harrow ['hærou]. I. s. herse f. II. v.tr. herser; to h. s.o.'s feelings, déchirer le cœur à qn. 'harrowing, a. poignant, navrant.

harsh [hɑːʃ], a. dur, rude; aigre, strident. -ly, adv. avec dureté; sévèrement. 'harshness, s. 1. dureté f, rudesse f; âpreté f; aigreur f. 2. sévérité f; rigueur f.

harvest ['hɑːvist]. I. s. moisson f; récolte f. II. v.tr. moissonner; récolter; abs. rentrer la moisson. 'harvester, s. (pers.) moissonneur, -euse. 2. (machine) moissonneuse (-lieuse) f.

hash [hæʃ]. I. s. Cu: hachis m. 2. F: to make a h. of sth., faire un beau gâchis de qch.; P: to settle s.o.'s h., régler son compte à qn.

haste [heist], s. hâte f. 'hastily, adv. à la hâte; sans réfléchir. 'hastiness, s. 1. précipitation f. 2. emportement m. 'hasty, a. (départ) précipité; (repas) sommaire. 2. emporté, vif.

hat [hæt], s. chapeau m; to pass round the h. (for s.o.), faire une quête (au profit de qn); F: keep it under your h., gardez ça pour vous; F: old h., vieux jeu. 'hatter, s. chapelier m.

hatch[1] [hætʃ], s. 1. Nau: écoutille f. 2. service h., passe-plats m.

hatch[2], v.tr. faire éclore (des pous-sins); ourdir (un complot). 2. v.i. éclore.

hatchet ['hætʃit], s. hachette f.

hate [heit]. I. s. haine f. II. v.tr. haïr, détester. 'hateful, a. odieux, détes-table. 'hatred, s. haine f.

haughty ['hɔːti], a. hautain, altier. -ily, adv. avec hauteur.

haul [hɔːl]. I. v.tr. tirer; traîner; remorquer; rouler (le charbon). II. s. Fish: coup m de filet; (b) prise f, pêche f; to make a good h., (i) faire une bonne pêche; (ii) F: (of burglar) emporter un fameux butin. 2. Aut: etc: parcours m, trajet m. 'haulage, s. 1. (a) camionnage m; h. contractor, entrepreneur m de transports; (b) traction f, remorquage m, halage m. 2. frais mpl de trans-port. 'haulier, s. camionneur m.

haunch [hɔ:n(t)ʃ], s. (a) hanche f; (b) Cu: cuissot m, quartier m (de chevreuil); (c) dog sitting on his haunches, chien assis sur son derrière.

haunt [hɔ:nt]. I. s. lieu m fréquenté (par qn, un animal); repaire m (d'un animal). II. v.tr. (a) fréquenter, hanter (un endroit); (b) (of ghost) hanter (une maison); this place is haunted, il y a des revenants ici; (c) haunted by memories, obsédé par des souvenirs.

†**have** [hæv], v.tr. 1. avoir, posséder; he had no friends, il n'avait pas d'amis. 2. to h. a child, avoir, donner naissance à, un enfant. 3. there was no work to be had, on ne pouvait pas obtenir de travail; to h. news from s.o., recevoir des nouvelles de qn; I must h. them by tomorrow, il me les faut pour demain; let me h. your keys, donnez-moi vos clefs; P: I had him h. it, (i) je lui ai dit son fait; (ii) je lui ai réglé son compte; P: you've had it! c'est loupé! 4. to h. lunch, déjeuner; will you h. some wine? voulez-vous prendre du vin? I had some more, j'en ai repris; to h. a cigar, fumer un cigare; P: I'm not having that, ça ne prend pas. 5. to h. measles, avoir la rougeole; to h. a dream, faire un rêve; to h. a bath, prendre un bain; to h. a pleasant evening, passer une soirée agréable. 6. F: you've been had, vous avez été refait. 7. to h. sth. done, faire faire qch.; to h. one's hair cut, se faire couper les cheveux; I had my watch stolen, on m'a volé ma montre. 8. which (one) will you h.? lequel voulez-vous? 9. to h. to do sth., être obligé de faire qch. 10. (aux. use) I h. given him the book, je lui ai donné le livre; I h. lived in London for three years, j'habite Londres depuis trois ans; You h. forgotten your gloves!—So I h.! Vous avez oublié vos gants!—en effet! You haven't done it!—I h.! Vous ne l'avez pas fait!—Si! 11. I had better say nothing, je ferais mieux de ne rien dire. 12. (a) F: to h. s.o. on, duper, faire marcher, qn; (b) to h. sth. on (a horse), faire un pari. 13. (a) to h. a tooth out, se faire arracher une dent; (b) F: to h. it out with s.o., vider une querelle avec qn. 14. F: to be had up, être cité devant les tribunaux.

haversack ['hævəsæk], s. havresac m.

havoc ['hævək], s. ravage m, dégâts mpl.

hawk [hɔ:k], s. faucon m.

hawker ['hɔ:kər], s. colporteur m, marchand m ambulant.

hawthorn ['hɔ:θɔ:n], s. aubépine f.

hay [hei], s. foin m. 'haycock, s., 'hayrick, s., 'haystack, s. meule f de foin. 'haymaking, s. fenaison f.

hazard ['hæzəd], s. 1. (a) hasard m; (b) risque m, péril m. 2. accident de terrain. 'hazardous, a. hasardeux, risqué.

haze [heiz], s. brume légère. 'hazy, a. (a) brumeux; (b) (of ideas) nébuleux, vague.

hazel ['heizl], s. noisetier m; h. nut, noisette f.

he [hi:], pers.pron. 1. (unstressed) il; here he comes, le voici qui vient; he is an honest man, c'est un honnête homme. 2. (a) (stressed) lui; he and I, lui et moi; 'he knows nothing about it, lui, il n'en sait rien; (b) celui; he believes, celui qui croit.

head [hed]. I. s. 1. tête f. 2. to win by a h., gagner d'une tête; F: I could do it standing on my h., c'est simple comme bonjour; F: to talk s.o.'s h. off, rompre les oreilles à qn. 2. to have a good h. for business, s'entendre aux affaires; it never entered my h. that . . ., il ne m'est pas venu à l'idée que . . .; his name has gone out of my h., j'ai complètement oublié son nom; to have a good h. for drink, bien porter le vin; to go off one's h., devenir fou; weak in the h., faible d'esprit. 3. pointe f (d'asperge); pied m (de céleri); tête f (de volcan); haut m (d'un escalier); tête, culasse f, fond m (de cylindre); chevet m (de lit); haut bout (de la table); to bring a matter to a h., faire aboutir une affaire. 4. tête (d'un cortège, d'une liste); chef m (de la famille, d'une entreprise); h. of department, chef de service; h. gardener, jardinier m en chef; h. office, bureau principal; h. wind, vent m contraire. 5. (a) (usu. inv.) thirty head of oxen, trente bœufs; (b) to pay so much a h., payer tant par tête, par personne. 6. (of coin) face f; F: I can't make h. or tail of it, je n'y comprends rien. 7. Civ.E: h. of water, colonne f d'eau. II. v. 1. v.tr. venir en tête (d'un cortège, Pol: du scrutin). 2. v.i. s'avancer, se diriger (vers un endroit); to be heading for ruin, aller tout droit vers la ruine. 'headache, s. mal m de tête; F: (of problem) casse-tête m. 'heading, s. rubrique f, en-tête m. 'headland, s. cap m, promontoire m. 'headlight, s. Aut: phare m. 'headlong. 1. adv. la tête la première; tête baissée. 2. a. précipité, irréfléchi. 'headmaster, s. directeur m (d'une école); proviseur m (d'un lycée). 'headmistress, s. directrice f. 'headquarters, s.pl. Mil: quartier m général; état-major m. 2. centre m (d'une banque, etc.), siège m social. 'headstrong, a. volontaire, têtu. 'headway, s. progrès m. 'heady, a. (vin, etc.) capiteux.

heal [hi:l]. 1. *v.tr.* guérir. 2. *v.i.* se guérir.

health [helθ], *s.* santé *f.* 'healthy, *a.* (*a*) sain; en bonne santé; bien portant; (*b*) salubre.

heap [hi:p]. I. *s.* tas *m*, monceau *m*. II. *v.tr.* 1. to h. (up), entasser, amonceler. 2. combler, remplir (with, de).

†**hear** [hiər], *v.tr.* 1. entendre; to h. s.o. say sth., entendre dire qch. à qn. 2. (= listen to) écouter; h.! h.! très bien! très bien! 3. apprendre (une nouvelle). 4. to h. from s.o., recevoir une lettre de qn; to h. of, about, s.o., avoir des nouvelles de qn, entendre parler de qn; he won't h. of it, il s'y oppose absolument. 'hearer, *s.* auditeur, -trice. 'hearing, *s.* 1. audition *f*, audience *f*. 2. ouïe *f*. 'hearsay, *s.* oui-dire *m inv.*

hearse [hə:s], *s.* corbillard *m*.

heart [hɑ:t], *s.* 1. cœur *m*. h. failure, défaillance *f* cardiaque. 2. (*a*) set your h. at rest, soyez tranquille; from the bottom of my h., de tout mon cœur; at h., au fond; he's a man after my own h., je le trouve très sympathique; (*b*) with all one's h., de tout son cœur; (*c*) to lose h., perdre courage. 3. cœur (d'un chou); fond *m* (d'artichaut); the h. of the matter, le vif de l'affaire. 4. (at cards) queen of hearts, dame *f* de cœur; have you any hearts? avez-vous du cœur? 'heart-breaking, *a.* navrant. 'heart-broken, *a.* navré. 'heartless, *a.* sans cœur, sans pitié.

hearth [hɑ:θ], *s.* foyer *m*, âtre *m*. 'hearthrug, *s.* tapis *m*, carpette *f*, de foyer.

hearty [hɑ:ti], *a.* 1. (accueil) cordial. 2. (*a*) vigoureux, robuste; (*b*) (repas) copieux. -ily, *adv.* 1. cordialement, sincèrement. 2. (manger) de bon appétit.

heat [hi:t]. I. *s.* 1. chaleur *f*; ardeur *f*. 2. *Sp:* épreuve *f*, manche *f*; dead h., course nulle. II. *v.tr.* & *i.* chauffer; (s')échauffer. 'heater, *s.* appareil *m* de chauffage; (water) h., chauffe-eau *m*; car h., chauffage *m* (de voiture). 'heating, *s.* chauffage *m*; central h., chauffage central. 'heat-resisting, *a.* calorifuge; thermorésistant. 'heat-wave, *s.* vague *f* de chaleur.

heath [hi:θ], *s.* 1. bruyère *f*. 2. lande *f*.

heathen ['hi:ð(ə)n], *a.* & *s.* païen, -ïenne.

heather ['heðər], *s.* bruyère *f*.

heave [hi:v]. I. *v.* 1. *v.tr.* (*a*) lever, soulever; (*b*) pousser (un soupir); (*c*) virer (un navire). 2. *v.i.* (*a*) (se) gonfler, se soulever; (*b*) (of pers.) avoir des haut-le-cœur; (*c*) (past: hove) *Nau:* to h. to, se mettre à la cape; to h. virer au cabestan. II. *s.* 1. soulèvement *m*, effort *m* (pour soulever). 2. haut-le-cœur *m*.

heaven ['hev(ə)n], *s.* ciel *m*; thank h.! dieu merci! 'heavenly, *a.* (*a*) céleste; (*b*) *F:* délicieux.

heavy ['hevi], *a.* 1. lourd. 2. h. meal, repas copieux; h. shower, grosse averse. 3. (travail) pénible, laborieux. -ily, *adv.* 1. lourdement; time hangs h. on his hands, le temps lui pèse. 2. h. underlined, fortement souligné; to lose h., perdre gros. 3. to sleep h., dormir profondément. 'heaviness, *s.* (*a*) lourdeur *f*, pesanteur *f*; (*b*) lassitude *f*. 'heavyweight, *s.* (boxer) poids *m* lourd.

Hebrew ['hi:bru:]. (*a*) *a.* & *s.* hébraïque (*mf*); israélite (*mf*); (*b*) *s.m. Ling:* l'hébreu *m*.

heckle [hekl], *v.tr.* (at public meetings) interpeller. 'heckler, *s.* interpellateur, -trice.

hectic ['hektik], *a.* agité, fiévreux.

hedge [hedʒ]. I. *s.* haie *f.* II. *v.i.* se réserver; chercher des échappatoires. 'hedgehog ['hedʒ(h)og], *s.* hérisson *m*.

heel [hi:l], *s.* talon *m*; to take to one's heels, prendre la fuite.

heifer ['hefər], *s.* génisse *f*.

height [hait], *s.* 1. hauteur *f*; taille *f*, grandeur *f* (de qn); altitude *f* (d'une montagne). 2. colline *f*, éminence *f*. 3. apogée *m* (de la fortune); comble *m* (de la folie); h. of fashion, dernière mode.

heir [eər], *s.* héritier *m*. 'heiress, *s.* héritière *f.* 'heirloom, *s.* meuble *m*, bijou *m*, de famille.

hell [hel], *s.* l'enfer *m.* 'hellish, *a.* infernal; diabolique.

helm [helm], *s.* Nau: barre *f*; gouvernail *m.* †'helmsman, *s.* homme *m* de barre; timonier *m*.

helmet ['helmit], *s.* casque *m*.

help [help]. I. *s.* 1. aide *f*, secours *m*; to cry for h., crier au secours. 2. (pers.) aide *mf*; daily h., femme *f* de ménage; mother's h., aide familiale. II. *v.tr.* 1. (*a*) aider, secourir; h.! au secours! (*b*) faciliter (le progrès). 2. (at table) servir; h. yourself, servez-vous. 3. (*a*) things which can't be helped, choses *f*, événements *m*; inévitables; I can't h. it, je n'y puis rien; it can't be helped, tant pis! (*b*) s'empêcher; I can't h. laughing, je ne puis pas m'empêcher de rire; I can't h. it, c'est plus fort que moi; (*c*) no longer than one can h., le moins de temps possible. 'helper, *s.* aide *mf*. 'helpful, *a.* (personne) serviable; (chose) utile. 'helping, *s.* portion *f* (de nourriture). 'helpless, *a.* sans ressource; sans initiative; faible, impuissant. 'helplessness, *s.* faiblesse *f*; manque *m* d'énergie, d'initiative.

hem [hem]. I. *s.* 1. bord *m*. 2. ourlet *m*. II. †*v.tr.* 1. ourler. 2. to be hemmed in, être entouré.

hemisphere ['hemisfiər], *s.* hémisphère *m.*

hemp [hemp], *s.* chanvre *m.*

hen [hen], *s.* poule *f*; F: h. party, réunion *f* entre femmes. 'henpecked, *a.* (mari) dont la femme porte la culotte.

hence [hens], *adv.* 1. five years h., dans cinq ans (d'ici). 2. h. his anger, de là sa fureur.

her¹ [hər, həːr], *pers. pron.* 1. (*direct object*) la, (*before vowel*) l'; (*indirect object*) lui; have you seen h.? l'avez-vous vue? look at h., regardez-la. 2. (*stressed, after prep.*) elle; I'm thinking of h., je pense à elle; I found Martin and h. at the station, je les ai trouvés, Martin et elle, à la gare.

her², *poss.a.* son, *f* sa, *pl.* ses.

heraldry ['herəldri], *s.* le blason. he'raldic, *a.* héraldique.

herb [həːb], *s.* (*a*) herbe *f*; (*b*) herbs (for seasoning), fines herbes.

herd [həːd]. I. *s.* (*a*) troupeau *m*; (*b*) foule *f* (de gens). II. *v.i.* to h. together, (i) (*of animals*) vivre en troupeaux, s'assembler en troupeau; (ii) (*of people*) s'assembler en foule.

here [hiər], *adv.* 1. (*a*) ici; in h., ici; h. goes! allons-y! (*b*) (at roll call) présent. 2. here's your hat, voici votre chapeau; h. you are, vous voici! 3. (*a*) h. and there, par-ci par-là; çà et là; (*b*) that's neither h. nor there, cela ne fait rien.

heredity [hi'rediti], *s.* hérédité *f.* he'reditary, *a.* héréditaire.

†heresy ['herəsi], *s.* hérésie *f.* 'heretic, *s.* hérétique *mf.*

herewith [hiə'wið], *adv.* avec ceci; ci-joint.

heritage ['heritidʒ], *s.* héritage *m.*

hermetic [həː'metik], *a.* (bouchage) hermétique. -ally, *adv.* hermétiquement.

hermit ['həːmit], *s.* ermite *m.* 'hermitage, *s.* ermitage *m.*

†hero ['hiərou], *s.* héros *m*; h. worship, culte *m* des héros. he'roic, *a.* héroïque. 'heroine, *s.* héroïne *f.* 'heroism, *s.* héroïsme *m.*

heroin ['herouin], *s. Med:* héroïne *f.*

herring ['heriŋ], *s.* hareng *m*; red h., (i) hareng saur; (ii) F: diversion *f.*

hers [həːz], *poss.pron.* le sien, la sienne, les siens, les siennes; this book is h., ce livre est à elle.

herself [həː'self], *pers.pron.* elle-même (*reflexive*) se.

hesitate ['heziteit], *v.i.* hésiter. 'hesitant, *a.* hésitant, irrésolu. 'hesitating, *a.* hésitant, incertain. 2. *s.* hésitation *f.* hesi'tation, *s.* hésitation *f.*

hibernate ['haibəneit], *v.i.* hiberner.

hiccough ['hikʌp]. I. *s.* hoquet *m.* II. *v.i.* avoir le hoquet.

†hide¹ [haid]. 1. *v.tr.* cacher (from, de); to h. one's face, se cacher la figure.

2. *v.i.* se cacher. 'hide and seek, *s.* (jeu (de) cache-cache m.) 'hiding¹, *s.* to go into h., se cacher; h. place, cachette *f.*

hide², *s.* peau *f*, dépouille *f*; cuir *m.* 'hidebound, *a.* aux vues étroites. 'hiding²', *s. F:* raclée *f*, rossée *f.*

hideous ['hidiəs], *a.* hideux, affreux, effroyable. 2. d'une laideur repoussante. -ly, *adv.* affreusement.

high [hai]. I. *a.* 1. haut; how h. is that tree? quelle est la hauteur de cet arbre? 2. élevé; (*a*) to play for h. stakes, jouer gros (jeu); (*b*) h. speed, grande vitesse; (*c*) h. wind, vent fort. 3. (*principal*) the H. Street, la grande rue; *Ecc:* h. mass, la grande messe. 4. (*a*) (*of meat*) avancé, gâté; (*of game*) faisandé; *F:* (*of pers.*) ivre, parti, éméché; (*b*) it's h. time he went to school, il est grand temps qu'il aille à l'école. 5. h. and dry, (i) (*of ship*) à sec; (ii) (*of pers.*) F: abandonné, en plan. II. *adv.* haut, en haut; to aim h., viser haut. III. *s.* 1. *Meteor:* zone *f* de haute pression. 2. *F:* all-time h., record le plus élevé. 'highball, *s. U.S:* (i) whisky m à l'eau; (ii) whisky-soda m. 'highbrow, *s. F:* intellectuel, -elle. 'high-'handed, *a.* (*action*) arbitraire; (*autorité*) tyrannique. 'highland. 1. *s.* pays montagneux. 2. *attrib:* (*a*) des montagnes; montagnard; (*b*) de la Haute Écosse. 'highlander, *s.* habitant *m* de la Haute Écosse. 'highlight. I. *s. F:* clou *m* (de la fête). II. *v.tr.* mettre en vedette. 'highly, *adv.* fort, très; h. amusing, très amusant; h. paid services, services largement rétribués; h. strung, (homme) nerveux, exalté. 'Highness, *s.* (*title*) Altesse *f.* †'highway, *s.* (*a*) grande route; (*b*) *Adm:* voie *f* publique; the H. Code, le Code de la route; (*c*) *U.S:* dual h., route à double piste; h. patrolman, motard *m.* †'highwayman, *s.* voleur *m* de grand chemin.

hike [haik]. I. *s.* excursion *f* à pied. II. *v.i.* faire une excursion à pied; to hitch-h., faire de l'auto-stop. 'hiker, *s.* excursionniste *mf* à pied; hitch- h., auto-stoppeur, -euse.

hilarious [hi'leəriəs], *a.* gai, joyeux, hilare. hi'larity, *s.* hilarité *f*, gaieté *f.*

hill [hil], *s.* 1. (*a*) colline *f*, coteau *m*; (*b*) éminence *f*; (*on road*) côte *f*; *P.N:* h. 1 in 10, pente de 10%. 'hillock, *s.* petite colline; butte *f.* 'hillside, *s.* (flanc *m* de) coteau *m.* 'hilly, *a.* (terrain) accidenté; (chemin) à fortes pentes.

hilt [hilt], *s.* poignée *f*, garde *f* (d'épée); to prove an assertion up to the h., démontrer surabondamment une assertion.

him [him], *pers.pron.* *(direct object)* le, *(before vowel)* l'; *(indirect, stressed)* lui; **call h.**, appelez-le; **I speak to h.**, je lui parle; **he took his luggage with h.**, il prit ses bagages avec lui. **him'self**, *pers.pron.* lui-même; *(reflexive)* se.

hind [haind], *a.* **h. legs**, jambes de derrière; **h. quarters**, arrière-train m.

hinder ['hindər], *v.tr.* 1. gêner, embarrasser; retarder. 2. empêcher. **'hindrance**, *s.* empêchement m; obstacle m.

Hindi ['hindi], *s. Ling:* le hindi.

Hindu [hin'du:], *a. & s.* hindou, -oue. **'Hinduism**, *s.* hindouisme m.

hinge [hind3]. I. *s.* 1. gond m. 2. charnière f. II. *v.i.* tourner, pivoter; dépendre (d'une réponse).

hint [hint]. I. *s.* 1. *(a)* insinuation f; **to give s.o. a h.**, toucher un mot à qn; *(b)* signe m, indication f. 2. **hints for housewives**, conseils m aux ménagères; **maintenance hints**, conseils pour l'entretien (d'un appareil). II. *v.tr. & i.* insinuer; **to h. at sth.**, laisser entendre qch.

hip [hip], *s. Anat:* hanche f.

hippopotamus [hipə'pɔtəməs], *s.* hippopotame m.

hire ['haiər]. I. *s.* louage m (d'une voiture), *U.S:* location f (d'une maison); **h. purchase**, (H.P.), vente f à crédit. II. louer (une voiture, *U.S:* un ouvrier); *U.S:* **hired girl**, bonne f, domestique f.

his [hiz]. I. *poss.a.* son f, sa, *pl.* ses; **he fell on his back**, il tomba sur le dos. II. *poss.pron.* le sien, la sienne, les siens, les siennes; **this book is his**, ce livre est à lui.

hiss [his]. I. *s.* *(a)* sifflement m; *(b)* sifflet m. II. *v.tr. & i.* siffler.

†history ['hist(ə)ri], *s.* (l')histoire f. **his'torical**, *a.* historique.

†hit [hit]. I. *s.* 1. *(a)* frapper (qch., qn); donner un coup à (qn, qch.); *(b)* **to h. against sth.**, cogner contre qch.; *(c)* atteindre, toucher; *F:* **he couldn't h. a haystack**, il raterait un éléphant dans un couloir; *(d) F:* **you've h. it!** vous avez deviné juste; *(e)* **to h. it off with s.o.**, s'accorder avec qn; **to h. out at s.o.**, décocher un coup à qn. II. *s.* 1. coup m; **that's a h. at you**, c'est vous qui êtes visé. 2. *Th: etc.* succès m.

hitch [hitʃ]. I. *s.* contretemps m, anicroche f; **without a h.**, sans à-coup. II. *v.tr.* accrocher, attacher, fixer; **to h. a ride**, voyager enau to-stop; *see* HIKE.

hive [haiv], *s.* ruche f.

hoard [hɔːd]. I. *s.* amas m, accumulation f. II. *v.tr.* amasser; accumuler.

hoarding ['hɔːdiŋ], *s.* panneau-réclame m.

hoarse [hɔːs], *a.* enroué, rauque. **-ly**, *adv.* d'une voix rauque. **'hoarseness**, *s.* enrouement m.

hoax [houks]. I. *s.* mystification f. II. *v.tr.* mystifier, attraper (qn).

hobble ['hɔbl]. 1. *v.i.* clocher, clopiner. 2. *v.tr.* entraver (un cheval).

'hobby ['hɔbi], *s.* passe-temps favori.

hobo ['houbou], *s. U.S: F:* chemineau m, clochard m.

hock¹ [hɔk], *s.* vin m du Rhin.

hock², *s.* jarret m (de quadrupède).

hockey ['hɔki], *s.* (jeu m de) hockey m.

hoe [hou]. I. *s.* houe f, binette f. II. *v.tr.* houer, biner; sarcler.

hog [hɔg]. I. *s.* 1. *(a)* cochon m; *(b)* porc châtré. 2. *(pers.) F:* goinfre m, glouton m. II. *†v.tr. & i. F:* *(a)* monopoliser (qch.); **to h. the limelight**, accaparer la vedette; *(b)* manger, boire, goulûment. **'hoggish**, *a. (of pers.)* glouton, grossier.

Hogmanay [hɔgmə'nei], *s. Scot:* la Saint-Sylvestre.

hogshead ['hɔgzhed], *s.* tonneau m, barrique f.

hoist [hɔist], *v.tr.* hisser.

†hold [hould]. I. *v.* 1. *v.tr.* *(a)* tenir (qch.); **to h. sth. tight**, tenir qch. serré; **to h. sth. in position**, tenir qch. en place; **to h. views**, professer des opinions; *(b)* **to h. one's ground**, tenir bon, ferme; **to h. one's drink**, bien porter le vin; **car that holds the road well**, voiture qui tient bien la route; *P.T.T:* **h. the line**, ne quittez pas; *(c)* contenir; **car that holds six people**, voiture à six places; *(d)* tenir (une séance); avoir (une consultation); **the Motor Show is held in October**, le Salon de l'automobile se tient au mois d'octobre; *(e)* retenir (l'attention); **to h. one's breath**, retenir son haleine; **to h. water**, (i) être étanche; (ii) *F: (of theory)* tenir debout; *(f)* **to h. s.o. responsible**, tenir qn responsable; *F:* **to h. the baby**, être, se trouver, responsable (d'un événement, etc.). 2. *v.i.* *(a) (of rope, etc.)* tenir (bon); *(b) (of weather)* se maintenir; *(c) (of promise, etc.)* **to h. good**, être valable. II. *s.* prise f; **to have a h. over s.o.**, avoir prise sur qn; *F:* **where did you get h. of that?** où avez-vous péché ça? **'hold-all**, *s.* (sac m) fourre-tout m. **hold 'back**. 1. *v.tr.* retenir (qn, ses larmes); cacher (la vérité). 2. *v.i.* rester en arrière; hésiter. **'holder**, *s.* 1. *(pers.)* titulaire mf. 2. support m; monture f. 3. récipient m. **'hold 'forth**, *v.i. F:* pérorer. **hold 'in**, *v.tr.* **to h. oneself in**, se contenir. **'holding**, *s.* *(a) Fin:* avoir m (en actions); *(b)* petite propriété f; terrain m. **hold 'off**, *v.tr. & i.* *(a)* tenir (qn) à distance; *(b)* **the rain is holding off**, jusqu'ici il ne pleut pas. **hold 'on**, *v.tr.* ne pas

lâcher, ne pas abandonner (qch.).
hold 'out. 1. *v.tr.* tendre, offrir.
2. *v.i.* durer, tenir; how long can you
h.o.? combien de temps pouvez-vous
tenir? **hold 'up,** *v.tr.* (*a*) soutenir
(qn, qch.); (*b*) lever (qch.) (en l'air);
(*c*) arrêter, gêner (la circulation);
(*d*) attaquer (qn). **'hold-up,** *s.* 1.
arrêt *m*, embarras *m* (de voitures).
2. attaque; coup *m* à main armée.
hole [houl], *s.* 1. trou *m*; creux *m*,
cavité *f*; terrier *m* (de lapin). 2.
orifice *m*, ouverture *f*; *E:* inspection
h., orifice de visite.
holiday ['holidei], *s.* (*a*) jour *m* férié;
public h., fête *f* légale; (*b*) congé *m*;
the holidays, les vacances *f*; **where did
you spend your h.?** où avez-vous passé
vos vacances?
holiness ['houlinis], *s.* sainteté *f*.
hollow ['holou]. I. *a.* 1. creux, caver-
neux, évidé; **h.-eyed,** aux yeux caves.
2. (son) sourd. II. *adv.* (sonner)
creux. III. *s.* creux *m*; cavité *f*;
excavation *f*. IV. *v.tr.* to h. (out),
creuser, évider.
holly [holi], *s.* houx *m*.
hollyhock ['holihok], *s.* rose *f* trémière.
holster ['houlstər], *s.* étui *m* de revolver.
holy ['houli], *a.* (*a*) saint, sacré; the H.
Ghost, le Saint-Esprit; h. water, eau
bénite; (*b*) (*pers.*) saint, pieux.
homage ['homidʒ], *s.* hommage *m*.
home [houm]. I. *s.* 1. (*a*) chez-soi *m
inv*; foyer *m*; (*b*) at h., à la maison,
chez soi; to stay at h., garder la
maison; to feel at h., se sentir à l'aise;
to make oneself at h., faire comme chez
soi. 2. patrie *f*; pays (natal). 3. to
take an example nearer h., sans aller
chercher si loin. 4. old people's h.,
maison de retraite; children's h.,
home *m* d'enfants; nursing h.,
clinique *f*. II. *adv.* 1. à la maison;
chez soi; to go h., rentrer (chez soi).
2. to bring sth. h. to s.o., faire sentir
qch. à qn; to strike h., frapper juste;
porter coup. III. *attrib. a.* 1. h. circle,
cercle de famille; h. address, adresse
personnelle; the h. counties, les
comtés avoisinant Londres; *Sp:* h.
ground, terrain du club. 2. h. trade,
commerce intérieur. IV. *v.i.* 1. (of
pigeon) revenir au colombier. 2. (of
missile) revenir par auto-guidage.
'homing. 1. *a.* (*a*) (*pigeon*) voyageur.
2. *s. Av:* auto-guidage *m*. **'homeless,**
a. sans foyer. **'homely,** *a.* 1. simple,
modeste. 2. *U.S:* (of *pers.*) sans
beauté; plutôt laid. **'homesick,** *a.*
nostalgique. **'homesickness,** *s.* nostalgie *f*, mal *m* du pays.
homicide ['homisaid], *s.* homicide *m*.
homi'cidal, *a.* homicide.
†**homily** ['homili], *s.* homélie *f*.
honest ['onist], *a.* (*a*) honnête, probe;
(*b*) vrai, sincère. **-ly,** *adv.* (*a*) honnête-

ment, loyalement; (*b*) sincèrement.
'honesty, *s.* (*a*) honnêteté *f*, probité *f*;
(*b*) véracité *f*, sincérité *f*.
honey ['hʌni], *s.* miel *m*. **'honeycomb,** *s.*
rayon *m* de miel. **'honeymoon,** *s.* lune
f de miel; voyage *m* de noces. **'honeysuckle,** *s.* chèvrefeuille *m*.
honorary ['onərəri], *a.* honoraire; non
rétribué, bénévole.
honour ['onər]. I. *s.* honneur *m*. 1. in
h. bound, obligé de l'honneur; on
one's h., engagé d'honneur. 2. distinction *f* honorifique. 3. Your H.,
Monsieur le juge. II. *v.tr.* honorer;
to h. one's signature, faire honneur à
sa signature. **'honourable,** *a.* honorable. **-bly,** *adv.* honorablement.
hood [hud], *s.* 1. capuchon *m*; capeline
f; *Sch:* = épitoge *f*. 2. *Aut:* (*a*)
capote *f*; (*b*) *U.S:* capot *m*.
hoodwink ['hudwink], *v.tr. F:* tromper;
donner le change à (qn).
†**hoof** [hu:f], *s.* 1. sabot *m* (de cheval,
etc.). II. *v.tr. F:* to h. s.o. out, chasser
qn à coups de pied.
hook [huk]. I. *s.* 1. crochet *m*, croc *m*;
(*a*) (for hanging clothes), patère *f*;
(*b*) agrafe *f*; h. and eye, agrafe et
œillet *m*. 2. *Fish:* hameçon *m*. II.
v.tr. 1. accrocher (qch. à qch.). 2. *Cl:*
to h. up, agrafer. 3. crocher, gaffer
(un objet flottant); prendre (un
poisson) à l'hameçon.
hooligan ['hu:ligən], *s.* voyou *m*.
hoop [hu:p], *s.* 1. cercle *m* (de tonneau).
2. cerceau *m*. **'hoopla,** *s.* jeu *m* des
anneaux.
hoot [hu:t]. I. *v.* 1. *v.i.* (of owl) ululer;
Aut: klaxonner; (of siren) mugir.
2. *v.tr.* huer, conspuer (qn); siffler
(une pièce de théâtre). II. *s.* ululement
(de hibou); coup *m* de sirène, de
klaxon. **'hooter,** *s.* sirène *f*; *Aut:*
avertisseur *m*, klaxon *m*.
hoover ['hu:vər], *v.tr. F:* passer l'aspirateur (sur qch.) (*from* Hoover
(*R.t.m.*), marque d'aspirateur).
†**hop** [hop]. I. *v.i.* sauter, sautiller. II.
s. (*a*) petit saut *m*; sautillement *m*;
F: to catch s.o. on the h., prendre qn
au pied levé; (*b*) *Av:* étape *f*.
hope [houp]. I. *v.i. & v.tr.* espérer; to h.
for sth., espérer qch. II. *s.* espérance
f; espoir *m*; *F:* what a h.! si vous
comptez là-dessus! **'hopeful,** *a.* plein
d'espoir; (avenir) qui donne de belles
espérances, qui promet. **-fully,** *adv.*
(travailler, etc.) avec bon espoir, avec
confiance. **'hopefulness,** *s.* (bon)
espoir *m*; confiance *f*. **'hopeless,** *a.*
sans espoir; désespéré (maladie)
incurable; (enfant, etc.) incorrigible;
it's a h. job, c'est désespérant. **-ly,**
adv. (vivre) sans espoir; regarder
(qn, qch.) avec désespoir; (vaincu)
irrémédiablement. **'hopelessness,** *s.*
état *m* désespéré.

hops [hops], s.pl. houblon m.

horizon [hə'raiz(ə)n], s. horizon m.

horizontal [hɔri'zɔnt(ə)l], a. horizontal. -ally, adv. horizontalement.

hormone ['hɔːmoun], s. hormone f.

horn [hɔːn], s. 1. corne f; bois m (d'un cerf); F: to draw in one's horns, en rabattre. 2. Mus: cor m; French h., cor d'harmonie. 3. Aut: avertisseur m, klaxon m. 'horny, a. corné, en corne; (of hands) calleux.

hornet ['hɔːnit], s. Z: frelon m.

horoscope ['hɔrəskoup], s. horoscope m.

horrify ['hɔrifai], v.tr. horrifier, faire horreur à (qn); F: scandaliser (qn). 'horrible, a. horrible, affreux. -ibly, adv. horriblement, affreusement. 'horrid, a. horrible, affreux; F: to be h. to s.o., être méchant envers qn. 'horror, s. 1. horreur f; h. film, film d'épouvante. 2. (a) chose f horrible, affreuse; F: it gives me the horrors, (a) cela me met les nerfs en pelote; (b) F: (of child) a little h., un petit diable. 'horror-stricken, -struck, a. saisi d'horreur.

horse [hɔːs], s. 1. cheval m; h. racing, courses fpl de chevaux; h. show, concours m hippique. 2. (vaulting) h., cheval de bois, d'arçons; (clothes) h., séchoir m. 'horseback, s. on h., à cheval; Cu: angels on h., friture f d'huîtres au lard. horse-'chestnut, s. marron m d'Inde; h.-c. (tree), marronnier m d'Inde. 'horsehair, s. crin m (de cheval). 'horseplay, s. jeu m brutal. 'horse power, s. (abbr. h.p.) cheval-vapeur m. 'horse-radish, s. Cu: raifort m. 'horseshoe, s. fer m à cheval. 'horsewhip. I. s. cravache f. II. v.tr. cravacher, sangler (qn). 'horsey, a. (of pers.) hippomane; qui affecte le langage, le costume, des grooms et des jockeys.

horticulture ['hɔːtikʌltʃər], s. horticulture f.

hose [houz], s. 1. Com: bas mpl. 2. manche f à eau.

hospitable [hɔs'pitəbl], a. hospitalier. -ibly, adv. d'une manière accueillante. hospi'tality, s. hospitalité f.

hospital [hɔs'pitl], s. hôpital m.

host [houst], s. 1. (a) hôte m; (b) hôtelier m. 2. Ecc: hostie f. 'hostess, s. (a) hôtesse f; (b) hôtelière f; (c) air h., hôtesse de l'air.

hostage ['hɔstidʒ], s. otage m.

hostel ['hɔstəl], s. (a) pension f, foyer m; (b) youth h., auberge f de la jeunesse. 'hosteller, s. youth h., ajiste mf. 'hostelling, s. youth h., ajisme m.

hostile ['hɔstail], a. hostile, ennemi, opposé (to, à). hos'tility, s. 1. hostilité f, animosité f. 2. pl. hostilités; état m de guerre.

hot [hɔt]. I. a. 1. (a) chaud; boiling h., bouillant; to be h., (i) (of pers.) avoir

chaud; (ii) (of weather) faire chaud; (b) brûlant; Cu: piquant. 2. (a) violent; to have a h. temper, s'emporter facilement; (b) (of struggle) acharné; (of resistance) vigoureux: Sp: h. favourite, grand favori. 3. F: to make it (too) h. for s.o., rendre la situation intenable à qn; h. car, voiture volée. II. v.tr. F: to h. sth. up, (i) chauffer, (ii) faire réchauffer, qch.; Aut: hotted-up engine, moteur gonflé. 'hothead, s. (pers.) tête f chaude, impétueux, exalté. 'hothouse, s. serre f chaude. 'hot-'tempered, a. emporté, vif. 'hot-'water bottle, s. bouillotte f.

hotel [hou'tel], s. hôtel m; private h., residential h., pension f de famille.

hotelier [(h)ou'teliei], s. hôtelier m.

hound [haund]. I. s. chien m courant; the hounds, la meute. II. v.tr. to h. s.o. down, poursuivre qn avec acharnement.

hour [auər], s. heure f; half an h., une demi-heure; a quarter of an h., un quart d'heure; h. by h., d'une heure à l'autre; to pay s.o. by the h., payer qn à l'heure; five miles an h., cinq milles à l'heure; D: to take hours over sth., mettre un temps interminable à faire qch.; in the small hours, fort avant dans la nuit; attrib. h. hand, petite aiguille (de montre). 'hourly, I. a. de toutes les heures; (salaire) à l'heure. II. adv. toutes les heures; d'heure en heure.

house. I. s. (haus). 1. (a) maison f; if you come to my h. this evening, si vous venez chez moi ce soir; to move h., déménager; to keep open h., tenir table ouverte; F: the H., Parl: la Chambre (i) des Communes, (ii) des Lords; Fin: la Bourse; (b) public h., café m, débit m de boissons; a drink on the h., consommation f payée aux frais de la maison. 2. famille f, dynastie f. 3. Th: auditoire m, assistance f; a good h., une salle pleine; first h., première séance f. 4. attrib. h. telephone, téléphone intérieur; h. coal, charbon m de ménage; under h. arrest, en résidence surveillée. II. v.tr. (hauz) loger, héberger (qn); pourvoir au logement de (la population); caser (un ustensile, etc.). 'house-agent, s. agent m immobilier. 'houseboat, s. péniche f (aménagée en habitation). 'housebreaker, s. 1. cambrioleur m. 2. Const: démolisseur m. 'housebreaking, s. 1. cambriolage m. 2. démolition f. 'housecoat, s. Cl: peignoir m; robe f d'intérieur. 'houseful, s. maisonnée f; pleine maison (d'invités, etc.). 'household, s. la famille; le ménage; h. expenses, frais mpl de ménage. 'housekeeper, s. 1. concierge mf. 2. femme f de charge; gouvernante f.

3. my wife's a good h., ma femme est bonne ménagère. **'housekeeping,** s. le ménage; les soins m du ménage. **'housemaid,** s. bonne f; femme f de chambre. **'housemaster,** s.m., **'housemistress,** s.f. Sch: professeur m chargé de la surveillance d'un internat. **'houseroom,** s. place f (pour loger qn, qch.). **'house-warming,** s. pendaison f de la crémaillère. †**housewife,** s. maîtresse f de maison; femme f d'intérieur. **'housework,** s. travaux mpl domestiques; **to do the h.,** faire le ménage. **'housing,** s. 1. logement m; **the h. problem,** la crise du logement. **2.** E: logement, bâti m, cage f; carter m, boîte f.

hovel ['hɔvl], s. taudis m.

hover ['hɔvər], v.i. (of bird) planer; (of pers.) errer, rôder (autour de qn). **'hovercraft,** s. aéroglisseur m.

how [hau], adv. 1. comment; **h. are you?** comment allez-vous? **2.** (a) **h. much, h. many,** combien (de); **h. old are you?** quel âge avez-vous? (b) **h. pretty she is!** comme elle est jolie! **h. I wish I could!** si seulement je pouvais!

however [hau'evər], adv. 1. (a) de quelque manière que; **h. that may be,** quoi qu'il en soit; (b) **h. good his work is,** quelque excellent que soit son travail; **h. little,** si peu que ce soit. **2.** toutefois, cependant, pourtant.

howl [haul]. **I.** v.i. & tr. hurler; mugir. **II.** s. (also **howling**) hurlement m; mugissement m. **'howler,** s. grosse gaffe f; Sch: perle f. **'howling** a., (tempête) furieuse; F: (succès) fou; F: (injustice) criante.

hub [hʌb], s. 1. moyeu m. 2. centre m d'activité.

hubbub ['hʌbʌb], s. remue-ménage m; vacarme m.

huddle ['hʌdl]. **I.** v.tr. & i. 1. entasser pêle-mêle; **to h. together, se** tasser. **2. huddled (up) in a corner,** blotti dans un coin. **II.** s. tas m confus; F: **to go into a h.,** tenir une séance secrète.

buff [hʌf], s. **to be in a h.,** être froissé. **'huffy,** a. 1. susceptible. 2. fâché.

†**hug** [hʌg]. **I.** v.tr. 1. étreindre, embrasser (qn). 2. Nau: **to h.** the shore, raser, longer, la côte; Aut: **to h.** the kerb, serrer le trottoir. **II.** s. étreinte f.

huge [hju:dʒ], a. énorme, vaste; immense.

hull [hʌl], s. coque f (de navire).

hullo [hʌ'lou], int. (a) ohé! holà! (b) bonjour! (c) P.T.T.: allô!

†**hum** [hʌm]. **I.** v. 1. v.i. bourdonner; ronfler. 2. v.tr. fredonner (un air). **II.** s. bourdonnement m; ronflement m; ronron m (d'un moteur).

human ['hju:mən]. **I.** a. humain. **2.** s. être humain. **hu'manity,** s. humanité f.

humane [hju(:)'mein], a. (a) humain, compatissant; (b) clément; qui évite de faire souffrir.

humble ['hʌmbl]. **I.** a. humble. **-bly,** adv. 1. humblement. 2. (vivre) modestement. **II.** v.tr. humilier, mortifier (qn); **to h. oneself,** s'abaisser.

humbug ['hʌmbʌg], s. 1. charlatanisme m; blague f. 2. charlatan m; blagueur m. 3. Cu: = bêtise f de Cambrai.

humdrum ['hʌmdrʌm], a. monotone.

†**humerus** ['hju:mərəs], s. Anat: humérus m.

humid ['hju:mid], a. humide. **hu'midify,** v.tr. humidificateur m. **hu'midity,** s. humidité f.

humiliate [hju(:)'milieit], v.tr. humilier, mortifier. **humili'ation,** s. humiliation f, affront m, mortification f. **hu'mility,** s. humilité f.

humour ['hju:mər]. **I.** s. 1. humeur f, disposition f; **in a good h.,** de bonne humeur. 2. humour m. **II.** v.tr. ménager (qn). **'humorist,** s. 1. farceur m. 2. Th: comique m. **'humorous,** a. plein d'humour; comique, drôle.

hump [hʌmp]. **I.** s. bosse f. **II.** v.tr. arquer, bomber (le dos). **'humpbacked,** a. (of pers.) bossu; (pont) en dos d'âne.

humus ['hju:məs], s. humus m; terreau m.

hunch [hʌn(t)ʃ]. **I.** v.tr. arrondir (le dos); voûter (les épaules). **II.** s. f: **to have a h. that . . .,** soupçonner que . . . **'hunchback,** s. (pers.) bossu, -ue.

hundred ['hʌndrəd], num. a. & s. cent (m); **about a h.,** une centaine (de). **'hundredth,** num. a. & s. centième (m). **'hundredweight,** s. (a) poids m de 112 livres; (b) U.S: poids de 100 livres.

Hungarian [hʌŋ'gɛəriən], a. & s. hongrois, -oise.

hunger ['hʌŋgər], s. faim f; h. strike, grève f de la faim. **'hungry,** a. affamé; **to be h.,** avoir faim. **-grily,** adv. avidement, voracement.

hunk [hʌŋk], s. gros morceau m (de fromage); quignon m (de pain).

hunt [hʌnt]. **I.** (a) chasser au chien courant; chasser à courre; (b) **to h. for sth.,** chercher (à découvrir) qch. **II.** s. 1. chasseur m; tueur m (de lions, etc.). 2. cheval m de chasse. **'hunt 'down,** v.tr. traquer (une bête); mettre (qn) aux abois. **'hunting,** s. (a) chasse f (à courre); (b) **bargain h.,** la chasse aux soldes; **to go house h.,** se mettre à la recherche d'une maison, d'un logement; (c) **h. ground,** (i) terrain m de chasse; (ii) endroit m propice (aux collectionneurs, etc.). **'hunt 'out,** v.tr. dénicher, déterrer (qch.). †**'huntsman,** s. 1. chasseur m (à courre). 2. veneur m, piqueur m.

hurdle ['hə:dl], s. 1. claie f. 2. Sp: barrière f, obstacle m; (horse racing) haie f.

hurl [hə:l], v.tr. lancer (qch.) avec violence (at, contre); to h. reproaches at s.o., cribler, accabler, qn de reproches.

hurrah [hu'rɑ:], **hurray** [hu'rei], int. & s. hourra m.

hurricane ['harikən], s. ouragan m, tornade f.

hurry ['hari]. I. v. 1. v.tr. hâter, presser, bousculer (qn); work that cannot be hurried, travail qui demande du temps. 2. v.i. se hâter, se presser, se dépêcher; h. up! dépêchez-vous! II. s. hâte f, précipitation f; to be in a h. être pressé, précipité; (travail) fait à la hâte. **'hurried**, a. (pas) pressé, précipité; (travail) fait à la hâte.

‡hurt [hə:t], v.tr. 1. faire du mal à, blesser (qn); to be, get, h., être blessé. 2. faire de la peine à (qn). 3. (of thing) nuire à, abîmer (qch.).

husband ['hazbənd], s. mari m, époux m.

hush [haʃ]. I. v. 1. v.tr. apaiser, faire taire. 2. v.i. se taire; faire silence. II. s. silence m, calme m. III. int. chut! silence! 'hush-hush, a. F: secret. **hush up**, v.tr. étouffer (un scandale).

husk [hask], s. cosse f, gousse f (de pois, etc.).

husky[1] ['haski], a. (of voice) enroué. **'huskiness**, s. enrouement m (de la voix).

†husky[2], s. chien m esquimau.

hustle ['hasl]. I. v.tr. bousculer; presser. 2. v.i. se dépêcher, se presser. II. s. hâte f.

hut [hat], s. hutte f, cabane f.

hutch [hatʃ], s. clapier m.

hyacinth ['haiəsinθ], s. jacinthe f.

hybrid ['haibrid], a. & s. hybride (m).

hydrangea [hai'drein(d)ʒə], s. hortensia m.

hydrant ['haidrənt], s. prise f d'eau; fire h., bouche f d'incendie.

hydraulic [hai'drɔ:lik], a. hydraulique.

hydrochloric [haidrə'klɔrik], a. (acide) chlorhydrique.

hydroelectric ['haidroui'lektrik], a. hydro-électrique. **hydroelec'tricity**, s. hydro-électricité f.

hydrogen ['haidrədʒ(ə)n], s. hydrogène m.

hydroplane ['haidrouplein], s. hydroglisseur m.

hyena [hai'i:nə], s. hyène f.

hygiene ['haidʒi:n], s. hygiène f. **hy'gienic**, a. hygiénique.

hymn [him], s. hymne f, cantique m.

hyphen ['haif(ə)n], s. trait m d'union. **'hyphenate**, v.tr. mettre un trait d'union à (un mot); **hyphenated word**, mot à trait d'union.

hypnotism ['hipnətism], s. hypnotisme m. **hyp'notic**, a. hypnotique. **'hypnotist**, s. hypnotiste mf. **'hypnotize**, v.tr. hypnotiser.

hypochondriac [haipou'kɔndriæk], s. malade mf imaginaire.

hypocrisy [hi'pɔkrisi], s. hypocrisie f. **'hypocrite**, s. hypocrite mf. **hypo'critical**, a. hypocrite.

hypotenuse [hai'pɔtinju:z], s. Mth: hypoténuse f.

hypothetical [haipə'θetikl], a. hypothétique, supposé. **hysteria** [his'tiəriə], s. hystérie f. **hys'terical**, a. (a) Med: hystérique; (b) sujet à des crises de nerfs; h. laugh, rire nerveux. **-ally**, adv. to laugh h., rire nerveusement; avoir le fou rire; to weep h., avoir une crise de larmes. **hys'terics**, s.pl. (a) crise f de nerfs; (b) fou rire m.

I

I[1], **i** [ai], s. (la lettre) I, i m; to dot one's i's, mettre les points sur les i.

I[2], pers. pron. (a) je, (before vowel sound) j'; I sing, je chante; (b) moi; it is I, c'est moi; (stressed) I'll do it, c'est moi qui le ferai.

ice [ais]. I. s. 1. glace f; my feet are like i., j'ai les pieds glacés; to break the i., (i) rompre la glace; (ii) faire cesser la contrainte; (ii) entamer un sujet (délicat); Ind: dry i., neige f carbonique. 2. Cu: (also ice-cream) strawberry i., glace à la fraise. 3. attrib. i. axe, piolet m; i. floe, banquise f; banc m de glace; i. hockey, hockey m sur glace; i. skating, patinage m (sur glace). II. v.tr. geler, congeler. 2. rafraîchir, frapper (une boisson). 3. glacer (un gâteau). 4. Av: to i. up, se givrer. **'iceberg**, s.

iceberg m. **'icicle**, s. glaçon m. **'icy**, a. glacial.

Icelander ['aislændər], s. Islandais, -aise. **Ice'landic**, a. (a) islandais, d'Islande; (b) s.m. Ling: Islandais m.

idea [ai'diə], s. idée f; to have some i. of chemistry, avoir des notions de chimie; I had no i. that . . ., j'ignorais absolument que . . . ; I have an i. that I've seen it, j'ai l'impression de l'avoir vu; F: what's the big i.? qu'est-ce qui vous prend?

ideal [ai'di:əl], a. & s. idéal (m). **i'dealist**, s. idéaliste mf. **i'dealize**, v.tr. idéaliser. **i'deally**, adv. idéalement.

identify [ai'dentifai], v.tr. 1. identifier (sth. with sth., qch. avec qch.). 2. constater, établir, l'identité de (qn). **i'dentical**, a. identique. **-ally**, adv.

identiquement. identifi'cation, s. identification *f.* i'dentity, s. identité *f*; i. card, carte *f* d'identité; mistaken i., erreur *f* sur la personne.

idiom [i'diəm], s. 1. idiome m. 2. idiotisme m. idio'matic, a. idiomatique; i. phrase, idiotisme m.

†idiosyncrasy [idiou'siŋkrəsi], s. idiosyncrasie *f*.

idiot ['idiət], s. (a) Med: idiot, -ote; (b) imbécile mf; F: you i.! espèce d'imbécile! 'idiocy, s. (a) idiotie *f* (congénitale); (b) stupidité *f*. idi'otic, a. bête. -ally, adv. bêtement.

idle ['aidl]. I. a. 1. (a) inoccupé, oisif; (of machine) au repos. 2. paresseux. 3. inutile; i. curiosity, simple curiosité. II. v.i. 1. fainéanter, paresser. 2. (of engine) tourner au ralenti. 'idleness, s. 1. oisiveté *f*, désœuvrement m. 2. paresse *f*. 'idler, s. 1. oisif, -ive; désœuvré, -ée. 2. paresseux, -euse. 'idly, adv. 1. sans travailler. 2. paresseusement.

idol ['aidl], s. idole *f*. 'idolize, v.tr. idolâtrer, adorer.

if [if], conj. 1. (a) si; if I'm late I apologise, si je suis en retard je fais mes excuses; if I am free I shall go out, si je suis libre je sortirai; if I were free I would go out, si j'étais libre je sortirais; (b) he will give you a shilling for it if anything, il vous en donnera un shilling, et encore! (c) if I were you, si j'étais vous, à votre place; (d) (exclamatory) if only I had known! si seulement je l'avais su! (e) as if, comme (si); as if by chance, comme par hasard. 2. (concessive) pleasant weather if cold, temps agréable bien que froid. 3. (= whether) do you know if he's at home? savez-vous s'il est chez lui? 4. your ifs and buts, vos si et vos mais.

ignite [ig'nait], 1. v.tr. mettre le feu à (qch.). 2. v.i. prendre feu. ig'nition, s. 1. ignition *f*. 2. Aut: allumage m.

ignoble [ig'noubl], a. ignoble; infâme, vil.

ignominious [ignə'miniəs], a. ignominieux. -ly, adv. avec ignominie.

ignore [ig'nɔːr], v.tr. ne tenir aucun compte de (qch.); to i. the facts, méconnaître les faits; to i. an invitation, ne pas répondre à une invitation. 'ignorance, s. ignorance *f*; i. of the law is no excuse, nul n'est censé ignorer la loi. 'ignorant, a. ignorant; to be i. of a fact, ignorer un fait.

ill [il]. I. a. 1. mauvais; of i. repute, mal famé. 2. malade; souffrant; i. health, mauvaise santé. II. s. mal m. III. adv. mal; i. informed, (i) mal renseigné; (ii) ignorant. ill-ad'vised, a. (pers.) malavisé; (action) peu judicieux. ill-con'sidered, a. peu réfléchi. ill-de'fined, a. mal défini. ill-dis-'posed, a. mal intentionné.

illegal [i'li:g(ə)l], a. illégal. -ally, adv. illégalement.

illegible [i'ledʒibl], a. illisible.

illegitimate [ili'dʒitimit], a. illégitime.

ill-feeling, s. ressentiment m, rancune *f*. ill-'gotten, a. (bien) mal acquis. ill-'humoured, a. de mauvaise humeur; maussade.

illicit [i'lisit], a. illicite; clandestin.

illiterate [i'litərit], a. illettré; analphabète.

ill-'mannered, a. grossier; impoli. ill-'natured, a. d'un mauvais caractère. 'illness, s. maladie *f*.

illogical [i'lɔdʒik(ə)l], a. illogique; peu logique. -ally, adv. illogiquement.

ill-'timed, a. mal à propos; inopportun. ill-'treat, v.tr. maltraiter; brutaliser.

illuminate [i'lju:mineit], v.tr. éclairer; illuminated sign, enseigne lumineuse. illumi'nation, s. (a) éclairage m; (b) illumination *f* (d'un édifice). il-'luminating, a. 1. éclairant. 2. (entretien) éclaircissant.

illusion [i'lu:ʒ(ə)n], s. illusion *f*. il-'lusionist, s. prestidigitateur m; illusionniste m. il'lusory, a. illusoire.

illustrate ['iləstreit], v.tr. 1. éclairer, expliquer (une règle). 2. illustrer. illus'tration, s. 1. explication *f*, exemple m. 2. illustration *f*, image *f*.

image ['imidʒ], s. image *f*. i'maginable, a. imaginable; F: imaginary, a. imaginaire. imagi'nation, s. imagination *f*; i'maginative, a. imaginatif. i'magine, v.tr. (a) imaginer, concevoir, se figurer (qch.); (b) croire (qu'on entend qch.).

imbecile ['imbisail, -si:l], s. imbécile mf; F: you i.! espèce d'idiot! imbe'cility, s. imbécillité *f*.

imitate ['imiteit], v.tr. imiter; copier. imi'tation, s. (a) imitation *f*; beware of imitations, méfiez-vous des contrefaçons; (b) attrib. factice; i. jewellery, bijouterie fausse. 'imitative, a. imitatif. 'imitator, s. imitateur, -trice.

immaculate [i'mækjulit], a. 1. immaculé; Ecc: the I. Conception, l'Immaculée Conception. 2. (of dress) irréprochable, impeccable.

immaterial [imə'tiəriəl], a. 1. immatériel. 2. peu important.

immature [imə'tjuər], a. pas mûr.

immediate [i'mi:djət], a. immédiat; the i. future, le proche avenir. im'mediately. I. adv. immédiatement; tout de suite. II. conj. dès que.

immense [i'mens], a. immense, vaste; (quantité) énorme. -ly, adv. F: énormément.

immerse [i'mə:s], v.tr. immerger, submerger, plonger (qch.) (dans un liquide); immersed in one's work, absorbé dans son travail. im'mersion, s. 1. immersion *f*; i. heater, (i) chauffe-eau m électrique; (ii) élément m chauffant. 2. absorption *f* (d'esprit).

imminent ['iminənt], a. imminent. 'imminence, s. imminence f.

immobile [i'moubail], a. fixe; immobile. immo'bility [-'bil-], s. immobilité f. immobili'zation [-bil-], s. immobilisation f. im'mobilize [-bil], v.tr. immobiliser.

immoderate [i'mɔd(ə)rit], a. immodéré.

immoral [i'mɔrəl], a. immoral; (of pers.) dissolu. immo'rality, s. immoralité f.

immortal [i'mɔːtl], a. & s. immortel (m). immor'tality, s. immortalité f.

immovable [i'muːvəbl], a. 1. fixe; à demeure. 2. (volonté) inébranlable.

immune [i'mjuːn], a. à l'abri d'une (contagion); immunisé. im'munity, s. immunité f. immuni'sation, s. immunisation f. 'immunize, v.tr. Med: immuniser.

imp [imp], s. diablotin m, lutin m; (of child) petit diable m.

impact ['impækt], s. choc m, impact m.

impair [im'pɛər], v.tr. affaiblir; altérer (la santé); diminuer (les forces).

impartial [im'pɑːʃ(ə)l], a. impartial. -ally, adv. impartialement. imparti'ality, s. impartialité f.

impassable [im'pɑːsəbl], a. infranchissable.

impassive [im'pæsiv], a. impassible.

impatience [im'peiʃ(ə)ns], s. impatience f. im'patient, a. impatient. -ly, adv. avec impatience.

impeccable [im'pekəbl], a. impeccable. -ly, adv. impeccablement.

impecunious [impi'kjuːniəs], a. impécunieux.

impede [im'piːd], v.tr. empêcher, entraver, gêner. im'pediment, s. empêchement m, obstacle m.

†impel [im'pei], v.tr. pousser, forcer.

impending [im'pendiŋ], a. (danger) imminent, menaçant.

impenetrable [im'penitrəbl], a. impénétrable.

impenitent [im'penit(ə)nt], a. impénitent.

imperative [im'perətiv], a. & s. impératif (m).

imperceptible [impə'septəbl], a. imperceptible; insaisissable. -ly, adv. imperceptiblement; insensiblement.

imperfect [im'pəːfikt], a. imparfait, incomplet, défectueux; a. Gram: imparfait m, -ly, adv. imparfaitement.

imperial [im'piəriəl], a. impérial. im-'perialism, s. impérialisme m.

†imperil [im'peril], v.tr. mettre en péril.

imperious [im'piəriəs], a. impérieux, arrogant. -ly, adv. impérieusement.

impermeable [im'pəːmiəbl], a. imperméable, étanche.

impersonal [im'pəːsənl], a. impersonnel.

impersonate [im'pəːsəneit], v.tr. se faire passer pour (qn). imperso'nation, s. imitation f (de qn). im'personator, s. imitateur, -trice.

impertinence [im'pəːtinəns], s. impertinence f, insolence f. im'pertinent, a. impertinent, insolent. -ly, adv. avec impertinence; d'un ton insolent.

impervious [im'pəːviəs], a. impénétrable. im'perviousness, s. impénétrabilité f.

impetigo [impi'taigou], s. Med: impétigo m.

impetuous [im'petjuəs], a. impétueux. -ly, adv. impétueusement. impetu'osity, im'petuousness, s. impétuosité f.

impetus ['impitəs], s. vitesse f acquise; élan m; impulsion f.

impinge [im'pin(d)ʒ], v.ind.tr. to i. on sth., se heurter à qch.; empiéter sur qch.

impious ['impiəs], a. impie.

implacable [im'plækəbl], a. implacable. -ly, adv. implacablement.

implement ['impliment], s. outil m, instrument m, ustensile m.

implicate ['implikeit], v.tr. impliquer. impli'cation, s. implication f (in, dans); insinuation f; portée f (d'un discours); by i., implicitement. im'plicit, a. (condition) implicite; (confiance) aveugle; (obéissance) absolue. -ly, adv. implicitement; (obéir) aveuglément.

implore [im'plɔːr], v.tr. implorer, supplier.

imply [im'plai], v.tr. impliquer. im-'plied, a. (consentement) implicite, tacite.

impolite [impə'lait], a. impoli (to, envers). -ly, adv. impoliment. impo'liteness, s. impolitesse f.

import. I. s. ['impɔːt] 1. sens m, signification f. 2. Com: imports, importations f; i. duty, droit m d'entrée. II. v. [im'pɔːt] Com: importer (des marchandises). im'portance, s. importance f. im'portant, a. important. impor'tation, s. importation f. im'porter, s. importateur, -trice.

importune [impɔː'tjuːn], v.tr. importuner. im'portunate, a. importun.

impose [im'pouz]. 1. v.tr. imposer. 2. v.i. to i. upon s.o., en imposer à qn; abuser de l'amabilité de qn. im-'posing, a. imposant; grandiose. impo'sition, s. imposition f; abus m (de la bonne volonté de qn).

impossible [im'pɔsəbl], a. impossible. impossi'bility, s. impossibilité f.

impostor [im'pɔstər], s. imposteur m. im'posture, s. imposture f.

impotence ['impət(ə)ns], s. (a) impuissance f; (b) impotence f. 'impotent, a. (a) impuissant; (b) impotent.

impoverish [im'pɔv(ə)riʃ], v.tr. appauvrir.

impracticable [im'præktikəbl], a. infaisable, impraticable.

impregnate ['impregneit], v.tr. imprégner, imbiber (with, de).

impress ['impres], v.tr. 1. faire impression sur, impressionner (qn); he impressed me, il m'a fait une impression favorable; I'm not impressed, cela me laisse froid. 2. to 1. sth. (up)on s.o., faire bien comprendre qch. à qn. im'pression, a. 1. impression f. 2. tirage m, édition f (d'un livre). im'pressionable, a. impressionnable, sensible. im'pressionism, s. A. & A: impressionnisme m. im'pressionist, s. impressionniste mf. impressio-'nistic, a. impressionniste. im'pressive, a. impressionnant.

imprint ['imprint], s. empreinte f; firme f, rubrique f (d'un éditeur).

imprison [im'prizn], v.tr. emprisonner. im'prisonment, s. emprisonnement m.

improbable [im'prɔbbl], a. improbable, invraisemblable. improba'bility, s. improbabilité f; invraisemblance f.

impromptu [im'prɔm(p)tjuː], a. adv. & s. impromptu (m).

improper [im'prɔpər], a. 1. inconvenant. 2. déplacé. impro'priety, s. (a) inconvenance f; (b) inconvenance f.

improve [im'pruːv]. 1. v.tr. (a) améliorer; perfectionner; (b) v.ind.tr. to i. (up)on, améliorer. 2. v.i. s'améliorer. im'provement, s. 1. amélioration f; perfectionnement m. 2. to be an i. on sth., surpasser qch.; my new car is a great i. on the old one, ma nouvelle voiture est bien supérieure à l'ancienne.

improvident [im'prɔvidənt], a. (a) imprévoyant; (b) prodigue.

improvise ['imprəvaiz], v.tr. improviser. improvi'sation, s. improvisation f.

imprudent [im'pruːd(ə)nt], a. imprudent. -ly, adv. imprudemment. im'prudence, s. imprudence f.

impudence ['impjud(ə)ns], s. impudence f, effronterie f. 'impudent, a. effronté, insolent. -ly, adv. effrontément.

impulse ['impʌls], s. impulsion f. im'pulsive, a. impulsif. -ly, adv. par impulsion.

impunity [im'pjuːniti], s. impunité f; with i., impunément.

impure [im'pjuər], a. impur. im'purity, s. 1. impureté f. 2. pl. saletés f; corps m étrangers.

impute [im'pjuːt], v.tr. imputer. impu-'tation, s. imputation f.

[in] 1. prep. 1. (a) en, à, dans; in Europe, en Europe; in Japan, au Japon; in Paris, à Paris; (b) in the crowd, dans la foule. 2. blind in one eye, aveugle d'un œil; two metres in length, long de deux mètres. 3. in ten, un sur dix. 4. (c) in the evening, le soir, pendant la soirée; in August, au mois d'août, en août; in the past, par le passé; never in my life, jamais de ma vie; (b) in a little while, sous peu. 5. in tears, en larmes; in despair, au désespoir. 6. dressed in white, habillé de blanc. 7. (a) in a gentle voice, d'une voix douce; to be in the fashion, être à la mode; (b) in alphabetical order, par ordre alphabétique; (c) in the form of, sous forme de. II. adv. 1. (a) à la maison, chez soi; (b) the train is in, le train est en gare; (c) is the fire still in? est-ce que le feu brûle encore? 2. (a) to be in with s.o., être en bons termes avec qn; (b) my luck is in, je suis en veine; F: to be in on sth., être dans le coup; (c) the Labour Party is in, le parti travailliste est au pouvoir; strawberries are in, c'est la saison des fraises. 3. we are in for a storm, nous aurons sûrement de l'orage; F: he's in for it! le voilà dans de beaux draps! 4. (a) day in day out, tout le long du jour; (b) all in, (i) (prix) tout compris; (ii) F: éreinté. III. s. the ins and outs, les coins et recoins (d'une affaire).

inability [inə'biliti], s. incapacité f; impuissance f.

inaccessible [inæk'sesəbl], a. inaccessible.

†inaccuracy [in'ækjurəsi], s. inexactitude f, imprécision f. in'accurate, a. inexact; imprécis; incorrect. -ly, adv. inexactement, incorrectement.

inactive [in'æktiv], a. inactif. in'action, s. inaction f.

inadequate [in'ædikwit], a. insuffisant.

inadmissible [inəd'misəbl], a. inadmissible.

inadvertence [inəd'vəːt(ə)ns], s. inadvertance f, étourderie f. inad'vertent, a. commis par inadvertance, par mégarde. -ly, adv. par inadvertance, par mégarde.

inadvisable [inəd'vaizəbl], a. peu sage; imprudent; à déconseiller.

inane [i'nein], a. inepte, stupide.

inanimate [in'ænimit], a. inanimé.

inappropriate [inə'proupriit], a. qui ne convient pas (to, à); (of word) impropre.

inaptitude [in'æptitjuːd], s. inaptitude f (for, à).

inarticulate [inɑː'tikjulit], a. incapable de parler.

inartistic [inɑː'tistik], a. sans valeur artistique; (of pers.) dépourvu de sens artistique.

inattentive [inə'tentiv], a. inattentif; distrait. ina'ttention, s. inattention f; distraction f.

inaudible [in'ɔːdəbl], a. (son) imperceptible; (voix) faible. -ibly, adv. sans bruit; (parler) de manière à ne pas être entendu.

inaugurate [i'nɔːgjureit], v.tr. inaugurer. inaugu'ration, s. inauguration f.

incalculable [in'kælkjuləbl], a. incalculable.

incandescent [inkæn'des(ə)nt], a. incandescent.

incapable [in'keipəbl], *a.* incapable; incompétent. **incapa'bility**, *s.* incapacité *f.*

incapacity [inkəp'æsiti], *s.* incapacité *f*; incompétence *f*; **inca'pacitate**, *v.tr.* rendre (qn) incapable (from, for, de).

incarnation [inka:'nei∫(ə)n], *s.* incarnation *f.* (du Christ). **in'carnate**, *a.* incarné, fait de chair; *(of Christ)* to become i., s'incarner.

incautious [in'kɔ:∫əs], *a.* imprudent; inconsidéré. **-ly,** *adv.* imprudemment.

incense[1] [in'sens], *s.* encens *m.*

incense[2] [in'sens], *v.tr.* exaspérer. **in'censed,** *a.* exaspéré.

incentive [in'sentiv], *s.* stimulant *m.*

incest ['insest], *s.* inceste *m.*

inch [in(t)∫], *s.* pouce *m*; by inches, peu à peu; he couldn't see an i. in front of him, il n'y voyait pas à deux pas devant lui.

incident ['insid(ə)nt], *s.* incident *m.* **inci'dental.** I *a.* (événement) fortuit, accidentel; 1. expenses, faux frais. **-ally,** *adv.* (a) accessoirement; (b) soit dit en passant. II. *s.pl.* faux frais *m.*

incision [in'siʒ(ə)n], *s.* incision *f.,* entaille *f.*

incisive [in'saisiv], *a.* incisif, tranchant.

incite [in'sait], *v.tr.* inciter. **in'citement,** *s.* incitation *f.*

incivility [insi'viliti], *s.* incivilité *f.*

incline. I. *v.i.* [in'klain] incliner, pencher; inclined at an angle of 45°, incliné à un angle de 45°. II. *s.* ['inklain] pente *f.,* déclivité *f.* **incli'nation,** *s.* inclination *f.* **in'clined,** *a.* 1. (plan) incliné. 2. enclin, porté (to, à); to be i. to do sth., avoir de l'inclination, une tendance, à faire qch.

include [in'klu:d], *v.tr.* comprendre, renfermer, embrasser, comporter. **in'clusion,** *s.* inclusion *f.* **in'clusive,** *a.* qui comprend, qui renferme; (somme) globale; (prix) tout compris.

incognito [in'kɔgnitou], *s.* & *adv.* incognito (*m*).

incoherence [inkou'hiər(ə)ns], *s.* incohérence *f.* **inco'herent,** *a.* incohérent; (style) décousu. **-ly,** *adv.* sans cohérence, sans suite.

incombustible [inkəm'bʌstəbl], *a.* incombustible.

income ['inkʌm], *s.* revenu(s) *m(pl)*; **i. tax,** impôt *m* sur le revenu.

incommunicado [inkəmjuni'ka:dou], *a.* tenu au secret.

incomparable [in'kɔmpərəbl], *a.* incomparable.

incompatible [inkəm'pætibl], *a.* incompatible, inconciliable. **incompati'bility,** *s.* incompatibilité *f.*

incompetence [in'kɔmpit(ə)ns], *s.* incompétence *f.;* incapacité *f.* **in'competent,** *a.* incompétent, incapable.

incomplete [inkəm'pli:t], *a.* incomplet, inachevé.

incomprehension [inkɔmpri'hen∫(ə)n], *s.* manque de compréhension. **incompre'hensible,** *a.* incompréhensible. **incompre'hensive,** *a.* 1. incomplet, non inclusif. 2. incompréhensif.

inconceivable [inkən'si:vəbl], *a.* inconcevable.

inconclusive [inkən'klu:siv], *a.* peu concluant. **-ly,** *adv.* d'une manière peu concluante.

incongruous [in'kɔngruəs], *a.* incongru, déplacé.

inconsequent [in'kɔnsikwənt], *a.* inconséquent.

inconsiderable [inkən'sid(ə)rəbl], *a.* insignifiant.

inconsiderate [inkən'sid(ə)rit], *a.* sans égards pour les autres.

inconsistent [inkən'sist(ə)nt], *a.* 1. incompatible. 2. inconsistant, inconséquent. **incon'sistency,** *s.* inconsistance *f;* contradiction *f.*

inconsolable [inkən'soulabl], *a.* inconsolable.

inconspicuous [inkən'spikjuəs], *a.* peu apparent; peu frappant.

inconstant [in'kɔnstənt], *a.* inconstant, volage. **in'constancy,** *s.* inconstance *f.*

incontestable [inkən'testəbl], *a.* incontestable.

inconvenience [inkən'vi:njəns]. I. *s.* incommodité *f,* contretemps *m;* inconvénient *m.* II. *v.tr.* déranger, gêner. **incon'venient,** *a.* malcommode; gênant; *(of time)* inopportun; if it's not i. for you, si cela ne vous dérange pas. **-ly,** *adv.* incommodément.

incorporate [in'kɔ:pəreit], *v.tr.* incorporer, unir (with, à avec); *Com:* constituer (une association) en société commerciale. **in'corporated,** *a.* 1. faisant corps (avec). 2. *Com:* (société) (i) constituée, (ii) *U.S:* anonyme.

incorrect [inkə'rekt], *a.* 1. inexact. 2. incorrect.

incorrigible [in'kɔridʒəbl], *a.* incorrigible.

incorruptible [inkə'rʌptəbl], *a.* incorruptible.

increase. I. *s.* ['inkri:s] augmentation *f;* accroissement *m;* redoublement *m* (d'efforts); to be on the i., être en augmentation; aller en croissant. II. *v.* [in'kri:s] 1. *v.i.* augmenter, s'agrandir; s'accroître; se multiplier. 2. *v.tr.* augmenter (la production); grossir (le nombre); accroître (sa fortune). **in'creasing,** *a.* croissant. **-ly,** *adv.* de plus en plus (difficile, etc.).

incredible [in'kredəbl], *a.* incroyable. **-bly,** *adv.* incroyablement.

incredulous [in'kredjuləs], *a.* incrédule. **incre'dulity,** *s.* incrédulité *f.*

increment ['inkrimənt], *s.* augmentation *f.*

incriminate [in'krimineit], *v.tr.* incriminer (qn); impliquer (qn) (dans une accusation). **incrimi'nation,** *s.* incrimination *f.* **in'criminating,** *s.* i. documents, pièces *f* à conviction.

incubate [in'kjubeit], *v.tr.* couver, incuber. **incu'bation,** *s.* incubation *f.* ‡**incubator,** *s.* incubateur *m;* couveuse *f; (for chickens)* éleveuse *f.*

‡**incur** [in'kə:r], *v.tr.* courir (un risque); encourir (des frais); contracter (des dettes).

incurable [in'kjuərəbl], *a.* incurable.

indebted [in'detid], *a.* **1.** endetté. **2.** redevable (à qn de qch.).

indecent [in'di:snt], *a.* peu décent, indécent.

indecision [indi'siʒ(ə)n], *s.* indécision *f.*

indecisive [indi'saisiv], *a.* indécisif; indécis.

indeed [in'di:d], *adv.* **1.** *(a)* en effet; vraiment; thank you very much i., merci infiniment. **2.** même; à vrai dire. **3.** yes i.! mais certainement! *(contradicting)* si fait!

indefatigable [indi'fætigəbl], *a.* infatigable. **-ly,** *adv.* infatigablement.

indefensible [indi'fensəbl], *a.* indéfendable; insoutenable.

indefinite [in'definit], *a.* indéfini; vague; indéterminé. **-ly,** *adv.* vaguement; indéfiniment.

indelible [in'delibl], *a.* indélébile; ineffaçable.

indelicate [in'delikit], *a.* indélicat; peu délicat; inconvenant.

indemnify [in'demnifai], *v.tr. (a)* garantir (qn contre qch.); *(b)* indemniser, dédommager (qn d'une perte). ‡**in'demnity,** *s. (a)* garantie *f,* assurance *f* (contre une perte); *(b)* indemnité *f,* dédommagement *m.*

indent [in'dent]. **1.** *v.tr.* denteler, découper (le bord de qch.); *(in printing)* (faire) rentrer (une ligne). **2.** *v.i.* to i. for sth., passer une commande pour qch. **inden'tation,** *s.* dentelure *f,* découpure *f;* empreinte creuse. **in'dented,** *a.* (bord) dentelé; *(littoral)* échancré; (ligne) en alinéa, en retrait.

independence [indi'pendəns], *s.* indépendance *f.* **inde'pendent,** *a.* indépendant; to be i., être son propre maître; to be (of) i. (means), vivre de ses rentes; i. school = école libre. **-ly,** *adv. (a)* indépendamment; *(b)* avec indépendance.

indescribable [indis'kraibəbl], *a.* indescriptible.

indestructible [indis'trʌktəbl], *a.* indestructible.

‡**index** ['indeks]. **I.** *s.* **1.** *(pl.* indexes*)* index *m,* premier doigt *m.* **2.** *(pl.* indices*)* indice *m;* signe *m* (indicateur). **3.** *(pl.* indexes*)* index; table *f* alpha-

bétique (d'un livre); card i., *(i)* fichier *m,* classeur *m; (ii)* catalogue *m* sur fiches; cost of living i., index du coût de la vie; *Ecc:* to put a book on the I., mettre un livre à l'Index. **II.** *v.tr.* faire l'index (d'un livre); classer (un article).

Indian ['indjən]. **1.** *(a)* a. de l'Inde; indien; *(b)* s. Indien, -ienne. **2.** Red Indians, Peaux-Rouges *m.*

india-rubber [indjə'rʌbər], *s.* gomme *f* (à effacer).

indicate ['indikeit], *v.tr.* indiquer. **indi'cation,** *s.* indice *m,* signe *m;* apparence *f.* **in'dicative,** *a. & s.* indicatif *(m).* **'indicator,** *s.* (tableau *m)* indicateur *m.*

indict [in'dait], *v.tr. Jur:* accuser, inculper (qn). **in'dictment,** *s.* accusation *f.*

indifference [in'difr(ə)ns], *s.* indifférence *f,* manque *m* d'intérêt. **in'different,** *a.* **1.** indifférent. **2.** médiocre, passable.

indigestion [indi'dʒest∫(ə)n], *s.* dyspepsie *f;* mauvaise digestion *f.* **indi'gestible,** *a.* indigeste.

indignation [indig'neiʃ(ə)n], *s.* indignation *f.* **in'dignant,** *a.* (air) indigné; (cri) d'indignation. **-ly,** *adv.* a'ec indignation.

‡**indignity** [in'digniti], *s.* indignité *f,* affront *m.*

indigo ['indigou], *s.* indigo *m.*

indirect [indi'rekt], *a.* indirect. **-ly,** *adv.* indirectement.

indiscreet [indis'kri:t], *a. (a)* indiscret; *(b)* peu judicieux, imprudent. **-ly,** *adv. (a)* indiscrètement; *(b)* sans considération. **indis'cretion,** *s. (a)* manque *m* de discrétion; *(b)* action inconsidérée.

indispensable [indis'pensəbl], *a.* indispensable.

indisposition [indispə'ziʃ(ə)n], *s.* indisposition *f,* malaise *m.* **indis'posed,** *a.* souffrant.

indisputable [indis'pju:təbl], *a.* incontestable.

indistinct [indis'tiŋkt], *a.* indistinct; confus; vague. **-ly,** *adv.* indistinctement.

indistinguishable [indis'tiŋgwi∫əbl], *a.* indistinguible.

individual [indi'vidju(ə)l]. **1.** *a. (a)* individuel; *(b)* particulier. **2.** *s.* individu *m.* **indivi'duality,** *s.* individualité *f.* **indi'vidualist,** *s.* individualiste *mf.*

indivisible [indi'vizibl], *a.* indivisible.

indolence ['indoləns], *s.* indolence *f,* paresse *f.* **'indolent,** *a.* indolent, paresseux.

Indonesian [ində'ni:ziən], *a. & s.* indonésien, -ienne.

indoor ['indo:r], *a.* (travail) d'intérieur; (plante) d'appartement; (jeux) de salon, de salle; (piscine) fermée. **in'doors,** *adv.* à la maison.

induce [in'dju:s], *v.tr.* 1. persuader à (qn de faire qch.). 2. produire, occasionner; provoquer (le sommeil). 3. *El:* amorcer (un courant). **in'ducement,** *s.* motif *m,* cause *f,* qui encourage qn à faire qch.; provocation *f* (au sommeil).

indulge [in'dʌldʒ]. 1. *v.tr.* gâter (qn); to i. oneself, s'écouter; ne rien se refuser. 2. *v.i.* to i. in sth., se livrer, s'adonner, à qch. **in'dulgence,** *s.* indulgence *f.* **in'dulgent,** *a.* indulgent.

†**industry** ['indastri], *s.* 1. application *f;* diligence *f.* 2. industrie *f.* **in'dustrial,** *a.* industriel; i. injuries, accidents *m* du travail; i. disputes, conflits *m* ouvriers. **in'dustrialism,** *s.* industrialisme *m.* **industriali'zation,** *s.* industrialisation *f.* **in'dustrialize,** *v.tr.* industrialiser. **in'dustrious,** *a.* travailleur, industrieux. **in'dustriousness,** *s.* assiduité *f* (au travail), application *f.* **in'dustry**

ineffectual [ini'fektju(ə)l], *a.* inefficace.

inefficient [ini'fiʃ(ə)nt], *a.* incompétent.

ineligible [in'elidʒəbl], *a.* inéligible.

inept [i'nept], *a.* 1. déplacé; mal à propos. 2. inepte, absurde.

inequality [ini(:)'kwoliti], *s.* inégalité *f.*

inequitable [in'ekwitəbl], *a.* inéquitable.

inert [i'nə:t], *a.* inerte. **in'ertia** [-ʃiə], *s.* inertie *f.*

inestimable [in'estiməbl], *a.* inestimable.

inevitable [in'evitəbl], *a.* (a) inévitable. (b) fatal; obligé. **-ly,** *adv.* inévitablement.

inexact [inig'zækt], *a.* inexact.

inexcusable [iniks'kju:zəbl], *a.* inexcusable.

inexhaustible [inig'zo:stəbl], *a.* inépuisable.

inexpensive [iniks'pensiv], *a.* pas cher, peu coûteux.

inexperienced [iniks'piəriənst], *a.* inexpérimenté.

inexplicable [in'eksplikəbl], *a.* inexplicable. **-bly,** *adv.* inexplicablement.

inextricable [in'ekstrikəbl], *a.* inextricable.

infallible [in'fæləbl], *a.* infaillible. **-bly,** *adv.* infailliblement.

infamous ['infəməs], *a.* infâme; abominable. **'infamy,** *s.* infamie *f.*

infant ['infənt], *s.* 1. enfant *mf* (en bas âge); i. mortality, mortalité infantile. 2. *Jur:* mineur, -eure. **'infancy,** *s.* 1. (première) enfance *f;* bas âge *m.* 2. *Jur:* minorité *f.* **'infantile,** *a.* 1. (esprit) d'enfant; (raisonnement) enfantin. 2. (maladie) infantile.

infantry ['infəntri], *s.* infanterie *f.*

infatuate [in'fætjueit], *v.tr.* to be infatuated with s.o., s'enticher de qn; être épris de qn. **infatu'ation,** *s.* engouement *m.*

infect [in'fekt], *v.tr.* 1. infecter, corrompre. 2. contaminer. **in'fection,** *s.* infection *f;* contagion *f.* **in'fectious,**

a. (a) infectieux; (b) contagieux, communicatif.

‡**infer** [in'fə:r], *v.tr.* 1. déduire (qch. de qch.). 2. impliquer. **'inference,** *s.* déduction *f,* conclusion *f.*

inferior [in'fiəriər]. 1. *a.* inférieur. 2. *s.* (a) inférieur, -e; (b) subordonné, -ée. **inferi'ority,** *s.* infériorité *f;* i. complex, complexe *m* d'infériorité.

infernal [in'fə:nl], *a.* infernal.

†**inferno** [in'fə:nou], *s.* enfer *m.*

infest [in'fest], *v.tr.* infester.

infidel ['infidəl], *a. & s.* incroyant, -ante.

infidelity [infi'deliti], *s.* infidélité *f.*

infiltrate ['infiltreit]. 1. *v.tr.* infiltrer; imprégner, pénétrer dans (qch.); *Pol:* noyauter. 2. *v.i.* s'infiltrer. **infil'tration,** *s.* infiltration *f;* *Pol:* noyautage *m.*

infinite ['infinit], *a.* infini. **-ly,** *adv.* infiniment. **in'finity,** *s.* infinité *f.* **infini'tesimal,** *a.* infinitésimal. **in'finitive,** *a. & s. Gram:* infinitif (*m*).

infirm [in'fə:m], *a.* infirme, débile. **in'firmary,** *s.* infirmerie *f;* hôpital *m.* **in'firmity,** *s.* infirmité *f.*

inflame [in'fleim], *v.i.* (a) prendre feu; (b) *Med:* s'enflammer. **in'flammable,** *a.* inflammable; *U.S:* ignifuge. **inflam'mation,** *s.* inflammation *f.*

inflate [in'fleit], *v.tr.* 1. gonfler (un pneu, etc.). 2. hausser, faire monter (les prix). **in'flated,** *a.* 1. gonflé. 2. (prix) exagéré. **in'flation,** *s.* 1. gonflement *m.* 2. inflation *f* fiduciaire.

inflexible [in'fleksəbl], *a.* inflexible. **inflexi'bility,** *s.* inflexibilité *f.*

inflict [in'flikt], *v.tr.* infliger (une punition à qn); occasionner (du chagrin à qn); imposer (sa compagnie à qn).

influence ['influəns]. I. *s.* influence *f.* II. *v.tr.* (of pers.) influencer (qn); (of thing) influer sur (qch.). **in'fluential,** *a.* influent.

influenza [influ'enzə], *s. Med:* grippe *f.*

influx ['inflʌks], *s.* affluence *f;* invasion *f.*

inform [in'fo:m]. 1. *v.tr.* informer, avertir (qn de qch.); renseigner (qn sur qch.); I regret to have to i. you that . . ., j'ai le regret de vous annoncer que . . . 2. *v.i.* to i. against s.o., dénoncer qn. **in'formant,** *s.* informateur, -trice. **infor'mation,** *s.* 1. renseignements *m pl;* pour i. à titre d'information; (computers) i. processing, informatique *f.* 2. savoir *m,* connaissances *f pl.* 3. dénonciation *f* (contre qn). **in'formative,** *a.* instructif. **in'formed,** *a.* bien renseigné. **in'former,** *s.* dénonciateur, -trice.

informal [in'fo:ml], *a.* 1. (dîner, etc.) sans cérémonie; (of meeting) non officiel. **-ally,** *adv.* sans cérémonie; à titre non officiel. **infor'mality,** *s.* absence *f* de cérémonie.

infra-black ['infrə'blæk], a. T.V: infra-noir.

infra-dig ['infrə'dig], a.phr. F: au-dessous de la dignité de (qn).

infra-red ['infrə'red], a. infra-rouge.

infrasonic ['infrə'sɔnik], a. infrasonore; i. vibration, infrason m.

infrastructure ['infrəstrʌktʃər], s. infrastructure f.

infrequent [in'fri:kwənt], a. rare; peu fréquent. -ly, adv. rarement.

infringe [in'frindʒ], v.tr. enfreindre, violer (une loi). infringement, s. infraction f (d'un règlement); violation (d'une loi); i. of patent, contrefaçon f.

infuriate [in'fjuərieit], v.tr. rendre furieux. in'furiated, a. furieux.

infuse [in'fju:z], v.tr. infuser.

infusion [in'fju:ʒ(ə)n], s. infusion f.

ingenious [in'dʒi:njəs], a. ingénieux. -ly, adv. ingénieusement. inge'nuity, s. ingéniosité f.

ingenuous [in'dʒenjuəs], a. ingénu; naïf.

ingot ['iŋgət], s. lingot m.

ingratiate [in'greiʃieit], v.tr. to i. oneself with s.o., s'insinuer dans les bonnes grâces de qn (in 'gratiating, a. insinuant.

ingratitude [in'grætitju:d], s. ingratitude f.

ingredient [in'gri:diənt], s. ingrédient m.

inhabit [in'hæbit], v.tr. habiter (dans). in'habitable, a. habitable. in'habitant, s. habitant, -ante.

inhale [in'heil], v.tr. aspirer, humer.

inherent [in'hiərənt], a. inhérent, naturel.

inherit [in'herit], v.tr. (a) hériter de (qch.); succéder à une fortune; (b) hériter (qch. de qn). in'heritance, s. 1. succession f. 2. héritage m.

inhospitable [inhɔs'pitəbl], a. inhospitalier.

inhuman [in'hju:mən], a. inhumain. inhu'manity, s. inhumanité f.

iniquitous [i'nikwitəs], a. inique. i'niquity, s. iniquité f.

initial [i'niʃ(ə)l]. I. 1. a. initial; premier. 2. s.pl. initiales fpl. II. v.tr. parapher (with correction).

initiate [i'niʃieit], v.tr. 1. commencer (des négociations); lancer (une mode). 2. initier (qn à un secret). initi'ation, s. 1. début(s) m (d'une entreprise). 2. initiation f (into, à). i'nitiative, s. initiative f. i'nitiator, s. initiateur, -trice; lanceur, -euse (d'une mode).

inject [in'dʒekt], v.tr. injecter. in'jection, s. injection f; piqûre f.

injudicious [indʒu(:)'diʃəs], a. peu judicieux.

injure ['in(d)ʒər], v.tr. 1. nuire à, faire tort à (qn). 2. blesser (qn); to i. oneself, se blesser, se faire du mal. 'injured, a. 1. the i. party, l'offensé, -ée. 2. (bras, etc.) blessé, estropié; s. the i., les blessés; (in accident) les

accidentés. in'jurious, a. nuisible, pernicieux. 'injury, s. 1. tort m, mal m. 2. blessure f; industrial injuries, accidents mpl du travail.

injustice [in'dʒʌstis], s. injustice f.

ink [iŋk]. I. s. encre f; Indian i., encre de Chine; written in i., écrit à l'encre. II. v.tr. encrer (des lettres). 'ink-fish, s. F: seiche f; calmar m. 'inkpot, s., 'inkwell, s. encrier m. 'inky, a. taché, barbouillé, d'encre.

inkling ['iŋkliŋ], s. soupçon m.

inland ['inlənd]. 1. s. (l')intérieur m (d'un pays). 2. attrib. intérieur; i. sea, mer intérieure, fermée; the I. Revenue, le fisc. 3. adv. vers l'intérieur; to go i., pénétrer dans les terres.

‡inlay ['inlei], v.tr. incruster (with, de); marqueter (une table, etc.). 'inlaid, a. incrusté, marqueté; i. work, marqueterie f.

inlet ['inlet], s. petit bras m de mer.

inn [in], s. auberge f; Jur: Inns of Court, les (quatre) Écoles de droit de Londres. 'innkeeper, s. aubergiste mf.

innate [i'neit], a. inné, naturel.

inner ['inər], a. intérieur; de dedans; i. meaning, sens intime; i. harbour, arrière-port m; Aut: i. tube, chambre f à air; F: the i. man, l'estomac m.

innings ['iniŋz], s. (at cricket) tour m de batte; F: he had a long i., il a fourni une longue carrière.

innocence ['inəsns], s. innocence f. 'innocent, a. innocent -ly, adv. innocemment.

innocuous [i'nɔkjuəs], a. inoffensif.

innovation [inou'veiʃ(ə)n], s. innovation f.

‡innuendo [inju(:)'endou], s. allusion f.

innumerable [i'nju:m(ə)rəbl], a. innombrable.

inoculate [i'nɔkjuleit], v.tr. inoculer. inocu'lation, s. inoculation f.

inoffensive [inə'fensiv], a. inoffensif.

inoperable [in'ɔp(ə)rəbl], a. Med: inopérable.

inopportune [in'ɔpətju:n], a. inopportun.

inordinate [i'nɔ:dinit], a. démesuré, immodéré.

inquest ['inkwest], s. enquête f; (coroner's) i., enquête judiciaire (en cas de mort suspecte).

inquire [in'kwaiər], v.tr. & i. se renseigner (sur qch.); s'informer (du prix de qch.); demander (son chemin); P.N.: i. within, s'adresser ici. in'quiring, a. curieux; (air) interrogateur. in'quiry, s. 1. enquête f. 2. demande f de renseignements; i. office, 'inquiries,' bureau m de renseignements.

Inquisition [inkwi'ziʃ(ə)n], s. Hist: the I., l'Inquisition f. in'quisitor, s. inquisiteur m.

inquisitive [in'kwizitiv], a. curieux. -ly, adv. avec curiosité. in'quisitiveness, s. curiosité f (indiscrète).

inrush ['inrʌʃ], s. irruption f.

insane [in'sein], a. fou; dérangé; s. the i., les aliénés m. in'sanity, s. folie f; démence f, aliénation f mentale.

insanitary [in'sænit(ə)ri], a. insalubre; antihygiénique.

insatiable [in'seiʃiəbl], a. insatiable.

inscription [in'skripʃ(ə)n], s. inscription f.

inscrutable [in'skruːtəbl], a. impénétrable, inscrutable.

insect ['insekt], s. insecte m. in'secticide, s. insecticide m.

insecure [insi'kjuər], a. 1. peu sûr; peu solide; mal affermi. 2. exposé au danger. -ly, adv. peu solidement; sans sécurité. inse'curity, s. insécurité f.

insensitive [in'sensitiv], a. insensible (to, à).

inseparable [in'sep(ə)rəbl], a. inséparable (from, de).

insert [in'səːt], v.tr. insérer, introduire (qch. dans qch.). in'sertion, s. insertion f.

inside [in'said]. 1. s. (a) dedans m, (côté m) intérieur m; on the i., au dedans; i. out, sens dessus dessous; (b) intérieur m (d'une maison, etc.); (c) F: ventre m, estomac m; (d) Sp: the insides, les centres. 2. a. ['insaid] intérieur; d'intérieur. 3. adv. intérieurement; en dedans. 4. prep. à l'intérieur de; dans.

insidious [in'sidiəs], a. insidieux.

insight ['insait], s. 1. perspicacité f; pénétration f. 2. aperçu m.

insignificance [insig'nifikəns], s. insignifiance f. insig'nificant, a. insignifiant.

insincere [insin'siər], a. (a) peu sincère; (b) faux. -ly, adv. sans sincérité. insin'cerity, s. manque m de sincérité.

insinuate [in'sinjueit], v.tr. insinuer; laisser entendre (que); s'insinuer (dans les bonnes grâces de qn). insin'ation, s. insinuation f.

insipid [in'sipid], a. insipide, fade. insi'pidity, s. insipidité f; fadeur f.

insist [in'sist], v.i. insister. in'sistence, s. insistance f; instance f. in'sistent, a. qui insiste, insistant; importun. -ly, adv. instamment; avec insistance.

insolence ['ins(ə)ləns], s. insolence f (to, envers). 'insolent, a. insolent. -ly, adv. insolemment.

insoluble [in'sɔljubl], a. insoluble.

insolvency [in'sɔlvənsi], s. (a) insolvabilité f; (b) faillite f. in'solvent, a. insolvable; en faillite.

insomnia [in'sɔmniə], s. insomnie f.

inspect [in'spekt], v.tr. inspecter; contrôler; vérifier. in'spection, s. inspection f; vérification f; contrôle m (des billets); (of book) i. copy, spécimen m. in'spector, s. inspecteur, -trice.

inspire [in'spaiər], v.tr. inspirer. inspi'ration, s. inspiration f.

instability [instə'biliti], s. instabilité f.

install [in'stɔːl], v.tr. installer. instal-'lation, s. installation f. in'stalment, s. acompte m; to pay in instalments, échelonner les paiements.

instance ['instəns], s. 1. exemple m, cas m. 2. for i., par exemple. 3. in the first i., en premier lieu.

instant ['instənt]. I. s. instant m, moment m. II. a. (abbr. inst.), Com: de ce mois; the 5th inst., le 5 courant. instan'taneous, a. instantané. in'stantly, adv. tout de suite.

instead [in'sted]. 1. prep.phr. i. of, au lieu de; à la place de. 2. adv. au lieu de cela; plutôt.

instep ['instep], s. cou-de-pied m.

instigate ['instigeit], v.tr. inciter, provoquer. insti'gation, s. instigation f, incitation f. 'instigator, s. instigateur -trice.

‡instil [in'stil], v.tr. instiller; faire pénétrer; infiltrer (une idée). instil-'lation, s. instillation f; inspiration f (d'une idée).

instinct ['instin(k)t], s. instinct m. in'stinctive, a. instinctif. -ly, adv. d'instinct; instinctivement.

institute ['institjuːt]. I. v.tr. instituer, établir. II. s. institut m. insti'tution, s. institution f. insti'tutional, a. institutionnel.

instruct [in'strʌkt], v.tr. instruire. 2. charger (qn de faire qch.). in'struction, s. 1. instruction f, enseignement m. 2. pl. indications f, instructions. in'structional, a. (école) d'application; (film) éducatif. in'structive, a. instructif. -ly, adv. d'une manière instructive. in'structor, s. maître m (enseignant); instructeur m; Sp: moniteur m; swimming i., professeur m de natation; Aut: driving i., moniteur de conduite.

instrument ['instrumənt], s. instrument m; appareil m; Av: i. flying, vol m sans visibilité. instru'mental, a. 1. contributif (to, in, à). 2. i. music, musique instrumentale. instru'mentalist, s. Mus: instrumentiste m. instrumen'tation, s. Mus: instrumentation f.

insubordinate [insə'bɔːdinit], a. insubordonné, insoumis. insubordi'nation, s. insubordination f, insoumission f.

insufferable [in'sʌf(ə)rəbl], a. insupportable.

insufficient [insə'fiʃ(ə)nt], a. insuffisant. -ly, adv. insuffisamment.

insular ['insjulər], a. (a) (climat) insulaire; (b) (esprit) étroit, borné. insu'larity, s. étroitesse f (d'esprit).

insulate ['insjuleit], v.tr. isoler; calorifuger (une chaudière); Cln: isonoriser. insu'lation, s. isolement m; calorifugeage m; Cln: insonorisation f. 'insulator, s. isolant m.

insult ['insʌlt]. I. s. insulte f, affront m. II. v.tr. insulter, in'sulting, a. offensant, injurieux.

insuperable [in'sju:p(ə)rəbl], a. insurmontable.

insure [in'juər], v.tr. (i) assurer, (ii) faire assurer (une maison, etc.). in'surance, s. assurance f; life i., assurance-vie f; Aut: third party, assurance au tiers, tous risques; Adm: National I., assurances sociales. in'surer, s. Com: assureur m.

insurgent [in'sə:dʒ(ə)nt], a. & s. insurgé, -ée.

insurmountable [insə(:)'mauntəbl], a. insurmontable.

insurrection [insə'rekʃ(ə)n], s. insurrection f, soulèvement m.

intact [in'tækt], a. intact.

intake ['inteik], s. 1. prise f, appel m (d'air); prise (d'eau); admission f (de vapeur). 2. consommation f.

intangible [in'tæn(d)ʒəbl], a. intangible, impalpable.

integral ['intigrəl]. 1. a. (a) to be an i. part of sth., faire corps avec qch.; (b) Mth: i. calculus, calcul intégral. 2. s. Mth: intégrale f. 'integrate, v.i. Pol: s'intégrer (dans un milieu). inte'gration, s. intégration f.

integrity [in'tegriti], s. intégrité f.

intellect ['intəlekt], s. intelligence f, esprit m. inte'llectual, a. intellectuel. -ally, adv. intellectuellement.

intelligence [in'telidʒəns], s. 1. intelligence f; i. test, test m d'habileté mentale. 2. renseignements mpl, nouvelles fpl, informations fpl; Mil: I. service = Deuxième Bureau m. in'telligent, a. intelligent, avisé. -ly, adv. intelligemment, avec intelligence. inte'lligible, a. intelligible. -bly, adv. intelligiblement.

intemperate [in'tempərit], a. 1. intempérant, immodéré. 2. adonné à la boisson.

intend [in'tend], v.tr. 1. avoir l'intention (de faire qch.). 2. destiner (qch. à qch.); he intends to be a schoolmaster, il se destine au professorat, il veut devenir professeur. 3. vouloir dire, entendre. in'tended, a. 1. (voyage) projeté. 2. voulu; intentionnel.

intense [in'tens], a. (a) vif, fort, intense; (b) d'un sérieux exagéré. -ly, adv. excessivement; profondément; avec intensité. in'tensify. 1. v.tr. intensifier, augmenter. 2. v.i. devenir plus intense. in'tensity, s. intensité f; force f; violence f (d'une douleur). in'tensive, a. intensif.

intent [in'tent]. I. a. i. on doing sth., résolu, déterminé, à faire qch. II. s. to all intents and purposes, virtuellement; en fait. in'tention, s. intention

f. in'tentional, a. intentionnel, voulu; fait exprès. -ally, adv. à dessein; exprès; intentionnellement.

interact [intə'rækt], v.i. réagir réciproquement.

intercede [intə'si:d], v.i. intercéder (auprès de qn).

intercept [intə'sept], v.tr. intercepter. inter'ception, s. interception f; captation f (de messages).

intercession [intə'seʃ(ə)n], s. intercession f.

interchangeable [intə'tʃeindʒəbl], a. interchangeable, permutable.

intercom [intə'kɔm], s. F: intercom m.

intercontinental [intəkɔnti'nentl], a. intercontinental.

intercourse ['intəkɔːs], s. (a) commerce m, relations fpl (humaines); (b) rapports mpl (sexuels).

interest ['intrest]. I. s. 1. Com: participation f. 2. avantage m, profit m. 3. Fin: intérêt m. II. v.tr. 1. intéresser (qn dans une affaire). 2. éveiller l'intérêt de (qn); to be interested in music, s'intéresser à la musique. 'interesting, a. intéressant.

interfere [intə'fiər], v.i. 1. intervenir (dans); se mêler (de); (of thing) to i. with sth., gêner qch. 2. Sc: interférer; Rad: brouiller. inter'ference, s. 1. intervention f, intrusion f. 2. Sc: interférence f; Rad: parasites mpl. inter'fering, a. (of pers.) importun; qui se mêle à tout.

interior [in'tiəriər], a. & s. intérieur (m).

interloper ['intələupər], s. intrus, -djue.

interlude ['intəlju:d], s. intermède m.

intermediary [intə'mi:djəri], s. intermédiaire m.

intermediate [intə'mi:djit], a. intermédiaire.

interminable [in'tə:minəbl], a. interminable, sans fin. -ably, adv. interminablement, sans fin.

intermittent [intə'mit(ə)nt], a. intermittent.

intern [in'tə:n], v.tr. interner. in'ternal, a. intérieur; interne; i. trade, commerce intérieur. -ally, adv. intérieurement; Med: not to be taken i., pour usage externe. in'ternment, s. internement m.

international [intə'næʃənl], a. international.

interphone ['intəfoun], s. interphone m, téléphone m intérieur.

interplanetary [intə'plænit(ə)ri], a. interplanétaire.

interplay ['intəplei], s. effet m réciproque; réaction f.

Interpol ['intəpɔl], s. Interpol m.

interpret [in'tə:prit], v.tr. interpréter. inter'pretation, s. interprétation f. in'terpreter, s. interprète mf.

interrogate [in'terəgeit], *v.tr.* interroger, questionner. **interro'gation**, *s.* interrogation *f.* **inter'rogative**, *a. & s.* interrogatif. interrogative, *a.* interrogateur; (pronom) interrogatif. **in'terrogator**, *s.* interrogateur, -trice.

interrupt [intə'rʌpt], *v.tr.* interrompre. **inter'ruption**, *s.* interruption *f*; dérangement *m.*

intersect [intə(:)'sekt]. 1. *v.tr.* entrecouper, intersecter. 2. *v.i.* (of lines) se couper, se croiser.

interval ['intəv(ə)l], *s.* intervalle *m*; at intervals, par intervalles; *Meteo:* bright intervals, belles éclaircies; *Th:* entracte *m*; *Sp:* la mi-temps.

intervene [intə(:)'vi:n], *v.i.* 1. intervenir, s'interposer. 2. (of event) survenir, arriver. **inter'vention**, *s.* intervention *f.*

interview ['intəvju:]. I. *s.* entrevue *f*; interview *m.* II. *v.tr.* interviewer. **'interviewer**, *s.* interviewe(u)r *m*; enquêteur, -trice.

intimate ['intimit], *a.* (ami) intime; (rapport) intime, étroit. -ly, *adv.* intimement; à fond. **'intimacy**, *s.* intimité *f.*

intimidate [in'timideit], *v.tr.* intimider. **in'timidating**, *a.* intimidant. **intimi'dation**, *s.* intimidation *f.*

into ['intu, 'intə], *prep.* dans, en; to fall is the hands of the enemy, tomber entre les mains de l'ennemi.

intolerable [in'tɔl(ə)rəbl], *a.* intolérable, insupportable.

intolerant [in'tɔlər(ə)nt], *a.* intolérant.

intoxicate [in'tɔksikeit], *v.tr.* enivrer, griser. **in'toxicated**, *a.* ivre; grisé (de succès). **in'toxicating**, *a.* enivrant; (boisson) alcoolique. **intoxi'cation**, *s.* ivresse *f*; *Med:* intoxication *f.*

†**intricacy** ['intrikəsi], *s.* complexité *f.* **'intricate**, *a.* compliqué.

intrigue [in'tri:g]. I. *v.i. & v.tr.* intriguer; éveiller la curiosité de (qn); mener des intrigues. II. *s.* intrigue *f.*

intrinsic [in'trinsik], *a.* intrinsèque.

introduce [intrə'dju:s], *v.tr.* 1. introduire. 2. présenter (qn à qn). **intro'duction**, *s.* 1. introduction *f.* présentation *f* (de qn à qn). 2. avant-propos *m*; prélude *m* (à une symphonie). **intro'ductory**, *a.* introductoire; (mots) d'introduction.

introspective [intrə'spektiv], *a.* introspectif.

intrude [in'tru:d], *v.i.* faire intrusion; être importun. **in'truder**, *s.* intrus, -use. **in'trusion**, *s.* intrusion *f.*

intuition [intju(:)'iʃ(ə)n], *s.* intuition *f.*

inundate ['inʌndeit], *v.tr.* inonder (with, de); to be inundated with requests, être débordé de requêtes. **inun'dation**, *s.* inondation *f.*

invade [in'veid], *v.tr.* envahir. **in'vader**, *s.* envahisseur *m.*

invalid ['invəlid, -li:d], *a. & s.* malade (mf)

invalid² [in'vælid], *a. Jur:* invalide; nul. **in'validate**, *v.tr. Jur:* invalider, rendre nul; vicier (un contrat).

invaluable [in'vælju(ə)bl], *a.* inestimable.

invariable [in'vɛəriəbl], *a.* invariable. -bly, *adv.* invariablement.

invasion [in'veiʒ(ə)n], *s.* invasion *f*, envahissement *m.*

invective [in'vektiv], *s.* invective *f.*

invent [in'vent], *v.tr.* inventer. **in'vention**, *s.* invention *f.* **in'ventive**, *a.* inventif. **in'ventor**, *s.* inventeur *m.*

inventory ['invəntri], *s.* inventaire *m.*

inverse ['invə:s], *a. & s.* inverse (*m*). -ly, *adv.* inversement.

invert [in'və:t], *v.tr.* renverser, retourner.

invest [in'vest], *v.tr. Fin:* placer, investir (des fonds); faire des placements. **in'vestment**, *s.* placement *m.* **in'vestor**, *s.* actionnaire *mf.*

investigate [in'vestigeit], *v.tr.* examiner, étudier (une question); faire une enquête sur (un crime). **investi'gation**, *s.* investigation *f*; enquête *f.* **in'vestigator**, *s.* investigateur, -trice.

inveterate [in'vet(ə)rit], *a.* invétéré; obstiné, acharné.

invidious [in'vidiəs], *a.* 1. odieux; ingrat. 2. qui suscite la jalousie.

invigorate [in'vigəreit], *v.tr.* fortifier.

invincible [in'vinsəbl], *a.* invincible.

invisible [in'vizəbl], *a.* invisible.

invite [in'vait], *v.tr.* inviter. **invi'tation**, *s.* invitation *f.* **in'viting**, *a.* invitant, attrayant; (of food) appétissant.

invoice ['invɔis]. I. *s. Com:* facture *f.* II. *v.tr.* facturer (des marchandises).

involuntary [in'vɔlənt(ə)ri], *a.* involontaire. -arily, *adv.* involontairement.

involve [in'vɔlv], *v.tr.* 1. (usu. passive) to be involved in (sth.), être engagé, impliqué, compromis, dans (une querelle, un complot, etc.); the forces involved, les forces en jeu. 2. comporter, entraîner, nécessiter; to i. great expense, entraîner de grands frais. **in'volved**, *a.* (style) compliqué, embrouillé.

invulnerable [in'vʌln(ə)rəbl], *a.* invulnérable.

inward ['inwəd]. 1. *a.* intérieur; interne; vers l'intérieur. 2. *adv.* (also **inwards**) vers l'intérieur; en dedans.

iodine ['aiədi:n], *s.* iode *m.*

ion ['aiən], *s. Sc:* ion *m.*

Iraki [i'rɑːki], *a. & s.* irakien, -ienne.

irate [ai'reit], *a.* courroucé; en colère.

iris ['aiəris], *s.* 1. *Anat:* (pl. irides) iris *m.* 2. *Bot:* (pl. irises) iris.

Irish ['aiəriʃ], *a.* irlandais; d'Irlande; *s.* the I., les Irlandais. †**'Irishman**, *s.* Irlandais *m.* †**'Irishwoman**, *s.* Irlandaise *f.*

irksome ['ə:ksəm], *a.* ennuyeux, ingrat.

iron ['aiən]. I. s. 1. fer m; cast i., fonte f. 2. fer à repasser. 3. pl. fers, chaînes f. II. v.tr. repasser (le linge); to i. out difficulties, aplanir les difficultés. **'ironing**, s. repassage m. **'ironmonger**, s. quincaillier m. **'ironmongery**, s. quincaillerie f.

†**irony** ['aiərəni], s. ironie f. **i'ronical**, a. ironique. **-ally**, adv. ironiquement.

irrational [i'ræʃnl], a. déraisonnable, absurde.

irreconcilable [irekən'sailəbl], a. 1. irréconciliable; implacable. 2. incompatible.

irrecoverable [iri'kʌv(ə)rəbl], a. irrécouvrable.

irredeemable [iri'di:məbl], a. (of pers.) incorrigible; (perte) irrémédiable; Fin: (obligations) non amortissables.

irregular [i'regjulər], a. irrégulier. **-ly**, adv. irrégulièrement. **irregu'larity**, s. irrégularité f.

irrelevant [i'relivənt], a. non pertinent; hors de propos. **ir'relevance**, s. manque m d'à-propos.

irremediable [iri'mi:diəbl], a. irrémédiable. **-ably**, adv. irrémédiablement.

irreparable [i'rep(ə)rəbl], a. irréparable.

irrepressible [iri'presəbl], a. irrésistible, irrépimable.

irresistible [iri'zistəbl], a. irrésistible.

irresolute [i'rezəljut], a. indécis; irrésolu.

irrespective [iri'spektiv], adv. i. of (sth.), indépendamment de (qch.).

irresponsible [iri'sponsəbl], a. irréfléchi; (of pers.) étourdi.

irretrievable [iri'tri:vəbl], a. irréparable, irrémédiable. **-bly**, adv. irréparablement; irrémédiablement.

irreverent [i'rev(ə)rənt], a. irrévérent, irrévérencieux.

irrevocable [i'revəkəbl], a. irrévocable.

irrigate ['irigeit], v.tr. irriguer (des champs); (of river) arroser (une région, une prairie). **irri'gation**, s. irrigation f.

irritate ['iriteit], v.tr. irriter; agacer. **'irritable**, a. irritable; irascible. **'irritant**, a. & s. irritant (m). **'irritating**, a. irritant; agaçant. **irri'tation**, s. irritation f; agacement m.

irruption [i'rʌp(ʃ)(ə)n], s. irruption f.

is [iz]. see BE.

Islamic [iz'læmik], a. islamique.

island ['ailənd], s. île f; (street) i., refuge m (pour piétons). **isle**, s. (used esp. in proper names) île f. **'islet**, s. îlot m.

isobar ['aisoubɑːr], s. isobare f.

isolate ['aisəleit], v.tr. isoler. **iso'lation**, s. isolement m. **iso'lationism**, s. Pol: isolationnisme m.

Israeli [iz'reili], a. & s. israélien, -ienne.

issue ['isjuː]. I. s. 1. issue f; résultat m; the point at i., la question pendante. 2. Fin: émission f (de billets de banque, etc.). 3. Jur: progéniture f, descendance f. II. v.tr. (a) émettre, mettre en circulation (des billets de banque); (b) lancer (un prospectus); (c) Jur: décerner (un mandat d'arrêt); (d) distribuer (des provisions); délivrer (un passeport).

isthmus ['isθməs], s. isthme m.

it [it], pers.pron. 1. (a) (subject) il; elle; (object) le, la; (indirect object) lui; (b) s. F: (i) le sex-appeal; (ii) he thinks he's 'it, il se croit sorti de la cuisse de Jupiter. 2. to face it, faire front; he hasn't got it in him to . . ., il n'est pas capable de . . .; to have a bad time of it, en voir de dures. 3. ce, cela, il; who is it? qui est-ce? that's it! (i) c'est ça! (ii) ça y est! it doesn't matter, cela ne fait rien; it's raining, il pleut. 4. it makes you think, cela vous fait réfléchir; it is said that . . ., on dit que . . .; how is it that . . .? d'où vient que . . .? 5. at it, in it, to it, y; above it, over it, au-dessus; dessus; under(neath) it, au-dessous; dessous; for it, en; pour lui, pour elle, pour cela; from it, en; far from it, tant s'en faut; of it, en; non, il y, dessus.

Italian [i'tæljən], 1. a. italien, d'Italie. 2. s. (a) Italien, -ienne; (b) Ling: l'italien m.

italics [i'tæliks], s.pl. italique m.

itch [itʃ]. I. v.i. démanger; éprouver des démangeaisons; to be itching to do sth., brûler d'envie de faire qch. II. s. (also itching) démangeaison f.

item ['aitəm], s. article m; détail m; news items, faits m divers; items on the agenda, questions f à l'ordre du jour.

†**itinerary** [i'tinərəri], s. itinéraire m. **i'tinerant**, a. (musicien) ambulant; (marchand) forain.

its [its], poss.a. son; f. sa, (before vowel) son; pl. ses.

it's [its]. F: = it is; it has.

itself [it'self], pers.pron. lui-même, elle-même; (reflexive) se.

I've [aiv]. F: = I have.

†**ivory** ['aiv(ə)ri], s. 1. ivoire m. 2. attrib. d'ivoire, en ivoire.

ivy ['aivi], s. lierre m.

J

J, j [dʒei], s. (la lettre) J, j m.

‡jab [dʒæb]. I. v.tr. piquer (qn) (du bout de qch.); *Med:* F: faire ure piqûre à qn. II. s. coup m (du bout de qch.); *Med:* F: piqûre f.

jack [dʒæk], s. 1. (pers.) j. of all trades, touche-à-tout m; j. tar, marin m. 2. (at cards) valet m. 3. *Aut:* 'cric m. **'jack 'up**, v.tr. soulever (une voiture) avec un cric.

jackal [dʒækɔ:l], s. chacal m.

jackdaw [dʒækdɔ:], s. choucas m (des tours).

jacket ['dʒækit], s. veston m; jaquette f; casaque f (de jockey).

jade [dʒeid], s. jade m.

jaded ['dʒeidid], a. surmené, éreinté.

jagged ['dʒægid], a. déchiqueté, ébréché.

jaguar ['dʒægjuər], s. jaguar m.

jam¹ [dʒæm]. I. ‡v. 1. v.tr. serrer, presser (qch. dans qch.); coincer (une machine). 2. v.i. se coincer; (of wheel) se caler; (of brake) se bloquer. II. s. (traffic) j. embouteillage m; F: to be in a j., être dans le pétrin. **'jamming**, s. *Rad:* brouillage m.

jam², s. confiture f; F: it's money for j., c'est donné.

Jamaican [dʒə'meik(ə)n], a. & s. jamaïquain,-quaine.

jamb [dʒæm], s. jambage m, montant m, chambranle m (de porte).

jangle ['dʒæŋgl], v.i. cliqueter; s'entrechoquer.

janitor ['dʒænitər], s. *U.S:* portier m, concierge m.

January ['dʒænjuəri], s. janvier m.

Japanese [dʒæpə'ni:z]. 1. a. & s. japonais, -aise. 2. s. *Ling:* le japonais.

‡jar¹ [dʒɑ:r]. I. v.i. heurter, cogner; taper sur les nerfs; (of colours) jurer. II. s. ébranlement m; choc m, secousse f. 'jarring, s. (of sound) discordant; (of blow) qui ébranle tout le corps.

jar², s. récipient m; pot m.

jasmine ['dʒæzmin], s. jasmin m.

jaundice ['dʒɔ:ndis], s. jaunisse f.

jaunt [dʒɔ:nt], s. balade f, sortie f.

jaunty ['dʒɔ:nti], a. 1. insouciant, désinvolte. 2. enjoué, vif.

jaw [dʒɔ:], s. mâchoire f.

jay [dʒei], s. geai m. **'jay-walker**, s. piéton m imprudent.

jazz [dʒæz], s. jazz m.

jealous ['dʒeləs], a. jaloux. **-ly**, adv. jalousement. **'jealousy**, s. jalousie f.

jeans [dʒi:nz], s.pl. *Cl:* blue-jean m.

jeep [dʒi:p], s. *Aut:* jeep f.

jeer [dʒiər]. I. v.i. se moquer de qn, de qch. II. s. raillerie f. **'jeering**. I. a. railleur. II. s. raillerie f, moquerie f.

‡jelly ['dʒeli], s. gelée f. **'jellyfish**, s. méduse f.

jeopardize ['dʒepədaiz], v.tr. mettre en péril.

jerk [dʒə:k]. I. s. saccade f, secousse f. II. v.tr. donner une secousse à (qch.); he jerked himself free, il s'est dégagé d'une secousse. **'jerky**, a. saccadé. **-ily**, adv. par saccades; par à-coups.

jerry ['dʒeri], s. P: pot m de chambre. **'jerrican**, s. jerricane f, jerrycan m. **'jerry-builder**, s. constructeur m de maisons de carton, de camelote. **'jerry-built**, a. (maison) de carton, de camelote.

jersey ['dʒə:zi], s. 1. *Cl:* jersey m; tricot m (de laine); *Sp:* maillot m. 2. j. (cloth) jersey.

jest [dʒest]. I. s. raillerie f, plaisanterie f; in j., en plaisantant. II. v.i. plaisanter; badiner. **'jesting**, s. raillerie f, badinage m. **'jester**, s. bouffon m (du roi, etc.).

jet¹ [dʒet], s. jais m; j. black, noir comme du jais.

jet², s. 1. jet m (d'eau, etc.). 2. ajutage m, jet (de tuyau d'arrosage); *Aut:* gicleur m; brûleur m (à gaz). 3. *Av:* j. engine, moteur m à réaction; j. (-propelled aircraft), avion m à réaction.

jettison ['dʒetis(ə)n], v.tr. jeter à la mer.

jetty ['dʒeti], s. jetée f, digue f.

Jew [dʒu:], s. Juif m. **'Jewess**, s. Juive f. **'Jewish**, a. juif.

jewel ['dʒuəl], s. 1. (a) bijou m, joyau m; (b) pl. pierres précieuses; pierrerie f. 2. (in watch) rubis m. **'jewelled**, a. (of watch) monté sur rubis. **'jeweller**, s. bijoutier m, joaillier m. **'jewellery**, 'jewelry, s. bijouterie f, joaillerie f; costume j. bijoux mpl de fantaisie.

‡jib [dʒib], v.i. (a) (of horse) refuser; (b) (of pers.) regimber.

jilt [dʒilt], v.tr. planter (là), plaquer (un amoureux).

jingle ['dʒiŋgl]. 1. v.i. tinter; cliqueter. 2. v.tr. faire tinter; faire sonner.

job [dʒɔb], s. 1. (a) tâche f, besogne f, travail m; to do odd jobs, bricoler; odd j. man, homme m à tout faire; F: it's a lovely j., c'est du beau travail; that's just the j., cela fait juste l'affaire; that's a good j.! ce n'est pas malheureux! j. lot, (lot m de) soldes mpl; (b) tâche difficile, corvée f; I had a j. to do it, j'ai eu du mal à le faire. 2. emploi m, place f; F: jobs for the boys, les planques fpl, l'assiette f au beurre; to be out of a j., chômer. **'jobber**, s. (on Stock Exchange) marchand m de titres. **'jobbing**, a. (tailleur) à façon; (jardinier) à la journée.

jockey ['dʒɔki], s. jockey m.

jocular ['dʒɔkjulər], a. facétieux.

jog [dʒɔg]. I. s. secousse f; cahot m. II. v.tr & i. pousser (le coude à qn); rafraîchir (la mémoire à qn); F: we're jogging along, on se défend.

join [dʒɔin]. I. s. joint m, jointure f. II. v.tr. 1. joindre, unir, réunir. 2. se joindre à, s'unir à (qn); entrer dans (un club); s'affilier à (un parti). 3. se joindre, s'unir, à (qch.); the footpath joins the road, le sentier rejoint la route. 'joiner, s. 1. menuisier m. 2. F: he's a j., il aime être membre des sociétés. 'joinery, s. menuiserie f. **joint.** I. s. 1. joint m, jointure f. 2. Anat: articulation f; out of j., (bras) disloqué, déboîté. 3. Cu: morceau m de viande, rôti m. 4. P: boîte f (louche). II. v.tr. 1. joindre, assembler (des pièces de bois). 2. découper (une volaille). 3. jointoyer (un mur). III. a. 1. en commun, combiné; j. commission, commission f mixte; Fin: j. shares, actions indivises; j. stock, capital social. 2. co-, associé; j. author, coauteur m; j. management, codirection f; j. owner, copropriétaire mf. -ly, adv. ensemble, conjointement; Jur: indivisément. 'jointed, a. articulé. **join 'up**, v.i. s'engager (dans l'armée).

joist [dʒɔist], s. solive f, poutre f.

joke [dʒouk]. I. s. plaisanterie f; farce f. II. v.i. plaisanter. 'joker, s. 1. farceur, -euse; practical j., mauvais plaisant. 2. (at cards) joker m. 'joking. 1. (ton) moqueur de, plaisanterie f. 2. s. plaisanterie f, badinage m.

jolly ['dʒɔli]. 1. a. joyeux, gai. 2. adv. F: rudement (content, etc.).

jolt [dʒoult]. I. s. cahot m, secousse f. II. v.tr. & i. cahoter.

jostle ['dʒɔsl], v.tr. bousculer, coudoyer.

jot [dʒɔt]. I. v.tr. to j. sth. down, noter, prendre note, de, qch. II. s. not a j., pas un iota.

journal ['dʒəːn(ə)l], s. journal m; revue f savante; Nau: journal de bord. 'journa'lese, s. F: style m de journaliste. 'journalism, s. journalisme m. 'journalist, s. journaliste mf.

journey ['dʒəːni], s. voyage m; trajet m.

jovial ['dʒouvjəl], a. jovial.

joy [dʒɔi], s. joie f, allégresse f. 'joyful, a. joyeux, heureux. -fully, adv. joyeusement. 'joy-ride, s. (a) balade f en auto (faite à l'insu du propriétaire); (b) promenade f agréable. 'joy-stick, s. Av: manche m à balai.

jubilant ['dʒuːbilənt], a. (a) réjoui; (b) joyeux, exultant. jubi'lation, s. joie f; jubilation f.

jubilee ['dʒuːbiliː], s. jubilé m; cinquantenaire m.

judge [dʒʌdʒ]. I. s. 1. juge m. 2. Sp: arbitre m. 3. connaisseur, -euse; to

be a good j. of wine, s'y connaître en vins. II. v.tr. 1. juger (un prisonnier); arbitrer (à un concours). 2. apprécier, estimer (une distance). 'judg(e)ment, s. 1. jugement m; décision f judiciaire. 2. opinion f, avis m. 3. bon sens m; discernement m. ju'dicial, a. judiciaire. ju'dicious, a. judicieux. -ly, adv. judicieusement.

jug [dʒʌg], s. 1. cruche f, broc m; pot m. 2. P: prison f, taule f. 'jugged, a. j. hare, civet m de lièvre.

juggle ['dʒʌgl], v.i. (a) jongler; (b) faire des tours de passe-passe. 'juggler, s. (a) jongleur, -euse; (b) prestidigitateur m.

juice [dʒuːs], s. jus m, suc m. 'juicy, a. succulent, juteux; plein de jus.

juke box ['dʒuːkbɔks], s. phonographe m à sous.

July [dʒuˈlai], s. juillet m.

jumble ['dʒʌmbl]. I. v.tr. brouiller, mêler. II. s. méli-mélo m, embrouillamini m; j. sale, vente f d'objets usagés (pour une œuvre de charité).

jump [dʒʌmp]. I. s. 1. saut m, bond m; saute f (dans les prix); Sp: high, long, j., saut en hauteur, en longueur. 2. sursaut m, haut-le-corps m. 3. Equit: obstacle m. II. v. 1. v.i. (a) sauter, bondir; (b) sursauter. 2. v.tr. (a) franchir, sauter (une haie); Rail: to j. the rails, sortir des rails; (b) to j. the queue, passer avant son tour; F: to j. the gun, (i) Sp: voler le départ; (ii) commencer à faire qch. avant son tour, prendre les devants. 'jumped-up, a. F: (bourgeois) parvenu. 'jumper[1], s. sauteur, -euse. **jump 'in**, v.i. entrer d'un bond; se jeter à l'eau; Aut: Rail: j. in! montez vite! **jump 'out**, v.i. sortir d'un bond; sauter à bas (du lit); F: I nearly jumped out of my skin, cela m'a fait sursauter. 'jumpy, a. F: agité, nerveux.

jumper[2] ['dʒʌmpər], s. Cl: 1. vareuse f (de marin). 2. tricot m; F: pull m (de femme). 3. U.S: (a) robe f à bretelles; (b) barboteuse f (pour enfants).

junction ['dʒʌŋ(k)ʃ(ə)n], s. 1. jonction f, confluent m; Nau: embranchement m; (b) gare f d'embranchement.

June [dʒuːn], s. juin m.

jungle ['dʒʌŋgl], s. jungle f.

junior ['dʒuːnjər], a. & s. 1. cadet, -ette; plus jeune. David Martin j., David Martin (i) le jeune, (ii) (fils) Sp: j. event, épreuve f des cadets. 2. moins ancien; subalterne (m); Jur: j. counsel, avocat m en second.

junk[1] [dʒʌŋk], s. Nau: jonque f.

junk[2], s. matériaux mpl de rebut; F: camelote f; j. dealer, marchand m de ferraille, de chiffons; fripier m; j. heap, dépotoir m; décharge f publique; I got it at a j. shop, je l'ai acheté chez un brocanteur.

junket ['dʒʌŋkit]. I. *s.* 1. lait caillé. 2. *F:* festin *m.* 3. *F: esp. U.S:* voyage *m* officiel, aux frais de la princesse. II. *v.i. F:* 1. festoyer. 2. *esp. U.S:* voyager aux frais de la princesse.

jurisdiction [dʒuəris'dik∫(ə)n], *s.* juridiction *f.*

†**jury** ['dʒuəri], *s.* jury *m*; jurés *mpl*; **j. box**, banc(s) *m(pl)* du jury. '**juror,** †'**juryman,** *s.* juré *m*, membre *m* du jury.

just [dʒʌst]. I. *a.* juste, équitable. **-ly,** *adv.* avec justice; équitablement; à juste titre. II. *s.pl.* **to sleep the sleep of the j.,** dormir du sommeil du juste. III. *adv.* 1. *(a)* juste, justement; au juste; **j. by the door,** tout près de la porte; **not ready j. yet,** pas encore tout à fait prêt; **that's j. it,** c'est bien cela; **j. so!** c'est bien cela! parfaitement! **very j. so,** très correct; **it's j. the same,** c'est tout un; *(b)* **j. as you please!** comme vous voudrez! **j. as** (he was leaving), au moment où (il partait); *(c)* **j. now,** (i) actuellement; pour le moment; (ii) tout à l'heure. 2. *(a)* immédiatement; *(b)* **he has j.** written to you, il vient de vous écrire; **he has j. come,** il ne fait que d'arriver;

(of book) **j. out,** vient de paraître. 3. sur le point de (partir, etc.); **I'm j. coming!** j'arrive! 4. **j. in time to,** à temps pour; **they j. missed the train,** ils ont manqué de peu le train. 5. *(a)* seulement; **j. once,** rien qu'une fois; **j. one, un seul;** *(b)* **j. listen!** écoutez donc!

justice ['dʒʌstis], *s.* 1. justice *f*; poetic **j.,** justice idéale; **the portrait did not do him j.,** le portrait ne l'avantageait pas; **to do j. to a meal,** faire honneur à un repas. 2. magistrat *m*; juge *m.*

justify ['dʒʌstifai], *v.tr.* justifier (qn, sa conduite); légitimer (une action). **justi'fiable,** *a.* justifiable; légitime. **justifi'cation,** *s.* justification *f.* '**justified,** *a.* justifié; (décision) bien fondée; **he was j. in the event,** l'événement lui donna raison.

‡**jut** [dʒʌt], *v.i.* **j.** (out), être en saillie, faire saillie.

jute [dʒuːt], *s.* jute *m.*

juvenile ['dʒuːvənail]. 1. *a.* juvénile; **j. books,** livres pour la jeunesse; **j. delinquency,** délinquance *f* juvénile; *Jur:* **j. offender,** accusé mineur. 2. *s.* jeune *mf.*

K

K, k [kei], *s.* (la lettre) K, k *m.*

kale [keil], *s.* chou frisé.

kangaroo [kæŋgə'ruː], *s.* kangourou *m.*

keel [kiːl], *s. Nau:* quille *f.*

keen [kiːn], *a.* 1. (couteau) affilé, aiguisé. 2. (froid) vif, perçant. 3. *(a)* ardent, zélé; *(b)* (concurrence) acharné. 4. (esprit) fin, pénétrant. **-ly,** *adv.* âprement; vivement. '**keenness,** *s.* 1. finesse *f*, acuité *f* (du tranchant d'un outil). 2. âpreté *f* (du froid). 3. ardeur *f*, zèle *m.*

‡**keep** [kiːp]. I. *v.* 1. *v.tr. (a)* observer (une règle); tenir (une promesse); ne pas manquer (un rendez-vous); *(b)* célébrer (une fête); observer (le Carême); *(c)* garder, protéger; subvenir aux besoins de (qn); **he has his parents to k.,** il a ses parents à sa charge; *(d)* avoir (une voiture); élever (des volailles); tenir (un hôtel); entretenir (une maîtresse); *(in shop)* **we don't keep cigars,** nous ne vendons pas de cigares; *(e)* maintenir (l'ordre); *(f)* retenir (qn à dîner); cacher (qch. à qn); **don't let me k. you,** que je ne vous retarde pas; **the noise keeps me from sleeping,** le bruit m'empêche de dormir; *(g)* **to k. one's seat,** rester assis; **I'll k. a seat for you,** je vais vous réserver une place; *(h)* **he can't k. a thing in his head,** il ne retient rien; **to k. one's figure,** garder la ligne; *(i)* **k. this to yourself,** gardez cela pour

vous; *(f)* **to k. warm,** (i) se tenir au chaud; (ii) se vêtir chaudement; **to k. s.o. waiting,** faire attendre qn. 2. *v.i. (a)* **to k. smiling,** garder le sourire; **to k. straight on,** suivre tout droit; *F:* **to k. at it,** travailler sans relâche; *(b) (of food)* se garder, se conserver. II. *s.* 1. donjon *m.* 2. nourriture *f*; frais *mpl* de subsistance; **to earn one's k.,** (i) gagner de quoi vivre; (ii) en faire pour son argent; **he isn't worth his k.,** il ne gagne pas sa nourriture. 3. *F:* **for keeps,** pour de bon. **keep a'way.** 1. *v.tr.* éloigner; tenir éloigné. 2. *v.i.* se tenir à l'écart. **keep 'back.** 1. *(a)* arrêter (l'ennemi); retenir (la foule); *(b)* retenir (une somme sur un compte). 2. *v.i.* **k.b.!** n'avancez pas! **keep 'in,** *v.tr.* retenir (qn) à la maison; mettre (un élève) en retenue; **to k. one's hand in,** s'entretenir la main. **keep 'off.** 1. *v.tr.* k.o. **the grass,** défense de marcher sur le gazon; **k. your hands off,** n'y touchez pas. 2. *v.i.* **if the rain keeps off,** s'il ne pleut pas. '**keep 'on,** *v.tr.* garder (son chapeau); ne pas congédier (un employé); continuer (de faire qch.). **keep 'out.** 1. *v.tr.* empêcher (qn) d'entrer. 2. *v.i. F:* **k.o. of this!** mêlez-vous de ce qui vous regarde! '**keep to,** *v.i.* s'en tenir à (une résolution); **to k. to the left,** tenir la gauche. **keep to'gether,** *v.i.* (*a*) rester ensemble; (*b*) rester unis. '**keep 'up. 1.** *v.tr.* entretenir (une route); maintenir (les prix); conserver (un usage); soutenir (l'intérêt); faire veiller (qn). **2.** *v.i.* to k. up appearances, sauver les apparences; to k. up with the times, se maintenir à la page; to k. up with the Joneses, rivaliser avec le voisin. '**keeper,** *s.* gardien *m*; conservateur *m.* (de musée). '**keeping,** *s.* in k., out of k., with, en accord, en désaccord, avec.

kennel ['ken(ə)l], *s.* niche *f* (à chien); *pl.* (i) établissement *m* d'élevage de chiens; (ii) pension *f* pour chiens et chats.

kerb [kə:b], *s.* **1.** bord *m* du trottoir. **2.** garde-feu *m.*

kernel ['kə:n(ə)l], *s.* amande *f* (de noisette).

kettle ['ketl], *s.* bouilloire *f.*

key [ki:]. **I.** *s.* **1.** clef *f*, clé *f*; k. man, homme *m* indispensable; k. money, pas *m* de porte; k. position, poste *m*, position *f* clef; k. ring, porte-clefs *m.* **2.** *Mus:* ton *m*; the k. of C, le ton d'ut. **3.** touche *f* (de piano, de machine à écrire). '**keyboard,** *s.* **1.** clavier *m* (de piano). **2.** (*in hotel*) porte-clefs *m*; tableau *m.* '**keyhole,** *s.* trou *m* de (la) serrure.

khaki ['ka:ki], *a. & s.* kaki (*m*).

kick [kik]. **I.** *v.* **1.** *v.i.* (*of animals*) ruer; (*of pers.*) to k. at, against, sth., regimber contre qch. **2.** *v.tr.* donner un coup de pied à (qn, qch.); *F:* I like kicking myself, je me serais donné des claques; *Sp:* to k. the ball, botter le ballon; to k. a goal, marquer un but; *P:* to k. the bucket, casser sa pipe. **II.** *s.* **1.** coup *m* de pied. **2.** *F:* he has no k., il est à plat; a drink with a k. in it, une boisson qui vous remonte. **3.** recul *m* (d'un fusil); retour *m* (de manivelle); **kick 'off,** *v.tr. Sp:* donner le coup d'envoi. '**kick-off,** *s.* coup *m* d'envoi.

kid¹ [kid], *s.* **1.** chevreau *m*, chevrette *f*; k. gloves, gants (en peau) de chevreau; to handle s.o. with k. gloves, ménager qn. **2.** *F:* gosse *mf*; my k. brother, mon petit frère.

‡**kid²,** *v.tr. F:* en conter à (qn); faire marcher (qn); no kidding! sans blague! to k. oneself that..., se faire accroire que...

‡**kidnap** ['kidnæp], *v.tr.* enlever (qn) de vive force; voler (un enfant); kidnapper. '**kidnapper,** *s.* auteur *m* de l'enlèvement; voleur, -euse (d'enfant). '**kidnapping,** *s.* enlèvement *m*, vol *m* (d'enfant).

kill [kil], *v.tr.* tuer; abattre (une bête); to k. time, tuer le temps. **II.** *s.* (*a*) mise *f* à mort (d'un renard, etc.); (*b*) le gibier tué, le tableau. '**killer,** *s.*

tueur, -euse; meurtrier *m.* '**killing. I.** *a.* **1.** (travail) tuant, écrasant. **2.** *F:* tordant, crevant. **II.** *s.* **1.** tuerie *f*, massacre *m*; abattage *m* (d'animaux). **2.** meurtre *m.* '**killjoy,** *s.* rabat-joie *m.*

kiln [kiln], *s.* four *m* (céramique, etc.).

kilogramme ['kiləgræm], *s.* kilogramme *m*; F: kilo *m.*

kilometre ['kiləmi:tər], *s.* kilomètre *m.*

kilt [kilt], *s. Cl:* kilt *m.*

†kimono [ki'mounu], *s.* kimono *m.*

kin [kin], *s.* (*a*) parents *mpl*; (*b*) to inform the next of k., prévenir la famille.

kind¹ [kaind], *s.* **1.** genre *m*, espèce *f*, sorte *f*; nothing of the k., rien de la sorte. **2.** in k., (paiement) en nature.

kind², *a.* bon, aimable, bienveillant; k.-hearted, bon, bienveillant. '**kindliness,** *s.* bonté *f*, bienveillance *f.* '**kindly. 1.** *a.* bon, bienveillant. **2.** *adv.* avec bonté; to take k. to s.o., prendre qn en amitié; *Com:* k. remit by cheque, prière de nous couvrir par chèque. '**kindness,** *s.* **1.** bonté *f*, amabilité *f.* **2.** a k., un service (rendu).

kindle ['kindl], *v.tr.* allumer.

king [kiŋ], *s.* **1.** roi *m*; K. Albert, le roi Albert. **2.** (*at chess, cards*) roi; (*at draughts*) dame *f.* '**kingcup,** *s. Bot:* bouton *m* d'or. '**kingdom,** *s.* **1.** royaume *m.* **2.** règne *m* (animal, végétal). **3.** *Ecc:* Thy k. come, que ton règne arrive. '**king-size(d),** *a. Com:* géant.

kingfisher ['kiŋfiʃər], *s.* martin-pêcheur *m.*

kink [kiŋk], *s.* (*a*) nœud *m*; faux pli; (*b*) *F:* lubie *f.*

kiosk ['kiɔsk], *s.* kiosque *m.*

kipper ['kipər], *s.* hareng salé et fumé, kipper *m.*

kiss [kis]. **I.** *s.* baiser *m.* **II.** *v.tr.* embrasser (qn); baiser (le front de qn).

kit [kit], *s.* **1.** (*a*) petit équipement; fourniment *m*; effets *mpl.* **2.** trousseau *m*, trousse *f* (d'outils); repair kit, nécessaire *m* de réparation. '**kit-bag,** *s.* musette *f*, sac *m* (de marin).

kitchen ['kitʃin], *s.* cuisine *f*; *attrib.* k. table, table *f* de cuisine; k. equipment, utensils, batterie *f* de cuisine; k. unit, bloc-cuisine *m*; k. garden, jardin *m* potager. **kitchen'ette,** *s.* petite cuisine *f.*

kite [kait], *s.* **1.** milan *m.* **2.** cerf-volant *m.*

kitten ['kitn], *s.* petit(e) chat(te).

kitty ['kiti], *s.* (*a*) cagnotte *f*; (*b*) *F:* magot *m.*

kiwi ['ki:wi:], *s.* aptéryx *m*, kiwi *m.*

kleptomania [kleptə'meiniə], *s.* kleptomanie *f.* **klepto'maniac,** *s.* kleptomane *mf.*

knack [næk], *s.* tour *m* de main; *F:* truc *m*; he has the k. of saying the right thing, il a le don de l'à-propos.

knapsack ['næpsæk], *s.* havresac *m;* sac *m* alpin.

knead [ni:d], *v.tr.* pétrir (la pâte).

knee [ni:], *s.* genou *m.* 'knee-cap, *s.* rotule *f.*

‡**kneel** [ni:l], *v.i.* s'agenouiller; se mettre à genoux. 'kneeling, *s.* agenouillement *m.*

knell [nel], *s.* glas *m.*

knickers ['nikəz], *s.pl.* culotte *f* (de femme).

knick-knack ['niknæk], *s.* bibelot *m.*

‡**knife** [naif]. I. *s.* couteau *m;* table k., couteau de table; flick k., couteau automatique; to have one's k. into s.o., s'acharner après, contre, qn. II. *v.tr.* donner un coup de couteau à (qn).

knight [nait]. I. *s.* 1. chevalier *m.* 2. (*at chess*) cavalier *m.* II. *v.tr.* faire, créer, (qn) chevalier. 'knighthood, *s.* titre *m* de chevalier.

‡**knit** [nit]. 1. *v.tr.* (a) tricoter; (b) to k. one's brows, froncer les sourcils. 2. *v.i.* (*of bones*) se souder. 'knitting, *s.* tricot *m;* tricotage *m;* k. needle, aiguille *f* à tricoter.

knob [nɔb], *s.* bosse *f;* protubérance *f;* bouton *m* (de porte, etc.); morceau *m* (de charbon, de sucre).

knock [nɔk]. I. *s.* coup *m;* heurt *m,* choc *m;* he got a k. on the head, il a reçu un coup sur la tête; there was a k. at the door, on a frappé à la porte. 2. *Aut:* cognement *m* (du moteur). II. *v.* 1. *v.tr.* frapper, heurter, cogner. 2. *v.i.* se heurter, se cogner (contre qch.); *Aut:* (*of engine*) cogner; to k. at the door, frapper à la porte. **knock a'bout.** 1. *v.tr.* bousculer, malmener (qn); maltraiter (qn, qch.). 2. *v.i.* parcourir le monde; rouler sa bosse. **knock 'down,** *v.tr.* jeter (qch.), étendre (qn), par terre; démolir (un mur, etc.); to be knocked down by a car, être renversé par une voiture. 'knocker, *s.* marteau *m* (de porte). 'knocking, *s.* 1. coups *mpl* (à la porte, etc.). 2. cognement *m* (d'un moteur). **knock-'kneed,** *a.* cagneux. **knock 'off.** 1. *v.tr.* faire tomber (qch.) (de la table, etc.). 2. *v.i.* *F:* cesser le travail. **knock 'out,** *v.tr.* faire sortir (qch.); chasser, repousser (un rivet); (*at boxing*) knockouter, mettre knock-out (l'adversaire); the blow knocked me out, le coup m'a fait perdre connaissance. **knock**

'over, *v.tr.* faire tomber, renverser (qch.). **knock 'up.** 1. *v.tr.* (a) réveiller, faire lever (qn); (b) I'm completely knocked up, je suis complètement éreinté. 2. *v.i.* to k. up against sth., se heurter contre qch., rencontrer qn par hasard.

knot [nɔt]. I. *s.* 1. nœud *m.* 2. groupe *m* (de personnes). II. ‡*v.tr. & i.* (se) nouer; faire des nœuds. 'knotty, *a.* plein de nœuds; noueux; (problème) difficile, délicat.

‡**know** [nou]. I. *v.tr.* 1. connaître (qn, un lieu); to get to k. s.o., faire la connaissance de qn. 2. savoir (un fait); connaître, posséder (un sujet); to k. how to do sth., savoir faire qch.; as far as I k., autant que je sache; not to k. sth., ne pas savoir qch., ignorer qch.; to get to k. sth., apprendre qch. *F:* he knows what's what, il est sûr de son fait; *F:* don't I k. it! à qui le dites-vous! *F:* not if I k. it! pour rien au monde! 3. you k. best, vous en êtes le meilleur juge; to k. better than to . . ., se bien garder de . . . 4. to k. about sth., être au courant (de qch.); I k. nothing about that, je n'en suis pas bien sûr! I k. nothing about it, je n'en sais rien. II. *s.* *F:* to be in the k., être au courant; être dans le secret. 'know-all, *s.* *F:* un je-sais-tout. 'know-how, *s.* tour *m* de main, méthode *f,* technique *f,* manière *f* (de s'y prendre). 'knowing. I. *a.* fin, malin, rusé; (sourire) entendu. -ly, *adv.* 1. sciemment. 2. habilement, d'un air rusé. II. *s.* there's no k. (how . . .), il n'y a pas moyen de savoir (comment . . .). 'knowledge ['nɔlidʒ], *s.* 1. connaissance *f* (d'un fait, d'une personne); lack of k., ignorance *f* (of, de); without my k., à mon insu *m;* not to my k., pas que je sache. 2. savoir *m,* connaissances *fpl;* to have a k. of several languages, connaître plusieurs langues. 'knowledgeable ['nɔl-], *a.* bien informé.

knuckle ['nʌkl]. I. *s.* 1. articulation *f,* jointure *f,* du doigt. 2. *Cu:* souris *f* (d'un gigot); jarret *m* (du veau). II. *v.i.* to k. down, s'y mettre sérieusement; to k. under, se soumettre; céder.

koala [kou'ɑ:lə], *s. Z:* koala *m.*

Korean [kɔ'riən], *a. & s.* coréen, -enne; the K. war, la guerre de Corée.

kudos ['kju:dɔs], *s. F:* la gloriole.

L

L, l [el], s. (la lettre) L, l m or f.
lab [læb], s, F: labo m.
label ['leibl]. I. s. 1. étiquette f. 2. *Com:* marque f, label m. II. ‡v.tr. étiqueter.
laboratory [lə'bɔːrətri], s. laboratoire m; l. assistant, laborantin, -tine.
laborious [lə'bɔːriəs], a. laborieux. **-ly,** *adv.* laborieusement.
labour ['leibər]. I. s. 1. travail m, labeur m, peine f. 2. (a) main-d'œuvre f; travailleurs mpl; l. troubles, agitation ouvrière; capital and l., le capital et la main d'œuvre; (b) the L. Party, le parti travailliste. 3. *Med:* couches fpl. II. *v.i.* (a) travailler, peiner; (b) to l. under a delusion, se faire illusion. **'laboured,** a. 1. (style) travaillé. 2. (respiration) pénible. **'labourer,** s. (a) travailleur m; (b) manœuvre m; (c) agricultural l., ouvrier m agricole.
labyrinth ['læbirinθ], s. labyrinthe m.
lace [leis]. I. s. 1. lacet m (de soulier); cordon m. 2. gold l., galon m, passement d'or. 3. dentelle f; Alençon l., point m d'Alençon. II. *v.tr.* lacer (ses chaussures); milk laced with rum, lait m au rhum.
lacerate ['læsəreit], v.tr. lacérer; déchirer (la chair, le cœur).
lack [læk]. I. s. manque m, défaut m (of, de); for l. of, faute de. II. v.tr. & i. to l. sth., manquer de qch.; ne pas avoir qch. **'lacking,** a. qui manque; manquant; l. in meaning, dénué de sens; F: he's a bit l., il est un peu simplet.
laconic [lə'kɔnik], a. laconique. **-ally,** *adv.* laconiquement.
lacquer ['lækər]. I. s. 1. vernis-laque m inv. 2. peinture laquée; cellulose l., laque m cellulosique. II. *v.tr.* 1. laquer. 2. vernir (des meubles).
lad [læd], s. jeune homme m; (jeune) garçon m.
ladder ['lædər]. I. s. 1. échelle f. 2. (in stocking) maille f qui file; to mend a l., rem(m)ailler un bas. **'ladder-proof,** a. (bas) indémaillable. II. *v.i.* (of stocking) se démailler.
ladle ['leidl], s. cuiller f à pot; soup l., louche f.
†lady ['leidi], s. dame f. 1. (a) femme bien élevée; (b) (woman) a l. and a gentleman, un monsieur et une dame; an old l., une vieille dame; (c) ladies' tailor, couturier m pour dames. 2. *Ecc:* Our L., Notre-Dame; my l., madame f (la comtesse, etc.). **'ladybird,** s. *Ent:* F: bête f à bon Dieu. **'ladyship,** s. her l., madame (la duchesse, etc.).

‡lag¹ [læg]. I. *v.i.* traîner; rester en arrière. II. s. (time) l., retard m.
‡lag², v.tr. revêtir (une chaudière, etc.) d'un calorifuge.
lager ['lɑːgər], s. bière f blonde allemande.
lagoon [lə'guːn], s. lagune f.
lair ['leər], s. tanière f, repaire m (de bête fauve).
lake [leik], s. lac m.
lamb [læm], s. agneau m.
lame [leim]. I. a. 1. boiteux; (through accident) estropié; l. excuse, faible (excuse). II. *v.tr.* rendre (qn) boiteux; estropier (qn). **'lameness,** s. 1. boitement m. 2. faiblesse f (d'une excuse, etc.).
lament [lə'ment]. I. s. lamentation f. II. *v.tr.* se lamenter, pleurer (sur qn, qch.). **'lamentable,** a. lamentable, déplorable. **-ably,** *adv.* lamentablement, déplorablement. **lamen'tation,** s. lamentation f. **la'mented,** a. the late l. X, le regretté X.
lamp [læmp], s. 1. (a) lampe f; (b) *Aut:* inspection l., baladeuse f; head l., phare m; side lamps, feux m de position. 2. standard l., lampadaire m; ceiling l., plafonnier m. **'lamp-post,** s. réverbère m. **'lamp-shade,** s. abat-jour m inv.
lance [lɑːns], s. lance f. **'lance-'corporal,** s. *Mil:* soldat m de première classe.
lancet ['lɑːnsit], s. *Med:* bistouri m.
land [lænd]. I. s. 1. (a) terre f; dry l., terre ferme; to see how the l. lies, tâter le terrain; (b) terre, sol m; waste l., terrain vague. 2. terre, pays m. II. *v.* 1. *v.tr.* (a) mettre (qn) à terre; débarquer (qn, qch.); (b) to l. a fish, amener un poisson à terre. 2. *v.i.* (of pers.) débarquer; (of aircraft) atterrir; faire escale (at, à). **'landing,** s. 1. (a) débarquement m; (b) *Mil:* Nau: descente f; (c) *Av:* atterrissage m; parachute l., parachutage m. 2. palier m (d'un escalier). **'landing-ground,** s. *Av:* terrain m d'atterrissage. **'landlady,** s. 1. logeuse f (en garni). 2. hôtelière f. **'landlord,** s. 1. propriétaire m. 2. aubergiste m, hôtelier m. **'landmark,** s. 1. (point m de) repère m. 2. point m décisif, événement m marquant. **'landowner,** s. propriétaire m (foncier). **'landscape,** s. paysage m. **'landslide,** s. 1. éboulement m (de terrain). 2. *Pol:* débâcle f.
lane [lein], s. 1. chemin m (vicinal, rural). 2. *Nau:* route f (de navigation); *Av:* voie f (aérienne). *Aut:* (traffic) l., voie f.

language ['læŋgwidʒ], s. 1. langue f (d'un peuple). 2. langage m; bad l., gros mots mpl.

languid ['læŋgwid], a. languissant; mou.

lanky ['læŋki], a. grand et maigre.

lantern ['læntən], s. lanterne f, falot m; fanal m; Chinese l., lanterne vénitienne.

lap[1] [læp], s. genou mpl; giron m; to sit on s.o.'s l., s'asseoir sur les genoux de qn. 'lap-dog, s. chien m de salon.

lap[2], s. Sp: tour m; circuit m de piste.

‡lap[3]. 1. v.tr. (of animal) laper (du lait, etc.). 2. v.i. (of water) clapoter.

lapel [lə'pel], s. revers m (d'un habit).

lapse [læps]. I. s. 1. erreur f, faute f; défaillance f (de mémoire); faux pas. 2. cours m, marche f (du temps); laps m de temps. II. v.i. 1. to l. from duty, manquer au devoir. 2. (of law, etc.) (se) périmer; cesser d'être en vigueur.

larceny ['lɑːsəni], s. vol m (simple).

larch [lɑːtʃ], s. mélèze m.

lard [lɑːd], s. saindoux m.

larder ['lɑːdər], s. garde-manger m inv.

large [lɑːdʒ]. I. a. (a) grand; gros; fort; to grow l., larger, grossir, grandir; (b) a l. sum, une forte somme; l. fortune, belle fortune; l. family, famille nombreuse; l. meal, repas copieux. -ly, adv. en grande partie; pour une large part. II. s. to be at l., être libre.

lark[1] [lɑːk], s. alouette f. 'larkspur, s. Bot: pied-d'alouette m.

lark[2]. I. s. F: farce f, blague f. II. v.i. F: to l. (about), faire des farces; rigoler.

‡larva ['lɑːvə], s. larve f.

lash[1] [læʃ]. I. s. 1. (a) coup m de fouet; (b) lanière f (de fouet). 2. cil m. II. v.tr. & i. (a) cingler (un cheval); fouetter (qn, un animal); (b) (of animal) to l. its tail, se battre les flancs avec la queue. lash 'out, v.i. (of horse) ruer; (of pers.) invectiver (at s.o., qn).

lash[2], v.tr. lier, attacher; Nau: amarrer.

lass [læs], s. jeune fille f.

lassitude ['læsitjuːd], s. lassitude f.

lasso ['læsou]. I. s. ‡s. lasso m. II. v.tr. prendre au lasso.

last[1] [lɑːst], s. forme f (à chaussure).

last[2]. I. a. dernier. 1. the l. but one, l'avant-dernier; l. but not least, enfin et surtout. 2. l. week, la semaine dernière; l. night, (i) la nuit dernière, (ii) hier soir. -ly, adv. pour finir; en dernier lieu. II. s. this is the l. of it, c'est la fin; to, till, the l., jusqu'au bout; at l., enfin. III. adv. (a) when I saw him l., la dernière fois que je l'ai vu; (b) he spoke l., il a parlé le dernier.

last[3], v.i. durer, se maintenir. 'lasting, a. durable.

latch [lætʃ]. I. s. (a) loquet m; (b) serrure f de sûreté. II. v.tr. fermer (la porte) au loquet. 'latch-key, s. clef f de maison.

late [leit]. I. a. 1. (a) en retard; the train is an hour l., le train a une heure de retard; (b) (delayed) retardé. 2. tard; it's getting l., il se fait tard; in l. summer, vers la fin de l'été; in later life, plus tard dans la vie. 3. (fruit, etc.) tardif. 4. (a) ancien, ex; the l. minister, l'ex-ministre; (b) my l. father, feu mon père. 5. récent, dernier; of l., dernièrement; depuis peu; latest news, dernières nouvelles. -ly, adv. dernièrement, récemment; depuis peu. II. adv. 1. en retard. 2. tard; to keep s.o. l., attarder qn; very l. at night, fort avant dans la nuit; l. in life, à un âge avancé; a moment later, l'instant d'après; F: see you later! à tout à l'heure! 'late-comer, s. retardataire mf.

latent ['leit(ə)nt], a. latent; caché.

lateral ['læt(ə)rəl], a. latéral. -ally, adv. latéralement.

lathe [leið], s. (tool) tour m.

lather ['lɑːðər]. I. s. 1. mousse f de savon. 2. écume f. II. v.tr. savonner. 2. v.i. (of soap) mousser.

latitude ['lætitjuːd], s. latitude f.

latter ['lætər], a. 1. dernier (des deux); the l., ce, le, dernier; celui-ci, ceux-ci. 2. the l. half of June, la seconde quinzaine de juin. -ly, adv. récemment.

lattice ['lætis], s. treillis m, treillage m; l. window, fenêtre f à losanges. 'lattice-work, s. treillis m; treillage m.

laudable ['lɔːdəbl], a. louable; digne d'éloges.

laugh [lɑːf]. I. s. rire m; with a l., en riant; to force a l., rire jaune. II. v.i. rire; (a) to l. heartily, rire de bon cœur; to l. to oneself, rire tout bas; to l. up one's sleeve, rire sous cape; to l. in s.o.'s face, rire au nez de qn; (b) to l. at, over, sth., rire de qch.; to l. at s.o., se moquer de qn. 'laughable, a. risible; ridicule. 'laughing, I. a. riant; rieur. -ly, adv. en riant. II. s. rires mpl; it's no l. matter, il n'y a pas de quoi rire. 'laughing-stock, s. risée f; to make a l.-s. of oneself, se faire moquer de soi. 'laughter, s. rires m(pl); to roar with l., rire aux éclats; F: to die with l., crever de rire.

launch [lɔːntʃ]. I. s. chaloupe f; motor l., vedette f à moteur; canot m automobile. II. v.tr. (a) lancer (un projectile, un coup); (b) mettre (une embarcation) à la mer; (c) lancer (une affaire); déclencher (une offensive). 'launching, s. lancement m (d'un navire, d'une affaire, d'une fusée); l. pad, aire f de lancement.

laundry ['lɔːndri], s. blanchisserie f. launde'rette, s. laverie f (automatique).

laurel ['lɔrəl], s. laurier m.

lava ['lɑːvə], s. lave f.

lavatory ['lævətri], s. cabinets mpl; toilette f; public l., W.C. public.

lavender ['lævindər], s. & a. lavande (f).

lavish ['læviʃ]. I. a. 1. prodigue (in, of de). 2. somptueux; abondant; l. expenditure, dépenses folles. **-ly**, adv. avec prodigalité. II. v.tr. prodiguer, répandre (son argent). **'lavishness**, s. prodigalité f.

law [lɔː], s. 1. loi f; the laws in force, la législation en vigueur. 2. to lay down the l., faire la loi (to s.o., à qn). 3. droit m; civil, criminal, l., le droit civil, criminel; to read l., faire son droit. 4. court of · l., cour f de justice; tribunal m. **'lawless**, a. sans loi; déréglé, désordonné. **'lawlessness**, s. dérèglement m, désordre m, anarchie f. **'lawsuit**, s. procès m. **'lawyer**, s. (a) homme m de loi, juriste m; (b) = (i) avocat m; (ii) avoué m; (iii) notaire m.

lawn [lɔːn], s. pelouse f; gazon m. **'lawn-mower**, s. tondeuse f (de gazon).

lax [læks], a. (of conduct) relâché; (of pers.) négligent; l. morals, morale f facile. **'laxative**, a. & s. laxatif (m).

†lay [lei], v.tr. 1. abattre (la poussière). 2. pondre (un œuf). 3. parier (une somme). 4. mettre (qch. sur qch.); poser (un tapis); asseoir (des fondements); ranger (des briques); préparer (le feu); to l. the table, mettre le couvert. **lay-by**, s. (on road) terre-plein m de) stationnement m. **lay 'down**, v.tr. (a) déposer (qch.); donner (sa vie); (b) établir (une règle); imposer (des conditions). **'layer**, s. couche f (de peinture); assise f, lit m (de béton). **lay 'in**, faire provision de (vivres, etc.). **lay 'off**, v.tr. congédier (des ouvriers). **lay 'out**, v.tr. (a) arranger (des objets); (b) dépenser (de l'argent); (c) to l. oneself out to do sth., se mettre en frais pour faire qch. **lay 'up**, v.tr. to be laid up, être alité.

lazy ['leizi], a. paresseux, fainéant. **-ily**, adv. paresseusement. **'laziness**, s. paresse f, fainéantise f.

lead¹ [led], s. 1. plomb m; attrib. de plomb; white l., céruse f; red l., minium m. 2. mine f (de crayon). 3. Nau: (plomb de) sonde f.

lead² [liːd]. I. s. 1. (a) to follow s.o.'s l., suivre l'exemple de qn; (b) to take the l., prendre la direction. 2. Th: vedette f; (cards) your l.! à vous de jouer. 3. (for dog) laisse f; El: câble m; branchement m. II. ‡v. 1. v.tr. (a) mener, conduire; to l. the way, (i) montrer le chemin; (ii) aller devant; (b) commander, diriger (un mouvement); (c) (cards) to l. clubs, entamer trèfle (2); (d) (in race) tenir la tête. 2. v.i. (of road) mener, conduire (to, à); to l. to nothing, n'aboutir à rien. **'lead a'way**, v.tr. emmener. **'lead back**, v.tr. ramener, reconduire.

'leader, s. 1. (a) conducteur, -trice; guide m; (b) chef m (d'un parti, etc.); F: leader m. 2. article de tête, de fond (d'un journal). **'leading**, a. premier; principal; a l. man, une personnalité; Th: etc: l. part, premier rôle; l. man, lady, vedette f.

†leaf [liːf], s. 1. feuille f (de plante, de papier). 2. feuillet m (de livre); to turn over a new l., changer de conduite. 3. rallonge f (de table). **'leaflet**, s. 1. feuillet m (de papier); papillon m (de publicité); prospectus m. **'leafy**, a. feuillu; couvert de feuilles.

league [liːg], s. ligue f; to be in l. with s.o., être de connivence avec qn; Fb: l. matches, matchs m de championnat.

leak [liːk]. I. s. (a) fuite f (d'un liquide); (b) infiltration f (d'eau, etc.). II. v.i. (of tank, etc.) avoir une fuite; (of liquid) fuir, couler; (of ship) faire eau; to l. away, se perdre; (of news, etc.) to l. out, s'ébruiter. **'leakage**, s. fuite f (d'eau, de gaz, etc.).

lean¹ [liːn]. I. a. maigre; amaigri, décharné. 2. s. maigre m (de la viande).

†lean². I. v.i. (a) s'appuyer (against, on, contre, sur, qch.); to l. on one's elbow, s'accouder; (b) se pencher (over, sur); (of wall etc.) incliner, pencher. 2. v.tr. appuyer (une échelle contre un mur). **'leaning**, s. inclination f (towards, pour); penchant m (towards, pour, vers); tendance f (towards, à). **'lean-to**, s. appentis m.

leap [liːp]. I. s. saut m, bond m. II. ‡v. (a) v.i. & tr. sauter; (b) (of flame, etc.) to l. (up), jaillir. **leap year**, s. année f bissextile.

†learn [lɔːn], v.tr. apprendre. **learned** ['lɔːnid], a. savant, instruit, érudit. **'learner**, s. 1. to be a quick l., apprendre facilement. 2. débutant, -ante; Aut: l.'s car = voiture f école. **'learning**, s. 1. étude f. 2. science f, instruction f.

lease [liːs]. I. s. bail m, pl. baux. II. v.tr. 1. louer; donner (une maison) à bail. 2. prendre (une maison) à bail; louer (une maison). **'leasehold**. I. s. (a) tenure f à bail; (b) immeuble loué à bail. 2. a. tenu à bail.

leash [liːʃ], s. (for dog) laisse f, attache f.

least [liːst]. 1. a. (le, la) moindre; (le) plus petit(e). 2. s. (the) l., (le) moins; to say the l., pour ne pas dire plus; at l., (tout) au moins; I can at l. try, je peux toujours essayer; not in the l., pas le moins du monde. 3. adv. moins.

leather ['leðər], s. cuir m.

leave [liːv]. I. s. 1. permission, autorisation f, permis m. 2. Mil: etc: l. (of absence), congé m; permission f. 3. to take one's l., prendre congé; faire ses adieux. II. ‡v.tr. 1. laisser; (a) left to oneself, livré à soi-même;

(b) to l. go of sth., lâcher qch.; (c) déposer (qch. quelque part); confier (qch. à qn); left-luggage office, consigne f; (d) l. it to me, laissez-moi faire; (e) to be left, rester. 2. (a) quitter (un endroit, qn); sortir de (la salle); abs. partir; (b) abandonner, quitter (sa famille). **'leave be'hind,** v.tr. laisser, oublier (qch.); partir sans (qn). **leave 'off.** 1. v.tr. (a) quitter (un vêtement d'hiver, une habitude); (b) cesser (le travail). 2. v.i. cesser, s'arrêter. **leave 'out,** v.tr. 1. exclure (qn). 2. (a) omettre (qch.); (b) oublier. **leave 'over,** v.tr. to be left over, rester. **'leavings,** s.pl. restes m; débris m.

lecture ['lektʃər]. I. s. 1. conférence f. 2. semonce f. II. v. 1. v.i. faire une, des, conférence(s); faire un cours. 2. v.tr. semoncer, réprimander (qn). **'lecturer,** s. conférencier, -ière; Sch: maître de conférences; chargé m de cours.

ledge [ledʒ], s. rebord m; (on building) corniche f.

ledger ['ledʒər], s. Com: grand livre m.

lee [li:], s. (a) Nau: côté m sous le vent; (b) abri m (contre le vent); leeward, Nau: 1. a. & adv. sous le vent. 2. s. côté m sous le vent. **'leeway,** s. Nau: dérive f; he has a lot of l. to make up, il a un fort retard à rattraper.

leek [li:k], s. poireau m.

left [left]. 1. a. gauche; on my l. hand, à ma gauche. 2. s. gauche f; on the l., à gauche; Pol: the L., la gauche.

leg [leg], s. 1. jambe f; patte f (de chien, d'oiseau, etc.); to pull s.o.'s l., se payer la tête de qn. 2. cuisse f (de volaille); l. of mutton, gigot m. 2. pied m (de table).

‡**legacy** ['legəsi], s. legs m; to come into a l., faire un héritage. **lega'tee,** s. légataire mf; residuary l., légataire (à titre) universel.

legal ['li:g(ə)l], a. légal; to take l. advice = consulter un avocat. **-ally,** adv. légalement; l. responsible, responsable en droit. **le'gality,** s. légalité f.

legend ['ledʒənd], s. 1. légende f, fable f. 2. explication f, légende (d'une carte, etc.). **'legendary,** a. légendaire.

leggings ['legiŋz], s.pl. Cl: jambières f; guêtres f.

legible ['ledʒibl], a. lisible. **-ibly,** adv. lisiblement. **legi'bility,** s. lisibilité f.

legion ['li:dʒ(ə)n], s. légion f.

legislation [ledʒis'leiʃ(ə)n], s. législation f. **'legislative,** a. législatif. **'legislator,** s. législateur m.

legitimate [li'dʒitimit], a. légitime. **-ly,** adv. légitimement.

leisure ['leʒər], s. loisir(s) m(pl); my l. moments, mes moments perdus; people of l., les désœuvrés. **'leisurely,**

a. (of pers.) qui n'est jamais pressé; in a l. fashion, sans se presser.

lemon ['lemən]. I. s. 1. citron m; l. squash, citronnade f; l. squeezer, presse-citrons m; l. (tree), citronnier m. 2. a. jaune citron. **lemon'ade,** s. limonade f; (still) citronnade f.

‡**lend** [lend], v.tr. prêter. **'lender,** s. prêteur, -euse. **'lending,** s. prêt m; Com: etc: prestation f (de capitaux); l. library, bibliothèque f de prêt.

length [leŋθ], s. 1. longueur f; the l. and breadth of the country, toute l'étendue du pays. 2. stay of some l., séjour assez prolongé; l. of service, (ancienneté f; at l., enfin, à la fin; (to speak) at some l., (parler) assez longuement. 3. to go to the l. of, aller jusqu'à (faire qch.). 4. morceau m, bout m (de ficelle, etc.); coupon m (de tissu). **'lengthen,** v. 1. v.tr. (r)allonger; prolonger (la vie, etc.). 2. v.i. s'allonger, se rallonger; augmenter, grandir. **'lengthening,** s. allongement m; prolongation f (d'un séjour, etc.). **'lengthy,** a. (discours) qui traîne en longueur; prolixe. **-ily,** adv. (parler) longuement, avec prolixité.

lenient ['li:niənt], a. clément; doux, indulgent (to, towards, envers, pour, qn). **-ly,** adv. avec clémence; avec douceur, indulgence. **'leniency,** s. clémence f; douceur f, indulgence f (to, towards, pour).

lens [lenz], s. (a) lentille f; verre m (de lunettes); (b) Phot: objectif m.

Lent [lent], s. Ecc: le carême.

leopard ['lepəd], s. léopard m.

less [les]. 1. a. (a) moindre; of l. value, de moindre valeur; sums l. than . . . , sommes au-dessous de . . .; to grow l., s'amoindrir; (b) eat l. meat, mangez moins de viande. 2. prep. moins (10%, etc.). 3. s. moins m; so much the l. to do, d'autant moins à faire. 4. adv. moins; one man l., un homme de moins; l. than six, moins de six; l. and l., de moins en moins. **'lessen.** 1. v.i. s'amoindrir, diminuer. 2. v.tr. amoindrir, diminuer; ralentir (son activité). **'lesser,** attrib. a. 1. petit. 2. moindre.

lessee [le'si:], s. locataire mf (à bail). **'lessor,** s. bailleur, -eresse.

lesson ['les(ə)n], s. leçon f.

lest [lest], conj. de peur que . . . (ne) + sub.

‡**let** [let]. 1. v.tr. (a) permettre; laisser; to l. s.o. do sth., laisser qn faire qch.; l. me tell you that . . . , permettez-moi de vous dire que . . .; to l. go, lâcher; (b) to l. s.o. know sth., faire savoir qch. à qn; (c) to l. s.o. through, laisser passer qn; (d) louer (sa maison etc.). II. v. aux. (supplying 1st & 3rd pers. of imperative) let's make haste!

dépêchons-nous! l. me see! voyons! attendez un peu! l. them all come! qu'ils viennent tous! let 'down, *v.tr.* 1. (*a*) baisser (la glace); (*b*) allonger (une robe). 2. I won't l. you down, vous pouvez compter sur moi. let 'in, *v.tr.* laisser entrer (qn, l'air, la pluie). let 'off, *v.tr.* 1. tirer, faire partir (un coup de feu). 2. (*a*) to l. s.o. off from doing sth., dispenser qn de faire qch. (*b*) faire grâce à qn. let 'out, *v.tr.* laisser sortir (qn); laisser échapper (un oiseau).

lethal ['li:θ(ə)l], *a.* mortel; l. weapon, arme meurtrière.

letter ['letər], *s.* 1. lettre *f*, caractère *m*; to obey to the l., obéir au pied de la lettre. 2. lettre, missive *f*; to open the letters, dépouiller le courrier. 'letter-box, *s.* boîte *f* aux lettres. 'letter-card, *s.* carte-lettre *f*.

lettuce ['letis], *s.* laitue *f*; *F:* salade *f*.

level ['lev(ə)l]. I. *s.* 1. niveau *m* (de la mer; de la société, etc.); on a l. with sth., à la hauteur de qch.; room on a l. with the garden, pièce de plain-pied avec le jardin; at ministerial l., à l'échelon ministériel. 2. terrain *m*, surface *f*, de niveau; on the l., (i) sur le plat; (ii) *F:* loyal; de bonne foi. II. *a.* 1. (*a*) (*not sloping*) (terrain) de niveau; (route) en palier; (*b*) (*flat*) égal; uni; (*c*) l. with ..., au niveau de ...; *Rail:* l. crossing, passage *m* à niveau. 2. to keep a l. head, garder son sang-froid. III. ‡*v.tr.* niveler, mettre (qch.) de niveau; to l. a house to the ground, raser une maison. level-'headed, *a.* (of pers.) qui garde son sang-froid. 'levelling, *s.* nivellement *m*; aplanissement *m* (d'une surface).

lever ['li:vər], *s.* levier *m*.

levy ['levi]. I. †*s.* levée *f* (d'un impôt). II. *v.tr.* lever, percevoir (un impôt).

†**liability** [laiə'biliti], *s.* 1. responsabilité *f*; joint l., responsabilité conjointe. *S. pl: Com:* etc: ensemble *m* des dettes; engagements *mpl.*, obligations *fpl.* 3. disposition *f*, tendance *f* (to sth., to do sth., à qch., à faire qch.). 'liable, *a.* 1. responsable (for, de). 2. passible (d'un impôt, d'une amende). 3. sujet, exposé (to, à); to be l. to colds, être susceptible de s'enrhumer.

liaison [li'eizon], *s.* liaison *f*. **li'aise**, *v.i.* *F:* faire, effectuer, la liaison.

liar ['laiər], *s.* menteur, -euse.

libel ['laibl]. I. *s.* diffamation *f*, calomnie *f*. II. ‡*v.tr.* diffamer (qn, par écrit); calomnier qn. 'libellous, *a.* (écrit) diffamatoire, calomnieux -ly, *adv.* calomnieusement.

liberal ['libərəl], *a.* 1. libéral; (of pers.) d'esprit large. 2. libéral, généreux; abondant. 3. *a.* & *s. Pol:* libéral (m).

-ally, *adv.* libéralement, généreusement. 'libe'rality, *s.* libéralité.

liberate ['libəreit], *v.tr.* libérer; mettre en liberté. **libe'ration**, *s.* libération *f*; mise en liberté.

†**liberty** ['libəti], *s.* liberté *f*; (*a*) at l., libre, disponible; at l. to do sth., libre de faire qch.; (*b*) to take the l. of, se permettre de; (*c*) to take liberties, prendre des libertés.

†**library** ['laibrəri], *s.* bibliothèque *f*; public l., bibliothèque municipale. record l., discothèque *f.* li'brarian, *s.* bibliothécaire *mf.*

licence ['lais(ə)ns], *s.* 1. permis *m*, autorisation *f*; patente *f*; marriage l., dispense *f* de bans; gun l., permis de port d'armes; *Aut:* car l. = carte grise; driving l., permis de conduire. 2. licence *f*. 'license, *v.tr.* accorder un permis, une patente, à (qn); patenter (qn); licensed house = débit *m* de boissons; *Av:* licensed pilot, pilote breveté. licen'see, *s.* patenté, -ée; détenteur *m* d'un permis; (of public house) gérant, -ante. li'centious, *a.* licencieux, dévergondé.

lick [lik]. I. *s.* coup *m* de langue. II. *v.tr.* lécher.

lid [lid], *s.* couvercle *m*.

lie[1] [lai]. I. *s.* mensonge *m*; to tell lies, mentir. II. *v.i.* mentir.

lie[2]. I. *s.* disposition *f* (du terrain, etc.). II. ‡*v.i.* 1. (*a*) être couché (à plat); to be l. asleep, être endormi; (*on gravestone*) here lies ..., ci-gît ...; (*b*) être, rester, se tenir; to l. still, rester tranquille. 2. (*of thg.*) être, se trouver. **lie 'down** *v.i.* 1. se coucher, s'étendre; l. down for a little, reposez-vous un peu. 2. *F:* he took it lying down, il n'a pas dit mot.

lieu [lju:], *s.* in l. of, au lieu de.

lieutenant [lef'tenənt], *s.* lieutenant *m*; *Nau:* lieutenant de vaisseau; l. commander, -sous-lieutenant *m*; l. colonel, lieutenant-colonel *m*; *Nau:* l. commander, capitaine *m* de corvette; l. general, général *m* de division; *Can:* l.-governor, lieutenant-gouverneur *m*.

†**life** [laif], *s.* vie *f*; to take s.o.'s l., tuer qn; to take one's own l., se suicider; to save s.o.'s l., sauver la vie à qn; to fly for one's l., s'enfuir à toutes jambes; to put new l. into s.o., sth., ranimer, *F:* galvaniser (qn, une entreprise). 2. (*a*) vie, vivant *m* (de qn); never in my l., jamais de la vie; tired of l., las de vivre; early l., enfance *f*; l. annuity, rente viagère; (*b*) biographie *f*; (*c*) durée *f* (d'une lampe, etc.); (*d*) he has seen l., il a beaucoup vécu. 'life-belt, *s.* ceinture *f* de sauvetage. 'lifeboat, *s.* *Nau:* canot *m* de sauvetage. 'lifeguard, *s.* *esp. U.S:* (on beach, etc.) maître-nageur *m.* 'lifeless, *a.* sans vie; (i)

mort; (ii) mou, sans entrain. 'lifelike, a. (portrait) vivant. 'lifelong, a. (amitié) de toute la vie; (ami) de toujours. life-size(d), a. (portrait) de grandeur naturelle. 'lifetime, s. vie f; in his l., de son vivant.

lift [lift]. I. 1. Aut: may I give you a l.? puis-je vous conduire quelque part? 2. ascenseur m; l. attendant, liftier m; goods l., monte-charge m inv; service l., monte-plats m inv. II. v. 1. v.tr. (a) lever, soulever (un poids); lever (les yeux); to l. up one's head, redresser la tête; to l. sth. down (from a shelf) descendre qch.; (b) Agr: arracher (les pommes de terre); (c) F: voler (du bétail, etc.). 2. v.i. (of fog) se lever, se dissiper.

light¹ [lait]. I. s. 1. lumière f; (a) by the l. of the sun, à la lumière du soleil; (b) it is l., il fait jour; (of crime, etc.) to come to l., se découvrir; to bring (sth.) to l., révéler (un crime); enhumer (des objets anciens); (c) éclairage m; jour m; (d) to throw l. on sth., jeter le jour sur qch., éclairer qch. 2. (a) lumière, lampe f; (b) feu m; traffic lights, feux de circulation. Aut: tail l., feu rouge; side lights, feux de position; Av: boundary l., feu de balisage; (c) the Portland l., le phare de Portland. II. ‡v.i. & tr. (a) (s')allumer; (b) (s')éclairer; (b) (s')illuminer. III. a. 1. clair; (bien) éclairé. 2. (of hair) blond; (of colour) clair. 'lighter, s. briquet m (à gaz, à essence). 'lighthouse, s. phare m. 'lighting, s. 1. allumage m. 2. éclairage m.

light², a. 1. léger. 2. to travel l., voyager avec peu de bagages. 3. to make l. of sth., traiter qch. à la légère. 4. adv. to sleep l., avoir le sommeil léger. -ly, adv. légèrement. 2. to get off l., s'en tirer à bon compte. 3. to speak l. of sth., parler de qch. à la légère. 'lighten, v.tr. alléger (un navire); réduire le poids de (qch.); soulager (une douleur). light-'hearted, a. au cœur léger; allègre. -ly, adv. gaiement. 'lightness, s. légèreté f.

lightning ['laitniŋ], s. éclairs m, foudre f; a flash of l., un éclair; l. progress, progrès mpl foudroyants; l. conductor, paratonnerre m; Ind: l. strike, grève f surprise.

like¹ [laik]. I. a. semblable, pareil, tel; l. father, l. son; tel père tel fils; a critic l. you, un critique tel que vous; I want to find one l. it, je veux trouver le pareil, la pareille; what's the weather l.? quel temps fait-il? what's he l.? comment est-il? that's just l. a woman! voilà bien les femmes! that's just l. me! c'est bien de moi! II. prep. comme. III. adv. F: l. enough, as l. as not, probablement, vraisemblablement. IV. s. semblable mf; pareil,

-eille. 'likelihood, s. probabilité f. 'likely. I. a. 1. vraisemblable. probable. 2. susceptible (de réussir). II. adv. very l., probablement; not l.! pas de danger! 'likeness, s. ressemblance f.

like². I. v.tr. aimer (bien); as much as you l., tant que vous voudrez; your father won't l. it, votre père ne sera pas content; how do you l. this coffee? comment trouvez-vous ce café? to do (just) as one likes, en faire à sa tête; would you l. some more? vous en prendrez encore un peu? II. s. likes and dislikes, (i) sympathies fpl et antipathies fpl; (ii) goûts mpl. 'likeable, a. agréable, sympathique. 'liking, s. goût m; sympathie f.

lilac ['lailək], a. & s. lilas (m).

†lily ['lili], s. 1. lis m. 2. l. of the valley, muguet m.

limb [lim], s. 1. Anat: membre m. 2. (grosse) branche f (d'un arbre).

lime¹ [laim], s. chaux f; limestone, s. calcaire m.

lime², s. limon m, citron m. 'lime-juice, s. jus de citron (doux).

lime³, s. l. (tree), tilleul m.

limelight ['laimlait], s. in the l., très en vue.

limit ['limit], s. limite f, borne f; a three-mile l., un rayon de trois milles; age l., limite d'âge; F: that's the l.! ça c'est le comble! II. v.tr. limiter, borner, restreindre. limi'tation, s. limitation f, restriction f.

limp¹ [limp]. I. s. boitement m; to walk with a l., boiter. II. v.i. boiter. 'limping, a. boiteux.

limp², a. mou; flasque.

limpet ['limpit], s. patelle f, bernique f.

line¹ [lain]. I. s. ligne f; compagnie f (de navigation, de transports aériens); file f, colonne f (d'autos); vers m (de poésie); Rail: voie f; to be working on the right lines, être en bonne voie; one must draw the l. somewhere, il y a limite à tout; F: it's hard lines, c'est dur; that's more in his l., c'est plus dans son genre; F: to drop s.o. a l., envoyer un petit mot à qn; Com: l. (of goods), série f (d'articles). II. v.tr. the troops lined the streets, les troupes formaient la haie; the street is lined with plane trees, la rue est bordée de platanes. 'lined¹, a. (of paper) réglé, rayé; (of face) ridé. line 'up, v.i. s'aligner.

line², v.tr. doubler (un vêtement). 'lined², a. doublé; fourré. 'lining, s. doublure f (d'un vêtement); Aut: garnitures f (de frein).

linen ['linin], s. 1. toile f (de lin). 2. linge m; lingerie f.

liner ['lainər], s. Nau: paquebot m; Atlantic l., transatlantique m.

ling [liŋ], s. bruyère (commune).

linger ['liŋgər], v.i. (a) tarder, s'attarder; to l. over (a meal), prolonger (un repas); (b) (of invalid) to l. (on), traîner. 'lingering, a. l. l. look, regard prolongé. 2. l. death, mort lente.

linguist ['liŋgwist], s. linguiste mf. linguistics, s.pl. la linguistique.

link [liŋk], I. s. 1. (a) chaînon m, maillon m, anneau m (d'une chaîne); (b) cuff-links, boutons jumelés. 2. lien m, trait m d'union (between, entre); air l., liaison aérienne. II. v.tr. enchaîner, (re)lier, unir (qch. avec qch.); to l. arms, se donner le bras.

links [liŋks], s.pl. terrain m de golf.

linnet ['linit], s. linotte f.

linoleum [li'nouljəm], s. linoléum m.

lint [lint], s. Med: tissu m de coton (pour pansements).

lion ['laiən], s. lion m. 'lioness, s. lionne f.

lip [lip], s. lèvre f; babine f (d'un animal). 'lipstick, s. rouge m à lèvres.

liquefy ['likwifai], 1. v.tr. liquéfier. 2. v.i. (of gas. etc.) se liquéfier; (of oil) se défiger.

liqueur [li'kjuər], s. liqueur f; l. brandy, fine f.

liquid ['likwid], 1. a. (a) liquide; (b) Com: etc: l. assets, valeurs f disponibles; liquidités f. 2. s. liquide m. 'liquidate, v.tr. liquider (une dette, F: une personne).

liquor ['likər], s. boisson f alcoolique.

liquorice ['likəris], s. réglisse f.

lisp [lisp]. I. s. zézayement m. II v.i. & tr. zézayer.

list [list]. I. s. liste f, rôle m, tableau m, état m; wine l., carte f des vins. II. v.tr. cataloguer (des articles).

listen ['lisn], v.ind.tr. to l. to s.o., sth., écouter qn, qch. 'listener, s. auditeur, -trice. listen 'in, v.i. écouter la radio.

listless ['listlis], a. nonchalant; apathique. -ly, adv. nonchalamment.

literal ['litərəl], a. (a) littéral; in the l. sense of the word, au sens propre du mot; (b) (of pers.) positif; prosaïque. -ally, adv. littéralement.

literature ['litrətʃər], s. littérature f; light l., lectures amusantes. 'literary, a. littéraire.

lithe [laið], a. souple, agile.

litigation [liti'geiʃ(ə)n], s. Jur: litige m.

litter ['litər], s. 1. litière f; civière f. 2. fouillis m, désordre m; papiers m etc. (jetés par terre). 3. portée f (d'un animal). 4. Agr: litière (de paille).

little ['litl]. I. a. 1. petit. 2. peu (de); l. money, un peu d'argent. 3. (esprit) mesquin. II. s. 1. peu m; he knows very l., il ne sait pas grand-chose; l. by l., peu à peu. 2. a l. un peu; for a l. (while), pendant un certain temps. III. adv. peu. 'littleness, s. (i) petitesse f; (ii) mesquinerie f.

live. I. a. [laiv]. 1. vivant; en vie; l. broadcast, émission f en direct. 2. l. wire, fil m en charge; F: he's a l. wire, il est dynamique. II. v. [liv]. 1. v.i. (a) vivre; (b) to l. on vegetables, se nourrir de légumes; he earns enough to l. on, il gagne de quoi vivre; (c) to l. in style, mener grand train; to l. well, faire bonne chère; (d) where do you l.? où habitez-vous? 2. v.tr. to l. a happy life, mener une vie heureuse. 'livelihood ['laiv-], s. gagne-pain m inv.; to make a l., gagner sa vie. 'liveliness ['laiv-], s. vivacité f, animation f; entrain m. 'lively ['laiv-], a. vif, animé, plein d'entrain; to take a l. interest in sth., s'intéresser vivement à qch. 'livestock ['laiv-], s. bétail m, bestiaux mpl. 'living ['liv-]. I. a. vivant, vif; en vie; s. the l., les vivants. II. s. 1. vie f; l. space, espace vital; standard of l., niveau m de vie. 2. to earn one's l., gagner sa vie. 3. Ecc: bénéfice m, cure f. 'living-room, s. salle f de séjour; Fr. C: vivoir m. 'liven ['laiv-], 1. v.tr. to l. s.o., sth. (up), animer qn, qch. 2. v.i. to l. up, s'animer.

liver ['livər], s. foie m.

livid ['livid], a. (teint) livide, blême.

lizard ['lizəd], s. lézard m.

load [loud]. I. s. 1. (a) fardeau m; (b) charge f (d'un canon); Aut: commercial l., charge utile; (c) -load; a lorry-l. of sand, une charge, un camion, de sable. 2. a l. on one's conscience, un poids sur la conscience. II. v. 1. v.tr. (a) charger (un camion); (b) charger (un fusil); Aut: armer (un graisseur). 2. v.i. to l. (up), charger, prendre un chargement.

†**loaf**[1] [louf], s.pl. loaves; miche f.

loaf[2], v.i. flâner. 'loafer, s. flâneur m; Pej: voyou m, voyou m.

loam [loum], s. terre f grasse.

loan [loun], s. 1. prêt m. 2. emprunt m.

loath [louθ], a. to be l. to do sth., faire qch. à contre-cœur.

loathe [louð], v.tr. détester, exécrer. 'loathing, s. dégoût m, répugnance f (for, pour). 'loathsome, a. repoussant, écœurant, dégoûtant.

†**lobby** ['lɔbi], s. vestibule m.

lobster ['lɔbstər], s. homard m; spiny l., rock l., langouste f.

local ['louk(ə)l]. 1. a. local, régional. 2. s. (a) habitant, -ante de l'endroit; (b) F: the l., le bistrot du coin. -ally, adv. localement; dans la région. lo'cality, s. localité f; voisinage m.

locate [lou'keit], v.tr. localiser (qch.); situer (qch.); découvrir, repérer (une faute, un défaut). lo'cation, s. 1. relève f, repérage m. 2. (a) situation f, emplacement m; (b) Cin: extérieurs mpl.

lock¹ [lɔk], s. mèche f, boucle f (de cheveux).

lock². I. s. 1. serrure f, fermeture f; under l. and key, sous clef. 2. platine f (de fusil). 3. écluse f. 4. Aut: (steering) l., angle m de braquage. II. v.tr. fermer à clef; to l. s.o. in a room, enfermer qn dans une pièce. **'lock-out**, s. Ind: lock-out m inv. **'locksmith**, s. serrurier m. **'lock 'up**, v.tr. mettre, enfermer (qn, qch.) sous clef; fermer (une maison) à clef.

locker ['lɔkər], s. armoire f; coffre m.

locket ['lɔkit], s. médaillon m (porté en parure).

locomotive [loukə'moutiv], a. locomotif. 2. s. locomotive f. **loco'motion**, s. locomotion f.

locust ['loukəst], s. criquet m (migrateur).

lode [loud], s. Min: filon m, veine f.

lodge [lɔdʒ]. I. s. 1. loge f (de concierge); maison f (de garde-chasse); pavillon m d'entrée (d'une propriété). 2. loge, atelier m (des franc-maçons). II. v. 1. v.tr. to l. a complaint, porter plainte. 2. v.i. (a) être en pension (chez qn); (b) (of thing) rester, se loger. **'lodger**, s. locataire mf, pensionnaire mf. **'lodgings**, s.pl. appartement m meublé; chambre f meublée.

loft [lɔft], s. grenier m, soupente f.

log [lɔg], s. 1. bûche f. 2. ship's l. (book), journal m de bord; l. book, (i) Av: carnet m de vol; (ii) Aut: F: = carte f grise.

logic ['lɔdʒik], s. logique f. **'logical**, a. logique. **-ally**, adv. logiquement.

loin [lɔin], s. 1. pl. reins m; l. cloth, pagne m. 2. Cu: filet m (de mouton, de veau); aloyau m et faux-filet (de bœuf).

loiter ['lɔitər], v.i. flâner, traîner; rôder (d'une manière suspecte). **'loiterer**, s. flâneur, -euse; rôdeur m.

loll [lɔl], v.i. to l. about, flâner, fainéanter; to l. (back) in an armchair, se prélasser dans un fauteuil.

†lolly ['lɔli], s. F: 1. sucette f; iced l., sucette glacée. 2. argent m, F: pognon m.

lonely ['lounli], a. solitaire, isolé; to feel very l., se sentir bien seul. **'loneliness**, s. 1. solitude f, isolement m. 2. sentiment m d'abandon.

long¹ [lɔŋ]. I. a. long. 1. to be six feet l., être long de six pieds; to make sth. longer, (r)allonger qch.; the longest way round, le chemin le plus long. 2. (in time) the days are getting longer. les jours augmentent; it will take a l. time, ce sera long; a l. time ago, il y a longtemps. II. s. before l., sous peu; for l., pendant longtemps; I won't take l., cela ne prendra pas longtemps. III. adv. 1. (a) longtemps; as l. as I live, tant que je vivrai; so l. as, pourvu que; he won't be l., il ne

tardera pas; (b) how l.? combien de temps? how l. have you been here? depuis quand êtes-vous ici? 2. l. before, after, longtemps avant, après; not l. before, after, peu de temps avant, après. 3. all day l., pendant toute la journée. 2. no longer, no . . . plus; how much longer? combien de temps encore? **'long-distance**, attrib. a. P.T.T.: l.-d. telephone, l'inter(urbain) m; Sp: l.-d. runner, coureur m de fond. **'long-drawn-'out**, a. prolongé. **'long-'lived**, a. qui a la vie longue; vivace; (erreur) persistante. **'long-'playing**, a. l.-p. record, microsillon m. **'long-'standing**, attrib. a. ancien; de longue date. **'long-'suffering**, a. patient, endurant. **'long-'term**, attrib. a. (politique, opération) à longue échéance, à long terme. **'long-'winded**, a. (of speaker) verbeux, intarissable.

long², v.i. to l. for, désirer (qch.) ardemment; avoir grande envie de (qch.). **'longing**, s. désir m ardent, grande envie f (for, de).

longitude ['lɔndʒitju:d], s. longitude f.

loo (the) [ðə'lu:], s. F: les cabinets m.

look [luk]. I. s. 1. regard m; to have a l. at sth., jeter un coup d'œil sur qch.; regarder qch.; to take a l. round the town, faire un tour de ville. 2. (a) aspect m, air m, apparence f; mine f; (b) pl. (good) looks, beauté f, mine f. II. v.i. & tr. 1. v.i. regarder; (a) to l. out of the window, regarder par la fenêtre; to l. the other way, détourner les yeux; l. (and see) what the time is, regardez quelle heure il est. 2. v.tr. to l. s.o. (full) in the face, regarder qn bien en face; dévisager qn; to l. s.o. up and down, toiser qn. 3. pred: avoir l'air, sembler; she looks her age, elle paraît bien son âge; what does he l. like? comment est-il? it looks like it, cela en a l'air; on le dirait. 4. F: l. here! dites donc! **look 'after**, v.ind.tr. soigner, s'occuper de (qn, qch.); to l. after oneself, (i) se dorloter; (ii) se débrouiller; to l. after a car, entretenir une voiture. **'look at**, v.ind.tr. regarder, considérer (qn, qch.); just l. at this! F: regardez-moi ça! to l. at him, one would say . . . à le voir on dirait. . . . **look a'way**, v.i. détourner les yeux. **look 'back**, v.i. regarder en arrière; se retourner. **look 'down**, v.i. regarder par terre; baisser les yeux; to l. down on s.o., dédaigner qn. **'look for**, v.ind.tr. 1. chercher (qn, qch.). 2. s'attendre à (qch.). **look 'forward**, v.i. (i) s'attendre (à qch.); (ii) envisager (qch.) avec plaisir. **'look-in**, s. F: he won't get a l.-in, il n'a pas la moindre chance. **'looking-glass**, s. miroir m. **look 'into**, v.ind.tr. examiner, étudier (une question). look 'out, v.i. (a) regarder au dehors; (b) veiller; guetter (for s.o., qn); (c) F: l. out! prenez garde! look 'over, v.tr. jeter un coup d'œil (sur qch.); examiner (qch.); visiter (une maison); repasser (un compte). look 'round, v.i. 1. regarder autour de soi. 2. se retourner (pour voir). look 'up. 1. v.i. (a) lever les yeux; (b) to l. up to s.o., respecter qn; (c) F: business is looking up, les affaires reprennent, vont mieux. 2. v.tr. to l. up a word, chercher un mot (dans le dictionnaire).

loom¹ [lu:m], s. métier m (à tisser).

loom², v.i. apparaître indistinctement.

loop [lu:p]. I. s. boucle f. II. v.tr. boucler (un ruban, un cordage); Av: to l. the loop, boucler la boucle, faire un looping. '**loophole**, s. 1. Mil: meurtrière f. 2. to find a l., trouver une échappatoire.

loose [lu:s]. a. 1. (a) mal assujetti; branlant; (détaché); (b) (of animal) déchaîné, lâché, échappé; (c) mobile; l. sheets (of paper), feuilles volantes; (d) l. cash, menue monnaie. 2. vague, peu exact; (style) décousu. 3. débauché, libertin; l. living, mauvaise vie. -ly, adv. 1. (tenir qch.) sans serrer. 2. inexactement. 'loose-leaf, attrib. a. (album, etc.) à feuilles mobiles. '**loosen.** 1. v.tr.(a) relâcher (un nœud); desserrer (un écrou, etc.). 2. v.i. se délier, se défaire; se desserrer; se relâcher.

loot [lu:t]. I. s. 1. pillage m. 2. butin m. II. v.tr. 1. piller, saccager (une ville). 2. voler (du bétail, etc.). '**looting,** s. pillage m.

‡**lop** [lɔp], v.tr. élaguer, tailler, émonder (un arbre). lop'sided, a. déjeté; de guingois.

lord [lɔːd], s. 1. seigneur m maître m. 2. (title) lord m. 'lordly, a. 1. noble, majestueux. 2. hautain, altier. 'lordship, s. your l., (to nobleman) monsieur le comte, etc.; (to bishop) monseigneur.

‡**lorry** ['lɔri], s. camion m; heavy l., poids lourd m.

‡**lose** [lu:z], v.tr. 1. (a) perdre; (b) he has lost an arm, il lui manque un bras; to l. one's voice, avoir, attraper, une extinction de voix; to l. one's strength, s'affaiblir, baisser; (c) to be lost at sea, périr en mer. to l. one's way, se perdre, s'égarer; to l. sight of s.o., perdre qn de vue. 3. (of clock) retarder. 4. manquer (le train, etc.). 'loser, s. 1. I'm the l. by it, j'y perds. 2. Sp: perdant, -ante; to be a bad l., être mauvais joueur. lost, a. perdu; l. property office, service m des objets trouvés.

loss [lɔs], s. perte f; dead l., perte sèche; to be at a l., être embarrassé, désorienté.

lot [lɔt], s. 1. to draw lots, tirer au sort. 2. (a) sort, part f, partage m; destin m, destinée f. 3. (a) (at auction, etc.) lot m; (b) U.S: lot (de terrain); Aut: parking l., parking m; (c) Com: to buy in one l., acheter en bloc; (d) F: a bad l., un mauvais garnement; (e) F: that's the l., c'est tout. 4. beaucoup; what a l. of people! que de gens! such a l., tellement.

†**lotion** ['lou(ə)n], s. lotion f.

†**lottery** ['lɔtri], s. loterie f.

loud [laud]. I. a. (a) bruyant, retentissant; l. laugh, gros rire; in a l. voice, à haute voix; (b) criard, voyant. 2. adv. (crier) haut, à haute voix. 'loud'ly, adv. (crier) fort, à haute voix; (rire) bruyamment. 2. l. dressed, à toilette tapageuse. 'loudness, s. force f (d'un bruit, etc.); grand bruit. '**loud-'speaker,** s. haut-parleur m, pl. haut-parleurs.

lounge [laundʒ]. I. s. (a) promenoir m; (in hotel) hall m; (in house) salon m; (b) Th: foyer m. II. v.i. flâner. 'lounger, s. flâneur, -euse. 'lounge-suit, s. complet veston m.

†**louse** [laus], s. pou m. '**lousy** [-zi], a. 1. pouilleux. 2. F: sale, P: moche.

lout [laut], s. rustre m, lourdaud m; voyou m.

love [lʌv]. I. s. 1. amour m; to fall in l. with s.o., s'éprendre de qn, tomber amoureux de qn; to make l. (to s.o.), (i) faire la cour à qn; (ii) faire l'amour; to marry for l., faire un mariage d'inclination; give my l. to your parents, faites mes amitiés à vos parents. 2. (at tennis) zéro m, rien m; l. all, égalité f à rien. II. v.tr. aimer (qn, qch.); adorer (faire qch.); I should l. to, je ne demande pas mieux. '**lovable,** a. aimable, sympathique. 'lovely, a. beau, ravissant; (of meal, etc.) excellent, F: épatant. 'lover, s. 1. (a) amoureux; (b) amant m. 2. amateur m (de qch.). 'loving, a. affectueux.

low¹ [lou]. I. a. (a) bas; l. tide, marée basse; l. ceiling, plafond bas, peu élevé; l. prices, prix bas; the lower jaw, la mâchoire inférieure; Mus: l. note, note basse; Ecc: l. mass, messe basse; (b) the lower animals, les animaux inférieurs; a l. trick, un sale coup; (c) to be in l. spirits, être abattu; F: avoir le cafard. II. adv. (perdre, etc.) bas; the lowest paid employee, les employés les moins payés. III. s. all-time l., record le plus bas. 'lower, v.tr. descendre (qch.); baisser (la voix); rabaisser, réduire (le prix de qch.). 'low-down. I. a. bas; ignoble; F: l.-d. trick, sale coup m. II. s. F: to give s.o. the l.-d., tuyauter qn. 'low'lying, a. (terrain) bas.

low², v.i. meugler.

lowering ['lauəriŋ], a. 1. (air) renfrogné. 2. (ciel) sombre, menaçant.

loyal ['lɔiəl], a. fidèle, dévoué; loyal (to, envers). **-ally,** adv. fidèlement. **'loyalty,** s. fidélité f.

lozenge ['lɔzindʒ], s. pastille f, tablette f.

lubricate ['lju:brikeit], v.tr. lubrifier; graisser; lubricating oil, huile f de graissage. **lubri'cation,** s. graissage m. **'lubricator,** s. graisseur m.

lucid ['lu:sid], a. 1. brillant, lumineux. 2. (esprit, style) lucide.

luck [lʌk], s. 1. hasard m, chance f, fortune f; worse l.! tant pis! hard l.! pas de chance! 2. bonheur m, (bonne) chance; to be in l., avoir de la chance. **'lucky,** a. (a) (of pers.) heureux, fortuné, chanceux; to be l., avoir de la chance; l. shot, coup m de veine; (b) (of thg.) to be l., porter bonheur. **-ily,** adv. heureusement; par bonheur.

ludicrous ['lju:dikrəs, 'lu:-], a. risible, grotesque.

luggage ['lʌgidʒ], s. bagage(s) m(pl); l. label, étiquette f à bagages; l. rack, porte-bagages m; Rail: l. van, fourgon m.

lukewarm ['lu:kwɔ:m], a. tiède.

lull [lʌl], s. moment m de calme; accalmie f. II. v.tr. (a) bercer, endormir (qn); (b) calmer (une douleur). **'lullaby,** s. Mus: berceuse f.

lumber ['lʌmbər]. I. s. 1. vieux meubles; fatras m. 2. U.S: bois m (en grume). II. v.tr. (a) encombrer, embarrasser (un lieu). †**lumberman,** s. U.S: (a) exploitant forestier; (b) bûcheron m. **'lumber yard,** s. U.S: chantier m de bois.

lumbering ['lʌmbriŋ], a. lourd, pesant.

luminous ['lu:minəs, 'lju:-], a. lumineux.

lump [lʌmp], s. (a) gros morceau m, bloc m (de pierre); motte f (d'argile); morceau (de sucre); (in porridge, etc.) grumeau m; l. sum, somme f globale; (b) bosse f (au front, etc.).

lunacy ['lu:nəsi], s. démence f; folie f. **'lunatic,** a. & s. fou, f folle; aliéné, -ée; dément, -ente.

lunch [lʌn(t)ʃ]. I. s. (also **'luncheon**) déjeuner m. II. v.i. déjeuner.

lung [lʌŋ], s. poumon m.

lurch[1] [lə:tʃ]. I. s. 1. embardée f (d'un navire); cahot m, embardée (d'une voiture). 2. pas titubant (d'un ivrogne). II. v.i. 1. (of ship, vehicle) faire une embardée. 2. (of pers.) to l. along, marcher en titubant.

lurch[2], s. to leave s.o. in the l., planter là qn.

lure ['ljuər, 'luər], v.tr. attirer, séduire (qn); détourner, entraîner (qn d'un devoir).

lurid ['ljuərid, 'lu-], a. blafard, sinistre.

lurk [lə:k], v.i. se cacher; rester tapi (dans un coin). **'lurking,** a. caché; a l. suspicion, un vague soupçon.

luscious ['lʌʃəs], a. succulent, savoureux.

lust [lʌst], s. appétit m (coupable); convoitise f.

lustre ['lʌstər], s. 1. éclat m, brillant m. 2. lustre m (de plafond).

lusty ['lʌsti], a. vigoureux, fort, robuste. **-ily,** adv. vigoureusement.

luxuriance [lʌg'zjuəriəns], s. luxuriance f, exubérance f. **lux'uriant,** a. exubérant, luxuriant.

†luxury ['lʌkʃəri], s. 1. luxe m. 2. (objet m de) luxe. **lux'urious,** a. (appartement) luxueux, somptueux.

lying[1] ['laiiŋ], a. faux.

lying[2], s. le mensonge.

lying[3], a. couché, étendu.

lyric ['lirik]. 1. a. lyrique. 2. s. poème m lyrique; Th: chanson m. **'lyrical,** a. lyrique.

M

M, m [em], s. (la lettre) M, m m.

mac [mæk], s. Cl: F: imper m.

macaroni [mækə'rouni], s. macaroni m.

macaroon [mækə'ru:n], s. macaron m.

Mach [mæk, mæʃ], s. Av: M. (number), (nombre m de) Mach.

machine [mə'ʃi:n], s. machine f, appareil m. **ma'chinery,** s. mécanisme m; machines fpl, machinerie f. **ma'chine-shop,** s. atelier m (i) de construction mécanique; (ii) d'usinage.

mackerel ['mæk(ə)rəl], s. Fish: maquereau m.

mackintosh ['mækintɔʃ], s. Cl: imperméable m.

mad [mæd], a. 1. fou; raving m., fou furieux. 2. m. for revenge, assoiffé de revanche; F: to be m. about, on s.o.,

sth., être fou, raffoler, de qn, qch. 3. F: to be m. with s.o., être furieux contre qn. 4. m. dog, chien enragé. **-ly,** adv. 1. follement; comme un fou. 2. (aimer) à la folie. 3. furieusement. **'madden,** v.tr. rendre fou, exaspérer (qn). **'maddening,** a. à rendre fou, exaspérant. **'madhouse,** s. F: the place is like a m., on se croirait chez les fous. †**madman,** s. fou m. **'madness,** s. folie f.

madam ['mædəm], s. (form of address) madame f, mademoiselle f.

made [meid], a. fait, fabriqué, confectionné; home-m., fait à la maison.

madeira [mə'diərə], s. vin m de Madère; m. cake = gâteau m de Savoie.

magazine [mægə'zi:n], *s.* 1. magasin *m* (d'armes, etc.); dépôt *m* (de munitions). 2. revue *f* périodique; magazine *m*.

maggot ['mægət], *s.* ver *m*, asticot *m*.

magic ['mædʒik], I. *s.* magie *f*, enchantement *m*. 2. *a.* magique, enchanté. 'magically, *adv.* comme par enchantement. ma'gician, *s.* magicien, -ienne.

magistrate ['mædʒistreit], *s.* magistrat *m*; juge *m*.

magnanimous [mæg'nænimos], *a.* magnanime.

magnate ['mægneit], *s.* magnat *m*; F: gros bonnet *m* (de l'industrie); roi *m* (du pétrole, etc.).

magnesium [mæg'ni:zjəm], *s.* magnésium *m*.

magnet ['mægnit], *s.* aimant *m*. **mag'netic.** 1. *a.* magnétique; aimanté. 2. *s.pl.* magnétisme *m*. -ally, *adv.* magnétiquement. 'magnetism, *s.* aimantation *f*. 'magnetize, *v.tr.* 1. magnétiser, attirer (qn). 2. aimanter (une aiguille, etc.).

magneto [mæg'ni:tou], *s. Aut: etc:* magnéto *f*.

magnificence [mæg'nifis(ə)ns], *s.* magnificence *f*. mag'nificent, *a.* magnifique; (repas) somptueux. -ly, *adv.* magnifiquement.

magnify ['mægnifai], *v.tr.* grossir, agrandir (une image); amplifier (un son); **magnifying glass,** loupe *f*. 'magnification, *s.* grossissement *m*; amplification *f*.

magnitude ['mægnitju:d], *s.* grandeur *f*.

magnum ['mægnəm], *s.* magnum *m*.

magpie ['mægpai], *s.* pie *f*.

mahogany [mə'hɔgəni], *s.* acajou *m*.

maid [meid], *s.* 1. old *m.*, vieille fille. 2. bonne *f*, domestique *f*; lady's *m.*, femme *f* de chambre. 'maiden, *s.* 1. (*a*) jeune fille *f*; (*b*) vierge *f*. 2. *attrib.* (*a*) *m.* aunt, tante non mariée; (*b*) *m.* name, nom de jeune fille; (*c*) *m.* voyage, premier voyage (d'un navire); *m.* speech, discours *m* de début (d'un député).

mail [meil]. I. *s. P.T.T:* 1. courrier *m*. 2. la poste; *Com:* m. order, commande *f* par poste; vente *f*, achat *m*, sur catalogue. II. *v.tr.* envoyer (qch.) par la poste. 'mailbag, *s.* sac *m* postal. 'mail box, *s. U.S:* boîte *f* aux lettres. 'mail train, *s.* train-poste *m*. 'mail-van, *s.* fourgon *m* postal.

maim [meim], *v.tr.* estropier, mutiler.

main [mein]. I. *s.* 1. in the *m.*, en général; en somme. *Civ.E:* canalisation *f* maîtresse; m. drainage, tout à l'égout *m*; *El:* câble *m* de distribution; to take power from the mains, brancher sur le secteur. II. *a.* principal, premier, essentiel; the *m.* body, le gros, the *m.* thing, l'essentiel *m*; *Cu:* m. course,

plat *m* de résistance; m. road, route *f* à grande circulation; m. street, rue *f* principale; *Rail:* m. line, grande ligne *f*. -ly, *adv.* 1. principalement, surtout. 2. en grande partie. 'mainland, *s.* continent *m*; terre *f* ferme. 'mainspring, *s.* ressort *m* moteur. 'mainstay, *s.* point *m* d'appui; soutien *m* principal.

maintain [mein'tein], *v.tr.* 1. maintenir (l'ordre); soutenir (la conversation). 2. entretenir, soutenir (une famille). 'maintenance, *s.* 1. maintien *m* (de l'ordre). 2. entretien *m* (d'une famille, d'une route).

maison(n)ette [meizo'net], *s.* appartement *m* à un ou deux étages.

maize [meiz], *s.* maïs *m*.

majesty ['mædʒisti], *s.* majesté *f*. ma'jestic, *a.* majestueux. -ally, *adv.* majestueusement.

major[1] ['meidʒər], *s. Mil:* commandant *m*. 'major-'general, *s. Mil:* général *m* de division.

major[2], *a.* majeur; m. road = route à priorité. ma'jority, *s.* majorité *f*.

make [meik]. I. *s.* 1. (*a*) façon *f*, fabrication *f* (d'un objet); (*b*) *Com: Ind:* marque *f* (d'un produit). 2. *F:* to be on the *m.*, chercher à faire fortune à tout prix. II. *v.* 1. (*a*) faire; construire (une machine); façonner (un vase); fabriquer (du papier); confectionner (des robes); what's it made of? en quoi est-ce? what do you *m.* of it? qu'en pensez-vous? to *m.* the bed, faire le lit; to *m.* one's escape, s'échapper; (*b*) établir, assurer (un raccordement); (*c*) gagner (de l'argent); to *m.* a name, se faire un nom; *F:* to *m.* it, réussir, y arriver; (*d*) to *m.* so happy, rendre qn heureux; to *m.* oneself comfortable, se mettre à l'aise; to *m.* oneself ill, se rendre malade; (*e*) what time do you *m.* it? quelle heure avez-vous? (*f*) you should *m.* him do it, vous devriez le forcer à le faire. 2. *v.i.* to *m.* for a place, se diriger vers un endroit. 'maker, *s. Ind:* fabricant *m*; constructeur *m* (de machines). 'make 'off, *v.i.* se sauver, décamper, filer. 'make 'out, *v.tr.* 1. faire, dresser (une liste, etc.); établir, relever (un compte); faire, tirer (un chèque). 2. établir, prouver (qch.). 3. comprendre (une énigme); déchiffrer (une écriture); I can't *m.* it out, je n'y comprends rien. 'make 'over, *v.tr.* céder, transférer (qch. à qn). 'makeshift, *s.* pis-aller *m*; moyen *m* de fortune. make 'up. I. *v.tr.* 1. compléter (une somme); combler (un déficit). 2. regagner (du terrain perdu); to *m.* it up to s.o., dédommager qn (de qch.); indemniser qn. 3. faire (un paquet); *Med:* exécuter (une ordonnance). 4. (*a*) faire, confectionner (des vêtements); (b) établir (un compte); (c) inventer (une histoire). 5. to m. (oneself) up, se maquiller. 6. to m. up one's mind, se décider, prendre son parti. 7. to m. it up, se réconcilier. II. *v.i.* to m. up for (sth.), rattraper (ses pertes, le temps perdu). 'make-up, s. maquillage *m.* 'make-weight, s. complément *m* de poids.

maladjusted [mælə'dʒʌstid], *a.* inadapté.

malaria [mə'lɛəriə], *s.* paludisme *m.*

male [meil]. **1.** *a.* mâle; masculin. **2.** *s.* mâle *m.*

malice ['mælis], *s.* malice *f,* méchanceté *f.* ma'licious, *a.* (a) méchant, malveillant; (b) rancunier. -ly, *adv.* (a) avec méchanceté; (b) par rancune.

malign [mə'lain], *v.tr.* calomnier, diffamer. ma'lignant, *a.* méchant; *Med:* malin.

mallet ['mælit], *s.* maillet *m.*

malnutrition [mælnju:'triʃ(ə)n], *s.* sous-alimentation *f;* alimentation *f* défectueuse.

malt [mɔːlt], *s.* malt *m.*

mamma [mə'mɑː], *s. F:* maman *f.*

mammal ['mæm(ə)l], *s. Z:* mammifère *m.*

mammoth ['mæməθ]. **1.** *s.* mammouth *m. Z:* attrib. *a. F:* géant, monstre.

†**man** [mæn], *s.* **1.** homme *m;* every m., tout le monde; chacun; any m., n'importe qui; no m., personne; few men, peu de gens; as many men ... , on dit que.... **2.** an old m., un vieillard; **the dead m.,** le mort; an important m., une personnalité. **3.** m. and wife, mari *m* et femme *f.* **4.** (a) domestique *m;* (b) *Ind: etc:* employé *m;* (delivery) m., livreur *m.* 'man-power, *s.* main-d'œuvre *f.* †'manservant, *s.* domestique *m.*

manage ['mænidʒ], *v.tr.* **1.** diriger; gérer (une entreprise, etc.); mener (une affaire). **2.** gouverner; tenir (des enfants, etc.); maîtriser, dompter (un animal). **3.** arranger, conduire (une affaire); to m. to do sth., trouver moyen de faire qch. **4.** *abs.* she manages well, elle sait s'y prendre. 'manageable, *a.* **1.** (outil) maniable; (canot) manœuvrable. **2.** (of pers.) traitable. 'management, *s.* **1.** (a) maniement *m* (d'un outil, des hommes); (b) direction *f,* conduite *f* (d'une affaire); gérance *f,* gestion *f* (d'une propriété). **2.** adresse *f;* savoir-faire *m.* **3.** *coll. Ind: etc:* l'administration *f,* la direction. 'manager, *s.* **1.** directeur *m,* administrateur *m;* gérant *m;* joint m., cogérant *m;* sales m., directeur commercial; department m., chef *m* de service; *Th:* imprésario *m; Cin: Sp:* manager *m.* 'manageress, *s.* directrice *f.* 'managing, *a.* directeur; m. director, administrateur *m* délégué.

mandarin(e) [mændə'ri:n], *s. Bot:* mandarine *f.*

mandate ['mændeit], *s.* mandat *m.*

mane [mein], *s.* crinière *f.*

mange ['meindʒ], *s.* gale *f.* 'mangy, *a.* (a) galeux; (b) *F:* minable, miteux, moche.

manger ['meindʒər], *s.* mangeoire *f.* crèche *f.*

mangle ['mæŋgl]. **I.** essoreuse *f* (à rouleaux). **II.** *v.tr.* **1.** essorer (le linge). déchirer, mutiler, lacérer (qn); charcuter (une volaille); déformer, estropier (un mot, une citation).

manhood ['mænhud], *s.* âge *m* d'homme; âge viril.

mania ['meiniə], *s.* **1.** manie *f;* folie *f.* **2.** to have a m. for doing sth., avoir la passion de qch. 'maniac, **1.** *a. & s.* fou *m* furieux. **2.** *s.* enragé, -ée (de qch.).

manicure ['mænikjuər]. **I.** *s.* **1.** soin *m* des mains; m. set, trousse *f* de manucure. **2.** manucure *mf.* **II.** *v.tr.* soigner les mains; se faire les ongles. 'manicurist, *s.* manucure *mf.*

manifest ['mænifest]. **I.** *v.tr.* manifester, témoigner (qch.). **II.** *a.* manifeste, évident. -ly, *adv.* manifestement. manifes'tation, *s.* manifestation *f.* mani'festo, *s. Pol:* proclamation *f.*

manipulate [mə'nipjuleit], *v.tr.* **1.** manipuler (un objet). **2.** *F:* to m. accounts, cuisiner les comptes. manipu'lation, *s.* **1.** manipulation *f.* **2.** *Pej:* tripotage *m.*

mankind [mæn'kaind], *s.inv.* le genre humain.

manly ['mænli], *a.* d'homme; mâle, viril. 'manliness, *s.* caractère *m* viril; virilité *f.*

mannequin ['mænikin], *s.* mannequin *m.*

manner ['mænər], *s.* **1.** manière *f,* façon *f* (de faire qch.); in such a m. that, de manière que, de sorte que. **2.** *pl.* mœurs *f,* usages *m* (d'un peuple). **3.** maintien *m,* air *m.* **4.** *pl.* manières; bad manners, mauvaises manières; to have bad manners, être mal élevé, manquer de savoir-vivre; good manners, politesse *f.*

manœuvre [mə'nuːvər]. **I.** *s.* manœuvre *f.* **II.** *v.tr. & i.* manœuvrer.

manor ['mænər], *s.* m. (house), manoir *m;* gentilhommière *f.*

mansion ['mænʃ(ə)n], *s.* (in country) château *m;* (in town) hôtel *m* (particulier).

manslaughter ['mænslɔːtər], *s.* homicide *m* involontaire; homicide sans préméditation.

mantelpiece ['mæntlpiːs], *s.* (manteau *m* de) cheminée *f.*

manual ['mænju(ə)l]. **1.** *a.* manuel; m. labour, travail manuel, de manœuvre. **2.** *s.* manuel *m;* aide-mémoire *m.* **3.** *s. Mus:* clavier *m* (d'un orgue).

manufacture [mænju'fækt∫ər]. I. s. fabrication f; confection f (de vêtements). II. v.tr. fabriquer (un produit industriel); confectionner (des vêtements); **manufacturing town**, ville f industrielle. **manu'facturer**, s. fabricant m, industriel m.

manure [mə'njuər]. I. s. engrais m; farmyard m., fumier m. II. v.tr. fumer, engraisser (la terre).

manuscript ['mænjuskript], a. & s. manuscrit (m).

many ['meni], a. & s. un grand nombre de; beaucoup de; bien des; plusieurs; ever so m. times, je ne sais combien de fois; m. of us, beaucoup d'entre nous; in so m. words, en propres termes; too m., trop de; how m.? combien de? as m. . . . as, autant de . . . que.

map [mæp]. I. s. carte f. II. †v.tr. (1) dresser une carte de (la région, etc.). 2. to m. out a route, tracer un itinéraire.

maple ['meipl], s. érable m.

maquis [mæ'ki:], s. maquis m.

marathon ['mærəθən], s. marathon m.

marble ['mɑ:bl], s. 1. marbre m; m. quarry, marbrière f. 2. bille f; to play marbles, jouer aux billes.

March¹ [mɑ:t∫], s. mars m.

march² [mɑ:t∫], I. s. 1. marche f; on the m., en marche; m. past, défilé m (devant qn); 2. marche, progrès m (des événements). II. v.i. marcher; to m. past (s.o.), défiler (devant qn).

marchioness [mɑ:'∫ənes], s. marquise f.

mare ['mɛər], s. jument f.

margarine [mɑ:dʒə'ri:n, mɑːgə'ri:n], s. margarine f.

margin ['mɑːdʒin], s. (a) marge f; (b) marge, écart m; to allow a m. for errors, calculer large, **'marginal**, a. marginal, en marge; Pol: m. seat, siège m chaudement disputé.

marigold ['mærigould], s. Bot: souci m; French m., œillet m d'Inde; African m., rose f d'Inde.

marijuana [mæri'wɑːnə], s. marijuana f.

marine [mə'ri:n]. 1. a. (a) (animal) marin; (b) m. insurance, assurance maritime. 2. s. (a) marine f; mercantile m., marine marchande; (b) soldat m de l'infanterie de marine. **maritime** ['mæritaim], a. maritime.

mark [mɑːk]. I. s. 1. but m, cible f; to hit the m., atteindre le but; frapper juste; wide of the m., loin de la vérité, du compte. 2. marque f; tache f (sur un vêtement, etc.); Sch: note f. II. v.tr. marquer; Sch: corriger (un devoir). 'marked, a. marqué; (of improvement) sensible. 'marking, s. 1. marquage m; Sch: correction f (des devoirs). 2. pl. marques f; (on animal) taches f, rayures f. †'marksman, s.

bon tireur m. 'marksmanship, s. habileté f au tir.

market ['mɑːkit]. I. s. marché m; (covered) marché couvert, halles fpl; black m., marché noir; the Common M., le marché commun; m. research, étude f du marché; Com: to find a m. for sth., trouver un débouché pour qch.; m. day, jour m de marché; m. garden, jardin m maraîcher; m. gardener, maraîcher, -ère. II. v.tr. trouver des débouchés pour (des marchandises); lancer (un article) sur le marché. 'marketable, a. vendable.

marmalade ['mɑːməleid], s. confiture f d'oranges.

marquee [mɑː'ki:], s. grande tente f.

marquess, marquis ['mɑːkwis], s. marquis m.

marriage ['mærid3], s. mariage m; m. certificate, acte m de mariage. **'marry**, v.tr. 1. (of priest, etc.) marier (qn). 2. épouser (qn); se marier (avec qn); abs. to get married, se marier.

marrow ['mærou], s. 1. moelle f. 2. (vegetable) m., courge f; courgette f.

marsh [mɑː∫], s. marais m, marécage m. **'marshy**, a. marécageux.

marshal ['mɑː∫(ə)l]. I. s. 1. (a) Mil: field-m., maréchal m; (b) Av: M. of the R.A.F. = Commandant m en Chef des Forces aériennes; Air Chief M., général m d'armée aérienne; Air M., général (de corps aérien). 2. maître m des cérémonies. II. ‡v.tr. placer (des personnes) en ordre, en rang; Rail: classer, trier (des wagons). **'marshalling**, s. 1. disposition f en ordre (de personnes & de choses). 2. Rail: classement m, manœuvre f (des wagons); m. yard, gare f de triage.

marten ['mɑːtin], s. Z: martre f; fouine f.

martial ['mɑː∫(ə)l], a. martial; guerrier.

martin ['mɑːtin], s. Z: martinet m.

martyr ['mɑːtər], s. martyr, f. martyre. **'martyrdom**, s. martyre m.

marvel ['mɑːv(ə)l]. I. s. merveille f. II. ‡v.i. s'émerveiller, s'étonner (at, de). **'marvellous**, a. merveilleux. -ly, adv. à merveille; merveilleusement.

mascot ['mæskət], s. mascotte f; porte-bonheur m.

masculine ['mæskjulin], a. masculin; mâle.

mash [mæ∫], v.tr. brasser, écraser (qch.). **mashed potatoes**, purée f de pommes de terre; pommes f mousseline. **'masher**, s. broyeur m; mélangeur m; H: presse-purée m inv.

mask [mɑːsk]. I. s. masque m. II. v.tr. 1. masquer. 2. cacher (ses pensées).

mason ['meisn], s. 1. maçon m. 2. franc-maçon m. **'masonry**, s. maçonnerie f.

masquerade [mæskə'reid]. I. s. mascarade f. II. v.i. se déguiser (en . . .); se faire passer (pour . . .).

mass¹ [mæs, mɑːs], *s. Ecc:* messe *f*.

mass² [mæs]. **I.** *s.* **1.** masse *f.* 2. foule *f* (de gens); the masses, la foule; m. protest, protestation *f* en masse; m. production, fabrication *f* en (grande) série. **II.** *v.tr. & i.* (se) masser. **'massive,** *a.* massif.

massacre ['mæsəkər]. **I.** *s.* massacre *m.* **II.** *v.tr.* massacrer.

massage ['mæsɑːʒ; *Fr.* 'mæsaːʒ]. **II.** *v.tr.* [mæ'saːʒ] masser (le corps). ma'sseur, ma'sseuse, *s.* masseur, -euse.

mast [mɑːst], *s.* **1.** *Nau:* mât *m.* 2. *Rad: etc:* pylône *m*.

master ['mɑːstər]. **I.** *s.* **1.** maître *m.* (= *employer*) patron *m; Sch:* professeur *m;* instituteur *m; attrib.* m. mind, esprit *m* supérieur; esprit dirigeant. **II.** *v.tr.* maîtriser; surmonter (une difficulté). **'masterful,** *a.* autoritaire. **'masterly,** *a.* de maître; magistral. **'masterpiece,** *s.* chef-d'œuvre *m*.

masticate ['mæstikeit], *v.tr.* mâcher, mastiquer.

mastiff ['mæstif], *s.* mâtin *m*.

mat [mæt], *s.* (*a*) natte *f*; (*b*) paillasson *m*; (*c*) carpette *f*; *F:* he's been on the m., on lui a passé un savon.

match¹ [mætʃ]. **I.** *s.* **1.** égal, -ale; pareil, -eille. 2. lutte *f,* partie *f,* match *m.* 3. mariage *m,* alliance *f.* **II.** *v.* **1.** *v.tr.* (*a*) égaler (qn); (*b*) apparier (des gants); assortir (des couleurs). 2. *v.i.* s'assortir; s'harmoniser. **'matching,** *s.* assortiment *m;* appariement *m.* **'matchless,** *a.* incomparable; sans égal; sans pareil.

match², *s.* allumette *f.* **'matchbox,** *s.* boîte *f* à allumettes.

mate [meit]. **I.** *s.* **1.** (*birds*) mâle *m,* femelle *f.* 2. *Ind:* compagnon *m; F:* camarade *mf.* 3. *Nau:* (*merchant navy*) officier *m;* first m., second *m;* second m., lieutenant *m;* (*b*) (*Navy*) second maître *m.* **II.** *v.i.* (*of birds*) s'accoupler.

material [mə'tiəriəl], *s.* **1.** *Tex:* tissu *m.* 2. *pl.* as *Ind:* raw materials, matières *f* premières; building materials, matériaux *m* de construction; *pl.* fournitures *fpl;* accessoires *mpl.* **ma'terialist,** *s.* matérialiste *mf.* **ma'terialize,** *v.i.* se matérialiser; (*of plan*) aboutir.

maternal [mə'tərnl], *a.* maternel. **ma'ternity,** *s.* maternité *f;* m. dress, robe *f* de grossesse; m. hospital, maternité *f*.

mathematics [mæθi'mætiks], *s.pl.* mathématiques *fpl.* **mathe'matical,** *a.* mathématique. **mathema'tician,** *s.* mathématicien, -ienne. **maths,** *s.pl. F:* math *fpl*.

matinée ['mætinei], *s. Th:* matinée *f*.

matins ['mætiŋz], *s.pl. Ecc:* matines *f*.

matrimony ['mætriməni], *s.* le mariage. **matri'monial,** *a.* matrimonial; conjugal.

matron ['meitrən], *s.* **1.** femme *f* mariée. 2. (*a*) intendante *f* (d'une école, etc.); (*b*) infirmière-major *f* (d'un hôpital).

matter ['mætər], *s.* **1.** matière *f;* substance *f;* sujet *m* (d'un discours); reading m., choses *f* à lire. 2. *Med:* pus *m.* 3. affaire *f,* chose *f,* cas *m;* what's the m.? qu'est-ce qu'il y a? qu'avez-vous? sth. must be the m., il doit y avoir qch. **II.** *v.i.* importer (à qn); it doesn't m., n'importe; cela ne fait rien. **'matter-of-fact,** *a.* pratique; prosaïque.

mattress ['mætris], *s.* matelas *m*.

mature [mə'tjuər]. **I.** *a.* mûr; *fig.* adv. mûrement. **II.** *v.tr.* mûrir (le vin, le fromage). 2. *v.i.* (*of fruit, etc.*) mûrir. **ma'turity,** *s.* maturité *f*.

maul [mɔːl], *v.tr.* meurtrir, malmener (qn).

Maundy Thursday ['mɔːndi'θəːzdi], *s.* le jeudi saint.

mauve [mouv], *a. & s.* mauve (*m*).

maxim ['mæksim], *s.* maxime *f,* dicton *m*.

†maximum ['mæksiməm], *a. & s.* maximum (*m*).

†may¹ [mei], *v.aux.* **1.** (*a*) I m., je peux; (*b*) it m. be that . . ., il se peut bien que . . .; be that as it m., quoi qu'il en soit; that's as m. be, c'est selon; run as he might, he couldn't catch me, il a eu beau courir, il n'a pas pu m'attraper; (*c*) we m. as well stay (here), autant vaut rester. 2. m. I? vous permettez? m. I come in?—you m., puis-je entrer?—mais certainement. 3. I hope it m. be true, pourvu que cela soit vrai! 4. much good m. it do you! grand bien vous fasse! **'maybe,** *adv.* peut-être.

May², *s.* **1.** (*month*) mai *m;* M. day, le premier mai. 2. **may**(tree), aubépine *f*.

mayor ['mεər], *s.* maire *m;* deputy m., adjoint *m.* **'mayoress,** *s.* femme *f* du maire.

maze [meiz], *s.* labyrinthe *m*.

me [mi, miː], *pers.pron., objective case.* **1.** me; moi; they hear me, ils m'entendent; listen to me! écoutez-moi! 2. (*stressed*) moi; come to me, venez à moi.

meadow ['medou], *s.* pré *m,* prairie *f*.

meagre ['miːgər], *a.* maigre; peu copieux.

meal¹ [miːl], *s.* farine *f* (d'avoine, de seigle, etc.).

meal², *s.* repas *m*.

mean¹ [miːn]. **I.** *s.* **1.** (*a*) milieu *m;* the happy m., le juste milieu; (*b*) *Mth:* moyenne *f.* 2. *pl.* moyen(s *m*)(*pl*), voie(s *f*)(*pl*); by all means! mais certainement! by means of sth., au moyen de qch. 2. *pl.* moyens (de vivre); resources *f;* private means, fortune *f* personnelle; means test, enquête *f* sur la situation (de fortune). **II.** *a.* moyen.

mean², *a.* 1. misérable, minable. 2. bas, méprisable; *a* m. trick, un vilain tour; un sale coup. 3. avare, mesquin. -ly, *adv.* 1. misérablement, pauvrement. 2. (se conduire) bassement. 3. mesquinement, chichement. 'meanness, *s.* 1. médiocrité *f*, pauvreté *f*; bassesse *f* (d'esprit). 2. mesquinerie *f*, avarice *f*.

‡**mean³**, *v.tr.* 1. (*a*) avoir l'intention (de faire qch.); se proposer (de faire qch.); what do you m. to do? que comptez-vous faire? he didn't m. it, il ne l'a pas fait exprès; without meaning it, sans le vouloir; (*b*) he means well, il a de bonnes intentions. 2. destiner (for, à qn). 3. (*a*) (*of words*) vouloir dire; signifier; (*b*) what do you m. by that? qu'entendez-vous par là? you don't m. it! vous plaisantez! I m. it, c'est sérieux. 'meaning. I. *a.* 1. well-m., bien intentionné. 2. (regard) significatif; (sourire) d'intelligence. -ly, *adv.* d'un air, d'un ton, significatif. II. *s.* (*a*) signification *f*, sens *m* (d'un mot); (*b*) you mistake my m., vous ne comprenez mal. 'meaningless, *a.* dénué de sens.

meander [mi'ændər], *v.i.* serpenter.

meantime ['mi:ntaim], **meanwhile** ['mi:n-(h)wail], *s. & adv.* dans l'intervalle; en attendant.

measles ['mi:zlz], *s.pl.* rougeole *f*. 'measly, *a. F:* insignifiant, misérable.

measure ['meʒər]. I. *s.* mesure *f*; made to m., fait sur mesure; (tape) m., mètre *m*; coal measures, gisements *m* houillers. II. *v.tr.* mesurer; métrer (un mur, etc.). 'measured, *a.* mesuré, déterminé; (pas) cadencé; (langage) modéré. 'measurement, *s.* mesure *f*; dimension *f*; hip m., tour *m* de hanches.

meat [mi:t], *s.* viande *f*.

mechanics [mi'kæniks], *s.pl.* la mécanique. me'chanic, *s.* mécanicien *m*; motor m., mécanicien garagiste *m*. me'chanical, *a.* 1. mécanique. 2. automatique. -ally, *adv.* 1. mécaniquement. 2. machinalement. 'mechanism, *s.* appareil *m*, dispositif *m*; mécanisme *m*. mechani'zation, *s.* mécanisation *f*. 'mechanize, *v.tr.* mécaniser; mechanized farming, motoculture *f*.

medal ['medl], *s.* médaille *f*. me'dallion, *s.* médaillon *m*.

meddle ['medl], *v.i.* se mêler (with, de); to m. with (sth.), toucher à (qch.). 'meddler, *s.* officieux, -euse; intrigant, -ante; touche-à-tout *m*. 'meddlesome, *a.* intrigant. 'meddling, *s.* intervention *f* (in, with, a matter, dans une affaire).

mediate ['mi:dieit], *v.i.* s'entremettre; servir de médiateur. medi'ation, *s.* médiation *f*; intervention *f* (amicale). 'mediator, *s.* médiateur, -trice.

medical ['medik(ə)l], *a.* médical; the m. profession, (i) le corps médical; (ii) la profession de médecin. -ally, *adv.* m. speaking, du point de vue médical; to be m. examined, subir un examen médical.

medicine ['meds(i)n], *s.* 1. la médecine. 2. médicament *m*; m. chest, armoire *f* à pharmacie. me'dicinal, *a.* médicinal.

medi(a)eval [medi'i:v(ə)l], *a.* du moyen âge; médiéval.

mediocre [mi:di'oukər], *a.* médiocre. medi'ocrity, *s.* médiocrité *f*.

meditate ['mediteit], *v.i.* (*a*) méditer (on, sur); (*b*) se recueillir. medi'tation, *s.* méditation *f*; recueillement *m*. 'meditative, *a.* méditatif; recueilli.

‡**medium** ['mi:diəm], *s.* 1. milieu *m*; happy m., juste milieu. 2. *Sc:* véhicule *m* (du son, etc.). 3. intermédiaire *m*; advertising m., organe *m* de publicité. 4. (*spiritualism*) médium *m*. *a.* moyen; m.-sized, de taille moyenne.

medley ['medli], *s.* mélange *m*; *Mus:* pot pourri *m*.

meek [mi:k], *a.* doux; humble. -ly, *adv.* avec douceur; humblement. 'meekness, *s.* douceur *f*, humilité *f*.

‡**meet** [mi:t]. 1. *v.tr. (a)* rencontrer (qn); se rencontrer avec (qn); (*b*) affronter (une difficulté); (*c*) rejoindre (qn); to go to m. s.o., aller au-devant de (qn); (*d*) faire la connaissance de (qn); (*e*) to m. s.o.'s eye, regarder qn en face; (*f*) se conformer (aux vues de qn); *F:* faire des concessions (à qn); (*g*) satisfaire à (un besoin); faire face à (une demande). 2. *v.i.* (*a*) se rencontrer, se voir; (*b*) (*of a society*) se réunir; (*c*) se joindre, se toucher; nos regards se croisèrent; (*d*) to m. with sth., rencontrer, trouver, qch.; to m. with losses, éprouver des pertes, essuyer un refus. 'meeting, *s.* 1. rencontre *f*. 2. assemblée *f*, réunion *f*. 'meeting-place, *s.* (lieu *m* de) rendez-vous *m*.

melancholy ['melənkəli]. 1. *s.* mélancolie *f*. 2. *a.* mélancolique; triste.

mellow ['melou], *a.* 1. (fruit) fondant, mûr. 2. (*of voice, wine*) moelleux; doux.

melodrama ['melədra:mə], *s.* mélodrame *m*. melodra'matic, *a.* mélodramatique.

melody ['melədi], *s.* mélodie *f*, air *m*, chant *m*. me'lodious, *a.* mélodieux.

melon ['melən], *s.* melon *m*.

melt [melt]. 1. *v.i.* fondre; se fondre. 2. *v.tr. (a)* (faire) fondre. 'melting. I. *a.* (*of snow*) fondant. II. *s.* fonte *f*, fusion *f*.

member ['membər], *s.* membre *m*.

memento [me'mentou], *s.* mémento *m*, souvenir *m*.

memo ['memou], *s. F:* note *f*; m.-pad, bloc-notes *m*.

memoir ['memwɑːr], s. (a) mémoire m, étude f; (b) notice f biographique; (c) pl. mémoires.

†memorandum [memə'rændəm], s. mémorandum m.

memory ['meməri], s. 1. mémoire f; loss of m., amnésie f. 2. souvenir m. 'memorable, a. mémorable. me-'morial. I. a. commémoratif. II. s. war m., monument m aux morts. 'memorize, v.tr. apprendre (qch.) par cœur.

menace ['menəs]. I. s. menace f. II. v.tr. menacer.

menagerie [mi'nædʒəri], s. ménagerie f.

mend [mend]. I. v.tr. raccommoder (un vêtement); réparer (qch.). II. s. 1. reprise f; raccommodage m. 2. Med: F: to be on the m., être en voie de guérison. 'mending, s. (a) raccommodage m; invisible m., stoppage m; (b) vêtements mpl à raccommoder.

menial ['miːniəl], a. servile; bas.

meningitis [menin'dʒaitis], s. Med: méningite f.

menopause ['menoupɔːz], s. Med: ménopause f.

menstruate ['menstrueit], v.i. (of woman) avoir ses règles. menstru'ation, s. menstruation f.

mental ['mentl], a. mental; de l'esprit; m. reservation, arrière-pensée f; m. arithmetic, calcul m de tête; m. home, clinique f psychiatrique; m. specialist, psychiatre m. -ally, adv. mentalement; m. deficient, anormal. men-'tality, s. mentalité f.

mention ['menʃ(ə)n]. I. s. mention f (de qch.). II. v.tr. mentionner, citer (qch.); I shall m. it to him, je lui en toucherai un mot; not to m . . ., sans parler de . . .

menu ['menjuː], s. menu m.

mercantile ['məːk(ə)ntail], a. marchand; m. nation, nation commerçante.

mercenary ['məːsin(ə)ri], a. & s. mercenaire (m).

merchant ['məːtʃ(ə)nt]. 1. s. négociant, -ante; commerçant, -ante. 2. a. marchand; du commerce. 'merchandise, s. marchandise(s) f(pl). 'merchandising, s. techniques fpl marchandes. 'merchant 'navy, 'service, s. Nau: marine f marchande.

mercy ['məːsi], s. miséricorde f, grâce f, pitié f; to be at s.o.'s m., être à la merci de qn. 'merciful, a. miséricordieux (to, pour); clément (to, envers). -fully, adv. miséricordieusement. 'merciless, a. impitoyable, sans pitié. -ly, adv. impitoyablement.

mere [miər], a. simple, pur, seul; he's a m. boy, ce n'est qu'un enfant. -ly, adv. simplement, seulement; tout bonnement.

merge [məːdʒ]. 1. v.tr. fondre, fusionner (deux systèmes). 2. v.i. se fondre, se perdre (in(to), dans); se confondre (in(to), avec); (of banks, etc.) s'amalgamer. 'merger, s. Com: fusion f (de plusieurs compagnies).

meringue [mə'ræŋ], s. meringue f.

merit ['merit]. I. s. 1. mérite m. 2. valeur f. II. v.tr. mériter.

mermaid ['məːmeid], s. sirène f.

merry ['meri], a. joyeux, gai. -ily, adv. gaiement, joyeusement. 'merriment, s. gaieté f, hilarité f.

mesmerize ['mezməraiz], v.tr. hypnotiser.

mesh [meʃ], s. 1. maille f (d'un filet); m. stocking, bas m indémaillable. 2. E: prise f, engrenage m.

meson ['mizɔn], s. Atom Ph: méson m.

mess [mes]. I. s. 1. saleté f. 2. fouillis m, gâchis m; to make a m. of it, tout gâcher. 3. Mil: table f, mess m. II. v. 1. v.tr. (a) salir, souiller (qch.); (b) gâcher (une affaire). 2. v.i. Mil: faire popote (avec qn). 'mess-up, s. F: 1. gâchis m. 2. malentendu m. 'messy, a. 1. sale; en désordre. 2. salissant.

message ['mesidʒ], s. (a) message m; to leave a m. for s.o., laisser un mot pour qn; (b) communication f (par téléphone); (c) commission f, course f. 'messenger, s. messager, -ère; (b) commissionnaire m; garçon m de bureau; (in hotel) chasseur m; telegraph m., facteur m des télégraphes. Queen's m., courrier m diplomatique.

metabolism [me'tæbɔlizm], s. métabolisme m.

metal ['metl], s. 1. métal m; sheet m., tôle f. 2. Civ.E: road m., cailloutis m. 3. pl. Rail: rails mpl. me'tallic, a. métallique. 'metallurgy, s. métallurgie f.

metamorphosis [metə'mɔːfɔsis], s. métamorphose f. meta'morphose, v.tr. métamorphoser, transformer (to, into, en).

metaphor ['metəfər], s. métaphore f; image f. meta'phoric(al), a. métaphorique. -ally, adv. métaphoriquement.

meteor ['miːtiər], s. météore m. mete'oric, a. météorique. 'meteorite, s. météorite f.

meteorology [miːtjərɔlɔdʒi], s. météorologie f. meteo'rologist, s. météorologue m. F: météo m.

meter ['miːtər], s. compteur m; parking m., compteur m de stationnement.

methane ['meθein], s. méthane m.

method ['meθəd], s. méthode f; manière f (de faire qch.); procédé m. me-'thodical, a. méthodique. m. life, vie réglée, ordonnée. -ally, adv. méthodiquement; avec méthode.

methyl ['meθil], s. Ch: méthyle m. 'methylated, a. m. spirits, alcool m à brûler.

meticulous [mi'tikjuləs], a. méticuleux.

metre[1] ['miːtər], s. Lit: mètre m, mesure f.

metre[2], s. mètre m; square, cubic, m., mètre carré, cube. **'metric**, a. (système) métrique.

mettle ['metl], s. to put s.o. on his m., piquer qn d'honneur.

mew [mjuː]. I. v.i. miauler. II. s. (also mewing) miaulement m.

mews [mjuːz], s.pl. écuries fpl; m. flat, appartement aménagé dans une ancienne écurie.

Mexican ['meksikən], a. & s. mexicain, -aine.

mezzanine ['mezəniːn], s. m. (floor), entresol m.

mica ['maikə], s. mica m.

Michaelmas ['miklməs], s. la Saint-Michel; m. daisy, aster m œil-du-Christ.

microbe ['maikroub], s. microbe m.

microfilm ['maikroufilm]. I. s. microfilm m. II. v.tr. microfilmer.

microphone ['maikrəfoun], s. microphone m; concealed m., espion m.

microscope ['maikrəskoup], s. microscope m; electron m., microscope électronique. **micro'scopic**, a. microscopique.

mid [mid], a. du milieu; mi-, moyen; in m. air, entre ciel et terre; m. June, la mi-juin. 'mid'day, s. midi m. 'middle'. 1. s. milieu m, centre m; in the m. of, au milieu de. 2. attrib. du milieu; central, moyen; m.-aged, d'un certain âge; the m. class(es), la bourgeoisie; m.-class, bourgeois. †'middleman', Com: revendeur m. 'middling, a. médiocre; passable; comme ci comme ça.

midge [midʒ], s. moucheron m; cousin m.

midget ['midʒit]. 1. s. nain, naine. 2. a. minuscule.

'**midland**. 1. a. du centre (de l'Angleterre). 2. s.pl. the Midlands, les comtés m du centre. 'mid'night, s. minuit m. †'midshipman', s. aspirant m (de marine). midst, s. in the m. of, au milieu de (la foule, etc.); in the m. of all this, sur ces entrefaites. 'mid'stream, s. in m., au milieu du courant. 'mid'summer, s. (a) plein m de l'été; (b) le solstice d'été; M. day, la Saint-Jean. 'mid'way, adv. à mi-chemin. 'mid'winter, s. milieu m, fort m, de l'hiver.

†**midwife** ['midwaif], s. sage-femme f. 'midwifery [-wif-], s. Med: obstétrique f.

might [mait], s. puissance f, force(s) f (pl). 'mighty, a. (a) puissant, fort; (b) grand, vaste; (c) F: to be in a m. hurry, être diablement pressé.

mignonette [minjo'net], s. réséda m odorant.

migraine ['miːgrein], s. migraine f.

migrate [mai'greit], v.i. émigrer. **mi'gration**, s. migration f. 'migratory, a. migrateur.

mike [maik], s. F: micro m.

mild [maild], a. doux. -ly, adv. doucement. 'mildness, s. 1. douceur f, clémence f (de qn, du temps). 2. caractère m bénin (d'une maladie).

mile [mail], s. mille m. 'mileage, s. distance en milles; Fr.C: millage m. 'milestone, s. borne f routière.

military ['milit(ə)ri]. 1. a. militaire; of m. age, en âge de servir. 2. s.pl.coll. the m., les militaires m; l'armée f. 'militant, a. militant.

milk [milk]. I. s. lait m; m. diet, régime lacté; m. bar, milk-bar m; m. jug, pot m à lait. II. v.tr. traire (une vache, etc.). †'milkman, s. laitier m. 'milky, a. laiteux; the M. Way, la Voie lactée.

mill [mil]. I. s. moulin m (à blé, à café, etc.); rolling m., laminoir m; cotton m., filature f de coton. II. v. 1. v.tr. moudre. 2. v.i. (of crowd) fourmiller; tourner en rond.

millet ['milit], s. Bot: millet m, mil m.

milligramme ['miligræm], s. milligramme m.

millimetre ['milimiːtər], s. millimètre m.

milliner ['milinər], s. modiste f. 'millinery, s. (articles mpl de) modes fpl.

million ['miljən], s. million m. millio'naire, a. & s. millionnaire (mf).

mimic ['mimik]. I. s. imitateur, -trice. II. †v.tr. imiter, mimer, contrefaire (qn, la nature). 'mimicry, s. mimique f, imitation f.

mince [mins]. I. s. Cu: hachis m. II. v.tr. 1. hacher (menu); minced meat, hachis m. 2. to m. (one's words), parler du bout des lèvres. 'mincemeat, s. (sorte de) compote f de raisins secs et de pommes. 'mincer, s. H: hachoir m (à viande, etc.). 'mincing, a. affecté, minaudier.

mind [maind]. I. s. 1. to bear sth. in m., ne pas oublier qch. 2. to know one's own m., savoir ce qu'on veut; to make up one's m., prendre son parti; se décider; I have a good m. to . . ., j'ai envie de . . .; to have sth. in m., avoir qch. en vue. 3. esprit m; to be out of one's m., avoir perdu la raison. II. v.tr. 1. faire attention à (qn, qch.). 2. s'occuper de, se mêler de (qch.). 3. (a) would you m. shutting the door? voudriez-vous bien fermer la porte? if you don't m., si cela vous est égal; (b) never m.! n'importe! 4. m. you don't fall! prenez garde de tomber! m. the step! attention à la marche! 5. soigner, avoir l'œil sur (des enfants); garder (des animaux, la maison).

mine[1] [main]. I. s. mine f. II. v.tr. & i. miner. 'minefield, s. Mil: champ m de mines. 'miner, s. Min: ouvrier m du fond. 'minesweeper, s. dragueur m de mines. 'mining, s. 1. Mil: pose f de mines. 2. Min: industrie f minière; m. village, village minier; m. engineer, ingénieur m des mines.

mine[2], poss.pron. le mien, la mienne, les miens, les miennes; this letter is m., cette lettre est à moi; a friend of m., un(e) de mes ami(e)s.

mineral ['minərəl], 1. a. minéral; m. waters (i) eaux f minérales; (ii) boissons f gazeuses. 2. s. minéral m; Min: minerai m; m. rights, droits miniers.

mingle ['miŋgl], 1. v.tr. mêler, mélanger. 2. v.i. se mêler, se confondre (with, avec).

mini- [mini-], a. mini-; m. skirt, mini-jupe f.

miniature ['miniə(t)ʃər]. 1. s. miniature f. 2. a. en miniature, en petit; m. model, maquette f.

†minimum ['miniməm], a. & s. minimum (m). 'minimize, v.tr. réduire au minimum; minimiser.

minister ['ministər], s. 1. Pol: ministre m. 2. Ecc: pasteur m. minis'terial, a. Pol: ministériel; du gouvernement. 'ministry, s. 1. ministère m, département m; the Air M., le Ministère de l'Air. 2. Ecc: he was intended for the m., il fut destiné à l'Église.

mink [miŋk], s. vison m.

minnow ['minou], s. Fish: vairon m.

minor ['mainər]. 1. a. petit; mineur; peu important; (rôle) subalterne; of m. interest, d'intérêt secondaire. 2. s. (pers.) mineur, -eure. mi'nority, s. minorité f.

mint[1] [mint], s. the M., la Monnaie. II. v.tr. frapper (de la monnaie).

mint[2] s. Bot: menthe f; Cu: m. sauce, vinaigrette f à la menthe.

minus ['mainəs]. 1. prep. moins. 2. a. m. (sign), moins m; m. quantity, quantité f négative.

minute[1] ['minit], s. 1. minute f; ten minutes past, to, trois heures dix, trois heures moins dix; m. hand, grande aiguille f (d'une montre); wait a m.! attendez un instant! 2. note f; procès-verbal m (d'une séance).

minute[2] [mai'njuːt], a. 1. tout petit; minuscule. 2. minutieux, détaillé. -ly, adv. minutieusement.

miracle ['mirəkl], s. miracle m. mi'raculous, a. (a) miraculeux; (b) extraordinaire.

mirage ['miraːʒ], s. mirage m.

mirror ['mirər], s. miroir m; glace f; Aut: driving m., rétroviseur m.

mirth [məːθ], s. gaieté f.

mis- [mis], prefix (used in combined forms) (a) mé-, més-; (b) mal (+ v.); mauvais (+ s.). misad'venture f; mésaventure f; contretemps m. misap-

pre'hension, s. malentendu m. mis-a'ppropriate, v.tr. détourner (des fonds). misappropri'ation, s. détournement m (de fonds). misbe'have, v.i. se mal conduire. mis'calculate. 1. v.tr. mal calculer. 2. v.i. se tromper. mis-calcu'lation, s. erreur f de calcul; mécompte m. mis'carriage, s. 1. avortement m, insuccès m (d'un projet); m. of justice, erreur f judiciaire. 2. Med: fausse couche f.

miscellaneous [misə'leiniəs], a. varié, mêlé, mélangé, divers.

mischief ['mistʃif], s. malice f; (of child) to get into m., faire des bêtises; to make m., semer la discorde. 'mischievous, a. (enfant) espiègle, malicieux. -ly, malicieusement; par espièglerie.

mis'conduct, s. mauvaise conduite f. miscon'duct, v.tr. mal diriger, mal gérer (une affaire). miscon'struction, s. fausse interprétation f. misdemeanour, s. Jur: délit m. misdi'rect, v.tr. mal diriger (une affaire); mal renseigner (qn).

miser ['maizər], s. avare mf. 'miserly, a. avare.

misery ['mizəri], s. 1. souffrances fpl. 2. misère f, détresse f. 'miserable, a. (a) (of pers.) malheureux, triste; (b) déplorable, abominable.

mis'fire, v.i. rater; Aut: (of engine) avoir des ratés. 'misfit, s. (a) vêtement m manqué; (b) (pers.) inadapté(e). mis'fortune, s. malheur m. mis'giving, s. doute m; crainte f. mis'guided, a. peu judicieux; (of attempt) malencontreux. 'mishap, s. contretemps m. misin'form, v.tr. mal renseigner (qn). misin'terpret, v.tr. mal interpréter. mis'judge, v.tr. mal juger; méconnaître (qn). mis'judged, a. (of pers.) mal compris. mis'lay, v.tr. égarer (qch.). ‡mis'lead, v.tr. induire (qn) en erreur; tromper (qn). mis-'leading, a. trompeur; fallacieux. mis-'manage, v.tr. mal administrer, mal gérer (une affaire). mis'management, s. mauvaise administration f; mauvaise gestion f. mis'place, v.tr. mal placer (sa confiance); déplacer (un objet). 'misprint, s. faute f d'impression, f: coquille f. mispro'nounce, v.tr. mal prononcer. mis'quote, v.tr. citer à faux. misrepre'sent, v.tr. mal représenter. misrepresen'tation, s. faux rapport m.

miss[1] [mis]. I. v.tr. 1. manquer (le but, un train, etc.); se tromper (de route); ne pas rencontrer (qn); to m. the point, ne pas comprendre; he just missed being killed, il a failli se faire tuer. 2. to m. (out) a word, sauter un mot. 3. remarquer, regretter, l'absence de (qn, qch.). II. s. coup m manqué; F: to give (s.o., sth.) a m., négliger de voir (qn, qch.), de visiter (qch.). 'missing, a. absent; perdu; Mil: disparu.

miss², s. (title) mademoiselle; pl. the Misses Martin, les demoiselles Martin.

missal [mis(ə)l], s. Ecc: missel m.

missile [misail], s. projectile m; engin m; guided m., missile m, engin m, téléguidé.

mission ['miʃ(ə)n], s. mission f. 'missionary, a. & s. missionnaire m.

mis'spelling, s. faute f d'orthographe.
mis'statement, s. rapport m inexact; erreur f (de fait).

mist [mist]. I. s. 1. brume f. 2. buée f. II. v.i. to m. over, se couvrir de buée. 'misty, a. brumeux.

mistake [mis'teik]. I. s. erreur f; faute f; to make a m., se tromper. II. ‡v.tr. 1. mal comprendre. 2. to m. s.o. for s.o., prendre qn pour qn. mis'taken, a. 1. to be m., se tromper. 2. (of opinion) erroné.

mistletoe ['mistlou], s. gui m.

mistress ['mistris], s. maîtresse f; Sch: (i) professeur m; (ii) institutrice f.

mis'trust, v.tr. se méfier de (qn, qch.).
‡misunder'stand, v.tr. 1. mal comprendre (qch.). 2. méconnaître (qn).
misunder'standing, s. 1. malentendu m. 2. mésentente f, brouille f. misunder'stood, a. 1. mal compris. 2. (of pers.) incompris. mis'use. I. s. [-juːs] abus m. II. v.tr. [-juːz] maltraiter (qn); abuser de (son autorité); to m. a word, employer un mot dans un sens abusif.

mix [miks]. I. v.tr. (a) mêler, mélanger; (b) préparer (un breuvage); (c) brasser (des billets de loterie); malaxer (le mortier); retourner (la salade); (d) confondre (des faits). 2. v.i. se mêler, se mélanger; to m. with people, fréquenter les gens. 'mixed, a. 1. mêlé, mélangé, mixte; m. sweets, bonbons assortis; m. ice, glace panachée; m. feelings, sentiments mitigés. 2. (of pers.) to get m., s'embrouiller; perdre la tête. 'mixer, s. 1. (machine) Ind: malaxeur m; H: (electric) m., batteur m (électrique). 2. he's a good, bad, m., (i) il est très sociable; (ii) il ne s'adapte pas. 'mixture s. mélange m. 'mix 'up, v.tr. mêler, mélanger; embrouiller (ses papiers); confondre (deux personnes). 'mix-up, s. 1. confusion f; embrouillement m, pagaille f. 2. F: bagarre f.

moan [moun]. I. s. gémissement m, plainte f. II. v.i. gémir, se lamenter. 'moaning, s. gémissement m.

moat [mout], s. fossé m, douve f.

mob [mob], s. 1. foule f; cohue f; bande f d'émeutiers.

mobile ['moubail], a. mobile. mo'bility, s. mobilité f.

mobilize ['moubilaiz]. 1. v.tr. mobiliser. 2. v.i. (of army) entrer en mobilisation. mobili'zation, s. mobilisation f (de troupes, de capitaux).

mock [mɔk]. I. attrib. a. d'imitation; contrefait; faux; m. modesty, fausse modestie; m. turtle soup, consommé m à la tête de veau. II. v.tr. & i. to m. (at) s.o., sth., se moquer de qn, qch.; railler qn, qch. 'mockery, s. 1. moquerie f, raillerie f. 2. sujet m de moquerie; objet m de risée. 'mocking, a. moqueur, railleur. -ly, adv. d'un ton moqueur, railleur; par dérision.

mode [moud], s. mode m; méthode f; m. of life, train m de vie.

model ['mɔdl]. I. s. 1. modèle m; to make a m., faire une maquette. 2. (artist's) m., modèle m. 3. (dressmaking) (a) modèle m, patron m; (b) mannequin m. II. ‡v.tr. modeler; to m. (fashions), être mannequin.

moderate ['mɔd(ə)rit], a. modéré; moyen, ordinaire; (résultat) médiocre; (prix) modique. -ly, adv. avec modération. moder'ation, s. mesure f, retenue f; in m., modérément.

modern ['mɔd(ə)n], a. moderne; m. languages, langues f vivantes. 'modernize, v.tr. moderniser; rénover.

modesty ['mɔdisti], s. modestie f; pudeur f. 'modest, a. modeste; peu exigeant; pudique, honnête. -ly, adv. modestement; sans prétentions; pudiquement.

modify ['mɔdifai], v.tr. modifier. modifi'cation, s. modification f.

modulation [mɔdju'leiʃ(ə)n], s. modulation f.

Mohammedan [mou'hæmid(ə)n], a. & s. musulman, -ane.

moist [mɔist], a. (chaleur) humide; (peau) moite. 'moisten, v.tr. humecter, mouiller. 'moisture, s. humidité f.

mole¹ [moul], s. grain m de beauté; nævus m.

mole², s. Z: taupe f. 'molehill, s. taupinière f.

mole³, s. môle m; brise-lames m.

molecule ['mɔlikjuːl], s. molécule f. mo'lecular, a. moléculaire.

molest [mɔ'lest], v.tr. molester (qn).

mollify ['mɔlifai], v.tr. adoucir, apaiser qn.

mollusc ['mɔləsk], s. mollusque m.

moment ['moumənt], s. moment m, instant m; at this m., en ce moment; actuellement. 'momentary, a. momentané, passager. mo'mentous, a. important.

momentum [mou'mentəm], s. 1. Ph: E: force f vive. 2. (impetus) vitesse f acquise; to lose m., perdre son élan.

monarch ['mɔnək], s. monarque m. 'monarchy, s. monarchie f.

monastery ['mɔnəstri], s. monastère m. mo'nastic, a. monastique.

Monday ['mʌndi], s. lundi m.

money ['mʌni], s. monnaie f; argent m; to pay in ready m., payer comptant; there's m. in it, c'est une bonne affaire; F: to be made of m., être cousu d'or. 'moneybox, s. 1. tirelire f. 2. caisse f. 'money-lender, s. Com: bailleur m de fonds.

mongrel ['mʌŋgrəl], s. & a. métis, -isse; (of dog) bâtard, -arde.

monitor ['mɔnitər]. I. s. moniteur, -trice. II. v.tr. Rad: etc: contrôler. 'monitoring, s. Rad: interception f; m. station, centre m d'écoute.

monk [mʌŋk], s. moine m, religieux m.

monkey ['mʌŋki], s. Z: singe m; female m., guenon f. monkey-wrench, s. U.S: clef f, anglaise, à molette.

mono- ['mɔnou-, mɔ'nɔ-], prefix (used in combined forms) mono-. 'monocle, s. monocle m. 'monocotyledon, s. Bot: monocotylédone f. 'monoculture, s. Agr: monoculture f. 'monogram, s. monogramme m, chiffre m. 'monologue, s. monologue m. mo'nopolist, s. monopolisateur m; accapareur, -euse. monopoli'zation, s. monopolisation f. mo'nopolize, v.tr. monopoliser, accaparer (une denrée); s'emparer de (la conversation). 'monorail, a. & s. monorail m. (m). 'monosyllable, s. monosyllabe f. mo'notonous, a. monotone. -ly, adv. monotonement.

monster ['mɔnstər]. 1. s. monstre m. 2. a. F: monstre; énorme. mon'strosity, s. monstruosité f. 'monstrous, a. monstrueux.

month [mʌnθ], s. mois m; by the m., au mois. **monthly**. I. a. mensuel; m. instalment, mensualité f. II. s. publication f mensuelle. III. adv. mensuellement; une fois par mois; tous les mois.

monument ['mɔnjumənt], s. monument m. monu'mental, a. monumental.

moo [muː], v.i. meugler, beugler.

mooch [muːtʃ], v.i. F: to m. about, flâner, traîner.

mood [muːd], s. 1. humeur f, disposition f. 2. Gram: mode m. 'moody, a. to be m., être maussade. -ily, adv. d'un air morose.

moon [muːn], s. lune f; to land on the m., alunir; once in a blue m., une fois par extraordinaire. 'moonbeam, s. rayon m de lune. 'moonlight, s. clair m de lune.

moor¹ [muər], s. lande f, bruyère f.

moor². 1. v.tr. amarrer (un navire); mouiller (une bouée). 'mooring, s. 1. amarrage m, mouillage m. 2. pl. ship her moorings, navire sur ses amarres. 3. v.i. s'amarrer.

moose [muːs], s. élan m; Fr.C: original m.

moot [muːt], a. m. point, point m discutable.

mop [mɔp]. I. s. balai m à franges; (dish-)m., lavette f; F: m. (of hair), tignasse f. II. ‡v.tr. to m. (up), éponger, essuyer.

mope [moup], v.i. être triste; s'ennuyer.

moped ['mouped], s. F: cyclomoteur m. moraine [mɔ'rein], s. moraine f.

moral ['mɔr(ə)l]. I. a. 1. moral. 2. conforme aux bonnes mœurs. -ally, adv. moralement. II. s. 1. morale f, moralité f (d'un conte). 2. pl. mœurs fpl. mo'rality, s. (a) moralité f; sens moral; (b) bonnes mœurs. 'moralize, v.i. moraliser, faire de la morale (on, sur).

morale [mɔ'rɑːl], s. moral m (d'une personne, d'un groupe).

morass [mɔ'ræs], s. marais m; fondrière f.

morbid ['mɔːbid], a. morbide; malsain, maladif; -ly, adv. morbidement, maladivement.

more [mɔːr]. 1. a. plus (de); m. than ten men, plus de dix hommes; one m., encore un; is there any m.? y en a-t-il encore? 2. s. or indef. pron. davantage; that's m. than enough, c'est plus qu'il n'en faut; what is m. . . ., qui plus est. . . 3. adv. (a) plus, davantage; m. and m., de plus en plus; (b) once m., encore une fois. 4. (a) a. he only does (the) m. harm, il n'en fait que plus de mal; (b) s. the m. one has, the m. one wants, plus on a, plus on désire avoir; (c) adv. all the m. . . ., d'autant plus . . . 5. no m. (a) a. I have no m. money, je n'ai plus d'argent; no m. soup, thank you, plus de potage, merci; (b) s. I have no m., je n'en ai plus; (c) adv. ne . . . plus. more'over, adv. d'ailleurs; du reste; et qui plus est.

moribund ['mɔriband], a. moribond.

morning ['mɔːniŋ], s. (a) matin m; the next m., le lendemain matin; the m. before, la veille au matin; four o'clock in the m., quatre heures du matin; early in the m., de grand matin; good m., bonjour; (b) matinée f; a morning's work, une matinée de travail.

morose [mɔ'rous], a. chagrin, morose. -ly, adv. d'un air chagrin. mo'roseness, s. humeur f chagrine.

morphia ['mɔːfjə], s. morphine f; m. addict, morphinomane mf.

morsel ['mɔːsəl], s. petit morceau m; choice m., morceau friand, de choix.

mortal ['mɔːtl], a. 1. mortel. 2. funeste, fatal (to, à); m. blow, coup mortel. 3. F: any m. thing, n'importe quoi. -ally, adv. mortellement. mor'tality, s. mortalité f (infantile, etc.).

mortar ['mɔːtər], s. mortier m.

mortgage ['mɔːgidʒ]. I. s. hypothèque f. II. v.tr. hypothéquer.

mortician [mɔː'tiʃ(ə)n], s. U.S: entrepreneur m de pompes funèbres.

mortify ['mɔ:tifai], *v.tr.* mortifier; humilier (qn). **mortifi'cation**, *s.* 1. mortification f (corporelle). 2. humiliation *f*, déconvenue *f*.

mortuary ['mɔ:tjuəri], *s.* morgue *f*.

mosaic [mə'zeiik], 1. *a.* (dallage, etc.) en mosaïque. 2. *s.* mosaïque *f*.

Moslem ['mɔzlem], *a. & s.* musulman, -ane.

mosque [mɔsk], *s.* mosquée *f*.

mosquito [mɔs'ki:tou], *s.* moustique *m*.

moss [mɔs], *s.* mousse *f*; m. rose, rose mousse; (*knitting*) m. stitch, point *m* de riz. **'mossy**, *a.* moussu.

most [moust]. 1. *a.* (a) le plus (de); (b) m. men, la plupart des hommes; for the m. part, (i) pour la plupart; (ii) le plus souvent. 2. *s. & indef. pron.* at (the) (very) m., au maximum; tout au plus. 3. *adv.* what I desire m., ce que je désire le plus, surtout, pardessus tout; the m. beautiful woman, la plus belle femme. 4. *adv.* très, fort, bien; m. likely, très probablement. **-ly**, *adv.* 1. pour la plupart. 2. le plus souvent; (pour) la plupart du temps.

motel [mou'tel], *s.* motel *m*.

moth [mɔθ], *s.* papillon *m* de nuit; phalène *f*; clothes m., mite *f*; m. balls, boules *f* de naphtaline. **'moth-eaten**, *a.* mité; *F:* (of pers.) miteux.

mother ['mʌðər], *s.* mère *f*. m. country, mère-patrie *f*; m. tongue, langue *f* maternelle. **'motherhood**, *s.* maternité *f*. **'mother-in-law**, *s.* belle-mère *f*. **'motherless**, *a.* sans mère; orphelin, -ine (de mère). **'motherly**, *a.* maternel.

motion ['mou∫(ə)n], *s.* 1. mouvement *m*, déplacement *m*; to set sth. in m., mettre qch. en marche. 2. signe *m*, geste *m*; to go through the motions, faire semblant (de faire qch.). 3. motion *f*, proposition *f*. **'motionless**, *a.* immobile.

motive ['moutiv]. 1. *a.* moteur; m. power, force motrice. 2. *s.* (a) motif *m* (for acting, of action); (b) mobile *m* (d'une action).

motley ['mɔtli], *a.* (a) bariolé, bigarré; (b) divers, mêlé.

motor ['moutər]. I. 1. *a.* moteur. 2. *s.* moteur *m*; two-stroke m., moteur à deux temps; **outboard** m., moteur hors-bord; m. show, salon *m* de l'automobile. II. 1. *v.i.* aller, voyager, en auto, en voiture. **'motorboat**, *s.* canot *m* automobile. **'motorcycle**, *F:* motorbike, *s.* motocyclette *f*, *F:* moto *f*. **'motoring**, *s.* automobilisme *m*; school of m., auto-école *f*. **'motorist**, *s.* automobiliste *mf*. **'motorize**, *v.tr.* motoriser. **'motorway**, *s.* autoroute *f*.

mottle ['mɔtl], *v.tr.* tacheter, marbrer.

motto ['mɔtou], *s.* devise *f*.

mould¹ [mould], *s.* terre *f* végétale; terreau *m*.

mould². I. *s.* moule *m*. II. *v.tr.* mouler; pétrir.

mould³, *s.* moisi *m*, moisissure *f*. **'moulder**, *v.i.* tomber en poussière; s'effriter; moisir. **'mouldy**, *a.* moisi; to go m., (se) moisir.

mound [maund], *s.* tertre *m*, butte *f*; monceau *m*, tas *m* (de pierres, etc.).

mount [maunt]. I. *s.* 1. (a) montage *m*, support *m*; monture *f*; (b) stamp m., charnière *f*. 2. monture *f* (d'un cavalier). II. *v.* 1. *v.i.* (a) monter (en haut d'une colline, etc.); (b) monter à cheval. 2. *v.tr. & i.* to m. (on) a chair, monter sur une chaise; to m. a bicycle, enfourcher un vélo. 3. *v.tr.* (a) monter, gravir (l'escalier); (b) to m. guard, monter la garde; (c) monter (un diamant); installer (une machine); entoiler (une carte). **'mount 'up**, *v.i.* (of costs) croître, augmenter.

mountain ['mauntin], *s.* montagne *f*; m. scenery, paysage montagneux; m. range, chaîne *f* de montagnes; m. ash, sorbier *m* des oiseaux. **mountain'eer**, *s.* alpiniste *mf*. **mountain'eering**, *s.* alpinisme *m*. **'mountainous**, *a.* (pays) montagneux.

mourn [mɔ:n], *v.i.* & *tr.* pleurer; (se) lamenter; to m. for, pleurer (qn, qch.). **'mourner**, *s.* affligé, -ée; the mourners, le convoi, le cortège funèbre. **'mournful**, *a.* lugubre, mélancolique. **-fully**, *adv.* lugubrement; avec mélancolie. **'mourning**, *s.* 1. affliction *f*, deuil *m*. 2. habits *mpl* de deuil; to go into m., prendre le deuil.

†mouse [maus], *s.* souris *f*; m. hole, trou *m* de souris. **'mousetrap**, *s.* souricière *f*; *F:* fromage *m* (de mauvaise qualité). **'mousy**, *a.* (a) timide; (b) de couleur indéterminée; (couleur) gris (de) souris.

moustache [məs'ta:∫], *s.* moustache(s) *f(pl)*.

mouth [mauθ], *s.* 1. bouche *f*. 2. gueule *f* (de chien, de carnivore). 3. (a) bouche (de puits); goulot *m* (de bouteille); ouverture *f*, entrée *f* (de tunnel); (b) embouchure *f* (de fleuve). **'mouthful**, *s.* bouchée *f*. **'mouthpiece**, *s.* 1. embouchure *f* (de clarinette, etc.). 2. porte-parole *m inv.* (d'un parti politique).

move [mu:v]. I. *s.* 1. démarche *f*; *F:* he's up to every m., il sait parer à tous les coups. 2. mouvement *m*; *F:* to get a m. on, se dépêcher. II. *v.* 1. *v.tr.* (a) déplacer (un objet); changer qch. de place; to m. (house), déménager; (b) remuer, bouger (la tête, etc.); mouvoir, animer (qch.); mettre (qch.) en mouvement; (c) émouvoir, toucher (qn); easily moved, émotionnable; (d) proposer (une motion). 2. *v.i.* (a) se mouvoir, se déplacer; keep moving! circulez! (b) bouger, (se) remuer 'movable, a. mobile. 'move a'bout. 1. v.tr. déplacer (qch.). 2. v.i. aller et venir. 'move a'way, v.i. s'éloigner, s'en aller. move 'back, v.i. (se) reculer; revenir en arrière. 'move 'forward. 1. v.tr. avancer, faire avancer (qn, qch.). 2. v.i. (s')avancer. 'movement, s. mouvement m. 'movie, s. F: esp. U.S: film m: the movies, le cinéma. 'moving, a. 1. en mouvement; en marche; mobile; m. staircase, escalier roulant. 2. (of force, etc.) moteur. 3. émouvant, touchant, attendrissant.

‡mow [mou], v.tr. 1. faucher. 2. tondre (le gazon). 'mowing-machine, s. 1. faucheuse f. 2. tondeuse f (de gazon).

Mr ['mistər], s. monsieur m.

Mrs ['misiz], s. madame f.

much [mʌtʃ]. I. a. (a) beaucoup (de); bien (du, de la, des); (b) how m.? combien (de)? 2. adv. beaucoup, bien; very m. better, beaucoup mieux; much worse, bien pis; it doesn't matter m., ça ne fait pas grand-chose; m. to my astonishment, à mon grand étonnement. 3. s. (a) this m., autant que ceci; that m. too big, trop grand de cela; (b) to make m. of s.o., faire fête à qn. 4. (a) as m., autant (de); as m. again, encore autant; (b) as m. as . . ., autant que . . .; (c) so m. the better, tant mieux; so m. so, à tel point; (d) too m., trop (de).

muck [mʌk], s. (a) fumier m; (b) ordures fpl.

mud [mʌd], s. boue f, bourbe f; (river) m., vase f. 'muddy, a. 1. boueux, bourbeux, vaseux. 2. (liquide) trouble; (couleur) sale; m. complexion, teint brouillé. 'mudguard, s. garde-boue m.

muddle ['mʌdl], s. I. confusion f, emmêlement m, fouillis m; to be in a m., être en désordre, en pagaille. II. v.tr. (em)brouiller (qch.). 'muddler, s. brouillon, -onne.

muffle ['mʌfl], v.tr. 1. emmitoufler (in. de). 2. assourdir (une cloche), étouffer (un son). 'muffler, s. 1. cache-nez m inv. 2. Aut: U.S: pot m d'échappement; silencieux m.

mug [mʌg], s. (for beer) chope f; (grosse) tasse f; m. in, timbale f.

muggy ['mʌgi], a. (temps) mou, lourd.

mulberry ['mʌlb(ə)ri], s. 1. mûre f. 2. mûrier m.

mule [mju:l], s. (he-)mule, mulet m; (she-)mule, mule f. 'mulish, a. têtu, comme un mulet. -ly, adv. avec entêtement.

multicoloured ['mʌltikʌləd], a. multicolore.

multiple ['mʌltipl], a. & s. multiple (m); m. store, maison f à succursales.

multipli'cation, s. multiplication f

'multiply. 1. v.tr. multiplier. 2. v.i. (of species, etc.) se multiplier.

multitude ['mʌltitju:d], s. multitude f; foule f.

mumble ['mʌmbl], v.tr. marmotter.

mummy¹ ['mʌmi], s. momie f.

mummy², s. F: maman f.

mumps [mʌmps], s.pl. Med: oreillons mpl.

munch [mʌn(t)ʃ], v.tr. mâcher, mâchonner.

municipal [mju:(')nisip(ə)l], a. municipal; m. buildings = hôtel m de ville. munici'pality, s. municipalité f.

munitions [mju:(')niʃ(ə)ns], s.usu.pl. munitions f (de guerre).

mural ['mjuərəl], a. mural; m. paintings, s. murals, peintures f murales.

murder ['mə:dər]. I. s. meurtre m; assassinat m. II. v.tr. assassiner (qn). 'murderer, s. meurtrier m, assassin m. 'murderess, s. meurtrière f. 'murderous, a. meurtrier.

murky ['mə:ki], a. ténébreux; (ciel) brouillé.

murmur ['mə:mər]. I. s. murmure m. II. v.tr. & i. murmurer, susurrer.

muscle ['mʌsl], s. muscle m. 'muscular, a. 1. (force) musculaire. 2. (homme) musculeux, musclé.

museum [mju:'ziəm], s. musée m.

mushroom ['mʌʃrum], s. champignon m.

music ['mju:zik], s. musique f. 'musical, a. 1. musical; m. instrument, instrument m de musique. 2. (of pers.) to be m., être (bon) musicien, (bonne) musicienne. 3. (of sounds) harmonieux, mélodieux. 'music-hall, s. music-hall m. mu'sician, s. musicien, -ienne.

Muslim ['mʌzlim], a. & s. musulman, -ane.

muslin ['mʌzlin], s. mousseline f.

musquash ['mʌskwɔʃ], s. Com: castor m du Canada.

mussel ['mʌsl], s. moule f.

‡must [mʌst], modal aux. v. (a) (obligation) you m. be ready, vous devrez être prêt; do so if you m., faites-le s'il le faut; (b) (probability) it must be the doctor, ce doit être le médecin; he m. have missed the train, il aura manqué le train.

mustard ['mʌstəd], s. moutarde f. 'mustard-'plaster, s. Med: sinapisme m. 'mustard-pot, s. moutardier m.

muster ['mʌstər]. 1. v.tr. rassembler (ses partisans, etc.). 2. v.i. se réunir, se rassembler.

musty ['mʌsti], a. (goût, odeur) de moisi; (of room) to smell m., sentir le renfermé. 'mustiness, s. goût m, odeur f de moisi.

mute [mju:t]. I. a. muet; Ling: 'h' m., 'h' muet. II. s. 1. (pers.) muet, -ette; employé m des pompes funèbres; Th: personnage muet. 2. Ling: consonne f sourde. 3. Mus: sourdine f.

mutilate ['mju:tileit], v.tr. mutiler, estropier. muti'lation, s. mutilation f.

mutiny ['mju:tini]. I. s. révolte f, mutinerie f. II. v.i. se révolter, se mutiner (against, contre). muti'neer, s. révolté m, mutiné m, mutin f. 'mutinous, a. rebelle, mutiné, mutin; (équipage) en révolte.

mutter ['mʌtər], v.tr. & i. marmotter; murmurer; to m. an oath, grommeler un juron. 'muttering, s. marmottage m; murmures mpl.

mutton ['mʌt(ə)n], s. mouton m; leg of m., gigot m; m. chop, côtelette f de mouton.

mutual ['mju:tjuəl], a. 1. mutuel, réciproque. 2. m. friend, ami commun. -ally, adv. mutuellement, réciproquement.

muzzle ['mʌzl]. I. s. 1. museau m (d'un animal). 2. bouche f, gueule f (d'une arme à feu). 3. muselière f (pour chiens). II. v.tr. museler (un chien, etc.; F: la presse).

my [mai], poss.a. mon, f. ma, pl. mes; I've broken my arm, je me suis cassé le bras.

myopia [mai'oupiə], s. Med: myopie f.

myosotis [maiə'soutis], s. Bot: myosotis m.

myself [mai'self], pers.pron. (emphatic) moi (-même); (reflexive) me.

mystery ['mistəri], s. mystère m. mys'terious, a. mystérieux. -ly, adv. mystérieusement. 'mystic. 1. a. mystique. 2. (of power) occulte; (of formula) magique. 2. s. mystique mf. 'mysticism, s. mysticisme m. mystifi-'cation, s. mystification f. 2. désorientation f. 'mystify, v.tr. 1. mystifier, intriguer (qn). 2. désorienter, dérouter (qn).

myth [miθ], s. mythe m. 'mythical, a. mythique. mytho'logical, a. mythologique. my'thology, s. mythologie f.

myxomatosis [miksəmə'tousis], s. myxomatose f.

N

N, n, [en], s. (la lettre) N, n, m.

‡nab [næb], v.tr. P: saisir, arrêter, P: pincer (qn); to get nabbed, se faire pincer.

‡nag [næg], v.tr. & i. quereller (qn); gronder (qn) sans cesse. 'nagging, a. 1. (of pers.) querelleur, grondeur. 2. (of pain) agaçant, énervant.

nail [neil]. I. s. 1. ongle m (de doigt). 2. clou m. II. v.tr. to n. (sth. up, down), clouer (qch.).

naive [nɑː'iːv], a. naïf; ingénu. -ly, adv. naïvement, ingénument.

naked ['neikid], a. nu. 'nakedness, s. nudité f.

name [neim]. I. s. 1. nom m; full n., nom et prénoms; Christian n., U.S: given n., nom de baptême; prénom m; my n. is ..., je m'appelle ... 2. réputation f, renommée f. II. v.tr. 1. nommer; désigner (qn, qch.) par son nom. 2. fixer (le jour, l'heure). 'nameless, a. 1. sans nom; inconnu. 2. anonyme. 3. (of fear, etc.) inexprimable. 'namely, adv. (à savoir; c'est-à-dire.

nanny ['næni], s. 1. n. (goat), chèvre f. 2. nurse f, bonne f d'enfants.

nap [næp], s. petit somme m; afternoon n., sieste f.

napalm ['næpɑːm], s. napalm m.

nape [neip], s. the n. of the neck, la nuque.

napkin ['næpkin], s. 1. serviette f (de table). 2. (baby's) n., F: ‡nappy, couche f.

‡narcissus [nɑː'sisəs], s. narcisse m.

narcotic [nɑː'kɔtik], a. & s. narcotique (m), stupéfiant (m).

narrate [nə'reit], v.tr. narrer, raconter

(qch.). 'narrative. 1. a. narratif. 2. récit m, narration f. na'rrator, s. narrateur, -trice.

narrow ['nærou]. I. a. (a) (chemin), étroit; (b) (esprit) borné. -ly, adv. 1. étroitement, strictement; (examiner qch.) de près. 2. tout juste; he n. missed injury, il faillit se blesser. II. v. 1. v.tr. resserrer, rétrécir. 2. v.i. devenir plus étroit. narrow-'minded, a. borné.

nasal ['neiz(ə)l], a. nasal; n. accent, accent nasillard.

nasturtium [nə'stə:ʃəm], s. capucine f.

nasty ['nɑːsti], a. désagréable. dégoûtant; sale (temps); (accident) sérieux. nation ['neiʃ(ə)n], s. nation f. 'national, a. national. -ally, adv. au point de vue national. 'nationalism, s. nationalisme m. natio'nality, s. nationalité f. nationali'zation, s. nationalisation f. native ['neitiv]. 1. a. (of place) natal, de naissance; n. language, langue maternelle; n. land, patrie f. 2. s. natif, -ive; indigène mf.

nativity [nə'tiviti], s. nativité f.

Nato ['neitou], s. Mil: Otan m.

natter ['nætər], v.i. F: bavarder.

natural ['nætʃər(ə)l], a. naturel. -ally, adv. naturellement.

naturalize ['nætʃərəlaiz], v.tr. naturaliser (un étranger); acclimater (une plante, un animal). naturali'zation, naturalisation f (d'un étranger); acclimatation f (d'une plante).

nature ['neitʃər], s. nature f; something in the n. of ..., une sorte, une espèce, de ... 'naturalist, s. naturaliste mf.

naughty ['nɔːti], a. (of child) vilain, méchant.

nauseate ['nɔːsieit], v.tr. écœurer, dégoûter (qn). '**nauseating**, a. dégoûtant, écœurant.

nautical ['nɔːtik(ə)l], a. nautique, marin.

naval ['neiv(ə)l], a. naval; n. officer, officier m de marine; n. college, école f navale.

nave [neiv], s. nef f (d'église).

navigate ['nævigeit]. 1. v.i. naviguer. 2. v.tr. a) parcourir (les mers, l'espace); b) gouverner, diriger (un navire). '**navigable**, a. (fleuve) navigable; (navire) en état de navigabilité. navi'**gation**, s. navigation f; the N. Laws, le Code maritime. '**navigator**, s. navigateur m.

†**navvy** ['nævi], s. terrassier m.

†**navy** ['neivi], s. marine f de guerre; n. blue, bleu m marine.

near [niər]. I. adv. près, proche; to draw n., s'approcher (to, de); in. at hand, tout près. II. prep. près de, auprès de; to be n. the end, toucher à la fin. III. a. 1. (of relative) proche; (of friend) cher, intime. 2. Aut: the n. side, (in Eng.) le côté gauche; (in Fr: US: etc:) le côté droit. -ly, adv. 1. (of) près. 2. presque, à peu près; très n., peu s'en faut; I n. fell, j'ai failli tomber. '**near by**, adv. & prep. tout près (de), tout proche (de).

neat [niːt], a. 1. (of spirits) pur; sans eau; n. whisky, whisky sec. 2. simple et de bon goût; (of room) bien rangé, en ordre. -ly, adv. (rangé) avec soin. '**neatness**, s. 1. simplicité f, bon goût m; netteté f (d'écriture). 2. (of pers.) ordre m.

nebulous ['nebjuləs], a. nébuleux.

necessary ['nesəs(ə)ri]. 1. a. a) nécessaire, indispensable; it is n. to (do sth.), il faut (faire qch.); if n., s'il le faut; au besoin; b) inévitable. 2. s. usu. pl. le nécessaire (à l'existence); F: the n., de l'argent; F: to do the n., payer la note. -ly, adv. nécessairement, forcément. ne'**cessitate**, v.tr. nécessiter (qch.). ne'**cessity**, s. nécessité f.

neck [nek]. I. s. 1. (a) cou m; Sp: to win by a n., gagner d'une encolure; (b) encolure f (de robe); low n., décolleté m. 2. (a) goulot m (de bouteille); (b) langue f (de terre). II. v.tr. & i. P: bécoter. '**necklace**, s. collier m (de diamants, etc.).

nectarine ['nektərin], s. brugnon m.

need [niːd]. I. s. 1. besoin m; to be in n. of sth., avoir besoin de qch. 2. adversité f; embarras m; besoin, indigence f. II. v. 1. v.tr. (a) avoir besoin de, réclamer, exiger, demander (qch.); (b) être obligé de (faire qch.). 2. ‡(modal aux.) n. he go? a-t-il besoin d'y aller? you n. not wait, inutile d'attendre. '**needless**, a. inutile, superflu. '**needy**, a. nécessiteux, besogneux.

needle ['niːdl], s. aiguille f. †'**needle-woman**, s. she's a good n., elle travaille

adroitement à l'aiguille. '**needlework**, s. travaux mpl à l'aiguille; bring your n., apportez votre ouvrage.

negative ['negətiv], a. & s. négatif (m).

neglect [ni'glekt]. I. s. 1. manque m d'égards (of, envers qn.); manque de soins(s); mauvais entretien m (d'une machine). 2. négligence f, inattention f. II. v.tr. 1. manquer d'égards envers (qn); manquer de soins pour (qn). 2. négliger, oublier (ses devoirs, etc.); laisser échapper (une occasion); omettre (de faire qch.). ne'**glected**, a. négligé; (jardin) mal tenu, à l'abandon.

negligence ['neglidʒəns], s. négligence f. '**negligent**, a. 1. négligent. 2. (air, ton) insouciant, nonchalant. -ly, adv. négligemment; avec négligence. '**negligible**, a. négligeable.

negotiate [ni'gouʃieit]. 1. v.tr. négocier (une affaire); conclure (un traité). 2. v.i. to n. for peace, entreprendre des pourparlers de paix. ne'**gotiable**, a. Com: (effet) négociable. negoti'**ation**, s. négociation f; price a matter for n., prix à débattre. ne'**gotiator**, s. négociateur, -trice.

negress ['niːgres], s. négresse f, noire f. †**negro** ['niːgrou], a. & s. nègre (m), noir (m).

neigh [nei]. I. s. hennissement m. II. v.i. hennir. '**neighing**, s. hennissement m.

neighbour ['neibər], s. voisin, -ine. '**neighbourhood**, s. 1. voisinage m; to live in the n. of ..., habiter à proximité de ... 2. alentours mpl (d'un lieu); voisinage, quartier m. '**neighbouring**, a. voisin; proche. '**neighbourly**, a. amical.

neither ['naiðər, 'niːðər]. I. adv. & conj. (a) n. ... nor, ni ... ni; (b) if you don't go, n. shall I, si vous n'y allez pas, je n'irai pas non plus. 2. a. & pron. ni l'un(e) ni l'autre; aucun(e).

neon ['niːon], s. néon m.

nephew ['nevju], s. neveu m.

nerve [nəːv], s. 1. (a) nerf m; (b) assurance f; courage m; to lose one's n., perdre son sang-froid; (c) audace f, aplomb m; P: you've got a n.! tu en as un toupet! 2. nervure f. 3. to strain every n., déployer tous ses efforts. II. v.tr. to n. oneself, s'enhardir (à parler). '**nerveless**, a. inerte, sans force; (style) mou. '**nerve-racking**, a. horripilant. '**nerviness**, s. F: nervosité f. '**nervous**, a. 1. (a) irritable; (b) inquiet; (c) timide. 2. Anat: the n. system, le système nerveux. -ly, adv. timidement; craintivement. '**nervousness**, s. (a) nervosité f; (b) timidité f.

nest [nest]. I. s. 1. nid m. 2. nichée f (d'oiseaux); n. of tables, table f gigogne. II. v.i. faire son nid. '**nestling**, s. oisillon m.

nestle ['nesl], *v.i.* se serrer (contre qn); se blottir (dans un fauteuil).

net[1] [net]. I. *s.* filet *m.* II. *v.tr.* prendre (des poissons, etc.) au filet.

net[2], *a.* (of price, weight) net.

network ['netwə:k], *s.* 1. treillis *f.* 2. réseau *m.* (routier, etc.).

neuralgia [njuə'reidʒə], *s.* névralgie *f.*

neuritis [njuə'raitis], *s.* névrite *f.*

†neurosis [njuə'rousis], *s. Med:* névrose *f.* **neu'rologist**, *s.* neurologie *m.* **neu-'rotic**, *a. & s.* névrosé, -ée.

neuter ['nju:tər], *a. & s.* neutre (*m*); (animal) châtré.

neutral ['nju:trl], *a. & s.* neutre (*m*); *Aut:* in n., au point mort. **neu'trality**, *s. Pol:* neutralité *f.* **'neutralize**, *v.tr.* neutraliser.

never ['nevər], *adv. (a)* (ne . . .) jamais; I n. go there, je n'y vais jamais; *(b)* (emphatic negative) he n. said a word about it, il n'en a pas dit le moindre mot; *(c)* n. mind! ne vous en faites pas! **'never-'ending**, *a.* perpétuel; qui n'en finit plus. **'never-'never**, *s. F:* to buy sth. on the n.-n., acheter qch. à crédit. **never'the'less**, *adv.* néanmoins, quand même, toutefois, pourtant.

new [nju:], *a.* 1. nouveau. 2. (vêtement) neuf; non usagé. 3. (pain) frais; n. potatoes, pommes de terre nouvelles. **-ly**, *adv.* récemment, nouvellement. **'newcomer**, *s.* nouveau venu *m.* **'new-laid**, *a.* (œuf) du jour. **'newness**, *s.* 1. nouveauté *f* (d'une mode). 2. inexpérience *f* (d'un employé). 2. état neuf (d'un objet). 'New 'Year, *s.* nouvel an *m;* nouvelle année *f; N.Y.'s day,* le jour de l'an; *N.Y.'s eve,* la Saint-Sylvestre.

news [nju:z], *s.* nouvelle(s) *f.* 1. what (is the) n.? quelles nouvelles? 2. *Cin: Rad:* the n., les actualités *fpl.* **'news-agent**, *s.* marchand *m* de journaux. **'newspaper**, *s.* journal *m.*

next [nekst]. I. *a.* 1. (of place) prochain; le plus proche; the n. room, la chambre voisine; seated n. to me, assis à côté de moi. 2. (of time) prochain, suivant; the n. day, le lendemain; the n. day but one, le surlendemain; n. year, l'année prochaine; the year after n., dans deux ans; (of order) suivant; who comes n.? à qui le tour? the n. size (in shoes), la pointure au-dessus. II. *adv.* 1. ensuite, après. 2. la prochaine fois; when I n. saw him, quand je le revis. III. *prep.* auprès de, à côté de (qn, qch.). **'next 'door**, *adv. & a.* (d')à côté.

nib ['nib], *s.* (bec *m* de) plume *f.*

nibble ['nibl], *v.tr. & i.* grignoter.

nice [nais], *a.* (a) *(of pers.)* gentil; sympathique; to be n. to s.o., se montrer aimable avec qn; *(b) (of thg.)* joli;

bon; n. and cool, d'une fraîcheur agréable. **-ly**, *adv.* joliment, gentiment, bien. **'niceness**, *s.* gentillesse *f* (de qn). **'nicety**, *s.* 1. to a n., exactement, à la perfection. 2. *pl.* niceties, minuties *f;* finesses *f* (d'un métier).

niche [nitʃ], *s.* niche *f.*

nick [nik], *s.* 1. entaille *f,* encoche *f.* 2. in the n. of time, juste à temps.

nickel ['nikl], *s.* 1. nickel *m.* 2. *U.S:* pièce *f* de cinq cents.

nickname. I. *s.* surnom *m;* sobriquet *m.* II. *v.tr.* surnommer (qn).

nicotine ['nikəti:n], *s.* nicotine *f.*

niece [ni:s], *s.* nièce *f.*

nigger ['nigər], *s. P: Pej:* nègre, *f.* négresse.

niggle ['nigl], *v.i.* vétiller; tatillonner. **'niggling**, *a.* n. details, détails insignifiants.

night [nait], *s.* 1. (a) nuit *f,* soir *m;* the n. before, la veille (au soir); good n.! bonsoir! bonne nuit! at n., la nuit; by n., de nuit; n. watchman, gardien *m* de nuit; *(b) Th:* first n., première *f.* 2. obscurité *f.* **'night-club**, *s.* boîte *f* de nuit. **'nightdress**, *U.S:* -robe, *s.* chemise *f* de nuit; *Fr:C:* jaquette *f.* **'nightfall**, *s.* tombée *f* de la nuit; at n., à la nuit tombante. **'nightingale**, *s.* rossignol *m.* **'nightly**, *adv.* tous les soirs, toutes les nuits. **'nightmare**, *s:* cauchemar *m.* **'nightshade**, *s.* (deadly) n., belladone *f.*

nil [nil], *s.* rien *m;* néant *m;* zéro *m.*

nine [nain], *num. a. & s.* neuf (*m*). **'nine-pin**, *s.* 1. *pl.* (jeu *m* de) quilles *fpl.* 2. quille *f.* **'nine'teen**, *num. a. & s.* dix-neuf (*m*). **'nine'teenth**, *num. a. & s.* dix-neuvième (*mf*). **'nine'tieth**, *num. a. & s.* quatre-vingt-dixième (*mf*). **'ninety**, *num. a. & s.* quatre-vingt-dix (*m*); **'n.-one**, quatre-vingt-onze. **'ninth**, *num. a. & s.* neuvième (*mf*).

nip [nip]. I. *s.* 1. pincement *m.* 2. morsure *f* (du froid). II. *v.* 1. *v.tr.* pincer; se pincer (le doigt, etc.); (of cold) piquer, mordre; brûler (les bourgeons). 2. *v.i. F:* just n. round to the baker's, cours vite chez le boulanger. **'nipper**, *s. F:* gamin *m,* gosse *m.* **'nippy**, *a. F:* 1. alerte, vif. 2. (vent) âpre.

nitrogen ['naitrədʒən], *s.* azote *m.* **'nitrate**, *s.* nitrate *m.* **'nitric**, *a.* (acide) nitrique, azotique.

no [nou]. I. *a.* 1. nul, pas de, point de, aucun; he made no reply, il ne fit aucune réponse; of no interest, sans intérêt; no nonsense! pas de bêtises! *P:N:* no admittance, entrée interdite; no smoking, défense de fumer. 2. peu; no . . . pas; he's no artist, il n'est pas artiste. 3. no one, *pron.* personne *m,* nul *m,* aucun *m.* II. *adv.* 1. whether or no, dans tous les cas. 2. (with comp.) I'm no richer than he (is), je ne suis pas plus riche que lui. III. *adv.* non; have you seen him? no . . ., l'avez vous vu? non . . . 2. †s. *(in voting)* ayes and noes, voix pour et contre.

noble ['noubl], *a.* & *s.* noble (*m*). **-bly**, *adv.* 1. noblement. 2. magnifiquement, superbement. **no'bility**, *s.* noblesse *f.* † **'nobleman**, *s.* noble *m*; gentilhomme *m*.

†**nobody** ['noubədi]. 1. *pron.* personne *m*, nul *m*, aucun *m*; who is there? n., qui est là? personne; n. is perfect, nul n'est parfait. 2. *s.* nullité *f*; zéro *m*; they are (mere) nobodies, ce sont des gens de rien.

nocturne ['nɔktəːn], *s. Mus:* nocturne *m*.

nod [nɔd]. I. *s.* inclination *f* de la tête; signe (de tête) affirmatif. II. *v.tr.* & *i.* 1. faire un signe de tête; incliner la tête. 2. somnoler, sommeiller.

noise [nɔiz], *s.* 1. bruit *m*; tapage *m*, vacarme *m*, fracas *m*. 2. son *m*. **'noiseless**, *a.* sans bruit; silencieux. **-ly**, *adv.* silencieusement; sans bruit. **'noisy**, *a.* bruyant, tapageur; (enfant) turbulent; to be n., faire du bruit, du tapage. **-ily**, *adv.* bruyamment, à grand bruit.

nomad ['nouməd], *a.* & *s.* nomade (*mf*). **no'madic**, *a.* nomade.

nominal ['nɔmin(ə)l], *a.* nominal. **-ally**, *adv.* nominalement; de nom.

nominate ['nɔmineit], *v.tr.* (*a*) nommer, choisir (qn à un emploi, etc.); (*b*) proposer, présenter (un candidat). **nomi'nation**, *s.* 1. nomination *f* (de qn à un emploi). 2. présentation *f* (d'un candidat). **nomi'nee**, *s.* candidat *m* désigné, choisi.

non- [nɔn-]. *prefix (used in compounds)* (i) non- (ii) in-; sans. **non-com'missioned**, *a. Mil:* n-c. officer, sous-officier *m*, gradé *m*. **'non-co'mmittal**, *a.* (réponse, etc.) qui n'engage à rien. **'non-'dazzle**, *a.* anti-éblouissant. **'non-descript**, *a.* indéfinissable; (style) quelconque.

none [nʌn]. 1. *pron.* (*a*) aucun; n. at all, pas un(e) seul(e); (*b*) personne; n. can tell, nul ne le sait. 2. *adv.* he was n. too soon, il arriva juste à temps.

non'entity, *s.* personne *f* insignifiante; nullité *f.* **non-ex'istent**, *a.* inexistant. **non-'iron**, *a.* (tissu) n'exigeant aucun repassage. **non-'ladder**, *a.* (bas) indémaillable. **'nonsense**, *s.* 1. nonsens *m.* 2. absurdité *f*; to talk n., dire des bêtises; n.! pas possible! **non'sensical**, *a.* absurde. **non-'skid**, *a.* anti-dérapant. **'non-'stop**. I. *a.* (train) direct; *Av:* sans escale. II. *adv.* sans arrêt, sans escale; to talk n-s., parler sans arrêt. **non-'union**, *a.* (ouvrier) non-syndiqué.

noodles ['nuːdlz], *s.pl. Cu:* nouilles *f*.

nook [nuk], *s.* coin *m*, recoin *m*.

noon [nuːn], *s.* midi *m*.

noose [nuːs], *s.* nœud *m* coulant; lacet *m*.

nor [nɔːr], *conj.* (ne, ni . . .) ni; neither you n. I, ni vous ni moi; n. you either, ni vous non plus.

norm [nɔːm], *s.* norme *f.* 'normal. 1. *a.* normal, régulier, ordinaire. 2. *s.* normale *f.* **-ally**, *adv.* normalement.

Norman ['nɔːmən], *a.* & *s.* normand. **-ande;** N. architecture, l'architecture romane (anglaise).

north [nɔːθ]. 1. *s.* nord *m.* 2. *adv.* au nord; vers le nord. 3. *a.* nord; exposé au nord. **north-'east.** 1. *s.* nord-est *m.* 2. *a.* (du) nord-est. 3. *adv.* vers le nord-est. **'northerly** [ð], *a.* (of wind) du nord; (of direction) (du, au) nord; vers le nord. **'northern** [ð], *a.* (du) nord; septentrional; N. lights, aurore *f* boréale. **'northwards**, *adv.* vers le nord. **north-'west.** 1. *s.* nord-ouest *m.* 2. (*a*) (du) nord-ouest. 3. *adv.* vers le nord-ouest. **north-'westerly, north-'western**, *a.* du nord-ouest.

Norwegian [nɔː'wiːdʒ(ə)n]. 1. *a.* & *s.* norvégien, -ienne. 2. *s. Ling:* le norvégien.

nose [nouz]. I. *s.* nez *m;* (of many animals) museau *m;* to blow one's n., se moucher. II. *v.tr. F:* to n. sth. out, découvrir (qch.); flairer (qch.). **'nose-dive.** I. *s. Av:* (*of* plane) piqué *m.* II. *v.i. Av:* piquer du nez; descendre en piqué. **'nosy**, *a. F:* fouinard; fureteur.

nostalgia [nɔs'tældʒiə], *s.* nostalgie *f.*

nostril ['nɔstril], *s.* (of pers.) narine *f.* (of horse, etc.) naseau *m.*

not [nɔt], *adv.* (ne) pas, (ne) point; he will, n., won't, come, il ne viendra pas; n. at all, pas du tout; I think n., je crois que non; n. negotiable, non-négociable; n. including, sans compter; F: n. to worry! ne vous en faites pas!

notable ['noutəbl], *a.* notable, considérable, insigne. **-ably**, *adv.* 1. notablement. 2. notamment, particulièrement. **nota'bility**, *s.* (pers.) célébrité *f*, personnalité *f.*

notch [nɔtʃ]. I. *s.* entaille *f*, encoche *f*; cran *m.* II. *v.tr.* entailler, encocher (un bâton); ébrécher (une lame).

note [nout]. I. *s.* note *f*; touche *f* (d'un piano); (bank) n., billet *m* (de banque); I'll send him a n., je lui enverrai un mot. II. *v.tr.* noter (qch.); remarquer (qch.). **'notebook**, *s.* carnet *m*, calepin *m;* bloc-notes *m.* **'notecase**, *s.* porte-billets *m.* **'noted**, *a.* distingué, éminent; célèbre (par qch.). **'note-paper**, *s.* papier *m* à lettres. **'note-worthy**, *a.* remarquable; digne d'attention.

nothing ['nʌθiŋ]. I. *s. or pron.* rien; to say n., ne rien dire; to say n. of . . ; sans parler de . . ; n. new, rien de nouveau; n. much, pas grand-chose; that's n. to do with you, cela ne vous regarde pas; n. else, rien d'autre; I've n. to do with it, je n'y suis pour rien; to think n. of sth., ne faire aucun cas de qch. II. s. 1. *Mth:* zéro m. 2. rien m; (*of plan*) to come to n., ne pas aboutir.

notice ['noutis]. I. s. 1. (a) avis m; (b) préavis m, avertissement m; (c) avis formel, instructions f formelles; (d) at short n., à court délai; (e) n. to quit, congé m; to give n. (to employer), donner sa démission. 2. (a) affiche f; (b) (*in newspaper*) annonce f. 3. to take n. of sth., tenir compte, prendre connaissance de qch; to attract n., se faire remarquer; *F:* to sit up and take n., dresser l'oreille. II. v.tr. observer, remarquer, s'apercevoir de (qn, qch.), prendre garde à (qn, qch.). 'noticeable, a. 1. digne d'attention, de remarque. 2. perceptible, sensible. -ably, adv. perceptiblement, sensiblement. 'notice-board, s. (a) écriteau m; (b) tableau m d'annonces.

notify ['noutifai], v.tr. annoncer, notifier (qch.); déclarer (une naissance); to n. s.o. of sth., aviser qn de qch. notifi-'cation, s. avis m, annonce f; déclaration f (de naissance, etc.).

notion ['nouʃ(ə)n], s. (a) notion f, idée f; (b) opinion f, pensée f.

notorious [nou'tɔːriəs], a. d'une triste notoriété; (menteur) insigne; (endroit) mal famé. -ly, adv. notoirement; n. cruel, connu pour sa cruauté. noto-'riety, s. notoriété f de mauvais aloi.

nought [nɔːt], s. *Mth:* zéro m.

noun [naun], s. *Gram:* substantif m, nom m.

nourish ['nʌriʃ], v.tr. nourrir; alimenter. 'nourishing, a. nourrissant, nutritif. 'nourishment, s. 1. alimentation f, nourriture f. 2. aliments mpl.

nous [naus], s. *F:* intelligence f.

novel[1] ['nɔv(ə)l], s. roman m. 'novelist, s. romancier, -ière.

novel[2], a. nouveau; original; singulier. 'novelty, s. chose f nouvelle; innovation f; *Com:* (article m de) nouveauté f.

November [nou'vembər], s. novembre m.

novice ['nɔvis], s. novice mf; débutant, -ante.

now [nau]. I. adv. 1. maintenant; (a) en ce moment, actuellement; (b) tout de suite; (c) n. and then, de temps en temps; n. . . . n. . . ., tantôt . . . tantôt . . . 2. (a) or; déjà; n. it happened that . . ., or il advint que . . . (b) what's the matter n.? qu'avez vous donc? well n.! eh bien! II. conj. maintenant que, à présent que. III. s. in three days from n., d'ici trois jours; until n., jusqu'ici, jusqu'à présent; from n. (on), dès maintenant; 'nowadays, adv. de nos jours; aujourd'hui.

nowhere ['nou(h)wεər], adv. nulle part.

nozzle ['nɔzl], s. ajutage m; jet m; lance f (de tuyau); bec m; *Av:* injecteur m; *Aut:* gicleur m.

†**nucleus** ['njuːkliəs], s. noyau m (de cellule, etc.). 'nuclear, a. nucléaire. n. power, énergie f atomique; n. reaction, réaction f nucléaire; n. war(fare), guerre f atomique.

nude [njuːd]. 1. a. nu. 2. s. nudité f; to draw from the n., dessiner d'après le nu. 'nudist, s. nudiste mf.

nudge [nʌdʒ]. I. s. coup de coude. II. v.tr. pousser (qn) du coude.

nuisance ['njuːs(ə)ns], s. (a) peste f; fléau m; he's a perfect n., il est assommant; (b) what a n.! que c'est embêtant!

null [nʌl], a. *Jur:* n. and void, nul et sans effet.

numb [nʌm]. I. a. engourdi. II. v.tr. engourdir. 'numbness, s. engourdissement m.

number ['nʌmbər]. I. s. 1. nombre m; a n. of people, plusieurs personnes; in small numbers, en petit nombre; one of their n., (l'un) d'entre eux. 2. chiffre m. 3. numéro m (d'une maison, etc.). II. v.tr. 1. compter, dénombrer. 2. numéroter (des maisons, etc.). 'numberless, a. innombrable; sans nombre.

numeral ['njuːmərəl], s. 1. a. numéral. 2. s. chiffre m, nombre m. nu'merical, a. numérique; a. nombreux.

nun [nʌn], s. religieuse f; *F:* the nuns, les (bonnes) sœurs. 'nunnery, s. couvent m.

nuptial ['nʌpʃəl], a. nuptial.

nurse [nəːs]. I. s. infirmière f; garde-malade mf; male n., infirmier m; children's n., bonne f d'enfants. II. v.tr. 1. soigner (un malade). 2. nourrir (un espoir, un chagrin); entretenir, cultiver (des plantes, les électeurs); mijoter (un projet). 3. bercer (un enfant); tenir (qn, qch.) dans ses bras. 'nursemaid, s. bonne f d'enfants. 'nursery, s. 1. (a) chambre f des enfants; nursery f; (b) crèche f; garderie f; resident n., pouponnière f; n. school, maternelle f. 2. *Agr:* pépinière f. 'nursery-gardener, †'nurseryman, s. pépiniériste m. 'nursing, s. soins mpl (d'une garde-malade); profession f d'infirmière. 'nursing home, s. clinique f.

nutrition [nju:'triʃ(ə)n], s. nutrition f. nu'tritious, nu'tritive, a. nutritif, -f.

nylon ['nailɔn], s. nylon m; n. stockings, bas mpl nylon.

nut [nʌt], s. 1. (a) noix f; hazel-n., noisette f. 2. écrou m. 'nutcrackers, s.pl. casse-noisette(s) m. 'nutmeg, s. (noix f) muscade. 'nutshell, s. coquille f de noix; in a n., en un mot.

nymph [nimf], s. nymphe f.

O

O, o [ou], s. 1. (la lettre) O, o, m. 2. P.T.T.: zéro m; 3103 [θri:wənouθri:] = 31.03 [trɑ̃teʒerotrwɑ:].

†**oaf** [ouf], s. lourdaud m.

oak [ouk], s. (a) o.(-tree), chêne m; o. apple, pomme f de chêne; (b) (bois m de) chêne.

oar [ɔːr], s. aviron m, rame f. '**oarlock**, s. U.S: dame f de nage; tolet m. †'**oarsman**, s. rameur m.

†**oasis** [ou'eisis], s. oasis f.

oath [ouθ], s. 1. serment m; on o., sous serment. 2. juron m; gros mot.

oats [outs], s.pl. avoine f. '**oatmeal**, s. farine f d'avoine.

obdurate ['obdjurit], a. (a) endurci, opiniâtre, têtu; (b) inflexible.

obedience [ə'bi:djəns], s. obéissance f. o'**bedient**, a. obéissant; soumis, docile. -**ly**, adv. avec obéissance, avec soumission.

obelisk ['ɔbilisk], s. obélisque m.

obese [ou'bi:s], a. obèse. o'**besity**, s. obésité f.

obey [ə'bei], v.tr. & i. obéir à.

†**obituary** [ə'bitjuəri], a. & s. nécrologie m; obituaire m. | o. notice, notice nécrologique.

object. I. s. ['ɔbdʒikt] 1. objet m; chose f. but m, objectif m. 3. Gram: complément m, objet. II. v.i. [əb'dʒekt] faire objection, trouver à redire (à qch.). ob'**jection**, s. 1. objection f; if you have no o. si cela ne vous fait rien. 2. obstacle m, inconvénient m; I see no o. (to it), je n'y vois pas d'inconvénient. ob'**jectionable**, a. 1. répréhensible, inacceptable. 2. désagréable. ob'**jective**, a. (a) but m, objectif m; (b) Phot: objectif m. ob'**jector**, s. protestataire mf.

oblige [ə'blaidʒ], v.tr. 1. obliger, astreindre (qn à faire qch.). 2. (a) rendre service à (qn); (b) to be obliged to s.o., être reconnaissant à qn. obli'**gation**, s. (a) obligation f; Ecc: day of o., fête f d'obligation; (b) dette f de reconnaissance; Com: engagement(s) m(pl). o'**bligatory**, a. obligatoire. o'**bliging**, a. obligeant, complaisant, serviable.

oblique [ə'bli:k], a. oblique, de biais. -**ly**, adv. obliquement, de biais.

obliterate [ə'blitəreit], v.tr. effacer, faire disparaître. oblite'**ration**, s. effaçage m; rature f.

oblivion [ə'bliviən], s. oubli m. o'**blivious**, a. oublieux; to be (completely) o. of sth., ignorer qch.

oblong ['ɔblɔŋ], 1. a. oblong. 2. s. rectangle m.

obnoxious [əb'nɔkʃəs], a. (a) odieux; antipathique; (b) repoussant, désagréable.

oboe ['oubou], s. hautbois m.

obscene [əb'si:n], a. obscène. ob'**scenity**, s. obscénité f.

obscure [əb'skjuər]. I. a. obscur. -**ly**, adv. obscurément. II. v.tr. obscurcir. ob'**scurity**, s. obscurité f.

obsequious [əb'zevz], a. obséquieux.

observe [əb'zəːv], v.tr. 1. observer (la loi, etc.). 2. remarquer, noter (qch.). 3. dire, remarquer (que . . .). ob'**servant**, a. observateur; he's very o., rien ne lui échappe. obser'**vation**, s. observation f; remarquer f. ob'**servatory**, s. observatoire m. ob'**server**, s. observateur, -trice.

obsess [əb'ses], v.tr. obséder. ob'**session**, s. obsession f.

obsolete ['ɔbsəlit], a. désuet; hors d'usage; suranné. obso'**lescent**, a. qui tombe en désuétude; (mot) vieilli.

obstacle ['ɔbstəkl], s. obstacle m.

obstetrics [ɔb'stetriks], s.pl. obstétrique f.

obstinate ['ɔbstinit], a. obstiné; entêté; opiniâtre. -**ly**, adv. obstinément, opiniâtrement. '**obstinacy**, s. obstination f, entêtement m, opiniâtreté f.

obstreperous [əb'strepərəs], a. bruyant, tapageur; turbulent.

obstruct [əb'strakt], v.tr. (a) obstruer; encombrer (la rue, etc.); boucher (un tuyau); (b) gêner, entraver (les mouvements de qn). ob'**struction**, s. 1. (a) engorgement m (d'un tuyau); (b) empêchement m (de qn). 2. encombrement m (dans la rue); Rail: o. on the line, obstacle m sur la voie. ob'**structionist**, s. Pol: obstructionniste m. ob'**structive**, a. obstructif.

obtain [əb'tein], v.tr. obtenir; se procurer (qch.). ob'**tainable**, a. procurable.

obtrude [əb'tru:d], v.tr. & i. mettre (qch.) en avant. ob'**trusion**, s. intrusion f; importunité f. ob'**trusive**, a. importun, indiscret; (of smell, etc.) pénétrant.

obtuse [əb'tju:s], a. obtus.

obvious ['ɔbviəs], a. évident, manifeste, clair. -**ly**, adv. évidemment, clairement. '**obviate**, v.tr. éviter (une difficulté); prévenir (des scrupules).

occasion [ə'keiʒ(ə)n], s. occasion f; I've no o. for complaint, je n'ai pas à me plaindre; if the o. arises, s'il y a lieu; le cas échéant. o'**casional**, a. o. showers, averses éparses; an o. visitor, un visiteur qui vient de temps en temps; o. table, petite table de salon. -**ally**, adv. de temps en temps.

occupy ['ɔkjupai], v.tr. occuper (qn, une maison); remplir (un espace). '**occupant**, '**occupier**, s. occupant, -ante;

locataire *mf* (d'une maison). occu'pation, *s.* (a) occupation *f*; (b) emploi *m*, métier *m*. occu'pational, *a.* (maladie) professionnelle; (thérapie) rééducative; o. hazards, risques *mpl* du métier.

‡occur [ə'kəːr], *v.i.* 1. (*of event*) avoir lieu; arriver; se produire. 2. se rencontrer, se trouver; this word occurs twice, ce mot se rencontre deux fois. 3. it occurs to me, il me vient à l'idée. oc'currence, *s.* événement *m*.

ocean ['ouʃ(ə)n], *s.* océan *m*; o. currents, courants océaniques. oce'anic, *a.* océanique. ocean'ography, *s.* océanographie *f*.

ochre ['oukər], *s.* ocre *f*.

o'clock [ə'klɔk], *adv.phr.* two o'c., deux heures; twelve o'c., midi *m*; minuit *m*.

octagon ['ɔktəgən], *s.* octogone *m*. oc'tagonal, *a.* octagonal.

octave ['ɔktiv, 'ɔkteiv], *s.* octave *f*.

octavo [ɔk'teivou], *a. & s.* in-octavo (*m*).

October [ɔk'toubər], *s.* octobre *m*.

octogenarian ['ɔktoudʒi'nɛəriən], *a. & s.* octogénaire (*mf*).

octopus ['ɔktəpəs], *s.* poulpe *m*; pieuvre *f*.

oculist ['ɔkjulist], *s.* oculiste *m*.

odd [ɔd], *a.* 1. (*a*) (nombre) impair; (*b*) a hundred o., une centaine de moutons; fifty thousand o., cinquante mille et quelques centaines. 2. (*a*) dépareillé; (*b*) at o. times, par-ci par-là; o. moments, moments de loisir; *Com:* o. lot, solde *m*. 3. singulier, drôle; excentrique. -ly, *adv.* singulièrement; o. enough nobody arrived, chose singulière, personne n'est arrivé. 'oddity, *s.* 1. singularité *f*, bizarrerie *f*. 2. (*a*) personne *f* excentrique; original, -aie; (*b*) chose *f* bizarre. 'oddness, *s.* singularité *f*, bizarrerie *f*. odds, *s.pl.* 1. (*a*) avantage *m*; chances *fpl*; the o. are against him, les chances sont contre lui; (*b*) différence *f*; it makes no o., ça ne fait rien; (*c*) *Sp:* o. on, against, a horse, cote *f* d'un cheval. 2. to be at o. with s.o., ne pas être d'accord avec qn. 3. o. and ends, petits bouts; restes *mpl*.

ode [oud], *s.* ode *f*.

odious ['oudjəs], *a.* odieux; détestable.

odour ['oudər], *s.* (a) odeur *f*; (b) parfum *m*. 'odourless, *a.* inodore; sans odeur.

of [accented ɔv, unaccented əv, v, f], *prep.* de. 1. (*a*) (*separation*) south of, au sud de; free of, libre de; *U.S:* five minutes of one, une heure moins cinq; (*b*) (*origin, cause*) the works of Shakespeare, l'œuvre de Shakespeare; of necessity, par nécessité; to die of a wound, mourir (des suites) d'une blessure. 2. it is very kind of you, c'est bien aimable de votre part. 3.

made of wood, fait de, en, bois. 4. (*a*) to think of s.o., penser à qn; (*b*) guilty of, coupable de; (*c*) doctor of medicine, docteur en médecine; bachelor of arts = licencié(e)-ès-lettres. 5. the town of Rouen, la ville de Rouen; a child of ten, un enfant de dix ans; hard of hearing, (un peu) sourd; that fool of a sergeant, cet imbécile de sergent; all of a sudden, tout d'un coup. 6. (*partitive*) how much of it do you want? combien en voulez-vous? two of them, deux d'entre eux; there were several of us, nous étions plusieurs; the best of men, le meilleur des hommes. 7. the first of June, le premier juin; a friend of mine, un de mes amis; it's no business of yours, cela ne vous regarde pas.

off [ɔf]. I. *adv.* 1. (*a*) (*away*) house a mile o., maison à un mille de distance; I'm o. to London, je pars pour Londres; to go to sleep, s'endormir; (*b*) *Th:* à la cantonnade. 2. (*removal*) (on gas, electric, stove, etc.) fermé; to take o. one's coat, ôter son manteau; the deal is o., le marché ne se fera pas; (*in restaurant*) chicken is o., il n'y a plus de poulet; (*b*) (*of food*) qui n'est plus frais; (*c*) to finish sth. off, parachever qch. 3. to be well o., être riche; être prospère; he's better o. where he is, il est bien mieux où il est; he is worse o., sa situation a empiré. 4. on and o., par intervalles. II. *prep.* 1. (*a*) to fall o. sth., tomber de qch.; door o. its hinges, porte qui est hors de ses gonds; to take sth. o. the table, prendre qch. sur la table; (*b*) écarté de, éloigné de; house o. the road, maison éloignée de la route; (*c*) *Nau:* o. side, hors jeu; (*c*) *F:* to be o. one's food, ne pas avoir d'appétit; to be o. colour, ne pas être dans son assiette. 2. *Nau:* o. the Cape, au large du Cap; o. Calais, devant Calais. III. *a. Aut:* o. side, côté *m* extérieur; côté droit, *U.S:* gauche; o. season, saison *f* morte. 'off-'hand, *a.* brusque, cavalier; désinvolte. 'off-licence, *s.* licence *f* permettant exclusivement la vente des boissons à emporter. 'off-'peak, o.-p. hours, heures creuses; o.-p. tariff, tarif *m* de nuit.

offal ['ɔfl], *s.* déchets *mpl* d'abattage (de boucherie); abats *mpl*.

offend [ə'fend], *v.tr.* o. offenser, froisser (qn); to be offended at sth., se fâcher de qch.; (b) to o. the eye, choquer les regards. o'ffence, *s.* 1. to take o. at sth., se froisser de qch. 2. offense *f*, faute *f*; *Jur:* crime *m*, délit *m*; minor o., contravention *f*. o'ffender, *s.* 1. *Jur:* délinquant, -ante: the chief o., le grand coupable. 2. offenseur *m*.

o'**ffending**, a. offensant, fautif. o'**ffensive**. I. a. offensant, choquant; (odeur) nauséabonde; to be o. to s.o., insulter qn. II. s. Mil: etc. offensive f.

offer ['ɔfər]. I. s. offre f; o. of marriage, demande f en mariage. II. v. 1. v.tr. offrir (qch. à qn). 2. v.i. s'offrir, se présenter, s. offre f. 'offering, 'offertory, s. Ecc: 1. offertoire m. 2. quête f.

office ['ɔfis], s. 1. bureau m; Com: head o., siège m social; the Foreign O. = ministère m des affaires étrangères; o. boy, garçon m de courses; U.S: o. holder, fonctionnaire m. 2. fonctions fpl; (of government) to be in o., être au pouvoir.

officer ['ɔfisər], s. officier m; police o., agent m de police; Mil: staff o., officier m d'état-major; Av: pilot o., sous-lieutenant m (aviateur); flying o., lieutenant m.

official [ə'fiʃ(ə)l]. 1. a. officiel. 2. s. fonctionnaire m. -ly, adv. officiellement. **official'ese**, s. F: jargon m administratif. o'**fficiate**, v.i. 1. Ecc: officier. 2. remplir les fonctions de (président, etc.). o'**fficious**, a. empressé; trop zélé. o'**fficiousness**, s. excès m de zèle.

offset ['ɔfset], v.tr. compenser (ses pertes).

offspring ['ɔfspriŋ], s. coll. progéniture f, descendants mpl.

often ['ɔfn], adv. souvent, fréquemment; how o.? (i) combien de fois? (ii) tous les combien?

oil [ɔil]. I. s. huile f; mineral o., pétrole m, huile minérale; o. -bearing, pétrolifère; o. heating, chauffage m au mazout; vegetable o., huile végétale; olive o., huile d'olive. II. v. 1. o.tr. huiler, graisser, lubrifier (une machine). 2. v.i. Nau: faire le plein de mazout. 'oiling, s. F: graissage m, lubrification f. 'oil painting, s. (a) peinture f à l'huile; (b) tableau m peint à l'huile. 'oilskins, s.pl Cl: ciré m. 'oily, a. huileux, gras, graisseux; (of manner) onctueux.

O.K. (also okay) F: I. int. très bien, d'accord, O.K. II. a. that's O.K., ça colle; everything's O.K., tout est en règle. III. s. approbation f; to give the O.K., donner le feu vert. IV. v.tr. passer, approuver (un projet).

old [ould], a. 1. vieux; âgé; an old man, un vieillard; an o. woman, une vieille; an o. maid, une vieille fille; o. age, la vieillesse. 2. how o. are you? quel âge avez-vous? to be five years o., avoir cinq ans. 3. (long-established) vieux, ancien; an o. friend of mine, un de mes vieux amis; an o. dodge, un coup classique. 4. (former) ancien; Sch: an o. boy, un ancien élève. 5. F: any

o. thing, n'importe quoi; the o. man, (i) papa, (ii) le patron. old-'fashioned, a. (a) à l'ancienne mode; (b) démodé, passé de mode. 2. (of ideas) vieux jeu. F: an o-f. look, un regard de travers.

†**oligarchy** ['ɔligɑːki], s. oligarchie f.

olive ['ɔliv], s. 1. olive f; o. (tree), olivier m; o. grove, olivette f, oliraie f. 2. Cu: (beef, etc.) o., paupiette f.

Olympic [o'limpik], a. the O. Games, les jeux olympiques.

omelet(te) ['ɔmlit], s. omelette f.

omen ['oumən], s. présage m, augure m. **'ominous** ['ɔm-], a. de mauvais augure; sinistre; inquiétant.

‡**omit** [o'mit], v.tr. omettre. o'**mission**, s. omission f.

omnipotence [ɔm'nipotəns], s. omnipotence f. om'**nipotent**, a. omnipotent.

omnivorous [ɔm'niv(ə)rəs], a. omnivore.

on [ɔn]. I. prep. 1. (a) sur; do not tread on it, ne marchez pas dessus; to be on the telephone, (i) être abonné au téléphone; (ii) parler au téléphone; (b) on foot, à pied; (c) to be on the staff, faire partie du personnel. 2. hanging on the wall, pendu au mur; on page four, à la page quatre. 3. on the right, à droite; on this side, de ce côté. 4. (a) on Sundays, le dimanche; on April 3rd, le trois avril; (b) on and after Monday, à partir de lundi; on application, sur demande; on examination, après examen. 5. on the sly, en sourdine. 6. on sale, en vente. 7. I'm here on business, je suis ici pour affaires; on holiday, en vacances. 8. F: the drinks are on me, c'est moi qui paie cette tournée. 9. to put on a horse, parier sur un cheval. II. adv. 1. to put the kettle on, mettre la bouilloire à chauffer; (of actor) to be on, être en scène; F: it's simply not on, il n'y a pas moyen. 2. to fly on, work on, continuer son vol, son travail; to drive on, talk on, continuer à parler; go on! (i) continuez! (ii) P: pas vrai! and so on, et ainsi de suite. 3. later on, plus tard; F: to have s.o. on, monter un bateau à qn. 4. to turn on the tap, ouvrir le robinet; the brakes are on, les freins sont serrés; this film was on last week, ce film a passé la semaine dernière; have you anything on this evening? êtes-vous occupé ce soir? 5. F: I'm on! ça me va! the police are on to him, la police est sur sa piste; he's always on at me, il s'en prend toujours à moi.

once [wʌns], adv. 1. une fois; o. only, une seule fois; o. a week, tous les huit jours; o. and for all, une fois pour toutes. 2. autrefois. 3. at o. (a) tout de suite; sur-le-champ; (b) à la fois.

one [wʌn]. I. *num.a.* 1. un; that's o. comfort, c'est déjà une consolation. 2. (*a*) seul, unique; (*b*) même; it's all o., cela revient au même. 3. there is only o. left, il n'en reste qu'un; number o., (i) numéro un; (ii) F: soi-même; the last but o., l'avant-dernier. III. *dem.pron.* (*a*) this o., celui-là, *f.* celle-là; which o. do you prefer? lequel, laquelle, préférez-vous? she is the o. who helped him, c'est elle qui l'a aidé; (*b*) our dear ones, ceux qui nous sont chers; *F:* that's a good one! en voilà une bonne. IV. *indef. a.* o. day, un jour; o. stormy evening, par une soirée tempétueuse. V. *indef.pron.* 1. (pl. some, any) I haven't a pencil, have you got one? je n'ai pas de crayon, en avez-vous un? o. of them, (i) l'un d'entre eux; (ii) *P:* un homosexuel; he's o. of the family, il est de la famille; o. by o., un(e) à un(e). 2. I for o. shall come, quant à moi, je viendrai; I'm not o. to . . ., je ne suis pas de ceux qui . . .; *F:* I'm not much of a o. for sweets, je ne suis pas grand amateur de bonbons. 3. (*subject*) on, (*object*) vous; o. cannot always be right, on ne peut pas toujours avoir raison; it's enough to kill o., il y a de quoi se faire mourir. 4. one's, son, sa, ses; votre, vos; to cut one's finger, se couper le doigt. 'one-armed, *a.* manchot; *F:* o.-a. bandit, tire-pognon *m.* 'one-eyed, *a.* borgne. 'one-horse, *a.* F: o.-h. town, petit bourg de rien du tout.

onerous ['ɔnərəs], *a.* onéreux; pénible.

one'self, *pron.* soi(-même); (*reflexive*) se. 'one-'sided, *a.* (*of bargain*) inégal, inéquitable; (*of judgement*) partial, injuste. 'one-track, *a.* F: (*esprit*) obsédé par une seule idée. one-'upmanship, *s.* F: l'art *m* de surpasser les autres. 'one-'way, *a.* (rue) à sens unique.

onion ['ʌnjən], *s.* oignon *m*; spring o., ciboule *f*.

onlooker ['ɔnlukər], *s.* spectateur, -trice; the onlookers, les assistants *m*.

only ['ounli]. I. *a.* seul, unique. II. *adv.* seulement, ne . . . que; I have o. three, je n'en ai que trois; o. he can say, lui seul saurait le dire; o. to think of it, rien que d'y penser; o. yesterday, pas plus tard qu'hier. III. *conj.* mais, seulement; interesting, o. too long, intéressant, mais trop long.

onslaught ['ɔnslɔːt], *s.* assaut *m*, attaque *f*.

onus ['ounəs], *s.* responsabilité *f*, charge *f*.

onwards ['ɔnwədz], *adv.* en avant.

ooze [uːz]. I. *s.* vase *f*, limon *m*. II. *v.i.* suinter. 'oozing, *s.* suintement *m*.

op [ɔp], *s.* F: 1. *Med:* opération *f*. 2. *Mil:* combined op(s), opération (i) amphibie, (ii) inter-armées.

opal ['oup(ə)l], *s.* opale *f*.

opaque [ou'peik], *a.* opaque.

open ['oup(ə)n]. I. *a.* ouvert. 1. (*a*) half o., entrouvert, entrebâillé; (*b*) (*of box*) ouvert; (*of bottle*) débouché; (*c*) o. to the public, ouvert, accessible, au public. 2. sans limites; sans bornes; in the o. air, en plein air; the o. sea, le large. 3. (*a*) o. car, voiture découverte; (*b*) o. to every wind, exposé à tous les vents; o. to conviction, accessible à la conviction; o. to improvement, susceptible d'amélioration. 4. (*a*) manifeste; public; (*b*) franc; o. admiration, franche admiration. 5. o. wound, plaie béante. 6. non obstrué; o. road, chemin libre. 7. non résolu; o. question, question discutable; to keep an o. mind, rester sans parti pris. 8. *Com:* o. account, compte ouvert; compte courant; o. cheque, chèque ouvert, non barré. -ly, *adv.* ouvertement, franchement. II. *v.* 1. *v.tr.* (*a*) ouvrir (une porte), déboucher, entamer (une bouteille); inaugurer (une fête, etc.); (*b*) commencer, entamer (une conversation); (*c*) *Com:* ouvrir (un compte). 2. *v.i.* (*a*) s'ouvrir; (*of view*) s'étendre; (*of flower*) s'épanouir; (*b*) (*of play, etc.*) commencer. 'opener, *s.* can, tin, o., ouvre-boîte(s) *m.* 'opening, *s.* 1. ouverture *f*; débouchage *m* (d'une bouteille); inauguration *f* (d'une fête, etc.); (*at cards*) attaque *f*. 2. trou *m*, orifice *m*. 3. occasion *f* favorable, débouché *m* (pour une marchandise, etc.). 4. *attrib.* d'ouverture; inaugural; o. sentence, phrase de début. 'open-'minded, *a.* qui a l'esprit ouvert, large; impartial. open 'out, *v.i.* (*of view, etc.*) s'ouvrir, s'étendre. open 'up, 1. *v.tr.* exposer, révéler (une perspective); frayer (un chemin); ouvrir (un pays au commerce). 2. *v.i. F:* to make s.o. o. up, délier la langue à qn.

opera ['ɔp(ə)rə], *s.* opéra *m*; o. glasses, jumelles *fpl* de théâtre; o. house, opéra, opér'atic, *a.* d'opéra.

operate ['ɔpəreit]. 1. *v.i.* opérer; (*of machinery*) fonctionner. 2. *v.tr.* faire manœuvrer (une machine). 'operating, *attrib. a. Med:* o. table, theatre, table *f*, salle *f*, d'opération. oper'ation, *s.* 1. fonctionnement *m*; (*of machinery*) to be in o., être en marche. 2. *Mil: etc:* opération *f*. *Med:* opération, intervention *f* chirurgicale. oper'ational, *a.* opérationnel. 'operative. 1. *a.* opératif; (*of law*) to become o., entrer en vigueur; the o. word, le mot qui compte. 2. *s.* ouvrier, -ière. 'operator, *s.* opérateur, -trice.

opinion ['ə'pinjən], s. opinion f, avis m; in my o., à mon avis; to ask s.o.'s o., consulter qn. ○'pinionated, a. opiniâtre.

opium ['oupjəm], s. opium m.

opossum [ə'pɔsəm], s. Z: opossum m.

opponent [ə'pounənt], s. adversaire m.

opportunity [ɔpə'tjuːniti], s. occasion f.

oppose [ə'pouz], v.tr. s'opposer à (qn, qch.); résister à (qn, qch.). ○'pposed, a. opposé, hostile. ○'pposing, a. (of characters, etc.) opposant. 'opposite. I. a. (a) opposé; vis-à-vis (to, de); en face (to, de); (b) contraire; the o. sex, l'autre sexe; in the o. direction, en sens inverse. 2. s. opposé m; just the o., tout le contraire. 3. adv. vis-à-vis; en face. 4. prep. en face de, vis-à-vis (de). oppo'sition, s. opposition f.

oppress [ə'pres], v.tr. (a) opprimer; (b) oppresser, accabler. o'ppression, s. (a) oppression f; (b) accablement m. o'ppressive, a. 1. oppressif, opprimant. 2. (a) (of atmosphere) lourd, étouffant; (b) (of grief) accablant. o'ppressor, s. (a) oppresseur m; (b) opprimeur m.

optical ['ɔptik(ə)l], a. 1. optique. 2. o. illusion, illusion d'optique. op'tician, s. opticien m. 'optics, s.pl. l'optique f.

optimism ['ɔptimizm], s. optimisme m. 'optimist, s. optimiste mf. opti'mistic, a. optimiste. -ally, adv. avec optimisme.

option ['ɔpʃ(ə)n], s. option f, choix m. 'optional, a. facultatif.

opulence ['ɔpjuləns], s. opulence f, richesse f. 'opulent, a. opulent.

or [ɔːr], conj. (a) ou; (with neg.) ni; without money or luggage, sans argent ni bagages; a mile or so, environ un mille; (b) sinon; don't move or I'll shoot, ne bougez pas, sinon je tire.

oracle ['ɔrəkl], s. oracle m.

oral ['ɔːr(ə)l], a. oral. -ally, adv. oralement, de vive voix.

orange ['ɔrin(d)ʒ], s. 1. orange f. 2. o.(tree), oranger m. 3. a. & s. (colour) orangé (m); orange (m) inv.

oration [ə'reiʃ(ə)n], s. allocution f, discours m. 'orator, s. orateur m. 'oratory[1], s. l'art m oratoire; l'éloquence.

oratorio [ərə'tɔːriou], s. oratorio m.

†**oratory**[2] ['ɔrət(ə)ri], s. Ecc: 1. oratoire m. 2. (les pères de) l'Oratoire.

orb [ɔːb], s. orbe m; globe m, sphère f.

orbit ['ɔːbit], s. 1. orbite f; to put a satellite, a man, into o., mettre un satellite, un homme, en orbite; the Russian o., la sphère d'influence soviétique. II. v.tr. décrire une orbite (autour d'une planète).

orchard ['ɔːtʃəd], s. verger m.

orchestra ['ɔːkistrə], s. orchestre m. or'chestral, a. orchestral. 'orches-

trate, v.tr. orchestrer, instrumenter. orches'tration, s. orchestration f, instrumentation f.

orchid ['ɔːkid], s. orchidée f.

ordain ['ɔːdein], v.tr. ordonner.

ordeal [ɔːdiːl], s. épreuve f.

order ['ɔːdər]. I. s. 1. ordre m. 2. succession f, suite f; in alphabetical o., par ordre alphabétique. 3. is your passport in o.? votre passeport est-il en règle? out of o., en mauvais état. 4. law and o., l'ordre public. 5. in o. to do sth., afin de, pour, faire qch.; in o. that, afin que, pour que. 6. (a) commandement m, instruction f; until further orders, jusqu'à nouvel ordre; (b) Com: commande f; suit made to o., complet fait sur mesure. 7. (a) arrêt m, arrêté m; (b) money o., postal o. = mandat-poste m. II. v.tr. (a) ordonner, commander, à (qn de faire qch.); (b) prescrire, ordonner; (c) Com: commander. 'orderly. 1. a. (a) ordonné, méthodique; rangé; (b) tranquille, discipliné. 2. s. Mil: planton m; hospital o., aide-infirmier m.

ordinal ['ɔːdinl], a. & s. ordinal.

ordinance ['ɔːdinəns], s. ordonnance f, décret m; règlement m.

ordinary ['ɔːdin(ə)ri]. I. a. ordinaire; coutumier; normal. -rily, adv. ordinairement, normalement; d'ordinaire; d'habitude. II. s. ordinaire m; out of the o., exceptionnel; peu ordinaire.

ordnance ['ɔːdnəns], s. 1. artillerie f. 2. O. Survey, service m topographique.

ore [ɔːr], s. minerai m.

organ ['ɔːgən], s. 1. Mus: (a) orgue m; (b) street o., orgue de Barbarie. 2. Anat: etc. organe m. or'ganic, a. organique. 'organism, s. organisme m. 'organist, s. organiste m/f.

organize ['ɔːgənaiz], v.tr. organiser. organi'zation, s. 1. organisation f. 2. organisme m (politique, etc.). 'organizer, s. organisateur, -trice.

†**orgy** ['ɔːdʒi], s. orgie f.

oriental [ɔːri'entl]. 1. a. oriental; d'orient. 2. s. oriental, -ale.

origin ['ɔridʒin], s. origine f. o'riginal. 1.a. original; o. meaning of a word, sens premier d'un mot. 2. s.(a) original m (d'un tableau, etc.); (b) personne f originale; original, -ale; type m à part. -ally, adv. (a) à l'origine; (b) dès l'origine. o'riginality, s. originalité f. o'riginate, v.i. tirer son origine, dériver, provenir (from, in, de).

ornament ['ɔːnəmənt]. I. s. ornement m. II. v.tr. orner, décorer. orna'mental, a. ornemental.

ornate [ɔː'neit], a. orné; surchargé d'ornements.

ornithology [ɔːni'θɔlədʒi], s. ornithologie f.

orphan ['ɔːf(ə)n], s. orphelin, -ine. 'orphanage, s. orphelinat m.

orthodox ['ɔːθədɔks], a. orthodoxe.

orthography [ɔː'θɔgrəfi], s. orthographe f.

orthopaedic [ɔːθəˈpiːdik], a. orthopédique.

oscillate ['ɔsileit], v.i. osciller. **oscillation**, s. oscillation f.

ostensible [ɔsˈtensəbl], a. prétendu; soidisant; feint. **-bly**, adv. en apparence; censément.

ostentation [ɔstenˈteiʃ(ə)n], s. ostentation f. **osten'tatious**, a. plein d'ostentation. **-ly**, adv. avec ostentation.

osteopath ['ɔstiəpæθ], s. chiropracteur m.

ostracize ['ɔstrəsaiz], v.tr. ostraciser.

ostrich ['ɔstritʃ], s. autruche f.

other ['ʌðər]. 1. a. autre; (a) o. things being equal, toutes choses égales; (b) o. people, d'autres; autrui m. 2. pron. autre; (a) I have no o., je n'en ai pas d'autre; one or o. of us, l'un de nous; (b) pl. d'autres; autrui. 3. adv. autrement. 'otherwise, adv. 1. autrement; except where o. stated, sauf indication contraire. 2. autrement; sans quoi, sans cela. 3. sous d'autres rapports; par ailleurs.

otter ['ɔtər], s. loutre f.

‡ought [ɔːt], v.aux. (with present and past meaning inv.) devoir, falloir. 1. (obligation) one o. not to do that, il ne faut, on ne doit, pas faire cela; I thought I o. to tell you, j'ai cru devoir vous en faire part. 2. (vague desirability) you o. not to have waited, vous n'auriez pas dû attendre; you o. to see the exhibition, vous devriez aller voir l'exposition. 3. (probability) your horse o. to win, votre cheval a de grandes chances de gagner.

our ['auər], poss.a. notre, pl. nos. **ours**, poss.pron. le nôtre, la nôtre, les nôtres; this is o., ceci est à nous; ceci nous appartient; a friend of o., un(e) de nos ami(e)s. **our'selves**, pers.pron.pl. nous (-mêmes).

oust [aust], v.tr. 1. déloger. 2. évincer.

out [aut], adv. 1. dehors; (a) the voyage o., l'aller m; (b) my father is o., mon père est sorti; o. at sea, au large; o. there, là-bas; the tide is o., la marée est basse. 2. to lean o., se pencher au dehors. 3. (a) découvert, exposé; the sun is o., il fait du soleil; the book is just o., le livre vient de paraître; (b) to o. loud, tout haut, à haute voix. 4. Sp: hors jeu; F: to be o. on one's feet, tituber de fatigue; to be o. in one's calculations, être loin de compte. 5. (of fire) éteint. 6. à bout; achevé. 7. o. of, hors de; dans; par; parmi; d'entre; to be o. of one's mind, avoir perdu la raison; to throw sth. o. of the window, jeter qch. par la fenêtre; to drink o. of a glass, boire dans un verre; one o. of three, un sur trois; o. of respect, par respect; to be o. of tea, ne plus avoir de thé.

'outback, s. Austr: l'intérieur m.

out'bid, v.tr. (at auction) renchérir sur (qn). **'outboard**, a. Nau: (moteur) hors-bord. **'outbreak**, s. 1. Med: éruption f. 2. révolte f, émeute f. **'outbuilding**, s. bâtiment m extérieur; annexe f; pl. communs m, dépendances f. **'outburst**, s. explosion f. **'outcast**, a. & s. exilé, -ée; proscrit, -ite. **'outcaste** (mf). **'outcome**, s. issue f, résultat m, dénouement m. **'outcry**, s. réclamations fpl indignées. **out'distance**, v.tr. distancer (un concurrent). **‡out'do**, v.tr. surpasser (qn); l'emporter sur (qn). **'outdoor**, a. extérieur (jeux, etc.); en plein air; to put on one's o. clothes, s'habiller pour sortir; **'outer**, a. extérieur, externe; o. space, l'espace intersidéral m. **'outfit**, s. équipement m; Cl: trousseau m, effets mpl; repair o., nécessaire m, trousse f, à réparations. **'outfitter**, s. marchand m de confections. **'outflow**, s. écoulement m. **'outgoings**, s.pl. dépenses fpl. **‡out'grow**, v.tr. devenir trop grand pour (ses vêtements); perdre (une habitude). **'outing**, s. promenade f; excursion f; sortie f. **out'landish**, a. bizarre, étrange. **'outlaw**, s. hors-la-loi m; proscrit, -ite. **'outlay**, s. débours mpl, frais mpl, dépenses fpl. **'outlet**, s. issue f; Com: débouché m (pour marchandises). **'outline**. I. s. contour m, profil m; general o. of a plan, aperçu m d'un projet. II. v.tr. esquisser. **out'live**, v.tr. survivre à (qn). **'outlook**, s. vue f, perspective f; point m de vue. **'outlying**, a. éloigné, écarté. **out'number**, v.tr. surpasser en nombre. **out-of-'date**, a. démodé, dépassé (billet, etc.) périmé. **out-of-'doors**, adv. dehors; en plein air. **out-of-the-'way**, a. (a) (of place, etc.) écarté; (b) peu ordinaire; pas commun; (of price) not o., pas exorbitant. **'output**, s. rendement m; production f.

outrage ['autreidʒ]. I. s. outrage m, atteinte f; attentat m. II. v.tr. outrager, faire outrage à. **out'rageous**, a. outrageant, outrageux; (conduite) atroce; (prix) exorbitant.

'outright. I. adv. 1. complètement; du premier coup; to buy sth. o., acheter qch. comptant, à forfait; to kill s.o. o., tuer qn raide. 2. franchement, carrément. II. a. 1. (vente) à forfait. 2. (of manner) franc; carré. **'outset**, s. commencement m. **out'shine**, v.tr. surpasser; dépasser; éclipser. **'outside**. I. s. extérieur m. II. a. (a) extérieur; (b) (avis) étranger, du dehors; (c) (prix) maximum; (d) F: it was an o. chance, il y avait tout juste une chance (de réussir). III. adv. [aut'said] (en) dehors, à l'extérieur. IV. *prep.* en dehors de, à l'extérieur de. out'sider, *s. F:* étranger, -ère, intrus *m. F: (horse racing)* cheval *m* non classé; outsider *m.* 'outsize, *a. Com:* dimension *f,* pointure *f,* hors série. 'outskirts, *s.pl.* abords *m;* banlieue *f,* approches *fpl* (d'une ville). out'spoken, *a. (of pers.)* franc; carré. out'standing, *a.* 1. (trait) saillant; (incident) marquant; (artiste, etc.) éminent. 2. (affaire) en suspens; (compte) impayé, dû; (paiement) en retard. out'stay, *v.tr.* to o. one's welcome, lasser l'amabilité de ses hôtes. out'stretched, *a.* déployé, étendu; (bras) tendu. 'outward, *a.* extérieur; de dehors; the o. voyage, l'aller *m.* -ly. *adv.* en apparence. 'outwards, *adv.* au dehors; vers l'extérieur. out'vote, *v.tr.* obtenir une majorité sur, l'emporter sur (qn). 'out'wit, *v.tr.* circonvenir (qn); déjouer les intentions de (qn); dépister (la police).

oval ['ouv(ə)l], *a. & s.* ovale (*m*). 'ovalize, *v.tr. a. I: E:* (s')ovaliser.

†ovary ['ouvəri], *s.* ovaire *m.*

ovation [ou'veiʃ(ə)n], *s.* ovation *f.*

oven ['ʌv(ə)n], *s.* four *m;* to cook sth. in a slow o., cuire qch. à feu doux. 'ovenware, *s.* vaisselle *f* allant au four.

over ['ouvər]. I. *prep.* 1. (*a*) sur, dessus, pardessus. (*b*) all o. the world, par tout le monde. 2. au-dessus de (qch.). 3. o. the border, au delà de la frontière; the house o. the way, la maison d'en face; the bridge o. the river, le pont qui traverse la rivière. 4. plus de; au-dessus de; o. fifty pounds, plus de cinquante livres; he's o. fifty, il a dépassé la cinquantaine; o. and above, en sus de. II. *adv.* 1. (*a*) to be all o. dust, être tout couvert de poussière; (*b*) o. and o. again, à plusieurs reprises. 2. (*a*) par-dessus; (*b*) to lean o., se pencher; pencher. 3. to fall o., tomber à la renverse; se renverser; to knock s.o. o., renverser qn. 4. to cross o., traverser; o. there, là-bas. 5. (*a*) en plus, en excès; I have a card o., j'ai une carte de trop. o. and above, en outre; (*b*) (*in compounds*) trop; à l'excès; o.-ripe, trop mûr. 6. fini, achevé; the danger is o., le danger est passé. 'overall. 1. *a.* total, global; o. length, longueur *f* hors tout. 2. *s. Cl:* blouse *f.* 'overarm, *a.* (nage) à l'indienne; (*at tennis*) (service) par le haut. over'bearing, *a.* arrogant, autoritaire. 'overboard, *adv. Nau:* to fall o., tomber à la mer. over'burden, *v.tr.* surcharger, accabler (with, de); *F:* he's not overburdened with brains, ce n'est pas l'intelligence qui l'écrase. 'overcast, *a.* (ciel) couvert, sombre. over'charge, *v.tr.* faire payer trop cher (qch. à qn). 'overcoat, *s.*

pardessus *m.* †over'come. I. *v.tr.* vaincre (ses adversaires); venir à bout de (ses difficultés); dominer, maîtriser (son émotion). II. *a.* accablé (de douleur); transi (de peur). over'crowded, *a.* trop rempli (with, de); surpeuplé. over'crowding, *s.* 1. encombrement *m.* 2. surpeuplement *m.* †over'do, *v.tr.* 1. to o. things, se surmener. 2. *Cu:* trop cuire (qch.). 'overdose, *s.* trop forte dose; dose (i) nuisible, (ii) mortelle. 'overdraft, *s.* découvert *m;* solde *m* débiteur. 'overdrawn, *a.* (compte) découvert. 'overdrive, *s. Aut:* (vitesse) surmultipliée *f.* †over'due, *a.* arriéré *m;* en retard. †over'eat, *v.i.* trop manger. over-'estimate, *v.tr.* surestimer; exagérer (le danger, etc.). over'fed, *a.* (chien, etc.) qui mange trop. over'flow, *v.tr. & i.* déborder. over'grown, *a.* (jardin) envahi de mauvaises herbes. over'haul, *v.tr.* réparer, réviser, remettre en état. 'overhaul, *s.* révision *f* (d'une machine); remise *f* en état. 'over'head, *adv.* au-dessus (de la tête); en haut, en l'air. 'overhead. (*a*) (câble) aérien; (*b*) *Aut:* (soupapes) en tête; (*c*) *Com:* o. expenses, *s.* overheads, frais *mpl* généraux. over'heat, *v.tr.* surchauffer. †over'hear, *v.tr.* surprendre (une conversation). 'overland, *a.* o. route, voie *f* de terre. over'lap, *v.tr. & i.* 1. recouvrir (partiellement); chevaucher. 2. dépasser (l'extrémité de qch.). 3. faire double emploi avec qch. 'over'leaf, *adv.* au dos, au verso (de la page). over'load, *v.tr.* surcharger (un camion); surmener (une machine). 'over'look, *v.tr.* 1. (*of building*) dominer (une vallée, etc.); donner sur (la rue). 2. (*a*) oublier, négliger (qch.); (*b*) fermer les yeux sur (qch.); laisser passer (une erreur). over'night, *adv.* to stay o. in Paris, passer une nuit à Paris; he became famous o., il est devenu célèbre du jour au lendemain. 'overnight o. stay, séjour *m* d'une seule nuit; o. bag, sac *m* de voyage. 'overpass, *s. CivE: U.S:* enjambement *m,* passage *m* supérieur. over'power, *v.tr.* maîtriser, dominer, vaincre, accabler. over-'powering, *a.* accablant; (désir) irrésistible. 'over'rate, *v.tr.* surestimer. over'rider, *s. Aut:* sabot *m* (de pare-choc). over'rule, *v.tr.* décider contre (l'avis de qn); rejeter (une réclamation); passer outre à (une difficulté); passer à l'ordre du jour sur (une objection). †over'run, *v.tr. (of enemy)* envahir (un pays); *(of mice)* infester (une maison). 'over'seas. 1. *adv.* par delà les mers. 2. *a.* d'outre-mer. over'shadow, *v.tr.* couvrir de son ombre; éclipser (qn). †over'shoot, *v.tr.* dépasser (le point d'arrêt); *Av:* se présenter trop long (sur la piste) to o. the mark, dépasser le but. 'oversight, *s.* oubli *m,* omission *f,* inadvertance *f.* ‡over'sleep, *v.i.* dormir trop tard. ‡over'steer, *v.i. Aut:* survirer. ‡over'step, *v.tr.* dépasser (les bornes). ‡over'take, *v.tr.* rattraper (qn); doubler, dépasser (une voiture, etc.). over'taking, *s. P.N: Aut:* no o., défense de doubler. 'over'tax, *v.tr.* trop exiger (de qn); to o. one's strength, se surmener; abuser de ses forces. ‡over'throw, défaire, vaincre (qn); renverser (un ministère, etc.). 'overtime, *s. & adv.* heures *f* supplémentaires (de travail). overture ['ouvətʃər], *s.* ouverture *f.* over'whelm, *v.tr.* accabler (l'ennemi); combler (qn de bontés). over'whelming, *a.* accablant; (majorité) écrasante. 'over'work, *v.tr. & i.* (se) surmener.

owe [ou], *v.tr.* devoir. 'owing. 1. *a.* dû; the money o. to me, l'argent qui m'est

dû. 2. *prep.phr.* o. to, à cause de, par suite de, en raison de.

owl [aul], *s.* hibou *m.*

own [oun]. I. *v.tr.* 1. posséder. 2. reconnaître, avouer (une erreur). II. *a.* (*a*) propre; my o. money, mon propre argent; (*b*) le mien, le tien, etc.; à moi, à toi, etc.; my time is my o., mon temps est à moi. III. *s.* my o., his o., *etc:* (*a*) le mien, le sien, etc.; I have money of my o., j'ai de l'argent à moi; (*b*) to do sth. on one's o., faire qch. (i) de sa propre initiative, (ii) indépendamment; I'm on my o. today, je suis seul aujourd'hui. 'owner, *s.* propriétaire *mf.*

‡ox [ɔks], *s.* bœuf *m.* 'ox-tail, *s.* queue *f* de bœuf; o. soup, crème *f* de queue de bœuf.

oxide ['ɔksaid], *s. Ch:* oxyde *m.* 'oxidize, *v.tr. & i.* (s')oxyder.

oxygen ['ɔksidʒin], *s.* oxygène *m.*

oyster ['ɔistər], *s.* huître *f.*

ozone ['ouzoun], *s.* ozone *m.*

P

P, p [pi:], *s.* (la lettre) P, p *m;* to mind one's P's and Q's, se surveiller.

pace [peis]. I. *s.* 1. pas *m.* 2. vitesse *f,* train *m,* allure *f.* II. *v.i.* to p. up and down, faire les cent pas.

pacify ['pæsifai], *v.tr.* pacifier: apaiser. 'pacifist, *a. pacifist mf.*

pack [pæk]. I. *v.tr.* 1. emballer, empaqueter; *abs.* faire ses malles. 2. tasser; serrer. 3. remplir, bourrer; the train was packed, le train était bondé. 4. to p. a child off to bed, envoyer un enfant au lit; *F:* to send s.o. packing, envoyer promener qn. II. *s.* 1. paquet *m;* balle *f* (de coton); p. of lies, tissu *m* de mensonges. 2. bande *f* (de loups); the p. (of hounds), la meute; *Sp:* (*Rugby*) le pack. 3. jeu *m* (de cartes). 'package, I. *s.* 1. empaquetage *m,* emballage *m.* 2. paquet *m,* colis *m.* 3. *attrib.* p. deal, contrat *m* global; p. tour, voyage *m* organisé. II. *v.tr. Com:* conditionner (des marchandises). 'packaged, *a. Com:* préconditionné. 'packaging, *s. Com:* conditionnement *m.* 'packer, *s.* emballeur, -euse. 'packet, *s.* paquet *m;* colis *m.* 'packing, *s.* 1. emballage *m,* empaquetage *m;* to do one's p., faire ses malles; p. case, caisse *f* d'emballage; p. paper, papier *m* d'emballage. 2. (*a*) matière *f* pour emballage; (*b*) garniture *f* (d'un piston, etc.).

pact [pækt], *s.* pacte *m,* convention *f.*

pad [pæd]. I. *s.* 1. (*a*) bourrelet *m,* coussinet *m;* (*b*) tampon *m.* 2. bloc *m* (de papier). II. ‡*v.tr.* rembourrer (un coussin); capitonner (un meuble); to

p. a speech, délayer un discours. 'padding, *s.* (*a*) rembourrage *m;* (*b*) délayage *m* (d'un discours), *F:* blabla-bla *m;* (*c*) ouate *f,* bourre *f.*

paddle ['pædl]. I. *s.* pagaie *f.* II. *v.i.* 1. *v.tr.* à pagayer; (*rowing*) tirer en. 2. *v.i.* barboter.

padlock ['pædlɔk]. I. *s.* cadenas *m.* II. *v.tr.* cadenasser.

pagan ['peigən], *a. & s.* païen, -ïenne.

page[1] [peidʒ], *s.* 1. page *m.* 2. chasseur *m* (d'hôtel).

page[2], *s.* page *f;* on p. 6, à la page 6.

paid [peid], *a.* (emploi rétribué; (*of bill*) payé, réglé.

pail [peil], *s.* seau *m.*

pain [pein]. 1. douleur *f,* souffrance *f;* peine *f; F:* he's a p. in the neck, il est enquiquinant. 2. to take pains to do sth., se donner de la peine, du mal, pour faire qch. 'pained, *a.* to look p., avoir l'air blessé, froissé. 'painful, *a.* 1. douloureux. 2. (*of effort, etc.*) pénible. **-fully,** *adv.* 1. douloureusement; (*b*) péniblement. 'painless, *a.* sans douleur; indolore. 'painstaking, *a.* 1. soigneux, assidu; (élève) appliqué; (travail) soigné. 2. s. soin *m.*

paint [peint]. I. *s.* (*a*) peinture *f;* p. brush, pinceau *m;* (*b*) box of paints, boîte *f* de couleurs. II. *v.tr.* 1. (*a*) peindre; (*b*) *abs.* faire de la peinture. 2. dépeindre. 3. *Med:* badigeonner (la gorge, etc.). 'painter[1], *s.* 1. (artiste-)peintre *m.* 2. (house) p., peintre en bâtiments, peintre décorateur. 'painting, *s.* 1. to study p., étudier la peinture. 2. peinture, tableau *m.* 'paintwork, *s.* les peintures *f.*

painter[2], s. *Nau:* amarre f.

pair[1]. I. s. (a) paire f; (b) (*man & wife*) couple m; (c) pictures which make a p., tableaux qui font pendant. II. v. 1. v.tr. apparecller, assortir (des gants, etc.); accoupler (des oiseaux, etc.). 2. v.i. *Parl:* s'absenter après entente avec un adversaire qui désire s'absenter. **'pairing,** s. conjugaison f (des machines, etc.); accouplement m (d'animaux mâle et femelle); *T.V:* pairage m.

pair[2]. *used in phr.* **an au p.** (student), un(e) étudiant(e) au pair.

pajamas [pə'dʒɑːməz], *s.pl. U.S:* pyjama m.

Pakistani [pɑːkis'tɑːni], a. & s. pakistanais, -aise.

pal [pæl], s. F: camarade mf.

palace ['pæləs], s. palais m.

palate ['pælit], s. *Anat:* palais m. **'palatable,** a. agréable au goût.

palatial [pə'leiʃ(ə)l], a. magnifique, grandiose.

pale [peil], a. (a) pâle, blême; **to turn p.,** pâlir; (b) (*of colour*) clair. **'paleness,** s. pâleur f.

palette ['pælit], s. palette f.

paling ['peiliŋ], s. palissade f.

pall [pɔːl], s. drap m mortuaire.

palliative ['pæliətiv], s. palliatif m, lénitif m.

pallid ['pælid], a. (a) pâle, décoloré; (b) blafard; (c) blême.

pallor ['pælər], s. pâleur f.

p.lm[1] [pɑːm], s. 1. palmier m. 2. P. Sunday, le dimanche des Rameaux.

palm[2], s. paume f (de la main). **'palmistry,** s. chiromancie f.

palpable ['pælpəbl], a. palpable.

palpitate ['pælpiteit], v.tr. palpiter. **palpi'tation,** s. palpitation f.

paltry ['pɔːltri], a. misérable, mesquin.

pamper ['pæmpər], v.tr. choyer, dorloter.

pamphlet ['pæmflit], s. brochure f.

pan[1] [pæn], s. 1. casserole f, poêlon m; frying p., poêle f. 2. (a) plateau m (d'une balance); (b) cuvette f (de W.C.). **'pancake,** s. crêpe f; p. day, mardi gras.

‡pan[2], v.i. things did not p. out as he intended, les choses ne se sont pas passées comme il l'aurait voulu.

pan-African ['pæn'æfrikən], a. panafricain.

pan-American ['pænə'merikən], a. panaméricain. **pan-A'mericanism,** s. panaméricanisme m.

panchromatic [pænkrou'mætik], a. *Phot:* panchromatique.

pancreas ['pæŋkriəs], s. *Anat:* pancréas m.

panda ['pændə], s. *Z:* panda m.

pander ['pændər], v.i. **to p. to** (a taste, etc.), flatter (bassement) (un goût).

pane [pein], s. vitre f, carreau m (de fenêtre).

panel ['pænl]. I. s. 1. panneau m; *Aut: Av:* instrument p., tableau m de bord. 2. *Jur: T.V: etc:* the p., le jury. II. ‡v.tr. recouvrir en panneaux; lambrisser (un mur). **'panelling,** s. lambris m, boiserie f (en bois); p. of oak p., panneaux mpl de chêne.

pang [pæŋ], s. angoisse subite; douleur f.

panic ['pænik]. I. s. panique f; affolement m. II. ‡v.i. être pris de panique; s'affoler. **'panicky,** a. F: sujet à la panique; alarmiste.

panorama [pænə'rɑːmə], s. panorama m. **pano'ramic,** a. panoramique.

†pansy ['pænzi], s. pensée f.

pant [pænt], v.i. panteler; palpiter; p. haleter.

panther ['pænθər], s. panthère f.

pantomime ['pæntəmaim], s. revue-féerie f.

†pantry ['pæntri], s. garde-manger m inv.

pants [pænts], s.pl. caleçon m; F: pantalon m.

papal ['peip(ə)l], a. papal.

paper ['peipər]. I. s. 1. papier m; brown p., papier gris. 2. document m, pièce f. 3. étude f, mémoire m. 4. *Sch:* composition f (d'examen); épreuve f (écrite). 5. journal m. 6. p. fastener, attache f métallique; p. knife, coupe-papier m. II. v.tr. tapisser (une salle). **'paperback,** s. livre m de poche.

par [pɑːr], s. pair m, égalité f; F: **to feel below p.,** ne pas être dans son assiette.

parachute ['pærəʃuːt], s. parachute m; p. regiment, régiment m de parachutistes. **'parachutist,** s. parachutiste mf.

parade [pə'reid]. I. s. 1. parade f. 2. *Mil:* (a) rassemblement m; (b) exercice m. 3. défilé m (des troupes, etc.). 4. esplanade f. II. v. 1. v.tr. faire parade de (ses connaissances); *Mil:* faire l'inspection (des troupes). 2. v.i. défiler (dans les rues).

paradise ['pærədais], s. paradis m; bird of p., oiseau m de paradis.

paradox ['pærədɔks], s. paradoxe m. **para'doxical,** a. paradoxal. **-ally,** adv. paradoxalement

paraffin ['pærəfin], s. 1. paraffine f; liquid p., huile f de paraffine. 2. pétrole m (lampant).

paragon ['pærəgən], s. modèle m (de vertu, etc.).

paragraph ['pærəgrɑːf, -græf], s. paragraphe m, alinéa m.

parallel ['pærəlel]. I. a. 1. parallèle. 2. semblable; (cas) analogue. II. s. parallèle m.

paralyse ['pærəlaiz], v.tr. paralyser. **pa'ralysis,** s. paralysie f. **para'lytic,** a. & s. paralytique (mf).

paramount ['pærəmaunt], a. (d'une importance) suprême.

parapet ['pærəpit], *s.* parapet *m*; garde-fou *m.*

paraphernalia [pærəfə'neiliə], *s.pl. F:* (a) effets *m*; affaires *f*; (b) attirail *m*, appareil *m.*

paraphrase ['pærəfreiz], *v.tr.* paraphraser.

parasite ['pærəsait], *s.* parasite *m.*

paratrooper ['pærətru:pər], *s.* (soldat) parachutiste *m*. **'paratroops**, *s.pl.* (soldats) parachutistes *mpl.*

parcel ['pɑːs(ə)l], *s.* paquet *m*, colis *m*; p. post, service *m* des colis postaux.

parch [pɑːtʃ], *v.tr.* (*of wind*) dessécher (l'herbe, etc.); to be parched (with thirst), avoir une soif ardente.

parchment ['pɑːtʃmənt], *s.* parchemin *m.*

pardon ['pɑːd(ə)n], I. *s.* pardon *m*; I beg your p.! je vous demande pardon! II. *v.tr.* pardonner (à qn).

parent ['pɛərənt], *s.* père *m*, mère *f*; *pl.* parents *m*, les père et mère. **'parentage**, *s.* origine *f*, naissance *f.*

parenthesis [pə'renθəsis], *s.* parenthèse *f*; in parentheses, entre parenthèses.

parish ['pæriʃ], *s.* paroisse *f*; p. church, église paroissiale. **pa'rishioner**, *s.* paroissien, -ienne.

park [pɑːk]. I. *s.* parc *m*; car p., parc à voitures, parking *m*. II. *v.tr.* (a) garer (une auto); *abs.* stationner; (b) F: p. it there! mets-le là! 'parking, *s.* parcage *m*; *P.N:* no p., défense de stationner; *U.S:* to b(e), parking *m*; p. meter, compteur *m* de stationnement, *Fr.C:* parcomètre *m*; p. lights, feux *m* de position.

parliament ['pɑːləmənt], *s.* le parlement. **'parliamentary**, *a.* parlementaire; p. election, élection *f* législative.

parochial [pə'roukiəl], *a.* (a) *Ecc:* paroissial; (b) *Pej:* provincial.

parody ['pærədi]. I. *s.* parodie *f.* II. *v.tr.* parodier.

parole [pə'roul]. I. *s.* parole *f* (d'honneur); prisoner on p., prisonnier sur parole. II. *v.tr.* libérer un prisonnier (i) sur parole, (ii) conditionnellement.

parquet ['pɑːkei], *s.* p. (floor), parquet *m*; p. flooring, parquetage *m.*

parrot ['pærət], *s.* perroquet *m.*

parry ['pæri], *v.tr.* parer, détourner (un coup).

parsimonious [pɑːsi'mouniəs], *a.* parcimonieux.

parsley ['pɑːsli], *s.* persil *m.*

parsnip ['pɑːsnip], *s.* panais *m.*

parson ['pɑːs(ə)n], *s.* prêtre *m*; pasteur *m*. **'parsonage**, *s.* = presbytère *m*, cure *f.*

part¹ [pɑːt]. I. *s.* 1. (a) partie *f*; good in parts, bon en partie, (b) *Ind:* spare parts, pièces *f* de rechange; (c) *Gram:* parts of speech, parties du discours. 2. (a) part *f*; to take p. in sth., prendre part à qch.; (b) *Th:* rôle *m*, personnage *m*. 3. (a) to take s.o.'s p.,

prendre le parti de qn; (b) on the p. of, de la part de; for my p., quant à moi. II. *adv.* partiellement; en partie. III. *v.* 1. *v.tr.* séparer (from, de); to p. one's hair, se faire une raie. 2. *v.i.* se diviser; (*of two people*) se quitter; to p. with one's money, débourser. **'parting**, *s.* 1. séparation *f*; départ *m.* 2. (*in hair*) raie *f.*

partial ['pɑːʃ(ə)l], *a.* 1. partial. 2. partiel; en partie. **-ally**, *adv.* 1. avec partialité. 2. en partie. **parti'ality**, *s.* partialité *f*; favoritisme *m.*

participate [pɑː'tisipeit], *v.i.* participer (in, à). **partici'pation**, *s.* participation *f.*

participle ['pɑːtisipl], *s.* participe *m.*

particle ['pɑːtikl], *s.* particule *f*, parcelle *f.*

particular [pə'tikjulər]. I. *a.* 1. particulier; spécial; for no p. reason, sans raison précise. 2. méticuleux; pointilleux. **-ly**, *adv.* particulièrement; I want it for tomorrow, il me le faut absolument pour demain. II. *s.* détail *m*, particularité *f*; for further particulars apply to . . ., pour plus amples renseignements s'adresser à. . . .

partisan [pɑːti'zæn], *s.* partisan *m.*

partition [pɑː'tiʃ(ə)n], *s.* (a) cloison *f*; (b) compartiment *m* (d'une cale, etc.).

partly ['pɑːtli], *adv.* partiellement; en partie.

partner ['pɑːtnər], *s.* (a) associé, -ée; (b) *Sp:* partenaire *mf*; (c) cavalier, -ière. **'partnership**, *s.* 1. association *f*; *Com:* to go into p. with s.o., s'associer avec qn. 2. société *f* (en commandite, etc.).

partridge ['pɑːtridʒ], *s.* (a) perdrix *f*; *Cu:* perdreau *m.*

†**party** ['pɑːti], *s.* 1. parti *m* (politique); to follow the p. line, obéir aux directives du parti. 2. réunion *f* intime; réception *f*; soirée *f.* 3. groupe *m* (de voyageurs); rescue p., équipe *f* de secours. 4. (a) *Jur:* p. to a dispute, partie *f*; (b) third p. insurance, assurance *f* (au) tiers; (c) *P.T.T:* p. line, ligne *f* partagée.

pass [pɑːs]. I. *v.* 1. *v.i.* passer; the procession passed slowly, le cortège défilait lentement; when 5 minutes had passed, au bout de 5 minutes. 2. *v.tr.* (a) croiser (qn dans la rue); passer devant (une fenêtre); doubler (une autre voiture); (b) être reçu à (un examen); (c) passer (le temps); (d) *Jur:* to sentence, prononcer le jugement; (e) *Fin:* to p. the buck, se débrouiller sur le voisin. II. *s.* 1. col *m*, défilé *m.* 2. *Sch:* to obtain a p., être reçu. 3. laisser-passer *m.* 4. *Sp:* passe *f*; *F:* to make a p. at s.o., faire des avances amoureuses à qn. **'passable**, *a.* passable, assez bon.

'passage, s. 1. passage m. 2. couloir m, corridor m. 'passenger, s. voyageur, -euse. passer-'by, s. passant, -ante. 'passing. I. a. (a) passager, p. remark, remarque en passant; (b) passager, éphémère. II. s. passage (d'un train); doublement m (d'une autre voiture); écoulement m (du temps).

passion ['pæʃ(ə)n], s. 1. passion f. 2. colère f, emportement m. 'passionate, a. 1. emporté, véhément. 2. passionné. -ly, adv. 1. passionnément. 2. avec colère.

passive ['pæsiv], a. & s. passif (m). -ly, adv. passivement.

pass 'off. 1. v.i. (of pain) disparaître; everything passed off well, tout s'est bien passé. 2. v.tr. to p. sth. off on (to) s.o., repasser (qch. à qn. pass 'on, v.tr. remettre (une commande). pass 'over. 1. v.i. passer (qch.) sous silence; (of storm) se dissiper. 2. v.tr. to p. s.o. over (for promotion), passer par-dessus le dos à qn. 'passport, s. passeport m. 'password, s. mot m de passe. past. I. a. passé, ancien; for some time p., depuis quelque temps. II. s. passé m. III. prep. (a) au delà de; to walk p. s.o., passer devant qn; (b) plus de; quarter p. four, quatre heures un quart. IV. adv. to walk, go, p., passer.

paste [peist]. I. s. 1. (a) tooth p., dentifrice f; (b) anchovy p., beurre m d'anchois; (c) colle f. 2. (of jewellery) it's only p., c'est du toc. II. v.tr. coller (une affiche, etc.).

pastime ['pɑːstaim, 'pʌs-], s. passe-temps m.

†pastry ['peistri], s. 1. pâte f (de pâtisserie). 2. pâtisserie f.

pasture ['pɑːstjər], s. 1. pâturage m. II. v.i. & tr. (faire) paître.

pasty¹ ['peisti], a. pâteux; p. face, visage terreux.

†pasty² ['pæsti], s. (petit) pâté m (en croûte).

pat [pæt]. I. s. 1. coup m léger; caresse f. 2. rondelle f, médaillon m (de beurre). II. †v.tr. taper, tapoter; caresser; to p. s.o. on the back, encourager qn; to p. oneself on the back, s'applaudir.

patch [pætʃ]. I. s. 1. pièce f (pour raccommoder). 2. tache f (de couleur). 3. morceau m, parcelle f (de terre). II. v.tr. rapiécer, raccommoder; to p. sth. up, rapetasser, rafistoler (qch.). 'patchwork, s. ouvrage m fait de pièces et de morceaux. 'patchy, a. inégal.

pâté ['pætei], s. Cu: pâté m.

patent ['peit(ə)nt, 'pæt-]. I. a. 1. breveté; p. medicine, spécialité pharmaceutique; p. leather, cuir verni. 2. patent, manifeste. II. s. (a) brevet m d'invention; (b) invention f brevetée. III. v.tr. faire breveter.

paternity [pə'tɜːniti], s. paternité f. pa'ternal, a. paternel.

path [pɑːθ], s. 1. chemin m; sentier m; allée f. 2. course f; trajet m.

pathetic [pə'θetik], a. pathétique. -ally, adv. pathétiquement.

pathology [pə'θɔlədʒi], s. pathologie f. patho'logical, a. pathologique. pa'thologist, s. (a) pathologiste m; (b) médecin m légiste.

pathos ['peiθɔs], s. pathétique m.

patience ['peiʃ(ə)ns], s. 1. patience f. 2. (game) réussite f. 'patient. I. a. patient, endurant. II. s. malade mf. -ly, adv. patiemment.

patriot ['peitriət, 'pæt-], s. patriote mf. patri'otic, a. patriote; (discours) patriotique. -ally, adv. patriotiquement. 'patriotism, s. patriotisme m.

patrol [pə'troul]. I. s. patrouille f; (scouting) troupe f; U.S: p. wagon, voiture f cellulaire. II. †v. 1. v.tr. patrouiller. 2. v.tr. faire la patrouille dans (un quartier). †pa'trolman, s. U.S: 1. patrouilleur m. 2. agent m de police.

patron ['peitrən], s. 1. protecteur m (des arts); patron m (d'une œuvre de charité); p. saint, patron, -onne. f. Com: client, -ente. patronage ['pæ-], s. patronage m. patronize ['pæ-], v.tr. 1. protéger (un artiste); traiter (qn) d'un air protecteur. 2. faire ses achats (à un magasin); fréquenter (un cinéma). 'patronizing ['pæ-], a. protecteur; (ton) de condescendance.

patter ['pætər]. I. v.i. trottiner, marcher à petits pas rapides; (of rain) crépiter, fouetter. II. s. petit bruit m (de pas). fouettement m (de la pluie).

pattern ['pætərn], s. 1. modèle m; dessin m; patron m (en papier); dresses of different patterns, robes de coupes différentes. 2. échantillon m.

†patty ['pæti], s. Cu: = bouchée f à la reine.

paunch [pɔːn(t)ʃ], s. panse f; ventre m.

pause [pɔːz]. I. s. pause f, arrêt m; Mus: point m d'orgue. II. v.i. faire une pause; pauser; s'arrêter un instant; hésiter.

pave [peiv], v.tr. paver (une rue); carreler (une cour); to p. the way, préparer le terrain. pavement, s. trottoir m; U.S: chaussée f. 'paving, s. 1. ravage m, dallage m; carrelage m. 2. pavé m; dalles f pl.

pavilion [pə'viljən], s. pavillon m.

paw [pɔː]. I. s. patte f (d'animal onguiculé, F: d'une personne). II. v.tr. donner des coups de patte à (qn, qch.); F: (of pers.) tripoter (qn, qch.); (of horse) to p. (the ground), piaffer.

pawn¹ [pɔ:n]. I. s. gage m. II. v.tr. mettre (qch.) en gage; engager (qch.). **'pawnbroker,** s. prêteur, -euse, sur gages; commissionnaire m au crédit municipal.

pawn², s. (at chess) pion m.

‡pay [pei]. I. v.tr. payer (qch. à qn, une dette); to p. a bill, solder, régler, un compte; *Adm:* p. as you earn, retenue f de l'impôt à la source; (on *receipted bill*) paid, pour acquit; F: to p. through the nose, payer un prix excessif; to p. s.o. a visit, faire, rendre, une visite à qn; F: to p. a visit, aller faire pipi; to p. s.o. back, (i) rembourser qn; (ii) rendre la pareille à qn; to p. for sth., payer qch.; how much did you p. for it? combien l'avez-vous payé? to p. in a cheque, mettre un chèque à l'encaissement; to p. off a debt, solder, régler, une dette. II. s. paie f, salaire m; traitement m; holidays with p., congés m payés. **'payable,** a. payable, acquittable. **'paying.** I. a. 1. rémunérateur; qui rapporte. 2. p. guest, pensionnaire mf. II. s. versement m (d'argent); remboursement m (d'un créancier); règlement m (d'une dette). **'payment,** s. versement m; règlement m; rémunération f (de services rendus).

pea [pi:], s. green peas, petits pois m; sweet peas, pois de senteur; p. green, vert feuille; p. soup, crème f de pois (cassés); purée f de pois.

peace [pi:s], s. 1. paix f; at p., en paix. 2. ordre m public; justice of the p. = juge m d'instance. 3. tranquillité f. **'peaceful.** a. 1. paisible, tranquille. 2. pacifique. **-fully,** adv. 1. paisiblement. 2. pacifiquement. **'peacefulness,** s. tranquillité f.

peach [pi:tʃ], s. pêche f; p. (tree), pêcher m.

peacock ['pi:kɔk], s. paon m. **'peahen,** s. paonne f.

peak [pi:k], s. 1. visière f (de casquette). 2. (a) pic m, cime f (de montagne); (b) El: p. load, charge f maximum (d'un générateur); Ind: p. output, record m (de production); Rail: etc: p. hours, heures f d'affluence.

peal [pi:l]. I. s. 1. carillon m. 2. coup m (de tonnerre). 3. éclat m (de rire). II. v.i. 1. (of bells) carillonner. 2. (of thunder) retentir. 3. (of laughter) résonner.

peanut ['pi:nʌt], s. arachide f, cacahuète f.

pear [pɛər], s. poire f; p. (tree), poirier m.

pearl [pə:l], s. 1. perle f. 2. mother of p., nacre f; p. button, bouton de nacre. 3. p. barley, orge m perlé.

peat [pi:t], s. tourbe f.

pebble ['pebl], s. caillou m; galet m. **'pebbly,** a. cailouteux; à galets.

peck [pek]. I. s. coup m de bec. II. v.tr. picoter, becqueter, donner un coup de bec à (qch.).

peculiar [pi'kju:liər], a. (a) particulier; spécial, of p. interest, d'un intérêt tout particulier; (b) étrange; bizarre, singulier. **-ly,** adv. 1. particulièrement. 2. étrangement. **†peculi'arity,** s. 1. trait m distinctif; particularité f. 2. bizarrerie f, singularité f.

pecuniary [pi'kju:niəri], a. pécuniaire.

pedal ['ped(ə)l]. I. s. pédale f. II. v.i. pédaler.

pedant ['ped(ə)nt], s. pédant, -ante. **pe'dantic,** a. pédantesque.

peddle ['pedl], v.tr. to p. drugs, faire le trafic des stupéfiants. **'peddler,** s. (drug) p., trafiquant m (de stupéfiants).

pedestal ['pedist(ə)l], s. piédestal m; socle m.

pedestrian [pi'destriən]. 1. a. pédestre. 2. s. piéton m; p. crossing, passage m clouté, à piétons.

pedigree ['pedigri], s. pedigree m (d'un animal); p. dog, chien de race.

peel [pi:l]. I. s. pelure f; écorce f, peau f; candied p., zeste confit. II. v. 1. v.tr. peler (un fruit); éplucher (des pommes de terre). 2. v.i. (of paint) s'écailler; (of skin) se desquamer; (of nose) peler. **'peeler,** s. éplucheur m; rasoir m à légumes. **'peelings,** s.pl. épluchures f.

peep [pi:p]. I. v.i. 1. to p. at sth., regarder qch. à la dérobée. 2. to p. out, se laisser entrevoir. II. s. coup m d'œil (furtif).

peer¹ [piər], s. pair m; *peerage* m, les pairs; la noblesse. **'peeress,** s. pairesse f.

peer², v.i. to p. at s.o., sth., scruter qn, qch., du regard.

peevish ['pi:viʃ], a. irritable, geignard, maussade.

peewit ['pi:wit], s. vanneau m (huppé).

peg [peg]. I. s. cheville f (de bois); fiche f; piquet m (de tente); (hat) p., patère f; he's a square p. in a round hole, il n'est pas dans son emploi; F: to take s.o. down a p. or two, rabattre le caquet de qn; to buy a suit off the p., acheter un complet de confection. II. ‡v.tr. 1. cheviller (un assemblage). 2. to p. prices, indexer les prix. 3. P: to p. out, mourir, P: casser sa pipe.

pelican ['pelikən], s. pélican m.

pellet ['pelit], s. (a) boulette f (de papier); (b) grain m de plomb.

pell-mell ['pel'mel]. 1. adv. pêle-mêle. 2. a. en confusion.

pelt [pelt]. 1. v.tr. lancer une volée (de pierres) à (qn). 2. v.i. pelting rain, pluie battante.

pen¹ [pen], s. parc m, enclos m (à moutons); submarine p., abri m, nid m, de sous-marins.

pen², s. plume f (pour écrire); fountain p., stylo m; ball-point p., stylo à bille.

penal ['piːn(ə)l], a. pénal. 1. p. servitude, travaux m forcés. 'penalize, v.tr. 1. sanctionner (un délit) d'une peine. 2. Sp: (i) pénaliser, (ii) handicaper (un joueur). †'penalty [-i]. I. s. 1. peine f; (in contract) p. clause, clause f pénale. 2. Sp: pénalisation f; p. kick, shot, penalty m. II. a. U.S: p. mail, courrier m en franchise (au service de l'État).

penance ['penəns], s. pénitence f.

pencil ['pens(i)l], s. crayon m; p. sharpener, taille-crayon m.

pending ['pendiŋ]. 1. a. (procès, etc.) pendant. 2. prep. p. the negotiations, en attendant la conclusion des négociations.

pendulum ['pendjuləm], s. pendule m, balancier m.

penetrate ['penitreit], v.tr. & i. pénétrer. 'penetrating, a. pénétrant; (son) mordant. pene'tration, s. pénétration f.

penguin ['pengwin], s. manchot m; pingouin m.

penicillin ['peni'silin], s. pénicilline f.

peninsula [pə'ninsjulə], s. péninsule f; presqu'île f.

penitence ['penit(ə)ns], s. pénitence f. 'penitent, a. & s. pénitent, -ente. -ly, adv. d'un air contrit. †peni'tentiary, s. U.S: prison f.

penknife ['pennaif], s. canif m.

†**penny** ['peni], s. = deux sous m; in p. numbers, en petites quantités; that will cost a pretty p., cela coûtera cher; F: a bad p., un mauvais sujet; F: the penny's dropped, on comprend, on y est. 'penniless, a. sans le sou, sans ressources.

pension ['penʃ(ə)n]. I. s. old age, retirement, p., retraite f de vieillesse. II. v.tr. pensionner (qn). 'pensionable, a. (of employment) qui donne droit à une retraite; (âge) de la mise à la retraite. 'pensioner, s. retraité, -ée.

pentagon ['pentəgən], s. pentagone m.

pensive ['pensiv], a. pensif, songeur.

penthouse ['penthaus], s. (a) appentis m; (b) appartement m tout en haut d'un immeuble.

people ['piːpl]. I. s.coll. gens mpl; monde m; F: my p., mes parents; the king and his p., le roi et ses sujets; p. say that . . ., on dit que; Pol: people's democracy, démocratie f populaire. II. v.tr. peupler (with, de).

pep [pep]. I. s. F: entrain m; p. pill, excitant m; p. talk, petit discours d'encouragement. II. †v.tr. F: to p. s.o., sth., up, regaillardir qn; donner de l'entrain à qch.

pepper ['pepər]. I. s. poivre m; p. mill, moulin à poivre. II. v.tr. poivrer.

'peppercorn, s. grain m de poivre.

'peppery, a. 1. poivré. 2. (of pers.) irascible.

per ['pəːr], prep. 1. (a) par; Com: as invoice, suivant facture; (b) ten francs p. pound, dix francs la livre. 2. p. annum, par an; p. cent, pour cent. per'centage, s. pourcentage m.

perambulator [pə'ræmbjuleitər], s. voiture f d'enfant, landau m.

perceive [pə'siːv], v.tr. s'apercevoir de (qch.). per'ceptible, a. perceptible. per'ception, s. perception f.

perch¹ [pəːtʃ]. I. s. perchoir m. II. v.i. (se) percher.

perch², s. Fish: perche f.

percolate ['pəːkəleit], v.i. s'infiltrer; (of coffee) filtrer. perco'lation, s. infiltration f. 'percolator, s. cafetière f automatique.

percussion [pə'kʌʃ(ə)n], s. percussion f; choc m.

peremptory [pə'rem(p)təri], a. péremptoire.

perfect. I. a. ['pəːfikt], parfait; Gram: s. the p., le parfait. -ly, adv. parfaitement. II. v.tr. [pə'fekt] rendre parfait; mettre (une invention) au point. per'fection, s. perfection f.

perfidy ['pəːfidi], s. perfidie f.

perforate ['pəːfəreit], v.tr. perforer; percer, transpercer. perfo'ration, s. perforation f.

perform [pə'fɔːm], v.tr. 1. s'acquitter de (son devoir). 2. Th: jouer (une pièce). per'formance, s. 1. fonctionnement m (d'une machine); Aut: rendement m; Sp: performance f. 2. Th: représentation f (d'une pièce); Cin: séance f. per'former, s. Th: etc: artiste mf; acteur, -trice.

perfume ['pəːfjuːm]. I. s. parfum m. II. v.tr. parfumer.

perfunctory [pə'fʌŋkt(ə)ri], a. 1. (examen) superficiel. 2. (of pers.) négligent; peu zélé.

perhaps [pə'hæps, præps], adv. peut-être; p. not, peut-être (bien) que non; p. I have it, il se peut que je l'aie.

peril ['peril], s. péril m, danger m. 'perilously, adv. dangereusement.

period ['piəriəd], s. 1. période f; Sch: heure f de cours; within the agreed p., dans le délai fixé. 2. époque f, âge m; p. furniture, meubles m de style. 3. point m (de ponctuation); F: he's no good, p., il est nul, tout court. F: règles fpl (d'une femme). peri'odical, a. & s. périodique (m). -ally, adv. périodiquement.

periscope ['periskoup], s. périscope m.

perish ['periʃ], v.i. (a) périr, mourir; (b) se détériorer. 'perishable. 1. a. périssable. 2. s.pl. perishables, marchandises fpl périssables. 'perished, a. (a) détérioré; (b) F: transi (de froid). 'perishing, a. (a) it's p., il fait un froid

de tous les diables; (b) P: p. idiot,
sacré idiot.

peritonitis [peritə'naitis], s. Med: péritonite f.

perjury ['pəːdʒəri], s. faux témoignage m. 'perjurer, s. parjure mf.

perk [pəːk], v.i. to p. up, se ranimer. 'perky, a. éveillé, guilleret.

perks [pəːks], s.pl. F: gratte f.

perm [pəːm]. I. s. F: permanente f. indéfrisable f. II. v.tr. F: to have one's hair permed, se faire faire une indéfrisable f.

permanent ['pəːmənənt], a. permanent; p. address, résidence fixe; p. wave, (ondulation) permanente f. -ly, adv. d'une façon permanente. 'permanency, s. emploi m permanent.

permeate ['pəːmieit], v.tr. & i. filtrer à travers (qch.).

permit. I. ʒ.v.r. [pə'mit] permettre. II. s. ['pəːmit] permis m; autorisation f. per'mission, s. permission f.

pernicious [pə'niʃəs], a. pernicieux.

pernickety [pə'nikiti], a. F: vétilleux; difficile; (of job) minutieux.

peroxide [pə'rɔksaid], s. peroxyde m.

perpendicular [pəːpən'dikjulər], a. & s. perpendiculaire (f). -ly, adv. perpendiculairement.

perpetrate ['pəːpitreit], v.tr. commettre, perpétrer (un crime). 'perpetrator, s. auteur m (d'un crime, d'une farce).

perpetual [pə'petjuəl], a. (a) perpétuel, éternel; (b) sans fin; continuel. -ally, adv. (a) perpétuellement; (b) sans cesse. per'petuate, v.tr. perpétuer.

perplex [pə'pleks], v.tr. embarrasser; mettre dans la perplexité. per'plexed, a. perplexe, embarrassé. per'plexing, a. embarrassant, troublant. per'plexity, s. perplexité f.

perquisite ['pəːkwizit], s. casuel m; pl. F: gratte f.

persecute ['pəːsikjuːt], v.tr. 1. persécuter. 2. tourmenter; harceler. perse'cution, s. persécution f; p. mania, délire m de la persécution. 'persecutor, s. persécuteur,-trice.

persevere [pəːsi'viər], v.i. persévérer. perse'verance, s. persévérance f. perse'vering, a. persévérant, assidu.

Persian ['pəːʃən]. 1. a. & s. persan, -ane; P: carpet, tapis m de Perse. 2. s. Ling: le persan.

persist [pə'sist], v.i. persister. per'sistence, s. persistance f. per'sistency, s. persistance f. per'sistent, a. persistant. -ly, adv. avec persistance.

person ['pəːs(ə)n], s. personne f; individu m; pl. gens m. 'personable, a. qui se présente bien. personage, s. personnage m; personnalité f. 'personal, a. personnel; don't be p., ne faites pas de personnalités; to make a p. application, se présenter en personne. -ally, adv. personnellement;

p. I think . . ., quant à moi, je pense . . . perso'nality, s. personnalité f. 'personalized, a. Com: F: personnalisé. personi'fication, s. personnification f. per'sonify, v.tr. personnifier. person'nel, s.coll: personnel m.

perspective [pə'spektiv], s. perspective f.

perspire [pə'spaiər], v.i. transpirer, suer. perspi'ration, s. (a) transpiration f; (b) sueur f.

persuade [pə'sweid], v.tr. persuader (à qn de faire qch.); he persuaded me not to, il m'en a dissuadé. per'suasion, s. persuasion f; conviction f. per'suasive, a. persuasif.

pertinent ['pəːtinənt], a. pertinent; à propos.

perturb [pə'təːb], v.tr. troubler, inquiéter. pertur'bation, s. agitation f; inquiétude f.

peruse [pə'ruːz], v.tr. lire attentivement. pe'rusal, s. lecture f.

pervade [pə'veid], v.tr. s'infiltrer dans (qch.).

perverse [pə'vəːs], a. (a) pervers, méchant; (b) contrariant. per'verseness, s. (a) perversité f; (b) esprit m contraire. per'version, s. perversion f. per'vert. I. v.tr. pervertir; fausser (les faits). II. s. ['pəː-], perverti, -ie.

pessimism ['pesimizm], s. pessimisme m. 'pessimist, s. pessimiste mf. pessi'mistic, a. pessimiste. -ally, adv. avec pessimisme.

pest [pest], s. peste f, fléau m. 'pester, v.tr. tourmenter; F: empoisonner (qn). pesti'lential, a. pestilentiel; F: assommant, empoisonnant.

pestle ['pesl], s. pilon m.

pet ['pet]. I. s. (a) animal m familier, favori; (b) enfant gâté(e). II. attrib. choyé, favori. III. ‡v.tr. choyer.

petal ['petl], s. pétale m.

petition [pi'tiʃ(ə)n], s. pétition f, requête f; Jur: p. for a divorce, demande f en divorce.

petrify ['petrifai], v.tr. pétrifier.

petrol ['petr(ə)l], s. essence f. pe'troleum, s. pétrole m; the p. industry, l'industrie pétrolière.

petticoat ['petikout], s. jupe f de dessous; jupon m.

petty ['peti], a. 1. (a) petit, insignifiant; (b) mesquin. 2. p. cash, petite caisse. 3. Nau: p. officer, officier m marinier, F: gradé m. 'pettiness, s. petitesse f, mesquinerie f.

petulance ['petjuləns], s. irritabilité f. 'petulant, a. irritable.

pew [pjuː], s. banc m d'église.

pewter ['pjuːtər], s. étain m.

phantom ['fæntəm], s. fantôme m, spectre m.

pharmaceutical [fɑːmə'sjuːtikəl], a. pharmaceutique.

phase [feiz], s. phase f.

pheasant ['feznt], *s.* faisan, -ane.

phenobarbitone ['fi:nou'bɑ:bitoun], *s. Med:* barbiturique *m*, phénobarbital *m*.

†**phenomenon** [fi'nɔminən], *s.* phénomène *m.* phe'nomenal, *a.* phénoménal.

philanthropy [fi'lænθrəpi], *s.* philanthropie *f.* phi'lanthropist, *s.* philanthrope *mf.*

philately [fi'lætəli], *s.* philatélie *f.* phi'latelist, *s.* philatéliste *mf.*

philology [fi'lɔlədʒi], *s.* philologie *f.* phi'lologist, *s.* philologue *m.*

†**philosophy** [fi'lɔsəfi], *s.* philosophie *f.* phi'losopher, *s.* philosophe *m.* philo'sophical, *a.* 1. philosophique. 2. (*of pers.*) philosophe, calme. **-ally,** *adv.* philosophiquement.

phlegm [flem], *s.* flegme *m.*

phone [foun]. I. *s. F:* téléphone *m.* II. *v.tr. F:* téléphoner (à qn).

phonetic [fə'netik], *a.* phonétique. **-ally,** *adv.* phonétiquement. pho'netics, *s.pl.* la phonétique.

phosphate ['fɔsfeit], *s.* phosphate *m.*

phosphorus ['fɔsf(ə)rəs], *s.* phosphore *m.* phospho'rescent, *a.* phosphorescent.

photo- ['foutou-, fɔ'tɔ-], *prefix used in combined forms.* **photo-** 'photo-e'lectric, *a.* (cellule) photo-électrique. 'photo-'finish, *s. Sp:* décision *f* par photo. 'photo'genic, *a.* photogénique. 'photograph. I. *s.* photographie *f.* II. *v.tr.* photographier. pho'tographer, *s.* photographe *m.* 'photo'graphic, *a.* photographique; p. library, photothèque *f.* **-ally,** *adv.* photographiquement. pho'tography, *s.* la photographie. 'photomi'crography, *s.* la photomicrographie. 'photo-re'connaissance, *s. Av:* reconnaissance *f* par photo. 'photostat, *s.* photocopie *f,* photostat *m.* II. *v.tr.* photocopier.

phrase [freiz]. I. *s.* 1. locution *f;* tour *m* de phrase. 2. *Mus:* phrase *f,* période *f.* II. *v.tr.* 1. exprimer (sa pensée). 2. *Mus:* phraser. phrase'ology, *s.* phraséologie *f.*

physical ['fizik(ə)l], *a.* physique. **-ally,** *adv.* physiquement, matériellement; impossible; impossible; **a p. handicapped person,** un diminué physique.

physician [fi'ziʃ(ə)n], *s.* médecin *m.*

physics ['fiziks], *s.pl.* la physique. 'physicist, *s.* physicien, -ienne.

physiognomy [fizi'ɔnəmi], *s.* physionomie *f.*

physiology [fizi'ɔlədʒi], *s.* physiologie *f.* physio'logical, *a.* physiologique.

physique [fi'zi:k], *s.* physique *m* (de qn).

†**piano** [pi'ænou], *s.* piano *m;* grand p., piano à queue. 'pianist, *s.* pianiste *mf.*

pick [pik]. I. *v.tr.* 1. (*a*) piocher (la terre); (*b*) *F:* to p. holes in sth., trouver à redire à qch.; *F:* why p. on me? pourquoi m'accuser, moi? 2. (*also*

pick out) choisir. 3. cueillir (des fruits, etc.). II. *s.* 1. pic *m,* pioche *f.* 2. choix *m,* élite *f.* 'pickaxe, *s.* pioche *f.*

picket ['pikit]. I. *s.* piquet *m.* II. *v.tr. Ind:* installer des piquets de grève.

pickle ['pikl]. I. *s.* 1. marinade *f.* 2. *pl. Cu:* conserves *f* au vinaigre. 3. *F:* to be in a p., être dans de beaux draps. II. *v.tr. Cu:* mariner; conserver (au vinaigre).

'**pickpocket** ['pikpɔkit], *s.* voleur *m* à la tire, pickpocket *m.* 'pick 'up, 1. *v.tr.* (*a*) ramasser (qch.); (*in knitting*) relever (une maille); (*b*) to p. up a language, s'initier rapidement à une langue; (*c*) trouver; to p. sth. up cheap, acheter qch. à bon marché; (*d*) capter (un message, etc.); (*e*) *Aut:* to p. up (speed), reprendre. 2. *v.i.* (*a*) retrouver ses forces; se rétablir. 'pick-up, *s.* 1. connaissance *f* de rencontre. 2. *Aut:* reprise *f* (du moteur). 3. *Rec:* pick-up *m.* 4. (*electronics*) capteur *m.*

picnic ['piknik]. I. *s.* pique-nique *m; F:* the Korean campaign was no p., la campagne de Corée n'a guère été une partie de plaisir. II. †*v.i.* pique-niquer.

picture ['piktʃər], *s.* image *f;* tableau *m;* peinture *f;* gravure *f; F:* to be in the p., être au courant. pic'torial, *a.* & *s.* illustré (*m*). pictu'resque, *a.* pittoresque.

pie [pai], *s.* (*a*) meat p. = pâté en croûte; (*b*) fruit p., tourte *f.*

piebald ['paibɔld], *a.* & *s.* (cheval) pie *m.*

piece [pi:s], *s.* pièce *f.* 1. (*a*) morceau *m;* bout *m;* (*b*) fragment *m;* to come to pieces, s'en aller en morceaux. 2. partie *f;* to take to pieces, démonter, défaire. 3. all in one p., tout d'une pièce. 4. p. of advice, conseil *m.*

piecemeal ['pi:smi:l], *adv.* par morceaux.

pier [piər], *s.* 1. jetée *f;* quai *m.* 2. pilier *m.*

pierce [piəs], *v.tr.* percer, transpercer. 'piercing, *a.* (cri) aigu, perçant; (froid) pénétrant.

piety ['paiəti], *s.* piété *f.*

pig [pig], *s.* 1. (*a*) porc *m,* cochon *m;* suck(l)ing p., cochon de lait; *F:* to buy a p. in a poke, acheter chat en poche; (*b*) *F:* to make a p. of oneself, manger gloutonnement; you (dirty little) p.! petit sale! don't be a p.! voyons, sois chic! (*c*) *F:* (iron), fer *m* en fonte, en gueuse. pig'headed, *a. F:* obstiné, entêté. 'piglet, *s.* porcelet *m.* 'pigskin, *s.* peau *f* de porc. 'pigsty, *s.* porcherie *f.*

pigeon ['pidʒin], *s.* pigeon *m.* 'pigeonhole. 1. *s.* case *f,* alvéole *m* (de bureau). II. *v.tr.* classer (des papiers).

pigment ['pigmənt], *s.* matière *f* colorante; colorant *m.*

pike [paik], s. Fish: brochet m.

pile¹ [pail], s. pieu m; built on piles, bâti sur pilotis.

pile² I. s. tas m, monceau m; atomic p., pile f atomique; F: to make one's p., faire fortune. II. v. 1. v.tr. to p. (up), entasser; amasser (une fortune); empiler (du bois); F: to p. it on, exagérer. 2. v.i. to p. up, s'amonceler.

pile³, s. poil m (d'un tapis).

pilfer ['pilfər], v.tr. chiper (qch. à qn); abs. chaparder.

pilgrim ['pilgrim], s. pèlerin, -ine. 'pilgrimage, s. pèlerinage m.

pill [pil], s. pilule f.

pillage ['pilidʒ]. I. s. pillage m. II. v.tr. piller, saccager.

pillar ['pilər], s. pilier m; colonne f. 'pillar-box, s. boîte f aux lettres; p.-b. red, rouge drapeau.

pillion ['piljən], s. siège m arrière (d'une moto); to ride p., monter derrière.

pillow ['pilou], s. oreiller m; p.-case, -slip, taie f d'oreiller.

pilot ['pailət]. I. s. (a) pilote m; (b) guide m; (c) p. lamp, lampe f témoin. II. v.tr. piloter (un navire, un avion).

pimento [pi'mentou], s. piment m.

pimple ['pimpl], s. bouton m, pustule f.

pin [pin]. I. s. 1. épingle f. 2. goupille f, cheville f. II. v.tr. 1. épingler. 2. to p. s.o. down to facts, obliger qn à reconnaître les faits.

pinafore ['pinəfɔːr], s. tablier m.

pincers ['pinsəz], s.pl. pince f; tenailles fpl.

pinch [pin(t)ʃ]. I. v.tr. 1. pincer. 2. serrer, gêner. 3. P: voler, chiper. II. s. 1. pinçade f; the p. of poverty, la gêne; F: at a p., au besoin. 2. pincée f (de sel, etc.).

pine¹ [pain], s. pin m; p. cone, pomme f de pin.

pine², v.i. languir.

pineapple ['painæpl], s. ananas m.

pinion ['pinjən], s. E: pignon m.

pink [piŋk]. 1. s. œillet m. 2. a. & s. rose (m).

pinnacle ['pinəkl], s. cime f; pic m.

pioneer [paiə'niər], s. pionnier m.

pious ['paiəs], a. pieux.

pip¹ [pip], s. 1. Mil: F: = galon m (d'officier), F: ficelle f. 2. Rad: the pips, le signal horaire, F: les tops m.

pip², s. pépin m (de fruit).

pipe [paip], s. 1. tuyau m, conduit m. 2. pipe f (de fumeur). 'pipeline, s. conduite f, canalisation f; (for oil) pipeline m, oléoduc m; (for gas) gazoduc m, feeder m. 'piper, s. joueur m de cornemuse.

pippin ['pipin], s. (pomme f) reinette f.

pique [pik], s. pique f, ressentiment m. 'piquant, a. (of flavour, etc.) piquant.

pirate ['paiərət], s. pirate m. 'piracy, s. piraterie f. 2. contrefaçon f (d'un livre, etc.).

piss [pis]. 1. s. P: urine f. 2. v.i. P: uriner, pisser.

pistachio [pis'tɑːʃiou], s. pistache f.

pistol ['pistl], s. pistolet m.

piston ['pistən], s. E: piston m; Aut: p. ring, segment m de piston.

pit [pit], s. 1. (a) fosse f, trou m; Aut: inspection p., fosse à réparations; (b) puits m (d'une mine de charbon). 2. Th: parterre m. 3. le creux (de l'estomac).

pitch¹ [pitʃ], s. poix f; brai m; bitume m; p. black, dark, noir comme poix.

pitch². I. v. 1. v.tr. (a) dresser (une tente). (b) lancer (une balle). 2. v.i. (of ship) tanguer. II. s. 1. Mus: hauteur f (d'un son); diapason m (d'un instrument). 2. Nau: tangage m. 3. Sp: terrain m (de football, etc.). 4. degré m de pente (d'un toit). 'pitchfork, s. fourche f (à foin).

pitfall ['pitfɔːl], s. trappe f; piège m.

pith [piθ], s. 1. mœlle f. 2. sève f, ardeur f. 'pithy, a., concis; vigoureux.

pitiful ['pitiful], a. 1. compatissant; plein de pitié. 2. pitoyable; lamentable. -fully, adv. pitoyablement. 'pitiless, a. impitoyable, sans pitié. -ly, adv. sans pitié.

pittance ['pit(ə)ns], s. maigre salaire m.

pity ['piti]. I. s. pitié f; compassion f; what a p.! quel dommage! II. v.tr. plaindre (qn); avoir pitié de (qn).

pivot ['pivət], s. pivot m; axe m.

placard ['plækɑːd], s. écriteau m; affiche f.

placate [plə'keit], v.tr. apaiser, calmer (qn).

place [pleis]. I. s. 1. (a) lieu m, endroit m, localité f; in another p., autre part; ailleurs; this is no p. for you, vous n'avez que faire ici; (b) p. of residence, demeure f. 2. place f; to take a p., mettre un couvert; out of p., hors de propos, déplacé; to take p., avoir lieu; se passer. 3. place, rang m; in the first p., d'abord; to put s.o. in his p., remettre qn à sa place; to back a horse for a p., jouer un cheval placé; Mth: answer to three places of decimals, solution à trois décimales. II. v.tr. 1. placer, mettre, poser; Com: difficult to p., à vente difficile; to p. an order, passer une commande. F: I can't p. him, je ne le remets pas. 3. place, poste m, emploi m.

placid ['plæsid], a. placide, calme, tranquille. -ly, adv. tranquillement.

plagiarism ['pleidʒiərizm], s. plagiat m.

plague [pleig]. 1. s. 1. fléau m. 2. peste f. II. v.tr. F: tourmenter (qn).

plaice [pleis], s. Fish: carrelet m; plie f.

plain [plein]. I. *a.* 1. clair, évident; in p. figures, en chiffres connus. 2. (*a*) in p. clothes, en civil; (*b*) uni, lisse; (*c*) p. cooking, cuisine simple. 3. laid; sans beauté. II. *adv.* (*also* plainly) clairement, distinctement. III. *s.* plaine *f.* '**plainness,** *s.* 1. clarté *f* (de langage); netteté *f* (d'un objet lointain). 2. manque *m* de beauté.

plaintiff ['pleintif], *s.* Jur: plaignant, -ante.

plaintive ['pleintiv], *a.* plaintif. -ly, *adv.* d'un ton plaintif.

plait [plæt]. I. *s.* natte *f*, tresse *f.* II. *v.tr.* natter, tresser.

plan [plæn]. I. *s.* 1. plan *m*; cadre *m.* 2. projet *m*, plan; according to p., selon les prévisions. II. ‡*v.tr.* projeter (un voyage, etc.). '**planning,** *s.* dirigisme *m*; organisation *f*; town p., urbanisme *m*; family p., contrôle *m* des naissances, planning *m* familial.

plane¹ [plein]. I. *s.* 1. plan *m.* 2. avion *m.* II. *a.* plan, uni; plat.

plane². I. *s.* rabot *m.* II. *v.tr.* raboter; aplanir.

plane³, *s.* p. (tree), platane *m.*

planet ['plænit], *s.* planète *f.*

plank [plæŋk], *s.* planche *f*; madrier *m.*

plant [plɑːnt]. I. *s.* 1. plante *f.* 2. Ind: appareil(s) *m(pl)*; installation *f*; outillage *m.* II. *v.tr.* planter. '**plan-**'**tation,** *s.* plantation *f.* '**planter,** *s.* planteur *m.*

plaque [plɑːk], *s.* plaque *f.*

plaster ['plɑːstər]. I. *s.* 1. emplâtre *m*; adhesive p., sparadrap *m.* 2. plâtre *m*; p. of Paris, plâtre de moulage. II. *v.tr.* plâtrer (un mur, etc.); to be plastered with mud, être tout couvert de boue. '**plasterer,** *s.* plâtrier *m.*

plastic ['plæstik], *a.* 1. plastique; p. surgery, chirurgie *f* plastique. 2. *a. & s.* (matière *f*) plastique (*m*). 3. p. bomb, plastic *m*, plastique *m.*

plate [pleit], *s.* 1. plaque *f*, lame *f* (de métal). 2. H: hot p., (i) plaque (chauffante) (de cuisinière électrique), (ii) chauffe-assiettes *m*; Aut: clutch p., plateau *m* d'embrayage; Aut: number p., plaque d'immatriculation; (dental) p., dentier *m.* 3. (*a*) Phot: plaque *f*; (*b*) (in book) gravure *f*; (*c*) p. glass, verre *m* à glaces. 4. (*a*) vaisselle *f* d'or, d'argent; it's only p., c'est seulement de l'argenté; (*b*) Sp: coupe *f* (donnée en prix). 5. assiette *f*; soup p., assiette creuse. '**plateful,** *s.* assiettée *f.* '**platelayer,** *s.* Rail: ouvrier *m* de la voie.

†plateau ['plætou], *s.* plateau *m.*

platform ['plætfɔːm], *s.* 1. terrasse *f.* 2. (*a*) plateforme *f*; (*b*) Rail: quai *m.* 3. estrade *f*, tribune *f* (de réunion publique); Pol: programme *m* (d'un parti).

platinum ['plætinəm], *s.* platine *m.*

platitude ['plætitjuːd], *s.* platitude *f.*

platypus ['plætipəs], *s.* Z: ornithor-hynque *m.*

plausible ['plɔːzibl], *a.* 1. (*a*) plausible; (*b*) spécieux. 2. enjôleur. -bly, *adv.* plausiblement.

play [plei]. I. *s.* 1. jeu *m*; in full p., en pleine activité. 2. jeu, amusement *m.* 3. (*a*) pièce *f* de théâtre; (*b*) spectacle *m.* II. *v.* 1. *v.i.* jouer. 2. *v.tr.* to p. a match, disputer un match; to p. tennis, jouer au tennis; to p. the piano, jouer du piano; Th: to p. Macbeth, tenir le rôle de Macbeth; F: to p. the fool, faire des sottises. play 'down, *v.tr.* minimiser l'importance de (qn, qch.). '**player,** *s.* joueur, -euse. '**playful,** *a.* enjoué, folâtre. '**playground,** *s.* Sch: cour *f*, terrain *m*, de récréation. '**plaything,** *s.* jouet *m.* play 'up, *v.tr. F:* to p. up to s.o., flatter qn; to p. s.o. up, agacer qn; chahuter qn. '**playwright,** *s.* auteur *m* dramatique.

plea [pliː], *s.* 1. Jur: défense *f.* 2. (*a*) excuse *f*, prétexte *m*; (*b*) appel *m* (for, à).

plead [pliːd]. 1. *v.i.* plaider; to p. guilty, s'avouer coupable. 2. *v.tr.* (*a*) plaider (une cause); (*b*) prétexter (l'ignorance).

pleasant ['plez(ə)nt], *a.* 1. agréable, aimable. 2. (*of pers.*) affable. -ly, *adv.* 1. agréablement. 2. avec affabilité.

please [pliːz], *v.tr.* 1. plaire à (qn); faire plaisir à (qn); contenter (qn); hard to p., difficile; p. yourself! faites à votre guise. 2. (if you) p., s'il vous plaît; p. sit down, veuillez vous asseoir. 3. *abs.* do as you p., faites comme vous voudrez. '**pleased,** *a.* satisfait, content. '**pleasing,** *a.* agréable. '**pleasure** ['pleʒər], *s.* plaisir *m.*

pleat [pliːt]. I. *s.* pli *m.* II. *v.tr.* plisser.

plebiscite ['plebisait], *s.* plébiscite *m.*

pledge [pledʒ]. I. *s.* 1. gage *m.* 2. promesse *f*, vœu *m.* II. *v.tr.* 1. mettre (qch.) en gage. 2. engager (sa parole).

plenty ['plenti], *s.* abondance *f*; you have p. of time, vous avez largement le temps; to have p. to live on, avoir largement de quoi vivre. '**plentiful,** *a.* abondant, copieux.

pleurisy ['pluərisi], *s.* Med: pleurésie *f.*

pliable ['plaiəbl], *a.* 1. flexible; souple. 2. docile, complaisant.

pliers ['plaiəz], *s.pl.* pince *f*, tenaille *f.*

plinth [plinθ], *s.* plinthe *f*; socle *m.*

‡plod [plɔd], *v.i.* 1. marcher péniblement. 2. travailler laborieusement.

plonk¹ [plɔŋk]. I. *s.* bruit *m* sourd. II. *v.tr.* F: poser (qch.) bruyamment.

plonk², *s. P: Austr:* vin *m* ordinaire, pinard *m.*

plot [plɔt]. I. *s.* 1. (lot *m* de) terrain *m*; building p., terrain à bâtir, lotissement *m.* 2. intrigue *f*, action *f* (d'un roman). 3. complot *m*, conspiration *f.* II. ‡*v.tr. & i.* comploter, conspirer. '**plotter,** *s.* conspirateur, -trice.

plough [plau]. I. s. charrue f. II. v.tr. **1.** labourer. **2.** Com: to p. back (profits), reverser (les bénéfices dans l'entreprise).

plover ['plʌvər], s. pluvier m.

pluck [plʌk]. I. v.tr. **1.** arracher (des plumes); épiler (les sourcils). **2.** plumer (une volaille). II. s. courage m, F: cran m. '**plucky,** a. courageux.

plug [plʌg]. I. s. **1.** tampon m, bouchon m. **2.** (a) cheville f; fiche f de connexion; wall p., prise f de courant; (b) Aut: sparking p., bougie f. **3.** chasse f d'eau (du W.C.). II. v.tr. **1.** boucher, tamponner. **2.** Com: faire une publicité à tout casser (pour qch.).

plum [plʌm], s. prune f; p. tree, prunier m; p. cake, cake m; p. pudding, pudding m (de Noël).

plumage ['plu:midʒ], s. plumage m.

plumb [plʌm]. v.tr. **1.** sonder. **2.** plomber (une canalisation). '**plumber,** s. plombier m. '**plumbing,** s. **1.** plomberie f. **2.** coll: tuyauterie f.

plump [plʌmp], a. rebondi, grassouillet, dodu; bien en chair. '**plumpness,** s. embonpoint m, rondeur f.

plunder ['plʌndər]. I. s. butin m. II. v.tr. piller.

plunge [plʌndʒ]. I. v. **1.** v.tr. plonger (qch. dans l'eau). **2.** v.i. plonger (dans l'eau); se jeter à corps perdu (dans une affaire). II. s. plongeon m; to take the p., sauter le pas.

plural ['pluər(ə)l], a. & s. pluriel (m).

plus [plʌs]. **1.** prep. plus. **2.** s. plus m.

plush [plʌʃ], s. peluche f.

plutocrat ['plu:tokræt], s. ploutocrate m.

ply [plai], v.i. to p. for hire, faire un service de taxi.

ply², s. **1.** pli m (de contre-plaqué). **2.** fil m (de laine de corde); three p. wool, laine trois fils. '**plywood,** s. contre-plaqué m.

p.m. [pi:'em], de l'après-midi, du soir.

pneumatic [nju:'mætik], a. pneumatique.

pneumonia [nju:'mouniə], s. pneumonie f.

poach [poutʃ], v.tr. Cu: pocher.

poach², v.tr. & i. braconner. '**poacher,** s. braconnier m. '**poaching,** s. braconnage m.

pocket ['pɔkit]. I. s. **1.** (a) poche f (de money, argent m de poche; p. edition, édition de poche; (b) to be in p., être en bénéfice; I am out of p. by it, j'y suis de ma poche. **2.** (a) (at billiards) blouse f; (b) Av: (air) p., trou m d'air. II. v.tr. **1.** (a) empocher; mettre (qch.) dans sa poche; (b) Pej: soustraire (de l'argent). **2.** (at billiards) blouser (la bille). '**pocketful,** s. pleine poche f.

pod [pɔd], s. cosse f, gousse f.

poem ['pouim], s. poème m. '**poet,** s. poète m. po'**etic(al),** a. poétique. '**poetry,** s. poésie f.

point [pɔint]. I. s. **1.** point m; (a) decimal p., virgule f; (b) p. of view, point de vue; (c) the p., le sujet, la question; off the p., hors de propos; p. of interest, détail m intéressant; we disagree on that p., là-dessus nous ne sommes pas d'accord; to make a p. of doing sth., se faire un devoir de faire qch.; in p. of fact, par le fait; (d) I was on the p. of going, j'allais partir; up to a p., jusqu'à un certain point; (e) Sp: to win on points, gagner aux points; (f) policeman on p. duty, agent m de service; (g) to refuse p. blank, refuser net. **2.** (a) pointe f (d'une épingle); piquant m (d'une plaisanterie); (b) Rail: points, aiguillage m; (c) p. of the compass, aire f de vent. II. v. **1.** v.tr. braquer (une arme) (at, (at, sur). **2.** v.i. to p. at s.o., sth., montrer qn, qch., du doigt; (b) to p. sth. out, signaler qch. '**pointed,** a. **1.** pointu. **2.** (of remark) mordant. -**ly,** adv. d'un ton mordant, sarcastique. '**pointer,** s. **1.** chien m d'arrêt, pointer m. **2.** F: renseignement m, F: tuyau m. '**pointing,** s. jointement m (d'un mur). '**pointless,** a. (plaisanterie) fade; (observation) qui ne rime à rien. †**pointsman,** s. Rail: aiguilleur m.

poise [pɔiz]. I. s. **1.** équilibre m, aplomb m. **2.** port m (du corps). II. v.tr. (a) équilibrer; (b) balancer.

poison ['pɔizn]. I. s. poison m. II. v.tr. (a) empoisonner; (b) corrompre (l'esprit). '**poisoner,** s. empoisonneur, -euse. '**poisoning,** s. empoisonnement m. '**poisonous,** a. toxique; empoisonné; venimeux; vénéneux.

poke [pouk]. I. v.tr. (a) pousser (qn, qch.) du bras, du coude; (b) tisonner (le feu); (c) to p. fun at s.o., se moquer de qn. **2.** v.i. to p. about, fouiller (dans tous les coins); to p. into other people's business, fourrer son nez dans les affaires d'autrui.

poker¹ ['poukər], s. tisonnier m.

poker², s. (game of cards) poker m.

pole¹ [poul], s. (a) perche f; tent p., mât m, montant m de tente; (b) Nau: flèche f (de mât); (c) Sp: p. jumping, saut m à la perche.

pole², s. Geog: pôle m; the p. star, l'étoile f polaire. '**polar,** a. polaire; p. bear, ours m blanc.

Pole³, s. polonais, -aise.

police [pə'li:s], s. inv. the p., la police; (in country districts) = la gendarmerie; p. constable = (i) agent m de police; (ii) gendarme m; p. station = commissariat m de police; the Royal Canadian Mounted P., la Gendarmerie royale du Canada; F: the p. are after him, la police est à ses trousses. †**policeman,** s. (i) agent m de police; (ii) gendarme m. †**policewoman,** s. femme-agent f (de police).

†**policy¹** ['pɔlisi], s. politique f; ligne f de conduite.

†**policy²**, s. police f (d'assurance).

polish ['pɔliʃ]. I. s. 1. poli m, brillant m, lustre m. 2. nail p., vernis m pour les ongles. 3. belles manières fpl. II. v.tr. polir; cirer (le parquet). '**polished**, a. poli.

Polish ['pouliʃ], a. polonais.

polite [pə'lait], a. poli, courtois. -**ly**, adv. poliment. po'**liteness**, s. politesse f.

politics ['pɔlitiks], s.pl. la politique. po'**litical**, a. politique. poli'**tician**, s. homme m politique.

poll [poul], s. vote m; scrutin m; Gallup p., (sondage m) Gallup m. '**polling**, s. vote m; élections fpl; p. booth, isoloir m; p. station, centre m de vote.

pollute [pɔ'luːt], v.tr. polluer, corrompre. po'**llution**, s. pollution f.

polo ['poulou], s. 1. Sp: polo m; water p., polo nautique. 2. Cl: p. neck, col roulé.

poltergeist ['pɔltəgaist], s. esprit m frappeur.

polygamy [pɔ'ligəmi], s. polygamie f. po'**lygamist**, s. polygame mf.

polyglot ['pɔliglɔt], a. & s. polyglotte (mf).

polygon ['pɔligən], s. polygone m.

polyp ['pɔlip], s. polype m.

polytechnic [pɔli'teknik]. 1. a. polytechnique. 2. s. collège m d'enseignement technique.

pomegranate ['pɔm(i)grænit], s. grenade f.

pomp [pɔmp], s. pompe f, éclat m, splendeur f. '**pompous**, a. suffisant. -**ly**, adv. avec suffisance.

pond [pɔnd], s. étang m; mare f.

ponder ['pɔndər]. 1. v.tr. réfléchir sur (une question); ruminer. 2. v.i. méditer. '**ponderous**, a. lourd, pesant.

pontiff ['pɔntif], s. pontife m; pape m; évêque m. pon'**tifical**, a. pontifical.

pontoon [pɔn'tuːn], s. ponton m; p. bridge, pont m de bateaux.

†**pony** ['pouni], s. poney m.

poodle ['puːdl], s. caniche mf.

pool¹ [puːl], s. mare f; swimming p., piscine f.

pool². I. s. 1. (a) Com: fonds communs; masse commune; (b) typing p., équipe f de dactylos. 2. Sp: cagnotte f; football p., concours m de pronostics sportifs. II. v.tr. mettre en commun (des capitaux, etc.).

poop [puːp], s. poupe f.

poor [puər], a. pauvre. 1. (a) besogneux, malheureux; (b) s.pl. the p., les pauvres m, les indigents m. 2. de piètre qualité; p. quality, basse qualité; p. health, santé f débile. '**poorly**. 1. adv. pauvrement, médiocrement. 2. a. souffrant, indisposé.

pop¹ [pɔp]. I. ‡v.i. 1. éclater; sauter. 2. F: to p. round to the grocer's, faire un saut jusque chez l'épicier. II. s. 1. bruit m sec. 2. F: boisson f pétillante, gazeuse. III. int. to go off p., éclater. '**pop-gun**, s. pistolet m d'enfant. pop' '**off**, v.i. (a) F: filer, déguerpir; (b) F: mourir subitement.

pop², s. F: U.S: papa m.

pop³, a. F: (= popular) p. art, le pop'art; p. music, yé-yé m; p. song, chanson f en vogue.

pope [poup], s. pape m.

poplar ['pɔplər], s. peuplier m.

†**poppy** ['pɔpi], s. pavot m; field p., coquelicot m.

popular ['pɔpjulər], a. populaire; (style, etc.) en vogue, à la mode; Pol: P. Front, front m populaire, coalition f de gauche. popu'**larity**, s. popularité f. '**popularize**, v.tr. populariser; vulgariser.

populate ['pɔpjuleit], v.tr. peupler. popu'**lation**, s. population f.

porcelain ['pɔːslin], s. porcelaine f.

porch [pɔːtʃ], s. (a) porche m, portique m; (b) U.S: véranda f, Fr.C: galerie f.

porcupine ['pɔːkjupain], s. porc-épic m.

pore¹ ['pɔːr], s. pore m.

pore², v.i. to p. over a book, être plongé dans un livre.

pork [pɔːk], s. Cu: porc m; p. pie, pâté m de porc (en croûte); p. butcher, charcutier m.

porous ['pɔːrəs], a. poreux, perméable.

porpoise ['pɔːpəs], s. marsouin m.

porridge ['pɔridʒ], s. bouillie f d'avoine.

port¹ [pɔːt], s. port m.

port², s. Nau: bâbord m.

port³, s. vin m de porto; porto m.

portable ['pɔːtəbl], a. portatif; mobile.

portal ['pɔːtl], s. (a) portail m; (b) portique m.

porter¹ ['pɔːtər], s. portier m, concierge m.

porter², s. porteur m; chasseur m (d'hôtel). '**porterage**, s. (prix m de) transport m.

†**portfolio** [pɔːt'fouljou], s. (a) serviette f (pour documents); (b) chemise f (de carton); (c) Pol: portefeuille m.

porthole ['pɔːthoul], s. hublot m.

†**portico** ['pɔːtikou], s. portique m.

portion ['pɔːʃ(ə)n], s. (a) partie f; part f; (b) portion f, ration f.

portly ['pɔːtli], a. corpulent, ventru.

portrait ['pɔːtrit], s. portrait m. por'**tray**, v.tr. dépeindre, décrire.

Portuguese [pɔːtju'giːz]. 1. a. & s. portugais, -aise. 2. s. Ling: le portugais.

pose [pouz]. I. s. 1. pose f, attitude f. 2. affectation f. II. v.i. & tr. poser.

position [pə'ziʃ(ə)n], s. 1. position f; attitude f. 2. position f; place f; situation f. 3. (a) état m, condition f; to be in a p. to do sth., être à même de faire qch.; (b) rang m social. 4. emploi m, poste m.

positive ['pozitiv], *a.* 1. positif, affirmatif. 2. (*a*) convaincu, certain; (*b*) (ton) absolu, tranchant. -ly, *adv.* 1. positivement. 2. assurément.

possess [pə'zes], *v.tr.* 1. avoir, posséder. 2. what possessed you? qu'est-ce qui vous a pris? po'ssession, *s.* possession *f.*

possible ['posəbl], *a.* possible; as far as p., dans la mesure du possible; as early as p., le plus tôt possible. -ibly, *adv.* 1. I can't p. do it, il ne m'est pas possible de le faire; as often as I, he, p. can, aussi souvent que possible. 2. peut-être; c'est possible! cela se peut. possi'bility, *s.* 1. possibilité *f.* 2. éventualité *f.*

post¹ [poust], *s.* 1. poteau *m*, pieu *m*; as deaf as a p., sourd comme un pot. 2. *Sp:* starting, winning, p., poteau de départ, d'arrivée.

post², *v.tr.* afficher (un avis); coller (des affiches); *P.N:* p. no bills, défense d'afficher. 'poster, *s.* affiche *f* (murale).

post³. I. *s.* 1. poste *m* (de sentinelle, etc.). 2. poste, emploi *m*. II. *v.tr. Mil:* 1. poster (une sentinelle). 2. to be posted, être affecté (à une unité).

post⁴, *s. Mil:* the last p., (i) la retraite (au clairon); (ii) la sonnerie aux morts.

post⁵. I. *s.* 1. courrier *m*; by return of p., par retour du courrier. 2. to send sth. by p., envoyer qch. par la poste. 3. p. office, bureau *m* de poste. II. *v.tr.* (*a*) mettre (une lettre) à la poste; poster (une lettre); (*b*) to keep oneself posted, se tenir au courant. 'postage, *s.* affranchissement *m* (d'une lettre); p. paid, port payé. 'postal, *a.* postal. 'postcard, *s.* carte *f* postale. †'postman, *s.* facteur *m.* 'postmark, *s.* (timbre *m* d')oblitération *f.* 'postmaster, -mistress, *s.* receveur, -euse, des Postes.

post- [poust, post-], *prefix used in combined forms.* post-. post'date, *v.tr.* postdater (un chèque). pos'terity [pos-], *s.* postérité *f.* post'humous ['pos-], *a.* posthume. post-im'pressionism, *s.* post-impressionnisme *m.* post-'mortem, *s.* autopsie *f* (cadavérique). post'pone, *v.tr.* remettre, différer. post'ponement, *s.* remise *f* à plus tard, ajournement *m.* 'postscript, *s.* (*abbr.* P.S.) post-scriptum *m.* post-'war, *a.* d'après guerre.

posture ['postʃər], *s.* posture *f*, attitude *f.*

pot [pot], *s.* (*a*) pot *m*; (*b*) marmite *f*, pots and pans, batterie *f* de cuisine. 'pot-holing, *s. F:* spéléologie *f.*

potash ['potæʃ], *s.* potasse *f.*

potassium [pə'tæsiəm], *s.* potassium *m.*

†potato [pə'teitou], *s.* pomme *f* de terre.

potency ['pout(ə)nsi], *s.* force *f*, puissance *f.* 'potent, *a.* efficace; puissant.

potential [pə'tenʃ(ə)l]. 1. *a.* (*a*) en puissance; virtuel; latent; (*b*) potentiel. 2. *s.* potentiel *m.* -ally, *adv.* potentiellement, virtuellement. poten'tiality, *s.* potentialité *f.*

potion ['pouʃ(ə)n], *s.* potion *f*; dose *f.*

pottery ['potəri], *s.* 1. poterie *f.* 2. vaisselle *f* de terre. 'potter, *s.* potier *m.*

potty ['poti], *a. F:* 1. petit, insignifiant. 2. toqué, timbré.

pouch [pautʃ], *s.* 1. petit sac *m*; bourse *f.* 2. poche *f* ventrale (des marsupiaux).

poultice ['poultis], *s.* cataplasme *m.*

poultry ['poultri], *s. coll.* volaille *f.* p. yard, basse-cour *f.* 'poulterer, *s.* marchand *m* de volaille.

pounce [pauns], *v.i.* (*a*) fondre, s'abattre (sur la proie); (*b*) se jeter (sur qch.).

pound¹ [paund], *s.* 1. livre *f* (sterling ou poids).

pound² [paund], *v.tr.* broyer, piler.

pour ['pɔ:r], 1. *v.tr.* verser. 2. *v.i.* (*of rain*) tomber à verse. 'pour 'out. 1. *v.tr.* verser. 2. *v.i.* sortir à flots.

pout [paut]. I. *s.* moue *f.* II. *v.i.* (*a*) faire la moue; (*b*) bouder.

poverty ['povəti], *s.* pauvreté *f.*

powder ['paudər], 1. *s.* poudre *f.* II. *v.tr.* saupoudrer (with, de). 2. se poudrer (le visage). 3. réduire en poudre.

power ['pauər], *s.* 1. pouvoir *m.* 2. faculté *f*, capacité *f.* 3. vigueur *f*, force *f.* 4. puissance *f*; force; p. station, centrale *f* électrique. 5. pouvoir, influence *f*, autorité *f.* 'powerful, *a.* (*a*) puissant; (*b*) fort, vigoureux. -fully, *adv.* puissamment; fortement. 'powerless, *a.* impuissant.

practicable ['præktikəbl], *a.* praticable. practica'bility, *s.* praticabilité *f.*

practical ['præktik(ə)l], *a.* pratique. -ally, *adv.* 1. pratiquement, en pratique. 2. pour ainsi dire; p. cured, presque guéri.

practice ['præktis], *s.* 1. pratique *f.* 2. habitude *f*, coutume *f.* 3. exercice *m*; usage *m*; *Sp:* entraînement *m.* 4. pratique, clientèle *f* (de médecin); étude *f* (d'avoué). 5. *pl.* pratiques, menées *fpl.*

practise ['præktis], *v.tr.* 1. pratiquer (une vertu); mettre en pratique (un principe). 2. pratiquer, exercer (une profession). prac'titioner, *s.* (general) p., médecin *m.*

prairie ['preəri], *s. usu. pl.* the prairies, la prairie (de l'Amérique du Nord).

praise [preiz]. I. *s.* éloge *m*; louange *f.* II. *v.tr.* louer, faire l'éloge de (qch., qn).

prance [prɑ:ns], *v.i.* 1. (*of horse*) fringuer; piaffer. 2. (*of pers.*) se pavaner; se carrer.

prank [præŋk], *s.* 1. escapade *f*, frasque *f*, fredaine *f.* 2. tour *m*, farce *f.*

prawn [prɔːn], s. crevette f rose, rouge; Dublin Bay p., langoustine f.

pray [prei], v.tr. & i. prier. '**prayer**, s. prière f (à Dieu); the Lord's P., l'oraison f dominicale; the P. Book, le rituel de l'Église anglicane; p. wheel (of Buddhists), moulin m, cylindre m, à prières.

preach [priːtʃ], v.i. & tr. prêcher. '**preacher**, s. prédicateur m.

precarious [priˈkɛəriəs], a. précaire, incertain. -**ly**, adv. précairement.

precaution [priˈkɔːʃ(ə)n], s. précaution f.

precede [pri(ː)ˈsiːd], v.tr. 1. précéder. 2. avoir le pas, la préséance, sur (qn). '**precedence**, s. (droit m de) priorité f. '**precedent**, s. précédent m. **preˈceding**, a. précédent; the p. day, la veille.

precept [ˈpriːsept], s. précepte m.

precinct [ˈpriːsiŋ(k)t], s. enceinte f, enclos m; pl. pourtour m (d'une cathédrale); **shopping** p., centre m commercial (fermé à la circulation automobile).

precious [ˈpreʃəs], a. précieux.

precipice [ˈpresipis], s. précipice m.

precipitate [priˈsipiteit], v.tr. (a) Ch: précipiter; (b) accélérer, hâter, précipiter (un événement). **precipiˈtation**, s. précipitation f.

précis [ˈpreisiː], s. précis m, résumé m.

precise [priˈsais], a. 1. précis; exact. 2. méticuleux. -**ly**, adv. 1. avec précision; at six (o'clock) p., à six heures précises. 2. parfaitement. **preˈciseness**, s. 1. précision f. 2. méticulosité f. **preˈcision**, s. précision f.

precocious [priˈkouʃəs], a. précoce.

preconceive [priːkənˈsiːv], v.tr. préconcevoir; **preconceived idea**, idée f préconçue.

preconcerted [priːkənˈsɔːtid], a. arrangé d'avance.

precursor [pri(ː)ˈkəːsər], s. précurseur m.

predecease [ˈpriːdiˈsiːs], v.tr. prédécéder, mourir avant (qn). '**predecessor**, s. prédécesseur m.

predicament [priˈdikəmənt], s. situation f difficile.

predict [priˈdikt], v.tr. prédire. **preˈdiction**, s. prédiction f.

predilection [priːdiˈlekʃ(ə)n], s. prédilection f.

predisposition [ˈpriːdispəˈziʃ(ə)n], s. prédisposition f.

predominate [priˈdɔmineit], v.i. prédominer.

prefabricate [ˈpriːˈfæbrikeit], v.tr. préfabriquer. **prefabriˈcation**, s. préfabrication f.

preface [ˈprefis], s. préface f; avant-propos m.

prefect [ˈpriːfekt], s. 1. préfet m; Sch: élève choisi(e) pour aider à maintenir la discipline.

‡**prefer** [priˈfəːr], v.tr. préférer, aimer mieux. '**preferable** [ˈpref-], a. pré-férable. -**bly**, adv. préférablement, par préférence. '**preference** [ˈpref-], s. préférence f; p. clause, pacte m de préférence; Fin: p. shares, actions f privilégiées. **preˈferential** [ˈpref-], a. (traitement) préférentiel; (tarif) de faveur.

prefix [ˈpriːfiks], s. préfixe m.

pregnancy [ˈpregnənsi], s. grossesse f; (of animal) gestation f. '**pregnant**, a. enceinte; (of cow, etc.) pleine.

prehensile [priˈhensail], a. préhensile. -

prehistory [priːˈhist(ə)ri], s. préhistoire f. **prehisˈtoric**, a. préhistorique.

prejudice [ˈpredʒudis]. I. s. préjugé m. II. v.tr. 1. nuire à (une réputation). 2. prévenir, prédisposer (qn contre qn). '**prejudiced**, a. prévenu (against, contre); to be p., avoir des préjugés. **prejuˈdicial**, a. préjudiciable.

prelate [ˈprelit], s. prélat m.

‡**preliminary** [priˈliminəri]. 1. a. préliminaire, préalable. 2. s. (a) préable m; (b) pl. préliminaires m.

prelude [ˈpreljuːd], s. prélude m (to, de).

premature [ˈpremətjuər], a. prématuré. -**ly**, adv. prématurément.

premeditate [priːˈmediteit], v.tr. préméditer. **preˈmeditated**, a. prémédité; réfléchi; p. insolence, insolence calculée. **premediˈtation**, s. préméditation f.

premier [ˈpriːmiər]. 1. a. premier. 2. s. premier ministre m.

première [ˈpremiɛər], s. Th: première f.

premises [ˈpremisiz], s.pl. local; on the p., sur les lieux.

premium [ˈpriːmiəm], s. 1. 'prix m, récompense f; prime f. 2. prix convenu, indemnité f; insurance p., prime d'assurance. 3. to be at a p., faire prime; être très recherché.

premonition [priːmoˈniʃ(ə)n], s. prémonition f.

preoccupation [priːɔkjuˈpeiʃ(ə)n], s. préoccupation f. **preˈoccupied**, a. préoccupé; absorbé.

prep [prep]. 1. s. Sch: F: étude f, devoirs mpl (du soir). 2. a. p. school, école f préparatoire (pour élèves de 8 à 13 ans).

prepare [priˈpɛər]. 1. v.tr. préparer. 2. v.i. se préparer, se disposer. **preˈparation**, s. 1. préparation f. 2. pl. préparatifs mpl. 3. Sch: étude f, devoirs mpl (du soir). **preˈparatory**, a. préparatoire, préalable; p. school, école f préparatoire (pour élèves de 8 à 13 ans).

prepay [ˈpriːˈpei], v.tr. payer d'avance; affranchir.

preponderant [priˈpɔndərənt], a. prépondérant.

preposition [prepəˈziʃ(ə)n], s. préposition f.

preposterous [priˈpɔst(ə)rəs], a. absurde.

prerogative [priˈrɔgətiv], s. prérogative f.

prescribe [pri'skraib], v.tr. prescrire, ordonner. **pre'scription**, s. Med: ordonnance f.

presence ['prez(ə)ns], s. 1. présence f. 2. air m, mine f. **present¹.** I. a. 1. présent; nobody else was p., personne d'autre n'était là. 2. (a) (also present-day) actuel; d'aujourd'hui; at p., actuellement; (b) en question; que voici. II. s. le présent; at p., à présent, maintenant. **'presently,** adv. (a) bientôt; plus tard; (b) U.S: maintenant, actuellement.

present². I. s. ['prezənt], s. cadeau m, don m; it's for a p., c'est pour offrir. II. [pri'zent], v.tr. présenter. **pre'sentable** [pri-], a. présentable. **pre-sen'tation** [pre-], s. présentation f.

presentiment [pri'zentimənt], s. pressentiment m.

preserve [pri'zə:v]. I. v.tr. 1. préserver, garantir. 2. conserver. 3. she's well preserved, elle ne marque pas son âge. II. s. 1. réserve f; (game) p., chasse gardée. 2. pl. (a) conserves fpl; (b) conserves fpl. **preser'vation**, s. conservation f. **pre'servative**, s. préservatif m; agent m de conservation.

preside [pri'zaid], v.i. présider. **'president,** s. président m (d'une république, U.S: d'une société anonyme).

press [pres]. I. s. (a) presse f (d'imprimerie, hydraulique, etc.); (b) imprimerie f; to pass a proof for p., donner le bon à tirer; (c) la presse, les journaux m; p. agency, agence f de presse, d'informations; to write for the p., faire du journalisme. II. v. 1. v.tr. (a) presser; appuyer sur (qch.); to p. a suit, donner un coup de fer à un complet; (b) to p. a point, insister sur un point; F: he didn't need much pressing, il ne se fit pas trop prier; (c) abs. time presses, le temps presse. 2. v.i. (a) to p. on sth., appuyer sur qch.; (b) to p. on, forcer le pas; F: p. on regardless! avançons et tant pis pour les autres! **'pressed,** a. p. for time, à court de temps; to be hard p., être aux abois, à la dernière extrémité. **'pressing.** I. a. (travail) urgent; (invitation) instante. II. s. calandrage m (du papier); E: emboutissage m; repassage m (d'un vêtement). **'pressure,** s. 1. (a) pression f; (b) blood p., tension f artérielle. 2. to bring p. to bear, exercer une pression; p. of business, presse f des affaires. **'pressurize,** v.tr. pressuriser.

prestige [pres'ti:3], s. prestige m.

presume [pri'zju:m]. 1. v.tr. (a) présumer; supposer; (b) prendre la liberté, présumer. 2. v.i. (a) abs. se montrer présomptueux; (b) to p. on, abuser de l'amitié de qn, etc.). **pre'sumably,** adv. probablement. **pre'sumption,** s. présomption f. **pre'sumptuous,** a. présomptueux.

pretend [pri'tend]. 1. v.tr. (a) feindre, simuler; (b) prétendre; I can't p. to advise you, je n'ai pas la prétention de vous conseiller. 2. v.i. faire semblant; jouer la comédie. **pre'tence,** s. 1. (faux) semblant m; simulation f; false pretences, moyens m frauduleux. 2. prétention f. **pre'tender,** s. Hist: The Young P., le Jeune Prétendant. **pre'tension,** s. prétention f. **pre'tentious,** a. prétentieux.

pretext ['pri:tekst], s. prétexte m.

pretty ['priti]. 1. a. joli; beau; gentil. 2. adv. assez, passablement. **'prettiness,** s. gentillesse f.

prevail [pri'veil], v.i. 1. prévaloir; l'emporter. 2. to p. on, amener, décider (qn à faire qch.). 3. prédominer, régner; the conditions prevailing in France, les conditions qui règnent en France. **pre'vailing,** a. (vent) dominant; p. opinion, opinion courante. **'prevalence,** s. prédominance f; fréquence f. **'prevalent,** a. répandu, général.

prevaricate [pri'værikeit], v.i. 1. équivoquer, tergiverser. 2. mentir. **prevari'cation,** s. 1. équivoques fpl. 2. mensonge m.

prevent [pri'vent], v.tr. empêcher, mettre obstacle à (qch.). 2. (a) prévenir, détourner (un malheur); (b) éviter (que qch. se passe). **pre'vention,** s. empêchement m; précautions fpl (contre les accidents); prévention f (de la maladie). **pre'ventive,** a. (médicament, etc.) préventif.

previous ['pri:viəs]. 1. a. préalable; antérieur; précédent. 2. adv. p. to, avant. **-ly,** adv. préalablement; auparavant.

prevision [pri'vi:ʒ(ə)n], s. prévision f.

pre-war ['pri:'wɔ:r], attrib. a. d'avant-guerre.

prey [prei]. I. s. proie f. II. v.i. to p. upon sth., faire sa proie de qch.; sth. is preying upon his mind, il y a qch. qui le travaille.

price [prais]. I. s. 1. prix m. II. 1. mettre un prix à (qch.). 2. s'informer du prix de (qch.). **'priceless,** a. (a) hors de prix, inestimable; (b) F: (of joke, etc.) impayable.

prick [prik]. I. s. piqûre f. II. v.tr. 1. piquer. 2. to p. (up) one's ears, (i) (of animal) dresser les oreilles; (ii) (of pers.) dresser l'oreille. **'prickle,** s. piquant m; épine f; (of plant) aiguillon m. **'prickly,** a. hérissé; épineux.

pride [praid]. I. s. orgueil m; (a) fierté f, morgue f; false p., vanité f; (b) amour-propre m. II. v.pr. to p. oneself on (doing) sth., s'enorgueillir de, se vanter, de (faire) qch.

priest [pri:st], s. prêtre m; parish p. = curé m. **'priesthood,** s. prêtrise f; to enter the p., se faire prêtre.

prig [prig], *s.* poseur *m.* **'priggish**, *a.* poseur, suffisant.

prim [prim], *a.* collet monté *inv*; guindé.

primary ['praiməri], *a.* premier, primitif; **p.** education, enseignement *m* primaire; *Geog*: **p.** era, ère *f* primaire; **p.** cause, cause première.

prime[1] [praim]. I. *a.* 1. premier; principal; of **p.** importance, de toute première importance. 2. **p.** (quality) meat, viande (de) choix.

prime[2], *v.tr.* 1. amorcer (une pompe, etc.). 2. mettre (qn) au courant.

primitive ['primitiv], *a.* primitif.

primrose ['primrouz], *s.* primevère *f.*

prince [prins], *s.* prince *m.* **prin'cess**, *s.* princesse *f.* **princi'pality**, *s.* principauté *f.*

principal ['prinsip(ə)l]. I. *a.* principal. **-ally**, *adv.* principalement. II. *s.* 1. (*pers.*) directeur, -trice (d'école); chef *m*, patron, -onne. 2. *Fin*: capital *m.*

principle ['prinsipl], *s.* principe *m*; on **p.**, par principe.

print [print]. I. *s.* 1. empreinte *f*, impression *f.* 2. (*a*) matière *f* imprimée; (*of book*) out of **p.**, épuisé; (*b*) large **p.**, gros caractères. 3. gravure *f*, image *f.* 4. (*a*) *Phot*: épreuve *f*; copie *f*; (*b*) blue **p.**, dessin négatif, *F*: bleu *m.* 5. indienne *f*, cotonnade *f.* II. *v.tr.* 1. imprimer; **printed matter**, imprimés *mpl.* 2. *Phot*: tirer une épreuve (d'un cliché). **'printer**, *s.* imprimeur *m*; **p.'s error**, faute *f* d'impression. **'printing**, *s.* impression *f*; tirage *m* (d'un livre). **p. press**, presse *f* d'imprimerie.

prior[1] ['praiər]. 1. *a.* préalable, précédent; antérieur. 2. *adv.* antérieurement. **pri'ority**, *s.* priorité *f.*

prior[2], *s.* prieur *m.* **'prioress**, *s.* prieure *f.* **'priory**, *s.* prieuré *m.*

prism ['priz(ə)m], *s.* prisme *m.* **pris'matic**, *a.* prismatique.

prison ['priz(ə)n], *s.* prison *f.* **'prisoner**, *s.* prisonnier, -ière.

private ['praivit]. I. *a.* privé, particulier. 1. **p.** persons, (simples) particuliers. 2. secret. 3. in my **p.** opinion, à mon avis personnel. 4. *P.N*: **p.**, entrée interdite au public; **p.** income, rentes *fpl.* II. *s.* 1. in **p.**, (i) en famille, dans l'intimité; (ii) sans témoins. 2. *Mil*: simple soldat *m.* **'privacy**, *s.* intimité *f*; there's no **p.** here, on n'est jamais seul ici. **'privately**, *adv.* en (simple) particulier; à titre confidentiel; **sold p.**, vendu à l'amiable.

privation [prai'veiʃ(ə)n], *s.* privation *f.*

privet ['privit], *s.* troène *m.*

privilege ['privilidʒ], *s.* privilège *m.* **'privileged**, *a.* privilégié.

prize [praiz]. I. *s.* 1. prix *m.* 2. (*in lottery*) lot *m.* 3. **p.** fighter, boxeur professionnel. II. *v.tr.* estimer, priser.

pro[1] [prou], *Latin prep*. 1. **pro forma**, pour la forme. 2. **pro tem**(pore), temporairement. 3. *s.* **the pros and cons**, le pour et le contre.

pro[2], *s. Sp: F*: professionnel, -elle.

probable ['probəbl], *a.* probable. **-bly**, *adv.* probablement. **proba'bility**, *s.* probabilité *f.*

probate ['proubeit], *s. Jur*: validation *f*, homologation *f* (d'un testament). **pro'bation**, *s.* 1. épreuve *f*, stage *m*; *Ecc*: probation *f* (d'un novice). 2. *Jur*: mise *f* en liberté sous surveillance; **p. officer**, délégué(e) à la liberté surveillée. **pro'bationer**, *s.* stagiaire *mf.*

probe [proub]. I. *v.tr.* 1. sonder, explorer. 2. approfondir, fouiller (un mystère). II. *s. Med*: sonde *f.* 3. *v.i.* to **p. into**, sonder (le passé, etc.).

problem ['problom], *s.* problème *m*; **the housing p.**, la crise du logement; **p. child**, enfant *mf* difficile. **proble'matic**(al), *a.* problématique.

procedure [prə'si:dʒər], *s.* procédé *m.* 2. procédure *f.*

proceed [prə'si:d], *v.i.* 1. (*a*) continuer; before we **p.** any farther, avant d'aller plus loin; (*b*) how shall we **p.**? quelle est la marche à suivre? (*c*) se mettre à (faire qch.). 2. (se) continuer, se poursuivre; **things are proceeding as usual**, les choses suivent leur cours. **pro'ceedings**, *s.pl.* (*a*) débats *m* (d'une assemblée); (*b*) *Jur*: to take **p.** against s.o., intenter un procès à qn. **'proceeds**, *s.pl.* produit *m*, montant *m* (d'une vente).

process ['prouses]. I. *s.* 1. (*a*) processus *m*; it's a slow **p.**, c'est un travail long; (*b*) cours *m*, avancement *m*; in **p.** of moving, en train de déménager. 2. méthode *f*; procédé *m.* II. *v.tr. Ind*: traiter, transformer (qch.). **'processing**, *s.* traitement *m* (d'une matière première); **food p.**, l'industrie *f* alimentaire; (*automation*) **data p.**, traitement *m* des informations. **pro'cession**, *s.* cortège *m*; défilé *m.*

proclaim [prə'kleim], *v.tr.* proclamer; déclarer (publiquement). **procla'mation**, *s.* proclamation *f.*

proclivity [prə'kliviti], *s.* penchant *m*, tendance *f*, inclination *f.*

procrastinate [prou'kræstineit], *v.i.* remettre les affaires à plus tard; temporiser. **procrasti'nation**, *s.* temporisation *f.*

procure [prə'kjuər], *v.tr.* obtenir, procurer. **pro'curable**, *a.* procurable. **pro'curer**, **-ess**, *s.* entremetteur, -euse, proxénète *m.*

‡prod [prod]. I. *v.tr.* 1. pousser (qch.). 2. aiguillonner, stimuler (qn). II. *s.* coup *m*; *F*: **give him a p.**, aiguillonnez-le un peu.

prodigal ['prɔdig(ə)l], a. & s. prodigue (f). **prodi'gality**, s. prodigalité f.
prodigy ['prɔdidʒi], s. 1. prodige m; merveille f. **pro'digious**, a. prodigieux. **pro'digiously**, adv. prodigieusement.
produce. I. v.tr. [prə'djus]. 1. (a) présenter (des documents, etc.); (b) to p. a play, mettre une pièce en scène. 2. Ind: fabriquer; éditer (un livre); produire; causer (un effet). 3. rapporter, rendre (un profit). II. s. ['prɔdjus] produit m (de son travail); coll: denrées fpl, produits; farm p., produits agricoles. **pro'ducer**, s. producteur, -trice f.; Th: metteur en scène; Cin: directeur de productions; Rad: T.V: metteur en ondes. **'product**, s. produit m. **pro'duction**, s. production f; fabrication f (de marchandises); Th: mise f en scène; Rad: T.V: mise en ondes. **pro'ductive**, a. productif; (of land) fécond. **produc'tivity**, s. productivité f; rendement m.
profane [prə'fein], a. profane; impie. **pro'fanity**, s. impiété f.
profess [prə'fes], v.tr. professer; to p. oneself satisfied, se déclarer satisfait; I do not p. to be a scholar, je ne prétends pas être savant. **pro'fessed**, a. (ennemi) déclaré; prétendu; soi-disant (savant, etc.). **pro'fessedly** [prə'fesidli], adv. de son propre aveu; ouvertement. **pro'fession**, s. profession f. **pro'fessional**, I. a. professionnel; de métier. II. s. (a) expert m; (b) Sp: professionnel, -elle. **-ally**, adv. professionnellement; dans l'exercice de sa profession, de son métier. **pro'fessionalism**, s. Sp: professionnalisme m. **pro'fessor**, s. professeur m (de faculté).
proficiency [prə'fiʃənsi], s. capacité f, compétence f. **pro'ficient**, a. capable, compétent.
profile ['proufail]. s. profil m.
profit ['prɔfit]. I. s. profit m, bénéfice m; avantage m. II. v.tr. & i. profiter (à qn, de qch.). **'profitable**, a. profitable, avantageux. **-ably**, adv. profitablement, avantageusement. **profi'teer**. I. s. profiteur m, mercanti m. II. v.i. faire des bénéfices excessifs. **profi'teering**, s. mercantilisme m.
profound [prə'faund], a. profond. **-ly**, adv. profondément.
profuse [prə'fjus], a. 1. to be p. in one's apologies, se confondre en excuses. 2. profus, abondant, excessif. **-ly**, adv. profusément. **pro'fusion**, s. profusion f.
progeny ['prɔdʒini], s. 1. progéniture f. 2. descendants mpl.
program(me) ['prougræm]. I. s. programme m. II. v.tr. programmer; programmed teaching, enseignement m programmé. **'programmer**, s.

(computers, etc.) (a) (pers.) programmeur, -euse; (b) (machine) programmateur m. **'programming**, s. programmation f.
progress. I. s. ['prougres] (a) marche en avant; avancement m (d'un travail); cours m (des événements); (b) progrès m. II. v.i. [prə'gres] (a) s'avancer; (b) faire des progrès. **pro'gression**, s. progression f. **pro'gressive**, a. progressif. **-ly**, adv. progressivement; au fur et à mesure.
prohibit [prə'hibit], v.tr. 1. prohiber, défendre, interdire (qch.). 2. empêcher (qn de faire qch.). **prohi'bition**, s. prohibition f, défense f. **pro'hibitive**, a. (prix) prohibitif, inabordable.
project. I. s. [prə'dʒekt]. I. v.tr. projeter. 2. v.i. faire saillie. II. s. ['prɔdʒekt] projet m. **pro'jectile**, s. projectile m. **pro'jecting**, a. saillant; en saillie. **pro'jection**, s. projection f 2. saillie f. **pro'jector**, s. projecteur m.
proletariat [prouli'tɛəriət], s. prolétariat m.
prolific [prə'lifik], a. prolifique; fécond.
prologue ['proulɔg], s. prologue m.
prolong [prə'lɔn], v.tr. prolonger. **prolon'gation**, s. prolongation f.
promenade [prɔmə'nɑːd], s. 1. promenade f. 2. (a) esplanade f; (b) promenoir m.
prominence ['prɔminəns], s. 1. (a) proéminence f; relief m; (b) saillie f. 2. éminence f. **'prominent**, a. 1. saillant. 2. remarquable; éminent.
promiscuous [prə'miskjuəs], a. 1. confus, mêlé. 2. casuel. **-ly**, adv. 1. confusément. 2. casuellement. **promis'cuity**, s. promiscuité f.
promise ['prɔmis]. I. s. promesse f; to show great p., donner de belles espérances. II. v.tr. promettre (qch. à qn). **'promising**, a. plein de promesses; qui s'annonce bien.
†**promontory** ['prɔmənt(ə)ri], s. promontoire m.
promote [prə'mout], v.tr. 1. donner de l'avancement à (qn); to be promoted, être promu. 2. (a) encourager (l'amitié); avancer (les intérêts de qn); (b) lancer (une entreprise). **pro'moter**, s. fondateur m (d'une société anonyme). **pro'motion**, s. promotion f, avancement m.
prompt [prɔm(p)t]. I. a. prompt; (a) vif, rapide; (b) immédiat. **-ly**, adv. promptement; ponctuellement. II. v.tr. 1. inciter (qn à faire qch.). 2. souffler (un acteur, un élève). **'prompter**, s. Th: souffleur, -euse. **'promptness**, s. promptitude f, empressement m.
prone [proun], a. 1. couché sur le ventre. 2. enclin (à faire qch.); accident p., prédisposé aux accidents.

prong [prɔŋ], s. fourchon m (de fourche), dent f (de fourchette).

pronoun ['prəunaun], s. pronom m.

pronounce [prə'nauns], v.tr. 1. (a) déclarer; (b) prononcer (un jugement). 2. prononcer, articuler (un mot). pro'nounced, a. prononcé, marqué; p. taste of garlic, goût d'ail très fort. pro'nouncement, s. déclaration f. pro'nunciation [-'nʌn-], s. prononciation f.

proof [pru:f]. I. s. 1. preuve f; to give p. of, témoigner. 2. (a) épreuve f; to put sth. to the p., mettre qch. à l'épreuve; (b) teneur f en alcool (d'un spiritueux). 3. (printer's) p., épreuve; p. reading, correction f sur épreuves. II. a. p. against sth., résistant à qch., à l'épreuve de qch.; insensible à qch.

prop [prɔp]. I. s. appui m, support m. II. v.tr. to p. up sth. up, appuyer, soutenir, qch.; étayer (un mur).

propaganda [prɔpə'gændə], s. propagande f.

propagate ['prɔpəgeit]. 1. v.tr. propager. 2. v.pr. & i. se propager, se reproduire. propa'gation, s. propagation f, réproduction f.

‡propel [prə'pel], v.tr. propulser; pousser en avant. pro'pellant, s. combustible m; (rockets) propergol m. pro'peller, s. 1. propulseur m; Aut: p. shaft, arbre m de transmission. 2. hélice f.

propensity [prə'pensiti], s. propension f, penchant m, inclination f, tendance f.

proper ['prɔpər], a. 1. propre. 2. vrai, juste, approprié. 3. (a) convenable; at the p. time, en temps opportun; (b) comme il faut; bienséant, correct. -ly, adv. 1. (a) correctement; (b) bien. 2. convenablement; comme il faut.

‡property ['prɔpəti], s. 1. (a) propriété f biens mpl, avoir m; that's my p., cela m'appartient; (b) immeuble(s) m(pl). 2. Th: accessoire m. 3. propriété; qualité f.

prophecy ['prɔfisi], s. prophétie f.

prophesy ['prɔfisai]. 1. v.i. prophétiser. 2. v.tr. prophétiser, prédire.

prophet ['prɔfit], s. prophète m. pro'phetic, a. prophétique.

propitiate [prə'piʃieit], v.tr. apaiser (qn); se faire pardonner par (qn). propiti'ation, s. 1. propitiation f. 2. apaisement m. pro'pitious, a. propice, favorable.

proportion [prə'pɔ:ʃ(ə)n], s. 1. partie f; portion f; part f. 2. rapport m, proportion f; out of p., mal proportionné. 3. pl. proportions; dimensions f. pro'portional, a. proportionnel. pro'portionate, a. proportionné (to, à).

propose [prə'pəuz], v.tr. 1. (a) proposer; (b) to p. a toast, porter un toast; (c) se proposer; what do you p. to do? que comptez-vous faire? 2. abs. faire la demande en mariage. pro'posal, s.

1. (a) proposition f, offre f; (b) demande f en mariage. 2. dessein m, projet m. pro'pose, s. proposeur, -euse. propo'sition, s. proposition f, offre f; paying p., affaire qui rapporte; it's a tough p., c'est une question difficile à résoudre; F: he's a tough p., il n'est guère commode.

proprietor [prə'praiətər], s. propriétaire. mf; garage p., garagiste m. pro-'prietary, a. Com: p. article, spécialité f; produit m breveté.

†propriety [prə'praiəti], s. 1. propriété f, justesse f, rectitude f. 2. bienséance f, convenance f.

propulsion [prə'pʌlʃ(ə)n], s. propulsion f.

prose [prəuz], s. prose f; Sch: French p., thème français. pro'saic, a. prosaïque.

prosecute ['prɔsikju:t], v.tr. poursuivre (qn en justice). prose'cution, s. Jur: poursuites fpl judiciaires; the p., les plaignants mpl; witness for the p., témoin m à charge. 'prosecutor, s. 1. plaignant, -ante. 2. the Public P. = le procureur de la République.

prospect ['prɔspekt], s. 1. vue f; perspective f. 2. perspective; expectative f; to have sth. in p., avoir qch. en vue. 3. pl. espérances fpl. pros'pective, a. en perspective; prospectif; a p. buyer, un acheteur éventuel. pros'pector, s. chercheur m (d'or, etc.).

prospectus [prə'spektəs], s. prospectus m.

prosper ['prɔspər], v.i. prospérer, réussir. pros'perity, s. prospérité f. 'prosperous, a. prospère, florissant.

prostate ['prɔsteit], s. Anat: prostate f.

prostitute ['prɔstitju:t], s. prostituée f.

prostration [prɔs'treiʃ(ə)n], s. abattement m; nervous p., dépression f nerveuse. 'prostrate, a. 1. couché; étendu. 2. abattu, accablé. pros'trated, a. accablé.

protagonist [prou'tægənist], s. protagoniste m.

protect [prə'tekt], v.tr. protéger (qn, qch.); sauvegarder (les intérêts de qn). pro'tection, s. protection f; abri m. pro'tector, s. protecteur m. pro'tectorate, s. protectorat m.

protégé [prɔ'teʒei], s. protégé, -ée.

protein ['prouti:n], s. protéine f.

protest. I. s. ['proutest]. 1. protestation f; under p., (i) sous réserve, (ii) en protestant. II. v.tr. & i. [prə'test], protester. 'protestant. & s. Ecc: protestant, -ante. protes'tation, s. protestation f.

protract [prə'trækt], v.tr. prolonger, allonger.

protrude [prə'tru:d], v.i. s'avancer, faire saillie. pro'trusion, s. saillie f; protubérance f.

protuberance [prə'tju:bərəns], s. protubérance f. pro'tuberant, a. pro-tubérant.

proud [praud], *a.* fier, orgueilleux. -**ly,** *adv.* fièrement, orgueilleusement.

prove [pruːv]. 1. *v.tr.* (*a*) éprouver, mettre à l'épreuve; (*b*) prouver, démontrer, établir (la vérité, etc.); it remains to be proved, cela n'est pas encore prouvé; (*c*) *Jur:* établir la validité d'un testament). 2. *v.i.* se montrer, se trouver, être; to p. useful, se trouver utile.

proverb ['prɔvəːb], *s.* proverbe *m.* **pro'verbial,** *a.* proverbial.

provide [prə'vaid]. 1. *v.i.* to p. against sth., se pourvoir contre qch. 2. (*a*) *v.tr.* fournir; (*b*) *v.i.* pourvoir à l'entretien (for, de); (*c*) *v.i.* subvenir (for, à). **pro'vided.** 1. *v.a.* pourvu, muni (with, de). 2. *conj.* p. (that), pourvu que; à condition que.

providence ['prɔvid(ə)ns], *s.* 1. prévoyance *f*, prudence *f.* 2. providence *f.* **provi'dential,** *a.* providentiel.

province ['prɔvins], *s.* 1. province *f*; in the provinces, en province. 2. that's not (within) my p., cela sort de mon domaine, de ma compétence. **pro'vincial,** *a. & s.* provincial, -ale.

provision [prə'viʒ(ə)n], *s.* 1. to make p. for sth., pourvoir à qch. 2. (*a*) provision *f*; (*b*) *pl.* provisions; vivres *m.* 3. article *m.* stipulation *f.* **pro'visional,** *a.* provisoire. -**ally,** *adv.* provisoirement.

†**proviso** [prə'vaizou], *s.* clause conditionnelle; condition *f*; stipulation *f.*

provoke [prə'vouk], *v.tr.* 1. (*a*) provoquer, inciter; (*b*) irriter, agacer. 2. exciter (la curiosité, etc.). **provo'cation,** *s.* provocation *f.* **pro'vocative** [-'vɔk-], *a.* provocant; agaçant. **pro'voking,** *a.* irritant, exaspérant.

prow [prau], *s.* proue *f.*

prowl [praul], *v.i.* to p. (about), rôder. **'prowler,** *s.* rôdeur, -euse.

proximity [prɔk'simiti], *s.* proximité *f.*

†**proxy** ['prɔksi], *s.* 1. to vote by p., voter par procuration. 2. mandataire *mf.*

prude [pruːd], *s.* prude *f.* '**prudery,** *s.* pruderie *f.* '**prudish,** *a.* prude.

prudence ['pruːd(ə)ns], *s.* prudence *f*, sagesse *f.* '**prudent,** *a.* prudent, sage. -**ly,** *adv.* prudemment, sagement.

prune[1] [pruːn], *s.* pruneau *m.*

prune[2], *v.tr.* tailler (un rosier, etc.). '**pruning,** *s.* taille *f*; p. **knife,** serpette *f.*

pry [prai], *v.i.* fureter, fouiller. '**prying,** *a.* curieux, indiscret.

psalm [saːm], *s.* psaume *m.*

pseudonym ['sjuːdənim], *s.* pseudonyme *m.*

psychiatry [sə'kaiətri], *s.* psychiatrie *f.* **psy'chiatrist,** *s.* psychiatre *mf.*

psychic ['saikik], *a.* psychique.

psychology [sai'kɔlɔʒi], *s.* psychologie *f.* **psycho'logical,** *a.* psychologique. **psy'chologist,** *s.* psychologue *m.*

psychopath ['saikoupæθ], *s.* psychopathe *mf.*

pub [pʌb], *s. F:* = bistrot *m*; to do a p. crawl, *v.i.* to p. crawl, faire la tournée des bistrots.

puberty ['pjuːbəti], *s.* puberté *f.*

pubis ['pjuːbis], *s. Anat:* pubis *m.*

public ['pʌblik]. I. *a.* public (*f.* publique); **p. holiday,** fête *f* légale; **p. utility service,** service *m* public; **p. library,** bibliothèque *f* municipale; **p. house** = débit *m* de boissons, café *m.* -**ly,** *adv.* publiquement; en public. II. *s.* public *m*; in p., en public. **'publican,** *s.* = débitant *m* de boissons, patron, -onne, de café. **publi'cation,** *s.* publication *f.* **'publicity,** *s.* publicité *f.* '**publicize,** *v.tr.* faire connaître au public. **'publish,** *v.tr.* publier. **'publisher,** *s.* éditeur *m.* **'publishing,** *s.* 1. publication *f.* 2. l'édition *f.*

pucker ['pʌkər]. I. *s.* ride *f*, pli *m.* II. *v.tr.* rider, plisser.

pudding ['pudiŋ], *s.* pudding *m*, pouding *m*; rice p. = gâteau *m* de riz; black p., boudin *m.*

puddle ['pʌdl], *s.* flaque *f* d'eau.

puerile ['pjuərail], *a.* puéril.

puff [pʌf]. I. 1. *s.* souffle *m*; bouffée *f.* 2. **powder p.,** houppe *f*, houppette *f.* 3. *Cu:* (*a*) **pastry,** pâte *f* feuilletée; (*b*) **gâteau** *m* feuilleté (fourré de confiture, etc.). II. *v.i.* souffler; haleter. '**puffed,** *a. F:* essoufflé. '**puffy,** *a.* bouffi, boursouflé.

pug [pʌg], *s.* carlin *m*; roquet *m.*

pugnacious [pʌg'neiʃəs], *a.* querelleur, batailleur.

pull [pul]. I. *s.* 1. (*a*) traction *f*; to give a p., tirer; (*b*) effort *m* de traction. 2. avantage *m.* II. *v.tr.* 1. tirer. 2. to p. a face, faire une grimace. 3. *F:* to p. a fast one, avoir qn. *Adv. phr.* **pull down,** *v.tr.* baisser (un store); démolir (une maison); (*of illness*) abattre, affaiblir (qn). **pull in.** 1. *v.tr. F:* (*of police*) arrêter (un suspect), rafler (un gang). 2. *v.i.* (*of train*) entrer en gare; *Aut:* to p. in to the kerb, se ranger près du trottoir. **'pull-in,** *s.* 1. parking *m* (près d'un café, etc.). 2. café *m*, restaurant *m* (pour routiers). **pull off,** *v.tr.* (*a*) enlever, ôter (un vêtement); (*b*) *Sp: F:* décrocher (un prix); (*c*) *F:* réussir à faire (qch.); venir à bout (qch.). **'pullover,** *s. Cl:* pullover *m*, *F:* pull *m.* **pull out,** (*a*) *v.tr.* arracher; (*b*) *v.i. Aut:* déboîter. **pull through,** *v.i.* guérir (d'une maladie); se remettre. **pull up.** 1. *v.tr.* remonter; relever (qch.); to p. up one's socks, (i) remonter ses chaussettes; (ii) *F:* se dégourdir, s'activer; *Aut:* to be pulled up (by the police), se faire siffler (par l'agent). 2. *v.i.* s'arrêter. **'pull-up,** *s.* 1. café *m*, restaurant *m* (pour routiers). 2. (*mountaineering*) tirée *f.*

pullet ['pulit], s. poulette f.

pulley ['puli], s. poulie f.

Pullman ['pulmən], Pr.n. Rail: P. car, voiture f Pullman.

pulp [pʌlp]. I. s. 1. pulpe f. II. v.tr. réduire en pulpe; mettre (des livres) au pilon.

pulpit ['pulpit], s. chaire f (de prédicateur).

pulse [pʌls], s. 1. pouls m. 2. El: pulse m; p. radar, radar m à impulsions. **pul'sate**, v.i. (a) (of heart) battre; (b) palpiter. **pul'sation**, s. pulsation f; battement f.

pulverize ['pʌlvəraiz], v.tr. pulvériser; broyer. **'pulverizer**, s. pulvérisateur m, atomiseur m. **pulveri'zation**, s. pulvérisation f.

pumice ['pʌmis], s. ponce f.

pump [pʌmp]. I. s. pompe f. II. v.tr. & i. pomper.

pumpkin ['pʌm(p)kin], s. potiron m; citrouille f.

pun [pʌn], s. calembour m; jeu m de mots.

punch¹ [pʌntʃ]. I. s. 1. (a) poinçon m; pointeau m (de mécanicien); chasse-clou m; (for piercing) perçoir m; découpoir m; (b) Rail: etc: poinçon (p. de contrôleur); pince f de contrôle; (p. card, carte f perforée. 2. (a) coup m de poing; (b) F: force f, énergie f. II. v.tr. 1. percer; découper; poinçonner. 2. donner un coup de poing (à qn).

punch², s. 1. Cu: punch m. 2. p. bowl, cuvette f (entre collines).

Punch³, Pr.n. = polichinelle m; guignol m.

punctilious [pʌŋk'tiliəs], a. pointilleux.

punctual ['pʌŋktju(ə)l], a. ponctuel, exact. **-ally**, adv. ponctuellement. **punctu-'ality**, s. ponctualité f, exactitude f.

punctuate ['pʌŋktjueit], v.tr. ponctuer. **punctu'ation**, s. ponctuation f.

puncture ['pʌŋktʃər]. I. s. 1. crevaison f. 2. (hole) piqûre f, perforation f. II. v.tr. perforer (un pneu); (with passive force) (of tyre) crever.

pungent ['pʌndʒənt], a. 1. mordant, caustique. 2. âcre, irritant. **'pungency**, s. 1. goût m piquant; odeur f forte. 2. âcreté f.

punish ['pʌniʃ], v.tr. punir; corriger (un enfant); Aut: to p. the engine, fatiguer le moteur. **'punishment**, s. punition f; châtiment m; capital p., peine f capitale.

punt [pʌnt], s. bateau m plat (conduit à la perche); p. pole, gaffe f, perche f.

puny ['pjuːni], a. 1. (a) petit, menu; (b) mesquin. 2. chétif, faible.

pup [pʌp], s. petit chien m, jeune chien m; F: to sell s.o. a p., tromper, rouler, qn. †**puppy**, s. jeune chien m; p. fat, adiposité f d'enfance, d'adolescence.

pupil¹ ['pjuːp(i)l], s. élève mf; écolier, -ière.

pupil², s. pupille f (de l'œil).

puppet ['pʌpit], s. marionnette f; pantin m.

purchase ['pəːtʃəs]. I. s. 1. achat m, acquisition f. 2. prise f. II. v.tr. acheter, acquérir. **'purchaser**, s. acheteur, -euse.

pure ['pjuər], a. pur; p. silk, soie naturelle. **-ly**, adv. purement.

purgatory ['pəːgət(ə)ri], s. le purgatoire.

purge [pəːdʒ], v.tr. 1. purger. 2. purifier. **'purgative** [-gə-], a. & s. purgatif (m).

purify ['pjuərifai], v.tr. purifier. **purifi-'cation**, s. purification f. **'purity**, s. pureté f. **'purist**, s. puriste mf.

puritan ['pjuəritən], s. puritain, -aine. **puri'tanical**, a. de puritain.

purl [pəːl]. (knitting) I. s. maille f à l'envers. II. v.tr. faire des mailles à l'envers.

purple ['pəːpl], a. & s. violet (m); pourpre (m).

purpose ['pəːpəs], s. 1. (a) dessein m, objet m; but m, intention f; on p., exprès, à dessein; (b) résolution f. 2. destination f, fin f; to answer the p., répondre au but; for this p., à cet effet. 3. to the p., à propos. 4. to some p., utilement. **'purposely**, adv. 1. à dessein, de propos délibéré. 2. exprès.

purr [pəːr]. I. v.i. ronronner. II. s. ronron m.

purse [pəːs], s. I. bourse f, porte-monnaie m. II. v.tr. to p. (up) one's lips, pincer les lèvres.

purser ['pəːsər], s. Nau: commissaire m.

pursue [pə'sjuː], v.tr. 1. (a) poursuivre (qn); (b) rechercher (le plaisir). 2. suivre (une ligne de conduite). **pur'suer**, s. poursuivant, -ante. **pur-'suit**, s. poursuite f; in p. of sth., à la recherche de qch.

purveyor [pə'veiər], s. fournisseur, -euse.

push [puʃ]. I. s. I. poussée f, impulsion f; F: to give s.o. the p., donner son congé à qn. 2. effort m; F: to have plenty of p., avoir du dynamisme, Pej: être un arriviste. 3. F: at a p., dans une extrémité; au besoin. II. v. 1. v.tr. (a) pousser; don't p. (me)! ne (me) bousculez pas! to p. (s.o., sth.) aside, écarter (qn, qch.); to p. (s.o., sth.) back, repousser (qn, qch.); faire reculer (qn); to p. in (a door), enfoncer (une porte); (b) pousser la vente de (ses marchandises); (c) I'm pushed for time, le temps me manque. 2. v.i. (a) avancer (avec difficulté); (b) pousser, exercer une pression. **'pusher**, s. F: arriviste mf. **'pushing**, a. (a) débrouillard, entreprenant; (b) indiscret.

‡put [put]. 1. v.tr. mettre; (a) to p. s.o. in his place, remettre qn à sa place; to p. the matter right, arranger l'affaire; (b) poser (une question); to p. it bluntly, pour parler franc; (c) to p. s.o. to bed, mettre qn au lit; coucher qn; (d) to p. s.o. to sleep, endormir qn. 2. v.i. to p. to sea, prendre le large; to p. into port, faire relâche. put a'way, v.tr. 1. (a) serrer; ranger; (b) mettre de côté. put 'back, v.tr. (a) remettre à sa place; (b) retarder (une pendule). put 'by, v.tr. mettre en réserve, de côté. put 'down, v.tr. 1. déposer, poser. 2. supprimer (une révolte). 3. (a) noter; p. it down to my account, mettez-le à mon compte. (b) tuer, abattre (un animal). put 'forward, v.tr. 1. (a) émettre, avancer, proposer (un projet); (b) to p. oneself forward, se mettre en avant, en évidence. 2. avancer. put in. 1. v.tr. to p. in a good word for s.o., dire un mot en faveur de qn; to p. in an hour's work, faire une heure de travail. 2. v.i. faire escale (in a port). put 'off, v.tr. (a) retirer, ôter; (b) remettre, différer; (c) to p. s.o. off, intimider qn. put 'on, v.tr. 1. monter (une pièce de théâtre). 2. mettre; chausser; p. on your hat, couvrez-vous. 3. avancer (la pendule). 4. to p. on the light, mettre la lumière; allumer. put 'out, v.tr. 1. avancer, étendre (le bras, etc.). 2. mettre dehors. 3. éteindre (la lumière). 4. déconcerter; ennuyer, contrarier; incommoder, gêner (qn). put 'up, v.tr. 1. (a) lever; dresser; put up your hands, haut les mains; (b) afficher (un avis). 2. augmenter (les prix). 3. (a) héberger (qn); v.i. to p. up at an hotel, descendre à un hôtel. 4. abs. to p. up with sth., s'accommoder de (qch.). 'put-up, a. F: a p.-up job, un coup monté.

putrefy ['pju:trifai], v.i. se putréfier, pourrir.

putrid ['pju:trid], a. 1. putride; infect. 2. P: moche.

putt [pʌt]. I. (at golf) putt m. II. v.tr. jouer sur le putting (-green).

putty ['pʌti], s. mastic m, enduit m; p. knife, spatule f de vitrier.

puzzle ['pʌzl]. I. s. 1. embarras m; perplexité f. 2. énigme f; problème m. 3. devinette f; crossword p., (problème de mots) croisés. II. v. 1. v.tr. embarrasser, intriguer. 2. v.i. se creuser la tête (pour comprendre qch.). 'puzzling, a. embarrassant, intriguant.

†pygmy ['pigmi]. 1. s. pygmée m. 2. attrib. pygméen.

pyjamas [pi'dʒɑːməz], s.pl. pyjama m, pyjama m.

pylon ['pailən], s. pylône m.

pyramid ['pirəmid], s. pyramide f.

pyrites [pai'raitiz], s. Min: pyrite f.

python ['paiθ(ə)n], s. python m.

Q

Q, q [kju:], s. (la lettre) Q, q m.

quack[1] [kwæk]. I. s. & int. couin-couin (m). II. v.i. (of duck) crier, faire couin-couin.

quack[2], s. (a) e. (doctor) charlatan m; (b) F: the q., le toubib.

quad [kwɔd], s. Sch: F: cour f (carrée).

Quadragesima [kwɔdrə'dʒesimə], s. Ecc: la Quadragésime.

quadrangle ['kwɔdræŋgl], s. Sch: cour f (carrée).

quadratic [kwɔ'drætik], a. q. equation, équation f du second degré.

quadrilateral [kwɔdri'læt(ə)rəl], s. quadrilatère m.

quadruped ['kwɔdruped], s. quadrupède m.

quadruple ['kwɔdrupl], a. & s. quadruple (m). 'quadruplets, F: quads, s.pl. quadruplé(e)s. quad'ruplicate. 1. s. in q., en quatre exemplaires. II. v.tr. quadrupler; faire quatre exemplaires (de qch.).

quagmire ['kwægmaiər, 'kwɔg-], s. fondrière f; marécage m.

quail [kweil], s. caille f.

quaint [kweint], a. étrange, bizarre; singulier.

quake [kweik], v.i. trembler (with fear, de peur).

Quaker ['kweikər], s. Ecc: Quaker, m.

qualify ['kwɔlifai]. 1. v.tr. (a) Gram: qualifier; (b) apporter des réserves à (un consentement); modifier, atténuer (une affirmation). 2. v.i. se qualifier (for, pour); to q. as a doctor, a pilot, être reçu médecin; passer son brevet de pilote. qualifi'cation, s. qualifications f; qualifications for an appointment, titres m à un emploi; to accept without q., accepter (i) sans réserve, (ii) sans conditions. 'qualified, a. 1. to be q. for a job, avoir les titres, les diplômes, nécessaires pour un emploi; to be q. to vote, avoir droit d'électeur. 2. q. approval, approbation modérée.

†quality ['kwɔliti], s. qualité f.

qualm [kwɑːm, kwɔːm], s. scrupule m, remords m.

quandary ['kwɔndəri], s. to be in a q., ne trop savoir que faire.

†quantity ['kwɔntiti], s. quantité f; Civ. E: q. surveying, toisé m, métrage m; q. surveyor, métreur m (vérificateur).

quarantine ['kwɔrəntiːn]. I. s. quarantaine f. II. v.tr. mettre en quarantaine.

quarrel ['kwɔrəl]. I. s. querelle f, dispute f. II. v.i. 1. to q. with s.o., trouver à redire à qch. 'quarrelling, s. querelles fpl, disputes fpl. 'quarrelsome, a. querelleur.

†**quarry**[1] ['kwɔri], s. proie f.

†**quarry**[2]. I. s. carrière f. II. v.tr. extraire (la pierre) de la carrière.

quart [kwɔːt], s. approx. = litre m.

quarter ['kwɔːtər]. I. s. 1. (a) quart m; (b) Cu: quartier m (de bœuf, etc.); hind quarters, arrière-train m (d'une bête). 2. (a) trimestre m; terme m; (b) a to six, six heures moins le quart. 3. from all quarters, de tous côtés; in high quarters, en haut lieu. 4. pl. résidence f; Mil: quartier. 5. pl. Mil: v.tr. Mil: cantonner, loger (les troupes). 'quarter-'final, a. Sp: quart m de finale. 'quarterly, 1. a. trimestriel. 2. adv. tous les trois mois.

quartet(te) [kwɔː'tet], s. Mus: quatuor m.

quarto ['kwɔːtou], a. & s. in-quarto (m).

quartz [kwɔːts], s. quartz m.

quaver[1] ['kweivər], s. 1. Mus: croche f. 2. (a) trille m; (b) tremblement m.

quay [kiː], s. quai m.

queasy ['kwiːzi], a. sujet à des nausées. 'queasiness, s. malaise m; nausées fpl.

queen [kwiːn], s. 1. reine f. 2. (at cards) dame f. 3. chatte f. 'queen-'bee, s. abeille f mère, reine f.

queer ['kwiər], a. 1. (a) étrange, singulier; (b) suspect; (c) a. & s.P: homosexuel m. 2. F: I feel very q., je me sens tout chose. -ly, adv. étrangement, bizarrement. II. v.tr. F: to q. s.o.'s pitch, faire échouer les plans de qn. 'queerness, s. étrangeté f, bizarrerie f.

quell [kwel], v.tr. calmer, dompter (une émotion); réprimer (une révolte).

quench [kwenʃ], v.tr. to q. one's thirst, se désaltérer.

querulous ['kwer(j)uləs], a. plaintif et maussade.

†**query** ['kwiəri]. I. s. question f. II. v.tr. mettre en question.

quest [kwest], s. recherche f.

question ['kwestʃ(ə)n]. I. s. question f; without q., sans aucun doute; the matter in q., l'affaire en question, dont il s'agit; to ask s.o. a q., poser une question à qn; q. mark, point m d'interrogation. II. v.tr. 1. questionner, interroger (qn). 2. mettre qch. en question, en doute. 'questionable, a. contestable, discutable. 2. in q. taste, d'un goût douteux. 'questioner, s. interrogateur, -trice. question-'naire, s. questionnaire m.

queue [kjuː]. I. s. queue f (de personnes, etc.). II. v.i. faire (la) queue; (of cars) prendre la file.

quibble ['kwibl]. I. s. argutie f; chicane f des mots; faux-fuyant m. II. v.i. chicaner; user d'équivoque. 'quibbler, s. chicaneur, -euse.

quick [kwik]. I. a. (a) rapide; the quickest way, le chemin le plus court; as q. as lightning, comme un éclair; be q.! dépêchez-vous! (b) (enfant) vif, éveillé; q. ear, oreille fine; to have a q. temper, s'emporter facilement. -ly, adv. vite. II. s. to be hurt to the q., être blessé au vif. 'quickness, s. vitesse f, rapidité f. 'quicksand, s. sable m mouvant; lise f.

quid [kwid], s. P: livre f (sterling); five q., cinq livres.

quiet ['kwaiət]. I. s. 1. tranquillité f, repos m, calme m. 2. F: to do sth. on the q., faire qch. en cachette; I'm telling you that on the q., je vous dis ça entre nous deux. II. a. 1. tranquille, calme, silencieux; be q.! taisez-vous! q. wedding, mariage célébré dans l'intimité; to have a q. dig at s.o., faire une allusion discrète à qn. -ly, adv. tranquillement, doucement; silencieusement. III. ‡v.tr. apaiser, calmer. 'quietness, s. tranquillité f, repos m.

quill [kwil], s. tuyau m (de plume).

quilt [kwilt]. I. s. couverture f piquée; couvre-pied(s) m. II. v.tr. piquer, capitonner (un vêtement).

quince [kwins], s. coing m; q. tree, cognassier m.

quintuple ['kwintjupl], a. & s. quintuple (m). 'quin'tuplet, s. 1. groupe m de cinq. 2. pl. quintuplets, F: quins, quintuplé(e)s.

quire [kwaiər], s. = main f (de papier).

quit [kwit]. I. a. quitte; to be q. of sth., être débarrassé de qch. II. ‡v.tr. quitter (qn, un endroit); F: to q. one's job, démissionner; U:S: to q. doing sth., cesser de faire qch.

quite [kwait], adv. 1. tout à fait, entièrement; q. new, tout nouveau; tout neuf; q. enough, bien assez; q. right, très bien; I q. understand, j'ai bien compris; je me rends parfaitement compte. 2. it's q. interesting, cela ne manque pas d'intérêt; q. a surprise, une véritable surprise; I q. believe that . . ., je veux bien croire que . . .

quiver[1] ['kwivər], s. carquois m.

quiver[2]. s. 1. tremblement m, frisson m; q. of the eyelid, battement m de paupière. II. v.i. trembler; frémir, frissonner; (of voice) trembloter.

quixotic [kwik'sɔtik], a. exalté, visionnaire.

quiz [kwiz], s. Rad: etc: devinette f.

quod [kwɔd], s. P: prison f, P: taule f.

quorum ['kwɔrəm], s. quorum m, nombre m voulu.

quota ['kwouta], s. quote-part f, quotité f; electoral q., quotient m électoral; **to fix quotas for an import**, contingenter une importation.

quote [kwout]. I. v.tr. 1. citer (un auteur). 2. Com: établir, faire (un prix). II. v.i. F: 1. citation f. 2. pl. quotes, guillemets mpl. **quo'tation**, s. 1. citation f; sq. marks, guillemets mpl. 2. cote f, cours m, prix m.

quotient ['kwouʃ(ə)nt], s. quotient m.

R

R, r [ɑːr], s. (la lettre) R, r f.

rabbi ['ræbai], s. rabbin m.

rabbit ['ræbit], s. 1. lapin m; wild r., lapin de garenne; r. hutch, clapier m; r. warren, garenne f. 2. Welsh r., fondue f au fromage sur canapé.

rabble ['ræbl], s. 1. cohue f; foule f. 2. the r., la canaille.

rabid ['ræbid], a. 1. (a) furieux; r. enemy, ennemi acharné; (b) ou-trancier. 2. (chien) enragé. **rabies** ['reibiz], s. rage f.

race¹ [reis]. I. s. 1. course f; **to run a r.**, disputer une course. 2. (in sea) raz m de courant; (in river) canal m, bief m. 3. E: ball r., (i) voie f de roulement; (ii) cage f à billes. II. v. 1. v.i. lutter de vitesse (with, avec); (of engine) s'emballer; (of propeller) s'affoler; (of pulse) battre la fièvre. 2. v.tr. faire courir (un cheval); Aut: emballer (le moteur). **'racecourse**, s. champ m de courses. **'racehorse**, s. cheval m de course. **'racing**, s. courses fpl; r. stable, écurie f de courses. **'racy**, a. vif, piquant; (style) plein de verve.

race², s. 1. race f; the human r., la race humaine; r. hatred, haine f raciale. 2. descendance f; lignée f. **'racial**, a. de (la) race; r. minorities, les races en minorité. **'racialism**, s. racisme m.

rack¹ [ræk], s. (a) râtelier m; (b) bomb r., lance-bombes m; luggage r., porte-bagages m; filet m (à bagages); Aut: roof r., galerie f.

rack², v.tr. tourmenter, torturer; **to r. one's brains**, se creuser la cervelle.

racket¹ ['rækit], s. raquette f; pl. (game) rackets, la raquette.

racket², s. F: 1. tapage m, vacarme m; **to stand the r.**, subvenir aux dépenses. 2. affaire f véreuse; escroquerie f. **racke'teer**, s. F: gangster m; com-binard m; trafiquant m.

radar ['reidɑr], s. radar m.

radiate ['reidieit], v. 1. v.i. rayonner, irradier. 2. v.tr. émettre, dégager (de la chaleur, etc.). **'radiance**, s. rayon-nement m. **'radiant**, a. radieux, rayonnant; r. heat, chaleur rayon-nante. **radi'ation**, s. 1. irradiation f; rayonnement m. 2. radiation f (du radium); nuclear r., rayonnement nucléaire. **'radiator**, s. radiateur m.

radical ['rædik(ə)l], a. & s. radical (m). -ally, adv. radicalement, foncièrement.

radio ['reidiou]. I. s. 1. la radio; r. (set), poste m, radio f. 2. (radio-telegraphy) radio m. 3. Av: r. beacon, radio-balise f; r. control, téléguidage m; r. direction, radioguidage m. 4. F: (i) radiographie f. F: radio f; (ii) radiologie f. F: radio f. II. v.tr. envoyer (un message) par radio. **radio'active**, a. radio-actif. **radioac'tivity**, s. radio-activité f. **radiode'tection**, s. radiodétection f. **'radiogram**, s. 1. radiogramme m. 2. combiné m (radiophone). **'radio-graph**. I. s. Med: radiogramme m, radiographie f. II. v.tr. radiographier. **radi'ographer**, s. assistant, -ante d'un radiologue. **radi'ography**, s. Med: radiographie f. **radi'ologist**, s. radio-logue mf. **radi'ology**, s. radiologie f. **radio'sonde**, s. radiosonde f.

radish ['rædiʃ], s. radis m.

radium ['reidiəm], s. radium m.

radius ['reidiəs], s. rayon m.

raft [rɑːft], s. radeau m; timber, U.S: lumber, r., train m de bois.

rafter ['rɑːftər], s. chevron m (d'un comble).

rag¹ [ræg], s. 1. chiffon m; lambeau m. 2. pl. haillons m, guenilles f, loques f. 3. the r. trade, l'industrie f de l'habillement. **'ragged** [-gid], a. en lambeaux; en haillons.

rag², s. F: Sch: (a) farce f; (b) chahut m. II. v.tr. F: (a) brimer (un camarade); (b) chahuter (un professeur); chambarder les effets (d'un étudiant).

rage [reidʒ]. I. s. 1. rage f, fureur f; **to fly into a r.**, s'emporter. 2. **to be all the r.**, faire fureur. II. v.i. être furieux; (of wind) faire rage; (of epidemic) sévir.

raid [reid]. I. s. (a) razzia f (de bandits); (b) (police) r., rafle f; (c) Mil: raid m; air r., bombardement m aérien. II. v. 1. v.i. faire une razzia, un raid. 2. v.tr. razzier (une tribu); (of police) faire une rafle dans (un quartier). **'raider**, s. maraudeur m, pillard m.

rail¹ [reil], s. 1. (a) barre f; (b) barre d'appui; rampe f. 2. pl. grille f. 3. (a) rail m; live r., rail de contact; **to leave the rails**, dérailler; (b) chemin m de fer. **'rail-car**, s. autorail m. **'railings**, s. 1. grille f. 2. balustrade f; rampe f. **'railway**, U.S: **'railroad**, s.

chemin *m* de fer; r., *U.S:* railroad, station, gare *f.* †railwayman, *s.* cheminot *m.*

rain [rein]. I. *s.* pluie *f.* II. *v.tr.* & *i.* pleuvoir; it's raining, il pleut. 'rainbow, *s.* arc-en-ciel *m.* 'raincoat, *s.* imperméable *m, F:* imper. 'rainfall, *s.* précipitation *f.* 'rainproof, *a.* imperméable *f.* 'rainwear, *s.* vêtements *mpl* de pluie. 'rainy, *a.* pluvieux.

raise [reiz], *v.tr.* 1. (a) dresser, mettre debout; relever; (b) soulever. 2. élever (une famille); cultiver (des légumes). 3. produire (de la vapeur); pousser (un cri); soulever (une objection). 4. lever (le bras); porter (son verre à ses lèvres); to r. s.o.'s hopes, donner de l'espoir à qn. 5. relever (un store); hausser (les prix). 6. to r. money, se procurer de l'argent.

raisin ['reizn], *s.* raisin *m* sec.

rake [reik]. I. *s.* râteau *m.* II. *v.tr.* ratisser (les feuilles); râteler (le sol); gratter, racler (une surface).

rally ['ræli]. I. *s.* 1. (a) ralliement *m;* (b) réunion *f* (de scouts); (c) *Aut:* rallye *m* automobile. 2. reprise *f* (des forces); *Sp:* dernier effort *m* (pour gagner le match). II. *v.* 1. *v.tr.* rallier (ses partisans). 2. *v.i.* (of troops) se reformer; (of pers.) reprendre ses forces; se remettre (d'une maladie).

ram [ræm]. I. *s.* 1. *Z:* bélier *m.* 2. bélier hydraulique; *(b)* mouton *m,* pilon *m* (de marteau-pilon). II. *v.tr.* 1. battre, tasser (le sol); enfoncer (un pieu). 2. éperonner (un navire); tamponner (une voiture).

ramjet ['ræmdʒet], *s. Av:* statoréacteur *m.*

ramble ['ræmbl]. I. *s.* 1. promenade *f.* 2. discours *m* incohérent. II. *v.i.* 1. errer à l'aventure. 2. parler sans suite; to r. on, dire mille inconséquences. 'rambling, *s.* 1. (discours) décousu, sans suite. 2. *r. house,* maison pleine de coins et de recoins.

ramify ['ræmifai], *v.i.* se ramifier.

ramp¹ [ræmp], *s.* rampe *f;* pente *f; Aut:* (repair) r., ponton *m* de visite, pont *m* élévateur; *P.N: Aut:* beware r.! dénivellation *f.*

ramp², [ræmp], *s. F:* supercherie *f;* it's a r., c'est un coup monté.

rampage [ræm'peidʒ], *v.i. F:* se comporter comme un fou.

rampart ['ræmpɑ:t], *s.* rempart *m.*

ramshackle ['ræmʃækl], *a.* délabré.

ranch [rɑ:n(t)ʃ], *s. U.S:* ranch *m,* ferme *f* d'élevage.

rancid ['rænsid], *a.* rance.

random ['rændəm]. 1. *s.* at r., au hasard. 2. *a.* r. shot, coup tiré au hasard.

range [reindʒ]. I. *s.* 1. (a) rangée *f;* (b) chaîne *f* (de montagnes). 2. (a) étendue *f;* r. of action, champ d'ac-

tivité; (b) r. of colours, gamme *f* de couleurs. 3. (a) distance *f;* (b) portée *f* (d'une arme à feu). 4. fourneau *m* de cuisine. II. *v.* 1. *v.tr.* ranger; classer. 2. *v.i.* se ranger; s'échelonner.

rank¹ [ræŋk]. I. *s.* 1. *Mil:* (a) rang *m;* (b) *pl.* the (other) ranks, les (simples) soldats; to rise from the ranks, sortir du rang, passer officier; (c) the r. and file, (i) *Mil:* la troupe; (ii) le commun des mortels. 2. (a) rang (social); (b) *Mil: etc:* grade *m.* 3. (taxi) r., station *f* (de taxis). II. *v.* 1. *v.tr.* ranger, compter (qn, qch.) (among, parmi). 2. *v.i.* se ranger, être classé.

rank², *a.* 1. (trop) luxuriant, exubérant. 2. *(of injustice)* criant.

rankle ['ræŋkl], *v.i.* to r. in s.o.'s mind, rester sur le cœur de qn.

ransack ['rænsæk], *v.tr.* 1. fouiller. 2. saccager, piller.

ransom ['rænsəm]. I. *s.* rançon *f.* II. *v.tr.* 1. payer la rançon de (qn). 2. mettre (qn) à rançon.

rant [rænt], *v.i.* déclamer, tempêter, tonitruer.

rap [ræp]. I. *s.* petit coup *m* sec et dur. II. *v.tr.* & *i.* frapper.

rapacious [ra'peiʃəs], *a.* rapace. ra'pacity, *s.* rapacité *f.*

rape [reip]. I. *s.* viol *m.* II. *v.tr.* violer (une femme).

rapid ['ræpid]. I. *a.* & *s.* rapide (*m*). -ly, *adv.* ra'pidity, *s.* rapidité *f.*

rapier ['reipiər], *s.* rapière *f.*

rapture ['ræptʃər], *s.* ravissement *m,* extase *m;* to go into raptures, s'extasier.

rare ['reər], *a.* rare. -ly, *adv.* rarement. 'rarefied, *a.* raréfié. 'rarity, *s.* 1. rareté *f.* 2. objet *m* rare; événement *m* rare.

rascal ['rɑ:sk(ə)l], *s.* coquin *m,* mauvais sujet *m; (of child)* polisson *m.*

rash¹ [ræʃ], *s. Med:* éruption *f.*

rash², *a.* téméraire; irréfléchi. -ly, *adv.* inconsidérément; (parler) à la légère. 'rashness, *s.* témérité *f;* étourderie *f.*

rasher ['ræʃər], *s.* tranche *f* de lard.

rasp [rɑ:sp]. I. *s. Tls:* râpe *f* (du bois). 2. *v.i.* grincer II. *v.tr.* râper. 'rasping, *a.* (son) grinçant.

raspberry ['rɑ:zb(ə)ri], *s.* framboise *f;* r. bush, framboisier *m.*

rat [ræt]. I. *s.* 1. rat *m.* 2. *Ind: F:* jaune *m;* renard *m.* II. †*v.i. 1. (of dog, etc.)* to go ratting, faire la chasse aux rats. 2. *F:* faire le jaune, le renard; to r. on s.o., vendre qn.

ratchet ['rætʃit], *s.* cliquet *m.*

rate [reit]. I. *s.* 1. quantité proportionnelle; birth, death, r, (taux *m* de la) natalité *f,* mortalité *f.* 2. (a) r. of growth, taux d'accroissement; (b) allure *f,* vitesse *f; (c) Fin:* taux; cours *m;* the bank r., le taux de la banque; *Com:* market rates, cours du marché;

advertising rates, tarif *m* de publicité. 2. *Adm:* impôt *m* local; contribution *f* foncière. **II.** *v.* **1.** *v.tr.* estimer, évaluer (qch.); classer (un navire, une auto); considérer (qch.), (as, comme). **2.** *v.i.* être classé (as, comme).

'rateable, *a. Adm:* **r. value** = valeur *f* locative imposable (d'un immeuble).

'ratepayer, *s.* contribuable *m.* **'rating,** *s.* **1.** évaluation *f;* *Aut:* calcul *m* de la puissance (des moteurs); *Adm:* répartition *f* des impôts locaux. **2.** *Sp:* classe *f,* catégorie *f.* **3.** *pl. Nau:* **the ratings,** les matelots et gradés.

rather ['rɑːðər], *adv.* **1.** plutôt. 2. un peu; assez; **r. plain,** plutôt laid; **I r. think,** je crois bien (que); **I'd r. come,** j'aimerais mieux venir.

ratify ['rætifai], *v.tr.* ratifier. **ratifi'cation,** *s.* ratification *f.*

†ratio ['reiʃiou], *s.* raison *f,* proportion *f.*

ration ['ræʃ(ə)n]. **I.** *s.* ration *f.* **II.** *v.tr.* rationner.

rational ['ræʃən(ə)l], *a.* (*a*) raisonnable; doué de raison; (*b*) raisonné. -ally, *adv.* raisonnablement.

rattle ['rætl]. **I.** *s.* **1.** (*a*) hochet *m* (d'enfant). 2. bruit *m,* fracas *m;* tapotis *m; Med:* (death) râle *m.* **II.** *v.* **1.** *v.i.* (*of car*) ferrailler; (*of hail*) crépiter; (*of window*) trembler. 2. *v.tr.* agiter (qch.) avec bruit; faire cliqueter (des clefs); *F:* bouleverser (qn); **he never gets rattled,** il ne s'épate jamais. **'rattlesnake,** *s.* serpent *m* à sonnettes.

raucous ['rɔːkəs], *a.* rauque.

ravage ['rævidʒ], *v.tr.* ravager, dévaster.

rave [reiv], *v.i.* (*a*) être en délire; battre la campagne; (*b*) to **r. at s.o.,** pester contre qn; **raving lunatic,** fou *m* furieux; (*c*) être en furie. **'raving,** *s.* délire *m; pl.* paroles *f* incohérentes.

raven ['reiv(ə)n], *s.* (grand) corbeau *m.*

ravenous ['ræv(ə)nəs], *a.* vorace. -ly, *adv.* voracement.

ravine [rə'viːn], *s.* ravin *m.*

raw [rɔː], *a.* **1.** cru. **2.** *Ind:* **r. materials,** matières *f* premières. **3.** sans expérience; **a r. hand,** un novice. **4.** **r. wound,** plaie *f* vive. **'rawness,** *s.* **1.** crudité *f.* **2.** inexpérience *f.* **3.** froid *m* humide.

ray [rei], *s.* rayon *m;* **X rays,** rayons X.

rayon ['reiən], *s.* rayonne *f.*

raze [reiz], *v.tr.* raser (un édifice).

razor ['reizər], *s.* rasoir *m;* **safety r.,** rasoir de sûreté; **electric r.,** rasoir électrique; **r. blade,** lame *f* de rasoir.

re [riː], *prep. Com:* relativement à, au sujet de.

re- ['riː-], *prefix;* re-; ré-; de nouveau; **to re-read,** relire; **to reprint,** réimprimer; **to revisit,** revisiter, visiter de nouveau.

reach [riːtʃ]. **I.** *s.* **1.** (*a*) portée *f,* atteinte *f;* **out of r.,** hors de portée;

(*b*) **within easy r. of the station,** à proximité *f,* près de, la gare. **2.** partie *f* droite (d'un fleuve) entre deux coudes; bief *m* (d'un canal). **II.** *v.* **1.** *v.tr.* (*a*) to **r. out,** étendre, avancer (la main); (*b*) atteindre (qch.); arriver à (un endroit); aboutir à (un accord). **2.** *v.i.* s'étendre; **as far as the eye could r.,** à perte de vue; to **r. out for sth.,** étendre la main pour prendre qch.

react [ri'ækt], *v.i.* réagir. **re'action,** *s.* réaction *f.* **re'actionary,** *a.* & *s.* réactionnaire (*mf*). **re'actor,** *s.* réacteur *m;* **atomic r.,** réacteur atomique.

‡read [riːd]. **I.** *v.tr.* lire; **the clause reads both ways,** l'article peut s'interpréter dans les deux sens; to **r. through sth.,** (*i*) parcourir qch., (*ii*) lire qch. en entier. **II.** *s.* to **have a quiet r.,** lire tranquillement. **III.** *a.* [red] **well-r.,** instruit, savant; qui a beaucoup lu. **'readable,** *a.* lisible. **'reader,** *s.* **1.** lecteur, -trice; *proof r.,* correcteur, -trice; d'épreuves. **2.** *Sch:* = professeur *m* de faculté. **3.** *Sch:* livre *m* de lecture. **'reading,** *s.* **1.** lecture *f;* **the r. public,** le public qui lit. **II.** *s.* la lecture.

readjust ['riːə'dʒʌst], *v.tr.* rajuster. **rea'djustment,** *s.* rajustement *m.*

ready ['redi], *a.* **1.** (*a*) prêt; to **get r.,** se préparer; (*b*) **r. to hand,** sous la main; **r. money,** argent comptant. **2.** prêt, disposé. **3.** prompt, facile. **II.** *adv.* **r. dressed,** tout habillé. **'readily,** *adv.* (*a*) faire qch.) volontiers; (imaginer qch.) aisément, facilement. **'readiness,** *s.* **1.** empressement *m* (à faire qch.); bonne volonté *f.* **2.** facilité *f* (de parole); vivacité *f* (d'esprit). **'ready-'made,** *a.* tout fait; **r.-m. clothes,** la confection.

real [riəl], *a.* **1.** (*a*) vrai; **r. silk,** soie naturelle; (*b*) véritable, réel. **2. r. estate,** propriété immobilière. -ly, *adv.* vraiment; réellement; en effet; **not r.!** pas possible! **'realism,** *s.* réalisme *m.* **'realist,** *s.* réaliste *mf.* **rea'listic,** *a.* réaliste. -ally, *adv.* avec réalisme. **re'ality,** *s.* la réalité.

realize ['riəlaiz], *v.tr.* **1.** réaliser (un projet, etc.). **2.** se rendre compte de (qch.). **reali'zation,** *s.* réalisation *f.*

realm [relm], *s.* royaume *m.*

ream [riːm], *s.* rame *f* (de papier).

reanimate ['riː'ænimeit], *v.tr.* ranimer.

reap [riːp], *v.tr.* (*a*) moissonner (le blé, etc.); (*b*) to **r. profit from sth.,** tirer profit de qch. **'reaper,** *s.* **1.** (*pers.*) moissonneur, -euse. **2.** (*machine*) moissonneuse *f;* **r. binder,** moissonneuse-lieuse *f.*

reappear [riːə'piər], *v.i.* reparaître. **rea'ppearance,** *s.* réapparition *f.*

rear¹ [riər]. **I.** *s.* **1.** *Mil:* (*also* **rear-guard**) arrière-garde *f* (d'une armée).

2. (a) arrière m (d'une maison); dernier rang m (d'un cortège); (b) P: a kick in the r., un coup de pied au derrière. II. a. d'arrière; de queue; postérieur. 'rear-'admiral, s. contreamiral m. 'rear-'engined, a. Aut: avec moteur à l'arrière.

rear². I. v.tr. élever (une famille, des animaux); cultiver (des plantes). 2. v.i. (of horse) se cabrer.

rearm ['ri:'ɑ:m], v.tr. réarmer. re'armament, s. réarmement m.

rearrange ['ri:ə'reindʒ], v.tr. arranger de nouveau; remettre en ordre. rea'rrangement, s. nouvel arrangement m; remise f en ordre.

reason ['ri:z(ə)n]. I. s. 1. raison f, cause f; for no r., sans motif, sans cause; the r. why, le pourquoi. 2. to lose one's r., perdre la raison. 3. raison; bon sens m; it stands to r., cela va sans dire. II. v.i. raisonner; déduire des conclusions. 'reasonable, a. raisonnable. -bly, adv. raisonnablement. 'reasoning, s. raisonnement m.

reassure [ri:(ə)'ʃuər], v.tr. rassurer (qn). rea'ssuring, a. rassurant.

rebate ['ri:bət], s. rabais m, escompte m; ristourne f.

rebel. I. ['reb(ə)l]. 1. a. insurgé. 2. s. rebelle mf; révolté, -ée; insurgé, -ée. II. ‡v.i. [ri'bel] se rebeller, se soulever (against, contre). re'bellion, s. rébellion f, révolte f. re'bellious, a. rebelle.

rebore [ri:'bɔ:r]. I. v.tr. Aut: réaléser. II. s. Aut: F: réalésage m.

rebound. I. v.i. [ri'baund] rebondir. II. s. ['ri:baund] rebondissement m; ricochet m.

rebuff [ri'bʌf]. I. s. rebuffade f; échec m. II. v.tr. repousser, rebuter (qn).

rebuild [ri:'bild], v.tr. rebâtir, reconstruire.

rebuke [ri'bju:k]. I. s. réprimande f, blâme m. II. v.tr. réprimander, blâmer (qn).

recall [ri'kɔ:l]. I. v.tr. rappeler (qn, qch.) se souvenir de (qch.). II. s. rappel m (de qn); decision beyond r., décision irrévocable.

recapitulate ['ri:kə'pitjuleit], v.tr. (F: ‡recap) faire un résumé. 'recapi'tulation, s. (F: 'recap) récapitulation f.

recapture [ri:'kæptʃər], v.tr. reprendre.

recede [ri'si:d], v.i. s'éloigner, reculer. re'ceding, a. (a) qui s'éloigne; (b) (front, etc.) fuyant.

receipt [ri'si:t]. I. s. Com: 1. (a) recette f; (b) réception f (d'une lettre). 2. reçu, quittance f. II. v.tr. Com: acquitter (une facture).

receive [ri'si:v], v.tr. 1. (a) recevoir; Com: received with thanks, pour acquit; (b) receler (un objet volé). 2. recevoir, accueillir (des invités). re'ceiver, s. 1. destinataire mf (d'une

lettre); receleur m (d'objets volés). 2. récepteur m (de téléphone).

recent ['ri:sənt], a. récent. -ly, adv. récemment; tout dernièrement.

receptacle ['ri'septəkl], s. récipient m.

reception [ri'sepʃn], s. 1. (a) réception f; (b) (in hotel, etc.) r. desk, la réception. 2. accueil m. re'ceptionist, s. préposée(e) à la réception (dans un hôtel); réceptionniste f (dans un salon de beauté, etc.).

receptive [ri'septiv], a. réceptif.

recess [ri'ses], s. 1. Jur: vacances fpl Pol: intersession f. 2. (a) recoin m; (b) embrasure f; niche f. re'cession, s. Com: récession f.

recipe ['resipi], s. recette f.

recipient [ri'sipiənt], s. (a) (object) récipient m; (b) (pers.) donataire mf; destinataire mf (d'une lettre).

reciprocate [ri'siprəkeit]. 1. v.tr. payer de retour (un sentiment); rendre mutuellement (des services). 2. v.i. retourner le compliment. re'ciprocal, a. réciproque; mutuel. -ally, adv. réciproquement; mutuellement. reci'procity, s. réciprocité f.

recite [ri'sait], v.tr. & i. réciter, déclamer. re'cital, s. Mus: audition f. reci'tation, s. récitation f. recita'tive, s. Mus: récitatif m.

reckless ['reklis], a. insouciant; téméraire; r. driving, conduite imprudente. -ly, adv. témérairement; avec insouciance. 'recklessness, s. imprudence f, témérité f.

reckon ['rekn]. (a) v.tr. & i. compter, calculer; (b) v.tr. estimer, juger; (c) to have to r. with s.o., avoir à compter avec qn. 'reckoning, s. (a) compte m, calcul m; (b) to the best of my r., autant que j'en puis juger.

reclaim [ri'kleim], v.tr. défricher (du terrain); mettre (un terrain) en valeur; récupérer (un sous-produit). recla-'mation, s. défrichement m (d'un terrain); récupération f (des sousproduits); assèchement m (des terres).

recline [ri'klain], v.i. être couché; reposer.

recluse [ri'klu:s], s. reclus,-use.

recognize ['rekəgnaiz], v.tr. reconnaître. recog'nition, s. reconnaissance f. 'recog'nizable, a. reconnaissable. 'recognized, a. reconnu, admis; (terme) consacré.

recoil [ri'kɔil]. I. v.i. (a) (of spring) se détendre; (b) (of firearm) reculer. 2. (of pers.) reculer; se révolter.

recollect [rekə'lekt], v.tr. se rappeler; se souvenir de (qch.). reco'llection, s. souvenir m, mémoire f.

recommend [rekə'mend], v.tr. recommander; conseiller (à qn de faire qch.); not to be recommended, à déconseiller. recommen'dation, s. recommandation f.

recompense ['rekəmpens]. I. s. 1. récompense f (for, de). 2. dédommagement m (for, de). II. v.tr. 1. récompenser (for, de). 2. dédommager (for, de).

reconcile ['rekənsail], v.tr. 1. réconcilier. 2. to r. oneself, se résigner (à qch.). 3. concilier, faire accorder (des faits). **reconcilable**, a. conciliable. **reconcili'ation**, s. réconciliation f.

recondition ['ri:kən'diʃ(ə)n], v.tr. rénover, remettre en état; Com: reconditionner; Aut: reconditioned engine, moteur révisé.

reconnaissance [ri'kɔnis(ə)ns], s. reconnaissance f.

reconnoitre [rekə'nɔitər], v.tr. reconnaître (le terrain); abs: faire une reconnaissance.

reconsider ['ri:kən'sidər], v.tr. 1. considérer de nouveau. 2. revenir sur (une décision). **reconside'ration**, s. reconsidération f (d'une question); révision f (d'un jugement).

reconstruct ['ri:kən'strʌkt], v.tr. 1. reconstruire. 2. reconstituer (un crime). **recon'struction**, s. 1. reconstruction f. 2. reconstitution f (d'un crime).

record. I. s. ['rekɔ:d] 1. enregistrement m (d'un fait); to be on r., être enregistré; F: off the r., en secret, entre nous. 2. to make, keep, a r. of sth., noter qch. 3. pl. archives f. 4. dossier m (de qn); police r., casier m judiciaire. 5. Sp: etc: record m. 6. disque m; long-playing r., microsillon m. II. v.tr. [ri'kɔ:d] 1. enregistrer (un fait); to r. one's vote, voter. 2. enregistrer, graver (une chanson); to r. on tape, enregistrer sur bande. **re'corder**, s. 1. Jur: = juge m. 2. tape r., magnétophone (R.t.m.); Aut: trip r., enregistreur m de distance. 3. Mus: flûte f à bec. **re'cording**, s. enregistrement m.

recount[1] [ri'kaunt], v.tr. raconter.

recount[2] ['ri:kaunt]. I. v.tr. recompter. II. s. Pol: nouveau dépouillement m du scrutin.

recoup [ri'ku:p], v.tr. abs. se dédommager (de ses pertes).

recourse [ri'kɔ:s], s. 1. recours m. 2. expédient m.

recover[1] [ri'kʌvər], v.tr. 1. recouvrer, retrouver (un objet perdu); to r. one's breath, reprendre haleine. 2. to r. lost ground, reprendre du terrain perdu; se rattraper. 3. v.i. guérir (d'une maladie). **re'covery**, s. 1. recouvrement m (d'un objet perdu). 2. guérison m (d'une maladie); redressement m (économique).

recover[2] ['ri:'kʌvər], v.tr. recouvrir.

recreation [rekri'eiʃ(ə)n], s. récréation f, divertissement m; r. ground, terrain m de jeux, de sports.

recriminate [ri'krimineit], v.i. récriminer. **recrimi'nation**, s. récrimination f.

recruit [ri'kru:t]. I. s. recrue f. II. v.tr. recruter.

rectangle ['rektæŋgl], s. rectangle m. **rec'tangular**, a. rectangulaire.

rectify ['rektifai], v.tr. rectifier, corriger. **rectifi'cation**, s. rectification f.

rector ['rektər], s. 1. = curé m. 2. recteur m (d'une université). †'rectory, s. = presbytère m.

recumbent [ri'kʌmbənt], a. couché, étendu; r. figure (on tomb), gisant m.

recuperate [ri'kju:pəreit], v.tr. Ind: etc: récupérer. 2. v.i. se remettre (d'une maladie). **recupe'ration**, s. 1. Med: rétablissement m. 2. Ind: récupération f.

‡**recur** [ri'kə:r], v.i. 1. revenir. 2. se renouveler. **re'currence** [-'kar-], s. réapparition f, renouvellement m, retour m. **re'current** [-'kar-], a. périodique; récurrent m. **re'curring**, a. périodique; r. decimal, fraction f décimale périodique.

red [red], a. & s. rouge m; (of hair) roux; to turn r., rougir; to be caught r-handed, être pris en flagrant délit; r. tape, (i) bolduc m (rouge); (ii) F: bureaucratie f. **'redbrick**, a. F: r. university, université f provinciale moderne. **'redden**, v.tr. & i. rougir.

redeem [ri'di:m], v.tr. 1. racheter; amortir (une dette). 2. libérer, racheter (qn). **re'deemer**, s. the R., le Rédempteur. **re'demption**, s. 1. Fin: remboursement m, amortissement m. 2. rédemption f (du genre humain).

redoubtable [ri'dautbl], a. redoutable, formidable.

redress [ri'dres]. I. s. réparation f, redressement m. II. v.tr. 1. rétablir (l'équilibre); redresser, réparer (un tort).

reduce [ri'dju:s], v.tr. 1. réduire; diminuer; to r. speed, ralentir la marche. 2. to r. sth. to ashes, réduire qch. en cendres. 3. to r. s.o. to silence, faire taire qn. **re'duced**, a. réduit; at r. prices, au rabais; en solde; in r. circumstances, dans la gêne. **re'duction**, s. réduction f; diminution f (des prix); Com: to make a r., faire une remise.

redundancy [ri'dʌndənsi], s. 1. surabondance f. 2. surplus m; excédent m; (of workers) surnombre m; r. payments, compensation f pour perte d'emploi faite aux ouvriers en surnombre. **re'dundant**, a. surabondant; superflu; (ouvriers) en surnombre.

re-echo [ri:'(i)ekou], 1. v.tr. répéter, renvoyer (un son). 2. v.i. retentir, résonner.

reed [ri:d], s. roseau m.

re-education ['ri:dju'keiʃ(ə)n], s. Med: rééducation f (physique) (d'un accidenté, etc.).

reef [ri:f], s. récif m.

reek [riːk]. I. *s.* odeur *f* forte, âcre; relent *m.* II. *v.i.* exhaler une mauvaise odeur; to r. of garlic, empester, puer, l'ail.

reel [riːl]. I. *s.* 1. dévidoir *m;* bobine *f.* 2. moulinet *m* (de canne à pêche); *F:* straight off the r., (tout) d'une traite; d'affilée. 3. bande *f* écossaise. II. *v.* 1. *v.tr.* dévider, bobiner (le fil). 2. *v.i.* (*a*) tournoyer; my head's reeling, la tête me tourne; (*b*) chanceler; (*of drunken man*) tituber.

re-elect [riːiˈlekt], *v.tr.* réélire. 're-e'lection, *s.* réélection *f.*

re-eligible [riːˈelidʒibl], *a.* rééligible.

re-embark [riːimˈbɑːk], *v.tr. & i.* rembarquer.

†**refer** [riˈfəːr]. 1. *v.tr.* soumettre (une affaire à qn); renvoyer (qn à qn); the reader is referred to ..., se rapporter à .... 2. se référer (à une autorité); (*of pers.*) faire allusion (à qn, qch.); (*of statement*) to r. to sth., se rapporter, avoir rapport, à qch. refe'ree, *s.* (*F:* ref) *Sp:* arbitre *m.* 'reference, *s.* 1. renvoi *m,* référence *f;* terms of r., mandat *m* (d'une commission, etc.). 2. work of r., ouvrage *m* à consulter; with r. to my letter, me référant à, comme suite à, ma lettre. 3. r. was made (to this), on a fait allusion à cette affaire). 4. renvoi *m* (dans un livre). 5. renseignements *mpl* sur qn); to give s.o. as a r., se recommander de qn.

referendum [refəˈrendəm], *s.* référendum *m.*

refill. I. *s.* ['riːfil] pile *f,* mine *f,* de rechange. II. *v.tr.* ['riːˈfil] remplir (qch.) (à nouveau).

refine [riˈfain], *v.tr.* raffiner; affiner (les métaux). re'fined, *a.* 1. (or) fin, affiné; (sucre) raffiné. 2. (goût) raffiné, délicat; (homme) distingué, cultivé. re'finement, *s.* raffinement *m.* re'fining, *s.* affinage *m* (des métaux); raffinage *m* (du sucre, du pétrole). re'finery, *s.* raffinerie *f.*

reflect [riˈflekt]. I. *v.tr.* réfléchir. refléter. II. *v.i.* méditer; réfléchir. re'flection, *s.* 1. réflexion *f,* reflet *m,* image *f.* 2. to cast reflections on s.o., censurer, critiquer, qn. 3. on r., toute réflexion faite. re'flector, *s.* réflecteur *m; Aut:* catadioptre *m,* cataphote *m* (R.t.m.).

reflex ['riːfleks]. I. *s.* réflexe *m.* II. *a.* 1. (*of movement*) réflexe. 2. *Phot:* r. camera, (appareil *m*) reflex *m.* 3. *Mth:* r. angle, angle *m* rentrant.

reflexive [riˈfleksiv], *a. Gram:* (verbe) réfléchi, pronominal.

reform [riˈfɔːm]. I. *v.tr.* réformer. II. *v.i.* se réformer. II. *s.* réforme *f.* refor'mation, *s.* réforme *f; Ecc:* the R., la Réforme. re'former, *s.* réformateur, -trice.

refrain [riˈfrein]. I. *s.* refrain *m.* II. *v.i.* se retenir, s'abstenir (from, de).

refresh [riˈfreʃ], *v.tr.* rafraîchir. re'freshing, *a.* rafraîchissant. re'fresher, *s.* 1. *F:* let's have a r., on va boire quelque chose. 2. *Sch:* r. course, cours *m* de perfectionnement. re'freshment, *s.* rafraîchissement *m; Rail:* r. room, buffet *m.*

refrigerator [riˈfridʒəreitər], *s.* réfrigérateur *m.*

†**refuel** ['riːˈfjuəl], *v.i. Nau: Av:* se réapprovisionner, se ravitailler, en combustible.

refuge [ˈrefjuːdʒ], *s.* 1. refuge *m,* abri *m* (from, contre); to take r., se réfugier. 2. lieu de refuge, asile *m;* street r., refuge. refu'gee, *s.* réfugié, -iée.

refund. I. *v.tr.* [riˈfʌnd] rembourser (de l'argent). II. *s.* ['riːfʌnd] remboursement *m.*

refuse. I. ['refjuːs], *s.* rebut *m;* déchets *mpl;* r. dump, la décharge publique.

refuse [riˈfjuːz], *v.tr.* 1. refuser. 2. rejeter, repousser (une requête). re'fusal, *s.* refus *m.*

refute [riˈfjuːt], *v.tr.* réfuter.

regain [riˈgein], *v.tr.* regagner; recouvrer (la liberté).

regal [ˈriːg(ə)l], *a.* royal.

regale [riˈgeil], *v.tr.* régaler.

regard [riˈgɑːd]. I. *s.* 1. with r. to, quant à. 2. égard *m:* attention *f;* to have no r. for human life, faire peu de cas de la vie humaine. 3. (*a*) respect *m;* estime *m;* (*b*) with kind regards from ..., avec les sincères amitiés de .... II. *v.tr.* regarder, considérer (qch.); to r. sth. with suspicion, avoir des soupçons au sujet de qch. re'gardless, *a.* r. of, peu soigneux of, de); inattentif (of, à); r. of expense, sans regarder à la dépense.

regatta [riˈgætə], *s.* régate *f.*

†**regency** [ˈriːdʒənsi], *s.* régence *f.* 'regent, *s.* régent, -ente.

regeneration [ridʒenəˈreiʃ(ə)n], *s.* régénération *f.*

regime [reiˈʒiːm], *s.* régime *m.*

regiment [ˈredʒimənt], *s.* régiment *m.* regi'mental. 1. *a.* du régiment, régimentaire. 2. *s.pl.* uniforme *m.*

region [ˈriːdʒ(ə)n], *s.* région *f.*

register [ˈredʒistər]. I. *s.* registre *m.* II. *v.* 1. *v.tr.* enregistrer; inscrire (un nom); déclarer (une naissance); recommander (une lettre); *Fig:* it didn't r. (with her), elle n'a rien pigé. 2. *v.i.* s'inscrire sur le registre (d'un hôtel, etc.). 'registered, *a.* (paquet) recommandé; state r. nurse, infirmière *f* diplômée d'État. regis'trar, *s.* 1. *Jur:* greffier *m.* 2. officier *m* de l'état civil. 3. secrétaire *m* et archiviste *m* (d'une université). regis'tration, *s.* enregistrement *m;* recommandation *f* (d'une lettre); r. number,

numéro *m* matricule, minéralogique.
'registry, *s. r.* (office), (i) bureau *m* de l'état civil; to get married at a r. office = se marier civilement; (ii) bureau, agence *f*, de placement (de domestiques).

regret [ri'gret]. I. *s.* regret *m*. II. †*v.tr.* regretter. re'gretfully, *adv.* avec regret, à regret. re'grettable, *a.* regrettable; à regretter.

regular ['regjulər]. I. *a.* régulier. 1. as r. as clockwork, exact comme une horloge. 2. réglé, rangé. 3. dans les règles; réglementaire; (verbe) régulier. 4. *F:* vrai, véritable. -ly, *adv.* 1. régulièrement. 2. *F:* véritablement, franchement. II. *s.* 1. *Mil:* militaire *m* de carrière. 2. *F:* habitué, -ée; bon client, bonne cliente. regu'larity, *s.* régularité *f.* 'regularize, *v.tr.* régulariser. 'regulate, *v.tr.* régler. regu'lation, *s.* 1. réglage *m* (d'une machine). 2. (*a*) règlement, arrêté *m*; (*b*) *attrib.* réglementaire, *s.* régulateur *m.*

rehabilitation [ri:həbili'teiʃ(ə)n], *s.* réhabilitation *f*; rééducation *f* (des mutilés); réadaptation *f* (des mutilés).

rehearse [ri'həːs], *v.tr. Th:* répéter (une pièce). re'hearsal, *s. Th:* répétition *f*; the dress r., la répétition générale.

reign [rein]. I. *s.* règne *m*. II. *v.i.* régner.

reimburse [ri:im'bəːs], *v.tr.* rembourser. reim'bursement, *s.* remboursement *m.*

rein [rein], *s.* rêne *f*; guide *f.*

reindeer ['reindiər], *s.* renne *m.*

reinforce [ri:in'fɔːs], *v.tr.* renforcer; consolider (un bâtiment); reinforced concrete, béton *m* armé. reinforcements, *s.pl. Mil:* renfort(s) *m.*

reinstate [ri:in'steit], *v.tr.* 1. réintégrer; rétablir (qn). 2. remettre, rétablir (qch.). rein'statement, *s.* 1. réintégration *f* (de qn). 2. rétablissement *m* (de qch.).

reiterate [ri:'itəreit], *v.tr.* réitérer. reite'ration, *s.* réitération *f.*

reject. I. *v.tr.* rejeter, repousser (qch.); refuser (qch., un candidat). II. *s.* ['ri:dʒekt] pièce *f* de rebut; export r., article impropre, non destiné, à l'exportation.

rejoice [ri'dʒɔis], *v.i.* se réjouir (at, de).

rejoin¹ [ri'dʒɔin], *v.i.* répliquer, répondre.

rejoin², *v.tr.* rejoindre (qn, son régiment).

rejuvenation [ridʒu:vi'neiʃ(ə)n], *s.* rajeunissement *m.*

relapse [ri'læps], *s.* rechute *f.*

relate [ri'leit]. 1. *v.tr.* raconter, conter. 2. *v.i.* se rapporter, avoir rapport (to, à). re'lated, *a.* 1. ayant rapport (to, à). 2. apparenté; parent (to, de); (by marriage) allié (to, à). re'lation, *s.* 1. relation *f*; rapport *m*; in r. to . . ., par rapport à . . .; *Adm: Com:*

public relations, service *m* des relations avec le public. 2. parent, -ente; r. by marriage, allié, -iée. re'lationship, *s.* 1. rapport *m*. 2. parenté *f.*

relative ['relativ]. I. *a.* relatif; r. pronoun, pronom relatif. 2. *s.* parent, -ente. -ly, *adv.* relativement.

relax [ri'læks]. 1. *v.tr.* relâcher; détendre. 2. *v.i.* se relâcher; se détendre. relax'ation, *s.* 1. relâchement *m* (de la discipline). 2. délassement *m*, repos *m*, relaxation *f.* re'laxing, *a.* (climat) énervant, débilitant; (séjour) décontractant, relaxant.

relay. 1. *v.tr.* [ri'lei] relayer; transmettre (un message). II. *s.* ['ri:lei]. 1. relais *m*; relève *f*; *Sp:* race, course *f* à, de, relais. 2. *Rad:* radio-diffusion *f* relayée.

release [ri'li:s]. I. *s.* 1. (*a*) délivrance *f*; libération *f*; (*b*) mise *f* en liberté. 2. lâchage *m* (d'une bombe); échappement *m* (de la vapeur); lancement *m* (d'un parachute), dégagement *m* (d'un frein). II. *v.tr.* 1. libérer; mettre en vente (un produit). 2. lâcher (une bombe); lancer (un parachute); desserrer (le frein); to r. one's hold, lâcher prise.

relegate ['religeit], *v.tr.* reléguer.

relent [ri'lent], *v.i.* se laisser attendrir re'lentless, *a.* implacable, impitoyable. -ly, *adv.* implacablement, impitoyablement. re'lentlessness, *s.* inflexibilité *f*, implacabilité *f.*

relevant ['relivənt], *a.* pertinent; à propos. 'relevance, *s.* pertinence *f*; à-propos *m.*

reliable [ri'laiəbl], *a.* sûr; sérieux; (machine) d'un fonctionnement sûr. relia'bility, *s.* sûreté *f*; honnêteté *f*; sécurité *f* du fonctionnement; régularité *f* de marche (d'une machine).

reliance [ri'laiəns], *s.* confiance *f.* re'liant, *a.* confiant; qui dépend (de qn pour qch.).

relic ['relik], *s.* 1. relique *f.* 2. *pl.* restes *m*; relics of the past, vestiges *m* du passé.

relief¹ [ri'li:f], *s.* 1. soulagement *m*; allégement *m.* 2. secours *m*. 3. réparation *f* (d'un grief). re'lieve, *v.tr.* 1. soulager, alléger; tranquilliser (l'esprit de qn); dissiper (l'ennui). 2. dégager (qn d'une obligation). 3. *Mil:* dégager, débloquer (une ville).

relief², *s.* relief *m*; to stand out in r., ressortir, se détacher.

religion [ri'lidʒən], *s.* religion *f*; culte *m.* re'ligious, *a.* religieux; pieux. -ly, *adv.* religieusement; scrupuleusement.

relinquish [ri'liŋkwiʃ], *v.tr.* abandonner; renoncer à (un projet).

†reliquary ['relikwəri], *s.* reliquaire *m.*

relish ['reliʃ]. I. *s.* (*a*) goût *m*, saveur *f*; (*b*) assaisonnement *m.* II. *v.tr.* goûter, savourer.

reluctance [ri'lʌktəns], s. répugnance f (à faire qch.); with r., à regret, à contre-cœur. **re'luctant**, a. (a) peu disposé (à faire qch.); (b) (consentement) donné à contre-cœur. **-ly**, adv. à contre-cœur.

rely [ri'lai], v.i. compter (sur qn, qch.); se fier (à qn).

remain [ri'mein], v.i. rester; it remains to be seen whether . . ., reste à savoir si . . .; to r. behind, rester; ne pas partir; the weather remains fine, le temps se maintient au beau; (in letter) I remain, your truly, agréez, Monsieur, mes salutations distinguées. **re'mainder**, s. 1. reste m, restant m. 2. coll. the r., les autres; Com: remainders, (i) invendus m soldés, (ii) (of books) solde m d'édition. II. v.tr. Com: solder (une édition). **re'mains**, s.pl. restes mpl; vestiges mpl.

remark [ri'ma:k]. I. s. remarque f, observation f. II. v. 1. v.tr. remarquer, observer. 2. v.i. faire une remarque. **re'markable**, a. remarquable. **-ably**, adv. remarquablement.

†remedy ['remidi], s. remède m.

remember [ri'membər], v.tr. 1. (a) se souvenir de (qch.); se rappeler (qch.); as far as I r., autant qu'il m'en souvient; (b) that's worth remembering, cela est à noter. 2. r. me to them, rappelez-moi à leur bon souvenir. **re'membrance**, s. souvenir m; mémoire f; in r. of s.o., en souvenir de qn.

remind [ri'maind], v.tr. to r. s.o. of sth., rappeler qch. à qn; that reminds me! à propos! **re'minder**, s. mémento m; Com: rappel m de compte, d'échéance; I'll send him a r., je vais lui rafraîchir la mémoire.

reminiscence [remi'nis(ə)ns], s. 1. réminiscence f. 2. pl. souvenirs m. **remi'nisce**, v.i. F: raconter ses souvenirs. **remi'niscent**, a. qui se souvient; r. of sth., qui rappelle qch.

remiss [ri'mis], a. négligent, insouciant. **re'mission**, s. 1. pardon m, rémission f (des péchés). 2. remise f (d'une peine, d'une dette).

‡remit [ri'mit], v.tr. Com: remettre, envoyer (de l'argent à qn); abs. kindly r., prière de nous couvrir. **re'mittance**, s. remise f (d'argent); envoi m de fonds.

remnant ['remnənt], s. 1. reste m, restant m. 2. r. sale, solde m de coupons.

remonstrate ['remənstreit], v.i. faire des remontrances (with s.o.); protester.

remorse [ri'mɔ:s], s. remords m; without r., sans aucune componction. **re'morseful**, a. plein de remords; repentant. **re'morseless**, a. sans remords; impitoyable.

remote [ri'mout], a. 1. lointain; éloigné, écarté; in a r. future, dans un avenir lointain; r. **control**, télécommande f. 2. a r. resemblance, une vague ressemblance; I haven't the remotest idea, je n'ai pas la moindre idée.

remove [ri'mu:v], v.tr. enlever, effacer (une tache), écarter (un obstacle); supprimer (un abus); enlever, retirer (son chapeau, etc.). **re'moval**, s. 1. enlèvement m (d'une tache, etc.); suppression f (d'un abus). 2. déménagement m. **re'mover**, s. 1. (furniture) r., déménageur m. 2. (varnish, paint) r., décapant m (pour vernis, pour peinture); make-up r., démaquillant m; superfluous hair r., pâte f dépilatoire; nail-varnish r., dissolvant m (pour ongles).

remunerate [ri'mju:nəreit], v.tr. rémunérer. **remune'ration**, s. rémunération f. **re'munerative**, a. (travail, etc.) rémunérateur.

renaissance [rə'neis(ə)ns], s. renaissance f.

render ['rendər], v.tr. rendre.

rendezvous ['rɒndivu:]. I. s. rendez-vous m. II. ‡v.i. F: se rencontrer.

renew [ri'nju:], v.tr. (a) renouveler; (b) to r. acquaintance, renouer connaissance. **re'newal**, s. renouvellement m.

renounce [ri'nauns], v.tr. renoncer à, abandonner. **re'nouncement**, s. renoncement m.

renovate ['renəveit], v.tr. remettre à neuf. **reno'vation**, s. rénovation f.

renown [ri'naun], s. renommée f, renom m.

rent[1] [rent], s. déchirure f, accroc m.

rent[2]. I. s. loyer m; location f. II. v.tr. louer (une maison). **rental**, s. 1. loyer m; valeur f locative (d'une maison). 2. fixed r., redevances fpl d'abonnement (d'un téléphone).

renunciation [rinʌnsi'eiʃ(ə)n], s. renoncement m, renonciation f.

reopen ['ri:'oup(ə)n], v.tr. & i. rouvrir; reprendre (les hostilités).

reorganize ['ri:'ɔ:gənaiz], 1. v.tr. réorganiser. 2. v.i. se réorganiser. **reorgani'zation**, s. réorganisation f.

repair [ri'pɛər]. I. s. 1. réparation f. 2. in good r., en bon état; in poor r., mal entretenu. II. v.tr. réparer, remettre en état; raccommoder (un vêtement). **re'pairer**, s. réparateur, -trice f; shoe r., cordonnier m.

repartee [repɑ:'ti:], s. repartie f.

repatriate [ri:'pætrieit], v.tr. rapatrier.

repay [ri:'pei], v.tr. 1. rendre (de l'argent). 2. rembourser (qn); récompenser (qn). **re'payment**, s. 1. remboursement m. 2. récompense f (d'un service).

repeal [ri'pi:l]. I. s. abrogation f (d'une loi), révocation f (d'un décret). II. v.tr. abroger, annuler (une loi); révoquer (un décret).

repeat [ri'pi:t], v.tr. (a) répéter; réitérer; (b) renouveler (une commande). re'peated, a. répété, réitéré, redoublé. -ly, adv. à plusieurs reprises.

‡repel [ri'pel], v.tr. repousser (qn); répugner à (qn). re'pellent. 1. a. répulsif; répugnant, repoussant. 2. s. insect r., insectifuge m.

repent [ri'pent], v.i. se repentir. re'pentance, s. repentir m. re'pentant, a. repentant, repenti.

repercussion [ri:pə'kʌʃ(ə)n], s. répercussion f.

repertoire ['repətwɑːr], s. répertoire m.

repetition [repi'tiʃ(ə)n], s. répétition f.

†repertory ['repət(ə)ri], s. Th: r. theatre, company, théâtre m, troupe f. de province.

replace [ri'pleis], v.tr. 1. replacer; remettre en place. 2. remplacer. re'placement, s. (a) remplacement m, substitution f; (b) (pers.) remplaçant, -ante; (c) Ind: pl. pièces f de rechange.

replenish [ri'pleniʃ], v.tr. remplir (with, de).

replica ['replikə], s. réplique f, double m.

reply [ri'plai]. I. †s. réponse f. II. v.i. & tr. répondre, répliquer.

repoint [ri'point], v.tr. rejointoyer (un mur).

report [ri'pɔːt]. I. s. 1. (a) rapport m; compte rendu; (b) weather r., bulletin m météorologique. 2. bruit m qui court; rumeur f. 3. détonation f; coup m. II. v.tr. rapporter (un fait); rendre compte de (qch.); (of journalist) faire le reportage de (qch.); to r. an accident to the police, signaler un accident à la police; Mil: reported missing, porté manquant. re'porter, s. journaliste mf, reporter m. re'porting, s. reportage m; comptes mpl rendus.

repose [ri'pouz]. I. s. repos m. II. v.i. (se) reposer.

reprehensible [repri'hensəbl], a. répréhensible, blâmable.

represent [repri'zent], v.tr. représenter. represen'tation, s. représentation f; Pol: proportional r., représentation proportionnelle. repre'sentative. I. a. représentatif. II. s. (a) représentant, -ante; (b) U.S: Pol: = député m.

repress [ri'pres], v.tr. réprimer. re'pression, s. répression f.

reprieve [ri'priːv]. I. s. 1. commutation f de la peine capitale. 2. répit m, délai m. II. v.tr. 1. accorder une commutation de la peine capitale. 2. accorder un délai (à qn).

reprimand ['reprimɑːnd]. I. s. réprimande f. II. v.tr. réprimander.

reprint. I. v.tr. [ri'print] réimprimer. II. s. ['riːprint] réimpression f.

reprisals [ri'praiz(ə)lz], s.pl. représailles f.

reproach [ri'proutʃ]. I. s. reproche m, blâme m. II. v.tr. reprocher (qch. à

qn). re'proachful, a. réprobateur; plein de reproche(s). -fully, adv. d'un ton, d'un air, de reproche.

reprobate ['reprəbeit], s. vaurien m.

reproduce [ri:prə'djuːs], v.tr. reproduire. repro'duction, s. reproduction f; copie f, imitation f.

reproof [ri'pruːf], s. reproche m; réprimande f.

reptile ['reptail], s. reptile m.

republic [ri'pʌblik], s. république f. re'publican, a. & s. républicain, -aine.

repudiate [ri'pjuːdieit], v.tr. répudier.

repugnance [ri'pʌgnəns], s. répugnance f, antipathie f. re'pugnant, a. répugnant.

repulse [ri'pʌls], v.tr. repousser (un ennemi, etc.). re'pulsive, a. répulsif; repoussant.

repute [ri'pjuːt], s. réputation f, renom m. 'reputable, a. honorable; estimé. repu'tation, s. réputation f; renom m. re'puted, a. réputé, censé, supposé; a r. Hogarth, un tableau attribué à Hogarth.

request [ri'kwest]. I. s. 1. demande f; requête f; samples sent on r., échantillons sur demande; P.N: r. stop, arrêt facultatif; Rad: r. programme, programme m des auditeurs. II. v.tr. demander (qch. à qn, à qn de faire qch.); Com: as requested, conformément à vos instructions.

requiem ['rekwiem], s. requiem m.

require [ri'kwaiər], v.tr. 1. demander; exiger, réclamer; work which requires patience, travail qui nécessite de la patience; have you everything you r.? avez-vous tout ce qu'il vous faut? you won't r. a coat, vous n'aurez pas besoin d'un manteau. re'quired, a. exigé, demandé; in the r. time, dans le délai prescrit. re'quirement, s. 1. demande f. 2. besoin m; exigence f.

requisite ['rekwizit]. 1. a. requis (to, pour); nécessaire. 2. s. (a) condition requise; (b) chose f nécessaire; accessoire m.

requisition [rekwi'ziʃ(ə)n]. I. s. demande f; Mil: réquisition f. II. v.tr. réquisitionner.

reredos ['riərədos], s. retable m.

rescind [ri'sind], v.tr. Jur: Adm: rescinder; annuler.

rescue ['reskjuː]. I. s. délivrance f; sauvetage m. II. v.tr. sauver, délivrer, secourir. 'rescuer, s. libérateur, -trice; sauveteur m.

research [ri'səːtʃ], s. recherche f; Ind: r. department, service m de recherches.

resemble [ri'zembl], v.tr. ressembler à (qn, qch.). re'semblance, s. ressemblance f.

resent [ri'zent], v.tr. 1. être offensé de (qch.). 2. s'offenser de (qch.); ressentir (une critique). re'sentful, a. 1. plein de ressentiment. 2. froissé, irrité. -**fully**, *adv.* avec ressentiment; d'un ton, d'un air, froissé. **re'sent-ment**, *s.* ressentiment *m.*

reserve [ri'zə:v]. I. *v.tr.* réserver; retenir (une place). II. *s.* réserve *f.* **reser'vation**, *s.* réserve *f.*; *Rail:* seat r., location *f* des places; to accept sth. without r., accepter qch. (i) sans réserve, (ii) sans arrière-pensée. **re'served**, *a.* (*a*) r. seats, places réservées; (*b*) (homme) réservé, renfermé, peu communicatif.

reservoir ['rezəvwɑ:r], *s.* réservoir *m.*

reside [ri'zaid], *v.i.* résider. **'residence**, *s.* résidence *f*, demeure *f*; *Com:* desirable r. for sale, belle propriété à vendre. **'resident.** I. *a.* qui réside; *Sch:* r. master = maître *m* d'internat. II. *s.* habitant, -ante; (*in hotel, etc.*) pensionnaire *mf.* **resi'dential**, *a.* (quartier) résidentiel.

residue ['rezidju], *s.* résidu *m*; reste *m.* **re'siduary**, *a.* résiduaire, résiduel; qui reste; *Jur:* (légataire) universel.

resign [ri'zain], *v.tr.* résigner; *abs.* démissionner; to r. oneself to doing sth., se résigner à faire qch. **resig'nation**, *s.* 1. démission *f* (d'un emploi). 2. résignation *f*, soumission *f* (à qch.). **re'signed**, *a.* résigné (à qch.).

resilient [ri'ziliənt], *a.* rebondissant, élastique.

resin ['rezin], *s.* 1. résine *f.* 2. colophane *f.* 'resinous, *a.* résineux.

resist [ri'zist], *v.tr.* résister à (qch.); repousser (une suggestion). **re'sis-tance**, *s.* résistance *f.*

resolute ['rezəlut], *a.* résolu, déterminé. **reso'lution** [-lu:ʃ(ə)n], *s.* résolution *f.* **resolve** [ri'zɔlv], *v.tr. & i.* (*a*) résoudre.

resonant ['rezənənt], *a.* résonnant.

resort [ri'zɔ:t]. I. *s.* 1. (*a*) ressource *f*; (*b*) recours *m.* 2. lieu *m* de séjour, de rendez-vous; seaside r., station *f* balnéaire; plage *f.* II. *v.i.* avoir recours à (la force, etc.).

resound [ri'zaund], *v.i.* résonner; retentir.

resource [ri'sɔ:s], *s.* ressource *f.* **re-'sourceful**, *a.* fertile en ressources, *F:* débrouillard.

respect [ri'spekt]. I. *s.* 1. rapport *m*, égard *m*; in many respects, à bien des égards. 2. respect *m*; estime *f.* II. *v.tr.* respecter. **respecta'bility**, *s.* respectabilité *f.* **re'spectable**, *a.* respectable; honorable. **-ably**, *adv.* 1. (vêtu) convenablement. 2. pas mal, passablement. **re'spectful**, *a.* respectueux. **-fully**, *adv.* avec respect. **re'spective**, *a.* respectif. **-ly**, *adv.* respectivement.

respiration [respə'reiʃ(ə)n], *s.* respiration *f.*

respite ['respait], *s.* répit *m*, relâche *m.*

respond [ri'spɔnd], *v.i.* répondre. **res'ponse**, *s.* réponse *f*; *Ecc:* répons *m.*

responsi'bility, *s.* responsabilité *f.* **res'ponsible**, *a.* 1. responsable. 2. capable, compétent. **res'ponsive**, *a.* impressionnable; sensible; *Aut:* (moteur) nerveux.

rest¹ [rest]. I. *s.* 1. repos *m*; to take a r., se reposer; to come to r., s'arrêter, s'immobiliser. 2. *Mus:* pause *f*, silence *m.* 3. support *m.* II. *v.* 1. *v.i.* (*a*) se reposer; (*b*) there the matter rests, les choses en sont là. 2. *v.tr.* appuyer (qch. sur qch.); déposer (qch.) quelque part). **'restful**, *a.* paisible, tranquille; reposant. **'rest-ing**, *a.* au repos; (*of actor*) en chômage. **'restless**, *a.* agité. **'restless-ness**, *s.* agitation *f*; nervosité *f.*

rest², *s.* 1. reste *m*, restant *m.* 2. the r., les autres *mpl.*

restaurant ['rest(ə)rɔŋ], *s.* restaurant *m*; *Rail:* r. car, wagon-restaurant *m.*

restitution [resti'tju:ʃ(ə)n], *s.* restitution *f.*

restive ['restiv], *a.* rétif.

restore [ri'stɔ:r], *v.tr.* 1. restituer, rendre. 2. restaurer (un bâtiment); réparer (un tableau). 3. rétablir (l'ordre). **resto'ration**, *s.* restauration *f.*

restrain [ri'strein], *v.tr.* retenir, empêcher (qn de faire qch.); retenir (sa curiosité). **res'traint**, *s.* contrainte *f*, frein *m.*

restrict [ri'strikt], *v.tr.* restreindre; limiter (le pouvoir de qn). **res'tric-tion**, *s.* restriction *f.* **res'trictive**, *a.* restrictif.

result [ri'zʌlt]. I. *s.* résultat *m.* II. *v.i.* résulter, provenir (from, de); aboutir (à une découverte, etc.).

resume [ri'zju:m], *v.tr.* reprendre. **re-'sumption**, *s.* reprise *f* (de négociations, etc.).

resumé [re'zju:mei], *s.* résumé *m.*

resurface [ri'sə:fis], 1. *v.tr.* refaire le revêtement (d'une route). 2. *v.i.* (*of submarine, etc.*) faire surface.

resurrection [rezə'rekʃ(ə)n], *s.* résurrection *f.*

resuscitate [ri'sasiteit], *v.tr. & i.* ressusciter. **resusci'tation**, *s.* résuscitation *f.*

retail ['ri:teil]. I. *s.* détail *m*; vente *f* au détail. II. *v.tr.* détailler; vendre au détail. **'retailer**, *s.* détaillant *m*, marchand *m* au détail.

retain [ri'tein], *v.tr.* 1. retenir. 2. conserver, garder. **re'tainer**, *s. Com:* arrhes *fpl*; *Jur:* avance *f.*

retaliate [ri'tælieit], *v.i.* rendre la pareille (à qn); user de représailles (envers qn). **retali'ation**, *s.* revanche *f*, représailles *fpl.*

retention [ri'tenʃ(ə)n], *s.* rétention *f*; conservation *f* (d'un usage). **re'ten-tive**, *a.* (mémoire) tenace, fidèle.

reticence ['retis(ə)ns], *s.* réticence *f.* **'reticent**, *a.* réticent, peu communi-catif.

retinue ['retinju:], s. suite f (d'un prince, etc.).

retire [ri'taiər], v.i. se retirer; to r. (on a pension), prendre sa retraite. re'tired, a. (of place) retiré; (of pers.) en retraite. re'tirement, s. la retraite f. re'tiring, a. (of pers.) réservé.

retort [ri'tɔːt]. I. s. réplique f, riposte f. II. v.tr. répliquer; riposter.

retrace [ri'treis], v.tr. to r. one's steps, revenir sur ses pas.

retract [ri'trækt], v.tr. rétracter; abs. se rétracter; se dédire. re'tractable, a. Av: r. undercarriage, train d'atterrissage escamotable.

retread. I. v.tr. ['ri:'tred] Aut: rechaper (un pneu). II. s. F: ['ri:tred] pneu m rechapé.

retreat [ri'tri:t]. I. s. retraite f. II. v.i. se retirer; Mil: battre en retraite.

retribution [retri'bju:ʃ(ə)n], s. châtiment m; jugement.

retrieve [ri'triːv], v.tr. (of dog) rapporter (le gibier); recouvrer (des biens); retrouver (un objet perdu). re'triever, s. (dog) retriever m.

retrograde ['retrogreid], a. rétrograde.

retrospect ['retrouspekt], s. coup d'œil m rétrospectif. retro'spective, a. rétrospectif, (loi) avec effect rétroactif.

return [ri'tə:n]. I. s. 1. retour m; r. (ticket), (billet m d') aller et retour m. 2. Com: profit m; pl. recettes f. 3. renvoi m (de marchandises achetées, etc.); restitution f (d'un objet volé, etc.); Com: pl. returns, rendus m. 4. in r. for . . ., en retour, en récompense, de . . .; Sp: r. match, match retour. 5. income tax r., déclaration f de revenu. II. v. 1. v.i. revenir; retourner; to r. home, rentrer. 2. v.tr. rendre (un objet emprunté); restituer (un objet volé); rembourser (un emprunt); Pol: élire (un député).

reunion [ri:'ju:njən], s. réunion f, assemblée f.

rev[1] [rev]. I. s. F: Aut: 4,000 revs a minute, 4.000 tours m à la minute. II. v.tr. F: Aut: to r. up (the engine), faire emballer le moteur.

Rev.[2], a. Ecc: (as title) le révérend.

reveal [ri'viːl], v.tr. révéler, découvrir; dévoiler (un mystère). reve'lation, s. révélation f.

reveille [ri'veli], s. Mil: le réveil, la diane.

‡**revel** ['revl], v.i. se délecter (in, à). 'revelry, s. divertissements mpl; orgie f.

revenge [ri'vendʒ], s. vengeance f; revanche f; in r., pour se venger.

revenue ['revinju:], s. revenu m, rentes fpl.

reverberate [ri'və:b(ə)reit], v.i. retentir, résonner. reverbe'ration, s. renvoi m, répercussion f (d'un son).

revere [ri'viər], v.tr. révérer, vénérer. 'reverence, s. révérence f, vénération f. 'reverend, a. Ecc: (as title) le révérend; the R. Mother Superior, la révérende mère supérieure. 'reverent, a. respectueux. -ly, adv. avec respect.

reverie ['revəri], s. rêverie f.

reverse [ri'və:s]. I. a. inverse, contraire. II. s. 1. inverse m, contraire m; Aut: marche f arrière. 2. revers m (d'une médaille; de fortune). III. v.tr. renverser; abs. Aut: faire marche arrière. re'versible, a. (drap) à deux endroits; (vêtement) à double face.

revert [ri'vəːt], v.i. revenir, retourner (to, à). re'version, s. retour m; réversion f.

review [ri'vjuː]. I. s. Mil: 1. revue f. 2. examen m; critique f (d'un livre). 3. revue (périodique). II. v.tr. réviser (un procédé); passer (les troupes) en revue; faire la critique (d'un livre). re'viewer, s. critique m (littéraire).

revise [ri'vaiz], v.tr. revoir, relire; corriger, réviser. re'vision, s. révision f.

revive [ri'vaiv], v.i. (of courage) se ranimer; (of feelings) renaître; (of trade, customs) reprendre; (of arts) renaître. re'vival, s. renaissance f (des arts); reprise f (des affaires); religious r., renouveau m religieux.

revocation [revə'keiʃ(ə)n], s. révocation f.

revoke [ri'vouk]. 1. v.tr. révoquer (un ordre, etc.). 2. v.i. (at cards) faire une fausse renonce.

revolt [ri'voult]. I. s. révolte f. II. v.i. se révolter, se soulever. re'volting, a. F: révoltant, dégoûtant.

revolution [revə'lu:ʃ(ə)n], s. révolution f; rotation f (autour d'un axe); Aut: r. counter, compte-tours m. revo'lutionary, a. & s. révolutionnaire m.

revolve [ri'volvər], v.i. tourner, pivoter.

revolver [ri'volvər], s. revolver m.

revue [ri'vju:], s. revue f.

revulsion [ri'valʃ(ə)n], s. révulsion f; F: écœurement m.

reward [ri'wɔ:d]. I. s. récompense f. II. v.tr. récompenser (for, de).

†**rhapsody** ['ræpsədi], s. rhapsodie f.

rhesus ['ri:səs], attrib. a. Med: r. factor, facteur m rhésus (du sang).

rhetoric ['retərik], s. rhétorique f. rhe'torical, a. (question) pour la forme.

rheumatism ['ru:mətizm], s. rhumatisme m. rheu'matic, a. rhumatismal.

rhinoceros [rai'nɔsərəs], s. rhinocéros m.

rhubarb ['ru:bɑːb], s. rhubarbe f.

rhyme [raim]. I. s. rime f; in r., en vers. II. v.i. rimer.

rhythm ['riθ(ə)m], s. rythme m, cadence f. 'rhythmic, a. rythmique, cadencé.

rib [rib], s. Anat: côte f.

ribald ['ribəld], *a.* licencieux, impudique.

ribbon ['ribən], *s.* ruban *m.*

rice [rais], *s.* riz *m; Cu:* r. pudding = gâteau *m* de riz.

rich [ritʃ], *a.* riche; (*of soil*) fertile. -ly, *adv.* richement; *F:* he r. deserves it, il l'a joliment bien mérité. '**riches**, *s.pl.* richesse(s)*f*(*pl*). '**richness**, *s.* richesse *f.*

rick [rik], *s.* meule *f* (de foin).

rickets ['rikits], *s.pl.* rachitisme *m.*

rickety ['rikiti], *a. F:* branlant; délabré.

‡**rid** [rid], *v.tr.* to get rid of, se débarrasser de (qn, qch.).

riddance ['rid(ə)ns], *s.* débarras *m.*

riddle¹ ['ridl], *s.* énigme *f*, devinette *f.*

riddle², *v.tr.* cribler (qn, qch., de balles).

ride [raid]. I. *s.* promenade *f* (à cheval); promenade, voyage *m* (en auto); to r. away, partir (à cheval); *F:* to take s.o. for a r., (i) assassiner qn; (ii) faire marcher, duper, qn. II. ‡*v.* 1. *v.i.* se promener, monter, à cheval; *Nau:* to r. at anchor, être mouillé. 2. *v.tr.* to r. a horse, monter à cheval; to r. an idea to death, être féru d'une idée. 'rider, *s.* 1. cavalier, -ière; (*horse-racing*) jockey *m.* 2. annexe *f* (d'un document). 'riding, *s.* équitation *f;* r. habit, amazone *f;* r. breeches culotte *f* de cheval; r. school, école *f* d'équitation; manège *m.* ride 'up, *v.tr.* (*of garment*) remonter.

ridge [ridʒ], *s.* crête *f* (d'une chaîne de montagnes, d'un comble); strie *f* (sur une surface); ride *f* (sur le sable).

ridicule ['ridikju:l]. I. *s.* moquerie *f*, raillerie *f*, dérision *f.* II. *v.tr.* se moquer de, ridiculiser (qn, qch.). ri'**diculous**, *a.* ridicule. -ly, *adv.* d'une façon ridicule.

rifle¹ ['raifl], *v.tr.* piller.

rifle², *s.* fusil *m.*

rift [rift], *s.* fente *f;* fissure *f.*

rig [rig], *s.* tour *f* de forage, derrick *m.* 'rigging, *s* gréement *m* (d'un navire). ‡**rig 'up**, *v.tr. F:* monter, installer (un appareil).

right [rait]. I. *a.* 1. bon, honnête, droit; it's only r., il n'est que juste, 2. correct, juste, exact; to put sth. r., corriger, rectifier, qch.; to be r., avoir raison; the r. thing to do, ce qu'il y a de mieux à faire; that's r.! c'est bien cela! r.! bon! d'accord! he's on the r. side of forty, il n'a pas encore quarante ans. 3. to be in one's r. mind, avoir toute sa raison; to set things r., rétablir les choses; all r., très bien. 4. (côté droit. -ly, *adv.* correctement; r. or wrongly, à tort ou à raison. II. *s.* 1. le droit; le bien; to be in the r., avoir raison. 2. droit, titre *m; by rights,* en toute justice; within one's rights, dans son droit. 3 droite *f;* côté *m* droit; on the r., à droite. III. *adv.* 1. (a) droit; to go r. on, continuer tout droit; (b)

r. away, sur-le-champ. 2. r. at the top, tout en haut; r. in the middle, au beau milieu. 3. to do r., bien faire; if I remember r., si je me souviens bien. 4. à droite; he owes money r. and left, il doit de l'argent de tous les côtés. IV. *v.tr.* redresser, réparer (un tort). '**right-angled**, *a.* à angle droit. '**righteous**, *a.* juste, vertueux. '**righteousness**, *s.* droiture *f*, vertu *f.* '**rightful**, *a.* légitime. '**right-hand**, *s.* à droite. '**right-handed**, *a.* (*of pers.*) droitier; (*of blow*) du droit.

rigid ['ridʒid], *a.* rigide, raide. -ly, *adv.* rigidement. ri'**gidity**, *s.* rigidité *f.*

rigour ['rigər], *s.* rigueur *f*, sévérité *f.* '**rigorous**, *a.* rigoureux. -ly, *adv.* rigoureusement.

rim [rim], *s.* 1. jante *f* (d'une roue). 2. bord *m* (d'un vase, etc.).

rind [raind], *s.* peau *f;* pelure *f;* couenne *f* (de lard).

ring¹ [riŋ], *s.* 1. anneau *m;* bague *f.* 2. rond *m*, anneau (de métal, etc.); segment *m* (de piston). 3. *Com:* syndicat *m*, cartel *m.* 4. arène *f*, piste *f* (de cirque); ring *m* (de boxe). 5. r. road, route *f* de ceinture (autour d'une ville). '**ringleader**, *s.* meneur *m* de révolte; chef *m* d'émeute. '**ringlet**, *s.* boucle *f* (de cheveux).

ring², I. *s.* 1. sonnerie *f;* tintement *m* (de cloches). 2. (a) coup *m* de sonnette; (b) appel *m* téléphonique; I'll give you a r., je vous téléphonerai. II. ‡*v.* 1. *v.i.* (*of bell*) sonner. 2. *v.tr.* sonner (une cloche, *abs.* à la porte); *abs.* to r. for the lift, appeler l'ascenseur. 'ringing, *a.* (son) sonore, retentissant. ring 'off, *v.tr. P.T.T:* abs. raccrocher (l'appareil). ring 'up, *v.tr.* donner un coup de téléphone à (qn).

rinse [rins]. I. *v.tr.* rincer. II. *s.* (*for hair*) rinçage *m* (de couleur).

riot ['raiət]. I. *s.* 1. émeute *f.* 2. orgie *f* (de couleurs). 3. (a) to run r., se déchaîner; (*of plants*) pulluler; (*b) F:* it's, he's, a r., c'est rigolo; c'est un rigolo. II. *v.i.* s'ameuter; bagarrer. '**rioter**, *s.* émeutier *m*, séditieux, -euse. '**riotous**, *a.* séditieux; tumultueux; turbulent.

‡**rip** [rip], *v.tr.* fendre; déchirer. rip 'off, *v.tr.* arracher.

ripe [raip], *a.* mûr. 'ripen, *v.tr.* & *i.* mûrir.

ripple ['ripl], *s.* ride *f* (sur l'eau); ondulation *f.*

rise [raiz]. I. *v.i.* (*of pers., sun, wind*) se lever; (*of pers.*) se mettre debout; (*of ground, smoke*) monter, s'élever; (*of prices*) être à la hausse; (*of river*) prendre sa source; to r. to the occasion, se montrer à la hauteur de la situation. II. *s.* montée *f*, côté *f* (sur une route); élévation *f* (de température); augmentation *f*, hausse *f* (de prix); to give r. to sth., faire naître, occasionner, qch.; the r. of Napoleon, l'essor *m* de Napoléon; F: to get a r. out of s.o., se payer la tête de qn. 'rising, I. *a.* (soleil) levant; (route) qui monte; (prix) en hausse; (vent) qui se lève; r. tide, marée *f* montante. II. *s.* ameutement *s*, soulèvement *m*.

risk [risk]. I. *s.* risque *m*, péril *m*. II. *v.tr.* risquer; aventurer. 'risky, *a.* hasardeux, chanceux.

rissole ['risoul], *s. Cu:* croquette *f*.

rite [rait], *s.* rite *m*.

ritual ['ritjuəl]. I. *a.* rituel. 2. *s.* rites *mpl.*

rival ['raiv(ə)l]. I. *a.* & *s.* rival, -ale *f*; concurrent, -ente. II. *v.tr.* rivaliser avec (qn). 'rivalry, *s.* rivalité *f*.

river ['rivər], *s.* fleuve *m*, rivière *f*.

rivet ['rivit]. I. *s.* rivet *m*. II. *v.tr.* river, riveter; fixer (l'attention). 'riveter, *s.* riveteur *m*, riveur *m*.

road [roud], *s.* 1. route *f*, chemin *m*, voie *f*; 'A' r. = route nationale; 'B' r. = route départementale; r. transport, transports routiers; *Com:* to be on the r., (i) F: être représentant; (ii) (of traveller) être en tournée; the r. to success, le chemin du succès. 2. chaussée *f*; (of car) to hold the r. well, bien tenir la route; r. test, essai *m* (de voiture) sur route. 3. *Nau:* roads (also roadstead), rade *f*. †roadman, *s.* cantonnier *m*. 'roadside, *s.* bord *m* de la route. 'roadway, *s.* chaussée *f*. 'roadworthy, *a.* (of car) en état de marche.

roam [roum], *v.i.* errer, rôder.

roar [rɔːr]. I. *s.* hurlement *m*; rugissement *m*; roars of laughter, grands éclats de rire. II. *v.i.* hurler; rugir.

roast [roust]. I. *v.* 1. *v.tr.* (a) rôtir, faire rôtir; (b) griller, torréfier (le café). 2. *v.i.* (of meat) rôtir; (of pers.) griller (au soleil). II. *s. Cu:* rôti *m*. III. *a.* rôti; r. beef, rôti *m* de bœuf; rosbif *m*. 'roasting, *s.* rôtissage *m*, cuisson *f* (de la viande); r. chicken, poulet *m* à rôtir.

†rob [rɔb], *v.tr.* voler; to rob s.o. of sth., voler qch. à qn. 'robbery, *s.* vol *m* (qualifié); F: it's sheer r., c'est de l'escroquerie.

robe [roub], *s.* 1. robe *f* (de cérémonie). 2. bath r., peignoir *m* de bain.

robin ['rɔbin], *s.* rouge-gorge *m*.

robot ['roubɔt], *s.* robot *m*.

robust [rou'bʌst], *a.* robuste, solide.

rock[1] [rɔk], *s.* 1. (a) rocher *m*, roc *m*; F: to be on the rocks, être dans la dèche; (b) roche *f*; volcanic r., roche volcanique. 3. *Cu:* r. cake, petit gâteau aux raisins secs; (Brighton, etc.) r., bâton *m* de sucrerie; whisky on the rocks, whisky avec glaçons. 4. (attrib.) r. drawings, dessins rupestres; r. plant, plante *f* alpine.

'rockery, *s.* jardin *m* de rocaille.

rock[2]. 1. *v.tr.* (a) bercer, balancer; basculer; (b) ébranler. 2. *v.i.* balancer. 'rocking, *a.* oscillant, branlant; r. chair, horse, fauteuil *m*, cheval *m*, à bascule.

rocket ['rɔkit]. I. *s.* fusée *f*; r. launcher, (i) lance-fusée *m*; (ii) rampe *f* de lancement de fusées. II. *v.i.* F: (of prices) monter en flèche.

rod [rɔd], *s.* 1. baguette *f*. 2. verge *f*. 3. r. and line, ligne *f* de pêche. 4. stair r., tringle *f* d'escalier.

rodent ['roud(ə)nt], *s. Z:* rongeur *m*.

roe [rou], *s. Fish:* (a) hard r., œufs *mpl*; (b) soft r., laite *f*, laitance *f*.

rogue [roug], *s.* 1. coquin, -ine; fripon, -onne. 2. malin, -igne; espiègle *mf*.

rôle [roul], *s. Th: etc.* rôle *m*.

roll [roul], *s.* 1. (a) petit pain *m* (de papier, etc.); (b) petit pain *m* 2. rôle *m*, liste *f*; to call the r., faire l'appel. 3. *Nau:* coup *m* de roulis. II. *v.tr.* & *i.* rouler. 'roller, *s.* 1. rouleau *m*. 2. E: cylindre *m*; laminoir *m*. 3. *Nau:* lame *f* de houle. 4. attrib. r. skates, patins *m* à roulettes; r. towel, essuie-mains *m* à rouleau. 'rolling. I. *a.* roulant. II. *s.* 1. roulement *m*; r. pin, rouleau *m* (à pâtisserie); r. mill, laminoir *m*; Rail: r. stock, matériel *m* roulant. 2. *Nau:* roulis *m*. 'roll-on, *s. Cl:* gaine *f* (élastique extensible). 'roll 'over, *v.i.* se retourner (en roulant). roll 'up. 1. *v.tr.* enrouler (une carte); retrousser (ses manches). 2. *v.i.* F: arriver, s'amener.

Roman ['roumən], *a.* & *s.* romain, -aine; R. nose, nez aquilin; R. Catholic, *a.* & *s.* catholique (mf).

romance [ro'mæns], *s.* histoire *f* romanesque; it's quite a r., c'est tout un roman. ro'mantic, *a.* 1. (histoire) romanesque. 2. *Lit:* romantique.

romp [rɔmp], *v.i.* s'ébattre; F: to r. in, home, gagner haut la main.

roof [ruːf], *s.* 1. †*s.* 1. toit *m*, toiture *f*, comble *m*. 2. r. of the mouth, palais *m*. 3. *Aut:* sunshine r., toit ouvrant; r. rack, galerie *f*; r. light, plafonnier *m*. II. *v.tr.* couvrir (une maison).

rook[1] [ruk], *s. Z:* freux *m*.

rook[2], *s.* (chess) tour *f*.

rook[3], *v.tr.* refaire, rouler (qn).

room [ruːm, rum], *s.* 1. place *f*, espace *m*. 2. there is r. for improvement, cela laisse à désirer. 3. (a) pièce *f*; salle *f*; (bed) r., chambre *f*; (b) pl. appartement *m*; furnished rooms to let, chambres garnies à louer. II. *v.i. U.S:* vivre en garni; partager un logement (avec qn). 'roomy, *a.* spacieux; ample.

roost [ruːst], *s.* 1. juchoir *m*, perchoir *m*. II. *v.i.* (of hens) se percher; se jucher. 'rooster, *s. U.S:* coq *m*.

root [ruːt]. I. s. 1. racine f. 2. source f, fondement m. II. v. 1. v.tr. to be rooted to the spot, être cloué sur place. 2. v.i. (a) (of plant) s'enraciner, prendre racine; (b) fouiller. 'rooted, a. (préjugé) enraciné, invétéré.

rope [roup]. I. s. corde f, cordage m; to know the ropes, connaître son affaire. II. v.tr. 1. corder. 2. (of climbers) roped together, en cordée.

rosary ['rouzəri], s. rosaire m; chapelet m.

rose [rouz], s. 1. rose f; r. bush, rosier m. 2. pomme f (d'arrosoir). 'rosebud, s. bouton m de rose. 'rosy, a. (de) rose. 'rosewood, s. palissandre m.

rosemary ['rouzməri], s. romarin m.

rosette [rou'zet], s. cocarde f, rosette f.

rosin ['rozin], s. colophane f.

rostrum ['rostrəm], s. tribune f.

rot [rot]. I. s. 1. pourriture f, carie f. 2. démoralisation f. II. v. (rotted) 1. v.i. (se) pourrir. 2. v.tr. pourrir, faire pourrir. 'rotten, a. pourri; carié. 'rotter, s. F: raté m; sale type m.

rota ['routə], s. tableau m (de service).

rotate [ro'teit]. 1. v.i. tourner. 2. v.tr. faire tourner. 'rotary, a. rotatif, rotatoire; r. dryer, essoreuse f centrifuge; r. (printing) press, rotative f; R. club, Rotary m. ro'tation, s. rotation f; in r., à tour de rôle. 'rotor, s. E: Av: rotor m; Aut: balai m rotatif (du distributeur).

rotund [ro'tʌnd], a. rond, arrondi.

rouge [ruːʒ], s. rouge m; fard m.

rough [rʌf]. I. a. 1. (of surface) rêche, rugueux, rude; (of road) raboteux. 2. grossier, brutal; r. sea, mer agitée; r. crossing, mauvaise traversée; r. play, jeu brutal; F: a r. customer, un sale type. 3. approximatif; r. sketch, esquisse f; Sch: r. work, brouillon m. -ly, adv. 1. rudement; brutalement. 2. grossièrement. 3. approximativement, à peu près; r. speaking, en général. II. s. 1. terrain m accidenté. 2. to take the r. with the smooth, prendre le bénéfice avec les charges. 3. (pers.) voyou m. III. adv. rudement; to play r., jouer brutalement. IV. v.tr. F: to r. it, vivre à la dure. 'rough and 'ready, a. fait à la hâte; (installation) de fortune. 'rough-house, s. F: chahut m, bousculade f. 'roughneck, s. F: U.S: voyou m. 'roughness, s. rudesse f; rugosité f; grossièreté f; brutalité f. 'roughshod, a. to ride r. over s.o., traiter qn sans ménagement.

roulette [ruː'let], s. roulette f.

round [raund]. I. a. rond, circulaire; r.-table conference, table f ronde, réunion f paritaire; r. shoulders, épaules voûtées; in r. figures, en chiffres ronds. II. s. 1. cercle m, rond m; r. of beef, gîte m; r. of toast,

rôtie f. 2. tournée f (d'un médecin, d'un facteur); Mil: (inspection); r. of golf, tournée de golf; to stand a r. (of drinks), payer une tournée (générale); the story went the rounds, l'histoire a passé de bouche en bouche; r. of applause, salve f d'applaudissements. 3. Mus: canon m. III. adv. 1. to go r., tourner; to turn r., se retourner; all the year r., toute l'année. 2. garden with a wall r., jardin avec un mur tout autour. 3. to hand (sth.) r., faire circuler (qch.); there's not enough to go r., il n'y en a pas pour tout le monde. 4. it's a long way r., cela fait un détour; to ask s.o., inviter qn (chez soi). IV. prep. autour de (la table, etc.); to go r. a museum, visiter le musée; to r. an obstacle, contourner un obstacle; F: to go r. the bend, devenir fou. V. v. 1. v.tr. arrondir; contourner (un obstacle); Nau: doubler, franchir (un cap). 2. v.i. s'arrondir; F: to r. on s.o., prendre à qn. 'roundabout, s. 1. chevaux mpl de bois; manège m. 2. Aut: rond-point m. II. a. détourné; indirect; 'rounded, a. arrondi. 'round-'shouldered, a. au dos voûté, bombé. 'round-'up, v.tr. rassembler; rafler (des malfaiteurs).

rouse [rauz], v.tr. 1. (a) réveiller (qn); secouer (qn); inciter (qn à agir); (b) mettre (qn) en colère. 2. soulever (l'indignation); susciter (l'admiration). 'rousing, a. (discours) vibrant; (applaudissements) chaleureux.

rout [raut]. I. s. Mil: déroute f. II. v.tr. mettre (une armée) en déroute.

route [ruːt], s. itinéraire m; route f.

routine [ruː'tiːn], s. routine f.

row¹ [rou], s. rang m, rangée f; ligne f.

row² [rou]. 1. v.i. (a) ramer; nager; to r. a race, faire une course d'aviron; (b) canoter. 2. v.tr. conduire à l'aviron. II. s. to go for a r., faire une promenade en canot. 'rower, s. rameur, -euse. 'rowing, s. canotage m; r. boat, canot m à l'aviron.

row³ [rau], s. 1. tapage m, vacarme m. 2. rixe f, scène f. 3. réprimande f; to get into a r., se faire attraper.

rowdy ['raudi]. 1. a. tapageur, crâne. 2. s. voyou m.

rowlocks ['rɒləks], s.pl. dames f de nage.

royal ['roiəl], a. royal. 'royalist, a. & s. royaliste (mf). 'royalty, s. 1. royauté f. 2. pl. redevance f (due à un inventeur); droits m d'auteur; Ind: (on patent, for use of oil pipeline) royalties fpl.

rub [rʌb]. I. v.tr. frotter. 2. v.i. frotter; se frotter. II. s. frottement m, friction f. 'rub 'down, v.tr. (a) panser; (b) frictionner. 'rubber¹, s. 1. caoutchouc m; (India) r., gomme f. 2. pl.

U.S.: (*overshoes*) caoutchoucs. **rub 'out,** *v.tr.* effacer. **rub 'up,** *v.tr.* astiquer, fourbir.

rubber², *s.* (*at bridge*) robre *m*; the r. game, la belle.

rubbish ['rʌbiʃ], *s.* 1. (*a*) immondices *fpl*, détritus *mpl*; ordures *fpl* (ménagères); (*b*) choses *fpl* sans valeur; (*c*) camelote *f.* 2. bêtises *f.* '**rubbishy,** *a.* sans valeur; de camelote.

rubble ['rʌbl], *s.* 1. blocaille *f.* 2. décombres *mpl.*

ruby ['ruːbi], *s.* rubis *m.*

rucksack ['rʌksæk], *s.* sac *m* à dos.

rudder ['rʌdər], *s. Nau:* gouvernail *m.*

ruddy ['rʌdi], *a.* 1. (*a*) coloré, haut en couleur; (*b*) rougeâtre. 2. *P:* (= bloody) a r. liar, un sacré menteur.

rude [ruːd], *a.* 1. primitif, rude; (*b*) grossier. 2. brusque; *r.* shock, choc violent. 3. impoli; mal élevé. -ly, *adv.* 1. brusquement. 2. impoliment. '**rudeness,** *s.* impolitesse *f.*

rudiment ['ruːdimənt], *s.* rudiment *m.* **rudi'mentary,** *a.* rudimentaire.

ruffian ['rʌfjən], *s.* bandit *m*, brute *f.*

ruffle ['rʌfl], *v.tr.* ébouriffer (ses cheveux); (*of bird*) hérisser (ses plumes); contrarier (qn); nothing ever ruffles him, rien ne le trouble jamais.

rug [rʌg], *s.* 1. couverture *f.* 2. carpette *f*; descente *f* de lit.

rugby ['rʌgbi], *s. r.* (football), *F:* rugger, le rugby.

rugged ['rʌgid], *a.* 1. raboteux, accidenté, inégal; 2. *r.* features, traits irréguliers.

ruin ['ruːin], *s.* I. ruine *f*; to look for (sth.) among the ruins, chercher (qch.) dans les décombres. II. *v.tr.* ruiner; abîmer (son chapeau, etc.). **ruin'ation,** *s.* ruine *f*, perte *f.* '**ruinous,** *a.* (*prix*) ruineux. -ly, *adv.* r. expensive, ruineux.

rule [ruːl], *s.* I. *s.* 1. règle *f*; règlement *m.* 2. empire *m*, autorité *f.* II. *v.tr.* 1. (*a*) gouverner (un état); régner sur (une nation); (*b*) tracer (une ligne) à la règle. 2. *v.i.* the prices ruling in London, les prix qui se pratiquent à Londres. '**ruler,** *s.* 1. souverain, -aine. 2. règle *f*; mètre *m.* '**ruling,** I. *a.* 1. souverain, dominant. 2. r. price, prix *m* pratiqué; prix du jour. II. *s.* ordonnance *f*; décision *f* (d'un juge).

rum [rʌm], *s.* rhum *m.*

rumble ['rʌmbl]. I. *s.* grondement *m.* II. *v.* 1. *v.i.* gronder (sourdement). 2. *v.tr. P:* flairer (qch.); se douter de (qch., qn).

ruminate ['ruːmineit], *v.i.* (*of cow*) ruminer; (*of pers.*) ruminer, méditer. '**ruminant,** *a.* & *s. Z:* ruminant (*m*).

rummage ['rʌmidʒ]. I. *v.tr.* & *i.* fouiller. II. *s.* objets *mpl* de rebut; r. sale, vente *f* d'objets usagés (pour une œuvre charitable).

rumour ['ruːmər], *s.* rumeur *f*, bruit *m* (qui court).

rump [rʌmp], *s. Z:* croupe *f*; *F:* (*of pers.*) postérieur *m*, derrière *m*; *Cu:* r. steak, rum(p)-steak *m*, romsteck *m.*

rumple ['rʌmpl], *v.tr.* chiffonner (une robe); ébouriffer (les cheveux).

rumpus ['rʌmpəs], *s. F:* chahut *m*, vacarme *m.*

run [rʌn]. I. *v.* 1. *v.i.* a to courir; to r. down, up, the street, descendre, monter, la rue en courant. 2. (*a*) fuir, se sauver; we must r. for it! sauvons-nous! (*b*) *Nau:* to r. before the wind, courir vent arrière; fuir devant le vent; (*d*) aller, marcher; circuler; train running to Paris, train à destination de Paris; the train is not running today, le train est supprimé aujourd'hui; *F:* I can't r. to that, c'est au-dessus de mes moyens; (*e*) fonctionner; the engine is running, le moteur est en marche; *f:* (*of colour*) déteindre; couler (au lavage). (*g*) (*of nose*) couler; (*of eyes*) pleurer; money runs through his fingers, l'argent lui fond entre les mains. 2. *v.tr.* (*a*) to r. s.o. close, serrer qn de près; (*b*) to r. the car into the garage, rentrer la voiture dans le garage; to r. s.o. into town, conduire qn en ville; *F:* I can't afford to r. a car, je n'ai pas les moyens d'entretenir une voiture; my car is cheap to r., ma voiture est économique; (*c*) tenir (un magasin, un hôtel); (*e*) to r. a thorn into one's finger, s'enfoncer une épine dans le doigt; to r. one's eyes over sth., parcourir qch. II. *s.* (*a*) at a r., au pas de course; *Sp:* (*cricket*) to make ten runs, marquer dix points; (*b*) promenade *f* (en auto); *Aut:* take-off r., course *f* d'essai; *Av:* take-off r., parcours *m* au décollage; (*c*) to have a r. of luck, être en veine; (*d*) there is a r. on that novel, on demande beaucoup ce roman; (*e*) libre accès *m*; to give s.o. the r. of one's library, mettre sa bibliothèque à la disposition de qn; (*f*) ski r., descente *f* à ski; toboggan r., piste *f* de toboggan. **run a'cross,** *v.i.* (*a*) traverser en courant; (*b*) rencontrer (qn) par hasard. **run a'way,** *v.i.* s'enfuir, se sauver. '**runaway,** *s.* fugitif *m.* **run 'down,** *v.tr.* 1. heurter, renverser (qn); *Aut:* écraser (qn). 2. dépister (un voleur, etc.). 3. dénigrer (qn).

rung [rʌŋ], *s.* échelon *m*; barreau *m*, (barre *f* de) traverse *f* (d'une échelle); bâton *m* (d'une chaise).

run 'in, *v.tr.* 1. *Aut:* roder (un moteur); running in, en rodage. 2. (*of police*) arrêter (qn). **run 'into,** *v.i.* to r. i. sth., entrer en collision avec qch.; to r.i. s.o., se trouver nez à nez

avec qn; to r.i. debt, faire des dettes; book that has r.i. five editions, livre dont on a publié cinq éditions.
'runner, s. I. coureur, -euse. 2. scarlet r., haricot m d'Espagne. 3. patin m (de traîneau). 4. curseur m. 5. chariot m de roulement. 'runner-'up, s. Sp: second, -onde. 'running. I. a. r. water, eau vive, (in room) eau courante; r. expenses, dépenses courantes; r. commentary, reportage en direct; three days r., trois jours de suite. II. s. I. courses fpl. 2. marche f, fonctionnement m (d'une machine); in r. order, prêt au service. 3. écoulement m (de l'eau). run 'off, v.i. fuir, se sauver. run 'over, v.i. 1. parcourir (un document); Aut: passer sur le corps de (qn); he has been r.o., il a été écrasé. 2. (of liquid) déborder. run 'up. 1. v.i. monter en courant; accourir; to r. up against s.o., (i) rencontrer (qn) par hasard; (ii) F: être en conflit avec qn. 2. v.tr. laisser monter (un compte); laisser accumuler (des dettes); confectionner (une robe) à la hâte. 'runway, s. Av: piste f d'envol.
rupture ['rʌptʃər]. I. s. rupture f; brouille f; hernie f. II. v.tr. rompre

(des relations); se rompre, claquer (un tendon). 'ruptured, a. (intestin) hernié.
rural ['ruərəl], a. rural; champêtre.
ruse [ruːz], s. ruse f, stratagème m.
rush¹ [rʌʃ], s. jonc m.
rush². [rʌʃ]. I. s. (a) course f précipitée; to make a r. at sth., se précipiter sur qch; (b) r. hours, heures d'affluence. II. v.tr. 1. v.i. se précipiter; s'élancer; to r. at s.o., sth., se jeter sur qn, qch. 2. v.tr. pousser vivement; dépêcher (un travail); exécuter (une commande) d'urgence; to be rushed to hospital, être transporté d'urgence à l'hôpital.
russet ['rʌsit]. I. s. (apple) reinette f grise.
Russian ['rʌʃən]. 1. s. (a) Russe mf; (b) Ling: le russe. 2. a. de Russie; russe.
rust [rʌst]. I. s. rouille f. II. v.i. se rouiller. 'rusty, a. rouillé.
rustic ['rʌstik], a. rustique; agreste.
rustle ['rʌsl]. I. s. bruissement m. II. v. 1. v.i. bruire; faire frou-frou. 2. v.tr. faire bruire.
rut [rʌt], s. ornière f.
ruthless ['ruːθlis], a. impitoyable. -ly, adv. sans pitié, sans merci.
rye [rai], s. (a) seigle m; (b) U.S: F: whisky m.

S

S, s [es], s. (la lettre) S, s m or f.
Sabbath ['sæbəθ], s. (a) Sabbat m (des Juifs); (b) dimanche m.
sable ['seibl], s. (fur) zibeline f.
sabotage ['sæbətɑːʒ]. I. s. sabotage m. II. v.tr. saboter. sabo'teur, s. saboteur, -euse.
saccharin ['sækərin, -riːn], s. saccharine f.
sachet ['sæʃei], s. sachet m.
sack¹ [sæk]. I. s. 1. (grand) sac m. 2. F: to give s.o. the s., congédier qn. II. v.tr. F: congédier (qn). 'sackcloth, s. toile f à sac.
sack², v.tr. saccager, mettre au pillage.
sacrament ['sækrəmənt], s. sacrement m.
sacred ['seikrid], a. sacré; s. music, musique religieuse.
sacrifice ['sækrifais]. I. s. 1. (a) sacrifice m; (b) victime f. 2. Com: at a s., à perte. II. v.tr. sacrifier; renoncer à (qch.).
sacrilege ['sækrilidʒ], s. sacrilège m.
†sacristy ['sækristi], s. sacristie f. 'sacristan, s. sacristain m.
sad [sæd], a. triste. -ly, adv. tristement. 'sadness, s. tristesse f, mélancolie f.
saddle ['sædl]. I. s. selle f. II. v.tr. (a) seller (un cheval); (b) F: charger, encombrer (qn de qch.).
sadist ['seidist], s. sadique mf. sa'distic, a. sadique.
safe [seif]. I. a. 1. en sûreté; à l'abri; s. and sound, sain et sauf. 2. sûr, sans

danger; (pont, etc.) solide; to be on the s. side, être du bon côté. -ly, adv. 1. sans accident; sain et sauf. 2. sûrement, sans danger, sans risque. II. s. 1. coffre-fort m. 2. gardemanger m. 'safeguard, v.tr. sauvegarder, protéger. 'safety, s. sûreté f, sécurité f; in a place of s., en lieu sûr; Ind: s. factor, coefficient m de sécurité; Av: Aut: s. belt, ceinture f de sécurité; s. catch, cran m d'arrêt; s. pin, épingle f de nourrice; E: s. valve, soupape f de sûreté.
saffron ['sæfrən], s. safran m.
†sag [sæg], v.i. s'affaisser, fléchir.
sage¹ [seidʒ]. 1. a. sage, prudent. 2. s. philosophe m, sage m.
sage², n. Bot: sauge f.
sago ['seigou], s. sagou m.
sail [seil]. I. s. Nau: 1. voile f. 2. to go for a s., faire une promenade à la voile. II. v.i. (a) (of sailing ship) faire de la voile; (of steamer) naviguer, faire route; (b) partir, appareiller; prendre la mer. 'sailcloth, s. toile f (à voile).
'sailor, s. marin m; to be a good s., avoir le pied marin; to be a bad s., être sujet au mal de mer.
saint [seint] (before Pr.n. usu. sənt), abbr. St., S.), s. saint, sainte; All Saints' Day, la Toussaint; St. Peter's, (l'église) Saint-Pierre. St. Bernard, s. (chien m) saint-bernard m.

sake [seik], *s.* for the s. of, à cause de; for my s., pour moi.

salad [ˈsæləd], *s.* salade *f*; fruit s., macédoine *f* de fruits; s. bowl, saladier *m*; s. shaker, panier *m* à salade.

†**salary** [ˈsæləri], *s.* traitement *m*, appointements *mpl*.

sale [seil], *s.* 1. vente *f*; débit *m*, mise *f* en vente; for s., à vendre; s. price, prix de solde. 'saleable, *a.* vendable; de vente facile. 'salesclerk, *s. U.S:* vendeur, -euse. †'salesman, *s.* 1. vendeur *m*. 2. représentant *m* (de commerce). 'salesmanship, *s.* l'art *m* de vendre. †'saleswoman, *s.* vendeuse *f*.

salient [ˈseiliənt], *a.* saillant.

saliva [səˈlaivə], *s.* salive *f*.

sallow [ˈsælou], *a.* jaunâtre, olivâtre. 'sallowness, *s.* teint *m* jaunâtre.

†**salmon** [ˈsæmən], *s.* saumon *m*; s. trout, truite *f* saumonée.

salon [ˈsælɔ̃], *s.* salon *m*; beauty s., institut *m* de beauté.

saloon [səˈluːn], *s.* (*a*) salon *m* (de paquebot); (*b*) *U.S:* café *m* (*in Eng.*) s. bar = bar *m*; billiard s., salle *f* de billard; (*c*) *Aut:* s. (car), conduite *f* intérieure, berline *f*.

salt [sɔlt]. I. *s.* sel *m*; s. cellar, salière *f*; to take a story with a pinch of s., prendre l'histoire avec un grain de sel. II. *a.* salé. III. *v.tr.* saler; saupoudrer (qch.) de sel. 'saltness, *s.* salure *f*; salinité *f*. 'salty, *a.* (trop) salé.

salubrious [səˈluːbriəs], *a.* salubre, sain.

salute [səˈluːt]. I. *s.* salut *m*, salutation *f*. II. *v.tr.* saluer (qn). salu'tation, *s.* salutation *f*.

salvage [ˈsælvidʒ]. I. *s.* sauvetage *m* (d'un navire); objets *mpl* sauvés (d'un incendie, etc.); récupération *f* (de matières pour l'industrie). II. *v.tr.* sauver; récupérer.

salvation [sælˈveiʃ(ə)n], *s.* salut *m*.

salvia [ˈselviə], *s. Bot:* sauge *f*.

†**salvo** [ˈselvou], *s.* salve *f*.

same [seim]. 1. *a.* & *pron.* (le, la) même, (les) mêmes; of the s. kind, similaire; in the s. way, de même; at the s. time, (i) en même temps; (ii) à la fois; it's all the s., c'est tout un; it's all the s. to me, ça m'est égal. 2. *adv.* to think the s., penser de même; all the same, malgré tout; quand même.

sample [ˈsɑːmpl]. I. *s.* échantillon *m*; s. survey, enquête *f* par sondage. II. *v.tr.* déguster (un vin); goûter (un plat); essayer (un nouveau restaurant).

†**sanatorium** [sænəˈtɔːriəm], *s.* sanatorium *m*; *Sch:* infirmerie *f*.

sanctify [ˈsæŋktifai], *v.tr.* sanctifier; consacrer.

sanctimonious [sæŋk(t)iˈmouniəs], *a.* béat, *F:* bondieusard.

sanction [ˈsæŋkʃ(ə)n]. I. *s.* sanction *f*. II. *v.tr.* sanctionner; sanctioned by usage, consacré par l'usage.

sanctity [ˈsæŋ(k)titi], *s.* 1. sainteté *f*. 2. inviolabilité *f*; caractère *m* sacré.

†**sanctuary** [ˈsæŋ(k)tjuəri], *s.* sanctuaire *m*.

sand [sænd], *s.* 1. sable *m*. 2. *pl.* plage *f*, grève *f*. 'sandbag, *s.* 1. sac *m* de sable. 2. *F:* assommoir *m*; boudin *m*. II. *v.tr.* 1. protéger (un bâtiment) avec des sacs de sables. 2. *F:* assommer (qn). 'sandbank, *s.* banc *m* de sable. 'sandpaper. I. *s.* papier *m* de verre. II. *v.tr.* poncer, douvir (une surface). 'sandstone, *s.* grès *m*. 'sandy, *a.* 1. sableux, sablonneux. 2. (*of hair*) roux pâle.

sandal [ˈsænd(ə)l], *s.* sandale *f*.

sandwich [ˈsænwidʒ]. I. *s.* sandwich *m*; ham sandwiches, sandwichs au jambon. II. *v.tr.* serrer, intercaler (between, entre). †'sandwichman, *s.* homme-sandwich *m*.

sane [sein], *a.* sain d'esprit; sensé. 'sanity, *s.* santé *f* d'esprit.

sanguine [ˈsæŋgwin], *a.* (*a*) sanguin; (*b*) confiant, optimiste.

sanitation [sæniˈteiʃ(ə)n], *s.* hygiène *f*; système *m* sanitaire; aménagements *mpl* sanitaires. 'sanitary, *a.* hygiénique.

sap[1] [sæp], *s.* sève *f*.

‡**sap**[2], *v.tr.* & *i.* saper, miner. 'sapper, *s. Mil:* sapeur *m*; *F:* the Sappers, le génie.

sapling [ˈsæpliŋ], *s.* jeune arbre *m*; baliveau *m*.

sapphire [ˈsæfaiər], *s.* saphir *m*.

sarcasm [ˈsɑːkæzm], *s.* 1. ironie *f*; esprit *m* sarcastique. 2. sarcasme *m*. sar'castic, *a.* sarcastique, mordant. -ally, *adv.* d'une manière sarcastique.

sarcoma [sɑːˈkoumə], *s. Med:* sarcome *m*.

sardine [sɑːˈdiːn], *s.* sardine *f*.

sardonic [sɑːˈdɔnik], *a.* sardonique.

sash[1] [sæʃ], *s.* écharpe *f*; ceinture *f*.

sash[2], *s.* cadre *m* (d'une fenêtre à guillotine).

satchel [ˈsætʃ(ə)l], *s.* cartable *m*.

satellite [ˈsætilait], *s.* satellite *m*; s. town, agglomération *f* satellite; s. state, état *m*, pays *m* satellite.

satiate [ˈseiʃieit], *v.tr.* rassasier (with, de); blaser (with, de). sati'ation, *s.* rassasiement *m*. 2. satiété *f*.

satin [ˈsætin], *s.* satin *m*.

satire [ˈsætaiər], *s.* satire *f*, sarcasme *m*. sa'tirical, *a.* 1. satirique. 2. sarcastique.

satisfaction [sætisˈfækʃ(ə)n], *s.* satisfaction *f*, contentement *m*. satis'factory, *a.* satisfaisant. -torily, *adv.* de façon satisfaisante.

satisfy [ˈsætisfai], *v.tr.* satisfaire; convaincre (qn d'un fait). 'satisfied, *a.* 1. content, satisfait. 2. convaincu. 'satisfying, *a.* satisfaisant; (*of food*) nourrissant; (*of argument*) convaincant.

saturate ['sætjureit], *v.tr.* saturer (with, de). **satu'ration**, *s.* saturation *f*; *Com:* the market has reached s. point, le marché est saturé.

Saturday ['sætədi], *s.* samedi *m.*

sauce [sɔːs], *s.* (*a*) sauce *f*; (*b*) assaisonnement *m*; condiment *m*; (*c*) *P:* culot *m*, toupet *m.* '**saucy**, *a.* impertinent, effronté.

saucepan ['sɔːspən], *s.* casserole *f.*

saucer ['sɔːsər], *s.* soucoupe *f*; *F:* flying s. soucoupe volante.

saunter ['sɔːntər], *v.i.* flâner; déambuler.

sausage ['sɔsidʒ], *s.* (*a*) (*eaten hot*) saucisse *f*; s. meat, chair *f* à saucisse; s. roll = friand *m*; (*b*) (*preserved, eaten cold*) saucisson *m.*

savage ['sævidʒ]. I. *a.* (*a*) sauvage, barbare; (*b*) (*animal*) féroce. **-ly**, *adv.* férocement; furieusement. II. *v.tr.* (*of animal*) attaquer (qn).

save [seiv], *v.tr.* 1. sauver; to s. appearances, sauver les apparences. 2. (*a*) mettre de côté; réserver; (*b*) économiser, épargner; *abs.* économiser pour l'avenir. 3. ménager; éviter (une dépense, de la peine); to s. time, gagner du temps. 4. to s. s.o. sth., éviter, épargner, qch. à qn. '**savings**, *s.pl.* économies *fpl*; s. bank, caisse *f* d'épargne.

saviour ['seivjər], *s.* sauveur *m.*

savoury ['seivəri]. 1. *a.* savoureux, appétissant; succulent; s. omelette, omelette aux fines herbes. 2. †*s.* entremets *m* non sucré.

saw [sɔː]. I. *s.* scie *f.* II. *v.tr.* scier; to s. up wood, débiter du bois. '**sawdust**, *s.* sciure *f.* '**sawmill**, *s.* scierie *f.*

saxophone ['sæksəfoun], *s.* saxophone *m.*

say [sei]. I. *v.tr.* dire; faire (ses prières); dire (la messe); to s. sth. again, répéter qch.; he says [sez] not, il dit que non; so to s., pour ainsi dire; I must s. that . . ., j'avoue que . . .; franchement . . .; have you said anything about it to him? lui en avez-vous parlé? there is sth. to be said on both sides, il y a du pour et du contre; they s. that . . ., it is said that . . ., on dit que . . .; I should s. so, je crois que oui; didn't I s. so? quand je vous le disais! come soon, s. Sunday, venez bientôt, disons dimanche; I s.! (i) dites donc! (ii) pas possible! *F:* what do you s. to a drink? si on buvait un verre? the less said the better, moins nous parlerons, mieux cela vaudra. II. s. to have one's s., dire son mot. '**saying**, *s.* 1. that goes without s. cela va sans dire; there's no s. (when . . .), impossible de dire (quand . . .). 2. dicton *m.*

scab [skæb], *s.* (*on wound*) croûte *f.*

scaffold ['skæf(ə)ld], *s.* échafaud *m.* '**scaffolding**, *s.* échafaudage *m.*

scald [skɔːld]. I. *v.tr.* échauder. II. *s.* échaudure *f.* '**scalding**, *a.* s. hot, tout bouillant.

scale[1] [skeil]. I. *s.* écaille *f.* II. *v.tr.* (*a*) écailler (un poisson); (*b*) détartrer, désincruster (une chaudière, etc.).

scale[2], *s.* 1. (*a*) (*of map, etc.*) échelle *f*; (*b*) (*of disaster, etc.*) étendue *f*; large-s. business, grosse affaire *f*; to do things on a large s. faire les choses en grand. 2. *Mus:* gamme *f.*

scale[3], *v.tr.* escalader (un mur, etc.).

scales [skeilz], *s.pl.* balance *f*; bathroom s., pèse-personne *m.*

scallop ['skɔləp], *s.* 1. coquille *f* Saint-Jacques. 2. feston *m*, dentelure *f.*

scalp [skælp]. *s.* 1. cuir *m* chevelu. 2. scalp(e) *m.* II. *v.tr.* scalper (un ennemi).

scalpel ['skælp(ə)l], *s.* scalpel *m.*

scamp [skæmp]. I. *s. F:* vaurien *m*; garnement *m.* II. *v.tr. F:* bâcler (un travail).

scamper ['skæmpər], *v.i.* (*a*) courir vite; (*b*) to s. off, se sauver à toutes jambes.

scampi ['skæmpi], *s.pl. Cu:* langoustines *fpl.*

‡**scan** [skæn]. I. *v.* 1. *v.i.* (*of verse*) se scander. 2. *v.tr.* examiner, scruter; *T.V:* balayer (l'image). II. *s. T.V: Radar:* s. axis, axe *m* radioélectrique. '**scanning**, *s.* 1. scansion *f* (de vers). 2. *Cin: T.V:* balayage *m.* '**scanner**, *s.* radar s., déchiffreur *m* de radar.

scandal ['skænd(ə)l], *s.* 1. scandale *m*; honte *f.* 2. médisance *f.* '**scandalize**, *v.tr.* scandaliser. '**scandalous**, *a.* scandaleux, infâme, honteux. **-ly**, *adv.* scandaleusement.

scant [skænt], *a.* insuffisant; with s. courtesy, peu poliment. **-ily**, *adv.* insuffisamment; s. clad, à peine vêtu. '**scantiness**, *s.* insuffisance *f*; pauvreté *f* (de la végétation); étroitesse *f* (d'un vêtement). '**scanty**, *a.* insuffisant; (vêtement) étroit, étriqué; s. meal, maigre repas.

scapegoat ['skeipgout], *s.* bouc *m* émissaire.

scar [skɑːr]. I. *s.* cicatrice *f.* II. ‡*v.tr.* marquer d'une cicatrice.

scarce [skɛəs], *a.* rare; peu abondant. **-ly**, *adv.* à peine; presque pas; s. ever, presque jamais. '**scarcity**, s. **scarceness**, s. rareté *f*, manque *m*, pénurie *f.*

scare [skɛər]. I. *s.* panique *f*, alarme *f.* II. *v.tr.* effrayer, effarer, alarmer; to s. away, effaroucher. '**scarecrow**, s. épouvantail *m.* '**scaremonger**, s. alarmiste *mf.*

†**scarf** [skɑːf], *s.* écharpe *f*; fichu *m*; cache-col *m inv*; foulard *m.*

scarlet ['skɑːlit], *a.* & *s.* écarlate (*f*); s. fever (*also* scarlatina), scarlatine *f.*

scathing ['skeiðiŋ], *a.* acerbe, cinglant, caustique.

scatter ['skætər]. 1. *v.tr.* (*a*) disperser, mettre en fuite; (*b*) éparpiller. 2. *v.i.* se disperser; s'éparpiller. '**scattered**, *a.* dispersé, éparpillé; épars.

scavenger ['skævindʒər], *s.* insecte *m*, animal *m*, nécrophage.

scenario [si'nɑːriou], *s.* scénario *m*.

scene [siːn], *s.* scène *f*; (*a*) *Th:* (i) Act III, Scene 2, Acte III, Scène II; (ii) behind the scenes, dans la coulisse; s. shifter, machiniste *m*; (iii) the s. is laid in London, l'action/se passe à Londres; (*b*) the s. of operations, le théâtre des opérations; on the s. of the disaster, sur les lieux du sinistre; (*c*) *F:* to make a s., faire une scène; faire de l'esclandre. '**scenery**, *s.* 1. paysage *m*. 2. *Th:* décors *mpl*. '**scenic**, *a.* 1. *U.S:* s. road, route *f* touristique. 2. s. railway, montagnes *fpl* russes.

scent [sent]. I. *s.* 1. parfum *m*; (*a*) (of fox, etc.) fumet *m*, vent *m*; (*b*) (of hounds) to be on the (right) s., être sur la piste. 2. odorat *m*, flair *m* (d'un chien). II. *v.tr.* 1. (of hounds) flairer, éventer (le gibier); (of pers.) flairer (des ennuis). 2. (of flowers) parfumer, embaumer (l'air). '**scented**, *a.* parfumé.

sceptic ['skeptik], *s.* sceptique *mf*. '**sceptical**, *a.* sceptique. **-ally**, *adv.* avec scepticisme. '**scepticism**, *s.* scepticisme *m*.

sceptre ['septər], *s.* sceptre *m*.

schedule ['ʃedjuːl]. I. *s.* 1. inventaire *m*; barème *m* (des prix). 2. plan *m* (d'exécution d'un travail, etc.); everything went according to s., tout a marché selon les prévisions; (of train) up to s., à l'heure; ahead of s., en avance. II. *v.tr.* 1. inscrire (qch.) sur l'inventaire; scheduled as a place of historic interest, classé comme monument historique. 2. dresser le programme de (qch.); the train is scheduled to arrive at midnight, selon l'indicateur le train arrive à minuit.

scheme [skiːm]. I. *s.* 1. arrangement *m*; colour s., combinaison *f* de couleurs; the s. of things, l'ordre des choses. 2. (*a*) plan *m*, projet *m*; (*b*) *Pej:* intrigue *f*; complot *m*; combine *f*. II. *v.i.* intriguer, ruser, comploter. **sche'matic**, *a.* schématique. '**scheming**, *s. Pej:* machinations *fpl*, intrigues *fpl*, combines *fpl*. '**schemer**, *s. Pej:* intrigant, -ante.

schism ['sizm], *s.* schisme *m*.

schist [ʃist], *s.* schiste *m*.

schnorkel ['ʃnɔːkl], *s.* schnorkel *m*.

scholar ['skɔlər], *s.* 1. élève *mf*; écolier, -ière. 2. savant *m*, érudit *m*; he's no s., son éducation laisse à désirer. '**scholarly**, *a.* savant, érudit. '**scholarship**, *s.* 1. savoir *m*, érudition *f*. 2.

bourse *f* (d'études). **scho'lastic**, *a.* the s. profession, l'enseignement *m*.

school [skuːl], *s.* (*a*) école *f*; to go to s., aller en classe; s. leaving age, âge *m* de fin de scolarité; nursery s., école maternelle; primary s., école primaire; secondary modern s. = collège *m* d'enseignement général; grammar, high, s. = lycée *m*; comprehensive s. = centre *m* d'études secondaires; independent, private, s., école libre; public s., (i) collège privé (avec internat); (ii) *U.S:* école d'État; preparatory s., institution *f* pour élèves de 8 à 13 ans; what s. were you at? où avez-vous fait vos études? s. year, année scolaire; *U.S:* to teach s., être dans l'enseignement; s. bus service, service *m* de ramassage scolaire; (*b*) s. of art, école des beaux-arts; *A. & A:* the Italian s., l'école italienne; s. of dancing, cours *m* de danse; s. of music, académie *f* de musique; conservatoire *m*; summer s., cours de vacances; s. of motoring, auto-école *f*. '**schoolbook**, *s.* livre *m* de classe. '**schoolboy**, *s.* écolier *m*, élève *m*; s. slang, argot *m* scolaire. '**schoolgirl**, *s.* écolière *f*; élève *f*. '**schooling**, *s.* instruction *f*, éducation *f*. '**schoolma'am**, **-marm**, *s.* (*a*) *U.S:* institutrice *f*; (*b*) *F:* a real s., (i) une pédante, (ii) une vraie prude. '**schoolmaster**, *s.* professeur *m*; instituteur *m*. '**schoolmistress**, *s.* professeur *m*; institutrice *f*. '**schoolroom**, *s.* (salle *f* de) classe *f*. '**schoolteacher**, *s.* instituteur *m*, institutrice *f*.

schooner[1] ['skuːnər], *s. Nau:* schooner *m*; goélette *f*.

schooner[2], *s.* (*a*) grande flûte *f* (pour bière); (*b*) (in Eng. approx.) demi-litre *m* (de bière); (*c*) grand verre *m* (à porto, à vin de Xérès).

science ['saiəns], *s.* science *f*; *Sch:* s. master, mistress, professeur *m* de sciences; s. fiction, science-fiction *f*. **scien'tific**, *a.* scientifique; s. instruments, instruments *m* de précision. '**scientist**, *s.* savant, -ante, scientifique.

scintillate ['sintileit], *v.i.* scintiller, étinceler.

scissors ['sizəz], *s.pl.* ciseaux *mpl*.

sclerosis [sklia'rousis], *s. Med:* sclérose *f*.

scoff [skɔf], *v.i.* se moquer. '**scoffer**, *s.* moqueur, -euse; railleur, -euse.

scold [skould], *v.tr.* gronder, réprimander (qn). '**scolding**, *s.* réprimande *f*.

scone [skɔn, skoun], *s.* pain *m* au lait.

scoop [skuːp]. I. *v.tr.* to s. (out), excaver; évider; to s. up, ramasser à la pelle. II. *s.* 1. (*a*) pelle *f* à main; (*b*) seau *m* à charbon (coupé en biseau). 2. at one s., d'un seul coup. 3. *F:* scoop *m*, reportage *m* sensationnel.

scooter ['sku:tər], s. 1. trottinette f, patinette f (d'enfant). 2. Aut: scooter m.

scope [skoup], s. (a) portée f, étendue f; (b) espace m, place f; full s., libre carrière f.

scorch [skɔːtʃ]. 1. v.tr. roussir, brûler légèrement; (of sun) rôtir, flétrir. 2. v.i. roussir. 3. v.i. F: Aut: brûler le pavé. 'scorched, a. roussi, légèrement brûlé; (of grass) desséché; s. earth policy, politique f de la terre brûlée. 'scorching. I. a. brûlant, ardent. II. adv. s. hot, tout brûlant. III. s. roussissement m; dessèchement m.

score ['skɔːr]. I. s. 1. éraflure f, entaille f. 2. old scores, vieux comptes. 3. points mpl; what's the s.? où en est le jeu? 4. Mus: partition f. 5. (a) inv. vingt, vingtaine f; (b) pl. F: un grand nombre. 6. point m, sujet m; on the s. of, pour cause de. II. v.tr. 1. érafler; strier; rayer. 2. Sp: compter, marquer (les points); to s. a goal, marquer un but; that's where he scores, c'est par là qu'il l'emporte. 3. Mus: orchestrer (une composition). 'scorer, s. Sp: marqueur m. 'scoring, s. 1. éraflement m; striation f. 2. Sp: marque f (des points). 3. Mus: orchestration f. 'score 'off, v.tr. F: river son clou (à qn).

scorn [skɔːn]. I. s. dédain m, mépris m. II. v.tr. dédaigner, mépriser. 'scornful, a. dédaigneux, méprisant. -fully, adv. dédaigneusement; avec mépris.

scorpion ['skɔːpjən], s. scorpion m.

Scot [skɔt], s. Écossais m, -aise. Scotch. I. a. (not used of pers. in Scot.) écossais; S. terrier, scotch-terrier m; S. broth, soupe f comprenant du mouton, des légumes et de l'orge; S. mist, bruine f; S. woodcock, œufs aux anchois sur canapé. II. s. (a) dialecte m écossais (de l'anglais); (b) whisky m écossais; a (glass of) s., un whisky, un scotch. †'Scotchman, †-woman, s. (not used in Scot.) Écossais, Écossaise. Scots, a. écossais, -aise. †'Scotsman, †-woman, s. Écossais, Écossaise; Rail: the Flying Scotsman, le rapide de Londres à Édimbourg. 'Scottish, a. écossais.

scotch [skɔtʃ], v.tr. mettre à néant, faire avorter (un projet).

scot-free ['skɔt'fri:], a. 1. to get off s.-f., s'en tirer indemne, sain et sauf. 2. sans frais.

scoundrel ['skaundrəl], s. scélérat m; escroc m.

scour [skauər], v.tr. nettoyer, récurer (une casserole).

scout [skaut]. I. s. 1. Mil: etc: éclaireur m; s. car, plane, véhicule m, avion m, de reconnaissance. 2. (boy) s., (catholic) scout m; (non-catholic) éclaireur m; U.S: girl s.,

---

scowl [skaul]. I. s. air m menaçant, renfrogné; froncement m des sourcils. II. v.i. se renfrogner; froncer les sourcils.

scramble ['skræmbl]. I. v. 1. v.i. to s. up, down, monter, descendre, à quatre pattes; to s. for sth., se bousculer pour avoir qch. 2. v.tr. (a) P.T.T: brouiller (un message); (b) scrambled eggs, œufs brouillés. II. s. mêlée f, bousculade f.

scrap¹ [skræp]. I. s. 1. petit morceau m; bout m, chiffon m; s. book, album m (de découpures, etc.). 2. (a) pl. restes mpl; bribes fpl; (b) s. metal, ferraille f; s. heap, tas m de ferraille; to throw sth. on the s. heap, mettre qch. au rebut. II. ‡v.tr. mettre (qch.) au rebut; mettre au rancart (une théorie). 'scrappy, a. s. knowledge, bribes fpl de connaissances; s. meal, maigre repas m.

scrap², s. querelle f, rixe f.

scrape [skreip]. I. s. 1. coup m de grattoir, de racloir. 2. F: mauvaise affaire f. II. v. 1. v.tr. (a) érafler, écorcher; (b) racler, gratter; F: to s. the barrel, racler les fonds de tiroir. 2. v.i. (a) gratter; (b) grincer; (c) to s. clear, échapper tout juste. scrape a'long, v.i. F: vivoter péniblement.

scratch [skrætʃ]. I. s. 1. (a) coup m d'ongle, de griffe; (b) égratignure f, éraflure f. 2. (a) grattement m; (b) grincement m. 3. Sp: scratch m; to start from s., partir de zéro; to come up to s., se montrer à la hauteur (de l'occasion). II. v. 1. v.tr. (a) égratigner, griffer; (b) gratter; (c) Sp: décommander (un match); abs. déclarer forfait. 2. v.i. (of pen, etc.) grincer, gratter. III. a. (repas, etc.) improvisé; sommaire; Sp: s. team, équipe improvisée. 'scratch 'out, v.tr. rayer, biffer (un mot).

scrawl [skrɔːl]. I. v.tr. griffonner. II. s. griffonnage m.

scream [skri:m]. I. s. (a) cri m perçant; (b) éclat m (de rire); (c) F: chose f amusante, grotesque. II. v.i. (a) pousser un cri perçant; crier; to s. with laughter, rire aux éclats. 'screamingly, adv. F: s. funny, tordant, crevant.

scree [skri:], s. éboulis m.

screech [skri:tʃ]. I. s. cri m perçant; cri rauque. II. v.i. pousser des cris perçants, des cris rauques.

screen [skri:n]. I. s. (draught) s., paravent m; A. & A: choir s., jubé m; s. of trees, rideau m d'arbres; Av:

blast s., déflecteur *m* de souffle; *Mil: etc:* to form a s., former un écran (against, contre). 2. *Cin: T.V:* écran *m*; the s. (considered as profession), le cinéma. 3. gravel s., crible *m* à gravier. II. *v.tr.* 1. cacher, masquer (qch.); protéger (qch. du vent). 2. examiner et interroger (une personne suspecte). 3. *Cin:* mettre (un roman) à l'écran; projeter (un film); *T.V:* passer (une émission) sur l'écran. 4. filtrer, cribler (un gravier). 'screening, s. 1. protection *f* (from, against); dissimulation *f* (d'un défaut). 2. examen *m* et interrogatoire *m* (d'une personne suspecte). 3. criblage *m*; filtrage *m*. 'screenwriter, s. *Cin:* dialoguiste *mf*.

screw [skru:]. I. s. 1. *(a)* vis *f*; s.-topped jar, bocal à couvercle à vis; *F:* to have a s. loose, être un peu timbré; *(b)* tour *m* de vis. 2. *Av: Nau:* hélice *f*. 3. *F:* salaire *m*. II. *v.* 1. *v.tr.* visser; to s. (sth.) down, visser (un couvercle, etc.); to s. (sth.) on, visser, fixer (qch.); *F:* his head's screwed on the right way, il a du bon sens; to s. up one's handkerchief, tirebouchonner son mouchoir; to s. up one's eyes, plisser les yeux; to s. up one's courage, prendre son courage à deux mains. 3. *v.i.* fermer à vis. 'screwdriver, s. tournevis *m*.

scribble ['skribl]. I. *v.tr.* griffonner. II. *s.* griffonnage *m*; mauvaise écriture *f*. 'scribbling, s. griffonnage *m*; s. paper, papier *m* à brouillon.

script [skript], s. *(a)* manuscrit *m*; *Sch:* copie *f* d'examen; *(c) Cin:* scénario *m*; s. girl, script-girl *f*; s. writer, scénariste *mf*.

scripture ['skript∫ər], s. the Scriptures, l'Écriture *f* sainte; *Sch:* s. (lesson), (leçon d')histoire sainte.

scroll [skroul], s. rouleau *m* (de parchemin).

‡scrub¹ [skrʌb], *v.tr.* nettoyer, frotter (avec une brosse dure). 'scrubbing, s. nettoyage *m* (avec une brosse dure); s. brush, brosse dure.

scrub², s. broussailles *fpl*; brousse *f*. 'scrubby, a. *(a)* couvert de broussailles; *(b) F:* (of pers.) insignifiant; chétif; piètre.

scruff [skrʌf], s. to seize an animal by the s. of the neck, saisir un animal par la peau du cou.

scruffy ['skrʌfi], a. *F:* mal soigné.

scrum [skrʌm], s. *(a) Sp:* (Rugby) mêlée *f*; s. half, demi *m* de mêlée; *(b) F:* bousculade *f*.

scruple ['skru:pl], s. scrupule *m*. 'scrupulous, a. scrupuleux; méticuleux. -ly, *adv.* scrupuleusement; méticuleusement. 'scrupulousness, s. esprit *m* scrupuleux.

scrutinize ['skru:tinaiz], *v.tr.* scruter; examiner minutieusement. 'scrutiny, s. examen *m* minutieux.

scuffle ['skʌfl]. I. *s.* mêlée *f*, bousculade *f*. II. *v.i.* *(a)* se bousculer; *(b)* traîner les pieds.

scull [skʌl]. I. *s.* 1. aviron *m* de couple; rame *f*. 2. godille *f*. II. *v.i.* 1. ramer, nager, en couple. 2. godiller. 'sculler, s. 1. rameur *m* de couple. 2. godilleur *m*.

‡scullery ['skʌləri], s. arrière-cuisine *f*.

sculptor ['skʌlptər], s. sculpteur *m*.

'sculpture, s. sculpture *f*.

scum [skʌm], s. écume *f*, mousse *f* (à la surface d'un liquide).

scurf [skə:f], s. pellicules *fpl* (sur la tête).

scuttle¹ ['skʌtl], s. seau *m* à charbon.

scuttle², *v.tr.* saborder (un navire).

scuttle³, *v.i.* to s. off, déguerpir, filer.

scythe [saið], s. faux *f*.

sea [si:], s. 1. mer *f*; s. bathing, bains *mpl* de mer; (of ship) to put (out) to s., prendre la mer; *F:* to be all at s., être tout désorienté. 2. heavy s., grosse mer; to ship a s., embarquer une paquet de mer. 'seafarer, s. homme *m* de mer, marin *m*. 'seafood, s. = fruits *mpl* de mer. 'seafront, s. bord *m* de mer; esplanade *f*; a house on the s., une maison qui donne sur la mer. 'seagull, s. mouette *f*; goéland *m*.

seal¹ [si:l], s. *Z:* phoque *m*. 'sealskin, s. *Com:* (fur) loutre *f*.

seal², I. s. sceau *m*; cachet *m*. II. *v.tr.* sceller; cacheter. 'sealing-wax, s. cire *f* à cacheter.

seam [si:m], s. 1. *(a)* couture *f*; *French* s., couture double; *(b) E:* couture, joint *m*; s. welding, soudage *m* à molettes. 2. *Min:* couche *f*, gisement *m*. 'seamless, a. 1. sans couture. 2. sans soudure.

†'seaman, s. 1. marin *m*; matelot *m*. 2. a good s., un bon navigateur. 'seamanship, s. *Nau:* la manœuvre. 'seaplane, hydravion *m*. 'seaport, s. port *m* de mer.

search [sə:t∫]. I. s. 1. recherche(s) *f(pl)*; in s. of, à la recherche de. 2. visite *f* (à la douane); *Jur:* perquisition *f*; s. warrant, mandat *m* de perquisition. 3. fouille *f* (dans un tiroir). II. *v.* 1. *v.tr.* chercher dans (un endroit); fouiller (un suspect); *(at Customs)* visiter (les valises de qn); *Jur:* perquisitionner dans (une maison); *P:* s. me! je n'ai pas la moindre idée! 2. *v.i.* to s. for sth., (re)chercher qch. 'searching, a. (examen) minutieux; (regard) pénétrant, scrutateur. 'searchlight, s. projecteur *m*.

seasick, a. to be s., avoir le mal de mer. 'seasickness, s. mal *m* de mer. 'seaside, s. bord *m* de la mer; s. resort, station *f* balnéaire; plage *f*.

season¹ ['si:zn], s. 1. saison f. 2. période f, temps m; s. ticket, F: season, carte f d'abonnement. '**seasonable**, a. de (la) saison. '**seasonal**, a. (changements) des saisons; (commerce) saisonnier.

season². 1. v.tr. assaisonner (un mets); conditionner (le bois). 2. v.i. (of wood) sécher. '**seasoned**, a. 1. assaisonné. 2. (of wood) sec. 'seasoning, s. Cu: assaisonnement m.

seat [si:t]. I. s. 1. siège m; banquette f; lunette f (de w.c.); place f (assise). 2. siège, fond m (d'une chaise); F: postérieur m, derrière m. 3. (of horseman) to have a good s., bien se tenir en selle. II. v.tr. 1. placer (qn); trouver place pour (qn); this table seats twelve, on tient douze à cette table. 2. (re)mettre le siège à (une chaise). 'seating, s. allocation f des places; s. capacity, nombre m de places (assises).

seaway, s. voie f maritime. '**seaweed**, s. algue f; goémon m; varech m. '**seaworthy**, a. (of ship) en (bon) état de navigabilité.

seclusion [si'klu:ʒ(ə)n], s. solitude f, retraite f. se'**cluded**, a. écarté, retiré.

second¹ ['sekənd], s. seconde f (de temps).

second². I. a. second, deuxième; the s. of May, le deux mai; Charles the S., Charles Deux; to travel s. class, voyager en seconde (classe); Aut: s. (gear), deuxième (vitesse); to be s. in command, commander en second. -ly, adv. deuxièmement, en second lieu. II. s. 1. le second, la seconde; le, la, deuxième. 2. pl. Com: articles m de deuxième qualité. III. v.tr. 1. seconder (qn); appuyer (qn); to s. a motion, appuyer une proposition. 2. Mil: [se'kɔnd] mettre (un officier) en disponibilité. '**secondary**, a. secondaire; s. road = route départementale. '**second'hand**, a. & adv. d'occasion. '**secondrate**, a. médiocre, inférieur; de second ordre.

secret ['si:krit]. I. a. secret; caché. -ly, adv. secrètement, en secret. II. s. secret m. 'secrecy, s. discrétion f; in s., en secret. secrete [si'kri:t], v.tr. cacher. '**secretive**, a. réservé; dissimulé.

†**secretary** ['sekrətri], s. (a) secrétaire mf; (b) S. of State, ministre m; secrétaire m d'État. secre'tarial, a. (travail) de secrétaire.

sect [sekt], s. secte f.

section ['sek[ə]n], s. section f; division f; vertical s., coupe f verticale. '**sectional**, a. (dessin) en coupe, en profil; s. bookcase, bibliothèque f démontable.

sector ['sektər], s. secteur m.

secular ['sekjulər], a. séculier; laïque.

secure [si'kjuər]. I. a. 1. sûr; assuré; to feel s. of victory, être certain de la victoire. 2. en sûreté, sauf. -ly, adv. sûrement; avec sécurité. II. v.tr. 1. fixer, retenir (qch. à sa place); verrouiller (la porte). 2. obtenir, se procurer (qch.). se'**curity**, s. 1. sécurité f. 2. (moyen m de) sécurité; sauvegarde f. 3. Jur: (a) caution f; (b) (pers.) (donneur m de) caution; garant m; (c) Fin: securities, titres m, valeurs f.

sedate [si'deit], a. posé, reposé; composé. -ly, adv. posément.

sedative ['sedətiv], a. & s. sédatif (m).

sedentary ['sedəntri], a. sédentaire.

sediment ['sediment], s. sédiment m, dépôt m. sedi'**mentary**, a. sédimentaire.

sedition [si'dif(ə)n], s. sédition f. se'**ditious**, a. séditieux.

seduce [si'dju:s], v.tr. séduire; corrompre. se'**duction**, s. séduction f. se'**ductive**, a. séduisant, attrayant.

†**see** [si:], v.tr. 1. voir; abs. as far as the eye can s., à perte de vue; to s. s.o. home, reconduire qn jusque chez lui; F: he'll never s. forty again, il a quarante ans sonnés. 2. (a) comprendre, saisir; (b) observer, remarquer; s'apercevoir de (qch.); (c) juger, apprécier; that's how I s. it, voilà comment j'envisage la chose. 3. examiner; regarder avec attention; let me see, (i) attendez un peu; (ii) faites voir! 4. (a) fréquenter, avoir des rapports avec; (b) to go and s. s.o., aller trouver qn; to s. the doctor, consulter le médecin; (c) recevoir (un visiteur). 'see about, v.ind.tr. s'occuper de (qch.); se charger de (qch.). 'see 'through. 1. v.i. (a) voir à travers; (b) pénétrer les intentions de; pénétrer. 2. v.tr. mener (qch.) à bonne fin. 'see to, v.ind.tr. s'occuper de (qch.); veiller à (qch.). 'seeing. 1. s. vue f, vision f; s. is believing, voir c'est croire; it's worth s., cela vaut la peine d'être vu. 2. conj. phr. s. that, puisque, vu que.

seed [si:d], s. (a) graine f; (b) coll. semence f; graine(s) (c) to go to s., (i) monter en graine; (ii) F: (of pers.) se ramollir. '**seeded**, a. Sp: (at tennis) s. players, têtes f de série.

‡**seek** [si:k], v.tr. chercher; rechercher.

seem [si:m], v.i. 1. sembler, paraître. 2. impers. it seems to me, il me semble; so it seems, à ce qu'il paraît. '**seeming**, a. apparent; soi-disant. -ly, adv. apparemment.

seep [si:p], v.i. suinter; s'infiltrer.

seer ['si(:)ər], s. prophète m.

see-saw ['si:so:], s. bascule f, balançoire f.

seethe [si:ð], v.i. (a) bouillonner; (b) (of crowd, etc.) s'agiter, grouiller.

segment ['segmənt], *s.* segment *m.*

segregate ['segrigeit], *v.tr.* isoler; mettre à part. **segre'gation**, *s.* ségrégation *f.*

seize [si:z]. **1.** *v.tr.* saisir. **2.** *v.i. E:* to s. (up), gripper, coincer; caler. **'seizure**, *s.* **1.** saisie *f* (de marchandises). **2.** *Med:* attaque *f.*

seldom ['seldəm], *adv.* rarement.

select [si'lekt]. **I.** *v.tr.* choisir (from, parmi). **II.** *a.* choisi; de (premier) choix. **se'lection**, *s.* choix *m*; sélection *f.*

†**self** [self]. **1.** *s.* le moi; one's better s., son meilleur côté. **2.** *pron.* (*on cheque*) pay s., payez à moi-même. **self-as'sertive**, *a.* outrecuidant; autoritaire. **self-as'surance**, *s.* **self-'confidence**, *s.* confiance *f* en soi; assurance *f*; aplomb *m.* **self-'confident**, *a.* sûr de soi; plein d'assurance. **self-'conscious**, *a.* embarrassé, gêné. **self-'consciousness**, *s.* contrainte *f*, embarras *m*, gêne *f.* **self-con'tained**, *a.* s.-c. flat, appartement *m* avec entrée particulière. **self-con'trol**, *s.* sang-froid *m*; maîtrise *f* de soi. **self-de'fence**, *s.* défense *f* personnelle; *Jur:* légitime défense. **self-de'nial**, *s.* (*a*) renoncement à soi; renoncement(s) *m(pl)*; (*b*) frugalité *f.* **self-em'ployed**, *a.* (travailleur) indépendant. **self-es'teem**, *s.* respect *m* de soi; amour-propre *m.* **self-'evident**, *a.* évident; qui saute aux yeux. **self-'government**, *s.* autonomie *f.* **self-im'portant**, *a.* suffisant, présomptueux. **self-in'dulgent**, *a.* qui ne se refuse rien. **'selfish**, *a.* égoïste, intéressé. **-ly**, *adv.* égoïstement; en égoïste. **'selfishness**, *s.* égoïsme *m.* **self-po'ssessed**, *a.* maître de soi; qui a du sang-froid. **self-po'ssession**, *s.* aplomb *m*, sang-froid *m.* **self-pro'pelled**, *a.* autopropulsé. **self-re'liance**, *s.* indépendance *f.* **self-re'liant**, *a.* indépendant. **self-re'spect**, *s.* respect *m* de soi; amour-propre *m.* **self-re'specting**, *a.* qui se respecte. **self-'satisfied**, *a.* content de soi; suffisant. **self-'service**, *a.* & *s. Com:* libre-service (*m*). **self-'starter**, *s. Aut:* démarreur *m.*

‡**sell** [sel], *v.tr.* **1.** (*a*) vendre; he sold it for ten shillings, il a vendu dix shillings; (*b*) *Com:* (of goods) to s. well, se placer facilement. **2.** trahir, vendre (un secret); *F:* you've been sold! on vous a refait. **'seller**, *s.* vendeur, -euse. **'selling**, *s.* vente *f*; s. price, prix *m* de vente. **sell off**, *v.tr.* solder (des marchandises). **sell out**, *v.tr.* (*a*) *Fin:* réaliser (des actions); (*b*) *Com:* vendre tout son stock de (qch.); the edition is sold out, l'édition est épuisée.

semaphore ['seməfɔ:r], *s.* sémaphore *m.*

semi- ['semi], *prefix.* semi-; demi-. **'semicircle**, *s.* demi-cercle *m.* **semi-'circular**, *a.* demi-circulaire. **'semi-'colon**, *s.* point-virgule *m.* **semi-de'tached**, *a.* (maison) jumelle, jumelée. **'semi-'final**, *s. Sp:* demi-finale *f.*

†**seminary** ['seminəri], *s.* séminaire *m.*

Semitic [si'mitik], *a.* sémitique.

semolina [semə'li:nə], *s.* semoule *f.*

senate ['senit], *s.* sénat *m.* **'senator**, *s.* sénateur *m.*

‡**send** [send], *v.tr.* **1.** envoyer (qn, qch.); expédier (un colis, etc.); *F:* to s. s.o. packing, envoyer promener qn. **2.** *abs.* to s. for s.o., sth., envoyer chercher qn, qch. **send a'way**, *v.tr.* (*a*) renvoyer, congédier; (*b*) expédier. **send 'back**, *v.tr.* renvoyer. **send 'off**, *v.tr.* (*a*) envoyer (qn); (*b*) expédier (une lettre, etc.). **send 'on**, *v.tr.* (*a*) faire suivre; (*b*) transmettre (un message). **send 'out**, *v.tr.* (*a*) faire sortir (qn); (*b*) lancer (des prospectus). **send 'round**, *v.tr.* envoyer (qn, qch.). **send 'up**, *v.tr.* (*a*) faire monter (qn, qch.); (*b*) faire hausser (les prix). **'sender**, *s.* expéditeur, -trice (d'une lettre).

senile ['si:nail], *a.* sénile. **se'nility** [sə'nil-], *s.* sénilité *f.*

senior ['si:njər]. **1.** *a.* (*a*) aîné; père; supérieur. **2.** *s.* (*a*) aîné, -ée; doyen, -enne; (*b*) to be s.o.'s s., être l'ancien, le doyen, de qn; *Sch:* the seniors, les grands. **seni'ority**, *s.* **1.** priorité *f* d'âge; supériorité *f* d'âge. **2.** to be promoted by s., avancer à l'ancienneté *f.*

sensation [sen'seiʃ(ə)n], *s.* sensation *f.* **1.** sentiment *m*; impression *f.* **2.** effet *m* sensationnel. **sen'sational**, *a.* sensationnel.

sense [sens]. **I.** *s.* **1.** sens *m.* **2.** *pl.* in one's (right) senses, sain d'esprit; (*b*) to lose one's senses, perdre connaissance *f.* **3.** sensation *f* (de plaisir, etc.); to have a good s. of time, avoir le sentiment de l'heure. **4.** bon sens, intelligence *f*; to talk s., parler raison. **5.** sens, signification *f* (d'un mot). **II.** *v.tr.* sentir (qch.) intuitivement; pressentir (qch.). **'senseless**, *a.* **1.** stupide, déraisonnable. **2.** to knock s.o. s., assommer qn. **'senselessness**, *s.* stupidité *f.* **'sensible**, *a.* sensé, raisonnable; (choix) judicieux. **-ibly**, *adv.* raisonnablement; judicieusement. **'sensitive**, *a.* sensible, sensitif; (of pers.) susceptible. **'sensual**, *a.* sensuel. **sensu'ality**, *s.* sensualité *f.* **'sensuous**, *a.* voluptueux.

sentence ['sentəns]. **I.** *s.* **1.** (*a*) jugement *m*; sentence *f*, condamnation *f*; peine *f.* **2.** *Gram:* phrase *f.* **II.** *v.tr. Jur:* condamner (qn).

sententious [sen'tenʃəs], *a.* sentencieux.

sentiment ['sentimənt], s. 1. sentiment m. 2. sentimentalité f. senti'mental, a. sentimental. -ally, adv. sentimentalement.

†**sentry** ['sentri], s. 1. (a) factionnaire m; (b) sentinelle f. 2. to stand s.: monter la garde. 'sentry-box, s. guérite f.

sepal ['sep(ə)l], s. sépale m.

separate, I. a. ['sep(ə)rət], (a) séparé, détaché; (b) distinct, indépendant. -ly, adv. séparément; à part. II. v.tr. & i. ['sepəreit] (se) séparer. sepa'ration, s. 1. séparation f. 2. écart m, distance f.

sepia ['si:pjə], s. sépia f.

September [sep'tembər], s. septembre m.

septic ['septik], a. septique; P: moche, infecte. septi'caemia, s. septicémie f.

sepulchre ['sep(ə)lkər], s. sépulcre m.

sequel ['si:kw(ə)l], s. suite f.

sequence ['si:kwəns], s. 1. (a) succession f; ordre m naturel; in s., en série; (b) suite f, série f; (c) Gram: concordance f (des temps). 2. (at cards) séquence f. 3. Cin: scène f.

sequoia [se'kwɔiə], s. Bot: séquoia m.

serenade [serə'neid], s. sérénade f.

serene [sə'ri:n], a. serein, calme. -ly, adv. tranquillement; avec sérénité. se'renity, s. sérénité f, calme m.

serge [sə:dʒ], s. serge f.

sergeant ['sɑ:dʒənt], s. (a) sergent m; maréchal m des logis; Av: flight s., sergent-chef m; (b) (police) s., brigadier m; 'sergeant-'major, s. = sergent-major m, adjudant m; regimental s.-m. = adjudant chef.

serial ['siəriəl], I. a. s. number, numéro de série. 2. s. feuilleton m.

series ['siəri:z], s. série f, suite f.

serious ['siəriəs], a. sérieux; s. injury, blessure f grave; I'm s., je ne plaisante pas. -ly, adv. sérieusement; s. ill, gravement malade. 'seriousness, s. 1. gravité f (d'une maladie, etc.). 2. sérieux m (de maintien, etc.); in all s., sérieusement.

sermon ['sə:mən], s. sermon m; homélie f.

serpent ['sə:p(ə)nt], s. serpent m.

serrated [se'reitid], a. dentelé.

serum ['siərəm], s. sérum m; immunisant m.

serve [sə:v]. 1. v.tr. (a) (of pers.) servir (un maître, un client, une cause, etc.); abs. servir (à table); (in shop) are you being served? est-ce qu'on s'occupe de vous? Jur: to s. on a jury, être du jury; (b) (of thing) être utile à (qn); it will s. the purpose, cela fera l'affaire; (c) it serves you right! c'est bien fait! vous ne l'avez pas volé; (d) (of bull, etc.) couvrir (une vache, etc.). 2. v.i. to s. as a pretext, servir de prétexte. 'servant, s. 1. domestique mf; bonne f. 2. civil s., fonctionnaire m. 'server, s. 1. (a) serveur, -euse;

(b) Ecc: acolyte m, répondant m. 2. salad, fish, servers, service m à salade, à poisson. 'service. I. s. 1. service m; public services, services publics; military s., service militaire. 2. the civil s., l'administration f; the foreign s., le service diplomatique; the (armed) services, les forces armées; the Senior S., la marine. 3. (domestic) s., service (domestique). s. flat, appartement m avec service; (in restaurant) s. charge, service. 4. to do s.o. a s., rendre (un) service à qn; I am at your s., je suis à votre disposition; social services, institutions f sociales. 5. Ecc: office m; culte m. 6. (at tennis) service. 7. tea s., service à thé. II. v.tr. entretenir et réparer (des autos, etc.). 'serviceable, a. (a) en état de fonctionner; utilisable; (b) pratique, commode. †'serviceman, s. soldat m, mobilisé m; disabled ex-s., mutilé m de guerre.

serviette [sə:vi'et], s. serviette f de table.

servile ['sə:vail], a. servile. ser'vility ['-vil-], s. servilité f.

servitude ['sə:vitju:d], s. servitude f.

session ['seʃən], s. session f; séance f.

set [set]. I. s. 1. (a) jeu m (d'outils); série f (de casseroles); batterie f (d'ustensiles de cuisine); service m (de porcelaine); train m (de pneus); (b) poste m (de radio, de télévision); (c) (at tennis) set m; (d) groupe m (de personnes). 2. (a) F: to make a dead s. at s.o., attaquer furieusement qn. (b) (for hair) mise f en plis. 3. (a) assiette f (d'une poutre); tournure f (d'un vêtement); voie f, chasse f (d'une scie). 4. Th: Cin: décor m; mise f en scène. II. v.tr. 1. (a) mettre, poser (qch. sur qch.); I haven't s. eyes on him, je ne l'ai pas vu; (b) to s. the table, mettre le couvert; (c) to s. the alarm for six o'clock, mettre le réveil sur six heures; Aut: to s. the speedometer to zero, ramener le compteur à zéro; (d) to have one's hair s., se faire faire une mise en plis; (e) Th: to s. a scene, monter un décor; (f) to s. a gem, sertir, enchâsser, une pierre; (g) to s. a trap, dresser, tendre, un piège; (h) to s. a chisel, affûter un ciseau; (i) to s. type, composer; (j) to s. the fashion, fixer, mener, la mode; (k) to s. a bone, remettre un os; (l) to s. one's teeth, serrer les dents; (m) to s. sth. going, mettre qch. en train; (n) to s. a good example, donner un bon exemple; to s. a problem, donner un problème à résoudre; Sch: to s. a book, mettre un livre au programme. 2. v.i. (a) (of sun) se coucher; (b) (of broken bone) se ressouder; (c) (of white of egg) se coaguler; (of jelly) prendre; (d) to s. to work, se mettre au travail. III. a. 1. (sourire) figé; to be all s., être prêt à commencer. 2. (prix) fixe; s. phrase, cliché m; Sch: the s. books, les auteurs m du programme. 3. to be s. on doing sth., être résolu, déterminé, à faire qch. **set a'bout**, v.i. to s.a. doing sth., se mettre à faire qch. **'set-back**, s. déconvenue f; revers m de fortune. **set 'down**, v.tr. poser (qch.); déposer (qn); coucher (qch. par écrit). **set 'in**, v.i. commencer; before winter sets in, avant le début de l'hiver. **set 'off**. 1. v.tr. faire partir (une fusée). 2. v.i. partir; se mettre en route. **set 'out**. 1. v.tr. arranger, disposer. 2. v.i. se mettre en route. **'set square**, s. équerre f. **'setting**, s. cadre m (d'un récit, etc.); Th: mise f en scène; monture f (d'un diamant); aiguisage m, affûtage m (d'un outil); mise f en plis (des cheveux); coucher m (du soleil); réduction f (d'une fracture); type s, composition f. **'set-to**, s. F: lutte f; combat m. **set 'up**, v.tr. monter (une machine); (of printer) composer (un manuscrit); établir (une agence, un record); organisation f.

settee [se'ti:], s. canapé m, causeuse f.

setter ['setər], s. chien m d'arrêt; setter m.

settle ['setl]. 1. v.tr. (a) établir, installer (qn); mettre ordre à (ses affaires); (b) dissiper (les doutes); calmer (les nerfs); (c) fixer, déterminer (une date); (d) résoudre, décider (une question); arranger, liquider (une affaire); that settles it! (i) voilà qui tranche la question! (ii) cela me décide! (e) payer, régler son compte. 2. v.i. (a) s'établir (dans un lieu); (of bird) se percher; (of snow) prendre, ne pas fondre; (b) (of liquid) se clarifier, déposer; (c) (of ground, pillar) prendre son assiette; se tasser; (of foundations) s'affaisser; (of weather) se calmer. **'settled**, a. (a) invariable, sûr; (of idea) enraciné; (of pers.) rangé; (of question) arrangé, décidé. **settle 'down**, v.i. (of pers.) se ranger; devenir sérieux; he's beginning to s.d. at school, il commence à s'habituer à l'école. **'settlement**, s. (also settling) 1. peuplement m (d'un pays). 2. règlement m (d'une affaire, d'un compte). 3. accord m amical. **'settler**, s. colon m; immigrant m.

seven ['sevn], num. a. & s. sept (m). **'seven'teen**, num. a. & s. dix-sept (m). **'seven'teenth**, num. a. & s. dix-septième (mf); the s. of March, le dix-sept mars. **'seventh**, num. a. & s. septième (mf); the s. of May, le sept mai. **'seventieth**, num. a. & s. soixante-dixième (mf). **'seventy**, num. a. & s. soixante-dix (m).

sever ['sevər], v.tr. désunir, disjoindre; rompre (une amitié).

several ['sevrəl], a. plusieurs; quelques.

severe [si'viər], a. 1. sévère, strict, rigoureux. 2. (a) (of weather) rigoureux, dur; (b) (of pain) vif; Med: s. cold, gros rhume. **-ly**, adv. 1. sévèrement; avec sévérité. 2. gravement (blessé). **se'verity**, s. sévérité f, rigueur f.

‡**sew** [sou], v.tr. coudre. **'sewing**, s. couture f; s. cotton, fil m à coudre; s. machine, machine f à coudre.

sewer ['sjuər], s. égout m. **'sewage**, s. eau f d'égout.

sex [seks], s. sexe m; s. appeal, charme m sensuel; F: sex-appeal m. **'sexless**, a. 1. asexué. 2. F: froid, frigide. **'sexual**, a. sexuel; s. intercourse, rapports m sexuels; s. reproduction, reproduction sexuée. **'sexy**, a. F: excitant, aguichant.

sextet [seks'tet], s. Mus: sextuor m.

sexton ['sekstən], s. (a) sacristain m; (b) fossoyeur m.

shabby ['ʃæbi], a. 1. pauvre, minable; to look s., avoir l'air râpé. 2. (of action) mesquin; peu honorable. **-ily**, adv. 1. pauvrement; s. dressed, miteux. 2. (se conduire) mesquinement. **'shabbiness**, s. 1. état m râpé, usé (d'un vêtement); apparence f pauvre, miteuse (de qn). 2. mesquinerie f (de conduite).

shade [ʃeid]. I. s. 1. ombre f. 2. nuance f; teinte f. 3. abat-jour m inv. II. v.tr. 1. ombrager; couvrir (qch.) d'ombre. 2. ombrer (un dessin); hachurer (une carte). **'shadiness**, s. 1. ombre f, ombrage m. 2. F: aspect m louche (d'une affaire). **'shady**, a. 1. ombragé; couvert d'ombre. 2. F: (affaire) louche.

shadow ['ʃædou]. I. s. ombre f; not the s. of a doubt, pas l'ombre d'un doute; Pol: s. cabinet, conseil m des ministres fantôme. II. v.tr. filer (qn). **'shadowing**, s. filature f (d'une personne suspecte). **'shadowy**, a. indécis, vague.

shaft[1] [ʃɑːft], s. 1. hampe f, bois m. 2. flèche f, trait m. 3. rayon m (de lumière). 4. fût m (d'une colonne). 5. Aut: etc: arbre m. 6. (of cart) brancard m.

shaft[2], s. puits m; cage f (d'un ascenseur).

shaggy ['ʃægi], a. poilu; (barbe) hirsute.

shake [ʃeik]. I. s. 1. secousse f; a s. of the head, un hochement de tête; to be all of a s., trembler de tous ses membres; F: in a s., en un rien de temps. 2. egg s., lait m de poule. 3. F: to be no great shakes, ne pas valoir grand-chose. II. †v. 1. v.tr. (a) secouer, agiter; to s. hands with s.o., serrer la main à qn; to s. oneself free, se dégager d'une secousse; (b) ébranler. 2. v.i. trembler. 'shake-down, s. F: lit m improvisé. 'shaken, a. secoué; émotionné. 'shaking. I. a. tremblant, branlant. II. s. secouement m; to get a good s. up, être pas mal secoué. shake 'off, v.tr. 1. venir à bout (d'un rhume). 2. se débarrasser de (qn). 'shaky, a. peu solide; faible; to feel s., ne pas être d'aplomb.

‡**shall** [ʃæl, ʃ(ə)l], modal aux. v. I. (implying command, insistence) 1. (a) all is as it should be, tout est très bien; (b) you s. do it! vous le ferez, je le veux! (c) you should do it, vous devriez le faire; you should have seen him, il fallait le voir! (d) I should think so! je crois bien! 2. s. I open the window? voulez-vous que j'ouvre la fenêtre? 3. if he should come, si par hasard il vient; should I be free, si je suis libre. II. (aux. of future or conditional) 1. you shan't have any! tu n'en auras pas! 2. (a) will you be there?—I s., y serez-vous?—oui (, j'y serai); (b) s. you come tomorrow? vous viendrez demain? 3. we should come if we were invited, nous viendrions si on nous invitait. 4. I should like a drink, je prendrais bien quelque chose.

shallot [ʃə'lɔt], s. échalote f.

shallow ['ʃæləu], I. a. (a) peu profond; plat; (b) superficiel, frivole; s. usu. pl. bas-fond m, haut-fond m. 'shallowness, s. (a) le peu de profondeur; (b) caractère m superficiel.

sham [ʃæm]. I. a. simulé, feint; faux, f. fausse. II. s. feinte f, trompe-l'œil m inv. III. ‡v.tr. feindre, simuler.

shambles ['ʃæmblz], s.pl. F: désordre m, gâchis m.

shame [ʃeim], I. s. 1. (a) honte f; (b) it's a s.! c'est honteux! what a s.! quel dommage! 2. v.tr. faire honte à, humilier (qn). 'shamefaced, a. honteux, embarrassé; penaud. 'shameful, a. honteux, scandaleux. 'shameless, a. (a) effronté, cynique; (b) honteux, scandaleux. -ly, adv. effrontément. 'shamelessness, s. 1. immodestie f. 2. effronterie f.

shampoo [ʃæm'pu:]. I. s. shampooing m. II. v.tr. se laver (la tête).

shamrock ['ʃæmrɔk], s. trèfle m d'Irlande.

shandy ['ʃændi], s. bière f panachée.

shan't [ʃɑːnt]. See SHALL.

‡**shanty** ['ʃænti], s. hutte f, cabane f; s. town, bidonville m.

shape [ʃeip], s. forme f; no communication in any s. or form, aucune communication de n'importe quelle sorte. 'shapeless, a. informe; difforme. 'shapelessness, s. manque m de forme. 'shapely, a. bien fait, bien tourné.

share [ʃɛər]. I. s. 1. part f, portion f; s. in profits, participation f aux bénéfices; to go shares, partager; s. and s. alike, en partageant également. 2. contribution f, écot m. 3. Fin: action f, titre m. II. v.tr. partager; prendre part à, participer à (qch.). 'share-cropping, s. Agr: métayage m. 'shareholder, s. Fin: actionnaire mf.

shark [ʃɑːk], s. requin m.

sharp [ʃɑːp]. I. a. 1. (a) tranchant, aiguisé; aigu, pointu; (b) (of features) anguleux; (c) (of outline) net; (of pers.) (a) fin; éveillé; pénétrant; (b) rusé, malin; s. practice, procédés peu honnêtes. 3. s. tongue, langue acérée. -ly, adv. brusquement; sévèrement. II. s. a. s.: dièse (m). III. adv. (a) turn s. to the right, prenez à droite, à angle droit; at four s., à quatre heures sonnantes. F: pile; F: look s.! grouille-toi! 'sharpen, v.tr. affiler, affûter, aiguiser; tailler (en pointe). 'sharpness, s. 1. acuité f; netteté f (d'un contour). 2. sévérité f, acerbité f (du ton).

shatter ['ʃætər], v.tr. fracasser; briser. 'shattering, s. (coup) écrasant.

shave [ʃeiv], v.tr.v. (se) raser. 'shaving, s. 1. action f de se raser; s. brush, blaireau m; s. soap, savon m à barbe. 2. pl. copeaux mpl (de bois).

shawl [ʃɔːl], s. châle m.

she [ʃi, ʃiː], pers. pron. 1. elle; here she comes, la voici (qui vient). 2. she who believes, celle qui croit. 3. (used as noun) F: femelle f; s. cat, chatte f.

‡**sheaf** [ʃiːf], s. 1. gerbe f (de blé, de fleurs). 2. liasse f (de papiers).

shear [ʃiər], v.tr. tondre (un mouton). 'shears, s.pl. cisaille(s) f(pl); grands ciseaux mpl.

sheath [ʃiːθ], s. fourreau m; gaine f.

shed¹ [ʃiːd], s. hangar m; appentis m; remise f.

‡**shed²**, v.tr. 1. perdre (ses feuilles). 2. répandre, verser (des larmes, la lumière); to s. light on a matter, éclairer une affaire. 3. El: to s. the load, délester.

sheen [ʃiːn], s. luisant m, lustre m.

‡**sheep** [ʃiːp], s. mouton m. 'sheepdog, s. chien m de berger. 'sheepish, a. penaud; gauche. -ly, adv. d'un air penaud, timide. 'sheepskin, s. peau f de mouton.

sheer¹ [ʃiər], v.i. Nau: embarder. sheer 'off, v.i. 1. Nau: larguer les amarres. 2. F: prendre la large.

sheer², a. (a) pur, véritable; absolu; a s. waste of time, une pure perte de temps; (b) (rocher) à pic; (c) (of silk, etc.) fin.

sheet [ʃiːt], s. 1. drap m (de lit). 2. feuille f (de papier, de plomb); s. iron, (fer m en) tôle f. 3. nappe f (d'eau); s. lightning, éclairs mpl diffus, en nappes.

†**shelf** [ʃelf], s. planche f; rayon m (de bibliothèque); F: to be on the s., être au rancart.

shell [ʃel]. I. s. 1. coquille f; coque f. 2. obus m. II. v.tr. 1. écosser (des pois). 2. Mil: bombarder. 'shellfish, s. coll: mollusques m et crustacés m; fruits m de mer. shell 'out, v.tr. F: payer (la note); débourser.

shelter ['ʃeltər]. I. s. abri m; asile m; under s., à l'abri, à couvert. II. v. 1. v.tr. abriter. 2. v.i. & pr. se mettre à l'abri, à couvert. 'sheltered, a. abrité.

shelve [ʃelv], v.tr. 1. mettre (des livres) sur des rayons. 2. ajourner, enterrer (une question). 'shelving, s. rayons mpl.

shepherd ['ʃepəd], s. berger m; Ecc: the Good S., le bon Pasteur. 'shepherdess, s. bergère f.

sheriff ['ʃerif], s. U.S: chef de la police (d'un comté).

†**sherry** ['ʃeri], s. vin m de Xérès; xérès m.

shield [ʃi:ld]. I. s. bouclier m. II. v.tr. protéger.

shift [ʃift]. I. s. 1. changement m de position. 2. (a) équipe f, poste m; to work in shifts, se relayer; (b) Ind: shift m. 3. Cl: (robe f) fourreau m. 4. expédient m. II. v. 1. v.tr. déplacer (qch.); Th: to s. the scenery, changer le décor. 2. v.i. (a) se déplacer; (b) the wind has shifted, le vent a tourné; (c) F: to s. for oneself, se débrouiller. 'shiftless, a. paresseux; peu débrouillard. 'shiftwork, s. Ind: travail m par équipes. 'shifty, a. roublard, retors; (regard) sournois.

shimmer ['ʃimər], v.i. miroiter; chatoyer.

shin [ʃin], s. devant m de la jambe; Cu: jarret m (de bœuf).

†**shine** [ʃain]. I. v.i. 1. briller; reluire; the sun is shining, il fait du soleil. 2. to s. on sth., éclairer, illuminer, qch. II. s. brillant m; luisant m. 'shining, a. brillant, (re)luisant. 'shiny, a. brillant, luisant; (vêtement) lustré par l'usage.

shingle ['ʃingl], s. galets mpl.

shingles ['ʃinglz], s.pl. Med: zona m.

ship [ʃip]. I. s. navire m; bâtiment m; on board s., à bord. II. †v.tr. 1. (i) embarquer,. (ii) expédier (des marchandises). 2. Nau: to s. a sea, embarquer (une lame). 'shipbuilder, s. constructeur m de navires. 'shipbuilding, s. construction f navale. 'shipment, s. 1. embarquement m; expédition f (de marchandises). 2. (goods shipped) chargement m. 'shipper, s. 1. chargeur m; expéditeur m. 2. affréteur m. 'shipping, s. 1. embarquement m; expédition f (de marchandises); s. agent, company, agence f maritime. 2. coll: navires mpl. 3. s. routes, routes f de navigation. 'shipshape, a. Nau: bien tenu; en bon ordre. 'shipwreck. I. s.

naufrage m. II. v.tr. to be shipwrecked, faire naufrage. 'shipyard, s. chantier m naval.

shire [ʃaiər, ʃ(ə)r], s. (usu. as ending of Pr.n.) comté m; Ayrshire, le comté d'Ayr.

shirk [ʃə:k], v.tr. manquer à, se dérober à (une obligation); abs. négliger son devoir. 'shirker, s. F: carotteur, -euse.

shirt [ʃə:t], s. chemise f; in one's shirt-sleeves, en bras de chemise; F: to put one's s. on a horse, parier tout ce qu'on possède sur un cheval; F: keep your s. on! ne vous emballez pas. 'shirt-'waist, s. chemisier m. 'shirt-'waister, s. robe f chemisier.

shiver ['ʃivər]. I. v.i. frissonner, grelotter, trembler. II. s. frisson m.

shoal [ʃoul], s. banc m voyageur (de poissons); tas m (de lettres).

shock [ʃɔk]. I. s. 1. choc m, heurt m. 2. (a) coup m, atteinte f; (b) electric s., secousse f électrique; (c) Med: choc; commotion f. II. v.tr. choquer, scandaliser (qn); bouleverser (qn). 'shocking, a. choquant; révoltant; affreux.

shoddy ['ʃɔdi], a. de mauvaise qualité, de camelote. 'shoddiness, s. mauvaise qualité f.

shoe [ʃu:], s. 1. soulier m; chaussure f; to put on one's shoes, se chausser. 'shoebrush, s. brosse f à souliers. 'shoehorn, s. chausse-pied m. 'shoemaker, s. (a) bottier m; (b) fabricant m de chaussures. 'shoestring, s. F: on a s., à peu de frais.

shoot [ʃu:t]. I. †v. 1. v.i. (a) se précipiter, se lancer; to s. ahead of s.o., devancer qn rapidement; (b) (of pain) lanciner, élancer; (c) (of tree, bud) pousser, bourgeonner; (of plant) germer. 2. v.tr. (a) franchir (un rapide); Aut: to s. the lights, brûler le feu rouge; (b) F: to s. a line, (i) exagérer son importance; (ii) baratiner; (c) lancer, tirer (une balle); décharger (un fusil); abs. tirer; to s. wide of the mark, (i) mal viser, (ii) être loin de la vérité; (d) tuer (qn) d'un coup de fusil; (e) chasser (le gibier); (f) Cin: tourner (un film); (g) Sp: to s. a goal, marquer un but. II. s. 1. pousse f (d'une plante); (of vine) sarment m; (of) Ind: couloir m, glissière f; goulotte f. 3. (a) partie f de chasse; (b) concours m de tir. 4. chasse f (gardée). S.F: the whole s., tout le bataclan. 'shooting, s. (a) s. incident, bagarre f avec coups de feu; (b) tir m (au pistolet); (c) la chasse; Aut: s. brake, break m (de chasse); canadienne f; s. stick, canne-siège f. 'shoot 'up. v.i. (of flame) jaillir; (of prices) augmenter rapidement; (of plant) pousser; (of child) grandir rapidement. 2. v.tr. Mil: Av:

shot [ʃɔt], s. 1. coll. projectiles mpl. 2. plomb m. 3. (a) coup m (de feu); (b) tireur, -euse. 'shot-gun, s. fusil m de chasse.

should. See SHALL.

shoulder ['ʃouldər], s. (a) épaule f; slung across the s., en bandoulière; s. blade, omoplate f; s. strap, bretelle f; épaulette f; (b) bas-côté m (d'une route).

shout [ʃaut]. I. s. (a) cri m; éclat m (de rire); (b) clameur f. II. v.i. & tr. crier; to s. s.o. down, huer qn. 'shouting, s. cris mpl; acclamations fpl.

shove [ʃʌv]. I. v.tr. F: pousser. II. s. F: coup m (d'épaule); poussée f.

shovel ['ʃʌv(ə)l]. I. s. pelle f. II. v.tr. pelleter; P: bâfrer (son repas). 'shovelful, s. pelletée f.

show [ʃou]. I. s. 1. étalage m (de qch.). 2. house, flat, maison f, appartement m, témoin. 2. (a) exposition f; motor s., salon m de l'automobile; fashion s., présentation f de collections; (b) Th: etc: spectacle m; film s., séance f de cinéma; to make a s. of oneself, se donner en spectacle; F: good s.! bravo! 3. (a) apparence f; semblant m; (b) parade f. 4. F: affaire f. II. ‡v. 1. v.tr. montrer; indiquer; to show s.o. to his room, conduire qn à sa chambre; to show s.o. round (the house), faire visiter (la maison), à qn; abs. time will s., qui vivra verra; F: I'll s. you (where you get off)! je vous apprendrai! 2. v.i. se montrer, se laisser voir; your slip's showing, votre jupon dépasse; to s. willing, faire preuve de bonne volonté. 'showcase, s. vitrine f. 'showdown, s. F: déballage m; if it comes to a s., s'il faut en venir au fait.

shower ['ʃauər]. I. s. (a) averse f; (b) volée f (de pierres); (c) douche f. II. v.tr. verser; accabler (qn d'invitations); to s. blows on s.o., faire pleuvoir des coups sur qn. 'showery, a. (temps) pluvieux.

showiness, s. prétention f; ostentation f. †'showman, s. forain m; he's a great s., c'est un as pour la mise en scène. 'showmanship, s. art m de la mise en scène. show 'off. 1. v.tr. (a) faire valoir (qch.); (b) faire étalage de (qch.). 2. v.i. poser, se pavaner. 'showpiece, s. article m d'exposition; monument m de grand intérêt. 'showroom, s. Com: salle f, magasin m, d'exposition. 'show 'up. 1. v.tr. démasquer (un imposteur); révéler (un défaut). 2. v.i. se détacher, ressortir (sur un fond); F: se présenter; faire acte de présence. 'showy, a. prétentieux, voyant.

shred [ʃred]. I. s. brin m; lambeau m, fragment m (d'étoffe). II. ‡v.tr.

---

mitrailler (un aérodrome, etc.); F: révolvériser (qn).

shop [ʃɔp]. I. s. 1. magasin m; (small) boutique f; s. assistant, vendeur, -euse; s. window, vitrine f; devanture f (de magasin); étalage m; mobile s., camionnette-boutique f; F: you've come to the wrong s., vous vous trompez d'adresse; F: all over the s., en confusion, en désordre. 2. Ind: workshop; s. closed, atelier fermé aux (ouvriers) non-syndiqués. 3. to talk s., parler métier. II. v.i. faire des achats. 'shopkeeper, s. commerçant, -ante; boutiquier, -ière. 'shop-lifting, s. vol m à l'étalage. 'shopper, s. acheteur, -euse. 'shopping, s. achats mpl; to go s., faire ses courses; to go window s., faire du lèche-vitrines. 'shop-soiled, a. (article) défraîchi. 'shopwalker, s. 1. chef m de rayon. 2. Ind: inspecteur, -trice.

shore¹ [ʃɔːr], s. rivage m; bord m (de la mer, d'un lac); on s. à terre; U.S: s. dinner, repas m composé de fruits de mer.

shore². I. s. étai m; contre-boutant m. II. v.tr. to s. up, étayer, contre-bouter (un mur).

short [ʃɔːt]. I. a. 1. court; de petite taille. 2. (of time) bref; s. story, nouvelle f; (of reply) brusque; sec. F: a s., un petit verre. 3. (of weight) insuffisant; I'm 20 francs s., il me manque 20 francs; to be s. of sth., être à court de qch. 4. Cu: s. pastry, pâte f brisée. -ly, adv. 1. brièvement; en peu de mots. 2. (répondre) brusquement, sèchement. 3. bientôt; s. after(wards), peu de temps après. II. s. 1. (a) the long and the s. of it, le fin mot de l'affaire; (b) pl. Cl: shorts, short m. 2. El: F: court-circuit m. 3. Cin: court métrage m. III. adv. 1. (s'arrêter) pile. 2. to fall s. of the mark, ne pas atteindre le but; s. of burning it, à moins de le brûler; to stop s. of crime, s'arrêter au seuil du crime. IV. v.tr. El: F: court-circuiter. 'shortage, s. insuffisance f; pénurie f; disette f. 'shortbread, s. Cu: = sablé m. short 'circuit, El: s. court-circuit m. II. v.tr. court-circuiter. 'shortcomings, spl. défauts m, imperfections f. 'shorten, v.i. & tr. raccourcir. 'shorthand, s. sténo(graphie) f; s. typist, sténo(dactylo) mf. short-handed, a. à court de main-d'œuvre, de personnel. short-'lived, a. éphémère, de courte durée. 'shortness, s. 1. peu m de longueur; brièveté f; brusquerie f (d'humeur). 2. manque m, insuffisance f (de vivres). short-'sighted. a. 1. myope. 2. imprévoyant. short-'tempered, a. vif; d'un caractère emporté. 'short-term, a. (placement, etc.) à court terme.

shy³. I. *v.tr.* F: lancer (une pierre, une balle). II. †*s.* (*at fair*) three shies for sixpence, trois coups m pour six pence.

Siamese [saiə'mi:z], *a. & s.* siamois, -oise.

sick [sik], *a.* I. malade: to be on the s. list, être malade. 2. to feel s., avoir mal au cœur; to be s., vomir; F: I'm s. of it! j'en ai plein le dos! '**sicken.** I. *v.i.* (*a*) to be sickening for an illness, couver une maladie; (*b*) se lasser (de qch.). 2. *v.tr.* F: it sickens me, ça me soulève le cœur. '**sickening,** *a.* F: écœurant. '**sickly,** *a.* maladif; s. smile, sourire pâle. '**sickness,** *s.* 1. maladie *f*; air, car, s., mal m de l'air, de voiture. 2. mal de cœur; nausées *fpl.*

sickle ['sikl], *s.* faucille *f*.

side [said], I. *s.* 1. flanc m; by the s. of, à côté de; s. by s., côte à côte. 2. (*a*) wrong s. out, à l'envers; (*b*) to hear both sides, entendre le pour et le contre. 3. on this s., de ce côté-ci; to move to one's, se ranger; F: to make sth. on the side, faire de la gratte. 4. (*a*) parti m; (*b*) section *f*, division *f*; (*c*) camp m, équipe *f*. 5. *attrib.* latéral, de côté; s. issue, question d'intérêt secondaire. II. *v.i.* to s. with s.o., se ranger du côté de qn. '**sideboard,** s. buffet m. '**sidelight,** s. lumière *f* oblique; aperçu m indirect. 2. *Aut:* feu m de position; *Nau:* feu de côté. '**sidewalk,** s. *U.S:* trottoir m. '**sideways,** *adv.* de côté; latéralement. '**siding,** s. Rail: voie *f* de garage.

sidle ['saidl], *v.i.* s'avancer de côté; to couler (auprès de qn).

siege [si:dʒ], *s.* siège m.

siesta [si'estə], *s.* sieste *f*.

sieve [siv]. I. *s.* crible m; tamis m. II. *v.tr.* passer au tamis.

sift [sift], *v.tr.* (*a*) passer au tamis; tamiser; (*b*) examiner minutieusement.

sigh [sai]. I. *s.* soupir m. II. *v.i.* soupirer.

sight [sait]. I. *s.* 1. vue *f*; to catch s. of, apercevoir; to lose s. of, perdre de vue; I can't bear the s. of him, je ne peux pas le sentir; at first s., au premier abord. 2. to come into s., (ap)paraître; out of s., caché aux regards. 3. spectacle m; chose *f* digne d'être vue; the sights, les monuments (de la ville); F: what a s. you are! comme vous voilà fait! II. *v.tr.* 1. *Nau:* relever (la terre). 2. pointer (un fusil). '**sightseeing,** s. to go s., visiter les monuments, les curiosités (d'une ville). '**sightseer,** s. touriste *mf*.

sign [sain]. I. *s.* signe m; indice m, indication *f*; shop s., enseigne *f*; international road signs, signalisation *f* routière internationale. II. *v.tr.* signer. **sign 'off,** *v.i.* (*of worker*) pointer au départ. **sign 'on.** I. *v.tr.* embaucher (un ouvrier); engager (un

----

shrewd [fru:d], *a.* sagace, perspicace; qui a du flair; s. blow, coup bien placé. **-ly,** *adv.* sagacement; avec finesse. '**shrewdness,** *s.* sagacité *f*; finesse *f*.

shriek [fri:k]. I. *s.* 1. cri m perçant; shrieks of laughter, grands éclats m de rire. 2. F: point m d'exclamation. II. *v.i.* pousser des cris aigus; to s. with laughter, rire aux éclats.

shrill [fril], *a.* aigu, strident.

shrimp [frimp], *s.* crevette *f* (grise).

shrine [frain], *s.* 1. tombeau m (de saint). 2. autel m (consacré à un saint).

‡**shrink** [friŋk], *v.i.* (*a*) se contracter; (se) rétrécir; (*b*) faire un mouvement de recul; to s. from doing sth., répugner à faire qch. '**shrinking.** 1. *v.tr.* (*a*) (capital) qui diminue. 2. timide, craintif. II. *s.* rétrécissement m (d'un tissu).

‡**shrivel** ['friv(ə)l]. 1. *v.tr.* brûler (les plantes). 2. *v.i.* se rider, se ratatiner.

shroud [fraud], *s.* linceul m, suaire m. '**shrouded,** *a.* enveloppé, voilé (de brume, etc.).

shrove [frouv] **S. Tuesday,** mardi m gras.

shrub [frʌb], *s.* arbrisseau m, arbuste m. '**shrubbery,** s. plantation *f* d'arbustes.

shrug [frʌg]. I. *v.tr.* hausser les épaules. II. *s.* haussement m d'épaules.

shrunken ['frʌŋkn], *a.* contracté; ratatiné.

shudder ['fʌdər]. I. *s.* frisson m; frémissement m. II. *v.i.* frissonner; frémir.

shuffle ['fʌfl]. I. *v.tr. & i.* traîner les pieds. 2. *v.tr.* (*at cards*) battre; mêler. 3. *v.i.* équivoquer.

‡**shun** [fʌn], *v.tr.* fuir, éviter.

shunt [fʌnt], *v.tr.* Rail: manœuvrer (un train). '**shunting,** s. manœuvre *f*; aiguillage m.

‡**shut** [fʌt]. 1. *v.tr.* fermer. 2. *v.i.* (se) fermer. **shut 'down,** *v.tr.* fermer (une usine, etc.). **shut 'in,** *v.tr.* (*a*) enfermer; (*b*) entourer, encercler (un endroit). **shut 'off,** *v.tr.* séparer, isoler (from, de). **shut 'out,** *v.tr.* (*a*) exclure (qn); (*b*) fermer la porte à (qn). '**shutter,** s. 1. volet m. 2. *Phot:* obturateur m. '**shut 'up.** 1. *v.tr.* enfermer (qn); fermer (une maison); F: réduire (qn) au silence. 2. *v.i.* F: se taire; s. up! la ferme!

shuttle ['fʌtl], *s.* navette *f*.

shy¹ [fai], *v.i.* (*of horse*) faire un écart; broncher.

shy². *a.* sauvage, farouche, timide; to fight s. of a job, éviter une besogne. **-ly,** *adv.* timidement. '**shyness,** *s.* timidité *f*; réserve *f*; sauvagerie *f*.

matelot). 2. v.i. (of worker) pointer à l'arrivée. 'signpost. I. s. poteau m indicateur. II. v.tr. F: signaliser (une route).

signal ['signl]. I. signal m; Aut: traffic signals, feux m de circulation. II. v. 1. v.i. Aut: to s. before stopping, avertir avant de stopper. 2. v.tr. signaler (un train); faire signe (à qn de s'arrêter). 'signal box, s. Rail: cabine f à signaux; poste m d'aiguillage. †'signalman, s. Rail: aiguilleur m.

signature ['signətʃər], s. signature f; s. tune, indicatif m musical.

signet ['signit], s. sceau m, cachet m; s. ring, (bague f) chevalière f.

significance [sig'nifikəns], s. 1. signification f. 2. importance f, conséquence f. sig'nificant, a. 1. significatif. 2. important. -ly, adv. d'une manière significative. 'signify. 1. v.tr. signifier; vouloir dire. 2. v.i. importer; it doesn't s., cela n'importe guère.

silence ['sailəns], s. 1. silence m. II. v.tr. réduire (qn) au silence; étouffer (les plaintes); Aut: to s. the exhaust, assourdir l'échappement. 'silencer, s. Aut: pot m d'échappement. 'silent, a. silencieux. -ly, adv. silencieusement.

silhouette [silu(:)'et], s. silhouette f.

silk [silk], s. soie f. 'silkworm, s. ver m à soie.

sill [sil], s. tablette f de fenêtre.

silly ['sili], a. sot, niais; to do sth. silly, faire une bêtise; to knock s.o. s., étourdir, assommer, qn; s. ass! imbécile! 'silliness, s. sottise f, niaiserie f.

silo ['sailou], s. 1. Agr: silo m. 2. launching s., puits m de lancement.

silt [silt], s. 1. dépôt m vaseux; vase f; limon m. II. v.tr. & i. to s. up, (s')envaser; (s')ensabler.

silver ['silvər], s. 1. argent m. 2. attrib. d'argent, en argent; s. mounted, monté en argent; s.-plated, argenté; s. paper, papier m d'étain. 3. argent monnayé. 4. argenterie f. 'silversmith, s. orfèvre m.

similar ['similər], a. semblable, pareil. -ly, adv. pareillement, semblablement. simi'larity, s. ressemblance f, similarité f.

simile ['simili], s. comparaison f, image f.

simmer ['simər], v.i. mijoter, bouillotter.

simple ['simpl], a. (a) simple, sans affectation; (b) naïf; crédule; niais; (c) it's s. robbery, c'est du vol pur et simple. -ply, adv. 1. (parler) simplement. 2. (a) absolument; the weather's s. terrible! il fait un temps de diable; (b) uniquement; I s. said that . . ., je me suis borné à dire que . . . sim'plicity, s. simplicité f. 'simplify, v.tr. simplifier.

simultaneous [sim(ə)l'teiniəs], a. simultané. -ly, adv. (a) simultanément; (b) en même temps (que).

sin [sin]. I. s. péché m; to live in s., F: vivre dans le collage. II. v.i. pécher. 'sinful, a. (plaisir) coupable; (gaspillage) scandaleux.

since [sins]. I. adv. depuis; ever s., depuis (lors). II. prep. depuis; he has been there s. five o'clock, il est là depuis cinq heures. III. conj. depuis que; s. I have been here, depuis que je suis ici; s. he is not of age, puisqu'il est mineur.

sincere [sin'siər], a. sincère; franc. -ly, adv. sincèrement; yours s., cordialement à vous. sin'cerity, s. sincérité f.

sinecure [sainikjuər], s. sinécure f.

sinew ['sinju], s. 1. tendon m. 2. pl. nerf m, force f.

‡sing [sin]. 1. v.tr. chanter. 2. v.i. (of ears) tinter, bourdonner; (of kettle) chanter. 'singer, s. chanteur m; chanteuse f; (operatic) cantatrice f; Ecc: chantre m. 'singing, s. 1. chant m. 2. bourdonnement m, tintement m (d'oreilles).

singe [sindʒ], v.tr. 1. brûler légèrement, roussir. 2. passer à la flamme.

single ['singl]. I. a. 1. (a) seul, unique; not a s. one, pas un seul; pas un; (b) individuel, particulier. 2. (a) s. bed, lit pour une personne; s. bedroom, chambre à un lit; (b) célibataire; non marié(e). -gly, adv. 1. séparément; un à un. 2. seul, sans aide. II. v.tr. to s. out, choisir (qn, qch.). 'single-handed, a. seul, sans aide. 'single-track, a. Rail: (ligne) à voie unique; to have a s.-t. mind, être incapable d'envisager deux idées à la fois.

singlet ['singlit], s. 1. gilet m de corps. 2. Sp: maillot m fin.

singular ['singjulər], a. & s. singulier (m). -ly, adv. singulièrement. singu'larity, s. singularité f.

sinister ['sinistər], a. sinistre.

sink¹ [sink], s. évier m.

‡sink² [sink], v. 1. v.i. (a) aller au fond; (of ship) couler au fond, sombrer; (b) s'enfoncer, pénétrer (into, dans); (c) (subside) s'affaisser; se tasser; (d) baisser (en valeur); diminuer. 2. v.tr. (a) faire sombrer (un navire); (b) enfoncer (un pieu, etc.); (c) creuser (un puits).

sinner ['sinər], s. pécheur, pécheresse. 'sinning, s. le péché.

sinuous ['sinjuəs], a. sinueux.

sinus ['sainəs], s. Anat: sinus m, antre m; Med: fistule f.

sip [sip]. I. s. petit coup m; petite gorgée f. II. ‡v.tr. boire à petits coups.

siphon ['saif(ə)n], s. siphon m.

sir [sər, sɔːr], s. 1. monsieur m; yes, s., oui, monsieur; (in letter) (Dear) S., Monsieur. 2. (title) Sir (ne s'emploie jamais sans le prénom).

siren ['saɪərən], s. sirène f.

sirloin ['sɔːlɔɪn], s. Cu: aloyau m.

sister ['sɪstər], s. 1. sœur f. 2. (a) Ecc: religieuse f.; sœur; (b) infirmière-major f. 'sister-in-law, s. belle-sœur f.

‡**sit** [sɪt], v. 1. v.i. (a) (of pers.) s'asseoir; être assis; rester assis; to s. for one's portrait, poser pour son portrait; (b) (of assembly, etc.) siéger; F: to s. on a project, laisser dormir un projet; (c) (of hen) couver (des œufs); (d) (of food) to s. heavy on the stomach, peser sur l'estomac. 2. v.tr. to s. a child on a chair, asseoir un enfant sur une chaise; to s. (oneself) down, s'asseoir. 'sit 'down, v.i. s'asseoir; to s. d. to table, se mettre à table. 'sit-down, s. -d. strike, grève f sur le tas. 'sitter, s. 1. (for artist) (a) modèle m; (b) client, -ente. 2. baby s., garde-bébé mf. 'sitting, s. séance f, réunion f (d'une commission, etc.); to paint a portrait in three sittings, faire un portrait en trois séances; to serve 200 people at one s., servir 200 personnes à la fois. 'sitting room, s. salle f de séjour, living-room m. 'sit 'up, v.i. 1. se tenir droit. 2. to s. up late, veiller tard; to s. up with an invalid, veiller un malade.

site [saɪt], s. 1. emplacement m (d'un édifice); caravan, camping s., camping m. 2. chantier m; building s., (i) terrain m à bâtir; (ii) chantier m de construction.

situation [sɪtjuˈeɪʃ(ə)n], s. 1. situation f. 2. emploi m. 'situated, a. 1. (of house) well s., bien situé. 2. this is how I am s., voici la situation dans laquelle je me trouve.

six [sɪks], num. a. & s. six (m); at sixes and sevens, en désordre. 'sixteen, num. a. & s. seize (m). 'sixteenth, num. a. & s. seizième (mf); (on the s. of May, le seize mai. sixth, num. a. & s. sixième (mf); (on the s. of June, le six juin. 'sixtieth, num. a. & s. soixantième (mf). 'sixty, num. a. & s. soixante (m).

size[1] [saɪz], s. 1. grandeur f, dimension f, grosseur f. 2. taille f; encolure f (de chemise); pointure f (de chaussures, de gants). II. v.tr. to s. s.o. up, classer, juger, qn.

size[2], s. apprêt m; colle f.

sizzle ['sɪzl], v.i. grésiller.

skate[1] [skeɪt], s. Fish: raie f.

skate[2]. I. s. patin m. II. v.i. patiner. 'skater, s. patineur, -euse. 'skating, s. patinage m; s. rink, (i) patinoire f; (ii) skating m, piste f de patinage.

skein [skeɪn], s. écheveau m (de laine).

skeleton ['skelɪt(ə)n], s. 1. squelette m. 2. charpente f, carcasse f (d'un navire, etc.); s. key, fausse clef f, F: rossignol m; s. staff of three, permanence f de trois employés.

sketch [sketʃ]. I. s. croquis m, esquisse f. II. v.tr. esquisser. 'sketchy, a. F: (of work) qui manque de précision; (of knowledge) superficiel.

skewer ['skjuː(ə)r], s. brochette f.

ski [skiː]. s. ski m; s. binding, fixation f; s. jump, saut m de ski; s. lift, remonte-pente m, téléski m. II. ‡v.i. faire du ski. 'skier, s. skieur, -euse. 'skiing, s. le ski.

‡**skid** [skɪd]. I. v.i. déraper; Av: glisser sur l'aile. II. s. (also skidding) dérapage m. 'skid-pan, s. Aut: piste f savonnée.

skiff [skɪf], s. Nau: 1. esquif m. 2. skiff m.

skill [skɪl], s. habileté f, adresse f, dextérité f. 'skilful, a. adroit, habile. -fully, adv. habilement, adroitement. 'skilled, a. habile; s. labour, main-d'œuvre f spécialisée.

‡**skim** [skɪm], v.tr. & i. 1. écumer; écrémer (le lait). 2. effleurer, raser (une surface); to s. (through) a novel, parcourir rapidement un roman.

skimpy ['skɪmpɪ], a. maigre (repas); (vêtement) étriqué.

skin [skɪn], s. peau f; soaked to the s., trempé jusqu'aux os. II. ‡v.tr. écorcher, dépouiller (un lapin, etc.); peler (un fruit). 'skinflint, s. avare mf. 'skinny, a. F: maigre, décharné.

‡**skip** [skɪp]. I. v.i. sauter, sautiller, gambader. 2. v.tr. & i. sauter, passer (un passage d'un livre); P: s. it! ça suffit!

skipper ['skɪpər], s. 1. Nau: patron m (de bateau). 2. Sp: chef m d'équipe.

skirmish ['skɜːmɪʃ], s. escarmouche f.

skirt [skɜːt]. I. s. (a) jupe f; mini s., mini-jupe f; (b) P: (i) femme f; (ii) poule f. II. v.tr. & i. contourner (un village, etc.); (of path) côtoyer (le bois, etc.).

skit [skɪt], s. satire f (on, de).

skittle ['skɪtl], s. 1. quille f. 2. pl. jeu m de quilles.

skull [skʌl], s. crâne m.

skunk [skʌŋk], s. 1. mouffette f. 2. (fur) sconce m, skunks m.

sky [skaɪ], s. ciel m. 'skylark, s. alouette f. 'skylight, s. châssis m vitré; lucarne f. 'skyline, s. horizon m. 'skyscraper, s. gratte-ciel m. 'skyway, s. 1. route f aérienne. 2. U.S: route f surélevée.

slab [slæb], s. plaque f, dalle f; tablette f (de chocolat); grosse tranche f (de gâteau).

slack [slæk]. I. a. 1. (a) mou, lâche, flasque; (b) faible, sans force. 2. négligent. 3. s. time, accalmie f; the s. season, la morte-saison. II. v.i. se relâcher; diminuer d'efforts. 'slacken. 1. v.tr. (a) ralentir (le pas); diminuer (de vitesse); (b) détendre (un cordage); desserrer (un écrou). 2. v.i. (of rope) prendre du mou. 'slacker, s. F:

paresseux, -euse; flemmard, -arde.
'slackness, s. 1. manque m d'énergie;
négligence f; fainéantise f. 2. mou m
(d'un cordage). 3. Com: stagnation m.
slacks, s.pl. pantalon m.

slag [slæg], s. scories fpl.; crasses fpl; s.
heap, crassier m.

slake [sleik], v.tr. 1. to s. one's thirst,
étancher sa soif. 2. éteindre, amortir
(la chaux).

slam¹ [slæm]. I. s. claquement m (d'une
porte). II. †v.tr. & i. claquer.

slam², s. (at bridge) chelem m.

slander ['slɑːndər]. I. s. calomnie f. II.
v.tr. calomnier; diffamer. **'slanderer,** s.
calomniateur, -trice; diffamateur,
-trice. **'slanderous,** a. calomnieux;
diffamatoire.

slang [slæŋ], s. argot m.

slant [slɑːnt]. I. s. 1. pente f, inclinaison f. 2. biais m, biseau m. 3.
point m de vue. II. v.i. (a) être en
pente; (s')incliner; (b) être oblique.
'slanting, a. (a) en pente, incliné; (b)
oblique.

slap [slæp]. I. s. claque f, tape f; s. in the
face, soufflet m, gifle f. II. †v.tr.
frapper (qn); donner une fessée à (un
enfant). **'slapdash,** a. & adv. sans soin;
s. work, travail bâclé. **'slap-happy,** a.
F: (a) (of boxer) sonné; (b) exalté,
transporté. **'slapstick,** s. a. (comedy)
farce f bouffonne. **'slap-up,** a. F:
fameux, chic, de premier ordre.

slash [slæʃ]. I. s. entaille f; balafre
f. II. v.tr. tailler; balafrer. **'slashing,**
a. mordant, cinglant.

slate [sleit], s. ardoise f; s. quarry, ardoisière f.

slaughter ['slɔːtər]. I. s. 1. abattage m
(de bétail); s. house, abattoir m. 2.
carnage m, massacre m. II. v.tr. 1.
abattre (des bêtes de boucherie). 2.
massacrer (des gens).

Slav [slɑːv], a. & s. slave (mf).

slave [sleiv]. I. s. esclave mf. II. v.i.
peiner, bûcher; s'éreinter (à un travail). **'slavery,** s. 1. esclavage m. 2.
travail m tuant. **'slavish,** a. (imitation) servile; (imiter) servilement.
-ly, adv. (obéir) en
esclave; (imiter) servilement.

†slay [slei], v.tr. tuer; mettre à mort.

sledge [sledʒ], s. traîneau m.

sledge-hammer ['sledʒhæmər], s. marteau m de forgeron.

sleek [sliːk], a. lisse, lissé. **'sleekness,**
s. luisant m.

sleep [sliːp]. I. s. 1. sommeil m; to go
to s., s'endormir; to send s.o. to s.,
endormir qn. 2. my foot's gone to s.,
j'ai le pied engourdi. II. †v.i. & tr. 1.
dormir; to s. like a log, dormir à
poings fermés. 2. to s. at an hotel,
coucher à un hôtel. **'sleeper,** s. 1.
dormeur, -euse; to be a light s., avoir
le sommeil léger. 2. Rail: traverse f.
3. Rail: wagon-lit m. **'sleepily,** adv.

d'un air endormi, somnolent. **'sleepiness,** s. 1. somnolence f. 2. indolence
f, léthargie f. **'sleeping.** I. a. 1.
dormant, endormi. 2. Com: s. partner,
commanditaire m. II. s. sommeil m;
s. draught, pills, somnifère m; Rail: s.
car, wagon-lit m; s. bag, sac m de
couchage. **'sleepless,** a. sans sommeil;
s. night, nuit blanche. **'sleep-
lessness,** s. insomnie f. **'sleepy,**
a. 1. somnolent; to feel s., avoir
sommeil; s. town, ville endormie. 2.
apathique, engourdi.

sleet [sliːt], s. grésil m.

sleeve [sliːv], s. 1. manche f. 2. E:
manchon m, douille f; bague f
d'assemblage.

sleigh [slei], s. traîneau m.

slender ['slendər], a. 1. mince, ténu;
svelte, élancé; fuselé. 2. (of hope)
faible; (of income) exigu. **'slenderness,**
s. 1. minceur f, sveltesse f. 2.
exiguïté f (d'une fortune); faiblesse f
(des ressources).

slice [slais]. I. s. 1. tranche f; s. of
bread and butter, tartine f de beurre. 2.
fish s., truelle f à poisson. II. v.tr. 1.
découper (qch.) en tranches. 2. (a)
(tennis) couper (la balle); (b) (golf)
faire dévier la balle à droite.

slide [slaid]. I. s. 1. glissade f, glissement m. 2. (for microscope)
lamelle f; (b) Phot: diapositive f. II.
†v.i. glisser. **'sliding,** a. glissant; s.
door, porte f à glissières; s. panel,
panneau m mobile; s. seat, siège m
amovible; Mth: etc: s. scale, échelle f
mobile.

slight [slait]. I. a. 1. mince, ténu; frêle.
2. léger; to some s. extent, quelque
peu; not the slightest danger, pas le
moindre danger; not in the slightest,
pas le moins du monde; -ly, adv. 1.
s. built, à la taille mince, svelte. 2.
légèrement, faiblement; s. better, un
petit peu mieux; I know him s., je le
connais un peu. II. s. affront m. III.
v.tr. traiter (qn) sans considération.
'slightingly, adv. dédaigneusement.

slim [slim]. I. a. svelte, élancé; mince.
II. †v.i. suivre un régime amaigrissant.
'slimness, s. sveltesse f; taille f mince.

slime [slaim], s. limon m, vase f. **'slimi-
ness,** s. état m vaseux. **'slimy,** a. 1.
vaseux; couvert de vase. 2. servile,
obséquieux.

sling [sliŋ]. I. s. 1. fronde f. 2. (a)
écharpe f; (b) bandoulière f; (c) (for
hoisting) élingue f. II. †v.tr. 1. lancer,
jeter. 2. suspendre (un hamac, etc.).

†slink [slink], v.i. to s. off, partir furtivement. **'slinking,** a. furtif. **'slinky,** a.
F: (forme) svelte; (vêtement) collant.

slip [slip]. I. s. 1. (a) glissade f, glissement m; faux pas m; (b) faute f,
erreur f d'inattention. 2. pillow s.,
taie f d'oreiller. 3. Cl: (a) combinai-

f (de femme); (b) slip m (d'homme).
4. *Nau:* cale f, chantier m (de construction). II. **‡v.** 1. *v.i.* (a) glisser; (b) to s. into the room, se glisser dans la salle; F: I slipped round to the baker's, j'ai fait un saut jusqu'à la boulangerie. 2. *v.tr.* (a) your name has slipped my memory, votre nom m'échappe; (b) *Aut:* to s. the clutch, laisser patiner l'embrayage. '**slipper,** *s. Cl:* pantoufle f; *Fr.C:* chaussette f. '**slippery,** *a.* 1. glissant. 2. (sujet) délicat. 3. rusé; he's a s. customer, on ne sait pas où le prendre. '**slipshod,** *a.* (pers.) mal soigné; (of work) négligé, bâclé. **slip 'up,** *v.i.* se tromper; faire une bourde; (of plan) échouer. '**slip-up,** *s. F:* erreur f, bévue f. '**slipway,** *s. Nau:* cale f; chantier m de construction.

slit [slit]. I. *s.* fente f; fissure f. II. **‡v.tr.** & i. (se) fendre.

slither ['sliðər], *v.i.* glisser.

sliver ['slivər], *s.* tranche f (mince); éclat m (de bois).

slobber ['slɔbər], *v.i.* (a) baver; (b) larmoyer.

sloe [slou], *s. Bot:* prunelle f.

‡slog [slɔg], *v.i. F:* turbiner; travailler avec acharnement (à qch.); to s. along, marcher d'un pas lourd. '**slogger,** *s.* bûcheur, -euse.

slogan ['slougən], *s.* slogan m; devise f.

‡slop [slɔp]. 1. *v.tr.* répandre (un liquide). 2. *v.i.* (of liquid) déborder; F: (of pers.) faire de la sensiblerie. '**sloppy,** *a.* (of pers.) mou; flasque; peu soigné (travail) fait sans soin; (roman) larmoyant; (vêtement) trop grand.

slope [sloup]. I. *s.* pente f. II. *v.i.* être en pente; incliner; pencher. '**sloping,** *a.* en pente; incliné.

slot [slɔt], *s.* entaille f, rainure f: s. machine, (i) distributeur m automatique; (ii) appareil m à jetons; s. meter, compteur m à paiement préalable.

slouch [slautʃ], *v.i.* manquer de tenue.

slovenly ['slʌvnli], *a.* 1. mal soigné. 2. (a) négligent; sans soin; (b) négligé. '**slovenliness,** *s.* manque m (i) de tenue; (ii) de soin.

slow [slou]. I. *a.* (a) lent; s. train, train omnibus m; (b) à l'esprit lourd; (enfant) arriéré; (c) my watch is s., ma montre retarde. -**ly,** *adv.* lentement. II. *adv. Ind:* to go s., faire la grève perlée; *P.N:* s.! ralentir! III. *v.tr.* & i. to s. down, ralentir. '**slowcoach,** *s. F:* lambin, -ine. '**slowness,** *s.* lenteur f.

slug [slʌg], *s.* limace f.

sluggish ['slʌgiʃ], *a.* paresseux, léthargique; *Aut:* (moteur) peu nerveux. '**sluggishness,** *s.* (a) paresse f; (b) lourdeur f.

sluice [slu:s], *s.* écluse f.

slum [slʌm], *s.* bas quartier m (d'une ville); rue f sordide; s. clearance, suppression f des taudis.

slumber ['slʌmbər], *s.* sommeil m; *Com:* s. wear, vêtements mpl de nuit.

slump [slʌmp]. I. *s. Com:* baisse f soudaine; crise f. II. *v.i.* (of prices) baisser tout à coup; dégringoler.

slur [slə:r], *s.* affront m.

slush [slʌʃ], *s.* fange f, bourbe f. '**slushy,** *a.* boueux.

slut [slʌt], *s.* souillon mf. '**sluttish,** *a.* malpropre, sale.

sly [slai], *a.* (a) matois, rusé; (b) sournois; (c) s. on the s., furtivement. 2. malin. -**ly,** *adv.* sournoisement. '**slyness,** *s.* 1. sournoiserie f. 2. malice f.

smack¹ [smæk]. I. *s.* 1. claquement m. 2. claque f. II. *v.tr.* frapper, taper (qn); donner une gifle à (qn).

smack², *s.* bateau m pêcheur.

small [smɔ:l]. I. *a.* petit; s. letters, minuscules f pl; s. change, menue monnaie f; s. income, mince revenu m; a s. coffee, une petite tasse de café; in a s. way, en petit; modestement. II. *adv.* (hacher) menu, en petits morceaux. small-**holding,** *s.* petite ferme f. '**smallpox,** *s.* variole f, petite vérole f. '**small-scale,** *a.* (modèle) réduit; s.-s. business, affaire peu importante.

smart [sma:t]. I. *s.* douleur f cuisante. II. *v.i.* (of wound) brûler; (of eyes) picoter. III. *a.* 1. (coup) cinglant; sec. 2. (of pace) vif. 3. habile; débrouillard; s. practice, escroquerie f. 4. élégant, distingué, chic. -**ly,** *adv.* 1. promptement. 2. (s'habiller) élégamment. '**smarten,** *v.tr.* to s. oneself up, se faire beau. '**smartness,** *s.* 1. vivacité f (d'esprit). 2. élégance f, chic m.

smash [smæʃ]. I. *s.* 1. coup m écrasant. 2. désastre m; (car) s., accident m. II. *v.* 1. *v.tr.* briser (qch.) (en morceaux). 2. *v.i.* éclater en morceaux. '**smashing,** *a.* 1. (coup) écrasant. 2. F: formidable, sensas.

smattering ['smætriŋ], *s.* légère connaissance f.

smear [smiər], *s.* 1. tache f, souillure f. II. *v.tr.* (a) barbouiller, salir (with, de); (b) enduire (with, de).

smell [smel]. I. *s.* 1. odorat m. 2. (a) odeur f; parfum m; (b) mauvaise odeur. II. **‡v.** 1. *v.tr.* flairer (qch.); sentir (une fleur); *abs.* avoir de l'odorat. 2. *v.i.* (a) (of flower, etc.) sentir; to s. pleasant, sentir bon; (b) sentir mauvais. '**smelly,** *a.* 1. malodorant.

smelt [smelt], *v.tr.* fondre (le minerai). 'smelting, *s.* fonte *f*, fonderie *f*.

smile [smail]. I. *s.* sourire *m.* II. *v.i.* sourire.

smithereens [smiðə'riːnz], *s.pl.* F: morceaux *m*, miettes *f*; to smash sth. to s., atomiser qch.

smock [smɔk], *s.* blouse *f*, sarrau *m.*

smog [smɔg], *s.* brouillard *m* enfumé.

smoke [smouk]. I. *s.* fumée *f.* II. *v.i.* & *tr.* fumer. 'smokeless, *a.* (combustible) sans fumée. 'smoker, *s.* fumeur, -euse. 'smoking, *s.* 1. fumage *m* (du jambon). 2. action *f*, habitude *f* de fumer (le tabac); *P/N:* no s., défense de fumer. 'smoky, *a.* (*of atmosphere*) fumeux; (*of room*) plein de fumée.

smooth [smuːð]. I. *a.* 1. lisse; uni; poli; (mer) calme. 2. doux; sans heurts. -ly, *adv.* 1. uniment, sans secousses. 2. (marcher, travailler) doucement. II. *v.tr.* 1. lisser (ses cheveux); aplanir (une planche); to s. the way for s.o., aplanir la voie pour qn. 3. adoucir (un angle). 'smoothness, *s.* 1. égalité *f* (d'une surface); calme *m* (de la mer). 2. douceur *f* (de la marche de la machine).

smother ['smʌðər], *v.tr.* étouffer; suffoquer.

smoulder ['smouldər], *v.i.* (*a*) brûler lentement; (*b*) couver (sous la cendre).

smudge [smʌdʒ]. I. *s.* tache *f*; noircissure *f.* II. *v.tr.* salir; barbouiller, maculer (son écriture).

smug [smʌg], *a.* suffisant. 'smugness, 'smugness, *s.* suffisance *f.*

smuggle ['smʌgl], *v.tr.* passer (qch.) en fraude, en contrebande; *abs.* faire de la contrebande. 'smuggler, *s.* contrebandier *m.* 'smuggling, *s.* contrebande *f.*

smut [smʌt], *s.* 1. tache *f* de suie. 2. *coll.* indécences *fpl*, ordures *fpl.* 'smutty, *a.* 1. noirci, sali. 2. (*of conversation*) malpropre, ordurier.

snack [snæk], *s.* léger repas *m*; cassecroûte *m*; to have a s., manger sur le pouce; s. bar, snack-bar *m.*

snag [snæg], *s.* to find a s., se heurter à un obstacle, rencontrer un pépin.

snail [sneil], *s.* limaçon *m*, escargot *m*, colimaçon *m.*

snake [sneik], *s.* serpent *m.*

snap [snæp]. I. *s.* 1. coup *m* de dents; bruit *m* sec. 2. fermoir *m*; bouton *m* à pression. 3. *Cu:* ginger s., biscuit *m* croquant de gingembre. II. *a.* imprévu; s. decision, décision prise sur le coup; *Pol:* s. division, vote *m* de surprise. III. *v.tr.* 1. happer (qch.). 2. F: to s. out of it, se secouer. 3. don't s. my head off! ne m'avalez pas! 4. to s. up a bargain, saisir une occasion. 'snappy, *a.* 1. irritable. 2. F: look s.! grouille-toi!

snare [snɛər], *s.* lacet *m*; piège *m*; a s. and a delusion, qch. de trompeur.

snarl¹ [snɑːl]. I. *v.i.* grogner, gronder. II. *s.* grognement *m*, grondement *m.*

snarl², *s.* US: *Aut:* embouteillage *m.*

snatch [snætʃ], *v.tr.* 1. saisir, empoigner; to s. a meal, manger un morceau sur le pouce. 2. arracher (qch. de qn).

sneak [sniːk]. I. *v.* 1. *v.i.* (*a*) to s. off, partir furtivement; (*b*) *Sch:* F: moucharder. 2. *v.tr.* F: chiper, chaparder. II. *s.* *Sch:* F: mouchard *m*; rapporteur, -euse. 'sneaking, *a.* (*a*) furtif; (*b*) a s. liking for sth., un penchant inavoué pour qch.

sneer [sniər]. I. *s.* 1. sourire *m* de mépris; ricanement *m.* 2. sarcasme *m.* II. *v.i.* ricaner; lancer des sarcasmes.

sneeze [sniːz]. I. *s.* éternuement *m.* II. *v.i.* éternuer.

sniff [snif]. I. *s.* reniflement *m.* II. *v.i.* & *tr.* renifler.

snigger ['snigər], *v.i.* rire sous cape. 'snigger, ricaner tout bas.

‡snip [snip]. I. *v.tr.* couper avec des ciseaux. II. *s.* 1. (*a*) morceau *m* coupé; petite entaille *f*; (*b*) coup *m* de ciseaux. 2. *P:* (*a*) certitude *f* (at horse race) gagnant *m* sûr; (*b*) affaire *f* avantageuse.

sniper ['snaipər], *s.* *Mil:* canardeur *m.*

‡snivel ['snivl], *v.i.* pleurnicher, larmoyer. 'snivelling. I. *a.* pleurnicheur, larmoyant. II. *s.* pleurnicherie *f.*

snob [snɔb], *s.* prétentieux, -euse; snob *mf*; (intellectual) s., poseur, -euse. 'snobbery, *s.* morgue *f*; snobisme *m.* 'snobbish, *a.* poseur; snob.

snooker ['snuːkər], *s.* (sorte de) jeu *m* de billard.

snoop [snuːp], *v.i.* fureter, fouiner. 'snooper, *s.* inquisiteur *m*; fouineur, -euse.

snooze [snuːz]. I. *s.* F: petit somme *m*, F: roupillon *m.*

snore [snɔːr]. I. *v.i.* ronfler. II. *s.* (also snoring) ronflement *m.*

snorkel ['snɔːkl], *s.* (*a*) schnorkel *m*; (*b*) masque *m* sous-marin.

snort [snɔːt], *v.i.* renifler fortement; (of horse) s'ébrouer. 'snorting, *s.* reniflement *m*; ébrouement *m.* 'snorter, *s.P:* (*a*) chose *f* épatante; (*b*) problème *m* qui donne du fil à retordre.

snout [snaut], *s.* museau *m*; *P:* nez *m*, groin *m.*

snow [snou]. I. *s.* neige *f.* II. *v.impers.* neiger; to be snowed up, (i) être bloqué, pris, par la neige; (ii) (*also under*) être submergé de besogne. 'snowball, *s.* boule *f* de neige. 'snowblindness, *s.* cécité *f* des neiges. 'snowbound, *a.* retenu, bloqué, par la neige. 'snowdrift, *s.* congère *f.* 'snowdrop, *s.* perce-neige *f.* 'snowfall, *s.* chute *f* de neige. 'snowflake, *s.* flocon *m* de neige. 'snowline, *s.* limite *f* des neiges éternelles. †'snowman, s. bonhomme m de neige; the abominable s., l'abominable homme des neiges. 'snowmobile, s. tracteur m automobile (pour expéditions polaires). 'snowplough, s. chasse-neige m. 'snowshoes, spl. raquettes fpl. 'snowstorm, s. tempête f de neige. 'snowy, a. neigeux; de neige.

snub¹ [snʌb]. I. s. mortification f, rebuffade f. ‡v.tr. infliger un affront à (qn).

snub², a. (nez) camus, retroussé.

snuff [snʌf], s. tabac m à priser; to take s., priser; a pinch of s., une prise.

snug [snʌg], a. confortable; F: little job, emploi m pépère. -ly, adv. confortablement, douillettement. 'snuggle, v.i. se pelotonner (contre qn); se blottir (dans son lit).

so [sou]. I. adv. 1. si, tellement; tant; aussi; so much, tellement, tant; he's so kind, il est si aimable. 2. (a) ainsi, de cette manière; so many, tant de; and so on, et ainsi de suite; so to speak, pour ainsi dire; (b) I think so, I believe so; so it seems, à ce qu'il paraît; I told you so! je vous l'avais bien dit! so much so that, à tel point que; is that so? vraiment? (c) perhaps so, cela se peut; quite so! parfaitement! a week or so, une semaine environ; (d) he's right and so are you, il a raison et vous aussi. 3. conj. so that; (a) pour que; (b) de sorte que. 4. conj. phr. so as to; (a) afin de; (b) de sorte que. II. conj. donc, c'est pourquoi; P: so what? (i) et puis quoi? (ii) ça te regarde, toi? 'so-and-so, s. F: (a) sale type m! (b) Mr. So-and-So, Monsieur Untel. 'so-called, a. soi-disant. 'so so, a. & adv. comme ci comme ça.

soak [souk]. I. v.tr. (a) tremper; (b) F: écorcher (un client). 2. v.i. s'infiltrer, s'imbiber; (b) P: boire comme une éponge. 'soaking, s. (a) trempage m (du linge); (b) (of pers.) to get a good s., se faire tremper.

soap [soup], s. savon m. 'soapflakes, s.pl. savon m en paillettes. 'soapy, a. savonneux; couvert de savon.

soar [sɔːr], v.i. prendre son essor; (of prices) monter.

sob [sɔb]. I. s. sanglot m. II. ‡v.i. sangloter.

sober ['soubər]. I. a. (a) sobre, modéré, tempéré; (b) calme, posé; (c) he's never s., il est toujours ivre. II. v.i. to s. down, s'assagir; to s. up, se dégriser. 'soberness, s. calme m, tranquillité f; modération f. so'briety, s. sobriété f; tempérance f.

soccer ['sɔkər], s. F: football m.

sociable ['souʃəbl], a. sociable. -bly, adv. sociablement, amicalement. socia'bility, s. sociabilité f.

social ['souʃ(ə)l], a. social; s. security, sécurité f sociale.

socialism ['souʃəlizm], s. socialisme m; 'socialist, a. & s. socialiste (mf).

society [sə'saiəti], s. société f.

sock [sɔk], s. 1. chaussette f. 2. semelle f intérieure (d'une chaussure).

socket ['sɔkit], s. 1. emboîture f, douille f. 2. (a) alvéole m (de dent); (b) orbite f (de l'œil).

soda ['soudə], s. 1. soude f; caustic s., soude caustique. 2. s. (water), eau f de seltz; soda m.

sodden ['sɔdn], a. détrempé.

sofa ['soufə], s. sofa m, canapé m.

soft [sɔft], a. 1. mou; Fin: s. currency, devise faible. 2. doux; s. heart, cœur tendre. -ly, adv. doucement, tendrement. soften ['sɔfn], v. 1. v.tr. amollir; assouplir (le cuir); adoucir (la voix). 2. v.i. s'amollir; s'attendrir. 'softener ['sɔfnər], v. water s., adoucisseur m d'eau. 'softness, s. douceur f.

soil [sɔil]. I. s. sol m, terrain m, terre f. II. v.tr. souiller, salir.

solar ['soulər], a. solaire.

solder ['sɔldər]. I. s. soudure f. II. v.tr. souder; ressouder.

soldier ['souldʒər], s. soldat m; militaire m.

sole¹ [soul]. I. s. 1. plante f (du pied). 2. semelle f (de chaussure). II. v.tr. ressemeler (des chaussures).

sole², s. Fish: sole f.

sole³, a. seul, unique; s. agent, agent exclusif. -ly, adv. uniquement.

solemn ['sɔləm], a. 1. solennel. 2. (of pers.) grave, sérieux. -ly, adv. 1. solennellement. 2. gravement. so'lemnity, s. 1. solennité f. 2. gravité f (de maintien). 'solemnize, v.tr. célébrer (un mariage).

solicit [sə'lisit], v.tr. 1. solliciter (une faveur). 2. (of prostitute) racoler, raccrocher. solici'tation, s. racolage m, raccrochage m.

solicitor [sə'lisitər], s. = avoué m.

solid ['sɔlid]. I. a. solide; s. mahogany table, table en acajou massif; s. vote, vote unanime. 2. s. solide m. soli'darity, s. solidarité f. soli'dification, s. solidification f. so'lidify, v.tr. & i. (se) solidifier. so'lidity, s. solidité f. 'solidly, adv. 1. solidement. 2. (voter) avec unanimité.

soliloquy [sə'liləkwi], s. soliloque m.

solitary ['sɔlit(ə)ri], a. solitaire. 'solitude, s. solitude f, isolement m.

solo ['soulou], s. 1. Mus: solo m. 2. whist m de Gand. 'soloist, s. soliste m.

solstice ['sɔlstis], s. solstice m.

soluble ['sɔljubl], a. soluble. solu'bility, s. solubilité f.

solution [sɔ'lju:ʃ(ə)n], s. solution f.

solve [sɔlv], v.tr. résoudre. 'solvency, s. solvabilité f. 'solvent. 1. a. Com:

solvable. 2. *s.* dissolvant *m*; solvant *m*.

sombre ['sɔmbər], *a.* sombre, morne.

some [sʌm]. I. *a.* 1. quelque, quelconque; *s.* day, un de ces jours; *s.* way or another, d'une manière ou d'une autre; to make *s.* sort of a reply, répondre d'une façon quelconque. 2. (*partitive*) de; to eat *s.* fruit, manger des fruits. 3. *s.* distance away, à quelque distance; after *s.* time, après un, au bout d'un, certain temps; *s.* days ago, il y a quelques jours. 4. *F:* (*intensive*) he's a doctor, comme médecin (i) c'est un as, (ii) *Pej:* il est plutôt quelconque. II. *pron.* 1. (*pers.*) certains. 2. I have *s.*, j'en ai; take *s.*! prenez-en! *s.* of them, quelques-uns d'entre eux. III. *adv.* environ, quelque (*ino*); *s.* twenty pounds, une vingtaine de livres. '**somebody**, '**someone**, *s.* or *pron.* quelqu'un; *F:* he thinks he's *s.*, il se croit quelqu'un. '**somehow**, *adv.* de façon ou d'autre; we'll manage *s.*, on se débrouillera.

somersault ['sʌməsɔːlt], *s.* saut *m* périlleux; to turn a *s.*, (i) (*of pers.*) faire la culbute; (ii) *Aut:* capoter.

'**something**. I. *s.* or *pron.* quelque chose *m*; say *s.*, dites quelque chose; to ask for *s.* to drink, demander à boire; *s.* else to do, autre chose à faire; he's *s.* of a miser, il est un peu, tant soit peu, avare; there's *s.* in what you say, il y a un fond de vérité dans ce que vous dites; there's *s.* in him, il a du fond. II. *adv.* quelque peu, tant soit peu; *F:* that's *s.* 'like a cigar! voilà un vrai cigare! '**sometimes**, *adv.* quelquefois, parfois. '**somewhat**, *adv.* un peu, quelque peu; tant soit peu. '**somewhere**, *adv.* quelque part; *s.* else, ailleurs, autre part; *s.* in the world, de par le monde; it's *s.* about fifty, il a environ cinquante ans.

'**somnolence** ['sɔmnələns], *s.* somnolence *f.* '**somnolent**, *a.* somnolent.

son [sʌn], *s.* fils *m.* '**son-in-law**, *s.* gendre *m*, beau-fils *m.*

sonata [sə'nɑːtə], *s.* sonate *f.*

sonde [sɔnd], *s. Meteor: etc:* sonde *f.*

song [sɔŋ], *s.* chant *m*; chanson *f.*; *s.* bird, oiseau *m* chanteur; *s.* thrush, grive *f* musicienne.

sonic ['sɔnik], *a.* sonique; *Nau:* s. depth-finder, sondeur *m* à écho; *Av:* s. barrier, mur *m* du son.

sonnet ['sɔnit], *s.* sonnet *m.*

sonorous ['sɔnərəs], *a.* sonore.

soon [suːn], *adv.* 1. bientôt, tôt; too *s.*, trop tôt, avant le temps; none too *s.*, juste à temps; how *s.* can you be ready? en combien de temps serez-vous prêt? 2. the **sooner the better**, le plus tôt sera le mieux; no sooner said than done, aussitôt dit, aussitôt fait; I'd sooner come, j'aimerais mieux venir.

soot [sut], *s.* suie *f.* '**sooty**, *a.* couvert de suie.

soothe [suːð], *v.tr.* calmer, apaiser; tranquilliser.

sophistication [səfisti'keiʃən], *s.* sophistication *f.*; savoir-vivre *m.* so'**phisticated**, *a.* aux goûts compliqués; blasé.

sophomore ['sɔfəmɔːr], *s. U.S: Sch:* étudiant, -ante, de seconde année.

soporific [sɔpə'rifik], *a.* & *s.* somnifère (*m*), soporifique (*m*).

sopping ['sɔpiŋ], *a. F:* wet, tout trempé.

†**soprano** [sə'prɑːnou], *s.* soprano *m.*

sorbet ['sɔːbei], *s. Cu:* sorbet *m.*

sorcery ['sɔːsəri], *s.* sorcellerie *f.*

sordid ['sɔːdid], *a.* sordide. '**sordidness**, *s.* sordidité *f.*

sore [sɔːr]. I. *a.* (*a*) douloureux, endolori; (*b*) enflammé, irrité; *s.* throat, mal *m* de gorge. II. *s.* plaie *f.* '**soreness**, *s.* endolorissement *m.*

sorrow ['sɔrou], *s.* peine *f*, chagrin *m*, tristesse *f.* '**sorrowful**, *a.* affligé, chagriné, triste. -**fully**, *adv.* tristement.

sorry ['sɔri], *a.* fâché, désolé, peiné; I'm *s.*! pardon! I'm *s.* for him, je le plains.

sort [sɔːt]. I. *s.* (*a*) sorte *f*, genre *m*, espèce *f*; nothing of the *s.*, pas du tout! I shall do nothing of the *s.*, je n'en ferai rien; (*b*) to be out of sorts, être indisposé. II. *v.tr.* trier; débrouiller (des papiers, etc.); (*at post office*) to *s.* the letters, router, trier, les lettres. '**sorter**, *s.* (*a*) trieur, -euse (de lettres); (*b*) (*machine*) trieuse *f.* '**sorting**, *s.* routage *m* (de lettres); *s.* office, bureau *m* de tri.

soul [soul], *s.* âme *f.*

sound[1] [saund]. I. *s.* son *m*; bruit *m*; *Av:* s. barrier, mur *m* du son; *Cin:* s. track, bande *f* sonore; s. wave, onde *f* sonore. II. *v.* 1. *v.i.* sonner; résonner; that sounds well, cela fait bon effet. 2. *v.tr.* (*a*) sonner (la cloche); (*b*) prononcer (une lettre); (*c*) *Med:* ausculter. '**sounding**, *s. Med:* auscultation *f.* '**sound-proof**. I. *a.* isolant; insonore. II. *v.tr.* insonoriser.

sound[2], *v.tr.* sonder. '**sounding**, *s. Nau:* sondage *m*; to take soundings, sonder, prendre le fond; *s.* balloon, ballon-sonde *m.*

sound[3], *s. Geog:* détroit *m*; goulet *m.*

sound[4], *a.* 1. sain; *s.* of mind, sain d'esprit. 2. *s.* financial position, situation financière solide; *s.* statesman, homme d'état au jugement sain; *s.* reasoning, raisonnement juste. 3. (*sommeil*) profond. -**ly**, *adv.* 1. sainement, judicieusement. 2. (*dormir*) à poings fermés. '**soundness**, *s.* 1. état *m* sain (d'esprit); bon état *m* (des marchandises). 2. solidité *f* (d'une maison de commerce, d'un argument).

soup [su:p], s. soupe f, potage m; thick s., crème f, purée f; clear s., consommé m; s. ladle, louche f; s. plate, assiette f creuse; s. tureen, soupière f. soup 'up, v.tr. P: gonfler, agrandir (la puissance de qch.), exagérer (une publicité, etc.); Aut: souped-up engine, moteur gonflé.

sour ['sauər], a. 1. aigre, acide, sur; to turn s., tourner à l'aigre. 2. (of pers.) revêche; aigre. 'sourness, s. aigreur f, acidité f (d'un fruit).

source [sɔ:s], s. source f.

south [sauθ]. I. a. & s. sud (m); the S. of France, le Midi (de la France); s. wind, vent du sud. 2. adv. au sud; vers le sud. South 'African, a. & s. sud-africain, -aine. south-'east. I. s. sud-est m. 2. a. du sud-est. 3. adv. vers le sud-est. south-'easterly, -eastern, a. du sud-est. southerly ['sʌð-], a. (vent du sud); (exposition) au sud. southern ['sʌð-], a. (du) sud; méridional; s. lights, aurore f australe; the S. Cross, la Croix du Sud. southerner ['sʌð-] s. habitant, -ante, du sud; méridional, -ale; U.S: Hist: sudiste mf. 'southwards, adv. vers le sud. south-'west. I. s. sud-ouest m. 2. a. du sud-ouest. 3. adv. vers le sud-ouest. south-'westerly, -western, a. du sud-ouest.

souvenir [su:və'ni:ər], s. souvenir m.

sovereign ['sɔvrin], s. 1. souverain, -aine. 2. souverain m (ancienne pièce d'or, valeur £1). 'sovereignty, s. souveraineté f.

soviet ['souviet], s. soviet m; S. Union, Union soviétique. 'sovietize, v.tr. soviétiser (un pays).

‡**sow**[1] [sou], v.tr. semer (des graines).

sow[2] [sau], s. truie f.

soya ['sɔiə], s. s. bean, soya m.

spa [spa:], s. ville f d'eau; station f thermale.

space [speis]. I. s. 1. espace m, intervalle m (de temps); in s., l'espace; attrib. spatial; s. flight, voyage m spatial; s. port, base f de lancement de fusées spatiales, d'astronefs; s. station, station f spatiale; s. suit, scaphandre m d'astronaute; vêtement m anti-g; s. travel, astronautique f. 3. étendue f, surface f; to take up a lot of s., occuper beaucoup de place. 4. blank s., blanc m; sign in the s. indicated, signez (votre nom) dans la case indiquée. II. v.tr. to s. (out), espacer; échelonner (des paiements). 'space-craft, s. astronef m. †'spaceman, s. (a) habitant m de l'espace; (b) cosmonaute m. 'space-saving, a. compact. 'spaceship, s. astronef m. 'spacing, s. (a) espacement m; échelonnement m; (b) (typing) in single, double s., à interligne simple, double. 'spacious, a.

spacieux; vaste. 'spaciousness, s. proportions fpl spacieuses (d'une salle).

spade[1] [speid], s. bêche f; (child's) pelle f; to call a s. a s., appeler les choses par leur nom; s. work, travaux m préliminaires (en vue d'une enquête, etc.).

spade[2], s. (at cards) pique m.

spaghetti [spə'geti], s. spaghetti mpl.

span [spæn]. I. s. 1. wing s. (of bird, aircraft), envergure f. 2. ouverture f, largeur f (d'une arche); écartement m (de deux piliers); travée f (d'un pont). II. v.tr. (of bridge, etc.) franchir, enjamber.

Spaniard ['spænjəd], s. Espagnol, -ole.

spaniel ['spænjəl], s. épagneul m.

Spanish ['spæniʃ]. 1. a. espagnol; d'Espagne. 2. s. Ling: l'espagnol m.

spank [spæŋk], v.tr. fesser (un enfant). 'spanking, s. fessée f.

spanner ['spænər], s. clef f (à écrous).

spar[1] [spa:r], s. 1. Nau: (a) espar m; (b) pl. the spars, la mâture. 2. Av: wing s., poutrelle f.

‡**spar**[2] v.i. faire un assaut de boxe amical (avec qn).

spare [spεər]. I. a. 1. in my s. time, à mes moments perdus; s. bedroom, chambre f d'ami(s). 2. s. parts, s. spares, pièces f détachées, de rechange; Aut: s. wheel, roue f de secours. II. v.tr. 1. épargner, ménager; to s. no expense, ne pas regarder à la dépense. 2. se passer de (qch.); can you s. it? je ne vous prive pas? to have no time to s., (i) ne pas avoir de temps libre; (ii) n'avoir que juste le temps (pour faire qch.). 3. to s. s.o.'s life, épargner la vie à qn; to s. s.o.'s feelings, ménager qn.

spark [spa:k]. I. s. étincelle f. II. v.i. émettre des étincelles. 'sparking plug, U.S: spark plug, s. Aut: bougie f.

sparkle ['spa:kl]. I. s. 1. brève lueur f. 2. étincellement m; éclat m. II. v.i. étinceler, scintiller. 'sparkling. a. (a) étincelant, brillant; (b) (vin) mousseux.

sparrow ['spærou], s. moineau m, passereau m. 'sparrowhawk, s. épervier m.

sparse [spa:s], a. clairsemé, épars. -ly, adv. peu abondamment; s. populated, peu peuplé.

spasm ['spæz(ə)m], s. Med: spasme m; accès m (de toux, de jalousie); to work in spasms, travailler par à-coups. spas'modic, a. 1. Med: spasmodique; (saut) involontaire. 2. (travail) fait par à-coups. -ally, adv. (travailler) par à-coups.

spastic ['spæstik], s. personne f atteinte de paralysie spasmodique.

spate [speit], s. crue f (d'une rivière); to have a s. of work, être débordé de travail.

spatial ['speiʃ(ə)l], a. spatial; dans l'espace.

spatter ['spætər], v.tr. éclabousser (qn, qch., de boue, etc.).

spawn [spɔːn]. I. s. frai m; œufs mpl (de poisson). II. v.i. (of fish) frayer.

‡speak [spiːk]. 1. v.i. (a) parler; without speaking, sans rien dire; speaking for myself, pour ma part; roughly speaking, approximativement; P.T.T: who's speaking? c'est de la part de qui? (b) faire un discours. 2. v.tr. (a) to s. the truth, dire la vérité; (b) to s. French, parler français. 'speaker, s. 1. parleur, -euse; orateur m; to be a fluent s., avoir la parole facile. 2. Pol: the S. = le Président (des Communes). 'speaking, s. parler m, discours m, parole f; plain s., francparler m; public s., l'art m oratoire. 'speak of, v.i. parler de (qn, qch.); it's nothing to s. of, cela ne vaut pas la peine d'en parler; she has no voice to s. of, elle n'a pour ainsi dire pas de voix, speak 'up, v.i. 1. parler plus haut. 2. parler en faveur (de qn).

spear [spiər], s. 1. lance f; javelot m, javeline f. 2. Fish: fœne f; harpon m.

special ['speʃl]. I. a. (a) spécial, particulier; s. price, prix m de faveur, d'ami; (b) s. friend, ami(e) m intime; a s. case, un cas d'espèce. -ally, adv. particulièrement; surtout. II. s. (a) édition f spéciale (d'un journal); (b) F: citoyen m faisant fonction d'agent de police; (c) (in restaurant) today's s., plat m du jour. 'specialist, s. spécialiste mf; heart s., cardiologue m. speci'ality, s. spécialité f. speciali'zation, s. spécialisation f. 'specialize, v.i. se spécialiser (in, dans).

species ['spiːʃiːz], s.inv. espèce f.

specify ['spesifai], v.tr. spécifier, déterminer. spe'cific, a. (a) spécifique; (b) (of statement) précis; (of order) explicite. specifi'cation, s. (a) spécification f (des détails); (b) pl. description f; caractéristiques fpl.

specimen ['spesimin], s. (a) spécimen m; (b) exemple m, échantillon m.

speck [spek], s. 1. petite tache f; moucheture f. 2. grain m, atome m, 'speckled, a. tacheté, moucheté.

spectacle ['spektəkl], s. 1. spectacle m. 2. pl. lunettes fpl. spec'tacular, a. spectaculaire. spec'tator, s. spectateur, -trice; assistant, -ante.

spectre ['spektər], s. spectre m, fantôme m.

spectrum ['spektrəm], s. Ph: spectre m.

speculate ['spekjuleit], v.i. 1. faire des conjectures (about, sur). 2. spéculer (in, sur). specu'lation, s. spéculation f. 'speculative, a. spéculatif. 'speculator, s. spéculateur, -trice; joueur m à la Bourse.

speech [spiːtʃ], s. 1. (a) la parole; (b) parts of s., parties f du discours. 2. langue f; parler m. 3. discours m. 4.

Sch: s. day, distribution f des prix. 'speechless, a. 1. incapable de parler. 2. interdit, interloqué; muet (de surprise).

speed [spiːd]. I. s. vitesse f; rapidité f; at full s., à toute vitesse; maximum s., vitesse limite; Aut: plafond m; P: s. cop, motard m; s. limit, vitesse f limite. II. v. 1. v.tr. to s. up the work, activer, accélérer, les travaux. 2. v.i. Aut: faire de la vitesse, foncer. 'speedboat, s. canot-automobile m; hors-bord m. 'speeding, s. Aut: excès m de vitesse. spee'dometer, s. indicateur m de vitesse; compteur m. 'speedway, s. Aut: 1. U.S: autoroute f. 2. piste f (d'autodrome). speedy, a. rapide, prompt.

spel(a)eology [spiːli'ɔlədʒi], s. spéléologie f. 'spel(a)eologist, s. spéléologue mf.

spell¹ [spel], s. formule f magique; charme m; to cast a s., jeter un sort (sur qn). 'spellbound, a. magnétisé; figé qui place.

spell², v.tr. épeler; to s. badly, faire des fautes d'orthographe; how is it spelt? comment cela s'écrit-il? 'spelling, s. orthographe f.

spell³, s. 1. tour m (de travail, etc.); three hours at a s., trois heures de suite. 2. a s. of cold weather, une période de froid.

‡spend [spend], v.tr. 1. dépenser; without spending a penny, sans rien débourser; F: to s. a penny, faire pipi. 2. passer, employer (son temps). 'spending, s. dépense f; s. power, pouvoir m d'achat. 'spendthrift, a. dépensier.

sperm [spɜːm], s. sperme m; s. whale, cachalot m.

sphere [sfiər], s. sphère f. spherical ['sfer-], a. sphérique.

sphinx [sfiŋks], s. sphinx m.

spice [spais]. I. s. épice f; aromate m. II. v.tr. épicer. 'spicy, a. 1. épicé; (goût) relevé. 2. (of story) (i) piquant; (ii) salé, épicé.

spider ['spaidər], s. araignée f.

spigot ['spigət], s. 1. fausset m. 2. U.S: robinet m.

spike [spaik], s. pointe f (de fer); piquant m (de fil barbelé).

‡spill [spil]. 1. v.tr. répandre, renverser; F: to s. the beans, (i) mettre les pieds dans le plat; (ii) gaffer; (iii) vendre la mèche. 2. v.i. (of liquid) se répandre.

‡spin [spin]. I. v.tr. filer (la laine, etc.). 2. v.i. (of top, etc.) tourner; (of aircraft) descendre en vrille; (of compass) s'affoler; my head's spinning, la tête me tourne. II. s. 1. tournoiement m; Av: (tail) s., vrille f; flat s., (i) Av: tonneau m; (ii) F: panique f. 'spindle, s. 1. Tex: fuseau m. 2. E: mandrin m; axe m (de pompe); arbre m (de tour). 'spin 'drier,

essoreuse f. **'spinner**, s. fileur, -euse. **'spinning**, filature f. **spin** 'dry, v.tr. délayer (un discours); faire traîner (une affaire).

spinach ['spinidʒ], s.ino. épinards mpl.

spine [spain], s. 1. colonne f vertébrale. 2. dos m (d'un livre). **'spineless**, a. F: (of pers.) mou; qui manque de caractère.

spinster ['spinstər], s.f. (a) Adm: célibataire f; (b) vieille fille f.

spiral ['spaiərəl]. I. s. (a) spirale f, hélice f; (b) Av: montée f, descente f, en spirale; (c) wage-price s., montée en flèche des prix et des salaires. II. a. spiral; s. staircase, escalier m en colimaçon.

spire [spaiər], s. aiguille f, flèche f (d'une église).

spirit ['spirit]. I. s. 1. esprit m, âme f; the Holy S., le Saint-Esprit, l'Esprit saint. 2. esprit, disposition f; party s., esprit de parti. To show s., montrer du caractère, du courage; to be in good spirits, être de bonne humeur; to be in low spirits, être accablé, abattu. 4. (a) pl. spiritueux mpl; alcool m; (b) surgical s. = alcool à 90°. II. v.tr. to s. sth. away, subtiliser, escamoter qch. **'spirited**, a. animé; vif. **'spiritualism**, s. spiritisme m. **'spiritualist**, s. spirite mf.

spit[1] [spit], s. 1. Cu: broche f. 2. Geog: flèche f.

‡spit[2]. I. v. 1. v.i. cracher. 2. v.tr. cracher (du sang); to s. sth. out, cracher qch; F: s. it out! dis-le. II. s. crachat m; F: he's the dead s. of his father, c'est son père tout craché, F: s. and polish, astiquage m. **'spitting**, s. crachement m; P.N: no s., défense de cracher.

spite [spait]. I. s. rancune f; malveillance f; dépit m; in s. of . . ., en dépit de . . ., malgré . . . II. v.tr. to do sth. to s. s.o., faire qch. pour contrarier qn. **'spiteful**, a. rancunier, vindicatif, méchant, malveillant. **-fully**, adv. ¶ par dépit; par rancune; par méchanceté. **'spitefulness**, s. méchanceté f; rancœur f; malveillance f.

splash [splæʃ]. I. s. 1. éclaboussement m; clapotis m. 2. (a) éclaboussure f; (b) tache f (de couleur). II. v. 1. v.tr. éclabousser (with, de); to s. one's money about, prodiguer son argent. 2. v.i. (of liquid) rejaillir en éclaboussures; (of waves) clapoter; (of tap) cracher; barboter, patauger (dans l'eau). **'splash-down**, s. amerrissage m (d'un engin spatial).

splendid ['splendid], a. magnifique; that's s.! à la bonne heure! **-ly**, adv. splendidement; magnifiquement. **'splendour**, s. splendeur f; éclat m.

splint [splint], s. Med: éclisse f.

splinter ['splintər]. I. s. 1. éclat m (de bois, etc.); écharde f (dans la peau). 2. Pol: s. group, groupe m fractionnaire. II. v.i. voler en éclats; **'splintered**, a. (bois) en éclats; (os) en esquilles.

split [split]. I. s. 1. fente f; fissure f. 2. division f; rupture f. 3. Cu: cream s., brioche f fourrée à la crème. 4. to do the splits, faire le grand écart. II. ‡v. 1. v.tr. fendre, déchirer (sa jupe); to s. the atom, désintégrer, diviser, l'atome. 2. v.i. se fendre; (of cloth) se déchirer; F: my head's splitting, j'ai un mal de tête fou; F: to s. on s.o., dénoncer qn. III. a. 1. fendu; in a s. second, en un rien de temps. 2. s. personality, dédoublement m de la personnalité. split 'up, v.tr. & i. (se) fractionner; (se) diviser.

splotch [splotʃ], s. F: tache f (de couleur, etc.).

splutter ['splʌtər], v.i. (a) (of pen) cracher; (b) (of pers.) bredouiller; (c) Aut: (of engine) bafouiller.

‡spoil [spoil]. I. v.tr. gâter, abîmer; endommager, gâcher (qch.); gâter (un enfant). 2. v.i. (of fruit, etc.) se gâter, s'abîmer. spoils, s.pl. butin m. **'spoil-sport**, s. gâte-tout m. **spoilt**, a. gâté, abîmé; avarié; s. child, enfant gâté.

spoke [spouk], s. rayon m (de roue).

spoken, a. (of language) parlé. **‡spokesman**, s. porte-parole m inv.

sponge [spʌn(d)ʒ]. I. s. 1. éponge f. 2. Cu: s. cake, (i) gâteau m de Savoie; (ii) = madeleine f; s. finger = biscuit m à la cuillère. II. v. 1. v.tr. éponger (qch.). 2. v.i. F: to s. on s.o., vivre aux crochets de qn; to s. on s.o. for drinks, se faire payer les tournées par qn. **'sponger**, s. F: parasite m; écornifleur, -euse. **'spongy**, a. spongieux.

sponsor ['sponsər]. I. s. 1. garant m, caution f. 2. parrain m, marraine f. II. v.tr. être le garant de (qn); parrainer (qn); T.V: etc: offrir (un programme).

spontaneous [spon'teinjəs], a. spontané.

spool [spuːl], s. bobine f.

spoon [spuːn]. I. s. cuiller f, cuillère f. II. v.i. P: (of couple) se faire des mamours. **‡spoon-feed**, v.tr. nourrir (un enfant) à la cuillère; F: mâcher les morceaux à (un élève); subventionner (une industrie). **'spoonful**, s. cuillerée f.

sporadic [spə'rædik], a. sporadique.

spore [spɔːr], s. spore f.

sport [spɔːt], s. 1. jeu m; divertissement m; to make s. of, se moquer de. 2. sport m; school sports, fête f sportive; Aut: sports car, model, voiture f, modèle m, grand sport; sports ground, terrain m de jeu; sports jacket, veston m sport. 3. he's a good s., (i) c'est un bon joueur; (ii) c'est un chic type. 'sporting, a. de sport; sportif; you've a s. chance, ça vaut la peine d'essayer le coup; I'll make you a s. offer, je vais vous faire une offre à laquelle vous ne perdrez rien. †'sportsman, s. 1. chasseur m; pêcheur m. 2. amateur m de sport. 3. a real s., un beau joueur.

spot [spot]. I. s. 1. endroit m, lieu m. adv.phr. on the s., sur-le-champ; immédiatement; F: to be on the s., (i) être très éveillé; (ii) être dans une situation dangereuse. 2. tache f. 3. pois m (de couleur); the blind s., Anat: la papille optique; (i) Aut: angle m aveugle; (radar) scanning s., spot m explorateur. 4. goutte f (de pluie); a s. of whisky, deux doigts de whisky; what about a s. of lunch? si nous allions déjeuner? II. ‡v.tr. 1. tacher, souiller (qch.). 2. repérer (qn, qch.); (at race) to s. the winner, prédire le gagnant. 'spot check, s. contrôle-surprise m. 'spotless, a. sans tache; immaculé; pur. -ly, adv. s. clean, d'une propreté irréprochable. 'spot-light, s. projecteur m; to put the s. on sth., mettre qch. en vedette. 'spot on, F: 1. a. exact, au point. 2. adv. au poil. 'spotted, a. tacheté, moucheté; Tex: à pois. 'spotty, a. tacheté, moucheté; (visage) couvert de boutons.

spout [spaut]. I. s. (a) tuyau m; (b) bec m (de théière). II. v. 1. v.i. (of liquid) jaillir. 2. v.tr. F: abs. parler à jet continu.

sprain [sprein]. I. s. entorse f, foulure f. II. v.tr. to s. one's wrist, se fouler le poignet; to s. one's ankle, se donner une entorse (à la cheville).

sprat [spræt], s. sprat, harenguet m.

sprawl [sprɔːl], v.i. s'étendre, s'étaler.

spray [sprei]. I. s. 1. embrun m. 2. (a) poussière f d'eau; (b) jet pulvérisé (de parfum). 3. gicleur m; vaporisateur m; s. gun, (also sprayer) vaporisateur m; pistolet m (à peinture, etc.). II. v.tr. 1. pulvériser, vaporiser, atomiser (un liquide). 2. asperger, arroser.

spread [spred]. I. s. 1. (a) étendue f; (b) envergure f. 2. diffusion f (d'une nouvelle); expansion f (des idées). II. ‡v. 1. v.tr. (a) étendre. (b) répandre. 2. v.i. (a) s'étendre, s'étaler; (b) se répandre, se propager.

sprig [sprig], s. brin m, brindille f; petite branche f.

spring [spriŋ]. I. s. 1. source f (d'eau). 2. printemps m; in s., au printemps; s. flowers, fleurs f printanières; s. tide, marée f de syzygie; grande marée. 3. saut m, bond m. 4. élasticité f. 5. ressort m. II. ‡v. 1. v.i. (a) bondir, sauter; F: where did you s. from?

d'où sortez-vous? the lid sprang open, le couvercle se releva instantanément; (b) (of water) jaillir. 2. v.tr. (a) Nau: to s. a leak, faire une voie d'eau; (b) to s. a surprise on s.o., prendre qn à l'improviste. 'springboard, s. tremplin m. 'springbok, s. Z: springbok m. spring'clean, v.tr. nettoyer à fond (une maison), Fr.C: faire le grand ménage. 'springiness, s. élasticité f. 'springlike, a. printanier. 'springy, a. élastique; (pas) alerte.

sprinkle ['spriŋkl], v.tr. (a) répandre, jeter (de l'eau, du sel); (b) arroser (d'eau); saupoudrer (de sel). 'sprinkler, s. arroseur m automatique rotatif. 'sprinkling, s. aspersion f, arrosage m; saupoudrage m; a s. of knowledge, quelques connaissances fpl.

sprint [sprint]. I. s. Sp: sprint m. II. v.i. sprinter. 'sprinter, s. sprinter m.

sprout [spraut]. I. v.i. (of plant) pousser, pointer; (of seed) germiner. II. s. Brussels sprouts, choux m de Bruxelles.

spruce[1] [spruːs], I. a. pimpant; soigné. II. v.tr. to s. oneself up, se faire beau.

spruce[2], s. Bot: épinette f; sapinette f.

spry [sprai], a. vif, actif.

spunk [spʌŋk], s. F: courage m; cran m.

spur [spəːr]. I. s. 1. éperon m. 2. coup m d'éperon; stimulant m; aiguillon m; on the s. of the moment, sous l'impulsion du moment. II. v.tr. 1. éperonner (un cheval). 2. to s. s.o. on, aiguillonner, stimuler (qn).

spurious ['spjuəriəs], a. faux; contrefait.

spurn [spəːn], v.tr. rejeter (une offre) avec mépris; traiter (qn) avec mépris.

spurt [spəːt]. I. s. 1. jaillissement m; jet m. 2. effort m soudain; Sp: to put on a s., démarrer. II. v.i. 1. to s. (up), jaillir. 2. Sp: démarrer, faire un effort de vitesse.

spy [spai]. I. s. †s. espion, -onne. II. v.i. espionner. 'spying, s. espionnage m.

squabble ['skwɔbl]. I. s. querelle f. II. v.i. se quereller. 'squabbling, s. querelles fpl.

squad [skwɔd], s. 1. Mil: etc: escouade f. 2. brigade f (de cheminots); the flying s., la brigade mobile (de la police).

squadron ['skwɔdrən], s. Mil: escadron m; Av: escadron, groupe m; s. leader, commandant m de groupe; Nau: escadre f.

squalid ['skwɔlid], a. sale; misérable; sordide. 'squalor, s. saleté f; misère f; aspect m sordide.

squall[1] ['skwɔːl], v.i. (of child, etc.) crier, brailler.

squall[2] ['skwɔːl], s. grain m; bourrasque f; rafale f; coup m de vent.

squander ['skwɔndər], v.tr. gaspiller (l'argent). 'squandering, s. gaspillage m.

square [skwɛər]. I. *s.* 1. carré *m.* 2. carreau *m* (de carte quadrillée); case *f* (d'échiquier); Cl: foulard *m*, carré. 3. place *f* (d'une ville). 4. set s., équerre *f* (à dessin). II. *a.* 1. carré; s. root, racine carrée. 2. to get things s., mettre tout en ordre; s. dealings, procédés *m* honnêtes. 3. F: (of pers.) vieux jeu; *a & s.*(personne) empesé(e). -ly, *adv.* 1. carrément. 2. loyalement. III. *adv.* 1. à angles droits; d'aplomb. 2. loyalement. IV. *v.tr.* 1. carrer, équarrir (la pierre, etc.) 2. arranger (qch.); balancer, régler (un compte); F: graisser la patte à (qn). 3. carrer (un nombre); quadriller (une carte). 'squared, *a.* (papier) quadrillé.

squash[1] [skwɔʃ]. I. *v.tr.* écraser; F: remettre (qn) à sa place. II. *s.* 1. cohue, presse *f.* 2. lemon, orange, s. citronnade *f*, orangeade *f.* 3. Sp: squash *m.* 'squashy, *a.* mou (et humide); détrempé.

squash[2], *s. Bot:* (*a*) gourde *f*; (*b*) *U.S:* courge *f*; courgette *f*.

‡squat [skwɔt]. I. *v.i.* 1. s'accroupir. 2. s'approprier un terrain. II. *a.* ramassé, trapu. 'squatter, s. squatter *m*.

squaw [skwɔ:], *s.* femme *f* peau-rouge.

squawk [skwɔ:k]. I. *s.* cri *m* rauque. II. *v.i.* pousser des cris rauques.

squeak [skwi:k]. I. *s.* cri *m* aigu; crissement *m.* II. *v.i.* pousser des cris aigus; crier; (*of floor*) grincer.

squeal [skwi:l]. I. *s.* cri *m* aigu; cri perçant. II. *v.i.* pousser des cris aigus.

squeeze [skwi:z]. I. *s.* 1. (*a*) compression *f*; (*b*) étreinte *f.* 2. presse *f*, cohue *f.* 3. F: credit s., restriction *f* du crédit. II. *v.tr.* 1. (*a*) presser; (*b*) étreindre. 2. se faufiler (par un trou, etc.); to s. up, se serrer, se tasser. 3. exercer une pression sur (qn); F: extorquer (de l'argent à qn).

squelch [skweltʃ], *v.i.* (*of water*) gargouiller; (*of pers.*) patauger (dans la boue, etc.)

squib [skwib], *s.* pétard *m.*

squint [skwint], *s.* strabisme *m.* II. *v.i.* loucher.

squirm [skwə:m], *v.i.* se tortiller; to make s.o s., mettre qn au supplice.

squirrel ['skwir(ə)l], *s.* écureuil *m.*

squirt [skwə:t]. I. *v.* 1. *v.tr.* faire jaillir (un liquide); injecter de l'huile. 2. *v.i.* (*of liquid*) jaillir; gicler. II. *s.* 1. jet *m*, giclée *f* (de liquide). 2. F: jeune insolent *m.*

stab [stæb]. I. ‡*v.tr.* poignarder (qn). II. *s.* coup *m* de poignard, de couteau.

stable[1] ['steibl]. I. *s.* écurie *f.* II. *v.tr.* loger (un cheval).

stable[2], *a.* 1. stable; solide, fixe. 2. constant, ferme. **sta'bility**, *s.* stabilité *f*; solidité *f.* **stabili'zation**, *s.* stabilisation *f.* 'stabilize, *v.tr.* stabiliser. 'stabilizer, *s.* stabilisateur *m*, équilibreur *m.*

stack [stæk]. I. *s.* 1. meule *f* (de foin); (*b*) pile *f*, tas *m.* 2. souche *f* de cheminée. II. *v.tr.* 1. mettre (le foin) en meule. 2. empiler, entasser (des objets).

staff [stɑ:f]. I. *s.* 1. bâton *m*; *Nau:* mât *m* (de pavillon). 2. *coll.* personnel *m*; *Mil:* état-major *m*; teaching s., personnel enseignant; editorial s., la rédaction; domestic s., les domestiques *m.* II. *v.tr.* pourvoir (un bureau, etc.) de personnel. 'staffwork, *s.* travail *m* d'organisation.

stag [stæg], *s.* 1. cerf *m.* 2. F: loup *m* (à la Bourse). 3. F: party, réunion *f* entre hommes.

stage [steidʒ]. I. *s.* 1. estrade *f*, platine *f* (d'un microscope); étage *m* (d'une fusée à exploration spatiale). 2. *Th:* scène *f*; s. play, pièce *f* de théâtre; s. door, entrée *f* des artistes; s. fright, trac *m*; s. hand, machiniste *m*; s. manager, régisseur *m*; s. whisper, aparté *m.* 3. phase *f*, période *f*, stade *m.* 4. étape *f* (d'un voyage); (*on bus route*) fare s., section *f.* II. *v.tr.* monter (une pièce); organiser (une démonstration). 'stager, *s.* F: old s., vieux routier *m.* 'staging, *s. Th:* mise *f* en scène. 'stagecraft, *s. Th:* technique *f* de la scène.

stagger ['stægər]. I. *v.* 1. *v.i.* chanceler, tituber. 2. *v.tr.* (*a*) consterner (qn); frapper (qn) de stupeur; (*b*) *Av:* décaler (les ailes); *E:* disposer (des rivets) en chicane; *El:* échelonner (les balais), étaler, échelonner (les vacances). II. *s.* 1. titubation *f.* 'staggered, *a.* holidays, congés échelonnés. 'staggering, *a.* (*of news*) renversant. II. *s.* 1. titubation *f.* 2. décalage *m*; échelonnement *m.*

stagnant ['stægnənt], *a.* stagnant; (*of trade*) en stagnation. **stag'nate**, *v.i.* être, devenir, stagnant. **stag'nation**, *s.* stagnation *f.*

stain [stein]. I. *s.* 1. tache *f*, souillure *f.* 2. couleur *f*, colorant *m.* II. *v.tr.* 1. tacher. 2. teindre, teinter (le bois). 'stainless, *a.* (acier) inoxydable.

stair [stɛər], *s.* 1. marche *f*, degré *m.* 2. *pl.* (*also* staircase) escalier *m.*

stake [steik]. I. *s.* 1. pieu *m*, poteau *m*; (*for plant*) tuteur *m.* 2. (*gaming*) mise *f*, enjeu *m*; the interests at s., les intérêts en jeu. II. *v.tr.* 1. ramer (des haricots); tuteurer (des tomates). 2. mettre (qch.) en jeu; jouer, miser (une somme).

stakhanovite [stæk'hɑ:nouvait], *s.* stakhanoviste *mf.*

stalactite ['stælæktait], *s.* stalactite *f.*

stalagmite ['stælægmait], *s.* stalagmite *f.*

stale [steil], *a.* 1. (pain) rassis; (œuf) qui n'est pas frais; (air) vicié; to s. smell, odeur *f* de renfermé; remugle *m.* 2. s. joke, vieille plaisanterie *f*; s. news nouvelle *f* déjà connue. 3. F: it's

gone s. on me, ça ne me plaît plus.
'stalemate, s. (a) (at chess) pat m;
(b) impasse f.

stalk¹ [stɔːk]. 1. v.i. to s. along, marcher
d'un pas majestueux; marcher à
grands pas. 2. v.tr. traquer (une bête)
à l'approche; filer (qn). 'stalking, s.
(deep) s., chasse f à l'approche.

stalk², s. tige f (de plante).

stall [stɔːl]. I. s. 1. stalle f (d'écurie);
case f (d'étable). 2. étalage m (en
plein vent); (at exhibition) stand m.
3. Ecc: stalle f; Th: (orchestra) stalls,
fauteuils m d'orchestre. II. v. 1. v.tr.
Aut: caler (le moteur); Av: mettre
(l'appareil) en perte de vitesse. 2. v.i.
(a) (of engine) caler; (b) (of pers.)
chercher à gagner du temps.

stallion ['stæljən], s. étalon m; cheval m
entier.

stamen ['steimen], s. Bot: étamine f.

stamina ['stæminə], s. vigueur f, résistance f.

stammer ['stæmər]. I. v.i. bégayer;
balbutier. II. s. (also stammering)
bégaiement m; balbutiement m.
'stammerer, s. bègue mf; balbutieur,
-euse.

stamp [stæmp]. I. s. 1. battement m de
pied; trépignement m. 2. timbre m;
(postage) s., timbre(-poste) m;
collector, philatéliste mf; revenue s.,
timbre du fisc; s. duty, droit m de
timbre; National Insurance s.,
cotisation f de la sécurité sociale. 2.
découpoir m (à emporte-pièce);
étampe f, poinçon m. II. v.tr. 1.
frapper (du pied); trépigner. 2. frapper,
imprimer, une marque (sur qch.). 3.
timbrer (un document); viser (un
passeport); timbrer, affranchir (une
lettre). 4. étamper, matricer (des
objets en métal).

stampede [stæm'piːd]. I. s. fuite f précipitée; panique f; ruée f. II. v.i.
fuir en désordre; se ruer, se précipiter
(en masse).

stand [stænd]. I. 1v. v.i. (a) être, se
tenir, rester, debout; to s. (up), se
lever; (b) to s. trouver, être; the house
stands on a hill, la maison se dresse, se
trouve, sur une colline; to s. talking,
rester à causer; (c) the contract
stands, le contrat tient; the objection
stands, cette objection subsiste; (d)
to s. in need of sth., avoir besoin de
qch.; to s. in danger of being killed,
s'exposer à se faire tuer; (e) to s. as a
candidate, se porter candidat; (f) how
do we s.? où en sont nos comptes?
as things s., au point où en sont les
choses; (g) to let a liquid s., laisser
reposer un liquide. 2. v.tr. (a) to s.
sth. against a wall, dresser qch. contre
un mur; (b) to s. one's ground, tenir
bon, ferme; (c) supporter (le froid,
etc.); résister à (des manipulations

brutales); F: I can't s. him, je ne peux
pas le sentir; (d) F: to s. s.o. a drink,
payer à boire à qn; payer une tournée.
II. s. 1. to take a firm s., se montrer
résolu; to make a s. against s.o.,
résister à qn. 2. support m, pied m
(de lampe); dessous m (de carafe). 3.
étalage m; (at exhibition) stand m. 4.
Sp: tribune f; stand m. 'stand a'side,
v.i. s'écarter, se ranger; se désister (en
faveur de qn). 'stand 'by, v.i. rester
fidèle à (sa promesse); tenir à (ce
qu'on dit); soutenir, défendre (qn).
'stand-by, s. 1. (pers.) soutien m. 2.
ressource f. 'stand-in, s. remplaçant
m (temporaire). 'standing. I. a. 1.
to be left s., être laissé sur place. 2.
s. crops, récoltes f sur pied. 3. s.
water, eau f stagnante. 4. s. joke,
plaisanterie f courante, traditionnelle.
II. s. 1. station f (debout); s. room,
place(s) f debout. 2. friend of long s.,
ami de longue date. 3. rang m,
position f; standing m. stand 'off,
v.tr. Ind: congédier (des employés).
stand-'offish, a. F: (of pers.) distant,
réservé. stand 'out, v.i. 1. résister (à
qch.); tenir bon (contre qch.). 2. se
détacher (sur qch.); his character
makes him s.o. from the crowd, sa
personnalité le détache de la foule.
'standpoint, s. point m de vue.
'standstill, s. immobilisation f; to
come to a s., s'arrêter.

standard ['stændəd], s. 1. bannière f;
Mil: étendard m; Nau: pavillon m;
Fin: the gold s., l'étalon m d'or. 2.
modèle m, type m; s. of living, niveau
m de vie. 3. degré m d'(excellence);
qualité f; up to s., à la hauteur; Com:
conforme à l'échantillon. 5. pylône m
d'éclairage. 6. attrib. s. size, de
taille courante; (of car) s. model,
voiture de série; s. English, l'anglais
des gens cultivés; Rail: s. gauge, voie
f normale; s. joke, plaisanterie f
classique. standardi'zation, s. étalon-
nage m (des poids); unification f (des
méthodes); standardisation f (d'une
machine). 'standardize, v.tr. étalon-
ner, unifier (des méthodes); Ind:
standardiser (les produits).

stanza ['stænzə], s. strophe f.

staple¹ ['steipl]. I. s. 1. crampon m, clou
m, à deux pointes; broche f (en fil de
fer). II. v.tr. agrafer, cramponner
(qch.); brocher (un livre). 'stapler,
s. agrafeuse f.

staple², attrib. a. s. diet, nourriture f de
base; s. industry, industrie f principale.

staple³, s. brin m, fibre f (de laine); soie
f (de coton).

star [staːr]. I. s. 1. étoile f; astre m. 2.
Cin: etc: vedette f, étoile, star f. II.
1v.i. Cin: etc: être en vedette. 'starlight, s. lumière f des étoiles. 'starry, a.
étoilé; semé d'étoiles.

starboard ['stɑ:bəd], s. Nau: tribord m.

starch [stɑ:tʃ]. I. s. amidon m. II. v.tr. empeser, amidonner. 'starchy, a. s. foods, féculents mpl.

stare [stɛər]. I. s. regard m fixe. II. v. 1. v.i. (a) regarder fixement; (b) écarquiller les yeux. 2. v.ind.tr. to s. at, regarder fixement; dévisager. 3. v.tr. to s. s.o. in the face, dévisager qn.

stark [stɑ:k]. adv. s. naked, tout nu; s. staring mad, complètement fou.

starling ['stɑ:liŋ], s. étourneau m.

start [stɑ:t]. I. s. 1. (a) tressaillement m, sursaut m; he gave a s., il sursauta; (b) saut m; mouvement m brusque. 2. (a) commencement m, début m; to make a good s., bien commencer; (b) départ m. II. v. 1. v.i. (a) tressaillir, sursauter; (b) commencer; débuter: to s. out, partir, se mettre en route; to s. back, reprendre le chemin (de la maison); (c) (of car) démarrer. 2. v.tr. (a) commencer (un travail, etc.); (b) lancer (une entreprise); fonder (un commerce); ouvrir (une école); provoquer (un incendie); (c) mettre (une machine) en marche; Aut: démarrer. 'starter, s. 1. Sp: partant m; you're an early s., vous partez de bonne heure. 2. Aut: (device) démarreur m. 'startle, v.tr. effrayer, alarmer (qn). 'startling, a. effrayant; (événement) sensationnel; (toilette) ébouriffante; (ressemblance) saisissante.

starve [stɑ:v]. 1. v.i. (a) to s. to death, mourir de faim; (b) manquer de nourriture. 2. v.tr. (a) faire mourir de faim; (b) priver de nourriture. star'vation, s. privation f, manque m, de nourriture; to die of s., mourir de faim: s. wages, salaire m de famine. 'starved, a. affamé; to s. of affection, privé d'affection.

state [steit]. I. s. 1. état m, condition f. 2. rang m, dignité f; to dine in s., dîner en grand gala; (of body) to lie in s., être exposé (sur un lit de parade); s. apartements, salons m d'apparat. 3. état m, nation f; s. forest, forêt domaniale; to establish s. control, étatiser; Secretary of S., (i) secrétaire d'État; (ii) U.S: = Ministre des Affaires étrangères. II. v.tr. déclarer, affirmer, faire connaître (qch.); I have seen it stated that . . ., j'ai lu quelque part que . . . 'stateless, a. Adm: s. person, apatride mf. 'stateliness, s. majesté f; dignité f. 'stately, a. majestueux; imposant; plein de dignité. 'statement, s. exposé m (des faits); rapport m, compte m rendu; affirmation f; Com: s. of account, état m, relevé m, de compte. †'statesman, s. homme m d'État. 'statesmanship, s. science f du gouvernement.

static ['stætik], a. statique.

station ['steiʃ(ə)n]. I. s. 1. position f, place f, poste m; Av: base f (aérienne); (in Austr:) sheep s., élevage m de moutons; El: power s., centrale f électrique; transformer s., transformateur m; Aut: service s., station-service f. 2. position f, rang m. 3. (railway) s., gare f; goods s., gare de marchandises; coach, bus, s., gare routière; underground, tube, s., station f de métro. 4. Ecc: the Stations of the Cross, le chemin de la Croix. II. v.tr. poster (des troupes, etc.). 'stationary, a. stationnaire, immobile; s. car, voiture en stationnement. 'stationmaster, s. chef m de gare.

stationer ['steiʃənər], s. papetier m; s.'s shop, papeterie f. 'stationery, s. fournitures fpl (de bureau, d'école).

statistics [stə'tistiks], s.pl. la statistique. sta'tistical, a. statistique. statis'tician, s. statisticien, -ienne.

statue ['stætju:], s. statue f.

stature ['stætjər], s. stature f; taille f.

status ['steitəs], s. statut m légal (de qn); condition f, position f; social s., rang m social; without official s., sans titre m officiel; s. quo, statu quo m inv.

statute ['stætju:t], s. 1. acte m du Parlement. 2. pl. statuts m, règlements m (d'une société). 'statutory, a. 1. réglementaire; s. holiday, fête f légale. 2. statutaire; conforme aux statuts.

staunch [stɔ:ntʃ], a. (of pers.) sûr; dévoué; ferme; (ami) solide. -ly, adv. avec résolution; avec dévotion.

stay [stei]. I. v.i. rester; séjourner (dans un endroit); descendre (à un hôtel). II. s. séjour m; visite f (chez un ami). stay a'way, v.i. s'absenter; ne pas venir. stay 'down, v.i. Sch: redoubler. stay 'in, v.i. (a) rester à la maison; (b) Sch: rester en retenue; (c) Ind: s. in strike, grève f sur le tas. 'staying, s. s. power, résistance f; endurance f. stay 'up, v.i. ne pas se coucher; veiller; to s. up late, veiller tard; (of child) se coucher plus tard que d'habitude.

stead [sted], s. to stand s.o. in good s., être fort utile à qn.

steady ['stedi]. I. a. (a) ferme, solide; fixe, rigide; (b) (travail, etc.) régulier, assidu; s. progress, progrès mpl soutenus; s. pulse, pouls égal; s. downpour, pluie f persistante. -ily, adv. (c) fermement; (b) régulièrement; (c) assidûment. II. adv. s. on! w. s.! ne bougez pas! s. (on)! doucement! du calme! III. v. 1. v.tr. raffermir, affermir; to s. oneself against sth., s'étayer contre qch. 2. v.i. (of market) reprendre son aplomb; (of pers.) to s. (down), se ranger. 'steadiness, s. 1. fermeté f. 2. assiduité f, persévérance f, application f. 3. stabilité f (des prix, etc.).

steak [steik], s. (a) tranche f (de viande, de poisson); (b) bifteck m; fillet s., tournedos m.

‡steal [sti:l], v.tr. (a) voler, dérober, soustraire (from, à); (b) to s. a march on s.o., devancer qn. *stealing, s. vol m.

stealthy ['stelθi], a. furtif. -ily, adv. furtivement.

steam [sti:m]. I. s. vapeur f; buée f; F: to let off s., (i) dépenser son superflu d'énergie; (ii) épancher sa bile. II. v. 1. v.tr. (faire) cuire à la vapeur. 2. v.i. jeter, exhaler, de la vapeur; fumer. 'steamer, s. 1. paquebot m. 2. marmite f à vapeur. steam 'roller, s. (a) rouleau m compresseur; (b) force f irrésistible. steam 'up, v.i. s'embuer. 'steamy, a. plein de buée; (of atmosphere) humide.

steel [sti:l]. I. s. 1. acier m; the iron and s. industry, l'industrie f sidérurgique; s. engraving, gravure f, estampe f, sur acier. 2. (for sharpening knives) affiloir m. II. v.tr. to s. oneself to do sth., s'armer de courage pour faire qch.

steep [sti:p], a. escarpé; à pic; raide. -ly, adv. en pente rapide; à pic. 'steepness, s. raideur f (d'une pente).

steeple ['sti:pl], s. (a) clocher m; (b) flèche f (de clocher).

steer [stiər], v.tr. gouverner (un navire); conduire (une auto); to s. clear of sth., éviter qch. 'steering, s. (a) Nau: manœuvre f de la barre; (b) Aut: direction f; s. column, colonne f de direction; s. wheel, volant m; (c) Pol: etc: s. committee, comité m d'organisation.

stem [stem]. I. s. (a) tige f (de plante); (b) pied m (de verre); (c) Ling: radical m (d'un mot). II. v.i. to s. from sth., être le résultat de qch. 'stembogen, s. Sp: stembogen m.

stench [stentʃ], s. odeur f infecte; puanteur f.

stencil ['stensil]. I. s. (a) patron m ajouré; (b) (typing) stencil m. II.. ‡v.tr. polycopier (un document).

sten gun ['stengʌn], s. = fusil-mitrailleur m.

stenographer [stə'nɔgrəfər], s. sténo(graphe) mf. 'steno'typist, s. sténotypiste mf.

step [step]. I. s. 1. pas m; to take steps to do sth., se préparer à faire qch. 2. marche f, degré m (d'un escalier); steps, escabeau m; s. ladder, échelle f double. II. ‡v.i. faire un pas, des pas; s. this way, venez par ici. 'stepbrother, s. frère m consanguin; demi-frère m. †'stepchild, s. enfant m/f d'un autre lit. 'stepdaughter, s. belle-fille f. 'stepfather, s. beau-père m. 'stepmother, s. belle-mère f. 'stepsister, s. sœur f consanguine; demi-sœur f.

'stepson, s. beau-fils m. 'step 'up, v.tr. augmenter (la production); El: survolter (le courant).

stereo ['stiəriou], s. & a. F: 1. (printing) cliché m. 2. stéréoscopique. 3. stéréophonique. 'stereo'graphic, a. stéréographique. stereo'phonic, a. stéréophonique. 'stereo'scope, s. stéréoscope. stereo'scopic, a. stéréoscopique. 'stereotype. I. s. cliché m. II. v.tr. stéréotyper, clicher. 'stereotyped, a. s. phrase, cliché m.

sterile ['sterail], a. stérile. ste'rility [-ril-], s. stérilité f. sterili'zation, s. stérilisation f. 'sterilize, v.tr. stériliser. 'sterilizer, s. stérilisateur m.

sterling ['stə:liŋ], a. pound s., livre f sterling; s. area, zone f sterling.

stern¹ [stə:n], a. sévère, dur. -ly, adv. sévèrement, durement.

stern², s. Nau: arrière m; poupe f.

sternum ['stə:nəm], s. Anat: sternum m.

‡stet [stet], v.tr. maintenir (un mot sur l'épreuve, sur le MS.); (imperative) s., bon; à maintenir.

stethoscope ['steθəskoup], s. stéthoscope m.

stevedore ['sti:vdɔ:r], s. Nau: arrimeur m; déchargeur m.

stew [stju:]. I. s. Cu: ragoût m; civet m. II. v. 1. v.tr. faire cuire en ragoût. 2. v.i. F: to let s.o. s. in his own juice, laisser qn mijoter (dans son jus). 'stewed, a. s. mutton, ragoût m de mouton; s. fruit, fruits m en compote; s. apples, marmelade f de pommes.

steward ['stjuəd], s. maître m d'hôtel (d'un cercle); Nau: (i) commis m aux vivres; (ii) garçon m de cabine, steward m; Av: steward; Ind: shop s., délégué m syndical. 'stewardess, s. Nau: femme f de chambre.

stick¹ [stik], s. bâton m; walking s., canne f; s. of celery, branche f de céleri; Sp: hockey s., crosse f; F: (of pers.) queer s., drôle m de type; Av: Mil: s. of bombs, chapelet m de bombes.

‡stick², v. 1. v.tr. (a) enfoncer (qch. dans qch.); F: (= put) mettre (qch. dans qch.); (b) coller; (c) F: I can't s. him, je ne peux pas le sentir. 2. v.i. (a) (se) coller, s'attacher, adhérer (to, à); (b) to s. to the facts, s'en tenir aux faits; F: to s. to one's guns, ne pas en démordre; (c) F: rester; (d) to s., to be stuck, être pris, engagé; (in mud) s'embourber; (of machine parts, etc.) coincer. 'stickiness, s. viscosité f; adhésivité f. 'sticking plaster, s. sparadrap m. 'stickler, s. rigoriste mf. stick 'out, v.i. faire saillie. stick 'up, v.i. se dresser; F: to s. up for s.o., prendre la défense de qn. 'sticky, a. collant, gluant; F: to be on a s. wicket, être dans une situation difficile. 2. F: difficile, désagréable.

stiff [stif]. I. *a.* (*a*) raide; rigide; dur; (*b*) ferme, consistant; (*c*) (examen, etc.) difficile; *F:* s. price, prix *m* salé; a s. whisky, un whisky bien tassé. II. *s. P:* 1. cadavre *m*, macchabée *m*. 2. big s., gros bêta *m*. '**stiffen,** *v.tr.* & *i.* (se) raidir; **'stiffly,** *adv.* 1. raidement. 2. d'un air guindé. '**stiffness,** *s.* (*a*) raideur *f*; rigidité *f*; (*b*) fermeté *f*, consistance *f*.

stifle [staifl]. 1. *v.tr.* (*a*) étouffer, suffoquer; (*b*) réprimer (une émotion, etc.). 2. *v.i.* suffoquer, étouffer. '**stifling,** *a.* étouffant, suffocant.

stigma ['stigmə], *s. Cl:* stigmate *m*, tache *f*. '**stigmatize,** *v.tr.* stigmatiser.

stile [stail], *s.* échalier *m*.

†stiletto [sti'letou], *s.* stylet *m*; s. heel, talon *m* aiguille.

still[1] [stil], *a.* tranquille; immobile; to keep s., ne pas bouger; s. life, nature morte. '**stillborn,** *a.* mort-né.

still[2]. 1. *adv.* encore; toujours. 2. *conj.* cependant, pourtant, toutefois.

still[3], *s.* alambic *m*, cornue *f*.

stilt [stilt], *s.* échasse *f*. '**stilted,** *a.* (*of style*) guindé.

stimulate ['stimjuleit], *v.tr.* stimuler; encourager (la production). '**stimulant,** *s.* stimulant *m*. s. '**stimulating,** *a.* stimulant; encourageant. **stimu'lation,** *s.* stimulation *f*. '**stimulus,** *s.* stimulant *m*; to give a s. to trade, donner de l'impulsion au commerce.

sting [stiŋ]. I. *s.* 1. dard *m*, aiguillon *m* (d'abeille, etc.). 2. piqûre *f*; (*b*) douleur *f* cuisante. II. *v.tr.* piquer; *F:* to be stung, attraper le coup de fusil.

stingy ['stin(d)ʒi], *a. F:* mesquin, chiche, ladre.

stink [stiŋk]. I. †*v.i.* puer; sentir mauvais; empester. '**stinker,** *s.* puanteur *f*; odeur *f* infecte. '**stinker,** *s. P:* 1. (*pers.*) sale type *m*. 2. to write a s., écrire une lettre carabinée.

stint [stint], *v.tr.* (*a*) to s. oneself, se refuser le nécessaire; (*b*) lésiner sur (qch.).

stipulate ['stipjuleit], *v.tr.* & *i.* stipuler. **stipu'lation,** *s.* stipulation *f*.

‡stir [stəːr], *v.tr.* & *i.* remuer; bouger; to s. up trouble, fomenter la dissension. '**stirring,** *a.* (discours) émouvant, entraînant.

stirrup ['stirəp], *s.* étrier *m*.

stitch [stitʃ]. I. *s.* (*a*) (*sewing*) point *m*, piqûre *f*; (*knitting*) maille *f*; (*b*) *Med:* point (de suture). II. *v.tr.* (*a*) coudre; (*b*) *Med:* suturer.

stoat [stout], *s.* hermine *f* d'été.

stock [stɔk]. I. *s.* 1. race *f*, famille *f*. 2. *Nau:* pl. chantier *m*; cale *f* de construction. 3. provision *f* (de bois, etc.); *Com:* marchandises *fpl*, stock *m*; in s., en magasin; *Agr:* bétail *m*; fat s., bétail de boucherie; s. farming,

élevage *m* (de bétail). 4. *Cu:* bouillon *m*. 5. *Fin:* fonds *mpl*, valeurs *fpl*, actions *fpl*; the S. Exchange, la Bourse. 6. *Bot:* girofflée *f* des jardins. 7. *attrib.* s. size, taille *f* courante; s. phrase, cliché *m*; *Sp:* s. car, stock-car *m*. II. *v.tr.* 1. monter (une ferme) en bétail; approvisionner (une ferme). (with, de). 2. stocker (des marchandises). '**stockbroker,** *s. Fin:* agent *m* de change. '**stockist,** *s. Com:* stockiste *m*. **†'stockman,** *s. Austr:* bouvier *m*. '**stockpile,** *s.* stocks *mpl* de réserve. II. *v.i.* & *tr.* stocker. '**stockpiling,** *s.* stockage *m*. '**stocktaking,** *s. Com:* inventaire *m*. '**stocky,** *a.* trapu.

stocking ['stɔkiŋ], *s. Cl:* bas *m*; fully-fashioned s., bas diminué.

stodge [stɔdʒ], *s. F:* aliment *m* bourrant, *esp.* pudding *m*. '**stodgy,** *a. F:* (repas) lourd; (livre) indigeste; (*of pers.*) lourd, rasoir.

stoical ['stouik(ə)l], *a.* stoïque. **-ally,** *adv.* stoïquement. '**stoicism,** *s.* stoïcisme *m*.

stoke [stouk], *v.tr.* charger (un foyer); chauffer (un four).

stole [stoul], *s.* étole *f*.

stolid ['stɔlid], *a.* lourd, lent, impassible. **-ly,** *adv.* avec flegme. **sto'lidity,** *s.* flegme *m*.

stomach ['stʌmək]. I. *s.* estomac *m*. II. *v.tr.* endurer, tolérer (qch.); digérer (une insulte); I can't s. it, j'en ai plein le dos.

†stone [stoun], *s.* 1. pierre *f*. 2. precious stones, pierres précieuses; pierreries *f*. 3. noyau *m* (de fruit). 4. *Med:* calcul *m*. 5. *inv.* 6 kg 348; to weigh 12 s. = peser 76 kilos. 6. *attrib.* de, en, pierre; de grès; s. blind, deaf, completement aveugle, sourd. '**stone-work,** *s.* (*a*) maçonnerie *f*; maçonnerie *f*; (*b*) ouvrage *m* en pierre. '**stony,** *a.* pierreux; couvert de pierres; *F:* s. (broke), dans la dèche.

stooge [stuːdʒ]. I. *s. F:* (*a*) *Th:* faire-valoir *m*; (*b*) subalterne *m*, nègre *m*; (*c*) police *m*, *P:* casserole *f*. II. *v.i. F:* (*a*) *Th:* servir de faire-valoir (à un acteur); (*b*) faire le nègre.

stool [stuːl], *s.* 1. tabouret *m*; folding s., pliant *m*. 2. *med. pl.* selles *f*.

stoop [stuːp], *v.i.* (*a*) se pencher, se baisser; (*b*) s'abaisser, descendre; (*c*) être voûté.

stop [stɔp]. I. ‡*v.* 1. *v.tr.* (*a*) boucher, fermer (un trou, etc.); plomber (une dent); (*b*) arrêter (qn, qch.); bloquer, stopper (un chèque); (*c*) cesser (ses efforts, etc.); arrêter (de parler); it's stopped raining, la pluie a cessé; (*d*) couper (l'électricité, le gaz). 2. *v.i.* s'arrêter; stopper; *P.N:* all buses to stop here, arrêt *m* fixe, obligatoire; *P.N: Aut:* stop, stop; (*b*) to s. at an hotel, descendre, séjourner, à un hôtel. II. *s.* 1. arrêt *m*; halte *f*; to come to a s., s'arrêter; bus s., arrêt d'autobus; request s., arrêt facultatif. 2. signe m de ponctuation; full s., point m. 'stopcock, s. robinet m d'arrêt, de fermeture. 'stopgap, s. bouche-trou m. 'stoplight, s. Aut: le (feu) stop. stop 'off, v.i. U.S: s'arrêter; faire étape. 'stoppage, s. obstruction f; interruption f (du travail). 'stopper, s. (a) bouchon m; (b) obturateur m. 'stopping, s. (a) plombage m (d'une dent); (b) s. place, arrêt m; escale f. 'stopwatch, s. compte-secondes m; chronomètre m.

store [stɔːr]. I. s. 1. provision f (de qch.); pl. stores, provisions, vivres m. 2. (a) entrepôt m, magasin m; (b) magasin; department s., grand magasin; the village store(s), l'alimentation f, l'épicerie f, du village. II. v.tr. 1. to s. (up), amasser, accumuler (qch.); emmagasiner (l'électricité, la chaleur). 2. mettre en dépôt (des meubles); mettre en grange (le blé, etc.). 'storehouse, s. magasin m, entrepôt m. 'storekeeper, s. 1. magasinier m. 2. U.S: boutiquier, -ière.

storey [stɔːri], s. étage m (d'une maison).

stork [stɔːk], s. cigogne f.

storm [stɔːm]. I. s. 1. orage m, pluie f (de projectiles); tempête f (d'injures). II. v. 1. v.i. (of pers.) tempêter, pester. II. v.tr. Mil: (i) livrer l'assaut à, (ii) prendre d'assaut (une place forte). 'stormy, a. orageux.

story[1] [stɔːri], s. histoire f; récit m; short s., nouvelle f; that's quite another s., c'est une autre paire de manches.

story[2], s. U.S: étage m (d'une maison).

stout[1] [staut], a. 1. (of thing) fort, solide. 2. (of pers.) gros, corpulent. 'stoutness, s. embonpoint m, corpulence f.

stout[2], s. stout m; bière f brune forte.

stove [stouv], s. (a) poêle m, fourneau m; slow-combustion s., calorifère m; (b) cuisinière f.

stow [stou], v.tr. to s. (away), mettre en place, ranger, serrer; Nau: arrimer.

straggler ['stræglər], s. traînard m. 'straggling, a. disséminé; s. village, village m aux maisons éparses.

straight [streit]. I. a. 1. droit; s. line, ligne droite. 2. honnête; s. answer, réponse franche, sans équivoque. 3. Pol: s. fight, campagne électorale à deux candidats; s. whisky, whisky sec. II. s. en ordre; to put things s., remettre de l'ordre; débrouiller (l'affaire); your tie's not s., votre cravate est de travers. III. s. 1. material cut on the s., tissu coupé de droit fil. 2. (horse racing) the s., le finish. III. adv. 1. droit; keep s. on, continuez tout droit; to read a book s. through, lire un livre

d'un bout à l'autre. 2. directement; to walk s. in, entrer sans frapper; s. away, tout de suite. 3. to look s.o. s. in the face, regarder qn bien en face; I tell you s., je vous le dis tout net. 'straighten, v.tr. redresser (qch.); arranger (qch.); mettre (qch.) en ordre. straight'forward, a. loyal, franc. -ly, adv. loyalement; franchement. straight'forwardness, s. honnêteté f, franchise f. 'straightness, s. rectitude f; droiture f.

strain[1] [strein]. I. s. 1. tension f; mental s., surmenage m intellectuel. 2. Med: entorse f, foulure f. II. v.tr. 1. tendre (un câble); se fatiguer (les yeux). 2. (a) Med: se forcer (le cœur); se fouler (l'épaule); (b) E: déformer (une pièce). 3. filtrer, passer (un liquide); faire égoutter (les légumes). 'strained, a. 1. s. relations, rapports m tendus; s. ankle, cheville f foulée; s. heart, cœur m fatigué. 2. filtré, tamisé. 'strainer, s. filtre m; tamis m; passoire f.

strain[2], s. (a) qualité f inhérente; tendance f; (b) race f, (of virus) souche f.

strait [streit], s. (a) détroit m; the Straits of Dover, le Pas de Calais; (b) to be in (great) straits, être dans l'embarras. 'strait-laced, a. prude; collet monté.

strand [strænd], s. brin m (de cordage, de fil à coudre).

stranded ['strændid], a. (of pers.) en panne; laissé en plan.

strange [strein(d)ʒ], a. 1. inconnu. 2. singulier, étrange. -ly, adv. étrangement, singulièrement. 'stranger, s. étranger, -ère; inconnu, -ue; I'm a s. here, je ne suis pas d'ici.

strangle ['strængl], v.tr. étrangler. strangu'lation, s. strangulation f.

strap [stræp], s. 1. courroie f; watch s., bracelet m pour montre. 2. bande f, sangle f (de cuir, etc.).

stratagem ['strætədʒəm], s. ruse f; stratagème m.

strategy ['strætədʒi], s. stratégie f. stra'tegic, a. stratégique. 'strategist, s. stratégiste m.

stratosphere ['strætəsfiər], s. stratosphère f.

†stratum ['strɑːtəm, 'streitəm], s. Geog: couche f.

straw [strɔː], s. paille f; F: it's the last s.! c'est le comble!

strawberry ['strɔːb(ə)ri], s. fraise f; s. (plant), fraisier m; wild s., fraise des bois; s. ice, glace à la fraise.

stray [strei]. I. a. 1. égaré, errant. 2. s. bullets, balles perdues. II. s. animal m égaré. III. v.i. s'égarer; errer.

streak [striːk], s. 1. raie f, bande f; trait m; s. of lightning, éclair m. 'streaking, s. T.V: traînage m. 'streaky, a. rayé, strié; (of bacon) entrelardé.

stream [striːm]. I. s. 1. cours m d'eau; ruisseau m. 2. coulée f (de lave); jet m (de sang, de lumière); défilé m interrompu (de voitures). 3. courant m; with the s., au fil de l'eau; against the s., à contre-courant. II. v.i. (of liquid) couler (à flots); ruisseler; (of hair, etc.) flotter (au vent). 'streamer, s. banderole f; paper streamers, serpentins m. 'streamline, v.tr. caréner (une auto); moderniser, rationaliser (des méthodes). 'streamlined, a. caréné, fuselé, profilé; aux formes élancées. s. economy, économie f réduite à l'essentiel. 'streamlining, s. (a) carénage m, profilage m; (b) modernisation f (des méthodes).

street [striːt]. s. rue f; the man in the s., l'homme moyen; s. level, rez-de-chaussée m inv. 'streetcar, s. U.S: tramway m.

strength [streŋθ]. s. 1. (a) force(s) f(pl); s. of mind, fermeté f d'esprit; s. of will, résolution f; on the s. of, sur la foi de; (b) solidité f. 2. Mil: effectifs mpl (d'un régiment). 'strengthen, v.tr. consolider; renforcer (une poutre); raffermir (l'autorité f de qn).

strenuous ['strenjuəs]. a. 1. (of pers.) actif, énergique. 2. (travail) acharné, ardu. -ly, adv. vigoureusement; énergiquement.

stress [stres]. I. s. 1. force f, contrainte f. 2. tension f. 3. insistance f; to lay s. on (sth.), insister sur (qch.). II. v.tr. appuyer, insister sur (qch.); souligner (un mot); accentuer (une syllabe).

stretch [stretʃ]. I. v. 1. v.tr. (a) tendre; (b) s'étirer; to s. one's legs, se dégourdir les jambes; (c) to s. a point, faire une concession. 2. v.i. (a) s'élargir, s'allonger; (of elastic) s'étendre; (of material) prêter; (of landscape) s'étendre. II. s. 1. élasticité f; attrib. (bas, etc.) extensible. 2. étendue f (de pays); (of time) at a s., tout d'un trait; d'affilée; P: to do a s., faire de la prison, P: de la taule. 'stretcher, s. brancard m.

strict [strikt], a. 1. exact; strict; précis; s. neutrality, neutralité f rigoureuse; s. discipline, discipline f sévère. 2. (of pers.) sévère. -ly, adv. 1. exactement, rigoureusement. 2. strictement; s. forbidden, absolument défendu. 3. sévèrement. 'strictness, s. sévérité f (de la discipline).

stride [straid]. I. s. enjambée f; to make great strides, faire de grands progrès. II. v.i. to s. along, avancer à grands pas.

strident ['straid(ə)nt], a. strident.

strife [straif], s. lutte f.

strike [straik]. I. ‡v. 1. v.tr. (a) frapper; (b) to s. a match, frotter une allumette; (c) to s. roots, prendre racine; (d) heurter (qch.); a thought strikes me, une idée me vient; he strikes me as being sincere, il me paraît sincère; that's how it struck me, voilà l'effet que cela m'a fait; (e) to s. oil, (i) rencontrer le pétrole; (ii) trouver le filon; (f) abs. Ind: se mettre en grève; (g) to s. an attitude, poser. 2. v.i. (of clock) sonner. II. s. 1. Ind: grève f; token s., grève symbolique; sympathy s., grève de solidarité; lightning s., grève surprise; go-slow s., grève perlée; sit-down s., grève sur le tas. 2. rencontre f (de pétrole, etc.); lucky s., coup m de veine. 'striker, s. Ind: gréviste mf. 'striking, a. 1. (pendule) à sonnerie. 2. (spectacle) frappant, remarquable.

string [striŋ]. I. s. 1. ficelle f; corde f; cordon m; to pull the strings, tirer les ficelles. 2. Mus: the strings, les instruments mpl à cordes. II. ‡v.tr. 1. corder (une raquette); monter (un violon). 2. enfiler (des perles). 'stringed, a. (instrument) à cordes. 'stringy, a. fibreux, filandreux.

stringent ['strindʒ(ə)nt], a. rigoureux, strict.

strip [strip]. I. s. bande f (de papier, etc.); s. cartoon, comic s., bande illustrée; P: to tear s.o. off a s., laver la tête à qn. II. ‡v. 1. v.tr. (a) mettre (qn) tout nu; stripped to the waist, le torse nu; (b) défruiter (un pommier, etc.); dégarnir (un lit). 2. v.i. se dévêtir.

stripe [straip], s. (a) raie f; rayure f; (b) Mil: galon m (de caporal). 'striped, a. rayé; (pelage) tigré, zébré.

‡**strive** [straiv], v.i. tâcher, s'efforcer (de faire qch.); rechercher (l'effet).

stroke [strouk]. I. s. 1. coup m; (a) coup (de férule, etc.); Sp: (rowing) coup d'aviron; (swimming) brassée f; (c) Aut: etc: mouvement m, course f (du piston); two-s. engine, (moteur à) deux temps m; (b) he hasn't done a s. of work, il n'a rien fait de ses dix doigts; (c) coup d'horloge); on the s. of nine, à neuf heures sonnant(es); (f) Med: F: attaque f (d'apoplexie); (g) coup de crayon, de pinceau; trait m de plume. 2. (rowing, pers.) chef m de nage. 3. caresse f de la main. II. v.tr. 1. Sp: to s. a boat, donner la nage. 2. caresser de la main; to s. the cat the wrong way, caresser le chat à rebrousse-poil.

stroll [stroul]. I. v.i. errer à l'aventure; flâner; se balader. II. s. petit tour m; bout m de promenade; balade f.

strong [stroŋ]. I. a. fort; solide; résistant; (of health) he's not very s., il est peu robuste; Com: s. market, marché m ferme; politeness is not his s. point, la politesse n'est pas son fort; (at cards) s. suit, couleur f longue; s.

cheese, fromage *m* qui pique; s. butter, beurre *m* rance; *Gram:* s. verb, verbe fort. II. *adv.* F: it's still going s., ça marche à merveille. -ly, *adv.* solidement; fermement; vigoureusement; énergiquement; I don't feel s. about it, je n'y attache pas une grande importance. '**strong-box**, s. coffre-fort *m.* '**stronghold**, s. forteresse *f*; citadelle *f*. strong-'minded, *a.* à l'esprit solide, résolu, décidé. '**strong-room**, s. cave *f* des coffres-forts.

structure ['strʌkt∫ər], s. 1. structure *f*. 2. édifice *m*, structure, bâtiment *m*. '**structural**, *a.* 1. de construction; s. iron, steel, charpentes *fpl* métalliques. 2. structural.

struggle ['strʌgl], I. *v.i.* lutter; se débattre. II. s. lutte *f*. '**struggler**, s. lutteur *m*. '**struggling**, *a.* (artiste, etc.) qui vit péniblement.

‡strum [strʌm], *v.tr.* taper (du piano); *abs.* pianoter; gratter (de la guitare).

‡strut¹ [strʌt], *v.i.* se pavaner, se rengorger; to s. in, out, entrer, sortir, d'un air important.

strut², s. support *m*, étai *m.*

strychnine ['strikni:n], s. strychnine *f.*

stub [stʌb]. I. s. 1. souche *f* (d'arbre); bout *m* (de crayon, de cigare). 2. souche, talon *m* (de chèque). II. *v.tr.* 1. to s. one's toe against sth., se cogner le pied contre qch. 2. to s. out a cigarette, éteindre une cigarette (en écrasant le bout).

stubble ['stʌbl], s. chaume *m.*

stubborn ['stʌbən], *a.* obstiné, opiniâtre, entêté, têtu. -ly, *adv.* obstinément, opiniâtrement. '**stubbornness**, s. entêtement *m*, obstination *f*, opiniâtreté *f.*

stucco ['stʌkou], s. stuc *m.*

stuck [stʌk], *a.* (a) s. pig, porc *m* égorgé; (b) F: immobilisé; en panne. '**stuck-'up**, *a.* prétentieux, guindé.

stud¹ [stʌd], s. 1. clou *m* à grosse tête. 2. bouton *m* (de chemise).

stud², s. écurie *f* (de chasse); (for breeding) haras *m*; s. book, registre *m* (des chevaux, etc.), stud-book *m.*

student ['stju:d(ə)nt], s. étudiant, -ante.

studio ['stju:diou], s. (a) (artist's) s., atelier *m*; (b) Cin: T.V: Rad: studio *m.*

studious ['stju:diəs], *a.* studieux, appliqué.

study ['stʌdi]. I. *v.tr.* étudier; to s. under s.o., suivre les cours de qn; to s. for an examination, préparer un examen; to s. economics, étudier les sciences économiques; to s. economy, viser à l'économie. II. s. 1. *s.* étude *f* (du français, etc.); to make a s. of sth., étudier qch. 2. cabinet *m* de travail; *Sch:* bedroom, chambre *f* d'étudiant(e). '**studied**, *a.* (a) étudié, recherché; (b) prémédité, calculé.

stuff [stʌf]. I. s. 1. matière *f*, substance *f*, étoffe *f*; F: he knows his s., il s'y connaît; s. and nonsense! quelle bêtise! 2. *Tex:* étoffe *f*, tissu *m.* II. *v.tr.* bourrer (with, de); rembourrer (un meuble); *Cu:* farcir (une volaille); empailler (un animal); F: to s. (oneself), se bourrer; bâfrer; to s. up a hole, boucher un trou; to s. sth. into sth., fourrer qch. dans qch. '**stuffing**, s. bourrage *m*, rembourrage *m*; empaillage *m*; *Cu:* farce *f*; P: to knock the s. out of s.o., flanquer une tripotée à qn.

stuffy ['stʌfi], *a.* 1. mal ventilé; mal aéré; qui sent le renfermé. 2. F: (of pers.) collet monté; don't be so s.! il n'y a pas de quoi te scandaliser! '**stuffiness**, s. manque *m* d'air; odeur *f* de renfermé.

stumble ['stʌmbl], *v.i.* trébucher; faire un faux pas. '**stumbling**, s. 1. trébuchement *m*; faux pas *m.* 2. s. block, pierre *f* d'achoppement.

stump [stʌmp]. I. s. 1. souche *f* (d'arbre); moignon *m* (de bras, de jambe); bout *m* (de crayon); mégot *m* (de cigarette). 2. *Cr:* (cricket) piquet *m* (du guichet); to draw stumps, cesser la partie. II. *v.* 1. *v.i.* to s. in, out, entrer, sortir, clopin-clopant. 2. *v.tr.* (a) F: coller (un candidat); réduire (qn) à quia; (b) at cricket master hors jeu (un batteur). '**stump 'up**, *v.i.* F: payer, casquer, s'exécuter. '**stumpy**, *a.* (of pers.) trapu.

‡stun [stʌn], *v.tr.* étourdir, assommer. 2. (of news, etc.) renverser, abasourdir.

stunt [stʌnt], s. F: 1. coup *m*, affaire *f*, de publicité. 2. tour *m* de force; *Cin:* s. man, acrobate (-doublure) *m.*

stunted ['stʌntid], *a.* rabougri, chétif.

stupefy ['stju:pifai], *v.tr.* stupéfier; hébéter; abasourdir; I'm absolutely stupefied (by it), je n'en reviens pas.

stupendous [stju:'pendəs], *a.* prodigieux; F: formidable.

stupid ['stju:pid], *a.* stupide; sot, bête. -ly, *adv.* stupidement; bêtement. stu'pidity, s. stupidité *f.*

stupor ['stju:pər], s. stupeur *f.*

sturdy ['stə:di], *a.* (a) vigoureux, robuste; (b) hardi, résolu, ferme. -ily, *adv.* (a) fortement; (b) vigoureusement. '**sturdiness**, s. vigueur *f.*

stutter ['stʌtər], I. *v.i. & tr.* bégayer, bredouiller. II. s. bégaiement *m.*

‡sty [stai], s. porcherie *f*; étable *f* (à porcs).

stye [stai], s. *Med:* orgelet *m.*

style [stail]. I. s. style *m*; to live in (great) s., mener grand train; furniture in Empire s., meubles *m* style Empire; *Com:* made in three styles, fabriqué sur trois modèles *m*; the latest s., la dernière mode; written in a humorous s., écrit sur un ton de plaisanterie. II. *v.tr.* Com: créer. 'stylish, *a.* élégant, chic. styli'zation, *s.* stylisation *f.* 'stylize, *v.tr.* styliser.

sub [sʌb]. I. *prefix (used in compounds)* sous-. II. *s: F: abbr. for* (i) SUBSCRIPTION, (ii) SUB-EDITOR, (iii) SUBSTITUTE, (iv) SUBMARINE. III. *v. F: abbr. for* (i) SUB-EDIT, (ii) SUBSTITUTE. 'suba'cute, *a. Med:* subaigu. 'subco'mmittee, *s.* sous-comité *m.* sub'conscious. 1. *a.* subconscient. 2. *s.* l'inconscient *m.* sub'contract. 1. *s.* sous-traité *m.* II. *v.tr.* ['sʌbkən'trækt], sous-traiter. 'subdi'vide, *v.tr. & i.* (se) subdiviser. 'subdi'vision, *s.* subdivision *f*; sous-division *f.*

subdue [səb'dju:], *v.tr.* 1. maîtriser, dompter; vaincre. 2. adoucir (la lumière, la voix). sub'dued, *a.* 1. (peuple) vaincu. 2. (*of pers.*) déprimé. 3. (*of light*) tamisé, atténué; (conversation) à voix basse.

sub'edit, *v.tr.* corriger, mettre au point (un article). 'sub-'editor, *s.* secrétaire *m* de la rédaction. **subject.** I. *s.* ['sʌbdʒikt] 1. (*pers.*) sujet, -ette. 2. sujet *m*; *Sch:* matière *f*. II. *v.tr.* [səb'dʒekt] soumettre (qn, qch. à qch.). III. *a.* ['sʌbdʒikt] 1. sujet, exposé, (à qch.); prices s. to 5% discount, prix qui comportent 5% d'escompte. 2. (*conditional*) s. to ratification, sous réserve de ratification. sub'jective, *a. & s. Gram:* subjonctif (m). 'sub'lease. I. *v.tr. (also sublet)* sous-louer. II. *s.* sous-bail *m*, sous-location *f.* 'sub-lieu'tenant [lef'tenənt], *s. Nau:* enseigne *m* (de vaisseau).

sublime [sə'blaim], *a. & s.* sublime (*m*).

submarine, *s.* sous-marin *m.* sub'merge. I. *v.tr.* submerger; inonder; noyer. 2. *v.i. (of submarine)* plonger. sub'mission, *s.* soumission *f*; résignation *f.* ‡sub'mit, *v.tr. & i.* (se) soumettre. sub'ordinate. I. *a.* inférieur, subalterne; (rôle) secondaire; *Gram:* subordonné. II. *s.* subordonné, -ée. III. *v.tr.* subordonner. sub'poena [-pi:nə], *Jur:* I. *s.* citation *f* de témoins sous peine d'amende. II. *v.tr.* citer qn à comparaître (sous peine d'amende). sub'scribe, *v.tr.* souscrire (pour une somme, à un emprunt). sub'scriber, *s.* abonné, -ée (à un journal, au téléphone). sub'scription, *s.* cotisation *f*; abonnement *m.* sub'sequent, *a.* subséquent, qui suit; at a s. meeting, à une séance ultérieure; sq, *adv.* plus tard; dans la suite. sub'side, *v.i.* s'affaisser, se tasser, s'enfoncer; (*of water, etc.*) baisser, diminuer; (*of storm, anger*) se calmer, s'apaiser. 'sub'sidence, *s.* affaissement *m*; effondrement *m.* sub'sidiary, *a.* subsidiaire, auxiliaire; s. company, *s.* subsidiary,

filiale *f.* 'subsidize, *v.tr.* subventionner. 'subsidy, *s.* subvention *f.* sub'sist, *v.i.* subsister. sub'sistence, *s.* 1. existence *f.* 2. means of s., moyens de subsistence *f.* 'subsoil, *s. Geog:* sous-sol *m.* 'sub'sonic, *a.* subsonique. 'substance, *s.* 1. substance *f.* 2. solidité *f.* sub'standard, *a.* inférieur (à la norme), sub'stantial, *a.* important; s. difference, une différence appréciable, sensible. 2. solide; s. meal, repas *m* copieux. -ally, *adv.* substantiellement; solidement; fortement; pour une grande part. sub'stantiate, *v.tr.* établir, justifier. 'substitute.' I. *s.* 1. (*pers.*) suppléant, -ante; remplaçant, -ante. 2. (*of foods, etc.*) succédané *m.* II. *v.* 1. *v.tr.* substituer. 2. *v.i.* s. for s.o., remplacer qn. 'sub'tenancy, *s.* sous-location *f.* 'sub'tenant, *s.* sous-locataire *mf.* 'subterfuge, *s.* subterfuge *m.* subter'ranean, *a.* souterrain. 'subtitle. I. *s.* sous-titre *m.* II. *v.tr. Cin:* sous-titrer.

subtle ['sʌtl], *a.* subtil. 'subtlety, *s.* ['sʌt-]. 1. subtilité *f.* 2. ruse *f*, astuce *f.*

sub'tract, *v.tr.* soustraire. sub'traction, *s.* soustraction *f.* 'suburb, *s.* banlieue *f*; the suburbs, la banlieue. sub'urban, *a.* suburbain; de banlieue. sub'urbanite, *s. F: Pej:* banlieusard, -arde. sub'urbia, *s.* la banlieue. 'subway, *s.* (*a*) passage *m* souterrain; (*b*) *U.S:* métro *m.*

succeed [sək'si:d], *v.tr. & i.* 1. (*a*) succéder (à qn, à qch., à la couronne); (*b*) suivre; day succeeds day, les jours se suivent. 2. *v.i.* réussir, succès, s. succès *m*, réussite *f*; issue *f* heureuse; to be a s., réussir; avoir du succès. suc'cessful, *a.* qui a du succès; (résultat) heureux; (portrait) réussi; s. candidate, candidat (i) élu, (ii) *Sch:* reçu. suc'cession, *s.* succession *f*; suite *f*; série *f*; in rapid s., coup sur coup; two years in s., deux années successives, consécutives. suc'cessive, *a.* successif, consécutif. suc'cessor, *s.* successeur *m.*

succulence ['sʌkjuləns], *s.* succulence *f.* 'succulent. 1. *a.* succulent. 2. *s.* plante *f* grasse.

succumb [sə'kʌm], *v.i.* succomber, céder (to, à).

such [sʌtʃ]. I. *a.* 1. tel, pareil, semblable; s. a man, un tel homme; **did you ever see s. a thing!** a-t-on jamais vu chose pareille! some s. plan, un projet de ce genre; I said no s. thing, je n'ai rien dit de semblable; on s. a date, à une certaine date; in s. (and s.) a place, en tel endroit; in s. a way that . . ., de telle sorte que . . .; de façon que . . . 2. (*intensive*) s. large houses, de si grandes maisons; s. a clever man, un homme si habile; I had s. a fright! j'ai eu une de ces peurs! II. *pron.* history as s. is often neglected, l'histoire en tant que telle est souvent négligée.

suck [sʌk], *v.tr. & i.* sucer. **suck 'down**, *v.tr.* engloutir; traîner au fond. **'sucker**, s. 1. *Bot:* rejeton m. 2. *P: (pers.)* poire *f.* **suck 'in**, *v.tr.* (*a*) sucer, absorber; (*b*) engloutir. **'suckle**, *v.tr.* allaiter (un enfant). **'suction**, s. succion *f;* aspiration *f;* appel m (d'air); s. fan, aspirateur m; s. valve, clapet m d'aspiration. **suck 'up.** 1. *v.tr.* sucer, aspirer; absorber (de l'eau). 2. *v.i. P:* to s. up to s.o., lécher les bottes à qn.

sudden ['sʌdn], *a.* soudain, subit; (mouvement) brusque; *adv.phr.* all of a s., soudain, tout à coup. **-ly**, *adv.* soudain, soudainement; subitement; tout à coup. **'suddenness**, s. soudaineté *f;* brusquerie *f.*

sue [s(j)u], *v.tr.* poursuivre (qn) en justice.

suède [sweid], s. (*for shoes*) daim m; (*for gloves*) suède m.

suet ['su:it], s. *Cu:* graisse *f* de rognon.

suffer ['sʌfər]. 1. *v.tr.* éprouver, souffrir (une perte); subir (une peine). 2. *v.i.* souffrir; subir une perte. **'sufferance**, s. on s., par tolérance. **'sufferer**, s. victime *f;* (*from illness*) malade *mf;* fellow-s., compagnon m d'infortune. **'suffering**, s. souffrances *fpl;* douleurs *fpl.*

suffice [sə'fais], *v.tr. & i.* suffire. **su'fficiency**, s. suffisance *f.* s. suffi- cient, *a.* assez; suffisant; one lamp is s., il suffit d'une lampe. **-ly**, *adv.* suffisamment; assez.

suffix ['sʌfiks], s. *Gram:* suffixe m.

suffocate ['sʌfəkeit], *v.i. & tr.* étouffer; suffoquer. **'suffocating**, *a.* étouffant, suffocant; it's s. here, on étouffe ici; **suffo'cation**, s. suffocation *f;* étouffe- ment m, asphyxie *f.*

suffrage ['sʌfridʒ], s. *Pol:* suffrage m.

sugar ['ʃugər]. I. s. sucre m; the s. industry, l'industrie *f* sucrière; s. cane, canne *f* à sucre; s. beet, betterave *f* à sucre; s. almond, dragée *f;* s. refinery, raffinerie *f* de sucre; s. basin, sucrier m; s. tongs, pince *f* à sucre. II. *v.tr.* sucrer (son café); to s. the pill, dorer la pilule. **'sugary**, *a.* (trop) sucré.

suggest [sə'dʒest], *v.tr.* 1. suggérer, proposer (qch. à qn). 2. inspirer (une idée). 3. insinuer. 4. évoquer, donner l'idée de (qch.). **sug'gesti- bility**, s. suggestibilité *f.* s. **sug'gestion**, s. suggestion *f.* s. **sug'gestive**, *a.* (*a*) suggestif, évocateur; (*b*) qui frise l'obscénité.

suicide ['su:isaid], s. suicide m; to commit s., se suicider. **su'icidal**, *a.* (tendances) au suicide; this would be s., ce serait un véritable suicide que d'agir de la sorte.

suit [sut]. I. s. 1. *Cl:* complet m (pour homme); tailleur m (pour femme). 2. (*at cards*) couleur *f;* to follow s., (i) (*at cards*) jouer dans la couleur; (ii) faire autant, de même. II. *v.tr.* conve- nir à, aller à (qn); this hat suits you, ce chapeau vous va bien; I shall do it when it suits me, je le ferai quand cela me conviendra. **suita'bility**, s. convenance *f;* à-propos m; aptitude *f* (de qn pour qch.). **'suitable**, *a.* conve- nable, qui convient; (exemple) approprié. **-ably**, *adv.* convenable- ment; (répondre) à propos; (agir) comme il convient. **'suitcase**, s. mallette *f,* valise *f.*

suite [swit], s. 1. suite *f* (d'un prince, etc.). 2. s. of furniture, ameublement m; dining-room s., salle *f* à manger; bathroom s., salle *f* de bains; s. of rooms), appartement m. 3. *Mus:* suite (d'orchestre).

sulk [sʌlk], *v.i.* bouder; faire la mine. **'sulkiness**, s. bouderie *f.* **'sulky**, *a.* boudeur, maussade. **-ily**, *adv.* en boudant.

sullen ['sʌlən], *a.* maussade, morose; sombre; (*silence*) obstiné, renfrogné; d'un air maussade. **'sullenness**, s. maussaderie *f;* air m renfrogné.

sulphate ['sʌlfeit], s. sulfate m.

sulphide ['sʌlfaid], s. sulfure m.

sulphur ['sʌlfər], s. soufre m. **sul- 'phuric**, *a.* sulfurique.

sultan ['sʌltən], s. sultan m.

sultana [sʌl'tɑ:nə], s. raisin m sec de Smyrne.

sultry ['sʌltri], *a.* étouffant, suffocant; it's s., il fait très lourd. **'sultriness**, s. chaleur *f* étouffante.

sum [sʌm]. I. s. 1. somme *f,* total m; montant m. 2. problème m (d'arith- métique); to do sums, faire le calcul. II. †*v.tr.* to s. up, résumer, faire un résumé de (qch.); évaluer (la situa- tion); juger, classer (qn). **'summarize**, *v.tr.* résumer. **'summary.** I *a.* som- maire. II. s. résumé m. **'summarily**, *adv.* sommairement.

summer ['sʌmər], s. été m; the s. holi- days, les grandes vacances; s. visitor, estivant, -ante; s. clothes, vêtements m d'été. **'summerhouse**, s. pavillon m, kiosque m.

summit ['sʌmit], s. sommet m, cime *f* (d'une montagne); *Pol:* s. meeting, conférence *f* au sommet.

summon ['sʌmən], *v.tr.* 1. appeler, faire venir (qn); convoquer (une assemblée); *Jur:* sommer (qn) de comparaître. 2. to s. up one's courage, faire appel à tout son courage. **'summons.** I. s. 1. appel m (fait d'autorité); convocation *f* urgente. 2. *Jur:* citation *f* (à comparaître); assignation *f.* II. *v.tr. Jur:* citer (qn) à comparaître; assigner (qn).

sump [sʌmp], s. Aut: etc: fond m de carter; cuvette f d'égouttage.

sumptuous ['sʌmptjuəs], a. somptueux.

sun [sʌn]. I. s. soleil m; the s.'s shining, il fait du soleil; s. glasses, lunettes f de soleil; s. lounge, solarium m; Aut: s. visor, pare-soleil m. II. v.tr. to s. oneself, prendre le soleil; se chauffer au soleil. '**sunbathe**, v.i. prendre des bains de soleil. '**sunbather**, s. personne f qui prend des bains de soleil. '**sunbathing**, s. bains mpl de soleil. '**sunbeam**, s. rayon m de soleil. '**sunburn**, s. 1. hâle m. 2. Med: coup m de soleil. '**sunburnt**, a. hâlé, basané. '**Sunday**, s. dimanche m; in one's S. best, dans ses habits du dimanche. '**sundial**, s. cadran m solaire. '**sunflower**, s. tournesol m, soleil m.

sundry ['sʌndri], s. (a) all and s., tous sans exception; he told all and s. about it, il le racontait à tout venant; (b) pl. sundries, (i) articles m divers; (ii) frais m divers.

sunk [sʌŋk], a. (a) (navire) sombré, coulé; (b) F: perdu, ruiné. '**sunken**, a. (a) (rocher) submergé; s. wreck, épave f sous-marine; (b) affaissé, enfoncé; s. cheeks, joues f creuses; (c) s. road, chemin m creux; s. garden, jardin m en contrebas.

sunless, a. sans soleil. '**sunlight**, s. lumière f du soleil; in the s., au soleil. '**sunlit**, a. ensoleillé. '**sunny**, a. (journée de) soleil; (endroit) ensoleillé, exposé au soleil; it's s., il fait du soleil. '**sunrise**, s. lever m du soleil. '**sunset**, s. coucher m du soleil. '**sunshade**, s. ombrelle f. '**sunshine**, s. clarté f, lumière f (du soleil); in the s., au soleil; Aut: s. roof, toit m ouvrant. '**sunstroke**, s. insolation f; coup m de soleil. '**sunsuit**, s. costume m bain de soleil.

super ['su:pər]. I. s. F: (a) abbr. for SUPERINTENDENT; (b) Aut: (petrol) super m. II. a. F: superbe; F: sensas. III. prefix (used in combined forms) super-, sur-. '**superable**, a. surmontable. super'**annuate**, v.tr. (a) retraiter (qn); (b) F: mettre au rancart (une vieille auto, etc.). superannu'**ation**, s. retraite f par limite d'âge; s. (contribution), retenue f pour la retraite.

superb [su:'pə:b], a. superbe, magnifique. -ly, adv. magnifiquement.

'**supercharger**, s. Aut: (sur)compresseur m. super'**cilious**, a. sourcilleux, hautain; (air) dédaigneux. -ly, adv. avec une nuance de dédain. super'**ficial**, a. superficiel. -ally, adv. superficiellement. su'**perfluous**, a. superflu. -ly, adv. d'une manière superflue, inutilement. '**superhighway**, s. U.S: autoroute f. super'**human**, a. surhumain. superim'**pose**, v.tr. super-

poser, surimposer; Cin: surimprimer. superin'**tend**, v.tr. diriger, surveiller. superin'**tendent**, s. directeur, -trice; surveillant, -ante; chef m (des travaux); police s. = commissaire m de police.

superior [su'piəriər], a. & s. supérieur, -eure; with a s. smile, avec un sourire suffisant. superi'**ority**, s. supériorité f. su'**perlative**. 1. a. suprême. 2. a. & s. Gram: superlatif (m). -ly, adv. F: au suprême degré. †'**superman**, s. surhomme m. '**supermarket**, s. supermarché m. super'**natural**, a. surnaturel. super'**sede**, v.tr. remplacer; prendre la place de (qn); supplanter (qn). super'**sonic**, a. 1. Ph: ultrasonore. 2. supersonique; s. bang, double bang m.

superstition [su:pə'stiʃ(ə)n], s. superstition f. super'**stitious**, a. superstitieux.

'**superstructure**, s. superstructure f. '**supertax**, s. surtaxe f. '**supervise**, v.tr. 1. surveiller. 2. diriger (une entreprise). super'**vision**, s. 1. surveillance f. 2. direction f (d'une entreprise). '**supervisor**, s. surveillant, -ante; directeur, -trice.

supper ['sʌpər], s. souper m; the Last S., la (Sainte) Cène.

supple ['sʌpl], a. souple.

supplement. I. s. ['sʌplimənt] supplément m. II. v.tr. [sʌpli'ment] ajouter à (un livre, etc.); augmenter (ses revenus en faisant qch.). supple'**mentary**, a. supplémentaire.

supplication [sʌpli'keiʃ(ə)n], s. supplication f.

supply [sə'plai]. I. v.tr. fournir, approvisionner (qn de qch.); réparer (une omission); répondre à (un besoin). II. s. 1. approvisionnement m, fourniture f. 2. provision f; pl. supplies, fournitures f; food supplies, vivres m; to get in supplies of sth., s'approvisionner en qch.; s. and demand, l'offre f et la demande; goods in short s., marchandises en manque. su'**pplier**, s. fournisseur, -euse.

support [sə'pɔ:t]. I. s. appui m, soutien m. II. v.tr. 1. supporter, soutenir (une voûte, etc.). 2. appuyer (qn); soutenir, corroborer (une théorie); faire une donation à (une œuvre de charité). 3. maintenir, faire subsister (une famille); to s. oneself, gagner sa vie. su'**pporter**, s. défenseur m; adhérent m (d'une cause); partisan m (de qn); Sp: supporter m. su'**pporting**, a. (mur) d'appui; Th: s. cast, la troupe qui seconde les premiers rôles.

suppose [sə'pəuz], v.tr. (a) supposer; (b) s'imaginer; croire, penser. suppo'**sition**, s. supposition f.

suppress [sə'pres], *v.tr.* 1. réprimer (une révolte); interdire (une publication); étouffer (un scandale), etc.). 2. supprimer (un fait); cacher, dissimuler (qch.). 3. T.V: etc: antiparasiter. **su'ppressed,** *a.* réprimé; (of excitement) contenu. **su'ppression,** *s.* 1. répression *f*; suppression *f*; étouffement *m* (d'un scandale). 2. dissimulation *f* (de la vérité). 3. T.V: etc: antiparasitage *m.* **su'ppressor;** *s.* Rad: **s.** grid, grille *f* de freinage; T.V: etc: appareil *m*, dispositif *m*, antiparasite.

supreme [su'pri:m], *a.* suprême; **s.** contempt, mépris souverain. **-ly,** *adv.* suprêmement. **su'premacy** ['prem-], *s.* suprématie *f.*

surcharge ['sə:tʃɑ:dʒ]. I. *s.* 1. droit *m* supplémentaire; surtaxe *f.* 2. surcharge *f* (sur un timbre-poste). II. *v.tr.* 1. surtaxer (une lettre). 2. surcharger (un timbre-poste).

sure [ʃuər]. 1. *a.* sûr, certain; it is **s.** to be fine, il fera sûrement beau; be **s.** not to lose it, prenez garde de le perdre. 2. *adv.* (a) U.S: vraiment, certainement; it **s.** was cold, il faisait vraiment froid; **s.!** mais oui! bien sûr! (b) **s.** enough he was there, il était bien là. **-ly,** *adv.* 1. sûrement. 2. assurément. **'sure-'footed,** *a.* au pied sûr. **'surety** *s.* (pers.) caution *f*; garant, -ante.

surf [sə:f]. I. *s.* ressac *m*; Sp: **s.** riding, (i) sport *m* de l'aquaplane; (ii) surfing *m*; **s.** rider, aquaplaniste *mf*; **s.** board, (i) aquaplane *m*, (ii) planche *f* de surfing. II. *v.i.* (a) se baigner dans le ressac; (b) faire du surfing. **'surf-boat,** *s.* surf-boat *m*; pirogue *f* de barre.

surface ['sə:fis]. I. *s.* surface *f.* II. *v.* 1. *v.tr.* apprêter la surface de (qch.); revêtir (une route). 2. *v.i.* (of submarine, etc.) faire surface.

surge [sə:dʒ]. I. *s.* Nau: houle *f*; **a s.** of anger, une vague de colère. II. *v.i.* (of sea) être houleux; (of crowd) se répandre en flots.

surgeon ['sə:dʒən], *s.* chirurgien, -ienne. **'surgery,** *s.* 1. chirurgie *f.* 2. cabinet *m* de consultation (d'un médecin); **s.** hours, heures de consultation. **'surgical,** *a.* chirurgical; **s.** instruments, instruments de chirurgie; **s.** appliances, appareils (i) chirurgicaux, (ii) orthopédiques.

surly ['sə:li], *a.* (a) bourru; (b) maussade.

surmise ['sə:maiz], *s.* conjecture *f*, supposition *f.*

surmount [sə:'maunt], *v.tr.* surmonter.

surname [sə:neim], *s.* nom *m* de famille.

surpass [sə'pɑ:s], *v.tr.* 1. to **s.** oneself, se surpasser. 2. dépasser (des espérances).

surplice ['sə:plis], *s.* surplis *m.*

surplus ['sə:pləs], *s.* 1. surplus *m*, excédent *m.* 2. *attrib.* de surplus; **s.** stock, soldes *mpl.*

surprise [sə'praiz], *s.* I. surprise *f*; étonnement *m*; to take s.o. by **s.**, prendre qn à l'improviste; to my great **s.**, à ma grande surprise; to give s.o. a **s.**, faire une surprise à qn. II. *v.tr.* surprendre; étonner; you **s.** me, vous me surprenez, vous m'étonnez. **sur'prising,** *a.* surprenant, étonnant.

surrealism [sə'riəlizm], *s.* surréalisme *m.* **su'rrealist,** *a. & s.* surréaliste (*mf*).

surrender [sə'rendər], *v.tr. & i.* (se) rendre.

surreptitious [sʌrəp'tiʃəs], *a.* subreptice, clandestin. **-ly,** *adv.* subrepticement, furtivement.

surround [sə'raund], *v.tr.* entourer. **su'rrounding,** *a.* entourant, environnant. **su'rroundings,** *s.pl.* 1. entourage *m*, milieu *m.* 2. environs *mpl*, alentours *mpl.*

surtax ['sə:tæks], *s.* surtaxe *f* (progressive sur le revenu).

surveillance [sə:'veiləns], *s.* surveillance *f*, contrôle *m.*

survey. I. *s.* ['sə:vei]. 1. aperçu *m*; vue *f* générale (d'un sujet); étude *f* (de la situation); inventaire *m* (de monuments historiques); **sample s.**, enquête *f* par sondage. 2. levé *m* (des plans, du terrain); to make a **s.**, lever un plan. 3. inspection *f*, visite *f*; expertise *f.* II. *v.tr.* [sə'vei] relever, faire le levé de (la ville, etc.); arpenter (un champ); to **s.** for quantities, métrer. **sur'veying,** *s.* levé *m* de plans, (land) **s.**, géodésie *f*; topographie *f*; **sur'veyor,** *s.* (architecte) expert *m*; quantity **s.**, métreur *m* (vérificateur).

survive [sə'vaiv], *v.i. & tr.* survivre; (of custom) subsister. **s.** to **s.** (a) survivance *f*; (b) Jur: etc: survie *f* (entre...). **sur'vivor,** *s.* survivant, survivante *f.*

susceptible [sə'septibl], *a.* 1. susceptible. 2. sensible, impressionnable. **suscepti'bility,** *s.* susceptibilité *f.*

suspect. I. *v.tr.* [səs'pekt] soupçonner; to **s.** danger, flairer le danger; I suspected as much, je m'en doutais. II. *a. & s.* ['sʌspekt] suspect, -e.

suspend [səs'pend], *v.tr.* suspendre. **sus'penders,** *s.pl.* (a) jarretelles *f*; sock **s.**, fixe-chaussettes *f*; (b) U.S: bretelles *f.* **su'spense,** *s.* suspens *m.* **su'spension,** *s.* suspension *f*; **s.** bridge, pont suspendu.

suspicion [sə'spiʃ(ə)n], *s.* soupçon *m*; I had my suspicions about it, je m'en doutais. **su'spicious,** *a.* 1. suspect; louche, équivoque. 2. (of pers.) méfiant, soupçonneux. **-ly,** *adv.* 1. d'une manière suspecte, louche. 2. d'un air méfiant.

sustain [sə'stein], v.tr. soutenir; supporter. **su'stained**, a. (of effort, etc.) soutenu; (of applause) prolongé. '**sustenance**, s. nourriture f.

swagger ['swægər]. I. v.i. crâner, se pavaner; fanfaronner. II. s. air m important, cavalier, désinvolte.

swallow¹ ['swɔlou], v.tr. avaler. '**swallow-hole**, s. aven m, gouffre m. swallow 'up, v.tr. (of sea, etc.) engloutir, engouffrer (qch.).

swallow², s. hirondelle f; Sp: s. dive, saut m d'ange.

swamp [swɔmp]. I. s. marais m, marécage m. II. v.tr. inonder, submerger. '**swampy**, a. marécageux.

swan [swɔn], s. cygne m.

swank [swæŋk], v.i. F: se donner des airs; faire de l'épate.

swap [swɔp]. I. ‡v.tr. F: échanger, troquer (qch. contre qch.). II. s. F: troc m, échange m; (stamp collecting) swaps, doubles mpl.

swarm [swɔːm]. I. s. essaim m. II. v.i. (a) essaimer; (b) pulluler, grouiller (with, de).

swarthy ['swɔːði], a. basané, bistré.

swastika ['swɔstikə], s. svastika m; croix f gammée.

‡swat [swɔt], v.tr. F: écraser (une mouche, etc.). '**swatter**, s. (fly) s., tue-mouches m.

swathe [sweið], v.tr. emmailloter, envelopper (in, de).

sway [swei]. I. v.i. se balancer, osciller; vaciller. 2. v.tr. influencer, entraîner (la foule).

swear [swɛər]. I. ‡v.tr. & i. jurer; to s. s.o. to secrecy, faire jurer le secret à qn; Jur: to be sworn in, prêter serment; to s. at s.o., maudire, injurier, qn; to s. to sth., attester qch. sous serment; I would s. to it, j'en jurerais. II. s. F: juron m. '**swearer**, s. homme m mal embouché; jureur m. '**swearing**, s. (a) attestation f sous serment; (b) assermentation f du (jury); (c) jurons mpl, gros mots mpl.

sweat [swet]. I. v.i. & tr. suer; transpirer. II. s. sueur f, transpiration f. '**sweated**, a. (travail) mal rétribué. '**sweating**, s. transpiration f; s. hands, mains f moites. '**sweaty**, a. en sueur; s. hands, mains f moites.

sweater ['swetər], s. Cl: chandail m; tricot m, sweater m.

Swede [swiːd], s. 1. (pers.) Suédois, -oise. 2. Agr: rutabaga m. '**Swedish**. 1. a. suédois. 2. s. Ling: le suédois.

sweep [swiːp]. I. ‡v.tr. 1. balayer (une salle); ramoner (une cheminée); (of current) to s. sth. along, entraîner qch.; bridge swept away by the torrent, pont emporté par le torrent. 2. v.i. to s. into a room, entrer dans une pièce d'un air majestueux. II. s. 1. coup m de balai; Mil: etc: balayage m; to make a clean s. of sth., faire table rase

de qch. 2. étendue f (de terrain); T.V: balayage m. 3. (chimney) s., ramoneur m. 4. F: escroc m. '**sweeper**, s. 1. (pers.) balayeur, -euse. 2. (machine) balayeuse f (mécanique). '**sweeping**. I. a. (déclaration) par trop générale; (réforme) complète; (changement) de fond en comble. II. s. balayage m; ramonage m (d'une cheminée). '**sweepstake**, s. Sp: sweepstake m.

sweet [swiːt]. I. a. doux; sucré; (ton) mélodieux; (of pers.) charmant; (of young animal, etc.) adorable. -ly, adv. doucement; agréablement; (chanter) mélodieusement. II. s. (a) bonbon m; (b) entremets m sucré. '**sweetbread**, s. Cu: ris m de veau. '**sweeten**, v.tr. sucrer (un plat); adoucir (la vie, etc.). '**sweetening**, s. 1. sucrage m. 2. substance f pour sucrer. '**sweetness**, s. 1. douceur f. 2. gentillesse f, charme m.

swell [swel]. I. ‡v.tr. & i. enfler, gonfler; (of sea) se soulever, houler. II. s. Nau: houle f. III. a. U.S: F: épatant. '**swelling**, s. 1. enflement m, gonflement m. 2. enflure f; tumeur f; grosseur f.

swelter ['sweltər], v.i. étouffer de chaleur. '**sweltering**, a. (of heat) étouffant, accablant.

swerve [swəːv]. I. s. écart m, déviation f; Aut: embardée f. II. v.i. faire un écart; (of horse) se dérober; (of car) faire une embardée.

swift [swift]. I. a. rapide; (of reply) prompt. -ly, adv. vite, rapidement. II. s. (bird) martinet m. '**swiftness**, s. rapidité f.

swig [swig]. I. s. P: grand trait m, lampée f (de bière). II. ‡v.tr. P: boire (un verre) à grands traits; obs. lamper.

swill [swil], v.tr. laver (le plancher) à grande eau; rincer (une cuvette, etc.).

swim [swim]. I. ‡v.i. nager; to s. across a river, traverser une rivière à la nage. II. s. 1. to go for a s., aller nager. 2. to be in the s., être dans le mouvement. '**swimmer**, s. nageur, -euse. '**swimming**, s. nage f, natation f; s. pool, bath(s), piscine f; s. costume, s. costume f, maillot m, de bain.

swindle ['swindl]. I. s. escroquerie f; duperie f; déception f. II. v.tr. escroquer, filouter, F: rouler (qn). '**swindler**, s. escroc m.

swing [swiŋ]. I. ‡v. 1. v.tr. se balancer; (of door) to s. open, s'ouvrir; to s. round, faire volte-face. 2. v.tr. (faire) balancer (qch.); faire tourner (qch.). II. s. 1. oscillation f (d'un pendule); to be in full s., (i) (of dance, etc.) battre son plein; (ii) (of factory) être en plein travail. 2. to walk with a s., marcher d'un pas rythmé; when you've got into the s. of things, quand vous serez au courant. 3. balançoire f.

swirl [swəːl]. I. s. remous m (de l'eau); tourbillon m (de poussière). II. v.i. tournoyer, tourbillonner.

Swiss [swis]. 1. a. suisse; helvétique. 2. s. Suisse, -esse; the S., les Suisses.

switch [switʃ]. I. s. El: interrupteur m; commutateur m; Aut: le contact; Rail: aiguille f; changement m de voie. II. v.tr. 1. (of animal) to s. its tail, battre l'air de sa queue. 2. to s. a train on to a branch line, aiguiller un train sur un embranchement. 3. to s. on, off, the light, the ignition, mettre, couper, le courant, le contact; to s. over to the offensive, passer à l'offensive. **'switchback**, s. montagnes f russes. **'switchboard**, s. P.T.T: standard m; s. operator, standardiste mf.

swivel ['swiv(ə)l]. I. s. (a) émerillon m; (b) pivot m; tourillon m. II. v.i. pivoter, tourner.

swollen ['swoul(ə)n], a. enflé, gonflé; (of river) en crue; F: s-headed, vaniteux, suffisant.

swoop [swuːp], v.i. to s. down, s'abattre, foncer (sur qch.).

sword [sɔːd], s. (a) épée f; (b) sabre m. **'swordfish**, s. espadon m.

sworn [swɔːn], a. 1. assermenté; s. enemies, ennemis jurés, acharnés. 2. (déclaration) sous serment.

swot [swɔt]. I. ‡v.tr. & i. F: Sch: bûcher, piocher. II. s. F: Sch: 1. (a) travail m intense; (b) corvée f. 2. (pers.) bûcheur, -euse.

sycamore ['sikəmɔːr], s. sycomore m.

syllable ['siləbl], s. syllabe f.

syllabus ['siləbəs], s. programme m.

symbol ['simb(ə)l], s. symbole m. **sym'bolic(al)**, a. symbolique. -ally, adv. symboliquement.

symmetry ['simətri], s. symétrie f. **sy'mmetrical**, a. symétrique. -ally, adv. symétriquement.

sympathize ['simpəθaiz], v.i. to s. with s.o., avoir de la compassion pour qn; abs. (i) comprendre le point de vue de qn; (ii) exprimer ses condoléances. **sympa'thetic**, a. compatissant; (auditoire) bien disposé; (paroles) de condoléance. -ally, adv. d'une manière compatissante. **'sympathy**, s. 1. compassion f. 2. sympathie f, solidarité f; s. strike, grève f de solidarité.

symphony ['simfəni], s. symphonie f; s. concert, concert m symphonique. **sym'phonic**, a. symphonique.

symptom ['simptəm], s. symptôme m; indice m.

synagogue ['sinəgɔg], s. synagogue f.

synchronize ['siŋkrənaiz]. I. v.tr. synchroniser. 2. v.i. (of events) arriver simultanément.

syndicate ['sindikit], s. syndicat m.

synonym ['sinənim], s. synonyme m. **sy'nonymous**, a. synonyme (with, de).

synopsis [si'nɔpsis], s. résumé m, sommaire m.

syntax ['sintæks], s. syntaxe f.

synthesis ['sinθəsis], s. synthèse f.

synthetic [sin'θetik], a. synthétique. -ally, adv. synthétiquement.

syringe [si'rindʒ]. I. s. seringue f. II. v.tr. seringuer.

syrup ['sirəp], s. 1. sirop m. 2. golden s., mélasse f raffinée.

system ['sistəm], s. 1. (a) système m; organisme m; (b) réseau m (routier, etc.). 2. méthode f. **syste'matic**, a. systématique, méthodique. -ally, adv. systématiquement; avec méthode.

T

T, t [tiː], (la lettre) T, t m.

tab [tæb], s. patte f (d'étoffe); étiquette f.

tabby ['tæbi], a. (chat) tigré.

table ['teibl]. I. s. 1. (a) table f; to lay the t., mettre la table; to clear the t., desservir; (b) attrib. de table; t. linen, linge m de table; t. mat, dessous m d'assiette; t. tennis, ping-pong m. 2. (list) table, tableau m. **'tablecloth**, s. nappe f. **'tablespoon**, s. cuillère f à servir.

tablet ['tæblit], s. 1. plaque f commémorative. 2. (a) Med: comprimé m; (b) t. of soap, savonnette f. 3. U.S: bloc-correspondance m.

taboo [tə'buː]. I. s. tabou m. II. pred.a. interdit, proscrit. III. v.tr. proscrire, interdire (qch.).

tabulate ['tæbjuleit], v.tr. classifier; cataloguer.

tacit ['tæsit], a. tacite, implicite. -ly, adv. tacitement.

taciturn ['tæsitəːn], a. taciturne.

tack [tæk]. I. s. 1. petit clou m; semence f. 2. Nau: to make a t., tirer une bordée; on the right t., sur la bonne voie. II. v. 1. v.tr. (a) to t. sth. (down), clouer qch.; F: to t. sth. (on) to sth., attacher qch. à qch.; (b) (needlework) faufiler, bâtir. 2. v.i. Nau: to t. (about), virer (de bord); louvoyer.

tackle ['tækl]. I. s. attirail m, appareil m, engins mpl. II. v.tr. (a) empoigner; saisir (qn) à bras-le-corps; s'attaquer à, aborder (un problème); (b) Fb: plaquer (un adversaire).

tact [tækt], s. tact m, savoir-faire m. **'tactful**, a. (homme) de tact; délicat; to be t., avoir du tact. -fully, adv. avec tact. **'tactless**, a. (a) dépourvu de tact; maladroit; (b) t. question, question indiscrète. -ly, adv. sans tact. **'tactlessness**, s. manque m de tact; maladresse f.

tactics ['tæktiks], *s.pl.* tactique *f.* '**tactical**, *a.* tactique.

tadpole ['tædpoul], *s.* têtard *m.*

tag [tæg], *s.* 1. (*a*) morceau *m* (d'étoffe) qui pend; (*b*) attache *f*; (*c*) ferret *m* (de lacet). 2. citation banale; cliché *m.*

tail [teil], *s.* 1. (*a*) queue *f* (d'animal); **to turn t.,** s'enfuir; (*b*) empennage *m* (d'un avion); pan *m* (d'un habit). 2. (*of coin*) pile *f*, revers *m.* 3. t. end, fin *f* (d'un orage, etc.); queue (d'un défilé).

tailor ['teilər]. I. *s.* tailleur *m.* II. *v.tr.* faire, façonner (un complet).

taint [teint], *s.* 1. corruption *f*; infection *f.* 2. tare *f* héréditaire. '**tainted,** *a.* infecté, corrompu; t. meat, viande gâtée.

talcum ['tælkəm], *s.* t. (powder), (poudre *f* de) talc *m.*

tale [teil], *s.* 1. conte *m*; récit *m*, histoire *f.* 2. rapport *m*; **to tell tales (about s.o.),** rapporter.

talent ['tælənt], *s.* talent *m*; aptitude *f*; *Cin: etc:* t. scout, dénicheur *m* de vedettes. '**talented,** *a.* doué.

talk [tɔːk]. I. *s.* 1. (*a*) paroles *fpl*; (*b*) bruit *m*, dires *mpl*; **it's all t.,** ce ne sont que des on-dit; (*c*) propos *mpl*; bavardage *m.* 2. entretien *m*; causerie *f.* II. *v.i. & tr.* parler; talking of that . . ., à propos de cela . . .; **to t. French,** parler français. '**talkative,** *a.* causeur; bavard. '**talker,** *s.* causeur, -euse; parleur, -euse; she's a great t., elle est bien bavarde. '**talking,** *s.* 1. discours *mpl*, propos *mpl.* 2. conversation *f*; bavardage *m.* **talk 'over,** discuter, débattre (une question).

tall [tɔːl], *a.* 1. (*of pers.*) grand; de haute taille. 2. (*of thg.*) haut, élevé.

tallow ['tælou], *s.* suif *m.*

tally ['tæli], *v.i.* correspondre (with, à); s'accorder (with, avec).

talon ['tælən], *s.* serre *f*; griffe *f.*

tambourine [tæmbə'riːn], *s.* tambour *m* de basque.

tame [teim]. I. *a.* (animal) apprivoisé, domestique. II. *v.tr.* (*a*) apprivoiser; (*b*) domestiquer (une bête); dompter (un lion). '**tamer,** *s.* dompteur, -euse (de lions, etc.). '**taming,** *s.* apprivoisement *m*; domestication *f.*

tamper ['tæmpər], *v.i.* **to t. with sth.,** toucher à qch.; falsifier (un registre).

‡**tan** [tæn]. 1. *v.tr.* (*a*) tanner (les peaux); (*b*) hâler, bronzer (la peau). 2. *v.i.* se hâler, se basaner.

tangent ['tæn(d)ʒ(ə)nt], *s.* tangente *f.*

tangerine [tæn(d)ʒə'riːn], *s.* mandarine *f.*

tangible ['tæn(d)ʒəbl], *a.* 1. tangible. 2. (différence) sensible.

tangle ['tæŋgl], *s.* 1. embrouillement *m*; emmêlement *m*; fouillis *m* (de broussailles). II. *v.tr.* embrouiller (qch.); emmêler.

tank [tæŋk], *s.* 1. réservoir *m* (à eau, etc.). 2. (*a*) *Mil:* char *m* de combat, tank *m*; (*b*) *Rail:* t. car, wagonciterne *m.*

tankard ['tæŋkəd], *s.* pot *m*, chope *f.*

‡**take** [teik], *v.* prendre. 1. *v.tr.* (*a*) to t. sth. from s.o., prendre qch. à qn; to t. sth. from the table, prendre qch. sur la table; to t. hold of s.o., saisir, empoigner, qn, qch.; to t. s.o. prisoner, faire qn prisonnier; to be taken ill, tomber malade; (*b*) to t. tickets, prendre les billets; to t. a paper, s'abonner à un journal; to t. the wrong road, se tromper de chemin; (*c*) gagner, remporter (un prix); to t. an examination, se présenter à un examen; (*d*) prendre (de la nourriture); **I cannot t. gin,** je ne supporte pas le gin; (*e*) faire (une promenade); prendre (un bain); **to have one's photograph taken,** se faire photographier; to t. sth. to pieces, démonter qch.; *Com:* what will you t. for it? combien en voulez-vous? (*f*) to t. a dislike to s.o., prendre qn en grippe; (*g*) **I t. that . . .,** je suppose que . . .; (*h*) (= require) the work took some doing, le travail a été dur; it won't long, ce sera tôt fait; **I t. sixes** (in gloves), j'ai six de pointure; (*i*) to t. s.o. somewhere, conduire qn à un endroit; to t. s.o. to hospital, transporter qn à l'hôpital. 2. *v.i.* avoir du succès; réussir; the vaccine didn't t., le vaccin n'a pas pris. **take 'away,** *v.tr.* enlever, emporter (qch.); emmener (qn). **take 'back,** *v.tr.* reconduire (qn); reporter (qch. à); retirer (ce qu'on a dit). **take 'down,** *v.tr.* descendre (qch.); démolir (un mur, etc.). **take 'in,** *v.tr.* 1. rentrer, faire entrer (qch.). 2. comprendre, se rendre compte de (qch.); to be taken in, se laisser attraper. '**takings,** *s.pl. Com:* recette *f.* **take 'off.** 1. *v.tr.* enlever, ôter (ses habits); rabattre (tant sur le prix de qch.); to t. oneself off, s'en aller. 2. *v.i. Av:* décoller. '**take-off,** *s.* (*a*) *Av:* décollage *m*; (*b*) *F:* caricature *f.* **take 'on,** *v.tr.* entreprendre (un travail); accepter (un défi); embaucher (un ouvrier). **take 'out,** *v.tr.* sortir (qch.); faire sortir (qn); enlever (une dent); contracter (une assurance). **take 'over,** *v.tr.* 1. prendre la suite (d'une affaire); *abs.* remplacer qn (dans ses fonctions). *Rad:* mettre en communication. '**take-over,** *s. Fin:* t.-o. bid, offre *m* de rachat. **take 'to,** *v.tr.* 1. prendre (la fuite). 2. s'adonner à (la boisson). 3. prendre (qn) en amitié. **take 'up,** *v.tr.* 1. raccourcir (une jupe, etc.). 2. adopter (une idée); embrasser (une carrière). 3. occuper (la place).

tanker ['tæŋkər], *s.* bateau-citerne *m*; pétrolier *m*; *Aut:* camion-citerne *m*.

tantalize ['tæntəlaiz], *v.tr.* taquiner qn; mettre (qn) au supplice. **'tantalizing,** *a.* tentant; (sourire) provocant.

tap[1] [tæp]. I. *s.* (*a*) fausset *m* (de fût); (*b*) robinet *m*. II. ‡*v.tr.* 1. percer (un fût); to t. wine, tirer du vin. 2. to t. a telephone, brancher un téléphone sur la table d'écoute.

tap[2]. I. *s.* tape *f*; petit coup *m*. II. ‡*v.tr.* frapper légèrement; taper, tapoter.

tape [teip]. I. *s.* (*a*) ruban *m*; ganse *f*; F: red t., fonctionnarisme *m*; *El:* insulating t., chatterton *m*; recording t., ruban magnétique; (*b*) *Sp:* bande *f* d'arrivée. II. *v.tr. Rec:* enregistrer sur bande. **'tape-machine,** *s.* téléimprimeur *m*. **'tape-measure,** *s.* mètre *m* (à ruban); centimètre *m* (de couturière). **'tape-recorder,** *s.* Magnétophone *m* (*R.t.m.*). **'tapeworm,** *s.* ver *m* solitaire.

taper ['teipər]. I. *s.* bougie filée; *Ecc:* cierge *m*. II. *v.* 1. *v.tr.* effiler; tailler en cône. 2. *v.i.* to t. (off), s'effiler; aller en diminuant. **'tapering,** *a.* en pointe; effilé, fuselé.

tapestry ['tæpistri], *s.* tapisserie *f*.

tapioca [tæpi'oukə], *s.* tapioca *m*.

tar [tɑːr]. I. *s.* goudron *m*. II. ‡*v.tr.* goudronner.

target ['tɑːgit], *s.* cible *f*; but *m*, objectif *m*.

tariff ['tærif], *s.* 1. tarif *m*. 2. tableau *m*, liste *f* des prix.

tarmac ['tɑːmæk], *s.* 1. *Civ.E:* goudron *m*. 2. *Av:* piste *f* d'envol.

tarnish ['tɑːniʃ], *v.tr.* & *i.* (se) ternir.

tarpaulin [tɑː'pɔːlin], *s.* bâche *f*.

tart[1] [tɑːt], *s.* 1. *Cu:* tarte *f*; (*small*) tartelette *f*. 2. *P:* fille *f*, poule *f*.

tart[2], *a.* (*a*) aigrelet, acerbe; (*b*) (*of answer*) mordant; acrimonieux.

task [tɑːsk], *s.* 1. tâche *f*; ouvrage *m*, besogne *f*. 2. to take s.o. to t., réprimander qn.

tassel ['tæs(ə)l], *s.* gland *m*; houppe *f*.

taste [teist]. I. *s.* goût *m*. II. *v.* 1. *v.tr.* goûter (qch.); déguster (du vin); sentir (de l'ail, etc.). 2. *v.i.* to t. of sth., avoir un goût de qch. **'tasteless,** *a.* 1. sans saveur, fade. 2. de mauvais goût, laid. **'tastelessness,** *s.* 1. insipidité *f*; fadeur *f*. 2. manque *m* de goût.

tattered ['tætəd], *a.* (vêtement) en loques (homme) déguenillé.

tatty ['tæti], *a. F:* défraîchi.

taunt [tɔːnt]. I. *s.* reproche *m* méprisant; sarcasme *m*. II. *v.tr.* (*a*) accabler (qn) de sarcasmes; (*b*) to t. s.o. with sth., reprocher qch. à qn (avec mépris). **'taunting,** *a.* (ton, air) de sarcasme.

taut [tɔːt], *a.* tendu, raidi.

tawny ['tɔːni], *a.* fauve; tirant sur le roux; **t. owl,** (i) chouette *f*, chat-huant *m*; (ii) assistante *f* (des Jeannettes).

tax [tæks]. I. *s.* 1. impôt *m*, contribution *f*, taxe *f*. 2. charge *f*; fardeau *m* (imposé à qn). II. *v.tr.* 1. (*a*) taxer; frapper (qch.) d'un impôt; (*b*) imposer (qn); (*c*) mettre à l'épreuve (la patience de qn). 2. to t. s.o. with doing sth., accuser qn d'avoir fait qch. **'taxable,** *a.* (revenu) imposable. **tax-'ation,** *s.* (*a*) imposition *f*; (*b*) charges *f* fiscales. **'tax-collector,** *s.* percepteur *m* (des contributions directes); receveur *m* (des contributions indirectes). **'tax-payer,** *s.* contribuable *m*.

taxi ['tæksi]. I. *s.* taxi *m*. II. *v.i.* (*of aircraft*) rouler au sol. **'taxi-driver,** *s.* chauffeur *m* de taxi. **'taximeter,** *s.* taximètre *m*.

tea [tiː], *s.* 1. (*a*) thé *m*; Indian t., thé de Ceylan; (*b*) (i) (afternoon) t., thé, goûter *m*; (ii) *Austr:* = dîner *m*; (*c*) *attrib.* **t. break** = pause-café *f*; **t. strainer,** passe-thé *m*; **t. trolley,** table *f* roulante. 2. tisane *f*, infusion *f*. **'teacloth,** *s.* torchon *m* (à vaisselle). **'teapot,** *s.* théière *f*. **'teaspoon,** *s.* cuillère *f* à café.

‡**teach** [tiːtʃ], *v.tr.* enseigner (qn, qch.); instruire (qn); to t. s.o. sth., enseigner, apprendre, qch. à qn. **'teacher,** *s.* instituteur, -trice; maître *m*, maîtresse *f* (d'école); professeur *m* (de lycée). **'teaching,** *s.* 1. enseignement *m*, instruction *f*. 2. doctrine *f*.

team [tiːm], *s.* 1. attelage *m* (de chevaux). 2. *Sp:* équipe *f* (de joueurs).

tear[1] [tiər], *s.* larme *f*; tearful, *a.* tout en pleurs. **-fully,** *adv.* en pleurant; les larmes aux yeux.

tear[2] [tɛər]. I. *s.* 1. déchirement *m*. 2. déchirure *f*, accroc *m* (dans un vêtement). II. ‡*v.tr.* déchirer; to t. a hole in sth., faire un trou, un accroc, à qch. **'tear a'way,** *v.tr.* arracher (qch.). **'tear 'down,** *v.tr.* arracher (une affiche). **tear 'up,** *v.tr.* déchirer; mettre (qch.) en pièces.

tease [tiːz], *v.tr.* taquiner, tourmenter, faire enrager (qn). **'teasing.** I. *a.* taquin. II. *s.* taquinerie *f*.

technique [tek'niːk], *s.* technique *f*. **'technical,** *a.* technique; **t. terms,** termes du métier. **-ally,** *adv.* techniquement; **tech'nicality,** *s.* détail *m* technique. **tech'nician,** *s.* technicien *m*. **tech'nology,** *s.* technologie *f*.

tedious ['tiːdiəs], *a.* fatigant; ennuyeux. **'tediousness,** **'tedium,** *s.* ennui *m*; manque *m* d'intérêt (d'un travail).

tee [tiː], *s. Sp:* tee *m*.

teem [tiːm], *v.i.* abonder (with, en); foisonner, fourmiller (with, de); **teeming rain,** pluie *f* torrentielle.

teenage ['ti:neidʒ], a. adolescent; de l'adolescence. **'teenager**, s. adolescent, -ente.

teethe [ti:ð], v.i. faire ses (premières) dents; **teething troubles**, difficultés f initiales.

teetotal [ti'toutl], a. antialcoolique. **tee-'totaller**, s. abstinent, -ente.

telecommunications ['telikəmju:ni'kei-ʃ(ə)nz], s.pl. télécommunications, fpl; **t. specialist**, télémécanicien m.

telegram ['teligræm], s. télégramme m; dépêche f; **radio t.**, radiotélégramme m.

telegraph ['teligræf, -ɑːf]. I. s. télégraphe m; **t. pole**, poteau m télégraphique. II. v.tr. & i. télégraphier; envoyer une dépêche. **tele'graphic**, a. télégraphique. **te'legraphist**, s. télégraphiste mf. **te'legraphy**, s. télégraphie f.

telepathy [ti'lepəθi], s. télépathie f.

telephone ['telifoun]. I. s. téléphone m; **automatic t.**, automatique m; **are you on the t.?** avez-vous le téléphone? **t. box**, cabine f téléphonique. II. v.i. & tr. téléphoner (s.o., à qn). **te'lephonist**, s. standardiste mf.

telescope ['teliskoup]. I. s. (a) lunette f; longuevue f; (b) télescope m. II. v. 1. v.tr. télescoper (un train, etc.). 2. v.i. (a) (of trains, etc.) se télescoper; (b) (of machine, etc., parts) s'emboîter. **tele'scopic**, a. télescopique; Phot: **t. lense**, téléobjectif m.

television ['telivi3(ə)n], s. télévision f; **t. set**, (poste m de) télévision; **t. screen**, le petit écran. **'televise**, v.tr. téléviser.

‡tell [tel]. I. v.tr. 1. (a) dire; (b) to s.o. sth., dire, apprendre, qch. à qn; **I told you so!** je vous l'avais bien dit! F: **you're telling me!** tu parles! (c) raconter, conter; (d) annoncer, proclamer (un fait); révéler (un secret). 2. **to s.o. about s.o.**, parler de qn à qn. 3. ordonner, dire, à (qn de faire qch.); **I told him not to**, je le lui ai défendu. 4. (a) discerner, distinguer, reconnaître; (b) savoir; **who can t.?** qui sait? **you never can tell**, on ne sait jamais. 5. **all told**, tout compris. II. v.i. (a) produire son effet; porter; **every shot tells**, chaque coup porte; (b) témoigner, militer (en faveur de qn). **'telling**. I. a. efficace; (style) énergique; **a t. effect**, un effet marqué. II. s. 1. récit m, narration f (d'une histoire); divulgation f (d'un secret). 2. **there's no t.**, on ne sait pas; qui sait? **'telling-off**, s. F: enguelade f. **tell 'off**, v.tr. F: réprimander (qn). **'telltale**, s. 1. rapporteur, -euse; Sch: F: cafard, -arde. 2. E: Aut: etc: indicateur m; **t. lamp**, lampe f témoin.

telly ['teli], s. Rad: P: télé f.

temper ['tempər]. I. s. 1. trempe f (de l'acier). 2. sangfroid m; **to keep one's t.**, rester calme; **to lose one's t.**, se fâcher. 3. humeur f (a) caractère m, tempérament m; (b) mauvaise humeur; **to be in a t.**, être en colère. II. v.tr. 1. tremper (de l'acier). 2. tempérer, modérer (son ardeur).

temperament ['temp(ə)rəmənt], s. tempérament m, humeur f. **tempera'mental**, a. capricieux.

temperance ['temp(ə)r(ə)ns], s. (a) tempérance f; modération f; sobriété f; (b) abstention f des boissons alcooliques. **'temperate**, a. 1. (of pers.) sobre. 2. (climat) tempéré.

temperature ['tempritʃər], s. température f; Med: **to have a t.**, avoir de la fièvre.

tempest ['tempist], s. tempête f. **tem-'pestuous**, a. tempétueux, de tempête; (of meeting) orageux.

temple¹ ['templ], s. temple m.

temple², s. Anat: tempe f.

tempo ['tempou], s. (a) Mus: tempo m; (b) rythme m (de la production, etc.).

temporary ['temp(ə)rəri], a. (a) temporaire, provisoire; (b) momentané. **-ily**, adv. (a) temporairement, provisoirement; (b) momentanément.

temporize ['tempəraiz], v.i. temporiser.

tempt [tem(p)t], v.tr. tenter. **temp'tation**, s. tentation f; **'tempting**, a. tentant, alléchant; (of offer) séduisant; (of dish) appétissant.

ten [ten], num. a. & s. dix (m); **about t. books**, une dizaine de livres.

tenacious [ti'neiʃəs], a. tenace. **-ly**, adv. obstinément; avec ténacité. **te-'nacity**, s. ténacité f.

tenancy ['tenənsi], s. location f. **'tenant**, s. locataire mf.

tend [tend], v.i. 1. tendre, se diriger (towards, vers). 2. **to t. to do sth.**, être sujet à faire qch.; **woollens that t. to shrink**, lainages qui ont tendance à rétrécir. **'tendency**, s. tendance f (to, à); penchant m (à qch.).

tender¹ ['tendər], a. tendre; (of plant) fragile. **'tenderness**, s. 1. sensibilité f (de la peau, etc.). 2. tendresse f, affection f.

tender². I. s. 1. Com: soumission f, offre f. 2. (of money) **to be legal t.**, avoir cours. II. v. 1. v.tr. offrir (ses services). 2. v.i. Com: soumissionner (pour qch.).

tender³, s. U.S: bar t., garçon m de comptoir, barman m.

tender⁴, s. Nau: bateau m annexe; Rail: tender m.

tendon ['tendən], s. Anat: tendon m.

tenfold ['tenfould]. 1. a. décuple. 2. adv. to increase t., décupler.

tennis ['tenis], s. tennis m.

tenor ['tenər], s. 1. teneur f; sens m général (d'un document). 2. Mus: ténor m.

tense¹ [tens], s. Gram: temps m.

tense², *a.* tendu, raide; **t. moment,** moment angoissant; **t. silence,** silence impressionnant. **'tenseness,** *s.* rigidité *f* (des muscles); tension *f* (nerveuse, etc.). **'tension,** *s.* (*a*) raideur *f*, rigidité *f* (d'une corde, des muscles); (*b*) tension *f* (nerveuse); (*c*) pression *f* (d'un gaz); (*d*) El: voltage *m*.

tent [tent], *s.* tente *f;* **t. peg,** piquet *m* de tente.

tentative [ˈtentətiv], *a.* expérimental; d'essai. **-ly,** *adv.* à titre d'essai.

tenth [tenθ], *num. a.* & *s.* dixième (*m*); (**on**) **the t. of March,** le dix mars.

tepid [ˈtepid], *a.* tiède.

term [təːm], *s.* 1. (*a*) terme *m*, période *f;* (*b*) Sch: trimestre *m.* 2. *pl.* conditions *f;* **to come to terms,** en venir à un accommodement. 3. *pl.* relations *f* (avec qn). 4. terme, mot *m.* Set: minal, *s.* 1. *Au:* aérogare *f.* 2. El: borne *f* (de prise de courant). **'termi-nate.** 1. *v.tr.* terminer; mettre fin à (un engagement); résilier (un contrat). 2. *v.i.* se terminer, finir (in, en, par); aboutir (in, à). **'terminus,** *s.* Rail: (gare *f*) terminus *m.*

terrace [ˈterəs], *s.* 1. terrasse *f;* (terre-plein *m.* 2. rangée *f* de maisons (de style uniforme).

terrestrial [tiˈrestriəl], *a.* terrestre.

terrible [ˈteribl], *a.* terrible; affreux. **-bly,** *adv.* terriblement, affreusement; *F:* **t. rich,** diablement riche.

terrier [ˈteriər], *s.* (chien *m*) terrier *m.*

terrific [təˈrifik], *a.* 1. terrifiant, épouvantable. 2. *F:* terrible; énorme; formidable. **-ally,** *adv.* 1. d'une manière terrifiante. 2. *F:* terriblement.

terrify [ˈterifai], *v.tr.* terrifier, effrayer, épouvanter. **'terrifying,** *a.* terrifiant, épouvantable.

territory [ˈterit(ə)ri], *s.* territoire *m.* **terri'torial,** *a.* (*a*) territorial; (*b*) terrien, foncier.

terror [ˈterər], *s.* 1. terreur *f,* effroi *m,* épouvante *f;* **to go in t. of s.o.,** avoir une peur bleue de qn. 2. **to be the t. of the village,** être la terreur du village; *F:* **he's a little t.,** c'est un enfant terrible. **'terrorism,** *s.* terrorisme *m.* **'terrorize,** *v.tr.* terroriser.

terse [təːs], *a.* (*a*) (style) concis; (*b*) (réponse) brusque.

terylene [ˈteriliːn], *s.* R.t.m. térylène *m.*

test [test]. I. *s.* 1. épreuve *f;* essai *m;* **blood t.,** analyse *f* du sang; **to put s.o. to the t.,** mettre qn à l'essai; **t. pilot,** pilote *m* d'essai; *Sc:* **t. tube,** éprouvette *f;* Sp: **t. match,** rencontre *f* internationale (de cricket). 2. examen *m;* **driving t.,** examen pour permis de conduire; **intelligence t.,** test *m* mental. II. *v.tr.* (*a*) éprouver; tester; mettre (qn, qch.) à l'épreuve; (*b*) essayer (une machine); contrôler, vérifier (des

poids); examiner (qn, qch.); analyser (l'eau).

testament [ˈtestəmənt], *s.* testament *m.*

testify [ˈtestifai], *v.tr.* Jur: affirmer sous serment.

testimonial [testiˈmouniəl], *s.* certificat *m;* (lettre *f* de) recommandation *f.*

tether [ˈteðər]. I. *s.* longe *f;* attache *f;* **to be at the end of one's t.,** être à bout de (i) forces, (ii) ressources. II. *v.tr.* attacher (un animal).

text [tekst], *s.* texte *m;* Sch: **t. book,** manuel *m.*

textile [ˈtekstail], *a.* & *s.* textile (*m*).

texture [ˈtekstjər], *s.* texture *f;* grain *m* (du bois).

than [ðæn, (*unaccentuated*) ðən], *conj.* que; (*with numbers*) de; **taller t. you,** plus grand que vous; **more t. twenty,** plus de vingt.

thank [θæŋk], *v.tr.* 1. (*a*) remercier (qn) (**for sth.,** de qch.); dire merci à (qn); **t. goodness!** Dieu merci! (*b*) **t. you,** merci; **no t. you,** merci! 2. **to have s.o. to t. for sth.,** devoir qch. à qn. **'thankful,** *a.* reconnaissant. **-fully,** *adv.* avec reconnaissance. **'thankful-ness,** *s.* reconnaissance *f,* gratitude *f.* **'thankless,** *a.* ingrat; **a t. task,** une vraie corvée. **'thanklessness,** *s.* 1. ingratitude *f.* 2. caractère ingrat (d'une tâche). **thanks,** *s.pl.* remerciements *m;* *F:* **many t.!** merci bien! **'thanksgiving,** *s.* action *f* de grâce(s).

that¹ [ðæt]. I. *dem. pron.,* *pl.* **those** [ðouz]. 1. cela, *F:* ça; ce; (*a*) **give me t.,** donnez-moi cela; **what is t.?** qu'est-ce (que c'est) que cela, que ça? **t. is my opinion,** voilà mon avis; **what do you mean by t.?** qu'entendez-vous par là? **t. is . . .,** c'est-à-dire . . .; (*b*) (*stressed*) **that's right!** c'est cela! **that's all,** voilà tout; **and that's t.!** et voilà! 2. (*opposed to* 'this', 'these') celui-là, *f.* celle-là, *pl.* ceux-là, *f.* celles là; **this is new, t. is old,** celui-ci est neuf, celui-là est vieux. 3. celui, *f.* celle, *pl.* ceux, *f.* celles; **those of whom I speak,** ceux dont je parle. II. *dem. a.,* *pl.* **those;** (*a*) ce, (*before vowel or h* 'mute') cet, *f.* cette, *pl.* ces; (*for emphasis and in opposition to* 'this') ce . . .-là; **t. book,** ce livre (-là); **t. one,** celui-là, celle-là; (*b*) **how's t. leg of yours?** eh bien, et cette jambe? (*c*) (*those* (*people*) *who* . . ., ceux qui . . . III. *dem. adv.* **t. high,** aussi haut que ça.

that² [ðət], *rel.pron. sg.* & *pl.* 1. (*subject*) qui; (*object*) que. 2. (*governed by prep.*) lequel, *f.* laquelle; *pl.* lesquels, *f.* lesquelles. 3. où; que.

that³ [ðæt, ðət], *conj.* (*introducing subordinate clause*) que; afin que, pour que.

thatch [θætʃ], *s.* chaume *m.* **thatched,** *a.* (toit *m*) de chaume; **t. cottage,** chaumière *f.*

thaw [θɔ:]. I. s. dégel m. II. 1. v.tr. dégeler; décongeler (la viande frigorifiée). 2. v.i. (a) (of snow) fondre; (of frozen meat) se décongeler; (b) impers. it's thawing, il dégèle.

the [ðə; before vowel ðiː]. I. def.art. 1. le, f. la; (before vowel or h 'mute') l'; pl. les; (a) I spoke to t. postman, j'ai parlé au facteur; give that to t. woman, donnez cela à la femme; he has gone to t. fields, il est allé aux champs; t. voice of t. people, la voix du peuple; t. roof of t. house, le toit de la maison; t. arrival of t. guests, l'arrivée des invités; Edward t. Seventh, Édouard Sept; (b) to work by t. day, travailler à la journée. 2. (demonstrative force) ce, cet, f. cette, pl. ces; at t. time, à cette époque. 3. [ðiː] (stressed) he's 'the surgeon here, c'est lui le grand chirurgien ici. II. adv. (preceding a comparative) t. sooner t. better, le plus tôt sera le mieux.

theatre [ˈθiətər], s. théâtre m. **the'atrical**, a. théâtral; t. company, troupe f d'acteurs; the a'tricals, s.pl. amateur t., spectacle m d'amateurs.

theft [θeft], s. (a) vol m; (b) petty t., larcin m.

their [ðɛər], poss.a. leur, pl. leurs.

theirs [ðɛəz], poss.pron. le leur, la leur, les leurs; he is a friend of t., c'est un de leurs amis.

them [ðem], pers.pron. pl. (object) 1. (direct) les mf; (indirect) leur mf; speak to t., parlez-leur. 2. eux, f. elles; many of t., plusieurs d'entre eux; give me half of t., donnez-m'en la moitié; every one of t. was killed, ils furent tous tués; neither of t., ni l'un ni l'autre. them'selves, pers.pron. pl. (a) [emphatic] eux m, elles f, eux-mêmes m, elles-mêmes f; (b) (reflexive) se.

theme [θiːm], s. sujet m, thème m. **'theme-song**, s. chanson f leitmotif.

then [ðen]. I. adv. 1. alors; en ce temps-là; t. and there, séance tenante. 2. puis, ensuite, alors. 3. d'ailleurs; aussi (bien); et puis. II. conj. en ce cas, donc, alors; but t . . ., mais c'est que. . . . III. quasi-s. ce temps-là; before t., avant cela; by t. they'd gone, ils étaient déjà partis; till t., (i) jusqu'alors; (ii) jusque-là; (ever) since t., depuis ce temps-là; between now and t., d'ici là.

theology [θiˈɔlədʒi], s. théologie f. **theo'logical**, a. théologique.

theorem [ˈθiərəm], s. théorème m.

theory [ˈθiəri], s. théorie f. **theo'retic(al)**, a. théorique. **-ally**, adv. théoriquement. **'theorize**, v.i. faire de la théorie.

there [ðɛər], I. adv. (a) là, y; put it t., mettez-le là; he's still t., il y est toujours; (b) [emphatic] hurry up t.!

---

dépêchez-vous là-bas! (c) (calling attention to sth.) t. is, are . . ., voilà. . . . 2. (a) (unstressed) t. is, are . . , il est, il y a . . .; (b) t. comes a time, arrive un moment. 3. (stressed) quant à cela; en cela. II. int. (stressed) voilà! là! III. quasi-s. in t., là-dedans; là. 'thereabouts, adv. 1. près de là, dans le voisinage. 2. à peu près; environ; it's four o'clock or t., il est quatre heures environ. 'thereby, adv. par ce moyen; de cette façon. 'therefore, adv. donc; par conséquent. there'upon, adv. 1. sur ce. 2. là-dessus, à ce sujet.

thermal [ˈθəːm(ə)l], a. 1. thermal; t. baths, thermes mpl. 2. Ph: thermal, thermique; t. efficiency, rendement m thermique.

thermometer [θəˈmɔmitər], s. thermomètre m.

thermonuclear [ˈθəːmouˈnjuːkliər], a. thermonucléaire.

Thermos [ˈθəːmɔs], s. R.t.m: bouteille Thermos.

thermostat [ˈθəːmɔstæt], s. thermostat m.

they [ðei]. pers.pron. pl. (subject) (a) ils, f. elles; here t. come, les voici (qui viennent); t. are rich people, ce sont des gens riches; (b) (stressed) eux, f. elles; it is t., ce sont eux; (c) ceux, celles. 2. indef.pron. on; t. say, on dit.

thick [θik]. I. a. épais; t. soup (potage m) crème f. -ly, adv. en couche épaisse; dru. II. s. 1. (la) partie charnue, le gras (de la jambe, etc.); in the t. of the fight, au (plus) fort de la mêlée. 2. to stick to s.o. through t. and thin, rester fidèle à qn à travers toutes les épreuves. III. adv. 1. to cut the bread t., couper le pain en tranches épaisses. 2. the blows fell t. and fast, les coups pleuvaient dru. 'thicken. 1. v.tr. épaissir; lier (une sauce). 2. v.i. (a) s'épaissir; (b) (of sauce) se lier; (of plot) se compliquer. 'thicket, s. hallier m, fourré m. 'thick'headed, a. F: stupide. 'thickness, s. 1. épaisseur f; abondance f (de la chevelure); consistance f (d'un liquide). 'thickset. a. (of pers.) trapu. 'thick-'skinned, a. 1. à la peau épaisse. 2. (of pers.) peu susceptible.

†thief [θiːf], s. voleur, -euse. thieve, v.tr. voler (qch.); abs. être voleur. 'thieving. 1. a. voleur. 2. s. vol m.

thigh [θai], s. cuisse f.

thimble [ˈθimbl], s. dé m (à coudre).

thin [θin]. I. a. 1. (a) mince; ténu; léger; (b) (of pers.) maigre, mince; to grow thinner, maigrir; s'amaigrir. 2. clairsemé, rare. -ly, adv. faible; (vêtu) insuffisamment. II. v.tr. amincir; délayer (la peinture); éclaircir (les arbres). 2. v.i. maigrir; s'amincir; s'effiler. 'thinness, s. 1. peu m d'épaisseur; minceur f; légèreté f (d'un voile); maigreur f. 2. rareté f (des cheveux). **'thin-'skinned,** a. (of pers.) susceptible.

thing [θiŋ], s. 1. chose f; (a) objet m, article m; (b) pl. vêtements m, effets m; tea things, service m à thé; (c) pl. affaires f, effets; to pack up one's things, (i) faire ses malles; (ii) ranger ses affaires. 2. être m, créature f; poor little things! pauvres petits! 3. (a) that's the very t., c'est juste ce qu'il faut; for one t., en premier lieu; (b) pl. things are going badly, les affaires vont mal.

†**think** [θiŋk], v.tr. & i. 1. penser, réfléchir. 2. songer, s'imaginer; one would have thought, c'était à croire; anyone would t., on dirait. 3. thinking to . . ., dans l'intention de . . . 4. (a) I t. so, je pense que oui; (b) penser, juger, trouver, penser. 5. I thought so, je m'y attendais. **'think about,** of,v.ind.tr. 1. penser à (qn, qch.); songer à (qch.). 2. s'imaginer, se figurer, songer. 3. considérer; to t. of the expense, regarder à la dépense. 4. (a) v.tr. what do you t. of it? qu'en pensez-vous? to t. too much of sth., attacher trop d'importance à qch.; (b) to t. well of s.o., estimer qn. **think 'out,** v.tr. 1. imaginer, méditer (qch.); to t. out a plan, élaborer un plan. 2. juger. **think 'over,** v.tr. réfléchir sur, aviser à (une question). **'thinker,** s. penseur, -euse. **'thinking.** I. a. pensant, qui pense. II. s. pensée(s) f(pl), réflexion f(pl.); to my t., à mon avis.

third [θə:d]. 1. num. a. troisième; t. person, (i) tierce personne, tiers m; (ii) Gram: troisième personne; the t. of March, le trois mars. 2. s. (a) Mus: (a) tierce f; (b) Aut: troisième (vitesse) f. 3. s. Mth: tiers m. -ly, adv. troisièmement; en troisième lieu. **'third-'rate,** a. très inférieur.

thirst [θə:st], s. soif f. **'thirsty,** a. altéré; to be t., avoir soif.

thirteen ['θə:'ti:n], num. a. & s. treize (m). **thir'teenth,** num. a. & s. treizième (m); (on) the t. of May, le treize mai.

thirty ['θə:ti], num. a. & s. trente (m); thirty-first, trente et unième; about t., une trentaine (de personnes, etc.). **'thirtieth,** num. a. & s. trentième (m); (on) the t. of June, le trente juin.

this [ðis]. I. dem.pron., pl. these [ði:z] 1. ceci; ce; who is t.? quelle est cette personne? before t., déjà; t. is curious, voici qui est curieux; t. is where he lives, c'est ici qu'il demeure. 2. (opposed to 'that') (a) will you have t. or that? voulez-vous ceci ou cela? speaking of t. or that, parlant de choses et d'autres; (b) celui-ci, f celle-ci, pl. ceux-ci, f celles-ci. II. dem.a., pl. these, ce, (before vowel or h 'mute') cet,

f. cette, pl. ces; (for emphasis) ce (etc.) . . . -ci; these books, ces livres-ci; in these days, de nos jours. III. dem.adv. t. high, aussi haut que ceci, que ça; t. far, jusqu' ici.

thistle ['θisl], s. chardon m.

thorn [θɔ:n], s. épine f. **'thorny,** a. épineux.

thorough ['θʌrə], a. 1. (a) (of search) minutieux; (of knowledge) profond; (of work) consciencieux; (b) a t. Frenchman, un vrai français; a t. republican, un républicain convaincu. -ly, adv. (épuiser) tout à fait; (comprendre) parfaitement; (renouveler) complètement; (nettoyer) à fond. **'thoroughbred.** 1. a. (cheval) pur sang; (chien) de race. 2. s. cheval pur sang m; animal m de race. **'thoroughfare,** s. voie f de communication; (of town) artère f; P.N: no t., passage interdit; t. far barrée.

though [ðou]. I. conj. 1. quoique, bien que, encore que + subj. 2. strange t. it may appear, si étrange que cela paraisse. 3. as t., comme si. II. adv. cependant, pourtant.

thought [θɔ:t], s. (la) pensée. 1. (a) idée f; (b) pl. esprit m, pensée f; his thoughts were elsewhere, son esprit était ailleurs. 3. (a) réflexion f; (b) pensées, rêverie f, méditation f. 4. intention f, dessein m; with the t. of . . ., dans le dessein de . . ., avec l'intention de . . . **'thoughtful,** a. 1. (a) pensif, méditatif; rêveur; (b) réfléchi. 2. prévenant (of, pour); to be t. of others, être plein d'égards pour les autres. -fully, adv. 1. pensivement. 2. d'une manière réfléchie. 3. avec prévenance. **'thoughtfulness,** s. 1. méditation f, recueillement m. 2. prudence f. 3. prévenance f, égards mpl (of qn, envers). **'thoughtless,** a. 1. irréfléchi, étourdi. 2. (of others, peu soucieux des autres. -ly, adv. étourdiment; (agir) à la légère. **'thoughtlessness,** s. 1. irréflexion f; étourderie f. 2. manque m d'égards (of, pour, envers).

†**thousand** ['θauz(ə)nd], num. a. & s. mille (m); a. millier m; the year 4000 B.C., l'an quatre mille avant J.-C. **'thousandth,** num. a. & s. millième (mf).

thrash [θræʃ], v.tr. battre (qn); F: rosser (qn). **'thrash 'out,** v.tr. débattre (une question). **'thrashing,** s. rossée f, correction f; Sp: défaite f.

thread [θred], s. 1. fil m. 2. (a) sewing t., fil à coudre. 3. filet m; pas m (de vis). II. v.tr. (a) enfiler (une aiguille, des perles); (b) to t. one's way (through a crowd), se faufiler (à travers la foule); (c) fileter (une vis). **'threadbare,** a. usé (jusqu') à la corde); (of clothes) râpé.

threat [θret], s. menace f. **'threaten,** v.tr. 1. menacer (qn). 2. **the sky threatens rain,** le ciel annonce la pluie; abs. a storm is threatening, l'orage menace.

three [θriː], num. a & s. trois (m). **'three-cornered,** a. triangulaire. **'three-engined,** a. Av: (avion) trimoteur. **'threefold.** 1. a. triple. 2. adv. trois fois autant. **threepence** ['θrep(ə)ns], s. (la somme de) trois pence m. **'threepenny,** attrib. a. (article) coûtant trois pence; t. bit, pièce f de trois pence. **'three-piece,** attrib. a. en trois pièces m; (lady's) t.-p. suit, trois-pièces m. **'three-ply,** attrib. a. 1. t.-p. wood, contre-plaqué m (à trois épaisseurs); 2. (laine f) à trois brins. **'three-speed,** attrib. a. à trois vitesses.

thresh [θreʃ], v.tr. battre (le blé). **'threshing,** s. battage m (des blés); t. machine, batteuse f.

threshold ['θreʃ(h)ould], s. seuil m, pas m (d'une porte).

thrift [θrift], s. 1. économie f, épargne f. **'thrifty,** a. économe, ménager; U.S: (of plant) vigoureux. **-ly,** adv. avec économie, frugalement. **'thriftiness,** s. économie f. **'thriftless,** a. dépensier, prodigue. **'thriftlessness,** s. 1. prodigalité f; 2. imprévoyance f.

thrill [θril]. I. s. (a) frisson m, tressaillement m; (b) (vive) émotion f. II. v.tr. faire frémir (qn); émouvoir (qn). 1. V: électriser (son auditoire). 2. v.i. tressaillir, frissonner, frémir. **'thriller,** s. roman m, film m, pièce f, à sensation; occ: roman policier. **'thrilling,** a. (spectacle) empoignant; (roman) sensationnel.

‡**thrive** [θraiv], v.i. (a) se (bien) développer; (b) prospérer. **'thriving,** a. vigoureux; prospère, florissant.

throat [θrout], s. gorge, gosier m.

throb [θrob]. I. s. pulsation f, battement m (du cœur); vrombissement m (d'une machine). II. v.i. (a) battre fort; palpiter; (of engine) vrombir; (b) my finger's throbbing, le doigt me lancine. **'throbbing,** s. battement m, pulsation f; vrombissement m (d'une machine); élancement m (d'un panaris).

thrombosis [θrɔm'bousis], s. Med: coronary t., infarctus m du myocarde.

throne [θroun], s. trône m.

throng [θrɔŋ]. I. s. foule f. II. v.i. 1. s'assembler en foule; affluer (dans un endroit). 2. v.tr. encombrer (les rues).

throttle [θrɔtl]. I. s. E: Aut: étrangleur m; to open out the t., mettre les gaz. II. v.tr. étrangler.

through [θruː]. I. prep. 1. (a) à travers; par; au travers d'(une haie); to speak t. one's nose, parler du nez; I've got t. this book, j'ai fini ce livre; (b) pendant, durant; U.S: Monday t. Friday, de lundi à vendredi. 2. par; par l'entremise de (qn). 3. en conséquence de, à cause de (qch.). II. adv. 1. à travers; to let s.o. t., laisser passer qn; t. and t., de bout en bout; de part en part; d'un bout à l'autre; jusqu'au bout. 2. directement; the train runs t. to Paris, le train est direct jusqu'à Paris; P.T.T: to get t. to s.o., obtenir la communication avec qn; I can't get t. to him, je ne peux pas l'avoir. III. attrib. a. Rail: t. carriage for . . ., voiture directe pour . . .; t. traffic, transit m. **through'out.** 1. prep. d'un bout à l'autre (du pays); t. France, partout en France; t. the year, (pendant) toute l'année. 2. adv. central heating t., chauffage (central) dans toutes les pièces. **'throughway,** s. U.S: autoroute f.

‡**throw** [θrou]. I. v.tr. 1. jeter, lancer (qch.); rejeter (la faute sur qn). 2. (of horse) démonter (qn). 3. F: to t. a party, inviter des amis à une réunion. II. s. jet m, lancement m (de qch.); within a stone's t., à quelques pas. **throw a'way,** v.tr. jeter (qch.); mettre (qch.) au rebut; gaspiller (son argent); laisser passer (une occasion). **throw 'in,** v.tr. 1. jeter (qch.) dans (qch.). 2. donner (qch.) par-dessus le marché. **throw 'off,** v.tr. 1. se débarrasser de (qn, qch.). 2. to t. s.o. off the scent, dépister qn. **throw 'out,** v.tr. F: se débarrasser de (qch.); mettre (qn) à la porte; rejeter (un projet de loi). **throw 'up,** v.tr. 1. jeter (qch.) en l'air. 2. abs. F: vomir. 3. renoncer à (un projet); to t. everything up, tout plaquer.

thrush [θrʌʃ], s. grive f.

thrust [θrʌst]. I. s. (a) poussée f; (b) coup m de pointe. II. ‡v.tr. pousser (avec force); fourrer (qch. dans qch.).

thud [θʌd]. I. s. bruit m sourd; floc m. II. v.i. tomber avec un bruit sourd; émettre un bruit mat.

thug [θʌg], s. F: assassin m; bandit m.

thumb [θʌm]. I. s. pouce m; to be under s.o.'s t., être sous la domination de qn. II. v.tr. F: to t. a lift, faire de l'auto-stop.

thump [θʌmp]. I. s. 1. coup m sourd. 2. coup m de poing, bourrade f. II. v.tr. & i. bourrer (qn) de coups; to t. (on) the table, frapper du poing sur la table; (of heart) battre fort.

thunder ['θʌndər]. I. s. tonnerre m. 2. foudre f. II. v.i. & tr. tonner; it's thundering, il tonne. **'thunderbolt,** s. 1. (coup m de) foudre f. 2. nouvelle f foudroyante. **'thundering,** a. 1. tonnant, fulminant. 2. to be in a t. rage, être dans une rage à tout casser. **'thunderstorm,** s. orage m. **'thunderstruck,** a. confondu, abasourdi; atterré.

Thursday ['θəːzdi], s. jeudi m; Maundy T., jeudi saint.

thus [ðʌs], *adv.* **1.** ainsi; de cette façon. **2.** ainsi, donc. **3.** t. far, jusqu'ici; jusque-là.

thwart [θwɔːt], *v.tr.* contrecarrer (qn); déjouer les menées de (qn); to be thwarted, essuyer un échec.

thyme [taim], *s.* thym *m*.

thyroid ['θaiərɔid], *a.* thyroïde.

tiara [ti'ɑːrə], *s.* tiare *f*.

tick¹ [tik]. I. *s.* **1.** (*a*) tic-tac *m*; F: on the t., à l'heure tapante; (*b*) F: moment *m*, instant *m*. **2.** marque *f*, pointage *m*. II. *v.i.* (*of clock*) faire tic-tac; F: what makes him t.? qu'est-ce qui le pousse? **2.** *v.tr.* to t. (off), (i) pointer (une liste); cocher (un nom); (ii) F: rembarrer (qn). 'ticker 'tape, *s.* bande *f* (de téléimprimeur). 'ticking, *s.* tic-tac *m*. tick 'over, *v.i.* Aut: etc: (*of engine*) tourner au (grand-)ralenti; marcher tout doucement.

tick², *s.* **1.** *Z:* tique *f*. **2.** *P:* petit salaud *m*.

tick³, *s.* F: on t., à crédit.

ticket ['tikit]. I. *s.* **1.** billet *m*; platform t., billet de quai; cloakroom t., numéro *m* de vestiaire; single t., aller *m*; return t., aller et retour *m*. **2.** étiquette *f*; facture *f*; *Aut: F:* to get a t., attraper une contravention. II. *v.tr.* étiqueter, marquer. 'ticket-collector, *s. Rail: etc:* contrôleur *m*. 'ticket-inspector, *s.* contrôleur *m* (d'autobus).

tickle ['tikl]. I. *s.* chatouillement *m*. II. *v.* **1.** *v.tr.* chatouiller; amuser; to be tickled to death, se tordre de rire; *Aut:* to t. the carburettor, amorcer le carburateur. **2.** *v.i.* my hand tickles, la main me démange. 'tickling, *s.* chatouillement *m*. 'ticklish, *a.* **1.** chatouilleux. **2.** (*of pers.*) susceptible; (*b*) (*of tasks, etc.*) délicat.

tide [taid], *s.* marée *f*. 'tidal, *a.* t. wave, raz *m* de marée; vague *f* de fond; t. river, fleuve *m* à marée. tide 'over, *v.tr.* permettre (à qn) de tenir le coup; dépanner (qn).

tidy ['taidi]. I. *a.* (*of room, etc.*) bien rangé, en bon ordre; (*of dress*) bien tenu; (*b*) (*of pers.*) ordonné; qui a de l'ordre. **-ily,** *adv.* proprement; avec ordre. II. *s.* sink t., coin *m* d'évier. III. *v.tr.* ranger; mettre de l'ordre dans (qch.); arranger (les choses); abs. to t. up, tout remettre en place. 'tidiness, *s.* bon ordre *m*; (*dress*) bonne tenue *f*.

tie [tai]. I. *s.* **1.** (*a*) lien *m*; attache *f*; (*b*) entrave *f*. **2.** lacet *m*, cordon *m*; (*b*) *Cl:* cravate *f*. **3.** *Sp:* match *m* nul. II. *v.* **1.** *v.tr.* (*a*) attacher; lier (qn à qch.); (*b*) lier, nouer (un lacet); faire (un nœud). **2.** *v.i. Sp: etc:* être, arriver, à égalité (with, avec). tie 'down, *v.tr.* immobiliser (qn); assujettir (qch.). tie 'on, *v.tr.* attacher (avec une ficelle). 'tie-pin, *s.* épingle *f* à cravate. tie 'up, *v.tr.* **1.** attacher,

ficeler (un paquet); bander, panser (une blessure). **2.** attacher (un animal); ligoter (qn). **3.** *F:* to get tied up (i) s'embrouiller; (ii) se marier.

tier [tiər], *s.* rangée *f*; étage *m*; in tiers, en amphithéâtre.

tiff [tif], *s.* petite querelle *f*.

tiger ['taigər], *s.* tigre *m*. 'tigress, *s.* tigresse *f*.

tight [tait]. I. *a.* (*a*) raide, tendu; to draw t.; (*b*) trop juste; (*c*) *F:* ivre, gris. **-ly,** *adv.* (*a*) fortement; (*b*) étroitement. II. *adv.* **1.** hermétiquement. **2.** (*a*) fortement, fermement; serré. 'tighten. **1.** *v.tr.* serrer, resserrer, renforcer (des restrictions); *Aut:* to t. the steering, rattraper le jeu de la direction. **2.** *v.i.* (*a*) se (res)serrer; (*b*) se tendre; raidir. 'tightness, *s.* **1.** tension *f*, raideur *f*. **2.** étroitesse *f* (d'un vêtement). tights, *s.pl. Cl:* collant *m*.

tile [tail]. I. *s.* **1.** tuile *f* (de toiture). **2.** carreau *m*. II. *v.tr.* **1.** couvrir (un comble) de tuiles. **2.** carreler (un plancher, etc.). 'tiled, *a.* **1.** (toit) en tuiles. **2.** (pavage) carrelé; (paroi) à carreaux.

till¹ [til], *v.tr.* labourer, cultiver.

till², *s.* tiroir-caisse *m*.

till³. **1.** *prep.* (*a*) jusqu'à; t. now, jusqu'ici; from morning t. night, du matin au soir; (*b*) not t., pas avant. **2.** *conj.* (*a*) jusqu'à ce que + *sub.*; to laugh t. one cries, rire aux larmes; (*b*) not t., pas avant que + *sub.*

tilt [tilt]. I. *s.* **1.** inclinaison *f*, pente *f*. **2.** (at) full t., à fond de train. II. *v.* **1.** *v.i.* to t. (up), s'incliner; pencher; to t. over, se renverser; (*of bench*) to t. up, basculer. **2.** *v.tr.* pencher, incliner; to t. one's chair back, se balancer sur sa chaise.

timber ['timbər], *s.* **1.** (*a*) bois *m* d'œuvre; bois de construction; (*b*) standing t., arbres *mpl* de haute futaie. **2.** poutre *f*, madrier *m*.

time [taim]. I. *s.* **1.** temps *m*; in (the course of) t., à la longue. **2.** within the required t., dans les délais voulus; in a short t., sous peu; for a long t. to come, d'ici là longtemps; for some t. past, depuis quelque temps; after a short t., peu après. **3.** (*a*) to lose t., perdre du temps; to take one's t. over sth., mettre le temps à faire qch.; (*b*) to serve one's t., faire son apprentissage. **4.** *usu. pl.* époque *f*; behind the times, arriéré. **5.** moment *m*; at that t., en ce temps-là; at the present t., à l'heure qu'il est; actuellement; at one t., autrefois, dans le temps; at no t., jamais; à aucun moment; at times, parfois; from that t., dès lors; depuis lors. **6.** heure *f*; (*a*) what's the t.? quelle heure est-il? (*b*) to be ahead of t., être en avance; to arrive on t., arriver à l'heure; in t., à temps; in good t., de bonne heure; (c) t. of the year, époque de l'année; saison f. 7. we had a good t., on s'est bien amusé. 8. fois f; t. after t., à maintes reprises. 9. adv.phr. at the same t., en même temps; (b) d'autre part. 10. Mus: mesure f. II. v.tr. 1. (a) fixer l'heure de (qch.); (b) mesurer (un coup); well-timed remark, observation f à propos; (c) E: régler, ajuster (l'allumage, etc.). 2. calculer la durée de (qch.). 3. Sp: chronométrer (qn, une course). 'time-exposure, s. Phot: pose f. 'time-lag, s. retard m. 'time-limit, s. 1. limite f de temps. 2. délai m (de paiement). 'timely, a. opportun, à propos. 'time-signal, s. Rad: signal m horaire. 'timetable, s. 1. horaire m; indicateur m. 2. Sch: emploi m du temps.

timid ['timid], a. timide, peureux. -ly, adv. timidement. ti'midity, s. timidité f.

tin [tin]. I. s. 1. étain m. 2. boîte f (en métal). II. v.tr. 1. étamer. 2. mettre (des conserves) en boîte. tin-foil, s. 1. feuille f d'étain. 2. papier m étain. 'tinker1, s. rétameur m. 'tinned, a. en conserve, en boîtes. 'tin-opener, s. ouvre-boîte(s) m. 'tin-plate, s. fer-blanc m.

tinge [tin(d)ʒ]. I. s. teinte f, nuance f. II. v.tr. teinter, nuancer.

tinker2 ['tiŋkər]. 1. v.tr. to t. (sth.) up, retaper, rafistoler (une machine). 2. v.i. to t. about, bricoler.

tinkle ['tiŋkl]. I. s. tintement m. II. v.i. tinter.

tinsel ['tins(ə)l], s. (a) lamé m, paillettes fpl.; (b) clinquant m.

tint [tint]. I. s. teinte f, nuance f. II. v.tr. teinter, colorer.

tiny ['taini], a. minuscule; a t. bit, un tout petit peu.

tip1 [tip]. I. s. 1. bout m, extrémité f, pointe f; asparagus tips, pointes d'asperges. 2. bout ferré, embout m (d'une canne, etc.). II. v.tr. mettre un bout, un embout (à qch.).

tip2. I. s. 1. pourboire m; the t. is included, le service est compris. 2. Sp: etc: tuyau m. 3. rubbish t., décharge f publique. II. v. 1. v.tr. (a) to t. (over), renverser (qch.); chavirer, verser (un canot, etc.); to t. (up), faire basculer; to t. (out), déverser, décharger; faire pencher; (b) donner un pourboire à (qn); (c) Sp: etc: tuyauter (qn). 2. v.i. to t. (over), se renverser, basculer; chavirer, verser; to t. (up), se soulever. 'tip-lorry, s. camion m à benne basculante. 'tipping, s. (distribution f de) pourboires mpl.

tipsy ['tipsi], a. gris, éméché, F: pompette; to get t., se griser.

tiptoe ['tiptou], s. & adv. on t., sur la pointe des pieds.

tire [taiər]. 1. v.tr. (a) fatiguer, lasser; (b) to t. out, épuiser, excéder (qn). 2. v.i. se lasser, se fatiguer. 'tired, a. fatigué; las; t. out, rompu de fatigue. 'tiredness, s. lassitude f, fatigue f. 'tireless, a. inlassable, infatigable. -ly, adv. infatigablement. 'tiresome, a. 1. fatigant; (discours) ennuyeux. 2. exaspérant; (enfant) assommant. 'tiring, a. 1. fatigant. 2. ennuyeux.

tissue ['tisju:], s. tissu m; étoffe f; t. paper, papier m de soie; papier pelure.

tit [tit], s. Z: mésange m.

titbit ['titbit], s. morceau m friand; friandise f.

titivate ['titiveit], v.i. F: se faire beau.

title ['taitl], s. titre m.

titter ['titər]. I. s. rire m étouffé; petit rire nerveux. II. v.i. rire nerveusement. 'tittering, s. petits rires.

to [tu:]. I. prep. à. 1. (a) he went to France, to Japan, to the U.S.A., il est allé en France, au Japon, aux États-Unis; I am going to the grocer's, je vais chez l'épicier; (b) the road to ruin, le chemin de la ruine. 2. vers; à; to the east, vers l'est. 3. ten minutes to six, six heures moins dix. 4. (a) to this, jusqu'à ce jour; (b) accurate to a millimetre, exact à un millimètre près. 5. to this end, à cet effet. 6. to put to flight, mettre en fuite. 7. (a) auprès de, à côté de; secretary to the manager, secrétaire du directeur; (b) six votes to four, six voix contre quatre; three goals to nil, trois buts à zéro. 8. to all appearances, selon les apparences. 9. to drink, to s.o., boire à la santé de qn. 10. (a) what's that to you? qu'est-ce que cela vous fait? (b) envers; pour; good to all, bon envers tous. II. (infinitive) 1. (a) (purpose, result) pour; so to speak, pour ainsi dire; (b) happy to do it, heureux de le faire; good to eat, bon à manger; (c) to look at her, à la voir. 2. (infin. used as a noun) to lie is shameful, il est honteux de mentir. 3. (infin. = finite clause) I wish him to do it, je veux qu'il le fasse. 4. (expressing futurity, obligation) you ought to do it, vous devriez le faire. III. adv. (stressed) to come to, reprendre connaissance; to go to and fro, aller et venir. to-'do, s. F: remue-ménage m; what a to-do! quelle affaire!

toad [toud], s. crapaud m.

toadstool ['toudstu:l], s. F: champignon m, esp. champignon vénéneux.

toast [toust]. I. s. 1. pain grillé, toast m; piece of t., rôtie f; anchovies on t., anchois sur canapé. 2. toast m; to give a t., boire à la santé de qn. II. v. 1. v.tr. (a) rôtir, griller (du pain); (b) porter un toast à (qn). 2. v.i. rôtir, griller. 'toaster, s. grille-pain m.

tobacco [tə'bækou], s. tabac m. to-'baconist, s. marchand m de tabac, buraliste mf; tobacconist's (shop), débit m de tabac.

toboggan [tə'bɔg(ə)n]. I. s. toboggan m, luge f. II. v.i. faire du toboggan.

today [tə'dei], adv. & s. aujourd'hui (m).

toddle ['tɔdl], v.i. marcher à petits pas; trottiner. 'toddler, s. a t., un tout petit.

toe [tou]. I. s. 1. orteil m; doigt m de pied. 2. bout m, pointe f (de chaussure). II. v.tr. F: to t. the line, se conformer au mot d'ordre. 'toecap, s. bout m rapporté (de chaussure). 'toenail, s. ongle m du pied.

toffee ['tɔfi], s. caramel m au beurre.

together [tə'geðər], adv. ensemble; (a) t. with, avec; en même temps que . . .; (b) to bring t., rassembler, réunir; (c) to act t., agir de concert; all t., tous à la fois; (d) for months t., pendant des mois entiers.

toil [tɔil]. I. s. labeur m, peine f; travail m pénible. II. v.i. travailler, peiner, se donner du mal.

toilet ['tɔilit], s. 1. (= washing, make-up) toilette f. 2. (in hotels, etc.) les toilettes, les cabinets m; t. paper, papier m hygiénique.

token ['touk(ə)n], s. 1. signe m, marque f (d'amitié, etc.). 2. flower t., chèque-fleurs m. 3. t. strike, grève f d'avertissement.

tolerance ['tɔlər(ə)ns], s. tolérance f. 'tolerable, a. (a) tolérable, supportable; (b) passable. -ably, adv. tolérablement; passablement. 'tolerant, a. tolérant. 'tolerate, v.tr. tolérer, supporter (la douleur). tole'ration, s. tolérance f (religieuse).

toll[1] [toul], s. péage m; t. bridge, road, pont m, route f, à péage.

toll[2], v.tr. & i. tinter, sonner (une cloche); to t. for the dead, sonner le glas. 'tolling, s. (a) tintement m; (b) glas m.

†**tomato** [tə'mɑːtou], s. tomate f.

tomb [tuːm], s. tombe f, tombeau m.

tome [toum], s. tome m; gros volume m.

tomfoolery [tɔm'fuːləri], s. bêtise(s) f(pl); niaiserie(s) f(pl).

tommy-gun ['tɔmigʌn], s. mitraillette f.

tomorrow [tə'mɔrou], adv. & s. demain (m); t. week, de demain en huit; the day after t., après-demain.

ton [tʌn], s. 1. tonne f. 2. Nau: tonneau m (de jauge). 'tonnage, s. Nau: tonnage m, jauge f.

tone [toun], s. 1. son m, accent m; timbre m (de la voix, etc.). 2. ton m, voix f. 3. ton, nuance f (d'une couleur).

tongs [tɔŋz], s.pl. 1. pincettes f. 2. pince(s) f(pl), tenailles fpl.

tongue [tʌŋ], s. 1. langue f; to find one's t., retrouver la parole; to have a ready t., avoir la langue bien pendue. 2. langue, idiome m. 3. languette f (de soulier); battant m (de cloche).

tongue-tied, a. muet (d'étonnement, etc.); interdit.

tonic ['tɔnik]. 1. a. tonique. 2. s. (a) Med: tonique m, fortifiant m; (b) Mus: tonique f.

tonight [tə'nait], adv. & s. cette nuit; ce soir.

tonsil ['tɔnsl], s. amygdale f. tonsil-'litis, s. angine f (tonsillaire).

too [tuː], adv. 1. trop, par trop; t. much money, trop d'argent; ten shillings t. much, dix shillings de trop; he was much t. strong for me, il était trop fort pour moi. 2. (also) aussi; également. 3. (moreover) d'ailleurs; de plus; en outre.

tool [tuːl]. I. s. 1. outil m; instrument m; gardening tools, matériel m de jardinage. 2. F: instrument, créature f; to make a t. of s.o., se servir de qn. II. v.tr. ciseler (une reliure); travailler (de l'argent); usiner (une pièce en acier). 'tooling, s. ciselage m; usinage m. 'tool-bag, -box, s. sac m, coffre m, à outils.

toot [tuːt]. I. s. Ind: Nau: coup m de sirène; Aut: coup m de klaxon. II. v.tr & i. Aut: corner, klaxonner.

†**tooth** [tuːθ], s. dent f; set of teeth, denture f; set of (false) teeth, dentier m; to fight t. and nail, se battre avec acharnement; F: to be long in the t., n'être plus jeune. 'toothache, s. mal m de dents. 'toothbrush, s. brosse f à dents. 'toothless, a. édenté. 'tooth-paste, s. pâte f dentifrice. 'toothpick, s. cure-dents m.

top[1] [tɔp]. I. s. 1. haut m, sommet m, cime f, faîte m (d'une montagne, d'un arbre); from t. to bottom, de haut en bas, de fond en comble; to come out on t., avoir le dessus. 2. surface f; dessus m (d'une table, etc.). tête f (de page, etc.). 4. haut bout m (de la table). 5. at the t. of one's voice, à tue-tête; to be on t. of one's form, être en pleine forme. II. attrib. a. 1. supérieur; de dessus, du haut, d'en haut; the t. floor, le dernier étage; Aut: t. gear, prise f (directe). 2. premier, principal; t. secret, ultra-secret. III. ‡v.tr. surmonter, couronner; coiffer (with, de). 2. dépasser, surpasser (qch. en hauteur). 'top 'coat, s. 1. pardessus m. 2. couche f de finition (de peinture). top-'heavy, a. trop lourd du haut. 'topmost, a. le plus haut. top 'up, v.tr. remplir (complètement); Aut: faire le plein (d'essence).

top[2], s. (toy) toupie f.

topaz ['toupæz], s. topaze f.

topic ['tɔpik], s. sujet m, thème m (de conversation); topics of the day, questions f d'actualités. 'topical, a. t. allusion, allusion f aux événements du jour; t. song, chanson f d'actualités.

topography [tə'pɔgrəfi], s. topographie f.

topple ['tɔpl], v.i. (a) to t. (over), tomber; (b) chanceler, branler.

topsy-turvy ['tɔpsi'tə:vi], adv. & adj. sens dessus dessous.

torch [tɔːtʃ], s. (a) torche f, flambeau m; (b) lampe f électrique, de poche.

torment, s. ['tɔːment] tourment m, torture f, supplice m. II. v.tr. [tɔː'ment] tourmenter, torturer (qn).

torpedo [tɔː'piːdou], s. I. †s. torpille f. II. v.tr. torpiller.

torrent ['tɔrent], s. torrent m. tor'rential, a. torrentiel.

torrid ['tɔrid], a. torride.

tortoise ['tɔːtəs], s. tortue f. 'tortoise-shell, s. écaille f.

tortuous ['tɔːtjuəs], a. tortueux.

torture ['tɔːtʃər]. I. s. torture f, supplice m. II. v.tr. torturer (qn); mettre (qn) au supplice.

toss [tɔs]. I. s. 1. action f de jeter (qch.) en l'air; (a) lancement m; (b) coup m de pile ou face. 2. t. of the head, mouvement m de tête dédaigneux. 3. chute f de cheval. II. v. 1. v.tr. (a) lancer, jeter (qch.) en l'air; (a') (of horse) démonter (son cavalier); (b) abs. to t. for sth., jouer qch. à pile ou face; (c) to t. one's head, relever la tête d'un air dédaigneux; (d) agiter, ballotter (qch.). 2. v.i. (a) s'agiter (dans son lit); (b) (of ship) to pitch and t., tanguer. 'toss-up, s. coup m de pile ou de face. 2. affaire f à issue douteuse.

tot [tɔt]. I. †v.tr. to t. up, additionner (des chiffres). II. s. 1. tiny t., bambin, -ine. 2. F: goutte f, petit verre m (de whisky, etc.).

total ['toutl]. I. a. total; complet; global. 2. s. total m; montant m; grand t., total global. -ally, adv. totalement, entièrement, complètement.

totalizator ['toutəlaizeitər], s. (F: tote) totalisateur m (des paris).

totter ['tɔtər], v.i. chanceler.

touch [tʌtʃ]. I. v. 1. v.tr. toucher; effleurer; atteindre (un niveau); émouvoir (qn); I never t. wine, jamais je ne bois de vin. 2. v.i. se toucher. II. s. 1. (le sens du) toucher m. 2. léger coup m. to give the finishing t., mettre la dernière main (à qch.). 3. pointe f; soupçon m. 4. in t. with s.o., en contact avec qn. 5. F: touche f. 'touch 'down, v.i. (a) Av: atterrir; faire escale; (b) Rugby Fb: toucher dans les buts. 'touched, a. 1. toqué, timbré. 'touching, a. touchant, attendrissant. touch 'up, v.tr. faire des retouches à (qch.); faire des raccords (à qch.). 'touchy, a. susceptible, ombrageux.

tough [tʌf]. I. a. dur; résistant; (tâche) rude, difficile. II. s. F: voyou m,

bandit m. 'toughen, v.tr. & i. durcir, (s')endurcir. 'toughness, s. dureté f; résistance f.

tour [tuər]. I. s. 1. tour m; excursion f. 2. t. of inspection, tournée f de visite. II. v.tr. faire le tour (d'un pays, etc.). 'tourist. I. s. touriste m/f. II. attrib. a. touristique.

tournament ['tuənəmənt], s. tournoi m (de tennis); concours m (d'échecs).

tow [tou], v.tr. remorquer. 'towing, s. remorque f, remorquage m. 'tow-path, s. chemin m de halage. 'tow-rope, s. remorque f.

towards [tə'wɔːdz], prep. 1. (of place) vers; du côté de qn. 2. envers; pour, à l'égard de (qn). 3. (of time) t. noon, vers midi; t. the end of his life . ., sur la fin de sa vie.

towel ['tauəl], s. serviette f (de toilette); essuie-main(s) m; (sanitary) t., serviette hygiénique.

tower ['tauər]. I. s. tour f; (church) t., clocher m; water t., château m d'eau. II. v.i. to t. over (s.o., sth.), dominer (qn, qch.). 'towering, a. très haut; F: in a t. rage, au paroxysme de la colère.

town [taun], s. 1. ville f; county t. = chef-lieu m de département; he works in T., il travaille à Londres. 2. attrib. de la ville; urbain; municipal; t. council, conseil m municipal; t. hall, hôtel m de ville; mairie f; t. planning, urbanisme m. 'township, s. esp. U.S: commune f.

toy [tɔi]. I. s. 1. jouet m. 2. attrib. tout petit; t. dog, bichon m, chien m de salon. II. v.i. to t. with sth., jouer avec qch.; to t. with one's food, manger du bout des dents. 'toyshop, s. magasin m de jouets.

trace [treis]. I. s. trace f, vestige m. II. v.tr. 1. tracer (un plan); esquisser (un projet. 2. calquer (un dessin). 3. to t. lost goods, recouvrer des objets perdus. 'tracery, s. A. & A: remplage m. 'tracing, s. 1. tracé m, calquage m. 2. dessin m calqué; calque m. t. paper, papier m à calquer.

track [træk], s. 1. trace f, piste f; to keep t. of s.o., ne pas perdre de vue. 2. chemin m; Sp: piste f; Rail: voie f. II. v.tr. to t. (down), traquer; dépister.

tract¹ [trækt], s. étendue f (de pays).

tract², s. brochure f; tract m.

tractor ['træktər], s. tracteur m.

trade [treid]. I. s. 1. emploi m; commerce m; métier m. 2. commerce, négoce m, affaires fpl. 3. attrib. t. price, prix marchand; t. name, appellation f. II. v. 1. v.i. faire le commerce, le négoce (in, de); trafiquer (in, en). 2. v.tr. troquer (qch. contre qch.). trade 'in, v.tr. donner (qch.) en reprise. 'trademark, s. marque *f* de fabrique; **registered t.-m.**, marque déposée. **'trader,** *s.* négociant, -ante; commerçant, -ante; marchand, -ande. †**'tradesman,** *s.* marchand *m*, fournisseur *m*. **trade- union,** *s.* syndicat *m* (ouvrier). **trade-'unionist,** *s.* syndiqué, -ée; syndicaliste *mf*. **'tradewind,** *s.* (vent) alizé *m*. **'trading,** *s.* commerce *m*, négoce *m*.

tradition [trə'diʃ(ə)n], *s.* tradition *f*. **tra-'ditional,** *a.* traditionnel. **-ally,** *adv.* traditionnellement.

traffic ['træfik]. **I.** *s.* **1.** traffic *m* (d'armes, etc.). **2.** mouvement *m*, circulation *f*; road t., circulation routière; *Aut:* t. indicator, indicateur *m* de direction; t. jam, embouteillage *m*; t. lights feux *mpl* de circulation. **II.** ‡*v.* **1.** *v.i.* trafiquer (*in, en*); faire le commerce (*in, de*). **2.** *v.tr. usu. Pej:* trafiquer de (qch.).

tragedy ['trædʒidi], *s.* tragédie *f*. **'tragic,** *a.* tragique. **-ally,** *adv.* tragiquement; au tragique.

trail [treil]. **I.** *s.* **1.** traînée *f* (de fumée, etc.). **2.** piste *f*. **II.** *v.tr. & i.* (se) traîner. **'trailer,** *s.* **1.** *Aut:* remorque *f*; *U.S:* caravane *f* (de camping). **2.** *Cin:* film *m* annonce.

train [trein]. **I.** *v.tr.* **1.** (a) former, instruire (qn); dresser (un animal); (b) *v.tr. & i. Sp:* (s')entraîner. **2.** pointer (un canon); braquer (une lunette). **II.** *s.* **1.** traîne *f*, queue *f* (d'une robe). **2.** succession *f* (d'événements); enchaînement *m* (d'idées). **3.** *Rail:* train *m*; rame *f* (du métro); t. ferry, ferry(-boat) *m*. **trai'nee,** *s.* élève *mf*; stagiaire *mf*. **'trainer,** *s.* **1.** dresseur *m* (d'animaux). **2.** *Sp:* entraîneur *m*. **'training,** *s.* (a) éducation *f*, instruction *f*; formation *f* (du caractère); (b) *Sp:* entraînement *m*; (c) dressage *m* (d'un animal).

trait [trei], *s.* trait *m* (de caractère).

traitor ['treitər], *s.* traître *m*.

trajectory [trə'dʒektəri], *s.* trajectoire *f*.

tram [træm], *s.* tramway *m*.

tramp [træmp]. **I.** *s.* **1.** bruit *m* de pas marqués. **2.** marche *f*; promenade *f* à pied. **3.** (*pers.*) chemineau *m*; clochard *m*. **4.** *Nau:* t. steamer, cargo *m*, tramp *m*. **II.** *v.i.* **1.** marcher lourdement. **2.** vagabonder; *v.tr.* to t. the streets, battre le pavé.

trample ['træmpl]. **1.** *v.i.* to t. on sth., s.o., piétiner, écraser (qch, qn. **2.** *v.tr.* to t. sth. under foot, fouler qch. aux pieds.

trance [trɑːns], *s.* (a) extase *f*; (b) transe *f*.

tranquil ['træŋkwil], *a.* tranquille; calme; paisible. **-illy,** *adv.* tranquillement. **tran'quillity,** tranquillité *f*; calme *m*. **'tranquillizer,** *s. Med:* tranquillisant *m*, calmant *m*.

trans- [træns,-, trænz-, trɑːns-, trɑːnz-], *prefix.* trans-. **trans'act,** *v.tr.* to t. business with s.o., faire des affaires, traiter une affaire, avec qn. **tran-'saction,** *s.* opération *f* (commerciale). **transat'lantic,** *a.* transatlantique. **trans'ceiver,** *s.* émetteur-récepteur *m*. **transconti'nental,** *a.* transcontinental. **trans'cribe,** *v.tr.* transcrire. **tran-'scription,** *s.* transcription *f*. **'transept,** *s. Arch: & A:* transept *m*. **'transfer. I.** *s.* **1.** (a) transport *m*, renvoi *m* (de qch. dans un autre endroit); déplacement *m* (d'un fonctionnaire); (b) *Jur:* transfert *m* (d'un droit); *Fin:* virement *m* (de fonds). **2.** *Jur:* (deed of) t., acte *m* de cession. **3.** (*in needlework, etc.*) décalque *m*. **II.** ‡*v.tr.* **1.** transférer; déplacer (un fonctionnaire); *Jur:* céder (une propriété); *Fin:* virer (une somme). **2.** (*needlework, etc.*) calquer. **trans'ferable,** *a.* transmissible; not t., strictement personnel. **trans'form,** *v.tr.* **1.** transformer, métamorphoser. **2.** *Sc: Ind:* convertir (*into, en*); *El:* transformer (le courant). **transfor'mation,** *s.* transformation *f*; métamorphose *f*; *Sc:* conversion *f* (de la chaleur en énergie). **trans'former,** *s. El:* transformateur *m* (de tension). **trans'fusion,** *s. Med:* blood t., transfusion *f* de sang. **tran'sistor,** *s. Rad:* transistor *m*. **'transit,** *s.* **1.** passage *m* (à travers un pays). **2.** transport *m* (de marchandises); damage in t., avarie(s) *f(pl)* en cours de route. **trans'late,** *v.tr.* traduire. **trans'lation,** *s.* traduction *f*. **trans'lator,** *s.* traducteur, -trice. **trans'mission,** *s.* transmission *f*. ‡**trans'mit,** *v.tr.* mettre. **trans'mitter,** *s. P.T.T:* metteur *m*; *Rad:* t. station, poste émetteur. **trans'parency,** *s.* **1.** transparence *f* (du verre); limpidité *f* (de l'eau). **2.** *Phot:* diapositive *f*. **trans'parent,** *a.* **1.** transparent; (eau) limpide. **2.** évident, clair. **-ly,** *adv.* d'une manière transparente; clairement. **tran'spire,** *v.i.* (*a*) transpirer; (*b*) (*of news*) s'ébruiter; (*c*) his account of what happened, sa version de ce qui s'était passé. **trans'plant. I.** *v.tr.* transplanter, repiquer (des plants). **II.** *s. Med:* greffe *f* (du cœur, etc.). **'trans-port. I.** *s.* **1.** (*also, esp. U.S:* transportation) transport *m* (de marchandises); t. cafe, restaurant *m* des routiers. **2.** *Nau:* t. (-ship), transport *m*; *Av:* t. plane, avion-cargo *m*. **II.** *v.tr.* transporter. **trans'porter,** *s.* transporteur *m*; t. bridge, (pont) transbordeur *m*; *Mil:* tank t., porte-chars *m inv.* **trans'pose,** *v.tr.* transposer. **trans'posing,** *s. Mus:* transposition *f*. **transubstanti'ation,** *s. Ecc:* transsubstantiation *f*. **'transverse,** *a.* transversal; en travers. **-ly,** *adv.* transversalement.

trap [træp]. I. *s.* piège *m.* II. ‡*v.tr.* prendre au piège. '**trap-door**, *s.* trappe *f.*

trapeze [trə'pi:z], *s.* trapèze *m.*

trappist [træpist], *a.* & *s.* Ecc: trappiste (*m*).

traps [træps], *s.pl.* F: effets *m* (personnels); to pack up one's t., plier bagage.

trapse [treips], *v.i.* traîner ça et là.

trash [træʃ], *s.* chose(s) *f(pl)* sans valeur; camelote *f.* '**trashy**, *a.* sans valeur; de camelote.

travel ['trævl]. I. ‡*v.i.* voyager. 2. être représentant (de commerce). II. *s.* voyages *mpl*; t: agency, agence *f* de voyages. '**traveller**, *s.* 1. voyageur, -euse; t's chèque, chèque *m* de voyage; Pol: fellow-t., communiste, -ante. 2. (commercial) t., représentant *m* (de commerce). '**travelogue**, *s.* Cin: documentaire *m* de voyage.

traverse ['trævəs], *v.tr.* traverser.

trawler ['trɔːlər], *s.* Nau: chalutier *m.*

tray [trei], *s.* plateau *m.*

treachery ['tretʃəri], *s.* trahison *f*, perfidie *f.* '**treacherous**, *a.* (homme) traître; (action) perfide. **-ly**, *adv.* (agir) en traître, perfidement.

treacle ['triːkl], *s.* mélasse *f.*

tread [tred]. I. *s.* 1. (*a*) pas *m*; (*b*) bruit *m* de pas. 2. (*a*) semelle *f* (de soulier); (*b*) Aut: bande *f* de roulement (d'un pneu). II. ‡*v.* 1. *v.i.* marcher; poser les pieds; to t. on sth., marcher sur qch. 2. *v.tr.* to t. sth. underfoot, écraser qch.; fouler qch. aux pieds.

treason ['triːzn], *s.* trahison *f*; reasonable, *a.* 1. de trahison. 2. traître, perfide.

treasure ['treʒər]. I. *s.* trésor *m.* II. *v.tr.* 1. tenir beaucoup (à qch.). 2. garder (qch.) soigneusement. '**treasurer**, *s.* trésorier, -ière. '**treasury**, *s.* trésor *m* (public); trésorerie *f.*

treat [triːt]. I. *s.* 1. régal *m*; festin *m*; fête *f.* 2. plaisir *m*; to give oneself a t., faire un petit extra. II. *v.i.* & *tr.* traiter; to t. oneself to sth., s'offrir qch. '**treatment**, *s.* traitement *m*; Med: cure *f.* '**treatise**, *s.* traité *m* (on, de). '**treaty**, *s.* 1. traité *m* (de paix). 2. Com: accord *m*, contrat *m.*

treble ['trebl]. I. *a.* 1. triple. 2. Mus: soprano. II. *s.* 1. triple *m.* 2. soprano *m.* III. *v.tr.* & *i.* (se) tripler.

tree [triː], *s.* arbre *m.*; apple, pear, t., pommier *m*, poirier *m.*

trefoil ['triːfɔil], *s.* trèfle *m.*

trek [trek], *s.* voyage *m* (long et difficile); it's quite a t., c'est bien loin.

trellis ['trelis], *s.* treillis *m*, treillage *m.*

tremble ['trembl], *v.i.* trembler. '**trembling**, *s.* tremblement *m.* '**tremor**, *s.* tremblement *m* (de terre). '**tremulous**, *a.* tremblotant; (of voice) chevrotant. **-ly**, *adv.* en tremblant.

tremendous [tri'mendəs], *a.* immense; a t. crowd, un monde fou.

trench [tren(t)ʃ], *s.* tranchée *f*; fossé *m.*

trend [trend], *s.* direction *f*; tendance *f* (de l'opinion, de la mode, etc.).

trespass ['trespəs], *v.i.* s'introduire sans autorisation sur la propriété de qn. '**trespasser**, *s.* intrus *m*; P.N: trespassers will be prosecuted, défense d'entrer sous peine d'amende.

trial ['traiəl], *s.* 1. (*a*) jugement *m* (d'un litige, d'un accusé); (*b*) procès *m*; famous trials, causes *f* célèbres. 2. essai *m*; (*a*) épreuve *f*; Sp: t. game, match *m* de sélection; (*b*) on t., à l'essai; Com: t. order, commande d'essai; Aut: t. run, course d'essai. 3. épreuve douloureuse.

triangle ['traiæŋgl], *s.* triangle *m.* tri'angular, *a.* triangulaire, en triangle.

tribe [traib], *s.* tribu *f.* '**tribal**, *a.* tribal, de tribu.

tribunal [tri'bjuːnl, trai-], *s.* tribunal *m*; cour *f* de justice; la cour.

tributary [tri'bjut(ə)ri]. 1. *a.* tributaire. 2. *s.* affluent *m* (d'un fleuve).

trick [trik]. I. *s.* 1. tour *m*; ruse *f*; farce *f*; (dishonest) supercherie *f*; conjuring t., tour de passe-passe; the tricks of the trade, les astuces *f* du métier. 2. (= habit) manie *f*, habitude *f.* 3. that'll do the t., cela fera l'affaire. 4. (at cards) levée *f.* II. *v.tr.* duper (qn). '**tricky**, *a.* compliqué; (of situation) délicat.

trickle ['trikl]. I. *s.* filet *m* (d'eau). II. *v.i.* couler (goutte à goutte).

tricycle ['traisikl], *s.* tricycle *m.*

tried [traid], *a.* (well) t., éprouvé.

trifle ['traifl]. I. *s.* 1. (*a*) bagatelle *f*, vétille *f*; (*b*) a t., un tout petit peu; un soupçon. 2. Cu: = diplomate *m.* II. *v.i.* jouer, badiner (with, avec). '**trifling**, *a.* insignifiant, peu important.

trigger ['trigər], *s.* détente *f*; gâchette *f* (de fusil, etc.); F: to be t.-happy, avoir la gâchette facile.

trim [trim]. I. *s.* 1. to be in good t., être en forme. 2. coupe *f* (de cheveux). II. ‡*v.tr.* 1. couper (les cheveux). 2. orner, parer, garnir. '**trimming**, *s.* garniture *f.*

Trinity ['triniti], *s.* la (sainte) Trinité; T. Sunday (fête *f*) de la Trinité.

trinket ['triŋkit], *s.* (*a*) petit objet de parure; breloque *f*; (*b*) bibelot *m.*

trio ['triːou], *s.* trio *m.*

trip [trip]. I. *v.* 1. *v.i.* to t. (up), (i) trébucher; faire un faux pas; (ii) se tromper. 2. *v.tr.* to t. s.o. (up), faire trébucher qn. II. *s.* excursion *f*; Aut: t. recorder, (totalisateur) journalier *m.* '**tripper**, *s.* excursionniste *m.*

tripe [traip], *s.* (*a*) Cu: tripes *f(pl)*; (*b*) F: fatras *m*, bêtises *fpl.*

triple ['tripl]. I. *a.* triple. **-ly**, *adv.* triplement. II. *v.tr.* & *i.* (se) tripler. '**triplicate**, *s.* triplicata *m*; triplicata *m*; in t., en triple exemplaire.

tripod ['traipod], s. trépied m.

trite [trait], a. banal; t. subject, sujet usé.

triumph ['traiəmf]. I. s. triomphe m, succès m. II. v.i. triompher (over, de). **tri'umphal**, a. triomphal; t. arch, arc m de triomphe. **tri'umphant**, a. triomphant. **-ly**, adv. triomphalement.

trivial ['triviəl], a. 1. insignifiant; sans importance. 2. banal.

trolley ['troli], s. 1. (a) chariot m; (b) (dinner) t., table f roulante. 2. trolley m (d'un tramway). **'trolley-bus**, s. trolleybus m.

trombone [trɔm'boun], s. trombone m.

troop [tru:p], s. 1. troupe f; bande f (de personnes); pl. troops, troupes, soldats m. II. v. 1. v.i. to t. together, s'attrouper, s'assembler. 2. v.tr. to t. the colour(s), présenter le drapeau.

trophy ['troufi], s. trophée m.

tropic ['tropik], s. Geog. tropique m; in the tropics, sous les tropiques. **'tropical**, a. tropical; des tropiques.

trot [trot]. I. s. trot m. II. v.i. trotter; aller au trot. **'trotting**, s. t. race, course f attelée.

trouble ['trʌbl]. I. s. 1. peine f, malheur m. 2. ennui m, difficulté f; soucis mpl; he's asking for t., il se prépare des ennuis; to make t., semer la discorde; there's going to be t., il y aura du grabuge; it's not worth the t., ce n'est pas la peine; it's no t.! il n'y a pas de quoi! 4. (a) Med: dérangement m; to have heart troubles, souffrir du coeur; (b) Aut: engine t., panne f de moteur; Ind: labour troubles, conflits m sociaux. II. v. 1. v.tr. (a) tourmenter, inquiéter (qn); (b) incommoder, gêner, déranger (qn); I'm sorry to t. you, excusez-moi de vous déranger. 2. v.i. s'inquiéter (about, au sujet de); don't t. to write, ne vous donnez pas la peine d'écrire. **'troublesome**, a. 1. ennuyeux; (enfant) énervant. 2. (tâche) difficile, pénible.

trough [trof], s. 1. auge f; drinking t., abreuvoir m. 2. t. of the wave, creux m de la lame. 3. t. of low pressure, zone f dépressionnaire.

trousers ['trauzəz], s.pl. (pair of) t., pantalon m.

trousseau ['tru:sou], s. trousseau m.

trout [traut], s.inv. truite f; salmon t., truite saumonnée.

trowel ['trau(ə)l], s. 1. truelle f. 2. Ag: déplantoir m.

truant ['tru:ənt], s. élève absent(e) (de l'école) sans permission; to play t., faire l'école buissonnière.

truce [tru:s], s. trêve f.

truck[1] [trʌk], s. (a) Aut: camion m; delivery t., camionnette f; t. driver, camionneur m; (b) luggage t., chariot m à bagages; diable f; (c) Rail: wagon m à marchandises (ouvert). **'trucking**, s. U.S: camionnage m.

truck[2], s. U.S: produits mpl maraîchers; t. farmer, maraîcher m; t. farming, culture f maraîchère.

trudge [trʌdʒ], v.i. marcher lourdement, péniblement.

true [tru:]. I. a. 1. vrai; exact; to come t., se réaliser. 2. véritable, réel, authentique. 3. (ami) fidèle, loyal. II. adv. 1. (chanter, viser) juste; to run t., tourner rond. III. s. out of t., (i) hors d'aplomb; (ii) (of wheel) décentré, excentré. **'truly**, adv. vraiment, véritablement; t. grateful, sincèrement reconnaissant; t.? vrai de vrai?

trump [trʌmp]. I. s. (at cards) atout m. II. v.tr. 1. couper (une carte); abs. jouer atout. 2. to t. up an excuse, inventer une excuse.

trumpet ['trʌmpit]. I. s. trompette f. II. v.i. 1. sonner de la trompette; (b) (of elephant) barrir.

truncheon ['trʌn(t)ʃ(ə)n], s. bâton m (d'agent de police).

trunk [trʌŋk], s. 1. (a) tronc m (d'arbre); (b) t. road, route nationale. 2. malle f, coffre m. 3. trompe f (d'éléphant). 4. pl. Cl: caleçon m court, slip m.

trust [trʌst]. I. s. 1. confiance f (in s.o., sth., en qn, qch.). 2. position of t., poste m de confiance. 3. trust m, syndicat m. II. v. 1. v.tr. se fier à (qn, qch.); mettre sa confiance en (qn); to t. s.o. with sth., confier qch. à qn. 2. v.i. (a) se confier (in, en); se fier (in, à); (b) to t. to luck, s'en remettre au hasard. **trus'tee**, s. Jur: fidéicommissaire m; mandataire mf; **'trustworthy**, a. 1. (of pers.) (digne) de confiance, de foi; honnête, fidèle. 2. (renseignement, etc.) digne de foi, exact.

truth [tru:θ], s. vérité f. **'truthful**, a. (of pers.) véridique; (portrait) fidèle. **-fully**, adv. 1. véridiquement; sans mentir. 2. fidèlement. **'truthfulness**, s. véracité f.

try [trai]. I. s. essai m, tentative f; at the first t., du premier coup; Rugby Fb: to score a t., marquer un essai. II. v. 1. v.tr. (a) éprouver (qn); mettre (qn, qch.) à l'épreuve; affliger (qn); to t. one's eyes, se fatiguer les yeux; (b) essayer, expérimenter (qch.); faire l'essai de qch.; to t. a dish, goûter un plat; (c) juger (une cause, un accusé); (d) essayer, tenter, tâcher (de faire qch.). 2. v.i. to t. for sth., tâcher d'obtenir qch. **'trying**, a. 1. difficile, dur; pénible. 2. vexant; contrariant; he's very t., il est insupportable. **'try on**, v.tr. essayer (un vêtement). **'try-on**, s. F: bluff m. **'try out**, v.tr. essayer (à fond) (une machine, etc.). **'try-out**, s. essai m.

tub [tʌb], *s.* baquet *m*, bac *m.* **'tubby**, *a.* F: (*of pers.*) boulot; gros et rond.

tube [tju:b], *s.* 1. tube *m*; tuyau *m; Aut:* inner t., chambre *f* à air; *T.V:* cathode-ray t., tube cathodique. 2. F: the t., le métro. **'tubeless**, *a.* (pneu) sans chambre.

tuberculosis [tju(:)bə:kju'lousis], *s.* tuberculose *f.*

tuck [tʌk], *s.* 1. (petit) pli *m*; rempli *m*, plissé *m.* II. *v.tr.* 1. faire des plis à, remplir (un vêtement); plisser, froncer (un tissu). 2. to t. a rug round s.o., envelopper qn d'une couverture. tuck 'in. 1. *v.tr.* serrer, rentrer, replier (qch.); to t. in the bedclothes, border le lit. 2 *v.i. F:* manger à belles dents.

Tuesday ['tju:zdi], *s.* mardi *m*; shrove T., (le) mardi gras.

tuft [tʌft], *s.* touffe *f* (d'herbe); mèche *f* (de laine, de cheveux).

tug [tʌg]. I. *s.* 1. traction *f* (subite); saccade *f*; to give a good t., tirer fort. 2. *Nau:* remorqueur *m.* II. *v.tr. & i.* tirer avec effort; tirer sur (qch.).

tuition [tju(:)'iʃ(ə)n], *s.* instruction *f*; private t., leçons *f* particulières.

tulip ['tju:lip], *s.* tulipe *f.*

tumble ['tʌmbl], *v.i.* tomber (par terre); (*of building*) to be tumbling down, s'écrouler. **'tumble-down**, *a. F:* croulant, délabré.

tumbler ['tʌmblər], *s.* verre *m* sans pied.

tummy ['tʌmi], *s. F:* estomac *m*, ventre *m*; t. ache, mal *m* au ventre.

tumour ['tju:mər], *s.* tumeur *f.*

tune [tju:n]. I *s.* 1. air *m* (de musique). 2. accord *m*; to sing out of t., chanter faux. II. *v.tr.* 1. accorder, mettre d'accord (un instrument); mettre au point (un moteur). 2. *Rad:* to t. in to a station, capter un poste; *abs.* to t. in, accorder le récepteur. **'tuneful**, *a.* mélodieux, harmonieux. **'tuning**, *s.* accordage *m* (d'un piano); E: réglage *m* (d'un moteur); Rad: réglage, syntonisation *f.*

tunic ['tju:nik], *s.* tunique *f.*

tunnel ['tʌnl], *s.* tunnel *m.*

tunny ['tʌni], *s.* thon *m.*

turbine ['tə:bain], *s.* turbine *f*; turbo-moteur *m.*

turbo-jet ['tə:bou'dʒet], *s.* Av: turbo-réacteur *m.*

turbot ['tə:bət], *s. Fish:* turbot *m.*

turbotrain ['tə:boutrein], *s.* turbotrain *m.*

turbulence ['tə:bjuləns], *s.* turbulence *f.* **'turbulent**, *a.* turbulent.

tureen [tə'ri:n], *s.* soupière *f.*

†**turf** [tə:f], *s.* 1. gazon *m.* 2. the t., le turf, le monde des courses.

Turk [tə:k], *s.* Turc, *f.* Turque. **Turkish** ['tə:kiʃ]. 1. *a.* turc, de Turquie; T. bath, bain turc; T. cigarettes, cigarettes d'orient; T. delight, rahat loukoum *m.* 2. *s. Ling:* le turc.

turkey ['tə:ki], *s.* dindon *m*; dinde *f*; (*young*) dindonneau *m.*

turmoil ['tə:mɔil], *s.* trouble *m*; agitation *f.*

turn [tə:n]. I. *v.* 1. *v.tr.* (*a*) tourner; faire tourner; retourner; to t. the key, donner un tour de clef; he's turned forty, il a passé la quarantaine; (*b*) changer, convertir, transformer (into, en); (*c*) *Techn:* tourner, façonner au tour. 2. *v.i.* (*a*) (se) tourner; se retourner; (*b*) to t. on s.o., s'en prendre à qn; (*b*) to t. upside down, (i) (*of boat*) chavirer; (ii) (*of car*) capoter; (*c*) s'adresser (à qn); avoir recours (à qn); (*d*) (*of tide*) changer; (*e*) se changer, se convertir, se transformer (into, en); it's turning to rain, le temps se met à la pluie; the milk has turned (sour), le lait a tourné; to t. socialist, devenir socialiste. II. *s.* 1. tour *m*, révolution *f* (d'une roue); *Cu:* done to a t., cuit à point. 2. (*a*) changement *m* de direction; *Aut:* virage *m*; (*b*) tournure *f* (des affaires); to take a tragic t., tourner au tragique; (*c*) renversement *m* (de la marée). 3. (*a*) tour; it's your t. (to play), (c'est à vous de jouer); in t., tour à tour; à tour de rôle. (*b*) *Th:* numéro *m.* 4. tournant *m*, coude *m*; sharp t., crochet *m*, tournant *m* brusque. turn a'way. 1. *v.tr.* détourner (les yeux); renvoyer (qn); se détourner. **turn 'back.** 1. *v.tr.* barrer le passage (à qn). 2. *v.i.* rebrousser chemin. **turn 'down**, *v.tr.* 1. baisser (le gaz). 2. repousser, refuser (une offre). **turn 'in**, *v.i. F:* (aller) se coucher. **'turning**, *s.* tournant *m* (d'une route); virage *m*; the first t. on the right, le premier (tournant), la première (route), à droite. **'turning-point**, *s.* moment *m* critique, décisif. **turn 'off.** 1. *v.tr.* fermer, couper (l'eau, le gaz). 2. *v.i.* changer de route; tourner (à droite, à gauche). **turn 'on**, *v.tr.* ouvrir (l'eau, le gaz); allumer (l'électricité). **turn 'out.** 1. *v.tr.* (*a*) mettre (qn) à la porte; (*b*) vider (un tiroir, etc.); (*c*) nettoyer (une pièce) à fond; (*d*) (*of pers.*) well turned out, élégant; (*e*) couper, éteindre (le gaz, etc.). 2. *v.i.* (*a*) sortir, paraître en public; (*b*) to t. out well, badly, tourner bien, mal; it turns out that ..., il se trouve que ... **turn 'over.** 1. *v.tr.* tourner, retourner (qch.). 2. *v.i.* se retourner; (*of car*) capoter. **'turn-over**, *s.* (*a*) *Com:* chiffre *m* d'affaires; (*b*) *Cu:* apple t.-o., chausson *m* aux pommes. **turn 'round**, *v.tr. & i.* (se) retourner. **'turnstile**, *s.* tourniquet (-compteur) *m* (pour entrées). **turn 'up.** 1. (*a*) relever (son col); retrousser (ses manches); (*b*) *F:* écœurer (qn). 2. *v.i.* arriver, se présenter.

turnip ['tə:nip], s. navet m.

turpentine ['tə:p(ə)ntain], s. térébenthine f.

turquoise ['tə:kwɑ:z,-kwɔiz], s. 1. turquoise f. 2. a. & s. t.(-blue), turquoise (m) inv.

turret ['tʌrit], s. tourelle f.

turtle ['tə:tl], s. tortue f de mer; t. soup, consommé m à la tortue. 'turtle-dove, s. tourterelle f.

tusk [tʌsk], s. défense f (d'éléphant).

tussle ['tʌsl], I. s. lutte f, mêlée f, bagarre f. II. v.i. lutter.

tutor ['tjuːtər], s. Sch: 1. directeur m des études (d'un groupe d'étudiants). 2. private t., précepteur m.

tuxedo [tʌk'siːdou], s. U.S: Cl: smoking m.

twaddle ['twɔdl], s. F: fadaises fpl.

twang [twæŋ], I. s. 1. son m vibrant (d'une harpe). 2. nasal t., ton m nasillard; to speak with a t., parler du nez. II. v. 1. v.tr. to t. a guitar, pincer, F: gratter, de la guitare. 2. v.i. Mus: (of string) vibrer, résonner.

tweak [twiːk], v.tr. pincer (l'oreille de qn).

tweed [twiːd], s. 1. tweed m, cheviotte f écossaise. 2. pl. Cl: complet m, tailleur m, de cheviotte.

tweezers ['twiːzəz], s.pl. petite pince f; brucelles fpl.

twelve [twelv], num. a. & s. douze (m); t. o'clock, (i) midi m; (ii) minuit m; half past t., midi et demi, minuit et demi. 'twelfth, num. a. & s. douzième (mf); (on) the t. of May, le douze mai; T. Night, jour m des Rois.

twenty ['twenti], num. a. & s. vingt (m); t.-first, vingt et unième; the t.-first of May, le vingt et un mai; about t. people, une vingtaine de gens. 'twentieth, num. a. & s. vingtième (mf); (on) the t. of June, le vingt juin.

twerp [twəːp], s. P: nouille f, pauvre type m.

twice [twais], adv. deux fois; t. as big as . . ., deux fois aussi grand que . . .; t. over, à deux reprises.

twig [twig], s. brindille f; ramille f.

twilight ['twailait], s. 1. crépuscule m. 2. attrib. crépusculaire.

twin [twin], a. & s. 1. jumeau,-elle. 2. a. t. beds, lits jumeaux; t. towns, villes jumelées. 'twin-engine, attrib. a. Av: (appareil) bimoteur m. 'twin-'jet, a. Av: t.-j. plane, biréacteur m.

twine [twain], I. s. ficelle f. II. v. 1. v.tr. tordre, tortiller (des fils); to t. sth. round sth., (en)rouler qch. autour de qch. 2. v.i. se tordre, se tortiller.

twinge [twin(d)ʒ], s. élancement m (de douleur); t. of conscience, remords m.

twinkle ['twiŋkl]. I. s. 1. scintillement m, clignotement m (des étoiles). 2. pétillement m (du regard). II. v.i. 1. (of light) scintiller, clignoter. 2. his eyes twinkled (with mischief), ses yeux pétillaient (de malice). 'twinkling, s. 1. scintillement m; pétillement m. 2. adv. phr. in a t., en un clin d'œil.

twirl [twəːl]. 1. v.tr. faire tournoyer. 2. v.i. tournoyer; (of dancer) pirouetter.

twist [twist]. I. s. 1. fil m retors; cordon m; cordonnet m. 2. to give sth. a t., exercer une torsion sur qch. 3. twists and turns, tours et retours. II. v. 1. v.tr. tordre, tortiller; to t. one's ankle, se fouler la cheville; (b) (of road) tourner, faire des détours, des lacets; (c) to t. and turn, serpenter. 'twisted, a. tordu, tors. 'twister, s. filou m.

twitch [twitʃ]. I. s. 1. saccade f; petit coup m sec. 2. mouvement m convulsif;(facial) tic m. II. v. 1. v.tr. vivement; donner une saccade à (qch.); contracter (les traits); crisper (les mains). 2. v.i. se contracter nerveusement; (of hands) se crisper; his face twitches, il a un tic.

twitter ['twitər]. I. s. gazouillement m; F: to be all of a t., être tout en émoi. II. v.i. gazouiller.

two [tuː], num. a. & s. deux (m). 'two-'seater, s. avion m, voiture f, à deux places. two-stroke, attrib. a. E: (moteur) (à) deux-temps. 'two-'timer, s. esp. U.S: (associé, etc.) malhonnête m; trompeur m. 'two-'way, a. (rue) à deux sens.

type [taip]. I. s. 1. type m; genre m. 2. (a) (for printing) caractère m; type; (b) coll. caractères. II. v.tr. taper (à la machine); dactylographier. 'type-script, s. manuscrit m dactylographié. 'typewriter, s. machine f à écrire. 'typing, s. dactylographie f. 'typist, s. dactylo mf.

typhoid ['taifɔid], a. & s. typhoïde (f).

typical ['tipik(ə)l], a. typique. -ally, adv. d'une manière typique, typiquement.

tyrant ['taiər(ə)nt], s. tyran m. 'tyranny, s. tyrannie f. ty'rannical, a. tyrannique. -ally, adv. tyranniquement; en tyran. 'tyrannize, v.i. faire le tyran; to t. over s.o., tyranniser qn.

tyre ['taiər], s. pneu m; radial-ply t., pneu m à carcasse radiale; t. lever, démonte-pneus m.

tyro ['taiərou], s. novice mf.

U

U, u [juː], s. (la lettre) U, u m.

udder [ˈʌdər], s. mamelle f, pis m (de vache, etc.).

ugly [ˈʌgli], a. laid; disgracieux; vilain; **to grow u.,** enlaidir; *F:* u. customer, vilain type. **'ugliness,** s. laideur f.

ulcer [ˈʌlsər], s. ulcère m.

ulterior [ʌlˈtiəriər], a. 1. ultérieur. 2. (motif) secret, caché; without u. motive, sans arrière-pensée.

ultimate [ˈʌltimit], a. final; dernier. **-ly,** adv. à la fin; en fin de compte.

†ultimatum [ʌlti'meitəm], s. ultimatum m.

ultra [ˈʌltrə], a. extrême. **ultrama'rine,** a. & s. (bleu m d')outremer (m). **'ultra'sonic,** a. ultrasonique; ultra-sonore.

umbrella [ʌmˈbrelə], s. parapluie m.

umpire [ˈʌmpaiər]. I. s. arbitre m, juge m. II. v.tr. arbitrer. **'umpiring,** s. arbitrage m.

un- [ʌn-], *prefix indicating negative.* dé(s)-; in-; non; nullement; peu, mal; (ne) pas; anti-; sans. **un'able,** a. incapable; **we are u. to help you,** nous ne pouvons pas vous aider; u. to attend, empêché. **unac'ceptable,** a. inacceptable; (théorie) irrecevable. **unac'companied,** a. non accompagné, seul; sans escorte; *Mus:* sans accompagnement. **unac'countable,** a. inexplicable; (conduite) bizarre. **-ly,** adv. inexplicablement. **unac'customed,** a. (of pers.) peu habitué (à qch.). **una'dulterated,** a. pur; *Com:* sans mélange; non frelaté. **una'ffected,** a. (a) sans affectation; (style) sans recherche; (b) inaltérable (à l'air, etc.). **-ly,** adv. sincèrement, simplement. **un'aided,** a. sans aide, tout seul. **un'altered,** a. inchangé; sans changement; tel quel. **unam'bitious,** a. sans ambition; sans prétention.

unanimous [juːˈnæniməs], a. unanime. **-ly,** adv. à l'unanimité; unanimement.

un'answerable, a. (argument) sans réplique. **un'appetizing,** a. peu appétissant. **una'pprochable,** a. inaccessible; (of pers.) inabordable. **un'armed,** a. sans armes. **una'shamed,** a. sans honte; éhonté. **un'asked,** a. to do sth. u., faire qch. spontanément. **unas'suming,** a. simple, modeste. **unat'tainable,** a. inaccessible (by, à); hors de la portée (by, de). **una'ttractive,** a. peu attrayant; (of pers.) peu sympathique. **un'authorized,** a. non autorisé; (commerce) illicite. **una'voidable,** a. inévitable; (événement) qu'on ne peut prévenir. **-ably,** adv. inévitablement. **u.** absent, empêché. **una'ware,** a. ignorant, pas au courant

(of sth., de qch.); **to be u. of sth.,** ignorer qch. **una'wares,** adv. (faire qch.) inconsciemment, par inadvertance; (prendre qn) au dépourvu. **un'balanced,** a. en équilibre instable; (esprit) déséquilibré. **un'bearable,** a. intolérable; u. agony, douleur f atroce. **-ably,** adv. insupportablement. **un'beatable,** a. imbattable. **unbe'coming,** a. (a) peu convenable; déplacé; (b) (of garment) peu seyant. **unbe'lievable,** a. incroyable. **‡un'bend,** v.i. se détendre. **un'bias(s)ed,** a. impartial; sans parti pris. **un'bleached,** a. *Com:* u. (linen) sheet, drap écru. **un'bounded,** a. sans bornes; illimité; (of conceit) démesuré. **un'breakable,** a. incassable. **un'broken,** a. (a) non brisé, non cassé; (b) intact; (c) *Sp:* u. record, record qui n'a pas été battu; (d) (of silence) ininterrompu. **un'burden,** v.tr. to u. oneself, s'épancher. **un'businesslike,** a. (a) peu commerçant; (b) (procédé) irrégulier; **to be u.,** manquer de méthode. **un'button,** v.tr. déboutonner. **un'canny,** a. (bruit) inquiétant, mystérieux; (lueur) sinistre. **un'cared for,** a. (enfant) peu soigné, délaissé; (jardin) à l'abandon. **unceré'monious,** a. (of pers.) sans façon, sans-gêne. **-ly,** adv. (a) sans cérémonie; (b) sans façons. **un'certain,** a. incertain. I. (of time, amount) indéterminé; (résultat) douteux. 2. u. temper, humeur f inégale. **un'certainty,** s. incertitude f. **un'challenged,** a. (droit, etc.) incontesté. **un'changeable,** a. immuable. **un'changed,** a. inchangé; toujours le même. **un'changing,** a. invariable, immuable. **un'civilized,** a. incivilisé, barbare. **un'claimed,** a. u. right, droit m non revendiqué; *P.T.T:* u. letter, lettre f au rebut.

uncle [ˈʌŋkl], s. oncle, m; yes, u.! oui, mon oncle!

un'clouded, a. (of sky) sans nuage; (of vision) clair; (of liquid) limpide. **un'coil,** v.tr. & i. (se) dérouler. **un'comfortable,** a. (a) inconfortable; peu confortable; incommode; (b) désagréable; gênant; (c) to feel u., être mal à l'aise. **-ably,** adv. (a) peu confortablement; incommodément; (b) désagréablement. **un'common,** a. peu commun; rare; (mot) peu usité; singulier. **unco'mmunicative,** a. renfermé, taciturne. **un'complaining,** a. patient, résigné. **uncompli'mentary,** a. peu flatteur. **un'compromising,** a. intransigeant; intraitable; u. sincerity, sincérité absolue. **uncon'cerned,** a. insouciant, indifférent; sans inquiétude;

u. air, air dégagé. **uncon'ditional,** *a.* absolu; (refus) catégorique. **-ally,** *adv.* **uncon'firmed,** *a.* non confirmé; (of news) sujet à caution. **uncon'genial,** *a.* (of pers.) peu sympathique; (travail) ingrat. **unco'nnected,** *a.* sans rapport, sans lien; (style) décousu, sans suite. **un'conscious,** *a.* 1. inconscient; to be u. of sth., ignorer qch. 2. sans connaissance; évanoui. 3. *s. Psy:* the u., l'inconscient *m.* **-ly,** *adv.* inconsciemment. **un'consciousness,** *s.* (a) inconscience *f* (of, de); (b) évanouissement *m.* **uncon'trollable,** *a.* (enfant) ingouvernable; (désir) irrésistible; u. laughter, fou rire *m.* **-ably,** *adv.* irrésistiblement. **uncon'ventional,** *a.* original, non-conformiste. **uncon'vinced,** *a.* sceptique (of, à l'égard de). **uncon'vincing,** *a.* peu convaincant, peu vraisemblable. **un'cooked,** *a.* (aliment) non cuit, cru. **un'cork,** *v.tr.* déboucher (une bouteille). **un'couth,** *a.* grossier; malappris, gauche. **un'cover,** *v.tr.* découvrir (qch.); mettre (qch.) à découvert. **un'crushable,** *a.* (tissu) infroissable. **un'cultivated,** *a.* (terrain) inculte; (personne) sans culture. **un'damaged,** *a.* non endommagé; indemne; intact. **unde'cided,** *a.* indécis; (of pers.) irrésolu, hésitant. **unde'cipherable,** *a.* (écriture) indéchiffrable. **unde'finable,** *a.* indéfinissable. **unde'fined,** *a.* non défini; indéterminé; vague. **unde'monstrative,** *a.* peu expansif; réservé. **unde'niable,** *a.* indéniable, incontestable. **-ably,** *adv.* incontestablement; indiscutablement.

under [ˈʌndər]. I. *prep.* 1. sous; audessous de u. water, sous l'eau; put it u. the table, mettez-le sous la table; to speak u. one's breath, parler à mi-voix; the u.-thirties, les moins de trente ans. 2. (a) u. lock and key, sous clef; u. these circumstances, dans ces conditions; u. his father's will, sous le testament de son père; to be u. the necessity of . . ., être dans la nécessité de . . . ; (b) to be u. s.o., être sous le commandement de qn. 3. u. repair, en réparation; patient u. treatment, malade en traitement. II. *adv.* 1. (au-)dessous; as u., comme ci-dessous. 2. (in compounds) trop peu; insuffisamment; to underpay, mal rétribuer. III. *a.* (used mainly in compounds) 1. de dessous; inférieur; **underlip,** lèvre inférieure. 2. subalterne; **u.-gardener,** aide-jardinier. 3. insuffisant; **under-dose,** dose *f* trop faible. **'undercarriage,** *s. Av:* train *m* d'atterrissage. **'underclothes,** *spl,* **underclothing,** *s.* linge *m* (de corps); lingerie *f* (féminine). **'underdog,** *s. coll.* the u., les

opprimés. **'under'done,** *a.* pas assez cuit; (bœuf) saignant. **'under'fed,** *a.* mal nourri; sous-alimenté. **'underfoot,** *adv.* sous les pieds; to trample sth. u., fouler qch. aux pieds. **'undergo,** *v.tr.* subir (un changement, une épreuve); éprouver (une perte, etc.). **under'graduate,** *s.* étudiant, -ante (d'université). **'underground.** 1. *adv.* (a) sous terre; (b) secrètement. 2. *a.* (a) souterrain; (b) clandestin. 3. *s.* the u., le métro. **'undergrowth,** *s.* broussailles *fpl;* sous-bois *m.* **'underhand,** *a.* secret; (of pers.) sournois. **'under'line,** *v.tr.* souligner. **'underlying,** *a.* au-dessous; (principe) fondamental. **'under'mine,** *v.tr.* miner, saper; s'abîmer lentement (la santé). **under'neath.** 1. *prep.* au-dessous de; sous. 2. *adv.* au-dessous; dessous; par-dessous. 3. *a.* de dessous; inférieur. **'under'paid,** *a.* mal rétribué. **'underpass,** *s.* passage *m* inférieur (sous une route). **'under'pay,** *v.tr.* mal rétribuer. **'under'privileged,** *a.* déshérité; économiquement faible. **'under'rate,** *v.tr.* sous-estimer. **under'signed,** *a.* & *s.* soussigné, -ée. **under'stand,** *v.tr.* comprendre. **under'standable,** *a.* compréhensible; that's u., cela se comprend. **under'standing.** I. *s.* 1. compréhension *f.* 2. accord *m,* entente *f.* II. *a.* qui comprend, compréhensif. **'understudy.** I. *v.tr. Th:* doubler (un rôle). II. *s. Th:* doublure *f.* ‡**'under'take,** *v.tr.* se charger de, assumer (une tâche). **'undertaker,** *s.* entrepreneur *m* de pompes funèbres. **'undertaking,** *s.* 1. entreprise *f.* 2. engagement *m,* promesse *f.* 3. métier *m* d'entrepreneur de pompes funèbres. **'underwear,** *F:* undies, *s.* linge *m* (de corps); lingerie *f.*

'unde'served, *a.* immérité. **unde'servedly** [-idli], *adv.* à tort; injustement. **unde'sirable,** *a.* & *s.* indésirable (mf). **'unde'veloped,** *a.* non développé; (terrain) inculte. **un'dignified,** *a.* peu digne; qui manque de dignité. **un'diplo'matic,** *a.* peu diplomatique; peu adroit. **un'disciplined,** *a.* indiscipliné. **undis'criminating,** *a.* (of pers.) sans discernement; (of taste) peu averti. **'undis'puted,** *a.* incontesté. **'undis'tinguishable,** *a.* 1. indiscernable (from, de). 2. imperceptible. **undis'tinguished,** *a.* médiocre; (représentation) quelconque. **undis'turbed,** *a.* tranquille; paisible; qui n'a pas été dérangé. ‡**un'do,** *v.tr.* défaire (qch.); dénouer (un nœud); réparer (le mal). **un'doing,** *s.* ruine *f;* perte *f.* **un'doubted,** *a.* indubitable, incontestable. **un'doubtedly** [-idli], *adv.* indubitablement; assurément; sans aucun doute. **un'dress,** *v.i. & tr.* (se) déshabiller. 'undue, a. (influence) illégitime; (optimisme) excessif, indu. undulate ['ʌndjuleit], v.tr. & i. onduler. 'undulating, a. onduleux. undu'lation, s. ondulation f.

un'duly, adv. 1. indûment. 2. à l'excès, outre mesure. un'earth, v.tr. déterrer, exhumer. un'earthly, a. (a) surnaturel; sinistre; (b) F: (bruit) de tous les diables; at an u. hour, à une heure indue. un'easiness, s. gêne f, malaise m; inquiétude f. un'easy, a. mal à l'aise, gêné; inquiet; (sommeil) agité. un'easily, adv. d'un air gêné; avec inquiétude. un'eatable, a. immangeable. uneco'nomic, a. non rentable. uneco'nomical, a. (of pers.) peu économe; (méthode) peu économique. un'educated, a. sans instruction; ignorant. unem'ployed, a. sans travail; s. the u., les chômeurs m. unem'ployment, s. chômage m. un'enviable, a. peu enviable. un'equal, a. inégal; to be u. to the task, ne pas être à la hauteur de sa tâche. -ally, adv. inégalement. un'equalled, a. sans égal. un'even, a. inégal; rugueux; irrégulier. un'eventful, a. sans incidents; (vie) calme. unex'ceptionable, a. irréprochable; (conduite) inattaquable. unex'pected, a. inattendu; (résultat) imprévu, inespéré. -ly, adv. de manière inattendue; inopinément. un'failing, a. 1. (moyen) infaillible, sûr; (bonne humeur) inaltérable. 2. (source) intarissable. un'fair, a. 1. (of pers.) injuste. 2. inéquitable; u. play, jeu déloyal. -ly, adv. injustement; inéquitablement. unfa'miliar, a. (visage) étranger, inconnu; peu familier. un'fashionable, a. démodé. un'fasten, v.tr. détacher (qch. de qch.); défaire (un vêtement). un'favourable, a. défavorable; (critique) adverse; (of terms) désavantageux (to, à). un'finished, a. inachevé; (ouvrage) imparfait; Ind: non façonné. un'fit, a. impropre (for, à) inapte (au service militaire); (of road) impraticable (aux voitures). un'flattering, a. peu flatteur. un'fold, v.tr. & i. déplier (un journal); (se) déployer; (se) dérouler. un'fore'seen, a. imprévu; inattendu. unfor'gettable, a. inoubliable. unfor'givable, a. impardonnable. unfor'giving, a. implacable, rancunier. unfor'gotten, a. inoublié. un'fortunate, a. malheureux; to be u., avoir de la malchance; (erreur) regrettable; how u.! quel malheur! quel dommage! -ly, adv. malheureusement; par malheur. un'founded, a. sans fondement. ‡un'freeze, v.tr. dégeler; Fin: débloquer. un'friendliness, s. hostilité (towards, contre). un'friendly, a. peu amical; mal disposé (envers qn). un'furnished, a. non meublé.

un'gainly, a. gauche, lourd. 'unget'-attable, a. F: inaccessible. un'graceful, a. disgracieux; gauche. -ly, adv. gauchement. un'gracious, a. peu aimable. -ly, adv. de mauvaise grâce. un'grateful, a. peu reconnaissant; ingrat. -fully, adv. avec ingratitude. un'gratefulness, s. ingratitude f. 'un'grudging, a. 1. donné de bon cœur. 2. libéral, généreux. -ly, adv. de bonne grâce; libéralement. 'un'guarded, a. 1. sans défense. 2. (of speech) inconsidéré; in an u. moment, dans un moment d'inattention. un'-happiness, s. chagrin m. un'happy, a. malheureux, triste; infortuné. -ily, adv. (a) malheureusement; (b) tristement. un'harmed, a. sain et sauf; indemne. un'healthy, a. malsain; insalubre; (of pers.) maladif. un'heard, a. 1. to condemn s.o. u., condamner qn sans l'entendre. 2. u. of, (i) inouï; (ii) inconnu. un'hesitating, a. sans hésitation; prompt; (réponse) ferme. -ly, adv. sans hésiter. un-i'dentified, a. non identifié.

uniform ['ju:nifɔ:m], a. & s. uniforme (m). -ly, adv. uniformément. uni'formity, s. uniformité f; unité f (de style); régularité f (de fonctionnement). uni'maginable, a. inimaginable. un-im'portant, a. sans importance. 'unin'habitable, a. inhabitable. 'unin'habited, a. inhabité. 'unin'telligent, a. à l'esprit borné. 'unin'telligible, a. inintelligible. 'unin'tentional, a. involontaire. -ally, adv. involontairement; sans le vouloir. un'interested, a. indifférent. un'interesting, a. peu intéressant; sans intérêt. 'unin'terrupted, a. 1. ininterrompu. 2. (of food) peu appétissant.

union ['ju:njən], s. 1. union f; concorde f, harmonie f. 2. (trade) u., syndicat m; customs u., union douanière. unique [ju'ni:k], a. unique. unit ['ju:nit], s. unité f; u. price, prix unitaire; u. furniture, mobilier m par éléments. unite [ju'nait], v.tr. unir. 'unity, s. unité f. universe ['ju:nivəːs], s. univers m. uni'versal, a. universel. university [ju:ni'vɔ:siti], s. université f; u. town, ville universitaire. un'just, a. injuste. -ly, adv. injustement. unjusti'fiable, a. injustifiable, inexcusable. un'justified, a. non justifié. un'kempt, a. mal soigné; mal tenu; (of hair) mal peigné. un'kind, a. (a) dur; cruel; (b) peu aimable. -ly, adv. méchamment; durement; sans bienveillance. un'kindness, s. méchanceté f; manque m de bienveillance. un'known, a. inconnu (to, à, de); ignoré (to, de).

unless [ʌn'les], conj. à moins que . . . (ne); u. I am mistaken, si je ne me trompe pas; u. I hear to the contrary, à moins d'avis contraire.

'un'like, a. différent (de qch.); not u., assez ressemblant (à qn, qch.); that's u. him! je ne le reconnais pas là! un'li(c)e)able, a. sympathique. un'likely, a. peu probable; invraisemblable. un'load, v.tr. décharger (un camion). un'lock, v.tr. ouvrir (la porte). un'lucky, a. malheureux; malencontreux; how u.! quelle malchance! it's u., cela porte malheur. -ily, adv. malheureusement. un-'manageable, a. 1. intraitable; (enfant) intenable. 2. difficile à manier. un'mannerly, a. malappris; grossier. 'un'marketable, a. invendable. un-'married, a. célibataire. un'merited, a. immérité. unmis'takable, a. clair; évident; facilement reconnaissable. -ably, adv. nettement, évidemment; à ne pas s'y méprendre. un'mounted, a. non monté; (of gem) non serti. un'necessary, a. inutile, superflu. -ily, adv. 1. sans nécessité; inutilement. 2. plus que de raison. un'noticed, a. inaperçu, inobservé. unob'servant, a. peu observateur. unob'tainable, a. impossible à obtenir, à se procurer. unob'trusive, a. discret; effacé, modeste. -ly, adv. discrètement. un-'occupied, a. 1. sans occupation. 2. inhabité. 3. (place) libre, disponible. uno'fficial, a. non officiel; non confirmé; (renseignement) officieux. un-'opposed, a. sans opposition. un'pack, v.tr. déballer, dépaqueter (des objets); défaire (une valise); abs. défaire ses bagages. un'paid, a. 1. non payé; (of post) non rétribué. 2. (of debt) impayé; non acquitté. un'palatable, a. désagréable. un'pardonable, a. impardonnable. unpatri'otic, a. (of pers.) peu patriotique; (of action) antipatriotique. un'perturbed, a. impassible; peu ému. un'pleasant, a. désagréable, déplaisant; fâcheux. -ly, adv. désagréablement; fâcheusement. un'pleasantness, s. (a) caractère m désagréable (de qch.); (b) désagrément m, ennui m. un'polished, a. (a) non poli; mat; (pierre) brut; (b) rude, grossier. un'popular, a. impopulaire; to make oneself u., se faire mal voir. un'practical, a. peu pratique; (projet) impraticable. un'precedented, a. (i) sans précédent; (ii) sans exemple; inédit. un'prejudiced, a. sans préjugés; désintéressé. unpre'pared, a. (discours) improvisé; to catch s.o. u., prendre qn au dépourvu. unpre'tentious, a. sans prétention; modeste. un'principled, a. sans principes; sans scrupule. un'profitable, a. Com: sans profit; peu rentable; (travail) inutile.

unpro'tected, a. (a) inabrité; sans défense; (b) Ind: E: exposé; sans carter; sans garde-fou. un'published, a. inédit; non publié. un'punctual, a. (a) inexact; (b) en retard; pas à l'heure. unpunctu'ality, s. inexactitude f; manque m de ponctualité. un'punished, a. impuni. un'qualified, a. 1. (a) incompétent; Jur: inhabile (à voter); (b) sans diplômes. 2. (éloges) sans réserve. un'questionable, a. indiscutable, indubitable; hors de doute. -ably, adv. indubitablement, sans aucun doute. un'questioning, a. (obéissance) aveugle; sans hésitation ni murmure. ‡un'ravel, v.tr. démêler. un'readable, a. illisible. unreason-able, a. déraisonnable; don't be u., soyez raisonnable; u. demand, demande f exorbitante. -ably, adv. d'une manière peu raisonnable. un'recognizable, a. méconnaissable. unre'lated, a. (of things) sans rapport; (of pers.) sans (aucun) lien de parenté. unre'lenting, a. (of pers.) implacable, impitoyable (towards, à, pour); (of persecution) acharné. unrelia'bility, s. instabilité (de qn). unre'liable, a. (homme) sur lequel on ne peut pas compter; (machine) d'un fonctionnement incertain; (carte) peu fidèle. unre'pentant, a. impénitent. unre-'served, a. (a) sans réserve; (b) u. seats, places fpl non réservées. unre'servedly [-idli], adv. sans réserve; franchement; entièrement. unre'sisting, a. soumis, docile. unre'sponsive, a. (of pers.) froid. unre'st, s. social u., malaise m social; labour u., agitation f ouvrière. unre'stricted, a. sans restriction. unre'warded, a. sans récompense. un'ripe, a. (fruit) vert, pas mûr; (blé) en herbe. un'rivalled, a. sans rival; sans pareil. un'roadworthy, a. Aut: inapte à rouler. un'roll, v.tr. & i. (se) dérouler. un'ruffled, a. calme. un-'safe, a. (a) dangereux, hasardeux; (b) exposé au danger. un'saleable, a. invendable. un'sanitary, a. peu hygiénique; insalubre. unsatis'factory, a. peu satisfaisant; (of explanation) peu convaincant. -ily, adv. d'une manière peu satisfaisante. un'satisfied, a. peu satisfait; (of appetite) inassouvi. unscien'tific, a. non scientifique; peu scientifique. un'screw, v.tr. dévisser. un'scrupulous, a. indélicat; sans scrupules. -ly, adv. peu scrupuleusement. un'seen, a. inaperçu, invisible; Sch: s. version f, (texte de) traduction f à livre ouvert. unself'conscious, a. naturel, sans contrainte. un'selfish, a. (of pers.) généreux; sans égoïsme; (motif) désintéressé. -ly, adv. généreusement. un'selfishness, s. générosité f; désintéressement m. un'settled, a. (a) (pays) troublé; (temps) variable; (esprit) inquiet; (b) (of question) indécis; (of bill) impayé; (c) (pays) sans habitants. un'settling, a. troublant. un'shakable, a. inébranlable; (amitié) à toute épreuve. un'shaken, a. inébranlé, ferme; to remain u., tenir bon. un'shrinkable, a. irrétrécissable. un'sightly, a. laid, vilain (à voir). un'signed, a. sans signature. un'sinkable, a. insubmersible. un'skilled, a. inexpérimenté (in, à); inexpert (in, dans, en); Ind.: u. worker, manœuvre m. un'sociable, a. insociable; sauvage, farouche. un'solved, a. (problème) non résolu; (mystère) impénétré. unso'phisticated, a. ingénu, naïf, simple. un'sparing, a. (effort) infatigable. un'speakable, a. inexprimable; F: détestable, au-dessous de tout. -ably, adv. ineffablement, indiciblement. un'spoken, a. sous-entendu, tacite. un'sportsmanlike, a. peu loyal. un'stable, a. (of thing) instable, peu sûr; (of pers.) inconstant; (of mind, etc.) déséquilibré. un'stamped, a. (lettre) non affranchi. un'steadiness, s. instabilité f. un'steady, a. peu stable; (of footsteps) chancelant; (of voice) mal assuré; (of character) inconstant. ‡un'stick, v.tr. décoller; (to come unstick, (i) se décoller; (ii) F: s'effondrer (of pers.) qui a échoué; (candidat) (i) refusé; (ii) non élu. -fully, adv. sans succès, vainement. un'suitable, a. (of pers.) inapte (for, à); (of thing) impropre, mal adapté (for, à); (of remark) déplacé. unsy'mmetrical, a. asymétrique. unsympa'thetic, a. froid, indifférent. -ally, adv. sans compassion, froidement. un'tamed, a. sauvage; indompté. un'thinkable, a. inimaginable; impensable. un'thinking, a. irréfléchi, étourdi. -ly, adv. sans (y) penser; étourdiment. un'tidiness, s. désordre m; manque m d'ordre. un'tidy, a. (of room) en désordre; (of hair) mal peigné; (of appearance) négligé; (of pers.) désordonné. -ily, adv. sans ordre; sans soin. un'tie, v.tr. dénouer; défaire (un nœud), détacher (un chien).

until [ʌn'til]. I. prep. jusqu'à; u. evening, jusqu'au soir; not u., pas avant. II. conj. jusqu'à ce que; not u., pas avant que.

un'tiring, a. inlassable, infatigable; (travail) assidu. un'told, a. (of wealth) immense; (of tale) non raconté. un'trained, a. inexpert, inexpérimenté; (animal) non dressé. un'troubled, a. calme, tranquille. un'true, a. (of statement) faux, mensonger. un'trustworthy, a. (of pers.) indigne de confiance; (témoin) récusable; (renseignement) douteux, sujet à caution. un'truthful, a. menteur, a. un'used, a.

1. [ʌn'juːzd] inutilisé; non employé. 2. [ʌn'juːst] (of pers.) peu habitué (to, à). un'usual, a. peu commun; insolite; inhabituel. un'varying, a. invariable; constant; monotone. un'veil, v.tr. dévoiler; inaugurer (une statue). un'wanted, a. non désiré, non voulu; superflu. un'warranted, a. (action) injustifiable. un'warranted, a. injustifié; (of insult) gratuit; (of remark) déplacé. un'welcome, a. (of news) fâcheux; (of pers.) importun. un'well, a. souffrant, désagréable. un'wholesome, a. (aliment) malsain. un'wieldy, a. peu maniable; peu servable; peu disposé (à faire qch.). -ly, adv. à contre-cœur; de mauvaise grâce; à regret. un'willingness, s. mauvaise volonté f; mauvaise grâce f; répugnance f (à faire qch.). un'wise, a. imprudent, peu sage; malavisé. -ly, adv. imprudemment. un'workable, a. (projet) impraticable. un'worthy, a. indigne; (conduite) méprisable; (travail) peu méritoire. ‡un'wrap, v.tr. défaire, désenvelopper. un'yielding, a. inébranlable, opiniâtre, inflexible.

up [ʌp]. I. adv. 1. (a) en montant; vers le haut; to go up, all the way up (the stairs), jusqu'au haut (de l'escalier); (b) to go up north, aller dans le nord; to go up to town, aller à Londres; to go up to the university, aller à l'université; (c) from five pounds up, à partir de cinq livres; from my youth up, dès ma jeunesse. 2. (a) en haut; up there, là-haut; up above eth, au-dessus de qch.; the moon is up, la lune est levée; P.N.: Road up, Travaux; (b) en dessus; (c) up in Yorkshire, au nord, dans le Yorkshire. 3. (a) to go up in price, subir une hausse de prix; things are looking up, les affaires sont à la hausse; Sp: to be one goal up, mener par un but; (b) to screw up, visser, serrer; his blood was up, il était monté; (c) to be well up in a subject, connaître un sujet à fond; (d) to praise s.o. up, vanter qn; to speak up, parler plus haut. 4. (a) debout, levé; to get up, se lever; hold yourself up! tenez-vous droit! (b) to be up all night, ne pas se coucher de la nuit; (c) to be up against (s.o., sth.), avoir affaire à (qn, qch.); F: to be up against it, avoir la déveine, la guigne. 5. F: what's up? que se passe-t-il? 6. time's up, il est l'heure (de finir, de fermer, etc.); c'est l'heure; his leave's up, sa permission est expirée; F: the game's up, tout est perdu. 7. up to; (a) jusqu'à; up up to now, to s.o., s'avancer vers qn; (b) up to now, to here, jusqu'ici; (c) to be up to a job, être à la hauteur d'une tâche. II. prep. 1. to be up the tree, être en haut de l'arbre. 2. up the river, en amont; **to walk up and down,** se promener de long en large. III. *attrib. a.* Rail: **up line,** voie paire; la voie en direction de Londres. IV. *s.* **the ups and downs of life,** les péripéties *f* de la vie. **'up-and-'coming,** *a.* (jeune homme) d'avenir. **'up-and-'up,** *s. F:* **to be on the u.-a.-u.,** (i) prospérer; (ii) être honnête. **'upbringing,** *s.* éducation *f* (d'un enfant). **up'heaval,** *s.* 1. soulèvement *m*; commotion *f*, bouleversement *m*. 2. agitation *f*, convulsion *f* (politique). **uphill.** 1. *a.* (of *road*) montant (*of task*) ardu, rude. 2. *adv.* **to go u.,** monter; aller en montant. **‡up'hold,** *v.tr.* supporter, soutenir, maintenir. **up'holstery,** *s.* (*a*) tapisserie *f* d'ameublement; (*b*) garniture *f* d'intérieur (d'une voiture). **'upkeep,** *s.* (frais *mpl* d')entretien *m*. **u'pon,** *prep.* sur. **'upper,** *a.* 1. supérieur; (plus)haut, (plus) élevé; de dessus; d'au-dessus; **the u. storey,** l'étage supérieur. 2. supérieur (en rang, etc.); **to have the u. hand,** avoir le dessus. **'uppermost.** 1. *a.* (*a*) le plus haut; le plus élevé; (*b*) de la plus grande importance; premier, **to be u.,** prédominer; tenir le premier rang; avoir l'avantage. 2. *adv.* face u., face en dessus. **'upright.** I. *a.* 1. vertical; perpendiculaire; droit; **to set sth. u.,** mettre qch. debout, d'aplomb. 2. (of *conduct*) droit, intègre, honnête. II. *s. Civ.E:* montant *m*; jambage *m*. **'uproar,** *s.* vacarme *m*, tapage *m*; **the town's in an u.,** la ville est en effervescence. **up'roarious,** *a.* tumultueux, tapageur. **-ly,** *adv.* tumultueusement. **up'root,** *v.tr.* déraciner, arracher (une plante, un mal). **'upset.** I. *s.* 1. renversement *m* (d'une voiture). 2. (*a*) bouleversement *m*; désordre *m*; (*b*) ennui *m*; (*c*) dérangement *m* (du corps). II. **‡up'set** 1. *v.tr.* (*a*) renverser (qch.); culbuter (qn); (*b*) désorganiser, déranger (les plans de qn); (*c*) dérégler, déranger (l'estomac); troubler (la digestion). 2. *v.i.* se renverser; (of *boat*) chavirer. **'upshot,** *s.* résultat *m*, dénouement *m* (d'une affaire, etc.). **'upside 'down,** *adv. phr.* (*a*) sens dessus dessous; la tête en bas; **to hold sth. u. d.,** tenir qch. à l'envers; (*b*) en désordre; bouleversé; **to turn everything u. d.,** tout bouleverser. **up'stairs.** 1. *adv.* en haut (de l'escalier); **to go u.,** monter. 2. *a.* (of *room*, etc.) d'en haut. **'uptake,** *s. F:* **to be slow, quick, in the u.,** (i) avoir la compréhension lente; (ii) avoir l'esprit vif. **'up-to-'date,** *attrib. a.* moderne, de son temps; *F:* à la page. **'upward,** *a.* (mouvement) ascensionnel; ascendant; **u.** gradient, montée *f*; (of *prices*) **u.** tendency, tendance *f* à la hausse. **'upwards,** *adv.* de bas en haut; vers

le haut; en montant. 2. en dessus; **to look u.,** regarder en haut, en l'air. 3. au-dessus; **£100 and u.,** cent livres et au-dessus; **from ten years old u.,** à partir de dix ans.

uranium [ju(ə)'reiniəm], *s.* uranium *m*.

urban [ə:'bən], *a.* urbain. **urbani'zation,** *s.* urbanisation *f*.

urbane [ə:'bein], *a.* courtois, poli.

urge [ə:dʒ]. I. *s.* incitation *f*; poussée *f*; **u.** to write, démangeaison *f* d'écrire. II. *v.tr.* encourager, (qn à faire qch.). **'urgency,** *s.* urgence *f*; extrémité *f* (d'un besoin). **'urgent,** *a.* urgent, pressant. **-ly,** *adv.* avec instance; avec insistance; instamment.

urn [ə:n], *s.* (tea-)u., fontaine *f* (à thé); samovar *m*.

us [ʌs, əs], *pers.pron.* (*object*) nous.

use. I. *s.* [ju:s]. 1. emploi *m*, usage *m*; utilisation *f*; **to make u. of sth.,** se servir de qch.; **ready for u.,** prêt à servir; **directions for u.,** mode d'emploi. 2. **to have the u. of sth.,** avoir le droit de se servir de qch.; **he has lost the u. of his left leg,** il a perdu l'usage de la jambe gauche. 3. utilité *f*; **it's no u.,** cela ne sert à rien; **to have no u. for sth.,** n'avoir que faire de qch.; **what's the u.?** à quoi bon? II. *v.tr.* [ju:z]. 1. se servir de (qch.); utiliser (qch.); employer (la force); **to u. discretion,** agir avec discrétion. 2. **to u. sth. up,** (i) épuiser, consommer (qch.); (ii) tirer parti de (qch.). 3. (*aux.*, *past tense*) **I used to do it,** j'avais l'habitude de le faire; **things aren't what they used to be,** ce n'est plus comme autrefois. **'usage** ['ju:z-], *s.* usage *m*, coutume *f*. **used,** *a.* 1. ['ju:zd] usagé; **u.** cars, voitures d'occasion. 2. ['ju:st] **to be u. to sth.,** accoutumé, habitué à qch. **'useful** ['ju:s-], *a.* utile. **-fully,** *adv.* utilement. **'usefulness** ['ju:s-], *s.* utilité *f*. **'useless** ['ju:s-], *a.* inutile; bon à rien; inefficace. **-ly,** *adv.* inutilement, en vain. **'uselessness,** *s.* inutilité *f*. **'user** ['ju:z-], *s.* usager, -ère. **'usual** ['ju:z-], *a.* usuel, habituel, ordinaire; **earlier than u.,** plus tôt que d'habitude; **as u.,** comme d'habitude. **-ally,** *adv.* ordinairement, habituellement, d'habitude.

usher ['ʌʃər], *v.tr.* introduire, faire entrer (qn); **to u. s.o. out,** reconduire qn. **ushe'rette,** *s. Cin:* ouvreuse *f*.

usurp [ju'zə:p], *v.tr.* usurper (from, sur); **to u. s.o.'s rights,** empiéter sur les droits de qn. **u'surper,** *s.* usurpateur, -trice.

utensil [ju(:)'tensl], *s.* ustensile *m*.

utilize ['ju:tilaiz], *v.tr.* utiliser, se servir de (qch.); tirer profit de (qch.). **util'tarian,** *a.* utilitaire. **u'tility,** *s.* (*a*) utilité *f*; (*b*) public u., service *m* public. **utili'zation,** *s.* utilisation *f*.

utter[1] ['ʌtər], a. complet, absolu; **an u. fool**, un parfait imbécile. **-ly**, adv. complètement, absolument, tout à fait. **'utmost** (also **uttermost**). I. a. extrême; dernier; **with the u. ease**, avec la plus grande facilité. II. s. dernière limite f; dernier degré m; **to the u. of my ability**, dans toute la mesure de mes moyens; **to do one's u.**, faire tout son possible. **utter**[2], v.tr. pousser (un cri); prononcer (un mot).

V

V, v [vi:], s. (la lettre) V, v m.

vacant ['veikənt], a. 1. vacant, vide, libre; **v. space**, place libre. 2. (regard) distrait, vague. **-ly**, adv. d'un air distrait, le regard perdu. **'vacancy**, s. poste m vacant; (on boarding house) **no vacancies!** complet! **va'cate**, v.tr. quitter (une chambre d'hôtel, etc.); évacuer (une maison). **va'cation**, s. vacances fpl.

vaccination [væksi'neiʃ(ə)n], s. vaccination f. **'vaccinate**, v.tr. vacciner. **'vaccine**, s. vaccin m.

vacuum ['vækjuəm], s. Ph: vide m; **v. packed**, emballé sous vide; **v. cleaner**, aspirateur m; **v. flask**, bouteille f isolante.

vagrant ['veigrənt], s. Jur: vagabond, -onde.

vague [veig], a. vague; imprécis; (of outline) estompé, flou; **I haven't the vaguest idea**, je n'en ai pas la moindre idée. **-ly**, adv. vaguement. **'vagueness**, s. vague m, imprécision f.

vain [vein], a. 1. vain; **in v.**, en vain. 2. vaniteux; (of woman) coquette. **-ly**, adv. vainement, en vain.

valet ['vælei], s. valet m de chambre.

valiant ['væljənt], a. vaillant.

valid ['vælid], a. valide, valable; bon; **no longer v.**, périmé. **va'lidity**, s. validité f (d'un document); force f (d'un argument).

†**valley** ['væli], s. vallée f.

value ['vælju:]. I. s. valeur f; of no v., sans valeur; Com: **market v.**, valeur marchande; **this article is very good v.**, cet article est très avantageux. II. v.tr. Com: 1. évaluer, estimer (un article). 2. estimer, tenir à (sa vie). **'valuable**. 1. a. (objet) précieux, de valeur, de prix. 2. s.pl. objets mpl de valeur, de prix. **valu'ation**, s. 1. évaluation f, estimation f; Jur: expertise f. 2. valeur f estimée. **'valueless**, a. sans valeur. **'valuer**, s. estimateur m, commissaire-priseur m, expert m.

valve [vælv], s. 1. soupape f, clapet m. 2. Rad: lampe f; tube m. 3. valvule f (du cœur).

van [væn], s. 1. Aut: camionnette f; fourgon m (de déménagement). 2. Rail: wagon m; fourgon.

vanadium [və'neidiəm], s. vanadium m.

vandalism ['vændəlizm], s. vandalisme m.

vanilla [və'nilə], s. vanille f; **v. ice**, glace à la vanille.

vanish ['væniʃ], v.i. disparaître.

vanity ['væniti], s. vanité f; orgueil m.

vaporize ['veipəraiz], v.tr. & i. (se) vaporiser. **'vaporizer**, s. pulvérisateur m; atomiseur m. **'vapour**, s. vapeur f.

varicose ['værikous], a. **v. vein**, varice f.

varnish ['vɑ:niʃ]. I. s. vernis m; **v. remover**, (i) Com: décapant m; (ii) (for nails) dissolvant m. II. v.tr. vernir; vernisser.

vary ['vɛəri], v.tr. & i. varier; v.i. différer (d'avis). **'variable**, a. variable. **vari'ation**, s. variation f; changement m. **'varied**, a. varié, divers. **'variegated**, a. 1. varié, divers. 2. bigarré, barriolé; panaché. **va'riety**, s. 1. variété f. 2. Th: **v. turns**, numéros m de music-hall. **'various**, a. 1. varié, divers. 2. différent; plusieurs; **for v. reasons**, pour plusieurs raisons; **at v. times**, à différentes reprises. **'varying**, a. variable, changeant; varié, divers.

vase [vɑ:z], s. vase m.

vast [vɑ:st], a. vaste, immense.

vat [væt], s. cuve f; bac m; bain m.

vault[1] [vɔ:lt], s. 1. voûte f. 2. souterrain m; **wine-v.**, cave f. **'vaulted**, a. voûté; en voûte.

vault[2], v.i. & tr. sauter (un obstacle).

veal [vi:l], s. Cu: veau m.

veer [viər], v.i. (a) (of wind) tourner; (b) (of pers.) **to v. round**, changer d'opinion; (c) Nau: filer (de la chaîne).

vegetable ['vedʒitəbl]. 1. a. végétal. 2. s. légume m; **early vegetables**, primeurs f; **v. garden**, potager m. **vege'tarian**, a. & s. végétarien, -ienne. **'vegetate**, v.i. végéter. **vege'tation**, s. végétation f.

vehemence ['vi:əməns], s. véhémence f. **'vehement**, a. véhément. **-ly**, adv. passionnément.

vehicle ['vi:ikl], s. véhicule m.

veil [veil]. I. s. voile m. II. v.tr. voiler.

vein [vein], s. 1. Anat: veine f. 2. nervure f (de feuille). 3. Min: filon m.

velocity [vi'lɔsiti], s. vitesse f.

velvet ['velvit], s. velours m. **'velvety**, a. velouté, velouteux.

vendor ['vendər], s. vendeur, -euse.

veneer [və'niər]. I. s. 1. placage m, revêtement m (de bois mince). 2. **a v. of politeness**, une politesse toute en surface. II. v.tr. plaquer (le bois).

venerate ['venəreit], v.tr. vénérer. **'venerable**, a. vénérable. **vene'ration**, s. vénération f (for, pour qn).

venereal [vi'niəriəl], a. Med: vénérien.

vengeance [ven(d)ʒ(ə)ns], s. vengeance f.; to take v., se venger (on s.o., sur qn, de qn).

venison ['venizn], s. chevreuil m.

venom ['venəm], s. venin m. 'venomous. a. 1. venimeux. 2. v. tongue, langue f de vipère. -ly, adv. d'une manière venimeuse.

vent [vent]. I. s. 1. trou m, orifice m. 2. to give v. to anger, donner libre cours à la colère. II. v.tr. to v. one's anger on s.o., passer sa colère sur qn.

ventilate ['ventileit], v.tr. aérer; ventiler. venti'lation, s. aération f, aérage m, ventilation f. 'ventilator, s. ventilateur m.

ventriloquist [ven'trilǝkwist], s. ventriloque mf.

venture ['ventʃər]. I. s. 1. entreprise f risquée; Com: spéculation f. 2. at a v., à l'aventure, au hasard. II. v. 1. v.tr. (a) oser (faire qch.); (b) hasarder, risquer (sa vie, son argent). 2. v.i. (a) to v. to do sth., se risquer à faire qch.; (b) s'aventurer (en pays inconnu); to v. out of doors, se risquer à sortir. 'venturesome, a. 1. aventureux, osé. 2. (of action) aventuré, risqué.

veranda(h) [və'rændə], s. véranda f.

verb [vəːb], s. verbe m. 'verbal, a. verbal, oral. -ally, adv. de vive voix.

verbatim [vəːˈbeitim], a. & adv. mot pour mot; (rapport, etc.) textuel.

verdict ['vəːdikt], s. 1. Jur: verdict m. 2. jugement m, décision f.

verge [vəːdʒ]. I. s. bord m; accotement m (d'une route); on the v. of ruin, à deux doigts de la ruine. II. v.i. to v. on sth., toucher à qch.; friser (la mauvaise foi).

verger ['vəːdʒər], s. Ecc: bedeau m.

verify ['verifai], v.tr. 1. confirmer (un fait). 2. vérifier, contrôler (des renseignements). verifi'cation, s. vérification f, contrôle m.

vermicelli [vəːmi'seli], s. vermicelle m.

vermilion [və'miljən]. 1. s. vermillon m, cinabre m. 2. a. (de) vermillon; vermeil.

vermin ['vəːmin], s. vermine f.

vermouth ['vəːməθ, 'vəːmuːt], s. vermouth(h) m.

versatile ['vəːsətail], a. (a) aux talents variés; (b) (esprit) souple.

verse [vəːs], s. (a) vers m (de poésie); (b) strophe f (d'un poème); (c) verset m (de la Bible); (d) coll. vers mpl; free v., vers libres.

version ['vəːʃ(ə)n], s. version f (des faits); according to his v., d'après lui.

versus ['vəːsəs], prep. esp. Jur: Sp: contre.

vertebrate ['vəːtibrit], a. & s. vertébré (m).

vertical ['vəːtik(ə)l], a. vertical; à pic. -ally, adv. verticalement; d'aplomb.

verve [vəːv], s. verve f.

very ['veri]. I. a. même; at that v. moment, à cet instant même; to the v. day, jour pour jour; at the v. beginning, tout au commencement. II. adv. 1. très; fort, bien; v. good, (i) très bon; (ii) très bien, fort bien; it isn't so v. difficult, ce n'est pas tellement difficile; v. much, beaucoup. 2. the v. first, le tout premier; the v. best, tout ce qu'il y a de meilleur, de mieux.

vespers ['vespəːz], s.pl. Ecc: vêpres f.

vessel ['vesl], s. 1. récipient m. 2. navire m.

vest [vest], s. (for men) gilet m (athlétique); (for women) chemise f américaine, Fr.C: camisole f.

vested ['vestid], a. dévolu; v. interests, droits acquis.

vestige ['vestidʒ], s. vestige m; not a v. of . . ., pas la moindre trace de . . .

vestment ['vestmənt], s. usu. pl. Ecc: vêtements m, ornements m, sacerdotaux. 'vestry, s. Ecc: sacristie f.

vet [vet]. I. s. F: vétérinaire m. II. †v.tr. F: (a) examiner (qn, une bête) (médicalement); (b) revoir, corriger (l'œuvre de qn).

veteran ['vet(ə)rən]. 1. s. vétéran m.; U.S: ancien combattant. 2. a. de vétéran; v. car, vieille voiture (1914-30).

veterinary ['vetrinri], a. v. surgeon, vétérinaire m.

veto ['viːtou]. I. †s. veto m. II. v.tr interdire (qch.); s'opposer à, mettre son veto à (qch.).

vex [veks], v.tr. vexer, fâcher, chagriner. vex'ation, s. (a) contrariété f, ennui m; (b) chagrin m, dépit m. 'vexed, a. 1. contrarié, chagrin. 2. v. question, question souvent débattue, non résolue.

via ['vaiə], prep. via; par la voie de; par (une route).

viaduct ['vaiədʌkt], s. viaduc m.

vibrate [vai'breit], v.i. vibrer; trépider. vi'brating, a. vibrant; (mouvement) vibratoire, oscillant. vi'bration, s. vibration f; oscillation f.

vicar ['vikər], s. Ecc: = curé m. 'vicarage, s. Ecc: = presbytère m; cure f.

vice¹ [vais], s. 1. vice m. 2. défaut m.

vice² [vais], s. étau m; bench-v., étau d'établi.

vice- [vais], prefix. vice-, †vice-'chairman, s. vice-président m. vice-'consul, s. vice-consul m; 'viceroy, s. vice-roi m.

vice versa ['vaisi'vəːsə], adv.phr. vice versa; réciproquement.

vicinity [vi'siniti], s. 1. voisinage m, proximité f (to, with, de). 2. abords mpl, alentours mpl (d'un lieu).

vicious ['viʃəs], a. vicieux; méchant. -ly, adv. 1. vicieusement. 2. méchamment. 'viciousness, s. 1. nature f vicieuse; vice m. 2. méchanceté f.

victim ['viktim], s. victime f. 'victimize, v.tr. 1. exercer des représailles contre (qn). 2. tromper, escroquer (qn).

victor ['viktər], s. vainqueur m. vic'torious, a. victorieux; vainqueur m. 'victory, s. victoire f.

vie [vaɪ], v.i. le disputer (with s.o., à qn); rivaliser (avec qn).

view [vju:]. I. s. vue f; on v., exposé; ouvert au public; field of v. (of telescope), champ m; point of v., point de vue; to hold extreme views, avoir des idées extrémistes; in my v., à mon avis; in v. of . ., en considération de . ., étant donné . .; to have sth. in v., avoir qch. en vue; whom have you in v.? à qui pensez-vous? II. v. 1. v.tr. (a) visiter (une maison à vendre); (b) envisager (qch.) (avec consternation, etc.). 2. v.i. T.V: regarder. 'viewer, s. 1. téléspectateur, -trice. Phot: visionneuse f. 'view-finder, s. Phot: viseur m. 'viewpoint, s. point m de vue.

vigilance ['vidʒiləns], s. vigilance f. 'vigilant, a. vigilant, éveillé, alerte.

vigour ['vigər], s. vigueur f, énergie f. 'vigorous, a. vigoureux, robuste. -ly, adv. vigoureusement.

vile [vaɪl], a. 1. vil; bas, infâme. 2. F: abominable, exécrable; v. temper, humeur massacrante.

villa ['vilə], s. villa f.

village ['vilidʒ], s. village m; attrib. de village, de campagne.

villain ['vilən], s. scélérat m; gredin m; bandit m; Th: etc: le traître. 'villainous, a. 1. vil, infâme. 2. F: abominable, exécrable.

vindicate ['vindikeit], v.tr. défendre (qn); justifier (sa conduite); maintenir (son dire). vindi'cation, s. défense f, apologie f.

vindictive [vin'diktiv], a. vindicatif; rancunier.

vine [vaɪn], s. vigne f; v. grower, viticulteur m; vigneron m; v. growing, viticulture f. v. stock, cep m de vigne. 'vineyard, s. clos m (de vigne); vigne f, vignoble m. 'vintage, s. 1. vendanges fpl; récolte f du raisin. 2. année f (de belle récolte); v. wine, grand vin; guaranteed v. appellation f contrôlée. 3. v. car, vieille voiture d'avant 1914. 'vintner, s. négociant m en vins.

vinegar ['vinigər], s. vinaigre m.

viola¹ [vi'oulə], s. Mus: alto m; v. player, altiste m/f.

viola², s. Bot: pensée f.

violate ['vaɪəleit], v.tr. violer; manquer à (une règle); enfreindre (la loi). vio'lation, s. violation f, infraction f.

violence ['vaɪələns], s. 1. violence f, intensité f (du vent). 2. robbery with v., vol m à main armée. 'violent, a. violent. v. dislike, vive aversion; v.

cold, gros rhume. -ly, adv. violemment; avec violence.

violet ['vaɪəlit]. 1. s. Bot: violette f. 2. a. & s. (colour) violet (m).

violin [vaɪə'lin], s. violon m. violinist, s. violoniste m/f.

violoncello [vaɪələn'tʃelou], s. violoncelle m. violon'cellist, s. violoncelliste m/f.

viper ['vaɪpər], s. vipère f.

virgin ['və:dʒin]. 1. s. vierge f; the Blessed V., la Sainte Vierge. 2. a. de vierge, virginal; v. forest, forêt f vierge.

virile ['virail], a. viril, mâle. v'rility, s. virilité f.

virtual ['və:tjuəl], a. de fait; en fait; to be the v. head of the business, être le vrai chef de la maison. -ally, adv. virtuellement.

virtue ['və:tju:], s. vertu f; by v. of, en vertu de, en raison de. 'virtuous, a. vertueux. -ly, adv. vertueusement.

virulence ['viruləns], s. virulence f. 'virulent, a. virulent. -ly, adv. avec virulence.

virus ['vaɪərəs], s. Med: virus m.

visa ['vi:zə]. I. s. visa m. II. v.tr. viser (un passeport).

viscount ['vaɪkaunt], s. vicomte m. 'viscountess, s. vicomtesse f.

viscous ['viskəs], a. visqueux; gluant.

visible ['vizəbl], a. visible; to become v., apparaître. -ibly, adv. visiblement, manifestement; à vue d'œil. visi'bility, s. visibilité f. 'vision, s. 1. vision f; vue f; field of v., champ visuel. 2. apparition f, fantôme m. 'visionary. I. a. (a) (of pers.) visionnaire; (b) (projet) chimérique. 2. s. visionnaire m/f, illuminé, -ée.

visit ['vizit]. I. s. visite f; séjour m. II. v.tr. visiter (un endroit); rendre visite à (qn); aller voir (qn, qch.). 'visiting, a. Sp: the v. team, les visiteurs m; v. card, carte f de visite; (at hospital) v. hours, heures f de visite. 'visitor, s. visiteur, -euse; summer visitors, estivants m; (at hotel) to sign the visitors' book = remplir sa fiche.

vista ['vistə], s. 1. échappée f (de vue). 2. perspective f (de hêtres, etc.); to open vistas, dégager les vues.

visual ['vizju(ə)l], a. visuel; Sch: teaching by v. aids, enseignement m par l'image. -ally, adv. visuellement. 'visualize, v.tr. se représenter (qch.); évoquer l'image de (qch.).

vital ['vaɪtl], a. vital; of v. importance, d'importance capitale. -ally, adv. d'une manière vitale. vi'tality, s. vitalité f; vigueur f.

vitamin ['vitəmin], s. vitamine f; v. deficiency, avitaminose f.

viva ['vaɪvə], s. Sch: F: (examen) oral m.

vivacious [vi'veiʃəs], *a.* vif, animé. **-ly,** *adv.* avec verve. **vi'vacity,** *s.* vivacité *f*; animation *f*.

vivid ['vivid], *a.* vif, éclatant. **-ly,** *adv.* vivement; avec éclat; (décrire qch.) d'une manière vivante. **'vividness,** *s.* vivacité *f*, éclat *m* (des couleurs).

vivisection [vivi'sek(ə)n], *s.* vivisection *f*.

vixen ['viksn], *s.* 1. *Z:* renarde *f.* 2. mégère *f.*

viz. [viz], *adv.* à savoir . . ; c'est-à-dire. . . .

vocabulary [və'kæbjuləri], *s.* vocabulaire *m.*

vocal ['vouk(ə)l], *a.* vocal. **-ally,** *adv.* vocalement, oralement. **'vocalist,** *s.* chanteur, -euse; cantatrice *f.*

vocation [və'keiʃ(ə)n], *s.* vocation *f.* **vo'cational,** *a.* (enseignement, etc.) professionnel.

vociferate [və'sifəreit], *v.i. & tr.* vociférer (against, contre). **vo'ciferous,** *a.* bruyant, criard, braillard. **-ly,** *adv.* bruyamment.

vogue [voug], *s.* vogue *f*, mode *f.*

voice [vɔis], *s.* 1. voix *f*; to lose one's v., attraper une extinction de voix. II. *v.tr.* exprimer, énoncer (une opinion).

void [vɔid], *a.* 1. *a.* (a) vide; (b) *Jur:* nul; (c) dépourvu, dénué (of, de). 2. *s.* vide *m*; to fill the v., combler le vide.

volcano [vɔl'keinou], *s.* volcan *m.* **vol'canic,** *a.* volcanique.

volition [və'liʃ(ə)n], *s.* volonté *f*; to do sth. of one's own v., faire qch. de son propre gré.

volley ['vɔli], *s.* volée *f.*

volt [voult], *s.* volt *m.* **'voltage,** *s.* tension *f* (en volts); high v., haute tension.

voluble ['vɔljubl], *a.* facile, aisé. **-bly,** *adv.* avec volubilité. **volu'bility,** *s.* volubilité *f.*

volume ['vɔljum], *s.* volume *m*; v. one, tome *m* premier.

volunteer [vɔlən'tiər]. I. *s.* volontaire *m.* II. v. 1. *v.tr.* offrir volontairement (ses services); donner spontanément (des renseignements). 2. *v.i. Mil:* s'engager (comme volontaire). **'voluntary,** *a.* volontaire, spontané; (organisation) bénévole.

voluptuous [və'lʌptjuəs], *a.* voluptueux.

vomit ['vɔmit], *v.tr. & i.* vomir, rendre. **'vomiting,** *s.* vomissement *m.*

voracious [və'reiʃəs], *a.* vorace, dévorant; v. appetite, appétit de loup. **vo'racity,** *s.* voracité *f.*

vote [vout]. I. *s.* 1. (a) vote *m*, scrutin *m*; to put a question to the v., mettre une question aux voix; to take the v., procéder au scrutin; (b) (individual) v., voix *f*, suffrage *m*; to have a v., avoir le droit de vote. 2. motion *f*, résolution *f.* II. *v.i. & tr.* voter. **'voting,** *s.* (participation *f* au) vote; scrutin *m.* **'voter,** *s.* électeur, -trice.

vouch [vautʃ], *v.i.* to v. for, répondre de (qn, la vérité de qch.); se porter garant de (qn). **'voucher,** *s.* *Com:* fiche *f*; reçu *m*, bon *m.*

vow [vau]. I. *s.* vœu *m*, serment *m.* II. *v.tr.* vouer, jurer.

vowel ['vauəl], *s.* voyelle *f.*

voyage ['vɔiidʒ], *s.* voyage *m* sur mer.

vulgar ['vʌlgər], *a.* vulgaire; commun. **-ly,** *adv.* vulgairement. **vul'garity,** *s.* vulgarité *f*, trivialité *f.*

vulnerable ['vʌln(ə)rəbl], *a.* vulnérable.

vulture ['vʌltʃər], *s.* vautour *m.*

W

W, w ['dʌblju:], *s.* (la lettre) W, w *m.*

wad [wɔd], *s.* (a) tampon *m* (d'ouate); (b) liasse *f* (de billets de banque). **'wadding,** *s.* ouate *f* (pour vêtements).

waddle ['wɔdl], *v.i.* se dandiner; marcher en canard.

wade [weid], *v.i.* marcher dans l'eau.

wafer ['weifər], *s.* 1. gaufrette *f.* 2. *Ecc:* hostie *f.*

‡wag [wæg]. I. *v.tr.* agiter, remuer. 2. *v.i.* s'agiter, se remuer.

wage¹ [weidʒ], *s.* gages *mpl*; salaire *m*, paie *f*; w. earner, (a) salarié, -iée; (b) le soutien (de la famille).

wage², *v.tr.* to w. war, faire la guerre.

wager ['weidʒər]. I. *s.* pari *m*; gageure *f.* II. *v.tr.* parier, gager.

wag(g)on ['wæg(ə)n], *s.* 1. charrette *f*; chariot *m.* 2. *Rail:* wagon *m*; fourgon *m.* 3. *F:* (a) to be on the w., s'abstenir de boissons alcooliques; (b) to jump on the band w., se ranger du bon côté.

wail [weil]. I. *v.i.* gémir. II. *s.* cri *m* plaintif; gémissement *m.*

wainscot ['weinskət], *s.* lambris *m.*

waist [weist], *s.* taille *f*, ceinture *f*; w. measurement, tour *m* de taille. **'waistcoat,** *s.* gilet *m.*

wait [weit]. I. *v.i.* (a) attendre; to keep s.o. waiting, faire attendre qn; to w. for s.o., attendre qn; (b) to w. at table, servir. II. *s.* 1. (a) attente *f*; (b) to lie in w., être à l'affût. 2. *pl.* waits, chanteurs *m* de noëls. **'waiter,** *s.* garçon *m* (de restaurant); head w., maître *m* d'hôtel. **'waiting,** *s.* 1. attente *f*; w. room, salle *f* d'attente; *Aut:* no w., stationnement interdit. 2. service *m.* **'waitress,** *s.* serveuse *f* (de restaurant).

waive [weiv], *v.tr.* renoncer à, abandonner; ne pas insister sur.

wake¹ [weik], *s. Nau:* sillage *m.*

‡wake² [weik]. I. *v.i.* to w. (up), se réveiller. 2. *v.tr.* to w. s.o. (up), réveiller qn. **'waken.** 1. *v.tr.* réveiller (qn); éveiller (une émotion). 2. *v.i.* se réveiller.

walk [wɔːk]. I. v.i. 1. marcher. 2. (as opposed to ride) aller à pied. 3. to w. in, out, entrer; sortir; F: to w. out on s.o., (i) abandonner qn; (ii) quitter qn en colère. II. s. 1. marche f. 2. promenade f (à pied). 3. démarche f. 4. allée f (de jardin); avenue f. '**walker**, s. marcheur, -euse; promeneur, -euse; he's a fast w., il marche vite. '**walkie-'talkie**, s. F: émetteur-récepteur m; poste m de radio portatif. '**walking**, s. marche f; promenades fpl à pied; it's within w. distance, on peut s'y rendre à pied; w. pace, allure f du pas; w. stick, canne f. '**walk-out**, s. F: grève f. '**walk-over**, s. victoire f facile; Sp: F: walk-over m.

wall [wɔːl], s. 1. (a) mur m; (b) muraille f; tariff w., barrière f douanière. 2. Min: paroi m d'une galerie). '**wall-paper**, s. papier m peint.

wallet ['wɔlit] s. portefeuille m.

wallaby ['wɔləbi], s. 1. Z: wallaby m. 2. F: Australien m.

wallflower ['wɔːlflauər], s. girofilée f des murailles.

Walloon [wə'luːn]. 1. a. & s. wallon, -onne. 2. s. Ling: wallon m.

wallow ['wɔlou], v.i. se vautrer; se rouler (dans la boue).

walnut ['wɔːlnʌt], s. 1. noix f. 2. w. (tree), noyer m.

walrus ['wɔːlrəs], s. morse m.

waltz [wɔːls]. I. s. valse f. II. v.i. valser.

wan [wɔn], a. blême; blafard; pâle.

wander ['wɔndər], v.i. (a) errer; se promener au hasard; (b) divaguer; avoir le délire. '**wanderer**, s. vagabond, -onde; voyageur, -euse.

wane [wein]. I. v.i. (of moon) décroître, décliner. II. s. moon on the w., lune f à son décours.

want [wɔnt]. I. v. v.i. (a) manquer (for, de); être dépourvu (de); (b) être dans le besoin. 2. v.tr. (a) manquer de, ne pas avoir (qch.); (b) avoir besoin de (qch.); have you all you w.? avez-vous tout ce qu'il vous faut? (c) désirer, vouloir; you are wanted on vous demande. II. s. 1. manque m, défaut m (de jugement, etc.). 2. indigence f, misère f. 3. besoin m; a long-felt w., une lacune à combler. '**wanted**, a. 1. désiré, voulu. 2. recherché par la police. '**wanting**, a. F: faible d'esprit; dépourvu d'intelligence. '**wanton**, a. w. destruction, destruction f pour le simple plaisir de détruire.

war [wɔːr]. I. s. guerre f; cold w., guerre froide. II. v.i. faire la guerre (à qch.). '**warfare**, s. la guerre.

warble ['wɔːbl], v.i. gazouiller. '**warbler**, s. oiseau m chanteur; fauvette f.

ward [wɔːd]. I. s. 1. pupille m. 2. (a) hospital w., salle f d'hôpital; (b) quartier m (de prison). 3. circonscription

f électorale. II. v.tr. to w. off a blow, parer un coup. '**warden**, s. (a) directeur m (d'une institution); (b) traffic w., contractuel m (qui surveille le stationnement des voitures). '**warder**, '**wardress**, s. gardien, -ienne, de prison. '**wardrobe**, s. armoire f; garde-robe f.

ware [wɛər], s. 1. coll: articles m fabriqués; ustensiles mpl (en aluminium, etc.). 2. pl. marchandises fpl. '**warehouse**, s. entrepôt m; magasin m.

warily ['wɛərili], adv. avec circonspection; prudemment.

warm [wɔːm]. I. a. 1. chaud; to be w., avoir chaud; it is w., il fait chaud. 2. (of welcome, etc.) chaleureux. -ly, adv. 1. chaudement. 2. chaleureusement. II. v. 1. v.tr. chauffer. 2. v.i. to w. up, s'échauffer; s'animer; (of pers.) devenir plus cordial. '**warming-pan**, s. bassinoire f. '**warmth**, s. 1. chaleur f. 2. cordialité f.

warn [wɔːn], v.tr. avertir. '**warning**. I. a. (geste) avertisseur; (écriteau, etc.) d'avertissement. II. s. avertissement m; air-raid w., alerte f; without w., sans préavis.

warp [wɔːp]. I. v. 1. v.tr. déjeter, gauchir; Tex: ourdir. 2. v.i. se déjeter, gauchir. II. s. Tex: chaîne f. '**warped**, a. (bois) déjeté, gauchi; (esprit) perverti. '**warping**, s. gauchissement m (du bois); gondolage m (de la tôle).

warrant ['wɔr(ə)nt]. I. s. (a) mandat m (d'arrêt); (b) ordonnance f (de paiement); travel w., feuille f de route. II. v.tr. justifier (une ligne de conduite). '**warranted**, a. Com: garanti. '**warrant officer**, s. (i) Mil: = adjudant-chef m; (ii) Nau: = maître m principal.

warren ['wɔrən], s. garenne f.

warrior ['wɔriər], s. guerrier m; the Unknown W., le Soldat inconnu.

wart [wɔːt], s. verrue f.

wary ['wɛəri], a. avisé, prudent; to be w. of sth., se méfier de qch.

wash [wɔʃ]. I. v.tr. laver; to w. one's hands, se laver les mains; sailor washed overboard, matelot enlevé par une vague; F: that story won't w.! ça ne prend pas. II. s. 1. to have a w., se laver, faire sa toilette. 2. colour w., badigeon m. 3. Nau: sillage m, remous m (d'un navire). '**washable**, a. lavable. '**washbasin**, s. lavabo m. '**washer**, s. machine f à laver; Aut: windscreen w., lave-glace m. '**washing**, s. 1. lavage m; ablutions fpl. 2. lessive f (du linge). 3. Aut: w. bay, installation f de lavage. wash '**out**, v.tr. (a) enlever (une tache); des. (of stain) partir au lavage; (b) laver, rincer (qch.). '**wash-out**, s. F: fiasco m; (of pers.) he's a w.o., c'est un raté. '**washstand**, s. 1. table f de toilette. 2.

U.S: Aut: installation f de lavage. **wash** 'up, v.tr. abs. faire la vaisselle. 'washing-'up, s. (lavage m de) la vaisselle; (in restaurant) plonge f. **washer²** ['wɔʃər], s. E: rondelle f. **waste** [weist]. I. v. 1. v.tr. gaspiller; perdre (du temps). 2. v.i. to w. away, dépérir. II. a. 1. w. land, (i) terre f inculte; (ii) (in town) terrain m vague; to lay w., dévaster, ravager (un pays). 2. (matière) de rebut; w. products, déchets m; w. paper basket, corbeille f à papier(s). III. s. 1. région f inculte. 2. gaspillage m. 3. déchets mpl, rebut m; H: w. disposal unit, broyeur m à ordures; w. pipe, (tuyau m de) trop-plein m. 'wastage, s. 1. gaspillage m. 2. coll. déchets mpl, rebuts mpl. 'wasteful, a. gaspilleur; prodigue. 'wastefulness, s. prodigalité f; gaspillage m. 'waster, s. (a) gaspilleur, -euse; time w., (i) personne f qui perd son temps; (ii) chose f qui vous fait perdre votre temps; (b) vaurien m.

watch [wɔtʃ]. I. s. 1. garde f; surveillance f; to be on the w. for, guetter. 2. Nau: quart m; (men) bordée f. 3. montre f. II. v. 1. v.i. (a) to w.(out), être sur ses gardes; w. out! prenez garde! attention! (b) to w. for s.o., attendre qn; guetter qn. 2. v.tr. (a) garder, veiller, sur (qn, qch.); (b) observer; regarder (attentivement); he needs watching, il a besoin d'être surveillé; (c) regarder (qn qui fait qch.); assister à (un match). 'watchdog, s. chien m de garde. 'watcher, s. veilleur, -euse; bird w., observateur m des mœurs des oiseaux. 'watchmaker, s. horloger m. †'watchman, s. Nau: homme m de garde; Ind: night w., veilleur m de nuit.

water ['wɔːtər]. I. s. 1. eau f; cold w., eau fraîche; to throw cold w. on a scheme, décourager un projet; fresh w., eau douce; drinking w., eau potable; to take the waters at Bath, faire une cure à Bath. 2. high w., marée haute; low w., marée basse; F: to be in low w., être dans la dèche. 3. to pass w., uriner. 4. w. hen, poule f d'eau; w. lily, nénuphar m; w. melon, pastèque f; w. polo, polo m nautique; w. skiing, ski m nautique; w. power, force f hydraulique. II. v. 1. v.tr. arroser; to w. down a statement, atténuer une affirmation. 2. v.i. (of eye) pleurer, larmoyer. 'water-colour, s. aquarelle f. 'watercress, s. cresson m. 'waterfall, s. chute f d'eau; cascade f. 'waterfowl, s. oiseau m aquatique. 'waterlogged, a. imbibé d'eau; détrempé. 'waterproof, a. & s. imperméable (m). 'watertight, a. étanche (à l'eau); (of regulation) qui a prévu tous les cas. 'waterworks,

s.pl. 1. usine f de distribution d'eau. 2. F: to turn on the w., pleurer. **watt** [wɔt], s. El: watt m. **wave** [weiv]. I. s. 1. vague f. 2. Sc: onde f; long waves, grandes ondes. 3. ondulation f (des cheveux). 4. geste m, signe m (de la main). II. 1. v.i. (a) to w. to s.o., faire signe à qn (en agitant le bras); (b) my hair waves naturally, mes cheveux ondulent naturellement. 2. v.tr. (a) agiter (le bras, un mouchoir); (b) to w. s.o. aside, écarter qn d'un geste; to w. s.o. on, faire signe à qn de continuer; (c) to have one's hair permanently waved, se faire faire une permanente. 'wavelength, s. longueur f d'onde. 'waver, v.i. vaciller; hésiter; être indécis. 'wavy, a. onduleux; (ligne) qui tremble; (of hair) ondoyant.

wax¹ [wæks]. I. s. cire f; (for skis) fart m. II. v.tr. cirer; farter (des skis). 'waxwork, s. figure f de cire.

wax², v.i. (of the moon) croître.

way [wei], s. 1. chemin m, route f, voie f. 2. (a) to show the w., montrer la route; to lose one's w., s'égarer; to go the wrong w., faire fausse route; on the w., chemin faisant; en chemin; (b) w. in, entrée f; w. out, sortie f; (c) to make one's w., se diriger; (d) to be in s.o.'s w., gêner qn; to get out of the w., se ranger; to keep out of the w., se tenir à l'écart; to make w. for s.o., faire place à qn. 3. all the w., jusqu'au bout; it's a long w. from here, c'est loin d'ici. 4. (a) côté m, direction f; this w., par ici; (b) sens m; the wrong w., à contre-sens. 5. moyen m. 6. (a) façon f, manière f; in one's own w., à sa guise; (b) to have one's (own) w., agir à sa guise. 7. in many ways, à bien des égards; in some ways, à certains points de vue. 8. (a) by the w., incidemment; en passant; by the w.! ah, j'y pense! (b) by w. of, à titre de. †**way**'lay, v.tr. arrêter (qn) au passage. 'wayside, s. bord m de la route.

we [wi(:)], pers. pron. (a) nous; (b) F: on. **weak** [wi:k], a. 1. faible; infirme; to grow w., s'affaiblir. 2. dilué; w. tea, thé léger. -ly, adv. (a) faiblement; (b) sans résolution. 'weaken. 1. v.tr. affaiblir. 2. v.i. s'affaiblir, faiblir. 'weakness, s. faiblesse f.

wealth [welθ], s. 1. richesse f. 2. abondance f, profusion f (de détails, etc.). 'wealthy, a. riche.

weapon ['wep(ə)n], s. arme f.

wear [wɛər]. I. 1. v.tr. (a) porter (un vêtement); (b) to w. holes in sth., faire des trous à qch. (à force d'usage); to w. oneself to death, se tuer à force de travail; (c) (passive force) to w. into holes, se trouer; to w. well, (i) faire bon usage; (ii) F: (of pers.) être bien conservé. 2. v.i. to w. out, s'user;

to w. off, s'effacer, disparaître. II. s. 1. usage m.; ladies' w., articles m pour dames. 2. usure f.

weary ['wiəri], a. fatigué; las. -ily, adv. d'un air, d'un ton, fatigué. 'weariness, s. lassitude f; fatigue f. 'wearisome, a. ennuyeux.

weasel ['wi:zl], s. belette f.

weather ['weðər]. I. s. temps m (qu'il fait); w. forecast, bulletin m météorologique, F: météo f. II. v.tr. 1. to w. a storm, (i) étaler à une tempête; (ii) (of pers.) se tirer d'affaire. 2. v.tr. & i. Geog: (se) désagréger. 'weatherboard, s. planche f à recouvrement. 'weathercock, s. girouette f.

‡weave [wi:v]. 1. v.tr. tisser. 2. v.i. se frayer un chemin (à travers qch.); P: to get weaving, s'y mettre. 'weaver, s. tisserand m. 'weaving, s. tissage m.

‡wed [wed], v.i. esp. U.S: se marier. 'wedding, s. mariage m; w. breakfast, repas m de noces; w. dress, robe f de mariée; w. ring, alliance f.

wedge [wedʒ]. I. s. coin m. II. v.tr. coincer, assujettir.

Wednesday ['wenzdi], s. mercredi m.

weed [wi:d]. I. s. mauvaise herbe. II. v.tr. sarcler; to w. out, éliminer. 'weeding, s. sarclage m; désherbage m. 'weedy, a. F: (of pers.) malingre.

week [wi:k], s. semaine f; today w., d'aujourd'hui en huit. 'weekday, s. jour m ouvrable; on weekdays, en semaine. weekend, s. weekend m. 'weekly. I. a. hebdomadaire (salaire) de la semaine. 2. s. journal m, revue f, hebdomadaire. 3. adv. tous les huit jours; par semaine.

weigh [wei]. 1. v.tr. (a) peser; soupeser; (b) to w. anchor, lever l'ancre. 2. v.i. peser; avoir du poids. 'weighing, s. pesée f (de qch.); w. machine, bascule f. weight, s. poids; m to pull one's w., y mettre du sien; that's a w. off my mind, voilà qui me soulage. 'weightiness, s. force f (d'une opinion). 'weighty, a. 1. pesant, lourd. 2. (motif) grave, sérieux.

weir [wiər], s. barrage m.

weird [wiəd], a. (a) surnaturel; mystérieux; (b) étrange, singulier.

welcome ['welkəm]. I. v.tr. souhaiter la bienvenue à (qn); recevoir (qch.) avec plaisir. II. s. (a) bienvenue f; (b) accueil m. III. a. (changement, etc.) bienvenu; you're w. to it, (i) c'est à votre disposition; (ii) Iron: grand bien vous fasse!

weld [weld], v.tr. souder. 'welding, s. soudage m, soudure f.

welfare ['welfɛər], s. bien-être m; social w., sécurité f sociale; child w., protection f de l'enfance; W. State, État m providence.

well¹ [wel], s. puits m.

well². I. adv. bien; to do as w. as one can, faire de son mieux; w. meant, fait à bonne intention; it's w. worth trying, ça vaut bien le coup; w. up (in sth.), calé; as w., aussi; as w. as, de même que; comme; w., as I was saying, donc; comme; je vous disais. II. a. (a) en bonne santé, bien portant; I don't feel w., je ne me sens pas bien; (b) it would be just as w. if . . ; il y aurait avantage à ce que . . . ; that's all very w. but . . , tout cela est bel et bon, mais . . . ; it's all very w. for you to say that, libre à vous de le dire. 'well-ad'vised, a (pers.) bien avisé; (action) sage, prudent. well-'known, a. bien connu; célèbre. well-'off, a. riche. well-'timed, a. bien calculé, opportun. 'well-to'-do, a. riche; dans l'aisance.

Welsh [welʃ]. 1. a. gallois; du pays de Galles. 2. s. (a) the W., les Gallois m; (b) Ling: le gallois. f 'Welshman, †-woman, s. Gallois, -oise.

west [west]. 1. s. ouest m, occident m. 2. adv. à l'ouest, à l'occident; vers l'ouest. 3. a. ouest inv.; d'ouest; occidental. 'westerly. 1. a. d'ouest. 2. adv. vers l'ouest. 'western, a. ouest inv., de l'ouest; occidental. 'westwards, adv. vers à, l'ouest.

wet [wet]. I. a. (a) mouillé, humide; w. through, trempé (jusqu'aux os); (b) (of weather) pluvieux. II. s. (a) to go out in the w., sortir sous la pluie; (b) P: (pers.) nouille f. III. ‡v.tr. mouiller. 'wetness, s. humidité f.

whale [(h)weil], s. baleine f. 'whaler, s. baleinier m. 'whaling, s. pêche f à la baleine.

wharf [(h)wɔ:f], s. débarcadère m, embarcadère m; quai m.

what [(h)wɔt]. I. a. 1. (interrog.) quel; w. time is it? quelle heure est-il? 2. (exclamatory) w. an idea! quelle idée! w. a fool he is! qu'il est bête! II. pron. 1. (rel. = that which) w.'s done is done, ce qui est fait est fait; w. I like is music, ce que j'aime c'est la musique; come w. may, advienne que pourra. 2. (interrog.) qu'est-ce que? que? quoi? w.'s his name? comment s'appelle-t-il? w. are you doing? qu'est-ce que vous faites? w.'s the French for dog? comment dit-on 'dog' en français? w. about it? eh bien, quoi? w. on earth for? mais pourquoi donc? 3. (indirect question, etc.) ce qui, ce que; tell me w.'s happening, dites-moi ce qui se passe; I don't know w. to do, je ne sais que faire. 4. (exclamatory) w.! comment! what'ever. 1. pron. w. you like, tout ce que vous voudrez; n'importe quoi. 2. a. aucun; no chance w., pas la moindre chance; nothing w., absolument rien.

wheat [(h)wi:t], s. blé m.

wheedle [(h)wi:dl], *v.tr.* enjôler, cajoler (qn).

wheel [(h)wi:l]. I. *s.* roue *f*; steering w., (i) *Aut:* volant *m*, (ii) *Nau:* barre *f*; potter's w., tour *m* de potier; w. chair, voiture *f* de malade. II. *v.* 1. *v.tr.* rouler (une brouette); pousser (un vélo). 2. *v.i.* to w. round, faire demi-tour; se retourner. 'wheelbase, *s.* *Aut:* etc: empattement *m*. 'wheelbarrow, *s.* brouette *f*.

wheeze [(h)wi:z]. I. *v.i.* respirer péniblement. II. *s.* 1. respiration *f* asthmatique. 2. *P:* truc *m*.

when [(h)wen]. I. *adv.* quand? II. *conj.* 1. quand, lorsque; w. one is young, quand on est jeune; w. I have finished, quand j'aurai fini. 2. the day w. I met you, le jour où je vous ai rencontré; at the very time w. ..; au moment même où ..; one day w. I was on duty, un jour que j'étais de service. when'ever, *adv.* toutes les fois que; chaque fois que; w. you like, quand vous voudrez.

where [(h)weər], *adv.* 1. où? w. am I? où suis-je? 2. (*relative*) I shall stay w. I am, je resterai là où je suis. 'whereabouts, *s.* lieu *m* où se trouve qn, qch.; nobody knows his w., personne ne sait où il est. 'wherefore, *s.* the why and the w., le pourquoi et le comment. where'ever, *adv.* partout où; n'importe où; w. you are, où que vous soyez. 'wherewithal, *s.* the w., le nécessaire; les moyens *m*; l'argent *m*.

‡**whet** [(h)wet], *v.tr.* 1. aiguiser (un outil). 2. stimuler (l'appétit, etc.).

whether [(h)weðər], *conj.* si; I don't know w. it's true, je ne sais pas si c'est vrai; w. he comes or not, qu'il vienne ou non.

which [(h)witʃ]. I. *a.* quel? etc.; w. colour do you like? quelle couleur aimez-vous? II. *pron.* 1. lequel? etc.; w. of the two houses is for sale? laquelle des deux maisons est à vendre? 2. qui, que, lequel; the house w. is for sale, la maison qui est à vendre; the house w. I sold, la maison que j'ai vendue; many books, all of w. were interesting, beaucoup de livres qui étaient tous intéressants; he looked like a colonel, w. indeed he was, il avait l'air d'un colonel, ce qu'il était en effet. 3. to w., at w., auquel, etc.; of w., from w., duquel, etc.; dont; the house of w. I was speaking, la maison dont, de laquelle, je parlais; the country to w. we are going, le pays où nous irons; after w. he went out, après quoi il est sorti. which'ever. 1. *a.* n'importe quel; take w. book you like, prenez n'importe quel livre. 2. *pron.* celui qui, celui que, n'importe lequel; take w. you like, prenez celui que vous voudrez, n'importe lequel.

whiff [(h)wif]. I. *s.* (a) bouffée *f* (de fumée); (b) *F:* mauvaise odeur *f*. II. *v.i.* *F:* puer.

while [(h)wail]. I. *s.* 1. after a w., après quelque temps; in a little w., sous peu; avant peu; a little w. ago, il y a peu de temps; a long w., longtemps. 2. to be worth w., valoir la peine. II. *v.tr.* to w. away the time, faire passer le temps. III. *conj.* 1. (a) pendant que; tandis que; w. he was here, pendant qu'il était ici; (b) (= as long as) tant que. 2. (= although) quoique, bien que.

whim [(h)wim], *s.* caprice *m*; fantaisie *f*.

whimper ['(h)wimpər], *v.i.* pleurnicher, geindre.

whine [(h)wain]. I. *v.i.* se plaindre; pleurnicher; geindre. II. *s.* (also whining) geignement *m*; plainte *f*.

whip [(h)wip]. I. *s.* fouet *m*. II. *v.tr. & i.* fouetter; to w. round the corner, tourner vivement le coin.

whirl [(h)wə:l]. I. *v.i.* tourbillonner, tournoyer. II. *s.* tourbillon *m*; my head's in a w., la tête me tourne. 'whirlpool, *s.* tourbillon *m* (d'eau). 'whirlwind, *s.* trombe *f*.

whirr [(h)wə:r]. I. *s.* bruissement *m*; ronronnement *m* (de machine). II. *v.i.* (*of machinery*) ronfler, ronronner.

whisk [(h)wisk]. I. *s.* (a) (*of cow*) agiter (sa queue); (b) to w. away, enlever qch. d'un geste rapide; (c) *Cu:* battre (des œufs); fouetter (la crème). II. *s.* 1. coup *m* (de queue). 2. *H:* (*for dusting*) époussette *f*; (b) batteur *m*, fouet *m* (à œufs).

whiskers ['(h)wiskəz], *s.pl.* moustache *f* (de chat, etc.).

whisky ['(h)wiski], *s.* whisky *m*.

whisper ['(h)wispər]. I. *s.* chuchotement *m*. II. *v.tr. & i.* chuchoter.

whist [(h)wist], *s.* whist *m*.

whistle [(h)wisl]. I. *s.* 1. sifflement *m*; coup *m* de sifflet. 2. sifflet *m*. II. *v.i. & tr.* siffler.

Whit [(h)wit], *a.* W. Sunday, (dimanche *m* de) la Pentecôte. 'Whitsun, *s.* la Pentecôte.

white [(h)wait]. I. *a.* blanc; as w. as a sheet, pâle comme la mort. II. *s.* 1. (*colour*) blanc *m*; w. of egg, blanc d'œuf. 2. (*pers.*) blanc, *f* blanche. 'whitebait, *s.* *Fish:* blanchaille *f*; a dish of w., une friture. 'whiten, *v.tr.* blanchir. 'whiteness, *s.* blancheur *f*. 'whitewash, *s.* lait *m* de chaux. II. *v.tr.* blanchir à la chaux. 'whiting, *s.* *Fish:* merlan *m*.

whizz [(h)wiz], *v.i.* siffler; to w. past, passer à toute vitesse.

who [hu:], *pron.* 1. qui? w. is she? qui est-elle? w. did it? qui est-ce qui l'a fait? 2. (*relative*) qui; my friend w. came, mon ami qui est venu. who'dunit, *s.* *F:* roman *m* policier.

who'ever, pron. 1. celui qui; quiconque; w. finds it, celui qui le trouvera. 2. w. you are, qui que vous soyez. 3. (object of sentence) w. she marries, celui qu'elle épousera.

whole [houl]. I. a. entier; complet; the w. truth, toute la vérité. II. s. tout m; as a w., dans son ensemble; en totalité; on the w., à tout prendre; en somme. 'whole**meal,** a. (pain) complet. 'whole**sale.** I. s. (vente f en) gros. II. a. 1. (commerce) de gros, en gros. 2. en masse. III. adv. (vendre) en gros. 'whole**saler,** s. grossiste m. 'whole**some,** a. (aliment) sain; (climat) salubre. 'whol**ly,** adv. 1. tout à fait; complètement. 2. intégralement, en totalité.

whom [hu:m], pron. (object) 1. qui? w. have you seen? qui avez-vous vu? 2. (a) (relative) que; the man w., I saw, l'homme que j'ai vu; (b) (after prep.) qui; (of whom) dont; lequel, etc.; the lady of w. I was speaking, la dame dont, de laquelle, je parlais; the lady to w. I was speaking, la dame à qui je parlais.

whoop [hu:p]. I. s. Med: quinte f (de la coqueluche). II. v.i. faire entendre une toux convulsive (de la coqueluche). 'whooping-cough, s. coqueluche f.

whose [hu:z], possessive pron. 1. de qui? 2. dont; de qui; duquel, etc.; the pupil w. work I showed you, l'élève dont je vous ai montré le travail.

why [(h)wai]. 1. adv. pourquoi? 2. s. pourquoi m. 3. int. w., what's the matter? mais qu'avez-vous donc?

wick [wik], s. mèche f (d'une lampe, etc.).

wicked ['wikid], a. mauvais, méchant. -**ly,** adv. méchamment. 'wicked**ness,** s. méchanceté f, perversité f.

wicket ['wikit], s. guichet m.

wide [waid]. I. a. 1. large; how w. is the room? quelle est la largeur de la pièce? 2. (of range, etc.) étendu, vaste; in a wider sense, par extension. 3. w. of the mark, loin de compte; (at cricket) w. (ball), balle f écartée. -**ly,** adv. largement; w. read, (journal) à grande circulation. II. adv. 1. loin; w. apart, bien espacé. 2. (ouvrir) largement, tout grand; w. open eyes, yeux grands ouverts. 'wi**den,** v.tr. & i. (s')élargir; (s')étendre. 'wide**spread,** a. étendu. 2. répandu. 'width, s. largeur f.

widow ['widou], s. veuve f. 'wid**ower,** s. veuf m.

wield [wi:ld], v.tr. manier; exercer (le pouvoir).

†**wife** [waif], s. femme f, épouse f.

wig [wig], s. perruque f.

wild [waild], a. 1. sauvage. 2. (a) a w. night, une nuit de tempête; (b) farouche, inapprivoisé; (c) dissipé, dissolu. 3. (a) affolé; w. with joy, fou de joie; (b) fantasque; insensé; au hasard; w. talk, propos en l'air. 4. s.pl. région f sauvage; in the wilds, dans la brousse. **wild-cat,** a. (of strike) non-officiel. 'wilder**ness** ['wil-], s. lieu m sauvage; terrain m inculte. 'wild**fire,** s. to spread like w., se répandre comme une traînée de poudre. 'wild**fowl,** s. coll. gibier m d'eau; sauvagine f.

wilful ['wilf(u)l], a. (of damage, etc.) fait exprès, intentionnel.

will [wil]. I. s. 1. volonté f; with a w., de bon cœur. 2. (a) décision f; volonté; (b) bon plaisir; gré m. 3. Jur: testament m. II. v.tr. vouloir; (a) (b) disposer (de qch.) par testament. III. 1 (modal) aux.v. 1. vouloir; (a) say what you w. . . ., quoi que vous disiez . . .; I would have it understood that . . ., je voudrais qu'il soit bien entendu que . . .; (b) the engine won't start, le moteur ne veut pas démarrer; would you please pass the salt? voudriez-vous, s'il vous plaît, me passer le sel? won't you sit down? asseyez-vous, je vous en prie; (c) (emphatic) accidents w. happen, on ne peut pas éviter les accidents. 2. (aux. of future tenses) (a) he w. be there, il y sera; you won't forget, he won't, vous n'oublierez pas, n'est-ce pas? (b) he would come if he were invited, il viendrait si on l'invitait. 'will**ing,** a. 1. de bonne volonté; bien disposé. 2. to be w. to do sth., vouloir bien faire qch.; F: to show w., faire preuve de bonne volonté. 'willing**ness,** s. bonne volonté f. 'will-power, s. volonté f.

willow ['wilou], s. saule m.

wilt [wilt], v.i. se flétrir, se faner.

wily ['waili], a. rusé, astucieux.

‡**win** [win], v.tr. & i. 1. gagner; remporter (une victoire). 2. acquérir (de la popularité); se faire (une réputation); to w. through, venir à bout (des difficultés).

wince [wins], v.i. faire une grimace de douleur.

wind [wind]. I. s. 1. vent m; F: to get the w. up, avoir le trac, la frousse; P: to raise the w., se procurer de l'argent. 2. Med: vent, flatuosité f. 3. souffle m, haleine f. 4. Mus: the w. the instruments m à vent. II. v.tr. couper le souffle à (qn), essouffler (qn). 'wind**cheater,** s. Cl: blouson m (de golf). 'wind**fall,** s. 1. fruit m tombé. 2. aubaine f. 'wind**mill,** s. moulin m à vent. 'wind**pipe,** s. Anat: trachée f. 'wind**screen,** U.S: 'wind**shield,** s. Aut: pare-brise m. 'wind**y,** a. venteux; exposé au vent.

‡**wind** [waind]. 1. *v.i.* serpenter. 2. *v.tr.* (a) enrouler; *Tex:* dévider (le fil); (b) remonter (une pendule). **windlass** ['windləs], *s.* treuil *m.* '**wind 'up**, *v.* 1. *v.tr.* enrouler (un cordage); remonter (une pendule); *Com:* liquider (une société); clôturer (un compte). 2. *v.i. F:* finir.

window ['windou], *s.* fenêtre *f*; French w., porte-fenêtre *f*; stained-glass w., vitrail *m*; (shop) w., vitrine *f*, devanture *f*; *Aut:* rear w., glace *f* (arrière; w. dressing, (i) l'art *m* de l'étalage; (ii) *F:* camouflage *m*, trompe-l'œil *m*; to go w. shopping, faire du lèche-vitrines.

wine [wain], *s.* vin *m*; w. cellar, cave *f* (au vin); w. glass, verre *m* à vin; (at restaurant) w. list, carte *f* des vins; w. merchant, négociant *m* en vins; w. waiter, sommelier *m.*

wing [wiŋ], *s.* 1. aile *f* (d'un oiseau, d'un avion). 2. (a) aile (d'un bâtiment); pavillon *m* (d'un hôpital); (b) *Av:* escadre *f* (aérienne); w. commander, lieutenant-colonel *m.* 3. *Th:* the wings, les coulisses *f.* 4. *Sp:* (pers.) ailier *m.*

wink [wiŋk]. I. s. clignement *m* d'œil; clin *m* d'œil. II. *v.i.* cligner de l'œil (à qn); *Aut:* winking indicator, clignotant *m.*

winkle ['wiŋkl], *s.* bigorneau *m.*

winner ['winər], *s.* gagnant, -ante. '**winning.** I. *a.* (numéro) gagnant, sortant. II. s. 1. *Sp:* w. post, poteau *m* d'arrivée. 2. *pl.* winnings, gains *m.*

winter ['wintər]. I. s. hiver *m*; w. resort, station *f* d'hiver; w. sports, sports *f* d'hiver. II. *v.i.* hiverner. '**wintry**, *a.* d'hiver; hivernal.

wipe [waip], *v.tr.* essuyer; to w. one's nose, se moucher. '**wipe 'out**, *v.tr.* (a) liquider (une dette); (b) exterminer (une armée). '**wiper**, *s. Aut:* windscreen w., essuie-glace *m.* '**wipe 'up**, *v.tr.* nettoyer (une saleté); *abs.* essuyer la vaisselle.

wire ['waiər]. I. s. 1. fil *m* métallique; copper w., fil de laiton; w. netting, treillage *m* en fil de fer; w. mattress, sommier *m* métallique; telegraph wires, fils télégraphiques. 2. télégramme *m*, dépêche *f.* II. *v.tr.* 1. poser l'électricité (dans une maison). 2. télégraphier. '**wireless**, *s.* radio *f.* '**wirepulling**, *s. F:* intrigues *fpl.* '**wiretapping**, *s.* écoute *f* téléphonique. '**wiring**, *s.* pose *f* de fils électriques; canalisation *f.* '**wiry**, *a.* (of hair) raide; (of pers.) sec et nerveux.

wise [waiz]. I. *a.* 1. sage; prudent. 2. he is none the wiser, il n'en est pas plus avancé; no one will be any the wiser, ni vu ni connu. **-ly**, *adv.* sagement, prudemment. II. *s.* manière *f*, façon *f*; *Com:* fashion w., du point de vue de la mode. '**wisdom**, *s.* sagesse *f.*

wish [wiʃ]. I. *v.* 1. *v.ind.tr.* to w. for, désirer, souhaiter. 2. *v.tr.* désirer, vouloir; I w. I were in your place, je voudrais bien être à votre place; to w. s.o. good night, dire bonsoir à qn. II. s. (a) désir *m*; vœu *m*; (b) souhait *m*, vœu. '**wishful**, *a.* that's w. thinking, c'est prendre ses désirs pour des réalités.

wishy-washy ['wiʃiwɔʃi], *a. F:* fade, insipide.

wisp [wisp], *s.* (a) bouchon *m*, poignée *f* (de paille); traînée *f* (de fumée); (b) w. of hair, mèche *f* de cheveux.

wistful ['wistf(u)l], *a.* désenchanté; w. smile, sourire pensif. **-fully**, *adv.* d'un air songeur et triste.

wit [wit], *s.* 1. esprit *m*, entendement *m*; intelligence *f*; to be at one's wits' end, ne plus savoir de quel côté se tourner. 2. homme *m*, femme *f*, d'esprit.

witch [witʃ], *s.* sorcière *f*; w. doctor, sorcier *m* guérisseur. '**witchcraft**, *s.* sorcellerie *f*; magie *f* noire.

with [wið], *prep.* avec. 1. (a) I shall be w. you in a moment, je serai à vous dans un moment; (b) girl w. blue eyes, jeune fille aux yeux bleus; (c) this decision rests w. you, c'est à vous de décider; (d) w. all his faults, malgré tous ses défauts. 2. (a) I can do nothing w. him, je ne peux rien en faire; it is a habit w. me, c'est une habitude chez moi; (b) w. these words, ce disant; (c) to fight w. s.o., se battre contre qn. 3. to part w. sth., se défaire de qch. 4. (a) to take sth. w. both hands, prendre qch. à deux mains; (b) to tremble w. rage, trembler de rage. 5. w. all due respect, sauf votre respect; I say so w. regret, je le dis à regret. 6. *F:* to be w. it, être dans le vent.

‡**withdraw** [wið'drɔː]. 1. *v.tr.* retirer; (b) soustraire (from, à). 2. *v.i.* se retirer; s'éloigner; to w. in favour of s.o., se désister en faveur de qn. **with'drawal**, *s.* retrait *m.*

wither ['wiðər]. 1. *v.i.* se dessécher, dépérir. 2. *v.tr.* dessécher, flétrir; foudroyer (qn du regard). '**withering**, *a.* qui dessèche; (regard) foudroyant, écrasant.

within [wið'in], *prep.* (a) à l'intérieur de, en dedans de; (b) to live w. one's income, ne pas dépenser plus que son revenu; w. a pound, à une livre près; (c) w. sight, en vue; w. call, à portée de la voix; w. two miles, à moins de deux milles; (d) w. an hour, dans une heure.

without [wið'aut], *prep.* sans; to go w. sth., se passer de qch.; *Ecc:* world w. end, pour les siècles des siècles.

‡**withstand** [wið'stænd], *v.tr.* résister à (la pression, etc.); soutenir (une attaque).

witness ['witnis]. I. s. témoin *m.* II. *v.* 1. *v.tr.* être témoin (d'un accident, etc.); certifier (une signature). 2. *v.i.*

to w. sth., témoigner de qch. 'witness-box, s. Jur: ≃ barre f des témoins.

witty ['witi], a. spirituel. -ily, adv. spirituellement.

wizard ['wizəd], s. sorcier m, magicien m.

wizened ['wiz(ə)nd], a. desséché, ratatiné.

wobble ['wɔbl], v.i. ballotter; branler.

woe [wou], s. malheur m, chagrin m. 'woe-begone, a. triste, désolé.

wog [wɔg], s. P: Pej: levantin m; Égyptien m; Arabe m, P: bicot m.

†wolf [wulf]. I. s. 1. loup m; she-w., louve f. 2. F: tombeur m (de femmes). II. v.tr. to w. one's food, avaler sa nourriture à grosses bouchées, bâfrer.

†woman ['wumən], s. 1. femme f; an old w., une vieille. 2. attrib. w. doctor, femme médecin.

wonder ['wʌndər]. I. s. 1. merveille f, prodige m; for a w., chose f remarquable; no w., rien d'étonnant. 2. étonnement m, surprise f. II. v. 1. v.i. s'étonner (at, de). 2. v.tr. se demander; I w. why, je voudrais bien savoir pourquoi. 'wonderful, a. merveilleux, prodigieux; to have a w. time, s'amuser bien; it was w.! c'était épatant! -fully, adv. merveilleusement.

wood [wud], s. bois m. 1. beer from the w., bière tirée au fût; w. carving, sculpture f sur bois; 'woodcut, s. gravure f sur bois. 'woodcutter, s. bûcheron m. 'wooded, a. boisé. 'wooden, a. 1. de bois, en bois. 2. F: w.-headed, stupide. 'woodland, s. pays m boisé, bois m. †'woodlouse, s. cloporte m. 'woodpecker, s. pic m; green w., pivert m. 'woodshed, s. bûcher m. 'wood-wind [-wind], s. Mus: les bois mpl. 'woodwork, s. 1. charpenterie f; menuiserie f. 2. boiserie f, charpente f; menuiserie f, ébénisterie f.

wool [wul], s. laine f; steel w., paille f de fer. 'wool-gathering, s. F: rêvasserie f. 'woollen, a. de laine; s. woollens, lainages m. 'woolly. 1. a. (a) laineux, de laine; (b) (contour) flou; F: (of ideas) vaseux. 2. s. F: tricot m.

wop [wɔp], s. P: Pej: Italien m, P: macaroni m.

word [wəːd], s. 1. mot m; (a) in other words, en d'autres termes; without a w., sans mot dire; with these words, ce disant; (c) to say a good w. for s.o., dire un mot en faveur de qn). 2. by w. of mouth, de vive voix; verbalement. 3. to keep one's w., tenir parole; to take s.o. at his w., prendre qn au mot. 4. w. of command, ordre m, commandement m. 'wording, s. mots mpl; langage m; termes mpl (d'un acte).

work [wəːk]. I. s. 1. travail m; hard at w., en plein travail. 2. travail, ouvrage m, besogne f, tâche f. 3. Lit: ouvrage m, œuvre f. 4. to be out of w., être sans

travail; chômer. 5. public works, travaux m publics; P.N: road works ahead! travaux! 6. pl. mécanisme m, mouvement m (d'une montre, etc.). 7. pl. usine f. II. v. 1. v.i. (a) travailler; (b) (of machinery, etc.) fonctionner, marcher; (c) Ind: to w. to rule, faire la grève du zèle. 2. v.tr. (a) to w. oneself to death, se tuer de travail; (b) faire marcher (une machine); faire opérer (un miracle); (c) to w. oneself into a rage, se mettre en colère; (d) exploiter (une mine); (e) to w. out a plan, élaborer un projet. 'worker, s. travailleur, -euse; ouvrier, -ière. 'working. I. a. 1. w. man, ouvrier m; w. party, équipe f. 2. (of machine, etc.) qui fonctionne; not w., hors d'action. II. s. 1. travail m. 2. in w. order, en état de service. 3. w. of s.o., machinations fpl. 'workman, s. ouvrier m; manœuvre m. 'workmanship, s. exécution f; façon f. 'workshop, s. atelier m.

world [wəːld], s. monde m. 1. map of the w., mappemonde f; all the w. over, dans le monde entier. 2. man of the w., homme m qui connaît la vie. 3. the theatrical w., le milieu du théâtre. 4. sth. out of this w., qch. d'extra-ordinaire, F: d'épatant. 'world-wide, a. universel; mondial.

worm [wəːm]. I. s. ver m. II. v.tr. to w. sth. out of s.o., tirer qch. de qn. 'worm-eaten, a. vermoulu.

worn out ['wɔːn'aut], a. 1. usé. 2. épuisé; exténué.

worry ['wʌri]. I. v. 1. v.tr. tourmenter, harceler. 2. v.i. se tourmenter, s'inquiéter; don't w.! soyez tranquille! II. s. ennui m; souci m. 'worried, a. soucieux, préoccupé.

worse [wəːs]. 1. a. & s. pire (m); plus mauvais; to make matters w., par surcroît de malheur; so much the w., tant pis. 2. s. to change for the w., s'altérer. 3. adv. pis; plus mal.

worship ['wəːʃip]. I. v.tr. adorer (Dieu); to w. money, faire son idole de l'argent. II. s. Ecc: culte m. 2. his W. the Mayor, monsieur le maire; yes, your W., oui, (i) monsieur le maire, (ii) monsieur le juge.

worst [wəːst]. 1. a. le (la) pire, (le) plus mauvais. 2. s. to get the w. of it, avoir le dessous; if the w. comes to the w., en mettant les choses au pis; do your w.! faites le pis que vous pourrez! that's the w. of cheap shoes, c'est l'inconvénient des souliers bon marché. 3. adv. (le) pis, (le) plus mal.

worth [wəːθ]. 1. pred.a. valant; (a) to be w., valoir. 2. s. valeur f. 'worthless, a. sans valeur. worth-while, a. qui en vaut la peine. 'worthy, a. digne.

wound [wu:nd]. I. s. (a) blessure f; (b) plaie f. II. v.tr. blesser.

woven ['wouv(ə)n], a. tissé.

wrangle ['ræŋgl], v.i. se disputer, se quereller.

‡wrap [ræp], v.tr. 1. envelopper. 2. enrouler (qch. autour de qch.). 'wrapper, s. couverture f (d'un livre); bande f (de journal). 'wrapping, s. w. paper, papier m d'emballage.

wreath [ri:θ], s. 1. couronne f; guirlande f. 2. volute f, panache m (de fumée).

wreck [rek]. I. s. 1. épave f. 2. naufrage m. II. v.tr. (a) to be wrecked, faire naufrage; (b) démolir; (c) saboter; ruiner; 'wreckage, s. épaves fpl; débris mpl.

wren [ren], s. roitelet m.

wrench [ren(t)ʃ]. I. s. 1. effort violent. 2. clef f; tourne-à-gauche m inv. II. v.tr. arracher (from, à).

wrestle ['resl], v.i. & tr. lutter. 'wrestler, s. lutteur m. 'wrestling, s. sport m de la lutte; all-in w., catch m.

wretch [retʃ], s. 1. malheureux, -euse; infortuné, -ée. 2. scélérat, -ate. 'wretched, a. 1. malheureux. 2. pitoyable. -ly, adv. misérablement; de façon lamentable.

wriggle ['rigl], v.i. (a) se tortiller; s'agiter; (b) to w. out of, se tirer de.

‡wring [riŋ], v.tr. tordre. 'wringing, a. w. wet, trempé jusqu'aux os; mouillé à tordre.

wrinkle ['riŋkl]. I. s. (a) ride f; (b) rugosité f; (c) (in garment) faux pli m; (d) renseignement m utile. II. v.i. & tr. (se) rider; (se) plisser.

wrist [rist], s. poignet m; w. watch, montre-bracelet f.

writ [rit], s. acte m judiciaire; mandat m.

‡write [rait], v.tr. écrire; rédiger. 'write down, v.tr. coucher par écrit; inscrire; marquer, noter. 'writer, s. auteur m; écrivain m. 'writing, s. 1. écriture f. 2. ouvrage m littéraire. 3. w. paper, papier m à lettres. 'write off, v.tr. Fin: réduire (le capital); Com: défalquer (une mauvaise créance); déduire (tant pour l'usure). 'write-off, s. F: perte f totale. 'write-up, s. article m (dans un journal); compte m rendu.

writhe [raið], v.i. se tordre; se tortiller.

wrong [rɔŋ]. I. a. 1. mauvais; mal inv. 2. (a) incorrect, inexact; faux; (b) to be w., avoir tort; se tromper. 3. (a) to drive on the w. side of the road, circuler à contre-voie; w. side up, sens dessus dessous; (b) to be on the w. track, suivre une mauvaise piste; to say the w. thing, commettre une gaffe; w. number, erreur f de numéro; w. note, fausse note. 4. what's w. with you? qu'avez-vous? II. s. 1. mal m. 2. tort, injustice f. 3. to be in the w., être dans son tort; avoir tort. III. adv. mal; (a) inexactement, incorrectement; (b) à tort. IV. v.tr. faire tort à (qn); être injuste pour, envers (qn). 'wrongful, a. injuste. -fully, adv. injustement; à tort. 'wrongly, adv. 1. à tort. 2. mal.

wrought [rɔ:t], a. w. iron, fer m forgé.

wry [rai], a. tordu; de travers; to pull a wry face, faire la grimace.

X

X, x [eks], s. 1. (la lettre) X, x m; Cin: X certificate = interdit aux moins de seize ans. 2. X rays, rayons m X. 'X-ray. I. attrib. a. (appareil) radiologique; X-r. examination, examen radiographique; X-r. treatment, radiothérapie f. II. v.tr. radiographier (qn).

Xmas ['krisməs], s. F: Noël m.

Y

Y, y [wai], s. (la lettre) Y, y m (i grec).

yacht [jɔt]. I. s. yacht m; y. club, yacht-club m. II. v.i. faire du yachting. 'yachting, s. yachting m. ‡'yachtsman, s. yachtman m

yank¹ [jæŋk], v.tr. F: tirer, arracher (d'un coup sec).

Yank², Yankee ['jæŋki], s. F: Américain, -aine (des États-Unis); Yankee m.

‡yap [jæp], v.i. japper.

yard¹ [jɑːd], s. yard m (0 mètre 914).

yard², s. 1. cour f (de maison); chantier m; builder's y., dépôt m de matériaux; Rail: marshalling y., gare f de triage.

yarn [jɑːn], s. 1. fil m; filé m. 2. histoire f, conte m.

yawn [jɔːn]. I. v.i. bâiller. II. s. bâillement m.

year [jəːr], s. an m; année f; in the y. 1850, en l'an 1850; last y., l'an dernier, l'année dernière; to be ten years old, avoir dix ans; calendar y., année civile; years ago, il y a bien des années. 'year-book, s. annuaire m. 'yearly. I. a. annuel. II. adv. annuellement.

yell [jel]. I. v.i. hurler; crier à tue-tête. II. s. hurlement m; cri m aigu.

yellow ['jelou]. 1. *a. & s.* jaune (*m*); *Aut:* y. band area = zone à stationnement interdit ou limité. 2. *a. F:* poltron, lâche. '**yellowhammer,** *s.* bruant *m* jaune.

yelp [jelp]. I. *v.i.* japper, glapir. II. *s.* (*also* **yelping**) jappement *m*.

yes [jes], *adv.* oui; (*contradicting*) si; (*interrogatively*) vraiment? '**yes-man,** *s. F:* beni-oui-oui *m*.

yesterday ['jestədi], *adv. & s.* hier (*m*); **the day before y.,** avant-hier (*m*); **y. week,** il y a eu hier huit jours.

yet [jet]. 1. *adv.* déjà; jusqu'ici; **not y., pas encore; as y.,** jusqu'à présent; **I'll do it y!,** j'y arriverai! 2. *conj.* néanmoins, cependant; tout de même.

yew [ju:], *s.* y. (**tree**), if *m*.

yield [ji:ld]. I. *s.* production *f*; rapport *m*; rendement *m*; récolte *f* (d'un champ). II. *v.* 1. *v.tr.* (*a*) rapporter, produire; (*b*) céder (un droit, etc.). 2. *v.i.* se rendre, faire sa soumission; succomber (à la tentation); (*b*) s'affaisser, fléchir, plier.

‡yodel ['joudl], *v.i.* iouler, yodler.

yoke [jouk]. I. *s.* 1. joug *m*. 2. empiècement *m* (d'une robe). II. *v.tr.* accoupler (des bœufs).

yolk [jouk], *s.* jaune *m* d'œuf.

you [ju:] *pers. pron.* (*a*) vous; *sg.* (*to relative, child*) (i) (*subject*) tu, (ii) (*object*) te, (iii) (*after prep.*) toi; if **I** were **y.,** à votre, ta, place; **y.** [**Englishmen, vous autres Anglais;** (*b*) (*indefinite*) on; **y. never can tell,** on ne sait jamais.

young [jʌŋ]. I. *a.* jeune; **younger son, daughter, fils cadet, fille cadette. II.** *s.pl.inv.* **the y.,** les jeunes; **books for the y.,** livres pour la jeunesse; **animal and its y.,** animal et ses petits. '**youngster,** *s.* (*a*) jeune homme *m*; (*b*) petit, -ite. *F:* gosse *mf*.

your [jɔ:r], *poss.a.* votre, vos; *sg.* (*of relative, child*) ton, ta, tes; **y. house, votre, ta, maison; y. turn!** à vous! à toi! (*b*) (*indefinite*) son, sa, ses; **you cannot alter y. nature,** on ne peut pas changer son caractère. **yours,** *poss. pron.* le vôtre; *sg.* (*of relative, child*) le tien, la tienne; **this is y.,** ceci est à vous, à toi; **a friend of y.,** un de vos, tes, amis. **†your'self,** *pers. pron.* vous-même; toi-même.

youth [ju:θ], *s.* 1. jeunesse *f*, adolescence *f*; **y. hostel, auberge *f* de la jeunesse; y. hosteller, ajiste *mf*, y. hostelling, ajisme *m*. 2. jeune homme *r.i,* adolescent *m*. '**youthful,** *a.* jeune; juvénile. '**youthfulness,** *s.* jeunesse *f*; air *m* de jeunesse.

Z

Z, z [zed, *U.S:* zi:], *s.* (la lettre) Z, z *m*.

zeal [zi:l], *s.* zèle *m*, ardeur *f*. '**zealous** ['ze-], *a.* zélé, empressé.

zebra ['zi:brə, 'zebrə], *s.* zèbre *m*; **z. crossing** = passage *m* pour piétons.

zenith ['zeniθ], *s.* zénith *m*.

zest [zest], *s.* enthousiasme *m*, entrain *m*.

zigzag ['zigzæg]. I. *s.* zigzag *m*. II. ‡*v.i.* zigzaguer.

zinc [ziŋk], *s.* zinc *m*.

zip [zip]. I. *s.* 1. *F:* énergie *f*. 2. **z. fastener,** fermeture *f* éclair (R.t.m.); (*in Belgium*) tirette-éclair *f*. II. ‡*v.i.* **to z. past,** passer comme un éclair.

zone [zoun]. I. *s.* zone *f*; *Aut:* **pink z. = zone bleue. II.** répartir (une ville, etc.) en zones; distribuer (des produits) par régions.

zoo [zu:], *s. F:* zoo *m*.

zoology [zou'ɔlədʒi], *s.* zoologie *f*. **zoo'logical,** *a.* zoologique. **zo'ologist,** *s.* zoologiste *m*.

APPENDICES

In order to keep the length of the appendices within reasonable limits, the following conventions have been observed:

(a) The list of geographical names has been limited to the names of the principal countries of the world, and the main islands, rivers and towns only when the form of the name differs in French and English. In order not to extend unduly the list of towns it has been found necessary to omit a certain number of Italian towns which have distinctive French and English forms (e.g. Padoue, Padua; Parme, Parma); and names such as Marseille or Lyon which are sometimes written with a final -s in English have not been included.

(b) The list of proper names is limited to the principal Christian names and historical names for which the form of the English and French names differ. English or French Christian names which have no equivalent in the other language have not been included, neither have diminutives.

Afin de ne pas accroître démesurément les appendices, nous avons adopté les limitations suivants:

(a) la liste des noms géographiques comprend les noms des principaux pays du monde et aussi les noms des îles, des fleuves ou des villes les plus importants si ceux-ci n'ont pas la même orthographe en français et en anglais. Pour que la liste des villes ne s'étende pas indéfiniment, il nous a paru nécessaire d'omettre les noms de certaines villes italiennes qui ont une orthographe différente en anglais et en français (*ex.* Padua, Padoue, Parma, Parme); sont omises également les villes telles que Marseille ou Lyon qui s'écrivent parfois en anglais avec un -s final.

(b) la liste des noms propres ne comprend que les principaux noms de baptême et noms historiques dont la forme anglaise est différente de celle du français. Sont omis également les noms de baptême anglaise ou français pour lesquels aucun équivalent n'existe dans l'autre langue, aussi bien que les diminutifs.

1

I. FRENCH-ENGLISH: FRANÇAIS-ANGLAIS

l'Abyssinie (f), Abyssinia
les Açores (f), the Azores
l'Adriatique (f), the Adriatic
l'Afghanistan (m), Afghanistan
l'Afrique (f), Africa; l'A. du Sud, South Africa
l'Albanie (f), Albania
Alger, Algiers
l'Algérie (f), Algeria
l'Allemagne (f), Germany
les Alpes (f), the Alps
l'Amazone (m), the (river) Amazon
l'Amérique (f), America
les Andes (f), the Andes
l'Andorre (f), Andorra
l'Angleterre (f), England
Anglo-Normandes (les îles), the Channel Islands
les Antilles (f), the West Indies; la Mer des A., the Caribbean (Sea)
Anvers, Antwerp
les Apennins (m), the Apennines
les Appalaches (m), the Appalachians
l'Arabie (f), Arabia; l'A. séoudite, Saudi Arabia
Argentine (la République), Argentina, the Argentine
l'Asie (f), Asia
Athènes, Athens
l'Atlantique (m), the Atlantic
Aurigny, Alderney
l'Australie (f), Australia
l'Autriche (f) Austria
Azur, la côte d', the (French) Riviera

Baffin (la Terre de), Baffin Island
Bâle, Basle, Basel
la Baltique, the Baltic (Sea)
la Barbade, Barbados
Barcelone, Barcelona
la Bavière, Bavaria
la Belgique, Belgium
le Bénélux, Benelux
les (îles) Bermudes (f), the Bermudas
Bethléem, Bethlehem
la Birmanie, Burma
la Bolivie, Bolivia
la Bourgogne, Burgundy
Brême, Bremen
le Brésil, Brazil
la Bretagne, Brittany
Britanniques, les îles (f), the British Isles
Bruxelles, Brussels
la Bulgarie, Bulgaria

le Cachemire, Kashmir
le Caire, Cairo
le Cambodge, Cambodia
Cameroun (la République du), (the Republic of) the Cameroons
le Canada, Canada
les (îles) Canaries (f), the Canary Islands, the Canaries

Cantorbéry, Canterbury
les Carpathes (f), the Carpathian Mountains, the Carpathians
le Cap, Capetown
la (mer) Caspienne, the Caspian (sea)
le Caucase, the Caucasus
Centrafricaine, la République, the Central African Republic
Ceylan (m), Ceylon
Changhaï, Shanghai
le Chili, Chile
la Chine, China
Chypre (f), Cyprus
Coblence, Coblenz
la Colombie, Colombia; la C. britannique, British Columbia
le Congo: (a) the (river) Congo; (b) la République du C., the Republic of the Congo; (c) la République démocratique du C., the Congolese Republic
Copenhague, Copenhagen
Cordoue, Cordoba
la Corée, Korea
la Corse, Corsica
la Cornouailles, Cornwall
la Côte d'Ivoire, the Ivory Coast
la Crète, Crete
la Crimée, the Crimea

Damas, Damascus
le Danemark, Denmark
le Danube, the Danube
Douvres, Dover
Dresde, Dresden
Dunkerque, Dunkirk

l'Èbre (m), the (river) Ebro
l'Écosse (f), Scotland
Édimbourg, Edinburgh
l'Égypte (f), Egypt
l'Eire (f), Eire
Elbe[1] (l'île d') (f), Elba
Elbe[2] (m), the (river) Elbe
l'Équateur (m), Ecuador
Érié (le lac), Lake Erie
l'Escaut (m), the (river) Scheldt
l'Espagne (f), Spain
les États-Unis (m), the United States
l'Éthiopie (f), Ethiopia
l'Europe (f), Europe

la Finlande, Finland
la Flandre, Flanders
Flessingue, Flushing
la Floride, Florida
la France, France
Francfort, Frankfurt

le Gabon, Gabo(o)n
Galles (le Pays de), Wales
la Gambie, the Gambia
Gand, Ghent
le Gange, the Ganges
la Gascogne, Gascony; le Golfe de G., the Bay of Biscay

Geographical Names

Gênes, Genoa
Genève, Geneva
le Ghana, Ghana
la Grande-Bretagne, Great Britain
la Grèce, Greece
le Groënland, Greenland
le Guatémala, Guatemala
Guernesey (m), Guernsey
la Guinée, Guinea
la Guyane, Guyana

Hambourg, Hamburg
la Havane, Havana
la Haye, the Hague
les Hébrides (f), the Hebrides
l'Himalaya (m), the Himalayas
la Hollande, Holland
la Hongrie, Hungary

l'Inde (f), India
l'Indonésie (f), Indonesia
l'Irak (m), Iraq
l'Iran (m), Iran
l'Irlande (f), Ireland; l'I. du Nord, Northern Ireland
l'Islande (f), Iceland
Israël (m), Israel
l'Italie (f), Italy

la Jamaïque, Jamaica
le Japon, Japan
Jersey (m), Jersey
Jérusalem, Jerusalem
la Jordanie, Jordan
le Jura, the Jura (Mountains)

Kaboul, Kabul
le Kénya, Kenya

la Laponie, Lapland
Léman (le lac), the lake of Geneva
le Liban, the Lebanon
le Libéria, Liberia
la Libye, Libya
Lisbonne, Lisbon
Livourne, Leghorn
Londres, London
le Luxembourg, Luxemburg

Madagascar (m), Madagascar
Madère (f), Madeira
Majorque (f), Majorca
la Malaisie, (i) Malaya; (ii) the Malay Archipelago
le Malawi, Malawi
Malgache (la République), (the Republic of) Madagascar, the Malagasy Republic
Mali (la République du), Mali
Malte (f), Malta
Man (l'île de), the Isle of Man
la Manche, the English Channel
Manille, Manilla
le Maroc, Morocco
Maurice (l'île), Mauritius
Mauritanie (la République islamique de), (the Islamic Republic of) Mauritania
Mayence, Mainz
la Mecque, Mecca

Méditerranée, la (mer), the Mediterranean
la Mélanésie, Melanesia
Mexico, Mexico (City)
le Mexique, Mexico (the country)
Minorque, Minorca
Montréal, Montreal
Moscou, Moscow

le Nicaragua, Nicaragua
le Niger, the (river) Niger; la République du N., the Niger Republic
le Nigeria, Nigeria
le Nil, the (river) Nile
Nord, la mer du, the North Sea
la Normandie, Normandy
la Norvège, Norway
le Nouveau-Brunswick, New Brunswick
la Nouvelle-Angleterre, New England
la Nouvelle-Calédonie, New Caledonia
la Nouvelle-Écosse, Nova Scotia
la Nouvelle-Galles du Sud, New South Wales
la Nouvelle-Guinée, New Guinea
les Nouvelles-Hébrides, the New Hebrides
la Nouvelle-Orléans, New Orleans
la Nouvelle-Zélande, New Zealand

les Orcades (f), the Orkneys
l'Océanie (f), Oceania
l'Orénoque (m), the (river) Orinoco
Ostende, Ostend
Ouessant, Ushant
l'Ouganda (m), Uganda
Oural (les Monts), the Urals

Pacifique (l'Océan), the Pacific (Ocean)
le Pakistan, Pakistan
le Panama, Panama
le Paraguay, Paraguay
les Pays-Bas (m), the Netherlands
la Pennsylvanie, Pennsylvania
le Pérou, Peru
la Perse, Persia
les Philippines (f), the Philippines
la Picardie, Picardy
la Pologne, Poland
la Polynésie, Polynesia
le Portugal, Portugal
la Prusse, Prussia
les Pyrénées (f), the Pyrenees

Quatre Cantons (lac des), Lake Lucerne
Québec, Quebec

la République Arabe Unie (R.A.U.), United Arab Republic (U.A.R.)
le Rhin, the (river) Rhine
la Rhodésie, Rhodesia
Rocheuses, les (montagnes), the Rockies, the Rocky Mountains
la Roumanie, R(o)umania
le Royaume-Uni, the United Kingdom
la Russie, Russia

Saint-Domingue, Santo Domingo
Sainte-Hélène, Saint Helena

3

le Saint-Laurent, the St. Lawrence (river)
Saint-Marin, San Marino
la Sardaigne, Sardinia
la Savoie, Savoy
la Saxe, Saxony
la Scandinavie, Scandinavia
Schaffhouse, Schaffhausen
le Sénégal, Senegal
Sercq, (the island of) Sark
la Sibérie, Siberia
la Sicile, Sicily
Singapour, Singapore
la Somalie (la République démocratique de), Somalia
Somalis (la Côte française des), French Somaliland
Sorlingues, les (îles) (*f*), the Scilly Islands
le Soudan, the Sudan
Sud-Africaine (la République), (the Republic of) South Africa
la Suède, Sweden
la Suisse, Switzerland
la Syrie, Syria

le Tage, the (river) Tagus
la Tamise, the (river) Thames
Tanger, Tangiers
la Tanzanie, Tanzania

la Tasmanie, Tasmania
le Tchad, (i) Lake Chad; (ii) (the Republic of) Chad
la Tchécoslovaquie, Czechoslovakia
Terre-Neuve (*f*), Newfoundland
la Thaïlande, Thailand, Siam
le Togo, (Republic of) Togo
Tolède, Toledo
la Trinité, Trinidad
la Tunisie, Tunisia
la Turquie, Turkey

l'U.R.S.S., *F:* l'Ursse (*f*), the U.S.S.R.
l'Uruguay, Uruguay

Valence, (i) Valence (France); (ii) Valencia (Spain)
le Vatican, the Vatican
Varsovie, Warsaw
le Venezuela, Venezuela
Venise, Venice
Vienne, (i) Vienna; (ii) Vienne (France)
le Vietnam, Vietnam
Vintimille, Ventimiglia

le Yémen, the Yemen
la Yougoslavie, Yugoslavia

le Zambèze, the Zambezi (river)
la Zambie, Zambia

II. ENGLISH-FRENCH: ANGLAIS-FRANÇAIS

Abyssinia, l'Abyssinie (f)
Adriatic (Sea) (the), (la mer) Adriatique (f)
Afghanistan, l'Afghanistan (m)
Africa, l'Afrique (f)
Albania, l'Albanie (f)
Alderney, Aurigny
Algeria, l'Algérie (f)
Algiers, Alger
Alps (the), les Alpes (f)
Amazon (the river)), l'Amazone (m)
America, l'Amérique (f)
Andes (the), les Andes (f)
Andorra, l'Andorre (f)
Antwerp, Anvers
Apennines (the), les Apennins (m)
Appalachians (the), les (monts) Appalaches (m)
Arabia, l'Arabie (f)
Argentina, the Argentine, (la République) Argentine
Asia, l'Asie (f)
Athens, Athènes
Atlantic (Ocean) (the), l'(Océan) Atlantique (m)
Australia, l'Australie (f)
Austria, l'Autriche (f)
Azores (the), les Açores (f)

Baffin Island, la Terre de Baffin
Baltic (Sea) (the), la (mer) Baltique (f)
Barbados, Barbade (f)
Barcelona, Barcelone
Basel, Basle, Bâle
Bavaria, la Bavière
Belgium, la Belgique
Benelux, le Bénélux
Bermudas (the), les (îles) Bermudes (f)
Bethlehem, Bethléem
Biscay (Bay of) (the), le Golfe de Gascogne
Bolivia, la Bolivie
Brazil, le Brésil
Bremen, Brême
British Isles (the), les Iles (f) britanniques
Brittany, la Bretagne
Brussels, Bruxelles
Bulgaria, la Bulgarie
Burgundy, la Bourgogne
Burma, la Birmanie

Cairo, le Caire
Cambodia, le Cambodge
Cameroons (the Republic of) (the), (la République du) Cameroun
Canada, le Canada
Canaries (the), the Canary Islands, les (Iles) Canaries (f)
Canterbury, Cantorbéry
Capetown, le Cap

Caribbean (the), la Mer des Antilles
Carpathians (the), the Carpathian Mountains, les Carpathes (m)
Caspian (Sea) (the), la (mer) Caspienne
Caucasus (the), le Caucase
Central African Republic (the), la République Centrafricaine
Ceylon, Ceylan (m)
Chad (Lake or Republic), le Tchad
Channel Islands (the), les îles Anglo-Normandes
Chile, le Chili
China, la Chine
Coblenz, Coblence
Colombia, la Colombie
Columbia (British), la Colombie britannique
Congo (river), le Congo; the Republic of the C., la République du Congo
Congolese Republic (the), la République démocratique du Congo
Copenhagen, Copenhague
Cordoba, Cordoue
Cornwall, la Cornouailles
Corsica, la Corse
Crete, Crète (f)
Crimea (the), la Crimée
Cyprus, Chypre (f)
Czechoslovakia, la Tchécoslovaquie

Damascus, Damas
Danube (the), le Danube
Denmark, le Danemark
Dover, Douvres
Dresden, Dresde

Ebro (the) (river), l'Ebre (m)
Ecuador, l'Équateur (m)
Edinburgh, Édimbourg
Egypt, l'Égypte (f)
Eire; l'Eire (f)
Elba, (l'île d') Elbe (f)
Elbe (the) (river), l'Elbe (m)
England, l'Angleterre (f)
English Channel (the), la Manche
Erie (Lake), le lac Erié
Ethiopia, l'Éthiopie (f)
Europe, l'Europe (f)

Finland, la Finlande
Flanders, la Flandre
Florida, la Floride
Flushing, Flessingue
France, la France
Frankfurt, Francfort

Gabo(o)n, le Gabon
Gambia, la Gambie
Ganges (the), le Gange
Gascony, la Gascogne
Geneva, Genève; the lake of G., le lac Léman

5

Geographical Names

Genoa, Gênes
Germany, l'Allemagne (f)
Ghana, le Ghana
Ghent, Gand
Great Britain, la Grande-Bretagne
Greece, la Grèce
Greenland, le Groënland
Guernsey, Guernesey (m)
Guinea, la Guinée
Guatemala, le Guatémala
Guyana, la Guyane

Hague (the), la Haye
Hamburg, Hambourg
Havana, la Havane
Hebrides (the), les Hébrides (f)
Himalayas (the), l'Himalaya
Holland, la Hollande
Hungary, la Hongrie

Iceland, l'Islande (f)
India, l'Inde (f)
Indonesia, l'Indonésie (f)
Iran, l'Iran (m)
Iraq, l'Irak (m)
Ireland, l'Irlande (f); Northern I.,
   l'Irlande du Nord
Lrsael, Israël (m)
Italy, l'Italie (f)
Ivory Coast (the), la Côte d'Ivoire

Jamaica, la Jamaïque
Japan, le Japon
Jersey, le Jersey
Jerusalem, Jérusalem
Jordan, la Jordanie
Jura (Mountains) (the), le Jura

Kabul, Kaboul
Kashmir, le Cachemire
Kenya, le Kenya
Korea, la Corée

Lapland, la Laponie
Lebanon (the), le Liban
Leghorn, Livourne
Liberia, le Libéria
Libya, la Libye
Lisbon, Lisbonne
London, Londres
Lucerne (Lake of), le lac des Quatre
   Cantons
Luxemburg, le Luxembourg

Madagascar, Madagascar (m); la
   République Malgache
Madeira, Madère (f)
Mainz, Mayence
Majorca, Majorque (f)
Malawi, le Malawi
Malaya, la Malaisie
Mali, (la République du) Mali
Malta, Malte (f)
Man (the Isle of), l'Ile de Man
Manilla, Manille
Mauritania (the Islamic Republic of), la
   (République islamique de) Mauritanie

Mauritius, l'Ile Maurice
Mecca, la Mecque
Mediterranean (Sea) (the), la (mer)
   Méditerranée
Melanesia, la Mélanésie
Mexico, le Mexique; M. (City), Mexico
Minorca, Minorque
Montreal, Montréal
Morocco, le Maroc
Moscow, Moscou

Netherlands (the), les Pays-Bas (m)
New Brunswick, le Nouveau-Brunswick
New Caledonia, la Nouvelle-Calédonie
New England, la Nouvelle-Angleterre
Newfoundland, Terre-Neuve (f)
New Guinea, la Nouvelle-Guinée
New Hebrides (the), les Nouvelles-
   Hébrides
New Orleans, la Nouvelle-Orléans
New South Wales, la Nouvelle-Galles
   du Sud
New Zealand, la Nouvelle-Zélande
Nicaragua, le Nicaragua
Niger (the), le Niger
Nigeria, le Nigeria
Nile (the), le Nil
Normandy, la Normandie
North Sea (the), la mer du Nord
Norway, la Norvège
Nova Scotia, la Nouvelle-Écosse

Oceania, l'Océanie (f)
Orinoco (the), l'Orénoque (m)
Orkneys (the), les Orcades (f)

Pacific (Ocean) (the), (l'Océan) Pacifique
   (m)
Pakistan, le Pakistan
Panama, le Panama
Paraguay, le Paraguay
Pennsylvania, la Pennsylvanie
Peru, le Pérou
Philippines (the), les Philippines (f)
Picardy, la Picardie
Poland, la Pologne
Polynesia, la Polynésie
Portugal, le Portugal
Prussia, la Prusse
Pyrenees (the), les Pyrénées (f)

Quebec, Québec

Rheims, Reims
Rhine (the), le Rhin
Rhodesia, la Rhodésie
Riviera (the), la Côte d'Azur
Rocky Mountains (the), the Rockies, les
   (montagnes) Rocheuses
R(o)umania, la Roumanie
Russia, la Russie

Saint Helena, Sainte-Hélène
St Lawrence (the), le Saint-Laurent
San Marino, Saint-Marin
Santo Domingo, Saint-Domingue

6

Sardinia, Sardaigne (*f*)
Sark, Sercq
Saudi Arabia, l'Arabie (*f*) séoudite
Savoy, la Savoie
Saxony, la Saxe
Scandinavia, la Scandinavie
Schaffhausen, Schaffhouse
Scilly Islands (the), les Sorlingues (*f*)
Scotland, l'Écosse (*f*)
Senegal, le Sénégal
Shanghai, Changhaï
Siberia, la Sibérie
Sicily, la Sicile
Singapore, Singapour
Somalia, (la République de) Somalie (*f*)
Somaliland (French), la Côte française des Somalis
South Africa (the Republic of), la République Sud-Africaine
Spain, l'Espagne (*f*)
Sweden, la Suède
Switzerland, la Suisse
Syria, la Syrie

Tagus (the), le Tage
Tanzania, la Tanzanie
Thailand, la Thaïlande
Thames (the), la Tamise
Togo (Republic of), le Togo
Toledo, Tolède

Trinidad, la Trinité, Trinidad
Tunisia, la Tunisie
Turkey, la Turquie

Uganda, l'Ouganda (*m*)
United Arab Republic (the) (U.A.R.), la République Arabe Unie (R.A.U.)
United Kingdom (the), le Royaume-Uni
United States (the), the U.S.A., les Etats-Unis
Urals (the), les Monts Oural
Uruguay, l'Uruguay (*m*)
Ushant, Ouessant
U.S.S.R. (the), l'U.R.S.S., F: l'Ursse (*f*)

Vatican (the), le Vatican
Venezuela, le Venezuela
Venice, Venise
Ventimiglia, Vintimille
Vienna, Vienne
Vietnam, le Vietnam

Wales, le Pays de Galles
Warsaw, Varsovie
West Indies (the), les Antilles (*f*)

Yemen (the), le Yémen
Yugoslavia, la Yougoslavie

Zambezi (the), le Zambèze
Zambia, la Zambie

1. FRENCH-ENGLISH: FRANÇAIS-ANGLAIS

Adèle, Adela
Adrien, (i) (*Rom. Hist.*) Hadrian; (ii) Adrian
Agnès, Agnes
Alain, Alan
Alexandre, Alexander
André, Andrew
Annibal, Hannibal
Antoine, Ant(h)ony
Aristote, Aristotle
Auguste, Augustus
Augustine, Augusta
Barthélemy, Bartholomew
Béatrice, Beatrice
Brigitte, Bridget
Benoît, Benedict
Camille, Camilla
Catherine, Catherine, Kathleen
Cécile, Cicely, Cecilia
Christine, Christina, Christine
Christophe, Christopher
Cicéron, Cicero
Claude, (i) (*m*) Claude; (ii) (*f*) Claudia
Cyrille, Cyril
Diane, Diana
Dominique, (i) (*m*) Dominic; (ii) (*f*) *no equivalent*
Dorothée, Dorothy, Dorothea
Édith, Edith
Edmond, Edmund
Édouard, Edward
Élisabeth, Elizabeth
Étienne, Stephen
Eustache, Eustace
Ève, Eva, Eve
François, Francis
Françoise, Frances
Frédéric, Frederic(k)
Gauthier, Walter
Geneviève, Genevieve
Gérard, Gerald, Gerard
Geoffroi, Geoffrey
Georges, George
Gilles, Giles
Grégoire, Gregory
Guillaume, William
Hélène, Helen
Henri, Henry
Henriette, Henrietta, Harriet
Hilaire, Hilary
Homère, Homer

Hugues, Hugh
Ignace, Ignatius
Irène, Irene
Isabelle, Isabel, Isabella
Jacques, James
Jean, John
Jeanne, Joan, Jean, Jane; J. d'Arc, Joan of Arc
Jeannette, Janet, Jeannette
Jérémie, Jeremy, Jeremiah
Joséphine, Josephine
Jules, Julius; J. César, Julius Caesar
Julie, Julia, Julie
Julien, Julian
Juliette, Juliet
Laurent, Laurence
Léon, Leo
Léonore, Leonora
Louis, Lewis, Louis
Louise, Louisa, Louise
Luc, Luke
Marguerite, Margaret, Marguerite
Marie, Mary, Marie, Maria
Marion, Marian
Marc, Mark
Marthe, Martha
Mathieu, Matthew
Michel, Michael
Moïse, Moses
Monique, Monica
Nicolas, Nicholas
Nicole, Nicola
Olivier, Oliver
Ovide, Ovid
Patrice, Patrick
Philippe, Philip
Pie, Pius
Pierre, Peter
Raoul, Ralph
Rodrigue, Roderick
Salomon, Solomon
Sophie, Sophia
Suzanne, Susan, Suzanne
Thérèse, T(h)eresa
Timothée, Timothy
Ursule, Ursula
Véronique, Veronica
Victoire, Victoria
Virgile, Virgil
Virginie, Virginia

2. ENGLISH-FRENCH: ANGLAIS-FRANÇAIS

Adela, Adèle
Adrian, Adrien
Agnes, Agnès
Alan, Alain
Alexander, Alexandre
Andrew, André
Ant(h)ony, Antoine
Aristotle, Aristote
Augusta, Augustine
Augustus, Auguste
Bartholomew, Barthélemy
Beatrice, Béatrice
Benedict, Benoît
Bridget, Brigitte
Camilla, Camille
Christina, Christine
Cecilia, Cécile
Christopher, Christophe
Cicely, Cécile
Cicero, Cicéron
Claudia, Claude
Cyril, Cyrille
Diana, Diane
Dominic, Dominique
Dorothea, Dorothy, Dorothée
Edith, Édith
Edmund, Edmond
Edward, Édouard
Elizabeth, Elisabeth
Eustace, Eustache
Eva, Eve, Ève
Frances, Françoise
Francis, François
Frederic(k), Frédéric
Genevieve, Geneviève
George, Georges
Gerald, Gerard, Gérard
Geoffrey, Geoffroi
Giles, Gilles
Gregory, Grégoire
Hadrian, Adrien
Hannibal, Annibal
Harriet, Henriette
Helen, Hélène
Henrietta, Henriette
Henry, Henri
Homer, Homère
Hilary, Hilaire
Hugh, Hugues
Ignatius, Ignace
Irene, Irène
Isabel(la), Isabelle

James, Jacques
Jane, Jeanne
Janet, Jeannette
Jean, Jeanne
Jeremy, Jeremiah, Jérémie
Joan, Jeanne; J. of Arc, Jeanne d'Arc
John, Jean
Josephine, Joséphine
Julia, Julie
Julian, Julien
Juliet, Juliette
Julius, Jules; J. Caesar, Jules César
Kathleen, Catherine
Laurence, Laurent
Leo, Léon
Leonora, Léonore
Lewis, Louis
Louisa, Louise
Luke, Luc
Margaret, Marguerite
Maria, Marie
Marian, Marion
Marc, Mark
Martha, Marthe
Mary, Marie
Matthew, Mathieu
Michael, Michel
Monica, Monique
Moses, Moïse
Nicholas, Nicolas
Nicola, Nicole
Oliver, Olivier
Ovid, Ovide
Patrick, Patrice, Patrick
Peter, Pierre
Philip, Philippe
Pius, Pie
Ralph, Raoul
Roderick, Rodrigue
Solomon, Salomon
Sophia, Sophie
Stephen, Étienne
Susan, Suzanne
T(h)eresa, Thérèse
Timothy, Timothée
Ursula, Ursule
Veronica, Véronique
Victoria, Victoire, Victoria
Virgil, Virgile
Virginia, Virginie
Walter, Gauthier
William, Guillaume

COINAGE—MONNAIES

WEIGHTS AND MEASURES—POIDS ET MESURES

In France and other French-speaking countries (Belgium, Switzerland, etc.) the metric system of weights and measures is used, the unit of length being the metre, of weight the gramme, of liquid measure the litre. The metric system is already widely used in English-speaking countries, especially by scientists. French-speaking people are, however, less familiar with the other weights and measures in current use in the English-speaking world, so tables of equivalents have been drawn up.

En France et dans les pays de langue française (la Belgique, la Suisse, etc.) on emploie le système métrique de poids et mesures (mètre, gramme, litre). Le système métrique est déjà utilisé dans les pays de langue anglaise, en particulier pour les mesures scientifiques, mais les autres poids et mesures qui sont d'usage courant dans le monde anglophone sont moins connus dans les pays francophones. Les tableaux suivants donnent une vue d'ensemble des équivalences.

1. Weights—Poids

(a) *Avoirdupois weights—Système avoirdupois*

ounce (oz.) (28,35 g)	U.S.
16 oz. = 1 pound (lb.) (453,6 g)	quintal (45,36 kg)
14 lb. = 1 stone (st.) (6,35 kg)	short ton (2,000 lb.) (907,18 kg)
112 lb. = 1 hundredweight (50,8 kg)	
20 cwt. = 1 ton (1017 kg)	

(b) *Troy weight (precious metals)—Système troy (métaux précieux)*

grain (0,064 g)	20 dwts = 1 oz. troy (31,1 g)
24 gr. = 1 pennyweight (dwt.) (1,555 g)	12 oz. = 1 lb. troy (373,2 g)

2. Long measure—Mesures de longueur

inch (in.) (2,54 cm)
12 inches (12″) = 1 foot (ft.) (30,48 cm)
3 feet (3′) = 1 yard (yd.) (0,914 m)
1760 yds. = 1 mile (1 km 6)   *Nau:* 6 feet = 1 fathom (1,8 m)

3. Square measure—Mesures de superficie

square inch (sq. in.)—6,45 cm²	square yard (sq. yd.)—0,836 m²
square foot (sq. ft.)—929 cm²	acre—0,4 hectare

4. Measures of volume—Mesures de volume

cubic inch (cu. in.)—16,4 cm³	cubic foot (cu. ft.)—28,315 dm³
cubic yard (cu. yd.)—764 dm³	

5. Measures of capacity—Mesures de capacité

G.B.	U.S.
Liquid and dry	*Liquid*
pint (pt.) (0,57 litres)	pint (0,47 litres)
2 pts. = 1 quart (qt) (1,14 litres)	quart (0,946 litres)
4 qts. = 1 gallon (gal.) (4,56 litres)	gallon (3,785 litres)
	barrel (119 litres)
	barrel (158,97 litres) (petroleum)
Dry	*Dry*
8 gall. = 1 bushel (bu.) (36,35 litres)	pint (0,55 litres)
8 bu. = 1 quarter (qr.) (290,8 litres)	quart (1,1 litres)
	gallon (4,4 litres)
	bushel (35,2 litres)

Note: French style punctuation is given for the metric equivalents, the decimal point being shown [,].

COINAGE—MONNAIES

1. Great Britain—Grande-Bretagne

> penny (1p)
> pound (£1)—100 pence (*une livre*)

Since 1971 the pound has been divided into 100 pence.

Depuis 1971 la livre est divisée en 100 pence.

2. United States—États-Unis

> cent (c.)
> nickel—5 cents
> dime—10 cents
> quarter—25 cents
> dollar ($)—100 cents

Dollars and cents are also used in Canada, Australia and New Zealand; the monetary unit of South Africa is the **rand**, divided into 100 cents.

On emploie également au Canada, en Australie et en Nouvelle-Zélande un dollar divisé en 100 cents; l'unité monétaire de l'Afrique du Sud est le **rand,** divisé en 100 cents.

11

Harrap's
French
and
English
Dictionaries

The famous Harrap family of bilingual dictionaries:

1. The **New Standard** (French-English) and **Standard** (English-French) for advanced students, translators and others needing a really comprehensive dictionary which can satisfy the highest demands.

2. The **New Shorter** for under-graduates, senior school students, executives and others who require a handy, modern work full enough for all normal needs.

3. The **Concise**, the ideal school and general purpose dictionary with its clear layout, adequate information and examples.

4. The **New Pocket**, a really modern, useful little dictionary which contains a remarkable amount of material, for use in schools, by the tourist and in the office as a quick reference.

Write for full details to: Harrap Books, 182-184 High Holborn, London WC1V 7AX.

Harrap's NEW STANDARD French and English Dictionary

Part One: French-English
Volume 1 (A-I), 597 pages
Volume 2 (J-Z), 556 pages
11¼'' x 8¾''   286 x 222mm

Harrap's STANDARD French and English Dictionary

Part Two: English-French
Complete in one volume,
1551 pages
11¼'' x 8¼''   286 x 210mm

"Reviewing **Harrap's New Standard French and English Dictionary** can probably be compared to road-testing the latest Rolls-Royce. In each case one knows that there is nothing better, that the product is unique, and that it is built on the experience of decades of thought and research. Equally important one knows that the purchase will have to give faithful service for many years."
The Times Higher Education Supplement

"The incomparable Standard bilingual dictionary"
Daily Telegraph

Harrap's NEW SHORTER French and English Dictionary

Part 1: French-English,
664 pages
Part 2: English-French,
872 pages
Complete in one volume
1524 pages
(The Complete dictionary is
also available in thumb indexed
and leather bound editions).
9½" x 6½"   242 x 166mm

"Use is the test of a dictionary and use over a period of some six months has proved to this reviewer that the New Shorter is almost impossible to fault. The definitions are exact and illuminating and they are lavishly illustrated by examples."
The Times Literary Supplement

"As welcome in the home as in the library."
Daily Telegraph

Harrap's CONCISE French and English Dictionary
New Edition 1978

Complete in one volume,
932 pages
8¾" x 5½" 222 x 141 mm

* A genuinely concise
dictionary for the student
* Entirely revised and extend-
ed with much new material
* Completely reset in a new
layout for greater clarity
* Fuller information about
each main entry than in comparable dictionaries
* Wealth of contemporary
examples to aid correct usage

The most up-to-date Concise
French and English Dictionary
in the world

Harrap's
NEW POCKET
French and English
Dictionary

**Complete in one volume,
525 pages
$7\frac{3}{8}'' \times 4\frac{5}{8}''$ 188 x 117mm**

"This volume has the qualities
one always finds in Harrap
dictionaries."
*The Times Educational
Supplement*

"Remarkably good value."
Daily Telegraph

Harrap's French ~ English Dictionary of Slang and Colloquialisms

256 pages
9¾" x 6½"   235 x 166mm

"Harrap's new dictionary is indispensable."
Cyril Connolly in the Sunday Times

Harrap's English ~ French Dictionary of Slang and Colloquialisms

"This is a delightful, sinewy and scholarly book." *The Times*

299 pages
9¾" x 6½"   235 x 166mm